HALSBURY'S

Laws of England

ANNUAL ABRIDGMENT

1978

HALSBURY'S

Laws of England

ANNUAL ABRIDGMENT

1978

EDITOR

K. H. MUGFORD
of Lincoln's Inn, Barrister

ASSISTANT EDITOR

PAUL BROWN BA

BUTTERWORTHS

LONDON

ENGLAND   Butterworth & Co (Publishers) Ltd
              88 Kingsway, London WC2AB

AUSTRALIA   Butterworth Pty Ltd
              586 Pacific Highway, Chatswood, Sydney,
              NSW 2067
              Also at Melbourne, Brisbane, Adelaide and Perth

CANADA   Butterworth & Co (Canada) Ltd
              2265 Midland Avenue, Scarborough,
              Toronto M1P 4S1

NEW ZEALAND   Butterworths of New Zealand Ltd
              T. & W. Young Building, 77–85 Customhouse
              Quay, Wellington

SOUTH AFRICA Butterworth & Co (South Africa) (Pty) Ltd
              152–154 Gale Street, Durban

USA   Butterworth & Co (Publishers) Inc
              10 Tower Office Park, Woburn, Boston,
              Mass 01801

ISBN 0 406 03361 7

PUBLISHERS' NOTE

This is the fifth Annual Abridgment and covers the year 1978. The Abridgment constitutes year by year a comprehensive survey of English case law, statute law and subordinate legislation. European Community law and decisions of Commonwealth courts are given attention commensurate with their importance. Further the Abridgment chronicles and tabulates topics which may be of interest to lawyers. Such topics are derived from government papers, reports of committees, the EEC official journal, legal periodicals and the daily press.

Each Annual Abridgment is complete without any recourse to any other publication.

The alphabetical arrangement, the comprehensive tables and index and the inclusion of destination and derivation tables of consolidation legislation make the work an ideal aid in research. At the same time, the typography and presentation have been so designed that the Abridgment is suitable for independent study. A section entitled "In Brief", which immediately follows the table of contents, shows at a glance the year's main developments.

When referring to this volume reference should be made to both the year and the relevant paragraph number: e.g. "1978 Halsbury's Abr para. 2039".

This volume covers the law made in 1978 and is compiled from sources available in London on 31st December 1978.

BUTTERWORTH LAW PUBLISHERS LTD

TABLE OF CONTENTS

Text of this Work arranged under Titles as follows:

IN BRIEF

A summary of the year's main developments

Bankruptcy

When making a criminal bankruptcy order, offences with which the offender has not been formally charged should only be taken into account with his consent: *DPP v Anderson*, para. 225.

Barristers

The House of Lords has narrowed the circumstances in which a barrister is immune from liability in negligence in relation to pre-trial advice or work: *Saif Ali v Sydney Mitchell & Co*, para. 241.

Companies

The limitation period for unclaimed dividends is six years and not twelve years: *Re Compania de Electricidad de la Provincia de Buenos Aires Ltd*, para. 382.

The extent of the jurisdiction of the Companies Court has been clarified: *Re Shilena Hosiery Co Ltd*, para. 350.

A pending action by a company ceases on the company's voluntary winding up and is not revived by an order declaring the dissolution void: *Foster Yates & Thom Ltd v H. W. Edgehill Equipment Ltd*, para. 383.

Conflict

The appropriate forum for actions is prima facie the country where the relevant events occurred: *MacShannon v Rockware Glass Ltd*, para. 442.

Constitutional law

The Scotland Act 1978, para. 437, provided for a directly elected assembly for Scotland, established constitutional and financial machinery for its operation and set out the powers of the assembly. The Wales Act 1978, para. 442, made similar provision for Wales.

Consumer protection

The Consumer Safety Act 1978, para. 449, enables provision to be made for the safety of certain goods to prevent or reduce the risk of death or personal injury from them.

Contract

The doctrine of contribution has been extended to persons liable for breach of contract: para. 835.

Damages for breach of contract may be awarded in the foreign currency best representing the plaintiff's loss: *Services Europe Atlantique Sud v Stockholms Rederiaktiebolag Svea*, para. 841.

County courts

The House of Lords has affirmed that an injunction may be granted to an unmarried woman under the Domestic Violence and Matrimonial Proceedings Act 1976 temporarily overriding the property rights of her partner: *Davis v Johnson*, para. 1522.

A time limit may be imposed on the operation of an injunction under the 1976 Act: para. 1520.

Criminal law

The Protection of Children Act 1978, para. 652, prohibits the exploitation of children by their use in the production of indecent photographs and penalises the distribution, showing and advertising of such photographs.

The Theft Act 1978, para. 667, amends the law relating to obtaining a pecuniary advantage by deception and creates the offence of making off without payment.

The Court of Appeal has laid down guidelines for the Crown Court concerning compensation orders: *R v Bunce*, para. 596.

The conviction for assault of a motorist who successfully resisted a forcible attempt to take her fingerprints has been quashed: *R v Jones*, para. 579.

Possession of a quantity of a controlled drug so small as to be unusable in any manner which the Misuse of Drugs Act 1971 was intended to prohibit will not support a conviction: *R v Carver*, para. 615.

When making a criminal bankruptcy order, offences with which the offender has not been formally charged should only be taken into account with his consent: *DPP v Anderson*, para. 225.

The Court of Appeal has laid down guidelines as to the burden of proof in conspiracy cases: *R v Bennett*, para. 601.

When the issue of provocation arises, the reasonable man has the power of self-control of an ordinary person of the accused's sex and age: *DPP v Camplin*, para. 638.

Criminal procedure

The Bail Act 1976 came into force on 17th April 1978, para. 588, and consequential amendments have been made to the Rules of the Supreme Court, para. 2205, the Magistrates' Courts Rules, para. 1884, the Magistrates' Courts (Forms) Rules, para. 1843 and the Crown Court Rules, para. 682.

A wife cannot be compelled to testify against a husband charged with violence on her: *Metropolitan Police Commissioner v Hoskyn*, para. 708.

The House of Lords has considered when two or more defendants may be said to be charged with the same offence: *R v Hills*, para. 722.

Damages

The Civil Liability (Contribution) Act 1978, para. 835, amends the law relating to contribution and to successive legal proceedings against persons liable for the same debt or damage.

The House of Lords has laid down guidelines for assessing damages in fatal accident cases: *Cookson v Knowles*, para. 863.

An award of damages to a person who is unconscious or insensible should include a sum for loss of future earnings: *Lim Poh Choo v Camden and Islington Area Health Authority*, para. 862.

Damages in tort and damages for breach of contract may be awarded in the foreign currency best representing the plaintiff's loss: *The Despina R; Services Europe Atlantique Sud v Stockholms Rederiaktiebolag Svea*, para. 841.

Damages may be awarded for loss of earnings during the "lost years" by which a person's life is shortened as a result of personal injury: *Pickett v British Rail Engineering Ltd*, para. 861.

Discovery

In a claim for personal injuries, an order for production of medical records must be for production to the applicant or his solicitor: *McIvor v Southern Health and Social Services Board, Northern Ireland*, para. 945.

Industrial tribunals should only order production of confidential reports where it is essential in the interests of justice: *Science Research Council v Nasse; Leyland Cars v Vyas*, para. 946.

Elections

The Representation of the People Act 1978, para. 1033, increases the limits on candidates' election expenses at parliamentary elections.

The European Assembly Elections Act 1978, para. 1208, gives effect to an EEC Council Decision concerning the election of representatives to the European Assembly.

Employment

The House of Lords has considered whether the dismissal of an employee for taking part in industrial action was unfair: *Stock v Frank Jones (Tipton) Ltd*, para. 2965.

Industrial tribunals have jurisdiction to consider a complaint of racial discrimination: *Zarczynska v Levy*, para. 2269.

European Communities

The European Assembly Elections Act 1978, para. 1208, gives effect to an EEC Council Decision on the election of representatives to the European Assembly by direct universal suffrage.

Evidence

Absolute privilege may attach to evidence given at certain tribunals which act in a manner similar to a court: *Trapp v Mackie*, para. 1287.

Executors and administrators

In order to establish a claim for maintenance under the Inheritance (Provision for Family and Dependants) Act 1975, a child of the deceased who was not a dependant must establish a moral claim beyond being a relative in need: *Re Coventry (deceased)*, para. 1294.

Extradition

The Suppression of Terrorism Act 1978 facilitates extradition from the United Kingdom by precluding the offender from claiming that certain offences are of a political character: para. 1321.

Foreign relations law

The Internationally Protected Persons Act 1978 gives the United Kingdom courts jurisdiction over certain serious offences committed abroad in relation to protected persons: para. 1411.

The State Immunity Act 1978 restricts the immunity from process in United Kingdom civil courts and tribunals enjoyed by sovereign states: para. 1421.

Hire purchase and consumer credit

The Consumer Safety Act 1978, para. 449, empowers the Secretary of State to make regulations preventing or reducing the risk of death or personal injury from certain goods including goods supplied under a hire purchase agreement.

Housing

The Home Purchase Assistance and Housing Corporation Guarantee Act 1978, para. 1484, authorises the use of public money for assisting first-time purchasers of house property.

The Homes Insulation Act 1978, para. 1489, provides for grants towards the cost of thermal insulation of private homes.

Husband and wife

The Domestic Proceedings and Magistrates' Courts Act 1978, para. 1509, makes new provision for matrimonial proceedings in magistrates' courts, replacing the Matrimonial Proceedings (Magistrates' Courts) Act 1960.

An injunction may be granted to an unmarried woman under the Domestic Violence and Matrimonial Proceedings Act 1976 temporarily overriding the property rights of her partner: *Davis v Johnson*, para. 1522.

A time limit may be imposed on the operation of an injunction under the 1976 Act: para. 1520.

Income taxation

An assessment to income tax must include a statement of the tax payable, not merely an assessment of the income liable to tax and information from which the amount of tax may be computed: *Hallamshire Industrial Finance Trust Ltd v Inland Revenue Commissioners*, para. 1552.

On appeal against an assessment to income tax by way of case stated, the court has jurisdiction to consider only the facts found by the Inland Revenue Commissioners: *Yoannou v Hall (Inspector of Taxes)*, para. 1566.

An employee's preferential right to acquire shares in the employing company is a taxable emolument from his employment: *Tyrer v Smart (Inspector of Taxes)*, para. 1614.

Injunctions

A time limit may be imposed on the operation of an injunction under the Domestic Violence and Matrimonial Proceedings Act 1976: para. 1520.

Landlord and tenant

A mortgagee's right to obtain possession of mortgaged premises may not be used as a device to evade the Rent Acts: *Quennell v Maltby*, para. 1736.

Where the Rent Acts would apply to a lease of a dwelling-house, the landlord may grant a licence of the premises if that is what the parties intend: *Somma v Hazelhurst*, para. 1726.

A joint tenant who is in sole occupation at the end of a protected tenancy is entitled to remain in possession as a statutory tenant: *Lloyd v Sadler*, para. 1752.

An adult who lives platonically with a person not related to him cannot succeed to a statutory tenancy: *Joram Developments Ltd v Sharratt*, para. 1753.

When a female statutory tenant dies a man who has lived with her for a long period does not necessarily succeed to the tenancy: *Helby v Rafferty*, para. 1754.

Where a lease is assigned and then disclaimed by the assignee's liquidator, the original lessee remains liable for the rent: *Warnford Investments Ltd v Duckworth*, para. 369.

Lessees' expenditure in making improvements to demised premises may not be taken into account when assessing a reasonable rent for the premises: *Ponsford v HMS (Aerosols) Ltd*, para. 1746.

Limitation of actions

The court has a general and unfettered discretion to override the time limits in personal injury actions: *Firman v Ellis*, para. 1795.

The limitation period for unclaimed dividends is six years and not twelve years: *Re Compania de Electricidad de la Provincia de Buenos Aires Ltd*, para. 382.

Local government

The Local Government Act 1978, para. 1814, enables local authorities to make payments to or provide benefits for persons suffering injustice as a result of maladministration.

Magistrates

The Domestic Proceedings and Magistrates' Courts Act 1978, para. 1509, makes new provision for matrimonial proceedings in magistrates' courts, replacing the Matrimonial Proceedings (Magistrates' Courts) Act 1960.

Minors

The Protection of Children Act 1978, para. 652, prohibits the exploitation of children by their use in the production of indecent photographs.

Mortgages

A mortgagee's right to obtain possession of mortgaged premises may not be used as a device to evade the Rent Acts: *Quennell v Maltby*, para. 1736.

Negligence

The court has no jurisdiction to make a finding of contributory negligence where it is not pleaded by the defendant: *Fookes v Slaytor*, para. 1997.

Patents

Remaining provisions of the Patents Act 1977, except those relating to Community patents, came into force on 1st June 1978: para. 2067.

Practice and procedure

The appropriate forum for actions is prima facie the country where the relevant events occurred: *MacShannon v Rockware Glass Ltd*, para. 422.

Race relations

Industrial tribunals have jurisdiction to consider a complaint of racial discrimination: *Zarczynska v Levy*, para. 2269.

Rating

The Rating (Disabled Persons) Act 1978, para. 2293, amends the law relating to relief from rates in respect of premises used by disabled persons.

Road traffic

Failure to comply with instructions does not vitiate a breath test unless the effect could be prejudicial to the motorist: *Attorney General's Reference (No. 1 of 1978)*, para. 2344.

Sale of goods

The Consumer Safety Act 1978, para. 449, enables provision to be made for the safety of goods. An order may prohibit the supply of unsafe goods or require the publication of a warning that goods are unsafe.

Sale of land

A completion notice issued under a condition of sale subsequent to a decree of specific performance is invalid: *Singh v Nazeer*, para. 2434.

A solicitor has no implied authority to exchange contracts by telephone or to dispense with actual exchange: *Domb v Isoz*, para. 2430.

Settlements

A beneficiary under a settlement may hold an interest in possession notwithstanding the trustees' power of accumulation: *Pearson v Inland Revenue Comrs*, para. 1442.

Tort

The doctrine of contribution is no longer restricted to tortfeasors, para. 835.

Damages in tort may be awarded in the foreign currency best representing the plaintiff's loss: *The Despina R*, para. 841.

Town and country planning

A second application may be made for approval of matters reserved under an outline planning permission, notwithstanding that those matters have already been approved: *Heron Corpn Ltd v Manchester City*, para. 2785.

When one building forming part of a complex is sold to a new owner, a new planning unit is not thereby created: *Kwik Save Discount Group Ltd v Secretary of State for Wales*, para. 2800.

Trover and detinue

Remaining provisions of the Torts (Interference with Goods) Act 1977 came into force on 1st June 1978: para. 2897.

Unfair dismissal

The House of Lords has considered whether the dismissal of an employee for taking part in industrial action was unfair: *Stock v Frank Jones (Tipton) Ltd*, para. 2965.

An agreement with employers to withdraw a complaint of unfair dismissal is void: *Naqvi v Stephens Jewellers Ltd*, para. 2929.

For unfair dismissal purposes, a fixed term contract of employment is one for a specified term, notwithstanding that it may be determinable by notice: *Dixon v British Broadcasting Corporation*, para. 2964.

When a company is voluntarily wound up, the instant dismissal of an employee is not necessarily unfair: *Fox Bros (Clothes) Ltd v Bryant*, para. 3005.

A woman over sixty but under the normal retiring age for her employment may present a claim for unfair dismissal: *Nothman v Barnet London Borough Council*, para. 2961.

REFERENCES AND ABBREVIATIONS

ACTR	Australian Capital Territory Reports
All ER	All England Law Reports
ALJ	Australian Law Journal
ALJR	Australian Law Journal Reports
ALR	Australian Law Reports
ATC	Annotated Tax Cases
BJAL	British Journal of Administrative Law
Brit J Criminol	British Journal of Criminology
BTR	British Tax Review
Business LR	Business Law Review
CCC	Canadian Criminal Cases
CLJ	Cambridge Law Journal
CLR	Commonwealth Law Reports (Australia)
CMLR	Common Market Law Reports
CML Review	Common Market Law Review
Conv	Conveyancer
Conv (NS)	Conveyancer and Property Lawyer
CPL	Current Property Law
Cr App Rep	Criminal Appeal Reports
Crim LR	Criminal Law Review
DLR	Dominion Law Reports (Canada)
EA	East Africa Law Reports
ECR	European Court Reports
EG	Estates Gazette
FR	Federal Court Reports (Canada)
FSR	Fleet Street Patent Reports
ICLQ	International and Comparative Law Quarterly
ICR	Industrial Court Reports
IJR	Irish Jurist Reports
ILJ	Industrial Law Journal
ILT	Irish Law Times
ILTR	Irish Law Times Reports
Imm AR	Immigration Appeals Reports
IR	Irish Reports
IRLR	Industrial Relations Law Reports
ITR	Industrial Tribunal Reports
JBL	Journal of Business Law
JCL	Journal of Criminal Law
JP	Justice of the Peace Reports
JP Jo	Justice of the Peace Journal
JPL	Journal of Planning and Environmental Law
JR	Juridical Review
JSPTL	Journal of the Society of Public Teachers of Law
KIR	Knight's Industrial Reports
LE	Legal Executive
LG	Law Guardian
LGC	Local Government Chronicle
LGR	Local Government Reports
Lloyd's Rep	Lloyd's Reports
LMCLQ	Lloyd's Maritime and Commercial Law Quarterly
LQR	Law Quarterly Review

LR	The Law Reports
LS Gaz	Law Society Gazette
L(TC)	Income Tax Leaflets
Med Sci & Law	Medicine Science & The Law
MLR	Modern Law Review
NI	Northern Ireland Reports
NILQ	Northern Ireland Law Quarterly
NLJ	New Law Journal
NSWLR	New South Wales Law Reports
NZLR	New Zealand Law Reports
OJC	Official Journal of the European Communities— communications and information series
OJL	Official Journal of the European Communities— legislation series
OR	Ontario Reports
PL	Public Law
P & CR	Property and Compensation Reports
RA	Rating Appeals
RPC	Reports of Patent Etc. Cases
RRC	Ryde's Rating Cases
RTR	Road Traffic Reports
RVR	Rating and Valuation Reporter
SASR	South Australian State Reports
SC	Session Cases
SCR	Supreme Court Reports (Canada)
SLG	Scottish Law Gazette
SLT	Scots Law Times
Sol Jo	Solicitors' Journal
STC	Simon's Tax Cases
TC	Tax Cases
TR	Taxation Reports
Traff Cas	Traffic Cases
VR	Victorian Reports
WAR	Western Australian Reports
WIR	West Indian Reports
WLR	Weekly Law Reports
WWR	Western Weekly Reports (Canada)

TABLE OF STATUTES

TABLE OF STATUTORY INSTRUMENTS

23

TABLE OF OTHER SUBORDINATE LEGISLATION

TABLE OF CASES

Decisions of the European Court of Justice are listed both alphabetically and numerically. The numerical table follows the alphabetical.

*Decisions of the European Court of Justice are listed below numerically.   These decisions are also included in the
preceding alphabetical table.*

HALSBURY'S

Annual Abridgment 1978

ADMINISTRATIVE LAW

Halsbury's Laws of England (4th edn.), Vol. 1, paras. 1–215

1   Articles

Parliamentary Commissioner's Annual Report for 1977, Henry E. Markson (a look at the Commissioner's annual report for 1977 (Second Report for Session 1977–78, HC 157)): 122 Sol Jo 275.

Planning Appeals: Parliamentary Ombudsman Cases, Henry E. Markson: 122 Sol Jo 801.

Public Inquiries and Disrupters, William Evans (the legal position of those who disrupt public inquiries and of those disrupted): 128 NLJ 291.

"Sound Administration Must Rest on a Sound Legal Basis", Janetta Harden and Nina Scott (the constitutional implications of enforcing a non-statutory incomes policy by unrelated statutory powers): 128 NLJ 4.

2   Certiorari—availability—application to quash decision of private disciplinary body

Prisoners who took part in a riot were disciplined by the prison board of visitors. They applied for leave to move for orders of certiorari to quash the board's awards as being in breach of natural justice. The applications were refused on the ground that such proceedings, which resulted in awards in respect of offences against discipline were not subject to judicial review. The prisoners appealed. *Held*, the first question was whether the Court of Appeal had jurisdiction to hear the appeal. Under Supreme Court of Judicature (Consolidation) Act 1925, s. 31 (1) (a) and Administration of Justice Act 1960, s. 1 (1) appeal from a decision of a Divisional Court of the Queen's Bench Division in a criminal cause or matter lay only to the House of Lords. The offences were described as offences against discipline. They were not offences against the public law and accordingly the decision was not in a criminal cause or matter and the Court of Appeal had jurisdiction.

The board had performed a judicial act and had a duty to act judicially. Certiorari would therefore normally lie. However the Divisional Court had decided that as the orders were made in private disciplinary proceedings by a closed body which had its own rules and power to impose sanctions within the scope of those rules the case fell within an exception to the general rule. The authority relied on to support this exception was doubtful. It was thus open to the court to consider as a matter of public policy whether certiorari should be allowed to go in respect of awards of boards of visitors. It was for the court, in the absence of any overriding statutory provisions, to say where the limits lay. In the general interest, including that of prisoners, certiorari should go in the present circumstances. The appeal would be allowed.

R v BOARD OF VISITORS OF HULL PRISON, EX PARTE ST. GERMAIN [1979] 2 WLR 42 (Court of Appeal: MEGAW, SHAW and WALLER LJJ). *Ex parte Fry* [1954] 1 WLR 730 doubted. Decision of Divisional Court of the Queen's Bench Division [1978] 2 All ER 198, 1977 Halsbury's Abr para. 3 reversed.

For comment on this case, see "The Courts intervene in the prison system," Justinian, Financial Times, 9th October 1978.

3 **—— public body—judicial discretion derived from prerogative— wrongful failure to exercise discretion**

A gang member injured in a fight applied for compensation to the Criminal Injuries Compensation Board. A clause of the Criminal Injuries Compensation Scheme required the Board to reduce compensation or reject a claim altogether if appropriate having regard to the applicant's conduct, character and way of life. In a previous policy statement interpreting the clause, the Board had stated that no award would be made to a gang member injured in a gang fight and that any such person injured in other circumstances would have to satisfy the Board that his injuries were unconnected with his gang membership. The Board, applying the policy statement, rejected the applicant's claim on the ground that he was a gang member and that he had failed to establish that his injuries were unconnected with his membership. The youth applied for an order of certiorari to quash the Board's decision on the ground that it had failed to exercise a judicial discretion. *Held*, (i) by its policy statement, the Board had wrongly deprived itself of a discretion derived from the prerogative to make a limited award notwithstanding the applicant's conduct or character. (ii) When deciding to exclude certain gang members, the Board was exercising a judicial and not an administrative function and therefore certiorari could issue to quash its decision. Accordingly the application would be allowed and the matter remitted to the Board for reconsideration.

R v CRIMINAL INJURIES COMPENSATION BOARD, EX PARTE RJC (AN INFANT) (1978) 122 Sol Jo 95 (Queen's Bench Division: LORD WIDGERY CJ, MELFORD STEVENSON and LLOYD JJ). Dicta of Diplock LJ in *R v Criminal Injuries Compensation Board, ex parte Lain* [1967] 2 QB 864 at 887, applied.

4 **Judicial control—exercise of discretion conferred by statute— abuse—failure to consider relevant factors**

See *Re D (a minor)*, para. 1930.

5 **Natural justice—bias—disciplinary tribunal—dual role of educa- tion officer**

See *Ellis v Inner London Education Authority*, para. 2999.

6 **—— —— private or domestic tribunal—prior involvement of chairman**

Two union members who had given evidence in a libel action brought on behalf of the union by the area president were subsequently charged under union rules with conduct detrimental to the union. According to the president's report to the union, the two members had contradicted in court statements made voluntarily to the union's solicitors. The disciplinary committee, of which the president acted as chairman, although without voting, found the charges proved and declared the members ineligible to hold office for two years. They sought appropriate injunctions and declarations. *Held*, actual bias was irrelevant. The president had appeared to be biased. He had borne the heat and burden of the libel action and it was manifestly unfair that he should have acted as chairman. The union's action in punishing witnesses was not a matter of contempt but of jurisdiction. A domestic tribunal had no power to punish a witness because his evidence did not come up to his proof. If it were to, no witness subject to the jurisdiction of a domestic tribunal would feel free to tell the unvarnished truth in court.

ROEBUCK AND O'BRIEN v NATIONAL UNION OF MINEWORKERS (YORKSHIRE AREA) [1978] LS Gaz R 343 (Chancery Division: TEMPLEMAN J).

For interlocutory proceedings in this matter see 1976 Halsbury's Abr para. 2.

7 **—— duty to act judicially or fairly—application for admission to educational institution**

The applicant, who was employed by a London borough as an education welfare officer, needed to obtain a Certificate of Qualification in Social Work to obtain promotion. His employers agreed that he should attend a course at a polytechnic. He was admitted to the course starting in 1975 without going through the normal selection procedure, but withdrew after lecturers refused to teach him. In 1976 he applied again and was rejected after going through the usual selection procedure. However, as a result of pressure from his employers the academic board of the polytechnic made arrangements for his admittance to the course without going through the agreed procedure. The applicant and others sought declarations that his initial rejection was improper and that proper consideration should be given to his application *Held*, an educational institution in considering an application for admission as a student was under no obligation to act judicially, nor was it bound to give a student a hearing or to assign reasons for refusing to admit him. However, the polytechnic in the present case did in fact interview the applicant and was thus under a duty to act fairly, for several reasons; since it was a publicly funded educational establishment, since the inability to obtain the certificate would seriously affect the applicant's career and since the polytechnic had published details of its selection procedure and supplied a copy to the applicant when he applied for the course. The treatment of him was unfair and his rejection invalid; nor had he been properly admitted by the action of the academic board. The declarations would be granted.

CENTRAL COUNCIL FOR EDUCATION AND TRAINING IN SOCIAL WORK V EDWARDS (1978) Times, 5th May (Chancery Division: SLADE J). *McInnes v Onslow-Fane* [1978] 3 All ER 211, para. 8 applied.

8   —— —— **application for licence**

The applicant made repeated applications to the boxing board for a boxing manager's licence. All his applications were turned down without reasons. The applicant sought a declaration that the board had acted in breach of natural justice in refusing to grant the licence and for failing to give reasons for doing so. He also objected that the board had failed to give him an oral hearing which he had requested. *Held*, in an application case, such as this, where a licence applied for had been refused, there was no obligation on the board to give its reasons for refusing the licence. There was no suggestion that the board had considered any alleged dishonesty or moral culpability on the part of the applicant. The decision was therefore no reflection on his character, but was merely a decision of the board on his suitability for a particular type of work. Taken that the decision was an honest one, in such matters the bodies closely concerned with sporting and other matters were the best judges of how such decisions should be made, not the courts. There was no obligation on the board to provide the applicant with an oral hearing.

McINNES V ONSLOW-FANE [1978] 3 All ER 211 (Chancery Division: MEGARRY V-C). *Nagle v Fielden* [1966] 2 QB 633, CA, *Enderby Town Football Club Ltd v Football Association Ltd* [1971] Ch 591, CA and, *Breen v Amalgamated Engineering Union* [1971] 2 QB 175, CA, applied.

9   —— **opportunity to be heard—internal disciplinary hearing—requirements**

See *Khanum v Mid-Glamorgan Area Health Authority*, para. 3000.

10   —— —— **local inquiry—objector's inability to attend**

A compulsory purchase order was made applying to houses owned by the applicant. After lodging an objection, the applicant was given ten or eleven weeks' notice of the date of the proposed inquiry, which was 21st April. On 1st April, the applicant informed the minister that she would not be able to attend the inquiry on that date for religious reasons, and requested a special hearing. The minister replied on 7th April that it was not possible to alter the date of the inquiry, but that the applicant could be represented at the inquiry. The applicant did not reply. At the inquiry, neither the applicant nor a representative appeared and the order was confirmed by the minister. The applicant complained that she had effectively been debarred from attending or being represented at the inquiry, and so had not had the opportunity to be heard. Her application for an order that the compulsory purchase order be quashed was refused. On appeal, *held*, it was an elementary principle of natural justice that the person conducting the inquiry should see that everything was done fairly. It was, however, a serious matter to adjourn an inquiry for one objector, as so many people were concerned. The minister had acted reasonably in arranging for the inquiry to be held on the day in question, especially since the objection was not raised until some time after the applicant had been informed, and the applicant had not made it clear that no one would attend on her behalf. There had been no want of natural justice and the appeal would be dismissed.

OSTREICHER V SECRETARY OF STATE FOR THE ENVIRONMENT [1978] 3 All ER 82 (Court of Appeal: LORD DENNING MR, SHAW and WALLER LJJ). Decision of Sir Douglas Frank QC sitting as a deputy High Court judge [1978] 1 All ER 591, 1977 Halsbury's Abr para. 443 affirmed.

11   —— —— **public inquiry—applicant denied opportunity to consider relevant documents**

A company applied to the local planning authority for planning permission to use land as a car park. Permission was refused and the company appealed to the Secretary of State. The authority refused to supply the company with copies of relevant documents before the inquiry. At the inquiry, the inspector refused the company's request for an adjournment to study the documents but allowed instead an extended lunch break. The Secretary of State dismissed the appeal and the company subsequently contended that his decision should be quashed on the ground that there had been a breach of procedural rules at the inquiry or alternatively a breach of natural justice. *Held*, (i) the authority was in breach of the inquiries procedure rules which required it to allow inspection of the documents before the inquiry; (ii) the inspector was in breach of the procedure rules and the rules of natural justice by refusing to give the company an adequate opportunity to study the documents at the hearing. There was a breach of natural justice even though there was only a risk that the inspector's refusal to allow a longer adjournment had substantially prejudiced the company's appeal. Accordingly the appeal would be allowed and the Secretary of State's decision quashed.

PERFORMANCE CARS LTD V SECRETARY OF STATE FOR THE ENVIRONMENT (1977) 34 P & CR 92 (Court of Appeal: LORD DENNING MR, BROWNE LJ and SIR JOHN PENNYCUICK). Decision of Sir Douglas Frank QC (1976) 240 EG 51, 1976 Halsbury's Abr para. 2542, reversed. *Hibernian Property Co Ltd v Secretary of State for the Environment* (1973) 27 P & CR 197, approved.

12   —— —— —— **applicant denied opportunity to rebut inspector's evidence**

An application by a firm of contractors for permission to extract gravel from agricultural land was refused by the local planning authority. The applicants appealed and a public inquiry was held. The Minister of Agriculture objected on the ground that extracting gravel and refilling the land would seriously affect the quality of the land for agriculture. Evidence was given by the Minister as to the importance of gravel in supplying moisture to the top soil but no evidence was given whether removal of gravel would disturb the moisture supply. The Secretary of State, following the inspector's recommendations, dismissed the appeal on the ground that removing gravel would adversely affect the moisture supply and reduce the potential yield of the land. The applicants sought an order of certiorari to quash the decision on the ground that there was no evidence to support the inspector's finding regarding soil moisture and that they had not had the opportunity of giving evidence on the matter. *Held*, even if there was sufficient evidence to support the finding, which was extremely doubtful, the Secretary of State was in breach of the rules of natural justice by acting on such evidence without allowing the applicants an opportunity to deal with it.

H. SABEY & CO LTD V SECRETARY OF STATE FOR THE ENVIRONMENT [1978] 1 All ER 586 (Queen's Bench Division: WILLIS J).

13 —————refusal of adjournment—finding of fraud against tax-payer by general commissioners

See *Ottley v Morris (Inspector of Taxes)*, para. 1554.

14 —————refusal of planning permission—applicant unaware of ground of objection

See *Lewis Thirkell Ltd v Secretary of State for the Environment*, para. 2797.

15 ————statutory power to authorise company investigation—exercise of power by Secretary of State—application of principles of natural justice

See *Norwest Holst Ltd v Department of Trade*, para. 357.

16 ———— suspension of local party officers pending inquiry—whether administrative necessity or punishment

In the course of a protracted and disruptive struggle between rival factions for control of a local constituency Labour party, the national executive decided to suspend the officers and committees of the constituency party and to appoint a national officer to run its affairs pending further inquiry and reorganisation. Officers facing suspension applied for injunctions restraining suspension on the ground that the national executive had acted beyond its powers and in denial of natural justice. *Held*, refusing the applications, under the party rules the national executive could suspend the officers and committees of a local party and appoint a national officer to act in their stead. The local party was in a state of chaos and for the mere restoration of order the balance of convenience required that the injuctions be refused. There was a distinction between suspensions effected by way of punishment and suspensions made as a holding operation pending inquiry. The latter were merely a matter of good administration and involved no denial of natural justice.

LEWIS V HEFFER [1978] 3 All ER 354 (Court of Appeal: LORD DENNING MR, ORMROD and GEOFFREY LANE LJJ).

17 ———— value added tax tribunal—jurisdiction

See *Coolisle Ltd v Customs and Excise Comrs*, para. 3071.

18 Parliamentary Commissioner—report

The Parliamentary Commissioner for Administration has published his annual report for 1977: H of C Paper (1977–78) No. 157. The Commissioner states that subject to the Select Committee's agreement he proposes to change his procedures to facilitate the progress of complaints sent to him direct. He proposes that he himself should offer to send such complaints to the constituent's member of parliament stating his willingness to start an investigation should the member wish him to do so. This the Commissioner believes would help to save trouble and lessen the risk of confusion about his ability to help.

ADMIRALTY

Halsbury's Laws of England (4th edn.), Vol. 1, paras. 301–600

19 Action in rem—arrest of vessel—appraisement and sale pendente lite—liability for cost of discharging cargo

A merchant bank made a loan to shipowners to purchase a vessel which was mortgaged as security. When the shipowners failed to pay the sums due under the mortgage, the bank arrested the vessel and successfully applied for an order for her appraisement and sale pendente lite. Under the order, the bank was made absolutely liable for the costs of discharging the cargo; the bank contended that the costs should be borne proportionately by the various cargo-owners. *Held*, as it was impossible to determine the rights and wrongs of the parties before trial, an intermediate course would be adopted and the order modified. Initially the bank would be liable for the costs of discharge but the court should protect any rights the bank might be found to have against the cargo-owners to recover the costs. Accordingly the cargo-owners would be allowed to take away their cargoes only if they paid the costs of discharge or else gave appropriate security for any amount ultimately held to be due from them.

THE MYRTO [1978] Lloyd's Rep 11 (Court of Appeal: LORD DENNING MR, ROSKILL and SHAW LJJ). Order of Brandon J [1977] 2 Lloyd's Rep 243, 1977 Halsbury's Abr para. 2559 varied in part.

20   —— —— caveat—effect

See *Re Aro Co Ltd*, para. 368.

21   —— —— release where security previously given

A collision occurred between a Polish ship and a West German ship carrying a cargo of timber. The cargo was lost and the English cargo-owners commenced an action in rem for damages against the Polish shipowner. On 30th May 1977 a sister-ship of the Polish ship was arrested in England. On 1st June the Polish shipowners paid a sum into a Polish court to constitute their limitation fund in respect of the collision. On 2nd June they gave security for the claim in the form of a written guarantee by their insurers, and the ship was released. They then sought the release of the letter of guarantee under the Merchant Shipping (Liability of Shipowners and Others) Act 1958, s. 5. Section 5 provides that where a ship is arrested in connection with a claim which appears to the court to be founded on a liability to which a limit is set by the Merchant Shipping Act 1894, s. 503, or security is given to prevent or obtain release from such an arrest, the court may order the release of the ship or security if certain conditions are fulfilled. One of the conditions is that satisfactory security must have previously been given in respect of the liability. *Held*, in order to fall within s. 5, the claim had to be one founded on a liability to which a limit was set by s. 503. The right of shipowners to limit their liability was conditional on the relevant occurrence having taken place without their actual fault or privity, and the burden of proof was on the shipowners. It was not enough for them to show that they had a prima facie or a reasonably arguable case that they were not at fault, and the Polish shipowners had not discharged their burden of proof. Thus the claim of the cargo-owners was not one which appeared to the court to be founded on a liability to which a limit was set within the meaning of the Act.

In addition, although the court's power under s. 5 to release a security extended to a written guarantee given by a third party, the payment into court in Poland on 1st June was not "security which had previously been given" within the meaning of s. 5. It had not been given previously to the arrest of the ship in England but only previously to the giving of further security in order to obtain her release from arrest. In order to fall within s. 5, the security had to be given before the arrest of the ship or before the giving of security to avoid such arrest. The Polish shipowners were therefore not entitled to the release of the security.

THE WLADYSLAW LOKOTIEK (1978) Times, 16th June (Queen's Bench Division: BRANDON J).

22   —— —— stay of proceedings—reference to arbitration—release of vessel

The owners of a ruined cargo of sugar began an action in rem against the ship which had carried it for the cargo's value plus interest and costs. The ship was arrested. The shipowner applied for a stay, contending that the dispute should have been referred to arbitration. The cargo-owners counter-claimed that their arbitration agreement was incapable of performance within the meaning of the Arbitration Act

1975, s. 1, and that the stay should be refused as the shipowners were not in a position to satisfy any award made against them. *Held*, (i) although the shipowners were incapable of meeting any award, it was possible that the P and I club of which they were a member could. Since the cargo-owners had failed to show that the club could not, the stay would be granted. However, the shipowners' contentions that the ship should automatically be released upon the grant of a stay, and that no security at all had to be provided for any claim against them, was wrong. The court had a discretion under RSC Ord. 75, r. 13 (4) to refuse to release the ship unless alternative security was provided. It was only proper to release a ship unconditionally where the stay would almost certainly be final and no judgment would subsequently be in need of satisfaction. This was not such a case.

(ii) The arbitration agreement was perfectly capable of performance; it was irrelevant for the purposes of the 1975 Act that a party was unable to satisfy an award made. The vital factor was whether that party was capable of involvement in the proceedings up until the date of award.

THE RENA K [1979] 1 All ER 397 (Queen's Bench Division: BRANDON J). *The Golden Trader* [1975] QB 348, 1974 Halsbury's Abr para. 3013 applied.

23   Jurisdiction—action in rem—power of court to determine beneficial owner

The plaintiffs were the consignees of a cargo of newsprint which was damaged by wetting during the voyage. The plaintiffs issued a writ for damages against the owners of the ship and the vessel was subsequently arrested under s. 3 (4) of the Administration of Justice Act 1956. That section provides that if in any action concerning a ship the person who would be liable in personam was the owner or charterer at the time when the cause of action arose, an action in rem could be invoked against the ship if, at the time the action was brought, the beneficial owner was that same person. At the time when the cargo was damaged the vessel was owned by a Panamanian company but ownership was later transferred to another company with the same parent company as the Panamanian company. The company owning the ship was subsequently purchased by a Singaporean company who transferred ownership of the vessel to another company which they had created. The defendants applied to have the writ and subsequent proceedings set aside on the ground that as the owners of the vessel at the time the action was brought were not the same beneficial owners as at the time the cause of action arose, the court had no jurisdiction. *Held*, s. 3 (4) empowered the court to look behind the registered owner to determine the true beneficial owner. In the present case there was no evidence to prove that the people owning the vessel were the same people who had beneficially owned it when the cause of action arose. Beneficial ownership had changed hands when the Singaporean company purchased the company owning the ship, and the proceedings would accordingly be set aside.

THE AVENTICUM [1978] 1 Lloyd's Rep 184 (Queen's Bench Division: SLYNN J).

AFFILIATION AND LEGITIMATION

Halsbury's Laws of England (4th edn.), Vol. 1, paras. 601–694

24   Article

Affiliation Proceedings, Gregory Knight (a summary of the procedure relating to the making of an affiliation order): 122 Sol Jo 171.

25   Paternity—blood tests

The Blood Tests (Evidence of Paternity) (Amendment) Regulations 1978, S.I. 1978 No. 1266 (in force on 25th September 1978), increase the fees payable under the Blood Tests (Evidence of Paternity) Regulations 1971 in respect of blood tests carried out for the purpose of determining paternity in civil proceedings.

AGENCY

Halsbury's Laws of England (4th edn.), Vol. 1, paras. 701–877

26   **Articles**

Commercial Agents: The Law Commission Report (a look at the Report on the Proposed EEC Directive on the Law relating to Commercial Agents (Cmnd 6948)): 128 NLJ 416.

Equity and Planning, R. N. D. Hamilton (accountability of purchaser of land who purports to act as agent for vendor: *English v Dedham Vale Properties* [1978] 1 All ER 382, 1977 Halsbury's Abr para. 22): 122 Sol Jo 751.

27   **Agent—authority—estate agent—authority to conclude tenancy agreement**

See *Walsh v Griffith Jones*, para. 1727.

28   **—— —— master of ship—authority to make salvage contract**

See *The Unique Mariner*, para. 2637.

29   **—— default of agent—acceptance of bribe—remedies of principal**

Malaysia

A property speculator and the agent of a housing society agreed that the former should acquire fifty-nine acres of land then cheaply available and resell it to the society at a vast profit. The agent was to pretend no knowledge of the speculator's acquisition when the land was resold. He received a substantial bribe for his compliance. The fraud was discovered and the agent convicted on two charges of corruption under Malaysian law. The housing society then instituted civil proceedings against him, claiming both the amount of the bribe as money had and received, and damages for its financial loss. The Federal Court of Malaysia found in the society's favour on both counts. On the agent's appeal, *held*, at common law a principal could claim either damages or the amount of the bribe, but not both. Malaysian statute recognised this right but did not extend it. Accordingly, the society had to elect at the time judgment was to be entered between its claim for the amount of the bribe and its claim for damages.

MAHESAN v MALAYSIA GOVERNMENT OFFICERS' CO-OPERATIVE HOUSING SOCIETY LTD [1978] 2 All ER 405 (Privy Council: LORD DIPLOCK, LORD EDMUND-DAVIES and LORD SCARMAN). *United Australia Ltd v Barclays Bank Ltd* [1941] AC 1, HL applied.

30   **—— fact of agency not disclosed—personal liability of agent**

In the correspondence which constituted the contract between a chartered civil engineer and a building company the engineer had not mentioned that he was acting on behalf of the owners of a property although the letters sent and received stated his professional qualifications. In an action by the building company the engineer was held to be personally liable. Although it was clear that he was not acting beneficially on his own account but had been professionally engaged on behalf of a client, that did not exclude his being personally liable. It was possible for a person who was in fact an agent, in that he had a principal standing behind him, to contract in such a way that he became personally liable to the other party. On the correspondence as it stood it was impossible to say that the engineer was acting as agent and the plaintiff was entitled to assume that he was not.

SIKA CONTRACTS LTD v GILL (1978) Times, 27th April (Queen's Bench Division: KERR J).

31   **—— insurance broker—interim insurance—whether broker agent of insurance company**

See *Stockton v Mason*, para. 1648.

32   —— liability of agent—insurance—failure to notify insured of cancellation of policy

See *Cherry Ltd v Allied Insurance Brokers Ltd*, para. 1646.

33   —— —— —— insured relying on agent to obtain full cover

See *Fine's Flowers Ltd v General Accident Assurance Company of Canada*, para. 1644.

34   —— powers of agent—receiver of company as agent—power to convey company property after liquidation

See *Sowman v David Samuel Trust Ltd (in liquidation)*, para. 2305.

AGRICULTURE

Halsbury's Laws of England (4th edn.), Vol. 1, paras. 1001–1853

35   **Article**

Farm Tenancy Succession, Andrew Densham (review of the tenancy succession provisions of the Agriculture (Miscellaneous Provisions) Act 1976): 247 EG 881.

36   **Agricultural holding—application for succession to tenancy of deceased tenant—Agricultural Land Tribunal decision**

HULME V EARL OF AYLESFORD AND TRUSTEES OF EARL OF AYLESFORD'S SETTLEMENT (1978) 245 EG 851: K. S. W. Mellor QC (application under Agriculture (Miscellaneous Provisions) Act 1976, s. 20, by widow and son of deceased tenant for tribunal's direction entitling them jointly and severally to tenancy; application by landlords for consent to notice to quit; landlords' contention that neither widow nor son eligible as, consequent on the death of the tenant, both were occupiers of a commercial unit within s. 18 (2) (c) rejected; status determined on death of tenant, and commercial unit not occupied by them prior to tenant's death; widow, however, ineligible as principal source of livelihood not derived from agricultural work on agricultural unit within s. 18 (2) (b) but from marital relationship with tenant; son eligible and suitable; son's application granted; landlords' application on grounds set out in Agricultural Holdings Act 1948, s. 25, dismissed as their case went simply to their financial position and had nothing to do with management of estate).

37   —— compensation to outgoing tenant—calculation

The Agricultural (Calculation of Value for Compensation) Regulations 1978, S.I. 1978 No. 809 (in force on 1st July 1978), make provision in respect of England and Wales for calculating the compensation payable to the outgoing tenant of an agricultural holding in respect of the improvements and other matters set out in the Fourth Schedule of the Agricultural Holdings Act 1948, as amended.

38   —— meaning—European Communities

See *Società Santa Anna Azienda Avicola v Instituto Nazionale della Previdenza Sociale* and *Servizio Contributi Agricoli Unificati*, para. 60.

39   —— notices—arbitration on notices

The Agricultural Holdings (Arbitration on Notices) Order 1978, S.I. 1978 No. 257 (in force 7th April 1978), specifies new questions to be determined by arbitration and confers additional powers on the arbitrator as a result of the coming into force of the Agricultural Holdings (Notices to Quit) Act 1977.

The Agriculture (Notices to Remedy and Notices to Quit) Order 1964 and the Agriculture (Notices to Quit) (Miscellaneous Provisions) Order 1972 are revoked.

40 ———— **forms of notices to remedy**

The Agriculture (Forms of Notices to Remedy) Regulations 1978, S.I. 1978 No. 258 (in force 7th April 1978), re-enact with amendments the Agriculture (Forms of Notices to Remedy) Regulations 1964. The forms are substantially the same but attention is drawn to the increased opportunities for arbitration as a result of the coming into force of the Agricultural Holdings (Arbitration on Notices) Order 1978, para. 39.

41 ———— **rent—whether rent paid by due date**

See *Beevers v Mason*, para. 1743.

42 ———— **term of agreement that tenant will not serve counter-notice—validity**

The terms of an agricultural lease precluded the tenant from serving a counter-notice under the Agricultral Holdings Act 1948, s. 24 (1) in the event of the landlords' serving notice to quit under s. 3 (1). When the landlords served notice upon the expiry of the tenancy, the tenant purported to serve a counter-notice. The former contended the counter-notice was ineffective because it was in breach of the lease. *Held*, the wording of s. 24 (1) was capable of one meaning only: it clearly provided that service of a counter-notice suspended the operation of a notice to quit until an Agricultural Land Tribunal had consented to its operation. Any agreement denying the effect of the provision was unenforceable. Any other interpretation would lead to the wholesale thwarting of Parliament's intention that tenant farmers should have a degree of security of tenure.

JOHNSON v MORETON [1978] 3 All ER 37 (House of Lords: LORD SALMON, LORD HAILSHAM OF ST MARYLEBONE, LORD SIMON OF GLAISDALE, LORD EDMOND-DAVIES and LORD RUSSELL OF KILLOWEN). Decision of Court of Appeal (1977) Times, 23rd February, 1977 Halsbury's Abr para. 34 affirmed.

43 **Agricultural Holdings Act 1948—variation**

The Agricultural Holdings Act 1948 (Variation of Fourth Schedule) Order 1978, S.I. 1978 No. 742 (in force on 1st July 1978) makes certain amendments and an addition to the Fourth Schedule to the Agricultural Holdings Act 1948. The Fourth Schedule lists the improvements and other matters for which a tenant of an agricultural holding may be entitled to compensation at the termination of the tenancy without requiring the consent of the landlord before the improvements are made.

44 **Agricultural Holdings (Notices to Quit) Act 1977—commencement**

The Agricultural Holdings (Notices to Quit) Act 1977 (Commencement) Order 1978, S.I. 1978 No. 256, brought the whole Act into force on 7th April 1978.

For provisions of the 1977 Act see 1977 Halsbury's Abr para. 35.

45 **Agricultural Land Tribunals—rules**

The Agricultural Land Tribunals (Rules) Order 1978, S.I. 1978 No. 259 (in force 7th April 1978), re-enacts with amendments necessitated by the coming into force of the Agricultural Holdings (Notices to Quit) Act 1977, the Agricultural Land Tribunals and Notices to Quit Order 1959.

46 **Agricultural levy—reliefs**

The Agricultural Levy Reliefs (Frozen Beef and Veal) Order 1978, S.I. 1978 No. 194 (in force on 14th February 1978), requires the Minister of Agriculture, Fisheries and Food to allocate the United Kingdom's share of a quota for the levy-free import of frozen beef and veal under the provisions of EEC Council Regulation 2861/77. Entitlement to relief is determined by the issue of licences.

47   Agricultural worker—accommodation provided by employer— registration of rent under Rent (Agriculture) Act 1976

See para. 1755.

48   —— —— security of tenure—meaning of agricultural work

The defendant's job as a gamekeeper involved keeping and rearing pheasants for sport. He appealed against an order for possession of his cottage in favour of his employer, contending that he was employed in agriculture and was therefore entitled to protection under the Rent (Agriculture) Act 1976. Section 1 of the Act provided for security of tenure for agricultural workers who were employed in the keeping of livestock for the production of food, wool, skins or fur for carrying on any agricultural activity. The defendant argued that the definition was not meant to be exhaustive and that as keeping pheasants was part of the rural scene it fell within the definition. *Held*, the definition was designed to include all activities involved in farming land for commercial purposes. As the pheasants were kept purely for sport, the defendant was employed in a rural activity but not an agricultural one. The appeal would be dismissed.

LORD GLENDYNE V RAPLEY [1978] 2 All ER 110 (Court of Appeal: LORD SCARMAN, MEGAW and ROSKILL LJJ).

49

A gamekeeper whose job was to rear pheasants for sport appealed against an order granting possession of his cottage to his employer. He contended that he was entitled to security of tenure as an agricultural worker under the Rent (Agriculture) Act 1976. Section 1 of the Act defines agriculture as including the keeping and breeding of livestock which in turn included any animal kept for the production of food or for the purpose of its use in any agricultural activity. *Held*, recent authority on the matter was to be found in the case of *Lord Glendyne v Rapley*. There, the Court of Appeal held that the definition of agriculture was not designed to cover every rural activity but included all activities involving farming land for commercial purposes. The Court of Appeal further held that pheasants were kept for sport and as a gamekeeper's occupation was to promote a field sport rather than agriculture, he was not protected by the Act. The gamekeeper's argument that his case was distinguishable from the authority on the ground that his employer shot pheasant as a commercial venture rather than a sport, could not be upheld. The appeal would be dismissed.

EARL OF NORMANTON V GILES (1978) 248 Estates Gazette 869 (Court of Appeal: STEPHENSON and LAWTON LJJ). *Lord Glendyne v Rapley* [1978] 2 All ER 110, CA, para. 48 applied.

50   Agriculture (Miscellaneous Provisions) Act 1968—amendment

The Agriculture (Miscellaneous Provisions) Act 1968 (Amendment) Regulations 1979, S.I. 1979 No. 25 (in force on 9th February 1979), amend the 1968 Act by substituting references to "area" and "areas" for references to "acreage" and "acreages" in s. 40 (3) (c), which provides for specifying the minimum amount of crop in respect of which payments may be made, and the manner in which the amounts of crop are to be determined for the purposes of a scheme made under s. 40 (1), (2).

51   Beef—premiums

See paras. 62, 63.

52   Butter and cream—subsidy

See paras. 66, 67.

53   Cereals Marketing Act 1965—amendment

The Cereals Marketing Act 1965 (Amendment) Regulations 1979, S.I. 1979 No. 26 (in force on 9th February 1979), further amend the Cereals Marketing Act 1965 by substituting references to "area" for references to "acreage" in ss. 13 (4), 15 (1) and 16 (6) (a), which provide for the specification of a rate of levy and its imposition.

54   Coffee and chicory extracts—metric quantities and quantity marking

See para. 3102.

55   Common agricultural policy—advance fixing of export refunds— advance payment

In an action against the EC Commission by malt producers for damages to compensate for losses they claimed to have suffered as a result of EEC Commission Regulation 413/76 which altered the system for advance fixing and payment of export refunds, the question arose as to the rights of the holder of an export licence fixing the refund in advance. *Held*, the aim of the rules relating to advance fixing of refunds was to enable exporters to be certain of the amount of the refund for which they might qualify when the export took place, in so far as they were actually carried out before the expiry of the export licence. A system of advance payment of export refunds was set up by EEC Commission Regulations 441/69 in respect of various products, including malt, in order to ensure equality of treatment with products originating in third countries. The rules governing advance fixing and advance payment pursued separate aims and could not be assimilated to one another. Although the holder of an export licence fixing the refund in advance had an established right to receive the refund when the export was carried out, in so far as it actually took place under the conditions laid down by the Community rules, he could not acquire from the issue of that licence a right to have the system for advance payment of the refund applied to him in accordance with the rules in force on the day of issue of the licence. In the light of conditions on the malt market, the applicants should have been prepared for an alteration in the advance fixing procedure and the applications would be dismissed.

Joined Cases 44–51/77: GROUPEMENT D'INTÉRÊT ECONOMIQUE 'UNION MALT' v EC COMMISSION [1978] ECR 57 (European Court of Justice).

56   —— —— calculation of refund

In the course of a dispute relating to the calculation of export refunds the European Court of Justice was asked to consider the question whether EEC Council Regulation 1380/75, art. 4 (3), read in conjunction with Regulation 2101/75, had to be taken as meaning that the export refund in the sugar sector, which is fixed in national currency for each exporter individually on the basis of a tender, had to be multiplied by the monetary co-efficient fixed by the Commission, which is derived from the percentage used to calculate monetary compensatory amounts. *Held*, in order for the co-efficient to be applied it would be necessary to show that refunds were fixed in units of account. It was clear that they were fixed in national currency and that conversion to units of account only took place when it was necessary to make various tenders comparable.

Case 108/77: HANS-OTTO WAGNER GmbH, AGRARHANDEL KG v HAUPTZOLLAMT HAMBURG-JONAS [1978] ECR 1187 (European Court of Justice).

57   —— —— whether compensation less favourable than right to cancel

Sugar traders had a large number of export licences in which their export refunds were fixed in advance. They alleged that EEC Council Regulation 1583/77, which fixed an amount of compensation payable under such licences if the exchange rate was altered was illegal because it ran contrary to the principle that parties who had obtained advance fixing of refunds should not be adversely affected by alterations. Unlike others engaged in agriculture sugar traders could no longer cancel licences already obtained, but could only claim compensation. *Held*, the payment of compensation was not of itself less favourable than the right to cancel and therefore the traders could claim compensation only in respect of the difference between the old exchange rate and the new.

Case 112/77: AUGUST TÖPFER & Co GmbH v EC COMMISSION [1978] ECR 1019 (European Court of Justice).

58 —— agricultural feeding stuffs—method of analysis

EEC Commission Directive 78/633 establishes Community methods of analysis for the official control of feeding stuffs to be brought into force not later than 1st January 1979.

59 —— Agricultural Guarantee and Guidance Fund—financing of interventions

EEC Council Regulation 1883/78 lays down general rules for the financing of interventions by the guarantee section of the Agricultural Guarantee and Guidance Fund.

60 —— agricultural holding—meaning

A company which carried on a business of raising poultry and laying-hens brought an action for a declaration of its right to be classified for the purpose of social security contributions as an agricultural and not an industrial undertaking. The national court asked the European Court of Justice to interpret the meaning of the term "agricultural holding". *Held*, it was impossible to find in the provisions of the EEC Treaty or in the rules of secondary Community law any general uniform Community definition of "agricultural holding" universally applicable to all the provisions laid down by law relating to agricultural production.

Case 85/77: SOCIETÀ SANTA ANNA AZIENDA AVICOLA v INSTITUTO NAZIONALE DELLA PREVIDENZA SOCIALE and SERVIZIO CONTRIBUTI AGRICOLI UNIFICATI [1978] 3 CMLR 67 (European Court of Justice).

61 —— agricultural statistics—method of analysis—Community typology of agricultural holdings

EEC Commission Decision 78/463 introduces a system of Community typology for the many different types of agricultural holdings to facilitate the analysis of statistics concerning their income and business operations. The system establishes a uniform classification of holdings, based on size and the type of farming carried on.

62 —— beef and veal—beef premium payments—protection

The Beef Premiums (Protection of Payments) Order 1978, S.I. 1978 No. 17 (in force for the purposes of art. 13 (power to require marking of animals brought into the United Kingdom) on 16th January 1978 and for all other purposes on 1st February 1978), re-enacts with modifications the Beef Premiums (Protection of Payments) Order 1975, 1975 Halsbury's Abr para. 60. It provides for the protection of premium payments under EEC arrangements for the regulation of the market in beef. The general supervision of the protection provisions, including arrangements for the examination, certification and marking of produce, continues to be undertaken by the Intervention Board for Agricultural Produce.

63 —— —— —— recovery powers

The Beef Premiums (Recovery Powers) Regulations 1978, S.I. 1978 No. 18 (in force on 1st February 1978), enable the Intervention Board for Agricultural Produce to recover a beef premium payment made under EEC arrangements if, contrary to the Beef Premiums (Protection of Payments) Order 1978, para. 62, the animal in respect of which it was paid has been retained in possession, sold, exported or used for breeding or milking.

64　　　　　———— monetary compensatory amounts

In 1971 the plaintiff meat importers entered into contracts with South American suppliers for the purchase and shipment to Italy of frozen meat. The price was to be paid by irrevocable banker's documentary credits. The earliest date of actual payment was December 1971 and the latest March 1972. The goods arrived and were cleared through customs in February and March 1972. In January 1972, monetary compensatory amounts were extended to Italy. The Italian customs authority levied compensatory amounts on the goods and the plaintiffs brought proceedings to recover the amounts paid. Questions were referred to the European Court of Justice concerning the applicability of monetary compensatory amounts. *Held*, since Italy had adopted for its currency an exchange rate exceeding the margins of fluctuation permitted by international agreement, the conditions for the application of compensatory amounts existed. The Commission was thus entitled to enact legislation establishing compensatory amounts applying to Italy. As to the period of reference for deciding whether compensatory amounts applied and what their amount was to be, reference should be made to each commercial operation individually; that is, to the date of import or export. Compensatory amounts were imposed by Community law enforceable in all member states and member states were not authorised to enact domestic legislation laying down criteria for the application of compensatory amounts to contracts made before the date when compensatory amounts were extended to that member state. As to the rules for payment in cases where an irrevocable credit had been opened to the exporter, the answer depended on the actual arrangements made in each case pursuant to the domestic law which applied to them.

　　Case 94/77: Fratelli Zerbone SNC v Amministrazione delle Finanze dello Stato [1978] ECR 99 (European Court of Justice).

65　　　　EEC Commission Regulation 2424/76 increased the levels of monetary compensatory amounts payable in respect of beef exported from the United Kingdom. Beef exporters commenced proceedings, claiming that the regulation did not apply to exports effected in pursuance of contracts concluded prior to the date of its promulgation; or alternatively, that it was invalid in relation to such exports. The matter was referred to the European Court of Justice. *Held*, in the absence of express provision to the contrary, the amounts to be levied were those fixed by rules in force at the moment of export, whatever the date of the contract. As there was no provision which exempted existing contracts from the charges, the regulation applied to contracts concluded prior to its promulgation. Furthermore, as the exporters were aware of the uncertainty of the situation, they had no legitimate expectations that the previous levels could be maintained. As the Commission had every right to fix new levels if the old ones were considered impracticable, the regulation was valid.

　　Case 146/77: British Beef Co Ltd v Intervention Board for Agricultural Produce [1978] 3 CMLR 47, ECJ (European Court of Justice).

66　　　　———— butter and cream—subsidy

The Butter Subsidy (Protection of Community Arrangements) Regulations 1978, S.I. 1978 No. 214 (in force on 20th March 1978), enable subsidy paid on butter under EEC Council Regulation 880/77 to be recovered where the butter has been exported from the United Kingdom or has, without the authority of the Intervention Board for Agricultural Produce, been used for manufacture.

67　　　　The Butter Subsidy (Protection of Community Arrangements) (Amendment) Regulations 1978, S.I. 1978 No. 960 (in force on 13th July 1978), amend the definition of "subsidy payment" in the Butter Subsidy (Protection of Community Arrangements) Regulations 1978, para. 66, by adding a reference to EEC Council Regulation 880/77 on the granting of a consumer subsidy for butter.

68   The Butter Subsidy (Protection of Community Arrangements) (Amendment No.
2) Regulations 1978, S.I. 1978 No. 1592 (in force on 9th November 1978), further
amend the definition of "subsidy payment" in the Butter Subsidy (Protection of
Community Arrangements) Regulations 1978, para. 66, by adding a reference to
EEC Council Regulation 2574/78, which has further amended Regulation 880/77
on the granting of a consumer subsidy for butter.

69   ──── **cereals—compound feeding stuffs—export refunds**

A German company was initially granted export refunds (in the form of levy free
import licences) on compound animal feeding-stuffs which contained only 2 per
cent of one of the products coming under the Community rules relating to the cereal
market as laid down in EEC Council Reg. 19. In proceedings by the German
authorities for the revocation of the export refunds the German court asked the
European Court whether under the system applicable to this class of feeding-stuffs
(laid down by EEC Council Reg. 116/64 and EEC Commission Reg. 171/64) the
refunds on such feeding-stuffs were related to the proportion in the mixture of
products coming under Reg. 19 or was it sufficient for the grant of the full refund if
only one product coming under Reg. 19 was contained therein and then only in very
small proportions. *Held*, the refund had to be proportionate to the amount of the
basic products subject to an organisation of the market in the composition of the
compound feeding-stuffs. A refund on the export of a compound feeding-stuff
under the regulations in question could be granted only where cereals or products to
which Reg. 19 applied were contained in the mixture in significant proportions.
    Case 125/76: CREMER v BUNDESANSTALT FÜR LANDWIRTSCHAFTLICHE MARK-
TORDNUNG [1977] ECR 1593 (European Court of Justice).

70   ──── **common organisation of markets—amendment of rules—
principle of protection of legitimate expectation**

See *Hellmut Stimming KG v Commission of the European Communities*, para. 1210.

71   ──── **exports—abolition of monetary compensatory amounts—
transitional provisions**

As from 4th June 1973 the system of monetary compensatory amounts on imports
and exports was in effect abolished by relating the basis of calculation from the
United States dollar to the central currencies of the "snake". However by EEC
Council Regulation 2042/73 the benefit of the former system was extended to
traders who had obtained the issue of export certificates before that date. The
plaintiff had exported various cereals after 4th June in respect of which he had
obtained certificates fixing refunds in advance before that date. In the course of
proceedings relating to the calculation of monetary compensatory amounts the
plaintiff challenged the legality of Reg. 2042/73 as contravening EEC Treaty arts. 7
and 40 by discriminating among traders who had obtained certificates fixing refunds
in advance depending on whether the exports had been made before or after that
date. The former attracted the whole of the compensatory payments of the old
system while the latter were affected by the traders' obligation to cover himself
against exchange risks and the effects of the devaluation of the dollar. *Held*, Reg.
2042/73 did not affect exports prior to 4th June which continued to be governed by
the rules applicable until that date. It constituted a transitional measure benefiting
traders who had obtained advance fixing prior to that date by granting them the
monetary compensatory amounts applicable on 3rd June. Such a transitional
measure could not be regarded as giving favourable treatment to exporters who had
performed their contracts before 4th June 1973.
    Case 27/77: COMPAGNIE CARGILL v OFFICE NATIONAL INTERPROFESSIONNEL DES
CÉRÉALES (ONIC) [1977] ECR 1535 (European Court of Justice).

72   ──── ──── **tax on exports of potatoes—foreseeability by prudent
trader**

After a fall in potato production in the European Communities a tax was imposed on the export of potatoes by EEC Council Regulation 348/76, which came into force almost immediately it was made. The plaintiffs were assessed to tax pursuant to this regulation after exporting potatoes to Sweden. The regulation had not been in force when the plaintiffs had entered into the contract of sale but they had learnt of its possible introduction by hearsay. They had made their calculations on the usual gross profit margin and were subsequently charged tax amounting to only slightly less than the contract selling price. The plaintiffs claimed that the tax amounted "virtually to expropriation" and that Regulation 348/76 had an illegal retroactive effect because it affected contracts concluded before its entry into force. *Held*, in view of the decrease in potato production there was an overriding public interest requiring the tax to be brought into effect immediately. A prudent trader should have foreseen the imposition of the tax, and the plaintiffs were therefore not able to plead legitimate expectation. When converting the tax into national currency the method of calculation used should be that which was less onerous to the taxpayer.

Case 78/77: FIRMA JOHANN LÜHRS v HAUPTZOLLAMT HAMBURG-JONAS [1978] ECR 169 (European Court of Justice).

73 ——— **fruit and vegetables**

EEC Council Regulation 1152/78 amends Regulation 516/77, 1977 Halsbury's Abr para. 58, relating to the common organisation of the market in products processed from fruit and vegetables, by introducing a system of production and to enable competition with the prices charged by major non-member producing countries. EEC Commission Regulation 1530/78 prescribes rules for the application of the system of aid.

74 EEC Council Regulation 1153/78 amends Regulation 2517/69 by lifting the ban on member states granting national aid for the replanting of apple, pear and peach orchards.

75 EEC Council Regulation 1154/78 makes various amendments to Regulations 2601/69 and 1035/72, including provisions dealing with the marketing period for fruit and vegetables and the payment of grant aid to certain producers' organisations.

76 ——— **import and export licences—advance fixing of levies**

EEC Commission Regulation 1624/78 amends Commission Regulation 193/75 laying down common detailed rules for the application of the system of import and export licences and advance fixing certificates for agricultural products.

77 ——— **Intervention Board for Agricultural Produce—power to require evidence of certain activities—persons engaged in activities**

The Common Agricultural Policy (Agricultural Procedure) (Protection of Community Arrangements) (Amendment) Order 1978, S.I. 1978 No. 1660 (in force on 23rd November 1978), provides that requirements under the Common Agricultural Policy (Agricultural Procedure) (Protection of Community Arrangements) (No. 2) Order 1973 as to the production of evidence of certain agricultural activities applies to any person engaged in any such activity, whether as principal or agent.

78 ——— **milk and milk products—measures to improve quality**

EEC Commission Regulation 1271/78 introduces certain measures to improve the quality of milk, including provisions for analysis of raw milk, testing of milking machines and training of qualified personnel.

79 ——— ——— **sale to school children**

EEC Commission Regulations 1057/78 and 1546/78 amend EEC Commission Regulation 1598/77 laying down detailed rules for the sale of milk and certain milk products at reduced prices to school children.

80   —— monetary compensatory amounts—exemption—natural justice clause

Applicants alleged that a decision of the Commission excluding contracts for the purchase of sugar from exemption from the French monetary compensatory amounts had been made in breach of the natural justice clause introduced by EEC Council Regulation 1608/74. That regulation gave member states a discretion to grant such exemption where a contract had been entered into more than three months before the compensation had been fixed. *Held*, the application of the natural justice clause was limited to those cases where the member state had informed the Commission of its intention to make use of it. As no such intention had been expressed in this case there had been no decision of the Commission on which an action could be based.

Case 132/77: Societe pour L'Exportation des Sucres SA v EC Commission [1978] ECR 1061 (European Court of Justice).

81   —— —— whether price of powdered whey dependent on that of skimmed milk

In the course of a dispute concerning a request for the cancellation of notices of assessment, a question was referred to the European Court of Justice as to whether monetary compensatory amounts could apply to the import of powdered whey. *Held*, compensatory amounts could only be charged in respect of products whose price was dependent on the price of products covered by intervention arrangements under the common arrangements of agricultural markets. Thus the question in this case was whether the price of powdered whey was dependent on that of skimmed milk. On the evidence it was clear that it was not and therefore monetary compensatory amounts could not apply to powdered whey.

Case 131/77: Firma Milac, Gross-und Aussenhandel Arnold Nöll v Hauptzollamt Saarbrücken [1978] ECR 1041 (European Court of Justice).

82   —— oils and fats—olive oil—meaning of producers

The relevant Italian intervention agency refused to pay an olive oil subsidy under EEC Council Regulation 136/66 to the manager of an oil-producing undertaking. He had in the year in question leased olive groves where the olives had already ripened and produced olive oil from the olives which he harvested himself. The subsidy was refused on the ground that he was not the "producer" of the olives within the meaning of the regulation since he had acquired the olive groves when the olives were already ripe. Questions were referred to the European Court of Justice on the meaning of "producers of olive oil" in Regulation 136/66. *Held*, Regulation 136/66, which established the common organisation of the market in oils and fats, drew a clear distinction between the cultivation of olive trees and the production of olive oil. The expression "producers of olive oil" must be interpreted as referring to the producers of the processed product, namely olive oil, and the olive oil subsidy for the year in question should therefore be granted to those producers.

Case 36/77: AIMA v Greco [1977] ECR 2059 (European Court of Justice).

83   —— production refunds—discrimination—abolition of refund on one of two products in comparable situations

On the common organisation of the market in cereals EEC Council Reg. 120/67, art. 11 provided for refunds for maize used in the manufacture of both quellmehl and pre-gelatinised starch on the ground that the two products were interchangeable and should therefore be commercially competitive. Subsequently art. 11 was amended by Reg. 1125/74 which, while retaining the refund for starch, abolished the refund for quellmehl on the ground that the opportunities for substituting quellmehl for starch were commercially negligible. German quellmehl producers disputed this view and took action against the German agricultural authority for recovery of unpaid refunds. The German court asked the European Court whether abolition of the refund infringed the prohibition of discrimination in EEC Treaty art. 40 (3) and if it did whether this gave the producers a direct claim to refunds or were measures by Community institutions necessary. *Held*, the prohibition of discrimination in EEC Treaty art. 40 (3) was a specific enunciation of the principle of equality fundamental to Community law. It required that similar situations should not be treated differently unless differentiation was objectively justified. Neither the Council nor the Commission had established that quellmehl and starch were no longer in comparable situations. In view of the length of time during which the two products had been given equality of treatment abolition of the refund for quellmehl was a disregard of the principle of equality and thus illegal.

However it was for the competent institution of the Community to adopt the measures necessary to correct this incompatibility.

Cases 117/76 and 16/77: ALBERT RUCKDESCHEL & CO AND HANSA-LAGERHAUS STRÖH & CO v HAUPTZOLLAMT HAMBURG-ST ANNEN; DIAMALT AG v HAUPTZOLLAMT ITZEHOE [1977] ECR 1753 (European Court of Justice).

The court reached the same conclusion with respect to claims for unpaid refunds where, after a long period of equal treatment the refund for maize groats and meal used for brewing was abolished while that for maize starch was retained. Here too the court felt that the objective circumstances which would have justified alteration of the existing system had not been established.

Cases 124/76 and 20/77: SA MOULINS ET HUILERIES DE PONT-À-MOUSSON v OFFICE NATIONAL INTERPROFESSIONNEL DES CÉRÉALES; SOCIÉTÉ COOPÉRATIVE "PROVIDENCE AGRICOLE DE LA CHAMPAGNE" v OFFICE NATIONAL INTERPROFESSIONNEL DES CÉRÉALES [1977] ECR 1795 (European Court of Justice).

84   —— **records—keeping of records by principals and agents**

The Common Agricultural Policy (Protection of Community Arrangements) (Amendment) Regulations 1978, S.I. 1978 No. 1330 (in force on 5th October 1978), amend the Common Agricultural Policy (Protection of Community Arrangments) Regulations 1973, as amended. Regulations 3 and 5 of the principal regulations provide for the keeping and production of certain records, and these regulations provide that those requirements apply to any person who is engaged in any of the relevant activities whether he is so engaged as principal or agent. They also extend the powers for the protection of the Community support system to cover feedingstuffs containing field beans or peas.

85   —— **sugar—monetary compensatory amounts—validity**

In 1976 the basic regulation applicable to the sugar trade in the European Communities was EEC Council Regulation 3330/74 which laid down quota arrangements for sugar products. Sugar produced over and above the maximum quota could not be disposed of on the internal market but had to be exported to non-member states by the manufacturers. No monetary compensatory amount was payable on such exports. Commission Regulation 458/73 provided a substitution arrangement whereby upon payment of a standard amount, a manufacturer could export sugar produced by other undertakings. Due to subsequent currency margins developing between member states the value of the standard payment varied when expressed in national currencies. The Commission claimed that Regulation 458/73 constituted a deflection in trade and adopted Regulation 101/77 to counteract benefits accruing to traders in countries where the currency had appreciated who assigned their export licences to traders in countries where the currency had depreciated. The Regulation provided that a monetary compensatory amount was payable on sugar exports pursuant to Regulation 3330/74 where customs export formalities were completed in a member state other than that in which the export licence was issued. A French court referred to the European Court for a preliminary ruling on the validity of Regulation 101/77. The questions for the Court were whether Regulation 101/77 constituted an amendment to the general Regulation 3330/74, whether the Commission was empowered to adopt such an amendment without authorisation from the Council and whether Regulation 458/73 should have been repealed. The Court also had to consider whether the Commission was empowered to introduce monetary compensatory amounts on exports of products which were expressly excluded from such arrangements. *Held*, the Commission was empowered to make Regulation 101/77. It did not amend Council Regulation 3330/74, but placed certain limitations on the authorised exports. It was not incompatible with Regulation 458/73 as it did not prohibit the transactions authorised by it, but merely imposed certain charges. Regulation 101/77 had to be adopted during the sugar marketing year in the interests of the Community, but it did not have a retroactive effect.

Case 96/77: SA Ancienne Maison Marcel Bauche v Administration Française des Douanes [1978] ECR 383 (European Court of Justice).

86 —— transitional provisions—quantitative restrictions on import of products not covered by common organisation of the market

In a case concerning restrictions on the import of potatoes in the United Kingdom, the question arose whether those restrictions could survive the end of the transitional period under the Act of Accession on 31st December 1977. The Act of Accession, art. 60 (2), provided that in respect of products not covered by a common organisation of the market, the provisions concerning abolition of quantitative restrictions should not apply until such a common organisation was implemented. It was conceded by the Dutch importer whose potatoes had been refused entry that until 31st December 1977 the restrictions could be justified under art. 60 (2). However, he contended that since art. 60 fell within the transitional measures of the Act of Accession, it came to an end on 31st December 1977 under art. 9 (2). The contrary view was expressed that art. 9 (2) only operated "subject to the dates, time limits and special provisions" provided for in the Act and the part of art. 60 (2) which said that it should apply until the common organisation of the market for the product was implemented, was such a time limit or special provision which kept art. 60 (2) alive notwithstanding art. 9 (2). *Held*, the question would be referred to the European Court of Justice.

Meijer BV v Department of Trade, Ministry of Agriculture, Fisheries and Food and Customs and Excise Commissioners [1978] 2 CMLR 563 (Queen's Bench Division: Donaldson J).

87 —— wine

The Common Agricultural Policy (Wine) Regulations 1978, S.I. 1978 No. 861 (in force on 24th July 1978) provide for the enforcement throughout the United Kingdom of specified EEC Regulations concerned with the production and marketing of wine and related products. The Regulations designate enforcement authorities, prescribe offences and a penalty and provide for specified defences, and largely re-enact with further amendments the Common Agricultural Policy (Wine) Regulations 1973.

88 —— —— monetary compensatory amounts—discretion of Commission

EEC Commission Regulation 2021/75 discontinued monetary compensatory amounts in relation to wine imports into all member states except the Federal Republic of Germany. The European Court of Justice was asked to consider whether the fixing of amounts in respect of only one country was discriminatory and whether the levy of compensatory amounts on imports from countries outside the Community was contrary to the prohibition against charges having an effect equivalent to customs duties. *Held*, the Commission had a wide discretion when considering the grant or levy of monetary compensatory amounts and had satisfied the court that the economic situations of the Federal Republic of Germany and other member states justified different treatments. It did not matter that the reason for this had not been expressly stated since the Commission had in fact retained the previous rule and it was assumed that the reason was the same as that for which it had been introduced originally. Nor were monetary compensatory amounts affected by the prohibition of charges having an effect equivalent to that of customs duties, because the reason for their adoption was to deal with any difficulties raised for the common agricultural policy by monetary instability.

Case 136/77: FIRMA A. RACKE V HAUPTZOLLAMT MAINZ [1978] ECR 1245 (European Court of Justice).

89 Damage by pests—prevention

The Prevention of Damage by Pests (Threshing and Dismantling of Ricks) (Revocation) Regulations 1978, S.I. 1978 No. 1614 (in force on 1st January 1979), revoke the Prevention of Damage by Pests (Threshing and Dismantling of Ricks) Regulations 1950, as amended.

90 Eggs—levy

The Eggs Authority (Rates of Levy) Order 1978, S.I. 1978 No. 389 (in force on 1st April 1978), specifies the rate of levy to be raised in respect of the accounting period beginning 1st April 1978 and ending 31st March 1979 to meet the aggregate of the amounts determined for financing the functions of the Eggs Authority.

91 —— marketing standards

The Eggs (Marketing Standards) (Amendment) Regulations 1978, S.I. 1978 No. 1248 (in force on 20th September 1978), amend the Eggs (Marketing Standards) Regulations 1973 by bringing up to date the Schedule of Community Regulations whose enforcement is provided for in the 1973 Regulations, deleting certain obsolete references and providing that contraventions of the 1973 Regulations shall be dealt with summarily.

92 Farm Capital Grant Scheme

The Farm Capital Grant (Variation) Scheme 1978, S.I. 1978 No. 380 (in force on 16th March 1978), varies further the Farm Capital Grant Scheme 1973 in order to provide for a grant at the rate of 50 per cent of expenditure incurred in cases where a programme of work is considered necessary to restore the productivity of land affected by flooding.

93

The Farm Capital Grant (Variation) (No. 2) Scheme 1978, S.I. 1978 No. 768 (in force on 7th June 1978), varies the Farm Capital Grant Scheme 1973 so as to provide grants at higher rates than at present to facilitate the replacement or reconditioning of buildings or other facilities destroyed or damaged by severe weather conditions during the period 1st October 1977 to 31st March 1978. Applications for the approval of proposals must be received on or after 7th June 1978 and not later than 31st July 1979, and written notification in relation to such destruction or damage must be received on or before 31st July 1978.

94 Fertilisers—sampling and analysis

The Fertilisers (Sampling and Analysis) Regulations 1978, S.I. 1978 No. 1108 (in force on 6th September 1978), supersede, insofar as they apply to fertilisers, certain provisions of the Fertilisers and Feeding Stuffs Regulations 1973 and of the Fertilisers and Feeding Stuffs (Amendment) Regulations 1976. The Regulations prescribe a number of matters required by the Agriculture Act 1970, Part IV and include provisions implementing EEC Commission Decision 77/535 as respects the sampling and analysis of fertilisers.

95 Home-Grown Cereals Authority—levy scheme

The Home-Grown Cereals Authority (Rate of Levy) Order 1978, S.I. 1978 No. 883 (in force on 1st August 1978), specifies the rate of levy to be raised in respect of home-grown wheat, barley and oats for the year starting 1st August 1978 and includes provisions as to the quantity of such wheat, barley and oats in respect of which the levy is to be imposed.

96   Hops—progressive wilt disease

The Progressive Wilt Disease of Hops Order 1978, S.I. 1978 No. 505 (in force on 28th April 1978), supersedes the Progressive Wilt Disease of Hops Order 1965 and requires occupiers to give the Minister of Agriculture, Fisheries and Food notice of the presence, or suspected presence, on their farms of this disease and to destroy dead or dying bines and leaves of hop plants on infected farms. The movement of hop plants is restricted, and other restrictions may be imposed. Failure to comply with the requirements of the Order is an offence punishable on summary conviction by a fine.

97   Horticulture—development

The Farm and Horticulture Development Regulations 1978, S.I. 1978 No. 1086 (in force on 4th September 1978), are made under s. 2 (2) of the European Communities Act 1972. They implement in the United Kingdom the provisions of EEC Council Directive 72/159 on the modernisation of farms, and EEC Council Directive 75/268 on mountain and hill farming in certain less-favoured areas. The Farm and Horticulture Development Regulations 1973 are superseded, except as regards any payment of grant made before 4th September 1978.

98   Livestock—intensive units—welfare

See para. 117.

99   Metrication

The Agriculture Act 1967 (Amendment) Regulations 1978, S.I. 1978 No. 244 (in force on 1st April 1978), amend the 1967 Act by substituting references to areas expressed in metric units for references to areas expressed in imperial units.

100   The Agricultural Holdings (England and Wales) (Amendment) Rules 1978, S.I. 1978 No. 444 (in force on 19th April 1978), amend the Agricultural Holdings (England and Wales) Rules 1948 by substituting references to areas expressed in metric units for references to areas expressed in imperial units.

101   The Agriculture Act 1947 (Amendment) Regulations 1978, S.I. 1978 No. 446 (in force on 19th April 1978), amend certain sections of the 1947 Act by substituting references to areas expressed in metric units for references to areas expressed in imperial units.

102   The Agricultural Holdings Act 1948 (Amendment) Regulations 1978, S.I. 1978 No. 447 (in force on 19th April 1978), amend certain sections of the 1948 Act by substituting references to areas expressed in metric units for references to areas expressed in imperial units.

103   Plant breeders' rights

The Plant Breeders' Rights Regulations 1978, S.I. 1978 No. 294 (in force on 1st April 1978), consolidate, with amendments, the Plant Breeders' Rights Regulations 1969, as amended. They prescribe the form and manner in which applications are to be made for grants of plant breeders' rights. The principal changes from the 1969 regulations are the specification of the plant material required to be delivered or produced in connection with applications for further plant varieties for which plant breeders' rights may be granted.

104   —— application for rights in designated countries

The Plant Breeders' Rights (Applications in Designated Countries) (Amendment) Order 1978, S.I. 1978 No. 1649 (in force on 20th November 1978), further amends the Plant Breeders' Rights (Applications in Designated Countries) Order 1968. The designated countries in respect of applications for plant breeders' rights are now extended.

105   —— fees

The Plant Breeders' Rights (Fees) Regulations 1978, S.I. 1978 No. 295 (in force on 1st April 1978), replace the Plant Breeders' Rights (Fees) Regulations 1977, 1977 Halsbury's Abr para. 99. They prescribe the fees payable to the Controller of Plant Variety Rights in regard to matters arising out of the application for granting and continuance of plant breeders' rights.

106   —— schemes

Schemes have been made prescribing the following plant varieties in respect of which grants of plant breeders' rights may be made:

	Relevant Statutory Instruments (1978)
Broad Beans and Field Beans	297
Brussels Sprouts	298
Cabbages	299
Celery (including Celeriac)	300
Fenugreek	301
Lupins	302
Maize	303
Marrows	304
Red Fescue (including Chewings Fescue)	305
Turnips	306
Velvet bent, Red top, Creeping bent and Brown top	307
Wood Meadow-Grass, Swamp Meadow-Grass, Smooth Stalked Meadow-Grass and Rough Stalked Meadow-Grass	308

107   Plant Varieties and Seeds Act 1964—commencement

The Plant Varieties and Seeds Act 1964 (Commencement No. 4) Order 1978, S.I. 1978 No. 1002 brings into force on 1st July 1979, s. 31 of the Plant Varieties and Seeds Act 1964 which provides for the repeal of the enactments listed in Sch. 6 to the Act.

108   —— repeals

The Plant Varieties and Seeds Act 1964 (Repeals) (Appointed Day) Order 1978, S.I. 1978 No. 1003, appoints 1st September 1978 as the day for the coming into force of the repeal of s. 32 of the Plant Varieties and Seeds Act 1964 and s. 2 (4) (a) of the Trade Descriptions Act 1968.

109   Potatoes—metric quantities and quantity marking

See para. 3107.

110   —— seed potatoes

The Seed Potatoes Regulations 1978, S.I. 1978 No. 215 (in force on 22nd March 1978), replace the Seed Potatoes Regulations 1963, which cease to have effect on 1st July 1978 in relation to seed potatoes being basic seed potatoes or certified seed potatoes and on 1st July 1979 in relation to any other seed potatoes. The regulations regulate the marketing of seed potatoes in Great Britain, but exclude seed potatoes used in scientific investigation or selection processes.

111 —— **fees**

The Seed Potatoes (Fees) Regulations 1978, S.I. 1978 No. 428 (in force on 13th April 1978), prescribe fees in respect of matters arising under the Seed Potatoes Regulations 1978, para. 110

112 Seeds—fees

The Seeds (National Lists of Varieties) (Fees) Regulations 1978, S.I. 1978 No. 296 (in force on 1st April 1978), replace the Seeds (National Lists of Varieties) (Fees) Regulations 1977, 1977 Halsbury's Abr para. 110. They prescribe fees in respect of matters arising under the Seeds (National Lists of Varieties) Regulations 1973. Provision is made for mitigation of fees for tests of a plant variety where that variety is the subject of an application for a grant of plant breeders' rights and fees for tests are being charged in respect of it in accordance with the Plant Breeders' Rights (Fees) Regulations 1978, para. 105.

113 The Seeds (Fees) Regulations 1978, S.I. 1978 No. 1010 (in force on 1st August 1978), supersede the Seeds (Fees) Regulations 1977, 1977 Halsbury's Abr para. 110.

The Regulations prescribe fees in respect of matters arising under the Vegetable Seeds Regulations 1975, the Cereal Seeds Regulations 1976, the Fodder Plant Seeds Regulations 1976, the Beet Seeds Regulations 1976, the Oil and Fibre Plant Seeds Regulations 1976 and the Seeds (Registration and Licensing) Regulations 1974, or any regulations amending or superseding any of those regulations.

114 Sugar beet—research and education

The Sugar Beet (Research and Education) Order 1978, S.I. 1978 No. 320 (in force on 1st April 1978), provides for the assessment and collection of contributions towards the programme of research and education for the year beginning 1st April 1978 from the British Sugar Corporation Ltd and growers of home-grown beet.

115 Tractors—approval of agricultural or forestry tractors—fees

The Agricultural or Forestry Tractors (Type Approval) (Fees) (Amendment) Regulations 1978, S.I. 1978 No. 62 (in force on 16th February 1978), amend the Agricultural or Forestry Tractors (Type Approval) (Fees) Regulations 1976, 1976 Halsbury's Abr para. 100, Sch. 1, which sets out the standard scale of fees for tests, and Sch. 2, which sets out the fees for the issue of documents, providing for an increase in all the fees. The Regulations also prescribe fees for the testing of agricultural or forestry tractors in connection with the type approval of such tractors for the purpose of Community Directives relating to braking devices and passenger seats, provision having been made for such type approval in the Agricultural or Forestry Tractors (Type Approval) (Amendment) Regulations 1976, 1976 Halsbury's Abr para. 99.

116 Wine—pre-packaging and labelling

See para. 3113.

ANIMALS

Halsbury's Laws of England (4th edn.), Vol. 2, paras. 201–497

117 Agricultural livestock—intensive units—welfare

The Welfare of Livestock (Intensive Units) Regulations 1978, S.I. 1978 No. 1800 (in force on 1st January 1979), make provision for the welfare of agricultural livestock kept in intensive units. The Regulations require daily inspections to be made to safeguard livestock in the units.

118   Diseases of animals—bees—importation

The Importation of Bees Order 1978, S.I. 1978 No. 683 (in force on 1st July 1978) prohibits the importation into Great Britain of bees in fixed-comb hives and bees which have not been certified to be free from disease by the responsible department of their country of origin. The importation of bees from the Isle of Man and Jersey is not affected.

119   —— cattle—brucellosis

The Brucellosis (England and Wales) Order 1978, S.I. 1978 No. 1480 (in force on 1st November 1978), which supersedes the Brucellosis (England and Wales) Order 1977, 1977 Halsbury's Abr para. 126, and subsequent orders, consolidates existing eradication and attested areas and declares certain new areas with effect from either 1st March 1979 or 1st November 1979. The Order sets out provisions which apply in such areas, including a prohibition on the movement of bovine animals into those areas, designed to prevent the introduction or spreading of brucellosis. The Minister or Secretary of State is enabled to require the slaughter on payment of compensation, of any animal infected or suspected of being so and to take any necessary incidental measures.

120   The Brucellosis (England and Wales) (Amendment) Order 1978, S.I. 1978 No. 541 (in force on 18th April 1978 except for art. 4 (2), which comes into force on 1st November 1978), further amends the Brucellosis (England and Wales) Order 1977, 1977 Halsbury's Abr paras. 126, 131. The order declares new eradication areas, consolidates Sch. 1, Parts I, II and III of the principal Order and adds certain livestock markets to the appropriate eradication areas.

This order has been revoked; see para. 119.

121   The Brucellosis (England and Wales) (Amendment) (No. 2) Order 1978, S.I. 1978 No. 689 (in force on 26th May 1978), amends the Brucellosis (England and Wales) Order 1977, 1977 Halsbury's Abr para. 126, as amended, in order to implement certain provisions of EEC Council Directive 78/52 relating to the accelerated eradication of brucellosis. New eradication areas are also declared, comprising all those parts of England and Wales which are not already included in an eradication or attested area.

This order has been revoked; see para. 119.

122   The Brucellosis Incentive Payments (Amendment) Scheme 1978, S.I. 1978 No. 594 (in force on 18th May 1978), amends the Brucellosis Incentive Payments Scheme 1977, 1977 Halsbury's Abr para. 132, to make it clear that incentive payments may only be recovered if it is established as a fact that they have been wrongly made.

123   —— —— brucellosis   and   tuberculosis—compensation   for slaughter

The Brucellosis and Tuberculosis (England and Wales) Compensation Order 1978, S.I. 1978 No. 1483 (in force on 8th November 1978), revokes and substantially re-enacts the Tuberculosis (Compensation) Order 1964, as amended, and the Brucellosis (England and Wales) Compensation Order 1972, as amended, and prescribes a scale of compensation for cattle slaughtered by order of the Minister or Secretary of State under the Diseases of Animals Act 1950, s. 17, in relation to their market value. The Order also sets out the method for the determination of the market value of animals.

124   —— —— enzootic bovine leukosis

The Enzootic Bovine Leukosis Order 1978, S.I. 1978 No. 975 (in force on 15th July 1978), applies the diseases of Animals Act 1950, which relates to the slaughter of animals on account of disease, to enzootic bovine leukosis and prescribes the notice to be served on the owner or the person in charge of the bovine animal which is intended to be slaughtered.

125 The Enzootic Bovine Leukosis (Compensation) Order 1978, S.I. 1978 No. 976 (in force on 15th July 1978), provides that the amount of compensation which has to be paid under the Diseases of Animals Act 1950, s. 17 (3), in respect of a bovine animal slaughtered on account of enzootic bovine leukosis shall be an amount equal to its market value.

126 —— **disinfectants**

The Diseases of Animals (Approved Disinfectants) Order 1978, S.I. 1978 No. 32 (in force on 31st January 1978), revokes and replaces the Diseases of Animals (Approved Disinfectants) Order 1972, as amended. The Order specifies disinfectants approved for use for the purposes of the Foot-and-Mouth Disease Orders, the Fowl Pest Orders, the Tuberculosis Orders and the Swine Vesicular Disease Order, or for use under general orders made under the Diseases of Animals Act 1950 in which there is a requirement for disinfection. The Order also provides for the testing of disinfectants and the marking of containers. Inspectors are empowered to take samples and by notice to require a particular method of disinfection.

127 The Diseases of Animals (Approved Disinfectants) (Amendment) Order 1979, S.I. 1979 No. 37 (in force on 31st January 1979), further amends the Diseases of Animals (Approved Disinfectants) Order 1978, 1978 Halsbury's Abridgment para. 126, by adding to the list of approved disinfectants specified newly approved disinfectants and by deleting certain disinfectants from the list. The disinfectants deleted may, however, continue to be used as approved disinfectants until 30th June 1979.

128 The Diseases of Animals (Fees for the Testing of Disinfectants) Order 1978, S.I. 1978 No. 708 (in force on 13th June 1978), replaces the Diseases of Animals (Fees for the Testing of Disinfectants) Order 1976, 1976 Halsbury's Abr para. 119. It prescribes revised fees payable for the testing of disinfectants for the purpose of determining their suitability for listing as approved disinfectants in the Diseases of Animals (Approved Disinfectants) Order 1978, para. 126.

129 The Diseases of Animals (Approved Disinfectants) (Amendment) Order 1978, S.I. 1978 No. 934 (in force on 25th July 1978), revokes and re-enacts with amendments the list of disinfectants approved in the Diseases of Animals (Approved Disinfectants) Order 1978, para. 126.

130 —— **export of animals and meat—export health certificates**

The Diseases of Animals (Export Health Certificates) Order 1978, S.I. 1978 No. 597 (in force on 9th May 1978), prohibits the exportation of bovine animals, swine, fresh meat and fresh poultry meat from Great Britain to other EEC member states unless an appropriate health certificate is in force. An appropriate health certificate is one in a form prescribed by the relevant EEC Directives, which are Council Directives 64/432, 64/433 and 71/118. See also Press Notice dated 19th April 1978 issued by the Ministry of Agriculture, Fisheries and Food.

131 —— **fees**

The Diseases of Animals (Miscellaneous Fees) Order 1978, S.I. 1978 No. 1188 (in force on 1st September 1978), revokes and re-enacts the Diseases of Animals (Miscellaneous Fees) Order 1976, as varied. Most of the fees payable have been increased and are payable to the Minister of Agriculture, Fisheries and Food or the Secretaries of State for Scotland and Wales.

132 —— **import of animals—responsible local authority**

The Designation of Local Authority (Southampton Port Health District) Order 1978, S.I. 1978 No. 163 (in force on 1st April 1978), makes the Southampton Port Health Authority (which is the Southampton District Council) the local authority in respect of the Southampton Port Health District for the purposes of the provisions of the Diseases of Animals Act 1950 which relate to imported animals.

133　　—— warble fly

The Warble Fly (England and Wales) Order 1978, S.I. 1978 No. 1197 (in force on 1st September 1978), makes infestation of cattle with the larva of the warble fly a disease for most purposes of the Diseases of Animals Act 1950, and makes provision for the inspection and treatment of affected cattle.

134　　Dogs—byelaw banning dogs from parks—validity

See *Burnley Borough Council v England*, para. 1802.

135　　Endangered Species (Import and Export) Act 1976—modification

The Endangered Species (Import and Export) Act 1976 (Modification) Order 1978, S.I. 1978 No. 1280 (in force on 29th September 1978), modifies the schedules to the 1976 Act to bring under control trade in certain parts and products of species which appear to be endangered by international trade or which are similar in appearance to such endangered species.

This order was subsequently revoked, by S.I. 1978 No. 1939, See para. 136.

136　　The Endangered Species (Import and Export) Act 1976 (Modification) (No. 2) Order 1978, S.I. 1978 No. 1939 (in force on 19th January 1979), modifies the Schedules to the Endangered Species (Import and Export) Act 1976, 1976 Halsbury's Abr para. 127, by bringing under control international trade in certain parts and products of species which appear to be endangered by the trade or which are similar in appearance to such endangered species.　The Order revokes the Endangered Species (Import and Export) Act 1976 (Modification) Order 1977, 1977 Halsbury's Abr para. 147 and the Endangered Species (Import and Export) Act 1976 (Modification) Order 1978, see para. 135.

137　　Farriers (Registration) Act 1975—commencement

The Farriers (Registration) Act 1975 (Commencement No. 2) Order 1978, S.I. 1978 No. 1928, brings s. 16 of the 1975 Act into force in England and Wales on 1st June 1979.

138　　Game—night poaching—meaning of night—evidence as to time of sunset

See *R v Crush*, para. 1285.

139　　—— —— rabbits

The defendant and other men were found trespassing at night on farm land.　They had with them four dogs, a motor-car spot lamp connected to motorcycle batteries and fifteen dead rabbits.　The defendant was charged with unlawfully taking or destroying rabbits by night in land occupied by the farmer, contrary to the Night Poaching Act 1828, s. 1.　The justices dismissed the information on the ground that the spot lamp, batteries and dogs were not "an engine or other instrument for the purpose of taking or destroying game".　On appeal by the prosecutor, *held*, s. 1 created two separate offences, that of unlawfully taking or destroying any game or rabbits and that of unlawfully entering or being in any land with any gun, net, engine or other instrument for the purpose of taking or destroying game.　"Game" did not include rabbits, and since the defendant was properly charged with the first type of offence under s. 1, it was irrelevant whether his apparatus fell within the items listed in the second part of s. 1.　The justices had erred and the case would be remitted to them for rehearing.

JONES v EVANS [1978] Crim LR 230 (Queen's Bench Division: LORD WIDGERY CJ, O'CONNOR and LLOYD JJ).

140   Horses and ponies—increases in minimum values

The Export of Horses and Ponies (Increase in Minimum Values) Order 1978, S.I. 1978 No. 1748 (in force on 27th December 1978), increases the minimum value of certain horses and of ponies for the purposes of the Diseases of Animals Act 1950, ss. 37 (3) and 37 (4A). The relevant authorities must be satisfied that horses and ponies for export are of not less than the minimum value.

141   Wild birds—protection

The Wild Birds (Little Owls) Order 1978, S.I. 1978 No. 1212 (in force on 4th September 1978), amends the Protection of Birds Act 1954 by adding the little owl to Schedule 4 (wild birds which may not be sold alive unless close-ringed and bred in captivity).

142   The Wild Birds (Special Protection in Severe Weather) Order 1979, S.I. 1979 No. 70 (in force on 26th January 1979), created periods of special protection for all wild birds listed in Schedule 3 to the Protection of Birds Act 1954 during which they were protected in the same manner as they are during the close season. The protection lasted for the short anticipated period of severe weather.

ARBITRATION

Halsbury's Laws of England (4th edn.), Vol. 2, paras. 501–653

143   Arbitration agreement—express and implied clauses—agreement to depart from strict rules of law

See *Eagle Star Insurance Co Ltd v Yuval Insurance Co Ltd.*, para. 159.

144   Arbitration clause—guarantee—whether right of action against guarantor without arbitration first

See *The Queen Frederica, Thermistocles Navegacion Societe Anonyme v Langton*, para. 2586.

145   Arbitrator—appointment—application by shipowner—whether shipowner's claim capable of going to arbitration

See *The Ioanna, Transamerican Ocean Contractors Inc v Transchemical Rotterdam BV*, para. 2585.

146   —— —— application for extension of time—whether right of action extinguished by delay

The charterers of a ship were time-barred from pursuing a claim against the defendants for short delivery of a consignment of timber by virtue of the Hague Rules, art. III, r. 6 which was incorporated in the charter by a clause paramount. They applied under the Arbitration Act 1950, s. 27 for an extension of time in which to appoint an arbitrator but were unsuccessful on the ground that they were guilty of excessive delay. On the charterer's appeal, the defendants contended that s. 27 had no application where the action was barred under the Hague Rules because the barring of an action under them extinguished not only the remedy but the right of action itself. *Held*, s. 27 could be invoked wherever an action had become time-barred; it contained nothing to exclude its application to cases where an action was barred under the Hague Rules. It was irrelevant what kind of bar was involved. Accordingly, the case had to be considered on its merits. Since the delay was occasioned by the defendants' insurers and since the defendants would not be prejudiced by the grant of an extension of time for the appointment of an arbitrator, the extension would be granted.

CONSOLIDATED INVESTMENTS AND CONTRACTING CO v SAPONARIA SHIPPING CO LTD [1978] 3 All ER 988 (Court of Appeal: LORD DENNING MR, ORMROD and GEOFFREY LANE LJJ).

147   —— —— time for appointment

See *Bunge SA v Schleswig-Holsteinische Landwirtschaftliche Hauptgenossenschaft Eingetr GmbH*, para. 2420.

148   —— jurisdiction—jurisdiction to award interest

See *The Finix*, para. 2602.

149   Award—appeal—compliance with rules

An agreement under a standard form contract of the Grain and Feed Trade Association provided for the sale of soya bean meal. It was to be shipped from Greece. The sellers obtained an export licence but before trading began the Greek authorities imposed an embargo on the export of soya bean meal. The buyers claimed damages for non-delivery but the sellers contended that they were protected from any untoward executive or legislative act by a prohibition clause in the contract. The dispute was referred to arbitration in accordance with the Association's rules and damages were awarded in the buyers' favour. The sellers appealed and were ordered to deposit the damages awarded against them within a certain time pending the hearing of the appeal. They were unable to comply with the order and successfully applied on two consecutive occasions for the time limit to be extended. At the hearing the Board of Appeal waived payment altogether and made an award for the sellers in the form of a special case. The buyers contended that the Board had no jurisdiction to make an award since only one time extension could be granted under the Association's rules and the sellers' appeal should be deemed to be withdrawn due to their failure to comply with the order for payment in time. Furthermore, they contended that the sellers could not rely on the prohibition clause as they had not taken steps to get the export licence restored. *Held*, (i) the Board of Appeal had an absolute discretion under the rules to extend time limits or dispense with the requirement for payment altogether; it could in effect determine the appeal as if all the conditions regarding payment had been complied with. (ii) The sellers were entitled to rely on the prohibition clause since they made persistent attempts to persuade the Greek authorities to restore their licence: there was no reasonable possibility of doing anything more to get the embargo lifted. Accordingly, the award in favour of the sellers would be upheld.

PROVIMI HELLAS AE v WARINCO AG [1978] 1 Lloyd's Rep 373 (Court of Appeal: MEGAW, LAWTON and SHAW LJJ). Decision of Mocatta J [1978] 1 Lloyd's Rep 67, affirmed.

150   —— foreign awards—parties to convention

The Arbitration (Foreign Awards) Order 1978, S.I. 1978 No. 186 (in force on 2nd March 1978), specifies the states which are parties to the 1927 Geneva Convention on the Execution of Foreign Arbitral Awards and revokes certain Arbitration (Foreign Awards) Orders 1931–1965 relating to those states. An arbitral award made in a Geneva Convention state is enforceable in the United Kingdom under the Arbitration Act 1950, Part II, except in so far as it is enforceable under the Arbitration Act 1975 when a state is also party to the 1958 New York Convention, 1975 Halsbury's Abr paras. 137, 138.

151   —— grounds for setting aside—error of law on face of award

The respondent architect had undertaken to build houses for the appellant council. A dispute arose under the contract and was referred to arbitration, the arbitrator advising the parties that the hearing would be restricted to specified issues. The council applied to have the subsequent interim award set aside or remitted on the grounds that it had not reached a finding on one of the specified issues, and that there had been technical misconduct on the part of the arbitrator. *Held*, in so far as an interim award reached conclusions it was binding, but the issues on which it did not make findings were still open. The reasons on which the arbitrator had reached his findings were listed on the face of the award and, on examination, it could be seen that the arbitrator had made an error of law and had considered a factor which he should not have taken into account. This error was sufficiently important for the court to exercise its jurisdiction and set aside the award.

The judge considered that courts should not usually interfere with the findings of an arbitrator, but ss. 22 and 23 of the Arbitration Act 1950 had given courts limited powers of interference to remit or set aside an award.

STOCKPORT METROPOLITAN BOROUGH COUNCIL v O'REILLY [1978] 1 Lloyd's Rep 595 (Queen's Bench Division: JUDGE EDGAR FAY QC sitting as a deputy High Court judge).

152 —— remission of award to arbitrator—alleged waiver of right of remission

Charterers contended that an award made by arbitrators in favour of the shipowners should be remitted on the ground that it had been arrived at unjustly as due to the arbitrators' misconduct in failing to notify them of relevant dates in the arbitration they did not have an opportunity to make certain submissions before the award was made. Even if there was no misconduct, there had been a serious procedural mishap which justified remitting the award. The shipowners argued that, by voluntarily paying the arbitrators' fees and taking up the award, the charterers had waived their right of objection. *Held*, an applicant for remission must show that the error in the arbitration proceedings had resulted in the award being unjust to him. He could discover whether the award was just only by taking it up himself or by allowing the other party to do so. It was reasonable for a party to pay arbitrators' fees and take up the award to see whether the decision was adverse to him, and such an action could not be regarded as a waiver of the right of remission. On the facts, the arbitrators were reasonably entitled to conclude from the stage of the proceedings reached and the absence of any indication to the contrary that the charterers' case was closed and that they were free to proceed. There had thus been no misconduct. The loss of the opportunity to put forward further material could be described as a procedural mishap. However, the charterers had not established that this caused injustice to them or that it might well have done so. The application for remission would accordingly be dismissed.

THE AROS, SOKRATIS ROKOPULOS v ESPERIA SpA [1978] 1 Lloyd's Rep 456 (Queen's Bench Division: BRANDON J).

153 —— second arbitration—res judicata

A dispute arose between buyers and sellers about the construction of a force majeure clause in a contract. The buyers referred the dispute to arbitration in terms limiting the reference to the issue of liability for non-delivery. The arbitrators found in favour of the buyers, who then submitted a debit note to the sellers in the amount of the damages which they claimed. The sellers refused payment and the buyers referred the claim for damages to arbitration. The sellers contended that having chosen to limit the first arbitration to the issue of liability, the buyers could not now pursue a claim for damages in a second arbitration. Arbitrators held in favour of the buyers but stated their award in the form of a special case. *Held*, the rule that there could not be serial claims for damages based upon the same cause of action did not apply to this case as there had not been two claims for damages. If the matter had arisen in litigation, regard would have to be had to the principle that no-one should be twice vexed by the same cause; however, in this case, there were two causes, the first being an alleged breach of an obligation to deliver and the second being concerned with remedies for that breach. Regard should also be had to the principle that there should be an end to litigation and to whether the right to claim damages had become merged in the declaration of liability. In any event, the buyers would

succeed because an award of damages could not have been made in the first
arbitration; its jurisdiction was consensual and depended on a reference of the dispute
to it, and the only dispute at that time was as to the application of the force majeure
clause. Therefore the buyers were not estopped from claiming damages by reason
of the previous proceedings.

COMPAGNIE GRANIERE SA v FRITZ KOPP AG [1978] 1 Lloyd's Rep 511 (Queen's
Bench Division: DONALDSON J).

154   —— special case—enforcement of award

In the course of an arbitration case in the Queen's Bench Division ([1978] 1 Lloyd's
Rep 652) DONALDSON J made a statement in the following terms: one of the
criticisms levelled at the special case procedure is that it delays the enforcement of the
award. This is based on the incorrect assumption that an award in the form of a
special case is not enforceable if an appeal is pending. The obligation to comply
with the award is not suspended by the giving of notice of appeal but is suspended
only by an order of the Commercial Court or Court of Appeal staying execution of
the award. Applications for such orders are considered on their merits and are not
granted automatically.

155   Costs of arbitration—order for costs against successful party

Various disputes between shipowners and charterers were referred to arbitration.
The owners' claim for certain sums and the charterers' counterclaim were fully
pleaded at the beginning of the arbitration. However, the owners' claim for
rectification of the charter was not made until the second day, as a result of which the
arbitration was adjourned. At the second arbitration the owners' claim for
rectification was allowed; the remainder of their claim and the charterers'
counterclaim were both successful in part and an award was made in the owners'
favour after setting-off the counterclaim against the claim. The arbitrator then
ordered the owners to pay all the costs of the arbitration. On appeal by the owners,
held, notwithstanding the general rule that costs should follow the event, the court
should not interfere with an arbitrator's discretion in the matter unless it was satisfied
that he had misdirected himself. The order for costs against the owners for the
whole period after the first arbitration was justified since their claim for rectification
ought to have been put forward before the arbitration began. However, when
deciding the question of costs up to and during the first arbitration, the arbitrator
had misdirected himself. He failed to consider whether the owners' claim was
justified and whether it was so inflated that it deterred the charterers from seeking a
settlement or else increased the costs of arbitration. The owners' claim was clearly
quite proper and the fact that it was more optimistic than the charterers' did not
justify the order for costs against them. As the arbitrator had misdirected himself in
part, the award would be remitted for reconsideration of the order.

TRAMOUNTANA ARMADORA SA v ATLANTIC SHIPPING CO SA [1978] 1 Lloyd's
Rep 319 (Queen's Bench Division: DONALDSON J).

156   Reference to arbitration—injunction restraining arbitration
proceedings

The chairman of a Singapore company entered into arrangements, nominally on
behalf of the company, to sell palm oil to a Pakistan corporation. A contract
providing for arbitration in London was concluded. When the company learnt of
the contract they took the point that the chairman had no actual or ostensible
authority to enter into it on their behalf. The Pakistan corporation commenced
arbitration and the Singapore company issued a writ and applied for an interlocutory
injunction to restrain the taking of steps in the arbitration. They were granted leave
to serve out of the jurisdiction. The corporation's application to set aside the writ
and claim to an interlocutory injunction were refused. On appeal, *held*, the court
had jurisdiction to grant an injunction to restrain arbitration proceedings pending

decision of a dispute as to the validity of the agreement to refer. The case was a proper one for service out of the jurisdiction. The appeal would be dismissed.

BEN & CO LTD v PAKISTAN EDIBLE OILS CORPN LTD (1978) Times, 13th July (Court of Appeal: LORD DENNING MR, EVELEIGH LJ and SIR DAVID CAIRNS). Dictum of Lindley LJ in *Kitts v Moore* [1895] 1 QB 253, CA at 260 applied.

157   Reference to independent tribunal—nature of reference—power of tribunal to state special case

A trade union complained that a company had failed to comply with the House of Commons Fair Wages Resolution of 1946 in the performance of a contract with the Ministry of Defence. In accordance with the Resolution, which was incorporated in the contract, the Secretary of State referred the complaint to an independent tribunal for decision. The company asked the tribunal to state its decision as a special case under the Arbitration Act 1950, s. 21. The tribunal refused on the ground that a reference to it under the 1946 Resolution was not a submission to arbitration and thus no special case could be stated. On the company's appeal, *held*, the reference under the Resolution did not amount to a submission to arbitration because (i) there was no suggestion that the tribunal would be performing any statutory function in deciding points raised, and (ii) issues could be referred for hearing by persons other than the contractual parties. Complaints could in fact be made where the parties were wholly in agreement with each other. A reference under the 1946 Resolution was accordingly not in the nature of a submission to arbitration.

IMPERIAL METAL INDUSTRIES (KYNOCH) LTD v AMALGAMATED UNION OF ENGINEERING WORKERS (TECHNICAL, ADMINISTRATIVE AND SUPERVISORY SECTION) (1978) Times, 19th July 1978 (Court of Appeal: STEPHENSON, ROSKILL and GEOFFREY LANE LJJ). *R v Industrial Court, ex parte A.S.S.E.T.* [1965] 1 QB 377, DC disapproved.

158   Stay of court proceedings—action in rem—when stay may be granted

See *The Rena K*, para. 22.

159   —— bar to application—whether defendant has taken a step in the proceedings

The plaintiffs, through their brokers, negotiated a reinsurance agreement with the defendants' agents in 1967. Under the agreement, the defendants were liable for a proportion of the claims made under policies issued by the plaintiffs and received a corresponding proportion of premiums, based on the plaintiffs' estimated premium income. The defendants were in fact agents for another company and were not the reinsurers. In 1969 the agents who had acted for the defendants in 1967 renegotiated the agreement with the plaintiffs, apparently without the defendants' authority or knowledge. The plaintiffs subsequently issued a writ against the defendants for certain sums allegedly due from them under the 1967 agreement. The statement of claim was defective and the defendants sought to have it struck out; the plaintiffs then issued a fresh writ and applied for summary judgment under RSC Ord. 14. The defendants applied to have the proceedings stayed and the dispute referred to arbitration under the terms of the agreement. *Held*, (i) the plaintiffs were not entitled to summary judgment since there were a number of matters which ought to be tried, such as the renegotiation of the agreement in 1969 and the plaintiffs' failure to inform the defendants that they had grossly underestimated their premium income. Moreover, it was questionable whether the plaintiffs could sue the defendants as principals on the 1967 agreement when their brokers ought to have known they were merely agents. (ii) Under the Arbitration Acts 1950 and 1975, an application to stay proceedings had to be made before the defendant had taken a step in the proceedings: he had not to have taken action which impliedly affirmed the correctness of the proceedings and his consent to be bound by the court's decision. The defendants had not taken a step in the proceedings since their action to have the defective statement of claim struck out was the opposite of affirming the correctness of the proceedings. (iii) A provision in the arbitration clause whereby arbitrators were not bound by the strict rules of law did not invalidate the clause. It merely dispensed with the need to observe the legal technicalities and did not oust the court's jurisdiction. The proceedings would be stayed and the dispute referred to arbitration.

EAGLE STAR INSURANCE CO LTD v YUVAL INSURANCE CO LTD [1978] 1 Lloyd's Rep 357 (Court of Appeal: LORD DENNING MR, GOFF and SHAW LJJ). Dicta of Lindley LJ in *Ives & Barker v Willans* [1894] 2 Ch 478, at 484, applied.

160　　—— non-domestic arbitration agreement—whether court has discretion to stay

The defendant companies entered into an agreement with the plaintiffs by which the defendants agreed to transport oil into Rhodesia by the plaintiffs' pipeline, and not to use any other method of transport. The agreement provided for arbitration in the case of dispute. The companies were excused from the agreement if prevented from using the pipeline by circumstances beyond their control, including government interference. After Rhodesia made a unilateral declaration of independence, the United Kingdom imposed sanctions and it became a criminal offence for a United Kingdom company to supply oil to Rhodesia. The plaintiffs claimed that the defendants were in breach of their contractual obligations by giving assurances to Rhodesia that oil would continue to be supplied even if the Beira pipeline could not be used, and brought actions in contract and tort. The defendants sought a stay of proceedings under the Arbitration Act 1975, s. 1. *Held*, the claims of the plaintiff in both tort and contract arose from or in connection with the agreement and were therefore subject to the arbitration clause. Section 1 was mandatory. It applied to all arbitration agreements and did not give the court discretion to refuse a stay of proceedings unless the agreement was void or inoperative. The defendants would be granted a stay of proceedings.

LONHRO LTD v SHELL PETROLEUM CO LTD (1978) Times, 1st February (Chancery Division: BRIGHTMAN J).

AUCTION

Halsbury's Laws of England (4th edn.), Vol. 2, paras. 701–756

161　　Auctioneer—liability for conversion

A publican who was buying a car on hire-purchase terms from the plaintiffs took the car to an auction to be sold, in breach of the terms of his hire-purchase agreement. The car was not sold under the hammer as it did not reach its reserve price. The highest bid was treated by the auctioneers as a "provisional bid" and the car was subsequently sold to the person who had made this bid. Provisional bids were an established feature of the auctioneer's trade.

Shortly afterwards the publican went bankrupt and neither the car, nor the purchaser, could be traced. The plaintiffs claimed from the auctioneers the £275 outstanding instalments on the car as damages for conversion. On appeal from the county court decision in favour of the plaintiffs, *held*, dismissing the appeal, where goods were sold by the intervention of an auctioneer under the hammer or as a result of a provisional bid, then if the seller had no title, the auctioneer was liable in conversion to the true owner however innocent he may have been in handling the goods.

R. H. WILLIS AND SON v BRITISH CAR AUCTIONS LTD [1978] 2 All ER 392 (Court of Appeal: LORD DENNING MR, ROSKILL and BROWNE LJJ).

162 The plaintiffs, a finance company, let a car on hire purchase and the hirer, in breach of the agreement, entered the car for an auction with the defendants, a firm of car auctioneers. The car was sold in an auction and the plaintiffs brought an action in conversion against the defendants. The defendants contended that auctioneers acting as they did could not in law be guilty of conversion. They also contended that the plaintiffs could not maintain the action as they had no right to immediate possession of the car; under the terms of the hire purchase agreement, even if the hirer was in breach of it, unless and until the plaintiffs served a notice of termination the right to immediate possession of the car remained in the hirer. *Held*, it was established that auctioneers could be liable for conversion in circumstances such as these. At common law, if a bailee acted in a way which destroyed the basis of the contract of bailment, the bailor became entitled at once to bring the contract to an end and thus at once acquired the right to immediate possession of the article bailed. This right was not affected by the terms of the contract conferring an express contractual right to bring the contract to an end only after notice of termination, since the contract did not expressly deprive the bailor of his common-law rights. The hirer had only a possessory title which he lost when he destroyed the agreement by acting dishonestly and therefore he could not convey any title to the auctioneer or to the innocent purchaser, and the defendants were liable in conversion.

UNION TRANSPORT FINANCE LTD v BRITISH CAR AUCTIONS LTD [1978] 2 All ER 385 (Court of Appeal: CAIRNS, ROSKILL and BRIDGE LJJ). *Hollins v Fowler* (1875) LR 7 HL 757, HL and *North Central Wagon & Finance Co Ltd v Graham* [1950] 2 KB 7, CA applied.

163   **Mock auction—sale by way of competitive bidding—meaning**

The defendant was charged with conducting a mock auction at which articles were offered for sale by competitive bidding and during the sale articles were sold to persons bidding for them at a price lower than their highest bid, and articles were given away or offered as gifts, contrary to the Mock Auctions Act 1961, s. 1. The defendant only disputed that there had been "competitive bidding". *Held*, the 1961 Act, s. 3, provided that competitive bidding included any mode of sale whereby prospective purchasers were enabled to compete for the purchase of articles, whether by way of increasing bids, or by the offer of articles to be bid for at successively decreasing prices, or otherwise. In this case, the audience was asked who would pay a certain sum for an article and hands were raised. The question was whether this amounted to competing for the purchase of articles "otherwise" within s. 3. Giving s. 3 a wide meaning that competitive bidding included any mode of sale whereby prospective purchasers might be enabled to compete for the purchase of articles in any way, the raising of hands constituted competitive bidding and the defendant was guilty of conducting a mock auction.

ALLEN v SIMMONS [1978] 3 All ER 662 (Queen's Bench Division: MELFORD STEVENSON, CANTLEY and CROOM-JOHNSON JJ). Dictum of Eveleigh J in *Clements v Rydeheard* [1978] 3 All ER 658, para. 164 followed.

164   The defendant was convicted of conducting a mock auction contrary to the Mock Auctions Act 1961, s. 1, having held a sale to which the Act applied. Initially he had offered lots at fixed prices well below their real value to all persons present, and had required them to raise their hands if they wished to purchase. The number of prospective purchasers always exceeded the number of lots offered, and the ones who raised their hands first were successful. He then offered a limited number of boxes for sale at a fixed price, and thereafter restricted the right to bid to purchasers of the boxes. His appeal against conviction to the Crown Court was allowed on the ground that the proceedings did not constitute a sale by way of competitive bidding. The prosecutor appealed. *Held*, the Act gave an extended meaning to "competitive bidding" so as to include any mode of sale whereby prospective purchasers might be enabled to compete for the purchase of articles in any way. Therefore, since only a limited number of people, selected in a competitive way, were allowed to conclude the final sales, the whole proceedings amounted to a mode of sale, and the method of selection of prospective purchasers constituted competitive bidding. The appeal would be allowed.

CLEMENTS v RYDEHEARD [1978] 3 All ER 658 (Queen's Bench Division: LORD WIDGERY CJ, EVELEIGH and BOREHAM JJ).

165   Sale by auction—exclusion clause—whether carried over to sale by private treaty

See *D & M Trailers (Halifax) Ltd v Stirling*, para. 2419.

AVIATION

Halsbury's Laws of England (4th edn.), Vol. 2, paras. 801–1423

166   Article

Terrorism and the Airline Passenger, Jonathan M. Barrett (the obligation on states party to the Tokyo, Hague and Montreal Conventions): 128 NLJ 499.

167   Air navigation—general regulations

The Air Navigation (Third Amendment) Order 1978, S.I. 1978 No. 284 (in force on 1st April 1978), amends the Air Navigation Order 1976, 1976 Halsbury's Abr para. 158, as amended. Changes include provisions that a Certificate of Airworthiness issued or received after 1st April 1978 may not specify the General Purpose Category; that the requirement of a certificate of compliance in respect of radio apparatus which has been overhauled, repaired or modified now applies to apparatus provided for use in any aircraft registered for use in the United Kingdom or in any survival craft carried therein; and that aircraft, engine and propellor log books are now required to be kept in respect of aircraft registered in the United Kingdom.

168   The Air Navigation (Fourth Amendment) Order 1978, S.I. 1978 No. 1627 (in force on 1st January 1979 except arts. 3 (2) and 3 (12) for which the date is 1st April 1979), amends the Air Navigation Order 1976, 1976 Halsbury's Abr para. 158, in connection with emergency exits from public transport aircraft; flights in the neighbourhood of an offshore installation and within the United Kingdom Flight Information region; regulations relating to the use of radio communication equipment; scales of equipment carried in helicopters and gyroplanes; navigation system requirements for aircraft flying in prescribed airspace and qualifications for helicopter pilots flying in controlled airspace.

169   The Air Navigation (General) (Second Amendment) Regulations 1978, S.I. 1978 No. 873 (in force on 17th July 1978), amend the Air Navigation (General) Regulations 1976, 1976 Halsbury's Abr para. 154, as amended. They permit public transport aircraft to use for landing or as alternate aerodromes, aerodromes provided with an aerodrome flight information service.

170   —— overseas territories

The Air Navigation (Overseas Territories) (Second Amendment) Order 1978, S.I. 1978 No. 1520 (in force on 22nd November 1978) amends the Air Navigation (Overseas Territories) Order 1977, 1977 Halsbury's Abr para. 188. The Order amends a number of the provisions of the 1977 Order including provisions relating to the airworthiness and equipment of aircraft, the licensing of aircraft crew, the operation of aircraft and the control of air traffic.

171   —— services—charges payable to Civil Aviation Authority

See paras. 182 et seq.

172   —— —— joint financing—Denmark and Iceland

The Civil Aviation (Joint Financing) Regulations 1978, S.I. 1978 No. 554 (in force on 10th May 1978), consolidate, with minor amendments, the Civil Aviation (Joint Financing) Regulations 1974, 1974 Halsbury's Abr paras. 148, 149, as amended. The Regulations make provision with respect to arrangements made between the United Kingdom Government and the Governments of Denmark and Iceland for the collection of charges for services which the Governments of Denmark and Iceland may impose under the 1956 Agreements on the Joint Financing of Certain Air Navigation Services.

173　Air traffic control—altitude regulations

The Rules of the Air and Air Traffic Control (Second Amendment) Regulations 1978, S.I. 1978 No. 140 (in force on 1st March 1978), amends the Rules of the Air and Air Traffic Control Regulations 1976, 1976 Halsbury's Abr Para. 152, as amended. An aircraft may now fly closer than 500 feet to persons, vessels, vehicles and structures if it is flying in accordance with an Aerial Application Certificate granted by the Civil Aviation Authority.

174

The Rules of the Air and Air Traffic Control (Third and Fourth Amendment) Regulations 1978, S.I. 1978 Nos. 877, 1391 (in force on 1st July and 2nd November 1978 respectively), further amend the Rules of the Air and Air Traffic Control Regulations 1976, 1976 Halsbury's Abr para. 180.

175　Aircraft—public health regulations

See para. 2245.

176　Airports policy—white paper

The Government have published a White paper entitled Airports Policy: Cmnd. 7084. In the present economic climate the Government consider that an important priority of any policy should be to establish the most effective use of existing airports' infrastructure and related investment. Under the present conditions of uncertainty rigid plans are inappropriate. The need is for a strategy which will balance conflicting interests and allow for change and adaptation.

177　Aviation Security Fund—contributions to fund—prescribed aerodromes

The Aviation Security Fund Regulations 1978, S.I. 1978 No. 769 (in force on 31st May 1978), require certain aerodrome authorities to pay contributions to the Aviation Security Fund. The aerodromes in respect of which contributions are required are those owned or managed by the Civil Aviation Authority or licensed by them for public use and which had more than 50,000 passengers in 1976. The regulations set out the method by which contributions are to be calculated.

178　Carriage by air—limitation of liability—conversion rate

The Carriage by Air (Sterling Equivalents) Order 1978, S.I. 1978 No. 31 (in force on 1st February 1978), specifies the sterling equivalents of amounts expressed in gold francs as the limit of the air carrier's liability both under the amended Warsaw Convention of 1929 and under corresponding provisions applying to carriage by air to which that convention does not apply. It supersedes the Carriage by Air (Sterling Equivalents) Order 1977, 1977 Halsbury's Abr para. 207.

179　————— sufficiency of notice of limitation

Canada
The plaintiff was a passenger on a scheduled flight of the defendant airline. The aircraft made a forced landing in the sea and commercial camera equipment belonging to the plaintiff was damaged by salt water. The airline admitted negligence but relied on a clause limiting liability in the terms and conditions of carriage printed on the reverse of the back page of the ticket. *Held*, the airline was

liable for the full amount. A person who wanted conditions of this kind incorporated in the contract had to take reasonable steps to bring them to the notice of the other party by, for example, putting a notice of the existence of the conditions on the face of the ticket. This the airline had failed to do. Furthermore it was an established principle that contracts of carriage ought to be construed strictly. The language of the relevant clause, which did not expressly refer to negligence, was not so plain that it should be construed as extending the exemption to negligence.

KOWALEWICH V AIRWEST AIRLINES LTD [1978] 2 WWR 60 (British Columbia Supreme Court).

180   —— parties to Convention

The Carriage by Air (Parties to Convention) (Supplementary) Order 1978, S.I. 1978 No. 1058 (made on 25th July 1978), certifies additional High Contracting Parties to the Warsaw Convention, relating to international carriage by air, and certifies the territories in respect of which they are parties.

181   Civil Aviation Act 1978

The Civil Aviation Act 1978 establishes a fund from which payments may be made in respect of expenses incurred for the purpose of protecting aircraft, aerodromes or air navigation installations against acts of violence or in connection with the policing of airports. It amends the law relating to the Civil Aviation Authority and the British Airways Board, and the law relating to noise, vibration and atmospheric pollution caused by aircraft. It makes various other amendments relating to aerodromes, aircraft and civil aviation. The Act received the royal assent on 23rd March 1978 and ss. 1 (1), (3)–(5), 2, 3, 13, 16 came into force on that day. Section 1 (2) came into force on 1st April 1978 for the defraying of expenses incurred on or after that date, and the remaining provisions came into force on 1st May 1978: Civil Aviation Act 1978 (Commencement) Order 1978, S.I. 1978 No. 486.

Section 1 establishes the Aviation Security Fund, out of which payments will normally be made in respect of expenses incurred in connection with the protection of aircraft, aerodromes and air navigation installations against acts of violence and the policing of aerodromes. Provision is made for the reimbursement of such expenses by the Protection of Aircraft Act 1973, s. 23, and the Policing of Airports Act 1974, s. 7. Section 2 provides that regulations may be made by the Secretary of State requiring aerodrome authorities to make contributions to the Fund calculated in a prescribed manner. Section 3 deals with the financing of the Fund and confers borrowing powers on the Secretary of State for the purposes of the Fund. Section 4 enables the Secretary of State to provide for the winding up of the Fund by order, whereupon ss. 1 and 2, supra, will cease to have effect.

Section 5 provides for an increase in the borrowing powers of the Civil Aviation Authority and the British Airways Board. The limit on the Authority is increased to £125 million, but it may borrow more to pay off a loan or the initial debt. The limit on borrowings by the British Airways Board may be increased by order to £850 million. The Civil Aviation Authority Act 1971 is also amended to allow the Authority to borrow temporarily from the Secretary of State as well as from others. Section 6 requires the Authority to act on lines approved by the Secretary of State in carrying out proposals involving substantial outlay on capital account and the hiring of equipment which if purchased outright would involve such an outlay. The Authority is permitted to enter into agreements for the payment to it of charges for air navigation services which are determined in pursuance of the agreement: s. 7.

Section 8 confers power on aerodrome authorities which are entitled to make byelaws to control the operation of aircraft within or directly above the aerodrome for the purpose of limiting or mitigating the effect of noise, vibration and atmospheric pollution caused by aircraft using the aerodrome. The Secretary of State has power in certain circumstances to revoke or vary such byelaws. Section 9 empowers aerodrome authorities to fix their charges by reference to the noise caused by aircraft and any inconvenience resulting from such noise in order to encourage the use of quieter aircraft and to diminish inconvenience from aircraft noise. Certain aerodrome authorities may be directed by order to fix their charges in this way. Section 10 enables the Secretary of State to give the Civil Aviation Authority general directions in the interests of national security which would override any conflicting provisions in the Civil Aviation Act 1971 except those made by order in time of war or national emergency. Section 11 amends the 1971 Act as to the mental element of the offence of contravening a term of an air transport licence. The British Airways Board Act 1977, s. 18, is repealed by s. 12, which provides that the Board may make pension arrangements for present and former employees and those of its subsidiaries and predecessors.

Section 13 governs the making of orders and regulations under the Act. Section 14 provides that the minor, consequential and consolidation amendments to the Civil Aviation Acts specified in Sch. 1, and the repeals to those Acts specified in Sch. 2, shall have effect. The Secretary of State is empowered to repeal or amend local Acts by order. Section 15 deals with interpretation and s. 16 with short title, commencement and extent.

182   Civil Aviation Authority—charges payable to Authority—navigation services

The Civil Aviation (Navigation Services Charges) (Amendment) Regulations 1978, S.I. 1978 No. 317 (in force on 1st April 1978), amend the Civil Aviation (Navigation Services Charges) Regulations 1977, 1977 Halsbury's Abr para. 200. The regulations increase the charges payable for navigation services provided in connection with the use of certain aerodromes. They require, in lieu of payment by operators of aircraft of charges for navigation services provided in connection with the use of certain aerodromes, the payment of a monthly charge by the aerodrome managers. They also provide for payment of a charge for flights made by helicopters from a point in the United Kingdom to an offshore installation in a specified area.

183   —— —— —— Canada

The Civil Aviation (Canadian Navigation Services) (Amendment) Regulations 1978, S.I. 1978 No. 245 (in force on 1st April 1978), amend the Civil Aviation (Canadian Navigation Services) Regulations 1977, 1977 Halsbury's Abr para. 202, by increasing the charge for air navigation services provided by the Government of Canada in the Gander Flight Information Region.

184   —— —— —— route charges

The Civil Aviation (Route Charges for Navigation Services) (Fourth Amendment) Regulations 1978, S.I. 1978 No. 241 (in force on 1st April 1978), further amend the Civil Aviation (Route Charges for Navigation Services) Regulations 1973 to provide a new tariff in relation to flights which enter the airspace defined in the 1973 Regulations where the United Kingdom provides air navigation services. The Regulations do not now apply to flights by helicopters between any point in the United Kindom and an offshore installation within a specified area.

This statutory instrument has been revoked and consolidated; see para 185.

185

The Civil Aviation (Route Charges for Navigation Services) Regulations 1978, S.I. 1978 No. 693 (in force on 12th June 1978), consolidate, with minor amendments, the Civil Aviation (Route Charges for Navigation Services) Regulations 1973, as amended. The only substantial amendment is that for the dates 1st November and 31st October, which were formerly the dates of the period for determination of the airways or routes most frequently used, are substituted 1st April and 31st March, in accordance with the current practice of Eurocontrol.

186

The Civil Aviation (Route Charges for Navigation Services) (Amendment) Regulations 1978, S.I. 1978 No. 837 (in force on 12th June 1978), corrects clerical errors in the Civil Aviation (Route Charges for Navigation Services) Regulations 1978, para. 185.

187   ——— revocation

The Civil Aviation Authority (Charges) (Revocation) Regulations 1978, S.I. 1978 No. 1633 (in force on 1st January 1979) revokes the Civil Aviation Authority (Charges) Regulations 1976, 1976 Halsbury's Abr para. 162 and the Civil Aviation Authority (Charges) (Amendment) Regulations 1977, 1977 Halsbury's Abr para. 198.

188   Hijacking—Bonn Agreement

The seven most industrialised nations in the West (Canada, France, Italy, Japan, the United Kingdom, the United States and West Germany) pledged themselves to take action against nations giving sanctuary to hijackers at the meeting of the heads of state and government at Bonn. The agreement states that where a country refuses the extradition or prosecution of those who have hijacked an aircraft and/or does not return the aircraft, the governments of the seven nations will take immediate action to cease all flights to that country. At the same time they will initiate action to halt all incoming flights from that country or from any other country by the airlines of the country concerned. The heads of state and government urge other governments to join them in this commitment: Times, 18 July 1978.

189   Hovercraft

See SHIPPING.

190   Navigation—general regulations

See para. 167.

191   ——— services—charges payable to Civil Aviation Authority

See paras. 182 et seq.

192   ——— ——— joint financing—Denmark and Iceland

See para. 172.

193   ——— joint financing

The Civil Aviation (Joint Financing) (Amendment) Regulations 1978, S.I. 1978 No. 1799 (in force on 1st January 1979) amend the Civil Aviation (Joint Financing) Regulations 1978 by increasing the charges payable by operators of aircraft to the Civil Aviation Authority in respect of crossings between Europe and North America. The charges are payable in pursuance of the Agreements on the Joint Financing of Certain Air Navigation Services in Greenland, Faroe Islands and Iceland.

194   Noise insulation grants

The Gatwick Airport–London Noise Insulation Grants (Second Amendment) Scheme 1978, S.I. 1978 No. 1797 (in force on 31st December 1978), varies the Gatwick Airport–London Noise Insulation Grants Scheme 1975, 1975 Halsbury's Abr para. 191 by extending, from 1st January 1979 to 1st July 1979, the time allowed for the completion of insulation work in respect of which a payment of grant under that Scheme may be made.

195   The Heathrow Airport–London Noise Insulation Grants (Second Amendment) 1978, S.I. 1978 No. 1798 (in force on 31st December 1978), varies the Heathrow Airport–London Noise Insulation Grants Scheme 1975, 1975 Halsbury's Abr para. 192, by extending from 1st January 1979 to 1st July 1979 the time allowed for completion of insulation work in respect of which a payment grant under that Scheme may be made.

196   Notices

The Civil Aviation (Notices) Regulations 1978, S.I. 1978 No. 1303 (in force on 1st October 1978), prescribe the manner of publishing and giving notices under the Civil Aviation Act 1971, s. 29, as amended by the Civil Aviation Act 1978, Sch. 1. The Civil Aviation (Notices) Regulations 1971, as amended, are revoked.

197   Registration of aircraft—interchange of Concorde to foreign carrier

The Air Navigation (Interchange of Concorde) Regulations 1978, S.I. 1978 No. 1631 (in force on 1st December 1978) amend the Air Navigation Order 1976, 1976 Halsbury's Abr para. 158, so that where a Concorde aircraft is interchanged to a foreign carrier and cannot be operated by that carrier under the law of the foreign state concerned unless it is temporarily transferred to the register of that state, art. 4 of the 1976 Order is modified so as to allow the commander of the aircraft to effect such a transfer.

198   Tokyo Convention

The Tokyo Convention (Certification of Countries) (Supplementary) Order 1978, S.I. 1978 No. 1534, (made on 24th October 1978), certifies additional countries in which the Tokyo Convention on Offences and certain other Acts Committed on board Aircraft is for the time being in force.

BAILMENT

Halsbury's Laws of England (4th edn.), Vol. 2, paras. 1501–1589

199   Articles

Authority to Delegate Under Bailments for Skill and Labour, N. E. Palmer (whether bailee is entitled to sub-contract performance of the work in favour of a competent third party): 128 NLJ 863.

Covenant and Contract in Bailment, N. E. Palmer (suggested method of enabling the bailee under an extended, non-contractual bailment by way of hire to exact promissory or semi-contractual obligations from the bailor): 128 NLJ 839.

Legal Problems of Involuntary Bailment, N. E. Palmer: 128 NLJ 763.

200   Bailee—bailee for reward—loss of goods—onus of proof

Malaysia
Ninety-three cases of pharmaceutical goods were shipped to a port. Sixty-four disappeared from the custody of the port authority and the consignees brought an action for damages for the loss. *Held*, the port authority were bailees for reward. At common law, the onus was always on the bailee, whether a bailee for reward or a gratuitous bailee, to prove that the loss of any goods bailed to him was not caused by any fault of his or of his servants or agents to whom he entrusted the goods for safekeeping. Accordingly, the onus of disproving negligence lay on the port authority. They had failed to discharge that onus as it was virtually certain that the cases had been stolen and could not have been stolen without the misconduct or negligence of the authority's servants who were employed to keep them in safe custody. The proposition that a master who was under a duty to guard another's goods was liable if the servant he sent to perform the duty for him performed it so negligently that thieves were enabled to steal the goods but was not liable if that servant joined in the theft was a mis-statement of the common law. The authority were thus liable in damages.

PORT SWETTENHAM AUTHORITY v T. W. WU & CO [1978] 3 All ER 337 (Privy Council: LORD WILBERFORCE, VISCOUNT DILHORNE, LORD SALMON, LORD FRASER OF TULLYBELTON and SIR GARFIELD BARWICK). *Hunt and Winterbotham Ltd v British*

Road Services [1962] 1 QB 617 and *Morris v C. W. Martin & Sons Ltd* [1966] 1 QB
716 applied, *Giblin v McMullen* (1868) LR 2 PC 317 doubted.

201   —— —— motor vehicle—whether bailee responsible for contents

Canada

A jeweller left his car in a hotel car park with an attaché case containing jewellery
locked in the boot. He gave the keys to the attendant and told him that there were
valuables in the boot. The case was stolen and the hotel was held liable as bailee for
reward of the car and the jewellery. On appeal on the ground that if the hotel was
liable as bailee for reward of the car it was not a bailee for reward of the jewellery,
held, a bailment for reward of a car would include both contents which could
reasonably be expected to be in the car and those of which the bailee had actual
knowledge. As the attendant had been told that there were valuables in the car, the
hotel was a bailee for reward of the jewellery.

MINICHIELLO v DEVONSHIRE HOTEL (1967) LTD [1978] 4 WWR 539 (Court of
Appeal of British Columbia). Decision of Supreme Court [1977] 5 WWR 502,
1977 Halsbury's Abr para. 223 affirmed.

202   —— gratuitous bailee—loss of goods—liability

Following their eviction from a council flat, a couple accepted the council's offer to
store their household chattels free of charge. Subsequently a meeting was arranged
at the couple's request to remove the property from storage but the council sent its
representative to the wrong place. The council was unable to contact the couple for
several days because their whereabouts were unknown. By the time another
meeting had been arranged the goods had been stolen from the lock-up garage where
they had been stored. It was agreed that a gratuitious bailee was bound to take
reasonable care of goods and deliver them up when a reasonable demand was made
and that if he failed to deliver he was liable for any loss unless he could show that
there had been no negligence on his part. *Held*, (i) the council had acted out of
kindness and was not negligent in storing the goods in the lock-up garage. (ii)
Although the court had sympathy with the council, its failure to send a representative
to the right place was negligent and from that time it was liable for the goods.

MITCHELL v EALING LONDON BOROUGH COUNCIL (1978) Times, 21st February
(Queen's Bench Division: O'CONNOR J). *Shaw & Co v Symmons & Sons* [1917] 1
KB 799 applied.

**203   —— standard of care—duty of garage in relation to customer's
vehicle**

The plaintiff owned a motor caravan, which had a defective gear-box making it
impossible to engage reverse gear. He asked the defendant garage owners to repair
the vehicle. He drove the vehicle to the garage and was requested to leave it in a cul-
de-sac, adjacent to the garage, which sloped downwards from the main road to its
closed end. The vehicle remained outside in the street and was stolen. The
defendants were held liable in negligence in allowing the vehicle to remain outside
their premises. On appeal, *held*, the standard of care expected of the defendants, as
prudent garage owners, was no greater than that standard exhibited by vehicle
owners who left their cars on the highway after providing for their immobilisation.
In view of the fact that the vehicle's condition and situation demanded that it would
take one man steering and three men pushing it backwards up hill in order to take
it away, this vehicle was as immobile as one could expect a vehicle to be and it was
wrong to hold the defendants guilty in negligence.

COWAN v BLACKWILL MOTOR CARAVAN CONVERSIONS LTD (trading as MATADOR
SERVICE STATION) [1978] RTR 421 (Court of Appeal: MEGAW, ORMROD and BRIDGE
LJJ).

**204   Bailor—right to sue third party—right to immediate possession—
hire purchase company**

See *Union Transport Finance Ltd v British Car Auctions Ltd*, para. 162.

BANKING

Halsbury's Laws of England (4th edn.), Vol. 3, paras. 1–182

205   **Bank—duty of care to surety—whether bank bound to minimise surety's financial obligation**

A client charged certain property in favour of the plaintiff bank, to secure an overdraft. The defendants acted as sureties. The bank sold the secured property when the client's overdraft reached £11,000, but realised only £6,500 on the sale. The defendants, who stood to repay the difference, contended that the bank had negligently failed to obtain the best sale price reasonably obtainable and that therefore, on the basis of *Cuckmere Brick Co Ltd v Mutual Finance Ltd* [1971] Ch 949, a case relating to the duty owed to a mortgagor by the mortgagee at sale, they were not liable as sureties. The bank contended that the contract of guarantee had given them full power to act as they saw fit and did not confer on the defendants any rights such as they claimed. *Held*, under the contract of guarantee the bank had wide discretionary powers to act in all matters as they saw fit. There were clearly no rights expressly given to the defendants, who consequently had no right to complain about any disposal. To extend the *Cuckmere Brick* case was unjustified: it would be going too far to extend a mortgagee's duty of care beyond the mortgagor to any person who might be affected by the former's acts. The defendants' liability as sureties was, therefore, undiminished.

BARCLAYS BANK LTD v THIENEL AND THIENEL (1978) 122 Sol Jo 472 (Queen's Bench Division: THESIGER J).

206   **Bank notes—fiduciary note issue—amount of issue**

The Fiduciary Note Issue (Extension of Period) Order 1978, S.I. 1978 No. 224 (in force on 14th March 1978), extends for a further two years the period during which the issue may exceed £1,575 million. The Fiduciary Note Issue (Extension of Period) Order 1976, 1976 Halsbury's Abr para. 188, is revoked.

207   **Interest—chargeable persons—persons receiving or entitled to income**

See *Dunmore v McGowan (Inspector of Taxes)*, para. 1589.

208   **Loan—security for loan—irrevocable letter of credit—default by principal debtor**

Australia

A firm of moneylenders (PIAL) borrowed a sum of money from a statutory corporation (SECV) and lent it to another company (FL). PIAL instructed its bank (CBC) to issue an irrevocable letter of credit in favour of SECV which could be drawn on upon production by SECV of a statement that payment of the principal had been demanded and not received. PIAL required its loan to FL to be secured by a letter of credit from another bank (BB) and this was issued on similar terms. With regard to both letters of credit, the obligation of the issuing banks arose only if the principal debtor defaulted in repayment upon demand at its due date. The letters of credit issued by PIAL also contained a clause providing that PIAL would indemnify CBC against default by PIAL in the repayment of its loan from SECV if it was caused by FL's failure to repay. There was no contractual provision for the security of CBC's loan in the event of PIAL's insolvency. PIAL went into liquidation and could not repay its loan to SECV who accordingly drew on CBC. FL was ready and able to repay its loan to PIAL. The question before the court was whether CBC had a proprietary interest in FL's debt to PIAL and were secured creditors for that amount. *Held*, there was nothing in the letter of credit issued by CBC that obliged PIAL to satisfy any calls of CBC out of moneys received from FL. The only contingency against which security was provided was a default by PIAL on its loan from SECV consequent upon a corresponding default by FL on its loan from

PIAL. There was no security against the contingency of default from any other cause. CBC thus had no proprietary interest in the debt owed to PIAL by FL.

COMMERCIAL BANKING CO OF SYDNEY LTD v PATRICK INTERMARINE ACCEPTANCES LTD (1978) 19 ALR 547 (Privy Council: LORD DIPLOCK, LORD FRASER OF TULLYBELTON, LORD RUSSELL OF KILLOWEN, LORD SCARMAN and SIR JOHN PENNYCUICK).

209 National Savings Bank—deposits

The National Savings Bank (Amendment) (No. 2) Regulations 1978, S.I. 1978 No. 1594 (in force on 6th December 1978) further amend the National Savings Bank Regulations 1972 by allowing deposits of less than 25p in the case of ordinary accounts and £1 in the case of investment accounts, providing they are presented directly to the principal office of the National Savings Bank.

210 —— —— investment deposits

The National Savings Bank (Investment Deposits) (Investment) Order 1978, S.I. 1978 No. 1839 (in force on 14th December 1978), specifies the investments in which the National Debt Commissioners may invest any balance in the National Savings Bank Investment Account Fund. The Order revokes the Post Office Savings Bank (Investment Deposits) (Investment) Order 1966.

211 —— —— repayment of deposits on death

The National Savings Bank (Amendment) Regulations 1978, S.I. 1978 No. 888 (in force on 14th July 1978), amend the National Savings Bank Regulations 1972 by increasing from £3,000 to £5,000 the limit on the amount which may be repaid on death without the necessity for proof from the Inland Revenue that no death duties or capital transfer tax are payable in respect of the deposits or that any death duties or capital transfer tax have been paid.

212 Savings banks—Registrar's fees

The Savings Banks (Registrar's Fees) (Amendment) Warrant 1978, S.I. 1978 No. 615 (in force on 25th April 1978), amends the Savings Banks (Registrar's Fees) Warrant 1976 in its application to England and Wales, the Isle of Man and the Channel Islands, by widening the definition of "the Registrar" to include a deputy appointed by the Chief Registrar of Friendly Societies. It replaces the Savings Banks (Registrar's Fees) (Amendment) Warrant 1977, 1977 Halsbury's Abr para. 236 which purported to make the same amendment in respect of the Savings Banks (Registrar's Fees) Warrant 1974.

213 Trustee savings banks—interest-bearing receipts

The Trustee Savings Banks (Interest-bearing Receipts) Order 1978, S.I. 1978 No. 605 (in force on 21st May 1978), reduces the rate of interest allowed to trustee savings banks on sums standing to their credit in the Fund for the Banks for Savings from £7·50 to £7·25 per cent per annum. The Trustee Savings Banks (Interest-bearing Receipts) Order 1977, 1977 Halsbury's Abr para. 239 is revoked.

214 —— transfer of stocks

The Trustee Savings Banks (Transfer of Stocks) Order 1978, S.I. 1978 No. 1718 (in force on 24th December 1978), provides that stocks registered in such parts of the National Savings Register as are kept by the trustees of trustee savings banks are to be transferred to that part of the Register kept by the Director of Savings. The relevant stocks and the respective dates of the transfers are specified in the Schedule to the Order.

215 Trustee Savings Banks Act 1976—commencement

The Trustee Savings Banks Act 1976 (Commencement No. 5) Order 1978, S.I. 1978

No. 533, brought into force on 28th April 1978 s. 10 (1), (3) of the 1976 Act. These provisions amend the Trustee Savings Banks Act 1969, s. 11, by removing the requirement for the consent of the National Debt Commissioners to the purchase and disposal of property by trustees and provide a saving for certificates issued under s. 11 (4) of the 1969 Act. Section 36 (part) and Sch. 6 (part) of the 1976 Act were also brought into force on 28th April 1978 so far as they relate to the repeal of the 1969 Act, s. 11 (1), (3), (4).

For provisions of the 1976 Act see 1976 Halsbury's Abr para. 198.

216   The Trustee Savings Bank Act 1976 (Commencement No. 6) Order 1978, S.I. 1978 No. 1079, brought into force on 18th August 1978 ss. 12 (part), 36 (part), Schs. 5 (part) and 6 (part) of the 1976 Act. These provisions relate to notification to depositors of transfers of ordinary deposits to another kind of account and minor amendments to and repeals of the Trustee Savings Banks Act 1969.

217   **Trustee Savings Banks Act 1978**

The Trustee Savings Banks Act 1978 clarifies and amends the law concerning investment and borrowing by trustee savings banks in certain minor respects. The Act received the royal assent on 30th June 1978 and came into force on that date.

Section 1 clarifies the investment and mortgage lending powers of trustee savings banks, removes any doubts as to the validity of mortgage loans made by trustee savings banks in the past and ensures that their validity will not in the future be subject to challenge by reference to whether or not a trustee savings bank has complied with the requirements of the Trustee Savings Banks Acts or its own rules in making a mortgage loan.

Section 2 enables the trustee savings banks to continue to receive deposits on wider terms than those permitted for ordinary deposits under Trustee Savings Bank Act 1969, s. 12.

Section 3 clarifies and limits the borrowing powers of trustee savings banks.

Sections 4 and 5 deal with extent and repeals.

BANKRUPTCY AND INSOLVENCY

Halsbury's Laws of England (4th edn.), Vol. 3, paras. 201–1062

218   **Article**

Criminal Bankruptcy, A. N. Khan (the success of the criminal bankruptcy provisions since their introduction in 1972): 122 Sol Jo 324.

219   **Appeal—appeal from county court—practice**

The following Practice Direction ([1978] 1 WLR 1060) has been issued by the Chancery Division.

1. It has been the practice hitherto for appeals from county courts in bankruptcy matters to be heard by Divisional Courts of the Chancery Division sitting on alternate Mondays, when required, throughout each term. This occasions disruption of the judges' work and interruption of the continuity of trials of other cases.

2. From the commencement of Hilary Term 1979 such appeals will normally be heard continuously during the second fortnight of each term (counting Easter Term and Trinity Term as a single term) or for such part of that fortnight as may be needed.

3. The Chief Clerk in Bankruptcy will during the last week of each term settle a list of the appeals to be heard during the following term. This will include all unheard appeals set down by that time. Any appeals set down between the settling of the list and the commencement of the sitting of the Divisional Court may be added to the list if time allows and the parties inform the chief clerk that they are ready.

4. The chief clerk will send a copy of the list to the solicitors to all parties to listed appeals (or to the parties themselves, if in person) not later than the first day of each term or, if appeals are added to the list pursuant to para. 3 above, forthwith on the inclusion of the appeal in the list.

5. Interlocutory applications may, while the Divisional Court is sitting, be made to that court instead of to the single judge pursuant to r. 133 of the Bankruptcy Rules 1952 (S.I. 1952 No. 2113).

6. If a sufficient case of urgency is made out a Divisional Court may be convened to hear an appeal at any time.

7. Motions and other bankruptcy matters in the High Court requiring to be heard by a single judge will continue to be heard on Mondays, when required, throughout each term, except when the Divisional Court is sitting. If a sufficient case of urgency is made out for the hearing of any such motion or matter during the sitting of the Divisional Court, it will be heard by one of the judges of that court.

220   Avoidance of settlement—purchaser in good faith and for valuable consideration—whether consideration sufficient

In 1975, the debtor executed a deed of arrangement with eight of his sixteen creditors. The deed assigned the debtor's property to the creditors in exchange for the right to seven days' notice of any further proceedings against him to enforce payment of his debts. The debtor became bankrupt in 1976 and his trustee in bankruptcy claimed that the deed of arrangement was void under the Bankruptcy Act 1914, s. 42, which provides that a settlement of property, not being a settlement made in favour of a purchaser in good faith and for valuable consideration, would be void against the trustee in bankruptcy if the settlor became bankrupt within two years of the settlement. *Held,* the question whether the creditors were purchasers for valuable consideration depended upon whether there had been a quid pro quo of commercial value for the assets which the debtor gave up. It appeared that nothing was given by the creditors except the obligation to give seven days' notice before taking proceedings against the debtor. The advantage secured by the debtor was a triviality and a quid pro quo of no commercial value whatsoever. It followed therefore, that the deed was void, under s. 42, against the trustee in bankruptcy.

TRUSTEE OF C. R. SPINKS (IN BANKRUPTCY) v DICKER (1978) 122 Sol Jo 791 (Chancery Division: BRIGHTMAN J). Dicta of Goff J in *Re Windle* [1975] 3 All ER 987, 1975 Halsbury's Abr para. 220 applied.

221   Bankruptcy rules—allowances—auctioneers and brokers

The Bankruptcy (Amendment No. 2) Rules 1978, S.I. 1978 No. 1224 (in force on 1st October 1978), amend the Bankruptcy Rules 1952 by revising the Scale of Allowances to Auctioneers and Brokers.

222   —— costs

The Bankruptcy (Amendment) Rules 1978, S.I. 1978 No. 544 (in force on 2nd May 1978) make various amendments to the Bankruptcy Rules 1952 as regards costs and their taxation. Rule 2 adds a rule allowing the Official Receiver or trustee in bankruptcy to meet certain costs and charges of less than £100 without taxation, while r. 3 increases the costs allowed in connection with calling of a creditors' meeting. Low value is no longer a requirement for disclaiming a lease without the leave of the court: r. 4. The level of debt below which creditors in summary cases are excluded in the Official Receiver's certificate on the bankrupt's application for discharge and do not receive certain notices has also been increased: r. 5. By r. 6, the financial limit on debtor's assets for the purposes of summary administration following the making of a receiving order under the Bankruptcy Act 1914 has been raised.

223   —— fees

The Bankruptcy Fees (Amendment) Order 1978, S.I. 1978 No. 570 (in force on 9th May 1978), adds a new fee to Table A (Fee No. 37), payable where a receiving order is made under the Insolvency Act 1976, s. 11. The Order also replaces Table B, Fees No. 18, 19, with an ad valorem fee payable by every trustee in bankruptcy on submission to the Secretary of State of accounts of receipts and payments under the Bankruptcy Act 1914, s. 92. Finally, the cost of insertion in the London Gazette of a notice authorised by the 1914 Act or Bankruptcy Rules 1952, is increased to £3·75.

224   The Bankruptcy Fees (Amendment No. 2) Order 1978, S.I. 1978 No. 704 (in force on 1st June 1978), amends the Bankruptcy Fees Order 1975, 1975 Halsbury's Abr para. 222, by providing for the payment of the amount of VAT in addition to the amount of any fee provided for in the Order where the tax is chargeable in respect of the service to which that fee relates.

The Bankruptcy Fees (Amendment No. 3) Order 1978, S.I. 1978 No. 1653 (in force on 1st December 1978), amends the Bankruptcy Fees Order 1975 by increasing certain fees contained in Sch. B of the 1975 Order taken by the Department of Trade in bankruptcy proceedings.

225   **Criminal bankruptcy—bankruptcy order—financial limit on juris-diction—relevant offences**

In making a bankruptcy order against the appellant, a convicted offender, the judge took into consideration the loss caused by offences with which he had not been formally charged. The appellant contended that the bankruptcy order should be set aside since the loss caused by offences with which he had been charged in the indictment did not amount to the £15,000 specified in the Powers of Criminal Courts Act 1973, s. 39 (1) as the limit for making such an order. *Held*, the practice of taking into consideration offences with which an offender had not been formally charged should only be followed with his express consent. The offender should be specifically informed of each offence intended to be taken into consideration, he should admit his guilt and agree to each offence being considered when determining his sentence. As this procedure had not been followed, the judge had no right to take account of the loss caused by offences not included in the indictment and therefore the limit of £15,000 had not been reached. The appeal would be allowed and the order set aside.

Director of Public Prosecutions v Anderson [1978] 2 All ER 512 (House of Lords: Lord Wilberforce, Lord Diplock, Lord Salmon, Lord Fraser of Tullybelton and Lord Keith of Kinkel). Decision of Court of Appeal [1978] 2 All ER 8, 1977 Halsbury's Abr para. 245 reversed.

226   **Forfeiture of lease—bankruptcy of surety—whether landlord required to serve a forfeiture notice**

See *Halliard Property Co Ltd v Jack Segal Ltd*, para. 1718.

227   **Insolvency Act 1976—commencement**

The Insolvency Act 1976 (Commencement No. 4) Order 1978, S.I. 1978 No. 139, brings into force on 1st March 1978 Insolvency Act 1976, s. 1976, s. 12, which transfers from the Lord Chancellor to the county courts rule committee the power to make county court rules relating to administration orders.

Section 14 and Sch, 3, containing consequential repeals, are also brought completely into force on that date.

For 1976 Act see 1976 Halsbury's Abr para. 206.

228   **Property available for distribution—property passing to trustee—protected transactions—payments into court under attachment of earnings order**

In June 1977 a consolidated attachment of earnings order was made against a debtor. Deductions by the employers were payable to the court monthly. Under Attachment of Earnings Act 1971, s. 13 sums paid under an order were to be dealt with as if paid by the debtor to satisfy the relevant adjudication, but in practice the court accumulated the sums paid in until a certain dividend could be paid. Sums were paid in each month from July to October and accumulated. On the same day as the last payment a receiving order was made against the debtor and he was later adjudicated bankrupt. The Official Receiver contended that the money in court should be paid to him as trustee of the bankrupt's estate. *Held*, the Attachment of Earnings Act 1971 did not effect an assignment of undistributed money to the judgment creditors. The payments into court before the date of receiving order were however protected for the judgment creditors by Bankruptcy Act 1914, s. 45, being payments made by the bankrupt to his creditors before the receiving order and at a time when they had no notice of any available act of bankruptcy committed before that time. The three payments from July to September belonged to the judgment creditors and the last to the Official Receiver as trustee.

RE GREEN (A BANKRUPT), EX PARTE OFFICIAL RECEIVER V CUTTING (1978) Times, 8th July (Chancery Division: WALTON J).

229   Receiving order under debenture—debt guaranteed by joint guarantors—effect of insolvency of one guarantor

See *Re Price*, para. 1450.

BARRISTERS

Halsbury's Laws of England (4th edn.), Vol. 3, paras. 1101–1221

230   Articles

Barristers' Immunity, A. Kewley (the extent to which a barrister should be liable for negligent pre-trial work): 122 Sol Jo 188.

The Future of the Bar: 128 NLJ 991.

The *Saif Ali* case: a New Liability for the Bar? Quentin Edwards (liability of barristers in the light of *Saif Ali v Sydney Mitchell & Co* [1978] 3 WLR 849: [1978] LS Gaz. 1185.

231   Chambers

Guidelines for the management and organisation of chambers are contained in the Annual Statement of the Senate of the Inns of Court and the Bar 1977–78, p. 45.

232   Change of professional address—notice of return to practice—opening of new chambers

The Bar Council rulings relating to the giving of notice of a change of professional address, notice of a return to practice and notice of the opening of a new set of chambers have been re-arranged by the Professional Conduct Committee and in their revised form are set out on p. 757 of the Guardian Gazette of 26th July 1978.

233   Conduct of case—application by client to dispense with counsel's services

A person being tried on a charge of perjury applied at the end of the prosecution case to dispense with his counsel's services. The judge refused the application after ascertaining that counsel was not forensically embarrassed in continuing to act. He also refused to hear the applicant's reasons. On appeal against conviction, *held*, in most cases a defendant would be allowed to give his reasons and the application would be allowed, but it was a matter for the judge's discretion. It was impossible to say that the exercise of the judge's discretion was invalidated by the fact that he did not allow the defendant to give his reasons.

R v LYONS (1978) Times, 13th July (Court of Appeal: LORD WIDGERY CJ, WALLER LJ and TUDOR EVANS J).

234 —— discussion of sentence—duty of defending counsel

Counsel may discuss the question of sentence of a defendant with a judge in accordance with the principles of *R v Turner* [1970] 2 QB 321. If the case becomes ineffective and is relisted before another judge there is no rule preventing counsel from raising the same matter with that other judge in accordance with the same principles. In that event it is not the duty of counsel to volunteer to disclose the previous judge's view or that the previous judge has been approached.

See ruling by the Bar Council, *Guardian Gazette*, 27th September 1978, p. 932.

235 —— non-attendance by instructing solicitor

A barrister should not appear in court unless his instructing solicitor is present. If, however, he arrives at court and finds neither the solicitor nor his representative present he may, when there is no practical alternative, conduct the case on behalf of the lay client and, exceptionally, interview supporting witnesses and take proofs of evidence if these are not already available. He should only take these steps if there are no grounds for seeking an adjournment. The Bar Council recognises that there are limits to what a counsel can effectively undertake in the absence of his instructing solicitor or his representative and suggest that in such circumstances counsel may feel obliged to seek an adjournment. See ruling by the Bar Council, Guardian Gazette, 28th June 1978, p. 638.

236 Counsel as witness

A barrister should not accept a retainer in a case in which he has reason to believe he will be a witness, and if being engaged in a case it becomes apparent that he is a witness on a material question of fact he ought not to continue to appear as counsel if he can retire without jeopardising his client's interests. If he continues in the case there is no rule of professional ethics which debars him from going into the witness box and being cross-examined.

See ruling of Bar Council (replacing the wording of the ruling in *Annual Statement* 1911, p. 11, paras. (1) and (2)), *Guardian Gazette*, 27th September 1978, p. 932.

237 Counsel's opinion—interrogatory to discover substance of opinion—legal professional privilege

See *Jones v G. D. Searle & Co Ltd*, para. 1796.

238 Foreign law and lawyers

The Bar Council has approved rules relating to the conditions on which foreign lawyers may be associated with chambers (superseding the rules in the *Annual Statement* 1973–74, p. 35) and the rules relating to practice by members of the Bar also qualified to practise in other systems of law. See the *Guardian Gazette*, 27th September 1978, p. 932.

239 Law centres

The current rules are contained in the Annual Statement of the Senate of the Inns of Court and the Bar 1977–78, pp. 49–51. They supersede those set out in the 1974–75 Annual Statement, 1975 Halsbury's Abr para. 239. No barrister may accept full-time or part-time employment at a centre other than a centre designated as such by the Bar Council. Subject to the rules a barrister who is employed at or attends a centre is bound by the rules of conduct and etiquette binding generally on barristers.

A barrister in full-time employment at a centre may appear as an advocate in a court or tribunal only on the instructions of a solicitor normally employed at that centre.

A barrister practising at the Bar from chambers may accept part-time employment at a centre.   Before accepting part-time employment a barrister must notify the Bar Council the terms of the employment and subsequently any variation.   He must receive no reward other than his remuneration as so notified.

A barrister whose primary occupation is employment at a centre is a practising barrister although he is not a member of chambers.   His remuneration may only be by way of salary.   Fees must be handed over to the centre.

A barrister who is employed part-time at or attends a centre and is in practice at the Bar from chambers may accept paid instructions from a solicitor for a lay client from the centre if he has not advised that client at a centre in relation to those proceedings.   Any fee must be paid over to the centre.

A barrister employed at a centre may not sue out any writ or process, instruct counsel or do any conveyancing.

A non-practising barrister may be employed at or attend a centre and advise clients but may not appear as a barrister in courts or tribunals.

A barrister whilst employed at a centre may appear as an advocate in courts or tribunals subject as follows:

(a) In centres other than law centres when neither private finance nor legal aid is available to a client or when no solicitor is prepared to accept his instructions or in cases of real emergency (the judge of which must be the barrister concerned) the employed barrister may appear as an advocate on the instructions of the centre in courts and tribunals in which a solicitor would have a right of audience and in applications for bail to a Judge in chambers: in all other cases where the services of an advocate is required the practice should be to refer the client to a solicitor selected from a list of solicitors provided at the centre.

(b) A barrister practising at the Bar from chambers in part-time employment at a law centre may, when neither private finance nor Legal Aid is available to a client or when no solicitor is prepared to accept his instructions or in cases of real emergency (the judge of which must be the barrister concerned) appear as an advocate on the instructions of the centre in courts or tribunals in which a solicitor would have a right of audience and in applications for bail to a Judge in chambers.

(c) A barrister in full-time employment at a law centre may appear as an advocate in courts and tribunals for clients of the centre provided that in cases in which a solicitor would have no right of audience he shall not appear without a solicitor or other representative of the centre in attendance.

(d) On each appearance as an advocate the employed barrister must have a backsheet prepared by and in the name of the centre marked with: (i) the name of the case or cases; (ii) the court or tribunal; (iii) the name of the barrister; (iv) the name of the centre; (v) the words "Legal Aid" where appropriate.

(e) The decision of the court or tribunal must be recorded on the backsheet.

(f) The barrister may interview and take statements from witnesses at his discretion and prepare his own brief.

(g) At all courts where counsel normally appear robed robes must be worn.

A barrister employed at or attending a centre may do any of the following without the instructions of a solicitor: (a) interview and take statements from clients and witnesses at his discretion; (b) write and sign letters on behalf of the centre provided that he does not add after his name the description "barrister" or "barrister at law"; (c) carry on correspondence with third parties and negotiate settlements on behalf of clients of the centre; (d) permit himself to be described as a barrister on letter headings and other official publications used at or distributed by the centre; (e) draft letters on behalf of the clients for signature by him; (f) draft pleadings on behalf of the client.

240   Legal services—provisions governing EEC lawyers practising in UK

See para. 1225.

241   Negligence—immunity from action—extent of immunity

In 1966 a solicitor's client was injured when the van in which he was travelling as passenger was involved in a collision with a car driven by a woman. On the advice of a barrister the solicitor advised the client to take action against the husband, the owner of the car, although he was not in the car at the time and his wife was not driving as his agent. Subsequently the action against the husband had to be discontinued but by then the limitation period for the action had expired and it was too late for the client to claim against anyone else. He claimed damages from the solicitor for professional negligence. The Court of Appeal dismissed the solicitor's application to join the barrister as third party to the action on the ground that the barrister's professional immunity extended to all acts connected with the conduct and management of litigation. On the question whether the third party action should be allowed to go to trial, *held*, it was no longer true to say that barristers enjoyed complete immunity for negligent acts and omissions. Their immunity from actions in relation to their conduct in court was dependent on public policy because they owed a duty to the court as well as to their client. The interests of public policy did not require that this immunity should extend to all acts connected with litigation, but only to those which were ultimately connected with the trial. In this case the acts complained of fell outside the scope of this immunity, and accordingly the barrister could be joined as third party to the action.

SAIF ALI v SYDNEY MITCHELL & CO [1978] 3 All ER 1033 (House of Lords: LORD WILBERFORCE, LORD DIPLOCK, LORD SALMON, LORD RUSSELL OF KILLOWEN and LORD KEITH OF KINKEL). Decision of the Court of Appeal, 1977 Halsbury's Abr para. 262, affirmed.

For a discussion of this case, see Problems in erosion of cherished notion, Justinian, Financial Times, 6th November 1978.

242   Overseas practice rules

The Bar Council have approved Overseas Practice Rules: Annual Statement of the Senate of the Inns of Court and the Bar 1977–78, p. 40. The rules supersede those set out in the 1973–74 Annual Statement, see 1974 Halsbury's Abr para. 220.

Subject to specified conditions and restrictions, barristers may accept instructions from practising foreign lawyers and from lay clients. They may negotiate fees for work done and if necessary enforce payment. They may also accept annual fees or retainers, fixed or contingent fees. A barrister may employ outside the United Kingdom anyone who is not a solicitor practising in England and Wales and may carry on practice outside the United Kingdom without the services of a clerk. A Queen's Counsel may draft documents in connection with proceedings outside the United Kingdom and appear in courts outside the United Kingdom with or without a junior. A barrister may enter into any association (including partnership) with a lawyer for the purpose of sharing any office or services outside the United Kingdom or for the purpose of doing, or sharing fees relating to, work of the kind for which he is entitled to accept instructions. However an association may not be created or subsist with a solicitor practising in the United Kingdom, or with a firm of solicitors so practising.

A practising barrister may not receive or handle clients' money or accept the status of an employee or of a commercial or business agent.

243   Professional misconduct—conviction for a serious offence

A barrister is under a professional obligation to report a conviction for a serious offence to the Senate. Serious offences include those involving dishonesty or which bring the profession into disrepute: Annual Statement of the Senate of the Inns of Court and the Bar 1977–78, p. 27.

244   —— disciplinary proceedings—powers of disciplinary body

Singapore
A remark made by an advocate to presiding judges was held by the Law Society of Singapore to constitute improper conduct. The Law Society, which was the

relevant disciplinary body, ordered him to pay a penalty under the Singapore Legal Profession Act. He applied to have the order set aside, contending that no conduct could be the subject of any disciplinary action unless it could be brought within certain heads of misconduct prescribed by the Act as reasons why an advocate was liable to be struck off, suspended or censured. The order was affirmed and he appealed. *Held*, the heads of misconduct enumerated in the Act were not exhaustive of the cases of professional misconduct that could be dealt with. The Act should not be construed so as to restrict the disciplinary powers it gave to the Law Society. Since the advocate's remark amounted to improper conduct, the order was justified and the appeal would be dismissed.

HILBORNE v LAW SOCIETY OF SINGAPORE [1978] 2 All ER 757 (Privy Council: LORD DIPLOCK, LORD FRASER OF TULLYBELTON and LORD RUSSELL OF KILLOWEN).

245　——— powers of Professional Conduct Committee of Bar Council

This Committee may now deal with minor cases of professional misconduct, incompetence and breach of etiquette. Annual Statement of the Senate of the Inns of Court and the Bar 1977–78, p. 25.

246　Pupillage

The duties of pupil-masters and pupils are set out in the Annual Statement of the Senate of the Inns of Court and the Bar 1977–78, p.52. Duties of pupil-masters include giving specific and detailed teaching instruction in the settling of pleadings and other documents, ensuring his pupil is well grounded in rules of conduct and etiquette, requiring his pupil to read his papers and attempt draft pleadings and other documents, requiring his pupil to accompany him frequently to court, and inviting him to sit on many conferences. Masters with essentially High Court practices should arrange for the pupil to accompany more junior members of chambers to lower courts. In the second six months the master should take a direct interest in the pupil's own work and in particular in his court appearances.

247　Tutorial services—overseas students—liability for value added tax

See *Webb v Customs and Excise Comrs*, para. 3087.

248　Visiting cards—use

The use of visiting cards by members of the Bar remains subject to the statement of principles set out in the *Annual Statement* 1973/74, p. 31, but under rules approved by the Bar Council cards may be used bearing (as appropriate) "Barrister" or "QC", other professional and academic qualifications and their professional address and telephone number. Barristers practising abroad must conform to the rules of the jurisdiction in which they practise. Notes have also been issued for guidance on these rules.

See the *Guardian Gazette*, 27th September 1978, p. 932.

BETTING, GAMING AND LOTTERIES

Halsbury's Laws of England (4th edn.), Vol. 4, paras. 1–190

249　Articles

A Case of Excessive Formalism: Gaming Act 1968, A. D. Science (applications for gaming licences and the attitude of the courts): 122 Sol Jo 218.

Report of the Royal Commission on Gambling, Gavin McFarlane: 128 NLJ 1061.

250   Bingo clubs—admission charges

See para. 318.

251   Gambling—report of Royal Commission

The recommendations of the Royal Commission on Gambling include the establishment (by the racing industry, if feasible) of a horse racing authority which would take over all the functions of the Horserace Betting Levy Board other than the assessment and collection of the levy, the establishment by the government of a gambling research unit; the establishment of a football board to collect and administer a fund raised from the pools; the establishment of a gaming review board to hear appeals from decisions of the Gaming Board given without reasons; the organisation of a nationwide lottery for good causes; the demise in July 1979 of the Pool Competitions Act 1971; the introduction of a casino betting duty; a reduction in football pool betting duty and an indexed-linked limit on the maximum football pool prize; and that betting offices should be allowed to sell light refreshments from vending machines.

Royal Commission on Gambling, Final Report, 2 volumes, HMSO. See Times, 13th July 1978.

252   Gaming—fees—variation

The Gaming Act (Variation of Fees) Order 1978, S.I. 1978 No. 1846 (in force on 1st May 1979), increases the fees payable under the Gaming Act 1968 for gaming licences and regulation of clubs and institutes.

253   Gaming club—application for licence—compliance with statutory requirements

See *R v Brighton Gaming Licensing Committee, ex parte Cotedale Ltd*, para. 317.

254   —— charges

See para. 318.

255   Gaming licence—notice of application—requirements of notice

See *R v Brighton Gaming Licensing Committee, ex parte Cotedale Ltd*, para. 317.

256   Gaming machines—licence duty

The Gaming Machine Licence Duty (Exemptions) Order 1978, S.I. 1978 No. 44 (in force on 20th February 1978), extends the exemption from gaming machine licence duty in respect of machines provided at pleasure fairs. The Gaming Machine Licence Duty (Exemptions) Order 1976, 1976 Halsbury's Abr para. 232 is revoked.

257   —— monetary limits

The Gaming Act (Variation of Monetary Limits) Order 1978, S.I. 1978 No. 37 (in force on 20th February 1978), increases the monetary limits specified in the Gaming Act 1968 on prizes at certain fairs, licensed club premises and other commercial entertainments.

258   General betting duty—estimate of duty payable—number of years over which assessment to be made

A bookmaker pleaded guilty to charges of being knowingly concerned in the fraudulent evasion of general betting duty in respect of bets made with him between September and December 1974. The Customs and Excise Comrs estimated the amount of duty unpaid by him between September 1971 and December 1974. The bookmaker paid the amount relating to the offences charged but contended that the estimate was invalid because it related to a period earlier than the first admitted offence. The commissioners sued for the balance. *Held*, the estimates were valid. Under the Betting and Gaming Duties Act 1972, Sch. 1, para. 11, where the commissioners were unable to ascertain the amount of duty due from a person because the accounts were incomplete and inaccurate, they were entitled to estimate the amount due and recover it. These powers of recovery were unrestricted as to time, so long as the commissioners acted in good faith and not arbitrarily.

CUSTOMS and EXCISE COMRS v GUINLE (1978) Times, 14th November (Queen's Bench Division: SHEEN J).

259   Horserace betting levy—settlement period

The Horserace Betting Levy Schemes (Variation of Settlement Period) Order 1978, S.I. 1978 No. 496 (in force on 1st May 1978), amends the Horserace Betting Levy Act 1969 by requiring the Secretary of State to determine an appropriate bookmakers' levy scheme if the recommendations of the Bookmakers' Committee have not been approved by the Horserace Betting Levy Board eight months before the beginning of the levy period.

260   Pools Competition Act 1971—continuation

The Pools Competition Act 1971 (Continuance) Order 1978, S.I. 1978 No. 778 (in force on 26th July 1978), continues in force the Pools Competition Act 1971 until and including, 26th July 1979.

BILLS OF EXCHANGE AND OTHER NEGOTIABLE INSTRUMENTS

Halsbury's Laws of England (4th edn.), Vol. 4, paras. 301–523

261   Bill of exchange—dishonour—parties entitled to judgment

The plaintiffs sold the defendants a quantity of steel and a bill of exchange was drawn on the defendants for the price. The bill was dishonoured by the defendants and the plaintiffs brought an action for the amount. As a general rule judgment is given when money is due under a bill of exchange but there is an exception giving rise to a discretion when the action is between the immediate parties. Although the plaintiffs were the drawers and the defendants were the acceptors the question in issue was whether the fact that the bill had left the plaintiffs' hands for a time excluded them from the definition of immediate parties. *Held*, the Bills of Exchange Act 1882, s. 29 (3) provided that the holder of a bill of exchange who derived his title through a holder in due course and who was not party to any fraud or illegality affecting it, had all the rights of a holder in due course with regard to the acceptor. In the present case the defendants had discounted the bill to a bank, who then became holder for value in due course, and when the bill was dishonoured the bank had passed it back to the plaintiffs. As the plaintiffs had derived their title through a holder in due course they had all the rights of a holder by virtue of s. 29 (3) and were entitled to immediate judgment for the full amount of the bill. The plaintiffs did not hold the bill in a dual capacity; when the bill was discounted they lost their original capacity as drawer, and they regained the bill in the capacity of holder which was now the dominant capacity.

JADE INTERNATIONAL STEEL STAHL UND EISEN GMBH & CO KG v ROBERT NICHOLAS (STEELS) LTD [1978] 3 All ER 104 (Court of Appeal: STEPHENSON, CUMMING-BRUCE and GEOFFREY LANE LJJ).

BRITISH NATIONALITY AND ALIENAGE

Halsbury's Laws of England (4th edn.), Vol. 4, paras. 901–973

262   British protectorates

The British Protectorates, Protected States and Protected Persons Order 1978, S.I. 1978 No. 1026 (in force on 16th August 1978), revokes S.I. 1974 No. 1895, 1974 Halsbury's Abr para. 234. The Order defines who are to be British protected persons for the purposes of the British Nationality Act 1948 by virtue of their connection with the former Solomon Islands protectorate, other than under the Solomon Islands Act 1978, or by virtue of their connection with any other former protectorate, any former Arabian protectorate or any former trust territory, or Brunei. It also provides for the registration as British protected persons of certain categories of persons who are stateless.

263   Citizenship—citizen by registration—registration by fraudulent means—validity of registration—power of Secretary of State to detain

A certificate of registration obtained by the fraudulent use of someone else's passport is null.

An immigrant obtained the passport and assumed the name of his dead cousin. He then obtained a certificate of registration and later a United Kingdom passport on the strength of the false passport. He was subsequently detained in pursuance of an order under the Immigration Act 1971, Sch. 2, para. 16. He contended his detention was unlawful because he was a citizen by registration and as such could only be deprived of his citizenship in the manner prescribed by the British Nationality Act 1948, s. 20. *Held*, before a person could rely on s. 20 he had to show he was a registered or naturalised citizen within s. 20 (1). The immigrant could not do so because his certificate of registration was a nullity. A certificate intended to confer citizenship on a person whom it transpired was dead at the relevant time conferred citizenship on no-one. Accordingly, the immigrant came within the scope of the Immigration Act 1971 and his detention was lawful.

R v Secretary of State for the Home Department, ex parte Sultan Mahmood (1978) Times, 2nd August (Court of Appeal: Stephenson, Roskill and Geoffrey Lane LJJ).

264   ——fees

The British Nationality (Amendment) Regulations 1978, S.I. 1978 No. 91 (in force at 1st March 1978), amend the British Nationality Regulations 1975, 1975 Halsbury's Abr para. 260, as amended, by increasing the fees payable in respect of the conferment of citizenship of the United Kingdom and Colonies by registration or naturalisation.

265   Immigration

See IMMIGRATION.

266   Race relations

See RACE RELATIONS.

BUILDING CONTRACTS, ARCHITECTS AND ENGINEERS

Halsbury's Laws of England (4th edn.), Vol. 4, paras. 1101–1369

267   Architect—duty of care—duty to advise clients of planning permission requirements

An architect was instructed by a company to design an office of under 10,000 square feet so that planning permission could be obtained without the need for a special office development permit under the Town and Country Planning Act 1971, s. 74. in reliance on a local planning officer's statement that a car park and caretaker's flat did not constitute office space, the architect's scheme for the office area alone covered 10,000 square feet. The company submitted a planning application to the council who purported to grant it planning permission. It was then discovered that the car park and flat should have been included in the office premises as defined by s. 73 (4) of the 1971 Act, which meant the area exceeded 10,000 square feet. Consequently, the planning permission was ineffective without the required office development permit and the planning permission was void. The company brought an action for damages against the architect. *Held*, the architect was aware of the requirements of s. 74 of the 1971 Act. He should have realised that planning permission could not be effective unless the planning application was within the exemption or was accompanied by an office development permit. While it was unfortunate that the council's policy with regard to computation of office space was wrong, the architect was liable for failing to warn the company that the planning permission would be ineffective unless the car park and flat could be excluded from the office area. The fact that the customers were professional men made no difference to the care and skill required of the architect.

B. L. HOLDINGS LTD v ROBERT J. WOOD AND PARTNERS (1978) 122 Sol Jo 525 (Queen's Bench Division: GIBSON J).

268   Building contract—breach of contract—breach by one party not discovered by other party until contract fulfilled—remedies

See *Morrison-Knudson Co Inc v British Columbia Hydro and Power Authority*, para. 479.

269   —— measure of damages

See *William Cory & Son Ltd v Wingate Investments (London Colney) Ltd*, para. 855.

270   —— construction—obligation to deliver drawings from time to time as work progresses—obligation to supply equipment

Canada

Under a contract for the installation of mining equipment the defendant undertook to deliver drawings to the contractor "from time to time as work progresses" and to "supply" certain equipment. The contract provided that the defendant was not bound by any implied term therein. The contractor failed to complete the work by the agreed completion date and the defendant terminated the contract. The contractor brought an action for breach of contract on the grounds that it was the defendant's delay in delivering the drawings and supplying the equipment which resulted in his failure to complete by the due date. The defendant contended that there was no breach of any express obligation and that the contract exempted him from liability under any term normally implied in contracts of a similar nature. *Held*, the true construction of the phrase "from time to time as work progresses" was at appropriate times in all the circumstances, including the completion date, and the obligation to "supply" was to be interpreted as an obligation to supply at an appropriate time. Thus the defendant was in breach of his express undertakings.

FISCHBACH AND MOORE OF CANADA LTD v NORANDA MINES LTD (1978) 84 DLR (3d) 465 (Court of Appeal of Saskatchewan).

271 —— sub-contractors—tax deduction scheme—certificate of exemption

See *Kirvell (Inspector of Taxes) v Guy*, para. 1572.

272 Surveyors—professional body—byelaws—validity of amendment

See *Merrills v Royal Institution of Chartered Surveyors*, para. 3092.

BUILDING SOCIETIES

Halsbury's Laws of England (4th edn.), Vol. 4, paras. 1501–1723

273 Fees

The Building Societies (Fees) Regulations 1978, S.I. 1978 No. 1752 (in force on 1st January 1978), increase fees payable in connection with the exercise by the Central Office and the Chief Registrar of their functions under the Building Societies Act 1962. The Building Societies (Fees) Regulations, 1977 Halsbury's Abr para. 289 are now superseded.

274 Powers—power to participate in arrangement to compensate investors in collapsed society

In the interest of maintaining the reputation of building societies for security and trustworthiness, the plaintiff building society and three other building societies agreed to participate in a rescue operation to prevent investors in a collapsed building society from bearing the substantial loss. A draft deed of arrangement was drawn up whereby each investor in the collapsed society would be credited on the books of the second plaintiff society with a sum equal to the value of his investment prior to the collapse. The real cost of the scheme would be borne equally between the five building societies and would have no effect on their rates of interest or the security of their own investors. The deed of arrangement was submitted for the statutory approval of the Chief Registrar of Friendly Societies. He withheld his consent pending judicial decisions on (i) whether s. 43 required any arrangement to embody mutual rights and obligations and (ii) whether the section could only apply to arrangements made in respect of future losses. *Held*, the section neither required mutuality nor was it confined to arrangements in respect of future losses. On the evidence the proposed arrangement was within the ambit of the section.

HALIFAX BUILDING SOCIETY v REGISTRY OF FRIENDLY SOCIETIES [1978] 3 All ER 403 (Chancery Division: TEMPLEMAN J).

CAPITAL GAINS TAXATION

Halsbury's Laws of England (4th edn.), Vol. 5, paras. 1–247

275 Article

Appointments and Advancements—A Capital Gains Tax Trap, V. R. Chapman (how to avoid the effect of the Finance Act 1965, s. 25 (3)): 128 NLJ 143.

276 Allowable loss—disposal of debt—debt on a security—waiver of unsecured loan

The taxpayer, a holding company which had bought all the shares in a subsidiary for £115,000 sold them to a purchaser for £250,000. A condition of the contract required the taxpayer to waive a loan of £500,000 made to the subsidiary. The taxpayer was assessed to corporation tax on the basis that it had made a chargeable

gain represented by the difference between the price received for the shares
(£250,000) over the price paid (£115,000). On appeal against the assessment the
taxpayer argued that the £250,000 had been paid for both the shares and the waiver
of the loan, as a composite transaction and that therefore there should be an
apportionment under the Finance Act 1965, Sch. 6, para. 21 (4). Alternatively it
was argued that as the taxpayer owned the subsidiary the loan to it was "a debt on a
security" within the terms of Sch. 7, paras. 11 (1) and 5 (3) (b) of the Act and
therefore disposal of the loan by waiver was an allowable loss. *Held*, (1) The
inclusive definition of "debt on a security" in Sch. 7, para. 5 (3) (b) was obscure but
a distinction could at least be drawn between a pure unsecured debt on the one hand
and a debt (which might be unsecured) which had, if not a marketable character, at
least such characteristics as enabled it to be dealt in and if necessary converted into
shares or other securities. The loan to the subsidiary was nothing but an unsecured
loan with no quality or characteristic which brought it within whatever special
category was meant by "debt on a security". (2) (VISCOUNT DILHORNE and LORD
RUSSELL OF KILLOWEN dissenting), on the true construction of the contract the
waiver of the loan was part of the consideration so that the £250,000 was paid for
both the transfer of the shares and waiver of the loan. On this point the appeal
would be allowed and the case remitted to the Commissioners for apportionment.

ABERDEEN CONSTRUCTION GROUP LTD v IRC [1978] 1 All ER 962 (House of
Lords: LORD WILBERFORCE, VISCOUNT DILHORNE, LORD FRASER OF TULLYBELTON,
LORD RUSSELL OF KILLOWEN and LORD KEITH OF KINKEL). Decision of Court of
Session (Inner House) 1977 STC 302, 1977 Halsbury's Abr para. 291 varied.

**277   Assessment—appeal—agreement with tax inspector to vary
assessment—whether agreement binding**

A taxpayer entered into correspondence with his tax inspector as to assessment of a
payment he had received. They initially agreed that the payment should be
apportioned partly to capital gains tax and partly under Schedule E, but they
disagreed as to the amount chargeable under Schedule E. The inspector subsequently
charged the whole payment to capital gains tax. The taxpayer appealed against the
assessment contending that the correspondence constituted an agreement within
Taxes Management Act 1970, s. 54 (1). *Held*, s. 54 (1) only applied to an agreement
to vary an assessment if the agreement specified the figures to be apportioned or at
the very least contained sufficient information to calculate them. The agreement in
question did neither and therefore s. 54 (1) did not apply. The appeal would be
dismissed.

DELBOURGO v FIELD (INSPECTOR OF TAXES) [1978] 2 All ER 193 (Court of Appeal:
STAMP, ORR and EVELEIGH LJJ). Decision of Foster J [1977] 1 All ER 323, 1976
Halsbury's Abr para. 270, affirmed.

**278   Disposal of assets—deemed disposal—capital sum derived from
assets—deferred consideration for shares**

In 1970 the taxpayers agreed to sell shares in a private company. The consideration
was partly a fixed sum per share to be paid immediately and partly a deferred
payment to be calculated in accordance with the agreement. The relevant date for
calculating the amount of the deferred consideration was 5th December 1972. On
the question of capital gains tax liability for the year of assessment 1970–1971 the
Revenue contended that the right to receive the deferred consideration was an asset
from which a capital sum was derived when the right matured on 5th December
1972 and that accordingly there was a deemed disposal under Finance Act 1965, s.
22 (3). *Held*, the right to receive the deferred consideration, being incorporeal
property, was a new asset. However, s. 22 (3) was confined to cases where no asset
was acquired in return for the capital sum whereas in the present case shares were
acquired in return for the deferred consideration. Accordingly s. 22 (3) did not give
rise to a deemed disposal.

MARREN (INSPECTOR OF TAXES) v INGLES [1979] STC 58 (Chancery Division:
SLADE J).

279   —— —— **transfer of assets by trustees to trustees—liability to tax**

In view of two recent cases concerning the treatment of resettled property for capital gains tax purposes (*Hart v Briscoe; Hoare Trustees v Gardner*, 1977 Halsbury's Abr para. 294), where new trustees become absolutely entitled to the settled property as against the old trustees, the Inland Revenue have stated how they will approach the questions raised by these cases in Statement of Practice SP 7/78. They will take the view that where a power of advancement or a general power of appointment is exercised irrevocably, the assets to which it applies will normally pass into a new settlement; a charge on a deemed disposal by the trustees of the original settlement will therefore arise under the Finance Act 1965, s. 25 (3). Where a special power of appointment is exercised, the Revenue consider that the assets to which the appointment applies will normally remain subject to the original settlement as modified by the appointment so that a deemed disposal for the purposes of s. 25 (3) does not result: Inland Revenue Press Release dated 14th November 1978.

280   —— **disposal of shares—transfer of value in shares—control of company**

The plaintiffs wished to sell their majority shareholding in an electronics company to an American company. In an attempt to avoid tax liability, a third company was created, with share capital divided into ordinary and preferred shares. The ordinary shares carried rights to most of the surplus assets upon a winding up. The plaintiffs' shares in the electronics company were sold to the third company in return for 100,000 of the third company's preferred shares. The latter resold its newly-acquired shares to the American company. Subsequently a fourth company, based in the Cayman Islands, applied for and received 100 preferred shares in the third company. The unissued ordinary shares in that company were then offered to the plaintiffs and the fourth company; the former refused but the latter accepted and became the sole ordinary shareholder in the third company. The third company was then wound up voluntarily and the majority of its assets went out of the country automatically, to the fourth company.

In the determination of whether capital gains tax was payable on the transaction, four questions arose: (i) whether the plaintiffs had made a disposal of their shares to the American company; (ii) whether the third company had obtained control of the electronics company for the purposes of the Finance Act 1965, Sch. 7, paras. 4 (2), 6 (1); (iii) whether the plaintiffs had exercised that control within Sch. 7, para. 15 (2); and (iv) whether, if they had, they had exercised it when the winding up resolution for the third company was passed. *Held*, (i), EVELEIGH LJ dissenting, the sale to the third company did not lose its character as a disposal merely because the shares were intended ultimately to go somewhere else; (ii) the third company had genuinely obtained control of the electronics company and therefore the whole transaction had to be treated as a reorganisation of capital. The third company's shares acquired by the plaintiffs had in consequence to be treated as the same as those they had had in the electronics company; (iii) although para. 15 (2) referred only to a single person's having control, it extended to cases of control by more than one person. On the facts, the plaintiffs had had control of the third company; and (iv), although absent when the winding up resolution was passed, it had been a part of the plaintiffs' preconceived plan and thus an exercise of their control. Accordingly, capital gains tax was payable.

FLOOR v DAVIS (INSPECTOR OF TAXES) [1978] 3 WLR 360 (Court of Appeal: BUCKLEY and EVELEIGH LJJ and SIR JOHN PENNYCUICK). Decision of Goulding J [1976] 3 All ER 314, 1976 Halsbury's Abr para. 284 reversed in part.

281   —— **surrender of rights—payment for release from service agreement**

An employer's rights under a service contract do not constitute an asset for the purposes of the Finance Act 1965, s. 22.

A sales director was released from his service contract with the taxpayer company in consideration of a payment from him of £50,000. The company was assessed to corporation tax on the amount, the Crown contending that the company's rights under the service agreement were incorporeal property generally for the purposes of the Finance Act 1965, s. 22 (1) (a). The company argued that the rights under the agreement were not assets for the purposes of the 1965 Act. *Held*, the answer depended on whether a chargeable gain accrued from an actual or notional disposal of any asset. The answer to that hung on whether the rights under the service contract disposed of were assets. The Crown's argument that such non-assignable rights were incorporeal property generally was wrong: prima facie the rights of an employer to personal services under a contract of employment were not property, and this was supported by the opinion of the House of Lords in *Nokes v Doncaster Amalgamated Collieries Ltd* [1940] AC 1014, where a contract of service was held not to be property for the purposes of the Companies Act 1929. Furthermore, the Crown's contention went against the proper construction of s. 22 (2) (b) of the 1965 Act, relating to disposals: if incorporeal property embraced all contractual rights, then every right under a contract was a separate asset even though the sum of the rights under it might be a composite asset. This resulted in the fallacy that the creation of a right over a composite asset was a disposal of a pre-existing asset, not the part-disposal ordained by the provision. Finally, the Crown could not rely on s. 22 (3) to show a notional disposal had been made because the sub-section related only to capital sums derived from assets which could be identified within the meaning of s. 22 (1).

O'BRIEN (INSPECTOR OF TAXES) v BENSON'S HOSIERY (HOLDINGS) LTD [1978] 3 All ER 1057 (Court of Appeal: BUCKLEY and BRIDGE LJJ and SIR DAVID CAIRNS). Decision of Fox J [1977] 3 All ER 352, 1977 Halsbury's Abr para. 295 reversed.

282 —— transfer to trustees—retention of life interest—sale of beneficial remainder—nature of disposal

A taxpayer executed a deed of settlement comprising two separate transactions: firstly he transferred shares and loan stock to a Guernsey company to be held on trust for his own benefit for life; secondly he sold the reversionary interest in the benefit of the trust to a Jersey company for £14,500. It was agreed that this sum represented the market value of the interest in remainder. He was assessed for capital gains tax on the basis that the transfer to the trustees was a total disposal of the property. He appealed, alleging that the sale of the interest in remainder was a part disposal within the Finance Act 1965, s. 22(2). The Revenue contended that the transfer to the trustees was a gift in settlement within s. 25(2) and so had to be deemed to be a disposal of the fund at market value either because the trustees had acquired the property otherwise than by way of a bargain made at arm's length within s. 22(4)(a) or because it was a disposal between connected persons within Sch. 7, para. 21. *Held*, even if the transfer had been a gift within s. 25(2) there was no basis on which the taxpayer's gain could be assessed apart from the sum paid by the Jersey company. On the facts s. 22(4)(a) could not apply because the transfer to the trustees was not otherwise than by way of a bargain made at arm's length. Nor could s. 22(4)(a) be supported by Sch. 7, para. 21 because the trustee company and the taxpayer were not connected persons for the purpose of that paragraph. The appeal would be allowed and the assessment reduced.

BERRY v WARNETT (INSPECTOR OF TAXES) [1978] 1 WLR 957 (Chancery Division: GOULDING J).

283 Exemptions and reliefs—annual payments due under covenants

The taxpayer company resolved to pay a dividend to its shareholders out of royalty payments from an American company. It was assessed to corporation tax on the notional gain arising from the distribution. The company contended that the payments were exempt under Finance Act 1965, Sch. 7, para. 12 (c), being annual payments due under a covenant. *Held*, the two questions to be decided were whether the royalty payments were "annual payments" and whether they were "due under a covenant" within para. 12 (c). Although royalty payments would not normally be annual payments because they would not be pure profit income in the payee's hands they were not incapable of being annual payments. In the present case the royalties were annual payments. In the context of para. 12 (c) the word "covenant" clearly bore its ordinary and primary meaning of a promise in a document executed by the promisor under seal. It followed that the payments were "due under a covenant".

RANK XEROX LTD v LANE (INSPECTOR OF TAXES) [1978] 2 All ER 1124 (Court of Appeal: BUCKLEY and BRIDGE LJJ and SIR DAVID CAIRNS). Decision of Slade J [1977] 3 All ER 593, 1977 Halsbury's Abr para. 296 reversed.

284   —— debt on a security—definition

The taxpayer company devised a scheme with the sole aim of avoiding liability for capital gains tax. It acquired a number of shares in an investment company on a premium with £5 payable on application and the balance on call. On the same day the taxpayers made two loans to the investment company, each of which carried interest of 11 per cent, but shortly afterwards the rate of interest on the first loan was reduced to zero and the rate on the second loan was increased to 22 per cent. The investment company then called for the balance due on the shares and shortly afterwards sold the second loan at its market value. The taxpayers appealed against an assessment for capital gains tax on the capital profit on the sale of the loan. The Commissioners contended that the sale was a "debt on a security" and therefore did not fall within the exemption in Sch. 7, para. 11 of the Finance Act 1965, which provides that where a person incurs a debt no chargeable gain shall accrue to the original creditor on a disposal of the debt, except in the case of a debt on a security. *Held*, the meaning of "debt on a security" had recently been considered in *Aberdeen Construction Group Ltd v Inland Revenue Commissioners* [1978] STC 127 where the House of Lords had held that there was no debt on a security without the "issue of a document or certificate by the debtor institutions which would represent a marketable security". As no document had been issued in the present case the Commissioners had erred in law in holding that the sale was a debt on a security. The appeal would be allowed even though the scheme was designed specifically to avoid liability for capital gains tax.

W. T. RAMSEY LTD v IRC [1978] 2 All ER 321 (Chancery Division: GOULDING J). Dicta of Lord Emslie and Lord Wilberforce in *Aberdeen Construction Group Ltd v Inland Revenue Commissioners* [1977] STC at 309, 1977 Halsbury's Abr para. 291 and [1978] STC at 133, para. 276 respectively applied.

285   —— gilt-edged securities

The Capital Gains Tax (Exempt Gilt-edged Securities) (No. 1) Order 1978, S.I. 1978 No. 141 (made on 30th January 1978), adds 12 per cent Treasury Stock 1995, 8¼ per cent Treasury Stock 1982, 3 per cent Exchequer Stock 1981, 10½ per cent Exchequer Stock 1997, 10 per cent Treasury Stock 1992 and 8¼ per cent Exchequer Stock 1981 to the category of stocks and bonds which are exempt from tax on capital gains if held for more than twelve months.

286   The Capital Gains Tax (Exempt Gilt-edged Securities) (No. 2) Order 1978, S.I. 1978 No. 1312 (made on 29th August 1978), adds 10½ per cent Treasury Stock 1999, 10¼ per cent Exchequer Stock 1995, 8¼ per cent Exchequer Stock 1983, 12 per cent Exchequer Stock 1998 and 9¼ per cent Exchequer Stock 1982 "A", to the category of stocks and bonds which are exempt from tax on capital gains if held for more than twelve months. The Order also rectifies an error in the Capital Gains Tax (Exempt gilt-edged Securities) (No. 4) Order 1977, 1977 Halsbury's Abr para. 300, by amending 9¼ per cent Exchequer Stock 1983 to 9¼ per cent Treasury Stock 1983.

287   The Capital Gains Tax (Exempt Gilt-edged Securities) (No. 3) Order 1978, S.I. 1978 No. 1838 (made on 12th December 1978), adds 12 per cent Exchequer Stock 2013–2017, 10 per cent Exchequer Stock 1983, 12 per cent Exchequer Stock 1999–2002, 12¼ per cent Exchequer Stock 1985, 12½ per cent Treasury Stock 2003–2005, 9¼ per cent Treasury Stock 1983 to the category of stocks and bonds which are exempt from tax on capital gains if held for more than twelve months.

288   —— retirement relief—disposal of shares in business

The Finance Act 1965, s. 34, gives relief from capital gains tax in respect of gains accruing to an individual in certain circumstances from the disposal of the whole or part of a business which he has owned throughout the period of ten years ending with the disposal. An extra-statutory concession by the Inland Revenue allows separate businesses owned during the ten-year period to be treated as the same business, provided that although carried on in different localities they were concerned with goods or services of the same kind. This condition is now to be dropped, and in future all separate businesses owned during the ten-year period will be treated as the same business for the purpose of s. 34: Inland Revenue Press Release, dated 13th March 1978.

289   —— transfer of shares—nominee property

Shareholders in a company transferred their shares to trustees to be held by them for a period of 15 years on the terms of an agreement. One of the shareholders appealed against a subsequent assessment to capital gains tax which had been made on the basis that the transfer of shares was a disposal giving rise to a chargeable gain. *Held*, the transfer was liable to tax unless it fell within the exemption contained in s. 22 (5) of the Finance Act 1965, which applied only if the trustees held the shares as nominees or as trustees for another person absolutely entitled as against them. Where there were several beneficial owners they fulfilled the requirements of the exemption if their interests were concurrent, and not successive, and if their interests were the same. As these requirements applied in the present case the shares were "nominee property", and not "settled property" for capital gains tax purposes and were within the s. 22 (5) exemption.

BOOTH v ELLARD (INSPECTOR OF TAXES) [1978] 3 All ER 298 (Chancery Division: GOULDING J). *Stephenson v Barclays Bank Trust Co Ltd* [1975] 1 All ER 625, 1975 Halsbury's Abr para 324, and *Kidson v MacDonald* [1974] Ch 339, 1974 Halsbury's Abr para. 269, applied.

290   Finance Act 1978

Finance Act 1978, Pt. III deals with capital gains tax; see further para. 2312.

291   Gain—computation—assets held on 6th April 1965—Lands Tribunal decision

GOOD (INSPECTOR OF TAXES) v GWYTHER [1978] RVR 135: R. C. Walmsley FRICS (taxpayer appealed against assessment to capital gains tax on sale of house; contended value in 1965 was £16,000 in light of condition it was in and offer made to him subsequently by an intending purchaser; valuation officer set value at £7,500 by reference to comparables; latter's valuation accepted because taxpayer could adduce no evidence to substantiate claim; valuation officer appeared to have been generous in any case in allowing taxpayer benefit of several doubtful points relating to value).

292   —— —— —— sales of land reflecting development value

The taxpayer sold some farming land at a price which reflected the expectation of planning permission being granted. Permission was not granted. He was assessed to tax under the Finance Act 1965, Sch. 6, para. 23, which provides that in certain circumstances the gain is to be computed by reference to the extent to which the consideration acquired on the disposal exceeds what the market value would have been if immediately before the disposal it had become unlawful to carry out any development. The taxpayer who proposed straight line apportionment under para. 24, argued that assessment under para. 23 was inappropriate as the condition on which the para. was based had not been met. Development had not become unlawful; it had remained unlawful. On appeal against the assessment *held*, what para. 23 supposed was not a change in the law whereby some particular development became unlawful but a change by the effect of which it had become unlawful to carry out any development over the land. The para. contemplated an absolute prohibition of all development with or without permission. Para. 23 applied and the appeal would be dismissed.

WATKINS v KIDSON (INSPECTOR OF TAXES) [1978] 2 All ER 785 (Court of Appeal: STAMP, ROSKILL and CUMMING-BRUCE LJJ). Decision of Fox J [1977] 3 All ER 545, 1977 Halsbury's Abr para. 305 affirmed.

Finance Act 1965, Sch. 6, para. 23, applies only to sales made before December 1973.

293   —— **gain arising from company's sale of subsidiary—scheme to avoid tax on gains—effectiveness**

The taxpayer company devised and executed a scheme to avoid tax on gains arising from the sale of a wholly-owned subsidiary for £4 million. Two companies were incorporated: the first had one hundred £1 shares, divided into seventy-six preference shares owned by the taxpayer, and twenty-four ordinary shares, carrying all the voting rights, held by the prospective purchaser; the second company had one hundred £1 shares, owned by the first company. The prospective purchaser lent £4 million to the second company, which purchased the subsidiary for that sum. The first company was then voluntarily wound up, £76 being paid to the taxpayer in respect of its preference shareholding, with the consequence that the second company became a wholly-owned subsidiary of the prospective purchaser and the registered shareholder of the purchased shares. *Held*, the scheme was valid and effective in avoiding the taxpayer's liability to capital gains tax on the gain arising from the disposal of the subsidiary. By virtue of the taxpayer's beneficial ownership of the seventy-six preference shares in the first company, that company and its wholly owned subsidiary were members of the same group of companies as the taxpayer and the disposal, being by one member of the group to another, was therefore within the exemption provided for by the Income and Corporation Taxes Act 1970, s. 273.

BURMAN (INSPECTOR OF TAXES) v HEDGES AND BUTLER LTD [1979] 1 WLR 160 (Chancery Division: WALTON J).

294   **Remission of tax—official error**

In response to a request for advance notification of a capital gains liability an error was made in the calculation and a wrong estimate supplied. This was later corrected and the taxpayer discovered that she was liable to pay a higher figure than she had anticipated. The Parliamentary Commissioner, investigating a complaint made to him, has stated that this type of error is not covered by the authority given in a white paper of 14th July 1971 (Cmnd. 4729) to remit tax in case of official error. That authority is concerned only with cases where some departmental error has given rise to arrears of tax and the question at issue is whether those arrears ought to be given up in whole or in part.

See *Case 1A/649/77* in the Fifth Report of the Parliamentary Commissioner for Administration for the Session 1977–78 (HC 524), p. 248.

CARRIERS

Halsbury's Laws of England (4th edn.), Vol. 5, paras. 301–484

295   **Article**

The Carriage of Dangerous Goods by Land, Dr. D. J. Hill (the position of carriers at common law and under the CMR Convention contained in the Carriage of Goods by Road Act 1965): [1978] 1 LMCLQ 74.

296   **Carriage by air**

See AVIATION.

297   **Carriage by sea**

See SHIPPING.

298   **Carriage of goods by road—liability of carrier—damages payable in respect of personal injury—whether carrier entitled to indemnity from owner of goods**

The plaintiff lorry driver was employed by the carriers to transport a heavy load. Because the carriers had failed to choose a suitable route for the journey having regard to the size of the load, the plaintiff was injured when the load hit a gantry and fell onto his driving cab. He successfully claimed damages from the carriers who then sought an indemnity from the owners of the load. They contended that a clause in the contract of carriage stating "transport only working RHA Conditions 1967 of carriage" incorporated into the contract the Road Haulage Association's Conditions, one condition of which required the owners to indemnify the carriers in respect of certain claims. *Held*, (i) although the clause was poorly drafted, it was reasonably clear in the circumstances that the carriers had contracted to transport the load in accordance with the RHA Conditions. (ii) The condition was intended to regulate the rights and liabilities arising out of the carriage of goods. However, the plaintiff made the claim as an employee against his employers for breach of their contractual duty to select an appropriate route. As the claim was outside the scope of the condition, the carriers were not entitled to an indemnity under it.

BOUGHEN v FREDERICK ATTWOOD LTD AND CRYOPLANTS LTD [1978] 1 Lloyd's Rep 413 (Queen's Bench Division: DONALDSON J.)

299   **National Freight Corporation—transferred employees—worsening of employees' position—compensation**

See *Tuck v National Freight Corporation*, para. 1152.

CHARITIES

Halsbury's Laws of England (4th edn.), Vol. 5, paras. 501–985

300   **Charitable gift—intention to benefit particular charities only—demise of donee—whether cy-près doctrine applicable**

A testatrix left half her residuary estate to a particular blind people's home and the other half to a particular old people's home, in both cases for the benefit of the patients. Although the former home was in existence and had a companion home elsewhere, the latter was defunct and had not been replaced. Questions arose as to the validity of the gifts. *Held*, (i) the gift to the blind people's home was unequivocally intended for the benefit of the patients of the particular home and would therefore be allowed. (ii) The gift to the old people's home could obviously not be applied as intended. It could only be applied at all if sufficient general charitable intention could be shown for the cy-près doctrine to operate. From the testatrix' will it was impossible to divine such an intention and accordingly the gift had to pass as on intestacy.

RE SPENCE'S WILL TRUSTS, OGDEN v SHACKLETON [1978] 3 All ER 92 (Chancery Division: MEGARRY V-C).

301   **Charitable institutions—rate relief**

See para. 2279.

302   **Charitable trust—charitable purposes—hostel for working men**

The testator gave the residue of his estate to the mayor or appropriate authority of Famagusta, Cyprus, on condition that the money be used for or towards the construction of a hostel for working men. The question for consideration of the court was whether there was a valid charitable trust or whether the gift failed for uncertainty. *Held*, the gift was a valid charitable trust for the relief of poverty. Poverty was not confined to the destitute but included those in the lower income bracket. "Working men" had some flavour of lower income, and "hostel" suggested modest accommodation for a limited period. In all the circumstances, the provision of a hostel would benefit the poor rather than the rich, and therefore the gift was charitable.

Re Niyazi's Will Trusts [1978] 3 All ER 765 (Chancery Division: Megarry V-C). *Re Lucas* [1922] 2 Ch 52 and *Guinness Trust (London Fund) Founded 1890, Registered 1902 v Green* [1955] 2 All ER 871, CA applied.

303   ——— —— trust for promotion of sport

The Court of Appeal by a majority has decided that a trust to provide facilities to encourage pupils of schools and universities to play Association football was not entitled to be registered as a charity. The additional object of providing facilities for physical recreation for young people in general did not alter the fact that the main object of the trust was to promote football.

IRC v Sir Stephen Andrew Stephen (1978) Times, 19th October. Decision of Walton J [1978] 1 All ER 230, 1977 Halsbury's Abr 326 affirmed.

304   ——— —— trust for showground purposes

Australia

A city council contracted to sell a piece of land which it had acquired on the condition that the area would be set aside permanently for a showground, park and recreational purposes. The land was held to be subject to a valid and enforceable charitable trust so that the council was not free to sell it. On appeal by the council, *held*, the condition that the land was to be set apart permanently for specified purposes showed an intention to create a trust binding the land in the council's ownership. It was only a valid charitable trust if it fell within the fourth class of charitable purposes defined in *Income Tax Special Purposes Comrs v Pemsel* [1891] AC 531, HL as a trust beneficial to the community. The activities included in "showground purposes" would operate to encourage agriculture and horticulture in the region and there was thus a trust for the promotion of agriculture, which type of trust had been held to be charitable. There was therefore a valid charitable trust. The appeal would be dismissed.

Brisbane City Council v A-G for Queensland [1978] 3 All ER 30 (Privy Council: Lord Wilberforce, Lord Hailsham of St Marylebone, Lord Russell of Killowen, Lord Keith of Kinkel and Sir John Pennycuick).

305   —— general charitable intention—worthy causes

A testatrix left a residuary gift to her trustees "to pay and divide the residue thereof between such worthy causes as have been communicated by me to my trustees in my lifetime". She had never communicated any worthy causes to her trustees. Her solicitor had prepared and signed a memorandum which disclosed that he and the testatrix had discussed the bequest in terms of the "charities" she wished to benefit. The solicitor had also sent a letter to the Treasury Solicitor in which he stated that "any worthy causes" was intended to include charitable institutions and any other institutions which were not strictly charitable. The question arose as to whether the residuary gift indicated a general charitable intent, or whether it was void for uncertainty. *Held*, neither the memorandum nor the letter to the Treasury Solicitor were admissible to show a general charitable intention. The letter stated the solicitor's view of the testatrix's intentions, while the memorandum showed that the testatrix had once used the term "worthy causes" in a particular context and did not indicate a general charitable intention. "Worthy causes" was not confined to charitable causes and the gift was void for uncertainty. The residue would pass to the next-of-kin as on an intestacy.

Re Atkinson's Will Trusts, Atkinson v Hall [1978] 1 All ER 1275 (Chancery Division: Megarry V-C).

306 —— trustees—appropriation of trust fund—university trust— alteration of beneficial interests

See *Re Freeston's Charity, Sylvester v University College, Oxford*, para. 1025.

307 Cy-près doctrine—general charitable intention—gift to defunct institution

See *Re Spence (deceased), Ogden v Shackleton*, para. 300.

308 Methodist Church—disposal of land subject to trusts

The Charities (Methodist Church) Regulations 1978, S.I. 1978 No. 1836 (in force on 1st February 1979) enable land held upon certain model trusts of the Methodist Church to be sold or otherwise disposed of without the necessity of the order of the court or the Charity Commissioners. The Regulations apply to both statutory trusts and to the fifth of the model deeds (the Wesleyan Methodist Secondary Schools' Trust Deed).

309 New College of Cobham—administration

The Charities (The New College of Cobham) Order 1978, S.I. 1978 No. 1155 (in force on 17th August 1978), gives effect to a Scheme of the Charity Commissioners for The New College of Cobham in Kent, an almshouse charity which is administered by a body corporate. The Scheme provides for the body corporate to be renamed and for its members to be increased from two to five. It also provides for the administration of the Charity and gives the body corporate power to charge Pensioners approved sums by way of contribution to the cost of maintaining the almshouses.

310 Official custodian—vesting of property

Under the Charities Act 1960, s. 16 (2), the agreement of the official custodian is required before personal property is transferred to him. The official custodian has indicated that stock transfers for registration in his name should be sent to his office at St Alban's House, 57–60 Haymarket, London SW1Y 4QX and not lodged direct with the registrar. Registrars have been asked to reject any stock transfer into the name of the official custodian which does not bear his stamp of acceptance. See the Law Society Gazette, 15th November 1978, p. 1131.

311 Rating—house owned by a charity—occupation by licensee— whether charity in rateable occupation

See *Forces Help Society and Lord Roberts Workshops v Canterbury City Council*, para. 2281.

312 Registration—exempt charity

The Exempt Charities Order 1978, S.I. 1978 No. 453 (in force on 1st May 1978), provides that University College London is an exempt charity for the purposes of the Charities Act 1960 and therefore not required to be registered with the Charity Commissioners.

313 —— London Welsh Association—whether class of beneficiaries a sufficient section of the public

A trust was set up to establish and maintain an institute and meeting place in London to be known as "The London Welsh Association" for the benefit of Welsh people resident in or near or visiting London with a view to creating a centre in London for promoting the moral, social, spiritual and educational welfare of Welsh people and fostering the study of the Welsh language and of Welsh history, literature, music and art. "Welsh people" were defined in the trust deed as meaning and including "persons of Welsh nationality by birth or descent or from or educated or at any time domiciled in the Principality of Wales or the County of Monmouth". The trustees' claim to exemption from income tax had been rejected by the House of Lords (*Williams Trustees v IRC* [1947] AC 447) on the ground that the trust was not established for charitable purposes only. The trustees applied for registration as a charity on the ground that since the decision of the House of Lords the law had been changed; under the deed they could use the property for purposes which were exclusively charitable or for non-charitable purposes and, accordingly, under the Charitable Trusts (Validation) Act 1954 they could claim registration. In the course of the claim for tax exemption the Court of Appeal had found that the potential beneficiaries lacked a common quality which united them into a charitable class; this had also been alluded to by the House of Lords but did not form part of the ratio decidendi. The Charity Commissioners found the beneficiary class to be imprecisely defined but ruled that it constituted a sufficient section of the public and did not preclude the trust property from being used exclusively for charitable purposes so as to attract the provisions of the 1954 Act. The trustees having agreed to some alterations proposed by the Commissioners, the trust was duly registered.

RE SIR HOWELL JONES WILLIAMS TRUST, see Report of the Charity Commissioners for 1977, paras. 71-80.

314   —— model railway club—requirement of public benefit

A model railway society was formed with the object of promoting railway modelling, providing facilities to enable its members to do railway modelling, and keeping a small museum of railways relics. Its membership was open to the public at large. It organised exhibitions to which the public were invited and raised funds for charity. It sought registration under the Charities Act 1960, s. 4, claiming inter alia that it was charitable under the Recreational Charities Act 1958 by virtue of the provision of facilities for recreation and leisure-time activities. The Charity Commissioners refused registration on the ground that the provision of such facilities was not in itself sufficient to justify registration. The facilities had to be provided with the object of improving the conditions of life either of the public generally or of a more limited class as defined in the Act who had need of those facilities by reason of their youth, age, etc. The facilities had also to be provided in the interests of social welfare. The commissioners found that the facilities were not provided for the benefit of the public generally or the benefit of any group who were in special need of them or in the interests of social welfare; they were provided for the mutual benefit of members of the society.

RE BLACKBURN AND EAST LANCASHIRE MODEL RAILWAY SOCIETY, see Report of the Charity Commissioners for 1977, paras. 64-66.

315   Visitor—jurisdiction—dispute as to membership of corporation

See *Patel v University of Bradford Senate*, para. 1026.

CHOSES IN ACTION

Halsbury's Laws of England (4th edn.), Vol. 6, paras. 1-89

316   Assignment of debt—assignment prohibited by contract— whether assignment valid

Under a contract for the carrying out of road works for a county council a contractor agreed not to assign the contract or any interest under it to any third party without the council's consent. The contractor fell into financial difficulties and assigned the amount payable by the council to the plaintiff. When the latter tried to enforce the debt the council, who had not consented to the assignment, refused to pay. The plaintiff brought an action to recover the sum due. *Held*, the debt was both a chose in action and an interest under the contract. The assignment of the debt was rendered invalid by the prohibition in the contract and therefore the council were entitled to refuse payment. The plaintiff could not claim that this would cause him hardship because he should have inquired as to the existence of such a prohibition before he purchased the debt.

HELSTAN SECURITIES LTD V HERTFORDSHIRE COUNTY COUNCIL [1978] 3 All ER 262 (Queen's Bench Division: CROOM-JOHNSON J).

CLUBS

Halsbury's Laws of England (4th edn.), Vol. 6, paras. 201–411

317　Gaming clubs—application for licence—compliance with statutory requirements

A company applied for a gaming licence and displayed a notice of application pursuant to the Gaming Act 1968, Sch. 2, para. 6 (2). Two objectors contended that the notice was bad on the ground that the name and address of the company secretary was included on it. This information was not required by para. 6 (2), and para. 6 (4) limited the matter published in notices of application to that required by para. 6 (2). Justices upheld the objection. The company applied for an order of mandamus that their application be heard and determined. *Held*, the notice was by a company and it was only right and proper for it to be authenticated by someone on the company's behalf. Para. 6 (4) was not to be construed so as to allow purely formalistic objections. The order would be granted.

R v BRIGHTON GAMING LICENSING COMMITTEE, EX PARTE COTEDALE LTD [1978] 3 All ER 897 (Court of Appeal: LORD DENNING MR, EVELEIGH LJ and SIR DAVID CAIRNS). *R v Newcastle upon Tyne Gaming Licensing Committee, ex parte White Hart Enterprises Ltd* [1977] 3 All ER 961, CA, 1977 Halsbury's Abr para. 330 applied.

318　——charges

The Gaming Clubs (Hours and Charges) (Amendment) Regulations 1978, S.I. 1978 No. 38 (in force on 20th February 1978), increase to £1·50 the maximum charges which may be made for admission to gaming on bingo club premises in England and Wales. The Gaming Clubs (Hours and Charges) (Amendment) Regulations 1976, 1976 Halsbury's Abr para. 311, are revoked.

COMMONS

Halsbury's Laws of England (4th edn.), Vol. 6, paras. 501–784

319　Registration—transfer of alleged rights to parish council—status of transferor

The applicant and other persons claimed grazing and other commoners' rights over a certain piece of land owned by the lords of the manor. To protect their rights, the alleged commoners signed a deed which purported to convey their rights to the parish council which would hold the rights on trust for the benefit of all individual commoners and their successors. The parish council then applied for registration of those rights under the Commons Registration Act 1965. Provisional registration of the rights was thus made. This led to objection by the owners of the land and the matter was referred to the Chief Commons Commissioner. At the hearing before the commissioner, the applicant was called to give evidence on behalf of the parish council. The Commissioner decided that there were no such rights as had been contended for by the parish council. The applicant then applied pursuant to the Commons Registration Act 1965, s. 18 (1) as a person aggrieved by the Commons commissioner's decision for the case to be stated for the opinion of the High Court on the ground that the Commissioner had erred in law in reaching his decision. His application was refused by the Commissioner on the ground that the applicant was not entitled to be heard at the hearing and was not an "aggrieved person" within the meaning of s. 18.   The applicant then applied for an order of mandamus directing the Commissioner to state a case.   *Held*, the main point to be considered was whether or not in the circumstances, the applicant could be said to be a person aggrieved by the Commissioner's decision.   The broad definition of an aggrieved person was someone who has a genuine grievance because an order had been made which prejudicially affected his interests.   It appeared that the applicant did in fact fall within that definition as he was someone who first claimed an interest in and a right over the land.   He was also a person who had an interest in the proceedings before the Commissioner.   Mandamus would go to direct the Commissioner to state a case in the terms sought.

R v Chief Commons Comr, ex parte Constable (1977) 76 LGR 127 (Queen's Bench Division: Lord Widgery CJ, Eveleigh and Boreham JJ).   *Attorney-General of the Gambia v N'Jie* [1961] AC 617 applied.

320   —— waste land of a manor—land no longer connected with manor

The appellant was owner of waste land which belonged to a manor over fifty years ago.   He appealed against an order that the land was common land and therefore registrable under the Commons Registration Act 1965.   *Held*, waste land could not be registered as common land by virtue of being waste land of a manor unless it was still owned by the lord of the manor at the date of registration.   Where the land had long ago ceased to have any connection with the manor, it was a misuse of language to describe it as "of a manor".   Moreover, as the land had no characteristics of common land apart from being open, uncultivated and unoccupied, it would not be expected to come within the ambit of the 1965 Act.   The appeal would be allowed.

Box Parish Council v Lacey (1978) 122 Sol Jo 394 (Court of Appeal: Stamp, Ormrod and Bridge LJJ).

COMMONWEALTH AND DEPENDENCIES

Halsbury's Laws of England (4th edn.), Vol. 6, paras. 801–1206

321   Australia—Director of Aboriginal and Islanders Advancement—power to distribute profits arising from mining leases—statutory provisions

Bauxite deposits were discovered under an aboriginal reserve in Queensland.   Acting in his capacity as trustee of the reserve, its director negotiated mining leases on behalf of the aborigines.   One of the terms of the lease was that three per cent of the profits of the operations would be paid to the director on behalf of all aborigines in Queensland.   The aborigines on the reserve contended that by entering such an agreement the director was in breach of his obligations to them.   *Held*, under the Aborigines Act 1971, ss. 29, 30, the director was given a general power to make mining agreements on whatever conditions he thought fit.   Section 30 (2) stated that accrued benefits could be distributed for the benefit of aborigines on a reserve or for other aborigines: this provision did not create two mutually exclusive classes of potential beneficiaries, but gave the director power to distribute for the benefit of all aborigines whether resident on the reserve or not.   He had done exactly that and accordingly the aborigines' claim would fail.

Director of Aboriginal and Islanders Advancement Corporation v Peinkinna (1978) 122 Sol Jo 95 (Privy Council: Lord Salmon, Lord Edmund-Davies, Lord Russell of Killowen, Lord Scarman and Sir Harry Gibbs).

322   Barbados—Court of Appeal—power to allow appeals

The Court of Appeal of Barbados allowed an appeal by a defendant who had been convicted of murder and ordered a new trial.   It gave leave for an appeal to the

Privy Council under the British Caribbean (Appeals to the Privy Council) Order-in-Council 1962, and the defendant lodged a petition for special leave to appeal on the ground that the interests of justice did not require a new trial. *Held*, the 1962 Order did not give the Court of Appeal of Barbados power to grant leave to appeal on a criminal matter. No special leave to appeal would be granted, because the court's power to order a new trial was unfettered.

HOLDER V R [1978] 3 WLR 817 (Privy Council: VISCOUNT DILHORNE, LORD EDMUND-DAVIES, LORD FRASER OF TULLYBELTON, LORD SCARMAN and SIR ROBIN COOKE).

323　　—— membership of Judicial Committee of the Privy Council

The Judicial Committee (Barbados) Order 1978, S.I. 1978 No. 620 (in force on 17th May 1978), names the Supreme Court of Barbados as a superior court for the purposes of the Judicial Committee Amendment Act 1895 which provides that any Chief Justice or judge of the supreme court or of a superior court of a specified dominion who is a member of the Privy Council shall be a member of the Judicial Committee of the Privy Council.

324　　Brunei—Independence

The Foreign Office has announced that Brunei will become fully independent in 1983: Times, 1st July 1978.

325　　Commonwealth Development Corporation Act 1978

The Commonwealth Development Corporation Act 1978 consolidates the Overseas Resources Development Act 1959 and related enactments. The Act received the royal assent on 23rd March 1978 and came into force on 23rd April 1978.

Tables showing the derivation of the Act and destination of enactments consolidated are set out on pages 69–71 following.

DESTINATION TABLE

This table shows in column (1) the enactments repealed by the Commonwealth Development Corporation Act 1978, and in column (2) the provisions of that Act corresponding thereto.

In certain cases the enactment in column (1), though having a corresponding provision in column (2), is not, or is not wholly, repealed as it is still required, or partly required, for the purposes of other legislation.

(1)	(2)	(1)	(2)
Overseas Resources Development Act 1959 (c. 23)	Commonwealth Development Corporation Act 1978 (c. 2)	Overseas Resources Development Act 1959 (c. 23)	Commonwealth Development Corporation Act 1978 (c. 2)
s. 1 (1)	ss. 1 (1), s. 2 (1)	s. 19 (1)	
(2)–(4)	s. 1 (2)–(4)	(2), (3)	Rep., 1968, c. 13, s. 24 (2), Sch. 6
2 (1)	2 (2), (3)	20 (a)	Omitted under the Consolidation of Enactments (Procedure) Act 1949
(2)	3 (1)		
(3)	4 (1)		
(4)	(3), (4)	(b)	s. 17 (1)
(5)	(2)	(2), (3)	(1), (2)
(6) (a), (b)	3 (2)	21 (1)	Rep., S.L.(R.)A. 1974
(c), (d)	4 (5)	(2), (3)	18 (2), (4)
3	3 (3)–(5)	(4)	(6)
4 (1)		22	————
(2)	18 (5) (a)	Sch. 1, para. 1	1 (1)
5 (1)	Rep., 1963 c. 40, s. 1 (5)	paras. 2–9	Sch. 1, paras. 1–9, 11
(2)	18 (5) (b)	Sch. 2	Rep., S.L. (R.)A. 1974
(3), (4)	Rep., 1963 c. 40, s. 1 (5)		
		Commonwealth Development Act 1963 (c. 21)	————
6	Omitted under the Consolidation of Enactments (Procedure) Act 1949	s. 1 (1)	ss. 1 (3), 17 (1), (3)
		(2)	1 (1), 17 (1)
7	Rep., 1969 c. 36, s. 3 (3)	(3)	Rep., 1969, c. 36, s. 3 (3)
8 (1)	8 (1)–(3)	2	Rep., S.L.(R.)A. 1976
(2)	(4)	3 (1), (2)	
(3)	————	(3)	Rep., S.L. (R.)A. 1976
9 (1)	7 (1)		
(2) (a)	(2)	**Overseas Aid Act 1966 (c. 21)**	
(b)	8 (5)		————
10 (1)	5 (1), Sch. 1, para. 10	s. 4	s. 13 (1), (2)
(2)–(4)	6		
11	5 (2), (3), (a), (b)	**National Loans Act 1968 (c. 13)**	————
12 (1)	9 (1)		
(2)	(2), (3)	s. 1 (8)†	s. 12 (4)
(3)–(5)	(4)–(6)	10 (3)	10 (3)
13 (1)	10 (1)		
(2)–(4)	11 (1)–(3)	**Overseas Resources Development Act 1969 (c. 36)**	
(5)	10 (2)		
14 (1)	12 (1)–(3)	s. 1	Rep., 1977, c. 6, s. 8 (3), Sch. 2
(2)	13 (3)		
(3)	12 (5)	2 (1)	2 (1), (2), 4 (2)–(4), 17 (1)
15 (1)	14 (1)		
(2)	(1)	(2)	2 (4)
(a)	(2)	(2A)‡	Sch. 1, para. 10
(b)	5 (2), (3) (c)	(3)	ss. 1 (3), 8 (1), (3)–(5)
16 (1)	15 (1), (3)	(4)	s. 4 (4) (a)
(2)	(2), (3)	3 (1)	————
17	16	(2)	7 (1)
18 (1)	Rep., 1968, c. 13, s. 24 (2), Sch. 6		
(2)	11 (4)		
	Rep. 1968, s. 13, s. 24 (2), Sch. 6		
(3)	12 (4)		

(1)	(2)	(1)	(2)
Overseas Resources Development Act 1959 (c. 23)	Commonwealth Development Corporation Act 1978 (c. 2)	International Finance, Trade and Aid Act 1977 (c. 6)	Commonwealth Development Corporation Act 1978 (c. 2)
s. 3 (3)	Rep., 1977, c. 6, s. 8 (3), Sch. 2	s. 5 (1)	s. 9 (4) (b)
		(2)	(6)
		(3)	10 (1), (2)
Ministers of the Crown Act 1975 (c. 26)		(4), (5)	
		6	Rep., 1975, c. 24, s. 10 (2), Sch. 3; 1975, c. 25, 25 s. 5 (2), Sch. 3, Part I
Sch. 2, Part I*	——	(4)	Rep., 1969, c. 36, s. 3 (3)
		(5)	

‡ Inserted under the Consolidation of Enactments (Procedure) Act 1949.
† Not repealed.
* Repealed in part.

TABLE OF DERIVATIONS

This table shows in the right hand column the legislative source from which the sections of the Commonwealth Development Corporation Act 1978 have been derived. In the table the following abbreviations are used:

1959 = The Overseas Resources Development Act 1959 c. 23.
1963 = The Commonwealth Development Act 1963 c. 40.
1966 = The Overseas Aid Act 1966 c. 21.
1968 = The National Loans Act 1968 c. 13
1969 = The Overseas Resources Development Act 1969 c. 36
1977 = The International Finance, Trade and Aid Act 1977 c. 6.

M followed by a number indicates an amendment proposed in the Memorandum under the Consolidation of Enactments (Procedure) Act 1949.

This table does not acknowledge the transfer of the functions conferred on the Secretaty of State by the 1959 and 1967 Acts to the Minister of Overseas Development by the Ministers of the Crown Act 1974 as re-enacted in the Ministers of the Crown Act 1975, s. 7 (2).

Section of Act	Derivation
1	1959 s. 1, Sch. 1 para. 1; 1963 s. 1 (1) and (2); 1969 s. 2 (3).
2	1959 ss. 1 (1) and 2 (1); 1969 s. 2 (1) and (2).
3	1959 ss. 2 (2) and (6) (a) and (b), 3.
4	1959 s. 2 (3), (4), (5) and (6) (c) and (d); 1969 s. 2 (1) and (4).
5	1959 ss. 10 (1), 11 and 15 (2) (b).
6	1959 s. 10 (2)–(4).
7	1959 s. 9 (1), (2) (a).
8	1959 ss. 8, 9 (2) (b); 1969 s. 2 (3).
9	1959 s. 12; 1977 s. 5 (2) and (3).
10	1959 s. 13 (1); 1968 s. 10 (3); 1977 s. 5 (4) and (5).
11	1959 ss. 13 (2)–(4), 18 (2).
12	1959 ss. 14 (1) and (3), 19 (1); 1968 s. 1 (8).
13	1959 s. 14 (2); 1966 s. 4.
14	1959 s. 15.
15	1959 s. 16.
16	1959 s. 17.
17	1959 s. 20 (a); 1963 s. 1 (1) and (2); 1969 s. 2 (1); M1.
18	1959 ss. 4 (2), 5 (2); M2.
19	——
Sch. 1	1959 Sch. 1 paras. 2–9, s. 10 (1); S.I. 1968/1656; M3.
Sch. 2	——

326   Dominica—constitution

The Commonwealth of Dominica Constitution Order 1978, S.I. 1978 No. 1027 (in force on 3rd November 1978), which is made at the request and with the consent of the Associated State of Dominica under the West Indies Act 1967, s. 5 (4), provides a new constitution for Dominica as a sovereign democratic republic within the Commonwealth styled the Commonwealth of Dominica. The new constitution is to come into effect on 3rd November 1978 upon the termination of the status of association of Dominica with the United Kingdom under the Act. Other enactments concerning the constitution of Dominica are revoked.

327   The Commonwealth of Dominica Constitution (Amendment) Order 1978, S.I. 1978 No. 1521 (in force on 3rd November 1978), which is made at the request and with the consent of the Associated State of Dominica under the West Indies Act 1967, s. 5 (4), amends the constitution established under that section for Dominica by the Commonwealth of Dominica Constitution Order 1978, S.I. 1978 No. 1027, para. 326, and the transitional provisions in Schedule 2 to that Order so as to effect various textual corrections as specified in the Schedule.

328   —— termination of association

The Dominica Termination of Association Order 1978, S.I. 1978 No. 1031 (in force on 3rd November 1978), terminates the status of association of Dominica with the United Kingdom, and provides that Dominica shall cease to form part of Her Majesty's dominions, with effect from 3rd November 1978.

329   The Dominica Modification of Enactments Order 1978, S.I. 1978 No. 1030 (in force on 3rd November 1978), effects amendments and modifications to certain enactments that appear to be necessary or expedient in consequence of the termination of the status of association of Dominica with the United Kingdom.

330   The Dominica Modification of Enactments (Amendment) Order 1978, S.I. 1978 No. 1622 (in force on 15th December 1978), makes certain corrections to the Dominica Modification of Enactments Order 1978, para. 329.

331   Gibraltar—Supreme Court—Admiralty jurisdiction

The Gibraltar Supreme Court (Admiralty Practice) Rules Order 1978, S.I. 1978 No. 276 (in force on a day to be appointed by the Government), made in pursuance of the Colonial Courts of Admiralty Act 1890, s. 7, approves Rules of Court regulating court fees and allowances to be taken and paid in the Supreme Court of Gibraltar in the exercise of the jurisdiction conferred by that Act.

332   Judicial Committee of the Privy Council—appeal—special leave to appeal in criminal case—whether appeal available from opinion given on Governor-General's reference

In considering the question whether an appeal would lie to the Judicial Committee of the Privy Council from an opinion of the Court of Appeal of New Zealand on a Governor General's reference under the Crimes Act 1961, s. 406 (b), *held*, an appeal would lie only if it fell within the ambit of the Judicial Committee Act 1833, s. 3. An opinion of the Court of Appeal neither affected any legal right of a defendant nor placed any fetter on the Governor General's exercise of the prerogative of mercy and accordingly it was not a determination for the purposes of the section.

THOMAS V R [1978] 3 WLR 927 (Privy Council: LORD WILBERFORCE, LORD HAILSHAM OF ST MARYLEBONE, LORD EDMUND-DAVIES, LORD FRASER OF TULLYBELTON, LORD SCARMAN). *Théberge v Landry* (1876) 2 App Cas 102, PC applied.

333   Malaysia—appeal to Privy Council

The Malaysia (Appeals to Privy Council) Order 1978, S.I. 1978 No. 182 (in force on

2nd March 1978), consolidates and amends orders conferring jurisdiction on the Judicial Committee of the Privy Council in respect of appeals from the Federal Court of Malaysia.

334   —— jurisdiction of Privy Council to hear appeals

The Judicial Committee of the Privy Council have ruled that they have no jurisdiction to hear appeals from Malaysia on criminal and constitutional matters unless the petition was lodged before 1st January 1978. It was not sufficient that a notice of intention to appeal had been lodged before that date.

LEE KOK ENG v PUBLIC PROSECUTOR (1978) Times, 31st October (Privy Council).

335   Saint Lucia—constitution

The Saint Lucia Constitution Order 1978, S.I. 1978 No. 1901 (in force on 22nd February 1979), provides a new constitution for Saint Lucia upon its attainment of responsible government within the Commonwealth at the termination of its status of association with the United Kingdom.

336   —— modification of enactments

The Saint Lucia Modification of Enactments Order 1978, S.I. 1978 No. 1899 (in force on 22nd February 1979), effects amendments and modifications to certain enactments, pursuant to the termination of association between the United Kingdom and Saint Lucia.

337   —— termination of association

The Saint Lucia Termination of Association Order 1978, S.I. 1978 No. 1900 (in force on 22nd February 1979), terminates the status of association of Saint Lucia with the United Kingdom with effect from 22nd February 1979.

338   Singapore—appeal to Privy Council—availability of defence not raised below

See *Mohamad Kunjo s/o Ramalan v Public Prosecutor*, para. 619.

339   Solomon Islands Act 1978

The Solomon Islands Act 1978 provides for the independence of the Solomon Islands within the Commonwealth and deals with various connected matters including citizenship. The Act received the royal assent on 25th May 1978, and came into force on that date.

Section 1 provides that the United Kingdom government ceases to be responsible for the Solomon Islands government on 7th July 1978. Certain citizens of the United Kingdom and Colonies being persons connected with the Solomon Islands or children of such persons, lose their citizenship on becoming citizens of the Solomon Islands: s. 2. Section 3 defines the persons who have a connection with the Solomon Islands. The circumstances in which a person may become, continue as or cease to be a British protected person are specified in s. 4. Section 5 deals with the position of married women. A woman who is a citizen of the United Kingdom and Colonies or a British protected person and is married to such a person, does not lose her citizenship or protection under ss. 2, 4 unless her husband does. Miscellaneous supplementary provisions are contained in ss. 6–10 and the Schedule.

340   —— constitution of Solomon Islands

The Solomon Islands Independence Order 1978, S.I. 1978 No. 783 (in force on 7th July 1978), provides for a Solomon Islands Constitution to come into effect on 7th July 1978, the day on which the Solomon Islands attain independence by virtue of the Solomon Islands Act 1978, para. 339. The Constitution deals with the legislature, the executive government, the legal system and the public service; it also contains provisions relating to citizenship of the Solomon Islands and the fundamental rights and freedoms of the individual.

341   Trinidad and Tobago—constitutional redress for contravention of fundamental human rights—compensation

A barrister who had been engaged in a case in the High Court of Trinidad and Tobago was committed to prison for contempt on the order of the judge. The barrister applied to the High Court, ex parte by notice of motion, naming the Attorney-General as respondent and claiming redress under s. 6 of the Constitution for infringement of his right under s. 1 not to be deprived of his liberty except by due process of law. The application was dismissed and the barrister appealed to the Court of Appeal. While this appeal was pending he received permission to appeal to the Judicial Committee of the Privy Council who quashed the original order committing the barrister to court on the basis that the judge had not explained the nature of the contempt sufficiently to give the barrister an opportunity to explain his conduct. The Court of Appeal subsequently dismissed the appeal from the High Court decision, contending that the judge's failure to specify the nature of the contempt did not contravene a right protected by the Constitution. On appeal against this decision *held*, under s. 6 (2) of the Constitution the High Court had original jurisdiction to determine any application alleging contravention of the human rights and fundamental freedom under s. 1. The judge's failure to give the barrister an adequate explanation of the nature of the alleged contempt amounted to a breach of natural justice and a contravention of his rights under the Constitution. He was therefore entitled to redress under s. 6. "Redress" in this context meant reparation or compensation, and that compensation should be measured in terms of the deprivation of liberty. It should include consequential loss of earning and recompense for the inconvenience and distress suffered as a result of the imprisonment.

MAHARAJ v A-G OF TRINIDAD AND TOBAGO (No. 2) [1978] 2 All ER 670 (Privy Council: LORD DIPLOCK, LORD HAILSHAM OF ST. MARYLEBONE, LORD SALMON, LORD RUSSELL OF KILLOWEN and LORD KEITH OF KINKEL).

For earlier proceedings before the Privy Council, see 1977 Halsbury's Abr para. 489.

342   Tuvalu Act 1978

The Tuvalu Act 1978 provides for the independence of Tuvalu, formerly the Ellice Islands, within the Commonwealth and for various connected matters, including nationality. The Act received the royal assent on 30th June 1978 and came into force on that date.

The government of the United Kingdom ceases to be responsible for the government of Tuvalu on 1st October 1978 and the powers of the Tuvalu legislature are enlarged: s. 1 and Sch. 1. Section 2 provides that any citizen of the United Kingdom and Colonies loses such citizenship on becoming a citizen of Tuvalu on independence, subject to certain exceptions in s. 3. Section 2 also prevents the wife of a United Kingdom and Colonies citizen from registering as such herself if her husband becomes a citizen of Tuvalu on independence. Section 3 provides for the retention of United Kingdom citizenship by certain citizens of Tuvalu, including those having a close connection with the United Kingdom. Supplementary provisions are contained in ss. 4–6 and Sch. 2.

COMPANIES

Halsbury's Laws of England (4th edn.), Vol. 7

343   Articles

Accounting Reference Periods, Kenneth C. K. Chow (accounting reference periods as introduced by the Companies Act 1976): 128 NLJ 1103.

After Bullock: Co-operation not Confrontation, Nicholas Bourne (analysis of Bullock proposals on worker participation, and assessment of possible legislation in that field): 128 NLJ 874.

Altering Objects Clauses, Henry E. Markson (alteration of clauses and their separate substantive nature): 122 Sol Jo 202.

Appointment of Company Inspectors and Natural Justice, A. N. Khan (whether rules of natural justice are observed in investigations under s. 165 of the Companies Act 1948): 122 Sol Jo 686.

Changes in Company Law—Directors' Duties, Barry A. K. Rider: 128 NLJ 1116.

Changes in Company Law—Director's Private Transactions, Barry A. K. Rider (discussion on dealings between director and company and the provision of loans to insiders): 128 NLJ 1138.

Companies Court Cases, Henry E. Markson: 128 NLJ 998.

Compensating Ex-Directors, Ralph Instone (Companies Act 1948, s. 191): 128 NLJ 54.

Compensation for Loss of Office, S. Dilwar Hussain (cases concerning compensation paid to directors for loss of office): 122 Sol Jo 187.

The Conduct of Company Directors, Barry A. K. Rider: 128 NLJ 27.

Crime and the Company, Brian Harris (offences requiring mens rea and those of strict liability): 142 JP Jo 65.

Draft Companies Bill: Implementation of the Second Directive, Keith Walmsley (proposed amendments to company law to implement the Second EEC Directive on Company Law): 128 NLJ 1051.

Golden Handshake to an Executive Director, G. Shapira (the position in the light of *Rowe v Taupo Totara Timber Co Ltd* [1977] 3 All ER 123, PC, 1977 Halsbury's Abr para. 369): [1977] NZLJ 437.

The Honest Director and Secret Profits, N. A. Bastin (company director's accountability for profits accruing to him by reason of his fiduciary relationship) 128 NLJ 527.

Insider Dealing and the Conduct of Directors, Keith Walmsley (the Government's White Paper, "The Conduct of Company Directors"): 128 NLJ 15.

Insider Trading Hong Kong Style, Barry A. K. Rider: 128 NLJ 897.

Loss of Office Compensation, Henry E. Markson (compensation for company directors for loss of office in the light of *Taupo Totara Timber Company Ltd v Rowe* [1977] 3 All ER 123, see 1977 Halsbury's Abr para. 369): 128 NLJ 925.

Mergers policy: a slight turn of the screw, Geoffrey Owen (a look at the Government's review of monopolies and mergers: a consultative document (HMSO, £2.85)), Financial Times, 11th May 1978.

Postponed Creditors Under the Partnership Act 1890, N. A. Bastin (examination of certain aspects of s. 3 of the Partnership Act 1890): 128 NLJ 1021.

Power to the Auditors, A. N. Khan (statutory duties of auditors as imposed by the Companies Act 1976): 122 Sol Jo 769.

Powers and Objects, Ralph Instone (scrutiny of decisions in *Charterbridge Corporation Ltd v Lloyds Bank Ltd* [1969] 2 All ER 1185 and *Re Introductions Ltd* [1969] 1 All ER 887): 128 NLJ 948.

Provisional Liquidator: Leave to Proceed, Henry E. Markson (position regarding proceedings involving provisional liquidators in the light of *Re Aro Co Ltd* (1978) Times, 20th June, See para. 368): 128 NLJ 866.

Winding Up, When Just and Equitable, Henry E. Markson (cases from Rhodesia, New Zealand and Australia citing *Re Westbourne Galleries Ltd* [1973] AC 360, HL): 128 NLJ 467.

Winding-Up: The Partnership Analogy, Henry E. Markson (Companies Act 1948, s. 222 (f) and the Partnership Act 1890, s. 35 (f)): 128 NLJ 115.

344   Accounts—contents

The Accounting Standards Committee of the Institute of Chartered Accountants has published Statement of Standard Accounting Practice No. 15 (SSAP 15) (replacing Exposure Draft 19) *Accounting for deferred taxation*. The SSAP15, which is to be applied to financial statements on or after 1st January 1979, supports the provision for deferred taxation but requires the provision to be made on the basis of the amounts which will probably become due rather than on the statutory rate of corporation tax, i.e. the amounts to be estimated by reference to investment and other incentives.

345   —— duty of external valuer to assist auditors

The Royal Institution of Chartered Surveyors has obtained legal advice on the extent of the responsibility of an external valuer to produce papers for examination by the company's auditors under the Companies Act 1967, s. 14 (5). Although the external valuer is under no statutory duty to assist the auditors the RICS, on the basis of the advice received, encourages valuers to co-operate reasonably and responsibly with any request from the auditors to avoid any qualification to the accounts and, perhaps, in their own interests if they should have been negligent or have included incorrect information in their valuation.

See RICS Guidance Note G2, *Accountancy*, July 1978, p. 116.

346   —— group accounts—presentation

Following the publication of International Accounting Standard No. 3 *Consolidated Financial Statements* ("IAS3"), the Accounting Standards Committee has published Statement of Standard Accounting Practice No. 14 ("SSAP 14") *Group Accounts* (formerly Exposure Draft 20). Compliance with SSAP14 will automatically ensure compliance with the requirements of IAS 3, except for paras 40 to 42 of the latter (which cover the basis for accounting for associated companies dealt with in SSAP1). SSAP14 is to come into force in respect of group accounts relating to periods starting on or after 1st January 1979. For the text of SSAP14 and a statement issued by the Accounting Standards Committee on its publication, see *Accountancy*, October 1978, p. 68.

347   Amalgamation—stamp duty on transaction—relief—meaning of "particular existing company"

The Finance Act 1927, s. 55, as amended, provides that relief from capital and transfer stamp duty is available on the reconstruction and amalgamation of a company where the commissioners are satisfied that the company is to be registered or has been incorporated or has increased its capital with a view to the acquisition either of the undertaking of, or not less than 90 per cent of the issued share capital of, any particular existing company.

The taxpayer increased its authorised capital with a view to acquiring a shareholding in an unlimited company. It paid stamp duty on the increase. It acquired the company by means of instruments of transfer. The Commissioners refused the company's claim for relief under s. 55 from capital duty and transfer on sale duty payable on the same transfer on the ground that "any particular existing company" was restricted to companies of limited liability only. *Held* (SIR DAVID CAIRNS dissenting), the words "particular existing company" were wide. They included existing companies of any kind incorporated under English law. The relief claimed by the company was therefore available and the appeal would be allowed.

CHELSEA LAND AND INVESTMENT CO LTD v IRC [1978] 2 All ER 113 (Court of Appeal: BUCKLEY and GOFF LJJ and SIR DAVID CAIRNS. Decision of Fox J [1977] 3 All ER 23, 1977 Halsbury's Abr para. 359, reversed.

Finance Act 1927, s. 55 (1)(A) (capital stamp duty) was repealed by Finance Act 1973, Sch. 22 with effect from 1st August 1973.

348   Annual return—company having share capital—prescribed form

The Companies (Annual Return) (Amendment) Regulations 1979, S.I. 1979 No. 54 (in force on 12th February 1979), amend the form of annual return to be made under the Companies Act 1948 by a company having a share capital. The amendment relates to entries to be made in the form where the company keeps its register of members or debenture holders otherwise than in a legible form.

349   Companies Court—applications in Long Vacation

See *Practice Direction*, para. 2159.

350   —— jurisdiction

A winding up order was made in respect of a company, following which the liquidator issued summonses against two associated companies seeking, inter alia, declarations that two transactions entered into by the company in liquidation were void as against the liquidator under the Law of Property Act 1925 s. 172 and should be set aside. The two companies claimed that, either the Companies Court lacked jurisdiction to hear the actions on the grounds that relief under s. 172 could be sought only in proceedings begun by writ or, should jurisdiction exist, the court should nevertheless exercise its discretion to decline to entertain the proceedings and require the claim to be made in proceedings begun by writ. The liquidator served notices of motion seeking declarations that the summons had been properly brought in the Companies Court and that the court had jurisdiction to grant the relief sought. *Held*, the Companies Court was not separate and distinct from the High Court but merely a way of describing the High Court when dealing with company matters originating in the chambers of the Bankruptcy Registrar. Similarly, the Companies judge was simply a way of describing a High Court judge dealing with such matters and he therefore had jurisdiction to grant relief under s. 172 in common with all High Court judges. Further, relief under s. 172 could be granted in proceedings begun by summons: the list of applications to be made by summons under the Companies (Winding-Up) Rules 1949, r. 68 was not exhaustive; RSC Ord. 5, r. 2 (b) dealing with proceedings which had to be begun by writ went to procedure not jurisdiction; and there were no grounds for holding that a claim against a stranger, incidental to the winding-up of a company, could only be brought by summons in the Companies Court if based upon a section of the Companies Act. As to the exercise of the court's discretion, since allegations of fraudulent preferences were commonly litigated within the Companies Court, there was no reason to require allegations of fraudulent companies to be litigated outside it. The declarations sought by the motions would be granted.

It was pointed out that the possibility of third party proceedings, which did not arise in the present case, could be grounds for claiming that proceedings under s. 172 should be begun by writ.

RE SHILENA HOSIERY CO LTD (1978) (Chancery Division: BRIGHTMAN J (judgment delivered 1st December)). *Re F & E Stanton Ltd* [1928] 1 KB 464 applied.

351   Conspiracy—agreement for company to give financial aid to purchasers of its shares—liability to company of directors entering into agreement on behalf of company—co-conspirators

The plaintiff company, represented by two of its directors, entered into an agreement in pursuance of which it purchased all the issued shares in a finance company for £500,000. The shareholders of that company then used the proceeds to purchase all the issued shares in the plaintiff company for £489,000. The agreement provided that the second transaction was to be conditional upon the completion of the first. Soon after the plaintiff company went into liquidation, and it was discovered that the real value of the shares in the finance company had been only £60,000. Through its receiver, the plaintiff company brought an action against all the parties to the transactions, including its two directors, claiming that by purchasing shares at an excess price the company had provided financial aid for the purchase of its own shares, contrary to the provisions of the Companies Act 1948, s. 54, and that the agreement to effect the transactions was therefore illegal and void. The company claimed damages for conspiracy on the grounds that the defendants had entered into an agreement to effect an unlawful purpose with knowledge of all the facts which constituted the illegality. In addition, during the trial of the action the plaintiffs asserted a claim in constructive trust against all the defendants. The trial judge dismissed the action, holding that since the plaintiff, through its directors, had been a party to the allegedly unlawful act, and knowledge of the illegality had been attributed to the directors, the plaintiff was precluded from suing its co-

conspirators. He further held that the claim in constructive trust required an amendment of the pleadings, but refused leave to amend. On appeal, *held*, since the company had been the victim of the conspiracy it could not be said that the knowledge of its directors had been notionally transmitted to it, and it was not, therefore, a co-conspirator. Alternatively, even if the company was found to have had knowledge of the illegal character of the agreement, the conspiracy alleged was not the agreement itself, but a conspiracy to enter into it, and since the company had not been a party to the negotiations preceding the agreement, it could not be held to have been a co-conspirator. To that extent the action had been wrongly dismissed. With respect to the claim in constructive trust, however, the trial judge had been right in holding that it could not be considered on the statement of claim as it then stood: although the word "dishonest" or "fraudulent" did not have to be specifically pleaded when knowledge of dishonesty was alleged, in the absence of such an unequivocal plea the pleading had to disclose the allegation with particularity, and it was not sufficient only to plead knowledge of facts constituting a statutory breach.

BELMONT FINANCE CORPN LTD v WILLIAMS FURNITURE LTD [1978] 3 WLR 712 (Court of Appeal: BUCKLEY, ORR and GOFF LJJ).

352   Corporate personality—lifting the veil

See *Woolfson v Strathclyde Regional Council*, para. 400.

353   Director—accountability for profits made from personal venture

Australia

The managing director of the appellant company, which had been incorporated for the purpose of financing the location and exploration of mineral deposits in Australia, obtained in his own name two mining exploration licences issued by the Tasmanian Government, as a result of which he made considerable profits from mining operations. Prior to the licences being granted a decision had been taken to "mothball" the company, and by the time they were granted funds were no longer available to finance the projects, although it was found as fact that the licences had been issued to the director on the strength of the company's resources and good name. The director was therefore faced with large personal obligations under the licences which, on resigning his place on the board, he expressed an intention to honour. He formed a new company, financed with his own capital, and subsequently made a substantial profit. The appellant company brought an action against him alleging a breach of the fiduciary duty owed by him to the company by virtue of his position as managing director and claiming an account of past and future profits made by him from the mining operations. The trial judge found in favour of the company and the director appealed to the Privy Council by leave of the Supreme Court of New South Wales. *Held*, since it was clear that the director's opportunity to earn a profit had arisen initially from the use made by him of his position in the company, he was accountable to the company unless he could show that the company, being fully informed as to the circumstances, had renounced its interest in the venture. On the facts the company had done so, and therefore the director had not acted in a way in which there was a real sensible possibility of conflict between his interests and the interests of the company. On the undisputed evidence the trial judge had erred in his conclusions and the appeal would be allowed.

QUEENSLAND MINES LTD v HUDSON (1978) 52 ALJR 399 (Privy Council: VISCOUNT DILHORNE, LORD HAILSHAM OF ST. MARYLEBONE, LORD SIMON OF GLAISDALE, LORD EDMUND-DAVIES and LORD SCARMAN). *Boardman v Phipps* [1967] 2 AC 46, HL and *Regal (Hastings) Ltd v Gulliver* [1967] 2 AC 134, HL applied.

354   Dividends—restrictions on increase—counter-inflation measures

See para. 1038.

355   Foreign company—locus standi to serve writ in United Kingdom

See *Bethlehem Steel Corporation v Universal Gas and Oil Co Inc*, para. 426.

356 ——**winding up—assets within jurisdiction—right of action against insurer**

Events occurred giving rise to a claim against a foreign unregistered company by the petitioners. Damages were awarded against the company, but it was unable to satisfy the judgment debt. It was insured against events such as that which had occurred, but failed to claim against the insurance association in respect of them. The petitioners then applied for the company to be wound up so that they could claim that its rights against the insurance association, the company's only asset within the jurisdiction, be transferred to them under the Third Parties (Rights against Insurers) Act 1930, s. 1 (1). The petition was opposed by the insurance association on the ground that the court had no jurisdiction to make the order, as the petitioners could not show for certain that the company had an asset within the jurisdiction which would be of benefit to them, since the rules of the association would inevitably cause the action to fail. *Held*, where the only alleged asset of the company was a right of action, it was not necessary for the petitioners to show that the action was bound to succeed, only that it had a reasonable possibility of success. Since it was common ground that there was a claim against the association, subject only to compliance with its rules, the onus was on the association to show that an action against it would not have any reasonable possibility of success. It had failed to do so and the court thus had jurisdiction to make a winding up order.

Re Allobrogia Steamship Corpn [1978] 3 All ER 423 (Chancery Division: Slade J). *Re Compania Merabelle San Nicholas SA* [1972] 3 All ER 448 applied.

357 **Investigation of company's affairs—appointment of inspectors**

Companies Act 1948, s. 165, gives the Department of Trade power to appoint inspectors to investigate the affairs of a company if it appears that persons concerned with the management of that company have been guilty of fraud, misfeasance or other misconduct towards it or its members. Companies Act 1967, s. 109, gives the Department power to require a company at any time to produce books and papers. For no reason apparent to the company or to objective observers, the Secretary of State for Trade authorized two officers under s. 109 to look at certain books and papers of a company and two of its subsidiaries. Subsequently, he appointed two inspectors under s. 165 to investigate the company's affairs. The company decided to challenge the Secretary of State's decision and commenced proceedings in which it sought a declaration that the appointment of the inspectors was ultra vires and invalid. A summons was taken out by the Department of Trade to strike out the proceedings. The company claimed that they knew of no reasons for the appointment of inspectors; no reasons had been given; reasons should have been given, at least in outline; and that therefore there had been a breach of natural justice. On appeal, *held*, there was nothing in the Companies Acts requiring the Secretary of State to give reasons. Once the s. 165 investigation had begun, it must be conducted in a fair and proper manner, but natural justice did not apply to the Secretary of State's decision to instigate an investigation. So long as he acted in good faith the Secretary of State did not have to disclose the material on which he had acted or the reasons for appointing inspectors. The action had been properly struck out and the appeal would be dismissed.

Norwest Holst Ltd v Department of Trade [1978] 3 All ER 280 (Court of Appeal: Lord Denning MR, Ormrod and Geoffrey Lane LJJ). Decision of Foster J (1977) Times, 6th August, 1977 Halsbury's Abr para. 379 affirmed.

358 **Monopolies and mergers—policy**

The Government has published a green paper entitled, A Review of Monopolies and Mergers Policy: Cmnd. 7198. This consultative document recommends that mergers should be shifted to a neutral position by means of three inter-related measures, that the case should be examined for extending the definition of a monopoly situation to include a definition of oligopoly in terms of market structure and that consideration should be given to dealing with uncompetitive practices by single firms outside the ambit of monopoly investigations.

359 Protection of depositors

The Protection of Depositors (Accounts) (Amendment) Regulations 1978, S.I. 1978 No. 1065 (in force on 1st September 1978) amend the Protection of Depositors (Accounts) Regulations 1976 to take account of amendments to the Companies Acts 1948 and 1967 made by the Companies Act 1976.

360 Register of members—company without share capital—members divided into classes—obligation to specify class of membership

A society, which was a limited company without share capital, divided its members into full, associate and provisional associate classes. The company register did not indicate membership status, but only full members were entitled to attend and vote at general meetings. An associate member wanted the society's constitution amended. In order to enable him to contact full members who would put forward his cause at a general meeting, he asked the society for a list of its full members. On the company's refusal, he applied for an order under Companies Act 1948, s. 113, for a copy of the part of the register containing the names of full members. The judge held that under s. 110 (1) (a) of the Act, a company without share capital, whose members were divided into different classes, was duty bound to specify in the register the class of membership of its members. The order was granted and the society appealed. *Held*, it was clear from the terms of s. 110, that a company with share capital was required to specify in its register matters which were not required in the case of a company without share capital. A company without share capital was only under a duty to enter in its register the names and addresses of its members. The other requirements in the section referred exclusively to companies with a share capital and were of no relevance to the present case. Further, the member was not entitled to obtain the names of the full members of the society by a requisition under s. 113. The section only required a company to disclose a part of its register which could be identified without reference to anything other than that which was on the register. In the present case, the information requested could only be obtained by reference to something which was neither bound to be, nor was, on the register i.e. the class of membership of the members. The appeal would therefore be allowed.

RE PERFORMING RIGHT SOCIETY LTD, LYTTLETON v PERFORMING RIGHT SOCIETY LTD [1978] 3 All ER 972 (Court of Appeal: BUCKLEY and GOFF LJJ and SIR DAVID CAIRNS). Decision of Brightman J [1978] 2 All ER 712, reversed.

361 Registrable charges—right to trace

See *Borden (UK) Ltd v Scottish Timber Products Ltd* para. 512.

362 Shares—untraceable shareholders—unclaimed dividends—limitation period for claims—winding up

See *Re Compania de Electricidad de la Provincia de Buenos Aires Ltd*, para 382.

363 Stamp duty—issue of loan capital—sums advanced to company without issue of written evidence

See *Agricultural Mortgage Corporation v IRC*, para. 2752.

364 Winding up—antecedent offences—fraudulent trading—intention to defraud

In January 1971 a company passed a resolution to cease trading. During the next two years its assets were got in and applied in discharge of its established debts except the claims of an Italian company for damages in respect of defective goods supplied to it by the company in 1966. In November 1973 the Italian company obtained judgment in Italy against the company, which had gone into liquidation in September 1973. The liquidator sought a declaration under the Companies Act 1948, s. 332, that between January 1971 and September 1973 the business of the company had been carried on with intent to defraud creditors, and an order that the former directors of the company and its parent company should pay to him a sum equal to the loss caused to the Italian company. The respondents applied to strike out the summons on the ground that it disclosed no reasonable cause of action. *Held*, "carrying on any business" in s. 332 was not synonymous with actually carrying on trade, and the collection and distribution of assets could constitute "any business". However, s. 332 required an intention to defraud and the only intent alleged was to prefer one creditor over another. The mere preference of one creditor over another where a person knew or had grounds to suspect that he would have insufficient assets to pay all creditors in full could not constitute fraudulent trading within s. 332. The summons would be struck out.

RE SARFLAX LTD [1979] 2 WLR 202 (Chancery Division: OLIVER J).

365 ——— **compliance with rules**

In giving judgment in the Companies Court, BRIGHTMAN J said that failure to comply with the Companies (Winding Up) Rules 1949, r. 33, which requires the petitioner or his solicitor to attend before the registrar on the appointed day to satisfy him that the papers are in order, was becoming too frequent. This impeded the operation of the Companies Registry and the Companies Court and therefore future petitions which did not comply with the rule would be struck out, save in exceptional circumstances: Times, 10th October 1978.

366 ——— **costs—priority—opposed petition**

A petition was presented to wind up a company. At the first hearing on 13th February 1978, the petition was opposed by the company and by an opposing creditor. The opposition was mainly prompted by the sole director of the company. After two adjournments, it was held that the opposition was not based on any substantial grounds and a winding up order was made. The petitioner sought an order that the director, who was not a party to the proceedings, be directed to pay the extra costs occasioned by the unjustified opposition personally. *Held*, the court had no jurisdiction to make the order as despite the appointment of a receiver a director retained the power to authorise the taking or defending of proceedings in the company's name. Although the court had a wide discretion as to costs, that did not assist the petitioner as the director was a complete stranger to the proceedings. However, an order would be made to the effect that the costs incurred after 13th February 1978 were not to be paid out of the company's assets in priority to payment in full of all unsecured creditors, the company being given liberty to apply for payment of the extra costs out of the surplus assets, if any.

RE REPROGRAPHIC EXPORTS (EUROMAT) LTD (1978) 122 Sol Jo 400 (Chancery Division: SLADE J). *Re Bathampton Properties Ltd* [1976] 3 All ER 200, 1976 Halsbury's Abr para. 354 applied.

367 ——— ——— **taxation—basis**

When a company was wound up, the liquidator took proceedings to determine issues as between the many claimants in the liquidation in order to enable speedy distribution of the company's assets. It was ordered that costs incurred in the proceedings be taxed on a trustee basis as the proceedings had been brought speedily to reduce hardship and costs had been incurred without stint. In an application to have the order reconsidered, the Department of Trade contended that the court had no power to order costs incurred in a liquidation to be taxed on a trustee basis and that in default of a direction to the contrary by the courts, taxing masters were required to tax costs in a liquidation on a solicitor and own client basis and not on a common fund basis. *Held*, the normal basis of taxation of costs incurred in a liquidation was the common fund basis. This had not been altered by the change in the categories of taxation by RSC Ord. 62. However, where costs had been incurred in the course of actual proceedings, the court had a discretion under RSC Ord. 62, r. 28, to order taxation on the trustee basis, although such an order would be made only in exceptional circumstances. If there were no proceedings, the taxing

master should apply the basis of common fund taxation as if he were the court under
the Companies (Winding Up) Rules 1949, r. 188. The order would stand.

RE NATION LIFE INSURANCE CO LTD (IN LIQUIDATION) [1978] 1 All ER 242
(Chancery Division: TEMPLEMAN J).

368   —— creditor—right to continue claim against company—whether
creditor secured

A creditor issued a writ in rem against a ship before its owners went into
liquidation. The ship had already been arrested by another set of creditors. The
creditor did not serve the writ nor arrest the vessel but entered a caveat in the
proceedings in rem commenced by the other creditors. After the winding up order
was made against the owners, the creditor applied under Companies Act 1948, s.
231, for the court's leave to continue the action started before the winding up,
contending that he was a secured creditor, having issued a writ in rem. *Held*, as the
creditor had not actually arrested the vessel, but had merely entered a caveat after it
had been arrested in someone else's action, a legal nexus between him and the ship
had not been established and he was not a secured creditor. If he was given leave to
proceed despite the winding up, it would enable an unsecured creditor to achieve
priority over other unsecured creditors. Accordingly, his application would fail.

RE ARO CO LTD [1979] 1 All ER 32 (Chancery Division: OLIVER J).

369   —— disclaimer by liquidator of lease assigned to company—
liability of original lessee for arrears of rent

The plaintiffs granted a lease of business premises to the defendants, who later, with
the plaintiffs' consent, assigned the lease to a company. The company then went into
voluntary liquidation and the liquidator subsequently disclaimed the lease. The
plaintiffs then sued the defendants as original lessees for rent falling due after the date
of the disclaimer. *Held*, under Companies Act 1948, s. 323 a disclaimer operated to
determine the liabilities of the company in respect of the property disclaimed but did
not affect the liabilities of any other person. Where a lease had been assigned, a
disclaimer by the liquidator of the assignee did not destroy the lease but left it in
existence. Accordingly, the original lessee remained liable for the rent throughout
the term.

The court added that the result would have been the same if the assignment had
been to an individual and the lease had been disclaimed by his trustee in bankruptcy.

WARNFORD INVESTMENTS LTD V DUCKWORTH [1978] 2 All ER 517 (Chancery
Division: MEGARRY V-C). *Hill v East and West India Dock Co* (1884) 9 App Cas
448, HL applied.

370   —— dismissal of employee pursuant to voluntary liquidation—
whether unfair

See *Fox Brothers (Clothes) Ltd v Bryant*, para. 3005.

371   —— distress for rates—date rate becomes due and payable—
whether local authority a priority creditor

A company entered into voluntary liquidation on 1st April 1974, without having
paid the general rate for 1973/1974 on certain property it had occupied. The local
authority claimed that under the Companies Act 1948, s. 319, it was a priority
creditor for the rates because they had been chargeable as of 1st April 1973, within
twelve months of liquidation. One of the liquidators rejected the claim on the
ground that the rate became due in March 1973 by virtue of a local authority
resolution to levy it, and that the debt had therefore not accrued within the twelve
months before liquidation. *Held*, a rate became payable from the date it was made
and published. To be properly due and payable it had to be legally enforceable and
the occupier had to be under a present liability to pay. The company in liquidation
was under no such obligation until 1st April 1973, when the valuation list was

published. Accordingly, the rate had become payable within the statutory twelve month period, and the local authority was a priority creditor.

Re Piccadilly Estate Hotels Ltd [1978] LS Gaz R 345 (Chancery Division: Slade J). *Thompson v Rating Authority for the Borough of Beckenham* [1947] 1 KB 802 applied.

372   —— distribution of assets—priority of payments

A capital gain arose in the course of the winding up of a company; the gain was liable to corporation tax under the Income and Corporation Taxes Act 1970, s. 238. Two questions arose; the first was whether the corporation tax was part of the "fees and expenses properly incurred in preserving, realising or getting in the assets" within the Companies (Winding-up) Rules 1949, r. 195(1); if it was, the tax would rank in front of the costs of the winding up petitition, the liquidator's remuneration and certain other matters. If it was not, but was part of the "necessary disbursements of the liquidator other than expenses properly incurred in preserving, realising or getting in the assets" within r. 195 (1), it would rank after the taxed costs of the petition and certain other matters, but in front of the liquidator's fees. The second question was whether the tax came within the expression "costs, charges and expenses incurred in the winding up" in the Companies Act 1948, s. 267. If it did, the court had power to make an order for payment of the tax out of the assets in such order of priority as it considered just and could therefore postpone the tax to the costs of the petition and the liquidator's fees. *Held*, (i) corporation tax was merely a possible consequence of the realisation of an asset at a profit. It was not an expense incurred by the liquidator for the purpose of realising the asset and therefore was not an "expense incurred in realising" it. However, it was clear that it was a "necessary disbursement" within r. 195 (1). (ii) There was authority for the proposition that Schedule D income tax was a charge or expense "incurred in the winding up" within the meaning of s. 267. Corporation tax was also such a charge or expense and on the facts the court would order that the liquidator's fees rank ahead of the liability for corporation tax.

Re Mesco Properties Ltd [1979] STC 11 (Chancery Division: Brightman J). *Re Beni-Felkai Mining Co Ltd* [1934] Ch 406 applied.

373   —— fees

The Companies (Department of Trade) Fees (Amendment) Order 1978, S.I. 1978, No. 569 (in force on 9th May 1978), substitutes an ad valorem fee, payable by every liquidator on the submission to the Secretary of State of amounts of their receipts and payments under the Companies Act 1948, s. 249, for Fees No. 7 and 10 (2) (iii). The Order also increases to £3·75 the fee payable for the insertion of notices in proceedings for the winding up of companies in the London Gazette.

374   The Companies (Department of Trade) Fees (Amendment No. 2) Order 1978, S.I. 1978 No. 705 (in force on 1st June 1978), provides for the payment of the amount of value added tax in addition to the amount of any fee provided for in the schedule to the Companies (Department of Trade) Fees Order 1975 where the tax is chargeable in respect of the service to which that fee relates.

375   The Companies (Department of Trade) Fees (Amendment No. 3) Order 1978. S.I. 1978 No. 1654 (in force on 1st December 1978), further amends the Companies (Department of Trade) Fees Order 1975, 1975 Halsbury's Abr para. 397 by increasing certain fees taken by the Department of Trade in proceedings for the winding up of companies.

376   —— foreign company—assets within jurisdiction

See *Re Allobrogia Steamship Corpn*, para. 356.

377   —— injunction to restrain—locus standi of petitioner

The plaintiff company sought an injunction to restrain the defendants from presenting a petition to wind up the company based on a debt of £39,068. The defendants' demand for the sum was served under the Companies Act 1948, s. 223, for the purpose of founding a winding up petition. It was alleged by the plaintiff company that the defendants had allowed credit of £20,000 in respect of goods sold and delivered to the said company, thereby precluding the defendants from claiming payment in respect of that amount. *Held*, the defendants, as prospective creditors in respect of at least £20,000, should be entitled to present a petition under s. 224 (1) of the 1948 Act. They were not to be deprived of this right on the basis of a substantial dispute as to the sum demanded. It was unnecessary for the defendants at this stage to make out a prima facie case for winding up under s. 224 (1) (c), since that was a matter for the Companies Court. Nor should the defendants be restrained from presenting a winding up petition otherwise than as prospective creditors. Provided a person had locus standi to present a petition, the determination of the validity of any allegations within that petition was a question for the Companies Court to decide. The injunction would be refused.

HOLT SOUTHEY LTD v CATNIC COMPONENTS LTD [1978] 2 All ER 276 (Chancery Division: GOULDING J). *Mann v Goldstein* [1968] 2 All ER 769 applied.

378   —— petition by creditor—summary dismissal—grounds

Scotland

An unsecured creditor petitioned for the winding up of a company. The business of the company was being carried on by a receiver appointed under a floating charge in favour of a bank. The receiver requested the court to dismiss the petition summarily on the ground that if the company were wound up the petitioner would receive no dividends, whereas if it were to continue in business there were prospects of a more advantageous realisation of its assets. *Held*, a petition should not be dismissed summarily where a creditor sought a winding-up order on the ground that a company was unable to pay its debts unless there were compelling reasons to do so. In this case, there were no such reasons justifying the refusal of an order for intimation, advertisement and service to the petitioner, who wished to question the accuracy of the receiver's statement of affairs. Whether or not a winding up order would be granted should await the expiry of the time for lodging of answers to the petition.

FOXHALL AND GYLE (NURSERIES) LTD, PETITIONERS 1978 SLT (NOTES) 29 (Outer House).

379   —— power of receiver under debenture—power to sell property after liquidation

See *Sowman v David Samuel Trust Ltd (in Liquidation)*, para. 2305.

380   —— property available for distribution—company's rights against insurers

See *Re Allobrogia Steamship Corpn*, para. 356.

381   —— rules

The Companies (Winding-up) (Amendment) Rules 1978, S.I. 1978 No. 543 (in force on 2nd May 1978), amend the Companies (Winding-up) Rules 1949 by increasing the costs allowed in connection with creditors' and contributories' meetings under r. 132 (3) and by increasing to £100 the costs, charges and expenses which the Official Receiver or liquidator may allow to be paid without taxation to any person employed by him under the proviso to r. 195 (2).

382   —— untraceable shareholders—unclaimed dividends—unclaimed capital on past reductions of capital—limitation period for claims

The liquidators of a company, which was being voluntarily wound up by its members, sought directions from the court as to how they should deal with the possible claims of untraceable shareholders to past dividends on shares and capital on past reductions of capital. There were sufficient assets to pay the claims in full. If the unascertainable shareholders could be regarded as creditors rather than members, the liquidators could exclude them from any distribution which might be made to the members of the company. But if they remained as members, moneys to meet potential claims would have to remain in the insolvency services account at the Bank of England. There was also a question of the length of the limitation period, if any, attaching to possible claims. *Held*, on any winding up, untraceable members who were owed money by the company as members must be treated as creditors, subject to the prior rights of ordinary creditors. This would greatly assist the liquidators who owed no duty to a creditor who failed to make a claim after proper advertisement of the winding up. On the question of the limitation period, the appropriate term for actions to enforce rights to unclaimed dividends on shares and rights to unclaimed capital on past reductions of capital was six years, as for actions founded on simple contract.

RE COMPANIA DE ELECTRICIDAD DE LA PROVINCIA DE BUENOS AIRES LTD [1978] 3 All ER 668 (Chancery Division: SLADE J). *Re Artisans' Land and Mortgage Corporation* [1904] 1 Ch. 796, not followed.

383   —— **voluntary winding up—limited liability company—pending action—revival of company—whether action held in abeyance**

A company went into a voluntary winding-up and its cause of action was purportedly assigned to another company after the first company had ceased to exist. A summons for directions was issued by the assignees. An order under the Companies Act 1948, s. 352 was later made declaring the dissolution void and the company resumed its legal existence. On a determination of whether the pending action ceased absolutely on the company's dissolution and whether it could be revived as a declaration that the dissolution was void, *held*, an action which was left incomplete or not assigned before the dissolution of the company was not held in abeyance. It died absolutely at the date of the winding-up and could not survive to become effective again by an order under s. 352.

FOSTER YATES AND THOM LTD v H. W. EDGEHILL EQUIPMENT LTD (1978) Times, 30th November (Court of Appeal: MEGAW, CUMMING-BRUCE LJJ and SIR BASIL NIELD). *Morris v Harris* [1927] AC 252, HL, followed.

COMPULSORY ACQUISITION OF LAND

Halsbury's Laws of England (4th edn.), Vol. 8, paras. 1–400

384   **Article**

Effect of Scheme where Part Only of Land of an Owner is Acquired, W. A. Leach (analysis of problems involved when part only of owner's land is compulsorily acquired): [1978] JPL 810.

385   **Compensation—assessment—effect of motorways**

Where a motorway is built and opened section by section, the Department of Transport regards each section as needing to be treated separately for claim purposes under the Land Compensation Act 1973, s. 4 (2). When assessing depreciation, the Department takes into account the use of the section of motorway on the first day of the claim period and any intensification of traffic which may then be reasonably expected of the motorway in the state it is in on that date.

See *Case 6/701/77* in the Fifth Report of the Parliamentary Commissioner for Administration for the Session 1977–78 (HC 524), p. 319.

386　　　— — Lands Tribunal decisions

ALI v SOUTHWARK LONDON BOROUGH (1977) 246 EG 663: E. C. Strathon FRICS (compulsory purchase of freehold dwelling-house let on two protected tenancies; tenants friends of owner who would vacate premises if he wished to reoccupy; owner contended house should be valued either on assumption that tenants would give up possession if house sold or with hope value to reflect likelihood of reasonably early possession; interest was encumbered by tenancies and understanding with tenants was irrelevant; nor would prospective purchaser raise bid on account of hope value; owner's valuations rejected; property should be valued on investment basis).

387　　　APPLEBY & IRELAND LTD v HAMPSHIRE COUNTY COUNCIL (1978) 247 Estates Gazette 1183: R. C. Walmsley FRICS (agreement for compulsory acquisition of engineering company's premises at Basingstoke made in 1973 and premises acquired in 1974; company relocated twelve miles away; claim for disturbance based on actual move; authority contended company could only recover compensation in respect of loss which would have been sustained if company had relocated within Basingstoke; question whether company could have mitigated loss by relocating within Basingstoke in 1973 when agreement made; valuations made on alternative bases of actual loss on move and estimated loss on move within Basingstoke; move within Basingstoke would have resulted in much smaller loss; since there was a choice of suitable premises in Basingstoke and company had sufficient finance for move in 1973, failure to do so amounted to unreasonable inaction resulting in avoidable loss; compensation would be reduced by amount of avoidable loss).

388　　　ARROW v BEXLEY LONDON BOROUGH COUNCIL [1978] RVR 25: R. C. Walmsley FRICS (house compulsorily purchased and entry taken in 1974; tenant had been rehoused by council in 1969; house not relet by claimant pending negotiations for sale to council; house extensively vandalised; claimant contended vandalism a direct consequence of house being unlet and therefore effect of vandalism on value of house should be ignored under "Pointe Gourde" principle since it was entirely due to council's scheme; house should be valued in actual state at relevant date because decrease in value not entirely due to scheme underlying acquisition, since decision not to relet was claimant's alone and he had done little to minimise risk; house not council's responsibility as risk of damage did not pass till authority took possession or compensation determined; council's valuation upheld).

389　　　HATHERELL v SEDGEMOOR DISTRICT COUNCIL [1978] RVR 28: Sir Douglas Frank QC (compulsory aquisition in 1976 of bungalow occupied on a protected tenancy and land; in 1965, claimant had obtained a s. 17 certificate for use of land for recreational purposes including car parking; planning permission for development of land as car park granted in 1970; in 1971, contractors constructing a motorway nearby extracted sand from land and deposited soil and clay on it; claimant contended bungalow should be valued with vacant possession and land valued with benefit of planning permission, which had not lapsed because development to which it related was begun when soil and clay were put on land; alternatively, the words "including car parking" in s. 17 certificate meant that car parking was a use for which planning permission might reasonably have been expected to be granted; bungalow should be valued subject to protected tenancy; planning permission had lapsed since laying of soil and clay was not commencement of development for which permission given; claimant's contention concerning s. 17 certificate upheld, but cost of developing car park exceeded value; council's valuation of land based on hope value for a car park accepted).

390　　　HONISETT v ROTHER DISTRICT COUNCIL [1978] RVR 139: J. D. Russell-Davis FRICS (compulsory purchase of leasehold interest in land with uncertain freehold title; dispute over compensation in respect of deductions from agreed freehold value of land; leaseholder claimed only deductions should be cost of acquiring freehold and attendant legal fees and insurance premium for indemnity against third party claiming freehold title; council claimed there should be deductions for cost of a lay-by constructed by them and alleged that as the freeholder would be the most likely purchaser of the leasehold interest there should be a deduction of his possible expenses plus half the remainder; compensation awarded in favour of leaseholder; a freeholder with an uncertain title would accept a fixed sum not claim a half interest; permissible deductions were that fixed sum, the cost of the lay-by, legal fees which would be incurred if acquiring freehold and insurance premiums).

391   IND COOPE (LONDON) LTD v ENFIELD LONDON BOROUGH (1977) 245 EG 942: J. D. Russell-Davis FRICS (off-licence premises with tied tenancy compulsorily acquired; offer of alternative accommodation a quarter of a mile away was refused by claimants on commercial grounds; tribunal said that refusal was reasonable; approach to valuation of compensation for off-licence was same as for other retail premises; special consideration should be given to tied trade which had greater security and therefore more value than free trade, or goodwill of any other business).

392   NATIONAL CARRIERS LTD v SECRETARY OF STATE FOR TRANSPORT (1978) 35 P & CR 245: V. G. Wellings QC (statutory undertakers sought compensation for compulsory acquisition of their premises under Town and Country Planning Act 1971, s. 238; s. 238 applies where acquisition effected without appropriate minister's certificate; no certificate obtained, although if claimants had made representations to minister they could have obtained one; authority contended s. 238 not applicable, since claimants could have acquired a certificate if they had made representations; s. 238 not applicable where no representations made to minister; premises should be valued on basis of open market value under Land Compensation Act 1961).

393   PANCHAL v PRESTON BOROUGH COUNCIL (1978) 247 EG 817: Sir Douglas Frank QC (claim for owner-occupier compensation after compulsory acquisition of house; owner had asked council about rights when house originally scheduled for clearance; advised to stay in possession; family moved to another house but left some furniture and owner returned each night to sleep; accepted that he had been in occupation; unlikely that he would have acted contrary to advice to stay in possession).

394   RATHGAR PROPERTY CO LTD v HARINGEY LONDON BOROUGH COUNCIL; MERRIDALE MOTORS LTD v HARINGEY LONDON BOROUGH COUNCIL [1978] RVR 44: W. H. Rees, FRICS (compulsory purchase of land forming part of a garage and petrol-filling station to form access to site subsequently developed by council; claimants contended valuation should take into account fact that land was only present access to site; council contended that fact should be ignored as it consisted of the special suitability of the land for a purpose to which the land could be applied only in pursuance of statutory powers, or for which there was no market apart from the special requirements of the purchasing authority; special quality of land should not be ignored, since purpose was not one to which land could be applied only in pursuance of statutory powers; there was a normal market for the land since there was more than one potential purchaser; other means of access to the site could be developed and the sum awarded would be the cost of development of one of them since a vendor of the claimants' land would regard that as the minimum price).

395   TAYLOR v CHELTENHAM BOROUGH COUNCIL (1978) 246 EG 923: R. C. Walmsley FRICS (local authority compulsorily acquired listed buildings in appalling condition; cost of repairs far outweighed value of house; low purchase price of £2,000 adopted as no-one would ever buy the house for their own occupation, and no speculator or builder would conceivably be prepared to pay more than £2,000).

396   WILLIAMSON v CAMBRIDGESHIRE COUNTY COUNCIL (1977) 34 P & CR 117: Sir Douglas Frank QC (compulsory acquisition of land for use as caravan site for gipsies; dispute over compensation; deemed planning permission taken into account when assessing compensation; authorised use of land as site for caravans occupied by gipsies; claimants contended deemed planning permission to be construed as allowing use for a general caravan site as no material change of use involved; "occupied by gipsies" strictly limited proposed use to gipsies only; use for general caravans would be material change of use).

397   —— —— potential use of land—severance loss

An Australian property developer appealed to the Privy Council against the refusal of the Supreme Court of Queensland to re-examine the assessment of compensation both for a strip of land compulsorily acquired to make way for a highway and for severance loss occasioned to a parcel of land consequently cut off from the remainder of the land he had owned. The Australian courts had disregarded both the fact that the developer had very profitably sold the land on one side of the highway for development and the development potential of the severed remnant which had disappeared when the strip was acquired. *Held*, compensation had to be assessed without reference to any diminution in the value of the land caused by the acquisition itself. This applied regardless of whether a landowner had known of the impending acquisition when he bought the land. Compensation accordingly had to be assessed by reference to the value of the whole area at one time owned by the developer as if it could all have been sold for development. The Supreme Court should have remitted the case to the Land Appeal Court on the ground that the latter's method of assessment had disregarded evidence of the value of the land. Such disregard amounted to an error of law.

MELWOOD UNITS PTY LTD V COMR OF MAIN ROADS [1978] 3 WLR 520 (Privy Council: LORD WILBERFORCE, LORD HAILSHAM OF ST MARYLEBONE, LORD SIMON OF GLAISDALE, LORD RUSSELL OF KILLOWEN and LORD KEITH OF KINKEL). *Pointe Gourde Quarrying and Transport Co Ltd v Sub-Intendent of Crown Lands* [1947] AC 565, PC applied.

398   —— disturbance—assessment—Lands Tribunal decisions

M. BLOOM (KOSHER) AND SONS LTD V TOWER HAMLETS LONDON BOROUGH COUNCIL (1977) 35 P & CR 423: V. G. Wellings QC (company foresaw compulsory acquisition of its premises and moved before it happened; when premises acquired, company sought large sum to compensate it for disturbance as move entirely prompted by possibility of compulsory purchase; only about half sum claimed for disturbance payable because no expenses incurred before notice to treat served in respect of old premises could be recovered as they were not consequential to compulsory acquisition).

399   SUCCAMORE V NEWHAM LONDON BOROUGH COUNCIL [1977] RVR 334; R. C. Walmsley FRICS (compulsory purchase of freehold house; compensation agreed for house; compensation for disturbance disputed by council; sums claimed included solicitor's fees for purchase of new house, building society fees, removal expenses, surveyor's fees for purchased house and for an abortive purchase, local search fees, carpets, curtains, travelling expenses; compensation claimed for cost of carpets and curtains reduced; other expenditure reimbursed in full).

400   —— —— occupier of premises

Scotland

The rateable occupier of a shop was a company in which the majority shareholding was vested in the owner of the building. There was no formal lease of the premises to the company. The building was compulsorily acquired and the owner's claim for compensation for disturbance was dismissed. He appealed, contending that he was in reality the only legal person involved in the entire business operation, being the major shareholder, and therefore should be entitled to compensation as the occupier of the premises. *Held*, the company had no control over the owner of the premises and he could not be treated as beneficially entitled to the whole shareholding of the company. Therefore, the principle of piercing the corporate veil where special circumstances indicated that it was a mere facade concealing the true facts, could not be applied. Further, as the company was the occupier of the premises and the business was carried on there, any loss suffered by the owner would be by virtue of his position as majority shareholder in the company and not as owner of the premises. Accordingly, the appeal would be dismissed.

WOOLFSON V STRATHCLYDE REGIONAL COUNCIL 1978 SLT 159 (House of Lords: LORD WILBERFORCE, LORD FRASER OF TULLYBELTON, LORD RUSSELL OF KILLOWEN and LORD KEITH OF KINKEL).   Decision of Inner House 1977 SLT 60, 1977 Halsbury's Abr para. 424 affirmed.   *Salomon v Salomon & Co Ltd* [1897] AC 22 applied; *D. H. N. Food Distributors Ltd v Tower Hamlets London Borough Council* [1976] 1 WLR 852, 1976 Halsbury's Abr para. 388 distinguished.

401   —— entry on to land—date of entry

COURAGE LTD V KINGSWOOD DISTRICT COUNCIL (1978) 35 P & CR 436: Sir Douglas Frank QC (compulsory purchase of land attached to public house; dispute over date of taking possession; council went onto land in July 1972, cleared it and erected a shed for workmen; in February 1973 claimant padlocked entrance to prevent unauthorised third parties going onto land and to ascertain precise date when council took possession; work council had done at that time was more than just surveying, it was part of the work for which the land was purchased; the date of possession was July 1972).

402   —— rate of interest after entry

The Acquisition of Land (Rate of Interest after Entry) Regulations 1978, S.I. 1978 No. 886 (in force on 20th July 1978) increased to $11\frac{1}{2}$ per cent per annum the rate of interest payable where entry is made, before payment of compensation, on land in England and Wales which is being purchased compulsorily.   The Acquisition of Land (Rate of Interest after Entry) (No. 4) Regulations 1977, 1977 Halsbury's Abr para. 433, are revoked.

These regulations were subsequently revoked, see para. 403.

403   The Acquisition of Land (Rate of Interest after Entry) (No. 2) Regulations 1978, S.I. 1978 No. 1418 (in force on 25th October 1978), increase to $12\frac{1}{2}$ per cent per annum the rate of interest payable where entry is made, before payment of compensation, on land in England and Wales which is being purchased compulsorily.   The Acquisition of Land (Rate of Interest after Entry) Regulations 1978, S.I. 1978 No. 886, are revoked.

These regulations were subsequently revoked, see para. 404.

404   The Acquisition of Land (Rate of Interest after Entry) (No. 3) Regulations 1978, S.I. 1978 No. 1741 (in force on 4th January 1979) increase from $12\frac{1}{2}$ per cent to 14 per cent the annual rate of interest payable on land in England and Wales which is being purchased compulsorily, where entry is made before payment of compensation.

405   —— time limit for claim—report of Parliamentary Commissioner for Administration

The Parliamentary Commissioner for Administration has criticised the Department of Transport for its failure to bring the rights of potential claimants of compensation under the Land Compensation Act 1973 adequately to their attention in time for them to make their claims.   Although the department is under no statutory duty to issue a public notice, the commissioner criticised it for having issued only one such notice, having issued it at holiday time and in an insufficiently "eye-catching" way. He also criticised the department's failure to monitor the effects of a press notice.   See Parliamentary Commissioner for Administration; Sixth Report for Session 1977–78 (Rochester Way, Bexley: Refusal to meet late claims for compensation.   HC 598).

406   Compensation for injury by works—assessment—Lands Tribunal decision

BARB AND BARB V SECRETARY OF STATE FOR TRANSPORT: RIGBY V SECRETARY OF STATE FOR TRANSPORT [1978] RVR 182: E. C. Strathon FRICS (claimants sought compensation for depreciation in the value of their properties caused by noise from motorway; their valuer brought evidence of asking and sale prices of other properties in the area; Secretary of State alleged there had been no depreciation; brought evidence of settlements of compensation for noise depreciation made in respect of comparable properties; there had been a depreciation; evidence of claimant's valuer as to asking and sale prices unsatisfactory as guideline for compensation; assessment made by reference to settlements with allowance for comparables' situation further from motorway).

407   Compulsory purchase order—confirmation by Secretary of State—effect of failure to give reasons for decision

See *Meravale Builders Ltd v Secretary of State for the Environment*, para. 410.

408   —— failure to serve notice on joint owner—whether substantial prejudice

The plaintiff and her husband jointly bought a house in 1967. In 1975 a compulsory purchase order was made in respect of it. Notice was served on the husband but not on the plaintiff. The plaintiff claimed that the order should be quashed on the grounds that the council had not complied with the Acquisition of Land (Authorisation Procedure) Act 1946, Sch. 1, para. 3 (1) (b), in that it had not served notice of the order on every owner of the land in question. The plaintiff contended that her interest had been substantially prejudiced by the failure to comply with that provision and accordingly the order should be quashed under Sch. 1, para. 15 (1) (b). The council denied that she had been prejudiced; she had known of the order but had made a conscious decision not to object in order to have it quashed on technical grounds. *Held*, there was insufficient evidence to establish that the plaintiff had known about the order but had decided not to object, especially as she was living apart from her husband when notice was served on him. The failure to serve notice on her deprived her of the chance of objecting to the order. The order would be quashed.

GEORGE V SECRETARY OF STATE FOR THE ENVIRONMENT (1978) 122 Sol Jo 437 (Queen's Bench Division: SIR DOUGLAS FRANK QC sitting as a deputy High Court judge).

409   —— notice to treat—notice relating to part of premises—church site

A church owned property used as a single unit comprising a church, a car park, rooms, halls, outbuildings and a caretaker's house. A notice to treat was served on the church by London Transport in pursuance of its powers under the London Transport Act 1975 to acquire compulsorily certain lands in respect of the land behind the church but not the church itself or the house. The church claimed that London Transport was obliged to purchase the whole property by virtue of the lands Clauses Consolidation Act 1845, s. 92, which provides that no party may be required to sell or convey a part of any house or other building if such party is willing to sell or convey the whole of it. London Transport sought a declaration that it was not so obliged. *Held*, the church had to show (i) that the church was a "house or other building" and (ii) that the land proposed to be taken was part of the "house or other building". (i) The church was a "house or other building" (and could be assumed to be an "other building") since the authorities did not impose any requirement of use for residential or domestic purposes. (ii) A "house" in s. 92 comprised all that would pass by grant of a house and this proposition applied also to "other buildings". The halls and outbuildings at least were part of the church property and should be treated as part of the church under s. 92. Therefore London Transport was not entitled to take only part of the church property. The summons would be dismissed.

LONDON TRANSPORT EXECUTIVE V CONGREGATIONAL UNION OF ENGLAND AND WALES (INCORPORATED) (1978) Times, 15th June (Chancery Division: GOULDING J).

410   —— order under Housing Acts—duality of purpose—whether one purpose ultra vires—effect on collateral purpose

A local housing authority made a compulsory purchase order in respect of sixty-eight acres of land on which it intended to build a housing estate. It was proposed that part of the land should be used by the highway authority to extend an existing major road, a proposal from which the new residents would derive no substantial advantage since the greater part of the development land was already accessible. The applicants, who owned land affected by the order, opposed it and their opposition was supported in the recommendations of the inspector. However, the order was confirmed by the Secretary of State. The applicant applied for the order to be quashed. *Held*, the power of local authorities under the Housing Act 1957, s. 107 to construct highways on land compulsorily acquired under Part V of that Act was subject to an implied restriction that any roads built accordingly had to be fairly and reasonably incidental to the provision of housing accommodation. Since it was admitted that the proposal to extend the road was a purpose independent of the building of the housing estate, the compulsory purchase order had been made for a purpose which was partly ultra vires and therefore should be quashed. Further, in confirming the order on the grounds that it was "not inappropriate" for land acquired under Part V of the Act to be used for the purpose of road improvement, the Secretary of State had differed from the inspector on a finding of fact: his failure to give written notification of the reasons for his decision had caused substantial prejudice to the applicants, and the order should be quashed on that ground also.

MERAVALE BUILDERS LTD V SECRETARY OF STATE FOR THE ENVIRONMENT (1978) 36 P & CR 87 (Queen's Bench Division: WILLIS J). *Galloway v London Corporation* (1866) LR 1 HL 34 and *Hanks v Minister of Housing and Local Government* [1963] 1 QB 999, applied.

411   —— procedure

The Department of the Environment has issued a booklet entitled "Compulsory Purchase Orders—a guide to procedure" which explains in simple terms all the steps involved in a compulsory acquisition. The booklet is intended primarily for those people whose property is included in a compulsory purchase order.

412   Development—certificates of appropriate alternative development—appeal from confirmation by Secretary of State—relevance of current planning policies

Applicants sought to quash two decisions of the Secretary of State confirming the issue of certificates of appropriate alternative development under the Land Compensation Act 1961, s. 17. On the question whether he should have had regard to planning circumstances which were current at the time of his decision but not at the time of the acquisition of the land, *held*, the Secretary of State should deal with such cases in the same way as planning appeals and have regard to those planning policies extant at the time of his decision.

ROBERT HITCHINS BUILDERS LTD V SECRETARY OF STATE FOR THE ENVIRONMENT; WAKELEY BROS (RAINHAM, KENT) LTD V SECRETARY OF STATE FOR THE ENVIRONMENT (1978) 248 Estates Gazette 689 (Queen's Bench Division: SIR DOUGLAS FRANK QC sitting as a deputy High Court judge).

413   Local inquiry—objector's inability to attend—opportunity to be heard

See *Ostreicher v Secretary of State for the Environment*, para. 10.

414   Planning blight—notices—Lands Tribunal decision

HOLMES V KNOWSLEY BOROUGH COUNCIL (1977) 35 P & CR 119: R. C. Walmsley FRICS (house-owner served blight notice on local authority when he found himself unable to sell house due to pending compulsory purchase; authority rejected it on ground that house was empty and thus he was not an owner-occupier; owner held not to be an owner-occupier since house stood to be regarded as unoccupied from time it was put on market which was more than twelve months before date of blight notice).

CONFLICT OF LAWS

Halsbury's Laws of England (4th edn.), Vol. 8, paras. 401–795

415   Adoption—international convention

The United Kingdom has ratified the Convention on Jurisdiction, Applicable Law and Recognition of Decrees Relating to Adoption (signed at The Hague on 15th November 1965), (in force on 23rd October 1978). The convention vests jurisdiction to grant adoptions in the authorities of the State where the adopter or the adopting spouses habitually reside, or of which he or they are nationals (art. 3). The applicable law relating to consents and consultations (other than those with respect to an adopter, his family or her spouse) is the national law of the child (art. 5); but in all other respects the applicable law is the internal law of the State with jurisdiction to grant the adoption (art. 4). The convention requires an adoption order to be made in the interest of the child and also requires thorough inquiries to be made before the order is made (art. 6). Article 7 deals with jurisdiction to annul or revoke an order and art. 8 requires an adoption order made in accordance with the convention to be recognised by all contracting States. The United Kingdom has by notification reserved specific provisions in its domestic law. The convention is published as Cmnd 7342.

416   Continental Shelf—jurisdiction

The Continental Shelf (Jurisdiction) (Amendment) Order 1978, S.I. 1978 No. 454 (in force on 24th April 1978), revokes the 1975 Order, 1975 Halsbury's Abr para. 440. It also includes the new areas designated as part of the Shelf by the Continental Shelf (Designation of Additional Areas) Orders 1977 and 1978 (as to which see respectively 1977 Halsbury's Abr para. 1856 and para. 1899 post), in the areas of the United Kingdom Continental Shelf treated respectively as English and Scottish areas for the purposes of the civil law of those countries and related matters.

417   The Continental Shelf (Jurisdiction) (Amendment) (No. 2) Order 1978, S.I. 1978 No. 1024 (in force on 23rd August 1978), includes in the areas of the United Kingdom Continental Shelf treated as English areas for the purposes of the civil law of England and Wales and related matters, the new areas designated as part of the Shelf by the Continental Shelf (Designation of Additional Areas) (No. 2) Order 1978, para. 1900.

418   Contract—damages—currency of award

See *Services Europe Atlantique Sud v Stockholms Rederiaktiebolag Svea*, para. 841.

419   Divorce—maintenance orders—reciprocal enforcement

See para. 968.

420   Jurisdiction—action involving foreign immovables—equitable jurisdiction in personam—discretion of court to stay proceedings

The plaintiffs, an American corporation, were the assignees of a judgment debt entered against the second defendant in New York following an action for fraud. They brought proceedings in England against the first and second defendants alleging conspiracy to defraud, claiming that the second defendant was keeping out of New York assets derived from the original fraud and likely to be of sufficient value to satisfy the judgment debt and that the first defendant had acquired a flat in Paris in his own name for the purpose of sheltering the second defendant's possessions. The plaintiffs applied for an order in personam against the first defendant authorising inspection of the Paris flat and its contents. The first defendant submitted, first, that the court had no jurisdiction to allow the action to continue since it related to the ownership of foreign immovables, and second, that even if the court had jurisdiction, it was bound to exercise its discretion to stay the proceedings since New York not

England was the natural forum. *Held*, the court had jurisdiction to hear the application since a personal equity had been created between the plaintiffs and the first defendant by the plaintiffs' allegation of fraud. Further, the court would not exercise its discretion to stay the proceedings, on the grounds (i) that since the first defendant spent as much time in England as New York, it was no more difficult for him to defend proceedings here than in New York, (ii) that the order sought by the plaintiffs was an order in personam and the first defendant was within the jurisdiction, and (iii) that speed was of the essence in this action and a possible inspection of the flat should not be delayed. The order would be granted accordingly.

Cook Industries Incorporated v Galliher [1978] 3 All ER 945 (Chancery Division: Templeman J).

For a discussion of this case, see Law travels abroad, Justinian, Financial Times, October 30th 1978.

421   —— **custody of children—Scottish mother and children temporarily resident in England**

See *Re Irving (Minors)*, para. 1935.

422   —— **selection of forum of action—conditions to be satisfied**

The plaintiffs claimed damages from their employers for personal injuries sustained in the course of their employment in factories in Scotland. In each case, the employer was a company whose head office was in England, and the employees brought their actions in England. The employers' applications to stay the proceedings were refused and the employers appealed. *Held*, in order to justify a stay two conditions had to be satisfied: (i) the defendant had to satisfy the court that there was another forum to whose jurisdiction he was amenable in which justice could be done between the parties at substantially less inconvenience or expense, and (ii) the stay must not deprive the plaintiff of a legitimate personal or juridical advantage which would be available to him if he invoked the jurisdiction of an English court. Since the injuries had occurred in Scotland and the plaintiffs and witnesses all lived and worked there, the Scottish courts were prima facie the natural or appropriate forum, and justice could be done there at substantially less expense and inconvenience. This threw on the plaintiffs the burden of showing that they would be deprived of a legitimate advantage which would have been available to them in England. The test whether such an advantage existed was objective; an unsubstantiated belief, although bona fide, was insufficient. In the Court of Appeal it was for the plaintiffs to prove any juridical advantages as a question of fact by expert evidence. In the House of Lords, however, this was not so as the House's jurisdiction extended to Scotland and their Lordships were entitled and bound to take judicial notice of Scots law. Comparing the length and expense of process and the likely measure of damages and amount of costs in the two countries, it could not be said that any advantage lay in bringing the actions in England. The appeal would be allowed.

MacShannon v Rockware Glass Ltd; Fyfe v Redpath Dorman Long Ltd; Jardine v British Steel Corpn; Paterson v Stone Manganese Marine Ltd [1978] 1 All ER 625 (House of Lords: Lord Diplock, Lord Salmon, Lord Fraser of Tullybelton, Lord Russell of Killowen and Lord Keith of Kinkel). Majority decision of the Court of Appeal [1977] 2 All ER 449, 1977 Halsbury's Abr para. 457 reversed. *The Atlantic Star* [1974] AC 436, HL applied.

423   —— **service of writ out of jurisdiction—leave**

See *Ben & Co Ltd v Pakistan Edible Oils Corpn Ltd*, para. 156.

424   —— **trespass to property abroad—movable and immovable property—power of English courts to intervene**

Two Greek companies which owned hotels in Turkish-occupied Cyprus appealed against a decision that they had no cause of action against a Turkish firm of travel agents and the London representative of the Turkish Federated State of Cyprus, who were advertising the hotels to British tourists, for conspiracy to procure trespass to the properties and their contents. *Held*, it was a well-established principle of English law that English courts had jurisdiction neither to determine title to immovable property situated abroad, nor to entertain an action for the recovery of damages for trespass to immovable property abroad. There was no distinction to be drawn between actions for trespass committed abroad and actions for conspiracy in the United Kingdom to commit trespass abroad because the latter action could not be sustained unless the court considered the right to possession of land situated abroad, which it could not do. However, the court could hear the action with regard to the chattels notwithstanding the fact that the companies were not in possession of them, since a valid claim could be laid in conversion and since the local laws of the area in which the hotels were situated had not been invoked to justify interference with the chattels. Accordingly, the appeal would be allowed to that extent.

HESPERIDES HOTELS LTD V MUFTIZADE [1978] 3 WLR 378 (House of Lords: LORD WILBERFORCE, VISCOUNT DILHORNE, LORD SALMON, LORD FRASER OF TULLYBELTON and LORD KEITH OF KINKEL). *British South Africa Co v Companhia de Moçambique* [1893] AC 602, HL followed. Decision of the Court of Appeal sub nom *Hesperides Hotels Ltd v Aegean Turkish Holidays Ltd* [1978] QB 205, 1977 Halsbury's Abr para. 458 reversed in part.

425   Procedure—parties—position of judicial administrator appointed under foreign law

In proceedings instituted in the Lebanon, a man whose brother had been missing since 1973 obtained a declaration that he was an absent person and was appointed his judicial administrator. He then sued the defendants in England for a debt due to his brother. *Held*, while under Lebanese law the plaintiff had good title to claim in his alleged representative capacity, such a right was not recognised by English law. The plaintiff could only have brought an action in his own name in England to recover the debts of an absent person, if he had obtained leave to swear death and had obtained an English grant of administration. Therefore, as the plaintiff's title was not recognised in England, his claim would be dismissed.

KAMOUH V ASSOCIATED ELECTRICAL INDUSTRIES INTERNATIONAL LTD (1978) 122 Sol Jo 714 (Queen's Bench Division: PARKER J)

426   Service of process—foreign corporation—locus standi to serve in United Kingdom

In order to recover money due under a contract, an American company delivered a writ to a London address which appeared on the defendant company's notepaper. The defendant company claimed that it was neither resident nor carrying on business in the United Kingdom and that the London address was that of a representative office only. The Court of Appeal decided that the American company was entitled to bring the action in the United Kingdom. On appeal, *held*, the American company had failed to establish that the defendant company was carrying on business from its London office and therefore it was not entitled to bring an action in the United Kingdom.

BETHLEHEM STEEL CORPN V UNIVERSAL GAS AND OIL CO INC (1978) Times, 3rd August (House of Lords: LORD WILBERFORCE, LORD SALMON, LORD RUSSELL OF KILLOWEN, LORD SCARMAN and LORD HAILSHAM OF ST MARYLEBONE).

427   Tort—damages—currency of award

See *The Despina R*, para. 841.

428   —— location of tort—fraudulent misrepresentation—service of writ out of jurisdiction

A London sugar broker wanted a bank reference for the other broker in a deal involving about one million tons of sugar. An employee of the Nassau branch of the respondent bank gave, by telephone and telex, a good reference on which the London broker relied. He turned down other offers and sold on half a million tons of sugar. Subsequently, the London broker said that the bank reference which he had been given was fraudulent. The bank employee had given the reference without justification for the fraudulent reason that he hoped to obtain commission for himself. The London broker sought to serve a writ out of the jurisdiction under RSC Order 11, r. 1 (1) (h). His application was refused on the ground that the alleged tort had not been committed within the jurisdiction. On appeal, *held*, the alleged fraudulent misrepresentations had been made by someone outside the jurisdiction by telephone conversations and by telex to someone within the jurisdiction. The tort had been committed in the place where the misrepresentations were received and acted upon by the recipient to his detriment. Leave to serve outside the jurisdiction could therefore be granted. However, the application failed because the appellant was unable to make out a good arguable case of fraudulent misrepresentation.

DIAMOND v BANK OF LONDON AND MONTREAL LTD [1979] 2 WLR 228 (Court of Appeal: LORD DENNING MR. STEPHENSON and SHAW LJJ).

CONSTITUTIONAL LAW

Halsbury's Laws of England (4th edn.), Vol. 8, paras. 801–1647

429   Articles

The Crown and the People, John Sweetman (characteristics of the British constitution): 122 Sol Jo 738.

Warning from the Joint Committee, Gavin Drewry (consideration of deficiencies in the system for scrutinising subordinate legislation): 128 NLJ 653.

430   Attorney General—refusal of consent to relator action—right of private individual to bring proceedings

See *Ex parte Island Records Ltd*, para. 524.

431   Coinage—Trial of the Pyx

The Trial of the Pyx (Amendment) Order 1978, S.I. 1978 No. 185 (in force on 10th February 1978), amends the Trial of the Pyx Order 1975, 1975 Halsbury's Abr para. 461, by giving to the Queen's Remembrancer the right to decide whether the whole or part only of the verdict of the jury shall be read out in his presence.

432   Consular fees

The Consular Fees Regulations 1978, S.I. 1978 No. 692 (in force on 25th May 1978), prescribe the manner in which a consular officer should carry out the duties imposed by the Consular Salaries and Fees Act 1891, s. 2 (2) and replace the Consular Fees Regulations 1971.

433   Emergency controls

See EMERGENCY CONTROLS.

434   Lord Chancellor—Pension—calculation of increases

See para. 2098.

435   Ministers—salaries

The Ministerial and other Salaries Order 1978, S.I. 1978 No. 1102 (in force on 31st July 1978), increases by ten per cent the annual salaries payable under the Ministerial and other Salaries Act 1975 to certain Ministers, Members of the Opposition and the Speaker of the House of Commons. It replaces the Ministerial and other Salaries Order 1977, 1977 Halsbury's Abr para. 468.

436   Northern Ireland

See NORTHERN IRELAND.

437   Scotland Act 1978

The Scotland Act 1978 received the royal assent on 31st July 1978 and comes into force on a day to be appointed. The Act gives effect for Scotland to proposals described in the White Papers "Our Changing Democracy: Devolution to Scotland and Wales" (Cmnd 6348) and "Devolution to Scotland and Wales: Supplementary Statement" (Cmnd 6585) and in the Lord President's Statement on Devolution on 26th July 1977 (Vol. 936 c. 313). It provides for a directly elected Assembly for Scotland, establishes the constitutional and financial machinery for its operation and sets out the powers which it will exercise.

Part I and Schedules 1 to 6 establish the Scottish Assembly and the Scottish Executive, and provide the main components of the constitutional framework within which they will operate.

Part II and Schedules 7 and 8 contain a number of provisions concerned with the relations between the devolved administration and the Government.

Part III and Schedule 9 contain the main provisions for financing the devolved services and for ensuring that expenditure on these services is subject to appropriate scrutiny.

Part IV and Schedules 10 to 12 define the principal matters for which the Scottish Assembly and the Scottish Secretaries are to be responsible.

Part V and Schedules 13 and 14 make provisions on a variety of topics including the status and remuneration of civil servants, rate support grants, tourism, and complaints of maladministration.

Part VI and Schedules 15 to 17 contain general and supplementary provisions.

438   —— referendum—date and conduct of referendum

The Scotland Act 1978 (Referendum) Order 1978, S.I. 1978 No. 1912 (in force on 20th December 1978), makes provision for the conduct of the referendum to beheld in Scotland under the Act and specifies the dates of the referendum as 1st March 1979. Schedules 1 and 2 specify the provisions of the Representation of the Peoples Acts 1949 and 1969 and other subordinate legislation which apply to the referendum together with appropriate modifications.

439   Secretary of State—transfer of functions—Wales

The Transfer of Functions (Wales) (No. 1) Order 1978, S.I. 1978 No. 272 (in force on 1st April 1978), transfers certain functions relating to agriculture, fisheries, water resources, water supply, land drainage and certain other matters. Under the order certain functions now exercisable by the Minister for Agriculture, Fisheries and Food or jointly by him and other ministers will be exercisable by the Secretary of State for Wales, either alone or jointly with the Minister or with him and other ministers. The Minister of Agriculture will exercise alone other functions now exercisable jointly by him and the Secretary of State.

440

The Transfer of Functions (Wales) (No. 2) Order 1978, S.I. 1978 No. 274 (in force on 1st April 1978), enables the Secretary of State for Wales to exercise in relation to Wales certain functions of the Secretary of State for Education and Science.

441   The Treasury—optimal control of policy

The committee (chairman R. J. Ball) appointed in 1976 to consider the present state of development of optimal control techniques as applied to macro-economic policy was required to make recommendations concerning the feasibility and value of applying these techniques within the Treasury. The Committee has published a report: Cmnd. 7148.

The committee recommend that the application of optimal control to the analysis of economic policy is feasible and recommend the establishment of a strong research unit with an independent advisory council to oversee the units programme.

442   Wales Act 1978

The Wales Act 1978 gives effect for Wales to proposals described in the White Papers "Our Changing Democracy: Devolution to Scotland and Wales" (Cmnd 6348) and "Devolution to Scotland and Wales: Supplementary Statement" (Cmnd 6585). It provides for a directly elected Assembly for Wales, establishes the constitutional and financial machinery for its operation and sets out the powers which it will exercise. The Act received the royal assent on 31st July 1978 and comes into force on a day to be appointed.

Part I and Schs. 1 to 3 establish the Welsh Assembly, define its principal functions and provide the main components of the constitutional framework within which it will operate.

Part II and Schs. 4 and 5 contain the provisions concerned with the relationship between the Welsh Assembly and the Government.

Part III and Sch. 6 contain the main provisions for financing the devolved services and for ensuring that the expenditure is subject to the appropriate scrutiny.

Part IV and Schs. 7 to 9 make provision on a variety of miscellaneous topics, including rate support and grants, tourism, water and land drainage, the Countryside Commission for Wales, status and remuneration of certain officers and servants, transfer of property, and complaints of maladministration.

Part V and Schs. 10 to 12 contain general and supplementary provisions.

443   —— referendum—date and conduct of referendum

The Wales Act 1978 (Referendum) Order 1978, S.I. 1978 No. 1915 (in force on 20th December 1978), makes provision for the conduct of the referendum to be held in Wales under the Act and specifies the date of the referendum as 1st March 1979. Schedules 1 and 2 specify the provisions of the Representation of the People Acts 1949 and 1969 and other subordinate legislation which apply to the referendum together with appropriate modifications.

444   —— —— form of referendum

The Wales Act 1978 (Referendum) (Welsh Forms) Order 1978, S.I. 1978 No. 1953 (in force on 22nd February 1979), prescribes both in English and Welsh, the form of the ballot paper, the elector's official poll card, the proxy's official poll card and the Declaration of Identity and Certificate of Employment used for the referendum held in Wales on 1st March 1979.

CONSUMER PROTECTION AND FAIR TRADING

Halsbury's Laws of England (3rd edn.), Vol. 38, paras. 94–185

445   Articles

Consumer Protection—For Whom?, Professor P. B. Fairest (circumstances in which a company may be a consumer): 128 NLJ 1127.

Consumer Protection and the Office of Fair Trading, R. G. Lawson (the consumer protection aspects of the Fair Trading Act 1973, Pts. II, III and XII): 128 NLJ 376.

Consumer Safety Act 1978, Alec Samuels: 122 Sol Jo 719.

Consumers Cannot Win, Patrick Eyre (statutory rights of consumers; methods of avoidance adopted by vendors): 128 NLJ 1159.

Judges lend their weight (usefulness of the Restrictive Practices Court and other tribunals composed of judges and laymen in the light of *Director General of Fair Trading v Smiths Bakeries (Westfield) Ltd*, para. 452): Justinian, Financial Times, 15th May 1978.

446   Babies' dummies—safety

The Babies' Dummies (Safety) Regulations 1978, S.I. 1978 No. 836 (Regulation 4 (3) in force on 1st January 1980; remainder in force on 1st January 1979 but in relation to goods sold, or in the possession of any person for the purpose of being sold, by the manufacturer or importer into Great Britain, in force on 1st October 1978) impose requirements relating to the safety of babies' dummies. The requirements are concerned with the materials and construction of dummies, their resistance to damage and their packaging and the instructions to be given with them for their safe use.

447   Balloon-making compounds—safety

The Balloon-Making Compounds (Safety) Order 1979, S.I. 1979 No. 44 (in force on 18th January 1979) prohibits persons from supplying, offering to supply, agreeing to supply, exposing for supply or possessing for supply, any substance for making balloons which contains Benzene, either as part of a balloon-making kit or separately.

448   Child's nightwear—safety

The Nightwear (Safety) Order 1978, S.I. 1978 No. 1728 (in force on 1st December 1978) prohibits the supply of child's nightwear which has been treated with or contains a certain chemical substance commonly known as Tris.

449   Consumer Safety Act 1978

The Consumer Safety Act 1978 gives the Secretary of State powers to make regulations preventing or reducing the risk of death or personal injury from certain goods, including goods supplied by way of sale or under a hire purchase agreement. The Act received the royal assent on 20th July 1978 and came into force on 28th September 1978 with the exception of s. 10 (1) and Sch. 3 (dealing with repeals) which come into force on a day to be appointed.

Section 1 specifies the provisions which may be contained in regulations made for the safety of any goods except food, fertilisers, animal feeding stuffs and medical products. Various offences in contravention of the safety regulations are contained in s. 2. The Secretary of State may make orders for a limited period prohibiting the supply of unsafe goods or may give notice to any person prohibiting the supply of such goods or requiring the publication of a warning that the goods are unsafe: s. 3. Schedule 1 sets out the procedure to be followed before making a prohibition order or serving a notice under s. 3. Section 4 enables the Secretary of State to obtain information necessary for the exercise of his powers under ss. 1, 3. Local weights and measures authorities are required to enforce safety regulations, prohibition orders and notices: s. 5. Powers of enforcement are contained in Sch. 2. Any person affected by a breach of any safety regulation, order or notice has a right of action in respect of the breach: s. 6. Supplementary provisions, repeals and transitional provisions are contained in ss. 7–12 and Sch. 3.

450   Consumer transactions—statement by vendor—restrictions

The Consumer Transactions (Restrictions on Statements) (Amendment) Order 1978, S.I. 1978 No. 127 (in force on 1st February 1978), amends the definition of "consumer transaction" in the Consumer Transactions (Restrictions on Statements) Order 1976, 1976 Halsbury's Abr para. 432. This is in consequence of the repeal and re-enactment by the Unfair Contract Terms Act 1977 of certain provisions of the Sale of Goods Act 1893 and the Supply of Goods (Implied Terms) Act 1973.

451 **Cosmetic products—safety**

The Cosmetic Products Regulations 1978, S.I. 1978 No. 1354 (in force on 15th October 1978) introduce requirements relating to cosmetic products in accordance with Council Directive No. 76/768/EEC. They impose a duty on manufacturers, importers and certain sellers not to sell or possess for sale any cosmetic product which could damage human health in normal use. They also provide that certain particulars are to be marked on cosmetic containers, and Schs. 1–4 list substances and colouring agents which may not be used or which may be used subject to restrictions.

452 **Course of conduct detrimental to interests of consumers—failure to give assurance—reference to Restrictive Practices Court**

A firm of bakers was convicted of forty-six offences under the Food and Drugs Act 1955 in three years. The Director General of Fair Trading failed to obtain a written assurance from the firm that it would refrain from continuing a course of conduct which appeared to him to be detrimental to the interests of, and unfair to, consumers. He therefore applied for an order under the 1973 Act, ss. 35 and 38 restraining the firm and its director, as an accessory, from continuing such a course of conduct. The firm and its director offered undertakings promising to take all reasonable precautions and to exercise all due diligence to refrain from the course of conduct complained of. The Director General contended that if the court made an order it had to be in absolute terms, but he was prepared to accept the conditional undertaking offered. *Held*, the court had the power to accept such undertakings instead of making an order, and this would accordingly be done.

DIRECTOR GENERAL OF FAIR TRADING v SMITHS BAKERIES (WESTFIELD) LTD (1978) Times, 12th May (Restrictive Practices Court: MOCATTA J presiding).

453 **Credit-sale agreements—agreements to which restrictions apply**

See para. 1477.

454 **Dangerous substances—packaging and labelling**

See para. 1454.

455 **Hire-purchase agreements—agreements to which restrictions apply**

See para. 1476.

456 **Perambulators and pushchairs—safety**

The Perambulators and Pushchairs (Safety) Regulations 1978, S.I. 1978 No. 1372 (in force in relation to goods sold by their manufacturer or importer on 1st January 1979 and in other cases on 1st July 1979) impose new requirements as to the safety of perambulators and pushchairs. These requirements relate to brakes, stability, harness attachment points and locking devices for folding perambulators and pushchairs.

457 **Price control—petrol**

The Petrol Prices (Display) (Amendment) Order 1979, S.I. 1979 No. 4 (in force on 1st February 1979), amends the 1978 Order to substitute a reference to the new British Standard Specification for petrol) and to amend those provisions relating to the display of prices on petrol pumps and related information on pumps and adjacent notices.

458 **Price marking—beds**

The Indication of Prices (Beds) Order 1978, S.I. 1978 No. 1716 (in force on 1st March 1979), prohibits any indication by a person that beds for sale by him may be sold by a person buying them at a particular price. The Order also provides that, except in certain prescribed circumstances, the dual price marking of beds is prohibited.

459   Price marking—food

See FOOD.

460   —— petrol

The Petrol Prices (Display) Order 1978, S.I. 1978 No. 1389 (articles one and five in force on 18th October 1978, articles two to four in force on 20th December 1978), introduces new requirements relating to the mode of display and legibility of petrol prices. The Petrol Prices (Display) Order 1977, 1977 Halsbury's Abr para. 483 is revoked.

461   Trade descriptions

See TRADE DESCRIPTIONS.

CONTEMPT OF COURT

Halsbury's Laws of England (4th edn.), Vol. 9, paras. 1–125

462   Article

Contempt—The Need for Reform, Antony Whitaker: 128 NLJ 1040.

463   Committal order—procedure—application for order—application by litigant in person

On an application by a litigant in person seeking a direction from the court as to its practice in contemplation of further applications which he proposed to make with a view to committing the opposing parties to the action to prison for alleged contempt of court, *held,* a litigant in person was at liberty to move for an order of committal for contempt of court not only in the Divisional Court of the Queen's Bench Division under RSC Ord. 52, r. 2, but also in a court other than the Divisional Court under RSC Ord. 52, r. 4.

BEVAN v HASTINGS JONES [1978] 1 All ER 479 (Chancery Division: GOULDING J). *Ex parte Liebrand* [1914] WN 310 and *Re G's Application for a Committal Order* [1954] 2 All ER 794 not followed.

464   In considering whether to allow an application by a litigant in person for an order of committal for contempt of court O'CONNOR J stated that as the Chancery Division had permitted such an application to be made a similar ruling would be made in the Queen's Bench Division, because it was undesirable that there should be a difference in practice between two divisions of the High Court.

DE VRIES v KAY (1978) Times, 7th October (Queen's Bench Division: O'CONNOR J).

465   —— validity—order lacking particularity

The parties were divorced in 1971 and an order was made for the sale of the matrimonial home. The husband refused to leave and an order was made for him to vacate the house. He failed to obey the order and was committed to prison for contempt of court. He appealed on the ground that the order for committal was bad for lack of particularity in that it did not state that he had not vacated the house. *Held,* this was carrying technicalities too far. The husband had defied the orders of the court and knew that he had done so. There was no need to put in

additional words other than that he was in breach of the order. The appeal would
be dismissed.

KAVANAGH v KAVANAGH (1978) Times, 26th July (Court of Appeal: LORD
DENNING MR, EVELEIGH LJ and SIR DAVID CAIRNS).

466   —— —— **order not in correct form**

See *Wellington v Wellington*, para. 1517, *Cinderby v Cinderby; Pekesin v Pekesin*, para.
1518.

467   **Criminal contempt—contempt in connection with proceedings in
an inferior court—local valuation court**

A religious sect sought to have its premises recognised as a place of public religious
worship, and a date was fixed for a hearing before the local valuation court. The
BBC had made a television programme about the sect, and the Attorney General and
others sought injunctions restraining the BBC from repeating the programme while
the hearing was pending. The point at issue was whether a local valuation court fell
within the Divisional Court's power to make an order in respect of a contempt
committed in connection with proceedings in an inferior court, within RSC Ord.
52, r. 1. The BBC undertook not to show the programme if the local valuation
court was found to be such an "inferior court". *Held*, to see if the tribunal was a
court, one had to look at the task performed, the procedure adopted, the method of
selecting members and how far its creation and duties were consistent with the
general idea of a court. Applying these criteria, a local valuation court was a clear
example of an inferior court, and thus fell within Ord. 52, r. 1.

A-G v BBC; DIBLE v BBC [1978] 3 All ER 731 (Queen's Bench Division: LORD
WIDGERY CJ, WIEN and KENNETH JONES JJ). Dictum of Fry LJ in *Royal Aquarium
and Summer and Winter Garden Society Ltd v Parkinson* [1892] 1 QB 431 at 447
applied.

468   —— **Crown Court—power to order committal**

An applicant for a job attended an interview at which he made it clear that he had
been called for jury service. He was given the job but was found to be quite
unsuitable and was dismissed. He attended at the court for jury service the following
week and said that he had been dismissed through his jury service. The matter was
reported to the judge, who gave instructions that the employer was to be brought
before him. Concluding that the dismissal was substantially prompted by the jury
service, the judge sentenced the employer for contempt. On appeal by the employer,
held, he should not have been convicted except on clear evidence establishing the
contempt beyond reasonable doubt. There was no such evidence, the proper
inference being that the employee was dismissed for unsuitability. The judge in this
case had assumed the role of prosecutor and cross-examined the employer. This was
undesirable. In a case such as this, the proper course would have been to deal with
it by motion to the Divisional Court. The appeal would be allowed.

ROONEY v SNARESBROOK CROWN COURT (1978) 122 Sol Jo 488 (Court of Appeal:
LORD DENNING MR and BROWNE LJ). *Balogh v St Albans Crown Court* [1975] 1 QB
73, 1974 Halsbury's Abr para. 470 applied.

469   —— **failure to surrender to bail—power of Crown Court to deal
with offence as criminal contempt of court**

See *R v Singh*, para. 683.

470   —— **leave to appeal to Court of Appeal—practice**

LORD WIDGERY CJ, in giving judgment in the criminal division of the Court of
Appeal on an application for leave to appeal against a finding of contempt in criminal
proceedings, stated that on an interpretation of the Administration of Justice Act
1960, s. 13 and the Criminal Appeal Act 1966, s. 1 (6) (c), any such application had

to be made in the civil division of the Court of Appeal, and it would therefore be refused.

R v TIBBITTS (1978) 122 Sol Jo 761 (Court of Appeal: LORD WIDGERY CJ, BRIDGE LJ and SMITH J).

471　　—— publication of name of witness granted anonymity—whether frustration of court's intention amounts to contempt

The Attorney General applied under RSC Ord. 52, r. 9 for an order against three newspapers for alleged contempt of court. The papers had published the name of an army officer called as a witness in a case concerning the Official Secrets Act 1920, whose name had been withheld in the interests of national security. The papers contended primarily that the court had merely requested that the witness' anonymity be preserved, and that as they were not in breach of any mandatory direction no offence had been committed. They further claimed that they could not be guilty unless disclosure of the officer's identity could be shown to have interfered with the course of justice. *Held*, all the staff on the newspapers concerned knew why the name of the officer had been withheld, yet they had deliberately set out to publish it. Primae facie this amounted to a contempt unless the papers could produce a successful defence. The defence proffered, that there had been no mandatory direction against disclosure and that therefore there was no offence, failed because the real basis for the Attorney General's application was the papers' flouting of the court's intention. Publication with a view to frustrating the ruling of a court amounted to contempt whether that ruling was intended to have direct effect just within the court or in the world at large.

The papers' second contention could not be upheld either: it was in the public interest that the courts should be protected from having their intentions disregarded or flouted. It did not matter whether the alleged contempt interfered with the course of justice or not in such circumstances.

A-G v LEVELLER MAGAZINE LTD [1978] 3 All ER 731 (Queen's Bench Division: LORD WIDGERY CJ, CROOM-JOHNSON and STOCKER JJ).

This decision was subsequently reversed on appeal to the House of Lords.

472　　—— publication prejudicing fair trial—publication of information not known to jury

A television company and a provincial newspaper were separately charged with contempt of court for publishing information about a criminal trial capable of revealing to the jury that the accused had committed other offences besides those charged on the indictment. The prosecution contended this tended to and was calculated to prejudice the administration of justice, the alleged contemnors that public policy required free reporting of legal proceedings and that this outweighed the private interest of an individual accused. *Held*, the disclosure of offences was a serious matter and automatically suggested contempt. Public policy governed the relevant law, whose purpose was the prevention of interference with the administration of justice. It was undesirable to limit freedom of speech more than necessary, but limits had to be imposed. The information published ought never to have been published, and any reporter should have realised it. The onus was not on the trial judge to ban reporting, but on reporters to understand so fundamental a rule of contempt.

R v BORDER TELEVISION LTD, EX PARTE THE ATTORNEY-GENERAL; R v NEWCASTLE CHRONICLE AND JOURNAL LTD, EX PARTE THE ATTORNEY-GENERAL (1978) 122 Sol Jo 162 (Queen's Bench Division: LORD WIDGERY CJ, MELFORD STEVENSON and LLOYD JJ).

473　　—— —— time of publication

Scotland

While a man was detained in police custody, in connection with a murder inquiry, a newspaper published an article about the inquiry and the man detained. The man was subsequently charged with murder, and committed for trial. He considered the article to be prejudicial to his case, and presented a petition claiming the article amounted to contempt of court. The newspaper proprietors argued that there was no contempt, as the court's jurisdiction could not arise until the man was committed for trial. *Held*, from the moment of arrest or from the moment that a warrant to arrest was granted, the person concerned was under the care and protection of the court; at either of these points relevant proceedings had commenced so as to bring into play the contempt jurisdiction of the court where prejudicial publication was concerned. The court thus had jurisdiction to deal with the case, and the newspaper was guilty of contempt.

HALL V ASSOCIATED NEWSPAPERS LTD, 1978 SLT 241 (High Court of Justiciary).

474   Custody order—party against whom order made present in court— whether personal service necessary

In the course of matrimonial proceedings in the county court the judge made an order in the morning that the father return the child of the marriage to the mother that afternoon. Immediately after the making of the order the father disappeared with the child. On appeal *held*, the judge had jurisdiction to order the father's arrest and subsequently to commit him to prison for contempt of court in disobeying the order despite the fact that the order had not been served on him or his solicitor before his disappearance. Under RSC Ord. 45, r. 7 (7) the court could dispense with service of a copy of an order if it was just to do so. Although there was no parallel rule in the county court, the High Court rule ought to be followed as it was not precluded by the county court rules. The father had known all about the order and had disappeared long before it had been drawn up and served. In these circumstances it was clearly just to dispense with service.

TURNER V TURNER (1978) Times, 16th September (Court of Appeal: LORD DENNING MR and EVELEIGH LJ).

475   Freedom of expression—uncertainty in the law

In the course of an address in support of an argument advanced by the Times and Sunday Times newspapers that a ban on the publication of articles about the drug thalidomide infringed the European Convention's guarantee of freedom of expression, the President of the European Commission of Human Rights described the English law of contempt as uncertain to an undesirable degree because it was not clear what criteria English courts should apply when an injunction against the Press was applied for: Times, 26th April 1978.

476   Phillimore Committee—discussion paper

A green paper on Contempt of Court has been published: Cmnd. 7145. This is a discussion paper concerned with the Report of the Phillimore Committee on Contempt of Court (1974): Cmnd. 5794, 1974 Halsbury's Abr para. 468. A summary of conclusions and recommendations of that Committee are annexed.

The Government have decided that satisfactory conclusions cannot be reached on the issues raised without informed Parliamentary and public discussion. Accordingly reactions to the green paper and comments on the Phillimore recommendations generally are welcomed by the Government.

CONTRACT

Halsbury's Laws of England (4th edn.), Vol. 9, paras. 201–699

477   Articles

Damages: Some Recent Developments, R. G. Lawson: 128 NLJ 600.
Fundamental Breach after the Unfair Contract Terms Act, Leslie Melville: 128 NLJ 127.

Fundamental Breach: a Rule Abolished, A. M. Tettenborn (Unfair Contract Terms Act 1977, s. 9 (1); unenforceable exception clause rendered effective): 122 Sol Jo 720.

Remoteness of Damage—Contract and Tort Reconciled?, Colin Manchester (questions relating to remoteness of damage in contract as raised in *H. Parsons (Livestock) Ltd v Uttley Ingham & Co Ltd* [1978] 1 All ER 525): 128 NLJ 1113.

The Unfair Contract Terms Act 1977, F. M. B. Reynolds (the provisions and aims of the Act): [1978] 1 LMCLQ 201.

The Unfair Contract Terms Act 1977: Some Practical Aspects, Peter J. Haycroft: 128 NLJ 176.

478   Breach of contract—anticipatory breach—time charterparty

See *The Lorfri; The Nanfri; The Benfri,* para. 2607.

479   —— breach undiscovered by injured party before fulfilment of contract—injured party's right to recover on a quantum meruit

Canada

The plaintiffs undertook the construction of a dam for the defendants. The latter committed several serious breaches of contract while construction was in progress, but the plaintiffs did not discover them until it had been completed. Upon discovering them, the plaintiffs sought compensation either under the terms of the contract or on the basis of a quantum meruit. At first instance they succeeded on the second ground. On the defendant's appeal, *held*, the plaintiffs were not entitled to recover on a quantum meruit because they had continued working on the dam after the breaches had occurred and, having completed the contract, had a perfectly good claim under it. Restitutionary remedies were not to be invoked where an adequate remedy already existed, particulary where by virtue of them a litigant might recover more than he could under the terms of the contract. Accordingly, the case would be remitted for determination of the contractual claim.

MORRISON-KNUDSON CO INC v BRITISH COLUMBIA HYDRO AND POWER AUTHORITY (1978) 85 DLR (3d) 186 (Court of Appeal of British Columbia).

480   —— fundamental breach—validity of exclusion clause—arson

See *Photo Production Ltd v Securicor Transport Ltd,* para. 494.

481   —— —— —— failure to deliver on time

A knitwear manufacturer who regularly used the defendants' delivery service was aware of a clause in the defendants' conditions of service limiting their liability in case of default. The defendants undertook to deliver high fashion knitwear by a certain date but were late with part of the consignment and the purchaser refused to accept. They admitted being in breach but sought to rely on the clause limiting their liability. *Held*, as there had been a total breach of the contract the defendants could not rely on the limiting condition. The contract was for the delivery of high fashion goods. It must have been reasonably within the contemplation of the parties that the result of late delivery would be loss of sale. As the market at place of delivery was lost and there was no other market the contract price was the proper measure of the value of the goods to the plaintiffs.

JOHN CURRIE SON & CO LTD v SECURICOR MOBILE LTD (1978) 122 Sol Jo 294 (Queen's Bench Division: FORBES J).

482   —— strike by employees—reinstatement pending inquiry—whether breach waived

See *Ellis v Inner London Education Authority,* para. 2999.

483   Building contract

See BUILDING CONTRACTS.

484   **Capacity of parties—inter-office trading transactions—whether genuine trading transactions**

The Hamburg and Munich offices of the sellers' company often traded independently of one another. The Hamburg office entered into a contract to sell a quantity of soya bean meal to the buyers. Subsequent contracts for the buying and selling of soya bean meal were made between the Hamburg and Munich offices. All the contracts were for shipment, c.i.f. Rotterdam and incorporated the terms of a standard form Grain and Feed Trade Association contract, which provided that shippers had to give notice of appropriation to the first buyers within ten days of the date of the bill of lading. Ten days after shipment was effected the Hamburg office, as shippers, gave notice of appropriation to the Munich office, as first buyers. The Munich office then gave notice to the Hamburg office, their buyers, and the Hamburg office, as subsequent sellers, gave notice to the buyers. As this notice arrived more than ten days after the date of the bill of lading the buyers claimed that it was out of time. They were prima facie correct, but the notice would be deemed to be in time if it had been given by the shipper within ten days and passed down a string of contracts within the requisite time limits. The buyers contended that, as the Hamburg and Munich offices were part of the same company, they could not enter into contracts with one another. *Held*, the Hamburg and Munich offices had entered into genuine transactions trading at arm's length, and the contracts were therefore valid. It was known in the trade that the sellers' offices often traded as separate legal entities, and the buyers should have envisaged that there might be a chain of contracts. Notice of appropriation was given in time.

BREMER HANDELGESELLSCHAFT MBH V TOEPFER [1978] 1 Lloyd's Rep 643 (Queen's Bench Division: DONALDSON J).

485   **Consideration—adequacy—performance of contractual duty—additional consideration**

Shipbuilders and shipowners entered into a contract to build a ship, the currency of the contract being US dollars. Under the contract, the builders undertook to open a letter of credit to provide security for repayment of instalments of the price if they defaulted in performing the contract. The US dollar was subsequently devalued and the builders threatened to terminate the contract unless the owners agreed that the price should be increased. Since they were anxious to use the ship to fulfil a charter, the owners agreed on condition that the letter of credit was correspondingly increased. The builders agreed. The increased price was paid and the ship delivered. Subsequently the owners claimed the return of the amount paid in excess of the original price, contending that the agreement to increase the price was void for lack of consideration, or alternatively that it was voidable as it had been made under economic duress. *Held*, (i) a promise by one party to fulfil an existing contractual obligation to the other party was not good consideration and thus the builders' original contractual liability to build the ship did not constitute good consideration. However, by undertaking to increase the letter of credit the builders had provided consideration, since this was an obligation additional to the existing contractual duty. Thus the contract was not void. (ii) It was possible to avoid contracts entered into as a result of economic duress, such as the threat to break the original contract in this case. However, the owners, by failing to make any protest, had affirmed the agreement and thus could not avoid it. They were thus not entitled to claim the return of the excess payment.

THE ATLANTIC BARON [1978] 3 All ER 1170 (Queen's Bench Division: MOCATTA J). *Stilk v Meyrick* (1809) 2 Camp 317 followed; dicta of Lord Denning MR in *D & C Builders Ltd v Rees* [1965] 3 All ER 837 at 841 and of Kerr J in *The Siboen and The Sibotre* [1976] 1 Lloyd's Rep 293 at 336, 1976 Halsbury's Abr para. 479 applied.

486   **Construction—charterparty—delay—whether breach of warranty**

See *Unitramp v Garnac Grain Co Inc*, para. 2513.

487   —— contract for the supply of oil

Australia

An oil company agreed to supply a mining company with oil for ten years. The contract contained provisions for adjustment of the base price in various circumstances. Clause A made provision after the first five years for possible adjustment of the base price in the event of substantial increases in the world FOB value of oil. Clause B provided for possible adjustment of the base price "at any time", inter alia, in the event that the oil company was only able to obtain the product from its usual sources on onerous terms. Within the five year period as a result of action by OPEC the price of oil rose dramatically and the oil company purported to increase the base price under clause B. The mining company argued that as the new price albeit drastically increased was no more than the world market price the requirement that it should be paid could not be regarded as onerous and that in any event the sole and exclusive provision touching variation of the base price in relation to movements in the world market price (FOB value) was clause A. *Held*, on the true construction of the contract the oil company was entitled to rely on clause B. Against the background of the contractual base price the drastic increase in the cost of the product to the oil company was well worthy of the word "onerous". There was no express term in clause A claiming exclusivity with respect to changes in the world price and none should be implied in the face of the generality of clause B which applied to an event occurring "at any time". Furthermore there was no reason why the oil company could not elect under which clause it would operate.

BP Australia Ltd v Nabalco Pty Ltd (1977) 16 ALR 207 (Privy Council: Lord Simon of Glaisdale, Lord Salmon, Lord Russell of Killowen, Lord Keith of Kinkel and Sir Richard Wild).

488   Contractual term—arbitration agreement—clause excusing arbitrator from strict rules of law—whether clause purported to oust jurisdiction of court

See *Eagle Star Insurance Co Ltd v Yuval Insurance Co Ltd*, para. 159.

489   —— express term—warranty—breach—material adverse change in company's assets

Due to a fall in trade caused primarily by their dress designer's illness, the plaintiff shareholders in a fashion company decided to sell the business to the defendants. The defendants were made aware that the company was trading at a loss and was in a traded-down state. In the agreement for sale, the plaintiffs warranted that, save as disclosed, there would be no material adverse change in the company's overall net assets other than normal trade fluctuations, prior to take over. It was agreed that an initial sum would be paid on completion and the balance by yearly instalments. After taking over the company, the defendants found that there had been a further decline in the company's assets amounting to £8,600 and a trading loss which they were able to offset against later profits, thereby obtaining a tax advantage. On the defendants' refusal to pay the instalments due to the reduction in the assets, the plaintiffs brought an action claiming payment. The defendants pleaded that the plaintiffs' breach of warranty entitled them to set off the sum of £8,600 against the amount owed and counterclaimed for damages. The plaintiffs contended that the adverse change in the company's assets was not a "material" change, or alternatively, it was a "normal trade fluctuation" and had in any event been disclosed to the defendants. *Held*, from the facts it was clear that there had been a material adverse change in the company's assets. The plaintiffs' disclosure of their designer's illness and the trading down of the company was more a general disclosure of a possible future loss than a disclosure of an actual drop in the company's net assets. Therefore, the disclosure did not protect the plaintiffs from being in breach of the warranty, as although the defendants were aware that there would be continuing losses, they did not know what the rate of loss would be. Further, as the loss had never occurred before, being entirely peculiar to the company, it was not a "normal trade fluctuation". However, the tax advantage received by the defendants was deductible from the damages of £8,600 payable by the plaintiffs because it arose out of the facts which caused the breach of warranty.

LEVISON v FARIN [1978] 2 All ER 1149 (Queen's Bench Division: GIBSON J). Dicta of Lord Reid in *British Transport Commission v Gourley* [1955] 3 All ER at 808 and Viscount Haldane LC in *British Westinghouse Electric and Manufacturing Co Ltd v Underground Electric Railways Co of London Ltd* [1911–13] All ER Rep at 69 applied.

490   —— innominate term—breach by seller—whether buyer entitled to reject goods

The sellers sold to the buyers 8,000 tonnes of barley f.o.b., the contract providing for 4 per cent foreign matter, weight and quality at loading as per Superintendence Company's Certificate, payment cash against documents on presentation. The buyers chartered a vessel, and 2,000 tonnes of barley were loaded. A certificate of quality then issued stated "Impurities and foreign substances 4·10 per cent". Discharge took place and the sellers presented the shipping documents, including the quality certificate, to the buyers, who refused to take up or pay for the goods on the ground that the quality certificate showed 4·10 per cent of foreign matter. It was agreed between the parties that the goods be sold "as is" for a net price less than the contract price. The sellers claimed the difference between the contract price and the proceeds of sale. Arbitrators found in favour of the buyers. On appeal, the Board of Appeal of GAFTA found in favour of the sellers but stated their award in the form of a special case. *Held*, in the absence of any clear agreement that the provision as to impurities was to be a condition, the court should lean in favour of construing it as an intermediate term, only a serious and substantial breach of which entitled the buyers to reject. If there had been no provision as to a quality final certificate, the breach would not have entitled rejection but would have entitled the buyers only to an allowance. However, the fact that there was a certificate showing a minor breach did not make any difference. The findings of the Board of Appeal showed that commercial men considered that this kind of deviation in quality would not be treated as entitling a rejection either of the quality final certificate or the goods. Therefore the buyers were not entitled automatically to reject the document. The excess of foreign matter was commercially insignificant and the sellers were accordingly entitled to damages against the buyers for non-acceptance, as property in the goods had not passed. The price of resale "as is" should be treated as the market price of the goods.

TRADAX INTERNATIONAL SA v GOLDSCHMIDT SA [1977] 2 Lloyd's Rep 604 (Queen's Bench Division: SLYNN J). *Cehave NV v Bremer Handelsgesellschaft mbH, The Hansa Nord* [1976] QB 44, CA, 1975 Halsbury's Abr para. 2955 and *Hong Kong Fir Shipping Co Ltd v Kawasaki Kisen Kaisha Ltd* [1962] 2 QB 26 applied.

491   —— term requiring payment against documents within certain time—whether obligation mutual

The sellers bought rapeseed c.i.f. Rotterdam/Europort and resold it to the buyers. The contract contained a special clause that payment in cash would be against documents and/or delivery order on arrival of the vessel at the port of discharge not later than twenty days after the date of bill of lading by telegraphic transfer. The bill of lading was dated 11th December 1974. However, the ship grounded en route necessitating repairs which delayed its arrival until April 1975. The sellers received the bill of lading in January and in February issued delivery orders to the buyers who rejected them on the ground that presentation was out of time, contending that the buyers were in default. It was decided that the payment clause related to the time of payment and imposed no obligation upon the sellers to present the documents in the stated time. The buyers appealed. *Held*, the two separate areas of dispute were firstly, whether the clause imposed obligations upon the sellers and secondly, if it did, whether those obligations were conditions, warranties or within a third category of innominate terms. It was indisputable that the obligations imposed by the clause were mutual. In commodity contracts it was law that provisions as to time were prima facie conditions. There was no reason to distinguish provisions as to time for the presentation of documents. Whether a contractual obligation entitled the other party to rescind the contract depended on the presumed or expressed intention of the parties at the date of the contract. The provisions as to time were of the essence of the contract and delay by the sellers in presenting shipping documents entitled the buyers to rescind. The appeal would be allowed.

ALFRED C. TOEPFER (HAMBURG) v VERHEIJDENS VEERVOEDER COMMISSIEHANDEL (ROTTERDAM); ALFRED C. TOEPFER (HAMBURG) v LENERSAN-POORTMAN NV— ROTTERDAM (1978) Times, 26th April (Queen's Bench Division: DONALDSON J).

492   Default—date of default

See *Bunge GmbH v Alfred C. Toepfer*, para. 500.

493   Exclusion clause—clause in ticket limiting liability—sufficiency of notice

See *Kowalewich v Airwest Airlines Ltd*, para. 179.

494   —— scope of clause—employer liable for negligence of employee—whether employer also liable for deliberate act of employee

An employee of the defendant security company deliberately set alight the plaintiff's premises in the course of his employment as a security patrolman. The defendants denied liability on the basis of limitation and exemption clauses contained in their contract with the plaintiffs. *Held*, although the clauses purported to absolve the defendants from liability for unforeseeable or unavoidable damage and fire damage attributable to anything but negligence on the part of the defendants' employees, it was unreasonable that they should escape liability solely because their employee had acted deliberately rather than negligently. In any event, the defendants had committed a fundamental breach of their contract in not protecting the premises and consequently could not rely on the exemption clauses. They were wholly liable for their employee's deliberate act.

PHOTO PRODUCTION LTD v SECURICOR TRANSPORT LTD [1978] 3 All ER 146 (Court of Appeal: LORD DENNING MR, SHAW and WALLER LJJ). *Suisse Atlantique Société d'Armement Maritime SA v NV Rotterdamsche Kolen Centrale* [1967] 1 AC 361, HL and *Harbutt's Plasticine Ltd v Wayne Tank and Pump Co Ltd* [1970] 1 QB 447, CA applied.

495   —— validity of clause—failure to deliver on time

See *John Currie & Co Ltd v Securicor Mobile Ltd*, para. 481.

496   Force majeure clause—construction—strikes

The sellers sold to the buyers a quantity of oil for shipment December/January. The contract contained a force majeure clause which provided for an extension of the shipment period. The oil was shipped at the beginning of February, but the bills of lading were dated January 31st. The buyers, believing that the oil had been shipped within the contract period, accepted the oil when it arrived. Neither the sellers nor the buyers were aware of the deception. When the buyers discovered the deception they claimed arbitration on the issue of whether the sellers had been in breach of contract. The sellers tried to rely on the force majeure clause, claiming that strikes had already affected the supply of oil to the port of loading and that therefore the shipment period was extended. *Held*, the sellers had to show that shipment had been prevented by a force majeure event. There was no evidence that shipment within the contract period had been made impossible by the strikes. The sellers were therefore liable to the buyers for damages for breach of contract.

THE KASTELLON, HUILERIE L'ABEILLE v SOCIETE DES HUILERIES DU NIGER [1978] 2 Lloyd's Rep 203 (Queen's Bench Division: DONALDSON J).

497 **Frustration—contract for the sale of land—inability to pay purchase price on completion date**

See *Universal Corpn v Five Ways Properties Ltd*, para. 2429.

498 —— **force majeure and prohibition clauses—liability of seller**

The sellers contracted to sell 1,000 tonnes of soya bean meal to the buyers, shipment to be from any Mediterranean port. The sellers acquired a quantity of soya bean meal from a third party who held an export licence for Piraeus. Before loading began the sellers learnt that the export licence had been suspended and that the export of soya during the contract period would be illegal. They tried, without success, to have the licence restored. The buyers claimed damages for non-delivery. The sellers contended that a prohibition clause in the contract protected them from non-delivery due to executive or legislative act of the country where the port of shipment was situated. At first instance the sellers' claim was upheld. On appeal by the buyers *held*, the sellers had undertaken to supply goods from any Mediterranean port and were not able to rely on an event included in an exception clause if the event affected only one of the ports. There was no reason why the prohibition clause should extend to the present situation when the sellers could have fulfilled their contractual obligations by exporting from another port.

Warinco AG v Fritz Mauthner [1978] 1 Lloyd's Rep 151 (Court of Appeal: Megaw, Bridge and Waller LJJ). Decision of Donaldson J [1977] 1 Lloyd's Rep 277, 1977 Halsbury's Abr para. 518 reversed. *Tradax Export SA v Andre & Cie SA* [1976] 1 Lloyd's Rep 416, CA 1975 Halsbury's Abr para. 537 distinguished.

499 A contract for the sale of soya bean meal from the United States provided for a specific quantity to be delivered each month. The contract contained a prohibition clause providing for the cancellation of any part of the contract if any government act prevented its fulfilment. Under a force majeure clause the sellers were required to notify the buyers of any relevant occurrence within a specified time, whereupon the time for delivery would be extended. After a two month extension, if performance was still impossible, the contract would be regarded as void.

The United States government imposed restrictions on the export of soya bean meal and on 29th June the sellers warned the buyers that the June instalment might be cancelled. The sellers then purported to give notice under the force majeure clause on 3rd July in order to extend the time for delivery and nominated "the usual ports on the Lakes/East Coast/Gulf" as shipping ports. On 9th July they gave notice of cancellation under the prohibition clause as a result of which the buyers claimed damages for non-delivery. The sellers contended that they were protected by the prohibition and force majeure clauses. *Held*, (i) the sellers were able to rely on the prohibition clause as their inability to deliver the June instalment in time was due to the government restrictions, not to any purported defect in the force majeure notice extending the time for delivery. (ii) The prohibition clause affected the whole of the June instalment not just the 60 per cent for which no licence was obtainable under a limited government export scheme introduced in July. (iii) The notice of 9th July, when read with the warning given on 29th June, constituted sufficient notice of cancellation as required by the prohibition clause. (iv) The force majeure notice was not defective through being late since under the contract, giving of notice meant its dispatch and it had been dispatched in time. However, the notice could only be effective if the sellers had intended to ship the meal from the nominated ports before the restrictions came into force. There was no evidence of intention to ship from East Coast ports and on that ground the notice was bad. (v) The buyers had waived any defect in the force majeure notice. They made no reference to any possible defect in their correspondence with the sellers and had acted on the basis that the notice was valid. Accordingly, the contract should be regarded as void and the sellers were not liable for non-delivery.

Bremer Handelsgesellschaft mbH v Vanden Avenne-Izegem PVBA [1978] 2 Lloyd's Rep 109 (House of Lords: Lord Wilberforce, Viscount Dilhorne, Lord Salmon, Lord Russell of Killowen and Lord Keith of Kinkel). *Tradax Export SA v Andre & Cie SA* [1976] 1 Lloyd's Rep 416, CA, 1975 Halsbury's Abr para. 537, applied. Decision of Court of Appeal [1977] 2 Lloyd's Rep 329, 1977 Halsbury's Abr para. 515 reversed.

500   Sellers contracted to sell to buyers 1,000 tonnes of extracted soya bean meal c.i.f. Rotterdam for shipment 500 tonnes each April and May 1973. The contract provided by cl. 9 that the sellers could extend the period of shipment by giving notice. Clause 22, a force majeure clause, also provided for an extension of time. In March and April 1973 flooding in the River Mississippi caused delays in the loading of the soya bean meal. The sellers purported to give notice under both cls. 9 and 22. In July, the buyers called for fulfilment of the April shipment with goods with a bill of lading dated the last day of the period of shipment as extended by cl. 22, failing which they would hold the sellers in default. The sellers never tendered any goods in respect of the April shipment. The dispute was referred to arbitration and the Board of Appeal of GAFTA, holding that the sellers were liable in damages for breach of contract, stated their award in the form of a special case. *Held*, the question was whether the purported extensions under cls. 9 and 22 were valid, in order to determine the date of default for the purpose of the assessment of damages. The purported notice under cl. 9 was invalid as it did not comply with the requirements of the clause. The buyers were not precluded from relying on such invalidity. The sellers' contention that because the buyers accepted the notice under cl. 22 as valid, although it was prima facie invalid as being out of time, they were bound also to treat as valid the notice under cl. 9, was incorrect. Firstly, it was not established that the notice under cl. 22 was out of time, and secondly both parties treated it as valid and acted on that basis. There was no such common attitude or conduct in relation to the notice under cl. 9, as the buyers never represented that they accepted it as a valid notice. The decision of the board would be upheld, the damages being assessed as at the date for shipment as extended by cl. 22 only.

BUNGE GMBH v ALFRED C. TOEPFER]1978] 1 Lloyd's Rep 506 (Queen's Bench Division: BRANDON J). *Panchaud Freres SA v Etablissements General Grain Co* [1970] 1 Lloyd's Rep 53 and *Toepfer v Cremer* [1975] 2 Lloyd's Rep 118, 1975 Halsbury's Abr para. 529 applied.

501   An English company contracted to buy sugar from a Polish state trading organisation. The contract was subject to the Refined Sugar Association's rules, r. 18 of which provided for the sellers' exemption from liability if governmental action frustrated the contract, and r. 21 of which stipulated that the sellers were to obtain any necessary export licence. Following the failure of the domestic sugar harvest, the Polish government banned all sugar exports and revoked all export licences. The contract had not been performed. The sellers pleaded force majeure under r. 18. The buyers contended the sellers were an organ of the Polish government and were thus not entitled to rely on r. 18, that the export ban was the result of a conspiracy between the sellers and their government to avoid the sellers' having to buy-in expensive sugar to fulfil the contract, and that r. 18 did not apply anyway as the sellers had failed to obtain the necessary export licence under r. 21. *Held*, English courts should be very reluctant to examine the motives of foreign governments. It seemed that the sellers were an independent body within Poland and that the ban on sugar exports had been imposed not to avoid the sellers' contractual liability but for domestic and logical reasons and to preserve foreign exchange. Accordingly, the sellers were protected under r. 18.

The duty under r. 21 to obtain the necessary export licence merely meant that the sellers had to get one, which they had done. They were not obliged to, nor could they, ensure its continuing validity.

LORD SALMON, dissenting on the second point, considered it incumbent on the sellers under r. 21 to ensure the contract goods received customs clearance and were loaded on board ship. He therefore considered the sellers were precluded from relying on the force majeure clause in r. 18.

C. CZARNIKOW LTD v CENTRALA HANDLU ZAGRANICZNEGO ROLIMPEX [1978] 2 All ER 1043 (House of Lords: LORD WILBERFORCE, VISCOUNT DILHORNE, LORD SALMON, LORD FRASER OF TULLYBELTON and LORD KEITH OF KINKEL). Decision of the Court of Appeal [1977] 1 All ER 81, 1977 Halsbury's Abr para. 516 affirmed.

502   The sellers agreed to sell wheat f.o.b. Argentina to the buyers in a contract which incorporated a GAFTA prohibition clause. The clause provided that the sellers could cancel the contract if government action made its performance impossible. Shortly afterwards, the Argentine state organ responsible for the purchase of all bread wheat extended its monopoly to include the type of wheat which the sellers had contracted to sell to the buyers. Thus, the sellers could only have performed the contract by buying wheat from the state at a much higher price than that for which they had contracted to resell it. They refused to do this on the grounds that they were exempted by the prohibition clause. The buyers claimed damages for non-performance. Arbitrators found in the buyers' favour because the sellers could have performed, albeit at a loss, but stated their award as a special case for the court. The sellers appealed from the court's decision to uphold the arbitrators' award. *Held*, it was impossible for the sellers to establish that they were excused from performance merely because they were prevented by an act of the government from buying from a particular seller. The prohibition clause could not be invoked simply because the contract could not be performed in the intended way. In the circumstances, the sellers could have bought the goods albeit at a higher price from another seller in the country. Accordingly, the appeal would be dismissed.

    EXPORTELISA SA v GUISEPPE AND FIGLI SOC COLL [1978] 1 Lloyd's Rep 433 (Court of Appeal: MEGAW, ROSKILL and CUMMING-BRUCE LJJ). Decision of Donaldson J [1977] 2 Lloyds Rep 494, 1977 Halsbury's Abr para. 521 affirmed. *Warinco AG v Fritz Mauthner* [1978] 1 Lloyd's Rep 151, CA, para. 498, applied.

503   Sellers of groundnut expellers failed to perform their side of a contract on time owing to both the failure of their supplier's distribution system and poor rail facilities. They pleaded force majeure. At the hearing of a special case, the court found that such events were too commonplace to constitute force majeure and that the sellers were accordingly liable. On appeal, *held*, the matter would be remitted to the arbitrators for them to establish whether or not the machinery breakdown alone would have resulted in the sellers' inability to deliver. To that extent, the appeal would be allowed.

    INTERTRADAX SA v LESIEUR-TOURTEAUX SARL [1978] LS Gaz R 712 (Court of Appeal: LORD DENNING MR, GOFF and CUMMING-BRUCE LJJ). Decision of Donaldson J [1977] 2 Lloyd's Rep 146, 1977 Halsbury's Abr para. 519 affirmed in part.

504   **Illegality—contract prima facie legal—right of party to raise additional issue without pleading illegality**

    See *Ibottson v Kushner*, para. 2908.

505   **Parties—implied authority**

    See *The Polyduke, Bahamas Oil Refining Co v Kristiansands Tankrederie A/S and Shell International Marine Ltd*, para. 2636.

506   **Performance—sufficiency—plaintiff required to obtain binding commitment letter—letter incomplete**

    Canada

    The defendant hired the plaintiff mortgage broker to obtain mortgage funds and agreed to pay him a commission if a "binding commitment letter" was obtained from an investor. The plaintiff received a letter from a potential investor which included the words "all moneys will be at seventeen per cent interest over a two-year period, interest only". The investor did not however go through with the transaction and the plaintiff sued the defendant for the commission on the ground that the letter had constituted a binding commitment. *Held*, as the letter also contained uncertainties such as the time when the funds were to be advanced and the personal guarantees required and did not state whether the interest was to be paid monthly or yearly, it did not constitute a binding commitment. As the plaintiff had not carried out the terms of the contract, the action would be dismissed.

    GREENBRIER MORTGAGE INVESTMENTS LTD v J. E. ONGMAN & SONS LTD [1978] 5 WWR 309 (Supreme Court of British Columbia).

507   Privity—clause conferring benefit on stranger to contract— whether party to contract can claim against stranger

See *The Elbe Maru, Nippon Yusen Kaisha v International Import and Export Co Ltd*, para. 2215.

508   Prohibition clause—construction

See *Exportelisa SA v Guiseppe & Figli Soc. Coll*, para. 502.

509   ————government embargo on export

See *Warinco AG v Fritz Mauthner*, para. 498.

510   —— provision for cancellation of contract—conditions for cancellation by seller in string

A contract was made between American sellers and English buyers for the sale of 4,000 long tons of yellow soya beans, c.i.f. Rotterdam, 1,000 tons to be shipped in each of four consecutive months. The contract incorporated the terms of a standard form contract (FOSFA No. 24), under which the sellers were entitled to cancel the contract should the performance of any part of it be rendered impossible by the imposition of a prohibition on export. Prior to the second shipment the U.S. government imposed a partial embargo on the export of soya beans and the sellers purported to cancel the contract. On a reference to arbitration the sellers, who were not the shippers but sellers in string, failed to show that there was a shipper at the head of the string with goods ready to ship within the shipment period, and were held to be liable to the buyers in damages. A special case was stated for the decision of the court. *Held*, to rely on the prohibition of export clause it was sufficient for the sellers to show that the prohibition in question was such that had performance of the contract been attempted it would have been prevented, regardless of whether they were in fact in a position to perform. However, the burden of proving that fulfilment of the contract had been rendered impossible by the prohibition remained with them, and was discharged only by showing first, that no goods of the contract description were available prior to the embargo for the performance of the contract and, second, that, following the embargo, it had not been reasonably possible to obtain any such goods. The test was applicable equally to sellers who were shippers and sellers in a string. On the facts the sellers had failed to discharge that burden of proof and the award would be upheld.

CONTINENTAL GRAIN EXPORT CORPN OF NEW YORK v STM GRAIN LTD (1978) (Queen's Bench Division: GOFF J (judgment delivered 30th November)). *Bremer Handelsgesellschaft mbH v Vanden Avenne-Izegem PVBA* [1978] 2 Lloyd's Rep 109, para. 499 HL considered.

511   Quantum meruit—right of injured party to recover where contract not repudiated

See *Morrison-Knudson Co Inc v British Columbia Hydro and Power Authority*, para. 479.

512   Restitution—equitable remedies—right to trace

A company supplied resin to a chipboard manufacturer, under a contractual term by which the supplier retained title to the goods until the manufacturer had paid all sums due to the supplier. The manufacturer went into liquidation, and the supplier brought an action in which it was claimed that the chipboard was the property of the supplier to the extent that it consisted of their resin or that it was charged to the same extent with payment due for resin supplied. *Held*, the supplier had no common law title to the goods, but the manufacturer was a bailee for the supplier and therefore a fiduciary relationship had been created between them. Consequently the equitable principle of tracing applied and the supplier was entitled to trace his resin into the chipboard. Furthermore the right to trace was not a charge within the scope of the

Companies Act 1948, s. 95 and thus was not void against the manufacturer's creditors for lack of registration.

BORDEN (UK) LTD v SCOTTISH TIMBER PRODUCTS LTD (1978) Times, 16th November (Chancery Division: Judge RUBIN sitting as a High Court judge). For a discussion of this case see "Goldfish bowl principle given forensic airing", Justinian, Financial Times, 20th November 1978.

513   Sale of goods
See SALE OF GOODS.

514   Sale of land
See SALE OF LAND.

515   Termination—effluxion of time—contract indefinite as to time
By virtue of a 1929 agreement between a water company and a health authority, the company agreed to supply a number of gallons of water a day free of cost to a hospital "at all times hereafter". The cost of supplying the water rose sharply over the years. The Water Act 1973 placed a statutory duty on the company to ensure that by 1981 its charges would not show preference to or discriminate against any class of persons. It was because of this duty, and bearing in mind the increased costs of supplying water, that the company sought to terminate the 1929 agreement. No express provision had been made in the agreement for termination by notice. *Held*, in the absence of any express provision, the agreement was impliedly terminable on reasonable notice. LORD DENNING MR said that the contract should be updated to take account of inflation. GOFF and CUMMING-BRUCE LJJ disagreed that a power to terminate the agreement could be inferred merely because no provision had been made for inflation. But they said that the power to terminate the agreement on notice was always impliedly there, because it substituted a simple arrangement for what would otherwise involve a complicated statutory procedure.

STAFFORDSHIRE AREA HEALTH AUTHORITY v SOUTH STAFFORDSHIRE WATERWORKS COMPANY [1978] 3 All ER 769 (Court of Appeal: LORD DENNING MR, GOFF and CUMMING-BRUCE LJJ). Decision of Foster J (1976) Times, 7th December, 1976 Halsbury's Abr para. 482 reversed.

516   Waiver—non-delivery of goods—whether waiver effective
The sellers of a quantity of soya bean meal were prevented from delivering a shipment of the beans by an embargo placed on the export of soya beans by the United States government. The sellers contended that the buyers had waived their right to reject. *Held*, a buyer could not lead a reasonable seller to believe that he would waive his right to reject upon non-delivery and then later rely upon that defect as a ground for rejecting the goods where it would be unfair or unjust to do so. The sellers had not discharged the burden of proving that they were prevented by the embargo from fulfilling the whole of the contract, but the buyer had waived his rights in relation to this particular shipment by his conduct.

BREMER HANDELSGESELLSCHAFT mbH v MACKPRANG (1978) Times, 17th November (Court of Appeal: LORD DENNING MR, SHAW and STEPHENSON LJJ). Decision of Goff J [1977] 2 Lloyd's Rep 467, 1977 Halsbury's Abr para. 541, reversed in part.

COPYRIGHT

Halsbury's Laws of England (4th edn.), Vol. 9, paras. 801–970

517   Article
Copyright in Engineering Drawings, Leslie Melville (examination of neglected

provisions of the Copyright Act 1956 and the Design Copyright Act 1968): 128 NLJ 1063.

518   Infringement—adoption of concept of copyright design—whether copying to be inferred

The plaintiffs brought an action for infringement of copyright in drawings relating to plastic knock-down drawers for the furniture industry. They alleged that the defendants had copied drawers manufactured by them in accordance with the drawings. The defendants contended that they had only taken the idea from the plaintiffs' drawings and the similar features were either common to the trade or arose from the commercial necessity for the defendants' drawers to be interchangeable with the plaintiffs'. On appeal by the defendants against a decision that there had been an infringement of copyright, *held*, the Copyright Act 1956 protected not the idea embodied in the work but the form in which it was expressed. Whether copying might be inferred from similarities between two products depended on whether the circumstances were such that it was more reasonable to infer copying than to attribute the similarities to other causes. In this case, analysis of the similarities showed that the defendants had adopted the plaintiffs' concept without copying, the similarities being a natural consequence of the adoption. The appeal would be allowed.

L.B. (PLASTICS) LTD v SWISH PRODUCTS LTD [1978] FSR 32 (Court of Appeal: BUCKLEY, GOFF and WALLER LJJ). Decision of Whitford J [1977] FSR 87, 1977 Halsbury's Abr para. 545 reversed.

This decision was subsequently reversed on appeal to the House of Lords.

519   —— architect's plan—whether substantial copying—interlocutory relief

The plaintiff was an architect who had drawn plans for the rebuilding of an hotel. When the work on the ground floor part of the building had been completed the construction company which had commissioned the plan went into receivership. The hotel was sold and the purchasers commissioned new architects who presented plans which were in certain respects admitted copies of the plaintiff's plans. The plaintiff sought an interlocutory injunction to restrain the proposed building work in accordance with the new architects' plans. *Held*, the plaintiff had a prima facie case, albeit a questionable one. There was doubt whether the copying was substantial and whether the company which had commissioned the plaintiff's plans could not use them in a modified form. However, no injunction would be granted, damages being an adequate remedy.

HUNTER v FITZROY ROBINSON AND PARTNERS [1978] FSR 167 (Chancery Division: OLIVER J).

520   —— interlocutory injunction—balance of convenience—adequacy of damages as remedy

The plaintiffs were large scale producers of ladies' dresses. They received complaints that the defendants were producing a virtually identical dress to one of their own designs and selling it at a lower price. In an action for infringement of copyright, the plaintiffs were granted an interim injunction restraining the defendants from selling, distributing or disposing of ladies' dresses which were substantially copied from the plaintiffs' designs. The defendants applied to discharge the injunction, denying the plaintiffs' allegation and contending that the design was neither original nor innovative but representative of a current trend among dress manufacturers. Their application was dismissed and they appealed against the continuance of the injunction. *Held*, the wide terms of the injunction would make it difficult and embarrassing for the defendants to comply with it as they would have difficulty in knowing what they could legitimately do. On the balance of convenience, it would be better to deal with the matter in damages, rather than stop the defendants from trading. The injunction would be discharged.

ALJOSE FASHIONS LTD (TRADING AS FIONA DRESSES) v ALFRED YOUNG & CO LTD [1978] FSR 364 (Court of Appeal: LORD DENNING MR, LAWTON and BRIDGE LJJ).

521　　　——reproduction of drawings—drawings part of patent specification

The plaintiff was the manufacturer and patent holder of steel lintels designed for use with cavity walls. The defendant received a brochure illustrating the plaintiff's lintels, and later began to manufacture lintels which differed only in that the rear support member was inclined at a slight angle and that there was no flange at the rear lower corner. The plaintiff brought an action alleging infringement of copyright in a number of the early drawings of their lintels and patent infringement. *Held*, with regard to the drawings (i) such details as the defendant had copied were not sufficient to infringe the copyright, (ii) the defendant had a defence under the Copyright Act 1956, s. 9 (8) in that the absence of the flange was an omission which would spring to the eye of one who was not an expert on lintels, (iii) a patentee abandoned copyright in drawings which were part of the patent specification. However, there had been an infringement of patent, because although there were differences between the two types of lintels they had essential features in common.

CATNIC COMPONENTS LTD v HILL AND SMITH LTD [1978] FSR 405 (Chancery Division: WHITFORD J).

522　　　——reproduction of textile design—knowledge of infringement—whether sale amounted to publication

The plaintiffs were involved in the design, manufacture and retail of printed textiles. At a meeting between the plaintiffs and a representative of the defendant company the latter expressed interest in one of the plaintiffs' designs and a further meeting was arranged. The representative then went to Hong Kong where he was shown an identical design, although he did not then fully recognise it as such. He arranged for shirts carrying that design to be manufactured and shipped to and distributed in England. The plaintiffs subsequently became aware of the defendant company's activities and wrote to it complaining of the infringement of copyright and requiring it to cease its activities. The company failed to comply and the plaintiffs sued for damages for infringement of copyright and conversion. *Held*, the plaintiffs could not recover in respect of the defendant company's activities up to a fortnight after receipt of the letter since they had failed to discharge the onus of proving its knowledge of the infringement as required by the Copyright Act 1956 ss. 5 (3) and 18. Further, selling did not constitute issuing copies to the public and therefore was not an offence under s. 3 (5) of the Act as contended by the plaintiffs: to construe s. 3 otherwise would be to deny the protection conferred by s. 5 (3). However, since it was agreed that knowledge of the infringement could be imputed to the defendant by a fortnight after receipt of the letter, the plaintiffs could succeed in respect of the defendant company's activities after that date.

INFABRICS LTD v JAYTEX SHIRT CO LTD [1978] FSR 451 (Chancery Division: WHITFORD J).

523　　　**International conventions**

The Copyright (International Conventions) (Amendment) Order 1978, S.I. 1978 No. 1060 (in force on 23rd August 1978) further amends the copyright (International Conventions) Order 1972 to take account of the accession of Costa Rica to the Berne Copyright Convention and the accession of Norway to the International Convention for the Protection of Performers, Producers of Phonograms and Broadcasting Organisations. The Order extends to dependent countries of the Commonwealth to which the 1972 Order extends.

524　　　**Protection of performers—alleged offence—whether a civil right of action conferred**

The defendants were "bootleggers" who had made unauthorised recordings of pop performances and had sold copies in the form of cassettes or records to small shopkeepers, who sold them to the public. A number of recording companies and pop performers applied ex parte for an order requiring the "bootleggers" to disclose all relevant material, preventing them disposing of their stock and enabling the plaintiffs to inspect it. Such orders had already been made, notably in *Anton Piller*

KG v Manufacturing Processes Ltd [1976] Ch 55, 1975 Halsbury's Abr para. 2623, against "pirates" who reproduced and sold existing records illicitly and in breach of copyright. On appeal by the plaintiffs from the judge's refusal to make the order on the ground that he had no jurisdiction, *held*, SHAW LJ dissenting, such orders, known as "Anton Piller" orders, could only be made against "bootleggers" if the performers and recording companies had a civil cause of action against them. Such an order could clearly be made against "pirates", since the latter were guilty of a civil wrong by infringing the copyright of the recording companies; however, there was no copyright in a performance. The making and selling of secret tapes and records of performances, if done without the performer's written consent, was a criminal offence under the Dramatic and Musical Performers' Protection Act 1958, s. 1. The question was whether the Act conferred a civil right of action. When an Act created a criminal offence, prescribing a penalty for its breach but not giving any civil remedy, generally a civil action in respect of it could only be brought by the Attorney General. Exceptionally, however, if a private individual could show that he had a private right being interfered with by the criminal act, causing him special damage, he could ask the court to restrain the offender from continuing the criminal act. In this case, the Attorney General had refused to bring a relator action, but the plaintiffs had particular rights which they were entitled to have protected, which were in the nature of property rights; the companies had the right to exploit the records made by them of the performances and the performers had the right to the royalty payable to them out of those records. Therefore the court had jurisdiction to grant an "Anton Piller" order in regard to "bootleggers". The appeal would be allowed and the case remitted to the judge to consider whether such an order should be made.

SHAW LJ considered that the interests of the companies and performers were too nebulous to be susceptible of legal protection.

Ex parte ISLAND RECORDS LTD [1978] 3 All ER 824 (Court of Appeal: LORD DENNING MR, SHAW and WALLER LJJ). *Anton Piller KG v Manufacturing Processes Ltd* [1976] Ch 55, 1975 Halsbury's Abr para. 2623, *Gouriet v Union of Post Office Workers* [1977] 3 All ER 70, HL, 1977 Halsbury's Abr para. 461 applied.

525　　Reversionary interest—ownership of interest—validity of assignments made before 1912

In the course of a complex copyright case involving the ownership of a multitude of reversionary interests under the Copyright Acts 1911 and 1956, GOFF J *held*, inter alia, (i) the words "express agreement" in the 1911 Act, s. 24 (1), proviso (a), included an agreement made before the commencement of that Act, so that the right substituted by s. 24 for that given under the Literary Copyright Act 1842 could effectively belong to a person other than the author if it had been assigned to that person under the 1842 Act; (ii) it was a question of construction whether an assignment made before 1912 of the copyright in a song operated to confer on the assignee the substituted copyright of the 1911 Act; (iii) a work the words and music of which were written by different persons was a collective work and accordingly the copyright did not vest in the authors' personal representatives twenty-five years after their deaths by virtue of the 1911 Act, s. 5 (2), proviso; and (iv) contracts assigning American renewal rights could be of a sufficiently general nature to transfer English reversionary rights even though at the time the contracts were made the parties were unaware of the existence of the English rights.

REDWOOD MUSIC LTD v FRANCIS DAY and HUNTER LTD [1978] RPC 429 (Queen's Bench Division: GOFF J.)

CORONERS

Halsbury's Laws of England (4th edn.), Vol. 9, paras. 1001–1184

526　　Article

No More Crime for Coroners, Anthony Morris (the substitution of the phrase "killed unlawfully" for murder, manslaughter or infanticide): 128 NLJ 393.

527   Inquest—application to quash verdict—whether verdict untenable

The deceased was arrested and force was used by the police to put him into a police van. In the course of the struggle one of the officers fell on his knees onto the deceased's abdomen. Medical evidence indicated that this was the probable cause of death. At the inquest, the jury returned a verdict of justifiable homicide under the Criminal Law Act 1967, s. 3 (1), whereby a person may use such force as is reasonable in the prevention of crime or in effecting or in assisting in the lawful arrest of offenders or of persons unlawfully at large. The Attorney General applied to quash the verdict on the ground that under s. 3 there had to be a deliberate application of force, whereas the evidence was that it was an accident and the verdict should have been one of accidental death. Counsel for the deceased's relatives agreed that a new inquest should be held; counsel for the coroner and the police adopted a neutral position. *Held*, as it was agreed that the verdict was untenable, justice required that a further investigation should take place. The verdict would be quashed and the case sent back for rehearing.

R v CORONER FOR DURHAM COUNTY, EX PARTE A-G (1978) Times, 29th June (Queen's Bench Division: LORD WIDGERY CJ, TALBOT and ACKNER JJ).

528   Pensions

See paras. 2088, 2095.

CORPORATIONS

Halsbury's Laws of England (4th edn.), Vol 9, paras. 1201–1407

529   Government of corporations—visitor—jurisdiction—university

See *Patel v University of Bradford Senate*, para. 1026.

530   Public corporation—alleged breach of statutory duty—action by private person—summons to dismiss action

See *Booth & Co (International) Ltd v National Enterprise Board*, para. 2755.

531   Trust set up by corporation—trust for accumulation of income—statutory restriction on accumulation—whether corporation a person

See *Re Dodwell & Co Ltd's Trust Deed*, para. 2138.

COUNTY COURTS

Halsbury's Laws of England (4th edn.), Vol. 10, paras. 1–684

532   Administration of Justice Act 1977—commencement

The Administration of Justice Act 1977 (Commencement No. 5) Order 1978, S.I. 1978 No. 810, brings into operation on 3rd July 1978 the following sub-sections of the Administration of Justice Act 1977, see 1977 Halsbury's Abr para. 580: s. 19 (2), which amends the County Courts Act 1959, s. 168, relating to rules as to funds in county courts; s. 19 (3), which substitutes a new s. 180 in the 1959 Act, relating to the taking charge of fees; and s. 19 (5), which amends the Attachment of Earnings Act 1971, s. 6, relating to the collecting officer of the court. These provisions enable the remaining administrative functions of county court registrars to be transferred to court officials.

533   Appeal—appeal to Court of Appeal—application for certiorari—availability

See *Pearlman v Keepers and Governors of Harrow School*, para. 1766.

534   Attachment of earnings order—meaning of earnings.

See *Miles v Miles*, para. 972.

535   Contempt of court—committal order—validity—failure to follow correct legal procedure

See *Wellington v Wellington*, para. 1517; *Cinderby v Cinderby; Pekesin v Pekesin*, para. 1518.

536   Costs—scale of costs—claim for damages for personal injuries exceeding specified sum—whether claim must be admitted or established

The plaintiff brought an action in the county court claiming damages for negligence and breach of statutory duty. The particulars of claim ended, "to include a claim for damages for personal injuries exceeding £5". The defendants paid a sum of money into court but did not admit that the plaintiff had suffered any personal injuries. The plaintiff accepted the sum paid in, but contended that part of the sum was for personal injuries. At the hearing, deciding the question of costs, and the scale of costs applicable, the issue arose as to whether "claim" in the County Court Rules, Ord. 47, r. 5 (4) (c), meant a claim which had been admitted or established, or merely a claim in the proceedings. *Held*, it was not necessary for a claim to be admitted or established either by the defendant's admission or a judicial decision. A mere claim in the proceedings was sufficient to satisfy the term "claim" in the rule.

VARLEY V TARMAC LTD (1978) 122 Sol Jo 540 (Court of Appeal: MEGAW, ROSKILL and CUMMING-BRUCE LJJ).

537   Districts

The County Court District (Devizes) Order 1978, S.I. 1978 No. 397 (in force on 1st April 1978), closes the Devizes County Court, divides its districts between those of neighbouring courts and provides for sittings of the Trowbridge County Court to be held at Devizes.

538   The County Court Districts (Warminster) Order 1978, S.I. 1978 No. 817 (in force on 1st July 1978), closes the Warminster County Court and divides its district between those of neighbouring courts.

539   Fees

The County Court Fees Order 1978, S.I. 1978 No. 1243 (in force on 2nd October 1978), revokes the County Court Fees Order 1975, 1975 Halsbury's Abr para. 579, as amended, amalgamates a large number of fees, and deletes a small number of fees no longer considered relevant. A number of fees are altered and increased.

540   Funds in court—rules—amendment

The County Court Funds (Amendment) Rules 1978, S.I. 1978 No. 750 (in force on 3rd July 1978), further amend the County Court Funds Rules 1965, to take account of the amendment of the County Courts Act 1959, s. 168, by the Administration of Justice Act 1977, s. 19 (2). The rules transfer to the chief clerk of the county court the administrative functions of the registrar in relation to funds in court. They also make a number of minor amendments to take into account changes in accounting procedure.

541   Jurisdiction—financial limit—family provision

See para. 1295.

542   —— **injunction—whether ancillary to claim for damages**

A contract of employment contained a provision restricting the employee's future employment in similar establishments within a specified distance of the employers' business. When the employee left, the employers applied to the county court for an interlocutory injunction to restrain her from entering into such employment pending the determination of the hearing. They also sought £1 damages for loss of goodwill. The employee submitted that the county court had no jurisdiction to entertain an application for an injunction unless that claim was ancillary to some other claim; in this case, the claim for an injunction was the primary claim and the claim for damages was ancillary, and therefore the county court had no jurisdiction. *Held*, it was irrelevant that the claim for damages was small. It was correct that the county courts' jurisdiction to grant an injunction was properly regarded as applying where the grant was ancillary to other relief sought, but that did not mean that one had to balance the size of the claim for damages against the claim for an injunction, to see which was the primary claim. The claim for damages was bona fide and the court had jurisdiction to grant the injunction.

HATT & CO (BATH) LTD v PEARCE [1978] 2 All ER 474 (Court of Appeal: MEGAW and ROSKILL LJJ).

543   —— **matrimonial home—grant of injunction—jurisdiction of court to attach power of arrest**

See *Lewis v Lewis*, para. 1521.

544   —— —— **home shared by unmarried couple—power of court to grant injunction excluding violent party**

See *Davis v Johnson*, para. 1522.

545   —— —— **power of court to grant injunction excluding spouse— duration of injunction**

See *Hopper v Hopper*, para. 1519.

546   —— **mobile home—application to determine dispute**

See *Taylor v Calvert*, para. 1729.

547   —— **service of default summons—extension of time limit—application for new business tenancy**

See *Lewis v Wolking Properties Ltd*, para. 1706.

548   **Litigant in person—form of pleadings—court's discretion to order costs**

The defendants in a possession action were litigants in person. The judge gave permission for the man who was their husband and father to present their case. As a result of unsatisfactory pleadings, the litigants sought an adjournment with a view to seeking legal representation and putting their pleadings into a proper form. The judge granted the adjournment, ordering the litigants to pay the arrears of rent and the plaintiff's costs of the adjournment taxed on a solicitor and own client basis. The defendants appealed against the refusal to accept the pleadings, and against the order of costs on a solicitor and own client basis. *Held*, a number of pleadings had been signed by the husband on behalf of his wife and son. This was irregular. All pleadings should be signed by either a solicitor, counsel, or a litigant in person. In the county court, all costs were in the discretion of the judge. He was free to decide on what basis to order them, whether party and party, common fund, solicitor and client, or whatever other basis he thought best.

GREENHOUSE v HETHERINGTON [1978] LS Gaz R 43 (Court of Appeal: MEGAW, ROSKILL and BROWNE LJJ).

549   Right of audience—legal executives

Legal executives have a limited right of audience in the county court from 1st April 1978. The right is limited to some 6,000 fellows of the Institute of Legal Executives. They may only appear in unopposed applications for adjournment or in applications for judgment by consent. This development is a consequence of the Administration of Justice Act 1977, s. 16, and is intended to speed up and reduce the cost of certain cases: County Courts (Right of Audience) Direction 1978.

550   Rules—amendment

The County Court (Amendment) Rules 1978, S.I. 1978 No. 682 (in force on 2nd June 1978), amend the County Court Rules 1936 to take into account provisions of the Torts (Interference with Goods) Act 1977. They also amend provisions relating to the Domestic Violence and Matrimonial Proceedings Act 1976. Applications for injunctions under s. 1 may now be served not less than 4 clear days before the return day and may be heard and determined in chambers. The rules also raise the amount of an unexecuted warrant in respect of which fortnightly returns must be made from £20 to £50.

551   The County Court (Amendment No. 2) Rules 1978, S.I. 1978 No. 794 (in force on 3rd July 1978), amend CCR Ord. 47, r. 5 by raising the amount of a claim on which no solicitors' costs are generally allowable from £100 to £200. Courts are however given a wide discretion to direct that the restriction will not apply where a claim exceeds £100. The method of applying for a direction is set out. The rules also correct anomalies in Appendix D and Appendix E relating to certificates for the postal service of summonses.

552   The County Court (Amendment No. 3) Rules 1978, S.I. 1978 No. 911 (in force on 3rd July 1978), provide that the restrictions on the allowance of costs imposed by the County Court (Amendment No. 2) Rules 1978, see para. 551, in cases involving sums between £100 and £200 shall not apply to proceedings commenced before 3rd July 1978.

553   The County Court (Amendment No. 4) Rules 1978, S.I. 1978 No. 1943 (in force, except for rr. 4, 5, on 5th February 1979; rr. 4, 5 in force on 12th March 1979), amend the County Court Rules. They allow a registrar, in appropriate cases, to waive the requirement that a solicitor acting for a minor should have his bill taxed. They provide for the service abroad of proceedings for the recovery of certain customs dues and levies. They change the procedure for the enforcement of injunctions in ways which assimilate the practice in the county court to that in the High Court; in particular the process of "attachment" is replaced by "committal". The form of summons to be used in forfeiture cases is amended and the amounts to be allowed by way of fixed costs in Appendix D, Parts I and II are raised.

COURTS

Halsbury's Laws of England (4th edn.), Vol. 10, paras. 701–991

554   Companies Court—jurisdiction

See *Re Shilena Hosiery Co Ltd*, para. 350.

555   Court of Appeal—appeal from divisional court on case stated by justices—whether criminal cause or matter disclosed

See *Camden London Borough Council v Herwald*, para. 2284.

556 —— judges—number

The Maximum Number of Judges Order 1978, S.I. 1978 No. 1057 (in force on 25th July 1978), increases the maximum number of ordinary judges of the Court of Appeal to eighteen.

557 Crown Court—appeal by case stated

The Lord Chief Justice issued the following Practice Direction on 4th December 1978.

It is desirable that there should be uniformity in cases stated by the Crown Court.

Pending any amendment of the relevant Rules, the content of any such case should comply with rule 68 of the Magistrates' Courts Rules 1968 and the form with form 148 of the Magistrates' Courts (Forms) Rules 1968, with necessary amendments only.

What that means, in a sentence, is that as regards appeals by case stated from the Crown Court the same form and content is required of the cases as is already prescribed for magistrates' cases.

558 —— bail—power to grant bail pending appeal

See *R v K*, para. 590.

559 —— contempt—power to order committal

See *Rooney v Snaresbrook Crown Court*, para. 468.

560 —— distribution of business—classification of offences

A Practice Direction, [1978] 2 All ER 912, which has been issued by LORD WIDGERY CJ with the concurrence of the Lord Chancellor, amends the directions on the distribution of Crown Court business ([1971] 3 All ER 829).

The main effect of the amendments is that offences are now classified as follows:

Class 1—The following offences, which are to be tried by a High Court judge: (1) any offences for which a person may be sentenced to death; (2) misprision of treason and treason felony; (3) murder; (4) genocide; (5) an offence under Official Secrets Act 1911, s. 1; (5) incitement, attempt or conspiracy to commit any of the above offences.

Class 2—The following offences, which are to be tried by a High Court judge unless a particular case is released by or on the authority of a presiding judge, that is to say, a High Court judge assigned to have special responsibility for a particular circuit; (1) manslaughter; (2) infanticide; (3) child destruction; (4) abortion (Offences against the Person Act 1861, s. 58); (5) rape; (6) sexual intercourse with girl under 13; (7) incest with girl under 13; (8) sedition; (9) an offence under the Geneva Conventions Act 1957, s. 1; (10) mutiny; (11) piracy; (12) incitement, attempt or conspiracy to commit any of the above offences.

Class 3—All offences triable only on indictment other than those in classes 1, 2 and 4. They may be listed for trial by a High Court judge or by a circuit judge or by a recorder.

Class 4—(a) wounding or causing grievous bodily harm with intent (Offences against the Person Act 1861, s. 18); (b) robbery or assault with intent to rob (Theft Act 1968, s. 8); (c) offences under para. (*a*) of s. 2 (2) of the Forgery Act 1913 where the amount of money or the value of goods exceeds £1,000; (d) offences under para. (*a*) of s. 7 of the Forgery Act 1913 where the amount of money or the value of the property exceeds £1,000; (e) incitement or attempt to commit any of the above offences; (f) conspiracy at common law or conspiracy to commit any offence other than one included in classes 1 and 2; (g) all offences triable either way and any offence in class 3, if included in class 4 in accordance with directions which may be either general or particular, given by a presiding judge or on his authority.

When tried on indictment offences in class 4 may be tried by a High Court judge, circuit judge or recorder but will normally be listed for trial by a circuit judge or recorder.

561   —— jurisdiction—appeal from justices on plea of guilty—power of court to inquire into proceedings before justices

On appeal against sentence in a case where the defendant had pleaded guilty the deputy circuit judge, after calling evidence and inquiring into the proceedings before the justices, sent the case back with a direction that pleas of not guilty be entered. The justices, who ruled that they were functi officio refused to hear the case and the prosecution applied for an order of certiorari to quash the Crown Court decision. *Held*, granting the application, unless the Crown Court learnt something which prima facie suggested that the justices should have exercised their discretion to permit a change of plea, it should not make inquiry and obtain evidence as to what went on before the justices. There was no prima facie evidence in the present case from which the Crown Court could properly have concluded that the justices could have considered exercising their discretion, let alone that they had exercised it wrongly.

R v COVENTRY CROWN COURT, EX PARTE MANSON [1978] LS Gaz R 343 (Queen's Bench Division: LORD WIDGERY CJ, O'CONNOR and LLOYD JJ).

562   —— late sittings

In dismissing appeals against sentences by appellants whose trial began at 4 p.m. and went on until 7.45 p.m., the Court of Appeal stressed that late sittings were to be avoided if at all possible.

R v HARRIES (1978) Times, 28th April (Court of Appeal).

563   —— rules—bail

See para. 682.

564   Funds in court—investment

The Funds in Court (Investment) (Amendment) Regulations 1978, S.I. 1978 No. 468 (in force on 25th April 1978), amend the Funds in Court (Investment) Regulations 1970 by adding to the list of prescribed securities the variable interest securities which are specified in the Trustee Investment Act 1961, Sch. 1, Pt. II, para. 9A, as added by the Trustee Investments (Additional Powers) (No. 2) Order 1977, S.I. 1977 No. 1878, 1977 Halsbury's Abr para. 3049.

565   Hearing in camera—grounds for hearing—sexual offences involving children

Canada

The defendant was convicted of two charges of illegal sexual intercourse with children. The Crown applied for the proceedings to be heard in camera on the grounds of protection of public morals, as the defendant was related to the children, and because schoolchildren might come into court during the trial. The defendant challenged the legality of the trial being held in camera. *Held*, if the fact that the defendant was related to the children became an important factor, or if children became present in the courtroom, an application for a hearing in camera could then be heard. The only circumstances in which a hearing could be held in camera were where the protection of public morals or the administration of justice so required it; a camera hearing could not be ordered on purely speculative grounds.

R v WARAWUK [1978] 5 WWR 389 (Supreme Court of Alberta).

566   House of Lords—costs—petition for leave to appeal

See *Procedure Direction*, para. 2193.

567   Judges—decisions against litigants appearing in person—need for giving clear reasons

Dismissing an appeal against an order for damages, the Court of Appeal emphasised that where a litigant appeared in person the judge should give clear reasons for his decision, and should be particularly careful when dealing with the case of the party against whom he decided.

BOWMAN v McKEOWN (1978) Times, 23rd November (Court of Appeal: BRANDON and STEPHENSON LJJ and SIR DAVID CAIRNS).

568 Judicial Committee of the Privy Council—appeals—Malaysia

See para. 333.

569 —— extension of membership—Barbados

See para. 323.

570 Judicial review—application—procedure

See *Uppal v Home Office* para. 2155.

571 Juvenile courts—citing of police cautions

See para. 761.

572 Local valuation court—whether an inferior court

See *A-G v BBC; Dible v BBC*, para. 467.

573 Practice and procedure

See PRACTICE AND PROCEDURE.

574 Tribunals—tribunals having similar attributes to court of justice— criteria for determining nature of tribunal

See *Trapp v Mackie*, para. 1287.

CREMATION AND BURIAL

Halsbury's Laws of England (4th edn.), Vol. 10, paras. 1001–1243

575 Funeral expenses—estate less than funeral expenses—liability of husband

Canada
On the death of a woman intestate in 1972, her parents, the plaintiffs, succeeded to her estate and paid her funeral expenses. The parents then brought an action for reimbursement of the cost of the funeral against her husband, who had been separated from her. *Held*, while at common law a husband was liable for the funeral expenses of his deceased wife, up to an amount befitting her station in life, since the Married Women's Property Act 1882, the reasons for this were no longer valid and his liability was limited to the difference between the estate and the amount of the funeral expenses. Accordingly, where a married woman's parents succeeded to her estate and paid her funeral expenses which exceeded the value of the estate, her husband, even though separated, was liable to pay them the difference.

PEARCE v DIENSTHUBER (1977) 17 OR (2d) 401 (Court of Appeal of Ontario). *Rees v Hughes* [1946] KB 517, DC applied.

576 Human remains—removal—licence fee

The Human Remains Removal Licence (Prescribed Fee) Order 1978, S.I. 1978 No. 239 (in force on 1st April 1978), increases from £4 to £5 the prescribed fee for a licence issued under Burial Act 1857, s. 25, for the removal of human remains interred in a place of burial.

CRIMINAL LAW

Halsbury's Laws of England (4th edn.), Vol. 11, paras. 1–1380

577　Articles

The Added Conspiracy Count, Glanville Williams (the effect of the Criminal Law Act 1977 on the practice of adding a conspiracy count to charges for consummated offences): 128 NLJ 24.

Assault (a series of articles covering assault, assault on the police, defences, the psychological effects of sexual assault and the Criminal Injuries Compensation Board): Court (Journal of Proceedings in Magistrates' Courts) Spring 1978.

Attempting the Impossible (discussion on whether it is an offence to attempt to commit the impossible, with reference to *Director of Public Prosecutions v Nock and Alsford*, see para. 598): 142 JP Jo 396.

Compounding the Confusion in Inchoate Offences, Glanville Williams (difficulties arising from prosecutions for attempt and for conspiracy to attempt impossible offences): 128 NLJ 724.

Criminal Compensation by an Offender, A. N. Khan (the statutory provisions relating to compensation by offenders and when a compensation order should be made): 122 Sol Jo 338.

The Criminal Injuries Compensation Scheme and Judicial Review (the attitude of the courts to the scheme and when they will intervene): 128 NLJ 200.

Criminal Injuries Compensation: Some Recent developments, A. N. Khan: 122 Sol Jo 549.

Defences of General Application, Law Commissioner's Report No. 83, (1) Duress, A. T. H. Smith, (2) Necessity, Glanville Williams, (3) Entrapment, A. J. Ashworth (consideration of Commission's proposals): [1978] Crim LR 122.

The Definition of an Alibi Defence, T. M. S. Tosswill: [1978] Crim LR 276.

The Drug Laws, W. T. West (a look at some recent cases): 122 Sol Jo 322.

Handling Stolen Goods—Theft Act 1968, s. 22, Alec Samuels (principal issues likely to arise in a handling trial): 142 JP Jo 437.

Identification and Alibi: the Duty of the Defending Solicitor, Alec Samuels (a look at the Devlin Report on Evidence of Identification in Criminal cases): 121 Sol Jo 841.

Impossible Attempts—An Alternative Solution, M. S. Rowell (problems in sentencing people who have attempted to commit crimes which are impossible of achievement): 128 NLJ 716.

Indecency Between Males and the Sexual Offences Act 1967, Roy Walmsley (discussion of the factors associated with the increase in recorded homosexual offences, and possible explanation for the offences); [1978] Crim LR 400.

Manslaughter and Omissions to Act, Lindsey E. Squire and Richard Painter (attitude of the courts towards manslaughter due to neglect in the light of *R v Stone and Dobinson* [1977] 2 All ER 341, 1976 Halsbury's Abr para. 632): 128 NLJ 994.

Protection of Children Act 1978: Indecent Photographing of Children, Alec Samuels (problem of defining "indecent" for purposes of Act): 122 Sol Jo 578.

Provocation and the Reasonable Man, Margaret Spencer (assessment of provocation and the reasonable man in the light of *DPP V Camplin* see para. 638): 128 NLJ 615.

Queue-Jumping and the Theft Bill, Jacques Parry (examination of the clause in the Theft Bill relating to criminal deception): 128 NLJ 663.

Reforming the Act—the End of the Beginning, Gavin Drewry (mechanism by which official information is revealed and concealed in the light of proposed reform of Official Secrets Act 1911): 128 NLJ 896.

Sexual Offences and the Trend in Crime 1949–76, Helena Campbell: 128 NLJ 748.

A Small New Liberty? D. W. Williams (the effect of the Criminal Law Act 1977, s. 62): 128 NLJ 9.

Strict Liability in Criminal Law: How Stands the Argument Now?, Stephen White (review of the arguments on strict liability in the light of recent studies of the enforcement of such legislation): 142 JP Jo 608.

Theft Act 1978, Alec Samuels: 122 Sol Jo 667.

Treason, Alan Wharman (comment on the law of treason): 128 NLJ 851.

Unauthorised Use of Electricity, J. Kodwo Bentil (examination of relevant law): 122 Sol Jo 706.

When is a Conspiracy like an Attempt—and Other Impossible Questions, Jennifer Temkin (discussion on attempts to commit impossible offences, and their relationship to the offences of conspiracy and incitement): (1978) 94 LQR 534.

578   Aiding and abetting—mens rea—degree of knowledge

Northern Ireland

A member of a terrorist organisation was convicted of unlawfully doing an act with the intention of causing an explosion, and of being in possession of a bomb. He had shown other members of the organisation the location of a public house in which the others had then placed a bomb. He appealed, contending that he had not possessed sufficient mens rea to be convicted as he had not known the precise nature of any offence that the other men might commit. *Held*, knowledge of the actual offence committed was unnecessary; it was enough that the accused knew of the type of offence contemplated or the essential matters constituting it. He knew he was participating in a military operation and with his knowledge of the organisation's methods he had to be taken to have foreseen the bombing attack and to have realised that the other persons involved were carrying a bomb or other weapon. Accordingly the appeal would be dismissed. The House considered that in cases of aiding and abetting, counselling and procuring, the indictment should make it clear that the accused was charged as principal in the second degree.

R v MAXWELL [1978] 1 WLR 1350 (House of Lords: VISCOUNT DILHORNE, LORD EDMUND-DAVIES, LORD SCARMAN, LORD HAILSHAM OF ST. MARYLEBONE and LORD FRASER OF TULLYBELTON). *R v Bainbridge* (1960) 1 QB 129, CCA, applied.

579   Assault—assault on constable in execution of duty—forcibly resisting attempt to take fingerprints

Following a minor incident in a car park involving two motorists and a policeman, a woman was arrested, charged and subsequently convicted of causing criminal damage, dangerous driving and assaulting two police constables. The assault charges had arisen from a spirited and successful attempt by the woman to resist the taking of her fingerprints by the police at the police station where she had been charged with the other offences and bailed. The police had obtained a magistrates' order for the taking of her fingerprints, but the relevant provision, Magistrates' Court Act 1952, s. 40 (2), required the prints to be taken either at the place where the court was sitting or, if the person had been remanded in custody, at the place to which that person had been committed. Reasonable force could be used by the police if necessary. On appeal, *held*, since she had been bailed, the woman was within her rights in refusing to allow her fingerprints to be taken at the police station. Although she had defended herself by biting and kicking the police, there was no suggestion that she had used more force than was reasonably necessary. She was innocent of the assault. It had been oppressive to charge her with dangerous driving, and the conviction for causing criminal damage was unsafe and unsatisfactory as quite possibly having been induced by the mass of evidence relating to the assaults. All the convictions would be quashed.

R v JONES (YVONNE) [1978] 3 All ER 1098 (Court of Appeal: SHAW LJ, MAIS and PETER PAIN JJ).

580   —— blow in face—whether occasioning actual bodily harm

The defendant was charged with assault occasioning actual bodily harm. Justices found that he had struck his victim in the face and convicted him because they considered it likely that the blow would have caused harm. The defendant appealed by way of case stated on the ground that it had not been proved that he had caused actual bodily harm. *Held*, the justices were justified in finding that the blow had caused harm even if it had only been slight. There should not in any case have been an appeal by way of case stated as there was no question of law involved.

TAYLOR V GRANVILLE [1978] Crim LR 482 (Queen's Bench Division: LORD WIDGERY CJ, BOREHAM and DRAKE JJ).

581   —— defence—consent—injury inflicted during lawful sport

During a game of rugby football the defendant punched a member of the opposing team and fractured his jaw. He was charged with inflicting grievous bodily harm and the question arose as to whether the injured player could be deemed to have consented to the risk of the injury. *Held*, rugby was a game of violence in which a player could be deemed to have consented to the risk of injury in some circumstances, but there was a limit on such consent. Where a player was assaulted in a part of the field away from the game he could not be said to have consented to the risk of the resulting injury.

R v BILLINGHURST [1978] Crim LR 553 (Crown Court at Newport: Judge RUTTER).

582   —— police officer—execution of duty—scope of duty—police intervening in attempted suicide

Canada

A police officer on duty approached a woman who was holding a knife and threatening to kill herself. She swung the knife at him and told him to leave her alone; they struggled and he eventually disarmed her. She was charged with assaulting a police officer in the execution of his duty. The charge was dismissed on the ground that as she was not doing anything illegal in attempting suicide, the officer was not acting in the execution of his duty after being told to go away. On appeal by the police, *held*, a police officer's duty extended beyond the prevention of crime and keeping the peace: it covered the case where he took reasonable steps to save the life of someone clearly intent on committing suicide. Therefore, as the officer was doing his duty the appeal would be allowed and the case remitted for further consideration.

R v DIETRICH (1978) 39 CCC (2d) 361 (Supreme Court of British Columbia). Dicta of Maugham LJ in *Haynes v Harwood* [1935] 1 KB 146, at 161, applied.

583   Attempt—attempt to incite perjury

The defendant had written a letter to another man asking whether the other man could persuade his wife to give false evidence at the defendant's trial for burglary. The statement of offence was "attempting to incite perjury" but the particulars of offence alleged an "attempt to incite [the other man] to procure perjury". The defendant appealed against conviction on the ground that the trial judge has misdirected the jury. *Held*, the judge had failed to leave to the jury whether what the defendant had done was sufficiently proximate to amount to an attempt. Nor was any direction given as to how the jury should approach the matter of attempt, which would have been difficult in any event in view of the confusion between the offence stated and the particulars of the offence. The appeal would be allowed.

R v CROMACK [1978] Crim LR 217 (Court of Appeal: EVELEIGH LJ, CUSACK and CROOM-JOHNSON JJ).

584   —— attempted theft—necessity for proof of intention

See *R v Hector*, para. 664; *R v Hussein*, para. 663.

585   —— attempting to drive with blood-alcohol concentration above prescribed limit—broken down vehicle

See *R v Farrance*, para. 2345; *R v Neilson*, para. 2346.

586   Automatism—insanity—dissociative state due to psychological blow

Canada

The defendant was charged with causing bodily harm with intent to wound after he had attacked his girlfriend with a rock. His defence was that of automatism; he claimed that he was in a "dissociative state", which was not a disease of the mind amounting to insanity, as it was induced by the psychological blow of discovering that the girl was no longer interested in him, and not by any underlying psychological condition or mental illness. The defendant was acquitted and the Crown appealed, contending that a dissociative state due to a psychological blow was a disease of the mind and thus the verdict should have been not guilty on account of insanity. *Held*, what mental states or conditions constituted a disease of the mind was a question of law. The distinction to be drawn between insanity and non-insane automatism was between a malfunctioning of the mind arising from some internal cause having its source in the accused's psychological or emotional make-up or in some organic pathology, as opposed to one which was the transient effect produced by some specific external factor. In this case, the emotional stress and disappointment could not amount to such an external factor, but the dissociative state must be considered as having its source primarily in the accused's psychological or emotional make-up, and it thus constituted a disease of the mind. The appeal would be allowed and a new trial ordered.

R v RABEY (1977) 17 OR (2d) 1 (Court of Appeal of Ontario).

587   —— —— mental state between the two—sufficiency as defence

The defendant was driving his van down a country road at night, swerving from side to side. A taxi driver attempted to overtake the defendant and there was a collision. On being told that the police had been called, the defendant drove off without lights, successfully evading police cars and a road block, and finally escaping on foot into a wood. When eventually caught, he said he could not remember the incident. Three days later he saw a psychiatrist who gave evidence at the trial that the defendant had been in a condition of hysterical amnesia or hysterical fatigue when his memory ceased to function and his subconscious mind took over, so that he was unaware of the implications of what he was doing. The defendant appealed against his conviction for dangerous driving on the basis that the judge had ruled that the psychiatrist's evidence provided no defence. *Held*, a defendant's mental state had to amount to either insanity or automatism to afford him a defence. The fact that the defendant in the case was driving and acting with a purpose—to get away—suggested that his mind was working to an extent sufficient to exclude both insanity and automatism. It may well have been that the defendant's mental state fell between the two recognised defences. If this was so, the psychiatric evidence was of value only in mitigation. The appeal would be dismissed.

R v ISITT [1978] Crim LR 159 (Court of Appeal: LAWTON LJ, SWANWICK and WIEN JJ).

588   Bail Act 1976—commencement

The Bail Act 1976 (Commencement) Order 1978, S.I. 1978 No. 132, brought the whole of the Act, see 1976 Halsbury's Abr para. 552, into force on 17th April 1978 apart from s. 13 which deals with commencement and came into force on 15th November 1976.

589   Bail—failure to surrender to bail—methods of punishment for offence

See *R v Singh* para. 683.

590   —— power of Crown Court to grant bail pending appeal—meaning of "in custody"

A juvenile court convicted a teenage boy of burglary and committed him to the care of a local authority by a care order made under the Children and Young Persons Act 1969. He was placed in an assessment centre. The boy appealed against the care order to the Crown Court, and applied for bail pending the appeal. Under the Courts Act 1971, s. 13 (4) the Crown Court has the power to admit to bail anyone who is in custody as the result of a sentence imposed by a magistrates' court. *Held*, a young person committed to the care of a local authority and placed in an assessment centre was not in custody within the meaning of s. 13 (4). The Crown Court therefore did not have the power to grant bail pending the determination of the appeal.

R v K [1978] 1 All ER 180 (Crown Court at Liverpool: JUDGE COLLINSON).

591   Blasphemous libel—intent

The editor of a newspaper and the newspaper itself were convicted of blasphemous libel. In his summing up the trial judge directed the jury that it was not necessary for the prosecution to prove an intent on the part of the accused to attack the Christian religion. On appeal *held*, dismissing the appeal, subjective intent was not an essential element of the offence. It was enough that the defendant deliberately published that which constituted the blasphemous material.

R v LEMON [1978] 1 All ER 175 (Court of Appeal: ROSKILL and EVELEIGH LJJ and STOCKER J).

This decision was affirmed by a bare majority on appeal to the House of Lords.

592   Burglary—burglary with intent to steal—need to prove intent

The defendant was seen leaving a flat in a public house. Nothing had been taken from the flat but he was charged with burglary with intent to steal. *Held*, a charge of burglary with intent to steal involved an undertaking by the prosecution to prove intent. In this case the most that could be said was either that the defendant had been too drunk to know what he was doing or that his intention had been to steal anything worth stealing. Neither proposition constituted an intent to steal and therefore there was no case for the defendant to answer.

R v BOZICKOVIC [1978] Crim LR 686 (Crown Court at Nottingham: MR RECORDER MCAULAY QC). *R v Hussein* [1978] Crim LR 219, applied.

593   Caravans—protection of occupier—whether site protected

The defendant used his land as a caravan site. He did not have planning permission to do this, and was therefore unable to obtain a site licence under the Caravan Sites and Control of Development Act 1960. He cut off the electricity supply to a caravan on his land and was charged with an offence under the Caravan Sites Act 1968, s. 3. That section makes it an offence persistently to withdraw a service reasonably required for the occupation of the caravan as a residence. The justices dismissed the case on the basis that since the defendant had no licence, the site was not a protected site, and consequently did not fall within the Caravan Sites Act 1968. On appeal, *held*, it was the defendant's own fault that he did not have a licence, because he had not obtained planning permission. It was false for the defendant to suppose that because he could not obtain a licence, he could avoid the requirements of the Caravan Sites Act 1968, s. 3. Cutting off the electricity constituted an offence under the section. The case would be remitted to the magistrates for reconsideration.

HOOPER v EAGLESTONE (1977) 76 LGR 308 (Queen's Bench Division: LORD WIDGERY CJ, CUMMING-BRUCE LJ, and PARK J).

594   Compensation order—amount of loss—figure neither agreed nor proved

The defendant took away a car, and while being chased by the police collided with another vehicle, causing damage to the car. He pleaded guilty to taking and driving away a motor vehicle without authority. He was sentenced to imprisonment and ordered to pay £100 compensation in respect of the damage. The only evidence of the damage was a statement by the car owner that he had received an estimate of £209 for repairs. The defendant appealed against the order, contending that he was not responsible for all the damage. *Held*, an order for compensation could not be made unless the figure was agreed or proved to be the loss suffered. In this case, the figure was merely an estimate which was disputed. The order should not have been made and would be quashed.

R v VIVIAN (1978) 122 Sol Jo 680 (Court of Appeal: BROWNE LJ and TALBOT and MICHAEL DAVIES JJ).

595   —— financial loss—power of court to include interest in order

The defendant was convicted of theft and obtaining property by deception. He was ordered to pay compensation under Powers of Criminal Courts Act 1973, s. 35 (1), of a sum which included an amount by way of interest. He applied to have the compensation order varied on the grounds that it should not have included the sum of interest. *Held*, s. 35 (1) provided that a convicted person could be required to pay compensation for any personal injury, loss or damage resulting from the offence. The word "loss" in s. 35 (1) should not be restricted to any particular kind of loss and included financial loss. The court had discretion to include in the order a sum by way of interest, equivalent to the amount of interest that might be awarded in a civil action. In exercising its discretion to include interest, the court should consider the amount of the loss and interest, the time which had elapsed since the loss was suffered and the convicted person's means. The application would be dismissed.

R v SCHOFIELD [1978] 2 All ER 705 (Court of Appeal: LORD WIDGERY CJ, SHAW LJ and LLOYD J).

596   —— payment and enforcement—guidelines for Crown Court

The Court of Appeal has laid down guidelines for the Crown Court as to times for payment of and enforcement of orders for compensation. The law is primarily contained in the Powers of Criminal Courts Act 1973, ss. 34–38. Extended time for payment and payment by instalments is permitted by s. 34 in the case of the Crown Court and by the Magistrates' Courts Act 1952, s. 63 in the case of magistrates' courts. Under the Administration of Justice Act 1970, s. 41 (1), as amended by the 1973 Act, a compensation order made by the Crown Court is enforceable in the same way as a sum adjudged to be payable on conviction by a magistrates' court. When passing sentence, the Crown Court may specify a period of imprisonment not exceeding twelve months in case of default if it considers the magistrates' power to sentence insufficient.

In the event of default the Crown Court may issue either a warrant of distress or a warrant committing the defaulter to prison. The maximum period of imprisonment by a magistrates' court is laid down in the 1952 Act, Sch. 3 as amended, and the minimum period is five days. The 1952 Act, s. 107 prohibits the imprisonment of a defaulter under the age of seventeen.

R v BUNCE (1978) 66 Cr App Rep 109 (Court of Appeal: ROSKILL and BROWNE LJJ, KERR J).

597   —— research study

See para. 2284.

598   Conspiracy—agreement to commit act believed to be unlawful—
                act not in fact unlawful

The appellants agreed together to obtain cocaine, a controlled drug, by separating it from other substances in a powder which they believed to contain cocaine. However, the powder did not contain cocaine and it would have been impossible to obtain the drug from it. They were convicted of conspiring to contravene the Misuse of Drugs Act 1971, s. 4 which made it an offence to produce a controlled drug. On appeal against conviction, *held*, the common law crime of conspiracy consisted of an agreement to do an unlawful act, the essence of the offence being agreement between the parties. However, it was also a "preliminary" crime in that it had to be possible for the act agreed upon to lead to the commission of an unlawful act. As it was impossible to produce cocaine from the powder, the appellants had agreed upon an act which was not unlawful and could not lead to the commission of the alleged offence. Common sense and justice required that they could not be guilty of conspiracy to commit a crime by agreeing, albeit unknowingly, to act lawfully. The appeal would be allowed.

DIRECTOR OF PUBLIC PROSECUTIONS v NOCK AND ALSFORD [1978] 2 All ER 654 (House of Lords: LORD DIPLOCK, LORD EDMUND-DAVIES, LORD RUSSELL OF KILLOWEN, LORD KEITH OF KINKEL and LORD SCARMAN). Decision of Court of Appeal (1978) Times, 1st February, reversed. *Haughton v Smith* [1975] AC 476, HL, applied.

The offence of conspiracy is now defined by Criminal Law Act 1977, s. 1.

599   —— agreement to commit act without knowledge of illegality— no overt act in pursuance of agreement after acquisition of knowledge

The appellant assisted two men who had arranged to buy cannabis abroad and sell it in this country. She helped to open a bank account in a bogus name and agreed to pay money which she would receive from one of the men into the bank. She was charged with conspiracy to supply a controlled drug. Her defence was that although she realised that something illegal was going on it was not until she had a talk with one of the men on 28th February 1976 that she knew that they were importing controlled drugs. Thereafter she did nothing to assist them. At the trial the prosecution presented their case in two ways. Firstly they contended that the appellant must have known all the time what the others were doing and that as she had helped them with guilty knowledge she was guilty of conspiracy. Secondly, on the basis of an admission that she would have paid in cheques after 28th February if asked, the prosecution contended that she was guilty even if she had first acquired knowledge on that date despite the fact that thereafter she did no overt act in pursuance of the agreement. The judge directed the jury in relation to the second contention that she was guilty on 28th February by reason of her secret and uncommunicated intention to deal as she had agreed with money which she might receive. On appeal against conviction, *held*, a secret and uncommunicated intention to join in an illegal enterprise should the occasion arise did not amount to an indictable conspiracy. Accordingly the judge's direction on the second contention was wrong.

As the jury might have accepted the appellant's defence and accordingly based their conclusion on the part of the summing up which was a misdirection the appeal would be allowed and the conviction quashed.

R v SCOTT (1978) 122 Sol Jo 523 (Court of Appeal: GEOFFREY LANE AND SHAW LJJ and CAULFIELD J).

The offence of conspiracy is now defined by Criminal Law Act 1977, s. 1.

600   —— conspiracy to steal—statutory or common law offence—form of indictment

In an attempt to explain whether conspiracy to steal was a common law offence or a statutory offence under the Criminal Law Act 1977, s. 1, *held*, s. 5 (1) preserved the common law offence of conspiracy to defraud; at common law this included an agreement by two or more persons by dishonesty to deprive another person of something belonging to him. Conspiracy to defraud included conspiracy to steal and the latter was therefore preserved as a common law offence by the Act. Further, it was acceptable for the indictment to state the offence as conspiracy to steal, rather than the larger version of conspiracy to defraud by conspiring to steal.

R v QUINN [1978] Crim LR 750 (Crown Court at Nottingham: DRAKE J).

601   —— whether agreement impossible to perform—meaning of "impossible"—burden of proof as to impossibility

The appellants agreed to buy cannabis from A. They were convicted of conspiring together to contravene the provisions of the Misuse of Drugs Act 1971 and appealed against conviction on the ground that it was for the prosecution to prove that it was possible for the agreement to be carried out as intended and that they had failed to do so. There was some doubt as to whether A had any cannabis to sell and it was submitted that if the carrying out of the agreement was thus impossible no criminal offence could have been committed and the appellants were not guilty. *Held*, (i) whether or not the performance of an agreement was possible had to be decided on the facts as they were at the time when the agreement was made. (ii) A distinction had to be drawn between an agreement which if carried out could not result in the commission of an offence because the result was physically or legally impossible and one which could not result in the commission of an offence because of the unwillingness or incompetence of a person not a party to the agreement or to some other frustrating factor. Only if the offence was impossible in the former sense could the accused be said to be innocent. In the present case there was no evidence that it was impossible, in that sense, for the agreement to be carried out. The appeal would be dismissed.

The court laid down the following guidelines as to the burden of proof in conspiracy cases. If the prosecution had evidence in their possession which showed that the carrying out of the agreement was physically impossible it was their duty either to call that evidence or make it available to the defence. If the prosecution had no such evidence it was not their duty in the first instance to show that the carrying out of the agreement would have been possible; the evidential burden of proving impossibility was then on the defence. The probative burden remained on the prosecution and if there was some evidence of impossibility the question should be left to the jury. If there was no evidence of impossibility the judge need not direct the jury about it.

R v Bennett (1978) Times, 11th August (Court of Appeal: Orr and Browne LJJ and Mais J). *DPP v Nock* [1978] 2 All ER 654, HL, para. 598 distinguished.

602   Corruption—recipient of gift not intending to carry out corrupt act

The defendant was the head of new work at the British Steel Corporation. He was convicted of corruption under the Prevention of Corruption Act 1906, s. 1, in that he had corruptly accepted holidays from the owner of an engineering company. It was alleged that the holidays were given to ensure that repair and construction work issuing from the corporation found its way to the company. The defendant appealed, contending that he had accepted the holidays not intending to carry out his side of the bargain and even if the donor had a corrupt motive, he was not corrupt in accepting the gifts since two persons could have entirely different intentions in one transaction. *Held*, under the Prevention of Corruption Act 1916, s. 2, the burden of proof was on the defendant to prove that the gifts were not corrupt. There was no evidence to support his contention that he intended to double-cross the donor. However, even if there had been such evidence, a recipient who took a gift knowing that it was intended as a bribe and intending to keep it entered into a corrupt bargain despite the fact that he might make a mental reservation not to carry out his side of the bargain. The appeal would be dismissed.

R v Mills (1978) Times, 14th June (Court of Appeal: Geoffrey Lane LJ, Milmo and Cantley JJ).

603   Criminal bankruptcy order—financial limit on jurisdiction—offences to be considered

See *DPP v Anderson*, para. 225.

604   Criminal capacity—child under fourteen—ability to distinguish between right and wrong—standard of proof of knowledge

Australia

A twelve-year-old boy was convicted of murder after killing another child by hitting him on the head with a brick. He then concealed the body. He appealed against conviction on the grounds that the trial judge had misdirected the jury both by stating that the presumption the boy was *doli incapax* could be rebutted by showing merely that he knew the difference between right and wrong, and in his explanation to the jury of how it should treat evidence of the boy's previous offences. *Held*, it was enough to rebut the presumption of *doli incapax* if it could be shown that a boy between the ages of ten and fourteen knew his act was wrong according to the principles of reasonable and ordinary men. On the second point, the evidence of previous offences had been given to assist the jury in determining whether the boy knew right from wrong, not in an attempt to show he had an evil disposition. Accordingly, the trial judge had acted correctly and the appeal would be dismissed.

R v M (1977) 16 SASR 589 (Supreme Court of South Australia).

605   Criminal damage—arson—lawful excuse—subjective or objective test—whether act capable of protecting property

The appellant was convicted under a charge of arson after he had set fire to a bed in an old people's home. He appealed on the ground that as he had intended to draw attention to a defective fire alarm he was entitled to raise the defence contained in Criminal Damage Act 1971, s. 5, that the act was done to prevent damage to the property. *Held*, the test in such cases was objective. The appellant's act was not capable of protecting property in itself, but could only draw attention to a need for protection. Therefore the defence in s. 5 was not available and the appeal would be dismissed.

R v HUNT (1978) 66 Cr App Rep 105 (Court of Appeal: ROSKILL LJ, WIEN and SLYNN JJ).

606   Criminal injuries—compensation—claim by relatives caring for dependants of the deceased

The mother of three children was strangled by their father. The children went to live with two aunts, who gave up their jobs and received boarding-out allowances from the local authorities for the children's maintenance. The Criminal Injuries Compensation Board awarded the aunts a sum which was the difference between their lost salaries and the boarding-out allowance. The aunts applied for an order of certiorari to quash the board's decision. *Held*, the aunts were not entitled to receive any sum under the Criminal Injuries Compensation Scheme. Any award had to be made to the children who were the dependants of the deceased. However, the board could exercise a discretionary power to pay to the aunts compensatory sums awarded to the children. The case would be remitted to the board for reassessment. In reassessing, the board should bear in mind that boarding-out allowances included a financial element which paid for outgoings and a sum for maternal services. In computing the children's loss, the board should take account of the aunts' lost salaries, and only set off against those sums the element of boarding-out allowance which could fairly be attributed to payment for maternal services.

R v CRIMINAL INJURIES COMPENSATION BOARD, EX PARTE MCGUFFIE [1978] Crim LR 160 (Queen's Bench Division: LORD WIDGERY CJ, CANTLEY and PETER PAIN JJ).

607   —— —— function of Board—discretion

See *R v Criminal Injuries Compensation Board, ex parte RJC (an infant)*, para. 3.

608   —— —— reform

A report on the Criminal Injuries Compensation Scheme by an interdepartmental working party recommends, inter alia, that the existing restriction on the payment of compensation to a victim living with his or her criminal assailant should be lifted provided that the assailant would not benefit from the award: Review of the Criminal Injuries Compensation Report of an Interdepartmental Working Party (Stationery Office, £2).

609   Dangerous drug—control—power of search—no legal warrant—admissibility of evidence obtained

Scotland

Cannabis resin was found in the defendant's room at an American military base by a search party acting under the authority of a purported warrant granted by a senior officer at the base. The warrant was not valid according to the code of American military law. The defendant submitted that as the warrant was illegal, the evidence obtained as a result of it should be excluded. The argument proceeded on the basis that there was no legal warrant according to the law of Scotland to authorise the search. *Held*, in the situation which had arisen there was an element of urgency and there was no one at the base who was entitled to obtain the statutory warrant under the Misuse of Drugs Act 1971, the police having taken no part in the proceedings. If the procedure in the Act for obtaining a warrant had been gone through, the evidence might have been lost. The evidence was admissible.

WALSH V MACPHAIL 1978 SLT 29 (High Court of Justiciary).

610   —— forfeiture order—time limit for imposing order

The appellant was charged with fraudulent evasion of the prohibition on the importation of cocaine. She pleaded guilty and was sentenced to a term of imprisonment. Four months later the judge made an order under Misuse of Drugs Act 1971, s. 27 or alternatively under Powers of Criminal Courts Act 1973, s. 43 for forfeiture of money found in her possession which was considered to relate to the offence. On appeal it was contended that a forfeiture order was a sentence or other order made by the Crown Court when dealing with an offender within Courts Act 1971, s. 11 (2) and accordingly could not be imposed outside the time limits for variation laid down by that provision. Those limits were less than four months. *Held*, the words "or other order made" were to be construed as denoting an order which while not forming part of the sentence was of the nature of a sentence. There was a difference between forfeiture under the Powers of Criminal Courts Act and under the Misuse of Drugs Act. In the former case the power was limited to property in the possession or control of the accused at the time of his arrest, and operated to deprive him of his rights in the property. Such an order was in the nature of a sentence. Misuse of Drugs Act 1971, s. 27 extended to anything shown to the satisfaction of the court to relate to the offence. The article could be forfeited, destroyed or otherwise dealt with. The object of such an order was the protection of the public and it was not in the nature of a sentence. Accordingly the time limits applied to an order under s. 43 of the 1973 Act but not to one under s. 27 of the 1971 Act. As the order had been made in the alternative under either provision that appeal would be dismissed.

R v MENOCAL [1978] 3 WLR 602 (Court of Appeal: ORR and CUMMING-BRUCE LJJ and WIEN J).

611   —— offer to supply a controlled drug—involvement at a distance

The police saw the second defendant approach a group of people in Piccadilly Circus and heard him ask them if they liked cannabis. When they asked him where they could get some, he took them to the flat of the first defendant. The first defendant pretended not to know the second defendant and went out when they arrived. Both defendants were convicted of being concerned in the making of an offer to supply a controlled drug, in contravention of s. 4 (3) (c) of the Misuse of Drugs Act 1971. The defence contended that, as the first defendant had not known of the offer made at Piccadilly Circus he could not be guilty of the offence. On appeal by the first defendant *held*, s. 4 (3) (c) had been widely drawn so as to include people who might be at some distance from the actual making of the offer. The appeal would be dismissed.

R v BLAKE; R v O'CONNOR (1978) Times, 4th May (Court of Appeal: ROSKILL, EVELEIGH LJJ and MICHAEL DAVIES J).

612   —— possession—cannabis

The defendant had been found in possession of cannabis leaves and stalk. He was charged with unlawful possession of controlled drugs, namely (i) cannabis, (ii) cannabis resin and (iii) a cannabinol derivative. He pleaded guilty to possessing cannabis but not guilty to possessing a cannabinol derivative, and that count was left on the file.   His appeal against conviction on the first count was allowed on the ground that the statutory definition of cannabis was restricted to the flowering or fruiting tops of the plant, and the leaf and stalk alone did not fall within the definition.

At a second trial on the count concerning the cannabinol derivative, as a result of the judge's ruling the defendant changed his plea to guilty.   The ruling was upheld on appeal and a point of law of general public importance was certified, namely, whether as the true construction of the Misuse of Drugs Act 1971 a person in possession of cannabis leaves and stalk only may thereby be in possession of a cannabinol derivative naturally contained in those leaves, in contravention of s. 5 (1).   *Held*, the offence of unlawful possession of any controlled drug described in Sch. 2 to the 1971 Act by its scientific name was not established by proof of possession of naturally occurring material of which the described drug was one of the constituents unseparated from the others.   Accordingly possession of cannabis leaves and stalk did not amount to possession of a cannabinol derivative.

DIRECTOR OF PUBLIC PROSECUTIONS v GOODCHILD [1978] 2 All ER 161 (House of Lords: LORD DIPLOCK, VISCOUNT DILHORNE, LORD SALMON, LORD FRASER OF TULLYBELTON and LORD SCARMAN).   Decision of the Court of Appeal sub nom *R v Goodchild (No 2)* [1978] 1 All ER 649, 1977 Halsbury's Abr para. 644 reversed.

Cannabis has been redefined by Criminal Law Act 1977, s. 52.

613   The defendant was found in possession of a quantity of cannabis resin, being the debris of a larger amount of either herbal cannabis or cannabis resin.   The prosecution relied on his possession of the debris as proof of previous possession of a larger quantity of cannabis resin, on a charge under the Misuse of Drugs Act 1971, s. 5 (2).   The Crown Court was not satisfied beyond reasonable doubt that the defendant had previously been in possession of cannabis resin, as specified in the charge, as opposed to herbal cannabis.   However, it dismissed the defendant's appeal against conviction, holding that the variance between the evidence and the charge was not substantial.   On appeal by the defendant, *held*, the appeal would be allowed as the defendant was entitled to have the case proved against him and if the prosecution could not satisfy the court that the substance was cannabis resin, then the court should have quashed the conviction.

MUIR v SMITH (1978) 122 Sol Jo 210 (Queen's Bench Division: LORD WIDGERY CJ, WIEN and KENNETH JONES JJ).

614   The defendant was convicted of possessing and supplying cannabis as he had in his possession the flowering top of the cannabis plant.   Misuse of Drugs Act 1971 s. 37 defined cannabis as the flowering or fruiting top of any cannabis plant from which the resin had not been extracted.   There was resin in the part of the plant in the defendant's possession but it would be very difficult to extract.   The question for the court was whether the plant satisfied the requirement of resin not being extracted.   *Held*, as the part of the plant in the defendant's possession contained resin he was rightly convicted.   It was immaterial that the resin was difficult or impossible to extract.

R v MALCOLM (1978) Times, 6th May (Court of Appeal: LORD WIDGERY CJ, CROOM-JOHNSON and STOCKER JJ).

Cannabis has been redefined by Criminal Law Act 1977, s. 52

615   —— —— —— **quantity so small as to be unusable**

The appellant was convicted of unlawful possession of cannabis resin under the Misuse of Drugs Act 1971, s. 5 (2).   He appealed on the grounds that the quantities of the drug, two milligrammes in all, were so minute that they could be equated with nothing and that since the mischief that the Act was aimed at was the use of dangerous drugs, possession of a quantity too small to be used ought to be ignored.   *Held*, while the de minimis maxim ought not to be relied on, the quantities of the drug found were too minute to amount to anything and were unusable in any manner which the 1971 Act intended to prohibit.   There was no evidence which justified the appellant's conviction because he was not demonstrated in law and on the evidence to have been "in unlawful possession of cannabis resin". The appeal would be allowed and the conviction quashed.

R v CARVER [1978] QB 472, [1978] 3 All ER 60 (Court of Appeal: LORD WIDGERY CJ, MICHAEL DAVIES and DRAKE JJ). *Bocking v Roberts* [1974] QB 307 explained.

616   —— **production—agreement to produce controlled drug**

See *DPP v Nock and Alsford*, para. 598.

617   **Defence—automatism—insanity—dissociative state due to psychological blow**

See *R v Rabey*, para. 586.

618   —— —— —— **mental state between the two**

See *R v Isitt*, para. 587.

619   —— **availability on appeal of defence not raised below**

Singapore

During a fight, the defendant hit his opponent with an exhaust pipe. The opponent died and the defendant was convicted of murder by two judges sitting together without a jury. He appealed, contending that on the evidence adduced at the trial, the defence of "sudden fight", which had not been raised at the trial and the burden of proving which was on the defendant, was available to him and should have been considered by the trial judges. *Held*, although a judge sitting without a jury to try a charge of murder did not have to refer to every possible defence, where the burden of proving the defence lay on the defendant and the defence was not raised below, as here, justice required that consideration should be given to whether there was sufficient evidence on which a reasonable tribunal could have found that the defence was made out. In this case, the defendant could not have established the defence in any event and there was no need for the trial judges to have referred to it in their judgment. The appeal would be dismissed.

KUNJO v PUBLIC PROSECUTOR [1978] 1 All ER 1209 (Privy Council: LORD ELWYN-JONES LC, LORD MORRIS OF BORTH-Y-GEST, LORD DIPLOCK, LORD FRASER OF TULLYBELTON and LORD SCARMAN).

620   **Electricity—abstraction—unauthorised connection of supply by consumer—whether consumer acting dishonestly**

Having failed to pay his electricity bill, the consumer's supply was disconnected by the Electricity Board. He reconnected the supply without the Board's authority although he informed them of his intention and ensured that his consumption would be accurately recorded. He was acquitted of dishonestly using electricity without due authority in contravention of the Theft Act 1968, s. 13. On appeal by the prosecution, *held*, the fact that the consumer knew he did not have the Board's authority did not of itself make his conduct dishonest. Whether a person acted dishonestly was a question of fact depending on his state of mind at the time of the act. Applying the standard of the ordinary decent man as laid down in *R v Feely* [1973] QB 530, the consumer did not act dishonestly. When he reconnected the supply he genuinely and reasonably believed he would be able to pay his next bill. Furthermore, he believed that by informing the Board of his intention to reconnect and ensuring that his consumption was recorded, he was not acting dishonestly. Accordingly the appeal would be dismissed.

BOGGELN v WILLIAMS [1978] 2 All ER 1061 (Queen's Bench Division: LORD WIDGERY CJ, O'CONNOR and LLOYD JJ). Dicta of Lawton LJ in *R v Feely* [1973] QB 530 at 535, approved.

621   **Employment of minor—illegal employment—liability of employer**

See *Portsea Island Mutual Co-operative Society Ltd v Leyland*, para 1156.

622   Evidence

See CRIMINAL PROCEDURE.

623   False accounting—production of document false in a material particular—false statement not material to accounting purpose

The defendent was convicted under the Theft Act 1968, s. 17 (1) (b), of producing a document made for accounting purposes which was false in a material particular, in that in furnishing information to a finance company he had produced a hire-purchase agreement which was false in that it purported to show that a named person had been a company director of a named company for eight years. He applied for leave to appeal against conviction, contending that the false statement had to be one which was material to an accounting purpose and also that, in any event, there was no evidence that the false statement was a material particular within s. 17 (1) (b). *Held*, under s. 17 (1) (b) the Crown had to show that the defendant dishonestly, with a view to gain for himself or another, or with intent to cause loss to another, in furnishing information for any purpose, produced or made use of any account or record or document which was made or required for any accounting purpose and which to his knowledge was or might be false or misleading in a material particular. There was no need for the material particular to be directly connected with the accounting purpose of the document; it was the document itself that had to be made for the accounting purpose and once that requirement was satisfied, any statement in it which was false in a material particular was sufficient. As to the argument that there was no evidence that a material particular was concerned, although in some cases evidence might be required to show why a hire purchase company wanted a particular piece of information and whether it was material, in this case the judge had directed the jury that a material particular meant "an important matter, a thing which mattered" and on the facts she was well justified in leaving the issue to the jury. The application would be refused.

R v MALLETT [1978] 3 All ER 10 (Court of Appeal: ROSKILL and EVELEIGH LJJ and MICHAEL DAVIES J).

624   Firearms

See FIREARMS.

625   Gross indecency—time limit for commencement of proceedings—evidence

A man was convicted of gross indecency with two others, who both gave evidence against him. However from their evidence it was not clear whether the offence had been committed within the twelve months before the commencement of the proceedings against him, as required by the Sexual Offences Act, 1967, s. 7 (1). He appealed against the conviction. *Held*, allowing the appeal, there was no compliance with s. 7 (1) where the evidence suggested that the offence might have been committed more than twelve months before the commencement of proceedings.

R v LEWIS (1978) Times, 11th November (Court of Appeal: ORR and BROWNE LJJ and PHILLIPS J).

626   Handling stolen goods—knowledge or belief that goods stolen—defendant believing goods stolen—whether goods in fact stolen—judge's direction to jury

The defendant was charged with handling stolen cigarette lighters and made a statement to the police that he had believed them to be stolen. The jury were directed that they could consider this statement in deciding whether the lighters were stolen goods. On the defendant's appeal on the grounds of a misdirection, *held*, the direction amounted to a statement that there was evidence that the lighters had been stolen, and although it would have been better not to refer to the defendant's opinion there had been no misdirection.

R v OVERINGTON [1978] Crim LR 692 (Court of Appeal: SHAW LJ, WATKINS and GIBSON JJ).

627 —— —— **test to be applied**

The defendant's handbag was found to contain jewellery which had been obtained by use of a stolen credit card. The defendant claimed that the jewellery was in a box and she did not know what it was; she said she was keeping it for a friend. In directing the jury as to the ingredient of knowledge at the time of receipt, the judge said that the standard to be applied was an objective one. On appeal against conviction, *held*, the test was a subjective one. Although the defendant's defence was not that she was unaware that the goods were stolen but that she was unaware of what they were, the jury had been misdirected regarding a material consideration on a matter which had to be proved by the prosecution and the appeal would be allowed.

R v STAGG [1978] Crim LR 227 (Court of Appeal: EVELEIGH LJ, CUSACK and WATKINS JJ). *Atwal v Massey* [1971] 3 All ER 881, DC followed.

628 On appeal against a conviction for handling stolen goods it was contended that the jury had been wrongly directed that proof of knowledge or belief would be established if they found that the appellant would have thought it more likely than not that the goods had been stolen. *Held*, there had been two errors in the direction. Firstly the jury should have been left to decide the meaning of belief for themselves. Secondly a belief that goods had probably been stolen was insufficient to justify a conviction. The jury had to be satisfied that the appellant had positively believed that the goods were stolen. The appeal would be allowed.

R v READER (1978) 66 Cr App Rep 33 (Court of Appeal: ORR and WALLER LJJ, MILMO J).

629 **Homicide—causation**

Scotland
A man convicted of culpable homicide when the victim died after a life-support machine had been switched off has had his appeal against conviction rejected. The Court of Criminal Appeal in Edinburgh unanimously held that the switching off of the machine by doctors did not constitute a break in the legal chain: R v FINLAYSON (1978) Times, 21st June.

630 **Illegal immigration**

See IMMIGRATION.

631 **Indecent photographs of children—offences**

See Protection of Children Act 1978, para. 652.

632 **Indictment—aiding and abetting—form of indictment**

See *R v Maxwell*, para. 578.

633 **Insanity—automatism—mental state between two—sufficiency as defence**

See *R v Isitt*, para. 587.

634 **Internationally Protected Persons Act 1978**

See para. 235.

635 **Kidnapping—ingredients of offence—whether carrying victim to intended place necessary**

The appellant approached a young couple on a common and told them that he was a police officer looking for drugs. He asked the boy to leave and said that he would escort the girl home. The girl accompanied the appellant about 100 yards to his car but before he could drive off, the boyfriend returned with friends and asked him for identification, whereupon he drove off. The appellant appealed against his conviction for kidnapping on the grounds that the trial judge had failed to direct the jury that it was necessary to prove that the victim was carried to the place where the kidnapper intended to carry her. *Held*, the essence of the offence was the taking and carrying away from the place where the victim wished to remain. It was unnecessary to prove that the kidnapper carried the victim to a place he intended. All that had to be proved was a deprivation of liberty, coupled with the carrying away from the place where the victim wished to be. The appeal would be dismissed.

R v WELLARD [1978] 3 All ER 161 (Court of Appeal: LAWTON LJ, THESIGER and LAWSON JJ).

636   Mens rea—specific or basic intent—effect of self-induced intoxication

The defendant's son died as a result of burns received when the defendant set fire to his lodgings. The defendant was charged with murder; his defence was that he was so drunk at the time that he was incapable of forming the necessary intent. The trial judge directed the jury that where the prosecution had to prove the defendant's intention or reckless state of mind, it was a defence to prove that the defendant was so affected by alcohol that he was incapable of forming that intention or of reaching that state of mind. The defendant was convicted of manslaughter based on the unlawful act of setting fire to the property of another. He applied for leave to appeal against conviction on the ground that the direction as to drunkenness was wrong. He contended that the offence of arson or malicious damage was a crime of specific intent, as opposed to a basic intent, in that it required a person to intend to do the damage or to be reckless as to whether the damage was done or not. *Held*, the unlawful act relied on by the trial judge of damaging the building of another by fire involved only a basic intent and thus the defence of drunkenness did not avail at all. The judge's summing-up was more favourable than necessary, and there were no grounds for interfering with the conviction.

R v O'DRISCOLL (1977) 65 Cr App Rep 50 (Court of Appeal: LORD WIDGERY CJ, WALLER LJ and ACKNER J). *DPP v Majewski* [1977] AC 443, HL, 1976 Halsbury's Abr para. 625 applied.

637   Murder—intent—malice aforethought

The two defendants, who were drunk, asked a man in the street for a light for a cigarette. He was unable to oblige, whereupon one of the defendants battered him to death while the other kept watch. The jury was directed that it was sufficient for a murder conviction that a man had an intention either to kill or to cause some really serious injury. On appeal against the direction, *held*, the direction was correct. The appeal would be dismissed.

R v ELLERTON [1978] Crim LR 166 (Court of Appeal: LAWTON LJ, SWANWICK and WIEN JJ). *R v Vickers* [1957] 2 All ER 741, CCA, followed.

638   —— provocation—defendant of tender years—reasonable man test

On appeal by the Director of Public Prosecutions against the substitution of a conviction of manslaughter for one of murder the Court of Appeal certified the following as involving a point of law of general public importance: whether on the prosecution of a boy of fifteen for murder, where the issue of provocation arises under the Homicide Act 1957, s. 3 the jury should be directed to consider whether the provocation was enough to make a reasonable man do as he did by reference to a reasonable adult or by reference to a reasonable boy of fifteen. *Held*, the reasonable man referred to was a person having the power of self control to be expected of an ordinary person of the sex and age of the accused but in other respects sharing such of the accused's characteristics as the jury thought would affect the gravity of the provocation to him. The question for the jury was not merely whether such a person would in like circumstances have been provoked to lose his self-control but would also have reacted to the provocation as the accused did.

DIRECTOR OF PUBLIC PROSECUTIONS V CAMPLIN [1978] 2 All ER 168 (House of Lords: LORD DIPLOCK, LORD MORRIS OF BORTH-Y-GEST, LORD SIMON OF GLAISDALE, LORD FRASER OF TULLYBELTON and LORD SCARMAN). Decision of Court of Appeal, sub nom. *R v Camplin* [1977] 3 WLR 929, 1977 Halsbury's Abr para. 700 affirmed. *Mancini v Director of Public Prosecutions* [1942] AC 1; *Holmes v Director of Public Prosecutions* [1946] AC 588 explained. *Bedder v Director of Public Prosecutions* [1954] 2 All ER 801 not followed.

639   Obscene   publications—defence—public   good—meaning   of learning

Obscene Publications Act 1959, s. 4 (1) provides a defence to a charge of publishing an obscene article that publication is for the public good as being in the interests of learning. On a reference by the Attorney-General of questions as to the meaning of learning and the admissibility of expert evidence called to establish a defence under s. 4, *held* (i) the meaning of learning was a product of scholarship. The argument that it meant teaching, education in its broadest sense was incorrect. (ii) It was imperative for a trial judge to instruct the jury that evidence called under s. 4 was not admissible on the issue whether the article was obscene or not under s. 1.

A-G's REFERENCE (No. 3 of 1977) [1978] 3 All ER 1166 (Court of Appeal: LORD WIDGERY CJ, WALLER LJ and TUDOR EVANS J). Dictum of Lord Wilberforce in *R v Jordan* [1977] AC 699 at 718–718, 1976 Halsbury's Abr para. 645 applied.

640   Obtaining a pecuniary advantage by deception—deferment of debt—false representation in hire purchase agreement

The defendant, under a false name, agreed to buy a car from motor dealers on hire purchase. After he had taken possession of the car, the dealers negotiated the hire purchase transaction with a finance company. Later, the defendant signed an agreement in the false name with the finance company undertaking to pay monthly instalments to it. However, after the first instalment, he defaulted and continued to use the car for over a year without payment. He was convicted of contravening the Theft Act 1968, ss. 15, 16 and he appealed. *Held,* (i) s. 15 dealt with the dishonest obtaining of property by deception. The prosecution had failed to prove that the dealers, who had parted with possession of the car before the hire purchase transaction, had been dishonestly led to do so by the defendant giving a false name. From the evidence, it appeared that the dealers would have acted in the same way if he had used his own name. The conviction under s. 15 would therefore be quashed. (ii) Section 16 was concerned with the dishonest obtaining of a pecuniary advantage by deception. The question was whether the defendant had obtained deferment of his debt by his false representations to the finance company. He had never made himself liable for a debt, which he deferred or evaded, by making the false representation because he had entered into the hire purchase transaction after gaining possession of the car. There was no reason to hold that by the fraud he obtained deferment of the debt. Thus the conviction under s. 16 would also be quashed and the appeal allowed.

R V CLOW (1978) Times, 9th August (Court of Appeal: ROSKILL LJ, ACKNER and STOCKER JJ).

From 20th October 1978 the Theft Act 1968, s. 16 (2) (a) is replaced by the Theft Act 1978, see para. 667.

641   —— evading a debt—deposit and rent payable in advance under tenancy agreement

The defendant signed a tenancy agreement to commence on the next day, which provided for a weekly rental payable monthly in advance and also for a returnable deposit. The defendant wrote out a cheque for one month's rent and the deposit and moved in the next day. He subsequently stopped the cheque; at that time there was no money in his bank account. He was convicted of obtaining a pecuniary advantage, namely the evasion of a debt, by deception, contrary to the Theft Act 1968, s. 16. He appealed, contending that both the returnable deposit and the rent in advance were unlawful payments under the Rent Act 1968 and could not constitute debts within s. 16. *Held*, the payment of the returnable deposit was not a premium within the Rent Act 1968, s. 92 (1). It was not a fine or "any other pecuniary consideration in addition to rent" as it was not part of the consideration for the grant of the tenancy but merely a deposit against damage and breakages. It could not therefore be an unlawful premium within the Rent Act 1968, 58 (1). As to the payment of rent, the defendant contended that it was void under the Rent Act 1968, s. 91 (1) because it was payable before the beginning of the rental period. He contended alternatively that the rental period was one week and even though it might have been lawful for one week's rent to be paid in advance, to ask for four weeks' rent was unlawful. Under the agreement, the rental period was clearly four weeks, and to hold that the payment of the rent the day before a tenancy was due to begin was void would be artificial. Thus there was no breach of requirements of the Rent Act and the obligations were debts to which the defendant had made himself liable. The appeal would be dismissed.

R v EWING (1976) 65 CR App Rep 4 (Court of Appeal: STEPHENSON and SHAW LJJ and LAWSON J).

Rent Act 1968, ss. 85 (1), 91 (1), 92 (1) now consolidated in Rent Act 1977, ss. 119, 126 (1), (2), 128, 152 (1).

Theft Act 1968, s. 16, replaced from 20th October 1978 by Theft Act 1978.

642   Obtaining property by deception—acceptance of rent by trespasser

See *R v Edwards*, para. 2891.

643   —— false name—causation

See *R v Clow*, para. 640.

644   Official Secrets Act—proposed changes

The government has published its proposals for replacing the Official Secrets Act 1911, s. 2, by legislation which would apply criminal sanctions to a more limited area of information: Reform of Section 2 of the Official Secrets Act 1911, HMSO, Cmnd. 7285.

645   Perjury—deliberate lying to court by solicitor

See *Re A Solicitor*, para. 2738.

646   Perverting the course of justice—attempt—assisting police suspect to avoid arrest—degree of knowledge required

The applicants had been convicted of the common law offence of attempting to pervert the course of public justice. According to the facts proved they had found themselves under observation by police in unmarked cars, and had given the registration numbers of the cars to another by way of assisting him to avoid arrest for robberies of which the police suspected him. During the trial they had successfully made a submission of no case to answer to charges under the Criminal Law Act 1967, s. 4 (1) of having impeded the apprehension of an arrestable offender, knowing or believing him to be guilty of an offence. They sought leave to appeal against conviction, on the ground that the withdrawal of the statutory charge implied that they neither knew nor believed the suspect to be guilty of any offence of which he was suspected, and that such lack of knowledge precluded a conviction for the common law offence. *Held*, it had been conclusively established that the fact of an unsuccessful prosecution under s. 4 (1) was irrelevant to a conviction for the common law offence. In the latter case it was sufficient to prove the doing of an act calculated to assist another to avoid arrest in the knowledge that that person was wanted by the police as a suspect. Since the facts clearly disclosed the offence and the jury had been given the proper directions, the applications would be refused.

R v Thomas; R v Ferguson [1979] 2 WLR 144 (Court of Appeal: Lord Widgery CJ, Bridge LJ and Wien J). *R v Bailey* [1956] NI 15 and *R v Britton* [1973] RTR 502, CA applied.

647   **Prevention of terrorism—temporary provisions—continuance**

The Prevention of Terrorism (Temporary Provisions) Act 1976 (Continuance) Order 1978, S.I. 1978 No. 487 (in force on 25th March 1978), continued in force the temporary provisions of the Prevention of Terrorism (Temporary Provisions) Act 1976, 1976 Halsbury's Abr para. 662, for a period of twelve months from 25th March 1978.

648   **Procedure**

See CRIMINAL PROCEDURE.

649   **Procuring execution of valuable securities by deception—evidence—adequacy**

See *R v Agbim*, para. 723.

650   **Prosecution of offences**

The Prosecution of Offences (Amendment) Regulations 1978, S.I. 1978 No. 1846 (in force on 1st January 1979), amend the Prosecution of Offences Regulations by deleting reg. 6 (1) (g) which required the full reporting by chief officers of police of offences involving obscene exhibitions and publications.

651   **Prostitution—living on earnings of prostitute—presumption—burden of proof**

The defendant had been seen frequently in the company of a prostitute, and evidence showed that he must have known that she was a prostitute. He was charged with living on the earnings of prostitution, and the judge directed the jury that the fact that the defendant was seen often in the prostitute's company gave rise to a conclusion that he was living on her earnings, under the Sexual Offences Act 1956, s. 30 (2). The judge did not differentiate between the burdens of proof on the prosecution and the defence; that the prosecution had to prove beyond reasonable doubt that the defendant was habitually in the company of a prostitute and then that the burden of proving on a balance of probabilities that he was not living on the earnings of prostitution lay on the defendant. On appeal against conviction, *held*, the essence of the case was that the defendant denied any association with the prostitute in circumstances in which he could properly be said to be living on her earnings, and it was open to the jury to reject that total denial. The judge had failed to explain the difference between the two burdens of proof, but applying the proviso, the appeal would be dismissed.

R v Bell [1978] Crim LR 233 (Court of Appeal: Lord Widgery CJ, Melford Stevenson and Lloyd JJ).

652   **Protection of Children Act 1978**

The Protection of Children Act 1978, which received the royal assent on 20th July 1978 and came into force on 20th August 1978, prevents the exploitation of children by their use in the production of indecent photographs and penalises the distribution, showing and advertising of such indecent photographs.

It is an offence for anyone to take or permit the taking of an indecent photograph of a child under the age of sixteen; or to distribute or show such indecent photographs or to possess them with a view to their being distributed or shown; or to publish or cause to be published any advertisement likely to convey that the advertiser distributes or shows such photographs or intends to do so: s. 1 (1). A person who parts with possession of an indecent photograph or who exposes or offers it for acquisition by another is to be regarded as distributing it: s. 1 (2). Proceedings may only be brought by or with the consent of the Director of Public Prosecutions: s. 1 (3). On a charge of distributing or showing indecent photographs or possessing them for such a purpose it is a defence for the accused to prove that he had a legitimate reason for so doing or that he had not seen the photographs and did not know nor have any cause to suspect them to be indecent: s. 1 (4). On a charge of taking or permitting the taking of indecent photographs of a child under the age of sixteen the husband or wife of the accused is a competent but not compellable witness: s. 2. Where a corporation is guilty of an offence under the Act and it is proved that the offence occurred with the consent or connivance of, or was due to the neglect of a director, manager, secretary or other officer of the corporation, that officer is also deemed to be guilty of the offence and is liable to be proceeded against: s. 3.

Powers of entry and search of premises, stalls and vehicles and of seizure and removal of articles are conferred by s. 4. Provisions as to orders for forfeiture and appeals against such orders are contained in s. 5.

Conviction on indictment is punishable by a fine or imprisonment for a maximum term of three years or both. Summary conviction is punishable by a maximum fine of £1,000 or imprisonment for a maximum term of six months or both: s. 6. Section 7 contains definitions. Section 8 relates to Northern Ireland. Section 9 contains formal provisions.

653 Public order—public place—front garden of house

The defendants fell into argument by the front door of a house which was one of several in a terrace. The houses each had small front gardens divided from the neighbouring gardens and the street by a low wall. The words used in the argument were clearly audible across the street. The defendants were convicted of using threatening, abusive or insulting words or behaviour in a public place with intent to provoke a breach of the peace or whereby a breach of the peace was likely to be caused contrary to the Public Order Act 1936, s. 5. On appeal that the garden was not a public place, *held*, the fact that members of the public had access to the garden to cross it to the front door on lawful business, did not make it a public place within the meaning of s. 5. It did not matter that the words had been audible across the street; where the person using the words and the person to whom they were addressed were in a private place, it was not possible for the offence to have been committed.

R v EDWARDS; R v ROBERTS (1978) 122 Sol Jo 177 (Court of Appeal: BRIDGE LJ, MICHAEL DAVIES and GIBSON JJ).

654 —— threatening behaviour—use of actual force—whether use of threatening behaviour appropriate charge—whether jury misdirected

The defendant was involved in a fight. He was subsequently charged with using threatening behaviour and also with assaulting a policeman who had attempted to break up the fight. He was convicted on the first count but not the second. He appealed, contending that he should have been charged with affray rather than use of threatening behaviour. He further contended that the judge in his summing up had wrongly failed to follow the prosecution's division of the case into acts prior to the alleged assault and the alleged assault itself. *Held*, (i) the fact that the defendant could have been charged with affray did not mean that he could not be charged with using threatening behaviour if evidence of threats existed, as it did here. (ii) The judge was not bound to follow the prosecution's analysis of a case. It was therefore incumbent upon the defendant to show that the verdict was unsafe. This he had not done and his conviction would accordingly stand.

R v OAKWELL [1978] 1 All ER 1223 (Court of Appeal: LORD WIDGERY CJ, MAIS and BOREHAM JJ).

655   Rape—cross-examination—character of complainant

On a conviction for rape, the defendant appealed on the grounds that the trial judge had refused to allow a cross-examination of the complainant concerning her previous sexual experiences. *Held*, there was a distinction to be made between a cross-examination designed to blacken the complainant's character and one which was designed to test the trustworthiness of her evidence. The latter kind only was permissible but only if the judge was satisfied that it would have been unfair to the accused to refuse to allow the cross-examination. The trial judge had exercised his discretion according to those principles and the decision would not be interfered with. The appeal would be dismissed.

R v MILLS (1978) Times, 21st November (Court of Appeal: ROSKILL LJ, LAWSON and NEILL JJ).

656   Rehabilitation of offenders—spent conviction—admissibility as evidence

See *Reynolds v Phoenix Assurance Co Ltd*, para. 726.

657   Road traffic offences

See ROAD TRAFFIC.

658   Sentencing

See SENTENCING.

659   Sexual offences—soliciting by a man—girls under sixteen years old—whether soliciting immoral

The appellant drove his car slowly past three fourteen-year-old girls inviting them to have sexual intercourse with him. He was convicted of persistently soliciting for an immoral purpose under the Sexual Offences Act 1956, s. 32. He appealed on the ground that the act of "kerb crawling" was not immoral. *Held*, although there might be instances where kerb crawling was not immoral, as where the woman was a prostitute, the fact that the girls in this case were only fourteen rendered the appellant's act not only immoral but also criminal, because sexual intercourse with a girl under the age of sixteen would have been an offence under the 1956 Act, s. 6 (1).

R v DODD (1978) 66 Cr App Rep 87 (Court of Appeal: GEOFFREY LANE LJ, CUSACK and CROOM-JOHNSON JJ). *Crook v Edmondson* [1966] 2 QB 81, DC distinguished.

660   Sexual Offences (Amendment) Act 1976—commencement

The Sexual Offences (Amendment) Act 1976 (Commencement) Order 1978, S.I. 1978 No. 485, brought into force on 22nd April 1978 the remaining provisions of the Sexual Offences (Amendment) Act 1976, 1976 Halsbury's Abr para. 678, being ss. 5 (1) (b) and 6 (4) (b), which restrict the publication or broadcasting in Northern Ireland of any matter likely to lead to the identification of the complainant or the accused in rape cases tried by court-martial.

661   Shipbuilding—breach of safety regulations

See *Lindsay v Vickers*, para. 1457.

662   Taking conveyance without authority—taking of horse—whether horse a conveyance

The respondent took three horses from a field and attached ropes as bridles. He was charged under Theft Act 1968, s. 12 with taking a conveyance and adapting it for the carriage of a person. The justices dismissed the informations on the ground that a horse was not a conveyance. On appeal, *held*, a horse was not a conveyance either in the ordinary meaning of the word or in the meaning in the statute, which seemed to be limited to machines. Bridling a horse did not adapt it for the carriage of a person within the section; it merely made it easier to ride.

NEAL v GRIBBLE [1978] RTR 409 (Queen's Bench Division: LORD WIDGERY CJ, CROOM-JOHNSON and STOCKER JJ).

663   Theft—attempted theft—necessity for proof of intention

The defendants were seen by police officers tampering with the rear door of a van. As the police officers approached, they ran off. Inside the van was a holdall containing valuable equipment. The defendants were charged with attempted theft. Their defence was that they were just curious. The judge in his summing up directed the jury that it was sufficient that the defendants were intending to look into the holdall and, if its contents were valuable, to steal it. The first defendant appealed against conviction on the ground that this was a misdirection. *Held*, the direction was wrong. It could not be said that one who had in mind to steal only if what he found was worth stealing had a present intention to steal.

R v HUSSEIN [1978] Crim LR 219 (Court of Appeal: VISCOUNT DILHORNE, LORD SCARMAN and CUSACK J). *R v Easom* [1971] 2 QB 315, CA applied.

664

The defendant entered a parked car without the owners' consent and was examining the contents when he was arrested and charged with the attempted theft of specified articles in the car. The defendant contended that he was not guilty as he was only looking to see if anything in the car was worth stealing. The trial judge did not direct the jury that the absence of an intention to steal the specified items was a defence to the charge, and the defendant was convicted. On appeal, *held*, if the defendant's intention to steal the specified items could not be proved, then the offence had not been committed. The jury had not been given an opportunity to consider the defence that the defendant had not intended to steal the specified items and the conviction would be quashed.

R v HECTOR [1978] LS Gaz R 103 (Court of Appeal: LAWTON LJ, SWANWICK and GIBSON JJ). *R v Easom* [1971] 2 QB 315, CA applied.

665   —— goods sold at undervalue—joint enterprise

The defendant, a supermarket cashier, underpriced items bought by a customer whom she knew by ringing up prices lower than those marked. Both the defendant and the customer were convicted of theft. The defendant appealed, contending that she could not be guilty of theft as she had not herself appropriated the property, and since the case fell within the Theft Act 1968, s. 16, in that it was a dishonest obtaining of a pecuniary advantage for another, a conviction for theft was not possible. *Held*, these contentions overlooked the Crown case that it was a joint dishonest enterprise and the act of one party was deemed to be the act of both. The customer had appropriated the goods and such an appropriation would sustain a charge of theft against both parties. The appeal would be dismissed.

R v BHACHU (1976) 65 Cr App Rep 261 (Court of Appeal: LORD WIDGERY CJ, TALBOT and SLYNN JJ).

Theft Act 1968, s. 16, replaced from 20th October 1978 by Theft Act 1978.

666   —— property belonging to another—supermarket goods—in whom ownership vested

A shopper acquired possession of goods in a supermarket from a counter-assistant who had bagged and weighed them. She was supposed then to pay a cashier in a different part of the shop before leaving, but she left without paying. Before justices she contended that ownership of the goods had passed to her with the transfer of possession and that unless it could be shown that she had not intended to pay she could not be convicted of theft. Justices accepted the submission. On the prosecutor's appeal, *held*, it was well-established that the property in goods held in shops was not intended to pass until the price was paid. The justices had come to the wrong conclusion and the case would be remitted for the hearing to continue.

DAVIES V LEIGHTON (1978) 122 Sol Jo 641 (Queen's Bench Division: LORD WIDGERY CJ, TALBOT and ACKNER JJ). *Lacis v Cashmarts* [1969] 2 QB 400 applied; *Edwards v Ddin* [1976] 3 All ER 705, 1976 Halsbury's Abr para. 682 distinguished.

667   **Theft Act 1978**

The Theft Act 1978 received the royal assent on 20th July 1978 and came into force on 20th October 1978. The Act replaces s. 16 (2) (a) of the Theft Act 1968 and implements the recommendations in the Criminal Law Revision Committee's Thirteenth Report on Section 16 of the Theft Act 1968 (Cmnd. 6733). It is an offence to obtain services by deception: s. 1 (1). This extends to situations where a person is induced to confer a benefit by doing or permitting some act on the understanding that the benefit has been or will be paid for: s. 1 (2). It is an offence dishonestly to secure the remission of, or intentionally make a permanent default in, any existing liability to make payment; or dishonestly to induce a creditor to wait for payment or to forgo it; or dishonestly to obtain any exemption from or abatement of such liability: s. 2 (1). "Liability" means legally enforceable liability: s. 2 (2). For the purposes of s. 2 (1), a creditor induced to take a cheque or other security by way of satisfaction of a liability is to be treated as being induced to wait for payment: s. 2 (3). "Obtains" includes obtaining for another or enabling another to obtain. It is an offence to make off without paying for any goods supplied or services rendered knowing that payment on the spot is expected: s. 3 (1). "Payment on the spot" includes payment at the time of collecting goods on which work has been done or in respect of which a service has been provided: s. 3 (2). Section 3 (1) does not apply where the supply of goods or services is unlawful or where payment is not legally enforceable: s. 3 (3). Any person may arrest without a warrant anyone whom he reasonably suspects to be making off without payment: s. 3 (4). All the offences under the Act are triable either on indictment or summarily; penalties are specified: s. 4. Supplementary and formal provisions are contained in ss. 5–7.

CRIMINAL PROCEDURE

Halsbury's Laws of England (4th edn.), Vol. 11, paras. 89–480, 611–810

668   **Articles**

Character and Antecedents, Billy Strachan (interpretation of character and antecedents and circumstances in which they should be taken into account when considering mode of trial): 122 Sol Jo 407.

Conditional Discharge: Recent Clarifications, A. N. Khan (clarification of legal issues in relation to an order for conditional discharge in the light of *R v Wehner* [1977] 1 WLR 1143, 1977 Halsbury's Abr para. 2503): 122 Sol Jo 447.

Corroboration and Self-Corroboration, Dr. A. J. Ashworth: 142 JP Jo 266.

Diminished Responsibility: the Jury's Function (review of the authorities relating to the function of the jury where there is evidence of diminished responsibility): 122 Sol Jo 427.

Fingerprinting—Some Aspects of Law and Practice, John Warner (consideration of the legal principles involved in fingerprinting): 128 NLJ 639.

The Fisher Report and the Judges' Rules, Phillip A. Thomas and Penny Smith (the right of persons in custody to communicate with a solicitor): 128 NLJ 548.

Identification Parades, James Morton (practical guidelines for solicitors taking suspects to identitication parades) 128 NLJ 526.

Judicial Warning in Identification Cases, A. N. Khan (consideration of the problems arising in identification cases): 122 Sol Jo 377.

The New Procedure for Selecting Mode of Trial (procedure for determining the mode of trial, either on indictment or summarily, in the light of the Criminal Law Act 1977): 142 JP Jo 381.

Preserving the Good Face of Justice: Some Recent Plea Bargain Cases, John Baldwin and Michael McConville: 128 NLJ 872.

Prosecutions: Procedural Errors or Errors of Substance, Billy Strachan (whether prosecutor can reopen his case when there has been an error in the proceedings): 122 Sol Jo 783.

Refreshing Memory, Michael Newark and Alec Samuels (conditions under which a witness should be allowed to refer to notes): [1978] Crim LR 408.

Restitution Orders, A. N. Khan (explanation of the relevant law of restitution): 122 Sol Jo 424.

Spouse Bashing—Wife not a Compellable Witness Against her Husband, J. Kodwo Bentil (examination of judicial authority on whether or not wife can be compelled to give evidence against her husband): 142 JP Jo 704.

The Use of Photographs for the Purpose of Identification, D. F. Libling: [1978] Crim LR 343.

669   Appeal—appeal against finding of contempt in criminal proceedings

See *R v Tibbits*, para. 470.

670   —— appeal against sentence—discretion of trial judge to see counsel privately—evidence

The appellant, who represented himself, was accused of several offences including living on the earnings of prostitution. During the trial a solicitor from whom he was taking advice asked to see the judge to obtain his views on the possible sentence. The judge agreed to see both the solicitor and counsel for the prosecution. During the interview he asked the prosecution counsel for an account of the sentences imposed in similar cases. Later in the trial when the judge was considering the sentence the police officer who was giving the appellant's antecedents introduced into evidence a document containing detailed information about police inquiries into his activities. The officer did not have personal knowledge about this information but had obtained it from his colleagues. The appellant had no chance to read the document before sentence was passed. On appeal against the sentence, *held*, the occasions when a judge could agree to see counsel in private were very limited, and even more limited were the occasions when he should agree to see prosecution counsel and a solicitor giving advice to a man who was representing himself. In such an interview the judge should not ask the advice of prosecution counsel as to a possible sentence, as was done here. Nor should any statement of antecedents of the kind given here have been admitted in evidence unless the police officer concerned could answer questions on it from his own personal knowledge. This was particularly important where the accused was conducting his own defence and had had no opportunity to read the document. The sentence would be varied.

R v WILKINS (1978) 66 Cr App Rep 49 (Court of Appeal: GEOFFREY LANE LJ, MACKENNA and CUSACK JJ).

671   —— appeal to House of Lords—costs—petition for leave to appeal

See *Procedure Direction*, para. 2193.

672   —— irregularity at trial—expert defence witness

Singapore

Under Singapore law the offence of trafficking in more than 30 grammes of morphine carries a mandatory death sentence. At the trial of a defendant for this offence the government chemist testified that the substance the defendant was carrying contained 46 gm of morphine. The defence chemist had not completed his analysis before the defence cross-examined the government chemist, nor before the defence chemist was himself called to give evidence. After he had been cross-examined, the defence applied for an adjournment until he had completed his analysis. The application was refused and the defendant convicted. On appeal *held*, although at first sight it might appear wrong to deny to the defendant an opportunity of presenting the results of a quantitative analysis by his own expert witness on consideration of the detailed evidence the refusal was justified. By the time the adjournment was asked for there was no basis for suggesting that any relevant evidence could become available as a result of the defence chemist's analysis. It was common ground that by the method of analysis used the margin of error was two per cent. It had never been suggested to the government chemist in cross-examination or by the defence chemist that an error of thirty-six per cent was within the bounds of possibility. Only an error of that order would have reduced the quantity of morphine below the critical figure of 30 grammes.

TEO HOOK SENG v PUBLIC PROSECUTOR [1978] LS Gaz R 343 (Privy Council: LORD DIPLOCK, LORD FRASER OF TULLYBELTON and LORD RUSSELL OF KILLOWEN).

673   —— leave to appeal—application out of time

The defendant's appeal against sentence was refused. While still unaware of this refusal, he absconded from police custody. The reason for his absconding was that his wife had to go to hospital for treatment for a suspected malignant disease. Notification of the refusal was sent to the defendant in prison and, when no renewal notice was received from him, a further notice was sent to the same address to the effect that the refusal was final. When the defendant was recaptured five months later he applied for extension of time to renew his application for leave to appeal. *Held*, the sole reason why he had not received the notification and why he had not been able to renew his application in time was that he had absconded. The circumstances did not justify his absconding and the appeal would be dismissed.

R v MARSHALL [1978] Crim LR 424 (Court of Appeal: BRIDGE LJ, MICHAEL DAVIES and GIBSON JJ).

674   —— reference by Home Secretary—fresh evidence

The defendants were convicted of burglary and robbery on the basis of the evidence of a scientific officer. He had expressed his conclusion at the trial that a shoe found at the house the defendants had occupied on the night of the robbery was the shoe which had made a mark in the soil found near the scene of the crime. The defendants' application for leave to appeal was refused. Subsequently fresh evidence was discovered. One of the witness's colleagues at the forensic science laboratory revealed that he had told the witness that the mark was only consistent with having been made by the shoe, and had not necessarily been made by it. Secondly, another scientific expert had subsequently examined the evidence and concluded that the shoe could have made the mark but could not be uniquely connected with it. The case was referred to the Court of Appeal by the Secretary of State under the Criminal Appeal Act 1968, s. 17 (1) (a). *Held*, the new evidence removed the foundation of the prosecution's case that the mark was made by the shoe. The appeal would be allowed and the conviction quashed.

R v MORGAN, BROWN and COWLEY (1978) Times, 9th June (Court of Appeal: LORD WIDGERY CJ, EVELEIGH LJ and WATKINS J).

675   —— rules

The Criminal Appeal (Amendment) Rules 1978, S.I. 1978 No. 1118 (in force on 2nd October 1978), amend the Criminal Appeal Rules 1968 in consequence of the Bail Act 1976, which came into force on 17th April 1978. In particular, the manner in which records of bail decisions are to be made under the 1976 Act, s. 5, is prescribed.

676   —— verdict unsafe or unsatisfactory—inconsistent verdicts

The defendant acquired a pistol during an evening spent at a social club. He became drunk and when the club closed he fired several shots at a car which was being driven away from the club. He was charged with possessing a firearm and ammunition without a certificate and with having a firearm in a public place. The jury were directed that lawful authority or reasonable excuse would be a defence to either charge. They acquitted him of the possession charge but not of the charge of having a firearm in a public place. He appealed on the ground that the verdicts on the two counts were inconsistent. *Held*, the fact that a jury had returned inconsistent verdicts was not in itself a ground for appeal. Inconsistent verdicts tended to show that a jury had been confused and therefore the verdicts might be considered unsafe, but here the jury could have reached their verdicts without confusion. They could have considered it unreasonable that the defendant should bring the pistol out in a public place but reasonable that he should not have a certificate because he had only acquired the pistol that evening. Although the verdicts had been inconsistent, the inconsistency did not go to the root of the conviction.

R v DAWES [1978] Crim LR 503 (Court of Appeal: LORD WIDGERY CJ, SHAW LJ and LLOYD J).

677 ——— **wrong decision in law—discretion of trial judge to order retrial**

During the defendant's trial for handling stolen goods his counsel unsuccessfully applied for a retrial on the ground that the prosecution had failed to disclose that it was a co-defendant who had informed the police that the stolen property was hidden in the defendant's premises. The defendant applied for leave to appeal against conviction on a purported point of law, namely that the judge should have ordered a retrial. *Held*, the question was not one of law but one of the judge's discretion and of alleged material irregularity in the prosecution not revealing the co-defendant's part as an informer, which were mixed questions of fact and law. There was no obligation on the prosecution to reveal their line of attack on the credibility of a defence witness. The application would be refused.

R v MADGE [1978] Crim LR 305 (Court of Appeal: EVELEIGH LJ and JUPP J).

678 **Arrest—arrest with warrant—warrant not in police officer's possession—arrest in civil matter**

A police officer purported to arrest the defendant on the strength of a warrant for non-payment of fines which was at the police station half a mile away. The defendant resisted arrest and was convicted of assaulting the officer in the execution of his duty. He appealed, contending that the officer was not acting in the execution of his duty, the arrest being unlawful because he did not have the warrant in his possession. *Held*, where a person was arrested on a warrant otherwise than for a criminal offence, as here, it was essential for the arresting officer to have the warrant in his possession, as the person arrested could then obtain his release by paying the sum stated on the warrant. In this case the officer clearly did not have the warrant in his possession; he merely believed it to be at the police station. The Magistrates' Courts Act 1952, s. 102 (4), which provided that a warrant to arrest a person charged with an offence could be executed notwithstanding that it was not in the police officer's possession at the time, applied only to criminal proceedings. The conviction would be quashed.

DE COSTA SMALL v KIRKPATRICK (1978) Times, 24th October (Queen's Bench Division: LORD WIDGERY CJ, WIEN AND SMITH JJ). *R v Purdy* [1975] QB 288, CA, 1974 Halsbury's Abr para. 830 applied.

679 ——— **arrest without warrant—common law power—breach of the peace committed or reasonably apprehended**

A police officer attempted to take a ring which he believed to be stolen property from a jeweller's shop without giving a receipt. The shop owner's brother refused to hand over the ring without a receipt and was arrested for wilfully obstructing a constable in the execution of his duty by the officer, who had no warrant. He contended that the arrest was unlawful. *Held*, the offence charged was not an arrestable offence under the Criminal Law Act 1967, s. 2. Any power of arrest therefore had to arise at common law, where it was only in cases when a breach of the peace had been committed or was reasonably apprehended that a police officer might arrest without a warrant. Thus an officer might only arrest without a warrant anyone who wilfully obstructed him in the execution of his duty if the nature of that obstruction was such that it actually caused or was likely to cause a breach of the peace, or was calculated to prevent the lawful arrest or detention of another. Whether the factual situation was such as to entitle a police officer to exercise this power had to be answered from the point of view of what the officer honestly believed on reasonable grounds. In this case there was no likelihood of a breach of the peace and the arrest was unlawful.

WERSHOF V METROPOLITAN POLICE COMMISSIONER [1978] 3 All ER 540 (Queen's Bench Division: MAY J).

680   —— use of force—justifiable homicide

See *R v Coroner for Durham County, ex parte Attorney General*, para. 527.

681   —— validity of arrest—defendant already under arrest for another offence

See *R v Hatton*, para. 2333.

682   **Bail—Crown Court rules**

The Crown Court (Amendment) Rules 1978, S.I. 1978 No. 439 (in force on 17th April 1978), amend the Crown Court Rules 1971 as a result of the Bail Act 1976, 1976 Halsbury's Abr para. 552. In particular, they prescribe the manner in which records of bail decisions are to be made and provide for seven days' notice to be given before a recognisance is estreated.

683   —— failure to surrender to bail—methods of punishing offence

The defendant failed to surrender to bail on the second day of his trial at Crown Court. The judge dealt with the matter summarily and, on the defendant admitting the offence of absconding from bail under the Bail Act 1976, s. 6, sentenced him to three months' imprisonment. He appealed against sentence on the grounds that he had not committed a contempt in the face of the court and the judge had neither the right nor the power to deal with the matter summarily. *Held*, the effect of s. 6 was to create a new offence, punishable in one of two ways: either as a summary offence triable only in a magistrates' court but with additional power to commit for sentence to the Crown Court; or as if it were a criminal contempt of court. The purpose of the section was to create swift and simple alternative remedies, and accordingly the trial judge had acted properly in dealing with the matter himself. However, the sentence was excessive and would be reduced to one month.

R v SINGH [1979] 2 WLR 100 (Court of Appeal: ROSKILL LJ, ACKNER and STOCKER JJ).

684   —— magistrates' courts rules

See paras 1843, 1844.

685   **Caution—cautioning of person taking part in affray—admissibility as evidence of statement made without caution**

See *R v Halford*, para. 710.

686   **Committal order—power of Crown Court to make order**

See *Rooney v Snaresbrook Crown Court*, para. 468.

687   **Committal proceedings—joinder without consent of defend-ants—power of magistrate to insist on concurrent committal proceedings**

See *R v Camberwell Green Justices, ex parte Christie*, para. 1829.

688   —— jurisdiction of justices

See MAGISTRATES.

689   Costs—appeal to House of Lords—petition for leave to appeal

See *Procedure Direction*, para. 2193.

690   —— order against convicted person—Crown Court—whether court required to limit costs payable

When considering the question of costs ordered against an offender, LAWTON LJ has stated that the rule of practice requiring the order to be for a fixed sum not exceeding a stated sum did not apply in all cases. The Costs in Criminal Cases Act 1973, s. 4 (1) provided that where a person was convicted on trial at the Crown Court, the court had the power to order him to pay the whole of the costs incurred in the prosecution. There was no reason why a rule of practice should amend statutory provisions and it was clearly a discretionary matter having regard to the means of the convicted person.

R v MOUNTAIN; R v KILMINSTER (1978) Times, 3rd May (Court of Appeal).

691   The appellant pleaded not guilty to a charge of driving with a blood-alcohol concentration above the prescribed limit. The case was adjourned owing to the illness of the police officer concerned. The appellant was then told that he was being charged with driving while unfit through drink to which he pleaded guilty. On his conviction he was fined, disqualified from driving for two years and ordered to pay the prosecution costs. On appeal, *held*, the fine and disqualification were fair in the circumstances, but the costs of both parties had been increased by the necessity for an adjournment. In such a case it would be proper to place an upper limit on the order for costs. The costs would be reduced accordingly.

R v NEWLOVE (1978) 66 Cr App Rep 1 (Court of Appeal: GEOFFREY LANE LJ, THESIGER and MICHAEL DAVIS JJ).

692   —— —— whether court required to limit costs payable

When an offender is ordered to pay costs, either the sum payable or the upper limit should be fixed.

R v SMITH (1978) Times, 12th April (Court of Appeal: LORD WIDGERY CJ, EVELEIGH LJ and DRAKE J). *R v Hier* (1976) 62 Cr App R 233, CA, 1976 Halsbury's Abr para. 564 applied.

693   Criminal Law Act 1977—commencement

The Criminal Law Act 1977 (Commencement No. 5) Order 1978, S.I. 1978 No. 712, brought s. 62 of the 1977 Act into force on 19th June 1978. Sections 14–26, 27–32 (except s. 31 (1), in force on 8th Sept. 1977), 34–37, 41, 42, 45, 46, 58, 61, 64 and Schs. 1–5, 8, 12 (insofar as not already in force) and 13 (part) came into force on 17th July 1978.

For 1977 Act, see 1977 Halsbury's Abr para. 635.

694   Crown Court—appeal by case stated

See para. 557.

695   —— distribution of business—classification of offences

See *Practice Direction*, para. 560.

696   Director of Public Prosecutions—powers—estoppel

See *Turner v Director of Public Prosecutions*, para. 738.

697 Evidence—character—character of accused

The appellant and another man had a heated discussion, which resulted in the appellant assaulting the other man. In cross examination it was submitted that the other man had been drinking heavily and had also been swearing. He claimed that these were imputations of bad character and made an application for permission to disclose the appellant's past record of assaults. The trial judge ruled that the requirements of the Criminal Evidence Act 1898 had been satisfied and allowed the application. On appeal *held*, saying that a man was drunk or swearing on a particular occasion did not amount to the sort of imputations of character upon which the Act was based. As there had been a fundamental mistake in the conduct of the proceedings, the appeal would be allowed.

R v McLean [1978] Crim LR 430 (Court of Appeal: Lord Widgery CJ, Shaw LJ and Lloyd J).

698

The defendant, who had been accused of threatening a man who owed him money, stated at the trial that his only previous conviction was for a driving offence. Counsel for the prosecution was permitted to cross-examine him about a previous charge of assault occasioning actual bodily harm, but this evidence was not referred to in the summing up for the jury. The defendant appealed against his conviction on the ground that the evidence had been inadmissible. *Held*, only where a defendant had expressly denied that he had been charged with another offence would cross-examination be permitted. In this case the jury might well have been prejudiced and therefore the conviction would be quashed.

R v Meehan and Meehan [1978] Crim LR 690 (Court of Appeal: Bridge LJ, Michael Davies and Jupp JJ).

699 —— —— —— trial judge's exercise of discretion

On the appellant's appeal against conviction for theft, it was conceded that his defence had involved imputations on the character of witnesses for the prosecution, but he submitted that the trial judge had been wrong in admitting evidence under the Criminal Evidence Act 1898 of two offences which he had committed subsequently but for which he had already been convicted. He contended that the trial judge should have exercised his discretion to exclude the evidence on the ground that its prejudicial effect outweighed any evidential value. *Held*, it was clear that in allowing evidence of the offences the trial judge had been aware that they had been committed subsequent to the offence being tried. There were no grounds for finding that, in such exercise of his discretion, the trial judge had either erred in principle or had made a decision for which there were no grounds. Therefore, the court was unable to interfere with the use of his discretion, and the appeal would be dismissed.

R v Coltress (1978) Times, 27th October (Court of Appeal: Orr and Browne LJJ and Phillips J). *Selvey v DPP* [1970] AC 304, HL applied.

700 —— child—need for corroboration—discretion of judge

At the defendant's trial for indecent assault on an eleven-year-old boy, evidence on oath was given by the boy, his brother, aged twelve, and another boy, aged sixteen. The defendant appealed against conviction, contending that no direction had been given by the trial judge that before accepting the evidence of the brother and the other boy the jury should look for corroboration because of their youth. *Held*, the case should be distinguished from cases in which several victims spoke of similar sexual assaults by the accused. In this case two boys who were not victims gave evidence. The trial judge was guilty of an omission in not warning the jury of the risk of acting on their uncorroborated evidence as he had done with regard to the evidence given by the victim. It was not possible to state as a general proposition what was the age above which it was unnecessary for the judge to give the warning, that was a matter of discretion for the trial judge. Although there had been an irregularity, there was no possibility of a miscarriage of justice and the appeal would be dismissed.

R v Morgan [1978] 3 All ER 13 (Court of Appeal: Roskill and Eveleigh LJJ and Michael Davies J).

701   —— confession—confession made in return for promise of bail—duty of judge

Following a statement by a police officer that bail would be granted if the accused persons admitted the offence, they conferred and were granted bail. The trial judge admitted the confessions as evidence. At the trial the police officer said that bail would not have been granted had they not confessed. The judge accepted that the statement to the accused was therefore a statement of fact and not an inducement to confess. On an appeal contending that the confessions were wrongly admitted, *held,* the trial judge should have first determined whether the police officer had made such a statement, instead of presuming he had and assuming it to be a statement of fact. The appeal would be allowed.

R v BAMFORD [1978] Crim LR 752 (Court of Appeal: ROSKILL LJ, ACKNER and STOCKER JJ).

702   —— corroboration—diaries of prosecution witness—value in support of oral evidence

A senior policeman appealed against several convictions of corruptly accepting bribes, on the ground that the trial judge had misdirected the jury as to the corroborative nature of certain dairies kept by a leading prosecution witness. The diaries has constantly been referred to during the trial in support of the witness' oral evidence. *Held,* it appeared that the diaries had played a substantial part in securing the appellant's convictions. It was possible that they had a disproportionately large effect on the jury because they had been so much the focus of attention. The real status of the diaries was limited to helping the witness give accurate dates; they did not constitute corroboration of his evidence. The judge's remarks that the diaries were the most important document in the prosecution's evidence and were important in relation to the oral evidence had therefore left the jury with a mistaken impression of their value. The appeal would accordingly be allowed.

R v VIRGO (1978) Times, 16th March (Court of Appeal: GEOFFREY LANE LJ, THOMPSON and BROWN JJ).

703   —— criminal libel—general bad reputation—admissibility at committal proceedings

See *R v Wells Street Justices, ex parte Deakin,* para. 1784.

704   —— documents—privilege—communication to counsel from client

At the defendant's trial for receiving stolen goods, a written communication from him to his counsel fell into the hands of the prosecuting counsel, who made use of it in cross-examination. The defendant appealed against conviction on the ground that the use of the information by the prosecution in breach of the privilege existing between counsel and client amounted to a breach of natural justice rendering the defendant's conviction unsafe and unsatisfactory. *Held,* privilege related only to production of a document, it did not determine its admissibility in evidence. Once the note was in the prosecution's possession it was in evidence. Admissibility depended on the relevance of the document, and the method of obtaining it was irrelevant. Even if the note itself had been inadmissible, counsel was entitled to put questions based on its contents. There was no breach of natural justice and the appeal would be dismissed.

R v TOMKINS [1978] Crim LR 290 (Court of Appeal: ORMROD LJ, THOMPSON and JUPP JJ). *Butler v Board of Trade* [1971] Ch 680, *R v Kuruma* [1955] AC 197 and *R v Rice* [1963] 1 QB 857 applied.

705   —— evidence irregularly obtained

The appellant got in touch with the police and offered to give them information about a theft of £2 million. After he had given them some details they suspected that he was involved in the theft. He was subsequently arrested pending further inquiries. He was held in police custody for five days during which time he was not allowed to communicate with anyone. He then made a written statement in which he confessed to dishonestly handling the stolen money and was charged with that offence. His statement was admitted as evidence at the trial and he was convicted. He appealed against conviction contending that he would not have made the statement but for the strain imposed by his isolation and since it had thus been unfairly obtained it should not have been admitted at his trial. *Held*, confessions which had been obtained in an oppressive manner, by force or by a trick should not be admitted. In the present case there was no evidence that the appellant had been kept in isolation with the object of getting him to crack under the strain. The object in keeping him isolated was to try and find out what had happened to the missing money. Nor was there any evidence that what had occurred had had any bearing on the appellant's decision to make his statement. He was an intelligent man, familiar with police methods and he had neither asked for nor been denied the advice of a solicitor. The appeal would be dismissed.

The Court stated that it was seriously concerned about the irregularities which had occurred and stressed the fact that police officers had no power to arrest anyone to enable inquiries to be made save under provisions concerned with the prevention of terrorism. It was possible that police officers should have such powers but it was for Parliament to decide.

R v HOUGHTON (1978) Times, 23rd June (Court of Appeal: LAWTON LJ, THESEIGER and LAWSON JJ).

The Criminal Law Act 1977, s. 62 now gives an arrested person the right to have someone informed of his arrest.

706   ——— ——— fingerprints taken illegally

Canada

At the trial of a juvenile the prosecution attempted to use in evidence finger prints taken from the boy. The trial judge refused to admit the evidence on the ground that it had been illegally obtained and the boy was acquitted. The prosecution suceeded in obtaining a retrial on the ground that the evidence had not been illegally obtained or, if it had, that it was admissible. On appeal *held*, although the taking of the fingerprints had been illegal, such evidence was admissible if any issue in the case was affected by it. It was immaterial that the fingerprints had been obtained in such a way that the administration of justice might be brought into question.

R v A.N. (1978) 83 DLR (3d) 370 (Court of Appeal of British Columbia).

707   ——— evidence obtained without search warrant—dangerous drugs

See *Walsh v MacPhail*, para. 609.

708   ——— evidence of spouse—whether spouse compellable witness

The appellant was convicted of wounding a woman with intent to do grievous bodily harm. Before the opening of the trial he and the woman were married. She was unwilling to give evidence against the appellant at the trial but was held to be a compellable witness. The appellant's appeal against conviction was dismissed but the Court of Appeal certified as a point of law of general public importance the question "whether a wife is a compellable witness against her husband in a case of violence on her by him". *Held*, LORD EDMUND-DAVIES dissenting, it was a fundamental principle of English law that a wife could not be compelled to give evidence against her husband. If this rule was to be changed it was for Parliament to do so.

LORD EDMUND-DAVIES considered that it was in the public interest that evidence of crime should be freely available to the court particularly where the spouse was the only person who could give such evidence. He did not accept that it had to be left to Parliament to decide whether spouses subjected to violence were to become compellable witnesses but considered that it was open to the House to state that such was already the law.

The appeal would be allowed and the conviction quashed.

METROPOLITAN POLICE COMMISSIONER v HOSKYN (1978) 142 JP 291 (House of

Lords: LORD WILBERFORCE, VISCOUNT DILHORNE, LORD SALMON, LORD EDMUND-
DAVIES and LORD KEITH OF KINKEL). *Leach v Rex* [1912] AC 305 applied; *R v
Lapworth* [1931] 1 KB 117 CCA overruled.

709   —— evidence probative of defendant's guilt—late introduction of
evidence

At the defendant's trial, after the close of the prosecution case, evidence of a
conversation between the defendant and the police officer in charge of the case
conducted without a caution was tendered during the cross-examination of the
defendant by counsel for the prosecution. The evidence was based on a record made
later by the officer, and the defence had no prior notice. In view of this, the
defendant applied to have the jury discharged. The application was refused, and the
defendant was convicted. On appeal, *held*, in general evidence capable of forming
part of the affirmative case for the prosecution should be tendered and led in the
course of that case. If it did not form part of the evidence upon which the defendant
was committed for trial, notice of it should be given to the defence before it was
tendered, giving the defence an opportunity to raise an objection. In this case, notice
should have been given to the defence, especially since the accuracy of the record had
not been acknowledged by the defendant. There had been a material irregularity
and as it was not a case for the proviso, the appeal would be allowed.

R v KANE (1977) 65 Cr App Rep 270 (Court of Appeal: SCARMAN and SHAW LJJ
and NIELD J).

710   —— evidence relating to defendant's credit—late introduction of
evidence

Uncautioned statements made by a man subsequently convicted of unlawful fighting
and making an affray were introduced in court by the prosecution after the close of
their case to test his credit. In seeking leave to appeal against conviction the defence
claimed the statements were introduced too late for them to be countered effectively
and that therefore there had either been a material procedural error or the jury's
verdict was unsafe. *Held*, all evidence which the prosecution considered probative
of a defendant's guilt had to be adduced before the end of the prosecution case if it
was available but that did not extend to non-probative evidence relating only to a
defendant's credit. The defence could not argue that prejudice had resulted from use
of the evidence and even if the use were wrong, which the court was not prepared
to say, no trace of injustice had resulted.

An alternative suggestion that cautions should have been given before the
statements used as evidence were made was wrong. It was impracticable for the
police to have to consider whether they had evidence against a person and therefore
had to give a caution, every time they wanted to speak to a person following an
affray.

R v HALFORD (1978) Times, 12th April (Court of Appeal: LORD WIDGERY CJ,
EVELEIGH LJ and DRAKE J). *R v Rice* [1963] 1 QB 857, CCA applied.

711   —— expert evidence—comparison of handwriting—standard of
proof

The defendant was convicted of assault with intent to rob, after tricking a woman
into allowing him on to her premises by representing himself as a postman. He was
carrying a parcel, which he left at the premises after the incident. The prosecution
sought to rely on a comparison by an expert witness of the writing on the parcel
with that found in the defendant's room and on his person after his arrest. The
appeal was brought on the ground that the documents found in the defendant's room
and on his person were not admissible evidence, as there was not sufficient proof that
they were written by him. The judge at first instance had ruled them admissible by
virtue of the Criminal Procedure Act 1865, s. 8; the defence claimed that they were
not admissible because the standard of proof required by s. 8 was proof beyond
reasonable doubt, not the civil standard of proof. *Held*, the decision of the judge at

first instance was correct. It was sufficient if the judge was satisfied that the writing was genuine. He was not required to be sure beyond reasonable doubt.

R v ANGELI [1978] 3 All ER 950 (Court of Appeal: BRIDGE LJ, THOMPSON and EASTHAM JJ).

712   —— fresh evidence after conviction—reference to Court of Appeal by Home Secretary—credibility of proposed alibi evidence

See *R v McMahon*, para. 748.

713   —— —— —— fresh scientific evidence

See *R v Morgan, Brown and Cowley*, para. 674.

714   —— identification

The Home Office has issued new rules for the conduct of identification parades together with administrative guidance, a form of notice to be given to the suspect before the parade, and forms for recording various aspects of the identification parade.   New rules have also been issued on the use of photographs for identification together with administrative guidance and a form to serve as a record of the use of photographs.   The Identification Parade Rules and the Use of Photographs for Identification Rules are now contained in separate codes.

The rules have been issued after consultation with the Lord Chief Justice and failure to observe their provisions may result in the judge commenting on the reliability of the evidence so obtained in the course of his summing up.   Home Office circular 9/1969 (which is superseded) has been cancelled: Home Office circular 109/1978 (HMSO).

715   —— —— proper approach for the court

The defendant was convicted of an offence on the basis of police identification and other circumstantial evidence.   In his summing up, the judge did not give the jury any warning as to the need for caution in cases where identification was in issue. The defendant appealed against his conviction.   *Held*, the judge had failed to direct the jury in accordance with the guidelines set out in *R v Turnbull* [1976] 3 All ER 549, 1976 Halsbury's Abr para. 601, concerning the need for caution when faced with identification evidence which was disputed.   In the present case, even though other evidence against the defendant might have been circumstantially strong irrespective of police evidence of identification, the jury should have been warned about the need for caution over the identification evidence.   It could not be said that that evidence had not affected the jury's decision.   Accordingly, the conviction would be quashed and the appeal allowed.

R v RAPHAEL (1978) Times, 13th October (Court of Appeal: LORD WIDGERY CJ, EVELEIGH LJ and SMITH J).

716   —— —— identification by finger-prints—justices' power to order finger-printing

The defendant who was charged with unlawfully damaging a car refused to allow the police to take his finger-prints for comparison with those on the car.   Under the Magistrates' Courts Act 1952, s. 40 justices may order the finger-printing of any person in custody who is not less than fourteen.   The defendant argued that finger-print evidence was so convincing it amounted to an oral or written confession and the justices had improperly exercised their discretion since a defendant could not be compelled by law to make a confession.   *Held*, the justices had properly exercised their discretion.   The conditions of s. 40 were satisfied and in such a case the justices had power to order finger-printing whenever they thought fit.

GEORGE v COOMBE [1978] Crim LR 47 (Queen's Bench Division: LORD WIDGERY CJ, TALBOT and BOREHAM JJ).

717   ———— identification by police officers—proper approach for the court

The defendant was convicted of conspiracy to possess and supply morphine on the identification evidence of police officers who had posed as buyers and claimed to have met the defendant in a public house together with his co-defendants, who were also convicted. After his arrest, some of the police officers had seen a photograph of the defendant before they picked him out at an identification parade. In his summing-up, the judge did not point out to the jury the dangers of relying on identification evidence, nor did he point out that the police officers might have identified the defendant at the identification parade from the photograph. The defendant appealed on the ground of misdirection by the judge. *Held*, the judge had omitted to direct the jury in accordance with the guidelines set out in *R v Turnbull* [1976] 3 All ER 549, CA, 1976 Halsbury's Abr para. 601, concerning the need for caution when faced with identification evidence. The fact that such warnings were not given adequately amounted to a misdirection. The court was not convinced that had the jury been correctly directed they would inevitably have come to the same conclusion and the conviction would be quashed.

R v HUNJAN (1978) Times, 13th June (Court of Appeal: GEOFFREY LANE LJ, MILMO and CANTLEY JJ).

718   ———— identification of assailant by victim—proper approach for the court

In a case where the issue turned on the identification of an assailant by his victim, the court said that it would be wrong to interpret or apply the guidelines laid down in *R v Turnbull* [1976] 3 All ER 549, CA, 1976 Halsbury's Abr para. 601, inflexibly. What that case did was to formulate a basic principle and sound practice. The principle was the special need for caution when the issue turned on the evidence of visual identification, and the practice was a careful summing-up, which not only contained a warning, but also exposed to the jury the weaknesses and dangers of identification evidence, both in general and in the circumstances of the particular case.

R v KEANE (1977) 65 Cr App Rep 247 (Court of Appeal: SCARMAN and BRIDGE LJJ and DONALDSON J).

719   ———— —— whether part of res gestae

When a car had to brake suddenly, the following car collided with it. The Crown case was that the defendant, the passenger in the following car, got out and assaulted the driver of the first car. When the police arrived soon afterwards, the driver told them that the defendant had hit him. The defendant was charged with assault. At the trial, the driver's identification of the defendant as his assailant to the police was admitted as part of the res gestae. The defendant appealed on the ground that the evidence was wrongly admitted. *Held*, it was difficult to imagine a more spontaneous identification. There was no opportunity for concoction and no chance of error. The evidence of identification was properly admitted and the appeal would be dismissed.

R v NYE AND LOAN [1978] Crim LR 94 (Court of Appeal: LAWTON LJ, PARK and MICHAEL DAVIES JJ). *R v Ratten* [1972] AC 378, PC applied.

720   ——— inadmissible statement—statement produced to test truth of defendant's evidence—duty of judge to warn jury of nature of statement

A defendant's statement was ruled inadmissible by the judge. When the defendant was giving evidence, his counsel examined him, not about the content of the statement, but about the circumstances in which it had come to be made. The judge then ordered that the statement be produced to the court, not as proof of its content, but as a test of the truth of the defendant's evidence. No warning was given that no weight should be attached to the evidence in the statement against the defendant's two co-accused, because of the hearsay rule. On appeal against conviction, *held*, although the judge had not been wrong to admit the statement, he should have warned the defendant's own counsel at a much earlier stage of the dangers of introducing in examination evidence of the making of a statement which had already been ruled inadmissible. The verdicts of all three men were unsatisfactory and the appeals would be allowed.

R v YOUNG AND ROBINSON [1978] Crim LR 163 (Court of Appeal: LAWTON LJ, MACKENNA and GIBSON JJ). *R v Treacy* [1944] 2 All ER 229, CCA, not applied.

721 —— **previous convictions—cross-examination about previous convictions—whether two separate defendants charged with same offence**

Two men were accused of assaulting each other. One was acquitted, the other convicted. The latter appealed, contending that as they had both been charged with the same offence the former should have been open to cross-examination about his previous convictions for violence. *Held*, it was stretching the concept of the same offence beyond its possible limits to construe two people charged with separate assaults as being charged with the same offence. The two men were in no sense co-defendants and accordingly the appeal would be dismissed.

R v LAUCHLIN (NOTE) (1976) [1978] RTR 326 (Court of Appeal: SHAW LJ, THESIGER and TALBOT JJ).

722 As a result of a collision between vehicles driven by the appellant and another man a pedestrian was killed. The two were both charged in successive counts in the same indictment with causing death by dangerous driving. During the trial, the appellant gave evidence against the other accused. A previous conviction of the appellant for dangerous driving was then admitted in evidence on the ground that he had given evidence against a person charged with the "same offence" within the Criminal Evidence Act 1898, s. 1 (f) (iii). The appellant appealed against conviction, contending that he and the other accused were not charged with the "same offence" since the the actus reus of the offence with which each was charged was different. *Held*, the appellant had driven too fast and not kept a proper lookout, while the other accused had turned into the path of an oncoming vehicle. For the offences charged to be regarded as the same, they had to be the same in all material respects, including the time at which the offence was alleged to have been committed, and a distinct and separate offence similar in all material respects to an offence committed later, no matter how short the interval between the two, could not properly be regarded as the "same offence". The counts in the indictment did not charge offences the same in all respects. The appeal would be allowed and the conviction quashed on the ground that there was a material irregularity in allowing the cross-examination of the appellant as to his character.

The court considered that the law in the matter was unsatisfactory and evidence as to character should be admissible wherever two accused were jointly tried and one gave evidence against the other, even though they were not charged with the same offence.

METROPOLITAN POLICE COMR v HILLS [1978] 2 All ER 1105 (House of Lords: LORD DIPLOCK, VISCOUNT DILHORNE, LORD SALMON, LORD RUSSELL OF KILLOWEN and LORD KEITH OF KINKEL). Decision of Court of Appeal (1978) Times, 2nd March, reversed. *R v Russell* [1971] 1 QB 151, CA overruled.

723 —— **proof of commission of offence—whether jury must agree that charge proved by same piece of evidence**

A doctor was charged under the Theft Act 1968, s. 20 (2), with procuring the execution of a valuable security by deception. It was contended that he had obtained cheques from the local area health authority by submitting claims for expenses to which he was entitled containing false statements of the gross pay received by staff employed by him. There were six counts and the prosecution led a mass of evidence to prove its case. He was convicted and appealed, contending that the judge had failed to direct the jury that they could not find that any one of the claim forms had not been a true or correct statement unless they were all agreed that the same piece of evidence proved falsity. *Held*, a jury had to consider whether on the evidence the charge had been made out. Each juror did not have to take the same view about the details of the evidence; they simply had to agree that the prosecution had proved the charge. The jury in this case had agreed and there was no reason to quash the verdict. The judge had not misdirected them and the appeal would be dismissed.

R v AGBIM (1978) Times, 24th October (Court of Appeal: LAWTON LJ, LAWSON and BOREHAM JJ).

724   —— similar facts

Following a series of thefts from a golf club changing room, police set a trap with a marked £1 note. The defendant was found with the marked note in his pocket. The prosecution obtained leave to call evidence of the other similar thefts to show the reason for setting the trap, but did not suggest that they were relevant to proving the case against the defendant. The trial judge, in his summing-up, referred to the evidence of the other thefts, but failed to warn the jury to disregard it so far as the defendant's guilt or innocence of the offence charged was concerned. On appeal against conviction, *held*, the judge should have explained precisely the limits of the evidence relating to previous thefts and its relevance. However, the jury would have come to the same conclusion if they had been properly directed, and so applying the proviso the appeal would be dismissed.

R v LARGE [1978] Crim LR 222 (Court of Appeal: GEOFFREY LANE LJ, MILMO and WATKINS JJ).

725   At the defendant's trial for rape, the prosecution sought to call three witnesses; the first was a woman who claimed also to have been raped by the defendant, and the second and third were women who claimed to have been accosted by the defendant. The evidence of all three witnesses was admitted under the similar fact rule. The first woman had failed to identify the defendant at an identification parade and had wrongly described his car to the police. She claimed to have identified the car in the police yard, and identified the defendant in the dock. The trial judge did not remind the jury of the discrepancy in the evidence about the car, nor did he warn them of the dangers of dock identification. On appeal against conviction, *held*, regarding the evidence of the second and third witnesses, it was not permissible to call evidence to show that a man had a propensity towards a particular type of crime; in this case approaching strange women and trying to get them into his car for the purpose of sexual intercourse. As to the evidence of the first witness, although the manner in which she had been raped bore a striking resemblance to this case, and was prima facie admissible, the only link was the unsatisfactory identification of the car, and the trial judge had failed to warn the jury of the dangers of dock identification. In view of these matters, the verdict was unsatisfactory and the appeal would be allowed.

R v TRICOGLUS (1976) 65 Cr App Rep 16 (Court of Appeal: LAWTON and WALLER LJJ and GRIFFITHS J).

726   —— spent conviction—admissibility

In 1972 the plaintiffs insured a building owned by them and in 1973 it was burnt down. The insurers disputed the amount claimed. The trial of the claim was postponed when the insurers discovered that one of the plaintiffs had been accused of conspiracy to defraud. The accused plaintiff was tried; he was found not guilty, but at the trial it was revealed that in 1961 he had been convicted of an offence and fined. The insurers then took the point that his conviction should have been disclosed when the policy was taken out, and sought to avoid the policy on the ground of non-disclosure. The trial judge refused to allow them to re-amend their defence to plead this, and the insurers appealed. *Held*, under the Rehabilitation of Offenders Act 1974, s. 4, once the rehabilitation period, of five years in this case, had elapsed, a conviction was spent. However, a judicial authority had power under the 1974 Act, s. 7 (3), to admit evidence of a spent conviction if justice could not be done in the case except by doing so. In this case, there would be no prejudice to the plaintiffs in allowing the amendment and as a matter of justice it ought to be allowed; the issue would then be brought before the Court and the judge could hear evidence as to whether the conviction was a material matter without evidence of which justice could not be done, as required by s. 7 (3). The appeal would be allowed.

REYNOLDS V PHOENIX ASSURANCE CO LTD (1978) 122 Sol Jo 161 (Court of Appeal: LORD DENNING MR, SHAW and WALLER JJ).

727   —— statement of co-accused prejudicial to accused

Three men were taken into custody. One of them, who pleaded guilty at the trial, made a statement damaging to the third defendant. During the interrogation that statement was read to the third defendant. The statement was admitted at the trial in order to show the third defendant's reaction to it. He appealed against conviction on the ground that it was wrongly admitted. *Held*, the statement was technically admissible but its prejudicial value far outweighed its probative value and for the jury to put it out of their minds would involve great difficulty. The verdict was unsatisfactory and as it was not a case for the proviso, the appeal would be allowed.

R v TAYLOR [1978] Crim LR 92 (Court of Appeal: LORD WIDGERY CJ, CANTLEY and PETER PAIN JJ). *R v Christie* [1914] AC 545, HL applied.

728   —— —— statement from dock

In the course of the trial of two men on charges of burglary and murder one of the co-accused made a statement prejudicial to the other. On appeal by the latter against his conviction, *held*, the trial judge had been correct to direct the jury that the statement was not to be regarded as evidence against the appellant because the co-accused could not have been cross-examined. In this respect statements from the dock were to be treated in the same way as statements made by a co-accused out of court.

R v GEORGE (1978) Times, 31st October (Court of Appeal: LORD WIDGERY CJ, BRIDGE LJ and WIEN J).

729   —— tape recording—re-recording

Canada

On a charge of conspiracy to extort money by deception and threats, the prosecution introduced tape recorded evidence which was in fact a re-recording of significant conversations from original tapes which had been destroyed. The tapes had been destroyed and the re-recording made by the police for the purpose of coping with the storage problem of a large number of tapes accumulated over a period, and for the purpose of re-use of those tapes. At the time of the re-recording it had not been police practice to use tape recorded evidence in court. *Held*, the original tapes had been destroyed in good faith. The "best evidence" rule therefore applied to permit the secondary re-recorded evidence to be given.

R v SWARTZ (1977) 37 CCC (2d) 409 (Court of Appeal of Ontario).

730   —— trade or business records—meaning of record

The defendants were charged with conspiracy to steal goods. One of the containers involved was short of the declared cargo when it arrived in England from Hong Kong. The Crown produced the bill of lading as evidence of the amount of cargo originally loaded. The defendants claimed that the bill of lading did not have a sufficient degree of permanence to be "a record relating to any trade or business" within the meaning of s. 1 (1) of the Criminal Evidence Act 1965. *Held*, a "record" did not have to be a permanent document, but was sufficient so long as it recorded the details of the transaction in issue, and was permanent for whatever period was commercially necessary. The operation of s. 1 (1) was not restricted to documents which had been compiled in this country. The bill of lading was a record within the meaning of the section and was therefore admissible as evidence.

R v JONES; R v SULLIVAN [1978] 2 All ER 718 (Court of Appeal: GEOFFREY LANE LJ, SWANWICK and WIEN JJ).

731   —— —— whether National Health Service hospital a business

The appellant was arrested for burglary and confessed to the police. He subsequently alleged that the police had used violence to obtain the confession and that his injuries had been examined in a National Health Service hospital. The prosecution successfully applied to have the hospital records admitted as evidence under the Criminal Evidence Act 1965 to support their contention that the appellant had not been injured by the police. Under the Act, a document is not admissible unless it is a record which relates to a trade or business; s. 1 (4) of the Act provides that business includes any public transport, public utility or similar undertaking carried on by a local authority and the Post Office. The appellant claimed that the records were not admissible as the hospital was not a "business". *Held*, business did not have a wide meaning under the Act. If the Act had intended to make government records in general admissible, it would not have enlarged the meaning of business in s. 1 (4) by including certain bodies only. Moreover, it was implicit that "business" had a commercial connotation; the main purpose of a National Health Service hospital could not be called commercial and therefore it was not a business within the meaning of the Act. The records were not admissible as they contained hearsay evidence and the Act did not apply. The appeal would be allowed.

R v CRAYDEN (1978) [1975] 2 All ER 700 (Court of Appeal: LAWTON LJ, SWANWICK and GIBSON JJ).

732   —— trial on several separate counts—admissibility of evidence of other alleged offences at trial of first count

A customs officer was charged with five offences of permitting airline stewardesses to unload duty free goods from aircraft. He refused to allow the charges to be heard together. At the hearing of the first case the prosecution sought to introduce evidence of the other charges to support their argument. The justices refused to admit the evidence and adjourned the case, so the prosecution applied for a judicial review of the refusal. *Held*, the prosecution should not have applied for a review because the first case had not been concluded and thus there were no facts on which a decision could be based. The trial should have been continued and if the prosecution had failed they should have appealed by way of case stated.

R v ROCHFORD JJ EX PARTE BUCK [1978] Crim LR 492 (Queen's Bench Division: LORD WIDGERY CJ, CROOM-JOHNSON and STOCKER JJ).

733   —— witness—power of judge to call witness

Although the judge in a criminal trial has the power to call a witness, ROSKILL LJ has stated that this power should be sparingly and rarely exercised. The decision as to who should be called to give evidence was primarily for prosecuting counsel: it was wrong for a trial judge to insist on calling a witness whom the prosecution was reluctant to call.

R v BALDWIN (1978) Times, 3rd May (Court of Appeal).

734   Indictment—amendment—court's power to amend

Canada

The defendant was charged with conspiracy to traffic in a restricted drug, trafficking in a restricted drug and having in his possession a restricted drug. He was acquitted on the first and third counts and his appeal against conviction on the second count was allowed on the ground that the substance in his possession was not the drug itself but a salt of it, trafficking in which constituted a separate offence which had not been charged in the indictment. The Crown appealed against the acquittal on the third count and the court amended the indictment to include possession of a salt of the drug. The defendant appealed against conviction, contending that the court had no power to amend the indictment to conform with the evidence. *Held*, the amendment did not charge a new offence, as it was no more than a particularisation of an ingredient of the main charge which was made necessary by the evidence which the court had already accepted. The defendant was not misled, as he knew that he was being charged with possession of a restricted drug for the purpose of trafficking. The appeal would be dismissed.

ELLIOTT v R (No. 2) [1978] 1 WWR 481 (Supreme Court of Canada).

For the appeal against conviction on the second count, see [1976] 4 WWR 285, 1976 Halsbury's Abr para. 576.

735   —— conviction of offence other than offence on indictment—validity

See *R v McCready; R v Hurd*, para. 758; *R v Nicholls*, para. 759.

736   —— form—effect of failure to comply with Indictment Rules

The defendant was charged with possessing an offensive weapon. The statement of offence in respect of that count in the indictment failed to state the statute which the defendant was alleged to have contravened, in breach of the Indictment Rules 1971. The trial judge refused to allow an amendment to the indictment. The defendant appealed against conviction, contending that the defect made the trial a nullity. *Held*, the indictment was not a nullity, as it could have been amended by the trial judge; it was merely defective. The Court of Appeal had no jurisdiction on appeal to amend the indictment, but it had power to consider a case where there had been a defect in the indictment because there had been a failure to comply with the Indictment Rules. As the summing-up was defective in relation to the count in question, the verdict was unsatisfactory and the conviction in respect of it would be quashed.

R v NELSON (1977) 65 Cr App Rep 119 (Court of Appeal: LAWTON LJ, MACKENNA and GIBSON JJ). *R v McVitie* [1960] 2 QB 483, CCA applied.

737   Institution of proceedings—criminal damage by wife—proceedings instituted by husband—whether consent of Director of Public Prosecutions required

A wife was granted a non-molestation order against her husband. Subsequently, the husband instituted proceedings against her alleging criminal damage to his property. The justices held that they had no jurisdiction to hear the case because, under Theft Act 1968, s. 30 (4), the institution of such proceedings between married couples required the consent of the Director of Public Prosecutions. The husband appealed on the ground that s. 30 (4) (a) (ii) of the Act provided that the Director's consent was not required where spouses were, by judicial order, no longer obliged to cohabit. *Held*, as the couple were no longer under an obligation to cohabit by virtue of the non-molestation order against the husband, the wife could not be protected by s. 30 (4) of the Theft Act against the institution of criminal proceedings by her husband. The case would be remitted to the justices for hearing.

WOODLEY v WOODLEY [1978] Crim LR 629 (Queen's Bench Division: LORD WIDGERY CJ, BOREHAM and DRAKE JJ).

738   —— private prosecution—undertaking by Director of Public Prosecutions that offender would not be prosecuted—effect

At a trial for robbery, the Director of Public Prosecutions decided in the public interest to call one of the participants as a witness for the prosecution rather than prosecute him for the offence. He was given a formal undertaking that he would not be prosecuted for the offences disclosed by his statements. The defendant in the case was convicted. Subsequently he launched a private prosecution of the witness in respect of the robbery. The DPP, considering that it was not in the interests of justice or the public for the prosecution to continue, intervened in pursuance of his powers under the Prosecution of Offences Acts 1879 and 1908 with a view to offering no evidence against the witness. The initiator of the private prosecution brought an action against the DPP, contending that he was acting unlawfully in the matter in that his proposed intervention in the conduct of the prosecution in order merely to offer no evidence and quash it was unlawful and ultra vires; that he was estopped from the proposed course of action by virtue of his statement to the jury at the original trial that it was open to any private individual to prosecute the witness; and that his purported exercise of a statutory power was void for bad faith. The DPP applied for the summons to be struck out as disclosing no reasonable cause of action and being vexatious and an abuse of the process of the court. *Held*, having regard to the wide powers conferred on the DPP by the Prosecution of Offences Acts and Regulations, it was impossible to argue that it was unlawful or ultra vires for him to intervene for the purpose of offering no evidence. As to estoppel, the DPP's statement was not a statement of fact but a correct statement of law, so far as it went, and could not found a plea of estoppel. Moreover, estoppel could not be raised to prevent the exercise of a statutory discretion, or excuse the performance of a statutory duty. The DPP had not acted in bad faith but in the public interest. The statement of claim would be struck out.

TURNER v DIRECTOR OF PUBLIC PROSECUTIONS (1978) Times, 8th August (Queen's Bench Division: MARS-JONES J).

739   —— undertaking by Director of Public Presecutions that offender would not be prosecuted—application for leave to apply for judicial review of immunity

The Director of Public Prosecutions granted immunity from prosecution in advance to a witness for the Crown in respect of committal proceedings against the defendant. The defendant applied to the Divisional Court for leave to apply for judicial review of the grant of immunity; he contended that the immunity was granted in such wide terms as to give the witness a charter to commit perjury under an unconditional promise of immunity from proceedings, and it would render the oath under which evidence was given nugatory. *Held*, it was for the trial judge, if the defendant were committed for trial, to deal with the question of the immunity in accordance with the law. The application would be refused.

RE THORPE (1978) Times, 17th November (Queen's Bench Division: LORD WIDGERY CJ, GRIFFITHS and GIBSON JJ).

740   Judges' Rules

The Judges' Rules have been reissued. The rules set out in Appendix A of the Home Office circular are identical to the rules issued in 1964. Appendix B contains the related administrative directions to the police which have been revised to take into account Home Office circulars issued since 1964. Administrative direction 4 (interviewing, fingerprinting and photographing children and young persons) has been revised to make it clear that it relates to all persons under 17 years. Administrative direction 7 (a) has been revised to make it clear that the sending of telegrams and letters by persons in police custody should be subject to the same provision as telephone communications to the person's solicitors and friends. A new administrative direction 4A incorporates guidance on the need for special care in the interrogation of mentally handicapped persons (formerly Home Office circular 109/1976). Appendix C of the new circular sets out arrangements for obtaining competent interpreters where police enquiries involve questioning a deaf person.

The Judges' Rules and Administrative Directions to the police (Home Office circular 89/1978) HMSO.

741   Judgment—variation of sentence or other order made by Crown Court—whether forfeiture order "other order"

See *R v Menocal*, para. 610.

742   Legal aid

See LEGAL AID.

743   **Oaths Act 1978**

The Oaths Act 1978 consolidates provisions relating to oaths and affirmations; see further para. 1283.

744   **Plea—plea bargaining—indictment charged after counsel informed defendant of judge's advice**

The defendant on a charge of robbery pleaded not guilty but admitted he would plead guilty to a charge of handling. During the trial the judge sent for the defendant's counsel and asked him privately if his client would plead guilty to handling. After both counsel for the defendant and Crown counsel had taken instructions, the judge gave leave to the court to add the charge of handling to the indictment. The defendant pleaded guilty to the charge and was sentenced to three years imprisonment. On appeal against this sentence, *held*, it was not excessive. The court once again drew attention to the undesirability of discussions taking place between counsel and the judge in private during the trial. Whilst this had been done for good reasons in order to shorten the length of the trial, the matter should have been dealt with in open court in the jury's absence.

R v WINTERFLOOD (1978) Times, 21st November (Court of Appeal: ROSKILL LJ, LAWSON and NEILL JJ).

745   —— —— **plea made under pressure**

The defendant was charged with damaging property, having an offensive weapon and assault. He told counsel he intended to plead not guilty. Counsel persuaded the defendant that, because of his mental condition, counsel should see the trial judge to ascertain what sentence he had in mind. The judge agreed with counsel that hospital treatment was needed and told counsel that on a plea of guilty he would consider a probation order or an order binding the defendant over on condition that hospital treatment was undergone. On hearing this the defendant decided to plead guilty. Fresh medical reports on him were then received and the defendant was sentenced to imprisonment. He applied for leave to appeal. *Held*, the judge was in difficulty because at the time he saw counsel he only knew part of the facts. It was clear that the defendant had pleaded guilty on the basis that he would not be sent to prison, in other words under pressure. Leave to appeal would be granted and a venire de novo ordered.

R v RYAN [1978] Crim LR 306 (Court of Appeal: WALLER LJ, TALBOT and MARS-JONES JJ).

746   —— —— **requirements of justice**

The defendant was charged with conspiracy to steal. Before the trial the judge had invited counsel for both sides to discuss the case. The defendant's counsel got the impression that the judge thought the defendant was guilty, and therefore advised his client to plead guilty. During the trial the defendant dismissed his counsel and solicitor and refused to continue with the case contending that, because of the previous discussions, he would not get a fair trial. He was convicted. On appeal *held*, pre-trial discussions were to be discouraged. There was no justification for the discussions to have taken place as they did and although the rest of the trial could not be faulted, justice had not been seen to be done. The conviction would be set aside.

R v LLEWELLYN (1978) Times, 3rd March (Court of Appeal: ROSKILL LJ, CHAPMAN and LAWSON JJ).

747   **Prosecution of offences—functions of Director of Public Prosecutions**

The Prosecution of Offences Regulations 1978, S.I. 1978 No. 1357 (in force on 1st January 1979), provide for the Director of Public Prosecutions to conduct certain criminal proceedings, to advise on criminal matters and to be supplied with information relating to criminal offences by chief officers of police and clerks to justices. The Regulations take into account changes in the law and in the type of case requiring action by the Director of Public Prosecutions by reason of their importance or difficulty. The Prosecution of Offences Regulations 1946 are revoked.

748　Reference by Home Secretary— admissibility of late evidence— statutory duty of Court of Appeal to admit

The Secretary of State referred to the Court of Appeal under the Criminal Appeal Act 1968, s. 17 (1) (b) a point arising in the case of a man convicted of killing a sub-postmaster. The point concerned the credibility of proposed alibi evidence, the specific question requiring an answer being whether, if the evidence of two men who claimed to have seen the accused on the day of the murder were tendered during an appeal arising from a reference under s. 17 (1) (a) of the 1968 Act, the court would consider itself bound by s. 23 (2) to receive it. *Held*, under s. 23 (2), the court was obliged to admit evidence unless it was satisfied the evidence would afford no ground for allowing the appeal. In this case, the evidence tendered was of no value because it did not show the accused to have been at such a distance from the place of the murder that he could not possibly have committed it.

R v McMAHON (1978) Times, 12th April (Court of Appeal: LORD WIDGERY CJ, EVELEIGH LJ and MILMO J).

749　—— appeal—fresh scientific evidence

See *R v Morgan, Brown and Cowley*, para. 674.

750　Seizure of property—powers of police—whether retention of property justified

The plaintiff, who had been charged with conspiracy and with handling stolen property, obtained a mandatory injunction for the return of bank notes which had been seized by the police when they searched his house. The Metropolitan Police Commissioner appealed on two grounds: either that the notes would be required as evidence in the trial; or that even if they were not required as evidence they could be retained for the payment of compensation if the plaintiff was convicted. *Held*, the retention of the notes was justified because it was possible that they would be required as evidence in the trial. If this had not been so there would have been no justification for retaining them because there was no express statutory provision conferring any right to deprive the plaintiff of his property.

MALONE v METROPOLITAN POLICE COMR [1978] 3 WLR 936 (Court of Appeal: STEPHENSON and ROSKILL LJJ).

751　Trial—application by accused to dispense with counsel's services—discretion of trial judge

See *R v Lyons*, para. 233.

752　—— hearing in camera—grounds for hearing——sexual offences involving children

See *R v Warawuk*, para. 565.

753　—— irregularity—non-disclosure of prosecution witnesses—certiorari

See *R v Leyland Justices, ex parte Hawthorn*, para. 763.

754　—— prosecution's right to closing speech—defendants neither giving nor calling evidence

When the two applicants and a co-defendant were tried on a joint charge of robbery, they were represented by counsel. The only evidence given was that of a witness on behalf of the co-defendant whose evidence could have discredited the evidence of the victim that he had been robbed by the three accused. In his closing speech, counsel for the prosecution commented on the case of all three accused, who were subsequently convicted. Application of leave to appeal against conviction was made on the ground that the prosecution should not have been permitted to make a closing speech against the applicants when they had neither given nor called evidence. Also, in the case of one applicant, a second ground of appeal was that the judge had misdirected the jury in stating that the evidence of his good character went to credibility and in the circumstances had little relevance to whether he had committed the offence. *Held*, where a defendant represented by counsel neither gave evidence nor called witnesses, the prosecution had a right to make the closing speech. However, that right should be sparingly exercised and where it was in fact exercised the speech should be brief. Further, that where defendants were jointly indicted for the same offence and evidence was adduced on behalf of only one defendant which affected the case of all defendants, the prosecution was entitled to refer to all the defendants' cases in his closing speech. The first ground of appeal would thus fail. On the second ground of appeal, although evidence of good character went primarily to the issue of credibility, it was also capable of being evidence in the cause. Therefore if the judge conveyed the impression to the jury that good character was only relevant when a defendant gave evidence, there had been a misdirection, but in the circumstances, such a misdirection could not render the verdict unsafe and unsatisfactory. Accordingly, leave to appeal would be refused.

R v BRYANT [1978] 2 All ER 689 (Court of Appeal: GEOFFREY LANE LJ, MILMO and WATKINS JJ). *R v Gardner* [1899] 1 QB 150 applied.

755 —— **summing up—duty of judge to follow distinction drawn by prosecution**

See *R v Oakwell*, para. 654.

756 —— —— **judge's comments on police evidence**

A police officer arrested the accused alleging that he was in possession of cannabis resin, which the accused denied. The issue for the jury was whether the officer was telling the truth. The judge's final summing-up drew attention to the fact that a police officer would not endanger his career by lying. On appeal on the ground that this was a material irregularity, *held*, the comment had not been made in very strong terms and was made at the end of an exemplary summing-up. The appeal would therefore be dismissed.

R v WELLWOOD-KERR [1978] Crim LR 760 (Court of Appeal: ROSKILL LJ, ACKNER and STOCKER JJ).

757 **Verdict—alternative counts—conviction on all counts**

The defendant was charged with theft and receiving and handling stolen goods in respect of the same goods. The jury were directed that if they convicted him of theft they need not consider the other two counts since they were alternative counts. The jury found the defendant guilty on all three counts. The judge failed to explain that this was contrary to his direction, and the defendant appealed. *Held*, the judge should not have purported to accept all three verdicts but should have reiterated his direction and sent the jury out again to decide on which of the three possible offences the defendant was to be convicted. Since the jury had failed to comply with the direction, it was impossible to say that the conviction for theft was safe or satisfactory. The appeal would be allowed and all three convictions quashed.

R v ALI [1978] Crim LR 245 (Court of Appeal: ORMROD and BRIDGE LJJ and JUPP J).

758 —— **conviction of offence other than that charged**

The defendants had been charged with causing grievous bodily harm with intent. The first defendant was convicted of common assault and the second defendant pleaded guilty to unlawful wounding. They appealed on the grounds that they could not be convicted of these offences under the indictment. *Held*, the Criminal Law Act 1967, s. 6 (3) provided that where a person was found not guilty of the offence as charged but the allegations in the indictment included, either expressly or impliedly, an allegation of another offence falling within the jurisdiction of the court the jury could find him guilty of that other offence or of another offence of which he could be found guilty if charged with it on indictment. Causing grievous bodily harm with intent did not necessarily involve wounding and, occasionally did not even involve an assault. Without an amendment of the original indictment the court could not accept pleas of unlawful wounding or assault and the appeals would be allowed.

The court considered that a clear distinction should be maintained between "causing" and "wounding". If there was reliable evidence that a wound had been inflicted the charge should be wounding with intent, and if there was no evidence of a wound the charge should be causing grievous bodily harm. If the indictment did not specify the way in which grievous bodily harm was caused there could be no plea to or verdict of unlawful wounding or assault occasioning actual bodily harm or common assault.

R v McCready; R v Hurd [1978] 3 All ER 967 (Court of Appeal: Lawton LJ, Mars-Jones and Gibson JJ). *R v Springfield* (1969) 53 Cr App R 608 applied.

759   The defendant was charged with causing grievous bodily harm with intent under the Offences against the Person Act 1861, s. 18. The judge, purporting to apply the Criminal Law Act 1967, s. 6 (3), directed the jury that there were alternative verdicts to a verdict of guilty under s. 18; namely, guilty under s. 20 or under s. 47. The defendant appealed against conviction for assault under s. 47. *Held*, a charge of causing grievous bodily harm with intent without any further particularisation of the manner in which the grievous bodily harm was caused did not necessarily involve the offence of assault occasioning actual bodily harm. The appeal would be allowed.

R v Nicholls [1978] Crim LR 247 (Court of Appeal: Roskill and Browne LJJ and Kerr J). *R v Austin* (1973) 58 Cr App Rep 163, CA followed.

760   —— jury—whether direction by judge amounted to coercion

Canada

At a trial the jury were asked to make their decision. After deliberation they returned noting that they all felt that the accused was guilty but that one of them felt himself unable to record that verdict. The judge reminded them of their oath and suggested that it would facilitate matters if they could reach a decision. He assured himself that there was no question of a deadlock, in which situation he would have dismissed the jurors. The jury returned with a unanimous verdict of guilty. Upon appeal contending that the trial judge had improperly coerced the jury into making a decision, *held* a judge had to avoid coercive language which would appear to interfere with the jury's right to make its decision without extraneous pressure. The trial judge had expressed himself strongly but not objectionably and had been prepared to accept a genuine disagreement. The appeal would be dismissed.

R v Littlejohn and Tirabasso (1978) 41 CCC (2d) 161 (Court of Appeal of Ontario).

761   Young offenders—police cautions—citing in juvenile courts

In an attempt to achieve greater uniformity of practice in the citing of police cautions before juvenile courts, the Home Office has issued a circular (No. 49/1978 (CS 9/78)) advocating the citing of any caution to the court by the police. The circular is the result of a conference convened by the Home Office especially to consider the issue of cautions: 128 NLJ 407.

CROWN PROCEEDINGS

Halsbury's Laws of England (4th edn.), Vol. 11, paras. 1401–1580

762   Certiorari—certiorari to quash order of justices—availability in cases of conflicting factual evidence

The applicant was convicted by magistrates of a road traffic offence. He sought an order of certiorari to set aside that conviction on the basis of his evidence that at the end of the proceedings the chairman of the magistrates said "we believe both witnesses". The implication was that it was merely the turn of the defence to lose. The chairman later claimed that she could not remember what she had said, but that the Bench had been satisfied that the charge was proved. *Held*, dismissing the application, it was an almost inflexible rule of the court that it did not attempt to deal with cases by certiorari which involved a conflict of evidence on fact. Such a case could not be solved on affidavit evidence alone without seeing the witnesses.

R v ABINGDON MAGISTRATES' COURT, EX PARTE CLIFFORD [1978] Crim LR 165 (Queen's Bench Division: LORD WIDGERY CJ, CANTLEY and PETER PAIN JJ).

763   —— —— non-disclosure of witnesses by prosecution—whether rules of natural justice infringed

A motorist applied for an order of certiorari to quash a conviction for driving without due care and attention on the ground that the prosecution had failed to notify him of the existence of witnesses whom it did not intend to call but who might have assisted the defence. The prosecution contended certiorari could not lie where the error was the prosecution's rather than the court's. *Held*, certiorari could not lie merely to enable a person to bring fresh evidence. However, a clear breach of the rules of natural justice had resulted from the prosecution's failure in that the motorist had been denied a fair trial. There was no reason why certiorari should not be granted to remedy a miscarriage of justice brought about by the prosecution and accordingly the motorist's conviction would be quashed.

R v LEYLAND JJ, EX PARTE HAWTHORN (1978) 122 Sol Jo 627 (Queen's Bench Division: LORD WIDGERY CJ, MAY and TUDOR EVANS JJ).

764   Habeas corpus—application for writ—child in local authority care—whether issue of writ appropriate

See *Re K (A Minor)*, para. 1925.

765   —— —— whether person wrongly detained—person mentally disordered—appointment of next friend

A woman who was seriously ill was a patient in a home for the disabled maintained by the health authority. Her husband claimed on her behalf, that she was being detained against her will and applied for a writ of habeas corpus so he could care for her at home. He appealed against the adjournment of his application, contending that as his wife's condition was so serious, she might die during the adjournment. *Held*, there were no grounds for the issue of a writ of habeas corpus. The patient was not imprisoned or detained against her will; the health authority was merely concerned for her welfare and was quite willing for her to leave if it was satisfied that she was mentally capable of deciding to do so. The appeal would be refused but the Official Solicitor would be invited to discover whether the patient wanted to return home. If that was the case, she should be allowed to leave.

The report of the Official Solicitor indicated that the woman both liked the hospital and had expressed a desire to go home. Unfortunately, she was mentally incapable of making a decision. In view of this, the reconvened court *held*, (i) for habeas corpus to lie it had to be applied for by the woman's next friend in view of her own incapacity; (ii) her husband was unsuitable to act as next friend because he was no longer able to exercise independent judgment as far as his wife was concerned; (iii) the issue would be referred back to the Divisional Court which had originally adjourned the application for habeas corpus, although such an application was clearly now inappropriate owing to the respective disabilities of the woman and her husband. For those proceedings to continue effectively, application would have to be made for the appointment of a suitable next friend.

FARR V SOUTH EAST THAMES REGIONAL HEALTH AUTHORITY (1978) Times, 27th April, 13th May (Court of Appeal: LORD DENNING MR, GOFF and CUMMING-BRUCE LJJ).

The husband subsequently had his right to act as her legal guardian taken away, see para. 1894.

766   —— Irish warrant—reason for issue

See *Re Lawlor*, para. 1306.

767   Judicial review—application—appropriate division of High Court

See *Uppal v Home Office*, para. 2155.

768   Mandamus—definition of aggrieved person

See *R v Chief Commons Commissioner, ex parte Constable*, para. 319.

769   —— order to justices to state case—power to make and file affidavit

After dismissing complaints against the defendants in respect of a failure to pay a rating surcharge, the justices refused to state a case for the opinion of the High Court. The council applied to the High Court for an order of mandamus requiring the justices to state a case. LORD WIDGERY CJ stated that where the decision of justices is called in question in a superior court, the justices have power under the Review of Justices Decisions Act 1872 to make and file an affidavit setting out the grounds of the decision and the facts on which it is based. In the interests of speed and efficiency, the justices should have filed such an affidavit in this case.

R v DAEJAN PROPERTIES LTD, EX PARTE MERTON LONDON BOROUGH COUNCIL (1978) Times, 25th April (Divisional Court of the Queen's Bench Division).

CUSTOMS AND EXCISE

Halsbury's Laws of England (4th edn), Vol. 12, paras. 501–1066

770   Anti-dumping and countervailing duties

The Anti-Dumping and Countervailing Duties Order 1978, S.I. 1978 No. 1147 (in force on 31st August 1978), implements in the law of the United Kingdom ECSC obligations on protection against dumping or the granting of bounties or subsidies by non-ECSC states in respect of products covered by the ECSC Treaty. The Order is made in consequence of ECSC Commission Recommendation 77/329, as amended.

The Customs Duties (ECSC) Anti-Dumping (No. 1) Order 1978, S.I. 1978 No. 78 (in force on 23rd January 1978), imposes an anti-dumping duty on imports of iron or steel coils for re-rolling originating in Czechoslovakia and Korea. Collection of duty is postponed in accordance with the Anti-Dumping and Countervailing Duties (Postponement of Collection) Regulations 1978, see para. 789, post, while in respect of goods from Czechoslovakia it has been suspended in pursuance of ECSC Commission Recommendation 859/78: Customs Duties (ECSC) Anti-Dumping (Amendment No. 2) Order 1978, see para. 792, post. The Order has been replaced as regards goods from Korea, see Customs Duties (ECSC) Anti-Dumping (No. 15) Order 1978, para. 785, post.

This order was subsequently revoked, see para. 797.

771   The Anti-Dumping Duty (Amendment) Order 1978, S.I. 1978 No. 1497 (in force on 10th November 1978), amends the Anti-Dumping Duty (No. 2) Order 1977, 1977 Halsbury's Abr para. 748, by amending the description of certain stainless steel originating in Spain which is subject to duty according to its metallurgical composition at the rate of 8 per cent imposed by the 1977 Order.

772   The Customs Duties (ECSC) Anti-Dumping (No. 2) Order 1978, S.I. 1978 No. 81 (in force on 24th January 1978), imposes duty on imports of certain iron and steel sheets and plates originating in Bulgaria, Czechoslovakia or Japan. Collection of duty is postponed in accordance with the Anti-Dumping and Countervailing Duties (Postponement of Collection) Regulations 1978, see para. 789, post, while in respect of goods from Czechoslovakia and Japan it is suspended in pursuance of ECSC Commission Recommendations 859/78, 714/78 respectively: Customs Duties (ECSC) Anti-Dumping (Amendment) and (Amendment No. 2) Orders 1978, see paras. 791, 792, post. The Order has been replaced as regards goods from Bulgaria, see Customs Duties (ECSC) Anti-Dumping (No. 15) Order 1978, para. 785, post.

773   The Customs Duties (ECSC) Anti-Dumping (No. 3) Order 1978, S.I. 1978 No. 82 (in force on 24th January 1978), imposed anti-dumping duty on certain haematite pig and cast iron imports from Canada. The Order was subsequently revoked, see Customs Duties (ECSC) Anti-Dumping (Revocation) (No. 1) Order 1978, para. 796, post.

774   The Customs Duties (ECSC) Anti-Dumping (No. 4) Order 1978, S.I. 1978 No. 83 (in force on 24th January 1978), imposes anti-dumping duty on certain steel and iron sheets and plates from Czechoslovakia. Collection of duty was suspended in pursuance of ECSC Commission Recommendation 859/78: Customs Duties (ECSC) Anti-Dumping (Amendment No. 2) Order 1978, see para. 792, post.
This order was subsequently revoked, see para. 797.

775   The Customs Duties (ECSC) Anti-Dumping (No. 5) Order 1978, S.I. 1978 No. 84 (in force on 24th January 1978), imposes anti-dumping duty on certain iron or steel wire rod from Czechoslovakia. Collection of duty was suspended in pursuance of ECSC Commission Recommendation 859/78: Customs Duties (ECSC) Anti-Dumping (Amendment No. 2) Order 1978, see para. 792, post.
This order was subsequently revoked, see para. 797.

776   The Customs Duties (ECSC) Anti-Dumping (No. 6) Order 1978, S.I. 1978 No. 85 (in force on 24th January 1978), imposes anti-dumping duty on certain zinc-coated iron and steel sheets and plates from Poland and Spain. Collection of duty is postponed in accordance with the Anti-Dumping and Countervailing Duties (Postponement of Collection) Regulations 1978, see para. 789, post, while in respect of goods from Spain it has been suspended in pursuance of ECSC Commission Recommendation 931/78: Customs Duties (ECSC) Anti-Dumping (Amendment No. 2) Order 1978, see para. 792, post.
This order was subsequently revoked, see para. 797.

777   The Customs Duties (ECSC) Anti-Dumping (No. 7) Order 1978, S.I. 1978 No. 109 (in force on 28th January), imposes anti-dumping duty on certain iron and steel angles, shapes and sections originating in Spain. Collection of duty was suspended in pursuance of ECSC Commission Recommendation 931/78: Customs Duties (ECSC) Anti-Dumping (Amendment No. 2) Order 1978, see para. 792, post.

778   The Customs Duties (ECSC) Anti-Dumping (No. 8) Order 1978, S.I. 1978 No. 110 (in force on 28th January 1978), imposed anti-dumping duty on certain iron and steel plates and sheets from East Germany, East Berlin, Romania and Spain. Collection of duty was postponed in accordance with the Anti-Dumping and Countervailing Duties (Postponement of Collection) Regulations 1978, see para. 789, post, while in respect of goods from Spain it was suspended in pursuance of ECSC Commission Recommendation 931/78: Customs Duties (ECSC) Anti-Dumping (Amendment No. 2) Order 1978, see para. 792, post. The Order was subsequently replaced as regards goods from all bar Spain, see Customs Duties (ECSC) Anti-Dumping (No. 15) Order 1978, para. 785, post.

779   The Customs Duties (ECSC) Anti-Dumping (No. 9) Order 1978, S.I. 1978 No. 111 (in force on 28th January 1978), imposes anti-dumping duty on iron and steel plates and sheets from Japan. Collection of duty was suspended in pursuance of ECSC

Commission Recommendation 714/78: Customs Duties (ECSC) Anti-Dumping (Amendment) Order 1978, see para. 791, post.

This order was subsequently revoked, see para. 797.

780   The Customs Duties (ECSC) Anti-Dumping (No. 10) Order 1978, S.I. 1978 No. 155 (in force on 6th February 1978), imposes anti-dumping duty on iron and steel coils for re-rolling originating from Bulgaria or Japan. Collection of duty is postponed in accordance with the Anti-Dumping and Countervailing Duties (Postponement of Collection) Regulations 1978, see para. 789, post, while in respect of goods from Japan it has been suspended altogether in pursuance of ECSC Commission Recommendation 714/78: Customs Duties (ECSC) Anti-Dumping (Amendment) Order 1978, see para. 791, post.

This order was subsequently revoked, see para. 797.

781   The Customs Duties (ECSC) Anti-Dumping (No. 11) Order 1978, S.I. 1978 No. 192 (in force on 9th February 1978), imposes anti-dumping duty on certain iron and steel angles, shapes and sections originating from Japan. Collection of duty was suspended in pursuance of ECSC Commission Recommendation 714/78: Customs Duties (ECSC) Anti-Dumping (Amendment) Order 1978, see para. 791, post.

This order was subsequently revoked, see para. 797.

782   The Customs Duties (ECSC) Anti-Dumping (No. 12) Order 1978, S.I. 1978 No. 193 (in force on 9th February 1978), enforces anti-dumping duty on certain iron and steel sheets and plates originating from Poland. Collection of duty is postponed in accordance with the Anti-Dumping and Countervailing Duties (Postponement of Collection) Regulations 1978, see para. 789, post.

783   The Customs Duties ECSC) Anti-Dumping (No. 13) Order 1978, S.I. 1978 No. 237 (in force on 21st February 1978), imposes anti-dumping duty on iron and steel coils for re-rolling originating from Australia. Collection of duty is postponed in accordance with the Anti-Dumping and countervailing Duties (Postponement of Collection) Regulations 1978, see para. 789, post.

The Order was subsequently revoked, see Customs Duties (ECSC) Anti-Dumping (Revocation) (No. 3) Order 1978, para. 798, post.

784   The Customs Duties (ECSC) Anti-Dumping (No. 14) Order 1978, S.I. 1978 No. 246 (in force on 22nd February 1978), imposes anti-dumping duty on certain zinc-coated sheets and plates of iron and steel originating in East Germany, East Berlin and Japan. Collection of duty is postponed in accordance with the Anti-Dumping and Countervailing Duties (Postponement of Collection) Regulations 1978, see para. 789, post, while in respect of goods from Japan it has been suspended in pursuance of ECSC Commission Recommendation 714/78: Customs Duties (ECSC) Anti-Dumping (Amendment) Order 1978, see para. 791, post.

785   The Customs Duties (ECSC) Anti-Dumping (No. 15) Order 1978, S.I. 1978 No. 641 (in force on 29th April 1978), imposes anti-dumping duty on iron and steel coils for re-rolling originating from Korea, and on iron and steel sheets and plates from Bulgaria, East Germany, East Berlin and Romania. The Order replaces the Customs Duties (ECSC) Anti-Dumping (Nos. 1, 2, 8) Orders 1978, see paras. 770, 772, 778, ante, insofar as those orders relate to the places subject to this order. Collection of duty is not postponed in this case.

786   The Customs Duties (ECSC) Anti-Dumping (No. 16) Order 1978, S.I. 1978 No. 698 (in force on 12th May 1978), imposes anti-dumping duty on imports of iron and steel coils for re-rolling originating in Bulgaria and accordingly replaces the Customs Duties (ESCC) Anti-Dumping No. 10 Order, see para. 780 in relation to such coils. The Order also provides for a reduction in the duty charged on imports from Poland under the Customs and Excise (ECSC) Anti-Dumping No. 12 Order 1978, see para. 782.

787 The Customs Duties (ECSC) Anti-Dumping (No. 17) Order 1978, S.I. 1978 No. 765 (in force on 27th May 1978), imposes anti-dumping duty on imports of certain zinc-coated sheets and plates of iron and steel from East Germany, and accordingly replaces the Customs and Excise (ECSC) Anti-Dumping (No. 14) Order 1978, see para. 784 in relation to such sheets.

The Order also provides for a reduction in the duty charged on imports from Australasia under the Customs Duties (ECSC) Anti-Dumping (No. 13) Order 1978, see para. 783.

788 The Customs Duties (ECSC) Anti-Dumping (No. 18) Order 1978, S.I. 1978 No. 1142 (in force on 4th August 1978), imposes anti-dumping duty on imports of certain zinc-coated iron and steel sheets and plates from Japan, certain iron and steel angles, shapes and sections from Spain, and miscellaneous iron and steel items from Czechoslovakia, Japan, Poland and Spain. The Customs Duties (ECSC) Anti-Dumping (Nos. 2, 7, 8, 12, 14) Order 1978, paras. 772, 777, 778, 782, and 784 respectively are replaced in part. Postponement of payment of duty on items from these countries by virtue of Anti-Dumping and Countervailing Duties (Postponement of Collection) Regulations 1978, see para. 789, is no longer possible.

789 **—— postponement of collection**

The Anti-Dumping and Countervailing Duties (Postponement of Collection) Regulations 1978, S.I. 1978 No. 77 (in force on 23rd January 1978), provide that if an importer gives security for payment of anti-dumping or countervailing duty charges under an order made under the European Communities Act 1972, s. 5 (1), collection of that duty is postponed so long as the charge of duty continues and the provisions of the regulations are complied with.

790 The Anti-Dumping and Countervailing Duties (Postponement of Collection) (Amendment) Regulations 1978, S.I. 1978 No. 598 (in force on 21st April 1978), amend the principal regulations, see para. 789, ante, by providing that where a provisional order charging duty expires, the postponement of collection of duty ends.

791 **—— revocation and suspension of duties**

The Customs Duties (ECSC) Anti-Dumping (Amendment) Order 1978, S.I. 1978 No. 601 (in force on 21st April 1978), suspends the liability of importers of certain Japanese iron and steel products to pay anti-dumping duty, in consequence of ECSC Commission Recommendation 714/78.

792 The Customs Duties (ECSC) Anti-Dumping (Amendment No. 2) Order 1978, S.I. 1978 No. 674 (in force on 6th May 1978), suspends the liability of importers of certain iron and steel products originating in Czechoslovakia and Spain to pay anti-dumping duty, in consequence of ECSC Commission Recommendations 859/78 and 931/78.

793 The Customs Duties (ECSC) Anti-Dumping (Amendment No. 3) Order 1978, S.I. 1978 No. 909 (in force on 30th June 1978), provides that in pursuance of ECSC Commission Recommendation 1235/78 no anti-dumping duty can be charged on certain Romanian iron and steel products, as previously provided for by the Customs Duties (ECSC) Anti-Dumping (No. 15) Order 1978, see para. 785.

794 The Customs Duties (ECSC Anti-Dumping (Amendment No. 4) Order 1978, S.I. 1978 No. 1143 (in force on 4th August 1978), lifts payment of duty under the Customs Duties (ECSC) Anti-Dumping (Nos. 13, 18) Orders 1978, see paras. 783, 788 respectively. Goods from Australia, Czechoslovakia, Japan, Poland and Spain may not be subjected to duty in consequence of ECSC Commission Recommendations 1704, 1715, 1716 and 1758/78.

795   The Customs Duties (ECSC) Anti-Dumping (Amendment No. 5) Order 1978, S.I. 1978 No. 1941 (in force on 29th December 1978), provides that no anti-dumping duty shall be charged on imports of certain iron and steel products originating in the Republic of Korea where such duty was imposed by the Customs Duties (ECSC) Anti-Dumping (No. 15) Order 1978, see para. 785.

796   The Customs Duties (ECSC) Anti-Dumping (Revocation) (No. 1) Order 1978, S.I. 1978 No. 640 (in force on 29th April 1978), revokes the Customs Duties (ECSC) Anti-Dumping (No. 3) Order 1978, see para. 773, ante. Revocation is in consequence of ECSC Commission Recommendations 77/329 and 117/78.

797   The Customs Duties (ECSC) Anti-Dumping (Revocation) (No. 2) Order 1978, S.I. 1978 No. 1205 (in force on 12th August 1978), revokes the Customs Duties (ECSC) Anti-Dumping (Nos. 1, 4, 5, 6, 9–11) Orders 1978, see supra, in consequence of various ECSC Commission Recommendations. No duty is now payable on goods imported into the United Kingdom originating in Czechoslovakia, Japan, Poland or Spain.

798   The Customs Duties (ECSC) Anti-Dumping (Revocation) (No. 3) Order 1978, S.I. 1978 No. 1342 (in force on 14th September 1978), revokes the Customs Duties (ECSC) Anti-Dumping (No. 13) Order 1978, para. 783, which imposed an anti-dumping duty on imports of certain iron or steel coils for re-rolling, originating in Australia.

799   **Beer—revenue control—regulations**

See paras. 1672, 1673.

800   **Common customs tariff**

See EUROPEAN COMMUNITIES.

801   **Customs duties—deferred payment**

The Customs Duties (Deferred Payment) (Amendment) Regulations 1978, S.I. 1978 No. 1725 (in force on 1st January 1979), amend the Customs Duties (Deferred Payment) Regulations 1976, 1976 Halsbury's Abr para. 717 in order to implement the obligations contained in EEC Council Directive 78/453 on duty deferment.

802   **—— educational, scientific and cultural materials**

The Customs Duties Relief Regulations 1978, S.I. 1978 No. 1704 (in force on 1st April 1979), repeals the Import Duties Act 1958, Sch. 4, para. 3, with the express provision that any direction under s. 6 of the 1958 Act remains unaffected. The Regulations remove articles intended to be used for scientific research, or for a purpose connected with the advancement of learning or art or with the promotion of sport, from the list of articles qualifying for relief from customs duties. Exemption from the duty, other than articles connected with the promotion of sport, is now effected on a Community basis by EEC Council Regulation 1798/75, 1975 Halsbury's Abr para. 1368.

803   **—— Greece**

See para. 1216.

804   **—— reliefs—personal reliefs**

The Customs Duty (Personal Reliefs) (No. 1) Order 1975 (Amendment) Order 1978, S.I. 1978 No. 1882 (in force on 1st January 1979), amends the Customs Duty (Personal Reliefs) (No. 1) Order 1975, 1975 Halsbury's Abr para. 925, by increasing from £25 to £70 the total value of goods on which an aggregate rate may be charged, in accordance with EEC Regulation No. 2780/78.

805   The Customs Duty (Personal Reliefs) (No. 1) Order 1968 (Amendment) Order 1978, S.I. 1978 No. 1883 (in force on 1st January 1979), gives legislative force to a higher scale of duty-free allowances.   On this scale the still wine allowance is increased from three to four litres and the "other goods" allowance is increased from £50 to £120.

The Customs Duty (Personal Reliefs) (No. 1) Order 1968, Sch. 1 is replaced.

806   —— —— **quota relief**

The Customs Duties (ECSC) (Quota and Other Reliefs) Order 1978, S.I. 1978 No. 1933 (in force on 1st January 1979), provides for reliefs from customs duty on certain iron and steel products which originate in the developing countries listed in Sch. 2.   The goods listed in Sch. 1, Part I are exempt from duty for one year and duty-free tariff quotas apply to those listed in Sch. 1, Part II.

807   The Customs Duties (Quota Relief) Order 1978, S.I. 1978 No. 878 (in force on 1st July 1978), provides for the administration of the United Kingdom's share of the tariff quota opened for the period July 1978–June 1979 by the EEC, providing exemption from customs duty for rum, arrack and tafia imported from various African, Caribbean and Pacific states.   The Order also provides that application for relief under the Customs Duties (Quota Relief) (Administration) Order 1976, see 1976 Halsbury's Abr para. 753, must be accompanied by the necessary origin documents.   Relief is restricted to goods imported for home use.

808   The Customs Duties (Quota Relief) (Paper, Paperboard and Printed Products) (Amendment) Order 1978, S.I. 1978 No. 820 (in force on 1st July 1978), amends the Customs Duties (Quota Relief) (Paper, Paperboard and Printed Products) Order 1977, 1977 Halsbury's Abr para. 772, by replacing the nine individual duty-free tariff quotas which the United Kingdom is entitled to under Protocol No. 1 to the Agreement between the EEC and Switzerland by a single quota.   The Order was made in consequence of EC Council Regulation 850/78.

809   The Customs Duties (Quota Relief) (Paper, Paperboard and Printed Products) Order 1978, S.I. 1978 No. 1866 (in force on 1st January 1979, provides for the opening during 1979 of duty-free tariff quotas for paper, paperboard and printed products originating in Austria, Iceland, Portugal, Sweden, Switzerland, Norway and Finland established in accordance with the Agreements between the EEC and those countries.

810   **Customs   procedure—international   arrangement—European decision**

EEC Council Decision 78/528 incorporates three Annexes concerning customs formalities, temporary storage of goods and free zones into an international convention on the simplification and harmonisation of customs procedures.   The convention was concluded by EEC Council Decision 75/199, 1975 Halsbury's Abr para. 1408.

811   **Excise duty—relief—alcoholic ingredients**

The Excise Duty (Relief on Alcoholic Ingredients) Regulations 1978, S.I. 1978 No. 1786 (in force on 1st January 1979), set out the conditions of the repayment of the excise duty paid in respect of beer, cider, made-wine and wine used as an ingredient in the production or manufacture of beverages and other articles of a low alcohol content and on wine converted into vinegar.

812   **Export of goods—control**

The Export of Goods (Control) (Amendment) Order 1978, S.I. 1978 No. 271 (in force on 24th March 1978), amends the Export of Goods (Control) Order 1970, Sch.

1, Group 1, by adding armour plate and certain riot control equipment to the list of goods the export of which is controlled.

The 1970 Regulations as amended were subsequently replaced, see para. 813, post.

813   The Export of Goods (Control) Order 1978, S.I. 1978 No. 796 (in force on 3rd July 1978), replaces the Export of Goods (Control) Order 1970, as amended. Subject to certain exceptions, the goods listed in Sch. 1 to the Order cannot be exported from the United Kingdom or shipped as ship's stores to specified Communist countries. The Customs and Excise Commissioners are empowered to demand evidence of the destinations which goods have reached.

814   The Export of Goods (Control) Order 1978 (Amendment) Order 1978, S.I. 1978 No. 945 (in force on 10th July 1978), amends the Export of Goods (Control) Order 1978, see para. 813, by including certain iron and steel products in the list of goods of which export to Austria, Finland, Norway, Portugal or Sweden is controlled.

This order is revoked by the Export of Goods (Control) Order 1978 (Amendment No. 4) Order 1978, para. 817.

815   The Export of Goods (Control) Order 1978 (Amendment No. 2) Order 1978, S.I. 1978 No. 1219 (in force on 14th September 1978), amends the Export of Goods (Control) Order 1978, see para. 813, by adding cobalt waste and scrap and depleted uranium to the goods the export of which is controlled.

816   The Export of Goods (Control) Order 1978 (Amendment No. 3) Order 1978, S.I. 1978 No. 1496 (in force on 9th November 1978), further amends the Export of Goods (Control) Order 1978, para. 813, by including specialised parts and components of the apparatus, appliances and equipment in Group 1 of Part II of Schedule 1 among the goods of which the export is controlled to South Africa and Namibia; by including certain types of frequency changes among the goods which are subject to export control in Group 3C of Part II of Schedule 1; and by ensuring that machines and apparatus capable of manufacturing semi-conductor devices are among the goods which are subject to export control in Group 3D.

817   The Export of Goods (Control) Order 1978 (Amendment No. 4) Order 1978, S.I. 1978 No. 1812 (in force on 13th December 1978) further amends the Export of Goods (Control) Order 1978, para. 813 and removes certain iron and steel products from the goods of which the export is controlled to Austria, Finland, Norway, Portugal or Sweden. The Export of Goods (Control) Order 1978 (Amendment) Order 1978, para. 814 is revoked.

818   Finance Act 1978

Finance Act 1978, Pt. I deals with revenue and excise duties; see further para. 2312.

819   Import duties—reliefs—inward and outward processing

The Customs Duties (Inward and Outward Processing Relief) Regulations 1978, S.I. 1978 No. 1148 (in force on 1st September 1978), make amendments to the Import Duties Act 1958, the Import Duties (Outward Processing Relief) Regulations 1976, 1976 Halsbury's Abr para. 743, and the Inward Processing Relief Regulations 1977, 1977 Halsbury's Abr para. 799, in consequence of the Finance Act 1978.

820   Import of goods—control

The Import of Goods (Control) (Amendment) Order 1978, S.I. 1978 No. 806 (in force on 3rd July 1978), further amends the Import of Goods Order 1954. Import licences for transit or transhipment can be granted provided that the goods are shipped to a specified destination or within a specified time. If any condition is contravened or not complied with the goods become liable to forfeiture.

821   **Import of indecent or obscene material—prohibition—validity of legislation**

See *R v Henn, R v Darby*, para. 1217.

822   **Offence—prohibition on export of restricted goods—evasion of prohibition—meaning of "evade"**

In a case where the defendant was charged under the Customs and Excise Act 1952, s. 56 (2), with being knowingly concerned in the exportation of goods with intent to evade prohibition on exportation, the court discussed the meaning of the word "evade" in that subsection. When not used in conjunction with "avoid", it should be given its normal English meaning of "to get round" or "to avoid"; it had no connotation of fraud or dishonesty, as it did in income tax law. The court also held that it was no defence to a charge under s. 56 (2) that a defendant genuinely believed that his conduct was lawful.

R v HURFORD-JONES (1977) 65 Cr App Rep 263 (Court of Appeal: LORD WIDGERY CJ, GEOFFREY LANE LJ and CAULFIELD J).

823   **Tobacco—higher tar cigarettes**

The Tobacco Products (Higher Tar Cigarettes) Regulations 1978, S.I. 1978 No. 1156 (in force on 4th September 1978), prescribe how tar yield is to be determined for the purpose of charging extra duty on higher tar cigarettes under the Finance Act 1978, s. 1. Provision is also made for the management and control of the additional duty.

824   **United Kingdom transit procedures—exemption of Community transit goods**

The Customs and Excise (Community Transit Goods) Regulations 1978, S.I. 1978 No. 1602 (in force on 8th December 1978) provide that goods in transit through the United Kingdom under cover of Community transit documents issued under EEC Council Reg. 222/77 are exempt from the Customs and Excise Act 1952, ss. 28, 47, 49 and 307 and the Finance Act 1971, Sch. 1. These regulations mean that Community transit goods are not subject to United Kingdom transit procedures and eliminates duplication of documents.

825   **Value added tax**

See VALUE ADDED TAX.

826   **Vehicle excise licence—abolition**

The government has announced its intention to abolish vehicle excise duties for the private motorist and to replace the lost revenue by an increase in the tax on petrol which is likely to be in the region of 19p per gallon (increase). Details of the proposals have yet to be worked out but it is expected that the changes will be introduced progressively and completed by 1983. The announcement was made in a written reply to a parliamentary question: see The Times, 22nd November 1978.

827   **—— whether required for moped used as pedal cycle**

See *McEachran v Hurst*, para. 2389.

828   **Warehousing—amendments**

The Customs and Excise (Warehouses) Regulations 1978, S.I. 1978 No. 1603 (in force on 8th December 1978), amends the Customs and Excise Act 1952 and related Acts to provide that warehouses be defined as either customs warehouses or excise warehouses so that different procedures may be applied to each type of warehouse. It also provides for warehouses to be approved for both purposes and for certain goods to be kept in a customs warehouse without being treated as warehoused goods. Provision is made for providing a legal basis for implementing EEC Council Reg. 69/74 relating to Customs Warehousing procedure.

DAMAGES AND COMPENSATION

Halsbury's Laws of England (4th edn.), Vol. 12, paras. 1101–1213

829   Articles
Civil Liability (Contribution) Act 1978, D. M. Morgan: 128 NLJ 1042.
Civil Liability (Contribution) Act 1978, Alec Samuels: 122 Sol Jo 799.
Economic Loss—An Australian Solution, Margaret Brazier (a possible solution to the problem of whether damages should be recoverable for economic loss resulting from negligence but unrelated to any physical injury): 128 NLJ 327.
Fatal Accidents: The Calculation of Awards, K. M. Stanton (the importance of the Court of Appeal's decision in *Cookson v Knowles* [1977] 2 All ER 820, 1977 Halsbury's Abr para. 838): 128 NLJ 81.
Marine Collisions and Foreign Currency, J. A. Knott (new developments in assessing damages where foreign currencies are involved with particular reference to claims in tort arising out of collisions between ships): 122 Sol Jo 443.
The Pearson Commission and Industrial Injuries Legislation, Roger Corke: 128 NLJ 1140.
The Pearson Report: An Appraisal, A. Kewley (examination of the major recommendations of the Report on when and to what extent compensation should be payable in respect of death or personal injury): 128 NLJ 651.

830   Aggravation—exemplary damages—prima facie case
In an action for libel against a reporter and a popular newspaper the plaintiff, a former cabinet minister, claimed exemplary damages in respect of an article naming him in connection with a notorious bribery and corruption scandal and alleging that he had been the subject of a report to the Director of Public Prosecutions. On an interlocutory application by the defendants to strike out the claim for exemplary damages, the plaintiff sought to justify the claim for this exceptional category of damages on the grounds that the article had relied on his distinguished name and record for its sensation value and had been published to make as much money as possible from the resulting circulation, that the defendants were utterly regardless of the harm they would do to his position and that the statements had been made recklessly as instanced by mention of the report to the DPP, the contents of which the defendants, in their pleadings, said they did not know. *Held*, dismissing the application, as the plaintiff had established prima facie the elements necessary to constitute a claim for exemplary damages he was entitled to put his points to the jury.
MAUDLING V SCOTT (1978) Times, 18th March (Court of Appeal: LORD DENNING MR, ORR and BRIDGE LJJ).

831   Assessment—car damaged in accident—basis of assessment
In 1975 the plaintiff's car, which he had bought new in 1972, was severely damaged in an accident caused by the defendant's admitted negligence. The plaintiff brought an action for damages and his insurance company's engineer gave evidence that the car was worth £795. Damages were awarded by assessing the pre-accident value of the car at £700 on the ground that the car was likely to fetch that price on the open market. On appeal, *held*, the correct approach was the cost to the plaintiff of putting himself back in the position in which he was immediately before the accident. The assessment of damages had to depend on the evidence before the court and not on the judge's own view of the probable value of the car. As the judge had applied the wrong test, the damages would be increased.
THATCHER V LITTLEJOHN [1978] RTR 369 (Court of Appeal: BUCKLEY and BRIDGE LJJ and SIR DAVID CAIRNS).

832   Award—appeal against award in libel action—application to strike out appeal as abuse of process of court

See *Obote v Judith, Countess of Listowel*, para. 2218.

833   Breach of contract—currency of award

See *Services Europe Atlantique Sud v Stockholms Rederiaktiebolag Svea*, para. 841.

834   —— sale of goods—exclusion clause—whether loss arising from late delivery consequential

Sellers contracted to supply masonry blocks to buyers who were the main contractors for the building of a school. The buyers claimed an indemnity from the sellers in respect of a claim against them by sub-contractors which arose from a late delivery of blocks by the sellers. The sellers alleged that under the terms of the contract they were excused from liability for any consequential loss arising from late delivery. The court gave judgment for the buyers and the sellers appealed. *Held*, the sellers could not rely on the exclusion in the contract because the buyers' loss had resulted directly and naturally from the sellers' breach and therefore could not have been consequential.

CROUDACE CONSTRUCTION LTD v CAWOODS CONCRETE PRODUCTS LTD [1978] 2 Lloyd's Rep 55 (Court of Appeal: MEGAW, LAWTON and BROWNE LJJ). *Millars Machinery Co Ltd v David Way and Son* (1934) 40 Com Cas 204 applied.

835   Civil Liability (Contribution) Act 1978

The Civil Liability (Contribution) Act 1978 gives effect with minor modifications to the Law Commission Report on Contribution (Law Com. No. 79). The Act amends the law relating to contribution and to successive legal proceedings against persons liable for the same debt or damage. It received the royal assent on 31st July 1978 and came into force on 1st January 1979: s. 10.

Section 1 provides that any person liable in respect of damage suffered by another may recover contribution from any other person liable in respect of the same damage. There is no restriction on the legal basis of liability. This replaces Law Reform (Married Women and Tortfeasors) Act 1935, s. 6 (1) (c) which applied the doctrine of contribution to tortfeasors. Under s. 1 (4) of the 1978 Act a person who has made a bona fide settlement of a claim is also entitled to recover contribution. Section 1 (5) prevents the re-opening in contribution proceedings of issues already determined in favour of the person from whom contribution is sought.

Section 2 provides that the amount of contribution recoverable is to be such as is found by the court to be just and equitable having regard to responsibility for the damage. A person may be exempt from liability to make contribution or may be required to provide a complete indemnity: s. 2 (2), but where the amount of damages was subject to a limit imposed by statute or agreement or to a reduction for contributory negligence he is not to be required to pay a greater amount than the amount of the damages as limited or reduced: s. 2 (3).

Sections 3 and 4 remove certain anomalies in the law relating to the effect of judgments. Section 3 provides that judgment recovered against a person liable in respect of any debt or damage will not be a bar to an action, or to continuance of an action, against any other person jointly liable in respect of the same debt or damage. This provision replaces 1935 Act, s. 6 (1) (a) which removed the bar in relation to joint liability in tort. Section 4 re-enacts that part of s. 6 (1) (b) of the 1935 Act which provides that a person who brings successive actions against persons liable for the same damage will not be entitled to costs in any action other than the first unless the court considers there was reasonable ground for bringing the action. The sanction in damages has been abolished.

Sections 5 to 10 contain supplemental provisions including application to the Crown, interpretation, savings, amendments and repeals (in Schs. 1 and 2), commencement and extent.

836　Compensation order—amount of compensation payable—whether estimate of amount sufficient

See *R v Vivian*, para. 594.

837　—— inclusion of interest—exercise of court's discretion

See *R v Schofield*, para. 595.

838　Criminal injuries—compensation

See CRIMINAL LAW.

839　—— —— function of Board—discretion

See *R v Criminal Injuries Compensation Board, ex parte RJC (an infant)*, para. 3.

840　Currency of award—demurrage—appropriate date of rate of exchange

See *The Bellami*, para. 2594.

841　—— tort and breach of contract

In the first case, a collision occurred between two ships, the *Eleftherotria* and the *Despina R*; it was agreed that the *Despina R* was 85 per cent to blame, and its owners were liable for that percentage of the loss and damage caused. The cost of repairs of the *Eleftherotria* was met by its owners in various foreign currencies; all payments on their behalf were made from a U.S. dollar account in New York, so all expenses incurred in foreign currencies other than U.S. dollars were met by transferring U.S. dollars from that account. The question arose whether, where the plaintiffs had suffered damage or sustained loss in a currency other than sterling, they were entitled to recover damages expressed in such other currency. The owners of the *Despina R* appealed against the Court of Appeal's decision that the plaintiffs were so entitled, and that the award would be made in U.S. dollars. *Held*, an English court had the power to give judgment or make an award in a foreign currency; a judgment in the currency in which the loss was sustained produced a more just result than one which fixed the plaintiff with a sum in sterling taken at the date of the breach or loss. The question arose whether the award should be made in the currency in which the expense or loss was immediately sustained ("the expenditure currency") or the currency in which the loss was effectively felt by the plaintiff, having regard to the currency in which he generally operated or with which he had the closest connection ("the plaintiff's currency"). Applying the normal principles in tort cases of restitutio in integrum and reasonable foreseeability of damage, the currency in which the loss was felt and which it was reasonably foreseeable the plaintiffs would have to spend was "the plaintiff's currency". In cases such as these, the burden was on the plaintiff to show that the loss was felt in "the plaintiff's currency". The Court of Appeal's decision was correct and the appeal would be dismissed.

The second case arose out of a charterparty under which Swedish shipowners chartered a ship to French charterers, the proper law of the contract being English. The cargo was damaged and the cargo receivers' claim was settled by the charterers in Brazilian cruzeiros, which they purchased with French francs. They then claimed against the owners for the French francs, the basis of the claim being damages for breach of the contract of affreightment. The owners appealed against the Court of Appeal's decision that the award would be made in French francs. *Held*, in contractual as in other cases a judgment or award could be given in a currency other than sterling. If the contract provided for a currency as the currency of account and payment in respect of all transactions arising under the contract, it was proper to award damages in that currency. If however there was no intention shown that damages for breach of the contract should be awarded in that currency, the plaintiff should be compensated for the expense or loss in the currency which most truly expressed his loss, in accordance with the principle of restitution and whether the parties must be taken reasonably to have had that in contemplation. In the present case, although English was the proper law of the contract, neither of the parties had any connection with sterling, so it was prima facie a case for judgment in a foreign currency. The charterers' loss was incurred in francs, and it was reasonably foreseeable that this would be so. Their recoverable loss was the sum of French francs they paid and the appeal would be dismissed.

THE DESPINA R [1978] 2 WLR 804 (House of Lords: LORD WILBERFORCE, LORD DIPLOCK, LORD SALMON, LORD RUSSELL OF KILLOWEN and LORD KEITH OF KINKEL). Decision of the Court of Appeal in *The Despina R* [1977] 3 All ER 874, 1977 Halsbury's Abr para. 907, and in *Services Europe Atlantique Sud v Stockholms Rederiaktiebolag Svea* [1978] 2 All ER 764 affirmed. *Miliangos v George Frank (Textiles) Ltd* [1976] AC 443, HL, 1975 Halsbury's Abr para. 1916 applied.

842   Exemplary damages—prima facie case

See *Maudling v Scott*, para. 830.

843   Injury to land—entitlement to replacement cost of buildings

Canada
Crude oil escaped from the defendant's pipeline saturating the plaintiffs' house and land. The defendant admitted liability and agreed to certain special damages. However the defendant maintained that the plaintiffs had no claim for damage to the house, soil and trees, because the property was in a commercial zone and if sold for commercial purposes would exceed its residential value, with or without the buildings. The defendant further maintained that if it was liable for the cost of replacement then this should be less depreciation, otherwise the plaintiffs would be benefiting at the defendant's expense by being provided with a new home. *Held*, the plaintiffs were entitled to the replacement cost of the house, soil and trees. The location was particularly suited to the plaintiffs, as it was next to their vintage car museum, they had lived in the house for a great many years and had no desire to move; furthermore they had obtained zoning approval to rebuild the house. There was no evidence that the new house would be worth anything more to them than the old house, consequently there would be no deduction for depreciation.

JENS AND JENS V MANNIX CO LTD [1978] 5 WWR 486 (Supreme Court of British Columbia).

844   Interest on recovery of damages—damages awarded by summary judgment—whether interest payable

The plaintiffs were given summary judgment for damages under RSC Ord. 14. They sought leave to appeal against the judge's refusal to award interest on the amount on the judgment. The Law Reform (Miscellaneous Provisions) Act 1934, s. 3 (1) provides that interest may be awarded, at the discretion of the court, in any proceedings for the recovery of debt or damages in any court of record. Summary judgments under RSC Ord. 14 have not been regarded as proceedings in a court of record as there is no trial. *Held*, trial could be defined as the conclusion of questions in issue in legal proceedings by any competent tribunal and summary judgment under Ord. 14 fell within this definition. The court would therefore exercise its discretion and order interest to be paid on the amount awarded to the plaintiffs.

GARDNER STEEL LTD V SHEFFIELD BROS (PROFILES) LTD [1978] 1 WLR 916 (Court of Appeal: STEPHENSON and ORMROD LJJ).

845   —— Law Commission report

See para. 1760.

846   Libel—compensatory damages—award by jury—whether award unreasonably high

See *Snyder v Montreal Gazette Ltd*, para. 1786.

847   Loss of expectation of life—exemplary damages—claim against estate of deceased wrongdoer

Canada

One man was fatally shot by another, who then committed suicide. In an action by the administrator of the former's estate for damages for loss of expectation of life and for exemplary damages, *held*, the estate would be awarded substantial damages under the former head of claim. Exemplary damages, however, could not be awarded where the wrongdoer himself would not suffer the punitive effect and where the deterrent effect of imposing such damages would be minimal.

BREITKREUTZ V PUBLIC TRUSTEE [1978] 5 WWR 544 (Supreme Court of Alberta).

848   Measure of damages—breach of contract—contract for sale of land—rule in Bain v Fothergill

The defendant, on becoming a junior partner with the plaintiff in a medical practice, bought a property comprising a private dwelling and a surgery, the conveyance being in the defendant's name and that of his wife. The partnership deed drawn up between the plaintiff and the defendant granted an option to the plaintiff to purchase the property, should the defendant cease to be partner. The partnership proved unworkable and the plaintiff gave notice to the defendant of the dissolution of the partnership, requiring the defendant to sell him the property under the option clause. The defendant refused and the plaintiff brought an action claiming specific performance of the contract and an injunction restraining the defendant from denying him the use of the surgery. At first instance the judge granted specific performance and continuing access to the surgery for the plaintiff. The Court of Appeal substituted for specific performance, a declaration that the option clause was valid, and refused access to the surgery on the basis of the defendant's wife's refusal to permit it. The defendant's wife confirmed that she would not agree to a sale or give access. The plaintiff brought an action claiming damages for breach of contract and the defendant contested the issue of the measure of damages only. The judge found on the evidence that the defendant had shown a marked lack of enthusiasm to carry out his obligations under the contract, but that as his wife would not agree to the sale the plaintiff's damages would be limited to his costs, under the rule in *Bain v Fothergill*, which operates where a vendor fails to convey the property to a purchaser because of his inability to do so resulting from a defect in his title. The plaintiff appealed. *Held*, allowing the appeal, the rule in *Bain v Fothergill* would only apply where the vendor had shown that he had used his best endeavours to fulfil his contractual obligations, and the onus of proof was on the vendor to show that he had done so. The inference from the evidence presented was that the defendants' failure to convey the property resulted from his own unwillingness to do so, rather than inability due to his wife's refusal to sell. There was no evidence that the defendant had attempted to persuade his wife to sell. Thus he had not discharged the onus on him and could not, therefore, claim the benefit of the rule in *Bain v Fothergill*. Full damages would therefore be awarded, the value of the property to be assessed at the date of the judgment not the date of the breach of contract; but the date should be moved back by one year due to the plaintiffs' delay in pursuing his claim. The plaintiff should also recover any loss to his medical practice that resulted from his inability to use the surgery.

MALHOTRA V CHOUDHURY [1978] 3 WLR 825 (Court of Appeal: STEPHENSON and CUMMING-BRUCE LJJ). *Bain v Fothergill* (1874) LR 7 HL 158, HL distinguished, *Day v Singleton* [1899] 2 Ch 320, CA applied.

849   —— —— tax benefit arising out of breach—set-off against damages

See *Levison v Farin*, para. 489.

850   —— damage to premises—date of assessment

The plaintiffs claimed damages for distortion of the framework of their garage premises due to vibrations during the construction of an adjoining multi-storey car park in 1968. They contended that they were entitled to have their damages, which were the cost of the repairs, assessed as at the date of the hearing in 1978, subject to it being proved against them that they had failed to act reasonably to mitigate their loss. *Held*, while the plaintiffs had proved that they had acted reasonably in postponing the repairs, the general principle was that damage had to be assessed at the date when it occurred. In the present case, the damage had been discovered in 1968, but experts on both sides had agreed that it was reasonable not to begin repairs until 1970. Accordingly, the measure of damages would be the cost of repairs as at 1970.

DODD PROPERTIES (KENT) LTD v CANTERBURY CITY COUNCIL (1978) 248 Estates Gazette 229 (Chancery Division: CANTLEY J).

851   —— loss of wife—entitlement to projected housekeeper's wages in lieu of actual loss

A forty-eight year old man who gave up work after his wife died following an abortion sought to have his damages calculated on the basis of the projected cost of a housekeeper to replace her rather than on his actual loss of earnings, which would have amounted to rather less. *Held*, the Fatal Accidents Act 1846 provided that the question had to be viewed through the eyes of a juryman not those of a judge. It would be repugnant to a juryman if a person were to make a profit from his wife's death, and in any event common sense directed that he be compensated for his actual loss. The appropriate measure would accordingly be his actual loss of earnings and he would be awarded some £26,000.

BAILEY v BARKING AND HAVERING AREA HEALTH AUTHORITY (1978) Times, 22nd July (Queen's Bench Division: PETER PAIN J).

852   —— negligence—solicitors

The vendor of property which was occupied by tenants instructed a firm of solicitors in connection with the sale. The solicitors prepared a contract which provided for vacant possession to be given on completion in May 1974. Although the tenants were protected, the solicitors wrongly believed the vendor had a right to evict them. In January 1974, when they discovered their mistake, the solicitors' advised the vendor to enter into a new agreement vesting title to the property in the purchasers as they wrongly believed the purchasers as landlords would have a right to evict the tenants. The purchasers were unable to do so and under a clause in the agreement, if the purchasers did not get vacant possession by a specified date, the vendor was required to repurchase the property for £90,000, the proportion of the purchase price he had already received. The purchasers claimed damages from the vendor who was unable to repurchase the property and the vendor claimed damages from the solicitors for their negligence. The solicitors contended that the agreement in January 1974 marked a cut-off point in their liability and any consequences arising from that agreement were due not to their negligence but to the vendor's failure to pay £90,000. *Held*, the solicitors were clearly negligent. Damages would be awarded under two heads: firstly, the vendor was to be placed in the same position financially as if the solicitors had advised him correctly. Therefore the measure of damages was the difference between £90,000 already received and £112,000, being the sum which the vendor would have received on a sale subject to the tenancies. Secondly, damages would be awarded for the loss which the solicitors ought to have realised was likely to result from their breach of duty. They must have foreseen that the vendor's ultimate liability to the purchasers was a likely result of their initial negligence, and therefore damages would be awarded according to the outcome of the purchasers' action for damages against the vendor.

RUMSEY v OWEN WHITE AND CATLIN (1978) 245 EG 225 (Court of Appeal: LORD DENNING MR, ROSKILL and SHAW LJJ). Decision of Sir Douglas Frank QC (1976) 241 EG 611, 1977 Halsbury's Abr para. 828 affirmed in part. *British Westinghouse Electric & Manufacturing Co Ltd Underground Electric Railways Co of London* [1912] AC 673, HL and dicta of Lord Reid in *Koufos v C. Czarnikow Ltd* [1969] 1 AC 350, HL at 382, 383, applied.

853 —— **personal injuries—loss of earnings—incapacity only partly due to injury**

Canada

As a result of injuries received in an accident caused by the defendant, the plaintiff was awarded special damages for loss of income for thirteen months following the accident. The defendant appealed on the ground that the damages should not have included compensation for three of the thirteen months as the plaintiff would not have been able to work during those months due to a heart condition unrelated to the accident. *Held*, the dominant rule in personal injury cases was that damages should be awarded which would put the injured party in the same position as he would have been had he not been injured. To include in the plaintiff's award damages for the three-month period in which she was disabled as a result of her heart condition would result in her being over-compensated for the injuries caused by the defendant. The original award for loss of income would be reduced.

PENNER V MITCHELL [1978] 5 WWR 328 (Supreme Court of Alberta). *Livingstone v Rawyards Coal Co* (1880) 5 App Cas 25, HL, applied.

854 —— —— **subsequent development of unconnected heart condition**

In 1971 the plaintiff, who was employed by the defendants, suffered injuries to his hand and fingers in the course of his employment. He underwent three amputations in successive years as the result of which he was left with a severely injured and disfigured hand. In 1976 he developed a serious heart condition unconnected with the injury. He became unfit for work from that date. He claimed damages for negligence from the defendants, contending that from 1976 he was entitled to his full notional pre-accident earnings for at least six months. For the balance of his expectation of life, which on account of the heart condition was limited, he claimed compensation for the difference between his pre-accident earnings and his earnings on light work. *Held*, the defendants were not liable for any loss of earnings from the time of the development of the heart condition in 1976. Where there was a second supervening non-tortious act which interrupted the effects of the first tortious act, the tortfeasor escaped the consequences of the second disability. Special damages with interest to 1976, when the heart condition developed, would be awarded. General damages for pain and suffering and loss of amenity from the date of injury to the end of the period of life expectancy would also be awarded.

HODGSON V GENERAL ELECTRICITY CO LTD [1978] 2 Lloyd's Rep 210 (Queen's Bench Division: LATEY J). *Cookson v Knowles* [1977] 2 All ER 820, CA, 1977 Halsbury's Abr para 812, and *Jones v National Coal Board* (unreported, 13th December 1976), applied.

855 —— **whether cost of exact replacement reasonable**

Defendants undertook to construct a distribution depot for the plaintiffs and undertook to lay a concrete surface in the parking area which the plaintiffs intended to use for heavy goods vehicles. The defendants' engineers specified a tarmacadam surface which was unsuitable for the purpose and would have required relaying at frequent intervals. The question arose as to whether an award of damages should be based on the cost of replacing the surface with concrete or with hot rolled asphalt, which was cheaper. *Held*, the rule in such cases was that a plaintiff should be entitled to such damages as would give him what he had contracted for, unless this led to an unreasonable result. Although the asphalt would require less maintenance than the tarmacadam it was considerably less suitable than the concrete and therefore the plaintiffs were entitled to an award of damages which would enable them to lay a concrete surface.

WILLIAM CORY & SON LTD V WINGATE INVESTMENTS (LONDON COLNEY) LTD (1978) 248 Estates Gazette 687 (Queen's Bench Division: SIR DOUGLAS FRANK QC sitting as a deputy High Court judge).

856   **Mitigation—two heads of damage—benefit accruing to plaintiff in respect of one head—set-off of benefit against damages arising from other head**

Premises were leased to the plaintiffs subject to an existing lease. The plaintiffs' solicitors served notice on his tenants terminating their tenancy, mistakenly stating that the plaintiffs would oppose the grant of a new tenancy. As a result, the tenants became entitled to compensation from the plaintiffs; they also vacated the premises. The plaintiffs brought an action against their solicitors alleging that they had been negligent in making the untrue statement and claiming damages in respect of their liability to pay compensation; they did not claim damages for loss of rent consequent on the vacation of the premises. The solicitors admitted negligence but contended that they were entitled to set off against the damages arising from the liability to pay compensation any benefit which might accrue to the plaintiffs by getting vacant possession of the premises, since that would be a benefit which resulted from their negligence. The plaintiffs argued that a benefit secured in mitigation of damage of one kind; that is, damage resulting from the vacation of the premises, could not be set off against damage of a different kind; that is, damage resulting from liability to pay compensation. *Held*, whether any benefit could be said to relate sufficiently closely to a particular head of damage as to be appropriate to set off against it was a question of fact. Since the plaintiffs were under a duty to mitigate any damage consequent on the negligence, which included damage resulting from the vacation of the premises, if it were established that a benefit had accrued to them from the vacation of the premises, the solicitors would be entitled to set off that benefit against the claim for damages in respect of the loss due to liability to pay compensation.

NADREPH LTD v WILLMETT & Co [1978] 1 All ER 746 (Chancery Division: WHITFORD J). *British Westinghouse Electric and Manufacturing Co Ltd v Underground Electric Railways Co of London Ltd* [1912] AC 693, HL applied.

857   **Penalty—carrying charges incurred due to late nomination of vessel**

Under a contract for the sale of maize, it was agreed that all carrying charges at loading incurred due to late arrival and/or late nomination of the vessel should be as per terms of the contract. Clause 6 provided that the buyers should nominate the vessel ten days prior to the date of shipment. Clause 13 provided for the extension of the shipping period on the buyers' application on specified payments being made. The buyers were late in nominating a vessel. The sellers claimed the payments under cl. 13 as representing the carrying charges which had been incurred at loading due to late nomination of the vessel. The buyers argued that the charges were penalties and did not constitute a genuine pre-estimate of the damages since they were quite distinct from the real cost of storage. The sellers claimed interest on the charges, since interest was part of the carrying charges. The dispute was referred to arbitration. The Board of Appeal of GAFTA found in favour of the sellers but stated the award in the form of a special case. *Held*, cl. 13 was not a provision whereby the parties had agreed that in the event of late arrival and/or late nomination a specified sum should be paid; it was a clause giving the buyers an option to apply for an extension of the shipping period on specific terms. The specified scale of charges represented the price to be paid for the extension. Even if the charges in cl.13 did not constitute a genuine pre-estimate of damages, this was irrelevant since the charges did not amount to a specified sum of money which the parties had agreed to pay in the event of a breach of contract. Thus the charges specified were not penalties. The board had concluded that interest was not within the ambit of carrying charges. Such charges were not defined in the contract, but were words in common commercial use to which the board had given its understanding of their commercial meaning. However, where there was a claim for interest and the tribunal had sufficient information to award it and no contention to the contrary, the arbitration should ordinarily include interest in an award of damages. The board's decision would be upheld and the award remitted in order that interest should be assessed on the sum awarded.

THOS. P. GONZALEZ CORPORATION v F. R. WARING (INTERNATIONAL) (PTY) LTD [1978] 1 Lloyd's Rep 494 (Queen's Bench Division: ACKNER J). *Panchaud Freres SA v R. Pagnan & Fratelli* [1974] 1 Lloyd's Rep 394 and *P. J. van der Zijden Wildhandel NV v Tucker & Cross Ltd* [1976] 1 Lloyd's Rep 341, 1976 Halsbury's Abr para. 147 applied.

858   Personal injury—action on behalf of minor—whether minor entitled to commence fresh action within extended limitation period

See *Tolley v Morris*, para. 2225.

859   —— assessment—factors to be considered

Canada

A fifteen-year old boy was injured while taking part in a gymnastics class and rendered quadriplegic, although his mind was unimpaired. The supervising teacher was found to be negligent and damages were awarded. The damages were reduced on the school authority's appeal, and the boy appealed. *Held*, the appeal would be allowed. In assessing general damages, the following factors should be taken into account; since the evidence indicated that the boy should be cared for at home rather than in an institution, the award for future care should be based on the reasonable cost of providing such care; deduction for basic necessities should be made in computing the award for loss of future income rather than in respect of future care; as to pain and suffering, loss of amenities and loss of expectation of life, the award under these non-economic related heads of damage should be a conventional award, adjusted to meet the individual circumstances.

THORNTON v BOARD OF SCHOOL TRUSTEES OF SCHOOL DISTRICT NO. 57 (PRINCE GEORGE) [1978] 1 WWR 607 (Supreme Court of Canada). Decision of Court of Appeal of British Columbia [1976] 5 WWR 240, 1976 Halsbury's Abr para. 1833 varied.

860   —— deduction in respect of attendance and mobility allowances

In an action for damages for personal injuries, the question arose whether the damages should be reduced in respect of attendance and mobility allowances received by the plaintiff under the Social Security Act 1975. *Held*, it was not the purpose of the legislation to deprive the plaintiff of damages awarded against the defendant. The allowances were payable independently of any compensation awarded and consequently the damages would not be reduced.

BOWKER v ROSE (1978) 122 Sol Jo 147 (Court of Appeal: LORD SCARMAN, MEGAW and ROSKILL LJJ). Dicta of Lord Reid in *Parry v Cleaver* [1970] AC 1 at 14, HL and *Daish v Waunton* [1972] 2 QB 262, CA applied. Decision of Talbot J (1977) 121 Sol Jo 274, affirmed.

861   —— injury leading to death—compensation for lost years— availability

An employee who contracted asbestosis in the course of his employment was awarded damages before his death and made an appeal against quantum which was heard after his death. Following the decision in *Oliver v Ashman* his claim for loss of earnings was limited to his life expectancy period and took no account of the years which he had lost as a result of the disease. On appeal, *held*, (LORD RUSSELL OF KILLOWEN dissenting) in *Oliver v Ashman* the Court of Appeal had erred in considering itself bound by a passage in *Benham v Gambling* [1941] AC 157, HL and had decided in effect that a man could not claim damages for loss of earnings in respect of years when he would not be there to earn them. The balance of authority suggested that this might not be so and on principle it seemed that, as the interest which a man had in the earnings he would have received in the lost years had a value which could be assessed, a rule which would allow a claim in respect of those earnings would come closer to his expectations. It would also bring the principles for assessment of claims made by an injured party into line with the provisions for claims by dependants in the Fatal Accidents Acts. However, his probable living expenses during the last years should be deducted in computing the damages. Accordingly the appeal would be allowed.

PICKETT v BRITISH RAIL ENGINEERING LTD [1978] 3 WLR 955 (House of Lords: LORD WILBERFORCE, LORD SALMON, LORD EDMUND-DAVIES, LORD RUSSELL OF KILLOWEN and LORD SCARMAN). *Pope v D. Murphy & Son Ltd* [1961] 1 QB 222 and *Skelton v Collins* (1966) 115 CLR 94 applied; *Harris v Brights Asphalt Contractors Ltd* [1953] 1 QB 617 and *Oliver v Ashman* [1962] 2 QB 210, CA overruled. Decision of the Court of Appeal (1977) Times, 17th November, 1977 Halsbury's Abr para. 832 reversed.

862 ——— **plaintiff unconscious or insensible—whether award should include sum for loss of future earnings**

A psychiatrist, now aged 41, suffered brain damage after a minor operation in 1973. She had been a senior registrar with good prospects of promotion to consultant psychiatrist within four or five years. The damage she suffered was diffuse, producing lack of co-ordination in all four limbs, depression and dementia. She was a helpless invalid who would require nursing for the rest of her life. There was no evidence that her expectation of life was reduced. She was awarded damages totalling £243,309, including £84,000 for loss of future earnings. The hospital authority appealed against the award, in particular contending that nothing should have been awarded for loss of future earnings. *Held*, LORD DENNING MR dissenting, it was well established that where a person suffered personal injury he should recover for loss of future earnings even though his injuries were so grave that he might be unconscious or insensible. Where a plaintiff was unlikely to be able to earn anything for the rest of his life the loss should be calculated on the basis of an assumed annuity. In the present case an allowance had correctly been made for inflation as the annuity was large enough to attract income tax at higher rates. It accordingly came within the exception to the general rule laid down by the House of Lords in *Cookson v Knowles* that no special allowance should be made for the prospect of inflation.

LORD DENNING, MR considered that large awards were in danger of injuring society. Where a plaintiff was unconscious or insensible compensation to be fair should not include an item for loss of earnings but an item for pecuniary loss suffered by the plaintiff's dependants.

LIM POH CHOO v CAMDEN AND ISLINGTON AREA HEALTH AUTHORITY [1978] 3 WLR 895 (Court of Appeal: LORD DENNING MR, LAWTON and BROWNE LJJ). Decision of Bristow J (1977) Times, 8th December, 1977 Halsbury's Abr para. 831 affirmed. *Phillips v London and South Western Railway Co* (1879) 5 CPD 280, CA; *H. West & Son Ltd v Shephard* [1964] AC 326, HL; and dictum of Lord Fraser of Tullybelton in *Cookson v Knowles* [1978] 2 WLR 978, 991, HL applied.

863 **Personal injury or death—damages under Fatal Accidents Acts— calculation of award—prospect of future inflation**

In an action under the Fatal Accident Acts a widow was awarded damages and interest on the whole of the sum awarded from the date of death to the date of judgment. On appeal the Court of Appeal reduced the damages and altered the award of interest, varying the guidelines laid down by that court in *Jefford v Gee* [1970] 2 QB 130. On further appeal, *held*, in fatal accident cases damages should normally be divided into two parts. The first part, the pre-trial pecuniary loss, was the total of the amounts assumed to have been lost for each week between death and trial. In calculating that amount the median rate of wages would normally be taken as the multiplicand, and where the deceased's age was such that he would probably have continued to have worked until the date of trial the multiplier would be the number of weeks between death and trial. On that part of the award interest should be awarded from the date of death to trial at half the current short term interest rate.

The second part was the future pecuniary loss of the dependants. In calculating that part the proper multiplicand should be based on the rate of wages at the date of trial. The multiplier should be related primarily to the deceased's age and hence to the probable length of his working life at the date of death. The sum should be such as prudently invested would provide the dependants with an annuity equal to the support probably lost through the deceased's death, the annuity being made up partly of income and partly of capital.

On the question of whether the prospect of future inflation should be taken into account in assessing damages the House considered that as awards were calculated on the basis of the low interest rates which capital would earn when the economy was stable, inflation was counterbalanced by the high rates of interest on gilt edged securities to which it gave rise. As long as a dependant was not liable for high rates of tax on her gross income she would be protected.

The House considered that the only circumstance in which it might be necessary to make a special allowance for future inflation was where the annuity was large enough to attract income tax at a high rate.

The House also considered that the principles relating to inflation and interest applied to claims for economic loss in personal injuries cases.

COOKSON V KNOWLES [1978] 2 All ER 604 (House of Lords: LORD DIPLOCK, VISCOUNT DILHORNE, LORD SALMON, LORD FRASER OF TULLYBELTON and LORD SCARMAN). Decision of the Court of Appeal [1977] QB 913, 1977 Halsbury's Abr para. 812, affirmed. Dicta of Lord Diplock in *Mallet v McMonagle* [1969] 2 All ER 178 at 190 and of Lord Pearson in *Taylor v O'Connor* [1970] 1 All ER 365 at 378 followed.

864   A doctor was killed in a road accident caused by the defendant's negligence. In assessing the damages payable to his widow the question arose whether future inflation should be considered. *Held*, from *Taylor v O'Connor* [1971] AC 115, HL it was possible to conclude that future inflation could be considered if economic circumstances required it. From the subsequent line of cases in the Court of Appeal, it was clear, however, that it was inappropriate to increase the multiplier applicable to counteract inflation, but that the court should do its best to minimise the effects of inflation where the conclusion could properly be drawn that inflation would adversely affect an award of damages. In the present circumstances, it could quite properly be concluded that inflation would continue at a minimum of seven per cent per annum until the end of the period prescribed by the multiplier. The dead man's income would have increased to take account of this and therefore the damages had to be increased pari passu if injustice were to be avoided.

DOYLE V NICHOLLS (1978) 122 Sol Jo 386 (Queen's Bench Division: BRISTOW J). *Taylor v O'Connor* [1971] AC 115, HL, *Mitchell v Mulholland* (No. 2) [1972] 1 QB 65, CA, *Young v Percival* [1974] 3 All ER 677, CA and *Cookson v Knowles* [1977] QB 913, CA, 1977 Halsbury's Abr para. 812 considered.

See now, however, *Cookson v Knowles* [1978] 2 All ER 604, HL, para. 863, ante.

865   —— **quantum of damages**

The following examples of awards of damages in personal injury or fatal accident cases are arranged in the following order, with cases involving more than one injury classified according to the major injury suffered.

Death	Internal injuries	Back and trunk
Brain damage and	Burns	Arms and hands
paralysis	Head	Legs and feet
Multiple injuries	Neck and shoulders	

DEATH

866   General damages: £50,530. Senior executive officer, 58, died of left ventricular failure with amoebic dysentery. Hospital treated him for ulcerative colitis and removed his colon. His widow, 61, claimed damages. Multiplier 10 years × £4,250 from date of trial onwards, £8,030 from date of death to trial. *Tuffill v Surrey Area Health Authority*, 14th March 1978 (Queen's Bench Division: Kenneth Jones J).

867   General damages: £3,000 (defendants' counter claim). Postman, single, 27, was killed in motor car accident. Mother suffers from multiple sclerosis, father, 58, also a postman. Parents partially dependent on son's earnings. *Lewis v Cuff*, 23rd June 1978 (Queen's Bench Division: Chapman J).

BRAIN DAMAGE AND PARALYSIS

868   General damages: £41,250. Waiter, single, 25, was passenger in van when it hit a tree. Sustained head injuries and compression fracture of 5th cervical vertebra with subluxation forward of 4th and 5th vertebrae. Required skull traction. He is now an incomplete tetraplegic and will never make a complete recovery, will always have to walk with sticks; bladder function impaired; sexual function and life expectancy impaired. Cannot undertake adult domestic pastimes and hobbies e.g. gardening, decorating. The above award was calculated as follows: £22,500 for pain and suffering etc., £15,000 (15 year multiplier) loss of future earning capacity, £250 p.a. for fifteen years for employment of skilled labour to carry out gardening, decorating, maintenance tasks. *Porter v Martin*, 23rd January 1978 (Queen's Bench Division: Judge E. H. Laughton Scott QC).

869   *Paraplegia*
General damages: £82,930. Warehouseman, bachelor, 55, fell 9 feet off a fork lift truck. Fractured thoracic spine at D10 resulting in complete paralysis below that level, haemothorax of the right lung, severe scalp laceration and depression. Unable to work again. Requires resident housekeeper and adapted living accommodation, an invalid car etc. Above sum includes £49,780 for future nursing care and amenities for a disabled person, and £10,900 for further loss of earnings. *Boulton v Sankey Building Supplies Ltd*, 17th October 1978 (Queen's Bench Division: Michael Davies J).

MULTIPLE INJURIES

870   General damages: £28,500. Secretary, 30, divorced, was injured in a motor car accident and sustained concussion, face lacerations, fracture of pelvis, strain of the left sacro-iliac joint, scalp abrasion. Post traumatic epilepsy, one fit every three weeks, blurring and reduction of vision, loss of memory, backache. She is registered as a disabled person. Loss of earning capacity and promotion prospects. Above sum includes £12,500 for loss of future earnings. *Horrell v Allen*, 10th February 1978 (Queen's Bench Division: Judge E. H. Laughton-Scott QC).

871   General damages: £75,000. Boy, 11, hit by car while crossing the road. Severe concussion, fractured left clavicle; right first and second ribs, right humerus, subtrochanteric fracture of right femur, fractures of both rami of left pelvis. Permanent residual spastic right hemiparesis; shortening of right leg and residual clumsiness of right arm and leg. He will always be at a grave disadvantage in obtaining employment. *Lawson v Ramsden*, 21st February 1978 (Queen's Bench Division: Lawson J).

872   General damages: £31,000. Bus company engineer supervisor, married, 54, was injured in a collision when he was riding a motor cycle. Fractured skull (right maxilla) causing brain damage, fracture of right lower ribs, fracture of right scapula. Permanent retrograde amnesia, photophobia, permanent squint, personality change (front lobe syndrome), 5 per cent risk of epilepsy, grave mental handicap, unemployable but may be able to earn "pin money" doing odd jobs. Above award includes £16,000 loss of future earnings, and £2,500 for loss of pension rights. *Williamson v Powell*, 9th May 1978 (Queen's Bench Division: Michael Davies J).

873   General damages: £61,000. Steel erector, 40, married, injured when a crane collapsed on him. Severe bruising of the skull, deep wound of left loin. Fracture of left acetabulum with inward displacement and distortion of the articular surface of left hip joint. Comminuted compound fracture of left femur involving the shaft and condyles and extending into left knee joint with marked distortion of its articular surface. Required a patellectomy and a pin inserted in the hip. He will require a new hip in 10–15 years. Permanently unfit to be a steel erector or for any heavy work. Severely handicapped in labour market. Above sum includes £51,000 future loss of earnings. *Hotchkiss v Pritchard International Corpn*, 28th June 1978 (Queen's bench Division: Neill J).

874   General damages: £9,000. Boy, 10, knocked down by a motor car when crossing the road. Head injury and brain damage, unconscious for five days, partial paralysis, partial loss of vision, bruised spleen, fractured right femur. Clumsy with his right hand, but he is left-handed. Right leg shortened by 1 inch. Has to wear bifocal glasses, cannot ride a bicycle. His eyes do not coordinate. Poor short term memory and frustration owing to his eye trouble. *Legg v Huggins*, 10th July 1978 (Queen's Bench Division: Judge Edgar Fay QC).

875   General damages: £1,750 (agreed). Auto-setter, 20, injured when his motor cycle plunged down 50 foot excavation beside road. Fractured both femurs, ruptured spleen and damaged left kidney. 17 inch scar on chest; 10 inch scar on right thigh. Shortening of right leg and limitation of hip rotation. *Corps v Costain Civil Engineering Ltd*, 8th December 1978 (Queen's Bench Division: Lawson J).

INTERNAL INJURIES

876   *Hernia*
General damages: £750. Fork lift truck driver, 53, sustained a right inguinal hernia when he was coupling trailer to the truck. Operative treatment complicated by a nerve adhesion to the scar tissue. Vulnerable to further straining injury. Thirty weeks off work. *Virgin v Bush Boake Allen Ltd*, 24th April 1978 (Queen's Bench Division: Croom-Johnson J).

877   *Lead absorption*
General damages: £750. Labourer, married, 44, absorbed excessive lead dust, fumes etc, causing gradual weakness and abdominal pain. *Djemal v H.J. Enthoven & Sons Ltd*, 7th November 1978 (Queen's Bench Division: Peter Pain J).

BURNS

878   General damages: £3,300 (agreed). Fireman injured in explosion when putting out fire in mobile van kitchen. Severe burns to face, neck and hands, face discoloured. Severe nervous shock causing an anxiety state with loss of confidence, poor concentration, dizziness, shaking, palpitations and headaches. Handicapped in work and everyday life. Uncertain whether he can resume fireman's full duties. *Imber v Bright*, 4th July 1978 (Queen's Bench Division: Chapman J).

HEAD

879   General damages: £75,000. Miner, 36, sustained injuries when his head was crushed in a digging machine. Fractured skull, loss of one eye, bone graft in scalp, injury to and loss of hearing in left ear. Above award includes a future loss of earnings of £15,000 (3 years as a tunneller) and £38,000 (as a labourer, multiplier 9½ at £4,000 p.a.). *McFadden v Kinnear Moodie (1973) Ltd*, 6th March 1978 (Queen's Bench Division: Kenneth Jones J).

880   General damages: £42,000. Married docker, 48, struck on head by lifting gear. Skull fractured, olfactory hallucinations (a symptom of epilepsy) very severe bilateral deafness, totally deaf in left ear and little hearing in right ear; tinnitus and headaches and dizzy spells, impairment of sense of smell. Permanently disabled for dock work and at a disadvantage in labour market. Unable to converse in company, cannot hear traffic on the roads, voices on the telephone, radio, bells etc. Gait rather unsteady, loss of confidence when going out alone, cannot ride motorcycle. Above sum includes £20,000 for loss of future earnings. *Price v Port of London Authority*, 26th July 1978 (Queen's Bench Division: Neill J).

881   *Head and arm*
General damages: £500. Medical equipment representative, 26, injured in motor car accident. Blow to right side of forehead, pieces of glass in right thumb and forearm, severe headaches. *Davison v Reid*, 17th March 1978 (Queen's Bench Division: Kenneth Jones J).

882   *Face*
General damages: £1,200. Married fitter, 19, a passenger in a motor car involved in an accident, sustained extensive laceration of face, back of left ear; ugly scar running across his left cheek across jawline on to his neck ½ ins wide × 4¼ in long, and depressed below the surface of surrounding skin. *Gregory v Kelly*, 13th March 1978 (Queen's Bench Division: Kenneth Jones J). As to liability see para. 2028.

883   General damages: £1,930. Accounting machine operator, single, 24, had three front teeth knocked out when her moped was in a collision. Her denture will require a bridge and she may require treatment for her jaw which had previously been treated for a deformity. *Holmes v Green*, 24th May 1978 (Queen's Bench Division: Judge Lymbery QC).

884   General damages: £565. Apprentice tool-maker, 18, riding a moped, was in collision with a motor car and crashed into a plate glass window. Lacerations to left side of chin and left side of neck. Disfiguring scars on chin, neck and all limbs. *Ford v Brooker*, 30th June 1978 (Queen's Bench Division: Judge Edgar Fay QC).

885   *Face and neck*
General damages: £2,000. Married canteen assistant, 45, received a whiplash injury and facial lacerations when she was in motorcar accident. Restricted neck movements, loss of sense of smell and taste, scars on face, scalp and neck, depression. *Edwards v Pantelic*, 27th October 1978 (Queen's Bench Division: Boreham J).

886   *Face, hip and leg*
General damages: £4,500 and £2,000. T.V. actor, 22, and girl, 20, injured in a motor car accident. He sustained a compound fracture of the left tibia, fibula and femur, nail inserted in the femur, permanent scarring on left leg. The girl had a forehead laceration which severed nerves conveying sensation to left side of top of scalp, permanently unsightly scar, some loss of memory. *Guy v Kelly*, 3rd October 1978, (Queen's Bench Division: Michael Davies J).

887   *Eye*
General damages: £9,600. Travelling salesman, 51, married. Had an operation on left eye to correct a squint. Surgery negligently performed resulting in perforation of eye. Entire nasal half of iris torn from its attachment to the cillary body. Pupil now slit-shaped. Lost sight of left eye, permanently and severely disfigured. Unable to pursue any recreational pursuits. Future earning capacity severely impaired. Above sum includes £4,000 for future loss of earnings. *Jackaman v Oxfordshire Area Health Authority*, 16th May 1978 (Queen's Bench Division: Drake J).

888   General damages: £6,000. Married area manager, 39, injured in a motor car accident. 95 per cent loss of vision in right eye, risk of retinal detachment glaucoma, perforating corneal scleral injury of right eye, deep vein thrombosis, fractured ribs and multiple facial lacerations. *Plate v Harris*, 6th December 1978, (Queen's Bench Division: Lawson J).

889   General damages: £23,836. Single apprentice engineer, 21, injured when a vehicle hit his motor cycle, resulting in the loss of vision of his left eye, and compound fractures to right tibia and fibula with extensive soft tissue injury and serious muscular and nerve damage. Continuing paralysis in right foot. Above sum includes £13,836 for future loss of earnings. *Holmes v Gillings*, 1st December 1978 (Queen's Bench Division: Swanwick J).

890   *Nose*
General damages: £5,716. Married fitter, 56, was hit across the face by a steel bar and his nose was fractured. Suffers from frequent headaches and has been forced to change jobs. Above sum includes £1,716 for future loss of earnings. *Hicks v London Borough of Lewisham*, 27th October 1978 (Queen's Bench Division: Peter Pain J).

NECK AND SHOULDERS

891   *Neck*
General damages: £1,000. Insurance claims manager, 30, married, sustained a whiplash injury to his cervical spine in a motor car accident. A disc lesion, bruising and injury to right shoulder. Osteo-arthritis is likely later. Intermittent pain when turning neck and stiffness when head has been in same position for some time. *Horne v Brooke*, 27th April 1978 (Queen's Bench Division: Bristow J).

892   Total agreed damages: £1,167. Married fireman, 38, suffered concussion and neck strain when a beam fell on him. Flexion of spine restricted. *Stone v Kent County Council*, 15th May 1978 (Queen's Bench Division: Michael Davies J).

893   General damages: £4,067. Stereotyper, 41, married, sustained whiplash injury in a motor car accident. Neck movement restricted permanently, discomfort from time to time; previous degenerative changes in neck. He cannot enjoy clay pigeon shooting because it is painful to tilt his head up. Above sum includes £1,567 for future loss of earnings. *Barlow v Stannard*, 25th May 1978 (Queen's Bench Division: Drake J).

894   *Shoulder*
General damages: £3,000. Costume designer, married, 60, slipped on wet paint on stage, sprained her right shoulder, bruised chest and upper right arm resulting in acute sub-deltoid bursitis and supra-spinatus. Still some restriction of movement, difficulty with household activities and swimming. She is right-handed. *Kerr v BBC*, 17th January 1978 (Queen's Bench Division: Judge E. H. Laughton Scott QC).

895   General damages: £1,200. Steel erector, 49, slipped as he was getting through a hole into some ducting. Strained his right shoulder, difficulty in using his right arm, and wielding a hammer. Three months off work. *Skeggs v Babcock & Wilcox (Operations) Ltd*, 17th January 1978 (Queen's Bench Division: Forbes J).

896   Total damages: £2,000 (agreed). Bus conductor, 58, married sustained capsulitis of the right shoulder when he fell as the driver braked suddenly. Continuing difficulty in fully stretching the shoulder. Limitation in physical activity of gardening and home decorating. *Pocock v Thames Valley & Aldershot Omnibus Co Ltd*, 21st March 1978 (Queen's Bench Division: Kenneth Jones J).

897   General damages: £2,000. Machinist, 50, stepped on a tilting duckboard and fell wrenching his shoulder. Some restriction of movement of shoulder and neck; pins and needles in his left hand when he grips hard; cannot reach up with left hand. Aggravation of pre-accident symptomless cervical spondylosis. Symptoms permanent. Cannot return to pre-accident work because he cannot carry heavy components. Five weeks off work. Unable to dig in the garden and difficulty carrying out home decoration. *Knell v Vauxhall Motors Ltd*, 11th July 1978 (Queen's Bench Division: May J).

898   General damages: £850. Machine operator, 55, was pulled on to machine when drill's arm caught in his sleeve, and strained shoulder muscles and groin and buttock muscles. Limited neck movement. *Charij v Dennis Motors Ltd*, 12th December 1978 (Queen's Bench Division: Gibson J).

899   *Shoulder, arm and ankle*
General damages: £7,000. Scientific officer at Harwell, 43, married, suffered a

fracture dislocation of right shoulder, fracture of right ankle and malleolus of right elbow in motor car accident. Some scarring on his head and restricted movement and stiffness in arm and shoulder; cannot put right arm behind his back or lift it higher than shoulder height which hampers him in his work, cannot drive for more than two hours. Can no longer engage in competitive sailing, and restricted in his hobbies, cannot swim properly. Increased risk of osteoarthritis. *Huxtable v Kearney*, 11th January 1978 (Queen's Bench Division: Judge E. H. Laughton Scott QC).

900 *Shoulder and leg*
General damages: £1,750 and £4,000. Husband, 82, and wife, 76, passengers in a motor car accident. Husband received a blow to the head and dislocated left shoulder, weakness in grip, cannot pick up a tea-pot. Wife received crushing lacerations to both legs, 8 inch wound on right leg requiring 23 stiches, oedema in ankles, wound discharged for 5 months, can only walk 100 yards with a frame, housebound and difficulty in doing household chores. Permanent unsightly scar on right leg, very mobile before accident. *Cleaver v Callaghan*, 13th July 1978 (Queen's Bench Division: Judge Lewis Hawser QC).

BACK AND TRUNK

901 *Back*
General damages: £200. Process operator, 40, strained back lifting a drum. Prolapse of lumbar intervertebral disc. Only fit for light work. *Weathers v Perox Chemicals Co Ltd*, 19th April 1978 (Queen's Bench Division: Croom-Johnson J).

902 Total Damages: £15,750 (agreed). Telephone engineer, 34, struck by sack of tools. Abrasions with severe bruising of buttocks and lower back. Flake fracture of right capitulum with damage restricting movement. Swelling and aching of left knee. Can no longer play football and golf. *Stoneham v The Post Office*, 25th April, 1978 (Queen's Bench Division: Croom-Johnson J).

903 General damages: £3,250. Gas conversion fitter, 41, married, fell off van steps and injured his back resulting in the removal of an intervertebral disc. Cannot perform heavy duties, cramp-like pain in buttocks which is aggravated by walking and driving. *Gray v Humphreys and Glasgow Ltd*, 3rd October 1978, (Queen's Bench Division: Wien J).

904 General damages: £350. Foreman fitter, 46, married, strained back muscles and ligaments when he fell backwards over a railing when a guard-dog leapt at him. Slight injury to the soft tissues of his right wrist. *Hinds v Roadshops Ltd* 23rd October 1978 (Queen's Bench Division: Judge Alan Lipfriend).

905 General damages: £1,000. Laboratory technician, 51, injured lower lumbar spine in a motor car collision. A soft tissue injury which exacerbated pre-existing back condition. Some impairment of mobility, difficulty driving his car owing to pain in right leg. *Reinman v Manning*, 3rd November 1978 (Queen's Bench Division: May J).

906 General damages: £7,500. Married pipe fitter, 36, injured his back lifting a motor pump; 18 months later he fell when a soakaway collapsed and re-injured his back resulting in a large central lumbar posterior disc protrusion requiring 2 operations. Limited leg and low back movements, only fit for light work. Above sum includes £2,500 for future loss of earnings. *Bawn v British Leyland (U.K.) Ltd*, 20th November 1978 (Queen's Bench Division: Swanwick J).

907 General damages: £2,250. Guillotine setter operator, 46, fell back on to the floor when his spanner spun loose as he was tightening a nut. He bruised his spine, exacerbating pre-existing spinal degeneration. Only fit for light work. *Hulton v Marconi Instruments Ltd*, 6th December 1978 (Queen's Bench Division: Swanwick J).

908   General damages: £750. Mobile repair welder, 41, strained his back lifting oxygen cylinder into a landrover. Prolapsed intervertebral disc, numbness in lower left leg and in 2 toes and sole of the left foot. Injury exacerbated previous back strain. *Harding v Poclain Ltd*, 11th December 1978 (Queen's Bench Division: Swanwick J).

909   *Back and wrist*
General damages: £1,400. Widow, factory worker, 53, fell over obstruction on factory floor. Strained back and right wrist. Reduction of grip, cannot do heavy lifting. Pre-existing back condition exacerbated. *Underwood v John J. Dunster & Son Ltd* 30th January 1978 (Queen's Bench Division: Judge E. H. Laughton-Scott QC).

910   *Pelvis*
Total damages £27,500 (agreed). Boy, 9, trapped pelvis between barrel and mounting of howitzer gun at a tattoo. Suffered a fracture dislocation of the pelvis and lumbar sacral plexis injury. Rupture of the urethra. Severe permanent limp and he will always be handicapped in labour market. *Woodhouse v Ministry of Defence*, 13th January 1978 (Queen's Bench Division: Judge Alan Lipfriend).

ARMS AND HANDS

911   *Arm and hand*
General damages: £7,500 (agreed). Hospital porter, 38, slipped in corridor and his arm went through a glass door panel. Severe lacerations of right hand and forearm involving damage to the tendons, arteries, nerves and muscles of hand and arm which required a number of operations. Right middle finger is bent; poor sensation over median nerve distribution of hand and palm which feels cold all the time; considerable disfiguring scars. *Bucho v City & East London Area Health Authority (Teaching)*, 25th October 1978 (Queen's Bench Division: Roy Beldam QC).

912   *Wrist*
General damages: £1,500. Married woman, 63, fell in the bus and fractured the lower end of left radius. Limitation of wrist movement and loss of grip. *Carter v Southdown Motor Services Ltd*, 19th April 1978 (Queen's Bench Division: Forbes J).

913   General damages: £1,250. Married crane driver, 43, slipped and fell on oily patch and strained "snuff-box" of right wrist. A scaphoid plaster was applied. Later degenerative osteoarthritis may develop. 14 weeks off work. *Parker v Attwoods Crane Hire Ltd*, 11th May 1978 (Queen's Bench Division: Michael Davies J).

914   General damages: £2,250. Married barmaid, 63, fell on slippery ramp and fractured lower end of left radius of wrist with gross deformity, aggravating a pre-accident wrist condition and resulting in loss of sensation in the fingers. Permanent loss of grip and radial deviation. Risk of grave injury to left hand owing to loss of sensation. *Brown v Bedfont & Hatton Royal British Legion Club Ltd*, 23rd May 1978 (Queen's Bench Division: Judge Lymbery QC)

915   *Wrist and hand*
General damages: £2,250. Technician, 44, sprained his right wrist and thumb when he fell over obstruction in workplace. Traction aggravated symptoms, psychological overlay. 146 weeks off work. *MacGregor v The Post Office*, 14th April 1978 (Queen's Bench Division: D. McNeill QC).

916   General damages: £600. Married woman, 65, fell over depressed and unstable paving stone and sustained a minor fracture of radial styloid process in left wrist, and fracture of base of first metacarpal bone in left hand, and twisted left ankle. Her ankle and left arm have developed osteo-arthritic changes. Spontaneous haemorrhage required physiotherapy. Permanent discomfort and pain in left thumb. *Lavers v London Borough of Redbridge*, 13th June 1978 (Queen's Bench Division: Kenneth Jones J).

917   *Hand*
General damages: £1,250. Foreman steel erector, 51, injured his hand when it was trapped when loading a welding set on to a lorry. Crush injury to left hand. He had pre-existing Dupuytren's Contracture of his hand which was exacerbated and advanced the necessity of an operation by 5 years. Substantial impairment of manual deftness and gripping ability of left hand. *Burns v Cozens and Sutcliffe (Erectors) Ltd*, 12th October 1978 (Queen's Bench Division: Wien J).

918   General damages: £7,150. Married steel erector, 63, injured his left hand when a grain auger started up when he was examining a fault. Laceration of the dorsum of thumb extending into the palm, division of 3 entensor tendons, division of radial artery, severance of thenar muscles, traumatic dislocation of trapezio-metacarpal joint of thumb, contusion of median nerve, division of digital nerve on radial side of middle finger. Permanent loss of dexterity and grip of left hand, stiffness in fingers resulting in 50 per cent work handicap. Above sum includes £3,400 for future loss of earnings. *Healey v Golden Produce Ltd*, 25th October 1978 (Queen's Bench Division: Sheen J).

919   General damages: £3,350. Married carpenter, 27, slipped and caught his left hand in a circular saw. Traumatic laceration of middle finger involving the interdigital cleft between index and middle fingers. Both flexor tendons severed, loss of soft tissue from end of index finger which is half an inch short, comminuted fracture of the terminal phalanx, joints of 2 fingers are stiff. *Ede v Greater London Council*, 26th October 1978 (Queen's Bench Division: Judge Alan Lipfriend).

920   General damages: £5,500. Labourer, 25, married, trapped his left hand between a wall and the cab of a mechanical shovel. Tearing injury of ulnar side of hand or the severance of the middle of the shafts of little and ring metacarpals, flexor tendons to the same fingers and ulnar nerve. Scarring and deformity of hand. Grip only 50 per cent normal. Permanently unable to do heavy bimanual activities. Fractures of 4th and 5th metacarpal bones are not united and may require more surgery. Handicapped in recreations of gardening and tennis. *Taylor v Ready Mixed Concrete Ltd*, 6th November 1978 (Queen's Bench Division: Kenneth Jones J).

LEGS AND FEET

921   *Hip and leg*
General Damages: £16,000. Storeman, 25, pillion passenger on Honda which was in a collision. Right leg amputated above knee. Fracture of right femur, intra medullary nail inserted. Artificial limb caused chafing, skin grafts on stump, skin problems continue, amputation required two operations. He is very conscious of his disability. *Gardiner v Allfield*, 6th April 1978 (Queen's Bench Division: Judge Edgar Fay QC.)

922   *Thigh and groin*
General Damages: £5,000. Unemployed man, married, 60 was shot in thigh and groin and hit on the head. He suffered a right orchidectomy, the gland of his penis was severely lacerated and some tissue lost. Required skin graft on thigh. Suffers from depression, tension, lost sexual desire and unable to have sexual intercourse. *Abbott v Jordanou* 28th April 1978 (Queen's Bench Division: Chapman J).

923   *Leg*
General damages: £3,500. Crane driver, married, 66, trapped his leg against some girders. Fracture of right lateral malleolus, disuseosteoporosis of right ankle and foot. Ankle mortice narrower at outer angle. Risk of osteoarthritis. His leg gave way six months after accident and he fell fracturing right wrist. Difficulty in decorating house, playing ukelele and painting with right hand. *Hawkins v Brown & Tawse Ltd*, 13th January 1978 (Queen's Bench Division: Ackner J).

924   General damages: £2,000. Drill operator, 52, married, fractured right tibia and fibula when he was struck by a falling rock. Deep vein thrombosis of left calf, right ulnar paresis due to elbow crutch pressure. Off work for 39 weeks. *Chambers v Amey Roadstone Corporation Ltd*, 3rd October 1978 (Queen's Bench Division: Forbes J).

925   *Leg and arm*
General damages: £6,000. Timekeeper, single, 18, was riding his moped when it was in collision with motor cycle. Compound fracture of left patella and kneecap and right wrist with gross deformity, severe concussion, greenstick fracture of left wrist, fracture of middle third of left leg. Cannot run, kneel or squat, or stand for long periods, some restricted movement in holding tools in right hand. No loss of future earnings. *Williams v Richards*, 20th March 1978 (Queen's Bench Division: Kenneth Jones J).

926   General damages: £5,000. Married female factory worker, 52, knocked off pedal cycle by motorist. Sustained bruises and grazes on left leg and buttock and left elbow. Since the accident she has suffered from constant double vision, a left convergent squint and headaches, left leg limp, incontinence and indigestion: post traumatic and functional symptoms. Unfit to work since accident. *Pietruszka v Simpkins*, 1st December 1978 (Queen's Bench Division: Griffiths J).

927   *Knee*
General damages: £4,500. Storeman, 64, fell over obstruction in gangway and sustained a torn meniscus of left knee, deep vein thrombosis, abrasions of left elbow. Off work for 12 months; has to walk with a stick, can only work at ground level. Thickening of left ankle, foot and calf. Permanent disability. Above sum includes £1,000 for future loss of earnings. *Benson v Spillers Ltd*, 22nd February 1978 (Queen's Bench Division: Lawson J).

928   General damages: £100. Car-deck attendant, single, 39, slipped on oil patch and bruised knee. Wasting of quadriceps muscle near left knee. Permanent limp, cannot play football or return to same job. 16 months off work. *Townsend v Townsend Car Ferries*, 10th April 1978 (Queen's Bench Division: Croom-Johnson J).

929   *Ankle*
General damages: £1,200. Docker, 47, married, struck on left ankle by swinging load. Fractured left inner ankle bone and bruised right arm. Six months off work. Permanent slight thickening of medial malleolus, still limps when tired and some aching at times. *Jackson v The Phoenix Timber Co Ltd*, 17th January 1978 (Queen's Bench Division: Michael Davies J).

930   General damages: £3,500. Test house supervisor, 50, slipped on a piece of metal and sustained a fracture dislocation of left ankle requiring surgical reduction and fixing with screws. Walks with a limp; permanent stiffness of the joint and strong likelihood of osteo-arthritis. *Brooks v KL Foundries Ltd*, 14th July 1978 (Queen's Bench Division: May J).

931   *Foot*
General damages: £2,000. General labourer, 51, fractured base of third metatarsal bone and fractured both phalanges of the big toe of the left foot when a steel plate fell on his foot. Soft tissues of his foot also injured. Arthritis at bases of 2nd and 3rd metatarsals and the cuneiform bones. Symptoms will continue and an arthrodesis may be necessary. *McGarrell v Bovis (Construction) Ltd*, 15th March 1978 (Queen's Bench Division: Judge Alan Lipfriend).

932   Total damages: £5,423 (agreed). Plumber, 44, injured when he fell from ladder in course of employment. Fracture of right oscaleis, extending into subtaloid joint. Complete loss of inversion and eversion of foot, and flexion of ankle reduced.

Suffers pain when walking on rough ground, and after walking several miles. Unable to run, crouch or climb ladders. Pre-accident hobby of cycling not affected, and able to continue working for previous employers. *Bate v Halton Borough Council,* 25th July 1978 (Queen's Bench Division: Hollings J).

933   **Tort—currency of award**

See *The Despina R*, para. 841.

DEEDS

Halsbury's Laws of England (4th edn.), Vol. 12, paras. 1301–1566

934   **Article**

Making a Deed, H. W. Wilkinson (effect of *First National Securities Ltd v Jones* [1978] 2 WLR 475, 1977 Halsbury's Abr para. 910): 128 NLJ 502

DEVELOPMENT LAND TAX

935   **Booklet**

The Inland Revenue have prepared a booklet (DLT 2) explaining the provisions of the Development Land Tax Act 1976 as amended by the Finance Act 1977. Copies may be obtained free of charge from the Development Land Tax Office, Corporation House, 73–75 Albert Road, Middlesbrough, Cleveland TS1 2RY or by personal callers at the Public Enquiry Room, Room 8, New Wing, Somerset House, Strand, London WC2R 1LB.

936   **Notification of disposals—forms**

The Inland Revenue have prepared two leaflets about the requirements of the Development Land Tax Act 1976 for notice to be given to them of certain disposals and other events which are likely to give rise to liability to development land tax. Leaflet DLT30 describes the types of disposals of interests in land and other events which are required to be notified to the Development Land Tax Office. Leaflet DLT300 contains information on the various prescribed notification forms and the circumstances in which each of them is to be used. Copies may be obtained free of charge from the Development Land Tax Office, Corporation House, 73–75 Albert Road, Middlesbrough, Cleveland TS1 2RY or by personal callers at the Public Enquiry Room, Room 8, New Wing, Somerset House, Strand, London WC2R 1LB: Inland Revenue Press Release dated 20th November 1978.

937   **Rates of tax—reduced rate—extension**

The Inland Revenue have issued a Press Release dated 28th June 1978 stating that the reduced rate of 66⅔ per cent on the £150,000 after the first £10,000 of development value realised in a financial year will operate for a further year. Accordingly, it will apply to disposals taking place on or before 31st March 1980. The necessary legislation will be included in the 1979 Finance Bill.

938   **Unpaid tax—interest**

Interest is payable on any unpaid development land tax from the reckonable date, that being the last day of the three-month period beginning on the date tax liability arose. Interest is paid on any repayment of tax from the later of the date of payment or the reckonable date. The relevant rate of interest is six per cent. Overpaid interest is refundable to taxpayers. See Inland Revenue Press Release dated 7th September 1978.

DISCOVERY, INSPECTION AND INTERROGATORIES

Halsbury's Laws of England (4th edn.), Vol. 13, paras. 1–142

939   Article

Discovery and Inspection in the High Court, Emlyn Williams (notes on procedure): 128 NLJ 429.

940   Default—failure to comply with order for discovery—acquisition of freehold by tenant

See *Nwojeki v Northumberland Court (Streatham) Ltd*, para. 1767.

941   Interrogatories—counsel's opinion—legal professional privilege

See *Jones v G. D. Searle & Co Ltd*, para. 1796.

942   Legal professional privilege—report on fatal accident—purpose of report

See *Waugh v British Railways Board*, para. 952.

943   Production of documents—appeals concerning children

In a case in the Family Division, Wood J stated that it was open to solicitors who were having difficulty in obtaining documents or justices' reasons in any appeal concerning a child, to apply to a single judge of the Family Division for an order for production so that further delay could be prevented.

Re B (A MINOR) (1978) Times, 26th October (Family Division: SIR GEORGE BAKER P and WOOD J).

944   ——— documents taken into account by rent officer—production in county court action

See *Legal & General Assurance Society Ltd v Keane*, para. 1742.

945   ——— medical records—production to party to action

The defendant to an action for damages for personal injuries applied under Administration of Justice Act 1970, s. 32 for an order for production of hospital records relating to treatment of the plaintiff before he was injured. The hospital authorities contended that production should be limited to medical advisers only. The Court of Appeal of Northern Ireland decided that there was no jurisdiction under s. 32 to make an order for production limited in that way. On appeal *held*, the power to make an order under s. 32 was discretionary and accordingly the court could decline to make an order if it was of the opinion that it was unnecessary or oppressive or not in the interests of justice or injurious to the public interest in some other way. However, where an order was made it should be for the production of the documents to the applicant, or if he was legally represented, to his solicitor.

The House also stated that the same principle applies to an order under s. 31 of the 1970 Act for disclosure by prospective parties to an action before it is begun.

McIVOR v SOUTHERN HEALTH AND SOCIAL SERVICES BOARD, NORTHERN IRELAND [1978] 2 All ER 625 (House of Lords: LORD DIPLOCK, LORD EDMUND-DAVIES, LORD RUSSELL OF KILLOWEN, LORD KEITH OF KINKEL and LORD SCARMAN). *Davidson v Lloyd Aircraft Services Ltd* [1974] 3 All ER 1, CA, 1974 Halsbury's Abr para. 1039, *Dunning v United Liverpool Hospitals* [1973] 2 All ER 454, CA and *Deistung v South Western Metropolitan Regional Hospital Board* [1975] 1 All ER 573, CA, 1974 Halsbury's Abr para. 1038 overruled.

For comment on this decision see, Making a breach in confidentiality, Justinian: Financial Times, 22nd May 1978.

946   —— order by industrial tribunal—complaint of race or sex discrimination—confidential reports

On the hearing of interlocutory appeals against orders for discovery of confidential reports made on complaints of sexual and racial discrimination, the Court of Appeal considered the conflict between the public interest in preserving confidentiality and the interest of a person who has presented a complaint of discrimination.

In the first case a woman civil servant who had not been considered for promotion when two of her colleagues had, claimed she had been overlooked because she was married and because of her trade union activities. An industrial tribunal ordered production of confidential reports on the two colleagues, and the order was confirmed by the Employment Appeal Tribunal. In the second case a coloured man was unsuccessful in his application for a transfer. He considered that he had been discriminated against because of his race. The Employment Appeal Tribunal on appeal from an industrial tribunal ordered production of confidential reports relating to the other applicants. On appeal against the orders, *held*, industrial tribunals should not order or permit the disclosure of reports or references given and received in confidence except where, after inspection of a particular document, the chairman decided that it was essential in the interests of justice that the confidence should be overridden. The appeals would be allowed.

SCIENCE RESEARCH COUNCIL v NASSE; LEYLAND CARS LTD v VYAS [1978] 3 WLR 754 (Court of Appeal: LORD DENNING MR, LAWTON and BROWNE LJJ). Decision of the Employment Appeal Tribunal in *Science Research Council v Nasse* [1978] 3 All ER 1195 reversed. *D v National Society for the Prevention of Cruelty to Children* [1978] AC 171, HL, 1977 Halsbury's Abr para. 916 applied.

947   In separate actions two female academics alleged that respective universities had discriminated against them on the grounds of their sex in relation to jobs for which they had applied. Both complainants made interlocutory applications to industrial tribunals for discovery of confidential reports and documents relating to other candidates for the posts. In the first case a general order for discovery was granted, but in the second the application was rejected. Both decisions were appealed against to the Employment Appeal Tribunal. *Held*, the Court of Appeal had recently emphasised the sacrosanct nature of confidential reports and documents, and had clearly decided that general orders for the discovery of such information should never be made. Only in exceptional cases should industrial tribunals, of their own volition, look at confidential documents, and even more rarely should they grant discovery to a complainant as a preliminary issue. The normal procedure to be adopted was for the complainant, during the hearing before the tribunal, to apply for discovery on the ground that to exclude the information would lead to injustice. Accordingly, the first appeal would be allowed and the second dismissed.

THE UNIVERSITY OF READING v MACCORMACK; BUSFIELD v THE UNIVERSITY OF ESSEX [1978] IRLR 490 (Employment Appeal Tribunal: KILNER BROWN J presiding). *Science Research Council v Nasse* [1978] 3 WLR 754, CA, para. 946 applied.

948   —— —— —— whether complainant entitled to discovery of all documents

The appellant applied for a post for which he was short-listed but not appointed. He claimed that this was because of his race and applied for discovery and inspection of the documents involved. He was granted discovery of documents relating to general procedure and qualifications of candidates interviewed but was refused others which related particularly to the short-listed candidates on the grounds that they were irrelevant to his case. He appealed. *Held*, the appellant was entitled to discovery of documents which would enable him to make a comparative analysis between his own qualifications and history and those of the other competitors for the job. It was justifiable that the appellant be given discovery of all the documents that related to the short-listed candidates so that the tribunal could legitimately decide whether his non-success was due to discrimination against him on racial grounds.

RASUL v COMMISSION FOR RACIAL EQUALITY [1978] IRLR 203 (Employment Appeal Tribunal: BRISTOW J presiding).

949   —— patent—documents discoverable

See *American Cyanamid Co v Ethicon Ltd*, para. 2056.

950   —— privilege—Crown privilege—non-disclosure on ground of public interest

The Bank of England acting under the directions of the government had entered into an agreement with a major oil company, in response to the company's acute financial difficulties. The agreement involved financial assistance by the Bank to which the company transferred a large quantity of stocks. The government had insisted that any re-sale of stocks should be non-profit sharing. Subsequently the value of the stocks increased substantially. In an action to have the agreement set aside the company applied for discovery of certain documents. Through the Attorney-General, intervening, the Chief Secretary of the Treasury had certified that production of the documents would be injurious to the public interest. *Held*, it was for the company to persuade the court to look at the documents and order production, and this it had failed to do. Such criticism of the certificate as there had been had only confirmed how carefully the Crown had decided what documents or parts of documents should not be produced. The company's contention that in the context of a commercial transaction any claim for privilege ought to be narrowly restricted was misconceived as this was a rescue operation rather than a bargain. It was not apparent that the company's case would be materially assisted by documents disclosing how the government, at the highest level, had decided what terms it would authorise the bank to offer. The documents were high level policy documents which it was necessary for the proper functioning of the public service to withhold from production.

BURMAH OIL LTD V BANK OF ENGLAND (1978) Times, 29th July (Chancery Division: FOSTER J).

This decision has been affirmed on appeal.

951   —— relevance of documents—evidence admissible as similar fact evidence

The plaintiffs owned the copyright of a musical work which, they alleged, had been copied in part for the sound track of a successful film. The third defendants in the case claimed to own the copyright in the sound track of the film, and had allegedly authorised the use of the music by the first defendants, the exhibitors and distributors of the film, and the second defendants, the makers of records of the sound track. The plaintiffs sought an order for discovery against the third defendants in respect of all documents relating to acts of infringement of copyright by them in previous legal actions, in particular in *Mood Music Publishing Co v de Wolfe Ltd*. The plaintiffs sought to discover such evidence on the basis that it would be admissible as similar fact evidence. *Held*, while in civil cases similar fact evidence may be admissible if it is thought to have some probative value, the discovery sought in this case did not bear directly on the issue in the trial; namely, whether the third defendants had authorised acts of infringement by the other defendants. The order would be refused.

E. G. MUSIC v S. F. (FILM) DISTRIBUTORS LTD [1978] FSR 121 (Chancery Division: WHITFORD J). *Mood Music Publishing Co v de Wolfe Ltd* reported at [1976] Ch D 119, 1975 Halsbury's Abr para. 1463.

952   —— report on fatal accident—whether report compiled for use in litigation or to establish cause of accident—legal professional privilege

The widow of a train driver killed in a rail accident sought discovery of a report compiled on the accident by British Rail. They claimed professional privilege for the report on the ground that it had been written partly to assist their legal department in any ensuing litigation. *Held*, LORD DENNING MR dissenting, the report had been compiled both to aid British Rail in defending any action arising and to ascertain the cause of the accident. The fact that it had been made for a dual purpose did not deprive it of the privilege that would have attached to it had it been made for the former purpose only. Discovery would thus be refused.

Lord Denning MR considered the report should be disclosed because its main purpose was to establish the cause of the accident, which was not privileged. Material should only be withheld when its main or sole purpose was to assist litigation. Justice demanded that such an important and useful piece of evidence be made available.

Waugh v British Railways Board (1978) 122 Sol Jo 730 (Court of Appeal: Lord Denning MR, Eveleigh LJ and Sir David Cairns).

953   —— requirement of physical possession or custody of documents sought—company documents—matrimonial proceedings

In the course of proceedings relating to the occupation of a matrimonial home, the husband was ordered under RSC Ord. 24 to grant discovery of certain documents relating both to expenditure on entertainment, travel and other domestic items incurred by him and a company of which he was managing director, and to the accounts of the company. On his appeal against the order, *held*, RSC Ord. 24 only gave the court power to order discovery of documents in the custody or physical control of the person against whom the order was sought. Since the husband's right to company documents arose solely from his position as a director and since the relevant documents were in the legal possession of the company, he had no power to disclose them and the order would be quashed in respect of them. However, the documents relating to domestic expenditure were in his custody and possession and the order would be upheld insofar as it related to them.

B v B (Matrimonial Proceedings: Discovery) [1978] 3 WLR 624 (Family Division: Dunn J). *Alfred Crompton Amusement Machines Ltd v Customs and Excise Commissioners (No. 2)* [1974] AC 405, HL and *Williams v Ingram* (1900) 16 TLR 451, CA applied.

954   —— use of documents disclosed—confidentiality—affidavit of means in family proceedings

See *Medway v Doublelock Ltd*, para. 967.

DISTRESS

Halsbury's Laws of England (4th edn.), Vol. 13, paras. 201–500

955   Distress for rates—date rate due and payable—whether local authority a priority creditor

See *Re Piccadilly Estate Hotels Ltd*, para. 371.

956   —— non-occupation of part of premises

See *Camden London Borough Council v Herwald*, para. 2284.

DIVORCE

Halsbury's Laws of England (4th edn.), Vol. 13, paras. 501–1352

957   Articles

Domestic Proceedings and Magistrates' Courts Act 1978, R. L. Waters: 122 Sol Jo 565.

Effect of Conduct on Matrimonial Relief, Margaret Spencer (an attempt to define obvious and gross conduct and the extent to which the courts take conduct into account): 128 NLJ 348.

Matrimonial Law Reform (the matrimonial jurisdiction of magistrates' courts and the provisions of the Domestic Proceedings and Magistrates' Courts Act): 142 JP Jo 95.

The New Matrimonial Law of Magistrates, Brian Harris (revision of magistrates' jurisdiction in matrimonial law; Domestic Proceedings and Magistrates' Courts Act 1978): 128 NLJ 1011.

Recognition of Foreign Divorce Decrees: Maintenance, R. L. Waters: 122 Sol Jo 326.

The Rôle of Solicitors in Divorce Proceedings, Mervyn Murch: (1978) 41 MLR 25.

Sale of Matrimonial Home, J. G. Miller (position in relation to a sale of the matrimonial home:) [1978] Conv. 301.

958   **Decree absolute—declaration concerning welfare of children— adequacy of financial provision for child**

See *Cook v Cook*, para. 975.

959   **Defended causes—request for directions for trial—pre-trial re- view—practice**

The following Practice Direction ([1979] 1 All ER 112) has been issued by the Family Division.

1. The proviso to r. 33 (4) of the Matrimonial Causes Rules 1977 enables a registrar to treat a request for directions for trial in a defended cause as a summons for directions under RSC Ord. 25. In that event, the registrar is required to give the parties notice of a date, time and place at which the request will be considered (a 'pre-trial review'). The provisions of RSC Ord. 34, r. 5 (3) (which provide for the parties to furnish the court with any information it may require as to the state of readiness of the case for trial) are applied to defended matrimonial causes by r. 46 (4) of the 1977 rules.

2. As from the beginning of the Hilary Term 1979 every request for directions for trial relating to a defended matrimonial cause proceeding in the Principal Registry will be referred to a registrar for a pre-trial review appointment to be fixed. Appointments are likely to be fixed for hearing from February onwards.

3. The prime objective behind the pre-trial review procedure is to enable the registrar to ascertain the true state of the case and to give such directions as are necessary for its 'just, expeditious and economic disposal'. In practice in those district registries where the system of pre-trial review has been applied to matrimonial causes, it has been found that under the registrar's guidance the parties are often able to compose their differences, or to drop unsubstantial charges and defences, and to concentrate on the main issues in dispute. Experience in the district registries has shown that, following pre-trial review, many cases proceed undefended under the special procedure, with consent orders as to financial provision or in respect of the custody of, or to access, to, the children. Where contested issues remain, the registrar is able to give directions to facilitate their expeditious determination at the subsequent hearing before the judge.

4. To avoid possible adjournments and delay it is especially important that the parties are represented on a pre-trial review hearing by their legal advisers who are fully conversant with the facts of the case, including counsel if he has been so instructed. The personal attendance of the parties on the review hearing is normally desirable.

960   **Discovery of documents—documents relating to one party's expenditure—requirement of physical possession by party from whom discovery sought**

See *B v B (Matrimonial Proceedings: Discovery)*, para. 953.

961   **Divorce county courts**

The Divorce County Courts Order 1978, S.I. 1978 No. 1759 (in force on 2nd January 1979), designates those courts which are to be divorce county courts and courts of trial for the purposes of the Matrimonial Causes Act 1967, s. 1 (1). Basingstoke, Bow, Camborne and Redruth, Chippenham, Consett, Neath and Port Talbot and Salisbury County Courts have been added to those designated as divorce county courts and courts of trial by previous orders, and Workington County Court has been made a court of trial. In the case of those courts mentioned in Sch. 2, column 1 of the Order, which are held in more than one place, the jurisdiction under the Act is exercisable only at the places specified in column 2.

The Order revokes the Divorce County Courts Order 1971, S.I. 1971 No. 1954, as amended: S.I. 1972 No. 1946; 1973 No. 1278; 1974 No. 1004, 1974 Halsbury's Abr para. 1056; 1975 Nos. 1002, 1869, 1975 Halsbury's Abr paras. 1110, 1111; 1976 Nos. 17, 676, 1222, 2233, 1976 Halsbury's Abr paras. 875–878; 1977 Nos. 938, 1624, 1977 Halsbury's Abr paras. 932, 933; 1978 No. 818, para. 962.

962   The Divorce County Courts (Amendment) Order 1978, S.I. 1978 No. 818 (in force on 1st July 1978), designates the Altrincham, Bishop Auckland, Gateshead, Llanelli, Macclesfield, North Shields, Rotherham, Runcorn, Skipton, South Shields and Welshpool County Courts as divorce county courts and adds them to the list of those at which undefended matrimonial causes may be tried.

This Order was subsequently revoked, see para. 961.

963   **Financial provision—application—relief not available at time of petition—whether leave required for subsequent application**

In 1970 a wife was granted a decree of divorce. In her petition she had applied for maintenance, child maintenance, a lump sum and/or secured provision. The court approved an agreement between the parties which provided inter alia for maintenance for the wife and children. In 1976 the wife applied for lump sum provision for the children. Under Matrimonial Causes Rules 1977, r. 68 leave must be obtained to make an application for relief which should have been made in the petition. On the question of whether leave was required the wife contended that the relief sought came within the terms of the petition. Alternatively she contended that she was a person having custody of a child within r. 69 of the 1977 Rules and accordingly did not require leave. *Held*, a person having custody of a child was a person other than the petitioner or the respondent. As the wife was the petitioner she could not apply under r. 69. Accordingly her application was under r. 68. Although it was difficult to regard the claim for a lump sum for the children as one which should have been made in the petition as there was no statutory provision for such a claim at the time of the petition, leave had nevertheless to be obtained as r. 68 was mandatory.

The court decided that in the circumstances leave would be refused.

McKay v Chapman [1978] 1 WLR 620 (Family Division: Lionel Swift QC sitting as a deputy High Court judge).

964   —— —— **remarriage of applicant**

Before the dissolution of her marriage, a woman gave notice in the required form that she intended to apply for periodical payments for the children of the marriage. After the dissolution and her remarriage, the woman was granted leave by the registrar to amend the application to add an application for ancillary relief for herself. It was objected that the registrar had no jurisdiction to do this. *Held*, Matrimonial Causes Act 1973, s. 28 (3), barred a wife from applying for ancillary relief after remarriage. The amendment was in effect a fresh application after remarriage and there was no jurisdiction to allow it.

Nixon v Fox (formerly Nixon) [1978] 3 WLR 565 (Family Division: Dunn J).

965   A former wife who had subsequently remarried applied to amend Form 6, the acknowledgment of service of the husband's petition for divorce, so as to comply with the wording of Form 11, the notice of application for ancillary relief. Dismissing the application on the ground that it was an attempt to defeat the Matrimonial Causes Act 1973, s. 28 (3), which expressly banned a former spouse from applying for ancillary relief from the other spouse after remarrying, WOOD J said that if on receipt of a petition the respondent decided not to file an answer, he or she should fill in a Form 11 application in lieu of an answer, thus avoiding the trap presented by s. 28 (3).

JENKINS V HARGOOD (FORMERLY JENKINS) [1978] 2 All ER 1001 (Family Division: WOOD J).

966   —— lump sum payment—matters to be considered

The parties were married in 1964. Shortly afterwards, the wife's father conveyed to her by deed of gift a farm which became the matrimonial home. Both husband and wife put great effort into improving the farm and ran the business as partners, though the freehold of the property remained in the wife's name. In 1976, the marriage was dissolved on a petition by the wife and she was given custody of the three children of the marriage. The husband, who had no other means of support, then applied for a lump sum and a transfer of property order of one half of the farm. The total overall value of the farm was estimated at approximately £102,000. An order was made for the wife to pay the husband a lump sum of £15,000 in three instalments, while he was to make nominal periodical payments to his wife and children. The husband appealed against the order on the ground that £15,000 was insufficient. *Held*, the valuation of the farm at £102,000 was purely an estimated valuer's figure and it would be quite unrealistic to view the wife as having assets amounting to that figure. In applying the Matrimonial Causes Act 1973, s. 25, care should be taken not to assume that justice required an equal division of the assets as the proportion of the division was dependent on the circumstances. In this case, it appeared that £15,000 was the largest capital sum that the wife could afford without having to sell the farm, bearing in mind the children involved and the need to provide for them. All the circumstances of the case had to be considered and £15,000 was an adequate amount for the husband to acquire new accommodation. The appeal would be dismissed.

P v P (FINANCIAL PROVISION: LUMP SUM) [1978] 3 All ER 70 (Court of Appeal: ROSKILL and ORMROD LJJ).

967   —— maintenance agreement—affidavit of means—disclosure of affidavit in unrelated proceedings

The plaintiff was involved in two separate actions in the High Court. In the Family Division, his former wife had made an application to vary a maintenance agreement. In the course of these proceedings, the plaintiff had sworn two affidavits of means. In the Queen's Bench Division, a company controlled by the plaintiff had applied for judgment against another company, which was applying for security for costs to be given by the plaintiff's company. To support that application, a director of the other company had sworn an affidavit in which were exhibited copies of the plaintiff's affidavits of means in the Family Division proceedings. The plaintiff brought an action in the Chancery Division for an injunction restraining the other company and its director from making use of his Family Division affidavits. *Held*, the public interest of confidentiality in the disclosure of means in family cases, outweighed the public interest of having a full disclosure of information in an application for security for costs. An injunction restraining the use of the affidavits for proceedings other than those in the Family Division would be granted.

MEDWAY V DOUBLELOCK LTD [1978] 1 All ER 1261 (Chancery Division: GOULDING J). *D v National Society for the Prevention of Cruelty to Children* [1977] 1 All ER 589, 1977 Halsbury's Abr para. 916, *Distillers Co (Biochemicals) Ltd v Times Newspapers Ltd* [1975] 1 All ER 41, 1975 Halsbury's Abr para. 1102, and *Riddick v Thames Board Mills Ltd* [1977] 3 All ER 677, 1977 Halsbury's Abr para. 918 applied.

968   —— maintenance orders—enforcement

The Recovery Abroad of Maintenance (Convention Countries) Order 1978, S.I.

1978 No. 279 (in force on 23rd March 1978), declares that Switzerland is a convention country for the purposes of the Maintenance Orders (Reciprocal Enforcement) Act 1972, and adds that country to the list of convention countries in the Recovery Abroad of Maintenance (Convention Countries) Order 1975, 1975 Halsbury's Abr para. 1135.

969 ——matters to be considered—effect of agreement between parties

When divorce proceedings were contemplated the parties agreed on financial provision for the wife. Each party signed the minutes of agreement to be submitted for the registrar's approval. A petition for dissolution was then filed by the husband. Subsequently it became clear that the wife was resiling from the agreement and she was ordered to show cause why the minutes of agreement should not be made an order of the court. *Held*, the court had an ultimate discretion concerning financial arrangements between the parties, whether the order was made under Matrimonial Causes Act 1973, s. 23 or s. 24, and in exercising that discretion it was the court's duty to consider the principles laid down in s. 25. In considering the conduct of the parties the fact of, and the nature of, the agreement voluntarily arrived at between them was a matter to be taken into account. The court had a duty to uphold an agreement especially if made at arm's length and negotiated by legal advisers, where there had been no change of circumstances and the agreement was not against public policy. The agreement would be approved.
Dean v Dean [1978] 3 All ER 758 (Family Division: Bush J).

970 —— periodical payments—agreement to waive future claims to maintenance

After the parties' divorce a consent order was made by which the husband was to convey the matrimonial home to the wife, and make a periodical payment of five pence per year until the conveyance. Payment was to cease upon completion of the conveyance, and in a collateral agreement the wife agreed to waive all further claims to maintenance. The wife subsequently became dissatisfied with the arrangements and applied for variation of the periodical payments, but the court held that it did not have jurisdiction to hear a fresh application. On the wife's appeal *held*, the court had no jurisdiction to hear a fresh application where it had already made financial provision on the merits of the case. The Matrimonial Causes Act 1973, s. 23 (1) empowered the court to achieve a final financial arrangement if it thought such finality was appropriate, practical and just. The consent order was such a final order and the appeal would be dismissed.
Minton v Minton [1979] 1 All ER 79 (House of Lords: Lord Wilberforce, Viscount Dilhorne, Lord Fraser of Tullybelton, Lord Russell of Killowen and Lord Scarman). Decision of Court of Appeal [1977] LS Gaz R 1129, 1977 Halsbury's Abr para. 939 affirmed.

971 —— —— appeal against order

See *Scott v Scott*, para. 974.

972 —— attachment of earnings

Following the parties' divorce the husband was ordered to make periodical payments to his former wife and son. The wife subsequently applied for an attachment of earnings order to secure payments in arrear. The husband had been forced to retire prematurely from his job as a fireman because of arthritis, and his pension under the Fireman's Pension Scheme Order 1973 was increased due to ill-health. He contended that the pension was paid in respect of a disability and therefore fell within the Attachment of Earnings Act 1971, s. 24 (2) (d) which provided that pensions payable in respect of disability or disablement were not earnings to which an attachment order could be made. At first instance the judge held the husband had failed to prove his increased pension was payable in respect of disablement. On appeal *held*, a pension payable to a fireman who had retired compulsorily because of disablement was not a pension payable in respect of disablement. The appellant's pension was calculated solely on the length of his pensionable service and was in no way connected with the extent or degree of his disablement. It fell within the definition of "earnings" in the Attachment of Earnings Act 1971 and was therefore liable to an attachment order.

MILES v MILES (1978) Times, 29th November (Court of Appeal: ORMROD, WALLER and BRANDON LJJ). Decision of Divisional Court of the Family Division (1978) Times, 21st July, affirmed.

973   —— —— low income of husband

A husband appealed against a court order requiring him to make periodical payments of £10 per week to his wife and child. *Held*, after paying statutory deductions, travelling expenses, tax, mortgage repayments, rates and the order the husband was left with £13·88 per week which was less than the minimum subsistence allowance for a single man. The husband's resources should not be depressed below subsistence level, but it was not right that the payments to the wife should be decreased to such an extent that the husband was living well above the minimum level. The court had to take into account the fact that the wife was entitled to rent and rate rebates. The husband required about £15 per week, so the payment to the wife would accordingly be reduced to £8.

WALKER v WALKER (1978) 122 Sol Jo 193 (Family Division: PURCHAS J).

974   —— periodical payments and transfer of property—appeal against orders—criteria for making orders

A husband and wife separated after seven years of marriage and were subsequently divorced. The wife had capital of £2,000, while the husband earned £3,400 per annum. Out of that, he was ordered to pay £6 per week for each of his three children, and £11 for his wife. The matrimonial home, valued at £7,000, was occupied by the wife and children subject to a trust for sale due to operate when all the children had reached their majorities. The husband was to take sixty per cent of the proceeds of sale, his wife forty per cent. The husband appealed. *Held*, in cases involving a small income and a small capital sum, the aim of any order relating to property should be to place both parties in a comparable position when they were thrown into the housing market. The order which had been made would enhance the capital position of the wife after the sale of the house, but that was correct in view of her inferior ability to obtain a mortgage. However, the weekly gross payments, which had been assessed on the basis of the one-third rule, would be reduced by £6 to ensure that both parties enjoyed a comparable standard of living. The rule was of no assistance in cases where a party was having to make mortgage payments to meet the priority needs of the children of the marriage.

SCOTT v SCOTT [1978] 3 All ER 65 (Court of Appeal: STEPHENSON and CUMMING-BRUCE LJJ).

975   —— provision for children—adequacy of provision—child dependant on supplementary benefit paid to wife

A wife had obtained a maintenance order for herself and her child. The Department of Health and Social Security collected the payments and paid the wife supplementary benefit and her rent. After pronouncing a decree nisi on the wife's undefended suit for divorce, the judge refused to make a declaration under the Matrimonial Causes Act 1973, s. 41 (1), that he was satisfied that the arrangements for financial provision for the child were adequate, on the grounds that the wife's means apart from supplementary benefit payments were inadequate to provide reasonable maintenance for the child; that the child's maintenance order, made over a year earlier, did not reflect the current level of earnings; and that it was not in the public interest or the child's that she should be dependent on the supplementary benefit paid to the wife, when no means were open to the department to obtain a review of the maintenance orders assigned to it. On appeal by the wife, *held*, the court was only concerned with investigating whether the child was being supported and whether there was a reasonable prospect of that support continuing. The adequacy of the financial provision for the child's general welfare was not a matter for investigation. There was no question of public policy involved, nor was it against the child's interests to be supported wholly or in part from public funds. There was no reason to suppose that any increase in the amount ordered to be paid would benefit the child, as it would still be less than the supplementary benefit paid. The appeal would be allowed and the declaration made.

Cook v Cook [1978] 1 WLR 994 (Court of Appeal: Buckley and Goff LJJ and Sir David Cairns).

976   —— transfer of property—application for order—failure to register application—effect of subsequent legal charge in favour of third party

See *Whittingham v Whittingham*, para. 1691.

977   Maintenance order—enforcement of order under Guardianship of Minors Act 1971—appeal

See *Re K (Minors)*, para. 1942.

978   Matrimonial causes—rules

The Matrimonial Causes (Amendment) Rules 1978, S.I. 1978 No. 527 (in force on 2nd May 1978 except for rr. 5, 8, 9, in force on 6th June 1978), amend the Matrimonial Causes Rules 1977. The registrar in a defended case may now treat a request for directions for trial as a summons for directions under RSC Ord. 25. He may also require information relating to the state of a defended cause which has been set down for trial, grant an order under the Matrimonial Causes Act 1973, s. 37 (2) (a), restraining a person from challenging a claim for financial relief, and allow temporary removal of children from the jurisdiction. Causes in which both parties are seeking a decree that neither opposes the grant of one to the other are to be treated as undefended.

The rules in addition facilitate disposal of causes in the special procedure list where there is an objection to paying any costs for which the petitioner prays and where there are children to whom the 1973 Act, s. 41 applies.

For 1977 Rules, see 1977 Halsbury's Abr para. 955.

979   —— costs

The Matrimonial Causes (Costs) (Amendment) Rules 1978, S.I. 1978 No. 922 (in force on 31st July 1978), amend the Matrimonial Causes (Costs) Rules 1977 by increasing the fixed costs and the prescribed sums to be allowed in average cases under the divorce scale applicable to matrimonial proceedings in divorce county courts.

For 1977 Rules, see 1977 Halsbury's Abr para. 956.

980   —— fees

The Matrimonial Causes Fees (Amendment) Order 1978, S.I. 1978 No. 1256 (in force on 2nd October 1978), amends the Matrimonial Causes Fees Order 1975, 1975 Halsbury's Abr para. 1139, by increasing the fee payable on the presentation of a petition to £20. It also makes consequential amendments in other fees to take into account the charges made by the County Court Fees Order 1978, para. 539 and the Supreme Court Fees (Amendment) Order 1978, para. 2220.

981   Matrimonial home—exclusion of spouse—power of arrest attached to injunction

See *Lewis v Lewis*, para. 1521.

982   —— occupation—production of documents—requirement of physical possession of documents

See *B v B (Matrimonial Proceedings: Discovery)*, para. 953.

983   **Nullity of marriage—impotence—degree of penetration required**

Scotland

The parties married in 1963 and separated in 1976. Although the couple had frequently attempted sexual intercourse, the husband had never achieved full penetration, apparently from reluctance to hurt his wife. The wife applied for a decree of nullity on the ground of her husband's impotence. *Held*, the capacity necessary to consummate a marriage was the capacity for full and complete intercourse. Capacity to achieve partial penetration only was insufficient and the wife was entitled to a decree of nullity on the ground of her husband's impotence.

J v J 1978 SLT 128 (Outer House).

984   **Petition—leave to present petition within three years—exceptional hardship or exceptional depravity**

After marriage a wife discovered that her husband was a homosexual and incapable of sustaining a sexual relationship with her. She applied under the Matrimonial Causes Act 1973, s. 3 (2) for leave to present a petition of divorce within three years on the grounds of either exceptional depravity on the part of the husband, or exceptional hardship suffered by her. At first instance the judge held that the wife had not made out her case on either ground. On the wife's appeal *held*, assessments of what constituted exceptional hardship and exceptional depravity involved value judgments of a subjective character. The courts were familiar with the concept of hardship but depravity was more difficult to define. As the judge was able to take various factors into account when considering the concept of hardship it was usually unnecessary to rely on exceptional depravity. The husband's homosexuality did not amount to exceptional depravity but, on the facts, the wife had proved that she had suffered exceptional hardship and she would be given leave to present a petition of divorce within three years.

C v C [1979] 2 WLR 95 (Court of Appeal: ORMROD, WALLER and BRANDON LJJ).

EASEMENTS

Halsbury's Laws of England (4th edn.), Vol. 14, paras. 1–300

985   **Article**

Right to Light, W. A. Greene (home improvements; position regarding amount of light to which neighbouring property is entitled): 122 Sol Jo 515.

986   **Extinguishment—doctrine of unity of ownership—effect on restrictive covenants**

See *Re Tiltwood, Sussex; Barrett v Bond*, para. 1171.

987   **Light—prescription—light required by greenhouse—requirement of sun's rays**

The plaintiffs were owners of a greenhouse which was put in shadow by a fence erected by the defendants. The plaintiffs brought an action for injunctions restraining the defendants from causing a nuisance by diminution of the access of light to the greenhouse. It was established that it had been used for the ordinary purposes of a greenhouse for at least twenty years and the plaintiffs claimed that they had acquired a prescriptive right to light. The defendants alleged that the plaintiff could only prescribe for an ordinary amount of light, which was less than that required by a greenhouse, and that a right to light consisted only in illumination and not in warmth and other properties of the sun's rays. *Held*, it was probable that the ordinary light required for a greenhouse was that light which would facilitate its use as such, but even if this was not so the plaintiffs had established a right to that amount of light by twenty years' user with the servient owner's knowledge. The user also entitled them to the right to the sun's rays, since without that right the nuisance would not be removed.

ALLEN v GREENWOOD [1979] 2 WLR 187 (Court of Appeal: BUCKLEY, ORR and GOFF LJJ).

988   Right of way—access to highway—visibility

See *Hayns v Secretary of State for the Environment*, para. 2789.

989   —— express grant—reservation of right to claim compensation—whether right extended to neighbouring land owned by grantor's successor

The claimants agreed to buy a parcel of land neighbouring their own in April 1973. In May the owners of the land executed a deed granting the respondents an easement to lay and maintain gas mains on the land and covenanted not to do any act which would interfere with that easement, but they reserved the right to claim compensation from the respondents if the covenant was to affect the grant of any planning permission. The measure of compensation was stated to be that which would have been payable if the respondents had served a notice of compulsory acquisition of the servient land. The claimants bought the servient land in June, and in November they sought planning permission to erect a warehouse and offices on both parcels of land. The question for the court was whether a claim could be made for compensation for the injurious effect of the covenant on the parcel of land which was not subject to it. *Held*, although the claimants had acquired the equitable interest in the servient land in April, the deed had not contemplated the grant of compensation in respect of the neighbouring land which they already owned, and accordingly they could only claim in respect of the servient land.

BLANDRENT INVESTMENT DEVELOPMENTS LTD v BRITISH GAS CORPN (1978) 248 Estates Gazette 131 (Court of Appeal: STEPHENSON, GEOFFREY LANE and CUMMING-BRUCE LJJ).

990   —— whether right of way capable of being occupied

See *Pitsea Access Road, Basildon, Essex: Land Reclamation Co Ltd v Basildon District Council*, para. 1712.

ECCLESIASTICAL LAW

Halsbury's Laws of England (4th edn.), Vol. 14, paras. 301–1435

991   Church of England (Miscellaneous Provisions) Measure 1978

The Church of England (Miscellaneous Provisions) Measure 1978 makes further provision with respect to the special majorities required for the final approval of certain measures; makes further provision with respect to the continuance in certain offices of persons in office at the commencement of the Ecclesiastical Offices (Age Limit) Measure 1975; makes provision for altering the financial year of the Church Commissioners; amends Schedule 1 to the Church Commissioners Measure 1947; provides for the diocesan member of the Central Board of Finance to be a voting member of the diocesan board of finance; amends the Parochial Registers and Records Measure 1978, s. 20; extends the New Parishes Measure 1943, s. 17; makes provisions for facilitating the conveyance of ecclesiastical property in certain circumstances; makes provision for extending the Inspection of Churches Measure

1955 and schemes made thereunder; amends the Cathedrals Measure 1963, s. 43 and the Endowments and Glebe Measure 1976, ss. 3 and 43 and repeals so much of the Queen Anne's Bounty Act 1714, s. 21, as requires certain documents to be enrolled in the High Court. The Measure received the royal assent on 30th June 1978 and came into force on 30th July 1978.

Section 1 makes necessary a two-thirds majority of those present and voting in each House of the General Synod to carry a motion for the final approval of a Measure providing for permanent changes in the Services of Baptism or Holy Communion or in the Ordinal.

Section 2 provides that the attainment of the age of seventy does not necessarily invalidate appointments to certain offices of persons who had attained that age and held office immediately before the passing of the Ecclesiastical Offices (Age Limit) Measures 1975, 1975 Halsbury's Abr para. 1165, which made seventy the age limit.

Section 3 enables the Church Commissioners to alter their financial year, currently running from 1st April to 31st March, to 1st January to 31st December, when they so decide.

Section 4 amends the constitution of the Church Commissioners, altering the requirements that at least two of the eight Commissioners shall be or shall have been counsel to Her Majesty, and making the length of time for which the Commissioners are appointed to office five years, or longer or shorter periods at the discretion of the General Synod.

Section 5 provides that diocesan members of the Central Board of Finance shall be voting members of the diocesan finance boards.

Section 6 restricts the power of an authority other than the local authority in control of diocesan record offices, to charge fees for searches, or the provision of copies. The fee must be the same as is payable to an incumbent for the same service, this being determined by order under the Ecclesiastical Fees Measure 1962.

Section 7 extends the powers of the Church Commissioners and other persons to dispose of land or buildings by sale or otherwise. These provisions shall now additionally apply to land no longer required for any of the following purposes for which it was acquired, namely, for providing access to or improving the amenities of a church, churchyard or burial ground or a house of residence of an incumbent.

Section 8 provides that where the fee simple of any ecclesiastical property is in abeyance, the fee simple shall, for the purposes of a compulsory acquisition, be treated as being vested in the Church Commissioners. Notices to treat must consequently be served on the Commissioners.

Section 9 extends the power of the bishop of a diocese, who has licensed a building for public worship, to direct that the Inspection of Churches Measure 1955, or any scheme made under it, shall apply to that building, with any modifications that he may specify.

Section 10 amends the Cathedrals Measure 1963, s. 43, so that non-residentiary canons in the cathedral church of Christ in Oxford shall, unless the bishop directs otherwise, vacate office on attaining the age of seventy years, or on ceasing to be beneficed, or licensed to serve, in the diocese of Oxford. The bishop may confer the title of canon emeritus on any person vacating the office of non-residentiary canon.

Section 11 makes minor corrections to the Endowments and Glebe Measure 1976.

Section 12 abolishes the requirement to enrol certain deeds in the High Court in accordance with the Queen Anne's Bounty Act 1714, s. 21.

Section 13 deals with citation, construction, commencement and extent.

992　　Clergy pensions scheme—Channel Islands

See para. 2085.

993　　Dioceses Measure 1978

The Dioceses Measure 1978 enables alterations to be made in the diocesan structure of the provinces of Canterbury and York. It additionally enables suffragan bishops to discharge certain functions hitherto discharged by diocesan bishops, abolishes the power to commission suffragan bishops, makes provision for the establishment of separate synods for diocesan areas, and makes further provision concerning the nomination of suffragan bishops and the discharge of the functions of diocesan bodies. The Measure received the royal assent on 2nd February 1978 and came into force on 2nd May 1978.

Section 1 provides for the appointment by the Standing Committee of the General Synod of a Diocesan Commission, whose main function is to advise on matters affecting the diocesan structure of the provinces of Canterbury and York: s. 2. Under s. 3 and the Schedule the Commission must prepare and make reorganisation schemes for the foundation of new bishoprics, the transfer of areas between dioceses, and the transfer of any diocese to another province. Sections 4–8 detail the procedure for making reorganisation schemes.

Section 9 invests the General Synod with power to make temporary provision with respect to the membership of the Convocations of Canterbury and York and of the House of Laity during the transitional period of any diocese created, transferred or modified by a reorganisation scheme.

Section 10 empowers diocesan bishops by instrument to delegate functions to suffragan bishops subject to such limitations as the former may impose. Section 11 provides for the making of schemes dividing dioceses into areas and dividing episcopal functions. Such schemes are to be made in accordance with s. 12, and may be varied or revoked by subsequent schemes: s. 13. Section 14 provides that any suffragan bishop's right to collate to any benefice is ineffective during a vacancy in the diocesan bishop's see.

The power of diocesan bishops to commission suffragan bishops is abolished: s. 15. Section 16 enables the functions vested in diocesan bishops by statute etc. to be exercised by suffragan bishops in consequence of reorganisation schemes. Section 17 provides for the constitution of area synods for episcopal areas, s. 18 deals with the creation or revival of suffragan sees. Sections 19, 20 make schemes for the discharge of the functions of diocesan bodies corporate and committees. Sections 21–24 are supplemental.

994   Endowments and Glebe Measure 1976—commencement

By an order of the Church Commissioners all provisions of the Endowments and Glebe Measure 1976, 1976 Halsbury's Abr para. 920 which were not then in force came into force on 1st April 1978.

995   Faculty—church building—reconstruction of organ—unlawful dismantling without faculty

The churchwarden and members of the congregation of a parish filed a petition for the reconstruction of the church organ. The diocesan advisory committee, to which the petitioners' proposals went, decided that the reconstruction was unnecessary. Without obtaining the required faculty, the petitioners authorised reconstruction work to begin. Even when it was realised that the work was illegal, the petitioners failed to stop it. During the hearing of the petition, the chancellor gave leave to amend it so that a confirmatory faculty for the work already done was sought, as well as a further faculty for the completion of the work. The archdeacon opposed the petition, and sought an order to have the organ restored to its former state. *Held*, the petitioners had acted in flagrant breach of the law in allowing the organ to be dismantled without a faculty to do so. Their petition would be dismissed with costs awarded against them. An order would be made for the restoration of the organ as far as was possible and advisable. The petitioners would bear the cost of the work.

RE ST MARY'S, BALHAM [1978] 1 All ER 993 (Southwark Consistory Court: GARTH MOORE Ch).

996   Parochial Registers and Records Measure 1978

The Parochial Registers and Records Measure 1978 consolidates with amendments the Parochial Registers Act 1812 and other enactments relating to the registration of baptisms and burials. Certain provisions are repealed without re-enactment. The Measure also replaces the Parochial Registers and Records Measure 1929 with fresh provisions relating to diocesan record offices and the deposit of register books and records. The Measure received the royal assent on 2nd February 1978 and came into force on 1st January 1979.

Sections 1–6 and Sch. 1 relate to the registration of baptism and burials.

Section 7 makes provision for diocesan record offices. By s. 8 such offices may be used as a place of deposit for manorial documents. Section 9 provides for the inspection of register books and records in parochial custody. Bishops must cause inspections of registers and records to be carried out within five years of the commencement of the Measure and thereafter every six years. Parish registers and records must in general be deposited in the diocesan record office when they are a hundred years old: ss. 10, 11, Sch. 2. In addition bishops retain their power to order the deposit of registers and records which are exposed to danger of loss or damage, or in respect of which directions under s. 11 as to safe-keeping, care and preservation have not been complied with: s. 12. Section 10 also enables persons with custody of registers and records in general to deposit them in a diocesan record office. Section 13 makes provision for the return to parochial custody of books and records deposited in such an office. Sections 14 and 15 relate to the custody and care of books and records deposited and for their transfer from one office to another.

Provision is made by ss. 16 to 18 for books and records in parochial custody or in diocesan record offices to be made available for exhibition and research.

Sections 19 to 27 deal with miscellaneous and supplemental matters including the disposal of books and records on the dissolution of a parish: s. 19, searches of register books: s. 20, the recovery of such books in the possession of unauthorised persons: s. 21, and special provisions relating to marriage registers deposited in a diocesan record office: s. 22.

997 Tithe redemption annuities—abolition

The Finance Act 1977, s. 56, provides for tithe redemption annuities to be extinguished from 2nd October 1977, and the Tithe Redemption Office will be closed on 31st December 1978. Collection of outstanding annuity payments will be transferred to the Inland Revenue Central Accounting Office and certain other statutory functions formerly carried out by the Tithe Redemption Office will continue to be carried out by the Inland Revenue at the new Tithe Records Office. The non-statutory service of the Tithe Redemption Office of answering postal inquiries about whether or not particular land appears to be subject to other "tithe charges" is to be discontinued from 31st December 1978. Inquiries should be received by 8th December 1978 at the latest. In future, searches for details of any current tithe charges may be made by callers in person at the new Tithe Records Office: Inland Revenue Press Release dated 24th October 1978.

998 Vacation of benefices—legal aid

The Vacation of Benefices (Legal Aid) Rules 1978, S.I. 1978 No. 951 (in force on 1st September 1978), make provision for the method of refund of costs out of the legal aid fund to an incumbent of a benefice and restrain other persons who are entitled to a refund in proceedings under the Incumbents (Vacation of Benefices) Measure 1977, Pt I, 1977 Halsbury's Abr para. 970.

EDUCATION

Halsbury's Laws of England (4th edn.), Vol. 15, paras. 1–400

999 Article

Schoolteachers' Position as to Corporal Punishment, A. K. Scutter: 122 Sol Jo 671.

1000 Awards

The Local Education Authority Awards Regulations 1978, S.I. 1978 No. 1097 (in force on 1st September 1978), consolidate, with amendments, the Local Education Authority Awards Regulations 1977, as amended, 1977 Halsbury's Abr para. 974. The principal amendments concern conditions as to residence, late applications for awards and transfer of awards held in respect of one course to another. Awards are increased and the means test applicable to the maintenance element of awards is relaxed.

1001   College of further education—scheme of government—division of powers between county council and board of governors

A departmental head at a college of further education sought a declaration that the board of governors of the college was acting ultra vires in setting up a subcommittee to appoint a disciplinary committee to hear charges against him, and that even if such an action was not ultra vires, the disciplinary committee did not have the power to dismiss him. The declaration was granted. On appeal by the local education authority and the governors, *held*, by the provisions of the Education (No. 2) Act 1968, s. 1 (3) and the scheme of government of the college, the governors had not acted ultra vires because the committee so appointed was intended to be a substitute for the committee of governors which had originally been appointed to make recommendations to the governing body which that body would be free to accept or reject. Further, the disciplinary committee would have the authority to dismiss the plaintiff in circumstances where the governors were unable to act and the local education authority had a duty to ensure the smooth running of the college. The appeal would be allowed.

WINDER v CAMBRIDGESHIRE COUNTY COUNCIL (1978) 76 LGR 549 (Court of Appeal: BROWNE, WALLER and STEPHENSON LJJ). Decision of Sir Douglas Frank QC (1977) 76 LGR 176, 1977 Halsbury's Abr para 978, reversed.

1002   Direct Grant Schools

The Direct Grant Schools (Amendment) Regulations 1978, S.I. 1978 No. 1145 (in force on 1st September 1978), amend the Direct Grant Schools Regulations 1959 in their application to schools other than grammar schools to take account of amendments to the Schools Regulations 1959, in particular the revocation of r. 6 and Sch. I. They also make provision for the Secretary of State to satisfy himself as to a teacher's health on his appointment. This provision replaces Schools Regulations 1959, Sch II, para. 1, as amended by Schools (Amendment) Regulations 1978, see para. 1017.

1003   Educational institution—application by student for admission—duty of institution in considering application

See *Central Council for Education and Training in Social Work v Edwards*, para. 7.

1004   Handicapped pupils and special schools

The Handicapped Pupils and Special Schools (Amendment) Regulations 1978, S.I. 1978 No. 1146 (in force on 1st September 1978), amend the Handicapped Pupils and Special Schools Regulations 1959. They take account of amendments to the Schools Regulations 1959, in particular the Schools (Amendment) Regulations 1978, see para. 1017, by making provision for the Secretary of State to be satisfied as to a teacher's health on his first appointment to a non-maintained special school.

1005   Headmaster—duty of care owed to pupils—when duty owed

See *Geyer v Downs*, para. 2016.

1006   Higher education—report

The Secretary of State for Education and Science established a working group in 1977 to consider measures to improve the system of management and control of higher education in the maintained sector of England and Wales and its better co-ordination with higher education in the universities.   Also to consider in the light of developments in relation to devolution and local authority finance what regional and national machinery might be established for these purposes.   The working group have now published a report: Cmnd. 7130.

1007   Local education authority—duty of care owed to pupils—when duty owed

See *Geyer v Downs*, para. 2016.

1008   —— duty to provide education—relevance of parents' wishes

A local authority agreed that a mentally handicapped child should attend an ordinary primary school for a trial period.   The arrangement was found to be unsuitable for the child and the local authority suggested to his parents that he attend a special school for mentally handicapped children.   His parents refused to have him removed and sought an injunction restraining the authority from excluding him from the school.   *Held*, local authorities were under a duty to provide sufficient schools under the Education Act 1944, s. 8 and parents were under a duty to ensure their children received full-time education under s. 36 of the Act.   Additionally s. 76 provided that as far as possible, children were to be educated in accordance with their parents' wishes.   However, a local authority was not bound to keep a child at a school which was unsuitable for his educational needs and in those circumstances, s. 76 did not apply.   Accordingly, the parents' claim for an injunction would fail.

WINWARD V CHESHIRE COUNTY COUNCIL (1978) Times, 21st July (Chancery Division: JUDGE MERVYN DAVIES QC sitting as a deputy High Court judge).

1009   —— ministerial control by direction—power of minister to direct authority to submit different proposals

Pursuant to directions by the Secretary of State under the Education Act 1976, s. 2 (1), a county council submitted proposals whereby two schools would become comprehensive but would remain separate schools.   The Secretary of State refused to approve the proposals under the Education Act 1944, s. 13, and directed the council to make fresh proposals for a single comprehensive school.   The council, contending that the minister could only call for substituted proposals if the originals failed to give effect to the comprehensive principle, sought a declaration that the request was ultra vires and void.   *Held*, under the 1976 Act, s. 2 (4), the minister was empowered to require further proposals if the originals appeared to him to be unsatisfactory.   These were general words with nothing to limit the ambit of the matters to which the minister could have regard in reaching a decision.   He could therefore have regard to other matters than compliance with the comprehensive principle.   The minister thus had power under s. 2 (4) to require the council to prepare further proposals for a single school, and the declaration would be refused.

NORTH YORKSHIRE COUNTY COUNCIL V SECRETARY OF STATE FOR EDUCATION AND SCIENCE (1978) 122 Sol Jo 348 (Chancery Division: BROWNE-WILKINSON J). *Secretary of State for Education and Science v Tameside Metropolitan Borough Council* [1977] AC 1014, HL, 1976 Halsbury's Abr para. 933 considered.

1010   Provision of milk and meals

The Provision of Milk and Meals (Amendment) Regulations 1978, S.I. 1978 No. 959 (in force on 1st August 1978), amend the Provision of Milk and Meals Regulations 1969.   No charge is to be made in respect of the provision of a third of a pint of milk a day where a local education authority chooses to exercise its power to provide milk in the case of pupils at primary and primary middle schools or in the case of pupils at secondary middle schools who are under the age of twelve or have attained that age during the current school year.   In those cases in which a charge continues to be made, it must be restricted to the cost of the milk.

1011   The Provision of Milk and Meals (Amendment) (No. 2) Regulations 1978, S.I. 1978

No. 1301 (in force on 13th November 1978), further amend the provision of Milk and Meals Regulations 1969. The amendments relate to the remission of charges for school meals; they raise the levels of net weekly income below which a parent qualifies for the remission and increase the amount which may be deducted from net income in respect of any special diet prescribed by a registered medical practitioner.

1012   Schools—independent schools—exemption from registration

The Independent Schools (Exemption from Registration) Order 1978, S.I. 1978 No. 467 (in force on 1st May 1978), revokes the Independent Schools (Exemption from Registration) Order 1957. A school which was exempt from registration under the 1957 Order continues to be exempt unless the proprietors are notified that the Secretary of State is no longer satisfied that sufficient information about the school has been supplied or that registration is unnecessary.

1013   —— —— recognition as efficient

A Press Notice dated 18th April 1978 issued by the Department of Education and Science draws attention to the Joint Circular "Ending of Arrangements for Recognition of Independent Schools as Efficient" (DES Circular 6/78 Welsh Office 60/78). Independent schools in England and Wales should not use the term "recognised as efficient by the Secretary of State" from 30th April 1978 as after that date it will have no meaning or validity. However, there will be no change in the statutory requirements concerning the registration and inspection of all independent schools. Being recognised as efficient has up to now been a condition for a school's entry to the teachers' superannuation scheme, but new regulations will be made to allow any finally registered school to apply for membership.

1014   Special education—report of Warnock committee

The Warnock report (Special Educational Needs; Report of the Committee of Enquiry into the Education of Handicapped Children and Young People (Cmnd. 7212)) recommends that local authorities should have to provide special education for those children now classed as remedial and educationally sub-normal, those with emotional or behavioural disorders and those with physical or mental disabilities. This would require amendment of the Education Act 1944. A special education element should be incorporated in all teacher training, coupled with short in-service courses on the subject. Priority should also be given to those under and over school age: Times, 25th May 1978.

1015   State awards

The State Awards Regulations 1978, S.I. 1978 No. 1096 (in force on 1st September 1978), consolidate with amendments the State Awards Regulations 1963 and other specified regulations relating to state scholarships, state bursaries, state bursaries for adult education and state scholarships for mature students. The revoked regulations continue to have effect in relation to state scholarships for mature students in respect of first degree and comparable courses awarded before the coming into operation of the present regulations as the provisions are not reproduced in the current regulations. State bursaries in respect of post-graduate and comparable courses may be awarded in respect of a course at a university or institution abroad as well as at one within the United Kingdom. The maximum duration of a state award is restricted in the case of a state person who has held some other statutory award in respect of his attendance at a post-graduate course.

1016   Students' dependants—allowances

The Students' Dependants Allowances Regulations 1978, S.I. 1978 No. 1098 (in force on 1st September 1978), consolidate the Students' Dependants' Allowances Regulations 1977, 1977 Halsbury's Abr para. 985, with amendments. They are drafted by reference to the Local Education Authority Awards Regulations 1978, para. 1000, which increase the amounts prescribed as a student's requirements. An allowance under the present Regulations is payable at a rate determined in part by reference to the principal Regulations and accordingly is payable at an increased rate. The means test for an allowance is relaxed so far as concerns the student's scholarship and similar income and the earned income of his spouse or a person living with him as his spouse.

1017   Teachers—health and physical capacity for teaching

The Schools (Amendment) Regulations 1978, S.I. 1978 No. 1144 (in force on 1st September 1978), amend the Schools Regulations 1959 which state that the Secretary of State should be satisfied by every teacher on his first employment as a qualified or student teacher as to his health and physical capacity for teaching. The question of a candidate's health and physical capacity may now be determined by the local education authority if it has not been considered by the Secretary of State.

1018   —— remuneration

The Remuneration of Teachers (Further Education) (Amendment) Order 1978, S.I. 1978 No. 1226 (in force on 25th August 1978), gives effect to the recommendations of a committee set up to consider the remuneration of teachers in further education establishments maintained by local authorites and certain other teachers on the staff of such authorities. It restores those teachers who suffered a loss or diminution in increment by reason of their salary exceeding £8,500 per annum to their position on the incremental scale. This order has retrospective effect from 1st August 1977.
    This Order has been revoked; see para. 1020.

1019

The Remuneration of Teachers (Further Education) (Amendment No. 2) Order 1978, S.I. 1978 No. 1773 (in force on 14th December 1978), gives effect to the recommendations made by the committee for the consideration of the pay of teachers in establishments of further education and other further education teachers on the staff of local education authorities, increases the amounts of the London area payments and also amends the salary scale applicable to teachers who are lecturers grade 1B in agricultural and horticultural establishments.

1020

The Remuneration of Teachers (Further Education) Order 1978, S.I. 1978 No. 1409 (in force on 28th September 1978), brings into operation the scales and other provisions relating to the remuneration of full-time teachers in all establishments of further education maintained by local education authorities, and of other such further education teachers on the staff of such authorities (except teachers seconded to bodies which reimburse the employing authorities the amount of their salaries) set out in a document published by Her Majesty's Stationery Office. This document gives effect to the recommendations made by the committee for the consideration of the remuneration of such teachers. The Order has retrospective effect from 1st April 1978. The Remuneration of Teachers (Further Education) Order 1976, 1976 Halsbury's Abr para. 940, as amended, is revoked.

1021

The Remuneration of Teachers (Primary and Secondary Schools) (Amendment) Order 1978, S.I. 1978 No. 982 (in force on 17th July 1978), gave effect to the recommendations agreed on by the Committee for the consideration of the remuneration of teachers in primary and secondary schools maintained by local education authorities and of certain other persons employed by local education authorities as teachers in the provision of primary or secondary education. It restored to their position on the incremental scale, with effect from 1st August 1977, teachers who suffered a loss or diminution of an increment by reason of their salary exceeding £8,500 p.a.
    This order was revoked by the Remuneration of Teachers (Primary and Secondary Schools) (No. 2) Order 1978, para. 1022.

1022

The Remuneration of Teachers (Primary and Secondary Schools) (No. 2) Order 1978, S.I. 1978 No. 1019 (in force on 28th July 1978), brings into operation the scales and other provisions relating to the remuneration of teachers in primary and secondary schools maintained by local education authorities and of certain other persons employed by local education authorities as teachers in the provision of primary or secondary education, set out in a document published by Her Majesty's Stationery Office.

This order revokes the Remuneration of Teachers (Primary and Secondary Schools) Order 1977, 1977 Halsbury's Abr para. 990, and the Remuneration of Teachers (Primary and Secondary Schools) (Amendment) Order 1977, para. 1021.

1023   —— teachers at schools designated as social priority schools— validity of designation

On February 1975 certain schools were designated as social priority schools by the Burnham Designating Committee under the Remuneration of Teachers (Primary and Secondary Schools) (Amendment) Order 1975, 1975 Halsbury's Abr, para. 1210. The Order established a Designating Committee (consisting mainly of Burnham Committee members), which reviewed the latter's decision approving its list of schools drawn up before the Order authorising the list was made. A local education authority refused to pay its teachers the additional remuneration due to them by virtue of their working in a designated school on the ground that the designation was invalid. In an action against it by a teacher at one of the designated schools, the local education authority contended that the designation had not been made by the Designating Committee constituted by the Order and further that even if it had been so made, the Order itself was ultra vires as an abuse of the Minister's power under the Education Act 1965, s. 2. *Held*, (i) whilst the original list had been drawn up by the Burnham Committee, the members of the Designating Committee had the knowledge of their previous deliberations and decisions as members of the Burnham Committee and it would be excessively technical to treat the lists submitted by the local education authorities to the Burnham Committee as not also being lists submitted to the Designating Committee; (ii) there was nothing in the Remuneration of Teachers Act 1965 which precluded the setting-up of a Designating Committee; it was established in pursuance of s. 7 (3) under which any order might contain such supplementary or incidental provisions as the Secretary of State thought necessary. Both the Order itself and the establishment of the Designating Committee were valid and the teacher was entitled to receive additional payment under the designation.

LEWIS v DYFED COUNTY COUNCIL (1978) Court of Appeal: LORD DENNING MR, SHAW and BRANDON LJJ. Decision of O' Connor J 1977 Halsbury's Abr para. 991 affirmed. See further 128 NLJ 1243.

1024   —— superannuation

See paras. 2122–2124.

1025   University—trusts—unification of trusts—alteration of beneficial interests

A university college was the sole trustee of a charitable trust fund of which the college and a school were the income beneficiaries. The college prepared a scheme under Universities and Colleges (Trusts) Act 1943 enabling all property held by it on trust to be administered together. On objection by the Minister of Education to the incorporation of the trust fund in the scheme the fund was divided into two parts, that for the college being retained in the scheme and that for the school being excluded. The college's part of the fund was invested in equities which produced better results than the school's half which remained in gilt-edged stocks. The governors of the school eventually disputed the appropriation and sought a declaration that they were entitled to half the income of the whole fund. The college contended that the severing of the fund and the appropriation of the two halves was not an alteration of the beneficial interests in the trust, and was authorised by the 1943 Act as being necessary for the better administration of all the trust funds in the hands of the college. *Held*, the income of half the fund as divided was different from half the income of the whole fund. There had accordingly been an alteration of the beneficial interests and there was nothing in the 1943 Act or the scheme under the Act to justify that alteration. The governors were entitled to the declaration sought, but as the college had acted innocently it would be called to account only from the first annual accounting period after the commencement of the proceedings.

RE FREESTON'S CHARITY, SYLVESTER v UNIVERSITY COLLEGE, OXFORD [1978] 1 WLR 741 (Court of Appeal: BUCKLEY and GOFF LJJ and SIR DAVID CAIRNS). *MacCulloch v Anderson* [1904] AC 55, HL and *Holder v Holder* [1968] Ch 353, CA applied. Decision of FOX J [1978] 1 WLR 120 affirmed.

1026   —— visitor—jurisdiction

A student at a university incorporated by royal charter failed his examinations and was required to withdraw from the university. His request to re-enter was refused and he brought an action against the university for declarations that it had arbitrarily, unreasonably and unlawfully refused him re-admission and lawful access, an injunction and exemplary damages. The university contended that the courts had no jurisdiction to hear the case as exclusive jurisdiction was in the visitor of the university. Under the university's charter the Crown had the right to appoint a visitor, but no such appointment had been made. *Held*, subject to any appointment by the Crown, the Crown itself was the visitor, the Lord Chancellor exercising visitatorial powers on its behalf. The visitor's jurisdiction over the internal affairs of the university was sole and exclusive; the courts had no jurisdiction over matters within his jurisdiction but could exercise control by means of prohibition or mandamus. The visitor's jurisdiction extended to disputes as to membership of the university. The student claimed access to the university as a member of it, and thus the matter fell within the visitor's jurisdiction; the claims for an injunction and damages were ancillary to that claim and therefore also fell within his jurisdiction. The appeal would be dismissed.

PATEL v UNIVERSITY OF BRADFORD SENATE [1978] 3 All ER 841 (Chancery Division: MEGARRY V-C). *R v Hertford College* (1878) 3 QBD 693 followed.

1027   Universities and colleges—disposal of land

The Universities and College Estates Act 1925 (Amendment) Regulations 1978, S.I. 1978 No. 443 (in force on 19th April 1978), amend the Universities and College Estates Act 1925 by reducing the area of land that may be granted by a university or college for public and charitable purposes.

ELECTIONS

Halsbury's Laws of England (4th edn.), Vol. 15, paras. 401–981

1028   European Assembly Elections Act 1978

See para. 1028.

1029   —— division of constituencies in United Kingdom

See para. 1207.

1030   Local Government Boundary Commission—revision of electoral arrangements—equality between voters

See *Enfield London Borough Council v Local Government Boundary Commission for England*, para. 1801.

1031   Propaganda—imprint on election publications—printer and publisher

A candidate in a local government election neglected to have printed on his election leaflets the printer's name and address. He admitted to an offence under the Representation of the People Act 1949, s. 95, but applied for relief from liability to prosecution under s. 145 on the basis that the offence was committed inadvertently and in good faith. *Held*, the candidate had been actively involved in two previous elections, and on both occasions he had been warned with regard to alleged offences of failing to declare election expenses. He had been told that any further infringements would lead to prosecution. Commission of an offence under s. 95 was a serious matter. The candidate was guilty of an illegal election practice. His applications for relief from prosecution under s. 145 would be refused.

RE BERRY (1978) Times, 11th February (Queen's Bench Division: DONALDSON J).

1032   Representation of the people—regulations

The Representation of the People (Amendment) Regulations 1978, S.I. 1978 No. 197 (in force on 15th February 1978), amend the Representation of the People Regulations 1974, reg. 23 so as to increase the fee payable for copies of the register of electors.

1033   Representation of the People Act 1978

The Representation of the People Act 1978 received the royal assent on 20th July 1978 and came into force on that date.

Section 1 amends s. 64 (2) (a) of the Representation of the People Act 1949 so as to increase the maximum amount which a candidate may incur as election expenses at a parliamentary election. Section 2 provides that the Secretary of State may, by order, vary the maximum amount of candidates' election expenses at parliamentary elections, local government elections and certain elections in the City of London so as to take account of any change in the value of money. Such an order must first be approved by Parliament.

EMERGENCY CONTROLS

1034   Counter-inflation—dividend control

The Counter-Inflation (Dividends) (Amendments) Order 1978, S.I. 1978 No. 1454 (in force on 11th October 1978) amends the Counter-Inflation (Dividends) Order 1973, which provides that the total amount of ordinary share dividend declared is not to exceed, by more than the prescribed percentage limit, the total amount of ordinary dividends declared for the previous financial year. The Order extends the kinds of dividends to be taken into account in assessing the percentage increase. It now includes dividends, other than ordinary or capital dividends, and interest payable on debentures which are issued after the commencement of the Order or for the benefit of holders of ordinary shares otherwise than for a payment in money or for a consideration less than their market value.

1035   —— price code—substituting provisions

The Counter-Inflation (Price Code) Order 1978, S.I. 1978 No. 1082 (in force on 1st August 1978), substitutes a new price code for that which has been in operation under the Counter-Inflation (Price Code) Order 1977, 1977 Halsbury's Abr para. 1008, which is revoked. The new Code differs in that it is addressed solely to the Price Commission in relation to its remaining functions under the Counter-Inflation Act 1973 and it does not make provision for controls on prices and profit margins since, after 31st July 1978, the Commission has no power to enforce such provisions.

1036   —— prices and charges—batteries

The Ever Ready Company (Great Britain) Limited (Prices) Order 1978, S.I. 1978 No. 445 (in force on 20th March 1978), restricts increases in the price of certain zinc carbon dry (primary) batteries to 2% of their price on 31st October 1977 and prohibits any further price increase before 1st September 1978.

1037 —— —— **increases**

The Prices and Charges (Notification of Increases) Order 1978, S.I. 1978 No. 1083 (in force on 1st August 1978), replaces the Prices and Charges (Notification of Increases and Information) Order 1977, 1977 Halsbury's Abr para. 1005. It makes provision for notification to the Price Commission of proposed increases in prices and charges. It no longer provides for the furnishing of periodic returns and for the keeping of records. The annual sales limits above which there is an obligation to notify are increased.

1038 **Dividends Act 1978**

The Dividends Act 1978, which received the royal assent on 31st July 1978 and came into force on that date, provides that the Counter-Inflation Act 1973, s. 10, dealing with the Treasury's restriction on company dividends, shall continue in force until the end of July 1979. The Act repeals the words in Sch. 2, para. 2 to the Prices Commission Act 1977 which are concerned with s. 10.

EMPLOYMENT

Halsbury's Laws of England (4th edn.), Vol. 16, paras. 501–1200

1039 **Articles**

Advisory, Conciliation and Arbitration Service: Recognition Issues, David Newell (examination of ACAS's functions in relation to the recognition of independent trade unions by employers): 122 Sol Jo 392.

The Certification Officer and Certificates of Employment, David Newell (criteria on which trade unions are granted certificates of independence and the test of independence) 122 Sol Jo 356.

Changing Trends in Employment: the Pregnant Employee, Anne Morris (rights of pregnant employees under Employment Protection Act 1975, Part I): 128 NLJ 1085.

Dismissing Strikers, Richard Kidner (the statutory provisions regulating dismissal and the relevant cases): 128 NLJ 203.

Employment Law and Management, N. J. Fagan (whether employers are inhibited by current legislation): 122 Sol Jo 255.

Fixed-Term Contracts, Victor Joffe (the fixed-term contract and provisions relating to unfair dismissal): 128 NLJ 580.

Frustration or Dismissal, Colin Manchester (circumstances in which a contract of employment is terminated by frustration): 128 NLJ 674.

Getting to Grips with handling Redundancies, Philip J. Circus (steps to be taken by and points for consideration of employers): 128 NLJ 254.

Industrial Tribunal Procedures: The New Rules, Philip J. Circus: 128 NLJ 817.

Pay Restraint: The Legal Constraints, R. B. Ferguson and A. C. Page (means open to the government in its attempts to curb wages): 128 NLJ 515.

Plant Hire: Liability, M. T. Lazarides (determination of liability in either contract or tort for acts done by the servant of the plant owner where one of the contracting parties had hired plant from the other): 122 Sol Jo 767.

Reinstatement of a Dismissed Employee, A. N. Khan (the reinstatement provisions of the Employment Protection Act 1975): 122 Sol Jo 88.

A Right to Work in the Contract of Employment, John McMullen (whether the employer is under a duty to provide the employee with work during period of contract of employment): 128 NLJ 848.

Temporary Workers and the Law, B. A. Hepple and B. W. Napier (legal status of temporary workers): (1978) 7 ILJ 84.

1040 **Advisory, Conciliation and Arbitration Service—statutory duties—validity of decision to defer enquiries pending judicial proceedings**

See *Engineers' and Managers' Association v ACAS*, para. 2872.

1041   Baking industry—Christmas and New Year

The Baking and Sausage Making (Christmas and New Year) Regulations 1978, S.I. 1978 No. 1516 (in force on 27th December 1978), enable women who have attained the age of eighteen to be employed on specified Saturday afternoons and Sundays in December 1978 and January 1979 in the manufacture of meat pies, sausages or cooked meats, in the pre-packing of bacon, and in the manufacture of bread or flour confectionery (including fruit pies but not biscuits), or in work incidental to such work.

1042   Central Arbitration Committee—remedies against its decisions— circumstances in which remedies are granted

The relevant union made a claim under the Employment Protection Act 1975, Sch. 11 in respect of the holiday entitlement of the company's employees. The union argued that comparisons should be made only with multi-plant groups whose structure was similar to the company's. The company contended that, as the claim related to a small service company, such comparisons were inappropriate. The Central Arbitration Committee accepted the union's proposition, and increased holiday entitlement. The company appealed to the High Court for an order of certiorari quashing the award. *Held*, the Employment Protection Act 1975, Sch. 11 did not provide a right of appeal against decisions of the Central Arbitration Committee. The only remedy against such decisions was an application for orders of mandamus or certiorari, but these were granted only in limited circumstances. The court could not interfere with decisions of the Central Arbitration Committee unless there had been an excess of jurisdiction, a breach of natural justice or an error of law apparent on the record of proceedings. None of these conditions was present in the instant case and the decision would be allowed to stand.

R v CENTRAL ARBITRATION COMMITTEE, EX PARTE TI TUBE DIVISION SERVICES LTD [1978] IRLR 183 (Queen's Bench Division: LORD WIDGERY CJ, WIEN and KENNETH JONES JJ).

1043   Compensation—right to claim compensation—existence of contract of employment

See *Airfix Footwear Ltd v Cope*, para. 1055.

1044   Continuity of employment—change of employer—meaning of associated employments

The appellants claimed compensation for unfair dismissal. They had been employed in the respondents' canteen, originally by another company who managed the canteen, but at the date of dismissal they were employed by the respondents who had taken over the canteen management. The industrial tribunal dismissed the claims on the grounds that the employees had not fulfilled the statutory requirement of twenty six weeks' continuous employment. On appeal *held*, the original canteen managers had been employed as sub-contractors. When the respondents took over the management of the canteen, the business had not been transferred within the meaning of the Contracts of Employment Act, 1972, Sch. 1, para. 9 (2). Paragraph 10 of the Act, however, provided that continuity of employment might be preserved if the two employments were associated, and employments were associated if one company controlled the other, or if both companies were under the control of the same third party. In the present case the same two men held more than 50 per cent of the shares in each of the companies and were therefore in a position to control both companies.

ZARB AND SAMUELS v BRITISH & BRAZILIAN PRODUCE CO (SALES) LTD [1978] IRLR 78 (Employment Appeal Tribunal: PHILLIPS J presiding).

1972 Act, Sch. 1, paras. 9, 10, now Employment Protection (Consolidation) Act 1978, Sch. 13, paras. 16–18.

1045 —— **dismissal with right of appeal—date of termination of employment**

A personnel research manager had been summarily dismissed on the grounds of gross misconduct; he exercised his right of appeal against dismissal in accordance with the company's own disciplinary procedure. He was removed from the company's payroll and he claimed unemployment benefit whilst awaiting their decision. If the appeal were allowed he would have been entitled to be reinstated with full back pay. His appeal was dismissed. To have completed the requisite period of employment to bring a complaint of unfair dismissal, the manager had to show that he was dismissed when his internal appeal was dismissed rather than on the date on which he was summarily dismissed. *Held*, when a notice of dismissal was given, it took immediate effect even if the manager had a right to appeal. The fact that the appeal was dismissed meant that the original dismissal would be affirmed. Further, the manager himself had treated the original dismissal as terminating his employment by claiming unemployment benefit. The manager had not therefore completed the requisite period of employment to present a claim for unfair dismissal.

SAINSBURY LTD v SAVAGE [1978] IRLR 479 (Employment Appeal Tribunal: SLYNN J presiding).

1046 —— **employee working for same employer in two different capacities**

A part-time supervisor who started working sixteen hours a week on 16th April 1977 became a full-time cleaner for the same employers on 2nd May while continuing his job as a supervisor. On 24th September he was imprisoned for twenty days. The employers' manager indicated that his job would be available on his release. When he returned to work on 17th October his supervisor's job was still available but not his cleaner's job. He refused an offer of another job and left. He subsequently presented a complaint of unfair dismissal. An industrial tribunal decided that the employee's job as a supervisor could be included with his job as a cleaner in deciding whether he had been employed continuously for twenty-six weeks and accordingly whether he was entitled to present a complaint. They also decided that his contract of employment had not been frustrated by his period in prison. On appeal, the employers contended that there was no continuity where an employee had carried on two separate jobs at the same time and had been dismissed from only one. *Held*, (i) there probably would be continuity in those circumstances, but in the present case there were not two distinct jobs and the period of continuity could begin when the employee started working sixteen hours a week as a supervisor. (ii) The short prison sentence did not frustrate the contract and the employers' conduct meant that they had not treated the contract as repudiated.

MECCA LTD v SHEPHERD [1978] LS Gaz R 825 (Employment Appeal Tribunal: PHILLIPS J presiding).

1047 —— **interruption due to sickness**

The employee was first employed by a company in February 1977. In June he fell ill and absented himself from work without informing the company. In July he was dismissed for non-attendance but was re-engaged on 1st August. He was dismissed a second time three weeks later. For the purposes of presenting his complaint of unfair dismissal, he had to show a continuous period of employment of twenty-six weeks and he relied on the Contracts of Employment Act 1972, Sch. 1, para. 5 (1) (a) which provides that continuity of employment is not broken if the interruption is caused by illness. *Held*, the first dismissal was not fatal to proving continuity of employment from February 1977 under para. 5 (1) (a). It did not have to be shown that the dismissal was expressly on account of incapacity to work in consequence of illness. The dismissal was not unrelated to para. 5 (1) (a). Accordingly, continuity from February 1977 had been established.

SCARLETT v GODFREY ABBOTT GROUP LTD [1978] IRLR 456 (Employment Appeal Tribunal: PHILLIPS J presiding).

1972 Act, Sch. 1, para. 5, now Employment Protection (Consolidation) Act 1978, Sch. 13, para. 9.

1048 —— part-time employment—whether normal working week of sixteen hours or more

During a period of employment lasting less than five years, the appellant worked alternately three days per week (20¼ hours) and two days per week (13½ hours) until she injured her back, after which she worked only two days per week. When she was dismissed she claimed compensation for unfair dismissal. Under the Contracts of Employment Act 1972, Sch. 1, para. 4A, she had to show that originally her contract had normally involved employment for sixteen hours or more weekly and that later it involved employment for eight hours or more. *Held*, a contract involving employment for sixteen hours or more was one which involved sixteen hours or more worked regularly. The hours could not be averaged out. Nor could the statute apply at the end of each fortnight. The claimant had not been employed for the requisite period and was not entitled to compensation.

OPIE v JOHN GUBBINS (INSURANCE BROKERS) LTD (1978) Times, 1st November (Employment Appeal Tribunal: KILNER BROWN J presiding).

1972 Act, Sch. 1, para. 4A, now Employment Protection (Consolidation) Act 1978, Sch. 13, para. 15.

1049 —— time of commencement of contract of employment—meaning of "week"

An industrial tribunal found that it had no jurisdiction to hear a complaint of unfair dismissal because the employee had not been employed for a continuous period of twenty-six weeks as required by the Trade Union and Labour Relations Act 1974, Sch. 1, para. 10 (a). She had begun work on Saturday, 15th January and the question was whether the week immediately preceding that date could be taken into account in computing the period. On appeal, *held*, since "week" in the Contracts of Employment Act 1972, Sch. 1, para. 4 meant a week ending with Saturday and since the week immediately prior to Saturday, January 15th when the employee started work, was a week which normally involved employment for sixteen hours or more as required by para. 4, that week was to be included in calculating the qualifying period of employment. The appeal would be allowed.

WYNNE v HAIR CONTROL [1978] ICR 870 (Employment Appeal Tribunal: SLYNN J presiding) *Coulson v City of London Polytechnic* [1976] ICR 433, EAT, 1976 Halsbury's Abr para. 2704 applied.

1972 Act, Sch. 1, para. 4, now Employment Protection (Consolidation) Act 1978, Sch. 13, para. 4. 1974 Act, Sch. 1, para. 10 (a) now 1978 Act, s. 64 (1).

1050 —— transfer of a part of a business—effect on employee

The appellant commenced employment, as a gas fitter with a company undertaking both gas fitting and plumbing contracts, in January 1966. In June 1973 he fell ill and did not return to work for over a year. In April 1974 the gas fitting part of the business was taken over by the respondents, by whom the appellant was employed upon his return to work in May 1974. In an attempt to establish that he had been continuously employed, he sought to rely on the Contracts of Employment Act 1972, Sch. 1, para. 9 (2), which provides that a transfer of a separate part of a business does not break the continuity of employment of an employee. *Held*, the gas fitting business was a recognisable and easily identifiable part of the whole of the first company and was thus transferable as a separate unit of the business within the meaning of para. 9 (2). Further, the period of sickness between the transfer in April, and the appellant's return to work in May, did not break the continuity of employment. Accordingly the appellant had been in continuous employment from January 1966.

GREEN v WAVERTREE HEATING AND PLUMBING CO LTD [1978] ICR 928 (Employment Appeal Tribunal: PHILLIPS J presiding).

1972 Act, Sch. 1, para. 9, now Employment Protection (Consolidation) Act 1978, Sch. 13, para. 17.

1051   —— transferred business not going concern

An insolvent company transferred its assets, premises and future contracts to new owners. The employee, who had worked for the insolvent company, was dismissed on the day of transfer and engaged by the new owners the same day. He was dismissed again three days later, and an industrial tribunal found that, at the time of the transfer, the employee had been employed by the insolvent company and could, therefore, include his employment with them in computing the total period of employment. It also found that he had been unfairly dismissed. The new employers appealed, on the ground that there had been no continuity of employment. Firstly they contended that there was no transfer of a business within the ambit of the Contracts of Employment Act 1972, Sch. 1, para. 9 (2), because it was necessary to show that the business was a "going concern", and in this case it had been insolvent at the time of the transfer. Secondly, there had been a break in the employment between the first dismissal and re-engagement. *Held*, dismissing the appeal, it was not essential that the business be a "going concern", although this was an important consideration in deciding whether there was in process a breaking up of that business and the transfer of assets piecemeal. This was not the case here, where the transferee had the financial ability to carry on the business intact, which the transferor had not.

As to the second ground, as the dismissal and the re-employment had taken place on the same day, the gap in employment would be disregarded in accordance with the doctrine that the law took no account of parts of a day. Accordingly the employee's employment with the insolvent company could be taken into account.

TEESSIDE TIMES LTD v DRURY [1978] ICR 822 (Employment Appeal Tribunal: PHILLIPS J presiding).

1972 Act, Sch. 1, para. 9, now Employment Protection (Consolidation) Act 1978, Sch. 13, para. 17.

1052   Contract of employment—bonus payments—breach of contract by employee—effect

The employee was promised a bonus of £200 p.a., but after one bonus of £25 he was told that no further payments would be made. He continued to work for the company until he was made redundant. The company appealed from an industrial tribunal's decision that under his contract of employment the employee was entitled to bonus payments. *Held*, there was no question of the employee being told that his job was at an end and accepting a new contract at reduced pay when he was informed that the bonus payments would stop. The company had merely told him that it could no longer pay the sum agreed, and the employee could either have treated the contract as at an end or regarded it as still subsisting. He had done the latter and so the company was liable for the accrued bonuses. The appeal would be dismissed.

W. P. M. RETAIL LTD v LANG (1978) 122 Sol Jo 296 (Employment Appeal Tribunal: BRISTOW J presiding). *Denmark Productions Ltd v Boscobel Productions Ltd* [1969] 1 QB 699, CA distinguished.

1053   —— construction

A sales representative was expressly engaged as a self-employed person by the company and worked as an agent on a commission basis only. His taxable income was assessed under Schedule D and he paid national insurance contributions as a self-employed person. When his engagement was terminated, he claimed he had been unfairly dismissed. The company appealed against an industrial tribunal's decision that he had been engaged under a contract of employment and was therefore entitled to bring an action for unfair dismissal. *Held*, the tribunal had carefully analysed all the characteristics of the case and had correctly directed itself on the law: there was no reason to interfere with its decision. The existence of a convenient arrangement for tax or insurance purposes did not indicate that a person was self-employed when the true relationship was one of employer and employee. The appeal would be dismissed.

TYNE & CLYDE WAREHOUSES LTD v HAMERTON (1978) 13 ITR 66 (Employment Appeal Tribunal: KILNER BROWN J presiding). *Ferguson v John Dawson & Partners (Contractors) Ltd* [1976] 3 All ER 817, CA, 1976 Halsbury's Abr para. 974, applied.

1054   —— —— **whether an employee or independent contractor**

A driving instructor was employed by the appellant company under a contract of service. Upon the re-organisation of the company, he entered into a new agreement which specifically stated that he was now self-employed, as an independent contractor. The Secretary of State ruled that for the purposes of national insurance contributions, he was an employee of the company. The questions on appeal were whether the decision of the Secretary of State was one on a question of law and appeal lay to the courts and, if so, whether he had been correct in his ruling. *Held*, whether a person worked under a contract of service or for services was a question of law and accordingly a right of appeal existed from the decision of the Secretary of State. Prima facie there was nothing improper in an employer and employee agreeing to change the latter's status; as there was no evidence in the case to show that the terms of the agreement were inconsistent with its nature or that it was a sham, it would be upheld and the appeal allowed.

BSM (1257) Ltd v Secretary of State For Social Services [1978] ICR 894 (Queen's Bench Division: Sir Douglas Frank QC sitting as a deputy High Court judge). *Global Plant Ltd v Secretary of State for Social Services* [1972] 1 QB 139 applied and *Massey v Crown Life Insurance Co* [1978] ICR 590 followed.

1055   —— **existence of contract—homeworker—right to claim compensation for unfair dismissal**

The claimant was a homeworker who made heels for a company's shoes. They gave her some training and supplied her with all the necessary materials daily for seven years, with occasional breaks when demand was low. They described her remuneration as wages, but did not deduct National Insurance contributions or income tax. On her claim for compensation for unfair dismissal an industrial tribunal rejected the company's contention that she was not employed under a contract of employment and therefore could not bring a claim. On appeal, *held*, the fact that the claimant had received daily supplies of materials over a long period with few breaks indicated a continuing relationship between the parties consistent with the existence of a contract of employment. The tribunal's decision would be upheld.

Airfix Footwear Ltd v Cope [1978] IRLR 396 (Employment Appeal Tribunal: Slynn J presiding).

1056   —— **frustration—imprisonment of employee**

See *Mecca Ltd v Shepherd*, para. 1046.

1057   —— **illegality—unenforceability**

The employee's claims for unfair dismissal and a redundancy payment were dismissed by an industrial tribunal after it discovered that, during her employment, she had received a weekly cash payment of £15 on which no tax had been paid. As this arrangement had been deliberately designed to defraud the Inland Revenue, the industrial tribunal held that it vitiated the whole contract of employment. On appeal, *held*, the scheme to defraud the Revenue had the effect of making the whole contract of employment illegal. A party to an illegal contract could not claim the statutory right to a redundancy payment or redress for unfair dismissal.

Tomlinson v Dick Evans U Drive Ltd [1978] IRLR 77 (Employment Appeal Tribunal: Bristow J presiding).

1058   —— **implied contract of service—determination of existence of contract**

See *Parsons v Albert J. Parsons & Sons Ltd*, para. 1091.

1059   —— **managing director—breach of fiduciary duty and disclosure of confidential information—test of confidential information**

The defendant had been employed as managing director by the plaintiff company under a ten year service contract starting in September 1972. The contract contained no provision for shortening the period of employment. Under the contract the defendant agreed not at any time to disclose confidential information obtained through his employment and not during his employment to be engaged or interested in any other business. In 1977 the company heard that the defendant was intending to leave his job and set up in competition with them. The defendant purported to resign but the company continued to regard the service agreement as being in force. The company subsequently discovered that, while supposedly engaged on company business, the defendant had been arranging purchases and sales of the type of goods in which the company dealt on his own behalf.

The company applied for interlocutory orders restraining the defendant from dealing with its customers and suppliers, and from disclosing or using confidential information obtained in the course of his employment. *Held*, the service contract was not terminated by the defendant's unilateral repudiation of it, and he was therefore still bound by the obligations arising from the contract. Although the court could not order specific performance of the contract it would restrain the defendant from committing other breaches of his obligations during the contract period. The defendant had acted in breach of his implied duty of fidelity and good faith, and in breach of the fiduciary duty of a director to apply the company's property for the company's benefit. Consequently he would also be restrained from using confidential information and trade secrets. Confidential information was information which the owner reasonably believed was confidential and the release of which he reasonably believed would damage his interests.

THOMAS MARSHALL (EXPORTS) LTD v GUINLE [1978] 3 All ER 193 (Chancery Division: MEGARRY V-C). *Lumley v Wagner* (1852) 1 De G. M. & G. 604, *William Robinson & Co Ltd v Heuer* [1898] 2 Ch 451, CA and *Warner Brothers Pictures Inc v Nelson* [1937] 1 KB 209 applied.

1060   —— outworker—whether employee or independent contractor

See *D'Ambrogio v Hyman Jacobs Ltd*, para. 1140.

1061   Dismissal—employer's duty to provide reasons on request —delay—whether delay amounted to unreasonable refusal

An employer appealed against a decision of an industrial tribunal awarding a dismissed employee a fortnight's pay for the employer's lateness in furnishing reasons for the dismissal. The tribunal had decided an oral request had been put to the employer on the employee's behalf and that no reasons had been given within the fortnight prescribed by the Employment Protection Act 1975, s. 70. The employer appealed. *Held*, there was sufficient evidence to show that the employer had unreasonably refused to provide reasons. Mere delay did not amount to unreasonable refusal, and accordingly no payment should have been made.

CHARLES LANG & SONS LTD v AUBREY [1978] ICR 168 (Employment Appeal Tribunal: LORD MACDONALD presiding).

1975 Act, s. 70 now Employment Protection (Consolidation) Act 1978, s. 53.

1062   —— reason for dismissal—employer's refusal to furnish reason in writing—reasonableness

An employee who was dismissed for an alleged theft from his employers made a request under the Employment Protection Act 1975, s. 70 for a written statement of the reasons for his dismissal. The employers refused because they had been asked by the police not to answer any correspondence in connection with the alleged offence while it was under investigation. An industrial tribunal held that this was an unreasonable refusal on the employers' part because, knowing that refusal to grant the request might incur a penalty, reasonable employers would have asked the police what they should do. The employers appealed against the tribunal's award of damages. *Held*, the question of whether the employers' refusal to supply a written statement was reasonable was one of fact for the tribunal. In order to succeed in their appeal, the employers had to show that no properly instructed tribunal would have found the refusal unreasonable and this they had failed to do. The appeal would be dismissed.

DAYNECOURT INSURANCE BROKERS LTD v ILES [1978] IRLR 335 (Employment Appeal Tribunal: PHILLIPS J presiding).

1975 Act, s. 70 now Employment Protection (Consolidation) Act 1978, s. 53.

1063   **Employee—meaning of employee—whether managing director employee of company**

The applicant, the chief accountant of a parent company, was appointed managing director of a subsidiary company. The subsidiary company passed a resolution confirming his appointment, but no mention was made of salary. There was no contract of service. The company nonetheless paid a salary to the applicant who in turn, performed the duties of managing director. After some months, he was dismissed. He complained to an industrial tribunal of unfair dismissal, but the tribunal found that he was not employed by the company, largely on the basis that no resolution in respect of salary had been passed. On appeal, *held*, where a company had appointed as managing director a director who then carried out the duties of a managing director in return for a regular salary from the company, he had to be considered an employee of the company even though he had no contract of service. The applicant in this case, although not a director, should be considered to be in a similar position. The case would be remitted to an industrial tribunal to be heard upon its merits.

FOLAMI v NIGERLINE (UK) LTD [1978] ICR 277 (Employment Appeal Tribunal: PHILLIPS J presiding). *Anderson v James Sutherland (Peterhead) Ltd* 1941 SC 203, applied.

1064   **Employer—contractual duty—duty to select appropriate route for carriage of goods**

See *Boughen v Frederick Attwood Ltd and Cryoplants Ltd*, para. 298.

1065   **—— contractual liability for negligence of employees—whether liable for deliberate acts of employees**

See *Photo Production Ltd v Securicor Transport Ltd*, para. 494.

1066   **—— duty of care—employee injured in payroll robbery—foreseeability**

Following an attack by thieves on employees collecting a firm's payroll from a bank their employers suggested variations in the method of collection, but these were never implemented. An employee who was injured in a later attack claimed damages from the employers on the ground that they had been in breach of their duty of care in that a security firm should have been employed to collect the wages. *Held*, employers were under a duty to take reasonable care that their employees were not subjected to a foreseeable risk of injury by criminals. Although no general rule could be made as to a size of payroll above which it would be sensible to employ a security firm, a reasonable employer having regard to past events would have done so in this case.

CHARLTON v FORREST PRINTING INK CO LTD (1978) 122 Sol Jo 730 (Queen's Bench Division: FORBES J).

1067   **Employer's liability policy—application for indemnity—whether employee acting in the course of his employment**

See *Paterson v Costain & Press (Overseas) Ltd*, para. 1661.

1068   **Employment agencies—au pairs—fees**

The Employment Agencies Act 1973 (Charging Fees to Au Pairs) Regulations 1978, S.I. 1978 No. 805 (in force on 10th July 1978), allows an employment agency to charge a fee to a person for finding him employment as an au pair outside the United Kingdom. The fee is chargeable where the agency uses someone acting from premises outside the United Kingdom to act for it in that connection and receives no fee from either that person or the intended employer. The fee should not exceed the amount of one week's pocket money payable to the au pair by the employer.

1069   Employment Appeal Tribunal—appeal procedure

The following Practice Direction ([1978] 2 All ER 293) has been issued by the President of the Employment Appeal Tribunal.

The practice direction dated 7th January 1977, *Practice Direction (EAT: Appeal Procedure)* [1977] 1 All ER 478, as amended on 9th March 1977, [1977] 1 All ER 880, is hereby revoked and replaced by the following.

1. The Employment Appeal Tribunal Rules 1976 (S.I. 1976 No. 322) (hereinafter called "the Rules") came into operation on 30th March 1976.

2. By virtue of paragraph 15 (2) of Schedule 6 to the Employment Protection Act 1975, the appeal tribunal has power, subject to the Rules, to regulate its own procedure.

3. Where the Rules do not otherwise provide the following procedure will be followed in all appeals to the appeal tribunal.

4. *Appeals out of time*
   (a) By virtue of r. 3 (1) of the Rules every appeal under s. 88 of the Employment Protection Act 1975 to the Employment Appeal Tribunal shall be instituted by serving on the tribunal, within 42 days of the date on which the document recording the decision or order appealed from was sent to the appellant, a notice of appeal as prescribed in the Rules.
   (b) Every notice of appeal not delivered within 42 days of the date on which the document recording the decision or order appealed from was sent to the appellant must be accompanied by an application for an extension of time, setting out the reasons for the delay.
   (c) Applications for an extension of time for appealing cannot be considered until a notice of appeal has been presented.
   (d) Unless otherwise ordered, the application for extension of time will be heard and determined by the registrar on a date appointed by him pursuant to r. 9 of the Rules.
   (e) In determining whether to extend the time for appealing, particular attention will be paid to the guidance contained in *Marshall v Harland & Wolff Ltd* [1972] ICR 97, and to whether any excuse for the delay has been shown.
   (f) It is not necessarily a good excuse for delay in appealing that legal aid has been applied for, or that support is being sought, e.g. from the Equal Opportunities Commission, or from a trade union. In such cases the intending appellant should at the earliest possible moment, and at the latest within the time limited for appealing, inform the registrar, and the other party, of his intentions, and seek the latter's agreement to an extension of time for appealing.
   (g) Time for appealing runs from the date on which the document recording the decision or order of the industrial tribunal was sent to the appellant, notwithstanding that the assessment of compensation had been adjourned, or an application has been made for a review.
   (h) In any case of doubt or difficulty, notice of appeal should be presented in time, and an application made to the registrar for directions.

5. *Institution of appeal*
   (a) Subject to r. 3 (2) of the Rules, if it appears to the registrar that a notice of appeal gives insufficient particulars or lacks clarity either as to the question of law or the grounds of an appeal, the registrar may postpone his decision under that rule pending amplification or clarification of the notice of appeal, as regards the question of law or grounds of appeal, by the intended appellant.
   (b) Upon the hearing of an appeal an appellant will not ordinarily be allowed

to contend that "the decision was contrary to the evidence" or "there was no evidence to support the decision," or to advance similar contentions, unless full and sufficient particulars identifying the particular matters relied upon have been supplied to the appeal tribunal.

(c) In any case where it appears to the registrar that the question raised by a notice of appeal, or the grounds of appeal stated therein and any further particulars given under (a) above, do not give the appeal tribunal jurisdiction to entertain the appeal, he will notify the appellant accordingly, informing him of the reasons for his decision.

(d) Where the appellant, having been notified of the registrar's decision under r. 3 (2), serves a fresh notice of appeal under r. 3 (3) within the time limited by that rule, the registrar may consider such fresh notice of appeal with regard to jurisdiction as though it were an original notice of appeal lodged pursuant to r. 3 (1).

(e) Where an appellant is dissatisfied with the reasons given by the registrar for his opinion that the grounds of appeal stated in the notice of appeal do not give the appeal tribunal jurisdiction to entertain the appeal, the registrar will place the papers before the President or a judge for his direction.

(f) It will not be open to the parties to reserve a right to amend, alter or add to any pleading. Any such right is not inherent and may only be exercised if permitted by order for which an interlocutory application should be made as soon as the need for alteration is known.

6. *New procedure*
(a) Where an appeal has not been rejected pursuant to r. 3 (2) but nevertheless the appeal tribunal considers that it is doubtful whether the grounds of appeal disclose an arguable point of law, the President or a judge may direct that the matter be set down before a division of the appeal tribunal for hearing of a preliminary point to enable the appellant to show cause why the appeal should not be dismissed on the ground that it does not disclose an arguable point of law.

(b) The respondent will be given notice of the hearing but since it will be limited to the preliminary point he will not be required to attend the hearing or permitted to take part in it.

(c) If the appellant succeeds in showing cause, the hearing will be adjourned and the appeal will be set down for hearing before a different division of the appeal tribunal in the usual way.

(d) If the appellant does not show cause, the appeal will be dismissed.

(e) The decision as to whether this procedure will be adopted in any particular case will be in the discretion of the President or a judge.

7. *Interlocutory applications*
(a) Every interlocutory application made to the appeal tribunal will be considered in the first place by the registrar who will have regard to the just and economical disposal of the application, and to the expense which may be incurred by the parties in attending an oral hearing.

(b) The registrar will submit a copy of the application to the other side together with notice of the time appointed for the hearing, and will indicate in the notice of appointment that if it is not intended to oppose the application it may be unnecessary for the parties to be heard and that the appropriate order may be made in their absence. Where the application is opposed the registrar will also in appropriate cases give the parties an opportunity of agreeing to the application being decided on the basis of written submissions.

(c) Save where the President or a judge directs otherwise, every interlocutory application to strike out pleadings or to debar a party from taking any further part in the proceedings pursuant to rr. 9 or 15 will be heard on the day appointed for the hearing of the appeal, but immediately preceding the hearing thereof.

8. *Meetings for directions*
On every appeal from the decision of the certification officer, and, if necessary, on

any other appeal, so soon as the answer is delivered, or if a cross-appeal, the reply, the registrar will appoint a day when the parties shall meet on an appointment for directions and the appeal tribunal will give such directions, including a date for hearing, as it deems necessary.

9. *Right to inspect the register and certain documents and to take copies*
Where, pursuant to the direction dated 31st March 1976, a document filed at the Employment Appeal Tribunal had been inspected and a photographic copy of the document is bespoken, a copying fee of 25p for each page will be charged.

10. *Listing of appeals*
Where the respondent's answer had been received and a copy served on the appellant both parties will be notified in writing of a date, between four and six weeks ahead, after which the hearing will take place. In the same letter the parties will be invited to apply for a date to be fixed for the hearing. For that purpose an application form will be enclosed, to be returned to the listing officer within 14 days on which solicitors (or if appropriate litigants in person) will be able to specify any dates they wish to be avoided. The date that has been fixed will then be notified to the parties with as much notice as possible.
If the application form is not returned to the Employment Appeal Tribunal within 14 days a party will have no right to ask for a fixed date. The case will in due course be listed for hearing (i.e. in the Warned List) and once this has been done it will be liable to be listed at a day's notice, though in practice it is hoped to be able to give much longer notice than that in the majority of cases. (Where either of the parties is appearing in person at least a week's notice will be given.) The Warned List will appear weekly in the Daily Cause List and it will also be displayed in room 6 at the Royal Courts of Justice. The onus will be on solicitors' or counsels' clerks to watch the Warned List; no date will be able to be vacated except by formal application to the tribunal.
The Warned List will accordingly contain (a) cases fixed for hearing during the coming week, with the date on which they are to be heard; (b) cases where the "not before date" has passed, no application has been made for a fixed date, and the date of hearing has not yet been fixed.
Cases where the "not before date" has not yet been reached, or cases in which an application has been made for a fixed date but the date has not yet been fixed; and cases that have been fixed for hearing beyond the following week will not be included in the Warned List. Normally a case estimated to take half a day or less will be listed together with another of the same duration for one court in one day, and when two or more courts are sitting "floaters" will also be listed as appropriate.

11. *Admissibility of documents*
  (a) Where, pursuant to rr. 9 or 13 an application is made by a party to an appeal to put in at the hearing of the appeal any document which was not before the industrial tribunal, including a note of evidence given before the industrial tribunal (other than the chairman's note), the application shall be submitted in writing with copies of the document(s) sought to be made admissible at the hearing.
  (b) The registrar will forthwith communicate the nature of the application and of the document(s) sought to be made admissible to the other party and where appropriate, to the chairman of the industrial tribunal, for comment.
  (c) A copy of the comment will be forwarded to the party making the application, by the registrar who will either dispose of it in accordance with the Rules or refer it to the appeal tribunal for a ruling at the hearing. In the case of comments received from the chairman of the industrial tribunal a copy will be sent to both parties.

12. *Complaints of bias, etc.*
  (a) The appeal tribunal will not normally consider complaints of bias or of the conduct of an industrial tribunal unless full and sufficient particulars are set out in the grounds of appeal.
  (b) In any such case the registrar may inquire of the party making the complaint

whether it is the intention to proceed with the complaint in which case the registrar will give appropriate directions for the hearing.

  (c) Such directions may include the filing of affidavits dealing with the matters upon the basis of which the complaint is made or for the giving of further particulars of the complaint on which the party will seek to rely.

  (d) On compliance with any such direction the registrar will communicate the complaint together with the matters relied on in support of the complaint to the chairman of the industrial tribunal so that he may have an opportunity of commenting upon it.

  (e) No such complaint will be permitted to be developed upon the hearing of the appeal, unless the appropriate procedure has been followed.

  (f) A copy of any affidavit or direction for particulars to be delivered thereunder will be communicated to the other side.

13. *Exhibits and documents for use at the hearing*

  (a) The appeal tribunal will prepare copies of all documents for use of the judges and members at the hearing in addition to those which the registrar is required to serve on the parties under the Rules.

  (b) There is no inherent right to a copy of the chairman's notes but copies will be sent to the parties as soon as they are available, unless in the discretion of the appeal tribunal, all or part of such notes is considered to be unnecessary for the purposes of the appeal. A chairman's notes are supplied for the use of the appeal tribunal and not for the parties to embark on a "fishing" expedition to establish further grounds of appeal.

  (c) It will be the responsibility of the parties or their advisers to ensure that all exhibits and documents used before the industrial tribunal, and which are considered to be relevant to the appeal, are sent to the appeal tribunal immediately on request. This will enable the appeal tribunal to number and prepare sufficient copies, together with an index, for the judges and members at least a week before the day appointed for the hearing.

  (d) A copy of the index will be sent to the parties or their representatives prior to the hearing so that they may prepare their bundles in the same order.

The Employment Protection Act 1975 has been consolidated in the Employment Protection (Consolidation) Act 1978.

1070   —— —— appeal alleging bias on part of industrial tribunal

In the course of an appeal against the decision of an industrial tribunal on the ground that it had been biased, the Employment Appeal Tribunal stated that notice of such an appeal had to give full particulars of the allegations, and that the chairman of the industrial tribunal should have a chance to comment or provide relevant information. The parties should keep in touch with the registrar, who would see that all necessary steps were taken.

    BHARWAJ v POST OFFICE [1978] ICR 144 (Employment Appeal Tribunal: PHILLIPS J presiding).

1071   —— costs—when employer should pay costs

Employers lodged an appeal against an industrial tribunal's finding that their dismissal of an employee had been unfair. They received notes of evidence taken at the tribunal hearing on April 19th 1978, but did not withdraw their appeal until July 12th, nine days before the hearing. *Held*, although parties should not be discouraged from withdrawing appeals, the employers in this case had delayed their decision to do so unreasonably, thereby causing the employee to incur unnecessary expense. Accordingly they would be ordered to pay costs.

    TVR ENGINEERING LTD v JOHNSON (1978) Times, 10th October (Employment Appeal Tribunal: SLYNN J presiding).

1072   —— fresh evidence—practice

On an application for a review or an appeal introducing fresh evidence, a statement of the new evidence must be lodged in the form of a proof. Only in that form can the tribunal properly measure the real value of the evidence.

VAUXHALL MOTORS LTD v HENRY (1978) Times, 6th April (Employment Appeal Tribunal: PHILLIPS J presiding).

1073   —— practice—relevance of documents produced

SLYNN J, President of the Employment Appeal Tribunal, has stated that it is the duty of the parties and their solicitors to ensure that all documents produced are necessary and relevant to the issue before the tribunal: Times, 10th November, 1978.

1074   —— time for appeal to Tribunal—enforcement

In proceedings before the Employment Appeal Tribunal, it has been stated that in future the forty-two day time limit for appealing from an industrial tribunal will be strictly enforced. Statistics testify to the accuracy and fairness of industrial tribunals, and employment cases require speedy final decisions.

HEM v SYKES AND SONS (SHEPLEY) LTD (1978) Times, 25th October (Employment Appeal Tribunal: KILNER BROWN J presiding).

1075   —— —— whether leave to appeal out of time should be granted

An industrial tribunal found an employer guilty of unfairly dismissing an employee and made a recommendation for reinstatement. A second tribunal subsequently made an order for compensation. The employer appealed against the latter decision and sought leave to appeal out of time against the earlier decision, but the registrar of the Appeal Tribunal rejected the claim on a strict interpretation of the Employment Appeal Tribunal Rules 1976, r. 3 of which prescribes a forty-two day limit for appeals. On the employer's appeal, *held*, normally the registrar's view was wholly correct: the time limit for appeal against any finding ran from the date that finding was made. However, in this case the employer should be entitled to make further submissions as it could be concluded from the reasons given by the first tribunal that its recommendation for reinstatement was not final. The employers would be given a further fourteen days in which to enter notice of an appeal.

FIRESTONE TYRE & RUBBER CO LTD v CHALLONER [1978] ICR 175 (Employment Appeal Tribunal: PHILLIPS J presiding). *Jowett v Earl of Bradford* [1977] ICR 342, EAT, 1976 Halsbury's Abr para. 100 applied.

1076   Employment (Continental Shelf) Act 1978

The Employment (Continental Shelf) Act 1978 enables the application of certain legislation to be extended to employment in some offshore areas. The Act received the royal assent on 31st July 1978 and came into force on that date.

Section 1 provides that specified employment legislation may be extended to cover activities connected with the exploration of certain petroleum fields in sectors of the continental shelf outside the territorial waters of any state. Miscellaneous supplementary provisions are contained in ss. 2, 3.

The provisions of the Act have been re-enacted in the Employment Protection (Consolidation) Act 1978, s. 137, which came into force on 1st November 1978.

1077   Employment Protection (Consolidation) Act 1978

The Employment Protection (Consolidation) Act 1978 received the royal assent on 31st July 1978 and came into force on 1st November 1978, with the exception of s. 139 (2) to (9) and the repeals of the Employment Protection Act 1975, s. 122 provided for in Sch. 17 to the present Act, which come into force on 1st January 1979. The Act consolidates certain enactments relating to rights of employees arising out of their employment and certain enactments relating to the insolvency of employers, to industrial tribunals, to recoupment of certain benefits, to conciliation officers and to the Employment Appeal Tribunal.

Tables showing the destination of enactments consolidated and the derivation of the new Act are set out on pages 231–246 following.

DESTINATION TABLE

This table shows in column (1) the enactments repealed by the Employment Protection (Consolidation) Act 1978, and in column (2) the provisions of that Act corresponding to the repealed provisions.

In certain cases the enactment in column (1), though having a corresponding provision in column (2), is not, or is not wholly, repealed, as it is still required, or partly required, for the purposes of other legislation.

(1)	(2)	(1)	(2)
Contracts of Employment Act 1963 (c. 49)	Employment Protection (Consolidation) Act 1978 (c. 44)	Redundancy Payments Act 1965 (c. 62)	Employment Protection (Consolidation) Act 1978 (c. 44)
Sch. 1, para. 1 (2)‡	Sch. 13, para. 21	s. 16 (6) (a)	s 149 (1), (a), (b), (2)
6‡	22	(b)	(1) (c), (d)
		(7)	154 (3), (4)
Industrial Training Act 1964 (c. 16		(8)	ss. 149 (4), 154 (1)
		17 (1), (2)	s. 141 (3), (4)
s. 12 (1)*	s. 128 (1)	(3)	Sch. 13, para. 14 (1)
(2B), (3)	Sch. 9, paras. 9, 10	(4)	(2)
(4)	s. 154 (2)	(4A), (4B)	(1)
		(5), (6)	(3)
Redundancy Payments Act 1965 (c. 62)			(4)
		(7)	Cf. Sch. 13, para. 14 (6)
		(8)	Sch. 13, para. 14 (5)
s. 1	81 (1), (2)	18	s. 102
2	82 (1)–(6)	19	100
3 (1), (2)	83	20 (1)	Sch. 13, para. 14 (6)
(3), (8)	84 (1)–(6)	(2)	s. 144 (3)
(9), (10)	90 (1), (3)	(3)	s. 144 (3), Sch. 13, para. 14 (6)
4 (1)	85 (1)	21	s. 101
(2)	ss. 85 (2), 90 (1) (e)	22	93
(3)–(5)	s. 85 (3)–(5)	23	150
5 (1), (2)	87 (1), (2)	24 (1)	Sch. 13, para. 12 (2) (a)
(2A)	Sch, 14, para. 7 (1) (j)	(2)	(1) (a)
(3)	s. 153 (1)	(3)	(3)
6 (1)	88 (1)	24A (1)	(2) (b)
(2)	90 (2)	(2)	(1) (a), (b)
(3)–(5)	88 (2)–(4)		
7	89	25 (1), (2)	s. 153 (1)
8 (1)	81 (4)	(3)	81 (3)
(2)	151 (1)	(4), (5)	140 (1), (2) (f), (h)
(3), (3A)	Sch. 13, para. 11 (2), (3)	26	103
(4)	1 (2)	30 (1), (2)	104 (1), (2)
9 (1)	ss. 91 (1), 128 (4)	(2A)	(3)
(2) (a)	s. 151 (2)	(3)–(8)	(4)–(9)
(b), (3)	91 (2), (3)	ss. 31–33	ss. 105–107
10	92 (1)–(4)	s. 34 (1)	s. 108 (1)
11	ss. 96, 154 (1)	(2)	ss. 108 (2), 128 (4)
12	s. 97	(3)	s. 108 (3)
13	94 (1)–(5), (7)	(3A), (4)	(4), (5)
13A	95	35 (1), (2)	109 (1), (2)
14	98	(3)	Rep., 1968 c. 13, s. 24 (2), Sch. 6, Part I
15 (1)	Sch. 15, para. 12		
(2)–(4)	s. 142 (2)–(4)	(4)	s. 109 (3)
(5)	Cf. s. 144 (3)	(5)	Rep., 1968 c. 13, s. 24 (2), Sch. 6, Part I
16 (1)	Rep., 1976 c. 79, s. 17 (4), Sch. 6	(6)	s. 154 (4)
		(7)	ss. 109 (4), 154 (1)
(2)	s. 144 (2)	36 (1)–(4)	Rep., 1973 c. 38, s. 100 (2) (b), Sch. 28
(3)	146 (1)		
(4), (5)	99		

‡ Repealed by the Contracts of Employment Act 1972, s. 13 (1), Sch. 3.
* Not repealed.

(1) Redundancy Payments Act 1965 (c. 62)	(2) Employment Protection (Consolidation) Act 1978 (c. 44)	(1) Redundancy Payments Act 1965 (c. 62)	(2) Employment Protection (Consolidation) Act 1978 (c. 44)
s. 36 (5), (6)	s. 153 (1)	para. 5	Rep., 1972 c. 58, s. 64, Sch. 7, Part II
ss. 37–39	Rep., 1972 c. 53, s. 13, Sch. 3	6	Rep., 1972 c. 58, s. 64, Sch. 7, Part II, and 1973 c. 32, s. 57, Sch. 5
40–42	ss. 110–112	paras. 7, 8	Sch. 5, paras. 3, 4
s. 43 (1), (1)A	s. 113 (1), (2)	4, paras. 1–5	Sch. 12, paras. 12–16
(2)–(5)	(3)–(6)	para. 6	Rep., 1975 c. 71, s. 125, Sch. 16, Part I, para. 25, Sch. 18
(6)	114	paras. 7–10	Sch. 12, paras. 17–20 s.
44	130	para. 11	153 (1)
46 (1)–(4)	Rep., 1971 c. 72, s. 169 (b), Sch. 9	12	Rep., 1975 c. 71, s. 125, Sch. 16, Part I, para. 27, Sch. 18
(5)	Sch. 9, para. 10	13	Sch. 12, para. 21
(6)	3	14	paras. 1, 4 (1)
(7)	———	15	1, 6
47	s. 118	paras. 16, 17	22, 23
48 (1)	ss. 82 (7), 84 (7), 142 (2)	para. 17A	para. 24
(2)	s. 94 (6)	paras. 18–20	paras. 25–27
(3)	81 (2)	para. 21	1, 4 (1)
(4)	153 (4)	21A (1)	1, 3 (1)
ss. 49–51	ss. 115–117	(2)	para. 3 (2)
s. 52	s. 120	(3)	s. 154
53	119	22 (1)	Sch. 12, para. 5
54 (1)	154 (1), (3)	(2)	28
(2)	(2)	5, para. 1	Cf. s. 153 (1), Sch. 13, para. 1 (1)
55 (1)–(3)	———	paras. 2–6	Sch. 6, paras. 1–5
(4)	Rep., 1969 c. 49, s. 141, Sch. 11	para. 7	s. 153 (1), Sch. 6, para. 6
(5), (6)†	s. 156 (2), (3)	paras. 8–12	Sch. 6, paras. 7–11
56 (1)	ss. 92 (5), 110 (9), 153 (1)	para. 13	Rep., 1975 c. 71, s. 125, Sch. 18
(2)	———	6, paras. 1, 2	Sch. 7
(3)	s. 114	para. 3	s. 153 (1)
(4)	153 (5)	7	Sch. 10
(5)	(7)	8	8
57	158	9	———
58 (1)–(3)	157 (1)–(3)	**Iron and Steel Act 1967 (c. 17)**	
(4)	Rep., 1973 c. 36, s. 41, Sch. 6		———
(5)	s. 157 (4)	s. 31 (3)†	Sch. 16. para. 3 (1)
59 (2)	———	(4) (b)	(2)
(3)†	160 (3)	(6)	———
Sch. 1, para. 1	Sch. 4, para. 1, Sch. 13, paras. 11 (2), (3), 13	**Superannuation (Miscellaneous Provisions) Act 1967 (c. 28)**	
paras. 2–4	Sch. 4, paras. 2–4	s. 9 (1)–(3)	Sch. 9, para. 11 (1)–(3)
para. 5 (1)	14, para. 7 (1) (l)	(4)	s. 154 (1), (2), Sch. 9, para. 11 (4)
(2)	(2)	(5)–(8)	Sch. 9, para. 11 (5)–(8)
(3)	(1) (k)	**National Loans Act 1968 (c. 13)**	
(4)	8 (1) (c)	Sch. 1†	s. 109 (1), (3)
(5)	s. 154 (1), Sch. 14 para. 8 (2)		
(6)	154 (3), (4)		
(7)	Sch. 14, para. 8 (4)		
paras. 6–8	Sch. 4, paras. 5–7		
para. 9	para. 2		
2	Rep., 1975 c. 91, s. 125, Sch. 18		
3, para. 1	Sch. 5, para. 1		
2	Rep., 1973 c. 32, s. 57, Sch. 5		
3	Rep., 1972 c. 58, s. 64, Sch. 7, Part II		
4	Sch. 5, para. 2		

† Repealed in part.

(1)	(2)
Redundancy Rebates Act 1969 (c. 8)	Employment Protection (Consolidation) Act 1978 (c. 44)
ss. 1, 2	Spent
Post Office Act 1969 (c. 48)	
Sch. 9, para. 34	Sch. 16, para. 8
Equal Pay Act 1970 (c. 41)	
s. 2 (7)	—
Civil Aviation Act 1971 (c. 75)	
Sch. 9, para. 2	Sch. 16, para. 12
Superannuation Act 1972 (c. 11)	
Sch. 6, para. 54	s. 99 (1) (a)
55	111 (2) (b), (3) (b), (6) (a)
Contracts of Employment Act 1972 (c. 53)	
s. 1 (1)–(4)	49 (1)–(4)
(5)	151 (1)
(6)	49 (5)
2 (1)–(3)	50
(4)	140 (1)
3	51
4 (1)	1 (1)–(3)
(2), (2A)	(4), (5)
(3)–(6)	2
(7)	ss. 3 (1), 147
(8)–(10)	s. 3 (2)–(4)
ss. 5, 6	ss. 4, 5
s. 7 (1)	s. 6
(2)	ss. 6, 154 (3), (4)
(3)	s. 154 (1), (2)
8 (1)–(3)	11 (1)–(3)
(4)–(6)	(5)–(7)
(7)	128 (4)
(8)	ss. 11 (9), 128 (4)
(9)	
9 (1)	Rep., 1976 c. 79, s. 17 (4), Sch. 6
(2) (a)	s. 144 (1) (a)
(b)	—
(c)	144 (1) (b)
(2A)	143 (3) (b), (4)
(3)	146 (1)
(4)	147
(5)	149 (1) (a), (c), (2)
(6)	154 (3), (4)
(7)	ss. 149 (4), 154 (1)
10 (1)	s. 7 (1)
(2)	Sch. 13, para. 8
(3)	s. 154 (3), (4)

(1)	(2)
Contracts of Employment Act 1972 (c. 53)	Employment Protection (Consolidation) Act 1978 (c. 44)
s. 10 (4)	ss. 7 (2), 154 (1)
11 (1)	s. 153 (1)
(2)	52
12 (1)	141 (1)
(2)	153 (5)
13 (1)	
(2)	Sch. 15, para. 8
(3), (4)	paras. 1, 2
(5)	13, para. 23; and cf. paras. 21, 22
(6)	15, para. 4 (a)
(7)	s. 159 (1)
14 (1)	
(2)	160 (3)
Sch. 1, paras. 1–4	Sch. 13, paras. 1–4
4A–4C	5–7
para. 5 (1), (2)	para. 9 (1), (2)
(3)	
5A	Sch. 13, para. 10
paras. 6, 7	15
8, 9	paras. 16, 17
para. 10 (1)	para. 18
(2)	s. 153 (4)
10A	Sch. 13, para. 19
11	24
2, para. 1 (1) (a)	Sch. 3, para. 1
(b)	s. 152
(2)	Sch. 14, para. 7 (1) (e)
2–7	3, paras. 2–7
3	—
British Library Act 1972 (c. 54)	
Schedule, para. 13 (2)†	—
National Health Service Reorganisation Act 1973 (c. 32)	
Sch. 4, para. 106	Sch. 5, para. 1
Social Security Act 1973 (c. 38)	
Sch. 27, para. 54	Rep., 1975 c. 71, s. 125 (3), Sch. 18
55	s. 103 (3)
56	105 (4)
57	153 (1)
58	113 (1)–(3), (5)
59	115 (1)
Employment and Training Act 1973 (c. 50)	
Sch. 2, Part 1, para. 15	Sch. 9, para. 9

† Repealed in part.

(1)	(2)	(1)	(2)
Trade Union and Labour Relations Act 1974 (c. 52)	Employment Protection (Consolidation) Act 1978 (c. 44)	Trade Union and Labour Relations Act 1974 (c. 52)	Employment Protection (Consolidation) Act 1978 (c. 44)
s. 1 (2) (b), (c), (d)†	—	para. 21 (4)	s. 67 (2)
26 (2)*–(4)*	ss. 154 (1), (2), (4)	(4A)	(4)
30 (1)†	ss. 146 (2), (3), 153 (1)	(5)	Sch. 9, para. 1 (5)
(3)*, (4)*	s. 153 (1)	(5A)	(6)
(5)*, (6)*	(4), (5)	(6)	(7)
31 (5)*	160 (3)	paras. 22–25	paras. 4–7
Sch. 1, para. 4 (1)	ss. 54 (1), 129	para. 26 (1)	Rep., 1975 c. 71, s. 125 (3), Sch. 18
(2)	s. 54 (2)	(2)–(4)	s. 134 (1)–(3)
5 (1)–(3)	55 (1)–(3)	(4A)	(4)
(4)	Rep., 1975 c. 71, s. 125, Sch. 16, Part III, para. 9, Sch. 18	(5)	(5)
(5), (6)	s. 55 (4), (5)	27	80
6 (1)–(3)	57 (1)–(3)	30 (1)	151 (1)
(4), (4A)	58 (1), (2)	(1A)	Sch. 13, para. 11 (1)
(5), (5A)	(3), (4)	(2)	s. 151 (2)
(6)	(5)	(3), (4)	Sch. 13, para. 20
(7)	59	32†	s. 140
(8)	57 (3)	33 (1)*	138 (1)
(9)	ss. 57 (4), 58 (6), 153 (2)	(2)*	(2), (3)
7 (1)–(3)	s. 62 (1)–(3)	(3)†	(7)
(4)	67 (3)	(4)*	(3)–(5)
(5)	62 (4)	(4A)	(6)
8	Rep., 1975 c. 71, Sch. 16, Part III, para. 13	(5)*	(4)
		Sch. 3, para. 16	
		4, para. 1	
9 (1) (a)	Rep., 1975 c. 71, s. 125, Sch. 16, Part III, para. 14 (1), Sch. 18	3	—
		6 (4)	Sch. 15, para. 1
		7*	4 (c)
(b)	s. 146 (1)		
(c)	Rep., 1976 c. 79, s. 17 (4), Sch. 6	Social Security (Consequential Provisions) Act 1975 (c. 18)	
(d)	s. 144 (2)		
(e)			—
(f)	Rep., 1975 c. 71, Sch. 16, Part III, para. 14 (1), Sch. 18	Sch. 2, para. 19	s. 113 (2)
		20	Rep., 1975 c. 71, s. 125 (3), Sch. 18
(2), (3)	s. 141 (2), (5)	21	s. 105 (4)
(4)	Rep., 1975 c. 71, s. 125, Sch. 16, Part III, para. 14 (2), Sch. 18	22	113 (2)
		23	115 (1)
(5)	—	Social Security Pensions Act 1975 (c. 60)	
10	s. 64 (1)		
11 (1)	(3)	s. 30 (5)	ss. 1 (4) (d), 11 (4) (b)
(2), (3)	149 (1) (c), (4)		
12 (a)	Sch. 15, para. 10 (1)	Employment Protection Act 1975 (c. 71)	
(b)	s. 142 (1)		
paras. 13, 14	ss. 65, 66	s. 22 (1), (2)	s. 12
para. 15	s. 63	(3)	143 (1)
16	128 (1), (2)	23	13
17 (1)	67 (1)	24 (1), (2)	14 (1), (2)
18	Sch. 9, para. 2	(3)	Sch. 14, para. 7 (1) (a)
20 (1)–(3)	s. 75	(4)	s. 14 (3), Sch. 14, para. 7 (1) (a)
(4)	154		
21 (1)	Sch. 9, para. 1 (1)	(5)	s. 153 (1)
(2) (a)	(2) (a)	ss. 25–28	ss. 15–18
(b)–(i)	(c)–(j)		
(3)	(3)		
(3A)	(4)		

† Repealed in part.   * Not Repealed.

(1)	(2)	(1)	(2)
Employment Protection Act 1975 (c. 71)	Employment Protection (Consolidation) Act 1978 (c. 44)	Employment Protection Act 1975 (c. 71)	Employment Protection (Consolidation) Act 1978 (c. 44)
s. 29 (1)–(3)	s. 19 (1)–(3)	s. 73	s. 72
(4)	64 (2)	74 (1)	73 (1)
30 (1)	143 (2)	(2) (a)	(2)
(2), (3)	20	(b)	(8)
31 (1)	21 (1)	(3)	(3)
(2)	Sch. 14, para. 7 (1) (b)	(4)	Sch. 13, para. 11 (1)
(3), (4)	s. 21 (2), (3)	(5)–(7)	s. 73 (4)–(6)
(5)	153 (1)	75 (1)	Sch. 14, para. 7 (1) (i)
32	22	(2)	(2)
33	61 (2)	(3)	(1) (h)
34 (1)–(5)	60	(4)–(6)	8 (1) (b),
(6)	Sch. 15, para. 10 (2)		(2), (3)
(7)	s. 65 (4)	(7)	s. 73 (7)
35 (1)	33 (1)	(8)	(9)
(2)–(5)	(3)–(6)	76	74
36	34	ss. 77–79	ss. 76–78
37 (1)–(4)	35	s. 80 (1)–(3)	s. 79
(5)	Sch. 14, para. 7 (1) (d)	(4)	Sch. 9, para. 8
ss. 38, 39	ss. 36, 37	ss. 81–83	ss. 8–10
41–47	38–44	s. 84 (1)–(3)	s. 11 (1), (2), (4)
s. 48 (1)	s. 45 (1)	(4)	(9)
(2) (a)	153 (1)	(5)	(8)
(b)	45 (2)	85 (1)	152
(3)	153 (1)	(2)	See against 1972 c. 53, Sch. 2, *ante*
(4), (5)	45 (3), (4)	86	s. 148
(6)	46	ss. 87, 88	ss. 135, 136
49	47	s. 108 (1)★	128 (4), 129
50 (1)	ss. 56, 86	(2)–(8)	s. 133
(2)	s. 33 (2)	109 (1)–(5)	131 (1)–(5)
51	61 (1)	(6)	Sch. 9, para. 1 (2) (b)
52	153 (1)	(7)–(9)	s. 131 (6)–(8)
53	23	110★	150
54	24	112 (1)	Sch. 16, para. 19 (2)
55 (1), (2)	25 (1), (2)	(2), (3)	s. 132 (2), (3)
(3), (4)	Sch. 9, para. 2	(4)	Sch. 16, para. 19 (1)
56	s. 26	(5), (6)	s. 132 (4), (5)
57 (1), (2)	s. 27 (1), (2)	(7)	(1)
(3)	Sch. 16, para. 23 (2) (b)	(8)	(6)
(4)–(8)	s. 27 (3)–(7)	117★	155
58 (1)–(3)	28 (1)–(3)	118†	140
(4)	Sch. 16, para. 23 (2) (c)	119 (2)	146 (1)
(5)	s. 28 (4)	(3)†	Rep., 1976 c. 79, s. 17 (4), Sch. 6
ss. 59, 60	ss. 29, 30	(4)†	s. 144 (2)
s. 61 (1)–(4)	s. 31 (1)–(4)	(5)†	141 (2)
(5)	Sch. 14, para. 7 (1) (c)	(6)★	(5)
(6)	s. 153 (1)	(7)†	143 (3), (4)
(7)–(13)	31 (5)–(11)	(8)–(11)	146 (4)–(7)
62 (a), (b)	32 (1)	(12)†, (13)★	144 (4), (5)
(c)	152	(15)★	149 (1)
ss. 63–69	ss. 121–127	(16)★	(4)
s. 70 (1)–(5)	s. 53	120 (1)	Sch. 13, para. 19
(6)	Sch. 14, para. 7 (1) (f), (g)	(2)	s. 95
71 (1)	s. 68 (1)	(3)	Sch. 13, para. 12
(2)–(7)	69	121†	s. 138
(8), (9)	70	122 (1)†	139 (1)
72 (1)–(4)	71 (1)–(4)	(3)	(2)
(5)	68 (2)	(4)†, (5)†	(3), (4)
(6)	71 (5)	(6)★, (7)★	(5), (6)
(7)	Sch. 14, para. 7 (1) (f), (g)	(7A)★, (7B)★	(7), (8)
(8)	8 (1) (a)	(8)★	(9)

★ Not repealed.

(1)	(2)	(1)	(2)
Employment Protection Act 1975 (c. 71)	Employment Protection (Consolidation) Act 1978 (c. 44)	New Towns (Amendment) Act 1976 (c. 68)	Employment Protection (Consolidation) Act 1978 (c. 44)
s. 123†	s. 154	s. 13 (5)†	—
124 (2)	—		
(3), (4)	156 (1), (2)	**Supplementary Benefits Act 1976 (c. 71)**	
126 (1)†	ss. 146 (2), (3), 153 (1)		
(2)★	s. 153 (1)		
(3)	—	Sch. 7, para. 40	132 (3) (e), (4) (b), (6)
(5)	151		
(8)★	153 (5)		
127†	137 (1)–(4)	**Race Relations Act 1976 (c. 74)**	
128†	157		
129 (2)			
(6)★	160 (3)	Sch. 3, para. 1 (2)	71 (3) (c)
Sch. 2	Sch. 1	(3)	76
3, para. 1	2, paras. 1, 3	(4)	136 (1) (d)
2	para. 2		
3	4	**Dock Work Regulation Act 1976 (c. 79)**	
4	6		
5	s. 48		
6	Sch. 2, para. 5		
7	7		
4, paras. 1–6	14, paras. 1–6		
para. 7	para. 9		
8 (a)	10	s. 14 (1), (2)	145 (3), (4)
(b)	s. 153 (1)	(3)	ss. 145 (4), 151
paras. 9, 10	Sch. 14, paras. 11, 12	(4)	s. 105 (2)
5	See against 1972 c. 53, Sch. 2, *ante*	(5)	145 (1)
6, paras. 1–7	Sch. 11, paras. 1–7	(6)†	145 (2)
para. 7A	para. 8	(7)★	ss. 149 (1) (c), (4), 154 (3)
8	9	ss. 14 (8)★, 15 (1)★	s. 145 (5)
para. 8A	10	Sch. 1, para. 17 (2)	—
paras. 9–23	paras. 11–25		
para. 23A	para. 26	**Social Security (Miscellaneous Provisions) Act 1977 (c. 5)**	
paras. 24, 25	paras. 27, 28		
12, para. 1†	12, para. 1		
paras. 2★–6★	paras. 2–6	s.16	132
8–12	7–11		
16, Parts I, II, Part III, paras. 8–30, 34 Part IV,	See against enactments amended, *ante*	**Redundancy Rebates Act 1977 (c. 22)**	
para. 14	Sch. 16, para. 11	s. 1 (1)	s. 154 (1), Sch. 6, para. 13 (1)
17, para. 7	15, para. 9	(2)	Sch. 16, para. 13 (1)
8	15 (1)	(3)	s. 154 (3), (4)
9, 10	—	(4)	Sch. 6, para. 13 (2)
16	Sch. 15, para. 11	2	Applies to Northern Ireland
17	17		
18★	4	3 (1), (2)	—
		(3)	s. 160 (3)
Trade Union and Labour Relations Amendment Act 1976 (c. 7)		Schedule	Sch. 6, para. 13 (1)
		Criminal Law Act 1977 (c. 45)	
s. 1 (e)	s. 58 (3)		
3 (3)★	153 (1)	s. 28 (2)★	ss. 104 (9), 107 (4)
(5)	58 (3)	(7)★	ss. 104 (10) (a), 107 (5) (a)
(6)	(6)		

★Not repealed.　　　　† Repealed in part.

(1)	(2)	(1)	(2)
Administration of Justice Act 1977 (c. 48)	Employment Protection (Consolidation) Act 1978 (c. 44)	House of Commons (Administration) Act 1978 (c. 36)	Employment Protection (Consolidation) Act 1978 (c. 44)
s. 6 32 (11)	Sch. 11, paras. 8, 10, 26 s. 160 (3)	Sch. 2, para. 4* 5*	s. 4 (4) (a) 139
Housing (Homeless Persons) Act 1977 (c. 48)		Employment (Continental Shelf) Act 1978 (c. 46)	
s. 14 (4) (b)†	—	s. 1 (1)* 2*	137 (2) (c) (5)

† Repealed in part.   * Not repealed.

TABLE OF DERIVATIONS

This table shows in the right hand column the legislative source from which the sections of the Employment Protection (Consolidation) Act 1978 in the left hand column have been derived. In the table the following abbreviations are used:

1965 = The Redundancy Payments Act 1965
     (1965 c. 62)
1972 = The Contracts of Employment Act 1972
     (1972 c. 53)
1974 = The Trade Union and Labour Relations Act 1974
     (1974 c. 52)
     (The reference to "para." indicates a paragraph of Schedule 1 to the Act.)
1975 = The Employment Protection Act 1975
     (1975 c. 71)
1977 = Redundancy Rebates Act 1977
     (1977 c. 22)
1977 Order = Redundancy Payments (Variation of Rebates) Order 1977
     (S.I. 1977/1321)
1977 Order (No. 2) = Employment Protection (Variation of Limits) Order 1977
     (S.I. 1977/2031)

This table does not acknowledge the transfer of the functions of the Minister of Labour to the Secretary of State for Employment by virtue of the Secretary of State for Employment and Productivity Order 1968.

Section of Act	Derivation
1	1972 s. 4 (1), (2) (2A); 1975 Sch. 16 Part II para. 4, 5, 6; Social Security Pensions Act 1975 (c. 60) s. 30 (5).
	1972 s. 4 (3) to (6).
3	1972 s. 4 (7) to (10); 1975 Sch. 16 Part II para. 7, 8.
4	1972 s. 5; 1975 Sch. 16 Part II para. 9; House of Commons (Administration) Act 1978 (c. 36) Sch. 2 para. 4.
5	1972 s. 6.
6	1972 s. 7 (1), (2).
7	1972 s. 10 (1), (4); 1975 Sch. 16 Part II para. 11.
8	1975 s. 81.
9	1975 s. 82.
10	1975 s. 83.
11	1972 s. 8; 1975 s. 84; Social Security Pensions Act 1975 (c. 60) s. 30 (5).
12	1975 s. 22 (1), (2).
13	1975 s. 23.
14	1975 s. 24 (1), (2), (4).
15	1975 s. 25; 1977 Order (No. 2) Art. 2.
16	1975 s. 26.

Section of Act	Derivation
17	1975 s. 27.
18	1975 s. 28.
19	1975 s. 29 (1) to (3).
20	1975 s. 30 (2), (3).
21	1975 s. 31 (1), (3), (4).
22	1975 s. 32.
23	1975 s. 53.
24	1975 s. 54.
25	1975 s. 55 (1), (2).
26	1975 s. 56.
27	1975 s. 57 (1), (2), (4) to (8).
28	1975 s. 58 (1) to (3), (5).
29	1975 s. 59.
30	1975 s. 60.
31	1975 s. 61 (1) to (4), (7) to (13).
32	1975 s. 62 (a) (b), 126 (1).
33	1975 s. 35, s. 50 (2).
34	1975 s. 36.
35	1975 s. 37 (1) to (4).
36	1975 s. 38.
37	1975 s. 39.
38	1975 s. 41.
39	1975 s. 42.
40	1975 s. 43.
41	1975 s. 44.
42	1975 s. 45.
43	1975 s. 46.
44	1975 s. 47.
45	1975 s. 48 (1), (2), (4), (5).
46	1975 s. 48 (6).

Section of Act	Derivation
47	1975 s. 49.
48	1975 Sch. 3 para. 5.
49	1972 s. 1 (1) to (4), (6); 1975 Sch. 16 Part II para. 1, 2, 3.
50	1972 s. 2 (1) to (3); 1975 Sch. 16 Part II para. 1.
51	1972 s. 3.
52	1972 s. 11 (2).
53	1975 s. 70 (1) to (5)
54	1974 para. 4.
55	1974 para. 5 (1) to (3), (5), (6); 1975 Sch. 16 Part III para. 8, 9, 10.
56	1975 s. 50 (1).
57	1974 para. 6 (1) to (3), (8), (9) (*a*) (*b*); 1974 s. 30 (1).
58	1974 para. 6 (4) to (6), (9); 1975 Sch. 16 Part III para. 11, 12; Trade Union and Labour Relations (Amendment) Act 1976 (c. 7) s. 1 (*e*), s. 3 (5), (6).
59	1974 para. 6 (7).
60	1975 s. 34 (1) to (5).
61	1975 ss. 33, 51.
62	1974 para. 7 (1) to (3), (5); 1975 Sch. 16 Part III para. 13.
63	1974 para. 15.
64	1974 para. 10; 1975 s. 29 (4); 1974 para. 11 (1); 1975 Sch. 16 Part III para. 15.
65	1974 para. 13; 1975 s. 34 (7).
66	1974 para. 14.
67	1974 paras. 17 (1), 21 (4), (4A), 7 (4); 1975 Sch. 16 Part III paras. 13, 16, 20, 21.
68	1975 s. 71 (1), s. 72 (5).
69	1975 s. 71 (2) to (7).
70	1975 s. 71 (8), (9).
71	1975 s. 72 (1) to (4); Race Relations Act 1976 (c. 74) Sch. 3 para. 1 (2).
72	1975 s. 73.
73	1975 s. 74 (1) to (3), (5) to (7); s. 75 (7), (8).
74	1975 s. 76.
75	1974 para. 20; 1975 Sch. 16 Part III para. 17.

Section of Act	Derivation
76	1975 s. 77; Race Relations Act 1976 (c. 74) Sch. 3 para. 1 (3).
77	1975 s. 78.
78	1975 s. 79.
79	1975 s. 80 (1) to (3).
80	1974 para. 27; 1975 Sch. 16 Part III para. 26, 27.
81	1965 s. 1, 48 (3), 25 (3), 8 (1); 1975 Sch. 16 Part I para. 1, 5 (1), 18.
81	1965 ss. 2, 48 (1); 1975 Sch. 16 Part I para. 2, 18.
83	1965 s. 3 (1), (2); 1975 Sch. 16 part I para. 3.
84	1965 ss. 3 (3) to (8), 48 (1); 1975 Sch. 16 Part I para. 3, 18.
85	1965 s. 4.
86	1975 s. 50 (1).
87	1965 s. 5 (1), (2); 1975 Sch. 16 Part I para. 4.
88	1965 s. 6 (1), (3) to (5).
89	1965 s. 7.
90	1965 s. 3 (9), s. 4 (2), s. 6 (2), s. 3 (10); 1975 sch. 16 Part I para. 3.
91	1965 s. 9 (1), (2) (b), (3).
92	1965 s. 10, s. 56 (1).
93	1965 s. 22; 1975 Sch. 16 Part I para. 10.
94	1965 s. 13, 48 (2); 1975 Sch. 16 Part I para. 7, 18.
95	1965 s. 13A; 1975 s. 120 (2).
96	1965 s. 11.
97	1965 s. 12; 1975 Sch. 16 Part I para. 6.
98	1965 s. 14.
99	1965 a. 16 (4), (5); Superannuation Act 1972 (c. 11) Sch. 6 para. 54.
100	1965 s. 19.
101	1965 s. 21; 1975 Sch. 16 Part I para. 9.
102	1965 s. 18.
103	1965 s. 26; Social Security Act 1973 (c. 38) Sch. 27 para. 55.
104	1965 s. 30; 1975 Sch. 16 Part I para. 12; Criminal Procedure (Scotland) Act 1975 (c. 21) s. 289B (1); Criminal Law Act 1977 (c. 45) s. 28 (2), Sch. 11 para. 5.

Section of Act	Derivation
105	1965 s. 31; Social Security Act 1973 Sch. 27 para. 56; Social Security (Consequential Provisions) Act 1975 (c. 18) Sch. 2 para. 21; 1975 Sch. 16 Part I para. 13; Dock Work Regulation Act 1976 (c. 79) s. 14 (4).
106	1965 s. 32; 1975 Sch. 16 Part I para. 14, 15.
107	1965 s. 33; Criminal Procedure (Scotland) Act 1975 (c. 21) s. 289B (1); Criminal Law Act 1977 (c. 45) s. 28 (2), Sch. 11 para. 5.
108	1965 s. 34; 1975 Sch. 16 Part I para. 16.
109	1965 s. 35 (1), (2), (4), (7); National Loans Act 1968 (c. 13) s. 5 (1), Sch. 1; 1975 Sch. 16 Part I para. 17.
110	1965 s. 40; s. 56 (1).
111	1965 s. 41; Superannuation Act 1972 (c. 11) Sch. 6 para. 55; Minister for the Civil Service order 1968 (S.I. 1968/1656).
112	1965 s. 42.
113	1965 s. 43 (1) to (5); Social Security Act 1973 (c. 38) Sch. 27 para. 58; Social Security (Consequential Provisions) Act 1975 (c. 18) Sch. 2 para. 22.
114	1965 s. 43 (6).
115	1965 s. 49; Social Security Act 1973 Sch. 27 para. 59; Social Security (Consequential Provisions) Act 1975 Sch. 2 para. 23.
116	1965 s. 50.
117	1965 s. 51.
118	1965 s. 47.
119	1965 s. 53.
120	1965 s. 52.
121	1975 s. 63.
122	1975 s. 64; 1977 Order (No. 2) Art. 2.
123	1975 s. 65.
124	1975 s. 66.
125	1975 s. 67.
126	1975 s. 68.
127	1975 s. 69.
128	1974 para. 16; Industrial Training Act 1964 (c. 16) s. 12 (1); 1965 s. 9 (1), 34 (2); 1972 s. 8 (7), (8); 1975 s. 108 (1).
129	1975 s. 108 (1); 1974 para. 4 (1).
130	1965 s. 44.

Section of Act	Derivation
131	1975 s. 109 (1) to (5), (7) to (9).
132	1975 s. 112 (2), (3), (5) to (8); Supplementary Benefits Act 1976 (c. 71) Sch. 7 para. 40; Social Security (Miscellaneous Provisions) Act 1977 (c. 5) s. 16.
133	1975 s. 108 (2) to (8).
134	1974 para. 26 (2), (3), (4), (4A), (5); 1975 Sch. 16 Part III para. 24, 25.
135	1975 s. 87.
136	1975 s. 88; Race Relations Act 1976 (c. 74) Sch. 3 para. 1 (4).
137	1975 s. 127 (1) (c) to (g), (2) to (4).
138	1974 para. 33; 1975 s. 121, Sch. 16 Part III para. 33, 34.
139	1975 s. 122 (1), (3) to (8); House of Commons (Administration) Act 1978 (c. 36) Sch. 2 para. 5.
140	1965 s. 25 (4), (5); 1972 s. 2 (4); 1974 para. 32; 1975 s. 118.
141	1972 s. 12 (1); 1974 para. 9 (2), (3); 1975 s. 119 (5), (6); 1965 s. 17 (1), (2).
142	1974 para. 12 (b); 1965 s. 15 (2) to (4).
143	1975 s. 22 (3), s. 30 (1), s. 119 (7); 1972 s. 9 (2A); 1975 Sch. 16 Part II para. 10 (a).
144	1972 s. 9 (2); 1975 s. 119 (4); 1974 para. 9 (1) (d); 1965 s. 16 (2), 20; 1975 s. 119 (12), (13).
145	Dock Work Regulation Act 1976 (c. 79) s. 14 (1) to (3), (5), (6), (8), s. 15 (1).
146 (1)	1972 s. 9 (3); 1975 s. 119 (2), Sch. 16 Part II para. 10 (b), Part III para. 14 (b); 1974 para. 9 (1) (b); 1965 s. 16 (3).
(2), (3)	1974 s. 30 (1); 1975 s. 126 (1).
(4) to (7)	1975 s. 119 (8) to (11).
147	1972 s. 4 (7), 9 (4).
148	1975 s. 86.
149	1965 s. 16 (6), (8); 1972 s. 9 (5), (7); 1974 para. 11 (2), (3); 1975 s. 119 (15), (16); Dock Work Regulation Act 1976 (c. 79) s. 14 (7).
150	1965 s. 23; 1975 s. 110.
151	1965 s. 8 (2), s. 9 (2) (a); 1972 s. 1 (5); 1974 para. 30 (1), (2); 1975 s. 126 (5); Dock Work Regulation Act 1976 (c. 79) s. 14 (3).
152	1972 Sch. 2 para. 1 (1) (b); 1975 s. 62 (c), 85, Sch. 5 para. 1 (1) (b).
153	1965 s. 5 (3), 25 (1), (2), 36 (5), (6), 48 (4), 56, Sch. 1 para. 9, Sch. 4 para. 11, Sch. 6 para. 3; 1972 s. 11 (1), 12 (2), Sch. 1 para. 10 (2); 1974 s. 30, Sch. 1 para. 6 (9) (c); 1975 s. 24 (5), 31 (5), 48 (2), (3), 52, 61 (6), 126, Sch. 4 para. 8 (b), Sch. 16 Part I para. 18, Part II para. 19, Part III para. 7 (2), (3), (4); Trade Union and Labour Relations (Amendment) Act 1976 (c. 7) s. 3 (3), (4).

Section of Act	Derivation
154	1965 s. 11 (4), s. 16 (7), (8), s. 35 (6), (7); Sch. 1 para. 5 (5), (6), Sch. 4 para. 21A (3); Superannuation (Miscellaneous Provisions) Act 1967 (c. 28) s. 9 (4); 1972 s. 7 (2), (3), s. 9 (6), (7), a. 10 (3), (4); 1974 s. 26, Sch. 1 para. 20 (4); 1975 s. 123, Sch. 16 Part I para. 21, 34, Part II para. 11; 1977 s. 1 (3).
155	1975 s. 117.
156	1975 s. 124 (3), (4); 1965 s. 55 (5), (6); National Loans Act 1968 (c. 13) Sch. 1.
157	1975 s. 128; 1965 s. 58.
158	1965 s. 57.
159	—
160	—
Sch. 1	1975 Sch. 2.
Sch. 2	1975 Sch. 3 paras. 1 to 4, 6, 7.
Sch. 3	1972 Sch. 2, subst. 1975 Sch. 5.
Sch. 4	1965 Sch. 1 paras. 1 to 4, 6 to 9; 1975 Sch. 16 Part I paras. 19, 20, 22.
Sch. 5	1965 Sch. 3; National Health Service Reorganisation Act 1973 (c. 32) Sch. 4 para. 106; National Health Service (Scotland) Act 1972 (c. 58) Sch. 6 para. 130.
Sch. 6	
para. 1, 2	1965 Sch. 5 paras. 2, 3; 1977 Order Art. 3.
3 to 7	1965 Sch. 5 paras. 4 to 8.
8	1965 Sch. 5 para. 9; 1977 Order Art. 3.
9, 10	1965 Sch. 5 paras. 10, 11.
11	1965 Sch. 5 para. 12; 1977 Order Art. 3.
12	1977 Order Art. 4.
13	1977 s. 1 (1), (2), (4), Sch.
Sch. 7	1965 Sch. 6 paras. 1, 2.
Sch. 8	1965 Sch. 8.
Sch. 9	
para. 1	1974 para. 21 (1) to (3A), (5), (5A), (6); 1975 s. 109 (6), Sch. 16 Part III para. 18, 19, 22, 23.
2	1975 s. 55 (3), (4); 1974 para. 18.
3	1965 s. 46 (6).
4	1974 para. 22.
5	1974 para. 23.
6	1974 para. 24.
7	1974 para. 25.
8	1975 s. 80 (4).
9, 10	Industrial Training Act 1964 (c. 16) s. 12 (2B), (3); 1965 s. 46 (5); Employment and Training Act 1973 (c. 50) Sch. 2 Part I para. 15; Minister for the Civil Service Order 1971 (S.I. 1971/2099).
11	Superannuation (Miscellaneous Provisions) Act 1967 (c. 28) s. 9; Minister for the Civil Service Order 1968 (S.I. 1968/1656).

Section of Act	Derivation
Sch. 10	1965 Sch. 7.
Sch. 11	1975 Sch. 6.
Sch. 12	1975 Sch. 12; 1965 Sch. 4, am. 1975 Sch. 16 Part I paras. 23 to 34.
	—
para. 1	
2	1975 Sch. 12 para. 2.
3	1975 Sch. 12 para. 3; 1965 Sch. 4 para. 21A (1), (2).
4	1975 Sch. 12 para. 4; 1965 Sch. 4 paras. 14, 21.
5	1975 Sch. 12 para. 5; 1965 Sch. 4 para. 22 (1).
6	1975 Sch. 12 para. 6; 1965 Sch. 4 para. 15.
7 to 11	1975 Sch. 12 paras. 8 to 12.
12 to 21	1965 Sch. 4 paras. 1 to 5, 7 to 10, 13.
22 to 28	1965 Sch. 4 paras. 16 to 20, 22 (2).
Sch. 13	1972 Sch. 1, am. 1975 Sch. 16 Part II paras. 12 to 19.
paras. 1 to 7	1972 Sch. 1 paras. 1 to 4C.
8	1972 s. 10 (2).
9	1972 Sch. 1 para. 5 (1), (2).
10	1972 Sch. 1 para. 5A.
11	1974 Sch. 1 para. 30 (1A); 1975 s. 74 (4); 1965 s. 8 (3), (3A), (4), Sch. 1 para. 1 (1) (*b*) (*c*); 1975 Sch. 16 Part I paras. 5, 19, 20, Part III para. 29.
12	1965 s. 24, s. 24A; 1975 s. 120 (3).
13	1965 Sch. 1 para. 1 (1) (*a*).
14	1965 s. 17 (3) to (8), 20 (1), (3); 1975 Sch. 16 Part I para. 8.
15	1972 Sch. 2 para. 6, 7.
16	1972 Sch. 1 para. 8.
17	1972 Sch. 1 para. 9.
18	1972 Sch. 1 para. 10.
19	1972 Sch. 1 para. 10A; 1975 s. 120 (1).
20	1974 para. 30 (3), (4); 1975 Sch. 16 Part III para. 30.
21	Contracts of Employment Act 1963 (c. 49) Sch. 1 para. 1 (2); 1972 s. 13 (5).
22	Contracts of Employment Act 1963 (c. 49) Sch. 1 para. 6; 1972 s. 13 (5).
23	1972 s. 13 (5).
24	1972 Sch. 1 para. 11.
Sch. 14	
para. 1 to 6	1975 Sch. 4 para. 1 to 6.
7 (1)	1975 s. 24 (3), (4), s. 31 (2), s. 37 (5), s. 61 (5); 1972 Sch. 2 para. 1 (2); 1975 s. 75 (3), s. 75 (1), s. 70 (6), s. 72 (7); 1965 s. 5 (2A), Sch. 5 para. 5 (1), (3); 1975 Sch. 5 para. 1 (2), Sch. 16 Part I paras. 4, 21.
(2)	1975 s. 75 (2); 1965 Sch. 1 para. 5 (2); 1975 Sch. 16 Part I para. 21.
8	1975 s. 75 (4) to (6), s. 72 (8), s. 86; 1965 Sch. 1 para. 5 (4), (5), (7); 1975 Sch. 16 Part I para. 21; 1977 Order (No. 2) Art. 2.
9	1975 Sch. 4 para. 7.
10	1975 Sch. 4 para. 8 (*a*).
11, 12	1975 Sch. 4 para. 9, 10.
Sch. 15	
para. 1 to 3	—
4	1975 Sch. 17 para. 18; 1974 Sch. 4 para. 7; 1972 s. 13 (6).
5	—
6	1977 Order (No. 2) Art. 3 (1).
7	Employment Protection Act 1975 (Commencement No. 4) Order 1976 (S.I. 1976/530); Employment Protection Act 1975 (Commencement No. 5) Order 1976 (S.I. 1976/1379).
8	1972 s. 13 (2).

Section of Act	Derivation
9	1975 Sch. 17 para. 7.
10 (1)	1974 para. 12 (*a*).
(2)	1975 s. 34 (6).
11	1975 Sch. 17 para. 16.
12	1965 s. 15 (1).
13	—
14	National Health Service (Preservation of Boards of Governors) Order 1974 (S.I. 1974/281).
15 (1)	1975 Sch. 17 para. 8.
(2)	1977 Order (No. 2) Art. 3 (2).

1078   —— **variation of limits**

The Employment Protection (Variation of Limits) Order 1978, S.I. 1978 No. 1777 (in force on 1st February 1979), increases certain limits in the Employment Protection (Consolidation) Act 1978 as follows: the amount of guarantee pay payable under s. 15(1) in respect of any day to £7·25; the amount for the purpose of calculating the sum payable under s. 122 in respect of a debt due to an employee whose employer becomes insolvent to £110; the amount of a "week's pay" for the purposes of calculating redundancy payments and basic and additional awards of compensation for unfair dismissal to £110.

1079   **Employment Subsidies Act 1978**

The Employment Subsidies Act 1978 empowers the Secretary of State to authorise payments to employers under schemes for the alleviation of high levels of unemployment. The Act received the royal assent on 23rd March 1978 and came into force on that date.

Schemes may be set up for making payments to employers to enable them to retain employees who would otherwise become unemployed, and to take on new employees: s. 1 (1). To set up the schemes, the appropriate employer and employee organisations must be consulted: s. 1 (2). The cost of any one scheme should not be more than £10 million a year, unless a resolution of the House of Commons decides otherwise: s. 2 (1). The Secretary of State has power to act without a resolution in cases of urgency: s. 2 (3). Schemes already set up under the Employment and Training Act 1973, s. 5, are authorised to continue: s. 3 (1). The Secretary of State's powers under s. 1 of the Act shall not be exercisable after the end of 1979 unless renewed by a resolution of the House of Commons: s. 3 (2), (3). Repeals are contained in s. 3 (7).

1080   **Guarantee payments—exemption**

Orders have been made excluding certain employees from guarantee payments in the following industries:

	Relevant Statutory Instruments
British Carbon Association	153
Card clothing	826
Furniture and Timber	940
Henry Wiggin and Co Ltd	429
Workshops for the Blind	737

1081   **Guarantee payment—right to payment—employee laid off because of trade dispute in associated company**

Industrial tribunal decision:

THOMSON V PRIEST (LINDLEY) LTD [1978] IRLR 99 (employee laid off for two days claimed guaranteed pay; employers contested claim on ground lay off was in consequence of trade dispute affecting an associated company within Employment Protection Act 1975, s. 23 (1); employee argued trade dispute only one of several reasons for lay off; employee not entitled to guaranteed pay as although not sole cause, there would have been no lay off without trade dispute).

1975 Act, s. 23 now Employment Protection (Consolidation) Act 1978, s. 13.

1082   —— —— **statutory conditions for entitlement**

Industrial tribunal decision:

MILLER V HARRY THORNTON (LOLLIES) LTD [1978] IRLR 430 (three female employees, having negotiated a maximum number of daily working hours, were required to work on any working day when called by employer; employer retained discretion to vary amount of work given according to demand for his products: power cuts were threatened due to a trade dispute and employees laid off for two days; employees entitled to guarantee payments under Employment Protection Act 1975, s. 22 (1); although hours of work not fixed, normal hours of work ascertainable as question of fact; days in question were days on which employees would normally be required to work under contracts of employment; a trade dispute constituted an "occurrence" within s. 22 (1) (b) of the Act).

1975 Act, s. 22 (1), now Employment Protection (Consolidation) Act 1978, s. 12.

1083   Health and safety at work

See HEALTH AND SAFETY AT WORK.

1084   Industrial democracy—Government proposals

The Government has published a White Paper entitled Industrial Democracy. The paper is the result of considerable study of foreign practice and of the report of the Bullock Committee.

The Government intends that employees and their representatives should participate in making corporate decisions which affect them. Legislation is to provide basic statutory rights for employees and trade unions, but details will be in the hands of individual companies. Those who employ more than 500 staff will be obliged to discuss with employees all important proposals affecting them. Joint representative committees (JRCs) should be formed by the unions in each company, with the right to require the board to discuss industrial strategy. The Government intends to discuss further the question of safeguarding the use of confidential information but warns against exaggerating the risks. JRCs should be empowered to compel companies to ballot employees on whether they want representation. Legislation is to be introduced giving companies the option of establishing a two tier board system comprising a policy board and a management board: employees should appoint up to a third of the members of the former. Employees of companies with more than 2,000 staff will have a statutory right to board representation. Only in special cases will exemption be granted to companies. The chairmen of nationalised industries have been asked to collaborate with unions to produce proposals for further improvements in consultation and participation by August 1978: White Paper entitled "Industrial Democracy" (Cmnd 7231) (HMSO: fifty pence).

1085   Industrial training—transfer of activities of establishments

The Industrial Training (Transfer of the Activities of Establishments) Order 1978, S.I. 1978 No. 448 (in force on 24th April 1978), transfers the activities of specified establishments for the purposes of the Industrial Training Act 1964 to other industrial training boards.

1086

The Industrial Training (Transfer of the Activities of Establishments) Order 1978, S.I. 1978 No. 1643 (in force on 12th December 1978), transfers the activities of specified establishments for the purposes of the Industrial Training Act 1964 to other industrial training boards.

1087

The Industrial Training (Transfer of the Activities of Establishments) (No. 2) Order 1978, S.I. 1978 No. 1225 (in force on 1st October 1978), transfers the activities of specified establishments to the industry of different industrial training boards.

1088   Industrial training levy

Levies have been imposed on employers in the following industries:

	Relevant Statutory Instruments (1978)
Air Transport and Travel	362
Carpet	1830
Ceramics, Glass and Mineral Products	1132
Chemical and Allied Products	773
Clothing and Allied Products	432
Construction	1471
Cotton and Allied Textiles	1021
Distributive	363
Engineering	612
Food, Drink and Tobacco	675
Footwear, Leather and Fur Skin	546
Hotel and Catering	547
Iron and Steel	223
Knitting, Lace and Net	242
Paper and Paper Products	613
Petroleum	57
Printing and Publishing	759
Road Transport	940
Rubber and Plastics Processing	1547
Shipbuilding	688
Wool, Jute and Flax	1305

A right to appeal to an industrial tribunal against an assessment is provided for.

1089   Industrial tribunal—costs

See *Rajguru v Top Order Ltd*, para. 2968.

1090   —— jurisdiction—declaration as to time off for public duties

An employee made a complaint under s. 59 of the Employment Protection Act 1975 that his employers did not give him enough time off to carry out his duties as a justice of the peace.   The industrial tribunal made a declaration to the effect that the employee should be allowed twenty-one days a year time off to attend to his duties as a justice of the peace, and that all days of absence over ten should be unpaid leave.   On appeal, *held*, the industrial tribunal had jurisdiction only to make a declaration on whether or not the employee should have time off.   It did not have the power to impose conditions as to how the time off should be granted.

CORNER v BUCKINGHAMSHIRE COUNTY COUNCIL [1978] ICR 421 (Employment Appeal Tribunal: SLYNN J presiding).

1975 Act s. 59 now Employment Protection (Consolidation) Act 1978, s. 29.

1091   —— —— determination of existence of contract of employment

In an action for compensation for unfair dismissal brought by a former director of a small family company, the industrial tribunal had held that it lacked jurisdiction to entertain the claim, on the ground that, in the absence of a contract of service, express or implied, between the director and the company, the director was not an employee within the Trade Union and Labour Relations Act 1974, s. 30, and therefore was not entitled to claim compensation for unfair dismissal under that Act.   The Employment Appeal Tribunal found that in considering whether a contract of service could be inferred from the relevant surrounding circumstances and facts the industrial tribunal had attached too much importance to the fact that the complainant's remuneration had been classified as "directors' emoluments" in the company's accounts, and remitted the case to another tribunal for rehearing.   The company appealed to the Court of Appeal.   *Held*, the industrial tribunal had not erred in law in finding that the applicant was not an employee within the meaning of the Act. They had been entitled to reach that decision and the appeal would be allowed.

PARSONS v ALBERT J. PARSONS & SONS LTD (1978) 122 Sol Jo 812 (Court of Appeal: LORD DENNING MR, STEPHENSON and SHAW LJJ).

For earlier proceedings, see 1977 Halsbury's Abr para. 1063.

1974 Act, s. 30 now Employment Protection (Consolidation) Act 1978, s. 153.

1092 —— —— jurisdiction to consider validity of improvement notice

See *Chrysler UK Ltd v McCarthy*, para. 1460.

1093 —— —— power to order discovery and inspection of documents

See *Science Research Council v Nasse*, para. 946; *University of Reading v MacCormack*, para. 947.

1094 —— —— racial discrimination—barmaid dismissed for serving coloured customers

See *Zarczynska v Levy*, para. 2269.

1095 —— —— when decision of tribunal is complete

The chairman of an industrial tribunal had delivered an oral judgment awarding the plaintiff a redundancy payment. Several weeks later, before the judgment had been put in writing, the chairman recalled the matter for further argument. On appeal by the plaintiff *held*, the issue turned on when the decision of an industrial tribunal was complete, so that it no longer had jurisdiction. In the civil courts the ordinary practice was that a decision was not complete until an order had been drawn up, and the same test should be applied to industrial tribunals. On the balance of convenience a chairman should be able to request further argument when an obvious mistake was discovered shortly after the hearing. The appeal would accordingly be dismissed.

HANKS v ACE HIGH PRODUCTIONS LTD [1978] ICR 1155 (Employment Appeal Tribunal: PHILLIPS J presiding).

1096 —— procedure

The Industrial Tribunals (Labour Relations) (Amendment) Regulations 1978, S.I. 1978 No. 991 (in force on 21st August 1978), amend the Industrial Tribunals (Labour Relations) Regulations 1974, 1974 Halsbury's Abr para. 1834. The Regulations empower a tribunal to require of its own motion a party to furnish further particulars, to review another tribunal's decision and to strike out originating applications for want of prosecutions.

1097 —— —— application for review

See *Blackpole Furniture Ltd v Sullivan*, para. 1118.

1098 —— —— notice of appearance—grounds for resisting application

See *Seldun Transport Services Ltd v Baker*, para. 2979.

1099 —— rectification of errors

In dismissing an appeal against an award of compensation for unfair dismissal, PHILLIPS J stated that it was better for errors to be corrected by a review than an appeal even where it meant the original decision would be overturned. He further considered that basic awards for unfair dismissal, fixed under the Employment Protection Act 1975, could prove excessive where the person dismissed found new employment quickly.

BRITISH MIDLAND AIRWAYS LTD v LEWIS [1978] ICR 782 (Employment Appeal Tribunal: PHILLIPS J presiding).

1975 Act now Employment Protection (Consolidation) Act 1978.

1100   —— review—fresh evidence—practice

See *Vauxhall Motors Ltd v Henry*, para. 1072.

1101   Itemised pay statement—deduction—adequacy of particulars

Industrial tribunal decision:

MILSOM v LEICESTERSHIRE COUNTY COUNCIL [1978] IRLR 433 (employee was advanced a sum of money by his employers to cover examination expenses, to be repaid on the employment ceasing; employee gave notice; received letter from employer requiring repayment; employee disputed the matter and denied willingness to have sum deducted from salary; next pay statement included deduction of sum in question, referred to as "miscellaneous deduction"; employee's claim that statement did not comply with requirements of Employment Protection Act 1975, s. 81 upheld; statement was not sufficiently specific to constitute an itemised pay statement under s. 81, and the deduction was not within s. 82 of the Act which was designed to cover cases of fixed deductions made at fixed regular intervals).

1975 Act, ss. 81, 82 now Employment Protection (Consolidation) Act 1978, ss. 8, 9.

1102   Job Release Act 1977—continuation

The Job Release Act 1977 (Continuation) Order 1978, S.I. 1978 No. 1007 (in force 30th September 1978), continues in force until 29th September 1979 s. 1 of the 1977 Act.

1103   Local government employee—loss of office—compensation

See *Mallet v Restormel Borough Council*, para. 1803; *Walsh v Rother District Council*, para. 1804.

1104   Managing director—absence of contract of service—whether an employee of company

See *Folami v Nigerline (UK) Ltd*, para. 1063.

1105   Maternity leave—employee's right to return to work

A full-time physiotherapist, grade 1, was absent from work on maternity leave. Before leaving, she made it clear that she did not wish to return to work on a full-time basis. She accepted an offer to return to work as a part-time physiotherapist, basic grade. On her return, she claimed that she was entitled under the Employment Protection Act 1975, s. 48, to a job as a part-time physiotherapist, grade 1, a job which was not available in the hospital. *Held*, she was not entitled under s. 48 to claim her old job back on a new basis. The contractual right to work part-time on basic grade was essentially indivisible and it was unreal to attempt to take part of it and combine it with another part extracted from the statutory right to return to her original job.

BOVEY v BOARD OF GOVERNORS OF THE HOSPITAL FOR SICK CHILDREN [1978] ICR 934 (Employment Appeal Tribunal: PHILLIPS J presiding).

1975 Act, s. 48 now Employment Protection (Consolidation) Act 1978, ss. 45, 46.

1106   —— —— adequacy of notice to employers

An employee, who failed to give her employers notice under Employment Protection Act 1975, s. 35, of her pregnancy and of her intention to return to work after the birth, at least three weeks before she went on maternity leave, was not given her job back after her confinement. Her claim of unfair dismissal was upheld by an industrial tribunal on the ground that she had given the employers notice as soon as it was reasonably practicable to do so. The employers appealed. *Held*, s. 35 gave an employee the right to return to her job after her confinement provided that notice was given at least three weeks before she left or as soon as it was reasonably practicable to do so. From the facts it appeared that the employee's reason for delaying matters was because she had not decided at the relevant time whether she would return to work. Section 35 was not intended to help someone who had not made up her mind. As the employee had known of her rights and the need to give her employers notice within the statutory period, the appeal would be allowed.

NU-SWIFT INTERNATIONAL LTD V MALLINSON (1978) 122 Sol Jo 744 (Employment Appeal Tribunal: SLYNN J presiding).

1975 Act, s. 35 now Employment Protection (Consolidation) Act 1978, s. 33.

1107 —— **period during which leave to be taken—whether employee has freedom of choice**

A teacher employed by the Inner London Education Authority (ILEA) informed them that she proposed to take maternity leave for three weeks before her confinement and three weeks after the birth. She applied for maternity pay for that period under Employment Protection Act 1975, s. 36, which provides that maternity pay is payable for a six-week period taken not earlier than the eleventh week before confinement. The ILEA claimed that she was bound by their staff code which was negotiated with the National Union of Teachers and which stipulated that the leave had to be taken at the beginning of the eleventh week. The question arose as to whether the freedom of choice given to an employee by the Act as to when to start maternity leave overrode the teacher's contractual obligation with the ILEA. *Held*, KILNER BROWN J dissenting, s. 36 of the 1975 Act by implication gave an employee a right of choice as to when her six weeks paid leave should start following the beginning of the eleventh week before the date of confinement. The teacher was therefore entitled to start her six weeks paid maternity leave at any time after the eleventh week despite the fact that she was contractually bound by the staff code to start her leave at the beginning of the eleventh week. The contractual term was a purported limitation upon the provisions of the Employment Protection Act, which gave an employee the freedom of choice, and the teacher could choose between the benefits under the code and those under the statute.

KILNER BROWN J considered that Parliament would wish to uphold the sanctity of contract particularly as it was devised between a trade union and an employing public authority.

INNER LONDON EDUCATION AUTHORITY v NASH (1978) 122 Sol Jo 860 (Employment Appeal Tribunal: KILNER BROWN J presiding).

1108 **Maternity pay—application of PAYE**

Under the Employment Protection Act 1975, payments of maternity pay may be made to an employee who stops work because of pregnancy. Such payments may be made at weekly intervals in the period following the cessation of employment or in a lump sum paid either in advance or arrear. Such payments are assessable to income tax under Schedule E if a contract of employment still exists at the time of payment, but under Schedule D, Case VI, of it does not. It was originally envisaged that employers would apply PAYE to all payments of maternity pay, but as from 6th April 1978 employers are not being asked to operate PAYE on Case VI payments, although no objection will be raised if they do so: Inland Revenue Statement of Practice (SP1/78) dated 18th July 1978.

1975 Act now consolidated in Employment Protection (Consolidation) Act 1978.

1109 **Pay statement—deduction**

See *Milsom v Leicestershire County Council*, para. 1101.

1110 **Racial discrimination**

See RACE RELATIONS.

1111 **Redundancy—amount of payment—deduction from basic hourly rate—whether deduction permissible**

A part-time teacher who had been dismissed on grounds of redundancy appealed against the assessment of her compensation, which was based on a lower hourly rate than that which she had been accustomed to be paid. The local authority claimed that part-time workers' hourly rates were reduced for the purpose of calculating redundancy pay to take account of the fact that a proportion of the hourly rate related to holiday periods for which no other payment was made. *Held*, the local authority could only have calculated redundancy pay on the reduced hourly rate if this had been agreed when the contract of employment was made or if it had been subsequently varied by mutual agreement. Accordingly the employee was entitled to a redundancy payment based on her full hourly rate.

COLE v CITY OF BIRMINGHAM DC [1978] IRLR 394 (Employment Appeal Tribunal: KILNER BROWN J presiding).

1112   —— **cessation of business— retirement of employer**

The employee was employed for six years by a sub-postmistress who retired and gave up the business at the sub-post office. The employee applied to an industrial tribunal for a redundancy payment which was refused on the basis that the business was that of Post Office which did not cease on the retirement of the sub-postmistress. On appeal, *held*, there was no need for the employer, who ceased to carry on business, to be an owner of the business in order to satisfy the Redundancy Payments Act 1965, s. 1 (2). The sub-postmistress, the employer, controlled the business and that was sufficient for a redundancy payment to be made. The case would be remitted for a rehearing.

THOMAS v JONES [1978] ICR 274 (Employment Appeal Tribunal: PHILLIPS J presiding).

1965 Act, s. 1 now Employment Protection (Consolidation) Act 1978, s. 81.

1113   —— **change in employer's place of business—employee transferred for trial period—time limit—effective date of dismissal**

Employers who transferred their staff to new premises were obliged to move their telephone switchboard from a third floor position with plenty of light and air to a basement. A switchboard operator who could not be required to transfer under her contract of employment was asked to consider moving and she agreed to accept a trial period. Two months later she decided that she did not like the new premises and left. An industrial tribunal upheld her claim that she had been unfairly dismissed. On appeal, *held*, although she had been entitled to make it a condition of her moving that she would have office accommodation of the kind she preferred, the employee was not entitled to compensation for unfair dismissal because the employers could not comply with her wishes. She was however entitled to a redundancy payment and did not lose her entitlement by virtue of the Redundancy Payments Act 1965, s. 3 (3) as amended, which limited trial periods to four weeks after the termination of the contract of employment where an employee accepted a new contract. In this case the original contract had not been terminated but the employee had postponed her decision to accept the employer's repudiation of the contract, and only when she had done so had there been a dismissal.

AIR CANADA v LEE [1978] IRLR 392 (Employment Appeal Tribunal: PHILLIPS J presiding).

1965 Act, s. 3 (3) now Employment Protection (Consolidation) Act 1978, s. 84 (1).

1114   —— **claim for payment—time limit—sufficiency of written notice of claim**

On 27th June 1975 the employee received a letter from his employers to the effect that his contract of employment would not be renewed. Negotiations took place, including oral discussions about a redundancy payment. On 23rd September 1975 the employee's solicitor wrote to the employers stating that he had not heard from them in respect of the employee's claim for a redundancy payment. No settlement was reached and on 1st October 1976 the employee applied to an industrial tribunal for a redundancy payment. The tribunal held that he was not entitled to such a payment as he had not made a claim for a payment by notice in writing to the employer within six months of his dismissal as required by the Redundancy Payments Act 1965, s. 21 (b); his contention that the letter of 23rd September constituted written notice within s. 21 (b) was rejected. On appeal, *held*, the letter did constitute notice within s. 21 (b). The test was whether the notice or writing relied on was of such a character that the recipient would reasonably understand in all the circumstances of the case that it was the employee's intention to seek a redundancy payment. The effect of the letter construed against the background of the oral discussions was that the employers should have understood that the employee was seeking a redundancy payment. The appeal would be allowed and the case remitted to a differently constituted tribunal.

PRICE V SMITHFIELD & ZWANENBERG GROUP LTD [1978] ICR 93 (Employment Appeal Tribunal: PHILLIPS J presiding). *Hetherington v Dependable Products Ltd* (1970) 9 KIR 183, CA followed.

1965 Act, s. 21, as amended by Employment Protection Act 1975, Sch. 16, Pt. I, para. 9 now consolidated in Employment Protection (Consolidation) Act 1978, s. 101.

1115   —— continuity of employment—change from permanent to temporary employment

The employee took up employment with the York City Council in 1973. Initially he worked temporarily in the York Festival Office and then joined the treasurer's department where he later obtained a permanent position. In 1975, he resigned to take up a year's temporary position with the Festival Office. He applied to return to the treasurer's department but was declared redundant as there were no available posts. The employee was only allowed redundancy payment for his final year by the industrial tribunal, and this decision was upheld by the Employment Appeal Tribunal. The employee appealed. *Held*, under the Redundancy Payments Act 1965, s. 9 (2), and Contracts of Employment Act 1972 Sched 1, a person's employment during any period should be presumed to have been continuous unless the contrary was proved. This applied where the terms of employment had changed or a new contract of employment had been agreed, provided that the employer remained the same. It also covered the case where the change was from permanent to temporary employment. The appeal would be allowed and payment awarded in respect of the whole of his employment.

WOOD V YORK CITY COUNCIL (1978) 122 Sol Jo 192 (Court of Appeal: LORD DENNING MR, SHAW and WALLER LJJ).

1965 and 1975 Acts now consolidated in Employment Protection (Consolidation) Act 1978.

1116   ——— employer's right to recover rebate

An employee was made redundant five years after transferring from a company to an associated company. At the time of his transfer he was given an assurance that his employment would be deemed continuous for the purpose of all rights and benefits. On the basis of the assurance an industrial tribunal awarded him a redundancy payment reflecting his total period of employment with the companies. However, the Secretary of State for Employment refused to give the employers a rebate on the whole of the payment under the Redundancy Payments Act 1965, s. 30 (1) (a), on the ground that the only payment for which they were "liable under the Act" within s. 30 (1) (a) was that in respect of the employee's five years' service with them. *Held*, where in the interests of good industrial relations a new employer gave an employee an assurance that this employment would be treated as continuous with his former employment, his liability to pay a redundancy payment for the whole period of employment was a liability arising "under the Act" within s. 30 (1) (a). Accordingly, the employers were entitled to a rebate on the full amount.

SECRETARY OF STATE FOR EMPLOYMENT V GLOBE ELASTIC THREAD CO LTD [1978] 3 All ER 954 (Court of Appeal: LORD DENNING MR, EVELEIGH LJ and SIR DAVID CAIRNS). *Evenden v Guildford City Association Football Club Ltd* [1975] QB 917, CA, 1975 Halsbury's Abr para. 1290 approved.

1965 Act, s. 30 now Employment Protection (Consolidation) Act 1978, s. 104.

1117 —— —— **hiving-down agreement**

The plaintiff employees had originally been employed by the defendants. The defendant company ran into financial difficulties and made a hiving-down agreement with another company which then became its wholly owned subsidiary. The business was sold as a going concern but the defendants retained the service of all employees and sub-contracted them to the subsidiary company. This company was subsequently acquired by Lonhro who later dismissed the employees for redundancy. In claims for redundancy payments and compensation for unfair dismissal, the employees contended that the effect of the hiving-down agreement was to transfer them to the employment of the subsequent proprietors of the business. An industrial tribunal found that the employees had remained in the defendants' employment. On appeal *held*, when the ownership of a big business was transferred it was often impossible to consider individual contracts of employment. It was wrong to conclude that there was no continuity of employment because there was no individual offer and acceptance of new contracts. It was necessary to look at all the circumstances and see whether the only reasonable conclusion was that the employees had agreed to work for the new proprietors. Hiving-down agreements could not be used as an excuse for avoiding consultation prior to redundancies. The appeals would be allowed and the applications submitted to different industrial tribunals for rehearing.

PAMBAKIAN v BRENTFORD NYLONS LTD [1978] ICR 665 (Employment Appeal Tribunal: PHILLIPS J presiding.)

1118 —— —— **temporary cessation of work—factors to be considered by industrial tribunal**

An employee worked for two separate periods before being made redundant; his entitlement to a redundancy payment depended on whether his absence between the two periods was due to a temporary cessation of work. An industrial tribunal, relying solely on guidelines issued by the Department of employment, decided that the cessation was temporary. The employers appealed against the redundancy payment and also applied for a review of the tribunal's decision; the application was refused in view of the pending appeal. On appeal against the refusal, *held*, (i) the tribunal's decision was defective since it was based entirely on guidelines which were not intended to be strict rules. In every case involving a cessation of work, the tribunal should use its own judgment, bearing in mind all the relevant circumstances such as the relative length of the periods of employment and the intervening absence. (ii) As a general rule, there was nothing improper in a tribunal considering an application to review its decision when that decision was under appeal. If the tribunal chairman felt it would be undesirable, he should consult with the registrar of the appeal tribunal. The employers' appeal would be allowed and the case remitted to a differently constituted tribunal.

BLACKPOLE FURNITURE LTD v SULLIVAN [1978] ICR 558 (Employment Appeal Tribunal: PHILLIPS J presiding). *Bentley Engineering Co Ltd v Crown* [1976] ICR 225, 1976 Halsbury's Abr para. 1019, applied.

For a discussion of this case see Equal Pay Sorted Out, Justinian; Financial Times, 17th July 1978.

1119 —— —— **transfer of business**

The first company agreed with the second company for the transfer of responsibility for the operation of a canteen for the first company's staff. The staff in the canteen became the employees of the second company; but they could not be made redundant without prior consultation with the first company. At the time of the transfer the second company wrote to the canteen staff telling them that the second company was "happy to continue with your present contract". Twenty-two months after the transfer, five employees were made redundant. On their application to a tribunal for redundancy pay, the tribunal held that there had been no change in the ownership of the business within the meaning of the Redundancy Payments Act 1965, s. 13, so that the employees had entered into new contracts with the second company and could not add the two periods of employment together. The employees had therefore failed to complete the qualifying period of 104 weeks required by s. 8. On appeal, *held*, although the second company had not intended the employees' original contracts to be continuous, there had been a change of ownership of the business within the meaning of s. 13. The employees were therefore entitled to redundancy payments as their periods of employment with both companies came to more than 104 weeks.

RASTILL v AUTOMATIC REFRESHMENT SERVICES LTD [1978] ICR 289 (Employment Appeal Tribunal: ARNOLD J presiding). *Evenden v Guildford City Association Football Club Ltd* [1975] QB 917, 1975 Halsbury's Abr para. 1290 and *Kenmir Ltd v Frizzell* [1968] 1 All ER 414, applied.

1965 Act, s. 13 now Employment Protection (Consolidation) Act 1978, s. 94.

1120 —— death of employer—employees' right to payment

Following the death of their employer, the employees continued to work for and be paid by the employer's widow who was his personal representative. Seven weeks after the death, a company assumed control of the business and the employees carried on working for the company. The employees subsequently claimed redundancy payments from the widow. An industrial tribunal decided that the employer's death had terminated the employees' contracts. They were accordingly treated as dismissed and were entitled to redundancy payments because the widow had not offered to renew their contracts in accordance with Redundancy Payments Act 1965, Sch. 4, para. 4. On appeal by the widow, *held*, the tribunal had based their decision on the wrong paragraph of Sch. 4. They should have applied para. 3 which provides that where a contract is renewed or an employee is re-engaged by a personal representative within eight weeks of the death the employee is not treated as having been dismissed. A contract would be renewed if a personal representative and the employee had agreed, or so acted that they were to be taken as having agreed, that despite the death matters should carry on as before. The case would be remitted for the tribunal to reach a conclusion on the facts.

RANGER v BROWN [1978] ICR 603 (Employment Appeal Tribunal: PHILLIPS J presiding).

1965 Act, Sch. 4 now Employment Protection (Consolidation) Act 1978, Sch. 12.

1121 —— dismissal by reason of redundancy—selection of redundant employees—whether unfair dismissal

See *Camper & Nicholson Ltd v Shaw*, para. 3007.

1122 —— employer's duty to consult trade union

See *Laffin and Callaghan v Fashion Industries (Hartlepool) Ltd*, para. 3010.

1123 —— —— dismissal of total of more than ten employees employed in several places—whether each place a separate establishment

A building company employed workers at several different sites. To meet a drop in demand, the company decided to reduce its labour force by dismissing some twenty four employees on eight sites with one week's notice. The union complained to an industrial tribunal and sought a declaration and protective award under the Employment Protection Act 1975, Pt. IV. The company maintained that each of the sites were separate establishments and were therefore outside the provisions of s. 99 (3) of the Act. This section requires, inter alia, consultation with the union sixty days in advance of a dismissal for redundancy of ten or more employees. The tribunal decided that the sites collectively were one establishment for the purposes of the Act, and that therefore the company was in breach of its obligations to consult. *Held*, the decision whether the sites were one establishment was a decision of fact. The tribunal's decision was a reasonable one and would not be upset. The appeal would be dismissed.

BARRATT DEVELOPMENTS (BRADFORD) LTD v UNION OF CONSTRUCTION, ALLIED TRADES AND TECHNICIANS [1978] ICR 319 (Employment Appeal Tribunal: BRISTOW J presiding).

1124   —— —— **effective date of consultation**

The defendant employers gave notice of dismissal for redundancy to a number of employees. The following day the employers started consultations about the redundancies with the recognised union. The union claimed that, by issuing the notices of dismissal before the commencement of consultations, the employers had failed to comply with the Employment Protection Act 1975, s. 99. An industrial tribunal dismissed the complaint and the union appealed. *Held*, s. 99 imposed an obligation to consult with the union when it was proposed to dismiss for redundancy. Consultation should have preceded the giving of notice of dismissal, and the appeal would be allowed.

NATIONAL UNION OF TEACHERS v AVON COUNTY COUNCIL [1978] IRLR 55 (Employment Appeal Tribunal: PHILLIPS J presiding).

1125   —— —— **effective date of proposals**

The defendant company was an autonomous company responsible for its own area while under the general control of a parent company. On 8th February 1977, the parent company informed the defendant company that there was to be a reorganisation which would involve redundancies. On 11th February, the defendant company informed the appropriate trade union that a statement concerning the redundancies would be made on 14th February. On 14th February, the union representatives were told that no detailed proposals had been considered and a meeting to discuss the proposals was arranged for 21st February. The union then made a complaint under Employment Protection Act 1975, s. 101, alleging non-compliance with s. 99 of the Act which required employers to consult trade unions about proposals for redundancy at the earliest opportunity. The complaint was dismissed by an industrial tribunal. The union appealed, contending that the parent company should be treated as the employer for the purposes of s. 99 and it had made proposals before 8th February. *Held*, as the defendant company and its parent company were not a single corporate entity, any contention that the proposals for dismissal came from the parent company, as employers within s. 99, on 8th February was unfounded. The earliest date on which a proposal could be said to have been made was 14th February. The company had consulted the union at the earliest opportunity and the appeal would be dismissed.

NATIONAL AND LOCAL GOVERNMENT OFFICERS ASSOCIATION v NATIONAL TRAVEL (MIDLANDS) LTD [1978] ICR 598 (Employment Appeal Tribunal: KILNER BROWN J presiding).

1126   —— —— **failure to consult—compensation**

An employer dismissed a number of employees on the ground of redundancy but failed to consult the relevant trade union. An industrial tribunal found the dismissals unfair but awarded only basic compensation because the dismissals were inevitable. On the employees' appeal, *held*, in the circumstances, a basic award was the appropriate compensation. It was highly unlikely that any of those dismissed could have been retained.

BARLEY v AMEY ROADSTONE CORPORATION LTD (No. 2) [1978] ICR 190 (Employment Appeal Tribunal: PHILLIPS J presiding).

1127   —— —— **recognition of union**

In 1975 all the employees of a company joined a trade union. In 1976 the joint council to which the company belonged agreed to a wage increase. The union representative informed the company, which agreed to comply and inform the employees. When twenty-one of the employees were made redundant, the union was granted a protective award for forty days in respect of the employees, as the company was in breach of its duty under the Employment Protection Act 1975, s. 99 (1), to consult union representatives before issuing redundancy notices. On appeal by the company, *held*, to be caught by s. 99 (1), the company had to have previously recognised the union for the purpose of collective bargaining; the wage increase negotiations amounted to an act of recognition with reference to the terms and conditions of employment. An escape clause was provided by s. 99 (8), if there were special circumstances which rendered it not reasonably practicable for the employer to comply with the requirement to consult the union. The question was whether the company's genuine belief that it had not recognised the union rendered it not reasonably practicable for consultation to take place. The company had to show that the belief was not only genuine but reasonable. In the circumstances, the company had been put on inquiry and the appeal would be dismissed.

JOSHUA WILSON AND BROS LTD v UNION OF SHOP DISTRIBUTIVE AND ALLIED WORKERS [1978] 3 All ER 4 (Employment Appeal Tribunal: KILNER BROWN J presiding). *Dedman v British Building & Engineering Appliances Ltd* [1974] 1 All ER 520, CA applied.

1128   A trade union contended that it had been recognised by a company for the purposes of collective bargaining on the strength of a short correspondence and one meeting held between them. It claimed that consequently it should have been consulted before the company made four employees redundant. The meeting and correspondence had arisen out of the company's alleged failure to meet the collective wages standard prescribed by an employer's federation of which the company was a member and which collectively recognised the union. Only eight out of the company's fifty-five employees were union members. Both an industrial tribunal and the Employment Appeal Tribunal concluded that on the facts the union had not been recognised and that the federation's agreement with the union was not binding on individual members in the absence of separate agreements made between those members and their employees. On the union's further appeal, *held*, the previous decisions contained no error in law. Recognition was such a crucial issue that it could not be assumed unless there was clear-cut evidence of mutual agreement, which in this case there was not. The union had not been recognised and therefore there was no duty on the company to consult the union before making staff redundant.

NATIONAL UNION OF GOLD, SILVER AND ALLIED TRADES v ALBURY BROTHERS LTD (1978) 122 Sol Jo 662 (Court of Appeal: LORD DENNING MR, EVELEIGH LJ and SIR DAVID CAIRNS). Decision of Employment Appeal Tribunal [1978] ICR 62, 1977 Halsbury's Abr para. 1093 affirmed.

1229   —— —— —— **company business transferred to partnership**
The employee was an apprentice carpenter and joiner with a building company. The company ceased the carpentry and joinery side of its business. The apprentice continued his training under a newly formed partnership. One of the partners was the managing director of the company. The offices of the partnership were next door to those of the company. After his apprenticeship had come to an end, the employee worked as an employee of the partnership. He was made redundant and the partnership office manager wrote to the employee's union informing it of the decision. The union sought a protective award under the Employment Protection Act 1975, s. 101, on the ground of the employer's failure to consult the union in accordance with s. 99. The tribunal dismissed the complaint on the ground that the partnership had not recognised the union for the purposes of s. 99. On appeal, *held*, although the partnership was a successor in business to the company, and despite the fact that the office manager had written to the union, the partnership was not bound to recognise the union on transfer of the carpentry and joinery side of the business from the company, and it had not done so. The appeal therefore failed.

UNION OF CONSTRUCTION, ALLIED TRADES AND TECHNICIANS v BURRAGE [1978] ICR 314 (Employment Appeal Tribunal: BRISTOW J presiding).

1130   —— —— **special circumstances preventing compliance**
An employer was wrongly advised by the Department of Employment that he could make a man redundant without first consulting that man's union. The Employment Protection Act 1975, s. 99 (1), imposes the duty to consult, but s. 99 (8) provides an escape clause where there are special circumstances rendering it not reasonably practicable for the employer to comply. The industrial tribunal decided

that the union's application for a protective award on behalf of the man failed, on the basis that the wrong advice from a government department was a special circumstance. The union appealed. *Held*, the fact that the employer had been misled was not a special circumstance rendering it not reasonably practicable for the employer to comply with his duty to consult. The appeal against the refusal of a protective award would be allowed.

UNION OF CONSTRUCTION ALLIED TRADES AND TECHNICIANS v H. ROOKE & SON LTD [1978] ICR 818 (Employment Appeal Tribunal: PHILLIPS J presiding).

1131 ——————— **reasonable expectation of sale of firm**

Scotland
An employer whose company fell into financial difficulties attempted to sell it as a going concern. When this failed he was forced to appoint a receiver, who immediately gave notice of redundancy to the workforce. The recognised trade union complained to an industrial tribunal that the employer had failed to comply with the consultation provisions laid down in the Employment Protection Act 1975, s. 99. The tribunal found that there were special circumstances rendering it not reasonably practicable to comply with the provisions. The union appealed. *Held*, the tribunal were correct in deciding that there had been special circumstances. The employer had acted reasonably in hoping to sell the business and avoid redundancies and had not proposed to dismiss employees as redundant prior to the appointment of the receiver. There had been no question of the employer's notifying the union earlier.

ASSOCIATION OF PATTERNMAKERS AND ALLIED CRAFTSMEN v KIRVIN [1978] IRLR 318 (Employment Appeal Tribunal: LORD McDONALD presiding).

1132 ——————— **whether insolvency a special circumstance**

When they became insolvent and ceased to trade the employers dismissed their employees without consulting the trade union. The union applied for a protective award. The employers contended that their insolvency was a special circumstance within the Employment Protection Act 1975, s. 99 (8), which rendered it not reasonably practicable for them to consult the union. *Held*, in order to be a special circumstance the factors surrounding the insolvency would have to be uncommon. Insolvency alone did not constitute a special circumstance. A sudden and unexpected event making it necessary for the company to cease trading could constitute a special circumstance; a gradual run down of the company, as in this case, could not. The employees were entitled to a protective award.

CLARKS OF HOVE LTD v BAKERS' UNION [1978] 1 All ER 152 (Court of Appeal: STEPHENSON, ROSKILL and GEOFFREY LANE LJJ). Decision of Employment Appeal Tribunal [1977] ICR 838, 1977 Halsbury's Abr para. 1096 reversed in part.

1133 —— **entitlement to payment—apprentice**

Following the refusal of the Secretary of State for Employment to give an employer a rebate for a supposed redundancy payment made to an apprentice journeyman fitter not retained beyond the end of his apprenticeship, a question arose as to the employer's liability to make the payment at all. *Held*, a contract of apprenticeship was a once-in-a-lifetime fixed term contract. The apprentice's dismissal was due to his not being offered a fresh contract as a fitter. Neither a redundancy payment nor compensation was payable on refusal to employ someone, even where a period of different employment had just been completed. The payment need not have been made and consequently no rebate was payable.

NORTH EAST COAST SHIPREPAIRERS LTD v SECRETARY OF STATE FOR EMPLOYMENT [1978] ICR 755 (Employment Appeal Tribunal: PHILLIPS J presiding).

1134 —— —— **contracting out of right to payment**

A lecturer was originally employed under a contract for eighteen months. On expiry, the contract was extended for a further seven months and an exclusion clause was included providing that failure to renew the contract would not give rise to a claim under the Redundancy Payments Act 1965 or to a complaint of unfair dismissal under the Trade Union and Labour Relations Act 1974. The contract was not renewed after the seven month extension. The employers, relying on the exclusion clause, appealed against a decision to grant the employee a redundancy payment and the employee cross-appealed against a decision that her complaint of unfair dismissal was time-barred. *Held*, (i) the 1965 and 1974 Acts permitted an employee under a fixed term contract for two years or more to contract out of her rights under those Acts. However, the employee's rights were not affected by the exclusion clause since the extension of her eighteen month contract by seven months did not constitute a fixed term contract for two years or more. Furthermore, such exclusion clauses only applied to a series of fixed term contracts if the final contract alone was for two years or more. (ii) The employee was fully aware of her rights and it was reasonably practicable for her to present her complaint of unfair dismissal within the statutory time limit. Accordingly both the appeal and the cross-appeal would be dismissed.

THE OPEN UNIVERSITY V TRIESMAN [1978] IRLR 114 (Employment Appeal Tribunal: PHILLIPS J presiding). Dicta of LORD DENNING MR in *BBC v Ioannou* [1975] 2 All ER 999, CA at 1006, 1975 Halsbury's Abr para. 1293, applied.

1965 and 1974 Acts now consolidated in Employment Protection (Consolidation) Act 1978.

1135   —— —— exclusion on account of pension rights—time for serving notice of exclusion

Having decided that the employee should be retired, the employers served a notice of dismissal on him which terminated on 31st July 1976, and his pension was assessed from then. On 5th October 1976 the employee claimed a redundancy payment. On 19th January 1977 the employers served him with a notice under the Redundancy Payments Pension Regulations 1965, reg. 5, claiming to exclude his right to a redundancy payment on the ground that the value of pension cancelled out any entitlement to a redundancy payment. The employee contended that the notice of exclusion was served too late. *Held*, no notice of claim for a redundancy payment could be made until the dismissal took effect, and the same applied when an employer wished to serve notice of exclusion of liability. The notice had to be served within a reasonable time. By 5th October 1976 the situation had matured sufficiently to require the notice to be served and as it was not served until January 1977 it was out of time. The employee was consequently entitled to a redundancy payment.

STOWE-WOODWARD BTR LTD V BEYNON [1978] ICR 609 (Employment Appeal Tribunal: KILNER BROWN J presiding).

1136   —— —— loss of right—change of ownership of business

Scotland

Due to a fall in demand for its products, a company disposed of one of its factories to another firm. The contract provided for the existing lease to be assigned to the firm, for the work in progress to be taken over and that the company's employees would be offered employment on approximately the same terms as before. The employees accepted the offer and claimed redundancy payments from the company. An industrial tribunal allowed their claim on the ground that although the employees were immediately re-engaged under new contracts on similar terms to their old contracts, there had not been a change of ownership of part of the company's business within the meaning of the Redundancy Payment Act 1965, s. 13 (1) and thus the employees were entitled to redundancy payments. The company appealed. *Held*, s. 13 provided that where a change occurred in the ownership of a business or part of it, an offer by the new owner to renew or extend an employee's contract on similar terms to the old one was to be treated as an offer by the previous owner. The tribunal had erred in law in finding that there had not been a change in ownership of part of the company's business within s. 13. Applying the test of severability, the factory could be separated from the company's other enterprises and sold as a going concern. The sale of the factory was therefore a transfer of a part of the company's business within s. 13 and the employees were not entitled to redundancy payments. Accordingly, the appeal would be allowed.

HECTOR POWE LTD v MELON [1978] IRLR 258 (Employment Appeal Tribunal: LORD MCDONALD presiding).

1965 Act, s. 13 now Employment Protection (Consolidation) Act 1978, s. 94.

1137   —— offer of alternative employment—reasonableness of refusal

The appellant had been employed as a teacher by the predecessors of the respondents for nine years. He subsequently worked for their educational television service until 1976 when the service was discontinued for economic reasons. The respondents offered the appellant a job as a teacher but he refused the offer and applied for a redundancy payment. An industrial tribunal dismissed the application on the ground that, by refusing the offer of a job, the appellant had acted unreasonably within the meaning of the Redundancy Payments Act 1965, s. 2. On appeal *held*, an industrial tribunal had to consider many factors when deciding whether an offer of alternative employment was suitable.

In the present case the employers had offered the only type of alternative employment which it was within their power to offer. The industrial tribunal had not erred in law in deciding that the employee had acted unreasonably, and that he was not, therefore, entitled to a redundancy payment.

FORRESTER v STRATHCLYDE REGIONAL COUNCIL (1977) 12 ITR 424 (Employment Appeal Tribunal: LORD MCDONALD presiding).

1965 Act, s. 2 now Employment Protection (Consolidation) Act 1978, s. 82.

1138   —— protective award—discretion to make award

An employer went into receivership and the receiver dismissed all the employees for redundancy without first consulting the trade union, in contravention of the Employment Protection Act 1975, s. 99. An industrial tribunal found that consultation with the union would not have resulted in a different decision being taken by the receiver. The default was thus merely technical and no protective award was made. The union appealed. *Held*, under the Employment Protection Act 1975, s. 101 (5) the industrial tribunal was not meant to consider only the employer's fault, but all the relevant factors, including the great disruption caused to employees by immediate dismissal. The case would therefore be remitted for consideration by the industrial tribunal of all the various factors.

TRANSPORT AND GENERAL WORKERS UNION v GAINSBOROUGH DISTRIBUTORS (UK) LTD [1978] IRLR 460 (Employment Appeal Tribunal: KILNER BROWN J presiding).

1139   —— selection of redundant employee

Industrial tribunal decision:

PICKERING v KINGSTON MOBILE UNITS [1978] IRLR 102 (employee joined firm in December 1976; six months later second employee joined to do same work; first employee, a bachelor, made redundant in preference to second employee, married man with four children; first employee unfairly dismissed as employers acted unreasonably in discriminating against employee with more experience because he was single).

1140   —— —— whether applicant an employee

Industrial tribunal decision:

D'AMBROGIO v HYMAN JACOBS LTD [1978] IRLR 236 (applicant employed as outworker for garment factory, working forty hours a week from home; employer visited her each day to provide her with materials and collect completed garments; business closed down, application for redundancy payment refused on ground that as she was an outworker she was not an employee; applicant entitled to payment; she was an employee with a contract of service, rather than a contract for services, as she was subject to the employer's control in her work).

1141   —— time off to look for work—entitlement to remuneration

See *Dutton v Hawker Siddeley Aviation Ltd*, para. 1150.

1142   Redundancy payments scheme—shipbuilding

The Shipbuilding (Redundancy Payments Scheme) (Great Britain) Order 1978, S.I. 1978 No. 1191 (in force on 4th August 1978), establishes under the Shipbuilding (Redundancy Payments) Act 1978 a scheme for the payment of benefits to employees of British shipbuilders who are made redundant or transferred to less well-paid employment during the period of two years beginning on 1st July 1977. The scheme prescribes the types of benefit, the class of persons eligible and the conditions qualifying them for benefit.

1143   Remuneration—teachers

See *Lewis v Dyfed County Council*, para. 1023.

1144   Sex discrimination

See SEX DISCRIMINATION.

1145   Shipbuilding (Redundancy Payments) Act 1978

The Shipbuilding (Redundancy Payments) Act 1978 received the royal assent on 5th May 1978 and came into force on that date. The Act empowers the Secretary of State to create redundancy schemes for the shipbuilding industry. There will be separate schemes for Great Britain and Northern Ireland. Under the British scheme employers of British Shipbuilders may benefit: s. 1. To qualify, the employees must be made redundant or be transferred to less well paid employment in the period of two years following the commencement of the scheme. The period can be extended by the Secretary of State: s. 2. Both the British and the Irish schemes will be financed by the government with Treasury approval: s. 3.

1146   Termination of employment—resignation or dismissal

An employee made the statement, "I am leaving, I want my cards", in a fit of temper. The statement was treated by the employer as a resignation. The employee claimed he was unfairly dismissed and sought compensation. On the question whether or not the employee had resigned, *held*, where the statement made was ambiguous the test was whether a reasonable employer would have taken the statement as a resignation. Where the statement was clear and unequivocal, as in this case, the test was subjective. Since the employer believed the employee to have resigned, he had not been dismissed in law.

GALE LTD v GILBERT [1978] IRLR 453 (Employment Appeal Tribunal: ARNOLD J presiding).

1147   —— whether employment terminated by agreement or dismissal

Employers at their discretion granted a period of leave to a Pakistani employee who wished to visit his sick mother in Pakistan. They gave their permission on condition that if he did not return on a specified date his contract of employment would terminate. When he failed to return because of sickness the employers treated the contract as terminated. The employee claimed that he had been unfairly dismissed. The employers appealed against the tribunal's finding that there had been a dismissal. *Held*, in granting the period of leave the employers had made it clear that there could be no extension of the term and the employee had agreed to this. Accordingly the contract had come to an end following a consensual termination, not a dismissal.

The Employment Appeal Tribunal observed that the problem caused where an employee failed to return after a period of discretionary leave was a common one. The solution attempted by the employers in this case was acceptable despite the fact that it could cause hardship, because it was always open to the employer to allow the employee to return.

BRITISH LEYLAND (UK) LTD V ASHRAF [1978] IRLR 330 (Employment Appeal Tribunal: PHILLIPS J presiding).

1148 Time off—time off for public duties

Industrial tribunal decision:

RATCLIFFE V DORSET COUNTY COUNCIL [1978] IRLR 191 (applicant employed as lecturer, was elected to borough council and had to take time off for council meetings; timetable altered but applicant still had to work at home in the evenings and at weekends to compensate; complaint under Employment Protection Act 1975, s. 59, that his right to take time off for public duties contravened, upheld; work load was not diminished as rearranging timetable did not amount to giving time off).

1149 —— time off for union duties and activities—industrial relations training—entitlement to pay during that period

Industrial tribunal decision;

VINE V DRG (UK) LTD [1978] IRLR 475 (employee, member of independent trade union, requested time off with pay to attend union training course; union officer entitled to be paid if duties concerned with industrial relations between employer and employee; employee member of branch committee concerned with internal union matters; duties were not the kind of duties for which official should be given paid time off).

1150 —— time off to look for work—entitlement to remuneration

The employee was made redundant. During his period of notice, he took time off to look for another job, but the employers refused to pay him for that time since he could not produce evidence of appointments for interviews. The employee claimed that he was entitled to payment under the Employment Protection Act 1975, s. 61, which provides that an employee who is made redundant is entitled to reasonable time off to look for new employment and is entitled to be paid for the period of absence. *Held*, there was no condition attached to the statutory right that an employee had to produce evidence of appointments for interviews. The employee was entitled to the payment.

DUTTON V HAWKER SIDDELEY AVIATION LTD [1978] ICR 105 (Employment Appeal Tribunal: PHILLIPS J presiding).

1975 Act, s. 61 now Employment Protection (Consolidation) Act 1978, s. 31.

1151 Trade unions

See TRADE UNIONS.

1152 Transfer of employment—worsening of position—whether worsening attributable to transfer—entitlement to compensation

The National Freight Corporation appealed against a decision that those of its staff who had been transferred to it from the British Railways Board under the Transport Act 1968, were entitled to compensation under the British Transport (Compensation of Employees) Regulations 1970. *Held* (LORD WILBERFORCE and VISCOUNT DILHORNE dissenting), the 1970 Regulations provided for the compensation of staff who had suffered loss, diminution or worsening of their position attributable to their transfer. The staff had claimed that the increase in their emoluments since their transfer had been less than if they had remained employed by the Board. The question was whether the worsening was to be judged by comparison with the Board's rates of pay. From the Regulations, it appeared that the words "worsening of his position" referred to one's own position and did not suggest comparison with anyone else's position or the position one might have been in. There was no express statement that that sort of comparison, which would be extremely laborious, was to be made and it could not be implied from the Act or the Regulations as a whole. Therefore, if the natural meaning of the word "worsening" was taken, it appeared that the staff had not suffered worsening of their position and the second point of it being attributable to the transfer did not arise. Accordingly, the appeal would be allowed.

Lord WILBERFORCE and VISCOUNT DILHORNE considered that the transfer was both a cause of the worsening and the factor for which protection was intended. The worsening therefore was properly attributable to the transfer.

TUCK v NATIONAL FREIGHT CORPORATION (1978) Times, November 28th (House of Lords: Lord WILBERFORCE, VISCOUNT DILHORNE, LORD FRASER OF TULLYBELTON, LORD RUSSELL OF KILLOWEN and LORD SCARMAN). Decision of Court of Appeal [1978] ICR 323, 1977 Halsbury's Abr para. 323, reversed.

1153   Unfair dismissal

See UNFAIR DISMISSAL.

1154   Vicarious liability—arson by employee—whether employer protected by exclusion clause

See *Photo Production Ltd v Securicor Transport Ltd*, para. 494.

1155   —— disclaimer of liability under local bye-law—Singapore

See *Karuppan Bhoomidas v Port of Singapore Authority*, para. 2032.

1156   —— employment of child under fourteen—employment by employee—whether employee acting in course of his employment

Justices convicted the appellants of employing a child under the age of fourteen before 9.00 am on a Saturday morning, in contravention of statute and local bye-laws. They found that the child had been taken on by the appellants' employee in the course of his employment to assist in the appellants' business, and held them vicariously liable for the employee's criminal act. On appeal, *held*, the appellants could only be liable if there was clear evidence that they or their authorised personnel manager or other such person had employed him. In this case it was clear that the appellants had had no knowledge of the child's employment and it was equally clear that the employee who had taken him on had not been authorised to hire staff. Accordingly, the appeal would be allowed.

PORTSEA ISLAND MUTUAL CO-OPERATIVE SOCIETY LTD v LAYLAND [1978] ICR 1195 (Queen's Bench Division: LORD WIDGERY CJ, TALBOT and WATKINS JJ). *Boyle v Smith* [1906] 1 KB 432 and *Robinson v Hill* [1910] 1 KB 94 applied.

1157   Wages—payments by health authorities—reimbursement of wages of doctor's staff—employment of member of doctor's family

See *Glanville v Secretary of State for Health and Social Services*, para. 1988.

1158   Wages councils—road haulage wages council

The Road Haulage Wages Council (Abolition) Order 1978, S.I. 1978 No. 966 (in force on 4th September 1978), abolishes the Road Haulage Wages Council.

ENVIRONMENT

1159   Conservation area—permission for demolition refused—relevance of proposed development

A local authority gave itself planning permission for redevelopment in a conservation area. The Secretary of State refused to allow demolition on the site on the ground that the proposed new development would not be acceptable. The council claimed that the quality of the proposed new development was not relevant to his decision, and that the Secretary of State could not refuse to allow the demolition because under the relevant regulations he was deemed to have granted the original permission. *Held*, the Secretary of State had been entitled to consider the effect of the proposed development as this was obviously relevant to the character of the area. Nor was his discretion fettered by the fact that the local planning authority's permission was deemed to have been given by him.

RICHMOND-UPON-THAMES LONDON BOROUGH COUNCIL v SECRETARY OF STATE FOR THE ENVIRONMENT (1978) Times, 2nd November (Queen's Bench Division: SIR DOUGLAS FRANK QC sitting as a deputy High Court judge).

1160   Gypsies—accommodation

The Department of the Environment has issued a circular outlining the Secretary of State's conclusions on the Cripps report on gypsy accommodation. The report was published in 1977 and advocated greater commitment on the part of government to the attainment of the purposes of the Caravan Sites Act 1968. For a full summary of those conclusion, see DoE Circular 57/78.

1161   Noise—motorway—depreciation in property value—compensation

See *Barb and Barb v Secretary of State for Transport*, para. 406.

1162   Nuclear fuels—erection of reprocessing plant—planning permission

The Town and Country Planning (Windscale and Calder Works) Special Development Order 1978, S.I. 1978 No. 523 (in force 15th May 1978) grants planning permission, subject to conditions, for the erection of a plant for the reprocessing of spent uranium oxide nuclear fuels, with support site services, on land owned by British Nuclear Fuels Ltd at the Windscale and Calder Works.

1163   Refuse Disposal (Amenity) Act 1978

The Refuse Disposal (Amenity) Act 1978 received the royal assent on 23rd March 1978 and came into force on 23rd April 1978 except for ss. 1 (8), 4 (2) and 6 (8) which come into force on a day to be appointed. The Act consolidates certain enactments relating to abandoned vehicles and other refuse.

Tables showing the destination of enactments consolidated and the derivation of the new Act are set out on pp. 266–268 following:

DESTINATION TABLE

This table shows in column (1) the enactments repealed by the Refuse Disposal (Amenity) Act 1978 and in column (2) the provisions of that Act corresponding thereto.

In certain cases the enactment in column (1), though having a corresponding provision in column (2), is not, or is not wholly, repealed as it is still required, or partly required, for the purposes of other legislation.

(1)	(2)	(1)	(2)
Civic Amenities Act 1967 (c. 69)	Refuse Disposal (Amenity) Act 1978 (c. 3)	Civic Amenities Act 1967 (c. 69)	Refuse Disposal (Amenity) Act 1978 (c. 3)
s. 18 (1)	s. 1 (1), (8)	s. 32 (3)★	s. 13 (5)
(2)–(4)	(2)–(4)		
(5)	(5), (6)	Vehicle and Driving Licences Act 1969 (c. 27)	
(6)	ss. 1 (7), 11 (1)		
(7)–(9)	———		
19	s. 2		
20(1)	3 (1)	s. 29 (3)	s. 4 (2)
(2)	(2), (3)	34 (1)★	10 (4), (5)
(3), (4)	(5), (6)	38 (2)★	13 (3), (4)
(4A)	(7)		
(5), (6)	(8), (9)	Town and Country Planning Act 1971 (c. 78)	
(7)	Applied to Scotland		
(8), (9)	———		
21 (1)	ss. 4 (1), (8), 11 (1)	Sch. 23, Part II†	8 (2), (3)
(2), (3)	s. 4 (3), (4)		
(4)	(5), (6)	Local Government Act 1972 (c. 70)	
(5)	(7)		
(6)	Applied to Scotland		
22 (1)	s. 5 (1)	s. 186 (2)	See against 1972 c. 70 Sch. 19, paras. 33–36 below
(2)	(2), (3)		
(3)	(4), (5)		
(4)	Applied to Scotland	Sch. 14, para. 45	ss. 1 (7), 11 (1)
23 (1)	s. 6 (1)	Sch. 19, para. 33	s. 3 (7), (8)
(2)	ss. 6 (2), 11 (1)	34	ss. 4 (1), (8), 11 (1)
(3)	s. 6 (3), (8)	35	s. 5 (4), (5) (b)
(4)	(4), (5)	36	7
(5)	(6)		
(6)	Applied to Scotland	Control of Pollution Act 1974 (c. 40)	
24	s. 7		
27 (1)	11 (1)		
(2)	10 (1), (2)		
(3)	(4), (5)	s. 104 (1)★	s. 10 (4). (5)
28	8	109 (2)★	13 (3)
29 (1)★	9	(a)★	(4)
(2)★	10 (2), (4)	(b)★	10 (3)
30 (1)†	11 (1)	Sch. 3, para. 25 (1)	1 (8)
(2)★	(2)	(2)	6 (8)

★ Not repealed   † Repealed in part

DERIVATION TABLE

The table on p. 268 shows in the right hand column the legislative source from which the sections of the Refuse Disposal (Amenity) Act 1978 in the left hand column have been derived. In the table the following abbreviations are used:

1967   = Civic Amenities Act 1967 (c. 69).
1969   = Vehicle and Driving Licences Act 1969 (c. 27).
1971   = Town and Country Planning Act 1971 (c. 78).
1972(S) = Town and Country Planning (Scotland) Act 1972 (c. 52).
1972   = Local Government Act 1972 (c. 70).
1973   = Local Government (Scotland) Act 1973 (c. 65).
1974   = Control of Pollution Act 1974 (c. 40).

This Table does not acknowledge:
   (a) the transfer of the functions of the Minister of Housing and Local Government and the Minister of Transport to the Secretary of State (Secretary of State for the Environment Order 1970, S.I. 1970/1681);
   (b) the transfer of the transport functions of the Secretary of State for the Environment to the Secretary of State for Transport (Secretary of State for Transport Order 1976, S.I. 1976/1775).

Section of Act	Derivation
1 (1)–(3)	1967 s. 18 (1)–(3).
(4)	1967 s. 18 (4); 1972 Sch. 30.
(5), (6)	1967 s. 18 (5).
(7)	1967 s. 18 (6); 1972 Sch. 14, para. 45.
(8)	1967 s. 18 (1); 1974 Sch. 3, para. 25 (1).
2	1967 s. 19.
3 (1)–(3)	1967 s. 20 (1), (2).
(4)	1967 s. 20 (7) (*a*).
(5), (6)	1967 s. 20 (3), (4).
(7)	1967 s. 20 (4A); 1972 Sch. 19, para. 33 (1).
(8)	1967 s. 20 (5); 1972 Sch. 19, para. 33 (2).
(9)	1967 s. 20 (6).
4 (1)	1967 s. 21 (1); 1972 Sch. 19, para. 34.
(2)	1969 s. 29 (3).
(3)–(7)	1967 s. 21 (2)–(5).
(8)	1967 s. 21 (1); 1972 Sch. 19, para. 34.
5 (1)–(3)	1967 s. 22 (1), (2).
(4), (5)	1967 s. 22 (3); 1972 Sch. 19, para. 35.
(6)	1967 s. 22 (4).
6 (1), (2)	1967 s. 23 (1), (2).
(3)	1967 s. 23 (3); 1972 Sch. 30.
(4), (5)	1967 s. 23 (4).
(6)	1967 s. 23 (5).
(7)	1967 s. 23 (6).
(8)	1974 Sch. 3, para. 25 (2), Sch. 4.
7	1967 s. 24; 1972 Sch. 19, para. 36.
8 (1)	1967 s. 28 (1); 1971 Sch. 25; 1972 (S) Sch. 23.
(2), (3)	1967 s. 28 (2), (3); 1971 Sch. 23, Pt. II.
(4)	1967 s. 28 (4); 1972 (S) Sch. 21, Pt. II.
9	1967 s. 29 (1).
10 (1), (2)	1967 ss. 27 (2), 29 (2).
(3)	1974 s. 109 (2) (*b*).
(4), (5)	1967 ss. 27 (3), 29 (2); 1969 s. 34 (1); 1974 s. 104 (1).
11 (1)	1967 ss. 27 (1), 30 (1); 1972 Sch. 30; 1973 Sch. 27, Pt. II, para. 169.
(2)	1967 s. 30 (2).
12	—
13 (1), (2)	—
(3), (4)	1969 s. 38 (2); 1974 s. 109 (2) (*a*).
(5)	1967 s. 32 (3).
Sch. 1	—
Sch. 2	—

1164   Smoke control areas—authorised fuels

The Smoke Control Areas (Authorised Fuels) Regulations 1978, S.I. 1978 No. 99 (in force on 24th February 1978) adds Palmalite ovoid briquettes to the authorised fuels under the Clean Air Act 1956, s. 11.

1165   —— exempted fireplaces

The Smoke Control Areas (Exempted Fireplaces) Order 1978, S.I. 1978 No. 1609 (in force on 11th December 1978), exempts, subject to conditions, a certain class of fireplace from the provisions of the Clean Air Act 1956, s. 11, which empowers a local authority to declare the whole or any part of their district to be a smoke control area.

EQUITY

Halsbury's Laws of England (4th edn.), Vol. 16, paras. 1201–1500

1166   Article

Acquiescence in Breach of Restrictive Covenant, F. Graham Glover (whether acquiescence can deprive a covenantee of his right, and if so, when): 128 NLJ 257.

1167   Election against will—effect on protected life interest

A testatrix bequeathed furniture, effects and £1,000 to the defendant and purportedly devised the house she had occupied to the plaintiff bank on trust for sale, subject to the condition that the defendant could occupy it for as long as he wanted. The proceeds of sale were to fall into the residue, one half of which was to be held on determinable statutory protective trusts for the defendant for life, the other half of which was to be held for his two daughters. The bank had a discretion in how it applied the income accruing under the trusts for the first twenty-one years.

The defendant had, however, been joint beneficial owner of the house purportedly devised to the bank. He elected against the will by selling the house, the freehold of which was his by survivorship. The bank applied to the court for rulings on the effect of the defendant's election against the will on his protected life interest and on whether that interest should be determined in an attempt to compensate the other beneficiaries. *Held*, for the doctrine of election to apply, the defendant had to have been granted an interest which he could use to compensate the other beneficiaries without having to forfeit his determinable life interest. In the present case, the only possible way in which the defendant could benefit the other beneficiaries was by forfeiting his life interest, but in fact the probable result of that would be to benefit his wife rather than them because she would become a member of the class of beneficiaries under the statutory discretionary trust arising from the determination of his life interest. Accordingly, the doctrine of election did not apply to the case at all.

RE GORDON'S WILL TRUSTS, NATIONAL WESTMINSTER BANK LTD v GORDON [1978] 2 All ER 969 (Court of Appeal: BUCKLEY and EVELEIGH LJJ and Sir JOHN PENNYCUICK). Decision of Goulding J [1977] Ch 27, 1977 Halsbury's Abr para. 1069 reversed. *Re Hargrove* [1915] 1 Ch 398 applied, *Carter v Silber* [1891] 3 Ch 553 overruled.

1168   Equitable licence—licence to occupy for life—determination by licensees' subsequent conduct

See *Williams v Staite*, para. 1725.

1169   Laches—application of doctrine of laches—dismissal of action for want of prosecution

See *Joyce v Joyce*, para. 2231.

1170   Restrictive covenant—modification

Lands Tribunal decision:

RE PEARSON'S APPLICATION (1978) 36 P & CR 285: V. G. WELLINGS QC (applicant sought to modify wording of restrictive covenant affecting his land so that he could convert his barn into an old people's home; company which owned benefited land objected on the ground that its chances of being able to obtain planning permission for increased industrial user of the land would be diminished; it would be the applicant's house, not the proposed old people's home, which would suffer from increased industrial user; the company could not object to the proposed modification because no injury would result).

1171   —— unity of ownership of benefited and burdened land—whether covenant extinguished

On the sale of a parcel of land attached to a mansion house, the purchaser covenanted not to use the land other than for agricultural purposes in order to preserve the view from the house. In 1952 the subsequent owner of the house purchased part of the burdened land. She subsequently sold her whole interest in several lots. The plaintiff, who purchased part of the burdened land from her, obtained planning permission for a housing development which the new owners of the benefited land claimed would be a breach of the covenant. The plaintiff sought a declaration that the covenant had been extinguished in 1952 when the land had come under a common owner. *Held*, the covenant had been extinguished when the fee simple of both the benefited and the burdened land had vested in the same owner. It could only have been revived if it had been re-created on the sale of the burdened land. As this had not been done, the plaintiff was entitled to the declaration.

RE TILTWOOD, SUSSEX; BARRETT v BOND [1978] 2 All ER 1091 (Chancery Division: FOSTER J).

1172   Tracing—where insolvent purchaser has not paid supplier for goods—supplier's right to recover as against other creditors

See *Borden (UK) Ltd v Scottish Timber Products Ltd*, para. 512.

ESTOPPEL

Halsbury's Laws of England (4th edn.), Vol. 16, paras. 1501–1641

1173   Estoppel against statute—estoppel against public body—whether body estopped from performing statutory duty

A company's application to the local planning authority for permission to build a factory was refused. The company contended that the authority was estopped from refusing planning permission because of representations made to the company by the authority's planning officers. It was also contended that the officers made certain determinations under the Town and Country Planning Act 1971, regarding the need for planning permission, which estopped the authority from exercising its own powers under the 1971 Act. *Held*, (i) estoppel could not be invoked against the authority since there had been no relevant representation which was acted on by the company to its detriment with the authority's knowledge. (ii) Even if there were grounds for estoppel, the company's contentions would have failed because of the general principle that a public body could not be estopped from performing its statutory duty. This principle was subject to limited exceptions which included the case where a planning authority delegated power to its officers to determine certain applications. However, the company did not have sufficient evidence to justify its belief that the officers had power to bind the authority: it was unaware of any relevant delegation of power to the officers except in relation to the determinations they had made under the 1971 Act. Moreover, there was no justification for extending the limited exceptions allowing estoppel against statute as that could have the effect of compelling an authority to allow development which contravened its planning policy or prejudiced members of the public. Accordingly, the authority was not estopped from refusing planning permission by its officers' representations.

WESTERN FISH PRODUCTS LTD v PENWITH DISTRICT COUNCIL (1978) 122 Sol Jo 471 (Court of Appeal: MEGAW, LAWTON and BROWNE LJJ). Dicta of Lord Widgery in *Brooks of Burton Ltd v Secretary of State for the Environment* (1976) 75 LGR 285 at 296, 1977 Halsbury's Abr para. 2801 applied.

1174   Issue estoppel—application to industrial tribunal—equal pay

See *McLaughlin v Gardans (Stockport) Ltd*, para. 2568.

1175   Promissory estoppel—estoppel against statute—statutory duty to collect value added tax

See *Medlam v Customs and Excise Commissioners*, para. 3043.

1176   Res judicata—action for possession of land—effect of previous magistrate's decision—Jamaica

The plaintiffs occupied five acres of land. A dispute over ownership had been running for many years between them and the alleged owners of the land. In 1962 a resident magistrate rejected the plaintiffs' claim to title. The plaintiffs remained in occupation but in the meantime the owners sold the land to the defendant developers, who began building works on the land without having obtained a warrant for possession. The plaintiffs issued a writ against them, which the defendants sought to have struck out on the basis that the ownership issue had been decided by the magistrate. The defendants' contention was upheld. On appeal, *held*, the relevant Jamaican law, the Landlord and Tenants Law, s. 54, made it clear that the order of a resident magistrate could not constitute a basis for a plea of res judicata on a matter of title. Therefore, the 1962 decision did not preclude the plaintiffs from instituting further proceedings and the appeal would be allowed.

PATRICK v BEVERLEY GARDENS DEVELOPMENT CO LTD [1978] 2 WLR 423 (Privy Council: LORD SALMON, LORD EDMUND-DAVIES, LORD RUSSELL OF KILLOWEN, LORD SCARMAN and SIR HARRY GIBBS).

1177   —— arbitration award

See *Compagnie Graniere SA v Fritz Kopp AG*, para. 153.

1178   Statutory duty or discretion—estoppel to prevent performance—Director of Public Prosecutions

See *Turner v Director of Public Prosecutions*, para. 738.

EUROPEAN COMMUNITIES

Halsbury's Laws of England (3rd edn.), Supp. Vol. 39A

1179   Articles

Direct Elections to the European Parliament, Gavin Drewry (consideration of the provisions of and issues arising from the European Assembly Elections Act 1978): 128 NLJ 578.

Equality, syrup, whisky and the EEC, A. H. Hermann (cases concerning equal pay for women, the Commission's power to amend subsidies and the effect of the Common Market on whisky): Financial Times, 19th January 1978.

EEC Anti-Trust Law: Fines for Breach, J. Kodwo Bentil (examination of nature and operation of the unit of account within the framework of EEC anti-trust law); 122 Sol Jo 519.

EEC Nationals in the United Kingdom 1: Rights of Entry and Residence, David Bennett: 128 NLJ 43.

Exclusive and Non-Exclusive Rights in Patent Licence Agreements, B. I. Cawthra (the legitimacy of the grant of exclusive rights from a competition point of view): 128 NLJ 37.

The Interpretation of EEC Legislation, Gavin McFarlane (consideration of the English courts' approach to legislation of the European Communities): 122 Sol Jo 463.

Joint Venture Agreements and Article 85, N. J. Byrne (recent decisions and the theoretical confusion currently prevailing): 128 NLJ 784.

Lawyers' Services within the Common Market, Rebecca M. M. Wallace (EC Council Directive 249/77 on the free movement of lawyers): 122 Sol Jo 843.

Lords' Consideration of EEC Proposals, Rebecca M. M. Wallace (Lords' report on "The Approximation of Laws Under Article 100 of the EEC Treaty"); 122 Sol Jo 498.

West Germany: New Law on Standard Contract Terms, Alan Greenwood: 128 NLJ 559.

1180   Commission

At a conference of the representatives of the Governments of member states Mr. Roy Jenkins was appointed President of the Commission of the European Communities for the period 6th January 1979 to 5th January 1981.

1181   Common customs tariff

See under FREE MOVEMENT OF GOODS, post.

1182   Community legislation—breach—pre-accession conduct—right of action before national court

The plaintiffs and defendants were manufacturers and dealers in camping gas equipment. The plaintiffs brought an action claiming damages from the defendants in respect of an alleged conspiracy to breach the EEC Treaty, arts. 85 and 86, relating to restrictive practices, and an injunction to restrain them from abusing their dominant market position. The actions complained of occurred between 1971 and 1973. The defendants brought a motion to strike out the claim as disclosing no reasonable cause of action, as it related to the defendants' conduct before the accession of the United Kingdom to the EEC. The plaintiffs contended that what the defendants did was a matter of concerted practice and the inference was that the activities going on before entry which subsequent to entry would be in breach of arts. 85 and 86 would have continued after entry. *Held*, there were no grounds for assuming that what was done after 1st January 1973 was the same as what was done before then. The case differed from cases where there was a written agreement to do the acts which continued in force after accession. Whatever might be the position before the EEC courts, pre-accession conduct which contravened EEC legislation would not found an action before an English court. The defendants' motion would accordingly succeed.

VALOR INTERNATIONAL LTD V APPLICATION DES GAZ SA AND EPI LEISURE LTD [1978] 2 CMLR 296 (Chancery Division: WHITFORD J).

For previous proceedings, see [1978] 1 CMLR 30, para. 2144.

1183   —— directive—direct applicability

A dispute arose between the customs authorities in the Netherlands and an importer as to the method of valuation of goods for customs purposes. The importer relied on EEC Council Directive 69/74 and the customs authorities relied on the incorporation of that provision in Dutch national law in slightly different language. They contended that the directive did not have direct effect and so the importer could not rely on the difference of wording between the two provisions so as to make that of the directive prevail. The matter was referred to the European Court of Justice. *Held*, Directive 69/74 might be relied on by parties concerned for the purpose of verifying whether the national measures adopted for its implementation were in accordance with it and the national courts should give it precedence over any national measures which were incompatible with it. The Court had no power either to interpret provisions of national law or to rule on their possible incompatibility with Community law, but in the context of interpretation of Community law it could provide the national court with criteria enabling it to deal with the action before it in particular as regards any incompatibility of national provisions with Community rules. Thus an interpretation on the meaning of Directive 69/74 could be given.

Case 38/77: ENKA BV V INSPECTEUR DER INVOERRECHTEN EN ACCIJNZEN, ARNHEM [1977] ECR 2203 (European Court of Justice).

1184 ———— **failure of state to implement directive**

The Netherlands did not put into force within the prescribed period, laws, regulations or administrative provisions needed to comply with the provisions of EEC Council Directive 71/347. The Directive related to the approximation of laws of member states relating to the measuring of grain. The EC Commission sought a declaration that the Netherlands had failed to fulfil an obligation under the EEC Treaty. The Netherlands tried to show that the common market had not been adversely effected by their failure. *Held*, for the purpose of trying to justify a failure to fulfil obligations under a harmonizing directive, a member state could not invoke the argument that the failure had had no adverse effect on the functioning of the market. The Netherlands had therefore failed to fulfil a Treaty obligation.

Case 95/77: COMMISSION OF THE EUROPEAN COMMUNITIES V THE NETHERLANDS [1978] ECR 863 (European Court of Justice).

1185 Italy did not put into force within the prescribed period, laws, regulations or administrative provisions needed to comply with EEC Council directives relating to the approximation of laws in the field of measuring instruments. The EC Commission sought a declaration that Italy had failed to fulfil its obligations under the directives. Italy tried to show that domestic difficulties and provisions of its national, legal and constitutional system, had prevented it from complying with its obligations. *Held*, for the purpose of trying to justify a failure to fulfil obligations arising from Council directives, a member state cannot rely upon domestic difficulties, or provisions of its national, legal or constitutional system. Italy had therefore failed to fulfil a Treaty obligation.

Case 100/77: COMMISSION OF THE EUROPEAN COMMUNITIES V ITALY [1978] ECR 879 (European Court of Justice).

1186 The Italian government failed to carry out a Council directive by the date laid down in the directive. The only step taken by the Italian authorities was to submit a bill to the Italian Senate, implementing the provisions of the directive. The Commission brought the matter before the European Court. The Italian government argued before the Court that observance of the objectives of the directive was already ensured by Royal Decree, but that the Government had introduced the bill in order to ensure precise application of the directive. Therefore the initial failure to comply with the directive did not adversely affect the functioning of the Common Market. *Held*, the obligation to implement directives was precise and absolute. It was no defence to a failure to implement a directive to claim that previous national legislation already ensured observance of the directive's objectives or that such failure had no adverse effect on the functioning of the Common Market. Italy had, therefore, failed to fulfil an obligation of the Treaty.

Case 147/77: RE THE ANIMAL SLAUGHTER DIRECTIVE 1974: COMMISSION OF THE EUROPEAN COMMUNITIES V ITALY [1978] 3 CMLR 428 (European Court of Justice).

1187 The EC Commission lodged an application for a declaration of failure on the part of the Italian Republic to comply with EEC Council Directive 73/23 on the harmonisation of laws on electrical equipment. The Directive did not lay down harmonisation standards but only transitional measures to ensure the free movement of electrical equipment between member states. The Italian authorities did not implement the Directive within the time limit specified, arguing that Italy's safety regulations were substantially the same as those in other member states and that the Directive's provisions were substantially met on the basis of existing Italian legislation. Thus in the absence of any harmonisation standards the Italian Republic was not required to take any further measures. *Held*, it was no defence to an action for failure to implement a Directive, that its provisions could not be applied until certain international or Community standards had been laid down, in the absence of which the time limit for implementation contained in the Directive lost its mandatory force; or that the requirements of the Directive were substantially applied on the basis of existing national legislation.

Thus Italy had failed to fulfil an obligation under the Treaty.

Case 123/76: RE THE ELECTRICAL EQUIPMENT DIRECTIVE 1973; EC COMMISSION V ITALY [1978] 3 CMLR 460 (European Court of Justice).

1188   —— interpretation

In a dispute between parties to a contract for the lease and the running of a shop, questions arose regarding the interpretation of the Convention of 27th September 1968 on Jurisdiction and the Enforcement of Judgments in Civil and Commercial Matters. The questions concerned Article 16 and were as follows: (1) Must "tenancies of immovable property" within the meaning of Art. 16 also include an agreement to rent, under a usufructuary lease, a retail business carried on in immovable property which was rented from a third party by the lessor? (2) If so does the exclusive jurisdiction of the courts of the State where the immovable property is situated also apply to a claim on the basis of such an agreement for (a) payment of rent of the retail premises under the usufructuary lease; or (b) payment by the tenant under the usufructuary lease of the head-rent owed by the lessor to the owners of the immovable property; or (c) payment of consideration for the goodwill of the retail business? (3) Is the answer to any of these questions affected by the fact that in the proceedings the defendant (the tenant under the usufructuary lease), contested the existence of the agreement. *Held*, in answer to questions (1) and (2), "tenancies of immovable property" did not include agreements to rent under a usufructuary lease a retail business carried on in immovable property rented from a third person by the lessor. In answer to (3), the fact that there was a dispute as to the existence of the agreement which formed the subject of the action did not effect the reply regarding the interpretation of Art. 16.

Case 73/77: SANDERS V VAN DER PUTTE [1977] ECR 2383 (European Court of Justice).

1189   —— —— EEC Treaty—implied provisions

The plaintiffs, sellers of gold and silver coins, were fraudulently induced to part with possession of 1,500 gold coins by three men who were subsequently convicted of being knowingly concerned in the fraudulent evasion of the prohibition on the importation of gold coins contrary to the Customs and Excise Act 1952, s. 304 (b). The Customs and Excise Commissioners claimed the right to forfeit the coins in accordance with the 1952 Act, s. 44 (f). The plaintiffs claimed the return of the coins on the ground that s. 44 (f) was inconsistent with the provisions of the EEC Treaty. They contended that the provisions of the Treaty concerning freedom of movement of goods imposed on member states an implied obligation not to confiscate property of a national of a member state without compensation, save as a penalty for the commission of a criminal offence, of which the plaintiffs were innocent. They sought the referral of the question to the European Court of Justice. *Held*, the EEC Treaty contained no implied articles relating to human rights and did not affect the 1952 Act, s. 44. It was not necessary to refer the question to the European Court of Justice and the coins were liable to forfeiture.

ALLGEMEINE GOLD UND SILBERSCHEIDEANSTALT V CUSTOMS AND EXCISE COMMISSIONERS [1978] 2 CMLR 292 (Queen's Bench Division; DONALDSON J).

For the convictions under s. 304 (b) and the appeal, see 1977 Halsbury's Abr paras. 1190, 1193.

1190 —— **legislation directly applicable—incompatibility of existing and subsequent national legislation—consequences for national courts**

An Italian company instituted proceedings against the Italian Finance Administration claiming repayment of fees levied in respect of inspections carried out on a consignment of beef imported from France. The inspections were required by Italian law, but the company contended that such inspections and the fees payable for them constituted obstacles to the free movement of goods and as such were forbidden under Community law. The Italian court referred certain questions to the European Court, and in the light of that court's ruling found that the fees had been illegally charged and ordered repayment. The Finance Administration appealed against the order, putting forward arguments which in the court's view raised the issue of the incompatibility of certain rules of Community law with a subsequent national law, namely that which fixed the scale of fees chargeable. Under Italian law, for the issue to be resolved the question of the constitutionality of that law would have had to be referred to the Constitutional Court. The court appreciated however that such a course, by reason of the procedure of the Constitutional Court, could have resulted in a lapse of the direct applicability of the relevant provisions of Community law. It therefore made a reference to the European Court for the determination of the question, inter alia, whether the consequence of EEC Treaty, art. 189 and the relevant established case law of the European Court in relation to directly applicable provisions of Community law was that subsequent conflicting national measures should be disregarded automatically, without waiting for eliminatory action to be taken by the appropriate national authority. *Held*, directly applicable provisions of Community law, being a direct source of rights and duties for all those affected thereby, had to be fully and uniformly applied in all member states for the whole period of their duration. Therefore, a national court, in applying provisions of community law, was under a duty to give full effect to those provisions, if necessary refusing of its own motion to apply any conflicting national measure, whether adopted prior to or after the relevant Community provision. It was not necessary for such conflicting national provisions to be expressly set aside, since, in accordance with the principle of the precedence of Community law, the entry into force of a directly applicable provision of Community law automatically superseded any existing conflicting national law and precluded the valid adoption of any new, incompatible national measure.

Case 106/77: AMMINISTRAZIONE DELLE FINANZE DELLO STATO v SIMMENTHAL SpA [1978] ECR 629 (European Court of Justice). For earlier proceedings, see 1977 Halsbury's Abr para. 55.

1191 —— **refusal of member state to grant discretionary relief—action against Commission—admissibility of action**

Following the decision of the French government to float the franc the Commission re-introduced a system of monetary compensatory amounts, which were subsequently increased several times. The applicants, French sugar exporters affected by these measures, applied to the appropriate national intervention agency for the exemption of certain contracts from the measures under EEC Commission Regulation No. 1608/74. Article 1 of that Regulation provides that member states shall have a discretion as to the implementation of monetary compensatory accounts where they have been introduced or increased as a result of national monetary changes, such discretion being unfettered with respect to contracts such as those for which the applicants sought relief. The agency denied the exemption on the grounds that the conditions precedent to the granting of discretionary relief had not been fulfilled, and its decision was reiterated by the Commission. Accordingly the applicants claimed damages against the Commission under arts. 178 and 215. The Commission submitted that the claim was inadmissible, on the ground that in this case the exercise of discretion under the regulation came within the decision-making power of member states. *Held*, since the action was in substance directed against measures taken by a national authority in pursuance of a provision of community

law, the conditions for bringing proceedings under arts. 178 and 215 had not been
satisfied. The claim would be dismissed as inadmissible.

Cases 12/77 and 18/77: DEBAYSER SA v EC COMMISSION [1978] ECR 553
(European Court of Justice).

**1192   —— regulations—action for annulment by natural or legal per-
sons—requirement of direct and individual concern**

By EEC Council Regulation 1092/77 imports into Italy of certain types of Japanese
motor-cycles were made subject to the production of an Italian import authorisation
in respect of each motor-cycle imported, the number of such authorisations to be
issued in 1977 being limited to 18,000. Prior to the adoption of the regulation in
July 1977, Italian law had allowed the unrestricted importation of motor cyles. The
applicants, representing Italian importers of motor-cycles from Japan, instituted
proceedings under EEC Treaty, art. 173 for the annulment of the regulation. The
Council raised the preliminary issue of admissibility, on the grounds that the
regulation was not of direct and individual concern to the applicants as required by
art. 173 (2). The applicants claimed that the condition was satisfied, in that both
prior to and after the adoption of the regulation they were the only persons interested
in importation, and as such were clearly the only persons affected by the restrictions
intoduced. *Held*, the condition laid down in art. 173 (2) had not been fulfilled and
the action was therefore inadmissible. The possibility of determining the number
or identity of persons to whom a measure applied did not imply that the measure was
of individual concern to them. The regulation would only be of concern to the
applicants in the event of a necessary authorisation being refused them pursuant to
it: the mere possibility of such a refusal did not provide a sufficient basis for
regarding the measure as being of individual concern to them.

Case 123/77: UNIONE NAZIONALE IMPORTATORI E COMMERCIANTI MOTOVEICOLI
ESTERI (UNICME) v EC COUNCIL [1978] ECR 845 (European Court of Justice).

**1193   —— —— liability of EEC for damage suffered as a result of
regulation**

The plaintiff companies brought proceedings under EEC Treaty, art 215 against the
Council and Commission for damages they claimed to have suffered as a result of an
increase in the price of chicken feeding stuffs consequential to the application of
Council Regulation 563/76. Case law had established that the regulation in question
was null and void as it had introduced arrangements constituting a discriminatory
distribution of the burden of costs between various agricultural sectors. *Held*, an
invalid legislative act was insufficient, in itself, as a basis for an action for damages
suffered by individuals. In the interests of the Community, individuals were
sometimes required to accept certain effects damaging to their economic interests.
The Community would be liable for such damage only if there had been a violation
of a superior law protecting the individual, or if the institution concerned had
ignored the limits imposed on its jurisdiction. In the present case the regulation,
although invalid, was not of a sufficiently detrimental effect to make the Community
liable for damage resulting from its application.

Cases 83 and 94/76; 4, 15 and 40/77 BAYERISCHE HNL VERMEHRUNGSBETRIEBE
GMBH AND CO KG v EC COUNCIL AND COMMISSION (1978) Times, 5th June
(European Court of Justice).

1194   A company sought compensation from the EEC for the injury which it claimed to
have suffered as a result of Commission Regulation No. 1947/76, the effect of which
was to modify certain compensatory amounts. The company claimed that as a
result of the modification it was prevented from performing in full contracts of sale,
entered into before the coming into force of the regulation, for the delivery to
companies within other EEC countries of products falling within a certain tariff
subheading, and was obliged to deliver alternative products under more onerous
conditions in return for partial termination of the original contracts. *Held*,
dismissing the application, the regulation was a legislative measure adopted by the
Community in the higher interest of the proper functioning of the common

organisation of the market. Although the desirability of protecting the legitimate interests of the trader could not be disregarded, nevertheless the Community could only be rendered liable for the damage suffered by such traders as a result of the adoption of legislative measures governing the system of compensatory amounts if, in the absence of any overriding public interest, the Commission were to abolish or modify the compensatory amounts applicable in a specific sector with immediate effect and without warning and in the absence of any appropriate transitional measures and if such abolition or modification was not forseeable by a prudent trader. None of those conditions had been satisfied in this instance. Accordingly the introduction of the regulation did not amount to a flagrant violation of a superior rule of law for the protection of the individual sufficient to incur the liability of the Community under EEC Treaty, art. 215, para. 2.

Case 97/76: MERKUR AUSSENHANDEL GMBH & CO KG V EC COMMISSION [1977] ECR 1063 (European Court of Justice).

1195 —— sex discrimination law—whether early retirement for women permissible

See Case 149/77; *Defrenne v Sabena*, para. 2571.

1196 Community proceedings—related action in national court—effect of proceedings on motion to dismiss action for want of prosecution

See *Aero Zipp Fasteners Ltd v YKK Fasteners Ltd; Opti Holdings AG v Yoshida Kogyo Kaboshiki Kaisha*, para. 2228.

1197 Community transport policy—air pollution—lead content of petrol

EEC Council Directive 78/611 specifies the maximum permitted lead content of petrol used in motor vehicles.

1198 —— transport undertaking—duty to keep record books—on whom duty lies

A Belgian labour sub-contracting firm which did not engage in transport activities itself but which hired out a driver to a client transport undertaking was prosecuted for not ensuring that the driver was carrying the individual driver's control book as required by EEC Council Regulation 543/69, art. 14, which provides that undertakings must keep a record of the individual drivers' record books. Questions were referred to the European Court of Justice as to the meaning of "undertakings" in that context. *Held*, "undertakings" referred to the transport undertaking for which the driver was driving the vehicle, and not to a labour sub-contractor which employed the man but did not itself engage in road transport activities. The position would be different only if national legislation adopted in pursuance of art, 14 were to impose that duty on an undertaking providing temporary labour.

Case 76/77: AUDITEUR DU TRAVAIL V DUFOUR [1978] 1 CMLR 265 (European Court of Justice).

1199 Competition policy—abuse of dominant position

The plaintiffs, who were in a dominant position in the banana market in a substantial part of the European Community, were charged with contravening Community competition policy by charging unfair and discriminatory prices for bananas, by forbidding their distributors to resell green bananas and by refusing to sell to a wholesaler. The plaintiffs appealed against the imposition of a fine in respect of these infringements. *Held*, the Commission had not produced sufficient evidence to support the allegation of unfair prices and the amount of the fine would be reduced accordingly. The remaining charges were held to be an abuse of the dominant position. A company was in a dominant position if it controlled a substantial area of the relevant market in a particular product. The cumulative effect of the advantages enjoyed by the plaintiffs ensured that they were in a dominant position in the relevant market, and they were abusing this position.

UNITED BRAND COMPANY v EC COMMISSION (1978) Times, 6th March (European Court of Justice).

1200 —— prevention of parallel imports—exclusive dealing agreement and trade mark agreement

In 1954 a British company, W, entered into an oral agreement with a distributor in the Netherlands, T, to the effect that T should be its exclusive distributor within the Netherlands. In 1963 T notified the Commission of the agreement, and were advised that on provisional examination of the notification the agreement fell within the exemption for exclusive dealing agreements provided by Regulation 67/67. T also had an oral agreement with W, granting T the exclusive right to use the trade marks of W's products in the Netherlands. In 1973, at the request of T, W withdrew the registration of these trade marks in its own name from the Benelux register, thus granting T the sole legal right to use the trade marks in the Netherlands. The Commission was not notified of the trade marks agreement, nor was it notified about W's instructions to the wholesalers W supplied in the UK, forbidding them to export W's products. In 1972 T commenced proceedings against other undertakings distributing W's products in the Netherlands. One of these undertakings applied to the Commission for a finding that there was an infringement of the provisions of EEC Treaty, art. 85. The Commission found that the agreements between T and W infringed art. 85 (1) and that T had supplied incorrect and misleading particulars in its notification of 1963, for which the Commission imposed a fine. T appealed. *Held*, from 1st January 1973 the agreements infringed art. 85 (1). Since the sale of W's products accounted for 15 per cent of the market in those products, the agreements affected trade between member states. The agreements had as their main object and effect the prevention of competition in the protected area, as they were designed to ensure T absolute territorial protection, by excluding all parallel imports. The agreements did not contribute either to improving production or distribution of the goods or to promoting technical and economic progress, and could not therefore be exempted under art. 85 (3).

There was no infringement prior to 1973 because the agreement only affected trade within one member state, the Netherlands, and between the Netherlands and the UK, which was not at that time a member state. It was not until the UK joined the Community that the agreement could be said to affect trade between two member states.

Case 28/77: TEPEA BV v EC COMMISSION [1978] 3 CMLR 392 (European Court of Justice).

1201 Co-operation agreements with non-member states

EEC Council Regulation 2213/78 approves the Co-operation Agreement between The EEC and the Arab Republic of Egypt relating to trade and economic matters.

1202

EEC Council Regulation 2214/78 approves the Co-operation Agreement between the EEC and the Lebanese Republic, relating to trade and economic matters.

1203

EEC Council Regulation 2215/78 brings into force the Co-operation Agreement between the EEC and the Hashemite Kingdom of Jordan relating to trade and economic matters.

1204

EEC Council Regulation 2216/78 approves the Co-operation Agreement between the EEC and the Syrian Arab Republic relating to trade and economic matters.

1205

EEC Council Regulation 2217/78 approves the Financial and Additional Protocols to the Agreement between the EEC and the State of Israel, concerning financial and economic co-operation.

1206   EEC Council Regulation 2237/78 approves the Financial and Additional Protocols to the Agreement between the EEC and the Portuguese Republic, concerning financial, trade and social co-operation.

1207   **European Assembly Constituencies**

The European Assembly Constituencies (England) Order 1978, S.I. 1978 No. 1903 (in force on 3rd January 1979), divides England into sixty-six European Assembly Constituencies for the purposes of the European Assembly elections.

Similar provisions are made in respect of Wales and Scotland: S.I. 1978 Nos. 1904, 1911.

1208   **European Assembly Elections Act 1978**

The European Assembly Elections Act 1978 gives effect to the EEC Council Decision concerning the election of representatives to the Assembly of the European Communities by direct universal suffrage. It also provides that any treaty providing for an increase in the powers of the Assembly is not to be ratified by the United Kingdom unless approved by an Act of Parliament. The Act received the royal assent on 5th May 1978 and came into force on that date.

The representatives of the United Kingdom are to be elected in accordance with the Act: s. 1. The number of representatives to be elected in each part of the United Kingdom is specified: s. 2. The elections are to be held under the simple majority system in Great Britain and under the single transferable vote system in Northern Ireland: s. 3, Sch. I. Double voting at general elections to the Assembly is forbidden: s. 4. Representatives to the Assembly are exempt from jury service in the United Kingdom: s. 5. Parliamentary approval is required for treaties increasing the power of the Assembly: s. 6. Section 7 provides for the payment of expenses incurred under the Act; s. 8 contains interpretation provisions and s. 9 provides for the exercise of the power to make orders and regulations. Schedule 2 provides that the respective Boundary Commissions shall divide Great Britain into Assembly constituencies.

1209   **European Court of Justice—procedure—rectification of judgments**

A party to an action before the European Court of Justice applied under the Rules of Procedure, art. 66 (1) for rectification of alleged clerical mistakes in the judgment. *Held*, art. 66 (1) provided that clerical mistakes or errors in calculation and obvious slips in a judgment could be rectified by the court. Two of the rectifications sought would be made, but the third would not, as it was designed to alter a legal decision in the judgment.

The court subsequently issued a second order rectifying the rectification.

Case 27/76: UNITED BRANDS CO AND UNITED BRANDS CONTINENTAAL BV v EC COMMISSION (RECTIFICATION) [1978] 3 CMLR 83, (European Court of Justice).

For a summary of the original decision, see (1978) Times, 6th March, para. 1199.

1210   **Free movement of goods—common customs tariff—amendment—principle of protection of legitimate expectation**

A German firm was importing quantities of Romanian meat under contract with the Romanian export agency. While the contract was still running, the European Commission adopted EEC Council regulations which had the effect of including the meat subject to the contract in a new tariff heading. This made the meat liable to an amended system of levies which effectively made it much more expensive. In consequence, the German firm stopped importing under their contract. The firm applied to the Commission for relief from the newly adopted regulations, or, alternatively, compensation for its consequent loss. *Held*, the German firm should have contemplated that the Commission might adopt the regulations at any time. There was evidence that it realised the Commission might act in the way it did. To protect its interests under the contract, the agricultural rules of the common market merely required the German firm to give notice to the Commission. The common market rules relating to tariff classifications could be changed by the Commission with impunity. The principle of the protection of the legitimate expectation of traders did not require further action by the Commission. Consequently the Commission could not be regarded as having caused the German firm any damage. The firm's application therefore failed.

Case 90/77: HELLMUT STIMMING KG v COMMISSION OF THE EUROPEAN COMMUNITIES [1978] ECR 995 (European Court of Justice).

1211 —— —— books for children—classification

A dispute arose as to the classification under the common customs tariff of books for children. The books consisted of pages almost entirely covered by coloured illustrations accompanied by captions or short passages of text. The national court held that the books should be classified under tariff heading 49.03 as "children's picture books and painting books". The importer contended that they should be classified under heading 49.01 as "printed books, booklets, brochures, pamphlets and leaflets". The matter was referred to the European Court of Justice. *Held*, Chapter 49, Note 5, provided that the expression "children's picture books" meant books for children in which the pictures dominate and are not subsidiary to the text. In the light of this, tariff heading 49.03 should be interpreted as referring to children's picture books in which the pictures covered almost the whole page and constituted the essential means by which the meaning was conveyed whilst the short captions served merely a simple explanatory purpose.

Case 62/77: CARLSEN VERLAG GMBH v OBERFINANZDIREKTION, COLOGNE [1978] 3 CMLR 14 (European Court of Justice).

1212 —— —— legislation

EEC Council Regulation 2800/78 and its Annexe (in force on 1st January 1979) replace the Annexe to EEC Council Regulation 950/68 as amended, setting out the common Customs Tariff.

1213 —— —— scientific apparatus—exemption

The plaintiffs claimed exemption from import duties for a piece of scientific apparatus under EEC Council Regulation 1798/75, which relates to the importation, free from common customs tariff duties, of scientific instruments or apparatus imported exclusively for educational purposes or scientific research. The tax authorities contended that as the apparatus in question could be used in industry and for other commercial purposes it did not fall within the scope of the exemption. The matter was referred to the European Court for interpretation of Regulation 1798/75. *Held*, "scientific instrument or apparatus" referred to an instrument or apparatus which, from an objective viewpoint, was particularly suitable for pure scientific research. The fact that the apparatus could be used for other purposes did not, in itself, exclude it from being of a scientific nature. So long as the other requirements of the Regulation were fulfilled the apparatus was exempt from the import duties.

Case 72/77: UNIVERSITEITSKLINIEK, UTRECHT v INSPECTEUR DER INVOERRECHTEN EN ACCIJNZEN [1978] ECR 189 (European Court of Justice).

1214 —— customs duties—charges having equivalent effect—elimination

EEC Council Regulation 816/70 established a system of organization of the wine trade in the common market. Acting under the Regulation, France imposed a charge on the importation of certain wines from Italy. The question arose of whether the Regulation, by allowing the imposition of charges on wines between member states, had authorized measures contrary to the rules of the EEC Treaty on the free movement of goods in the common market. *Held*, the abolition between member states of customs duties and charges having the equivalent effect was a fundamental principle of the common market applicable to all products and goods.

Any possible exception should therefore be clearly laid down. There was no exception for agricultural products in the EEC Treaty provisions. The article in the Regulation which permitted the imposition on wine of charges equivalent to customs duties was therefore incompatible with the EEC Treaty and was invalid.

Cases 80, 81/77: SOCIETE LES COMMISSIONAIRES REUNIS SARL V RECEVEUR DES DOUANES [1978] ECR 927 (European Court of Justice).

1215   —— —— goods sent by post—evaluation for customs purposes

EEC Commission Regulation 2741/78 provides that, from 1st January 1979, in determining the value of goods of a commercial nature sent by post for customs purposes, all postal charges levied on the goods up to the place of destination shall be included.

1216   —— —— non-member states—Greece

The Customs Duties (Greece) Order 1978, S.I. 1978 No. 1593 (in force on 1st January 1979) amends the Customs Duties (Greece) (No. 3) Order 1977, 1977 Halsbury's Abr para. 768, by altering the reference to degree of alcohol to the symbol "% vol" in the description of certain alcoholic drinks originating in Greece.

1217   —— quantitative restriction—exception on grounds of public policy or public morality—validity of English customs legislation

The defendants were convicted of being knowingly concerned in the fraudulent evasion of the prohibition in Customs Consolidation Act 1876, s. 42, on the importation of indecent or obscene material. The material in question was imported into the United Kingdom from Holland. The defendants appealed contending that since the entry of the United Kingdom into the EEC, the English legislation was void as being contrary to the provisions of the EEC Treaty prohibiting quantitative restrictions on the free movement of goods between member states. The Crown contended that the case fell within EEC Treaty, art. 36, which provided that the prohibition on such restrictions should not preclude prohibitions on imports justified on grounds of public morality, public policy or public security. *Held*, the plain purpose of art. 36 was to preserve prohibitions which had the plain purpose of supporting public morality. A prohibition on the introduction of obscene literature could not be otherwise than a prohibition justified on the grounds of public morality and public policy. No real question was raised in this case as to the meaning of "public morality" or "public policy" and there was no necessity for a reference to the European Court of Justice. The appeal would be dismissed.

R v HENN; R v DARBY [1978] 3 All ER 1190 (Court of Appeal: LORD WIDGERY CJ, WALLER LJ and MILMO J). Decision of Crown Court at Ipswich [1977] Crim LR 743, 1977 Halsbury's Abr para. 1191 affirmed.

1218   —— —— gold and silver coin—validity of English customs legislation

See *Allgemeine Gold und Silberscheideanstalt v Customs and Excise Commissioners*, para. 1189.

1219   —— —— —— whether goods or means of payment

The appellants were convicted by the Crown Court of fraudulently evading statutory prohibitions on the importation of gold coins into the U.K. and the export of silver alloy coins from the U.K. On appeal against conviction they contended that the statutory prohibitions infringed the EEC Treaty, arts. 30 and 34 which provide for the prohibition of quantitative restrictions on imports and exports respectively between member states. On a reference by the Court of Appeal under art. 177 to the European Court of Justice, *held*, since the purpose of the questions asked was to determine whether the coins in question constituted goods subject to the provisions of arts. 30 to 37 relating to the free movement of goods, or a means of payment, they should be considered in the context of the general system of the

Treaty. Articles 104 to 109, dealing with the overall balance of payments, related to all monetary movements and provided for the making of all monetary transfers necessary for the free movement of goods, services, persons and capital. Accordingly, by their very nature, coins which were either legal tender or regarded as being equivalent to currency constituted a means of payment and were not subject to the provisions of arts. 30 and 34. With respect to coins which by reason of their age were no longer legal tender, although they were goods subject to those provisions, statutory prohibitions on their disposal designed to prevent their disposal in the territory of another member state were justified on the grounds of public policy under art. 36.

R v THOMPSON (1978) Times, 28th November (European Court of Justice). For earlier proceedings see 1977 Halsbury's Abr para. 1193.

1220   —— —— import regulation—declaration of origin

Table grapes of Spanish origin were imported into France from Italy where they had been put into free circulation with a certificate declaring that they were of Italian origin. The importers were charged with importing prohibited goods by means of a false declaration of origin since the quota fixed for imports of Spanish grapes had been exhausted. They contended that the commercial agreement between the EEC and Spain prohibited France from laying down import quotas for Spanish table grapes. Questions were referred to the European Court of Justice concerning the application to the case of EEC Treaty, arts. 30 and 115 and EEC regulations laying down common quality standards for certain fruit and vegetable products. *Held*, the existence of a commercial agreement between the EEC and Spain formed no obstacle to the application to imports of table grapes of art. 115 which permitted derogation from the prohibition as quantitative restrictions imposed by art. 30. Any administrative or penal measure going beyond what was strictly necessary to enable an importing member state to obtain reasonably complete and accurate information on the movement of goods falling within specific measures of commercial policy had to be regarded as a measure having an effect equivalent to a quantitative restriction prohibited by art. 30. Similarly, the requirement of an import licence for the introduction into a member state of goods put into free circulation in another member state was incompatible with the provisions of the Treaty in so far as the goods were not the subject of a derogation authorised by the Commission by virtue of art. 115. EEC Council Regulation 158/66 relating to the control of quality of fruit and vegetables could not of itself justify a requirement to produce documents concerning the origin of the products. The regulation sought to penalise any infringement of it without distinction as to the origin of the product. National measures entailing such distinctions might therefore be regarded as discriminatory and thereby incompatible with art. 30.

Case 52/77: CAYROL V RIVOIRA & FIGLI [1977] ECR 2261 (European Court of Justice).

1221   —— —— national control of retail prices—compatibility with community law

A licensed victualler was convicted of offences against an order made in the Netherlands which laid down the minimum retail prices of spirits. The European Court of Justice was asked to determine two questions: firstly whether the imposition of minimum prices was prohibited by EEC Treaty, art. 30 as a quantitative restriction on imports, and secondly whether arts. 92 to 94 had to be interpreted as meaning that the imposition of price controls was an aid granted by the state and so incompatible with Community law. *Held*, for the prohibition in art. 30 to operate it would be sufficient that a measure was likely to hinder imports. The Dutch order was prohibited because although the minimum retail price had been imposed on both domestic and imported goods equally, it might have prevented any lower cost price of imported goods being reflected in their retail price. However the order plainly did not come within the concept of an aid as expressed in arts. 92 to 94 because it favoured all distributors, not just those in the Netherlands.

Case 82/77: OPENBAAR MINISTERIE (PUBLIC PROSECUTOR) v VAN TIGGELE [1978] 2 CMLR 528 (European Court of Justice).

1222   —— —— prices

See *G.B.-Inno-B.M. NV v Vereniging van de Kleinhandelaars in Tabak*, para. 1243.

1223   —— trade marked goods—effect of repackaging goods

The first plaintiff granted its subsidiary, the second plaintiff, a licence under which the second plaintiff manufactured Valium and sold it in Germany under the name Valium Roche. Both Valium and Roche are trade marks protected by international registration. The defendant, a German marketing company, purchased Valium Roche from its parent company in the Netherlands. The Netherlands company had bought the drug in Britain, where it had been put on the market by the British subsidiary of the first plaintiff, and had then repackaged it. The words Valium and Roche were put on the packages, as were the words "marketed by Centrafarm GmbH". The enclosed leaflet was identical to that used by the second plaintiff and was signed Hoffman-La Roche. The first plaintiff claimed that the defendant's conduct was an infringement of its trade mark rights, and the second plaintiff considered the defendant's conduct an infringement of its right to use its trade name. The question for the European Court was whether the person entitled to a trade mark right was empowered to prevent a parallel importer from acting as the defendant had done. The Court also had to consider the position of a proprietor of a trade mark who had acquired a dominant position within the market in one of the member states as a result of the prohibition of imports of a repackaged product. *Held*, although the EEC Treaty prohibited quantitative restrictions and measures having equivalent effect, art. 36 permitted exceptions to safeguard rights in the specific subject matter of property. In relation to trade marks the specific subject matter was the guarantee that the owner of the trade mark had the exclusive right to use that name. The holder of a trade mark was therefore justified in resisting the marketing of the product after it had been repackaged in a new container on which the trade mark had been placed by a third party. Such resistance did, however, amount to a disguised restriction if the holder's use of the trade mark contributed to the artificial partitioning of the markets between member states, if the repackaging did not affect the original condition of the product, if the holder of the trade mark received prior notice of the marketing and repackaging, and if the new wrapping mentioned that the product had been repackaged. In the present case, the use of the trade mark fell within the exception provided for in art. 36, as the holder of the trade mark had not used it as a means of abusing its dominant position on the market.

Case 102/77: HOFFMANN-LA ROCHE & CO AG v CENTRAFARM VERTRIEBSGESELLS-CHAFT PHARMAZEUTISCHER ERZEUGNISSE MBH [1978] 3 CMLR 217 (European Court of Justice).

1224   Free movement of persons—right of establishment—mutual recognition of qualifications—dental practitioners

EEC Council Directive 78/686 contains provisions dealing with the mutual recognition of diplomas, certificates and other evidence of the formal qualifications of dental practitioners.

EEC Council Directive 78/687 concerns the coordination of provisions laid down by law, regulation or administrative action in respect of the activities of dental practitioners.

EEC Council Decision 78/688 sets up an Advisory Committee on the Training of Dental Practitioners.

1225   Free movements of services—right to provide services—lawyers

The European Communities (Services of Lawyers) Order 1978, S.I. 1978 No. 1910 (in force on 1st March 1979), gives effect to the EC Council Directive 77/249, 1977 Halsbury's Abr para. 1204, on the services of lawyers, by enabling, under certain conditions, lawyers qualified in other EEC member States to provide services in the United Kingdom which could otherwise be provided only by advocates, barristers or solicitors.

1226   Harmonisation of laws—motor vehicle standards—statutory plates and inscriptions

EEC Commission Directive 78/507 adapts in view of technical progress EEC Council Directive 76/114 which provides for the approximation of the laws of member states relating to the position and method of attachment of statutory plates and inscriptions on motor vehicles and their trailers.

1227   Imports—abolition of exemption from import requirements—duty of Commission to provide transitional measures

See *Intercontinentale Fleischhandelsgesellschaft mbH & Co KG v EC Commission*, para. 1232.

1228   Iron and steel employees—re-adaptation benefits

The European Communities (Iron and Steel Employees Re-adaptation Benefits Scheme) (Amendment) Regulations 1978, S.I. 1978 No. 1122 (in force on 27th August 1978), further amend the scheme established by the European Communities (Iron and Steel Employees Re-adaptation Benefits Scheme) Regulations 1974, 1974 Halsbury's Abr para. 1326. The amendments provide for a new method of calculation of payments made under the scheme during retraining, based on previous earnings but with a deduction for income tax deducted from those earnings.

1229   Judgments—reciprocal enforcement in original member states

A judgment was delivered in Italy and sought to be enforced in Belgium. An appeal had been lodged before the Italian Court of Cassation against the Italian judgment. A stay of enforcement was sought in Belgium until the appeal was disposed of, under the 1968 Convention as Jurisdiction and the Enforcement of Judgments in Civil and Commercial Matters, arts. 30 and 38, which permit the court of execution to stay enforcement until an ordinary appeal against the original judgment has been disposed of. Questions on the meaning of "ordinary appeal" in arts. 30 and 38 were referred to the European Court of Justice. *Held*, the expression "ordinary appeal" in arts. 30 and 38 should be defined solely within the framework of the system of the Convention itself and not according to the law either of the state in which the judgment was given or of the state in which recognition or enforcement of that judgment was sought. Within that framework, an "ordinary appeal" was any appeal which might result in the annulment or amendment of the judgment which was the subject-matter of the proceedings for recognition or enforcement under the Convention and the lodging of which was subject in the state in which judgment was given to a limitation period laid down by law which started to run by virtue of that judgment.

Case 43/77: INDUSTRIAL DIAMOND SUPPLIES v RIVA [1978] 1 CMLR 349 (European Court of Justice).

1230   Jurisdiction—national courts of original member states—contract for sale of goods on instalment credit terms

A German company sold a machine tool to a French company, payment to be by two equal bills of exchange payable at sixty and ninety days. On the partial insolvency of the French company a German court gave judgment against the buyer in respect of the unpaid part of the purchase price. The lower French courts declared the judgment enforceable in France, and the buyer appealed, claiming that the sale constituted an instalment credit sale within the convention on Jurisdiction and the Enforcement of Judgments in Civil and Commercial Matters 1968, art. 13, and therefore the decision of the German court, which did not comply with the rule on jurisdiction in art. 14 relating to actions against credit buyers, could not be enforced in France. The Cour de Cassation referred the question whether the sale of the machine constituted a sale under art. 13 to the European Court of Justice. *Held*, although the concept of an instalment credit sale varied between member states, in the context of intra community relations it should be given a uniform substantive meaning in order to ensure the harmonious operation of arts. 13 and 14. From the relevant rules common to the laws of member states it was clear that a sale under art. 13 implied a transaction in which the price was discharged by way of several payments. Further, in keeping with the policy of the convention, art. 14 was to be given a restrictive interpretation, by confining its limitation on jurisdiction over actions by sellers against buyers to cases where the buyer was the final private consumer. In this case the sale by one company to another did not constitute an instalment credit sale within art. 13.

Case 150/77: SOCIETE BERTRAND v PAUL OTT KG [1978] 3 CMLR 499 (European Court of Justice).

1231 Legal aid—transmission of applications

The United Kingdom has ratified the European Agreement on the Transmission of Applications for Legal Aid and it came into force on 17th February 1978. The purpose of the agreement is to facilitate the steps which have to be taken by those of limited means in order to obtain legal aid in civil, commercial or administrative matters in a contracting state of the Council of Europe.

1232 Liability of the Community—abolition of exemption from import requirements—duty to provide transitional measures

Importers entered into a contract with a Romanian state corporation for the supply of seasoned meat, the import of which into the Community was at the time exempt from the requirement of EEC Commission Regulation 1090/75 that there should be countervailing export of an equivalent amount of meat. Due to alleged force majeure, there was a delay in supply of the meat until after the date when the exemption was abolished by EEC Commission Regulation 2033/75. The importers brought an action for damages against the Commission, claiming that it should have provided transitional measures preserving the exemption for imports under pre-existing contracts, or at least exempted that part of the transaction which was delayed through force majeure. *Held*, the Commission had conveyed nothing to importers which could have justified the expectation that regardless of the development of market conditions, the previous rules would be maintained without alteration during the time when prior contracts were to be performed. There was accordingly no obligation to provide transitional measures. The principle of force majeure applied only where the importer was under a legal obligation to complete the transaction within a time limit laid down in the import licence. In this case, the delay only meant that the imports would be subject to a less favourable system. This was a matter for private litigation between the contracting parties.

Case 68/77: INTERCONTINENTALE FLEISCHHANDELSGESELLSCHAFT MBH & CO KG v EC COMMISSION [1978] 2 CMLR 733 (European Court of Justice).

1233 Lomé Convention—accession of new states

EEC Council Regulation 2236/78 provides for the accession of the Republic of Cape Verde, Papua New Guinea and The Democratic Republic of Sao Tome and Principe to the ACP-EEC Convention of Lomé.

1234 Migrant workers—convention

The European Convention on the Legal Status of Migrant Workers was opened for signature on 24th November 1977. It requires five signatures before it comes into effect and was signed on 24th November 1977 by Spain and West Germany. Belgium signed on 7th February 1978.

1235 Monetary compensatory amounts—claim against Commission for loss caused by fluctuation

The applicant, a German firm, concluded a contract with an Italian firm for the sale of 1,000 tonnes of white sugar, to be delivered between January and June 1972. The price was calculated in accordance with Commission Regulation No. 2635/71, which amended the compensatory amounts in agriculture following the temporary widening of margins of fluctuation for the currencies of certain member states. After the contract was concluded, Italy adopted Commission Reg. No. 2887/71, which had the effect of reducing the compensation payable in Germany. As a result the German firm made a loss on the export. The firm claimed the difference in compensation from the Commission. *Held*, the Commission had not laid down in Reg. No. 2887/71 any transitional provisions for old agreements. However, previous regulations had similarly not provided transitional provisions for exports, but only for imports. It was foreseeable that a system of compensatory payments might soon have to apply to Italy. The principle of protection of the legitimate expectation of interested parties had therefore not been infringed. The application would be dismissed.

Case 126/76: DIETZ V COMMISSION OF THE EUROPEAN COMMUNITIES [1977] ECR 2431 (European Court of Justice).

1236 —— disturbances in trade in agriculture—review of Commission's discretion

The system of monetary compensatory amounts on imports and exports provided by EEC Council Reg. 947/71 where the exchange rate of the currency of a member state fluctuates beyond certain limits can be applied only if the absence of such compensatory amounts would lead to disturbances in trade in agriculture.

Early in 1976 France took the franc out of the "snake" and the Commission adopted Reg. 652/76 establishing monetary compensatory amounts on trade between France and other member states and non-member countries. The preamble to Reg. 652/76 stated only that the rates on the foreign exchange market of the franc had fallen appreciably and that accordingly the conditions justifying the application of monetary compensatory amounts had been met. The plaintiff, a French exporter of products derived from maize considered the requirement to pay such amounts on his exports as illegal and the French tribunal referred to the European Court for preliminary ruling questions relating to the validity of Reg. 974/71 and in particular its compatibility with EEC Treaty, art. 39 which sets out the various objectives of the common agricultural policy. *Held*, the possibilities of disturbances in trade in agricultural products were so numerous and diverse that the Commission could find there was a risk of disturbances merely on the basis of an appreciable fall in the rate of exchange of a currency. Where, as here, a complex economic situation had to be evaluated the administration enjoyed a wide discretion. In reviewing the exercise of such discretion, the court had to confine itself to examining whether it contained a manifest error or constituted a misuse of power or whether the authority had not clearly exceeded the bounds of its discretion. In pursuing the object of the common agricultural policy community institutions had to secure the permanent harmonization made necessary by any conflicts between these objectives taken individually and, where necessary allow any one of them temporary priority in order to satisfy the demands of the economic factors in view of which their decisions were made. If, because of the monetary situation preference happened to be given to the requirements of stabilizing the market, Reg. 974/71 did not thereby contravene EEC Treaty, art. 39.

Case 29/77: SA ROQUETTE FRERE V FRANCE [1977] ECR 1835 (European Court of Justice).

1237 National and community law—effect of community law prior to full membership

The respondents started proceedings against the appellants for infringement of copyright. They claimed an injunction to restrain the appellant from infringing the copyright, delivery up and destruction of all the infringing copies, and damages. The appellants counterclaimed for damages for breach of agreement; namely that they could manufacture the articles in return for royalties. Following the entry of the UK into the EEC and the coming into force of the European Communities Act 1972, the appellants amended their pleadings to include a claim of abuse of dominant market position in breach of Articles 85 and 86 of the Treaty of Rome. The respondents were subsequently relieved from an order that they deliver up certain documents relating to the abuse of dominant position claim in a period prior to the UK's membership of the EEC. On appeal, *held*, the EEC legislation was not retrospective in effect. As the delivery up related to a period prior to UK entry, the decision to relieve the respondents was correct. The appeal would be dismissed.

APPLICATION DES GAZ SA v FALKS VERITAS LIMITED [1978] 1 CMLR 383 (Court of Appeal: VISCOUNT DILHORNE, LORD EDMUND-DAVIES and LORD SCARMAN).

For previous proceedings in this matter, see 1974 Halsbury's Abr para. 1295.

1238   —— **incompatibility of national tax measure—supremacy of community law**

The defendants imported a quantity of beef into Italy. On entry it was subjected to a health tax levied under Italian legislation. The plaintiffs claimed that the tax was contrary to the provisions of the EEC Treaty abolishing quantitative restrictions. An Italian court gave judgment in their favour and ordered the plaintiffs to reimburse the defendants. The plaintiffs appealed, contending that under national legislation only the Italian Constitutional Court had the power to decide on the constitutionality of national measures. The question was referred to the European Court on whether enforceable Community law rules should be upheld without waiting for the repeal of obstructing national rules or a national court's rule of non-constitutionality. *Held*, Community law was an integral part of the national legal orders of member states and had priority over national law. It superseded national laws which were incompatible with it and prevented the valid enactment of subsequent national laws which were incompatible with it. A national court was under an obligation to apply Community rules even if it meant not applying a national law.

ITALIAN TAX AND REVENUE ADMINISTRATION v SIMMENTHAL (1978) Times, 13th March (European Court of Justice).

For the decision with regard to quantitative restrictions see 1977 Halsbury's Abr para. 55.

1239   **Pest control**

EEC Commission Decision 78/436 establishes a Scientific Committee for Pesticides. The Commission of the European Communities may consult the Committee on scientific and technical problems relating to the use and marketing of pesticides and, in particular, on questions concerning the safety of pesticides for plants, man, animals and the environment.

1240   **Research and development**

EEC Council Decision 78/263 adopts a multi-annual research and development programme for the European Economic Community in the field of primary raw materials from 1978 to 1981.

1241   EEC Council Decision 78/264 adopts a programme of research and development for the European Atomic Energy Community on uranium exploration and extraction for a period of three years from 1st January 1978.

1242   EEC Council Decision 78/384 adopts a multi-annual research and development programme (1978 to 1980) for the European Economic Community in the field of paper and board recycling.

1243   **Restrictive practices—abuse of dominant market position—abuse encouraged by national legislative provision**

A company which ran several supermarkets in Belgium was ordered by a Belgian national court to discontinue the selling or offering for sale of cigarettes at a price lower than that stated on the tax label contrary to Belgian national legislation. The company appealed and questions were referred to the European Court of Justice on the compatibility with Community law of the Belgian legislation in so far as under the latter a selling price determined by the manufacturers or importers was imposed for sales to the consumer. *Held*, EEC Treaty, art. 86, prohibited any abuse by undertakings of a dominant position, even if such abuse was encouraged by a national legislative provision. In order to assess the compatibility with this provision of the introduction or maintenance in force of a measure such as the one is question, it had to be determined, taking into account the obstacles to trade which might result from the fiscal arrangements to which those products were subject, whether, apart from any abuse of a dominant position which such arrangements might encourage, such introduction or maintenance in force was likely to affect trade between member states. Rules in a member state under which a fixed price freely chosen by the manufacturer or importer was imposed for the sale to the consumer of tobacco products could constitute a measure having an effect equivalent to a quantitative restriction on imports contrary to EEC Treaty, art. 30, but only if such a system of fixed prices was in fact likely to hinder imports between member states. EEC Council Directive 72/464 on taxes affecting the consumption of manufactured tobacco did not prohibit member states from introducing or maintaining in force legislation under which a selling price was imposed for the sale to the consumer of tobacco products, provided that that price was freely determined by the manufacturer or importer.

Case 13/77: G. B.-INNO-B. M. NV v VERENIGING VAN DE KLEINHANDELAARS IN TABAK [1978] 1 CMLR 283 (European Court of Justice).

1244 ———— pre-accession conduct

See *Valor International Ltd v Application des Gaz SA and EPI Leisure Ltd*, para. 2144.

1245 ——— restriction on delivery of goods—whether restriction an abuse

Dutch subsidiaries of British Petroleum cut their petrol deliveries to an occasional Dutch customer following the introduction of rationing by the Dutch government. All customers were affected, but irregular ones most markedly. The EC Commission found the subsidiaries to have abused their dominant market position but imposed no fine in the circumstances. To avoid the possibility of damages claims based on the finding, and to remove its stigma, the subsidaries sought to have it annulled. *Held*, the absence of pecuniary sanctions did not preclude the subsidiaries from commencing an action for annulment. An occasional customer could hardly complain that it had been treated less well than more regular customers during a crisis. In any event, the customer had managed to obtain a reasonable proportion of its normal quantity of fuel from other sources. Accordingly, the subsidiaries had not abused their dominant position and the finding would be annulled.

Case 77/77: BRITISH PETROLEUM MAATSCHAPPIJ NEDERLAND BV v EC COMMISSION [1978] 3 CMLR 174 (European Court of Justice).

1246 ——— old agreements—notification—provisional validity

In the context of a dispute between the grantee and the grantor of an exclusive sales concession, it was pleaded that the exclusive sales contract was void for violation of EEC Treaty, art. 85. The contract was an "old agreement" which had been notified to the Commission in proper time. The Commission had not made any decision in respect of it, because it considered that it was covered by the group exemption in Regulation 67/67. *Held*, once an "old agreement" had been notified in accordance with the legislation, it was then provisionally valid until the date of an actual individual decision relating to it. If the Commission had closed the file on an agreement, as in this case, that agreement would be indefinitely valid. It was not open to a litigant before a national court to plead that the Commission had acted unlawfully in closing the file.

Case 59/77: ETS A DE BLOOS, SPRL v BOUYER SCA [1978] 1 CMLR 511 (European Court of Justice). *Brasserie de Haecht v Wilkin* (No.2) (48/72) [1973] CMLR 287, and *Portelange SA v Smith Corona Marchant International SA* (10/69) [1974] 1 CMLR 397, 1974 Halsbury's Abr para. 1333, applied.

1247   —— restrictive trade agreement—licence agreement—effect of partial nullity

Under a licence agreement the licensees, a French company, agreed to pay an annual minimum royalty to the English company granting the licence. The amount due for 1974 was not paid and the English company obtained judgment in default of appearance for £5,000. The French company applied to have the judgment set aside, on the grounds that since certain clauses of the agreement infringed EEC Treaty, art. 85 (1) the whole agreement was void. The trial judge dismissed the motion and the company appealed. *Held*, it was clear that the nullity under art. 85 of certain provisions did not automatically invalidate the whole agreement: the agreement should be considered as a whole, less the prohibited provisions, and the relevant national law applied to the remaining provisions. In this case, although some clauses of the agreement were arguably void under art. 85 (1) and liable to be struck out, the minimum royalty clause on which the action had been brought was valid under community law and enforceable in the English courts, being an independent promise supported by consideration. The French company was therefore not entitled to have the judgment set aside.

CHEMIDUS WAVIN LTD v SOCIÉTÉ POUR LA TRANSFORMATION ET L'EXPLOITATION DES RESINES INDUSTRIELLES SA [1978] 3 CMLR 514 (Court of Appeal: BUCKLEY, ORR AND GOFF LJJ). Case 56/65: *La Technique Minière v Maschinenbau ULM GmbH* [1966] CMLR 357, ECJ applied. Decision of Walton J, [1976] 2 CMLR 387, 1976 Halsbury's Abr para. 1147 affirmed.

1248   —— —— prohibition on exports

A producer of records, cassettes and tapes, which were sold chiefly on the German market, entered into agreements with customers which provided that none of the producer's products might be exported to other countries. The EC Commission found that such a prohibition on export constituted an infringement of the EEC Treaty, art. 85 (1), as being a restrictive trade agreement. The producer appealed to the European Court of Justice. *Held*, by its very nature a clause prohibiting exports constituted a restriction on competition whether it was adopted at the instigation of the supplier or of the customer, since the agreed purpose of the contracting parties was the endeavour to isolate a part of the market. This was so even though in practice the supplier was not strict in enforcing the prohibition. The clauses in dispute were such as to be capable of affecting trade between member states and amounted to a breach of art. 85 (1). The appeal would be dismissed.

Case 19/77: MILLER INTERNATIONAL SCHALLPLATTEN GMBH v EC COMMISSION [1978] 2 CMLR 334 (European Court of Justice).

1249   —— selective distribution system—whether compatible with self-service wholesale trade

A general self-service wholesaler, M, applied to the European court for annulment of a decision of the EC Commission approving by negative clearance a selective distribution system established by S, a manufacturer of electronic equipment (radios, tape recorders etc.) for the leisure market. Because M would not accept the conditions on which S appoints its distributors, S had refused to appoint M. M contended that S's system was incompatible with the structure of the wholesale trade and that the obligations which it imposed on its distributors constituted restrictions on competition prohibited by EEC Treaty, art. 85 (1) which did not qualify for exemption under art. 85 (3). *Held*, the Commission had been justified in recognising that selective distribution systems constituted, together with others, an aspect of competition which accorded with art. 85 (1) provided that resellers were chosen on the basis of objective criteria of a qualitative nature relating to the technical qualifications of staff and suitability of premises and that such conditions were applied uniformly. The obligation on non-specialist wholesalers to open a specialist department was designed to ensure sale of the products under appropriate conditions and did not constitute a restriction on competition under art. 85 (1). Neither did the requirement that wholesalers forming part of S's network would supply only appointed resalers and would not supply private customers including large institutions. Such obligations were necessary to any marketing system based on selection of outlets and were essential to the separation of the functions of wholesaler and retailer without which the former would enjoy an unfair competitive advantage. The obligation to estimate supplies six months in advance and to achieve a certain turnover, while exceeding the essential requirements of selective distribution system, fulfilled the conditions for exemption under art. 85 (3). Distribution would be improved by ensuring stability of supply from which consumers would benefit through the continued availability of a wider range of goods. This could not be achieved through the occasional placement of orders. The obligation could be largely fulfilled without inconvenience to wholesale self-service undertakings.

Case 26/76: METRO SB-GROSSMARKTE GMBH & CO KG V EC COMMISSION [1977] ECR 1875 (European Court of Justice).

1250   Social security—attendance allowance—entitlement

National Insurance Commissioner's decision:

Decision CA 3/77: RE RESIDENCE CONDITIONS [1978] 2 CMLR 287 (claimant was of Irish nationality, and the widow of an Irish worker; she came to live in England; applied for an attendance allowance; application was refused because she had not satisfied the residence requirement for non-British citizens; EEC Council Regulation 1408/71 provided for the payment of benefit to workers and families of workers of member states, and superseded national legislation; claimant was therefore to be treated as if she were a British citizen, and had to satisfy only those provisions relating to British citizens; she was eligible for the attendance allowance).

1251   —— national benefits—claim made in member state—whether effective in another member state

National Insurance Commissioner's decision:

RE AN ITALIAN CLAIMANT [1978] 2 CMLR 331 (claimant resided in United Kingdom and from 1954 to 1964 paid social security contributions; returned to Italy as permanent resident and in 1974 claimed Italian invalidity benefit; claim forwarded to British authorities; whether claim effectively made in United Kingdom; where claim for invalidity benefit made by migrant worker to institution of place of permanent residence and in accordance with procedure specified by legislation of that place, no need to make new claim in another EEC member state; claim thus effectively made; claim disallowed as claimant did not satisfy British contribution conditions for relevant period).

1252   ———— employment in different member states—overlapping

An Italian national had worked in Italy and then for twenty years as a mineworker in Belgium. He satisfied all the conditions of the Belgian legislation for entitlement to a miners' invalidity pension. The worker was also awarded an Italian pension on the basis of aggregation of insurance periods completed in both member states and apportionment of the Italian benefit. Relying on EEC Council Reg. 1408/71, art. 46 (3) against overlapping of benefits the Belgian institution reduced the invalidity pension by the amount of the Italian benefit and claimed repayment. The Belgian court asked the European Court whether such a reduction was compatible with EEC Treaty, art. 51. *Held*, the aim of EEC Treaty, arts. 48 to 51 would not be attained if in the exercise of the right of freedom of movement thus conferred, workers were to lose social security benefits guaranteed to them by the legislation of a member state alone. An application of EEC Council Reg. 1408/71, art. 46 (3) which led to a diminution of the rights which the person concerned already enjoyed by virtue of the national legislation alone was incompatible with EEC Treaty, art. 51. The application of rules preventing the overlapping of benefits where there was duplication of insurance periods was possible only where for the acquisition or calculation of the worker's right it was necessary to have recourse to aggregation of the insurance periods and apportionment of the benefits. In the present case entitlement to the invalidity pension under the Belgian legislation had been acquired on the basis of the periods of work completed in Belgium alone.

Case 112/76: Manzoni v Fonds National de Retraite des Ouvries Mineurs [1977] ECR 1647 (European Court of Justice).

1253 An Italian national worked as a miner, in France for four years and then in Belgium for eleven years. The worker satisfied all the conditions for an invalidity pension under the Belgian legislation but his French pension was awarded on the basis of aggregation of periods completed in both member states and apportionment of benefit. Applying the national rules against overlapping of benefits the Belgian institution deducted the apportioned amount of the French benefit from the invalidity pension and sought a refund of the amount overpaid. The worker took action to oppose the deduction. The Belgian court asked the European Court whether EEC Council Reg. 1408/71 art. 12 authorising the overlapping of benefits had to take precedence over national rules against overlapping in cases in which the Community provisions resulted in a migrant worker being placed in a more favourable position than a non-migrant worker. *Held*, so long as a worker was receiving a pension by virtue of national legislation alone the provision of Reg. 1408/71 did not prevent the national legislation, including the national rules against overlapping, from being applied to him in its entirety but if the application of the national legislation proved less favourable than the rules regarding aggregation and apportionment then, under Reg. 1408/71, art. 46 (1) those rules had to be applied.

The charge that migrant workers obtained an advantage over workers who had never left their own country could not be accepted, since no discrimination could arise in legal situations which were not comparable.

Case 22/77: Fonds National de Retraite des Ouvries Mineurs v Mura [1977] ECR 1699 (European Court of Justice).

1254 An Italian worker resident in Italy had completed insurance periods in both Italy and Germany. He was granted an Italian pension and also satisfied the conditions for entitlement under German legislation alone. The amount of his German pension was initially calculated on that basis but subsequently the pension authority reduced the amount by applying EEC Council Reg. 1408/71, art. 46 (3) which purports to limit overlapping of benefits acquired in different member states. The worker disputed the reduction and in the resulting proceedings the German tribunal asked the European Court whether art. 46 (3) could be validly applied where the payment of benefit under national legislation alone could be realised only by waiving, under art. 10 residence requirements under national law. *Held*, article 46 (3) was applicable only in cases where, for the purposes of acquiring the right to benefit within the meaning of EEC Treaty, art. 51 (a), it was necessary to have recourse to the arrangements for aggregation of the periods of insurance. As the waiving of residence clauses pursuant to Reg. 1408/71, art. 10 had no effect on the acquisition of the right to benefit it could not involve the application of art. 46 (3).

Case 32/77: Giuliani v Landesversicherungsanstalt Schwaben [1977] ECR 1857 (European Court of Justice).

1255 An Italian national who had qualified for an invalidity pension under the Belgian legislation alone and an Italian pension on the basis of aggregation and apportionment took action against the Belgian institution to prevent deduction of the Italian benefit from the invalidity pension. The Belgian court asked the European Court whether EEC Council Reg. 1408/71 art. 12 (2) was compatible with the reduction of an invalidity pension granted under art. 46 (1) on the ground that similar benefits had been awarded by another member state, where the reduction was effected under the internal law of the state making the deduction. *Held*, where the worker was receiving a pension under national legislation alone Reg. 1408/71 did not prevent the application of national rules against overlapping unless the result would be less favourable than the application of aggregation and apportionment under art. 46 (1).

Case 37/77: Greco v Fonds National de Retraite des Ouvries Mineurs [1977] ECR 1711 (European Court of Justice).

1256 —— —— —— —— **applicability of national rules against overlapping of benefits**

In three cases before national courts concerning the overlapping of national social security benefits questions arose as to the applicability of both Community and national rules against such overlapping. References were made to the European Court for the interpretation of EEC Council Reg. 1408/71, art. 12 (2), which provides for the exemption of certain benefits awarded by two or more member states from national rules against overlapping and art. 46, which provides for the calculation of benefits to which workers are entitled solely by virtue of the national legislation of one member state, and EEC Council Reg. 574/72, which implements Community rules against overlapping. *Held*, where a worker received a benefit by virtue of national legislation alone, the provisions of Reg. 1408/71 did not exempt him from the application of national rules against the overlapping of benefits unless such application would prove less favourable to him than the application of art. 46 of that reg., in which case that article should be applied. Further, Reg. 574/72, art. 7, which lays down rules for the modification of overlapping benefits, applied only to benefits awarded by the application of the process of aggregation of insurance periods completed in different member states. It was also pointed out that an insurance period which was purchased pursuant to a right conferred by national legislation constituted a voluntary or optional period of insurance within art. 46 (2) of that reg., and as such was not to be taken into account for the purposes of aggregation.

Case 83/77: NASELLI V CAISSE AUXÍLIARE D'ASSURANCE MALADIE-INVALIDITÉ; Case 98/77: MAX SCHAAP V BESTUUR VAN DE BEDRIJFSVERENIGING VOOR BANK-EN VERZEKERINGSWEZEN, GROOTHANDEL EN VRIJE BEROEPEN; and Case 105/77: BESTUUR VAN DE SOCIALE VERZEKERINGSBANK V BOERBOOM-KERSJES [1978] ECR 683, 707, 717 (European Court of Justice).

1257 —— —— **family allowances—family resident in different member state from father**

The plaintiff was an Italian worker employed in Belgium. His wife and three children were resident in Italy where the wife was employed. The Belgian authorities refused the plaintiff payment of family allowances on account of the residence of the wife and children in Italy. The Belgian authorities relied on EEC Council Regulation 1408/71, which lays down rules of priority in cases of overlapping entitlement to family allowances. The question arose as to whether the fact that the wife was both a worker and resident with her children in Italy disentitled the husband, as head of the household, to Belgian social security. *Held*, pursuit of a professional or trade activity in the state in whose territory the members of the family were residing was not a sufficient condition for the suspension of entitlement to social security benefits in another state, since, in addition, it was necessary that family benefits should be payable under the laws of the member state. Under Italian law the wife, even though she worked in Italy, did not qualify for benefits. The Belgian authorities could not refuse, therefore, to pay benefits to the father.

Case 134/77: RAGAZZONI V CAISSE DE COMPENSATION POUR ALLOCATIONS FAMILIALES "ASSUBEL" [1978] ECR 963 (European Court of Justice).

1258 —— —— **language of claim**

The plaintiff was a Belgian national residing in France. In the course of her working life she had completed insurance periods in Belgium, Germany and France. Following a dispute with the Belgian social security office over her right to a retirement pension, she lodged an appeal in the Belgian courts. The appeal was written in French. The courts insisted that the language of judicial proceedings was Dutch and declared that the appeal was null and void because it was written in the wrong language. *Held*, EEC Council Reg. No. 1408/71, Art. 84 (4), required the authorities, institutions and tribunals of one member state to accept claims and documents submitted in the language of another member state. This rule was limited to the field of social security.   But, in this field, it was for the court to arrange for any documents to be translated.

Case 55/77: Reboulet (Maris) v Rijksdienst Voor Werknemerspensioenen [1977] ECR 2327 (European Court of Justice).

1259 —— —— **reimbursement of medical expenses incurred in another member state**

A Dutch court referred to the European Court of Justice, the question whether under EEC Council Reg. 1408/71, art. 22, a worker was entitled to recover expenses incurred for medical treatment given in a member state other than his state of residence when his state of residence could provide treatment, albeit inferior, itself. *Held*, art. 22 could be construed as applying not only where the country of residence could not provide treatment, but also where it was less effective than that which the claimant could obtain in another member state.   Accordingly, the treatment should have been authorised and the cost would be refunded in full.

Case 117/77: Bestuur Van Het Algemeen Ziekenfonds, Drenthe-Platteland v Pierik [1978] 3 CMLR 343 (European Court of Justice).

1260 —— **old age pension—increased rate payable to former French prisoners of war—applicability of community legislation**

A Belgian national employed in France claimed an advance old age pension under the French Social Security Code, which provided that insured persons who were former long-term prisoners of war were entitled to a pension equal to 50 per cent of their basic wage, as opposed to the normal rate of 25 per cent.   His application, made on the grounds that he had been a prisoner of war as a member of the Belgian armed forces and invoking the community principle of equality of treatment between national workers and workers who were nationals of another member state, was rejected by the social security institution, which pointed out that such a pension constituted a benefit scheme for victims of war or its consequences under EEC Council Regulation 1408/71, art. 4 (4) and was therefore excluded from the field of application of that regulation.   The worker's appeal against that decision was upheld and the Regional Director of Social Security appealed to the Cour d'Appel, which referred to the European Court of Justice the question whether the pension came within the exclusion of art. 4 (4).   *Held*, a consideration of the purposes of and conditions of entitlement to the pension showed that it did not exhibit the characteristics of a social security benefit within art. 4 (1): its insertion in national social security legislation was not in itself decisive as to its nature, and its purpose was clearly to show national gratitude to long-term prisoners of war.   Accordingly, the pension fell within the exclusion of art. 4 (4).

Case 9/78: Directeur Regional de la Securite Sociale de Nancy v Gillard [1978] 3 CMLR 554 (European Court of Justice).

1261 —— **orphans' pensions and family allowances—nature of benefits—interpretation of community provisions against overlapping benefits**

Two German minors, whose parents were divorced and whose father subsequently died, lived in Belgium with their German mother and Belgian step-father.   The appropriate German national authority granted them German orphans' pensions, but suspended their pension rights on the ground that their step-father was in receipt of Belgian family allowances in respect of them, by virtue of his Belgian occupation. On appeal by the children against the suspension, the German court referred the question of the interpretation of EEC Council Reg. 1408/71, art. 79 (3) to the European Court.   Article 79 (3) provides that rights to, inter alia, family allowances and orphans' pensions shall be suspended if the children become entitled to family benefits or allowances under the legislation of a member state by virtue of the pursuit of an occupation.   *Held*, there was a clear distinction between a family allowance, payable to a worker by virtue of his actual occupation, and an orphan's pension, payable to the orphan himself by virtue of a prior occupation which ceased on the death of the worker. Since it would be contrary to the overall policy of Community provisions against the overlapping of social security benefits if the grant of one benefit to one dependant could be adversely affected by the payment of a benefit to another dependant, rights to benefits susceptible to suspension under art. 79 (3) should be interpreted as referring to rights to benefits of the same kind existing in favour of one recipient alone, acquired by virtue of the pursuit of a professional or trade activity.

The court pointed out that, in accordance with art. 2, the application of Reg. 1408/71 extended to cases where the residence in another member state was that, not of the worker, but of a survivor of his.

Case 115/77: LAUMANN V LANDESVERSICHERUNGSANSTALT RHEINPROVINZ [1978] ECR 805 (European Court of Justice).

1262   —— retirement pension—entitlement—minimum pension

An application was made to the Belgian authorities for a retirement pension by a worker of Italian nationality residing in Belgium who worked in Italy from 1926 to 1942, and in 1946 and 1947, and in Belgium from 1949 to 1973. EEC Council Regulation 1408/71, art. 50, covers cases where the periods of employment under the legislation of the states to which the worker was subject were relatively short, with the result that the total amount of the benefits payable by those states does not provide a reasonable standard of living. It provides that in such cases where the legislation of the state of residence lays down a minimum benefit, the benefit payable by that state is to be increased by a supplement. The Belgian declaration stated that a minimum benefit did not exist as the calculation of benefits rested on the amount of wage or salary and on the duration of the insurance periods completed. The question was referred to the European Court of Justice. Held, art. 50 was applicable only in cases in which provision was made in the legislation of the member state in whose territory the worker resided for a minimum pension.

Case 64/77: TORRI V OFFICE NATIONAL DES PENSIONS POUR TRAVAILLEURS SALARIÉS [1977] ECR 2299 (European Court of Justice).

1263   —— sickness benefit—disqualifying act by worker outside United Kingdom

See Kenny v Insurance Officer, para. 2711.

1264   —— —— entitlement—claim by national of different member state

An Irish national claimed sickness benefit from the British authorities in respect of a period of illness suffered while he was imprisoned in Ireland. The national insurance commissioner referred to the European Court of Justice questions asking whether, notwithstanding Regulation 1408/71, arts. 19, 22, which prohibit discrimination, a member state could treat an act by an EEC national in a different member state as disqualifying that national from benefit if that act would have disqualified him had it been committed in its own territory. Held, it was for national authorities to decide impartially whether an act which would result in disqualification from benefit for its own nationals should equally disqualify the national of another member state.

Case 1/78: KENNY V NATIONAL INSURANCE COMMISSIONER, LIVERPOOL (1978) Times, 3rd July, ECJ.

For proceedings in which commissioner's reference to the European Court was made, see para. 2711.

1265   —— —— migrant worker—aggregation of insurance periods

After completing her schooling in France, the applicant stayed in Great Britain working as an au pair and attending evening classes. On her return to France, she applied for French sickness insurance benefits in respect of medical treatment received there. The benefits were refused as she had not completed the requisite number of hours of employment. The question was referred to the European Court of Justice whether she could claim the benefits under EEC Council Regulation 1408/71, as a migrant worker. *Held*, a national of a member state who in another member state had been subject to a social security scheme which was applicable to all residents could only benefit from Regulation 1408/71 if he could be identified as an employed person within art. 1 (a) (ii). As regards the United Kingdom, in the absence of any other criterion, such identification depended by virtue of Annex V on whether he was required to pay social security contributions as an employed person. Rights acquired by a person who could thus be identified had to be taken into account by any other member state as if they were periods required under its own legislation.

Case 84/77: CAISSE PRIMAIRE D'ASSURANCE MALADIE D'EURE-ET-LOIR v RECQ [1978] ECR 7 (European Court of Justice).

1266   —— unemployment benefit—entitlement—nature of benefit

The plaintiff left the Netherlands and took up residence in Belgium in 1976; there she applied for unemployment benefit, relying on EEC Council Regulation 1408/71 and the fact that in the Netherlands she had received unemployment benefit under the law relating to unemployment allowances. The national court was of the opinion that that law was not social security legislation but social assistance legislation, the administration of which was entrusted to the local authorities and not to the social security institutions. The matter was referred to the European Court of Justice. *Held*, the fact that a member state had specified a law in its declaration under Regulation 1408/71 had to be accepted as proof that the benefits granted on the basis of that law were social security benefits within the meaning of the regulation.

Case 35/77: BEERENS v RIJKSDIENST VOOR ARBEIDSVOORZIENING [1977] ECR 2249 (European Court of Justice).

1267   —— —— free movement of workers—national provisions

A Belgian national, who went to school in Belgium, completed his education by attending an engineering course in Holland. Returning to Belgium, he was unable to find work and applied for unemployment benefit to the relevant Belgian authority. He was refused benefit on the basis that he had failed to make his application, in compliance with Belgian law, within one year of completing his studies there. The period of further education in Holland was not taken into account. On appeal against this decision, a question was referred to the European Court as to whether under the EEC Treaty or the provisions of EEC Council Reg. No. 1408/71, the Belgian social security provisions were compatible with Community law which required coordination of national laws regarding unemployment benefit and which, more generally, sought to ensure free movement of workers within the Community. *Held*, European law had no application in the case of an unemployed person who had never been in employment and had never been treated as an employed person under national legislation. Furthermore, there was no requirement that, for the purposes of paying unemployment benefits to former students who had never been employed, the social security authority in one member state should treat studies completed in another member state, as though those studies had been completed in the competent paying state.

Case 66/77: KUYKEN v RIJKSDIENST VOOR ARBEIDSVOORZIENING [1977] ECR 2311 (European Court of Justice).

1268   —— voluntary or optional insurance—assimilation of periods of study and periods of employment

The plaintiff, a Belgian national now regularly employed in Belgium, applied to the Belgian insurance authority for assimilation of prior periods of study. Before his employment in Belgium the plaintiff had alternated periods of study in Belgium and France with periods of employment in France and elsewhere. The insurance authority rejected the application on the ground that under Belgian law assimilation could be granted only if a period of study was followed immediately by employment in Belgium. The tribunal considering the matter referred to the European Court the question of the applicability of EEC Council Regulation 1408/71, art. 9 (2) which provides that where under the legislation of a member state admission to voluntary or optional continued insurance is conditional upon completion of insurance periods, any periods completed under the legislation of another member state must be taken into account. *Held*, art. 9 (2) showed an intention to cover every type of insurance incorporating a voluntary element regardless of any continuance of existing insurance. Accordingly assimilation of periods of study and periods of employment had to be considered as admission to voluntary or optional continued insurance under art. 9 (2).

Case 93/76: LIEGEOIS V OFFICE NATIONAL DES PENSIONS POUR TRAVAILLEURS SALARIES [1977] 2 CMLR 757 (European Court of Justice).

1269   —————— insurance period purchased in exercise of national right

See *Max Schaap v Bestuur van de Bedrijfsvereniging voor Bank-en Verzekeringswezen*, para. 1256

1270   Treaties

The European Communities (Definition of Treaties) Order 1978, S.I. 1978 No. 617, the European Communities (Definition of Treaties) (Nos. 2–4) Order 1978, S.I. 1978 Nos. 618, 619, 781, the European Communities (Definition of Treaties) (No. 6) (International Development Association) Order 1978, S.I. 1978 No. 1103 and the European Communities (Definition of Treaties) (No. 7) (International Wheat Agreement) Order 1978, S.I. 1978 No. 1104 declare certain treaties to be community treaties as defined in the European Communities Act 1972, s. 1 (2). In respect of each treaty, the orders come into force on dates to be notified in the London Gazette.

1271   —— Joint European Torus

The European Communities (Definition of Treaties) (No. 5) (Joint European Torus) Order 1978, S.I. 1978 No. 1032 (in force 26th July 1978), declares the Exchange of Letters dated 3rd May 1978 between the Government of the United Kingdom and the European Atomic Energy Community regarding privileges to be granted to the Joint European Torus to be a Community Treaty as defined in the European Communities Act 1972. The principal effect of the declaration is to bring into play in relation to the exchange of letters the provisions of the European Communities Act 1972.

The European Communities (Privileges of the Joint European Torus) Order 1978, S.I. 1978 No. 1033 (in force on 26th July 1978), confers privileges on the Joint European Torus, as required by EC Council Decision 78/472 Euratom of 30th May 1978 and of the Exchange of Letters of 3rd May 1978 between the Government of the United Kingdom and the European Atomic Energy Community, supra.

1272   Weights and measures—units of measurement

See para. 3109.

1273   Wine—pre-packaging and labelling

See para. 3113.

EVIDENCE

Halsbury's Laws of England (4th edn.), Vol. 17, paras. 1–400

1274   Articles

Similar Facts, George W. Keeton (review of the latest cases on similar fact evidence): 142 JP Jo 126.

Unsilencing Your Hostile Witness, Victor Tunkel (the effect of *R v Thompson* (1977) 64 Cr App R 96, CA, 1976 Halsbury's Abr para. 597): 128 NLJ 478.

1275   Admissibility—estimate of arrears of income tax

See *Johnson v Scott (Inspector of Taxes)*, para. 1549.

1276   —— hearsay—statement of person beyond the seas—whether attempt to procure maker of statement as witness necessary

In an action against an underwriter, shipowners claimed to be indemnified under a policy of marine insurance for the total loss of their vessel which was allegedly sunk by a crew member. The underwriter served notices on the shipowners under RSC Ord. 38, r. 21, that he proposed to give in evidence statements made by the crew member to show fraud on the part of the shipowners, and stating that he might not be able to call the crew member as a witness as he was overseas. The shipowners served a counter-notice under Ord. 38, r. 26, requiring the crew member to be called as a witness. They contended that under Ord. 38, r. 25, the party seeking to introduce statements as evidence without calling their maker had to show that he had taken all reasonable steps to call him, and that the underwriter had not taken such steps. *Held*, where a party sought to give in evidence a statement by a person said to be beyond the seas, it was not necessary to show that efforts had been made to procure him to give evidence at the trial; the fact that he was abroad was in itself a sufficient reason for admitting the statement.

PIERMAY SHIPPING CO SA v CHESTER [1978] 1 All ER 1233 (Court of Appeal: MEGAW, LAWTON and EVELEIGH LJJ). *Rasool v West Midlands Passenger Transport Executive* [1974] 3 All ER 638, 1974 Halsbury's Abr para. 1358 approved.

1277   —— similar facts

The plaintiff brought an action against a bank for damages for loss of a diamond he alleged he had deposited there. He sought to introduce evidence of an event in 1969 when jewellery deposited at the bank by another customer had been removed to the flat of his bank's managing director and subsequently stolen. *Held*, there were two issues in this case; whether the diamond was deposited at the bank and whether the way the bank secured its customers' property was reasonably safe. The evidence in question was not relevant to the first issue but it was relevant to the second to show that experience had shown that the bank's system for securing customers' property was not reasonably safe. The evidence was admissible.

SATTIN v NATIONAL UNION BANK (1978) 122 Sol Jo 367, CA (Court of Appeal: MEGAW, LAWTON and BROWNE LJJ).

1278   Criminal cases

See CRIMINAL PROCEDURE.

1279   Foreign proceedings—Akrotiri and Dhekelia

The Evidence (Proceedings in Other Jurisdictions) (Sovereign Base Areas of Akrotiri and Dhekelia) Order 1978, S.I. 1978 No. 1920 (in force on 10th January 1979), extends the provisions of the Evidence (Proceedings in other Jurisdictions) Act 1975, which sets out a comprehensive code for the taking of evidence by courts on behalf of other courts, to the Sovereign Base Areas of Akrotiri and Dhekelia, with modifications.

1280   —— Cayman Islands

The Evidence (Proceedings in Other Jurisdictions) (Cayman Islands) Order 1978, S.I. 1978 No. 1890 (in force on 10th January 1979), extends the provisions of the Evidence (Proceedings in Other Jurisdictions) Act 1975, which sets out a comprehensive code for the taking of evidence by courts on behalf of other courts, to the Cayman Islands, with modifications.

1281   —— Falkland Islands

The Evidence (Proceedings in Other Jurisdictions) (Falkland Islands and Dependencies) Order 1978, S.I. 1978 No. 1891 (in force on 10th January 1979), extends the
provisions of the Evidence (Proceedings in Other Jurisdictions) Act 1975, which sets
out a comprehensive code for the taking of evidence by courts on behalf of other
courts, to the Falkland Islands and its Dependencies, with modifications.

1282   —— Gibraltar

The Evidence (Proceedings in Other Jurisdictions) (Gibraltar) Order 1978, S.I. 1978
No. 1892 (in force on 10th January 1979), extends to Gibraltar the provisions of the
Evidence (Proceedings in Other Jurisdictions) Act 1975 that provide for the repeal
of the Foreign Tribunals Evidence Act 1856, the Evidence by Commission Act
1859, the Extradition Act 1870, s. 24, the Evidence by Commission Act 1885 and
the Arbitration (International Investment Disputes) Act 1966, s. 3 (1) (b).

1283   Oaths Act 1978

The Oaths Act 1978 consolidates provisions relating to oaths and affirmations.   The
Act received the royal assent on 30th June 1978 and came into force on 30th July
1978.

Tables showing the derivation of the Act and the destination of enactments
consolidated are set out on page 299.

DESTINATION TABLE

This table shows in column (1) the enactments repealed by the Oaths Act 1978, and in column (2) the provisions of that Act corresponding thereto.

(1)	(2)	(1)	(2)
Oaths Act 1838 (c.105)	Oaths Act 1978 (c.19)	Oaths Act 1909 (c.39)	Oaths Act 1978 (c.19)
The entire Act	s.4(1)	ss. 1–3	s. 1
		Oaths Act 1961 (c.21)	
Oaths Act 1888 (c.46)			
		s. 1 (1), (2)	5 (2), (3)
s. 1	5 (1), (4)	The Administration of Justice Act 1977 c. 38	
2	6 (1)		
3	4 (2)		
4	6 (2)		
5	3	s. 8 (1)	5 (1), (4)

TABLE OF DERIVATIONS

This table shows in the right hand column the legislative source from which the sections of the Oaths Act 1978 have been derived. In the table the following abbreviations are used:

     1838   =   The Oaths Act 1838
                  (1 & 2 Vict. c. 105)
     1888   =   The Oaths Act 1888
                  (51 & 52 Vict. c. 46.)
     1909   =   The Oaths Act 1909
                  (9 Edw. 7 c. 39)
     1961   =   The Oaths Act 1961
                  (9 & 10 Eliz. 2 c. 21)
     1977   =   The Administration of Justice Act 1977
                  (1977 c. 38).

Section of Act	Derivation
1	1909 ss. 1–3.
2	[Consequential amendments.]
3	1888 s 5.
4(1)	1838.
(2)	1888 s. 3.
5(1)	1888 s. 1; 1977 s. 8(1).
(2), (3)	1961 s. 1(1), (2).
(4)	1888 s. 1; 1977 s. 8(1).
6(1)	1888 s. 2.
(2)	1888 s. 4.
7	[Repeals and savings.]
8	[Short title, extent and commencement.]
Sch.	[Enactments repealed.]

1284   Refreshing memory—requirement of contemporaneity—application in extradition proceedings

See *Re Miller*, para. 1312.

1285   Special modes of proof—judicial notice—time—time of sunset

The defendant was charged with an offence under the Night Poaching Act 1828. Such offences must be proved to have been committed by night, defined in s. 12 as commencing "at the expiration of the first hour after sunset and (concluding) at the beginning of the last hour before sunrise". In the present case it was important to establish the exact time of sunset on the day in question. The prosecution sought to adduce evidence of the time of sunset by putting in "Whitaker's Almanack". *Held*, the court could not take judicial notice of the time of sunset as evidenced by an almanac.

The prosecution was subsequently permitted to call an astronomer to prove the time of sunset at the place of the alleged offence.

R v CRUSH [1978] Crim LR 357 (Crown Court at Croydon: JUDGE DENNIS SMITH). *Tutton v Darke, Nixon v Freedom* (1860) 5 H & N 647 followed.

1286   Transcript of evidence—absence of transcript—admissibility of counsel's note of evidence

In a case in the Court of Appeal, LORD WIDGERY CJ stated that where no transcript of evidence was available from the shorthand writers, their Lordships had declined an offer to look at an abbreviated concentrated note of evidence taken by counsel at the trial because it was a dangerous practice to adopt.

R v WINTER (1978) Times, 28th November (Court of Appeal).

1287   Tribunals—privilege attaching to evidence of witnesses—judicial nature of tribunal

The headmaster of a Scottish school was dismissed by the local education authority. On the petition of the headmaster the Secretary of State, in exercise of his statutory powers, appointed a commissioner to hold a local inquiry into the reasons for the dismissal. In the course of the inquiry a witness gave allegedly maliciously false evidence in respect of which the headmaster sought reparation. The action was dismissed at first instance and by the Second Division of the Court of Session on the grounds that the occasion on which the relevant words were spoken was one which attracted absolute privilege. He appealed to the House of Lords. *Held*, it was a rule of both Scottish and English law that absolute privilege attached to words spoken or written in the course of giving evidence in proceedings in a court of justice or a tribunal which, having similar attributes to a court, acted in a similar manner. Accordingly, in deciding whether evidence given in the tribunal in question was absolutely privileged, it was necessary to consider, first, the authority under which the tribunal was acting; second, the nature of the question into which it was bound to inquire; third, the procedure adopted; and fourth, the legal consequences of its conclusion. In this case the tribunal had been set up under statutory authority, for the purpose of deciding an issue between the dismissed headmaster and the local education authority. Further a clearly judicial manner of proceeding had been adopted leading to a final determination of the issue. An examination of all the characteristics of the tribunal showed it to have been acting in a manner similar to a court. Evidence given in proceedings before it was therefore absolutely privileged. The appeal would be dismissed.

TRAPP V MACKIE [1979] 1 All ER 489 (House of Lords: LORD DIPLOCK, LORD SALMON, LORD EDMUND-DAVIES, LORD FRASER OF TULLYBELTON and LORD RUSSELL OF KILLOWEN (judgment delivered 13th December)). *Royal Aquarium Ltd v Parkinson* [1892] 1 QB 431, CA, and *O'Connor v Waldron* [1935] AC 76, HL applied.

EXECUTION

Halsbury's Laws of England (4th edn.), Vol. 17, paras. 401–700

1288   Stay of execution—courts' discretion

A football club had incurred enormous debts, including a debt for £7,561 to the plaintiffs for the price of football programmes. Many of the creditors agreed to take no action for a specified period, but the plaintiffs brought an action for the money due and judgment was given against the club. On appeal by the club, a stay of execution was granted on certain conditions under RSC Ord. 47, r. 1 (1), in that there were special circumstances rendering it inexpedient to enforce the judgment. On appeal by the plaintiffs, *held*, the court should not seek to limit its discretion under Ord. 47 by tabulating the circumstances under which it would exercise it. In this case, it would do little good to allow creditors to enforce their judgments as the club would have to close down. If execution did proceed against the club, all that it could do would be to ask for a formal moratorium under the Companies Act 1948, s. 206. To do so would cost about £5,000 and there would then be that much less for creditors. Therefore in the interests of the creditors, execution should be stayed and the appeal dismissed.

PRESTIGE PUBLICATIONS LTD v CHELSEA FOOTBALL AND ATHLETIC CO LTD (1978) 122 Sol Jo 436 (Court of Appeal: LORD DENNING MR, GOFF and CUMMING-BRUCE LJJ).

EXECUTORS AND ADMINISTRATORS

Halsbury's Laws of England (4th edn.), Vol. 17, paras. 701–1591

1289   Article

Provision for Dependants and Agreements for Testamentary Provision, J. Gareth Miller (the extension in the categories of persons entitled to apply for financial provision brought about by the Inheritance (Provision for Family and Dependants) Act 1975, 1975 Halsbury's Abr para. 1478): 128 NLJ 449.

1290   Action against personal representative—defence struck out—jurisdiction of court to amend pleading after judgment

On the death of the defendant in an action for an order of specific performance of an option agreement and damages, the action was continued against his personal representative, the applicant in the present proceedings. In the action against her, she failed to comply with an order for discovery of documents and her defence was struck out. The order for specific performance was refused, but an inquiry as to damages against the estate was directed and an order made that the applicant pay the damages found to be due. The estate amounted to £9,000 and the plaintiff's claim amounted to £100,000. Having failed to plead *plene administravit* or *plene administravit praeter* in the action, the applicant was precluded from raising a defence based on an insufficiency of assets in her hands and would become personally liable. She therefore sought an order that she be at liberty to serve a defence of *plene administrativit praeter* effectively limiting her liability to the value of the estate. *Held*, the court had jurisdiction to amend a pleading even after judgment. However, in this case there was no defence to amend as it had been struck out in circumstances amounting to contempt. The applicant relied on RSC Ord. 24, r. 17, which provided that an order for discovery could be revoked by a subsequent order made "at or before the trial of the cause or matter in connection with which the original order was made." Even if the court had jurisdiction to do so, the action had been fought to judgment without the benefit of discovery and it was now too late for a person in contempt to ask to be excused from the consequences of failure to give discovery when it could no longer be effectively given. In any event, the "original order" was in connection with the trial for specific performance and damages and that "trial" had taken place. All that remained was the inquiry as to damages and the court had no jurisdiction to revoke the order for discovery and thus leave the defence standing. The relief sought would be refused.

MIDLAND BANK TRUST CO LTD v GREEN (No. 2) (1978) Times, 5th July (Chancery Division: OLIVER J).

For proceedings in which the order of specific performance was sought, see 1977 Halsbury's Abr para. 1636.

1291 Administration of estates—distribution of estates—date of distribution

See *Royal Trust Company v East*, para. 3122.

1292 —— grant of administration—revocation of grant

See *Re Davies, deceased; Panton v Jones*, para. 3125.

1293 Family provision—application by wife of polygamous marriage—meaning of "wife"

The applicant married the deceased in India according to Hindu rites in 1937. In 1948, the deceased polygamously entered into a second marriage under Indian law. All three parties subsequently came to England and acquired an English domicile of choice. In 1970, the applicant ceased to live with the deceased and his second wife and was not in fact being maintained by him at the time of his death in 1976. The deceased's will, made in 1970, left the whole of his residuary estate to the second wife and the applicant applied under the Inheritance (Provision for Family and Dependants Act 1975, s. 1 (1) (a), for financial provision. *Held*, as there was no definition of wife in the 1975 Act, it was a question of construction whether the applicant came within the section. Although the rule in *Hyde v Hyde* (1866) 1 PD 130 provided that English courts did not recognise a polygamous marriage for the purpose of enforcing matrimonial duties or obtaining relief for a breach of matrimonial obligations, the situation was altered by the Matrimonial Causes Act 1973, s. 47, which provides that an English court should not be precluded from granting matrimonial relief or making a declaration concerning the validity of a marriage by reason only that the marriage was entered into under a law which permitted polygamy. It followed therefore, that "wife" in the 1975 Act should not be construed only in terms of a monogamous marriage. In any event, the question in this case was one of succession not one of matrimonial relief. The applicant, being the wife of a polygamous marriage, had therefore the right to claim financial provision from the estate of her deceased husband under the Inheritance (Provision for Family and Dependants) Act 1975. The claim would be allowed.

RE SEHOTA (DECEASED), KAUR v KAUR [1978] 3 All ER 385 (Chancery Division: FOSTER J).

For 1975 Act, see 1975 Halsbury's Abr para. 1478.

1294 —— child—child not dependent—meaning of "maintenance"

A widow whose husband died intestate claimed possession of his house, which comprised a substantial part of his estate. Their son claimed a maintenance payment from the estate under the Inheritance (Provision for Family and Dependants) Act 1975. He had been living with his father, but had not been dependent on him. The master upheld the son's claim and the widow appealed. *Held*, although the 1975 Act made fresh provisions expanding the class of potential applicants for financial provision so that a child could claim maintenance this did not lead to a more liberal approach to the meaning of "maintenance". A child who was not dependent had to establish a moral claim beyond the fact of his being a blood relative in need. The son in this case had failed to establish such a claim and accordingly the appeal would be allowed.

RE COVENTRY (DECEASED) (1978) Times, 14th November (Chancery Division: OLIVER J).

1295   —— county court jurisdiction

The County Courts Jurisdiction (Inheritance—Provision for Family and Dependants) Order 1978, S.I. 1978 No. 176 (in force 1st March 1978), increases to £15,000 the jurisdiction of county courts relating to claims on a deceased person's estate by a relative or dependant under the Inheritance (Provision for Family and Dependants) Act 1975, s. 2.

1296   —— person maintained by the deceased otherwise than for full valuable consideration

A woman who had lived with the testator as his common law wife after his divorce and had borne him a son claimed that she was entitled to provision from his estate, which was valued between £25,000 and £30,000. He had left all his property to his legitimate son who claimed that as the woman had originally gone to his father as a housekeeper she was not entitled to provision. *Held*, it was clear that a family relationship had existed between the woman and the testator and that she had become a de facto wife. As both she and the children were entitled to provision from the estate, she would be awarded a lump sum of £5,000 and the remainder would be divided equally between the sons.

CA v CC (1978) Times, 18th November (Family Division: SIR GEORGE BAKER P).

1297   —— procedure—appeal from master's decision

The following Practice Direction ([1978] 2 All ER 167) has been issued by the Chancery Division.

1. Applications under the Inheritance (Provision for Family and Dependants) Act 1975 are now frequently heard and disposed of by masters. The question arises how the case is to proceed if a party is dissatisfied with the master's decision.

2. It is open to the master, with the consent of the parties, to try the case in court under RSC Ord. 36, r. 9, and if he does so an appeal lies to the Court of Appeal under RSC Ord. 58, r. 3.

3. If, however, the case is heard in chambers a dissatisfied party must apply for an adjournment to the judge, in which case there must be a rehearing, normally in court.

4. Though the judge or the parties may require any cross-examination on affidavits or other oral evidence to be heard again in full, in most cases this should not be necessary if a full note or a transcript of the evidence before the master has been made.

5. A master hearing a case in chambers should therefore ensure, if possible, that the proceedings before him are recorded by a shorthand writer or a recording instrument. If he is unable to arrange this he should take as full a note as practicable of the oral evidence given before him. On the adjournment to the judge there should be sent to the judge, with the affidavits, a transcript or copy of the master's note of the oral evidence and a transcript or copy of the master's judgment.

6. No provision should be made for the attendance of witnesses at the rehearing before the judge unless a judge so directs. A party requiring such a direction should apply to the master to adjourn that question to a judge in chambers as a preliminary point.

1298   Intestacy—appropriation by personal representatives—matrimonial home—surviving spouse's interest in estate less than value of house

A husband died intestate. Prior to his death, he had lived with his wife in the matrimonial home which comprised part of his residuary estate. The value of the house was greater than the value of the wife's absolute interest in the estate. Pursuant to the Intestates' Estates Act 1952, Sch. 2, para. 1 (1), she gave notice to the husband's personal representatives requiring them to appropriate the house to her in or towards satisfaction of her interest in the estate. The question before the court was whether a surviving spouse could require appropriation of the matrimonial home where the value of the spouse's absolute interest in the estate was less than the value of the house. *Held*, the Act only gave the surviving spouse a right to require appropriation of the matrimonial home where the value of his or her absolute interest in the intestate spouse's estate was greater than the value of the house. The words "in or towards satisfaction" of any absolute interest did not contemplate the satisfaction being greater in value than the interest. The wife was therefore not entitled to require the house to be appropriated to her.

RE PHELPS (DECEASED), WELLS v PHELPS [1978] 3 All ER 395 (Chancery Division: FOSTER J).

1299   Practice—probate—non-contentious   probate—application   to pass over executors—suitability of non-contentious procedure

The wife of the deceased made an application under Supreme Court of Judicature (Consolidation) Act 1925, s. 162 (1) b, to pass over the executors appointed by the deceased's will and inviting the court to grant letters of administration with the will annexed to them. The application was made in accordance with the Non-Contentious Probate Rules 1954, rr. 51, 60. *Held*, the Non-Contentious Probate Rules were not well adapted to deal with such highly contentious matters. In the present case there had been numerous affidavits and an eleven-day hearing period. Much time and expense could have been saved at the outset, when it was apparent that the matter was contentious, if the applicants had particularized their circumstances and reasons and the registrar had directed that all further evidence should have been given orally before the judge. The application would accordingly be dismissed.

VAN HOORN v VAN HOORN (1978) Times, 30th November (Family Division: BALCOMBE J).

1300   —— —— —— fees

The Supreme Court (Non-contentious Probate) Fees (Amendment) Order 1978, S.I. 1978 No. 1298 (in force 2nd October 1978), amends the 1975 Order, 1975 Halsbury's Abr para. 1481 by substituting for the scale of charges in Fee No. 1 an ad valorem fee of £2.50 per £1,000 of the value of the estate, where it does not exceed £100,000 while raising from £1,000 to £2,000 the figure at which no fee is payable. Changes are also made in Fee Nos. 5, 6, 12 and 16.

1301   —— —— production of deed or other instrument—stamp duty

The following Practice Note ([1978] 1 All ER 1046) has been issued by the Family Division.

1. Where, for the purposes of applying for a grant of representation, it is necessary for the applicant to produce to the Principal or a District Registry an original deed or other instrument, it is the practice of the Registry to examine the instrument to ensure that it has been properly executed and duly stamped under the Stamp Act 1891 before proceeding with the application. Where there is any doubt whether the instrument is duly stamped, the applicant will be asked to present the instrument to the Controller of Stamps (Inland Revenue) for adjudication before the issue of the grant.

2. To avoid delay in the issue of the grant in such cases, the Commissioners of Inland Revenue have agreed that the applicant may, if so desired, submit the original instrument to the Adjudication Section of the Office of the Controller of Stamps for preliminary noting, endorsement and return, provided that a written undertaking is at the time given to the Controller by a solicitor applying for the grant of representation that he will, on or immediately after the issue of the grant, resubmit the original instrument to the Controller for formal adjudication and pay the stamp duty (if any) to which the instrument is adjudged liable.

3. In every case on the application for a grant, the original instrument (after inspection) will be returned as soon as practicable to the applicant, or his solicitor, by the probate registry. Practitioners are reminded, however, that where the application is for a grant to an assignee or assignees under r. 22 of the Non-

Contentious Probate Rules 1954, a copy of the original instrument of assignment must be lodged in the registry (see r. 22 (3)).

1302   Proceedings against estate—appointment of Official Solicitor to represent estate—judgment obtained after lapse of appointment

An Iranian diplomat died indebted to the plaintiff bank. No grant of probate or letters of administration had been obtained within the jurisdiction and the bank did not know whether personal representatives had been appointed in any other country. The bank commenced an action against the estate by issuing a specially indorsed writ in which the defendants were described as the personal representatives of the deceased. At the bank's request the Official Solicitor consented to being appointed to represent the estate for the purpose only of accepting service of the writ. He refused consent to an appointment which extended to his taking any further step in the proceedings. The court made an order in those terms. The writ was served on the Official Solicitor and his acceptance indorsed. The bank then obtained entry of judgment in default of appearance and sought to enforce that judgment. *Held*, proceedings against the estate of a deceased person were actions in personam. As with all such actions there had to be a natural or artificial person who was recognised by law as a defendant against whom steps in the action could be taken. The appointment of the Official Solicitor to act as defendant was strictly limited and lapsed as soon as he had accepted service of the writ. No one else had been appointed to take his place and accordingly the judgment was a nullity.

BANK MELLI, IRAN V PERSONAL REPRESENTATIVE OF AMIRTEYMOUR [1978] 3 All ER 637 (Court of Appeal: LORD DIPLOCK, VISCOUNT DILHORNE and LORD SCARMAN).

EXPLOSIVES

Halsbury's Laws of England (4th Edn.), Vol. 18, paras. 1–200

1303   Explosives Acts—restrictions on imports of explosives—acetylene

The Compressed Acetylene (Importation) Regulations 1978, S.I. 1978 No. 1723 (in force on 6th December 1978), makes acetylene at a pressure between 0·62 bar and 18·0 bar subject to the provisions of the Explosives Act 1875, s. 40 (9), which prohibits the import of explosives into the United Kingdom except under licence issued by the Health and Safety Executive Order in Council No. 30 S.R. & O. 1937 No. 54 is modified accordingly.

1304   Licensing of stores—fees

The Explosives (Licensing of Stores) Variation of Fees Regulations 1978, S.I. 1978 No. 270 (in force on 3rd April 1978), amend the Explosives Act 1875, ss. 15 and 18, by increasing the maximum fees payable for a store licence and for the renewal of a store licence to £17.50 in both cases.

EXTRADITION AND FUGITIVE OFFENDERS

Halsbury's Laws of England (4th edn.), Vol. 18, paras. 201–295

1305   Drug offences—France

The France (Extradition) (Amendment) Order 1978, S.I. 1978 No. 455 (in force on 16th April 1978), extends the application of the Extradition Acts 1870 to 1935 in the case of France to include drug offences.

1306   Fugitive offender—application for habeas corpus—Irish warrant—reason for issue

In 1972 the applicant was convicted of a minor offence in the Republic of Ireland but he failed to appear for sentencing. In 1977 he was arrested in England under a warrant issued in Ireland for his return for sentencing. He brought an application for habeas corpus under the Backing of Warrants (Republic of Ireland) Act 1965, s. 1 (3), alleging that the warrant had actually been issued to secure his attendance as a witness in a murder trial. An English court had refused to back an earlier warrant issued for that purpose. *Held*, there was no evidence that the Irish court had previously made any significant attempt to sentence the applicant for the 1972 offence. It appeared that the true reason for the issue of the 1977 warrant was to secure his attendance at the murder trial, and accordingly the English court could not back the warrant.

RE LAWLOR (1978) 66 Cr App Rep 75 (Queen's Bench Division: LORD WIDGERY CJ, MICHAEL DAVIES and GOFF JJ).

1307   —— —— nature of offence

The applicant, who had been convicted in Israel of assault occasioning bodily harm, broke bail pending sentence and became a fugitive offender. At the Moroccan embassy in Paris he gave information about military installations in Israel, and obtained a passport to travel to the United Kingdom where he was arrested in extradition proceedings requested by the Government of Israel. The extradition request was accompanied only by the judgment of conviction in Israel, and not by judgment of sentence and a statement of how much of the sentence had been carried out, as required by the Israel (Extradition) Order 1960, art. 8. The applicant sought a writ of habeas corpus, claiming that, because of the failure to comply with the Order, the request was bad in law. He also claimed that his admitted political offence at the Moroccan embassy in Paris exempted him from extradition under the Extradition Act 1870, s. 3 (1). *Held*, an instrument should be construed so as to give effect to it, rather than to create an absurdity. The requirement of judgment of sentence in art. 8 applied only where sentence had been passed. On the political offence issue, acts of international espionage were not offences of a political character for the purposes of the Extradition Acts. In any case, the extradition request was not made in respect of the political offence. The application would be dismissed.

R v GOVERNOR OF PENTONVILLE PRISON, EX PARTE REBOTT [1978] LS Gaz R 43 Court of Appeal: LORD WIDGERY CJ, CUMMING-BRUCE LJ and PARK J).

1308   —— —— second application

A businessman who was to have been extradited to Singapore after his application for habeas corpus had been dismissed by the House of Lords has been granted leave to make a second application for habeas corpus. In his first application he applied to be discharged from custody under Fugitive Offenders Act 1967, s. 8 (3) (a) and (c) alleging the trivial nature of the offences and that the Singapore government was acting in bad faith in bringing the charges. The new application will rely on s. 8 (3) (b) that by reason of the passage of time since the applicant was alleged to have committed the offences it would be unjust or oppressive to return him.

EX PARTE TARLING (1978) Times, 6th June (Queen's Bench Division: LORD WIDGERY CJ, TALBOT and WATKINS JJ).

1309   —— —— whether passage of time a bar to extradition

After a shooting in Cyprus in 1973, a warrant was issued for the arrest of the appellant, who was a member of a Cypriot political organisation. He went into hiding until July 1974, when the government was overthrown. He moved about freely and openly until September 1974, when he emigrated to England with the permission of the government then in power. He returned for a short time in 1975 and no attempt was made to arrest him by the former government, which had returned to power. In October 1975 the government changed its policy and decided to prosecute political opponents. As a result, in February 1976 extradition proceedings were commenced in Cyprus against the appellant. He was arrested in England in March 1977 and in the course of the extradition hearing he gave evidence that if he was tried in Cyprus he would rely on an alibi supported by a witness who had emigrated to England in 1975. The witness was no longer compellable and stated that he was unwilling to return to Cyprus. The appellant was committed to prison and applied for a writ of habeas corpus. In December 1977 the Divisional Court refused his application and he appealed, contending that he was entitled to be discharged under the Fugitive Offenders Act 1967, s. 8 (3) (b) because by reason of the passage of time since he was alleged to have committed the offence it would, having regard to all the circumstances, be unjust or oppressive to return him to Cyprus. *Held*, LORD KEITH OF KINKEL dissenting, having regard to all the circumstances it would be unjust or oppressive to return the appellant to Cyprus. It would be unjust because the witness was no longer compellable and his absence would detract significantly from the fairness of the trial. It would be oppressive because between July 1974 and his arrest in March 1977 the appellant was justified in believing that the Cyprus government had no intention of prosecuting him. The appeal would be allowed.

The court considered that delay in the commencement of extradition proceedings brought about by the accused by fleeing the country or going into hiding could not, save in exceptional circumstances, be relied on as a ground for holding it unjust or oppressive to return him.

KAKIS v GOVERNMENT OF THE REPUBLIC OF CYPRUS [1978] 2 All ER 634 (House of Lords: LORD DIPLOCK, LORD EDMUND-DAVIES, LORD RUSSELL OF KILLOWEN, LORD KEITH OF KINKEL and LORD SCARMAN). Decision of the Divisional Court of the Queen's Bench Division sub nom *R v Governor of Pentonville Prison, ex parte Kakis* (1977) Times, 17th December, 1977 Halsbury's Abr para. 1275 reversed.

1310   —— —— whether prima facie case against offender

A business man applied for a writ of habeas corpus to secure his release from prison. He had been committed to prison pending the making of an extradition order to Singapore, where he was to face charges arising out of his alleged fraud and dishonesty in the financial operations of a group of companies in the Far East. In considering whether under the Fugitive Offenders Act 1967 a prima facie case had been made out against him on the equivalent offences in English law, the Divisional Court found no prima facie case to support the charges of conspiracy to steal and defraud, or the first charge relating to offences under the Prevention of Fraud (Investments) Act 1958, s. 13. They did find a prima facie case to support the charges of failure to comply with certain provisions of the Singapore Companies Acts and the second charge of offences against the 1958 Act, s. 13. The applicant was granted leave to appeal against the finding in respect of the second charge concerning offences under s. 13, and the Singapore Government was granted leave to appeal against the findings in respect of the charges of conspiracy and the first charge under s. 13. On appeal, *held*, VISCOUNT DILHORNE and LORD EDMUND-DAVIES dissenting, (i) on the appeal by the Singapore Government, as to the charges relating to conspiracy, although the applicant's actions might amount to breach of fiduciary duty, exorbitant profit making and failure to comply with the law on company accounts, they did not amount to theft and fraud and the conclusion of the Divisional Court that no case of theft or fraud had been made out would be upheld.

In relation to the first charge of offences under s. 13, the facts were that certain profits of a company had failed to appear in the accounts. The applicant was in charge of the accounts, but the Divisional Court's finding that he had had no dishonest intention was correct. The appeal would be dismissed.

(ii) On the appeal by the applicant, since the Divisional Court found no sufficient evidence of dishonesty to support the first charge under s. 13, the second charge, which rested substantially on the same dishonesty, could not survive. The appeal on that would be allowed.

TARLING v GOVERNMENT OF THE REPUBLIC OF SINGAPORE (1978) Times, 20th April (House of Lords: LORD WILBERFORCE, VISCOUNT DILHORNE, LORD SALMON, LORD EDMUND-DAVIES and LORD KEITH OF KINKEL). Decision of the Divisional Court of the Queen's Bench Division (1977) Times, 30th July sub nom *R v Governor of Pentonville Prison, ex parte Tarling*, 1977 Halsbury's Abr para. 1271 affirmed in part and reversed in part.

Article: Law Lords draw boundary line, Justinian: Financial Times, 24th April 1978.

1311   —— designated Commonwealth countries

The Fugitive Offenders (Designated Commonwealth Countries) Order 1978, S.I. 1978 No. 1905 (in force on 24th January 1979), enables any country within the Commonwealth to be designated by Order in Council for the purposes of the Fugitive Offenders Act 1967, s. 1. The Commonwealth of Dominica, the Solomon Islands and Tuvalu for such purposes.

1312   —— extradition—application of evidential rules of practice

The applicant, having been committed to prison by the magistrate following extradition proceedings instituted by the Australian Government, applied to the Divisional Court for a writ of habeas corpus. He claimed that the magistrate had been wrong in admitting depositions from Australia made by witnesses who had refreshed their memories from statements made several weeks after the alleged offence. *Held*, rules connected with the refreshing of the memories of witnesses such as the requirement of contemporaneity were merely rules of practice which did not have to be followed in extradition proceedings. They should be distinguished from evidentiary rules of law which magistrates were obliged to apply in all cases. The depositions had therefore been rightly admitted and the application would be dismissed.

RE MILLER (1978) Times, 25th October (Queen's Bench Division: LORD WIDGERY CJ, WIEN and SMITH JJ).

1313   —— —— Israel

The Israel (Extradition) (Amendment) Order 1978, S.I. 1978 No. 1623 (in force on 14th December 1978), amends the Israel (Extradition) Order 1960, so as to reserve the right of the requested Government not to extradite its nationals in accordance with the Agreement for the reciprocal extradition of criminals between the United Kingdom and Israel.

1314   —— —— Germany

The Federal Republic of Germany (Extradition) (Amendment) Order 1978, S.I. 1978 No. 1403 (in force on 3rd October 1978), applies the Extradition Acts 1870 to 1935 in the case of the Federal Republic of Germany and Land Berlin (West Berlin) in accordance with the Treaty between the United Kingdom and Germany for the Mutual Surrender of Fugitive Criminals, signed at London on 14th May 1872, as reapplied, with amendments, by the Agreement for the Extradition of Fugitive Criminals concluded at Bonn on 23rd February 1960, and was further amended by Notes exchanged at London on 25th and 27th September 1978.

1315   —— —— Spain

The Spain (Extradition) (Revocation) Order 1978, S.I. 1978 No. 1523 (in force on 22nd November 1978), revokes the Orders in Council, dated 27th November 1878 and 28th May 1889, which applied the Extradition Acts 1870 and 1873 in the case of Spain, following the termination on 13th October 1978 of the Treaty for the Mutual Surrender of Fugitive Criminals between the United Kingdom and Spain.

1316   Genocide—specified states

The Extradition (Genocide) (Amendment) Order 1978, S.I. 1978 No. 782 (in force on 29th June 1978) adds Austria to the states with which the United Kingdom has extradition treaties and which are Contracting Parties to the Convention on the Prevention and Punishment of the Crime of Genocide and thereby applies the

Extradition Acts 1870 to 1935 as amended by the Genocide Act 1969 to the offence of genocide with respect to that State.

1317 The Extradition (Genocide) (Amendment No. 2) Order 1978, S.I. 1978 No. 1886 (in force on 25th January 1979), deletes the entry relating to Spain from the Extradition (Genocide) Order 1970, Sch. 2. The Order also amends Sch. 3 to the 1970 Order so as to omit the entries for those British possessions which have attained independence.

1318 **Hijacking—specified states**

The Extradition (Hijacking) (Amendment) Order 1978, S.I. 1978 No. 1887 (in force on 25th January 1979), deletes the entry for Spain from the Extradition (Hijacking) Order 1971, Sch. 2, and adds it to Sch. 3, Part I. The order further amends the 1971 Order by adding the names of specified foreign states which have become parties to the Convention for the Suppression of the Unlawful Seizure of Aircraft, and by omitting the entries for those territories which have attained independence.

1319 **Internationally Protected Persons Act 1978**

See para. 1411.

1320 **Protection of aircraft—specified states**

The Extradition (Protection of Aircraft) (Amendment) Order 1978, S.I. 1978 No. 1888 (in force on 25th January 1979), deletes the entry for Spain from the Extradition (Protection of Aircraft) Order 1973, Sch. 2 and adds it to Sch. 3, Part I. This Order further amends the 1973 Order by adding the names of specified foreign states which have become parties to the Convention for the Suppression of Unlawful Acts against the Safety of Civil Aviation. It also amends Sch. 4 of the 1973 Order in respect of Seychelles and Gilbert and Ellice Islands Colony.

1321 **Suppression of Terrorism Act 1978**

The main purpose of the Suppression of Terrorism Act 1978 was to enable the United Kingdom to ratify the European Convention on the Suppression of Terrorism, which was opened for signature on 27th January 1977 (Cmnd. 7031). The Act facilitates extradition from the United Kingdom to convention countries by precluding the offender from claiming that certain offences are of a political character, provides for safeguards in respect thereof and amends the legislation affected. The Act received the royal assent on 30th June 1978 and came into force on 21st August 1978.

By section 1 certain acts committed outside the United Kingdom which would constitute the offences listed in Schedule 1 are not to be regarded as offences of a political character, for which extradition is not permitted, for the purposes of extradition to convention countries under the Extradition Act 1870, the Fugitive Offenders Act 1967 and the Backing of Warrants (Republic of Ireland) Act 1965. There is corresponding provision for the taking of evidence in the United Kingdom under the Extradition Act 1873 and the Evidence (Proceedings in Other Jurisdictions) Act 1975 for use in criminal proceedings in convention countries and in certain circumstances the Republic of Ireland.

Sections 2 and 3 amend the relevant legislation to provide safeguards in respect of Schedule 1 offences for those fugitives who, if returned, might suffer on account of their race, religion, nationality or political opinions and to make extraditable any offence under the Explosive Substances Act 1883 and any indictable offence under the Firearms Act 1968.

Section 4 enables the United Kingdom courts to exercise jurisdiction in respect of certain offences committed outside the United Kingdom and section 5 empowers the Secretary of State to apply certain provisions of the Act to certain categories of states as if they were convention countries.

Section 6, which applies only to Northern Ireland, amends the Criminal Jurisdiction Act 1975 so as to extend the circumstances in which the operation of an order for the return to the Republic of Ireland, for trial, of a person accused of an extra-territorial offence is postponed thus bringing it into line with the corresponding Irish provision.

Section 7 provides for the extension of the Act to certain islands and territories, section 8 deals with interpretation and the making of orders by the Secretary of State and section 9 gives the short title and provides for repeals and commencement.

1322 —— application of Extradition Acts to specified states

The Extradition (Suppression of Terrorism) Order 1978, S.I. 1978 No. 1106 (in force on 25th October 1978), applies the Extradition Acts 1870 to 1935 as amended in the case of the states party to the European Convention on the Suppression of Terrorism (which was signed at Strasbourg on 27th January 1977) subject to and in accordance with the extradition treaties made with those states as supplemented by Articles 3 and 4 of the Convention which are set out in Schedule 1 of the Order. In particular the Order makes extraditable the offences mentioned in Articles 1 and 2 of the Convention in so far as they are not already extraditable.

1323 —— convention countries

The Suppression of Terrorism Act 1978 (Designation of Countries) Order 1978, S.I. 1978 No. 1245 (in force on 25th October 1978), designates Austria, Denmark, the Federal Republic of Germany and West Berlin and Sweden as parties to the European Convention on the Suppression of Terrorism so that they become convention countries within the meaning of the Suppression of Terrorism Act 1978, para. 1321.

1324 Tokyo Convention—specified states

The Extradition (Tokyo Convention) (Amendment) Order 1978, S.I. 1978 No. 1889 (in force on 25th January 1979), applies the Extradition Acts 1870 to 1932, as amended by the Tokyo Convention Act 1967, to offences committed on board aircraft in flight registered in Peru and removes Spain from the list of states to which the Acts apply. It also removes Tuvalu from the list of territories to which the application of the Tokyo Convention has been extended.

1325 Treaties—France

The treaty with France dated 14th August 1876 has been amended; see Exchange of Notes, TS 62 (1978); Cmnd. 7241.

FAMILY ARRANGEMENTS, UNDUE INFLUENCE AND VOIDABLE CONVEYANCES

Halsbury's Laws of England (4th edn.), Vol. 18, paras. 301–400

1326 Transfer of property—transfer of wife's interest in land to husband—failure to take independent advice—whether transaction fair, just and reasonable

After the dissolution of the parties' marriage, the plaintiff executed a deed of release and conveyed to her husband her joint interest in the matrimonial home. The husband subsequently sold the home. The plaintiff claimed a half share in the proceeds of sale, contending that the deed of release was of no effect against them. *Held*, for the plaintiff to succeed she had to show that she was poor and ignorant, that the disposal was at an undervalue and that she had not had independent advice. As a telephonist she was far from well-off, and she clearly had no conveyancing knowledge; the only consideration for her giving up her interest was release from liability under a mortgage on the property, under which some borrowed capital had been repaid. She had not received any sum in recognition of the capital sum repaid. There was no hint of her ever having taken independent advice; if she had she would almost certainly have acted differently. As she satisfied the three requirements, the action would succeed and the transaction would be set aside.

CRESSWELL v POTTER (NOTE) (1968) [1978] 1 WLR 255 (Chancery Division: MEGARRY J).

1327 —————— wife's financial entitlement

A wife left the matrimonial home to live with another man. She subsequently conveyed her half-interest in the former matrimonial home to her husband without taking advice. Following her divorce, she applied under the Matrimonial Causes Act 1973, s. 23 for a lump sum from her ex-husband and for a property transfer order relating to the home. *Held*, even if the transfer were valid, the court could ignore its effect as it had a discretionary power to make any order that would produce a just result. That power was contained in ss. 24, 25 of the 1973 Act. Under the circumstances, the wife should receive a lump sum equivalent to half the value of the home at the date she left it. It would be quite unfair to order the husband to sell the house to do this; the sum envisaged could be raised by way of a further mortgage.

The court considered it essential that a party in a position such as the wife's be encouraged to take independent advice before transferring her sole substantial asset. The courts should not encourage transactions made between parties of unequal bargaining power where the inequality was the result of emotional strain felt by one of them.

BACKHOUSE v BACKHOUSE [1978] 1 All ER 1158 (Family Division: BALCOMBE J). *Cresswell v Potter (Note)* [1978] 1 WLR 255, see para. 1326 considered.

For earlier summary of this case, sub nom *B v B*, see 1977 Halsbury's Abr para. 1284.

FIREARMS

Halsbury's Laws of England (4th edn.), Vol. 11, paras. 875–898

1328 Article

Firearms Law, W. T. West: 122 Sol Jo 753.

1329 Fees

The Firearms (Variation of Fees) Order 1978, S.I. 1978 No. 267 (in force on 1st April 1978), increases the fees for firearm certificates and shot gun certificates and for the registration of firearms dealers and the new registration certificates issued annually to firearms dealers. The Order extends only to England and Wales.

1330 Gun Barrel Proof Act 1978

See para. 2856.

1331 Shot-gun certificate—applicant with previous firearms conviction—exercise of discretion by Chief Officer of Police

The applicant, a Chief Officer of Police, considered a renewal application for a shot gun certificate from a person who had previously been convicted of armed poaching. The applicant carried out his normal policy of refusing to renew a certificate where the owner of the gun had a previous conviction involving guns. The Crown Court quashed the applicant's refusal to renew the certificate. On appeal, *held*, to be lawful the applicant's policy had to admit of individual consideration of every case. The policy was punitive. The punishment for poaching, and fitness to hold a shot-gun certificate were two different matters. The certificate would be granted.

R v WAKEFIELD CROWN COURT, EX PARTE OLDFIELD [1978] Crim LR 164 (Queen's Bench Division: LORD WIDGERY CJ, CUMMING-BRUCE LJ and PARK J).

FIRE SERVICES

1332   Appointments and promotions

The Fire Services (Appointments and Promotion) Regulations 1978, S.I. 1978 No. 436 (in force 1st June 1978), consolidate with amendments and revoke the following orders: S.I. 1965 No. 577; S.I. 1967 No. 1689; S.I. 1968 No. 614; S.I. 1970 No. 102; S.I. 1972 No. 932; S.I. 1976 No. 2017, 1976 Halsbury's Abr para. 1203.

The principal changes are in the specifications of the examinations which qualify for promotion to leading fireman, sub-officer and station officer and the transfer to the Fire Service Central Examinations Board of reponsibility for the examinations previously the responsibility of individual fire authorities.

1333   Pensions

See paras. 2089–2091.

FISHERIES

Halsbury's Laws of England (4th Edn.), Vol. 18, paras. 601–942

1334   Common organisation of fisheries—conservation of resources— incompatibility of national measures

By an EEC Council Resolution member states were allowed to adopt appropriate interim measures pending the adoption of common regulations for the protection of fishing resources. The Irish government had introduced measures prohibiting fishing boats of more than a certain size from fishing in Irish waters. The Commission brought an action for a declaration that Ireland had introduced discriminatory measures and accordingly had failed to fulfil its obligations under the Treaty. In further proceedings a number of Dutch trawler captains, who were prosecuted for breach of the Irish fishing measures, claimed that the Irish measures were incompatible with Community law. The question in issue was whether the Irish measures were genuine conservation measures or whether they were in contravention of the non-discrimination rule contained in EEC Treaty, art. 7, and EEC Council Regulation 101/76, which provides for equality of access to fishing grounds among Community fishermen. *Held*, although the Irish measures were based on apparently objective considerations such as size and power of boats, they discriminated against other member states. The Irish fishing fleet did not contain boats over the specified size whereas the measures would have the effect of excluding boats from other countries. As the Irish measures were contrary to Community law the conviction of the Dutch captains was also contrary to that law. It was not necessary to consider whether the Irish regulations were genuine conservation measures as they had already been found discriminatory.

Case 61/77: RE SEA FISHERY RESTRICTIONS: EC COMMISSION v IRELAND [1978] 2 CMLR 466 (European Court of Justice).

1335

The masters of ten Dutch trawlers were prosecuted for fishing in Irish waters within the limits laid down by two orders made to conserve fish stocks. Questions were referred to the European Court of Justice (i) as to whether Articles 102 and 103 of the Treaty of Accession precluded member states from making conservation orders in respect of national maritime waters, (ii) as to whether Article 7 of the Treaty of Rome and Articles 100 and 101 of the Treaty of Accession precluded Ireland from making orders which discriminated against other member states, and (iii) as to whether a conviction in the Irish courts would be incompatible with Community law. *Held,* (i) member states could make interim conservation orders in respect of national maritime waters in so far as they were compatible with Community law. (ii) As the orders favoured Irish fishermen over those of other member states they were discriminatory and were precluded by Article 7 of the Treaty of Rome and Articles 100 and 101 of the Treaty of Accession. (iii) Where a national law had been held to be contrary to Community law a conviction in proceedings under that law would be incompatible with Community law.

Case 88/77: MINISTER FOR FISHERIES v C. A. SCHONENBERG [1978] 2 CMLR 519 (European Court of Justice).

1336   Diseases of fish

The Diseases of Fish Order 1978, S.I. 1978 No. 1022 (in force on 15th August 1978), extends the provisions of the Diseases of Fish Act 1937 to bacterial kidney disease. This disease affects fish of the salmon family.

1337   Fishery limits—fishing boats—designated countries

The Fishing Boats (Faroe Islands) Designation Order, S.I. 1978 No. 191 (in force on 11th February 1978), designates the Faroe Islands as a country whose registered fishing boats may fish in the areas specified in the order for sea fish specified in relation to those areas. The order expired on 28th February 1978.

1338   The Fishing Boats (Faroe Islands) Designation (No. 2) Order 1978, S.I. 1978 No. 288 (in force on 3rd March 1978), designates the Faroe Islands as a country whose registered fishing boats may fish in the areas specified in the order for sea fish specified in relation to those areas. This order, due to expire on 1st April 1978, was extended until 1st June 1978 by S.I. 1978 No. 490 and to 1st August 1978 by S.I. 1978 No. 767.

1339   The Fishing Boats (Faroe Islands) Designation (No. 3) Order 1978, S.I. 1978 No. 1168 (in force on 9th August 1978), designates the Faroe Islands as a country whose registered boats may fish in the areas specified in the order for sea fish specified in relation to those areas. This order expired on 1st January 1979.

1340   The Fishing Boats (Faroe Islands) Designation (No. 3) (Variation) Order 1978, S.I. 1978 No. 1650 (in force on 21st November 1978) amends the Fishing Boats (Faroe Islands) Designation (No. 3) Order 1978 by permitting Faroese boats to fish for Norway pout and sprat in part of ICES area VIA.

1341   The Fishing Boats (Specified Countries) Designation (No. 3) (Variation) Order 1978, S.I. 1978 No. 772 (in force on 1st June 1978), extends the designated areas in which fishing boats registered in Sweden may fish and amends the descriptions of sea fish for which they may fish in those areas.

1342   The Fishing Boats (Specified Countries) Designation (No. 3) Order 1977 (Variation) (No. 2) Order 1978, S.I. 1978 No. 1651 (in force on 21st November 1978), further varies the Fishing Boats (specified countries) Designation (No. 3) Order 1977, 1977 Halsbury's Abr para. 1295, by adjusting the designated areas in which fishing boats registered in Spain and Sweden may fish, and amending the descriptions of sea fish for which they may fish in those areas.

1343   The Fishing Boats (Faroe islands) Designation (No. 4) Order 1978, S.I. 1978 No.

1950 (in force on 4th January 1979), designated the Faroe Islands as a country whose registered boats could fish in the areas specified in the order for sea fish specified in relation to those areas.   The Order expired on 28th February 1979.

1344   Fishing vessels—grants

The Fishing Vessels (Acquisition and Improvement) (Grants) (Variation) Scheme 1978, S.I. 1978 No. 1820 (in force on 9th December 1978), varies the Fishing Vessels (Acquisition and Improvement) (Grants) Scheme 1976, 1976 Halsbury's Abr para. 1222, by substituting 1st January 1980 as the date by which applications must be approved for the payment of grants under the 1976 scheme.

1345   —— safety provisions

The Fishing Vessels (Safety Provisions) (Amendment) Rules 1978, S.I. 1978 No. 1598 (in force on 17th December 1978), amend the Fishing Vessels (Safety Provisions) Rules 1975.   The requirement for all fishing vessels to have periodical inspections not less than 21 months and not more than 27 months after the issue of a fishing vessel certificate will continue to apply only to vessels to which Rule 1 (4) (a) (v) applies.   Other vessels will not require periodical inspection until after their fishing vessel certificates have been in force for 48 months and they have been satisfactorily surveyed and renewal certificates have been issued.

1346 The Fishing Vessels (Safety Provisions) (Amendment No. 2) Rules 1978, S.I. 1978 No. 1873 (in force on 1st February 1979), amend the Fishing Vessels (Safety Provisions) Rules 1975, 1975 Halsbury's Abr para. 1516, by prescribing requirements for lifebuoy marker smoke signals.   They also prescribe different requirements for line-throwing appliances, parachute distress rocket signals for lifeboats, liferafts and fishing vessels, hand-held distress flare signals for lifeboats and liferafts and buoyant smoke signals for lifeboats.

1347   Haddock—licensing

The Haddock (North Sea) Licensing Order 1978, S.I. 1978 No. 1285 (in force on 18th September 1978), prohibits fishing by British fishing boats registered in the United Kingdom for haddock in the North Sea except under licence.   Exempted from this prohibition is fishing by British fishing boats of registered length less than forty feet.   Enforcement powers are conferred on British sea fishery officers.

1348   —— prohibition

The Haddock (Restrictions on Landing) (Revocation) Order 1978, S.I. 1978 No. 1286 (in force on 11th September 1978), revokes the Haddock (Restrictions on Landing) Order 1977, 1977 Halsbury's Abr para. 1303.

1349 The Rockall Haddock (Restrictions on Landing) Order 1978, S.I. 1978 No. 1413 (in force on 9th October 1978), prohibits the landing in the United Kingdom of haddock caught in waters off Rockall by a British fishing boat.   Nothing in the provisions of the Order prevents the landing of any under-sized haddock which may be lawfully landed by virtue of an order made under the Sea Fish (Conservation) Act 1967, s. 1.   Enforcement powers are conferred on British sea fishery officers.

1350 The West Coast Haddock (Restrictions on Landing) Order 1978, S.I. 1978 No. 1287 (in force on 11th September 1978), prohibits the landing in the United Kingdom of haddock caught in waters off the West Coast of Scotland by a British fishing boat, but excepts from this prohibition the landing of specified quanties of haddock. Nothing in the provisions of the Order prevents the landing of under-sized haddock which may be lawfully landed by virtue of an order made under the Sea Fish (Conservation) Act 1967, s. 1.   Enforcement powers are conferred on British sea fishery officers.

1351   Herring—prohibition

The Irish Sea Herring (Prohibition of Fishing) Order 1978, S.I. 1978 No. 1374 (in force on 24th September 1978), prohibits fishing for herring in a specified sea area until 1st January 1979, and applies the powers of British sea-fishery officers for enforcement purposes.   The Order applies to all fishing boats, including foreign vessels.

1352   The West Coast Herring (Prohibition of Fishing) Order 1978, S.I. 1978 No. 930 (in force on 6th July 1978) prohibits fishing for herring in a specified area of sea within British fishery limits along the west coast of the British Isles.

1353   Mackerel—licensing

The Mackerel Licensing (Manx and Channel Islands Boats) Order 1978, S.I. 1978 No. 1537 (in force on 5th November 1978), prohibits fishing for mackerel by British fishing boats registered in the Isle of Man or the Channel Islands in specified areas unless the fishing is authorised by a licence.   There is excepted from the prohibition fishing by handline or by any British fishing boat having a registered length of less then forty feet.

1354   The Mackerel Licensing (Variation) Order 1978, S.I. 1978 No. 1538 (in force on 5th November 1978), varies the Mackerel Licensing Order 1977, 1977 Halsbury's Abr para. 1312, which prohibits fishing without a licence by British fishing boats registered in the United Kingdom for mackerel in specified areas.   The present order excepts from the prohibition fishing by handline or by British fishing boats whose registered length is less than forty feet.

1355   Nets—north-east Atlantic

The Fishing Nets (North-East Atlantic) (Variation) Order 1978, S.I. 1978 No. 946 (in force on 11th July 1978), amends the Fishing Nets (North-East Atlantic) Order 1977, 1977 Halsbury's Abr para. 1313 in those cases where a by-catch limit is fixed for fishing with small mesh nets.   It reduces the limit from twenty per cent of the catch to ten per cent, to be determined either on the basis of ten per cent of the total weight of the catch or by reference to a sample of at least 100 kilograms taken by a British Sea Fishery Officer.   It also provides that there shall be no limit where the net is being used for nephrops fishing in accordance with the order and makes minor amendments to the provisions relating to attachments which may be affixed to nets during fishing operations.

1356   Norway pout—prohibition

The Norway Pout (Prohibition of Fishing) (No. 3) (Variation) Order 1978, S.I. 1978 No. 1379 (in force on 1st October 1978), varies the Norway Pout (Prohibition of Fishing) (No. 3) Order 1977, 1977 Halsbury's Abr para. 1316, by redefining the area within which fishing for Norway Pout is prohibited.   During the months of October to March the area of sea in which such fishing is prohibited extends further eastwards than formerly defined and as defined for the other months of the year.

1357   Private fishery—fishery in tidal waters—origin—extent

The defendant and others removed mussels from mussel grounds.   The plaintiff sought a declaration that the defendant was not entitled to do so and that only the plaintiff, as lessee of the shell-fishing rights on the sea shore and in the sea bed belonging to the lord of the manor, was entitled to remove shellfish from the area. The declaration was granted and the defendant appealed.   *Held*, the first question was whether the present lord of the manor had a right of fishery.   Such a right existed by prescription, the enjoyment of the fishery resting on the presumption of a lost grant from before Magna Carta, there being nothing to show that the enjoyment of the fishery was modern.   The second question was the extent of the fishery.   The defendant's contention, that it was a rule of law that where a several fishery subsisted in tidal waters its seaward extent could not be further than the mean low water mark of the ordinary tides, was incorrect. Such a fishery could lawfully subsist in relation to areas seaward of mean low water mark of ordinary tides. In this case, the mussel grounds lay between low water mark at ordinary tides and low water mark at the spring tides. When the right of fishery was granted, it must have been granted where the right could be exploited. Thus the rights enjoyed by the plaintiff extended at least as far as mean low water mark of the spring tides. The defendant had taken mussels from the landward side of that line. The appeal would be dismissed and the declaration upheld.

LOOSE v CASTLETON (1978) 122 Sol Jo 487 (Court of Appeal; MEGAW, ORMROD and BRIDGE LJJ). *Malcolmson v O'Dea* (1863) 10 HL Cas 593 and *Gann v Free Fishers of Whitstable* (1865) 11 HL Cas 193 applied.

For previous proceedings, see para. 2198.

1358   Salmon and freshwater fisheries—taking salmon during close time—intention

A fisherman regularly staked out nets to catch plaice, cod, mullet and bass. During the weekly close time for salmon, he found a dead salmon in one net and a live one in another. He was charged under the Salmon and Freshwater Fisheries Act 1975, s. 19, with taking salmon during the weekly close time other than with a rod and line or putts and putchers. He was acquitted on the ground that he was fishing for other fish and had no intention of catching salmon. On appeal by the prosecutor, *held*, it was clear that an offence under s. 17 required an intention to catch salmon. The fisherman had not so intended and the appeal would be dismissed.

CAIN v CAMPBELL [1978] Crim LR 292 (Queen's Bench Division: LORD WIDGERY CJ, O'CONNOR and LLOYD JJ).

1359   Sea fishing—conservation—application to Channel Islands

The Sea Fish (Conservation) (Channel Islands Boats) Order 1978, S.I. 1978 No. 280 (in force on 8th March 1978) applies the Sea Fish (Conservation) Act 1967, s. 4 (as substituted by the Fishery Limits Act 1976, s. 3) which deals with the licensing of fishing boats, to British fishing boats registered in any of the Channel Islands as it applies in relation to British fishing boats registered in the United Kingdom.

1360   —— —— application to Isle of Man

The Sea Fish (Conservation) (Manx Boats) Order 1978, S.I. 1978 No. 281 (in force on 8th March 1978), applies the Sea Fish (Conservation) Act 1967, s. 4 (as substituted by the Fishery Limits Act 1976, s. 3) which deals with the licensing of fishing boats, to British fishing boats registered in the Isle of Man as it applies in relation to British fishing boats registered in the United Kingdom. The previous order, S.I. 1973 No. 1888 is revoked.

1361   —— industry—loans and grants—time limits

The Sea Fish Industry Act 1970 (Relaxation of Time Limits) Order 1978, S.I. 1978 No. 1822 (in force on 9th December 1978), relaxes time limits contained in certain provisions of the Sea Fish Industry Act 1970.

1362 The Sea Fishing (Specified Foreign Boats) Licensing (No. 3) Order 1977 (Variation) Order 1978, S.I. 1978 No. 1652 (in force on 21st November 1978), further varies the Sea Fishing (Specified Foreign Boats) Licensing (No. 3) Order 1977, 1977 Halsbury's Abr para. 1322 by bringing fishing boats registered in Sweden and the Faroe Islands within its terms and altering existing arrangements in relation to Spanish vessels.

1363   —— local fisheries districts

The Eastern Sea Fisheries District (Variation) Order 1978, S.I. 1978 No. 438 (in force 1st April 1978), enlarges the Eastern Sea Fisheries District created in 1893 by order of the Board of Trade under the Sea Fisheries Regulations Act 1888. The Order also varies the constitution of the Eastern Local Fisheries Committee.

1364   Seals—conservation

The Convention for the Conservation of Antarctic Seals entered into force on 11th March 1978 under art. 13 following the deposit of the seventh instrument of ratification or acceptance. See Convention for the Conservation of Antarctic Seals, Cmnd. 7209, Treaty Series No. 45 (1978).

1365   Southern sea fisheries district—variation

The Southern Sea Fisheries District (Variation) Order 1978, S.I. 1978 No. 1715 (in force on 1st December 1978) varies the description of the limits of the Southern Sea Fisheries District. The Order prescribes lines at or near the mouths of certain rivers or streams flowing into the sea or any estuary within the limits of the district above which the district is not to extend into such river or stream. In such areas the South West Water Authority, the Southern Water Authority and the Wessex Water Authority shall, within their respective areas, have the powers of a local fisheries committee.

1366   White Fish Authority—grants

The White Fish Authority (Research and Development Grants) Order 1978, S.I. 1978 No. 1821 (in force on 9th December 1978), raises to £6 million the limit imposed by the Sea Fish Industry Act 1970 in relation to the aggregate amount of any grants payable to the White Fish Authority for the purposes of research or experiment or in providing plants for making white fish or making ice.

FOOD, DAIRIES AND SLAUGHTERHOUSES

Halsbury's Laws of England (4th edn.), Vol. 18, paras. 1001–1351

1367   Antioxidant in food

The Antioxidants in Food Regulations 1978, S.I. 1978 No. 105 (in force on 28th February 1978), re-enacts with amendments the Antioxidant in Food Regulations 1974, 1974 Halsbury's Abr para. 1427. The Regulations substitute a revised definition of "dairy product"; extend the list of specified foods which may contain permitted antioxidants within specified maximum levels of use; permit the presence of diphenylamine on apples and pears at specified levels; and permit the presence in food for babies and children of BHA and BHT.

1368   Bread—prices

The Bread Prices (No. 2) Order 1976 (Amendment) (No. 5) Order 1978, S.I. 1978 No. 516 (in force on 3rd April 1978), varies the Bread Prices (No. 2) Order 1976, 1976 Halsbury's Abr para. 1242, by increasing the maximum retail price of most bread loaves of 28 oz. or less.

This Order has been revoked; see para. 1370.

1369

The Bread Prices (No. 2) Order 1976 (Amendment) (No. 6) Order 1978, S.I. 1978 No. 545 (in force on 2nd May 1978), varies the Bread Prices (No. 2) Order 1976, 1976 Halsbury's Abr para. 1242, as varied, by providing that the Order shall apply to bread loaves made for sale in metric quantities as it applies to bread loaves made for sale in the corresponding imperial quantities.

1370

The Bread Prices (No. 2) Order 1976 (Amendment) (No. 7) Order 1978, S.I. 1978

No. 1790 (in force on 11th December 1978), varies the Bread Prices (No. 2) Order 1976, 1976 Halsbury's Abr para. 1242, by increasing the maximum retail price of most bread loaves of 800g or less. The Bread Prices (No. 2) Order 1976 (Amendment) (No. 5) Order 1978, para. 1368 is revoked.

1371   Butter—prices

The Butter Prices Order 1978, S.I. 1978 No. 97 (in force on 16th February 1978), revokes the Butter Prices Order 1977, 1977 Halsbury's Abr para. 1325, and reproduces with modifications the provisions of that Order which regulated the maximum prices which may be charged for the sale of butter subsidised in pursuance of the EEC butter subsidy regulation.

1372   The Butter Prices (Amendment) Order 1978, S.I. 1978 No. 835 (in force on 1st July 1978), varies the Butter Prices Order 1978, see para. 1371, by increasing the maximum retail prices of butter.

1373   The Concentrated Butter Prices Order 1978, S.I. 1978 No. 971 (in force on 14th August 1978), regulates the maximum price which may be charged for the sale by retail of concentrated butter produced from butter sold from intervention stocks at a reduced price under the provisions of EEC Commission Regulation No. 649/78. The Order also requires retailers selling such concentrated butter to keep available information about the maximum prices.

1374   Cheese—prices

The Price Marking (Cheese) (Amendment) Order 1978, S.I. 1978 No. 133 (in force on 1st March 1978), amends the Price Marking (Cheese) Order 1977, 1977 Halsbury's Abr para. 1327, by providing that the obligation to indicate the unit price for pre-packed cheese applies only where the weight of the cheese is marked on the container, by exempting from the requirement to indicate the unit price certain natural cheese pre-packed in specified quantities and by postponing until 1st July 1978 the obligation to indicate the unit price for natural cheese pre-packed in a predetermined fixed weight pattern.

1375   The Cheese Prices Orders (Revocation) Order 1978, S.I. 1978 No. 98 (in force on 16th February 1978), revokes those provisions of the Cheese Prices Order 1976, 1976 Halsbury's Abr para. 1245, remaining unrevoked. It also revokes the Cheese Prices (Amendment) Order 1977, 1977 Halsbury's Abr para. 1326.

1376   Coffee and chicory extracts—metric quantities

See para. 3102.

1377   Colouring matter

The Colouring Matter in Food (Amendment) Regulations 1978, S.I. 1978 No. 1787 (in force on 1st January 1979), implement EEC Council Directive 78/144. The Regulations further amend the Colouring Matter in Food Regulations 1973 by altering the list of colouring matters permitted in or on food.

1378   Composition and labelling—coffee and coffee products

The Coffee and Coffee Products Regulations 1978, S.I. 1978 No. 1420 (regs. 1, 2 and 16 in force on 24th October 1978, remainder in force on 12th July 1980), implement Council Directive No. 77/436/EEC on the approximation of laws of member states relating to coffee extracts and chicory extracts. The regulations prescribe definitions and reserved descriptions for certain coffee products and lay down certain requirements as to advertising and labelling. The Coffee and Coffee Product Regulations 1967, S.I. 1967 No. 1865 are revoked.

1379   Labelling

The Labelling of Food (Amendment) Regulations 1978, S.I. 1978 No. 646 (in force on 30th May 1978, except for reg. 3 which comes into force on 1st April 1980), further amend the Labelling of Food Regulations 1970, as amended. The Regulations specify a new appropriate designation ("Pacific Pilchard") for the Californian Pilchard, the Chilean Pilchard and the Japanese Pilchard, and a new appropriate designation ("South Atlantic Pilchard") for the South African Pilchard.

1380   Materials in contact with food

The Materials and Articles in Contact with Food Regulations 1978, S.I. 1978 No. 1927 (in force on 26th November 1979), implement EEC Council Directive 76/893, 1976 Halsbury's Abr para. 1254, on the approximation of the laws of member states relating to materials and articles intended to come into contact with foodstuffs. Materials and articles which are in their finished state and are intended to come into contact with food must be manufactured in accordance with good manufacturing practice; that is, they must not transfer their constituents to food in quantities which could endanger human health or cause food to deteriorate. Such materials and articles are required to be described as suitable for use with food, and other specified particulars must be provided. The manner of marketing at all stages of marketing is prescribed.

1381   Meat inspection—authorised officers

The Authorised Officers (Meat Inspection) Regulations 1978, S.I. 1978 No. 884 (in force on 7th July 1978), prescribe the qualifications to be held by an officer of a council authorised under the Food and Drugs Act 1955 to act in relation to the examination and seizure of meat. They revoke and re-enact the Authorised Officers (Meat Inspection) Regulations 1974, 1974 Halsbury's Abr para. 1437, and prescribe one additional alternative qualification, that of a Certificate of Registration of the Environmental Health Officers Registration Board.

1382   Milk—prices

The Milk (Great Britain) (Amendment) Order 1978, S.I. 1978 No. 469 (in force on 1st April 1978), prescribed revised maximum prices for the sale in Great Britain of raw milk for heat treatment.
This Order has been revoked; see para. 1383.

1383   The Milk (Great Britain) (Amendment) (No. 2) Order 1978, S.I. 1978 No. 1382 (in force on 1st October 1978), amended the Milk (Great Britain) Order 1977, 1977 Halsbury's Abr para. 1339, by providing that the additional charge for Channel Islands and South Devon Milk could be made at the rate of 2·904p per litre for the months April to September inclusive, and at the rate of 3·124p per litre for the months October to March inclusive. The Milk (Great Britain) (Amendment) Order 1978, para. 1382 was revoked.

1384   The Milk (Great Britain) (Amendment) (No. 3) Order 1978, S.I. 1978 No. 1498 (in force on 5th November 1978), amends the Milk (Great Britain) Order 1977, 1977 Halsbury's Abr para. 1339. The regulations increase the maximum prices for the sale in Great Britain of raw milk for heat treatment and raise the maximum retail prices of milk by 1p per pint with effect from 5th November 1978 in England and Wales and from 3rd December 1978 in Scotland. The Milk (Great Britain) (Amendment) (No. 2) Order, para. 1383 is revoked.

1385   The Milk (Northern Ireland) (Amendment) (No. 2) Order 1978, S.I. 1978 No. 1491 (in force on 1st November 1978), amends the Milk (Northern Ireland) Order 1977, 1977 Halsbury's Abr para. 1340. It increases the maximum price for the sale in Northern Ireland of raw milk for heat treatment by 2·76p per litre and raises the maximum retail price of milk in Northern Ireland by 1p per pint.

1386   Potatoes—imperial quantities

See para. 3107.

1387   Poultry—humane slaughter

The Slaughter of Poultry Act 1967 Extension Order 1978, S.I. 1978 No. 201 (in force on 1st March), extends the Slaughter of Poultry Act 1967 to the slaughter of guinea-fowl, ducks and geese. The Act makes provision for the humane slaughter, for the purposes of preparation for sale for human consumption, of turkeys or domestic fowls kept in captivity.

1388   Prices

The Food (Prohibition of Repricing) Order 1978, S.I. 1978 No. 1014 (in force on 14th August 1978), prohibits the repricing of items of food which have been displayed for retail sale marked with a price. An exception is made for the withdrawal of special and introductory offer prices.

1389

The Price Marking (Food) Order 1978, S.I. 1978 No. 738 (in force on 1st July 1978), requires the display of prices for the sale of food and drink for human consumption when an indication is given on any premises or at any place (whether by display or by the giving of any kind of notice), that it is or may be for sale there by retail. The Order does not affect food already covered by orders requiring the display of unit prices for particular foods.

1390   Welfare food

See SOCIAL WELFARE.

1391   Wine—pre-packaging and labelling

See para. 3113.

FOREIGN RELATIONS LAW

Halsbury's Laws of England (4th edn.), Vol. 18, paras. 1401–1907

1392   Articles

Rolimpex: A Sweet Solution to Legal Status, Max Lesser (legal status of East European Foreign Trade Organisations which function as both exporters of local products and importers of Western goods): 128 NLJ 591.

Sovereign Immunity Revisited, Malcolm Shaw (whether doctrine of sovereign immunity applies to all transactions entered into by a governmental entity or whether it is restricted): 128 NLJ 983.

Sovereign Immunity and Cement, Hugh C. Collins (*Trendtex Trading Corpn v Central Bank of Nigeria* [1977] QB 529, CA, 1977 Halsbury's Abr para. 1356): 122 Sol Jo 105.

The State Immunity Act 1978, Malcolm Shaw: 128 NLJ 1136.

State Immunity Act 1978, Rebecca M. M. Wallace: 122 Sol Jo 735.

1393   Consular conventions

The consular convention concluded with Poland on 23rd February 1967 has been revised and expanded by an amending protocol. The text of the consular convention as revised has been published as Cmnd. 7373 (TS 100 (1978)). The instruments of ratification having been exchanged, the protocol entered into force on 23rd September 1978.

1394   Consular fees

The Consular Fees Order 1978, S.I. 1978 No. 177 (in force on 6th March 1978), increases most of the consular fees and makes minor amendments to the services for which fees are charged. The Consular Fees Order 1977, 1977 Halsbury's Abr para. 463, is revoked.

1395   Consular officers—immunities and privileges

The Commonwealth Countries and Republic of Ireland (Immunities and Privileges) (Amendment) Order 1978, S.I. No. 780 (in force on 29th June 1978), corrects an error in the Commonwealth Countries and Republic of Ireland (Immunities and Privileges) (Amendment) Order 1977, 1977 Halsbury's Abr para. 1350 which accorded partial relief from general rates to the Hong Kong Liaison Offices.

1396   Consular relations—merchant shipping and civil aviation

The Consular Relations (Merchant Shipping and Civil Aviation) (Polish People's Republic) Order 1978, S.I. 1978 No. 275 (in force on a date to be notified in the London, Edinburgh and Belfast Gazettes), provides for the limiting of the jurisdiction of the United Kingdom Courts to entertain proceedings relating to the remuneration under any contract of service of the master, commander or any crew member of a ship or aircraft (other than ships of war and military aircraft) of the Polish People's Republic. The Order also provides for the limiting of the jurisdiction of the courts in relation to offences committed on board Polish merchant ships by the master or a member of the crew, and that the detention on board of a member of the crew for a disciplinary offence shall be lawful except in certain cases.

1397   —— reciprocal extension of privileges

The Consular Relations (Privileges and Immunities) (Polish People's Republic) Order 1978, S.I. 1978 No. 1028 (in force on a date notified in the London Gazette), made pursuant to the Consular Relations Act 1968, gives effect to the relevant provisions of the Consular Convention between the United Kingdom and the Polish People's Republic signed at London on 23rd February 1967 (Cmnd. 4790), as amended by the Protocol signed at London on 16th December 1976 (Cmnd. 6740) by according to consular posts of the Polish People's Republic and persons connected with them certain privileges and immunities additional to those accorded by the 1968 Act, Sch. 1.

1398   Consuls' powers—administration of estates—Estonia

The Administration of Estates by Consular Officers (Estonia) (Revocation) Order 1978, S.I. 1978 No. 779 (in force on 21st June 1978), revokes the Administration of Estates by Consular Officers (Estonia) Order in Council 1939.

1399   Fisheries conventions

The North-East Atlantic Fisheries Convention 1959 has been modified. See the *Procès-Verbal* concerning modifications to Article 7 (1) of the North-East Atlantic Fisheries Convention signed at London on 24th January 1959 (TS 67 (1978); Cmnd. 7260).

1400   Foreign Compensation Commission

The Foreign Compensation (Financial Provisions) Order 1978, S.I. 1978 No. 180 (in force on 20th March 1978), directs the Commission to pay into the Exchequer amounts in respect of the Commission's expenses.

1401   High seas—pollution from land based sources

The United Kingdom instrument of ratification of the Convention for the Prevention of Marine Pollution from Land-Based Sources was deposited on 6th

April 1978 and the convention entered into force on 6th May 1978. Subsequently the text of the convention was re-issued as TS 64 (1978); Cmnd. 7251.

1402   Internal waters—international convention

The Annex to the Convention on the Facilitation of International Maritime Traffic 1965 has been amended. The amendments entered into force on 31st July 1978; see TS 63 (1978); Cmnd. 7243.

1403   International Development Association

The International Development Association (Fifth Replenishment) Order 1978, S.I. 1978 No. 472 (in force on 8th November 1978), provides for the payment to the International Development Association of £705,944.83 as an additional subscription carrying voting rights and of £474,065,631.70 as an additional contribution not carrying voting rights. It also provides for the redemption of non-interest bearing and non-negotiable notes issued by the Minister of Overseas Development in payment of the additional subscription and contribution and for the payment of certain sums received from the Association into the Consolidated Fund.

1404   International   organisations—immunities   and   privileges— conferment

An agreement has been reached under which the International Rubber Group whose headquarters will be established in the United Kingdom will be recognised as enjoying legal personality and, subject to waiver, specific immunity from jurisdiction. Provision is also made for, inter alia, exemption from direct taxation and customs duties. (See Headquarters Agreement, Cmnd. 7211, Treaty Series No. 51 (1978)). An agreement has also been reached with the Commission of the European Communities setting out privileges in relation to indirect taxation and immigration procedures which have been granted to the Joint European Torus (JET); see Exchange of Letters constituting an Agreement with Euratom, Cmnd. 7255, Treaty Series No. 66 (1978). See also S.I. 1978 No. 181, para. 1406.

1405   The European Patent Organisation (Immunities and Privileges) Order 1978, S.I. 1978 No. 179 (in force on 10th February 1978), confers privileges on the European Patent Organisation, representatives of its members, officers of the European Patent Office and experts.

1406   The International Rubber Study Group (Immunities and Privileges) Order 1978, S.I. 1978 No. 181 (in force on a date to be notified in the London, Edinburgh and Belfast Gazettes), confers privileges and immunities on the International Rubber Study Group, its officers, representatives of its members, and experts serving on committees or employed on missions on its behalf.

1407   The European Space Agency (Immunities and Privileges) Order 1978, S.I. 1978 No. 1105 (in force on a date to be notified in the London Gazette), supersedes the European Space Research Organisation (Immunities and Privileges) Order 1974, 1974 Halsbury's Abr para. 1456, and the European Launcher Development Organisation (Immunities and Privileges) Order 1965, and confers privileges and immunities upon the European Space Agency representatives of its member states, its officers and experts. These privileges and immunities are conferred in accordance with the Convention for the Establishment of a European Space Agency, Annex I (Cmnd. 6272) opened for signature in Paris on 30th May 1975.

1408   The African Development Bank (Privileges) Order 1978, S.I. 1978 No. 1884 (in force on 10th January 1979) confers the legal capacities of a body corporate upon the African Development Bank and grants it certain taxation exemptions, as required by the Exchange of Notes between the Government of the United Kingdom and the African Development Bank.

1409   The International Lead and Zinc Study Group (Immunities and Privileges) Order
1978, S.I. 1978 No. 1893 (in a force on a date to be notified) confers privileges and
immunities upon the International Lead and Zinc Study Groups, representatives of
its members and its officers and servants. See further, Cmnd. 7343, para. 1410.

1410   Agreement has been reached between the government and the International Lead
and Zinc Study Group which is to have its headquarters in the United Kingdom.
The agreement provides for the group to have legal personality and for its premises
to enjoy inviolability.   It will further enjoy immunity from jurisdiction and
execution except (i) so far as waived, (ii) in relation to damage caused by a motor
vehicle, (iii) in respect of the enforcement of certain arbitration awards, and (iv) in
respect of the judicial attachment of wages etc. owed to group employees.   The
group is also exempt from direct taxes and customs duties. See the draft headquarters
Agreement between the Government of the United Kingdom and the International
Lead and Zinc Study Group; Cmnd. 7343.

1411   ## Internationally Protected Persons Act 1978
The Internationally Protected Persons Bill 1978 enables the United Kingdom to
ratify the Convention on the Prevention and Punishment of Crimes against
Internationally Protected Persons (Cmnd. 6176), which was signed at New York on
behalf of the United Kingdom on 13th December 1974.   The Act received the royal
assent on 30th June 1978 and comes into force on a day to be appointed.
Section 1 gives jurisdiction to the United Kingdom courts over specified serious
offences committed outside the United Kingdom in relation to protected persons.
It also creates the offences of threatening to commit any of the specified offences
anywhere in the world.   A protected person is defined as a Head of State or
Government, a Foreign Minister, or a representative of a State or international
organisation who is entitled under international law to special protection.   Section
2 specifies that the consent of the Attorney General must be obtained before
proceedings under s. 1 are instituted.   This section also adds offences to clause 1 of the
Schedule in the Visiting Forces Act 1952, which, in certain circumstances, gives a
country primary jurisdiction over certain offences committed within the United
Kingdom jurisdiction by a member of that country's visiting force.   Section 3
amends the Extradition Act 1870 and the Fugitive Offencers Act 1967 to provide
for the new offence of threats to be an extraditable offence under the 1870 Act and
a returnable offence under the 1967 Act.   Where no extradition arrangement exists
with a State which is party to the Convention, an Order in Council may be made
applying the Extradition Act 1870 to that State as if the Convention itself constituted
an extradition arrangement.   For the purpose of extradition out of the United
Kingdom to a State, an offence under s. 1, wherever committed, is deemed to be
committed within the jurisdiction of that State.   Section 4 deals with extent.
Section 5 deals with interpretation and repeals, and provides for the commencement
of the Act.

1412   ## Outer space
The United Kingdom instrument of ratification of the Convention on Registration
of Objects launched into Outer Space was deposited and the convention entered into
force for the United Kingdom on 30th March 1978.   The text of the convention
was subsequently re-issued as TS 70 (1978); Cmnd. 7271.

1413   ## Prohibited transactions—South Africa
The South Africa (Prohibited Exports and Transactions) (Overseas Territories)
Order 1978, S.I. 1978 No. 1624 (in force on 14th December 1978), made under the
United Nations Act 1946, prohibits certain specified territories from the exportation
of certain goods to South Africa.   It also prohibits certain transactions relating to
patents, registered designs and industrial information or techniques for the
manufacture or maintenance of arms and specified associated goods in South
Africa.   The Order additionally confers powers to obtain evidence and information
for its purposes.

1414　　The South Africa (Prohibited Exports and Transactions) (Overseas Territories) (Amendment) Order 1978, S.I. 1978 No. 1894 (in force on 24th January 1979), amends the South Africa (Prohibited Exponents and Transactions) (Overseas Territories) Order 1978, para. 1413, arts. 4 and 5, by including among the goods to which those articles apply specialised parts and components of the apparatus, appliances and equipment in Sch. 2 to the principal Order.

1415　　The South Africa (United Nations Arms Embargo) (Prohibited Transactions) Order 1978, S.I. 1978 No. 277 (in force on 24th March 1978), prohibits certain transactions relating to patents, registered designs and industrial information or techniques for the manufacture or maintenance of arms and certain associated goods in South Africa. It confers powers to obtain evidence and information for the purposes of the Order.

1416　　The South Africa (United Nations Arms Embargo) (Prohibited Transactions) (Amendment) Order 1978, S.I. 1978 No. 1034 (in force on 24th August 1978), amends the principal Order, S.I. 1978 No. 277, para. 1415 ante, by replacing the reference in ibid. art. 3 (3) to the Export of Goods (Control) Order 1970 with a reference to the Export of Goods (Control) Order 1978 which revokes the 1970 Order.

1417　　The South Africa (United Nations Arms Embargo) (Prohibited Transactions) (Amendment No. 2) Order 1978, S.I. 1978 No. 1895 (in force on 24th January 1979), further amends the South Africa (United Nations Arms Embargo) (Prohibited Transactions) Order 1978, paras. 1415, 1416, supra art. 3, by including among the goods to which that article applies specialised parts and components of the apparatus, appliances and equipment in the Export of Goods (Control) Order 1978, as amended, paras. 812–816, Sch. 1, Part II, Group I.

1418　　The South Africa (United Nations Arms Embargo) (Prohibited Transactions) (Guernsey) Order 1978, S.I. 1978 No. 1052, the South Africa (United Nations Arms Embargo) (Prohibited Transactions) (Isle of Man) Order 1978, S.I. 1978 No. 1053 and the South Africa (United Nations Arms Embargo) (Prohibited Transactions) (Jersey) Order 1978, S.I. 1978 (in force on 1st September 1978), extend to the Bailiwick of Guernsey, the Isle of Man and the Bailiwick of Jersey respectively and, pursuant to United Nations Security Council Resolution No. 418 of 4th November 1978, prohibit certain transactions relating to patents, registered designs and industrial information or techniques for the manufacture or maintenance of arms and certain associated goods in South Africa. They may also confer powers to obtain evidence and information for the purposes of the Orders.

1419　　**Sovereign immunity—act of state—doctrine of restrictive immunity**

Canada

An action for damages against a sovereign state for breach of a commercial contract was dismissed on the basis of sovereign immunity. There was an appeal on the basis of the doctrine of restrictive immunity, which holds that a sovereign state is not immune from liability for acts other than legislative or international transactions. *Held*, the restrictive doctrine was part of the law of Canada. A Canadian company had suffered damage as the result of the breach of a commercial contract by a sovereign state. The sovereign state was therefore liable to action in the Canadian courts.

ZODIAK INTERNATIONAL PRODUCTS INC v POLISH PEOPLE'S REPUBLIC (1977) 81 DLR (3d) 656 (Court of Appeal of Quebec).

1420　　—— —— **immunity of state trading organisation—scope of force majeure clause**

See *C. Czarkinow Ltd v Rolimpex*, para. 501.

1421   **State Immunity Act 1978**

The State Immunity Act 1978 restricts the immunity from process in United Kingdom civil courts and tribunals enjoyed by sovereign states. The Act received the royal assent on 20th July 1978 and came into force on 22nd November 1978.

Section 1 confers a general right of immunity on sovereign states, which applies in any circumstances except those in which it is excluded by ss. 2–11. By s. 2 a state is not immune if it has waived its immunity, nor is it immune if the proceedings in which it is involved are of a commercial, industrial, financial, professional or similar nature or relate to a contractual obligation to be performed wholly or partly in the United Kingdom: s. 3. Section 4 excludes, with provisos, immunity in proceedings arising from a contract of employment made between the state and an individual where either the contract was made in the United Kingdom or is to be wholly or partly performed there.

Immunity does not extend to proceedings in respect of death, personal injury or damage to or loss of tangible property: s. 5. Nor are states immune from certain proceedings relating either to immovable property in the United Kingdom or to a state's interest in any property arising by way of succession, gift or bona vacantia: s. 6 (1), (2). Courts may exercise their jurisdiction over any property relating to the estates of deceased person or persons of unsound mind, to the insolvency or winding up of companies or to the administration of trusts, regardless of any interest or claim of a sovereign state in that property: s. 6 (3). By s. 7 a state is not immune from proceedings relating to patents, trade marks, designs or plant breeders' rights belonging to it and registered, protected or applied for in the United Kingdom. This also applies to any actions for infringement. Section 8 provides that a state is not immune from proceedings involving its membership of a body corporate, unincorporated body or partnership, nor is it immune from arbitration proceedings in the United Kingdom to which it has agreed to submit a dispute: s. 9. There is no immunity from proceedings relating to ships and cargo used for commercial purposes: s. 10. Finally, immunity does not extend to value added tax proceedings or proceedings arising from customs and excise duties or agricultural levies: s. 11.

Sections 12, 13 concern procedure. They regulate the service of process and transmission of judgments against states, extend time limits for taking various steps in the proceedings and confer certain other privileges on states. A state's consent is required before any order decreeing specific performance against it, imposing a penalty on it or granting an injunction against it is made. Similarly, a state's consent is required before execution against any of its property not used or intended for a commercial purpose can take place.

Section 14 identifies the bodies and organisations qualifying for immunity while s. 15 enables Orders in Council to be made extending or restricting immunity and privilege. Immunities or privileges conferred by the Diplomatic Privileges Act 1964 or the Consular Relations Act 1968 are not affected: s. 16. Section 17 contains definitions.

A judgment given against the United Kingdom by a state which is party to the European Convention on State Immunity is to be recognised by the United Kingdom if, in corresponding circumstances, a United Kingdom court would have entertained proceedings against the state giving judgment: s. 18. Section 19 specifies exceptions to that rule. Section 20 extends the Diplomatic Privileges Act 1964 to a sovereign or head of state, with necessary modifications, ss. 21–23 are supplementary.

1422   **United Nations—specialised agencies**

The convention for the Establishment of the Inter-Governmental Maritime Consulative Organisation 1948 has been further amended. The United Kingdom instrument of acceptance of the further amendments was deposited in 1975 and the amendments came into force on 1st April 1978. The text of the amendments was presented to Parliament in August 1978 as TS 69 (1978); Cmnd. 7262.

1423   The articles of agreement of the International Monetary Fund have been amended twice: see Cmnd. 7205 (TS 44 (1978)) and Cmnd. 7331 (TS 83 (1978)). The second amendment, which was adopted on 24th March 1976, came into operation on 1st April 1978. The revised text is set out in Cmnd. 7331.

FRIENDLY SOCIETIES

Halsbury's Laws of England (4th edn.), Vol. 19, paras. 101–400

1424   Benefit—increase of limits

The Friendly Societies (Limits of Benefits) Order 1978, S.I. 1978 No. 920 (in force on 31st July 1978), raises the limit on the amounts which members of registered friendly societies or branches may be entitled to receive from any one or more of such societies or branches under non-tax-exempt business. The new limits are £15,000 by way of gross sum under life or endowment business, whether or not any part of the entitlement is under any mortgage protection policy or policies, and £1,500 by way of annuity.

1425   Dissolution—division or appropriation of assets—power to apply assets for purposes outside society's objects

A society registered under the Friendly Societies Act 1896 had as its objects the provision by voluntary contributions for the relief of widows and orphans of members, the payment of money on a member's death and the relief of members during sickness and infirmity. In 1968 the society resolved to wind itself up. The instrument of dissolution provided that the funds and property of the society should be appropriated for the purchase of annuities for present beneficiaries, for the granting of a sum of money to a specified benevolent fund and for the donation of the balance to another fund. The society was dissolved and the first two proposals concerning the disposal of its assets were carried out, leaving the balance in the hands of the sole trustee of the society. He took out a summons to determine whether pursuant to the 1896 Act, s. 79 (4), and the execution of the instrument of dissolution, he was authorised to dispose of the funds in accordance with the instrument. *Held*, s. 79 (4) provided that the instrument of dissolution should not contain any provision for a division or appropriation of the funds of a society otherwise than for the purpose of carrying into effect the objects of the society unless the claim of every member was first satisfied. This impliedly authorised a division or appropriation for some purpose other than that of carrying into effect the objects of the society after the claims of members were satisfied, which in this case they had been by the purchase of the annuities. However, the authority to make a division or appropriation of the funds was not dispositive, enabling the funds to be given to anyone, but administrative, authorising the funds to be divided or appropriated between those who were otherwise entitled to them under the general law, even though this would not be carrying into effect the society's objects. Therefore, except for the purchase of the annuities for the beneficiaries, the trustee was not authorised to dispose of the assets in the manner proposed.

RE BUCKS CONSTABULARY WIDOWS' AND ORPHANS' FUND FRIENDLY SOCIETY; THOMPSON v HOLDSWORTH [1978] 1 WLR 641 (Chancery Division: MEGARRY V-C).

The 1896 Act, s. 79 (4), now Friendly Societies Act 1974, s. 94 (5).

1426   —— instrument of dissolution ineffective to dispose of assets— destination of assets

A society registered under the Friendly Societies Act 1896 had as its object the provision of relief for members in sickness and infirmity and for widows and orphans of members. In 1968 the society resolved to wind itself up and an instrument of dissolution provided for the disposal of its assets. The instrument was however held to be ineffective for that purpose (see para. 1425). The trustee took out a summons to establish the destination of the society's assets. The two main claimants were the Crown, as bona vacantia, and the members of the society as at the date of dissolution. *Held*, there was no provision in the society's rules for distribution of surplus assets on dissolution but as s. 49 of the 1896 Act vested property of registered societies in the trustees for the use and benefit of the society and its members there was no need. In default of a rule to the contrary, when a member of a society ceased to be a member he ceased to have any interest in its funds. Accordingly when a society was dissolved with members in existence the only persons interested in the property were those existing members. The assets of the society were held on trust for the members as at the date of dissolution to the total exclusion of any claim on behalf of the Crown.

RE BUCKS CONSTABULARY WIDOWS AND ORPHANS FUND FRIENDLY SOCIETY (No. 2) (1978) 122 Sol Jo 557 (Chancery Division: WALTON J).

Friendly Societies Act 1896, s. 49 now Friendly Societies Act 1974, s. 54.

1427   Fees

The Friendly Societies (Fees) Regulations 1978, S.I. 1978 No. 1717 (in force on 1st January 1979), replace the Friendly Societies Regulations 1975, Sch. 2, 1975 Halsbury's Abr para. 1600, thereby increasing the fees to be paid for matters to be transacted and for the inspection of documents under the Friendly Societies Act 1974, 1974 Halsbury's Abr para. 1478. The Friendly Societies (Fees) Regulations 1977, 1977 Halsbury's Abr para. 1360 are revoked.

FUEL AND ENERGY

Halsbury's Laws of England (4th edn.), Vol. 16, paras. 1–490 and Vol. 19, paras. 401–600

1428   Community energy policy—financial support

EEC Council Regulations 1302/78 and 1303/78 provide for the grant of financial support for projects to exploit alternative energy sources and for demonstration projects to reduce energy consumption.

1429   Conservation of energy—insulation of private dwellings

See para. 1489.

1430   Dangerous substances—packaging and labelling

See para. 1454.

1431   Electricity—unauthorised connection of supply by consumer—whether consumer acting "dishonestly"

See *Boggeln v Williams*, para. 620.

1432   Electricity board—works on highway—duty of care to pedestrians

See *Pitman v Southern Electricity Board*, para. 2022.

1433   Gas—consumers' deposits—rate of interest

The Gas (Consumers' Deposits) (Rate of Interest) Order 1978, S.I. 1978 No. 1848 (in force on 1st April 1979), increases to 7 per cent the yearly rate of interest payable by the British Gas Corporation on every sum of 50 p deposited with them by way of security under the Gas Act 1972, Sch. 4. The Gas (Consumers' Deposits) (Rate of Interest) Order 1950 is revoked.

1434   —— quality

The Gas Quality (Amendment) Regulations 1978, S.I. 1978 No. 230 (in force on 21st March 1978), substitutes a new table for the table contained in the schedule to the Gas Quality Regulations 1972. Gas is not to be supplied at a pressure less than that specified in relation to the Wobbe number of the gas as set out in the table.

1435   Nuclear fuels—erection of reprocessing plant—planning permission

See para. 1162.

1436   Nuclear installations—excepted matter

The Nuclear Installations (Excepted Matter) Regulations 1978, S.I. 1978 No. 1779 (in force on 1st January 1979), prescribe certain specified quantities and forms of nuclear matter which are excluded from the provisions of the Nuclear Installations Act 1965 and so do not attract the strict liability for damage which is imposed under the Act. Consignments of nuclear matter leaving a nuclear installation are also exempt if they do not exceed certain limits of activity and are packed in accordance with International Atomic Energy Agency regulations. The Nuclear Installations (Excepted Matter) Regulations 1965 are superseded by these Regulations.

1437   Nuclear Safeguards and Electricity (Finance) Act 1978

The Nuclear Safeguards and Electricity (Finance) Act 1978 which received the royal assent on 30th June 1978 and came into force on that date, gives effect to an agreement for the application of safeguards in connection with the Treaty of the Non-Proliferation of Nuclear Weapons (Cmnd. 6730).

Section 1 provides that effect is to be given to the safeguards agreement of 6th September 1976 between the United Kingdom, the European Atomic Energy Community and the International Atomic Energy Agency. Section 2 confers powers of entry to civil nuclear installations on inspectors of the Agency for the purposes of making inspections permitted by the Agreement. It also provides penalties for the obstruction of such inspections and for giving false information. Section 3 enables the Secretary of State to make regulations giving effect to specified provisions of the safeguard agreement. Section 4 relates to offences under these provisions by bodies corporate. Section 5 authorises the Secretary of State to make contributions, not exceeding an aggregate of £50 million, towards the expenditure of the Generating Board in connection with the construction of the Drax power station. Section 6 deals with citation and extent.

1438   Petroleum extraction—contracts—restrictive trade practices—exemption

See Participation Agreements Act 1978, para. 2840.

1439   Solid fuel—display of information

See para. 3108.

1440   Units of measurement—metrication

The Coal and Other Mines (Metrication) Regulations 1978, S.I. 1978 No. 1648 (in force on 12th December 1978), amend various specified instruments so as to substitute metric measurements for imperial measurements. The Regulations also amend the Coal and Other Mines (Working Plans) Rules 1956 to allow the use of Ordnance Datum as well as the hitherto used assumed level below Ordnance Datum.

GIFT AND ESTATE TAXATION

Halsbury's Laws of England (4th edn.), Vol. 19, paras. 601–926

1441   **Article**

Foreign Trusts Again, J. B. Morcom (capital transfer tax and excluded property): 128 NLJ 1044.

Capital Transfer Tax Appeals, J. B. Morcom (methods of resolving disputes concerning capital transfer tax): 128 NLJ 1161.

Taxation and the Small Business Sector with Special Reference to Capital Transfer Tax, Raymond K. Ashton: [1978] BTR 30.

1442   **Capital transfer tax—interest in possession—whether affected by power of accumulation**

The terms of a settlement provided that trustees were to hold the capital and income of the trust fund for such of the settlor's three daughters as attained the age of twenty-one or married under that age, subject to a power of accumulation vested in the trustees. The daughters all reached twenty-one by February 1974. The Revenue claimed that the trustees were liable to capital transfer tax in respect of an appointment made to one of the daughters in 1976. The trustees contended that her interest had become an interest in possession in February 1974, before the date on which dispositions became chargeable transfers under the Finance Act 1975. *Held*, in order for an interest to be an interest in possession it was sufficient that it was not an interest in reversion or remainder. The daughter had therefore obtained an interest in possession in February 1974, despite the trustees' power of accumulation, and the 1976 appointment was not subject to capital transfer tax.

PEARSON v IRC [1978] STC 627 (Chancery Division: FOX J).

1443   **Estate duty—exemption—member of armed forces—whether death caused by war wound**

After the death in 1967 of the fourth Duke of Westminster, his executors applied to the Defence Council for a certificate under the Finance Act 1952, s. 71 in respect of the estate. Section 71 provided that estate duty was not to be charged if it was certified by the Defence Council that the deceased died from a wound inflicted when he was a member of the Crown's armed forces on active service against the enemy. The executors claimed that the duke's wartime wound had caused the cancer from which he died, but which had been concealed by other complications and so had not received timely treatment. The Council contended that s. 71 was not intended to cover circumstances where death not directly caused by the wound occurred sooner than it might have done if the wound had not been suffered. The executors sought a declaration that the certificate should be granted. *Held*, the Council were wrong to conclude that the wound needed to have directly, pathologically and physiologically brought about the death. The question was whether the wound was a cause of the death, it did not have to be the only or direct pathological cause. Accordingly, the declaration would be granted.

BARTY-KING v MINISTRY OF DEFENCE (1978) Times, 13th October (Queen's Bench Division: MAY J). *R v Criminal Injuries Compensation Board, ex parte Ince* [1973] 3 All ER 808, CA, applied.

The corresponding provision relating to capital transfer tax is Finance Act 1975, Sch. 7, para. 1.

1444   **—— property passing on death—settled property—discretionary power to accumulate trust income**

Scotland

A settlor directed trustees to apply, during the trust period which covered the lives of his children and of the survivor of them, the whole of the income of the trust fund in such a manner as they might think fit for the benefit of the beneficiaries. The trustees were also given a discretionary power to accumulate any part or whole of the income. The settlor died before the trust period expired. The trustees had accumulated the whole of the income accruing to the trust fund from the time of its creation until the settlor's death. The Inland Revenue Commissioners claimed that the power to accumulate was void beyond the life of the settlor by virtue of the restrictions on the accumulation of income corresponding to the Law of Property Act 1925, s. 164. This rendered estate duty payable on the whole of the trust fund on the death of the settlor under the Finance Act 1894, s. 2 (1) (b). The trustees appealed, contending that the restrictions on accumulation did not render unlawful any discretionary power to accumulate beyond the permitted period if that power was one that the trustees were not obliged to exercise. Further, that as the power to accumulate did not involve the addition of income to capital but the retaining of it in order to distribute it to beneficiaries, it was an administrative power outside the scope of the restrictions and there was no termination of a power to accumulate on the death of the settlor. *Held*, an accumulation was caught by the restrictions if the deed was expressed in such a manner that a mandate to accumulate was given by the settlor. It did not matter whether the mandate flowed from an express or implied direction or an unfettered discretionary power. The accumulation therefore was only valid for the permitted period, which in this case was the duration of the settlor's life. In the context of the deed, "accumulate" did not mean "retain" but had its normal meaning of addition of income to capital. Accordingly, on the death of the settlor, there had been a termination of the power to accumulate causing estate duty to be payable on the whole of the trust fund. The appeal would be dismissed.

BAIRD V LORD ADVOCATE [1978] STC 282 (Inner House).

This decision was affirmed in part on appeal to the House of Lords: [1979] 2 WLR 369.

1445   —— property situate out of Great Britain—shares

The testatrix was born in England but she was domiciled and resident in Southern Rhodesia from 1951 until her death in 1969. During that time she bought shares in South Africa in two groups of companies which were registered in her name on registers kept in South Africa, and the dividends were always paid there. One of the groups of companies kept branch registers in England while the other kept a duplicate register there. In 1962, being apprehensive about the political situation, the testatrix sent the share certificates to a bank in England. In 1967 she was refused permission to transfer the certificates to South Africa due to exchange control restrictions. She never dealt with the shares in England. When she died, her executor, in order to determine whether estate duty was payable in England, sought the determination of the court whether the shares held in England were "property . . . which is situate out of Great Britain" within the Finance Act 1949, s. 28 (2), and were thus exempt from estate duty. *Held*, the shares in both groups of companies were property situate out of Great Britain; as to the group which kept duplicate registers in England, those registers were of no legal significance and were not branch registers where title to the shares could be dealt with. The shares could be effectively dealt with only where they were registered in South Africa and were therefore situate out of Great Britain. As to the other shares, they could be dealt with either in England or in South Africa. The court had to select one country as the place where in the ordinary course of affairs the testatrix would have dealt with them. That place would have been South Africa and accordingly those shares were also situate out of Great Britain.

STANDARD CHARTERED BANK LTD V INLAND REVENUE COMMISSIONERS [1978] STC 272 (Chancery Division: GOULDING J).

The corresponding provision relating to capital transfer tax is Finance Act 1975, s. 24(2).

GIFTS

Halsbury's Laws of England (4th edn.), Vol. 20, paras. 1–100

1446   Article

Gifts to Unincorporated Associations, H. K. Insall: [1977] NZLJ 489.

1447   **Testamentary gift—residuary gift—gift subject to life interest—date of distribution of estate**

See *Royal Trust Company v East*, para. 3122.

GUARANTEE AND INDEMNITY

Halsbury's Laws of England (4th edn.), Vol. 20, paras. 101–400

1448   **Guarantee—enforceability—allegation of undue influence and unenforceable transaction—consideration**

Canada

The plaintiff company, suppliers of materials to a company owned by the defendant, brought an action on a guarantee signed by the defendant personally in respect of past and future debts of his company. In his defence the defendant alleged, first, that the guarantee, not having been made under seal, was invalid, and second, that, having felt himself to be under pressure at the time of signing the guarantee, there had been undue influence or an unconscionable transaction. The defendant claimed that he had signed the guarantee on the understanding that only by doing so would he receive any further credit from the plaintiff company for materials which he badly needed and credit for which he could not obtain elsewhere. *Held*, as to the validity of the guarantee, despite the absence of a seal there was clear evidence of consideration for the past and future debts of the defendant's company: goods had been purchased following the signing of the guarantee and on the strength of it. As to the issues of undue influence and unconscionability, in the absence of proof that the plaintiff had known of the defendant's anxiety for his company, or that the plaintiff had attempted to charge more for goods purchased subsequently, or that the plaintiff had committed a fraudulent or wrongful act, or of the existence of a special relationship between the plaintiff and the defendant, there could be no undue influence. Further, since the normal price had been charged for the goods, in the absence of evidence that the plaintiff's request for a guarantee had been unreasonable, this was not a case of a stronger party exploiting a weaker one: the defendant had failed to discharge his onus of proving the unconscionable transaction alleged.

THERMO-FLO CORP LTD v KURYLUK (1978) 84 DLR (3d) 529 (Supreme Court of Nova Scotia).

1449   **Guarantor—duty owed to guarantor by bank at sale of debtor's property**

See *Barclays Bank Ltd v Thienel and Thienel*, para. 205.

1450   **—— joint guarantors—amount of contributions**

Canada

A company was placed in receivership under the terms of a debenture held by the company's bank. At the time of the receivership, the bank held varying guarantees in respect of the debt from the company's five shareholders. The question arose as to (i) whether the guarantors were bound to contribute equally or in proportion to the limit of their guarantees, and (ii) the effect of the insolvency of one of the guarantors. *Held*, where there were several guarantors of the same debt with varying limits on their respective guarantees, the burden was to be shared by them, not equally, but rateably in proportion to their respective liabilities. Where one guarantor was insolvent and unable to contribute, the liabilities of the others would be proportionately increased.

RE PRICE (1978) 85 DLR (3d) 554 (Supreme Court of Nova Scotia). *Ellesmere Brewery Co v Cooper* [1896] 1 QB 75, applied.

1451   —— liability of guarantor—initiation clause in charterparty—right of owners to claim against guarantor without arbitration first

See *The Queen Frederica, Thermistocles Navegacion Societe Anonyme v Langton*, para. 2586.

HEALTH AND SAFETY AT WORK

Halsbury's Laws of England (4th edn.), Vol. 20, paras. 401–801

1452   **Article**

Dangerous Machinery (the existence of a serious gap in the legislation): 122 Sol Jo 56.

Safety Representatives and Safety Committees—Power Without Responsibility, D. A. Castle: 128 NLJ 944.

1453   **Control of workplace hazards—air pollution, noise and vibration**

The Health and Safety Commission have published a consultative document setting out measures agreed by the General Conference of the International Labour Office to increase workers' protection against air pollution, noise and vibration: Health and Safety Bulletin, 7th March 1978.

The document, entitled "International Labour Conference: Convention and Recommendation concerning the Protection of Workers against Occupational Hazards in the Working Environment due to Air Pollution, Noise and Vibration", is obtainable from HMSO, price fifty pence.

1454   **Dangerous substances—packing and labelling**

The Packaging and Labelling of Dangerous Substances Regulations 1978, S.I. 1978 No. 209 (in force in relation to substances in containers of 200 litres capacity or more on 1st September 1978 and in any other case on 1st March 1979), impose requirements in respect of the containers in which prescribed dangerous substances are supplied, the particulars to be shown on those containers and method by which they are to be marked or labelled. Provision is also made for enforcement.

1455   —— —— relaxation of provisions of Poisons Rules

The Poisons (Amendment) Rules 1978, S.I. 1978 No. 672 (in force on 26th June 1978), amend the Poisons Rules 1978 (see para. 1889) so as to relieve from specified obligations of those rules poisons within the Packaging and Labelling of Dangerous Substances Regulations 1978 (see para. 1454). The labelling and packaging provisions of the Poisons Rules cease to have effect in general as from the dates on which the Packaging and Labelling of Dangerous Substances Regulations come into force but there are transitional provisions relating to the intermediate periods.

1456   **Employer—duty to keep floor free from obstruction—extent of duty**

A maintenance bricklayer working in a factory fell over a wire stretched across a badly lit passageway and was injured. He claimed that the employers were liable for the injury caused by the obstruction under Factories Act 1961, s. 28 (1). The employers argued that there was no way of knowing how the wire had come to be there and its presence had not been reasonably foreseeable. *Held*, the question of foreseeability was not relevant to the statutory duty to remove dangerous obstructions from passageways. It would have been reasonably practicable for the employers to have prevented or removed the obstruction and therefore they were liable for the bricklayer's injury.

BENNETT V RYLANDS WHITECROSS LTD [1978] ICR 1031 (Queen's Bench Division: KILNER BROWN J).

1457   ——— duty to maintain safe oxygen level—extent of duty

An employee charge-hand was overcome by lack of oxygen in a pressure vessel while working on his employers' ship. The employers were charged with contravention of the Shipbuilding and Ship-repairing Regulations 1960, reg. 50 (a) in that their employee entered a confined space in which there was reason to believe the oxygen level was too low. However, an employer is exempt from liability when the confined space has been adequately ventilated and a responsible person has tested it and certified it as safe for entry without breathing apparatus. The justices found that as a charge-hand could be termed a responsible person, his omission to follow the employers' own safety procedure, which complied with the regulation, excused the employers from liability. On appeal, *held*, since the vessel had not actually been tested or certified safe for entry by a responsible person, the exemption did not apply. Accordingly the case would be remitted to the justices with a direction to convict.

LINDSAY V VICKERS LTD [1978] Crim LR 55 (Queen's Bench Division: LORD WIDGERY CJ, CANTLEY and PETER PAIN JJ).

1458   Factories—standards of lighting

The Factories (Standards of Lighting) (Revocation) Regulations 1978, S.I. 1978 No. 1126 (in force on 1st October 1978), revoke the Factories (Standards of Lighting) Regulations 1941 which laid down a minimum standard for factory lighting and make a consequential amendment to the Woodworking Machines Regulations 1974.

1459   Genetic manipulation

The Health and Safety (Genetic Manipulation) Regulations 1978, S.I. 1978 No. 752 (in force on 1st August 1978), provide that no person may carry on genetic manipulation unless either he has given notice of his intention to do so both to the Health and Safety Executive and to the Genetic Manipulation Advisory Group, or he enjoys an exemption from giving such notice. The meaning of the word "work" in the Health and Safety at Work etc. Act 1974, Part I, is extended to include any activity involving genetic manipulation.

1460   Improvement notice—validity—jurisdiction of industrial tribunal to consider validity

Following a fire at a factory occupied by a company, two improvement notices were served on the company. The company contended they were invalid for being too vague. An industrial tribunal ruled, as a preliminary point, that the notices were not invalid for want of preciseness. The company appealed. *Held*, the tribunal had the jurisdiction to redraft any notice it found vague, after a determination of the facts. Accordingly, any decision relating to the notice before an investigation of the facts had taken place was inappropriate.

CHRYSLER UNITED KINGDOM LTD v MCCARTHY [1978] ICR 939 (Queen's Bench Division: LORD WIDGERY CJ, EVELEIGH and FORBES JJ).

1461   Petroleum—licences—fees

The Petroleum (Regulation) Acts 1928 and 1936 (Variation of Fees) Regulations 1978, S.I. 1978 No. 635 (in force on 1st July 1978), modify the Petroleum (Consolidation) Act 1928 by substituting a new Sch. 1 setting out the scale of fees payable in respect of licences to keep petroleum-spirit, and the Petroleum (Transfer of Licences) Act 1936 by increasing the fee payable for the transfer of a petroleum-spirit licence.

1462   Protective   clothing—provision—dispute—whether   a   trade dispute

See *Decision R (U) 5/77*, para. 2728.

HIGHWAYS, STREETS AND BRIDGES

Halsbury's Laws of England (3rd edn.), Vol. 19, paras. 1–822

1463 Article

Maintenance of Highways, J. F. Garner (liability of local authorities for accidents caused by defective condition of highways): 122 Sol Jo 705.

1464 Access from adjoining land—right of way—visibility

See *Hayns v Secretary of State for the Environment*, para. 2789.

1465 Diversion order—diversion of footpath—powers of local authority and Secretary of State

A developer obtained planning permission to erect buildings on a plot over which a public footpath ran. He diverted the path and began building before a diversion order had been made. He was twice convicted of obstruction. A diversion order was subsequently made by the local authority and confirmed by the Secretary of State. Two members of the Ramblers' Association applied to have the order quashed. *Held*, under the Town and Country Planning Act 1971, s. 210, local authorities were empowered to divert footpaths subject to the conditions applied by s. 209 to the making of authorisation orders by the Secretary of State. Section 209 limited the power to divert to cases where diversion was necessary to enable development to be carried out in accordance with planning permission granted under the Act; it had to be construed in the context of lawful, not unlawful, development. On that construction, s. 210 could be invoked by the local authority to render lawful that which had not been lawful and the application would be dismissed.

Ashby v Secretary of State for the Environment (1978) 122 Sol Jo 524 (Queen's Bench Division: Sir Douglas Frank QC sitting as a deputy High Court judge).

1466 Footpath—obstruction—discretion of council to take proceedings to prevent

An order of mandamus was sought against a local council in respect of the blocking of a footpath which the applicant alleged was a public path. There was no reference to the path in the definitive map. The council declined to exercise its powers under s. 116 of the Highways Act 1959 to have the path unblocked, on the ground that the owner of the land in question would contest the action. *Held*, although the council had a general duty to preserve highways in its district, it had a discretion as to whether to embark on legal proceedings and could decline to do so if it considered the prospects of success too small and the expense too great. The council could not be said to have exercised its discretion wrongly, and the order would be refused.

R v Lancashire County Council, ex parte Guyer (1978) 34 P & CR 264 (Queen's Bench Division: Lord Widgery CJ, Talbot and Boreham JJ). Dictum of Neville J in *Holloway v Egham Urban District Council* (1908) 72 JP 433 at 434 applied.

1467 Highway authority—duty of care—road works—obliteration of traffic sign

A motor accident resulting in injury occurred at the intersection of a priority road with an unclassified country lane. The motorist proceeding along the lane accepted responsibility for the accident but claimed a contribution from the county council as the highway authority. The intersection was "blind" and there was no traffic sign warning motorists of the priority road. The sign, in the form of white road markings, had been obliterated by the council during resurfacing and no temporary sign had been erected. *Held*, it would be obvious to a reasonably careful highway authority that if, in carrying out road repairs, widening or resurfacing, it was necessary to remove traffic signs then, unless care was taken to give warning by way of temporary signs, danger to road users would be created or increased. Where traffic signs were altered or removed the authority was under a duty to take reasonable steps to ensure that the situation so created was not dangerous or, if dangerous, to give reasonable warning of the danger. There would have been no difficulty in providing a temporary sign and if one had been provided the motorist in the lane would have been given the opportunity of slowing down and possibly avoiding the collision. Accordingly there had been a breach of duty which was causative. The council would be held one third responsible.

BIRD V PEARCE (1978) Times, 10th February (Queen's Bench Division: WOOD J).

1468 Local inquiries—procedure—report

The Department of Transport and the Department of the Environment have published their Report on the Review on Highway Inquiry Procedures (Cmnd. 7133), which re-examines the adequacy of the present procedures and considers possible improvements.

1469 Obstruction of highway—works by electricity board—duty of care to pedestrians

See *Pitman v Southern Electricity Board*, para. 2022.

1470 Reclassification—definitive map—evidence of previous use

In the course of a review of a definitive map the Secretary of State considered the upgrading of a footpath to a bridleway. He excluded evidence that the highway had been used as a bridleway before the definitive map was drawn up in 1953, on the ground that in order to establish a right of way the public were required to have used it within the twenty years preceding the date the use was brought into question. A member of the public claimed that the Secretary of State should have considered the excluded evidence. *Held*, the Secretary of State was incorrect in asserting that use within the last twenty years had to be established; for the purposes of the case, the date the use had been brought into question was 1953 because it was in that year that the status of the highway had originally been considered. There was therefore no burden on the claimant to establish use since 1953. There was, however, a burden on the Secretary of State under the National Parks and Access to the Countryside Act 1949, s. 33 (2) (e), to consider the applicant's evidence because it was evidence of matters to which a local authority had to have regard in carrying out a review of a definitive map: such evidence expressly included that concerning the classification of highways.

R V SECRETARY OF STATE FOR THE ENVIRONMENT, EX PARTE STEWART (1978) 122 Sol Jo 644 (Queen's Bench Division: LORD WIDGERY CJ, TALBOT and ACKNER JJ).

1471 Right of way—vehicular and pedestrian rights—conclusiveness of definitive map as evidence

When the definitive map of Suffolk was settled under the National Parks and Access to the Countryside Act 1949, a particular right of way was shown as a footpath only. There was no objection to this classification at the time but subsequent research showed that prior to the use as a footpath, the right of way had been used as a cartway for hundreds of years. The defendants who were the proprietors of an adjacent holiday camp, wished to establish the right of way as a public carriageway and the council took out a summons to determine whether, because of the definitive map it was a public footpath only. *Held*, under s. 32 (4) (a) of the Act the definitive map was conclusive evidence that the right of way was a footpath only. With respect to bridleways and roads, s. 32 (4) (b) provided for a qualification to the effect that the definitive map was conclusive only of the rights of way shown and not of whether the public had any other rights of way but there was no such qualification with respect to footpaths under s. 32 (4) (a). Under the review provisions of the Act the right of way could be reclassified as a public carriageway but until that was done the map had to be treated as conclusive.

SUFFOLK COUNTY COUNCIL V MASON [1978] 2 All ER 618 (Court of Appeal: LORD DENNING MR, ORMROD and GEOFFREY LANE LJJ). Decision of Sir Douglas Frank QC, (1977) 121 Sol Jo 375, 1977 Halsbury's Abr para. 1404 reversed.

1472   Skate boarding—accident prevention

In answer to a request for a list of statutory provisions which govern the safety of pedestrians and others against personal injury arising from skateboarders it was suggested that the following were relevant:—

The Highways Act 1835, s. 72 (driving a truck or sledge on footpath);
Offences against the Person Act 1861, s. 35 (furious driving);
The Public Health Act 1925, s. 74 (riding to endanger life or limb);
The Highways Act 1959, s. 140 (games on highway).

The power under the Local Government Act 1972, s. 235 to make byelaws for the prevention and suppression of nuisances was also pointed out (946 H. of C. Official Report, 17th March 1978, written answers, *col. 357.*

HIRE PURCHASE AND CONSUMER CREDIT

Halsbury's Laws of England (3rd edn.), Vol. 19, paras. 823–921

1473   Articles

Connected Lender Commencement Controversy, A. P. Dobson (whether Consumer Credit Act 1974, s. 75 applies to customers holding credit cards before 1st July 1977): 128 NLJ 448.

Connected Lender Substantive Controversy, A. P. Dobson (consideration of Consumer Credit Act 1974, s. 75): 128 NLJ 703.

The Concurrent Liability Conundrum, Professor P. B. Fairest and D. L. Rudkin (the overlap of ss. 56 and 75 of the Consumer Credit Act 1974): 128 NLJ 243.

Consumer Credit: Where Are We Now?, J. N. Adams (survey of the principal sections in force of the Consumer Credit Act 1974): 128 NLJ 604.

1474   Consumer credit—exempt agreements

The Consumer Credit (Exempt Agreements) (Amendment) Order 1978, S.I. 1978 No. 126 (in force on 1st March 1978), varies the Consumer Credit (Exempt Agreements) Order 1977, 1977 Halsbury's Abr para. 1415. The 1977 Order provides, inter alia, that certain consumer credit agreements secured on land where the creditor is a body specified in the Schedule to the Order are exempt agreements. The 1978 Order specifies further bodies to be included in the Schedule.

1475

The Consumer Credit (Exempt Agreements) (Amendment No. 2) Order 1978, S.I. 1978 No. 1616 (in force on 8th December 1978), amends the Consumer Credit (Exempt Agreements) Order 1977, 1977 Halsbury's Abr para. 1415, which provides, inter alia, that certain consumer credit agreements secured on land where the creditor is a body specified in the Schedule are exempt agreements. This is now extended by specifying further bodies to be included in the Schedule.

1476   Control of agreements—agreements to which restrictions apply— increase in limit of value

The Hire-Purchase (Increase of Limit of Value) (Great Britain) Order 1978, S.I. 1978 No. 461 (in force 1st June 1978), amends the Hire Purchase Act 1965, s. 2 so as to increase the financial limits of controlled agreements to £5,000.

1477   —— —— minimum value

The Hire-Purchase and Credit Sale Agreements (Control) (Amendment) Order 1978, S. I. 1978 No. 553 (in force on 2nd May 1978), varies the Hire-Purchase and Credit Sale Agreements (Control) Order 1976, 1976 Halsbury's Abr para. 1370, as varied by S. I. 1977 No. 771. The exemption from control of credit sale agreements is no longer limited by reference to specified minimum payments, but now applies where the cash price under the agreement does not exceed £1,000.

1478   **Disposition of vehicle subject to hire purchase contract—operation of presumptions in favour of private purchaser**

The defendants let a car to M on hire purchase terms. Some time later M delivered the car to S, who was a director of the plaintiffs, in return for £3,000 paid by S to M. Subsequently S purported to sell the car to L Ltd, who in turn sold it to D Finance Ltd, who themselves let it on hire purchase to the plaintiffs. The defendants terminated the agreement with M and took possession of the car from the plaintiffs. The plaintiffs brought an action against the defendants for the return of the car or its value in money, plus damages, claiming that there had been a disposition of the car to a private purchaser S, who had taken in good faith and without notice of the hire purchase agreement. However, the judge at first instance found on the evidence that the transaction between M and S was not a genuine sale by M to S, but a loan of the car as security, and he dismissed the action. The plaintiffs appealed, relying on the presumptions contained in the Hire Purchase Act 1964, ss. 28 (3), 29 (3), that unless proved to the contrary, the private purchaser was a purchaser in good faith and without notice of the hire purchase agreement. *Held*, where all the dispositions of a vehicle were known, as was the case in this instance, s. 27 (1), (2) were the only provisions of the Hire Purchase Act relevant to the transfer of title, and these sub-sections contained no presumptions in the private purchaser's favour. Section 28 only applied where some of the dispositions were not known. Section 29 (3) did not contain any presumption which could assist the plaintiffs and was merely a definition sub-section to the effect that notice of a hire purchase agreement meant actual notice. Thus as there were no presumptions in favour of S, because the trial judge had found that the transaction between M and S was not a genuine sale, no title had been passed to S. The appeal would be dismissed.

SONECO LTD v BARCROSS FINANCE LTD [1978] RTR 444 (Court of Appeal: STEPHENSON and ORR LJJ).

HOUSING

Halsbury's Laws of England (3rd edn.), Vol. 19, paras. 922–1218

1479   **Articles**

Accountability of Housing Associations, Austin Neville: 128 NLJ 946.

Council Tenants' Complaints and the Local Ombudsmen, David C. Hoath (necessity for statutory protection for council tenants): 128 NLJ 672.

Housing the Homeless? Peter Robson (assistance to the homeless in the light of the Housing (Homeless Persons) Act 1977, 1977 Halsbury's Abr para. 1427): 122 Sol Jo 614.

Housing (Homeless Persons) Act 1977: Two Views, A. J. Brown and Audrey Harvey (effects of 1977 Act from a local government point of view and a housing adviser's point of view): 122 Sol Jo 971.

Improving the National Housing Stock, W. A. Greene (the objects of housing policy and the grants available for rehabilitation): 122 Sol Jo 24.

Multiple (Paying) Occupation: Enforcement Problems, Alec Samuels (when do the changes in the use of a dwelling house constitute development requiring planning permission and sufficient to sustain an enforcement notice?): [1978] JPL 748.

1480   Assistance for house purchase and improvement—qualifying lenders

The Assistance for House Purchase and Improvement (Qualifying Lenders) Order 1978, S.I. 1978 No. 10 (in force 1st February 1978), prescribes a further body as a qualifying lender for the purposes of operating the option mortgage scheme under the Housing Subsidies Act 1967, Part II.

1481   —— variation of subsidy

The Assistance for House Purchase and Improvement (Variation of Subsidy) Order 1978, S.I. 1978 No. 1699 (in force on 4th December 1978), provides new scales of percentages in relation to option mortgage subsidy payable under the Housing Subsidies Act 1967, Part II in respect of interest payable under option mortgages for any period beginning on or after 1st January 1979 where the rate of interest for the time being exceeds 6·4 per cent per annum. The existing rates of subsidy are reduced by 0·1 per cent. The Order also revokes certain existing Orders dealing with previous rates of subsidy, but saves their operation in relation to any period ending before 1st January 1979.

1482   Clearance area—demolition of properties acquired for housing purposes

The Attorney General applied in a relator action on behalf of houseowners in a clearance area, whose houses were the subject of compulsory purchase orders, for an interlocutory injunction restraining the council from demolishing those properties. The relators argued that, having acquired the houses for housing purposes under the Housing Act 1957, s. 96 (b), the council was duty-bound under s. 105 (4), (4A), to use the properties as housing accommodation and that demolition was accordingly ultra vires. The council contended that the word "building" in s. 105 (4), which referred to "a building", and in s. 105 (4A), which was added by the Housing Act 1974 and referred to "a house or building", did not include a house, so that the duty only related to houses acquired after the 1974 Act came into force and in the absence of such a duty, the council was entitled to demolish. *Held*, it was clear from the 1957 Act, s. 49, that the council could include houses belonging to it in the clearance area, but only on the basis that the majority were unfit for human habitation. The council's submission as to the meaning of the word "building" was correct. On the evidence, the vast majority of the houses concerned were unfit for human habitation and on the balance of convenience the injunction would be refused.

ATTORNEY GENERAL (ON THE RELATION OF RIVERS-MOORE) v PORTSMOUTH CITY COUNCIL (1978) Times, 14th March (Chancery Division: WALTON J).

1483   Common lodging house—control order—whether house occupied by inmates

A local authority made a control order under Housing Act 1964, s. 73 (1), in respect of a common lodging house. The house had been registered for about fifty years until 1973, and was used on average by some seventy to seventy-five women who were accommodated there at any one time. Some of the women stayed for a short time, others for longer. The owner appealed against the order on the grounds that the house was not "occupied" by persons who did not form a single household within the meaning of the section and that in any case the inhabitants did not constitute a single household as the section required before it could operate. The claims were upheld. On the local authority's appeal, *held*, the word "occupied" was not restricted to mean occupied by exclusive possession, but had the ordinary wide meaning of "living in". Nor could it be said that the largely changing body of persons living in the house formed a single household. The house was therefore occupied by the inmates who did not form a single household, in satisfaction of the section.

SILBERS v SOUTHWARK LONDON BOROUGH COUNCIL (1977) 76 LGR 421 (Court of Appeal: STEPHENSON, GEOFFREY LANE and CUMMING-BRUCE LJJ). *Simmons v Pizzey* [1977] 2 All ER 432 HL, 1977 Halsbury's Abr para. 1436 followed.

1484   **Home Purchase Assistance and Housing Corporation Guarantee Act 1978**

The House Purchase Assistance and Housing Corporation Guarantee Act 1978 authorises the use of public money for assisting first-time purchasers of house property, and for connected purposes. The Act also increases the financial limit governing the Housing Corporation's power to guarantee loans to housing associations and others. The Act received the royal assent on 30th June 1978 and came into force on that day, except for ss. 1 to 3 which came into force on 1st December 1978.

Section 1 enables the Secretary of State to make advances to recognised lending institutions to enable them to provide assistance to those purchasing house property for the first time. The assistance will be limited to purchases made with a secured loan. Two forms of assistance may be provided: a loan of £600, interest free for five years, which the lending institution adds to the normal mortgage advance (but not so that the total loan exceeds the loan value of the property), and a cash bonus up to a maximum of £110. The price of properties must be within price limits which the Secretary of State may set from time to time by order. The amount of the secured loan must be at least £1,600 and not less than 25 per cent of the purchase price of the property. Certain savings conditions which purchasers must satisfy are set out. The Secretary of State may alter by order the benefits and savings conditions, and he may introduce a scale of values for the Government loan matched to a scale of savings.

Section 2 and the Schedule specify the recognised savings and lending institutions, and enable the Secretary of State to add institutions to, or remove them from, the lists. After consultation with savings and lending institutions, the Secretary of State may make directions settling the terms on which advances are to be made. Recommendations made by associations representing lending and savings institutions to their members about the manner of implementing the Act may be exempted from the provisions of the Restrictive Trade Practices Act 1976.

Section 3 makes consequential amendments to building society law. Section 4 enables an Order in Council under the Northern Ireland Act 1974 to make for Northern Ireland provision corresponding to ss. 1 to 3 of the present Act, without the need for affirmative resolutions.

Section 5 amends the Housing Act 1974 to increase the maximum loan guarantee limit of the Housing Corporation from £100 million to £300 million. It also provides for the Secretary of State, with the consent of the Treasury, to increase this ceiling by affirmative resolutions order to not more than £500 million.

Section 6 deals with citation and extent.

1485   **—— recognised savings institutions**

The Home Purchase Assistance (Recognised Savings Institutions) Order 1978, S.I. 1978 No. 1785 (in force on 5th December 1978), adds certain institutions to those specified in the Home Purchase Assistance and Housing Corporation Guarantee Act 1978 as being recognised savings institutions for the purpose of receiving assistance under the Act.

1486   **Homeless persons—duties of local authorities under Housing (Homeless Persons) Act 1977—time at which duties arise**

The applicant, having been classified by the housing authority as homeless and having a priority need according to the Housing (Homeless Persons) Act 1977, s. 1, sought an order of mandamus requiring the authority to carry out its duties under s. 4 of that Act to secure available accommodation. The authority contended that such a duty did not arise until the applicant had been notified of its decision as to her status. It further submitted that notification of its decision to another authority under s. 5 of the Act had not constituted constructive notice of its decision to the applicant. *Held*, the authority's duties under s. 4 arose as soon as it was satisfied that the applicant was homeless: the existence of such duties was not dependent on notification of the decision under s. 8 of the Act. Further, s. 5 (6) provided that notification by the authority of its decision to a second housing authority requiring the latter to take the responsibility of providing housing accommodation did not absolve the notifying authority from performing its duties under s. 4 of the Act until the issue of responsibility was finally determined. However, it was unnecessary to grant the order sought, and the application would be refused.

R v BEVERLEY BOROUGH COUNCIL, EX PARTE McPHEE (1978) Times, 27th October (Queen's Bench Division: LORD WIDGERY CJ, WIEN and SMITH JJ).

For 1977 Act see 1977 Halsbury's Abr para. 1427.

1487　　—— transfer of responsibility between housing authorities

The Housing (Homeless Persons) (Appropriate Arrangements) Order 1978, S.I. 1978 No. 69 (in force on 21st January 1978), directs that, for the purposes of the Housing (Homeless Persons) Act 1977, s. 5, which makes provision for the transfer between housing authorities of responsibility for a homeless person, the appropriate arrangements referred to in the section are to be arrangements set out in the Schedule to the Order. These arrangements provide for any disputed question under s. 5 to be determined either by a person agreed upon by the two authorities concerned or in default by a person appointed, from a panel to be drawn up by the named associations, by the Chairman or Chairmen of the association or associations representing those authorities.

1488　　The Housing (Homeless Persons) (Appropriate Arrangements) (No. 2) Order 1978, S.I. 1978 No. 661 (in force on 28th April 1978), provides for the appropriate arrangements for the determination of disputed questions under s. 5 of the Act as to the responsibility for a homeless person in cases involving disputes between Scottish authorities or between Scottish and English or Welsh authorities.

1489　　Homes Insulation Act 1978

The Homes Insulation Act 1978 provides for grants towards the cost of thermal insulation of private homes. The Act received the royal assent on 31st July 1978 and came into force on that date.

Section 1 enables the Secretary of State to prepare schemes requiring local authorities to make grants towards the improvement of insulation of dwellings. The schemes are to specify the improvements for which grants will be available and the categories of eligible dwellings and persons. The first scheme is to relate to roof insulation and water supply, the grant available being sixty six per cent of the cost involved or £50, whichever is less, but both amounts may be altered by the Secretary of State; for subsequent schemes, he is empowered to prescribe the percentage or amount. Section 2 provides for the local authorities to be fully reimbursed for grants within the prescribed yearly limit and allows for contribution towards the reasonable cost of their administrative expenses. Section 3 contains provisions applicable to Northern Ireland and s. 4 deals with citation and extent.

1490　　Housing association grants

The Department of the Environment has issued revised administration allowances for housing association grants under s. 29 (6) of the Housing Act 1974. The revised allowances apply to all housing projects completed on or after 1st November 1978 where the final grant has not been paid. The allowances applicable to any particular activity will reflect the scales operative at the time the activity took place. See Department of the Environment circular 73/78.

1491　　—— revision of administration allowances

The administration allowances for housing association grants have been revised in respect of all housing projects completed on or after 1st November 1977, where a final grant has not been paid. See Department of the Environment Circular 9/78.

1492   Housing finance—rent allowance subsidy

The Housing Finance (Rent Allowance Subsidy) Order 1978, S.I. 1978 No. 34 (in force on 14th February 1978), fixes the amount of rent allowance subsidy payable to a local authority for 1978–79 at 100 per cent of the authority's standard amount of rent allowances for the year.

1493   Housing subsidy—rent conditions—revocation

In an answer to a written parliamentary question, the Secretary of State for the Environment said that the rent condition attached to the high costs element of housing subsidy for 1978/79 was to be revoked. The subsidy had been paid only to those authorities who, inter alia, decided to raise their rents in the relevant financial year by a specified sum. Legal advice had shown that it might be held that the authorities were under a legal obligation to raise their rents in order to qualify for the subsidy. Since this would be contrary to Government policy, the rent condition attached to the high costs element of subsidy for the year 1978/79 would be revoked: Department of the Environment Press Notice dated 3rd March 1978.

1494   Local authority houses—management and control—notice to quit—common law rights of unprotected tenant

Tenants of a council house, who were not protected by the Rent Acts, fell into arrears with the rent. The local authority gave them notice to quit and commenced possession proceedings. According to its practice, the authority then made an informal agreement with the tenants whereby they undertook to pay off a certain amount of arrears every week. An order for possession was made, subject to the provision that it was unenforceable without leave of the court. The tenants failed to pay off the arrears as agreed and the authority applied for leave to issue a warrant for possession; by the time the application was heard, the tenants had paid some of the arrears. The authority appealed against an order that no warrant should issue providing the tenants paid the rent each week together with part of the arrears. *Held*, the common law rights of tenants not protected by the Rent Acts were strictly limited. The authority had served a valid notice to quit in accordance with its duties under the Housing Act 1957 and the tenants had failed to pay off the arrears in compliance with the agreement: the most the court could do in such circumstances was to allow the tenants sufficient time to leave the premises without undue hardship. Accordingly the appeal would be allowed and a warrant for possession issued immediately.

BRISTOL CITY COUNCIL v RAWLINS (1977) 34 P & CR 12 (Court of Appeal: ORR and GEOFFREY LANE LJJ). *Bristol District Council v Clark* [1975] 2 All ER 976 CA, 1975 Halsbury's Abr para. 1723, applied.

1495   Mobile home—security of tenure—application for extension of period of security

See *Taylor v Calvert*, para. 1729.

1496   Rent rebate and allowance schemes

The Rent Rebate and Rent Allowance Schemes (England and Wales) Regulations 1978, S.I. 1978 No. 217 (in force 21st March 1978), further vary the Housing Finance Act 1972, Sch. 4 by enabling authorities to set the period of a rent rebate or allowance, in the case of non-pensioners, at up to nine months where the grant of the rebate or allowance is notified during March or April in any year. They also enable authorities who have a shorter period to extend that period at any time up to the maximum applicable.

1497   The Rent Rebate and Rent Allowance Schemes (England and Wales) (No. 2) Regulations 1978, S.I. 1978 No. 1302 (in force on 30th September 1978) vary the Housing Finance Act 1972, Schs. 3 and 4. They increase the needs allowance and deductions in respect of non-dependants, which are used in calculating the amount of rebate or allowance, for any week in a rebate or allowance period beginning after 12th November 1978. They also empower local authorities to grant a rebate or allowance for a period commencing up to twelve months before receipt of a first application if the circumstances of the applicant are considered exceptional.

1498   The Rent Rebates and Rent Allowances (Students) (England and Wales) Regulations 1978, S.I. 1978 No. 1078 (in force on 1st September 1978), raise to £7.70 the deductions to be made in calculating the rent which is eligible to be met by a rent rebate or rent allowance under Housing Finance Act 1972, Part II, as amended, in the case of tenants who are students in receipt of certain awards or grants for the purpose of their further full-time education. The Rent Rebates and Rent Allowances (Students) (England and Wales) Regulations 1977, 1977 Halsbury's Abr para. 1440, are amended.

1499   **Repairs—requirement of substantial repairs—cost of repairs compared with value of property**

A local authority served notices under the Housing Act 1957, s. 9 (1A) on two property companies requiring them to do repairs to bring houses owned by them up to a reasonable standard. The houses were occupied by tenants. On appeal by the companies, it was held that since the value of the houses after repairs would be less than the capital sum spent on repairs, the notices should be quashed. On appeal by the local authority, *held*, the judge had not considered the possibility that the property companies could make a handsome profit by allowing the houses to get so dilapidated as to be condemned. In that situation the tenants would no longer be protected by the Rent Acts and the owners could evict them by giving an undertaking to the local authority under the 1957 Act, s. 16 (4), that the premises would not be used for human habitation and thus obtain vacant possession. Consequently the cost of repairs should be compared with the value of the property with vacant possession. The appeal would be allowed.

HILLBANK PROPERTIES LTD v HACKNEY LONDON BOROUGH COUNCIL; TALISMAN PROPERTIES LTD v HACKNEY LONDON BOROUGH COUNCIL [1978] 3 All ER 343 (Court of Appeal: LORD DENNING MR, GEOFFREY LANE and EVELEIGH LJJ).

HUMAN RIGHTS

Halsbury's Laws of England (4th edn.), Vol. 18, paras. 1625–1722

1500   **Birching—decision of European Court of Human Rights**

A young Manxman who had been birched in his schooldays for assaulting a school prefect sought a declaration from the European Court of Human Rights that birching constituted a degrading punishment in breach of the European Convention on Human Rights, art. 3. *Held*, SIR GERALD FITZMAURICE, the British judge, dissenting, for a punishment to be degrading it had to attain a particular level of debasement and humiliation, which was to be derived from its nature and its means of infliction. Birching constituted institutionalised violence which amounted to an assault in direct contravention of art. 3. The purpose of the article was the protection of a person's dignity and physical integrity.

TYRER v GOVERNMENT OF GREAT BRITAIN: Daily Telegraph, 26th April 1978 (European Court of Human Rights).

The decision imposes an obligation on Great Britain to bring about the abolition of birching.

For summary of the judgment in this case, see Council of Europe Press Release, Human Rights News C(78) 18, 25th April 1978.

1501   Complaint against West Germany—secret surveillance of mail and telecommunications—locus standi of petitioners—justification

Five West German citizens petitioned the European Commission of Human Rights to establish whether the secret surveillance of mail and telecommunications by the West German government was in violation of the European Convention on Human Rights and Fundamental Freedoms. It was not argued that such surveillance did not take place: the German government merely sought to establish it was justified on the grounds of national security and the prevention of disorder and crime. An intermediate issue arose as to whether the petitioners could be considered victims of a violation for the purposes of bringing a claim, when they could not show they had been subjected to surveillance themselves. On this and the substantive point, *held*, the petitioners were entitled to claim to be victims of a violation even though, because of the element of secrecy involved, they could not show they had actually suffered themselves.

The clear aim of the West German government in legitimising a prima facie breach of the rights to respect for private and family life and correspondence was the safeguarding of national security, especially in the light of the threats posed by sophisticated contemporary espionage and by terrorism. Accordingly, no breach of the Convention had been established.

KLASS v FEDERAL REPUBLIC OF GERMANY (European Court of Human Rights). See Council of Europe Press Release, Human Rights News C (78) 37, dated 6th September 1978.

1502   Complaint by Ireland—allegations of torture by British—findings of the European Court of Human Rights

In a judgment given on 18th January 1978 the European Court of Human Rights found the British Government not guilty of torturing internees detained by security forces in Ireland in 1971. The allegations had been made by the Government of the Republic of Ireland. However, Britain was found guilty of using five interrogation techniques which constituted degrading and inhuman treatment. Nevertheless, the court was unable to order the institution of proceedings against those involved in the violations: Times, 19th January 1978.

1503   Declaration on the mass media

The Member States of UNESCO have issued a Declaration on the Mass Media. The declaration is concerned with the use of the media for the strengthening of peace and international understanding, the promotion of human rights and the countering of racialism, apartheid and incitement to war. The declaration calls for journalists to be given freedom to report and the fullest possible facilities of access to information to enable them to provide to the public information guaranteed by the diversity of sources and means of information available (art. II. 2). The declaration also calls for the guaranteeing of the existence of favourable conditions for the operation of the mass media in conformity with the Universal Declaration of Human Rights and the principles proclaimed in the International Covenant on Civil and Political Rights (art. XI). For the text of the declaration, see The Times, 23rd November 1978.

1504   Petition by a prisoner—correspondence with legal adviser

See para. 2239.

1505   Pop festivals—public policy

See para. 2257.

HUSBAND AND WIFE

Halsbury's Laws of England (3rd edn.), Vol. 19, paras. 1219–1494

1506   Articles

Battered Cohabitee and Property Rights, A. N. Khan (the cases decided under the Domestic Violence and Matrimonial Proceedings Act 1976): 142 JP Jo 86.

Better Law for Battered Wives, A. N. Khan (analysis of the Domestic Violence and Matrimonial Proceedings Act 1976 in the light of judicial developments): 122 Sol Jo 391.

Consent to Marriage Obtained by Fraud, Frank Bates (the attitude of courts to marriages obtained by fraud): 128 NLJ 403.

Credit for Post-Separation Mortgage Repayments, Roderick L. Denyer (extent to which one spouse is to be credited by the other with the mortgage instalments paid after the separation): 128 NLJ 828.

The Domestic Proceedings and Magistrates' Courts Act 1978, Margaret Spencer (major changes made by the Act in the jurisdiction of magistrates' courts when granting matrimonial relief): 128 NLJ 727.

Domestic Violence and Cohabitees, Margaret Rutherford (cases under the Domestic Violence and Matrimonial Proceedings Act 1976): 128 NLJ 379.

Domestic Violence and Rights of Property, D. Lasok (cases under the Domestic Violence and Matrimonial Proceedings Act 1976): 128 NLJ 124.

The Effects of Tax on Maintenance Orders, David C. Robinson and Brian W. Hudson (principles to be applied when granting ancillary relief under ss. 22–25 of the Matrimonial Causes Act 1973): 128 NLJ 959.

Maintenance—From the Husband or the State? Joan Lunn (on a wife's application for maintenance what consideration should be given to the availability of social security benefits?): 128 NLJ 1112.

Violence in the Home—More New Legislation, M. D. A. Freeman (new remedies for domestic violence in the magistrates' court; Domestic Proceedings and Magistrates' Courts Act 1978): 128 NLJ 924.

1507   Abortion—wife seeking legal abortion—power of husband to prevent

A wife wished to have her pregnancy legally terminated. She obtained a certificate signed by two registered medical practitioners as required by the Abortion Act 1967. Her husband contended that she had no proper legal grounds for terminating the pregnancy and sought an injunction to prevent the operation being carried out without his consent. *Held*, there had to be a legal right enforceable in law or equity before an injunction restraining the infringement of that right would be granted. The husband had no such right. The Abortion Act 1967 did not give the father a right to be consulted and the courts had no power to enforce personal family obligations. The provisions of the Act had been complied with and the application would be dismissed.

PATON v TRUSTEES OF BRITISH PREGNANCY ADVISORY SERVICE [1978] 2 All ER 987 (Family Division: SIR GEORGE BAKER P).

1508   Criminal damage—institution of proceedings against wife by husband—whether consent of Director of Public Prosecutions required

See *Woodley v Woodley*, para. 737.

1509   Domestic Proceedings and Magistrates' Courts Act 1978

The Domestic Proceedings and Magistrates' Courts Act 1978 gives effect to the recommendations in the Law Commission's Report (Law Com. No. 77). It replaces the Matrimonial Proceedings (Magistrates' Courts) Act 1960 and amends certain other enactments relating to domestic proceedings in magistrates' courts. The Act received the royal assent on 30th June 1978 and comes into force on a day or days to be appointed except ss. 86, 88 (5), 89 (part), 90 and Schs. 1, 3 (part) which came into force on 18th July 1978: S.I. 1978 No. 997. The repeal of the Children Act 1975, Sch. 3, para. 26 and Adoption Act 1976, Sch. 1, para. 6, contained in Sch. 3 came into force on 20th November 1978.

Part I: Matrimonial Proceedings in Magistrates' Courts
Section 1 sets out the grounds of application by a spouse for financial provisions in a magistrates' court. The court may make an order for periodical payments or a lump sum for a spouse or child having considered certain matters: ss. 2, 3. Sections 4 and 5 specify the duration of orders and certain age limits on orders for a child. Orders may be made by agreement: s. 6. The court may also make a periodical payments order when spouses live apart by agreement and one has made periodical payments to the other or to a child: s. 7. When an application is made under ss. 2, 6 or 7, the court may make an order for the custody of a child under eighteen and place the child under the supervision of a local authority or probation officer: ss. 8, 9. The court may also commit a child under seventeen to the care of a local authority: s. 10. Provisions for the maintenance of a child under a custody order are contained in s. 11. Supplementary provisions relating to the court's powers under ss. 8–10 are contained in s. 12. Section 13 deals with disputes over a child's welfare between persons having joint custody. After making an order for the custody of a child under s. 8, the court may allow access to the child by his grandparents: s. 14. When exercising its powers, the court must treat a child's welfare as paramount: s. 15. Section 16 empowers the court to make orders protecting a spouse or child from violence and excluding a spouse from the matrimonial home. Section 17 contains supplementary provisions relating to orders under s. 16. Section 18 enables the court to attach a power of arrest to such orders. The court may make interim maintenance or custody orders: s. 19. Orders for periodical payments and custody may be varied and revoked: ss. 20, 21. Section 22 enables the instalments under a lump sum order to be varied. Supplementary provisions relating to the variation and revocation of orders are contained in s. 23. Proceedings under ss. 20, 21 may be brought by or against a person outside England and Wales: s. 24. Section 25 deals with the effect of cohabitation on certain orders. Before making an order under s. 2, the court must consider the possibility of a reconciliation: s. 26. The court may refuse to make an order under s. 2 if it considers any matter could be more conveniently dealt with by the High Court: s. 27. Section 28 empowers the High Court or a county court to terminate a magistrates' court order, except an order for a lump sum payment. Section 29 deals with appeals. Section 30 contains provisions relating to jurisdiction and procedure. When an application under s. 1 is adjourned, the court which resumes the hearing must include at least one of the original justices: s. 31. Sections 32 and 33 deal with the enforcement of orders for the payment of money and for custody. When making a custody order, the court may restrict the removal of a child from England and Wales: s. 34. The court may order the repayment of money paid under a periodical payments order after the payee's remarriage: s. 35.

Part II: Amendments of the Guardianship of Minors Acts 1971 and 1973
Various amendments and additions to the 1971 and 1973 Acts are made by ss. 36–48. These relate to the powers of a magistrates' court to make custody, access and maintenance orders in guardianship proceedings.

Part III: Amendments of other Enactments relating to Domestic Proceedings
Amendments and additions to the Affiliation Proceedings Act 1957 are made by ss. 49–53 which include matters dealing with the variation, revocation and provisions of affiliation orders.
  The Maintenance Orders (Reciprocal Enforcement) Act 1972 is amended and extended by ss. 54–61. These sections deal with a complaint for the recovery of maintenance in England and Wales by a spouse or former spouse outside the United Kingdom and with various miscellaneous provisions regarding Scotland and N. Ireland.

Sections 62 and 63 amend the Matrimonial Causes Act 1973, ss. 4, 27 which relate to desertion and failure to maintain.

Amendments and additions to the Children Act 1975, Part II are made by ss. 64–71 which deal with orders for financial provision and certain other orders in custodianship proceedings.

Section 72–74 amend and extend provisions of the Children Act 1975, Part I and the Adoption Act 1976 relating to supervision and care orders and the hearing of adoption proceedings in private.

Part IV: Amendments of the Magistrates' Courts Act 1952
The Magistrates' Courts Act 1952 is amended and extended by ss. 75–83 which include provisions dealing with the court's powers regarding periodical payments and the hearing of domestic proceedings.

Part V: Supplementary Provisions
Supplementary and transitional provisions, minor and consequential amendments and repeals are contained in ss. 84—90 and Schs. 1, 2 and 3.

1510 Maintenance order—appeal against amount—matters to be considered

The parties married in June 1977 and went to live with the wife's father. On her father's death the wife was granted rent-free life occupancy of the house. In August 1977, the husband left the wife and was subsequently ordered to pay her weekly maintenance of £20. He appealed against the amount payable on the ground that the shortness of the marriage warranted a nominal order only. *Held*, on marriage, the wife, who had previously been a widow, had given up her job as well as lost widow's pension rights and was receiving supplementary benefit because of her inability to find employment. Thus her position, even though she had rent-free accommodation, had changed for the worse. As the husband could afford the payment and as the marriage was still subsisting, it appeared that the correct principles had been applied and the order was justified.

ABDUREMAN V ABDUREMAN (1978) 122 Sol Jo 663 (Family Division: BALCOMBE J).

1511 —— appeal to Family Division—procedure

The following Practice Direction ([1978] 2 All ER 432) has been issued by the Family Division.

With effect from 1st June 1978 RSC Ord. 90, r. 16, is amended. Unless the President otherwise directs, an appeal under the Matrimonial Proceedings (Magistrates' Courts) Act 1960 to the Family Division of the High Court may be determined by a single judge, instead of by a Divisional Court in cases where the appeal relates only to the amount of any weekly payment ordered to be made. The President may also direct that such an appeal be heard and determined by a single judge at "a divorce town" within the meaning of the Matrimonial Causes Rules 1977. Consequential amendments are made to RSC Ord. 90, r. 16, concerning the number of copy documents required to be lodged where the appeal is to quantum only.

The practice to be followed in respect of any such appeal to a single judge of the Family Division will be that contained in the Practice Direction [1977] 2 All ER 543 subject to the following modifications: (i) one copy only of the various documents in support of the appeal need be lodged, unless the President directs that an appeal which has been listed before a single judge shall instead be heard by a Divisional Court when the Clerk of the Rules will notify the appellant's solicitor (or the appellant if acting in person) and request that he do lodge the additional copies required by Ord. 90, r. 16, and the Practice Direction [1977] 2 All ER 543 prior to the date fixed for the hearing; (ii) any request to fix an appeal for hearing by a single judge at a place other than at the Royal Courts of Justice should be made in writing to the Clerk of the Rules; (iii) where the president directs that the appeal be heard at a divorce town as defined by the Matrimonial Causes Rules 1977, the Clerk of the Rules will inform the appellant of the relevant town and will refer the papers to the listing officer of the appropriate Circuit Office for a date of hearing to be fixed and notified to the appellant.

It should be noted that every appeal under the Matrimonial Proceedings (Magistrates' Courts) Act 1960 must continue to be entered in the Principal Registry.

The Registrar's Direction dated 16th December 1971 (Divisional Court appeal: date of hearing) is hereby cancelled.

1512   —— enforcement—recovery of maintenance abroad

See para. 968.

1513   —— magistrates' court order—appeal to High Court

See para. 1511.

1514   —— variation by justices—appeal against variation—procedure

A wife appealed against a variation order made by justices reducing weekly maintenance payments for herself and her children from £62 to £15. In remitting the case to justices, SIR GEORGE BAKER P stated that practitioners were failing to use the new form of notice of motion on appeal as set out in the Appendix to the Practice Direction (Divisional Court: Appeal) [1977] 2 All ER 543, 1977 Halsbury's Abr para. 1462.

ADAMS V ADAMS (1978) 122 Sol Jo 348 (Family Division; SIR GEORGE BAKER P and WOOD J).

1515   Matrimonial home—domestic violence—exclusion of one party—children's interests paramount

An unmarried couple were joint tenants of a council house. Living with them were the woman's two young children, the man being the father of the younger. The woman left the man and took the children to live with friends. She applied to the county court for injunctions under the Domestic Violence and Matrimonial Proceeding Act 1976, s. 1 (1) (a), (b), (c), to restrain the man from molesting her or the children and to exclude him from the home. It was found that there had been no serious physical violence, but the injunctions sought were granted. On appeal by the man, *held*, under s. 1 (1) (c) the court's discretion to grant an injunction excluding one of the parties from the home was unfettered; it was not necessary for violence to have occurred. Since the relationship had broken down, the principal need was to provide for the children. For that reason, the order that the man should leave the house would be affirmed. The injunction against molestation would, however, be discharged.

SPINDLOW V SPINDLOW [1978] 3 WLR 777 (Court of Appeal: STAMP, LAWTON and ORMROD LJJ). *Davis v Johnson* [1978] 1 All ER 1132, HL, para. 1522 and *Bassett v Bassett* [1975] Fam 76, CA, 1974 Halsbury's Abr para. 1761 applied.

1516   —— —— —— committal for breach of order

See *Kavanagh v Kavanagh*, para. 465.

1517   —— —— —— —— validity of committal order

When a husband returned to the matrimonial home in breach of an injunction restraining him from returning there made under the Domestic Violence and Matrimonial Proceedings Act 1976, he was arrested under s. 2 of the Act and brought before a judge, who issued a warrant for attachment committing him for contempt for an unspecified period. The warrant did not follow the form specified by the County Court (Amendment No. 2) Rules 1977, 1977 Halsbury's Abr para. 1464. On appeal, *held*, every requirement of the law had to be strictly complied with before a man's liberty was taken away. The committal order was bad and the husband would be released at once.

WELLINGTON V WELLINGTON (1978) 122 Sol Jo 296 (Court of Appeal: LORD DENNING MR, ORR and BRIDGE LJJ). *McIlraith v Grady* [1968] 1 QB 468 applied.

1518   Injunctions under the Domestic Violence and Matrimonial Proceedings Act 1976 were issued against two husbands restraining them from molesting their wives and excluding them from the matrimonial home.   Both men failed to obey the injunctions and were committed to prison for contempt of court.   There were serious defects and omissions in the committal orders; in particular, the incorrect form of order was used, no time was specified and the grounds for committal were not stated.   In one case, a member of the court office, without reference to the judge, tried to correct the errors by typing in the missing details.   The Official Solicitor challenged the validity of the men's committal in view of the defective orders.   *Held*, whenever an individual's liberty was affected, all legal requirements had to be complied with at the time when the committal order was made.   Moreover, defects in the order could not be remedied after committal under the slip rule contained in CCR Ord 15, r. 12 or RSC Ord 20, r. 11 which allowed amendment of clerical or accidental mistakes.   Accordingly the committal orders were bad and would be set aside.

CINDERBY v CINDERBY; PEKESIN v PEKESIN (1978) 122 Sol Jo 436 (Court of Appeal: LORD DENNING MR, GOFF and CUMMING-BRUCE LJJ).   *Wellington v Wellington* (1978) 122 Sol Jo 296, para. 1517, applied.

1519   —— —— —— **duration of injunction**

An injunction was granted under the Domestic Violence and Matrimonial Proceedings Act 1976 excluding a husband from the matrimonial home.   The wife appealed against the limited duration of the injunction.   *Held*, an injunction under the 1976 Act was essentially a short-term remedy.   Unless there were exceptional circumstances, a party should not be excluded from his own property for more than a few months.   It should be made clear to both parties that the protection of the injunction would be withdrawn after a reasonable time, which meant a sufficient time for the wife to make arrangements for her accommodation.   The appeal would be dismissed.

HOPPER v HOPPER [1979] 1 All ER 181 (Court of Appeal: STAMP, ORMROD and LAWTON LJJ).   Dicta of Lord Salmon in *Davis v Johnson* [1978] 1 All ER 1132, HL at 1152, para. 1522, applied.

1520   The President of the Family Division has issued a Practice Note ([1978] 2 All ER 1056) in the following terms:

1. Section 1 (1) (c) of the Domestic Violence and Matrimonial Proceedings Act 1976, empowers a county court to include in an injunction provisions excluding a party from the matrimonial home or a part of the matrimonial home or from a specified area in which the matrimonial home is included.   Where a power of arrest under section 2 of the Act is attached to any injunction containing such provisions, the respondent is liable to be arrested if he enters the matrimonial home or part thereof or specified area at any time while the injunction remains in force.

2. It is within the discretion of the court to decide whether an injunction should be granted and, if so, for how long it should operate.   But whenever an injunction is granted excluding one of the parties from the matrimonial home (or a part thereof or specified area), consideration should be given to imposing a time limit on the operation of the injunction.   In most cases a period of up to three months is likely to suffice, at least in the first instance.   It will be open to the respondent in any event to apply for the discharge of the injunction before the expiry of the period fixed, for instance on the ground of reconciliation; and to the applicant to apply for an extension.

1521   —— —— —— **injunction in divorce proceedings—attachment of power of arrest**

A wife left the matrimonial home after her husband had caused her actual bodily harm.   In the course of divorce proceedings she applied for injunctions restraining her husband from molesting her and ordering him to vacate the matrimonial home.   She also applied for a power of arrest to be attached to the injunctions.   The county court judge granted the injunctions but dismissed the other application on the ground that the right to attach a power of arrest conferred on a judge by Domestic Violence and Matrimonial Proceedings Act 1976, s. 2 applied only where the application for the injunction had been made under s. 1.   On appeal, *held*, s. 2 was a general provision, not limited by s. 1.   It applied to any case where a High Court or county court judge granted an injunction in one or more of the forms set out in s. 2 (1).   Accordingly if the judge was satisfied that the husband had caused actual bodily harm to the applicant and considered that he was likely to do so again he could attach a power of arrest to the injunction.   He should do so however only if exceptional circumstances existed; the remedy was not to be regarded as routine.

The court considered that if an applicant intends to ask the court to attach a power of arrest notice of that intention should be given to the other side.

LEWIS v LEWIS [1978] 1 All ER 729 (Court of Appeal: ROSKILL and ORMROD LJJ).

1522   —— —— ——**jurisdiction of county court to override property rights**

The Court of Appeal, in allowing an appeal against a refusal to grant an injunction excluding a violent man from the council accommodation he shared as joint tenant with his common law wife, declined to follow earlier decisions of the court in *B v B* [1978] 2 WLR 160, and *Cantliff v Jenkins* [1978] 2 WLR 177, see 1977 Halsbury's Abr para. 575.   In these cases the court had decided that the property rights of a violent party could not be infringed, thus limiting the statutory powers to the rare cases where the woman is the sole tenant of the shared home.   On appeal, *held*, (i) (LORD DIPLOCK dissenting), the Domestic Violence and Matrimonial Proceedings Act 1976, s.1 was not concerned with property rights; it was intended to give protection from domestic violence and eviction and no distinction should be made in its application between married and unmarried couples.   Accordingly a county court had jurisdiction to exclude a violent lover from a home which he had a right to occupy.   An owner or tenant was not however to be permanently deprived of his proprietary rights and the county court's discretion to exclude him should be exercised only for a limited period until other arrangements could be made.   (ii) The doctrine of *stare decisis* expounded in *Young v Bristol Aeroplane Co Ltd* [1944] 1 KB 718, CA was binding on the Court of Appeal and that court had decided incorrectly in holding otherwise.   (iii) Just as it was an established rule that counsel could not refer to Hansard as an aid to the construction of a statute, it would be improper for a judge to allow Hansard to affect his decision.   The appeal would be dismissed.

LORD DIPLOCK concurred in the conclusion of the majority but on a narrower construction of s.1.

DAVIS v JOHNSON [1978] 1 All ER 1132 (House of Lords: LORD DIPLOCK, VISCOUNT DILHORNE, LORD KILBRANDON, LORD SALMON and LORD SCARMAN). Decision of Court of Appeal [1978] 2 WLR 182, 1977 Halsbury's Abr para. 573 affirmed.

1523   —— ——**injunction restraining husband from molesting wife— application to High Court**

An originating summons was issued in the High Court on behalf of a wife for an injunction to restrain the husband from molesting her and for a power of arrest without warrant to be attached to the injunction.   No proceedings claiming any other relief had been commenced.   *Held*, the Domestic Violence and Matrimonial Proceedings Act 1976, s. 1, provided that without prejudice to the jurisdiction of the High Court, a county court should have power to grant such an injunction whether or not any other relief was sought in the proceedings.   The words "whether or not any other relief is sought" applied only to applications in the county court.   The Act had not enlarged the jurisdiction of the High Court to grant the injunction itself. Accordingly, an injunction could be granted by the High Court under its statutory or inherent jurisdiction, but a power of arrest could be attached under the 1976 Act,

s. 2, only if proceedings for substantive relief had been started or an undertaking was given to start proceedings forthwith.

CRUTCHER V CRUTCHER (1978) Times, 18th July (Family Division: PAYNE J).

1524 —— home in joint names—unmarried couple—no financial contribution by one party—beneficial interest of that party

See *Ruff v Strobel*, para. 2909.

1525 —— occupation—production of documents—requirement of physical possession of documents

See *B v B (Matrimonial Proceedings: Discovery)*, para. 953.

1526 —— occupation by wife—rateable occupation—agreement between spouses—whether binding on rating authority

See *Charnwood Borough Council v Garner*, para. 2283.

1527 —— ownership of business and home—unmarried couple—property in name of one party—beneficial interest

Canada

A man and woman cohabited for almost twenty years. During that time the woman helped the man to establish himself in a bee-keeping business initially by keeping him financially, whilst he accumulated capital from his wages, then by working on an equal basis with him in the business and helping it to expand. She also assisted him in building their home. At first instance her claim for a half-share of the interest in the real property was rejected. She appealed. *Held*, the trial judge had underestimated the contribution she had made to the business and home, and she was entitled to a half of the property and assets under a constructive trust. It could not be said that the man held a share of the interest in the property for her on resulting trust as there was no evidence that it was the intention of both parties that she should have such an interest. Her interest arose under a constructive trust on the grounds that the man would be unjustly enriched if he were permitted to retain the property. In the absence of evidence as to the amount of the contribution of each party, the woman was entitled to half the interest in the property and assets on the principle that equality is equity.

BECKER V PETTKUS (1978) 20 OR (2d) 105 (Ontario Court of Appeal).

1528 —— rateable occupation—spouses judicially separated

See *Brown v Oxford City Council*, para. 2282.

1529 —— wife's unregistered interest—position of mortgagee

See *Williams & Glyn's Bank v Boland*, para. 1978, *Bird v Syme Thompson*, para. 1969.

1530 Non-molestation order—effect on institution of criminal proceedings by spouse

See *Woodley v Woodley*, para. 737.

1531 Polygamous marriage—application by wife for financial provision from estate

See *Re Sehota (deceased), Kaur v Kaur*, para. 1293.

1532 Transfer of property—transfer of wife's interest in matrimonial home to husband—failure to take independent advice—position of wife

See *Backhouse v Backhouse*, para. 1327; *Cresswell v Potter (Note)*, para. 1326.

IMMIGRATION

Halsbury's Laws of England (4th edn.), Vol. 4, paras. 974–1033

1533 **Article**

Immigration: Some Interpretations, A. N. Khan (interpretations of the Immigration Act 1971): 122 Sol Jo 785.

1534 **Appeal—application for extension of leave made after expiry of leave—refusal—jurisdiction to hear appeal**

A non-patrial remained in the United Kingdom after the date on which his leave to do so expired. He then applied to the Secretary of State for removal of the limitation on his leave, which was refused. On appeal, *held*, an immigrant whose leave to remain had expired before he applied for an extension had no right of appeal. To have given such a right would have furnished him with a defence to a charge of knowingly remaining beyond the time permitted by his leave.

R v HAMID (1978) Times, 19th October (Court of Appeal: LORD WIDGERY CJ, EVELEIGH LJ and SMITH J).

1535 —— **application for judicial review—procedure**

See *Uppal v Home Office* (CA), para. 2155.

1536 **Deportation order—deportation while petition to European Commission of Human Rights pending—whether deportation should be delayed**

An Indian couple, who had remained in the United Kingdom after their permission to do so expired, sought a declaration that they could not be deported while the final decision on their petition to the European Commission of Human Rights was pending. They relied heavily on article 25 of the Convention of Human Rights and Fundamental Freedoms, which imposed on those countries which recognised the Commission an undertaking not to hinder the exercise of the right to petition. *Held*, the applicants had not been hindered in their right to petition and had failed to establish that they had a legal right not to be deported. The basis of their claim was that their two children had been born in the United Kingdom but this had only been made possible by the breach of their conditions of entry. The most that could be claimed in the present case was that the Home Secretary should deal with the application fairly and this he had done. The declaration would be refused.

UPPAL v HOME OFFICE (1978) Times, 21st October (Chancery Division: MEGARRY V-C).

This decision was affirmed on different grounds on appeal; see para. 2155.

1537 —— **validity—order made after five years of ordinary residence**

The applicant, a Commonwealth citizen, was ordinarily resident in the United Kingdom for five years. During that time, he was notified of the Secretary of State's decision to deport him, but the deportation order was not made until after the five years had expired. The applicant sought leave to apply for a judicial review so that he might be released from custody on the ground that the Immigration Act 1971, s. 7, provided that where a Commonwealth citizen was ordinarily resident in the United Kingdom for five years he was not liable to deportation. *Held*, as the Secretary of State had decided to make the deportation order within the five-year period, the applicant was not entitled to the benefit of s. 7, even though the order was not actually made until the period had expired.

R v SECRETARY OF STATE FOR THE HOME OFFICE, EX PARTE UWABOR [1978] Crim LR 360 (Queen's Bench Division: LORD WIDGERY CJ, MELFORD STEVENSON and CANTLEY JJ).

1538   Detention order—validity—court's jurisdiction

An immigrant contended that he had been granted unconditional leave to remain in the United Kingdom, having arrived with his father in 1964. Inquiries later suggested that the man was not his father and that the applicant had entered the United Kingdom as an illegal immigrant in 1969 or 1970. He was detained under a detention order pursuant to the Immigration Act 1971, Sch. 2, para. 16, which specified alternative grounds for detention. The immigration officer deleted the wrong ground. An application for a writ of habeas corpus was made by the immigrant on the grounds that he had a right to remain in the United Kingdom and that, even if he had not, the detention was invalidated by the error on it. *Held*, BOREHAM J dissenting, if the Home Secretary had acted in good faith and on adequate evidence, the court would not inquire into the facts that had led to the conclusion that the immigrant was not entitled to remain here. Further, an incorrect deletion on the order did not render it a complete nullity. The court was entitled under the Habeas Corpus Act 1816, ss. 3 and 4, to inquire into the true state of the facts; in looking to the substance rather than the form, no injustice had been done. The application would therefore be refused.

RE SHAHID IQBAL [1978] 3 WLR 884 (Queen's Bench Division: LORD WIDGERY CJ, BOREHAM and DRAKE JJ). *R v Secretary of State for the Home Department, ex parte Hussain* [1978] 1 WLR 700, CA, 1977 Halsbury's Abr para. 1486, followed.

1539   Entry—application by dependant—person settled in UK—whether whole family settled in UK

The applicant, who was twenty, applied to accompany members of his family to the United Kingdom for permanent settlement as a dependant of his father, who was already settled here. He relied on the Statement of Immigration Rules for Control on Entry, para. 44, which provides that an unmarried and fully dependent son under twenty-one who formed part of the family unit overseas may be admitted if the whole family are settled in the UK or are being admitted for settlement. The applicant's unmarried elder brother was remaining in India to farm the family land. The adjudicator found that because of the elder brother in India, the applicant could not claim that the whole of his family was settled here within para. 44. The applicant applied for orders of certiorari and mandamus directing the Immigration Appeal Tribunal to hear the appeal, contending that "whole family" in para. 44 should be restricted to dependent members of the family. *Held*, if the elder son had left home, married and had his own family, he would not be part of the family unit. But as he was remaining to farm the family land, the adjudicator was entitled to find that he was still part of the family unit. The application would be dismissed.

HARMAIL SINGH V VICE-PRESIDENT OF THE IMMIGRATION APPEAL TRIBUNAL (1978) Times, 12th July (Court of Appeal: LORD DENNING MR, EVELEIGH LJ and SIR DAVID CAIRNS).

1540   ——— sponsor out of the country—whether sponsor's absence a bar to settlement

The applicant, a Kenyan citizen, came to the United Kingdom for a two month visit in 1972. He subsequently applied to stay as a dependant of his mother, who had been ordinarily resident in the United Kingdom but who had returned to Kenya in 1972. The immigration rules provided for the settlement of a dependant of a person who was already in the United Kingdom and was settled here. *Held*, the mother was not "already in the United Kingdom" at the time of the application. These words had to be construed in their ordinary sense and meant that the sponsor had physically to be in the United Kingdom.

R v IMMIGRATION APPEAL TRIBUNAL, EX PARTE MANEK [1978] 3 All ER 641 (Court of Appeal: LORD DENNING MR, GEOFFREY LANE and EVELEIGH LJJ). Decision of Divisional Court of the Queen's Bench Division (1978) Times, 24th January reversed.

1541   —— **permission to stay obtained by fraud—validity of permission—burden of proof**

A non-patrial under the Immigration Act 1971 was detained as an illegal immigrant by the Home Secretary pending his return to the country from which he came. The non-patrial had fraudulently obtained permission to stay indefinitely by means of a new passport which contained no record of the conditions under which he had originally been allowed to enter. He applied for an order of habeas corpus directed to the governor of the prison where he was being detained. *Held*, the burden of proving that he was not an illegal immigrant, and therefore that he should not be detained, rested on the detainee. He was unable to discharge that burden. The Home Secretary had acted reasonably and the court would not intervene. The detained person's remedy was by appeal under the Act when he had left the United Kingdom and not by an application for habeas corpus.

R v SECRETARY OF STATE FOR HOME DEPARTMENT EX PARTE CHOUDHARY [1978] 3 All ER 790 (Court of Appeal: LORD DENNING MR, GEOFFREY LANE and EVELEIGH LJJ). *R v Secretary of State for the Home Department, ex parte Hussain* [1978] 2 All ER 423, CA, 1977 Halsbury's Abr para 1486 applied.

1542   —— **permission to stay obtained by mistake—validity of permission**

An Indian citizen first entered the United Kingdom with limited permission to remain. On his return from one of several trips abroad he was given permission to remain for an indefinite period. On no occasion did he make any misrepresentation to the immigration officer as to his status. He was subsequently detained in prison as an illegal immigrant on the ground that, as he did not fall within any of the prescribed categories of legal immigrants, the immigration officer had no authority to grant him indefinite leave to stay. He claimed that he had been wrongfully detained and applied for a writ of habeas corpus. *Held*, the question for the court was whether in the circumstances the Secretary of State had acted reasonably in detaining him. The permission had not been granted as the result of any fraud or misrepresentation and it could not be said that the immigration officer's mistake vitiated his authority to grant indefinite leave. The writ would be granted.

R v SECRETARY OF STATE FOR HOME AFFAIRS, EX PARTE RAM [1979] 1 WLR 148 (Queen's Bench Division: LORD WIDGERY CJ, MAY and TUDOR EVANS JJ).

1543   —— **temporary admission—whether knowingly remaining after expiry of permission**

The defendant, who entered the United Kingdom with permission to stay for six months, was charged with knowingly remaining in the country after the expiry of the permitted period. He claimed that the death of his mother during that period had disturbed him to the extent that he did not realise that he had stayed beyond the permitted period. The trial judge ruled that this was not a defence known to law and the defendant was convicted. On appeal, *held*, the occasions when a judge could properly rule that a defence was not known to law were very limited. In this case there might have been questions of fact and degree as to the state of the defendant's mind. Probably a man could not claim to have done something without knowledge if he could recall the event to mind. However, there was evidence that the defendant had been unaffected by his mother's death in any other respect and therefore a conviction had been inevitable. The appeal would be dismissed.

R v BELLO [1978] Crim LR 551 (Court of Appeal: LORD WIDGERY CJ, SHAW LJ and LLOYD J). Dictum of Lindley J in *Macleay v Tait* [1906] AC 24 at 32 considered.

1544   **Registration with police—effect of expiry of leave to remain in United Kingdom**

An alien who had remained in the United Kingdom after his leave to remain expired was convicted of failing without reasonable excuse to furnish particulars to a registration officer as required by the Immigration (Registration with Police)

Regulations 1972, contrary to the Immigration Act 1971, s. 26 (1) (f). On appeal, *held*, the 1972 Regulations, reg. 3, provided that the regulations should apply in the case of an alien who had a limited leave to enter or remain in the United Kingdom. Thus the application of the regulations was restricted to the period of leave and once that period expired the regulations ceased to apply and different provisions came into operation. The appeal would be allowed and the conviction quashed.

R v NAIK (1978) Times, 26th July (Court of Appeal: SHAW LJ, JUPP and NEILL JJ).

1545 The defendant remained in the United Kingdom after the period of his leave to enter had expired. He was arrested and convicted of failing without reasonable excuse to furnish particulars to a registration officer, contrary to the Immigration Act 1971, s. 26, and the Immigration (Registration with Police) Regulations 1972. On appeal, *held*, the regulations applied to aliens with limited leave to enter or remain in the United Kingdom. Once the period of leave had expired, the regulations ceased to apply. Offences against the regulations committed after the date of expiry of the period of leave were not covered by those regulations. The appeal would be allowed and the conviction quashed.

R v MAOK [1978] LS Gaz R 857 (Court of Appeal: SHAW LJ, JUPP and NEILL JJ).

1546 —— fees

The Immigration (Registration with Police) (Amendment) Regulations 1978, S.I. 1978 No. 24 (in force on 1st March 1978), increase the fees payable by aliens, other than EEC nationals, required to register with the police.

1547 Select Committee—report

The report of the Commons Select Committee on Race Relations and Immigration has been published. Among its principal recommendations are the following: (i) an overall annual figure for admissions of immigrants from the Indian sub-continent should be announced; (ii) the applications for entry of wives and children of those immigrants in Britain before 1st January 1973 should receive priority; (iii) the admission of fiancés and fiancées should have low priority; (iv) there should be no further major primary immigration in the predictable future; (v) the immigration service intelligence unit, the police and other bodies should be given more resources to trace overstayers and deal with all aspects of illegal immigration; and (vi) entry applications of dependants, fiancés and fiancées should be made by their sponsors in the United Kingdom to reduce the temptation both to use false documents and obviate the need for agents: Times, 22nd March 1978.

INCOME TAXATION

Halsbury's Laws of England (4th edn.), Vol. 23.

1548 Articles

A Case for Reform, (legislation to nullify certain tax avoidance schemes). TAXATION, 17th June 1978, p. 205.

Finance Act 1978, Brian Harvey and Julia Kerr (taxation of personal income): 122 Sol Jo 598.

Tax Free Ex Gratia Payments, O. P. Wylie (when such payments are not taxable): TAXATION, 14th January 1978, p. 274.

Tax Havens: The Possible Application of United Kingdom Tax Legislation to the Channel Islands, St John Robilliard [1978] BTR 111.

1549   Assessment—appeal—admissibility of Crown evidence

A taxpayer appealed against assessments to Schedule D income tax covering an eight year period. The commissioners accepted statements of capital income and expenditure submitted by the tax inspector which showed that the taxpayer had failed to explain certain withdrawals from his bank account and that his estimates of his outgoings were remarkably low. They found that he had been neglectful in making his tax returns. The court rejected his claim that the commissioners had had no evidence on which to base their decision on the ground that they were entitled to accept the inspector's statements. *Held*, on the evidence shown the commissioners were entitled to find that the taxpayer had been neglectful in making his returns, as it was plain that he had been living above his declared income. There was nothing to suggest that the commissioners had based their decision on any improper material and it was not open to a taxpayer to obtain a rehearing of his appeal merely by suggesting that it was not possible to say whether the commissioners had acted on the basis of the proper material.

JOHNSON v SCOTT (INSPECTOR OF TAXES) [1978] STC 476 (Court of Appeal; BUCKLEY and BRIDGE LJJ and FOSTER J). Decision of Walton J [1978] STC 48, 1977 Halsbury's Abr para. 1499 affirmed.

1550   —— —— agreement with tax inspector to vary assessment— whether agreement binding

See *Delbourgo v Field (Inspector of Taxes)*, para. 277.

1551   —— —— failure to produce evidence

Estimated assessments were made on the taxpayer, a medical practitioner. He appealed, contending that the assessments were excessive, and sought postponement of payment of the tax. The Special Commissioners found that the taxpayer had produced no accounts for the relevant period, and there was no reason to believe that he had been overcharged or to postpone payment. The taxpayer required the commissioners to state a case for the High Court. They did so, but the case stated was signed by only one of the two commissioners who had heard the appeal. At the hearing of the appeal, the taxpayer contended that the case stated was defective since it was signed by only one commissioner, and that there was no evidence on which the commissioners could reasonably have reached their conclusion. His appeal was dismissed, and he appealed. *Held*, the taxpayer could not assert both that the case stated was valid for the purposes of conducting his appeal and that it was invalid, in which case no appeal would be competent. On the facts found by the commissioners, there was no information before them relating to the taxpayer's income and they could not have come to any other conclusion. The appeal would be dismissed.

PARIKH v CURRIE (INSPECTOR OF TAXES) [1978] STC 473 (Court of Appeal: STAMP, ROSKILL and CUMMING-BRUCE LJJ). Decision of Fox J [1977] STC 215, 1977 Halsbury's Abr para. 1500 affirmed.

1552   —— —— whether appeal finally determined

A taxpayer appealed to the Special Commissioners against assessments to income and profits tax by the Inland Revenue on the ground that they were excessive. The Revenue agreed that the taxpayer was not bound to pay the tax until final determination of the appeal. The Special Commissioners purported to determine the appeal by a decision in February 1973. The taxpayer sought a declaration that they had not finally determined his appeal on the ground that their determination was only a statement of the amount of the income and profits assessable to tax and did not include a statement of the tax payable. *Held*, the Taxes Management Act 1970, s. 31 (5), provided that a notice of appeal had to state its grounds and a taxpayer was not entitled, as of right, to rely on any grounds not so stated. The Commissioners' function was thus to determine the issues raised on appeal. In the present case, the actual issues of the appeal had been defined and the Commissioners had given their decision in February 1973 which was the date the appeal was determined. However, the Act did not provide that an assessment did not need to include a statement of the tax payable. A man should be told what tax he had to pay and not merely be given information from which the amount of tax payable had to be computed by a skilled adviser. As the appeal had been determined, the declaration would not be granted.

HALLAMSHIRE INDUSTRIAL FINANCE TRUST LTD v INLAND REVENUE COMMISSIONERS (1978) Times, 26th October (Chancery Division: BROWNE-WILKINSON J).

1553   —— settlement on children—income paid to children under deed of release and assignment—whether assessable as taxpayer's income

A taxpayer's wife was entitled to contingent reversionary life interests under settlements made by her father and sister. In 1959, the wife executed a deed of assignment and release of her interests under the settlements to the trustees thereof. She subsequently executed a deed of appointment in favour of her children. In 1974, she revoked the 1959 appointment and appointed in favour of her children and grand-children. However, since 1963, income had been paid out of the trust fund to her infant children. The Inland Revenue claimed that the income paid to the children was paid by virtue of a settlement constituted by the deeds of assignment and release and of appointment and should thus be treated as income of the settlor under Income and Corporation Taxes Act 1970, s. 437 (1). It therefore fell to be taxed as the taxpayer's income under s. 37 of the Act which provided for the aggregation of a wife's income. The taxpayer contended that the income could not be treated as his wife's because it originated from her father and sister. The Special Commissioners upheld the Revenue's claim and the taxpayer appealed. *Held*, what had to be considered was whether the deeds of assignment and release constituted a disposition in consequence of which the income had been paid to the children. From the facts it was clear that there had been such a disposition and s. 437 of the 1970 Act, which provided that income paid to a settlor's infant children was assessable in his hands, applied. Further, even if the wife had not made the disposition in favour of her children, the income would have belonged to her and thus been assessable under s. 442 of the Act as income which was provided directly or indirectly by her. The appeal would therefore be dismissed.

D'ABREU v INLAND REVENUE COMMISSIONERS [1978] STC 538 (Chancery Division: OLIVER J). *Inland Revenue Commissioners v Buchanan* [1957] 2 All ER 400 applied.

1554   —— time limit for assessment—fraud—finding of fraud made in absence of taxpayer

A taxpayer applied to the general commissioners for adjournment of the hearing of his case. The commissioners refused and went on to make a finding of fraud against him under Taxes Management Act 1970, s. 36. On appeal, *held*, although the taxpayer had acted casually in writing a letter to the commissioners and not appearing before them, he had obtained a previous adjournment in that way and might have thought it was appropriate. In relation to the finding of fraud, the taxpayer's evidence could have been crucial and the possibility of injustice far outweighed the inconvenience of an adjournment.

The court was satisfied that there had been injustice and the case would be remitted to the commissioners.

OTTLEY v MORRIS (INSPECTOR OF TAXES) [1978] STC 594 (Chancery Division: Fox J). *Rose v Humbles (Inspector of Taxes)* [1970] 2 All ER 519, followed.

1555   —— whether assessment to include statement of the tax payable

See *Hallamshire Industrial Finance Trust Ltd v Inland Revenue Commissioners*, para. 1552.

1556   **Avoidance—artificial transactions in land—tax advantage—consideration received in connection with distribution of profits by a company**

The taxpayers were equal shareholders in company A and company B. Company A owned land which it decided to sell. In order to reduce tax liability on the sale profits, the taxpayers entered into a tax avoidance scheme. The scheme vested the freehold interest in the land in company B and left company A with the profits of sale. The taxpayers then exchanged their shares in company A for shares in the specially incorporated company C. The two companies elected under the Income and Corporation Taxes Act 1970, s. 256, for tax-free dividends to be paid to company C by company A. A tax-free dividend of the same amount as the sale profits was subsequently paid to company C by company A. The land was then sold by company B. The taxpayers entered into a loan transaction which allowed them to hold the sums received on indefinite loan. They were served with notices, under s. 460 of the 1970 Act, which purported to cancel their tax advantage and assess them to income tax. The notices were upheld by the Special Commissioners and the taxpayers appealed. *Held*, s. 461 of the 1970 Act prescribed the circumstances under the tax advantages could be cancelled under s. 460. By receiving shares in company C, the taxpayers had obtained a tax advantage, the amount of which could be assessed by reference to the amount of tax-free dividends paid by company A to company C. Further, the exchange of shares in company C for those in company A enabled company A to distribute profits by way of dividend among the taxpayers. Accordingly, the share exchange between companies A and C was within the scope of s. 461, para. D, and the s. 460 notices and tax assessments were valid.

WILLIAMS v INLAND REVENUE COMMISSIONERS [1978] STC 379 (Chancery Division: BROWNE-WILKINSON J). *Anysz v Inland Revenue Commissioners* [1978] STC 296, 1977 Halsbury's Abr para. 1518 followed.

1557   **—— establishment of overseas partnership—income not remitted to United Kingdom**

The taxpayer, a prominent United Kingdom television personality, in anticipation of substantial earnings from overseas appearances, entered into partnership with a Bahamian "off the peg" company to exploit his talents on the basis that 95 per cent of the profits would go to him. All partnership activities took place abroad and no overseas earnings were remitted to the United Kingdom. The question was whether under the Income and Corporation Taxes Act 1970, Schedule D the taxpayer's share of the profits was taxable under Case II in respect of his profession or vocation or under Case V in respect of income arising from possessions out of the United Kingdom. Under Case II he would be taxable whether or not moneys had been brought into the United Kingdom whereas his liability under Case V was limited by s. 122 (2) (b) of the Act to sums actually received in the United Kingdom. *Held*, income from a business carried on exclusively abroad was income from a possession out of the United Kingdom and so came under Case V. It did not follow from the fact that the taxpayer had entered into partnership with a company and that a company could not appear on television that the taxpayer's television appearances had been made on his own behalf rather than on behalf of the partnership business. The business of the partnership was the exploitation of the taxpayer's talents. Its purposes had been widely stated and were all such as the company could pursue vicariously through its agents.

The fact that by setting up the partnership business the parties hoped to achieve a measure of tax avoidance did not import that the partnership business was not to be conducted for profit. A taxpayer was entitled to arrange his affairs to reduce his tax obligations provided the means adopted were legitimate and genuine. It had not been suggested in the present case that what had been done was a sham. The means were both legitimate and effective.

NEWSTEAD (INSPECTOR OF TAXES) v FROST [1978] 1 WLR 1441 (Court of Appeal: BUCKLEY, ROSKILL and GOFF LJJ). Decision of Browne-Wilkinson J [1978] 2 All ER 241, 1977 Halsbury's Abr para. 1504 affirmed. *Colquhoun v Brooks* (1889), 14 App Cas 493, HL applied.

Income and Corporation Taxes Act 1970, s. 122 (2) (b) has been repealed; see now Finance Act 1974, s. 23.

1558   **—— fund administered abroad—whether discretionary benefici-ary has power to enjoy income—statutory provisions**

The taxpayers, who resided in the United Kingdom were beneficiaries under a discretionary trust of overseas property settled on non-resident trustees. Under powers contained in the settlement appointments from capital of some £2·6m had been made for the taxpayers. The Inland Revenue contended that the taxpayers fell to be assessed under Income Tax Act 1952, s. 412 (1) (now Income and Corporation Taxes Act 1970, s. 478 (1)) which provides that where an individual ordinarily resident in the United Kingdom has, by means of a transfer of assets, acquired the power to enjoy any income of a non-resident person, that income is deemed to be income of the resident for the purposes of tax if it would have been taxable if received by him in the United Kingdom. *Held*, as the section was a final one it had to be construed strictly. Thus if the taxpayer had power to enjoy even a hundredth part of the income of the foreign trustees, the whole of their income was to be deemed his. But before s. 412 (1) could take effect the person sought to be charged must have acquired rights by virtue of which he had the power to enjoy any of that income. Although "power to enjoy" was defined in s. 412 (5) it was first necessary to see what "rights" had been acquired under the settlement by the taxpayers. The most relevant was the right to retain any sums properly paid to them by the trustees in the exercise of their discretionary powers but this was simply the negative right of being afforded a complete defence to any claim for repayment. Prior to actual payment, there was no right to the money at all. Accordingly none of the discretionary beneficiaries had any "right" to anything at all which could possibly bring s. 412 (1) into play.

VESTEY v INLAND REVENUE COMMISSIONERS (No. 2) [1978] 3 WLR 693 (Chancery Division: WALTON J).

For assessment of the above settlement under 1952 Act s. 412 (2) see *Vestey v Inland Revenue Commissioners* [1978] 2 WLR 136, 1977 Halsbury's Abr para. 1505.

1559   **Benefits—beneficial loans—official rate of interest**

The Income Tax (Official Rate of Interest on Beneficial Loans) Order 1978, S.I. 1978 No. 28 (in force 6th April 1978), prescribes that the official rate of interest for the purposes of the charge to income tax under the Finance Act 1976 in respect of certain cheap or interest-free loans which directors and higher-paid employees obtain by reason of their employment is 9 per cent per annum.

1560   **—— benefits in kind—scholarships for employees' children**

The Inland Revenue have issued a Press Release dated 14th June 1978 stating that henceforward they propose to contend for liability under the Finance Act 1976, s. 61, for scholarships awarded to a member of the family or household of a director or higher-paid employee when the award is made by reason of the latter's employment. They argue that those awards gave rise to benefits provided by reason of the employment and are therefore assessable on the parents under s. 61; the Income and Corporation Taxes Act 1970, s. 375, while exempting from tax the scholarship income in the scholar's hands, does not prevent the cost of providing the scholarship from being a benefit taxable under s. 61.

1561   **—— car benefits—prescription of cash equivalents**

The Income Tax (Cash Equivalents of Car Benefits) Order 1978, S.I. 1978 No. 434 (in force 6th April 1978), prescribes new amounts of cash equivalents on which directors and higher-paid employees are chargeable to income tax under the Finance Act 1976, s. 64 in respect of the benefit of a car made available for private use by reason of their employment. For this purpose higher-paid employees are those earning £7,500 a year or more.

1562   Capital allowance—first year allowance—expenditure incurred in provision of finance

A company borrowed large sums of money to finance the construction of an oil rig. Fees and interest payments were made on the loans and were charged to capital in the company's accounts. The company sought a first year capital allowance in respect of the fees and interest payments under the Finance Act 1971, s. 41, contending that they constituted capital expenditure on the provision of machinery or plant. Special commissioners and the High Court rejected the claim. On appeal direct to the House of Lords, *held*, LORD SALMON dissenting, the expenditure had not been incurred in the provision of machinery or plant, but in the provision of finance by means of which machinery and plant could be obtained. There was a distinction to be drawn between the two cases and therefore the appeal would be dismissed.

LORD SALMON considered the distinction artificial and the majority view contrary to the policy of the 1971 Act, which was to encourage re-investment in machinery and plant.

BEN-ODECO LTD v POWLSON (INSPECTOR OF TAXES) [1978] STC 460 (House of Lords: LORD WILBERFORCE, LORD HAILSHAM OF MARYLEBONE, LORD SALMON, LORD RUSSELL OF KILLOWEN and LORD SCARMAN). Decision of Brightman J [1978] 1 All ER 913, 1977 Halsbury's Abr para. 1508 affirmed.

1563   —— machinery or plant—restaurant ship

The taxpayer company purchased a vessel and spent a large sum converting and fitting it out as a restaurant. It was permanently moored and used as a restaurant until 1975. The company claimed capital allowances in respect of the expenditure; the question was whether the ship fell within the phrase "machinery or plant", within the Capital Allowances Act 1968. The Crown's contention was that one had to apply the "functional test", whether the object in dispute was part of the premises in which the business was carried on, or part of the plant with which it was carried on; in this case, the ship was only the premises. The company contended that where land or buildings were under consideration, to be "plant" the object had to play a part in the commercial process of the trade; where, however, it was a chattel, it was enough to ask whether it was kept for permanent employment in the business, and the ship fell within this definition. *Held*, the authorities did not support such a distinction. The ship was the premises in which the trade was carried on. It was not apparatus essential to the business, notwithstanding that the fact that it was a ship meant that it had a particular commercial utility. Accordingly, the expenditure did not qualify for the allowances.

BENSON (INSPECTOR OF TAXES) v THE YARD ARM CLUB LTD [1978] 2 All ER 958 (Chancery Division: GOULDING J).

1564   —— vehicle leasing

The Inland Revenue has given warning that it has advised its inspectors on the tax implications of certain types of vehicle leasing arrangement (see Times, 27th July 1978). Normally there are no problems with such arrangements from the tax point of view but the Inland Revenue may use existing powers to discourage arrangements whereby the vehicle is made available at the end of the lease to the lessee or his nominee at a price below the market value. In such arrangements, the vehicle might be regarded as stock-in-trade (thereby losing the 100 per cent capital allowance), or the lessor may be required to include the market value of the vehicle when sold into its calculations (rather than the lower sale price), or the rental payments might be disallowed for tax purposes or the final receipient might be taxed on the benefit received under Schedule E.

1565   Capital charge—machinery or plant—loss of ship through dumping of ammunition—whether insurance moneys liable to corporation tax

A dredger was carrying out operations in a fishing harbour when it dredged up ammunition dumped by the British Army at the end of the Second World War.

An explosion resulted and the dredger sank. The owners were assessed for corporation tax on the basis that the insurance money received for the loss should result in a balancing charge being made under the Capital Allowances Act, 1968. They appealed against the assessment, claiming that the loss of the ship was due to a war risk and therefore fell within the exemption contained in s. 33 (7) of the Act. Section 33 (7) provides that "war risk" is to be defined according to the meaning attached to the phrase in the agreement for re-insurance of British ships made by the Minister of War Transport in 1943. It was necessary to show by this definition that the dumping of the ammunition was a consequence of hostilities or warlike operations. The special commissioners hearing the appeal held this to be the case, but dismissed the appeal on the basis that the case fell within the exclusion contained in the re-insurance agreement for the loss of a ship due to contact with any fixed or floating object. The commissioners found that the ammunition which consisted of shells, was made up of fixed or floating objects. The owners appealed. *Held*, the dumping of the ammunition did not come within the ambit of s. 33 (7), although it might have done in other circumstances. In this case the dumping amounted to a destruction of war stores due to the advent of peace, thus it was an act of pacification, not a consequence of warlike operations. Nevertheless, even if s. 33 (7) had applied the exclusion contained in the re-insurance agreement would have taken the case out of the s. 33 (7) exemption; it could not be argued that merely because the shells were resting on the sea-bed they were not fixed or floating objects. The appeal would therefore be dismissed.

COSTAIN-BLANKEVOORT (UK) DREDGING CO LTD v DAVENPORT (INSPECTOR OF TAXES) (1978) 123 Sol Jo 35 (Chancery Division: WALTON J).

1566   Case stated—contents—jurisdiction of court to admit further evidence

The taxpayer appealed against assessment to income tax made in respect of his purported income from writing, from property and from letting accommodation. The commissioners reduced the assessments in respect of income from writing and discharged the assessments in respect of income from property but, on the evidence, they found that the taxpayer had been letting accommodation and increased the assessments in respect of income from that source. The taxpayer transmitted the case stated by the commissioners to the High Court, contending that it was inaccurate, that the proceedings before the commissioners had been conducted improperly and that the assessments should be discharged. *Held*, on appeal by case stated the court had jurisdiction to consider only the facts found by the commissioners and to determine only questions of law arising from those facts. They were not entitled to receive evidence from the taxpayer to supplement or override the case stated. On the facts as set out in the case stated, the conclusion reached was one at which any reasonable commissioner could have arrived. The court, therefore, could not interfere with the commissioners' decision and the appeal would be dismissed.

YOANNOU v HALL (INSPECTOR OF TAXES) [1978] STC 600 (Chancery Division: FOX J).

1567   Child allowance—apportionment—conflicting claims of mother and father

The husband and wife and their two children lived together in the matrimonial home until March 1975 when the husband left. Both parents claimed income tax relief in respect of the children for the tax years 1973–4 and 1974–5. The parties were not able to agree an apportionment. The commissioners found that the child relief should be apportioned at 60 per cent to the husband and 40 per cent to the wife for 1973–4, and 25 per cent to the husband and 75 per cent to the wife for 1974–5. The apportionment for the second year took into account the fact that for part of that period the husband had been making contributions under a court order and these were deductible in the assessment of his total income for tax purposes. On appeal by the husband *held*, it was not necessary to determine the exact amount spent on the children as long as the findings were expressed in percentages of the total expenditure on them. Once the commissioners had apportioned, as between the parents, the total expenditure on the children, they were entitled to apportion the child allowance on the same basis. As there was conflicting evidence as to how much each parent had spent on the children the commissioners were entitled to use their discretion to reach the conclusion they did and the appeal would be dismissed.

BUXTON v BUXTON AND INLAND REVENUE COMMISSIONERS [1978] STC 122 (Chancery Division: BRIGHTMAN J).

1568   —— entitlement—custody of child

When a university student was twenty-two her father declared that he relinquished all rights over her in favour of the taxpayer. The taxpayer subsequently maintained her at university and paid the fees, and she stayed with him during holidays. He claimed a child allowance in respect of her under the Income and Corporation Taxes Act 1970, s. 10 (1) (b), contending that she was in his custody, he maintained her at his own expense and she was receiving full-time education. *Held*, mere factual, not legal, custody was sufficient to satisfy the requirement of s. 10 (1) (b). However, at the beginning of the relevant period the student was twenty-three, an adult, and could not be in anybody's custody. When her father purported to relinquish his rights over her to the taxpayer, under English law he had no rights over her capable of being relinquished. The taxpayer's claim would fail.

NWAGBO v RISING (INSPECTOR OF TAXES) [1978] STC 558 (Chancery Division: Fox J). *Kirby v Leather* [1965] 2 QB 367, CA followed.

1569   ——— evidence

The taxpayer claimed child allowances in respect of four children whom he claimed were his. The taxpayer was a citizen of the Republic of the Yemen, and claimed that the children were his by one of his two wives under Mohammedan law. The General Commissioners found that the taxpayer had not proved on the balance of probabilities that the children were his and disallowed the claims for child allowances. The taxpayer required the Commissioners to state a case for the High Court. *Held*, the Commissioners had been faced with a difficult task on evidence which was unsatisfactory through no fault of the taxpayer, since there was no system of registration of births in the Republic of the Yemen. There was no question of law in the case and the court had no jurisdiction to reach any different findings of fact. The appeal would be dismissed.

MOHSIN v EDON (INSPECTOR OF TAXES) (NOTE) [1978] STC 163 (Chancery Division: BRIGHTMAN J).

1570   Close company—loans applied in acquiring interest in close company—tax relief on interest

The Finance Act 1974, Sch. 1, paras. 9 and 10, provides for relief from income tax in respect of interest on a loan applied in acquiring any part of the ordinary share capital of a close company or an associated close company. The Inland Revenue has now agreed that these provisions may be interpreted as not requiring the company to remain close at the time of paying the interest. The Inland Revenue's booklet entitled "Tax Treatment of Interest Paid", issued in 1974, is amended accordingly: Inland Revenue Press Release dated 19th October 1978 and Statement of Practice SP 3/78.

1571   —— shortfall in distributions—assessment to tax—exemption where distribution restricted by law

The Income and Corporation Taxes Act 1970, s. 289, provided for assessments to tax to be made on a close company which had a shortfall in the amount of the annual distribution of its income. Exemptions from s. 289 were provided by s. 290 (4) where a company was subjected to any restriction imposed by law with respect to the making of distributions. The taxpayer company's articles permitted a maximum distribution which fell short of the required standard laid down in s. 290 (1), and consequently shortfall assessments were made on the company. The company contended that it fell within s. 290 (4) because its articles prevented it from making further distributions, so that it was subject to a restriction "imposed by law" and accordingly the shortfall had to be disregarded. *Held*, it could not be said that restrictions imposed on a company by its articles were "imposed by law". A company assuming a constitution restricted its own powers, and could alter its articles at a general meeting. The assessment would be upheld.

NOBLE (INSPECTOR OF TAXES) v LAYGATE INVESTMENTS LTD [1978] 2 All ER 1067 (Chancery Division: OLIVER J).

In relation to accounting periods ending after 5th April 1973, shortfall assessments are replaced by apportionment provisions under the Finance Act 1972, s. 94, Sch. 16.

1572 Construction industry—sub-contractors—tax deduction scheme —certificate of exemption—jurisdiction of the commissioners

A sub-contractor had been refused a certificate of exemption from tax deductions by the Board of the Inland Revenue. He had exercised his right of appeal to the general commissioners under the Finance (No. 2) Act 1975. The Board had refused to grant the certificates on the grounds that he had failed to comply with the conditions outlined in the 1975 Act as to his obligations under the Income Tax Acts during the qualifying period. They refused to exercise their discretion to waive compliance with these conditions. The commissioners decided that the Board had been correct to refuse the certificate, but that they would issue it as the sub-contractor had since rectified his faults. The commissioners had no jurisdiction to hear an appeal from the Board relating to the latter's decision that an applicant had not satisfied the conditions. In deciding whether the Board had actually made a decision, *held*, on the facts of the case they had done so; even if they had not, the commissioners had no jurisdiction to waive the right of compliance with the conditions if the Board itself refused to do so, despite the fact that the sub-contractor had rectified his faults subsequently.

KIRVELL (INSPECTOR OF TAXES) v GUY (1978) Times, 29th November (Chancery Division: WALTON J).

1573 ———— —— rate of deduction

Under the Finance (No. 2) Act 1975, a deduction on account of tax is to be made by a contractor from amounts paid (less cost of materials) to a sub-contractor who does not hold a valid certificate authorising payment in full. The present rate of deduction is 34 per cent under the Finance Act 1977, s. 39. As a consequence of the reduction of the basic rate of income tax for 1978/79, the Finance Act 1978, s. 33, reduces the rate of deduction to 33 per cent. The new rate applies to all payments made on or after 6th November 1978. All contractors known to be operating the deduction scheme will be notified individually: Inland Revenue Press Release dated 3rd October 1978.

1574 Corporation tax—work-in-progress—change in method of valuation—effect on tax liability

During the 1960s the taxpayer company became engaged in large projects involving contracts which extended over several years. As a result, in 1969 the company adopted a new accounting method whereby a proportion of the anticipated profit on the contracts was taken into account for each year, as opposed to the old basis whereby no profit was included until a contract was completed. This change necessitated the revaluation of the work-in-progress at the beginning of 1969, which resulted in an excess of £579,874 over the old valuation. The company claimed that the figure did not reflect profit arising during the year ending December 1969 and was not assessable to corporation tax. *Held*, where a trader decided to write down his stock, that decision took effect for tax purposes in that year notwithstanding that the stock might have been going down in value in previous years. By analogy, the same thing applied where a trader attributed year by year a percentage of the contractual price agreed, thus effecting a writing-up of the work-in-progress.

Although the surplus brought into account in 1969 was partly referable to previous years, none of it could be attributable to a previous year any more than a bad debt could be attributed to a year earlier than that in which it was recognised to be bad. Thus the excess was a trading profit for the financial year 1969 and was assessable to corporation tax.

PEARCE (INSPECTOR OF TAXES) v WOODALL DUCKHAM LTD [1978] 2 All ER 793 (Court of Appeal: STAMP, ORR and EVELEIGH LJJ). Decision of Templeman J [1977] 1 All ER 753, 1976 Halsbury's Abr para. 1419 affirmed.

1575 Covenants in favour of charities—repayment procedure

Under the procedure introduced in 1973, when a charity claimed repayment of tax deducted from certain annual payments made under deeds of covenant, a form signed by the covenantor was produced in relation to net payments of £15 of less only on the occasion of the first claim. The limit was increased to £30 in 1976, see 1976 Halsbury's Abr para. 1420, and is further increased to £52 for payments due after 5th April 1978: Inland Revenue Press Release dated 9th November 1978.

1576 Double taxation—Nigeria

Nigeria has given notice terminating the Double Taxation Arrangement with the United Kingdom. The existing arrangement will accordingly cease to have effect in the United Kingdom from 6th April 1979 in respect of income tax and 1st January 1979 in respect of corporation tax: Inland Revenue Press Release dated 7th July 1978.

1577 —— relief—Botswana

The Double Taxation Relief (Taxes on Income) (Botswana) Order 1978, S.I. 1978 No. 183 (made on 9th February 1978 and taking effect as respects income tax for the tax year 1976–77 and subsequent years and as respects corporation tax for the financial year commencing 1st April 1976 and subsequent years), replaces the Arrangement made with Bechuanaland Protectorate in 1949 as amended. The 1978 Order sets out the new arrangements made between the United Kingdom and Botswana with a view to affording relief from double taxation in relation to income tax and corporation tax and taxes of a similar character imposed by the laws of Botswana.

1578 —— —— Ghana

The Double Taxation Relief (Taxes on Income) (Ghana) Order 1978, S.I. 1978 No. 785 (made on 31st May 1978), sets out the arrangements made between the United Kingdom and Ghana with a view to affording relief from double taxation in relation to income tax, corporation tax, capital gains tax or development land tax and taxes of a similar character imposed in Ghana.

1579 —— —— Hungary

The Double Taxation Relief (Taxes on Income) (Hungary) Order 1978, S.I. 1978 No. 1056 (made on 25th July 1978), sets out the arrangements made between the United Kingdom and Hungary with a view to affording relief from double taxation in relation to income tax, corporation tax, capital gains tax or development land tax and taxes of a similar character imposed in Hungary.

1580 —— —— Korea

The Double Taxation Relief (Taxes on Income) (Republic of Korea) Order 1978, S.I. 1978 No. 786 (made on 31st May 1978), sets out the arrangements made between the United Kingdom and Korea with a view to affording relief from double taxation in relation to income tax, corporation tax or capital gains tax and taxes of a similar character imposed in Korea.

1581   —— —— **Philippines**

The Double Taxation (Taxes on Income) (Philippines) Order 1978, S.I. 1978 No. 184 (made on 9th February 1978) sets out the arrangements made between the United Kingdom and the Philippines with a view to affording relief from double taxation in relation to income tax, corporation tax or capital gains tax and taxes of a similar character imposed by the laws of the Philippines.

1582   —— —— **Poland**

The Double Taxation Relief (Taxes on Income) (Poland) Order 1978, S.I. 1978 No. 282 (made on 1st March 1978), sets out the arrangements made between the United Kingdom and Poland with a view to affording relief from double taxation in relation to income tax, corporation tax or capital gains tax and taxes of a similar character imposed by the laws of Poland.

1583   —— —— **Singapore**

The Double Taxation Relief (Taxes on Income) (Singapore) Order 1978, S.I. 1978 No. 787 (made on 31st May 1978), sets out the arrangements made between the United Kingdom and Singapore with a view to affording relief from double taxation in relation to income tax, corporation tax or capital gains tax and taxes of a similar character imposed in Singapore.

1584   —— —— **Switzerland**

The Double Taxation Relief (Taxes on Income) (Switzerland) Order 1978, S.I. 1978 No. 1408 (made on 29th September 1978), sets out the arrangements made between the United Kingdom and Switzerland with a view to affording relief from double taxation in relation to income tax, corporation tax or capital gains tax and taxes of a similar character imposed by the law of Switzerland. The Convention scheduled to this order replaces the 1954 Convention.

1585   —— **United States**

The American Senate has ratified an Anglo-American Double Taxation Treaty, but British companies are not to be exempted from the need to pay state unitary taxes levied in Alaska, California and Oregon. A clause providing this exemption was rejected: Financial Times, 28th June 1978.

1586   **Exemption—trade unions—provident benefits**

Under the Income and Corporation Taxes Act 1970, s. 338, trade unions are exempt from tax on income used for the payment of provident benefits to members. The Statement of Practice 6/78 explains that certain legal expenses incurred by unions will in future be regarded as provident benefits for this purpose: Inland Revenue Press Release dated 13th November 1978.

1587   **Finance Act 1978**

Finance Act 1978, Pt. III deals with income tax and corporation tax; see further para. 2312.

1588   **Information—power of commissioners to require—whether any limitation period applicable**

Six associated companies appealed from a decision of special commissioners imposing penalties on them under the Taxes Management Act 1970, s. 98 (1) for non-compliance with notices issued under s. 20 requiring them to produce certain documents for inspection. They contended that the notices were invalid because, inter alia, (i) they related to periods going back as far as 1961 and as such ought to be deemed out of time notwithstanding the lack of a time limit in s. 20, and (ii) because they required information about periods for which four of the companies had not been asked to furnish returns despite the fact that notices could only be issued following failure to comply with a request to make returns. *Held*, (i) had Parliament intended a limitation period to apply to s. 20 it would have included one. The section could be very useful in the investigation of alleged fraud and wilful default, where normal limitation periods had no application. (ii) Despite the courts' critical attitude to technical defences, it was clear that the notices had, in respect of the four companies, required information which the Inland Revenue were not entitled to receive. It would be unjust for the companies effectively to be penalised for not having rewritten the notices. Accordingly, the appeal would be allowed to that extent.

B & S DISPLAYS LTD v INLAND REVENUE COMMISSIONERS [1978] STC 331 (Chancery Division: GOULDING J). *Dyson v Attorney-General* [1912] 1 Ch 158 applied.

1589   Interest—chargeable persons—persons receiving or entitled to income

A written agreement with a bank in 1965, guaranteed that the taxpayer would pay all moneys owed to the said bank by a company. In 1967, the taxpayer opened a deposit account in the bank's name on his behalf. In June 1967, he authorised the bank to transfer to a second deposit account in the bank's name a certain sum to be retained by them while he remained under any liability in respect of the guarantee. The balance from the first deposit account, including interest credited, was transferred to the second in July. This second account was credited with interest until July 1969 when it was closed and the balance was withdrawn. The taxpayer was assessed to income tax under Sch. D, Case III, as the person receiving or entitled to the interest in the relevant years of assessment. He appealed on the ground that the money in the second account was held by the bank as trustee during the period of the guarantee and also that under his June authorisation to the bank he did not receive and was not entitled to any interest at any time as he could not claim it. The assessment was upheld and the taxpayer appealed. *Held*, the interest was received when it was credited to the deposit account, which was a debt owed by the bank to the taxpayer, although subject to any claims that might arise under the guarantee. Interest which was credited to a person's deposit account was received by that person at the date when it was so credited, notwithstanding that it might not be paid to him until a future date and it belonged to him whether or not it was paid. Nor was the relationship between the bank and the taxpayer anything but one of banker and customer. There was no fiduciary element in the transaction. The appeal would be dismissed.

DUNMORE v McGOWAN (INSPECTOR OF TAXES) [1978] STC 217 (Court of Appeal: STAMP, ORR and EVELEIGH LJJ). Decision of Brightman J [1976] STC 433, 1976 Halsbury's Abr para. 1436 affirmed.

1590   Interest on overdue tax—rare and special circumstances in which interest waived

Under the Taxes Management Act 1970, s. 86 (as substituted by the Finance (No. 2) Act 1975, s. 46), interest is charged from a reckonable date on unpaid tax, irrespective of the cause of delay in payment. The Inland Revenue have no discretion, but they are prepared "in rare and special circumstances" to forgo payment of interest. In making reference to the rare and special circumstances the Parliamentary Commissioner has stated that what is meant by this expression is errors on the part of the Revenue that would make an interest charge altogether unconscionable, as might happen if the taxpayer had been led to pay tax later than the due date as a direct consequence of some wrong or misleading answer to a question as to what that date was.

See *Case 1B/637/77* and *Case 1A/720/77* in the Fifth Report of the Parliamentary Commissioner for Administration for the Session 1977–78 (HC 524), pp. 246, 256.

1591   One-parent families—divorced and separated persons—pamphlets

The Inland Revenue have issued two pamphlets, "Income Tax and One-Parent Families" (IR 29) and "Income Tax—Separation and Divorce" (IR 30). Both are available, free of charge, from any tax office from 10th November 1978.

1592   Overseas earnings—relief—partnerships

The Non-Contentious Business Committee of the Law Society queried with the Inland Revenue whether an individual who obtained relief under the Finance Act 1978, s. 28 (relief to an individual who carries on a trade or profession in the United Kingdom and who performs duties overseas), could share the relief with his partners. In reply the Inland Revenue has stated that the amount of any deduction due under s. 28 is calculated by reference to each individual partner's share of partnership profits (as defined) and to the number of qualifying days abroad. The deduction is then treated in the same way as a personal allowance due to the individual partner, and is reflected in the computation of tax in respect of the partnership profits as a whole. The Inland Revenue is not concerned should the tax relief due in respect of a period of absence abroad be shared among the partners by adjustments to their capital or drawing amounts. Such a sharing might in certain circumstances, however, be regarded as a gift for capital transfer tax purposes; but the likelihood of such a case not being a gift out of income or not falling within another exemption seemed remote. See exchange of correspondence in the *Law Society Gazette*, 19th October 1978, p. 1034.

1593   Pay As You Earn—assessment—directors' credited bonuses

An annual bonus was voted to the directors of a company. The company paid them a portion of the bonus and credited the rest to an account with the company. The directors were free to draw on the account at any time. An issue arose as to whether the money constituted payment of income for the purposes of the Pay As You Earn provisions of Sch. E. *Held*, the word payment had no strict definition and was to be construed on the facts of each particular case. If money was placed unreservedly at the disposal of the directors and they could have it at any moment they chose, it amounted to payment. The company was liable to pay income tax, as an employer, in respect of those payments that had been voted to the directors but not paid.

GARFORTH (INSPECTOR OF TAXES) v NEWSMITH STAINLESS LTD [1979] STC 129 (Chancery Division: WALTON J).

1594   —— multiple taxable incomes

The Income Tax (Employments) (No. 7) Regulations 1978, S.I. 1978 No. 326 (in force on 6th April 1978), amend the Income Tax (Employments) Regulations 1973. The additional personal relief allowable for certain persons under the Income and Corporation Taxes Act 1970, s. 14 becomes a relief for which no notice of coding need be given to an employee when the rate of relief is changed. Amendments are made to the provisions relating to the rate of tax specified in a PAYE code where an employee has a second source of Schedule E income to which PAYE does not apply. The limit of weekly or monthly pay above which an employer has to operate the PAYE scheme for every employee is increased and amendments are made to provisions dealing with employers' tax returns showing certain benefits received by employees.

1595   —— repayment to wives

The Income Tax (Employments) (No. 8) Regulations 1978, S.I. 1978 No. 1196 (in force on 8th September 1978), further amend the Income Tax (Employments) Regulations 1973. The Finance Act 1978, s. 22, para. 2312, provides that, in certain circumstances, where tax has been deducted from a wife's earned income under the PAYE scheme, any tax repayment due will be made to her, not her husband. Under the 1978 Regulations, if the amount repaid to a husband or wife exceeds the amount properly due, the excess may be recovered as unpaid tax through the PAYE scheme.

Provision is also made to take account of changes introduced by the Finance Act 1977, s. 31, 1977 Halsbury's Abr para. 2246, regarding the deduction of tax from emoluments for duties performed outside the United Kingdom.

1596   —— **temporary workers engaged through foreign agencies**

The Inland Revenue has issued a Press Release dated 6th April 1978 clarifying the position where a temporary worker is engaged through an agency which is not resident in the United Kingdom. Normally the agency through which the worker is employed is responsible for operating PAYE on his earnings. However, if the foreign agency does not have a branch or permanent agent in the United Kingdom, the person engaging the worker is responsible for applying PAYE to his remuneration.

1597   **Post-war credits—final claims**

The Post-War Credit (Income Tax) Order 1978, S.I. 1978 No. 662 (in force on 1st July 1978), prevents any person applying for repayment of a post-war credit after 31st December 1978 unless his application is supported by a post-war credit certificate. It also provides that no-one can demand that he be issued with such a certificate after that date.

1598   Although under S.I. 1978 No. 662 the final date for claiming repayment of post-war credits where the certificate cannot be produced was 31st December 1978, the Inland Revenue will in practice continue until 31st March 1979 to accept claims where the applicant can show reasonable excuse (e.g. because of prolonged illness, absence from home, residence abroad etc.) for having failed to make his claim within the published time limit: Inland Revenue Press Release dated 11th December 1978.

1599   **Profits—allowable deductions—annuity payments to charity— whether bona fide commercial transaction**

As part of a tax saving scheme, the taxpayer agreed to make five yearly payments to a registered charity of £500 each in consideration of payment to him of £2,480. Steps were taken to give the charity security against failure by the taxpayer to pay the instalments. He was assessed to surtax for the relevant years, but his appeal was allowed on the ground that the yearly payments were payments of "any annuity or other annual payment" within the Income and Corporation Taxes Act 1970, s. 52 (1), and were deductible from his total income. On appeal by the Crown, *held*, the whole transaction had to be looked at to ascertain the true character of the payments; the mere description of them in the agreement as "annuities" was not conclusive. The Crown's contention that the £2,480 was a loan and the repayments were of a capital nature was incorrect; they were income payments paid wholly out of profits or gains brought into charge to tax and thus fell within s. 52 (1).

The Crown's contention that the scheme was a settlement the income of which was to be treated as the income of the settlor under the 1970 Act, s. 457, was also incorrect, as the transaction was a commercial one without any element of bounty; the word "commercial" was not restricted to transactions effected in the course of business. Nor was the deduction to be disallowed under the 1970 Act, s. 434, as not being made for valuable and sufficient consideration. The fact that the sole object of the transaction was tax avoidance did not prevent this, since the parties anticipated that the taxpayer would be able to deduct the annuity payments from his total income and such considerations may have been taken into account in negotiating the price, which was a full and sufficient consideration for the annuity. The appeal would be dismissed.

INLAND REVENUE COMMISSIONERS v PLUMMER [1978] STC 517 (Court of Appeal: BUCKLEY and BRIDGE LJJ and FOSTER J). Decision of Walton J [1977] 3 All ER

1009, 1977 Halsbury's Abr para. 1537 affirmed. *Sothern-Smith v Clancy* [1941] 1 KB 276 followed.

Since March 1977, the Finance Act 1977, s. 48, has operated to make such schemes ineffective.

1600   —— —— capital or income receipts—sale of land acquired for investment

The liquidator of a group of companies formed to develop land claimed that the proceeds of the sale of much of the land when the companies' future looked bleak should not be subject to corporation tax on the ground that such proceeds were the realisation of an investment rather than trading receipts. Special commissioners held that the land was not likely to be retained by the companies whatever the circumstances and that the proceeds of sale were accordingly trading profits. On appeal, *held*, when the land had been acquired the companies had intended to establish a permanent investment portfolio suitable for the public company they hoped to become. The land was only sold when changed circumstances prevented execution of the plan. In such circumstances the disposals did not amount to transactions in the course of a trade or adventures in the nature of a trade and the proceeds did not amount to trading receipts. Accordingly, the appeal would be allowed.

SIMMONS (AS LIQUIDATOR OF LIONEL SIMMONS PROPERTIES LTD) V INLAND REVENUE COMMISSIONERS [1978] STC 344 (Chancery Division: GOULDING J).

1601   —— —— capital or revenue expenditure—mining companies

Expenditure by mining companies on unsuccessful applications for planning permission to extract minerals is capital expenditure which hitherto has not been regarded as eligible for any form of tax relief. The Inland Revenue have now decided that in future relief may be given under the mining capital allowances provisions of the Capital Allowances Act 1968, s. 62: Inland Revenue Press Release dated 6th November 1978 and Statement of Practice SP 4/78.

1602   —— —— —— obligation to pay gratuities to retiring employees

Scotland

The taxpayer company was resident in the United Kingdom but carried on business in West Bengal. Under a West Bengal Act which came into force on 14th June 1971 the company became liable to pay retirement gratuities to its employees, the amount of each gratuity being calculated by reference to salary and length of service. Service before the Act came into force had to be taken into account. The company decided to make an annual provision to meet its accruing liability in respect of gratuities. For the year ending 31st December 1971 the sum of £221,619 was debited, which sum took account of pre-1971 service of employees to whom the Act applied as well as their service in 1971. The company was assessed to corporation tax and appealed, contending that the provision for payment of gratuities should have been allowed as a deduction in computing its profits for that year. The Special Commissioners held that it was an allowable deduction and the Crown appealed, contending that the proportion of the £221,619 which related to pre-1971 service was a capital provision, and was not a proper debit item to be charged against trading receipts when computing the company's profits. *Held*, the sum in question was not a capital payment but revenue, and the entire £221,619 could be charged against profits for 1971. In debiting that sum, the company was showing the true amount by which its liabilities in respect of the employment of its workforce was increased in 1971. It could not have made provision earlier for the payments required by the Act for the years before 1971, as it was under no liability to pay gratuities until then. The appeal would be dismissed.

INLAND REVENUE COMMISSIONERS V TITAGHUR JUTE FACTORY CO LTD [1978] STC 166 (Inner House).

1603   —— —— —— **payment for improvement to lease**

On appeal by a company against a decision increasing its assessment to corporation tax, *held*, dismissing the appeal, a sum paid by a tenant to his landlord to renegotiate a term of a lease in favour of the tenant was expenditure of a capital nature and was not deductible in computing a company's profits for corporation tax purposes.

TUCKER (INSPECTOR OF TAXES) v GRANADA MOTORWAY SERVICES LTD [1978] STC 587 (Court of Appeal: STAMP and ORR LJJ and SIR DAVID CAIRNS). Decision of Templeman J [1977] 3 All ER 865, 1977 Halsbury's Abr para. 1539 affirmed.

1604   —— **bills and promissory notes discounted or bought by a bank— liability of anticipated profits to tax**

A bank's business included discounting or purchasing bills and notes issued by borrowers. In preparing its annual accounts, it followed normal accounting practice, which was to divide the total discount applicable to each bill or note by the number of days to which the discount related. The appropriate number of days' discount was then taken into the annual profit and loss account as part of the receipts or earnings for each year. Thus the amount of the discount was treated as accruing at an even rate over the whole period during which the bank held the note, although it did not in fact do so. When the bank sold a note before maturity, it brought into its accounts for that year the difference between the discounted value of the note at the beginning of that year and the sale price. The amounts thus taken into account each year were referred to as "accrued discount" or "earned discount". The bank was assessed to corporation tax on the basis of these accounts and appealed on the ground that for tax purposes it was incorrect to include in the profits a proportionate part of the anticipated profits from the bills, since profit should not be taxed until realised. The assessment was reduced and the Inland Revenue's appeal was dismissed. On further appeal, *held*, LORD DIPLOCK and LORD RUSSELL OF KILLOWEN dissenting, the question of what was profit was a question of fact ascertained by the tests applied in ordinary business. However, the Crown's contention that the assessment should be made on the basis of the bank's accounts, since the principles of commercial accounting should normally prevail, was of no assistance, as the accounts could also have been drawn up to exclude the "accrued discount" by a method which also accorded with the principles of commercial accounting. The answer to the problem depended on the true nature of what the bank was doing when it discounted a bill. What it did was to acquire an asset, and so long as it continued to hold the asset, it could not realise any profit or loss in respect of it. In taking credit for "accrued discount" while still holding the bill, the bank was anticipating a profit not yet realised, which was uncertain, as bills were sometimes sold before maturity for less than their value at maturity. There was a clear distinction between interest and discount, as the former accrued at fixed intervals and the latter did not. The bank's accounts were thus drawn up on the principle of anticipating future profits, and were not a proper basis for assessing liability to corporation tax. The appeal would be dismissed.

WILLINGALE (INSPECTOR OF TAXES) v INTERNATIONAL COMMERCIAL BANK LTD [1978] 1 All ER 754 (House of Lords: LORD DIPLOCK, LORD SALMON, LORD FRASER OF TULLYBELTON, LORD RUSSELL OF KILLOWEN and LORD KEITH OF KINKEL). Decision of the Court of Appeal [1977] 2 All ER 618, 1977 Halsbury's Abr para. 1540 affirmed. Dictum of Lord Reid in *BSC Footwear Ltd v Ridgway (Inspector of Taxes)* [1972] AC 544, HL, at 552 applied.

For a discussion of this case, see When promissory notes resemble commodities, Justinian: Financial Times, 6th February 1978.

1605   **Reliefs—life assurance**

The Income Tax (Life Assurance Premium Relief) Regulations 1978, S. I. 1978 No. 1159 (in force on 6th April 1979) supplement the Finance Act 1976, Sch. 4. From 6th April 1979 a person who pays a premium on which relief is due will normally be entitled to deduct the appropriate sum from the premium. Reg. 3 makes provisions relating to the information which a person making such a deduction must supply to the life office. Reg. 4 provides for the rounding of sums payable by way of net premium to a multiple of one new penny or halfpenny. Regs. 5–10 set out the procedure whereby the life office may claim reimbursement from the Revenue for the loss of receipts following such deductions. Regs. 11–12 give the Revenue power to obtain any necessary information from policy holders and life offices.

The Life Offices' Association and Associated Scottish Life Offices have issued a memorandum explaining this change; see 128 NLJ 831.

1606 Retirement annuity contracts—"open market" annuities—conditions for approval

Under the Finance Act 1978, s. 26, a retirement annuity contract approved by the Inland Revenue under the Income and Corporation Taxes Act 1970, s. 226, may include an option for the policyholder to require the transfer of funds representing his accrued rights to another specified Life Office to be applied as a premium under a similarly approved contract with the second Life Office. Section 26 authorises the Board to impose such conditions as they think proper in connection with the approval of a s. 226 contract conferring an "open market" option. Those conditions are set out in detail in a leaflet prepared by the Superannuation Funds Office entitled "Retirement Annuity Contracts—'Open Market' Annuities", copies of which may be obtained from the Enquiry Room, Joint Office of Inland Revenue Superannuation Funds Office and Occupational Pensions Board, Apex Tower, High Street, New Malden, Surrey KT3 4DN. Inland Revenue Press Release dated 15th December 1978.

1607 Returns—failure to deliver income tax returns—reasonable excuse for failure

The taxpayer failed to comply with statutory notices requiring him to make returns of his income for the years ending in April 1973, 1974 and 1975 respectively. He complained of misconduct on the part of his Inspector of Taxes such as to make further dealings with the inspector improper, but the commissioners, who held that even a legitimate grievance did not absolve a taxpayer of obligations under the taxing Acts, imposed a penalty of £25 in respect of each year for which no return had been made. Their decision was upheld on appeal and the taxpayer appealed to the Court of Appeal, relying on the Taxes Management Act 1970, s. 118 (2). *Held*, it was clear that the commissioners had properly found that there was no reasonable excuse for the failure to complete and submit the returns in question. The appeal based on s. 118 was entirely misconceived and would be dismissed.

Napier v IRC (1978) (Court of Appeal: Orr, Lawton and Cumming-Bruce LJJ (judgment delivered 30th November)). Decision of Brightman J [1977] TR 289 affirmed.

1608

A penalty of £10 was imposed on a taxpayer for failing to make a return of his income. He contended that he did not have to make a return because he was unemployed for a number of years. *Held*, the Revenue were entitled to require a return of income to be made regardless of one's state of employment. It was only after a return was made that a taxpayer might satisfy the Revenue that he had no taxable income. The penalty would be awarded.

Garnham v Inland Revenue Commissioners [1977] TR 307 (Chancery Division: Browne-Wilkinson, J).

1609 Schedule D—deductible expenses—travelling costs

A dentist travelled to and from his surgery each day by car. On the way, both morning and evening, he stopped at his laboratory to collect dentures and discuss work with the dental technicians who worked there. The dentist claimed the cost of travelling between the laboratory and the surgery as an expense against his tax. The tax commissioners upheld the deduction as an expense necessarily incurred in the course of the dentist's work. On appeal, *held*, the test was not whether the expense had been necessary, but whether it had been incurred wholly and exclusively for the purposes of the taxpayer's profession. The dentist undoubtedly stopped off at the laboratory for the purposes of his work, but it was also the case that the stop coincided with his journey to and from the surgery. The requirement was that the expense should be incurred exclusively for the purposes of work. The appeal succeeded and the travelling expenses would be disallowed.

SARGENT (INSPECTOR OF TAXES) v BARNES [1978] 2 All ER 737 (Chancery Division: OLIVER J).

1610   —— stock relief—building licences granted under Community Land Act 1975

The Inland Revenue have clarified their treatment of building licences granted under the Community Land Act 1975 for stock relief purposes. Provided that substantial development on the underlying land has begun, the cost of the licence will qualify for stock relief as work in progress. Full details are given in Statement of Practice SP 8/78: Inland Revenue Press Release dated 15th November 1978.

1611   —— trading profits—whether profits chargeable to tax

The taxpayer, who was a builder, decided to buy a piece of land because of its potential for building. A friend agreed to put up part of the purchase price and the land was conveyed to her and to the taxpayer's wife as tenants in common in equal shares. The title deeds were deposited in the taxpayer's bank. When the land was sold the wife's share of the proceeds was used to pay off the taxpayer's overdraft and the balance was paid into his deposit account. The Revenue claimed that the taxpayer had obtained his wife's share of the profits as part of his trading stock and that the profits were therefore chargeable to tax under the Income and Corporation Taxes Act 1970, Sch. D, Case 1 as part of his trading profits as a builder. On the taxpayer's appeal the Commissioners found that the taxpayer's wife was in the position of trustee for her husband and that her half share in the land formed part of his stock in trade. On appeal *held*, the appeal did not involve any question of law and, on the evidence, the Commissioners were justified in finding that the land formed part of the taxpayer's trading stock. Profits from the sale of the land were taxable under Case 1 as profits of the taxpayer's trade.

SMART v LOWNDES (INSPECTOR OF TAXES) [1978] STC 607 (Chancery Division: FOX J).

1612   Schedule E—benefits in kind—beneficial loan arrangements

The benefit from certain cheap bridging loans in excess of £25,000 made by employers to employees who have to change their residence as the result of a transfer from one post to another is liable to tax under the Finance Act 1976, s. 66. However, as an extra-statutory concession no assessment is made in respect of reasonable removal expenses borne by an employer on such a move. In practice, this concession covers the reimbursement in such circumstances of the interest payable on a bridging loan. The Revenue propose to extend this concession so as not to charge to tax under s. 66 the benefit from a bridging loan in excess of £25,000 provided the loan is made where the employee has had to change his residence as the result of a transfer within his employer's organisation or in order to take up a new employment, and the loan is outstanding for no more than twelve months, or such longer period as the Board may allow: Inland Revenue Press Release dated 6th December 1978.

1613   —— emoluments from office or employment—inspector holding public inquiries—whether holder of an office

A taxpayer was invited to act as an inspector whose function was to hold occasional public local inquiries under the Acquisition of Land (Authorities Procedure) Act 1946. Until 1973, the fees he received for holding inquiries were assessed to tax under Schedule D, Case II on the basis that he was self-employed. The Inland Revenue then decided that in his work as an inspector, the taxpayer was holding an office and thus was liable to be taxed under Schedule E, Case I. The general commissioners upheld the taxpayer's claim that he was taxable under Schedule D and the Revenue appealed. *Held*, from the authorities and the dictionary definition of "office" it appeared that in his position as an inspector, the taxpayer held a series of "offices" to which from time to time he was appointed by those having the power of appointment to such offices. Therefore, the taxpayer was the holder of "an office" and was accordingly taxable under Schedule E. The appeal would be allowed.

EDWARDS (INSPECTOR OF TAXES) v CLINCH (1978) Times, 30th November (Chancery Division: WALTON J).

1614   —— —— preferential right to acquire shares

The taxpayer, an employee of a subsidiary company, exercised his preferential right to purchase shares in the parent company, a right granted only to employees of at least five years' service. In consequence he gained a substantial financial benefit. The special commissioners of the Inland Revenue found as fact that the company's aim in making the shares available was to encourage employees to become shareholders in the parent company for the purpose of maintaining the quality of service given by the staff, and therefore the benefit which accrued to the employee was a taxable emolument from his employment, being an advantage afforded to him in return for acting as or being an employee. The trial judge found, however, that the commissioners had erred in law and held that the benefit thus obtained was not such an emolument. The decision was affirmed by the Court of Appeal and the Revenue appealed. *Held*, allowing the appeal, there were no grounds for saying that there was any error of law in the commissioners' decision which, on the evidence, was reasonable and not therefore susceptible to interference.

LORD SALMON pointed out that the policy of taxing employees on benefits resulting from the acquisition of shares under preference schemes should perhaps be reconsidered.

TYRER v SMART (Inspector of Taxes) [1979] STC 34 (House of Lords: LORD DIPLOCK, LORD SALMON, LORD EDMUND-DAVIES, LORD FRASER OF TULLYBELTON and LORD RUSSELL OF KILLOWEN). *Hochtrasser v Mayes* [1960] AC 373, HL and *Laidler v Perry* [1966] AC 16, HL applied. Decision of the Court of Appeal [1978] 1 All ER 1089 reversed. See further 128 NLJ 1245.

For a discussion of this case, see Tax on your Gifts, Justinian, Financial Times, 18th December 1978.

1615   —— expenses—working clothes

A surveyor claimed that cleaning and repairing expenses to clothes, incurred as a result of visits to construction sites, were tax deductible for the purposes of Schedule E income tax. *Held*, the clothes were not specially bought for that purpose but were his ordinary clothes. The money was not expended wholly in the performance of his duties and was therefore not tax deductible.

WARD (INSPECTOR OF TAXES) v DUNN [1979] STC 178 (Chancery Division: WALTON J).

1616   —— Pay As You Earn

See under PAY AS YOU EARN.

1617   —— repayment to wives

The Income Tax (Repayments to Wives) Regulations 1978, S.I. 1978 No. 1117 (in force 1st August 1978) supplement the provisions of the Finance Act 1978, s. 22, para. 2312, for the repayment of Schedule E tax in certain circumstances to married women.

1618   Schedule F—company distributions—year of payment

Scotland

The taxpayer company was assessed under the Finance Act 1965, s. 47, to Schedule F income tax for the year 1968–69 in the amount of £115,867, being the gross equivalent of £67,564. The company contended that the relevant distribution had not been made in that year. Loans had been made to the directors of the company which totalled £60,330 as at 31st March 1966. In the course of the year ended 31st March 1967, properties were sold by the company, realising a sum of £68,984. On the balance sheet for that year, there was shown on one side a capital distribution of £67,564 and on the other side the loans to the directors were deleted, the balance being shown as unclaimed capital distribution among current liabilities. The draft accounts were accepted at the Annual General Meeting on 5th August 1968. The Inland Revenue contended that although the capital distribution amounting to £67,564 was shown in the balance sheet for the year to 31st March 1967, it did not in fact take place until the Annual General Meeting in August 1968; that is, in the tax year 1968–69. *Held*, on the evidence, the Inland Revenue was entitled to hold that the distribution was made in August 1968. No evidence had been adduced by the taxpayer company that there had been a company decision to make the distribution before 31st March 1967; the company could not rely merely on the face of the balance sheet for that year. The Inland Revenue was entitled to take the view that the date of distribution could only be the date on which the taxpayer company authorised the making of the distribution.

JOHN PATERSON (MOTORS) LTD v INLAND REVENUE COMMISSIONERS [1978] STC 59 (Inner House).

As to Schedule F from 6th April 1973, see Finance Act 1972, s. 85.

1619　Tax advantage—cancellation

The Inland Revenue has announced that for a trial period of twelve months it has decided to modify its practice under s. 464 of the Income and Corporation Taxes Act 1970. Where a taxpayer has given full reasons for his transactions and has applied for clearance under s. 464 but the Inland Revenue refuse clearance, it will (where possible) indicate the main grounds for refusal. However it cannot undertake always to do so. Further, in appropriate cases where the Inland Revenue does not think it right to give reasons it will invite the principals and their advisers to an interview to ensure that it has fully appreciated the position. See *Accountancy*, July 1978, p. 8.

1620　———— procedure

Under the Income and Corporation Taxes Act 1970, s. 460 (6) the defendants notified the taxpayer that they had reason to believe s. 460, which provides for tax advantages to be counteracted in certain circumstances, applied to him in respect of specified transactions. Reasons for this belief were not given. The taxpayer made a statutory declaration that he had not obtained the tax advantages and this was sent to the appropriate tribunal together with the defendants' counter-statement made in accordance with s. 460 (7). On the basis of the counter-statement the tribunal decided there was a prima facie case for proceeding with the matter and the taxpayer was informed that his tax liability would be adjusted. Pending the determination of his appeal against the assessment the taxpayer brought proceedings in the High Court. He claimed declarations that the original notification was null and void as it did not set out the defendants' reasons, and that the tribunal's decision was also null and void and a breach of natural justice in that the tribunal had taken into account the counter-statement which was based on material not made known to the taxpayer. The court held that the taxpayer was not entitled to the declarations claimed. On appeal *held*, the defendants were not under a duty under s. 460 (6) to disclose their reasons to the taxpayer. Under s. 460 (7) the counter-statement was not confined to counteracting the issues raised by the taxpayer's statutory declaration and natural justice did not require that the taxpayer should be given an opportunity to answer the counter-statement. On the information before it the tribunal had correctly decided that there was a prima facie case for proceeding with the matter and the appeal would therefore be dismissed.

BALEN v INLAND REVENUE COMMISSIONERS [1978] STC 420 (Court of Appeal: STAMP, ORR and GEOFFREY LANE LJJ). Decision of Oliver J [1977] 2 All ER 406, 1977 Halsbury's Abr para. 1556 affirmed.

1621   —— transaction in securities—acquisition of company profits—matters to be considered

Taxpayers who were sole shareholders of a company dealing in picture frames came into possession of a valuable painting which they wished to sell to a fine art dealer. In order to do this they sold the company's other assets to another of their companies and then sold the company shares to the dealers. The Revenue alleged that this amounted to the obtaining of a tax advantage as a result of a transaction in securities and assessed them to income tax and surtax to counteract the advantage. The taxpayer appealed. *Held*, the question for the court was whether the transaction had resulted in the company profits going to the taxpayers in such a way that they would not pay tax. The obvious way for them to have obtained the profits would have been to have sold the painting and distributed the profits to themselves as dividend. Instead they had chosen to sell the shares and had accepted a price lower than the value of the painting because they believed that they would obtain the sum tax free. The Revenue's contentions were therefore correct and the assessment to income tax and surtax would be upheld.

IRC v WIGGINS (1978) 122 Sol Jo 863 (Chancery Division: WALTON J).

1622   —— —— exemption from adjustment to counteract tax advantage—whether transaction carried out for commercial reasons

The taxpayer, a farmer, owned 50 per cent of the shares in a private investment company which he proposed to sell in order to raise sufficient money to purchase an adjoining farm, in the interests of efficiency and profitability. The major asset of the investment company was a majority shareholding in a public company, and in order to keep control of that company within his family, the taxpayer and his brother who held the remaining shares in the investment company, agreed to sell their entire shareholding to a family trust company. The transaction was duly executed and the taxpayer used his half of the proceeds to purchase the farm. The Inland Revenue, finding that in consequence of the sale of shares the taxpayer had gained a tax advantage within the Income and Corporation Taxes Act 1970, s. 460, issued a notice under s. 460 (3) assessing him to income tax and surtax on the proceeds of sale, by way of counteracting the tax advantage obtained. Section 460 (1) provides that where a tax advantage has been so obtained adjustments shall be made to counteract it unless, inter alia, the taxpayer can show that the transaction was carried out for bona fide commercial reasons and that it did not have as its sale or main object the gaining of a tax advantage. The taxpayer appealed against the assessment to the Special Commissioners who found that although the gaining of a tax advantage was not the object of the transaction, it had not been carried out for a commercial reason, since the purpose of the transaction, namely the purchase of the farm, was unconnected with the taxpayer's interests in the companies involved in the transaction. The taxpayer appealed. *Held*, s. 460 (1) imposed no qualification as to the nature of the commercial reason for which the transaction must have been carried out: it was sufficient if, in the light of all the circumstances surrounding it, the transaction was carried out for a commercial reason which need not be intrinsic to the transaction. In this case the predominant reason for the taxpayer's sale of shares was the wholly commercial reason of purchasing the adjoining farm, and since there was no dispute as to the bona fide nature of the reason, he was entitled to the exemption from adjustment. The appeal would be allowed.

CLARK v INLAND REVENUE COMMISSIONERS [1978] STC 614 (Chancery Division: FOX J).

1623   Trading losses—losses incurred in relation to principal object of company—principal object discontinued and premises let—set-off of losses against rentals

Malaysia

A Malaysian company was incorporated with the principal object of carrying on a tobacco business. Its memorandum of association empowered it to grant licences over and generally deal with land and other property. In 1964 the company ceased trading in tobacco, having accumulated losses for income tax purposes. It granted licences to other companies to use its factory and warehouse at a monthly rental. When it was assessed to income tax on the rents, it claimed to be entitled to set off against these the losses incurred in the tobacco business on the ground that the rents were income from "a source consisting of a business" for the purposes of the Malaysian Income Tax Act 1967. The Inland Revenue contended that since the classes of taxable income specified in the Act were mutually exclusive, "rents" could not also be "gains or profits from a business", and that after 1964 the company, having ceased to operate the business for which it was incorporated, was no longer carrying on a business and therefore could not set off previous losses. On appeal to the Privy Council, *held*, the classes of income should be given their ordinary meaning, so they could overlap and rents could constitute gains or profits from a business. The rents, being received in the course of carrying on the business of putting the property to profitable use, could thus be described as gains or profits from a business. If a company was incorporated for the purpose of making profits, prima facie any gainful use to which it put its assets amounted to the carrying on of a business. The inference that letting out the properties for rent amounted to carrying on a business was not rebutted and the company was entitled to set off its previous losses against the rental income.

AMERICAN LEAF BLENDING CO SDN BHD V DIRECTOR-GENERAL OF INLAND REVENUE [1978] STC 561 (Privy Council: LORD DIPLOCK, VISCOUNT DILHORNE, LORD EDMUND-DAVIES, LORD RUSSELL OF KILLOWEN and SIR ROBIN COOKE).

1624   Wife's earnings—separate assessment—extension of time limit for making election

The Board of Inland Revenue ordinarily exercises its discretionary powers of extending the statutory time limit for the making of an election for separate assessment of wife's earnings in favour of cases involving the sickness or absence abroad of either spouse. Such powers may also be exercised where there are serious personal difficulties which prevent prompt attention to fix affairs at the critical time and where, through no fault of the taxpayer or his advisers, relevant information was not available for reaching a decision within the statutory time limit: 951 H. of C. Official Report, 14th June 1978, written answers, cols. *580, 581.*

INDUSTRIAL AND PROVIDENT SOCIETIES

Halsbury's Laws of England (4th edn.), Vol. 24, paras. 1–200

1625   Fees

The Industrial and Provident Societies (Amendment of Fees) Regulations 1978, S.I. 1978 No. 1729 (in force on 1st January 1979) increase the fees to be paid for matters to be transacted and for the inspection of documents under the Industrial and Provident Societies Acts 1965 and 1967. They amend the Industrial and Provident Societies Regulations 1967, superseding the Industrial and Provident Societies (Amendment of Fees) Regulations 1977, 1977 Halsbury's Abr para. 1562.

1626   Industrial and Provident Societies Act 1978

The Industrial and Provident Societies Act 1978 raises the amounts of deposits which an industrial and provident society may take without thereby carrying on the business of banking, and authorises the further alteration of those amounts from time to time. The Act received the royal assent on 20th July 1978 and came into force on 20th August 1978.

Section 1 amends the Industrial and Provident Societies Act 1965 so as to raise the limit of deposits which can be taken at any one time from £2 to £10, and the maximum amount which can be taken from any one depositor from £50 to £250. The committee of a registered society is empowered to pass a resolution within a specified period to increase the amount depositors are permitted to hold or deposit in any one payment under the registered rules of the society, within the increased limits. Under s. 2, the chief registrar may, with the consent of the Treasury, by order made by statutory instrument, substitute for the limits specified in the 1965 Act such other sums, not being less than £10, denoting the limit of the deposits which can be taken at any one time, and £250, denoting the maximum amount which can be taken from any one depositor. Section 3 deals with construction, citation, commencement and extent.

INJUNCTIONS

Halsbury's Laws of England (4th edn.), Vol. 24, paras. 901–1200

1627   Article

Superstuds and Confidence, Grant Hammond (when an injunction will be granted to restrain a breach of confidence in the light of *Woodward v Hutchins* [1977] 1 WLR 760, CA, 1977 Halsbury's Abr para. 1565); [1977] NZLJ 464.

1628   Contract of employment—repudiation by employee—disclosure and use of confidential information

See *Thomas Marshal (Exports) Ltd v Guinle*, para. 1059.

1629   County court—jurisdiction—claim for injunction

See *Hatt & Co (Bath) Ltd v Pearce*, para. 542.

1630   ———— exclusion of one party from matrimonial home

See *Davis v Johnson*, para. 1522.

1631   —————— duration of injunction

See *Hopper v Hopper*, para. 1519; *Practice Note*, para. 1520.

1632   Ex parte applications—Family Division

See *Practice Note*, para. 2192.

1633   Interlocutory injunction—balance of convenience—bank under obligation to fulfil contractual requirements

The sellers entered into a contract with the buyers, the first defendants, for the sale and delivery of equipment. The contract price was £500,000, of which £25,000 was payable in advance on presentation of a guarantee by the sellers' bank, the second defendants. A further £50,000 was to be paid by "irrevocable, unconfirmed letter of credit", and the balance of the price was payable under a financial agreement made with the defendant bank. The sellers received the advance payment, completed the manufacture of the goods and, in due course, received a substantial sum of money under the financial agreement. The buyers claimed repayment of the advance payment on the ground that the delivery had not been completed by the date specified in the bank's guarantee. The bank said that it was bound to honour its obligations under the guarantee. The sellers applied for an injunction to restrain the buyers from claiming under the guarantee. *Held*, a bank was under an obligation to perform its requirements under a particular contract. The obligation did not depend on the resolution of any dispute between the parties to the contract, but on whether the event giving rise to the obligation to pay had arisen. As the defendant bank felt that it was under an obligation to make a settlement with the sellers, it would be wrong for the court to interfere. To do so would involve the bank in an enquiry as to whether or not the parties had properly fulfilled their obligations under the contract of sale. Applying the principles laid down in *American Cyanamid v Ethicon* the balance of convenience was against the grant of the injunction requested by the buyers.

Howe Richardson Scale Co Ltd v Polimex-Cekop and National Westminster Bank Ltd [1978] 1 Lloyd's Rep 161 (Court of Appeal: Roskill and Cumming-Bruce LJJ). *American Cyanamid v Ethicon* [1975] 1 All ER 504, HL, 1975 Halsbury's Abr para. 1864 applied.

1634   —————— **criteria to be considered**

See *Corruplast Ltd v George Harrison (Agencies) Ltd*, para. 2058.

1635   —— **injunction restraining action in furtherance of trade dispute— balance of convenience**

See *The Camilla M*, para. 2871.

1636   —— **passing off—balance of convenience**

See *Morning Star Co-operative Society Ltd v Express Newspapers Ltd*, para. 2234.

1637   —— **restraint on disposition of assets within jurisdiction—nature of injunction**

In 1974, shipowners, who were incorporated in Cyprus, chartered a vessel to the charterers, who were incorporated in the Irish Republic. In 1975, the charterers executed a debenture in favour of the Ulster Bank creating a floating charge for all moneys due or to become due to the bank, which should rank as a first charge on the property. The debenture holder was empowered to appoint a receiver to collect property charged. Disputes arose between the charterers and the owners and were referred to arbitration. In April 1976, an injunction was granted to the owners restraining the charterers from removing any assets up to a specified limit out of the jurisdiction until fourteen days after publication of the award. The arbitration was compromised, but the charterers failed to pay the sum agreed. The owners obtained judgment for the amount outstanding, but the judgment remained unsatisfied. In September 1976, the guarantor of the foreign debenture was called on by the bank to honour his guarantee, and did so. The debenture was then assigned to him and he appointed a receiver. On a summons by the receiver, the injunction restraining the charterers from removing any assets from the jurisdiction was discharged. On appeal by the shipowners against the discharge of the injunction, *held,* the type of injunction in the present case, known as a "Mareva" injunction did not have to relate to specified assets, but if it related to unspecified assets, it had to be capable of applying to all the defendant's assets which might be in the jurisdiction while the injunction remained.

In this case, no asset was irremovable from the jurisdiction because the order only required assets up to a stated value to be kept within the jurisdiction. The procedure was therefore not a form of pre-trial attachment as it was not a seizure of assets; even if it related to a particular asset, a Mareva injunction was relief in personam and only prohibited the owner from doing certain things in relation to the asset. In this case, the charterers were already restrained from removing their assets outside the jurisdiction when the receiver was appointed and thus the receiver, as their agent, was also restrained. However, the debenture holder was not so bound; the appointment of the receiver crystallised the floating charge and the debenture holder became entitled to a fixed charge on the charterers' funds in the jurisdiction, as one of their assets, subject to his getting the injunction discharged so that the assets could be removed. Treating the debenture holder as an additional applicant in the receiver's summons to discharge the injunction, since the debenture holder was an equitable assignee of the fund and had priority over the owners if they attempted to levy execution on it, the order discharging the injunction would be affirmed and the appeal dismissed.

THE CRETAN HARMONY, CRETANOR MARITIME CO LTD v IRISH MARINE MANAGEMENT LTD [1978] 3 All ER 164 (Court of Appeal: BUCKLEY and GOFF LJJ and SIR DAVID CAIRNS).

1638   Mandatory injunction—preservation of property—ex parte application for search of premises—necessity for premises to be precisely described

See *Protector Alarms Ltd v Maxim Alarms Ltd*, para. 2200.

1639   Restraint of legal proceedings—injunction restraining arbitration proceedings

See *Ben & Co Ltd v Pakistan Edible Oils Corporation Ltd*, para. 156.

1640   Restrictive covenant—breach—balance of convenience

See *Richards v Levy*, para. 2736.

INSURANCE

Halsbury's Laws of England (4th edn.), Vol. 25, paras. 1–1000

1641   Articles

Duty to Disclose in Contracts of Insurance, St. John Robilliard (duty on insured to disclose factors which might influence terms of contract of insurance): 128 NLJ 739.

Insurance and the EEC, R. W. Hodgin (EEC co-ordination of provisions on the business of direct insurance other than life insurance): [1978] LCMLQ 621.

Insurance Intermediaries—Recent and Projected Developments—Insurance Brokers (Registration) Act 1977, Derek Morgan: [1978] 1 LMCLQ 39.

Property Insurance, H. W. Wilkinson (problems concerning property insurance, considered in the light of recent court decisions): 128 NLJ 602.

1642   European Community provisions

EEC Council Directive 78/473 provides for the co-ordination of laws, regulations and administrative provisions relating to the taking up and pursuit of business of direct insurance other than life insurance.

1643   Fire insurance—amount recoverable—basis of valuation

The plaintiff was the owner of old maltings which were destroyed by fire in 1973. The court was required to consider whether his loss should be calculated on the basis of (i) the market value of the property if it had been sold immediately before the fire, (ii) the cost of building an equivalent modern replacement, or (iii) the cost of reinstating the building in its old form. The second method was accepted as being an alternative way of stating the market value but the valuation based on the third method, which was made in 1974, was substantially higher. *Held*, although it was an accepted principle that an assured should never be more than fully indemnified, this did not mean that market value was always the appropriate method of evaluation. Each case would turn upon its own facts and there would be circumstances where a plaintiff was entitled to claim that his indemnity would be complete only upon reinstatement. This was such a case and therefore the plaintiff's indemnity would be based on the 1974 evaluation with an allowance for the loss caused by the rise in building costs since that date.

REYNOLDS v PHOENIX ASSURANCE CO LTD (1978) 247 Estates Gazette 995 (Queen's Bench Division: FORBES J).

1644   Insurance agent—duty of care—insured relying on agent to provide full coverage—liability of agent when risk not covered materialising

Canada

The plaintiff instructed an insurance agent to obtain "full coverage" for his horticultural business. The agent obtained coverage under a complex policy covering a number of risks, but not the one that occurred, namely damage to plants by freezing caused by the failure of a water pump. The agent was held liable at first instance for breach of contract and for breach of his duty to inform the plaintiff of the gap in coverage. On appeal, *held*, the undertaking to secure full coverage amounted to a contractual undertaking to keep the insured covered against all foreseeable, insurable, and normal risks to the property used in connection with the business. The loss had resulted from such a risk, and in this respect the agent was liable. The agent was also liable for failing to inform the plaintiff of the gap in coverage.

FINE'S FLOWERS LTD v GENERAL ACCIDENT ASSURANCE COMPANY OF CANADA (1977) 17 OR (2d) 529 (Court of Appeal of Ontario). Decision of the High Court of Ontario (1974) 5 OR (2d) 137, 1975 Halsbury's Abr para. 1888, affirmed.

1645   Insurance brokers—code of conduct

The Insurance Brokers Registration Council (Code of Conduct) Approval Order 1978, S.I. 1978 No. 1394 (in force on 20th October 1978), approves the code of conduct drawn up by the Registration Council for the purposes of the Insurance Brokers (Registration) Act 1977. The code is set out in the schedule to the Order.

1646   —— duty of care—duty to advise of cancellation of policy

Owing to dissatisfaction with the service offered them by the defendant insurance brokers, the plaintiffs stopped dealing through them. The defendants were instructed to cancel all policies they had taken out for the plaintiffs. One insurance company refused to cancel a policy insuring against loss consequential on the destruction of the plaintiffs' premises. On the defendants' advice, the plaintiffs kept the policy in being and cancelled new cover they had just arranged. The original insurers then agreed to cancel the policy and informed the defendants to that effect. The latter failed to notify the plaintiffs who, following heavy consequential loss resulting from a fire, sued the defendants for breach of contract and negligence. *Held*, the plaintiffs had cancelled new cover on the defendants' advice. That advice was rendered unsound by the failure to notify the plaintiffs of the insurers' subsequent agreement to cancel. Furthermore, the defendants had offered specialised knowledge realising or intending that it should be acted on and consequently were liable under the principle in *Hedley Byrne & Co Ltd v Heller & Partners*. Accordingly, the defendants were liable to pay damages, the measure of which would reflect the recompense forthcoming had the first insurance policy still been effective.

CHERRY LTD v ALLIED INSURANCE BROKERS LTD [1978] 1 Lloyd's Rep 274 (Queen's Bench Division: CANTLEY J). *Hedley Byrne & Co Ltd v Heller & Partners*, [1964] AC 465, HL, applied.

1647   —— —— duty to ensure that assured properly covered

The plaintiff was a property repairer and part-time musician. He went to a firm of insurance brokers to effect motor insurance; the brokers suggested an insurance company which it knew did not accept risks in certain categories, including part-time musicians. The plaintiff was asked by the brokers what his occupation was and replied that he was a property repairer. The policy was effected. Subsequently the plaintiff was involved in an accident and the insurance company avoided liability on the ground of non-disclosure of a fact regarded by the insurers as material, to the knowledge of the brokers as the plaintiff's agents. The plaintiff brought an action against the brokers on the ground that they had failed to use all reasonable care to see that he was properly covered. *Held*, the brokers had failed in that duty; the plaintiff should have been asked if he fell into any of the excluded categories. The brokers were therefore liable for breach of their duty of care towards him.

McNealy v Pennine Insurance Co Ltd [1978] 2 Lloyd's Rep 18 (Court of Appeal: Lord Denning MR, Shaw and Waller LJJ).

1648   —— interim insurance—whether agent of insurers

In an action for damages for personal injuries sustained in a road accident, the question arose whether there was a contract of interim insurance between the insurers and the car owner involved. Negotiations had taken place through a firm of insurance brokers who contended that they had been acting as agents for the insurance company. *Held*, insurance brokers were entitled to enter into temporary interim insurance contracts as agents for the insurers. When people contacted brokers on matters of insurance, they relied on the broker's statement that they were covered as constituting a contract. They spoke to the brokers as agents of the insurers, rather than as their own agents for the purpose of negotiating a contract with the insurers. Thus the brokers were the agents of the insurance company.

Stockton v Mason (1978) Times, 27th June (Court of Appeal: Lord Diplock, Viscount Dilhorne and Lord Scarman).

1649   —— registration and enrolment

The Insurance Brokers Registration Council (Registration and Enrolment) Rules Approval Order 1978, S.I. 1978 No. 1395 (in force on 20th October 1978) approves the rules made by the Registration Council in relation to the register and list of insurance brokers. The rules are set out in the schedule to the Order.

1650   Insurance Brokers (Registration) Act 1977—commencement

The Insurance Brokers (Registration) Act 1977 (Commencement No. 2) Order 1978, S.I. 1978 No. 1393 brought ss. 2–5, 9, 13–18, 19 (part) and 20 of the Act (see 1977 Halsbury's Abr para. 1590) into force on 20th October 1978.

1651   Insurance Brokers Registration Council—disciplinary committee—constitution

The Insurance Brokers Registration Council (Constitution of the Disciplinary Committee) Rules Approval Order 1978, S.I. 1978 No. 1457 (in force on 31st October 1978), approves rules made by the Insurance Brokers Registration Council as to the constitution of the Disciplinary Committee.

1652   —— —— legal assessor

The Insurance Brokers Registration Council (Disciplinary Committee) Legal Assessor Rules 1978, S.I. 1978 No. 1503 (in force on 10th November 1978), regulate the functions of the legal assessor appointed to advise the disciplinary committee of the Insurance Brokers Registration Council on questions of law under the Insurance Brokers (Registration) Act 1977, s. 20, 1977 Halsbury's Abr para. 1590.

1653   —— —— procedure

The Insurance Brokers Registration Council (Procedure of the Disciplinary Committee) Rules Approval Order 1978, S.I. 1978 No. 1458 (in force on 31st October 1978), approves rules made by the Insurance Brokers Registration Council as to the procedure to be followed in proceedings before the disciplinary committee.

1654   —— investigating committee—constitution

The Insurance Brokers Registration Council (Constitution of the Investigating Committee) Rules Approval Order 1978, S.I. 1978 No. 1456 (in force on 31st October 1978), approves rules made by the Insurance Brokers Registration Council as to the constitution of the Investigating Committee.

1655   Insurance companies—accounts and forms

The Insurance Companies (Accounts and Forms) (Amendment) Regulations 1978, S.I. 1978 No. 721 (in force on 31st July 1978), further amend the Insurance Companies (Accounts and Forms) Regulations 1968 by requiring an insurance company to reflect in its accounts submitted in respect of financial years ending on or after 31st July certain of the requirements of the Insurance Companies (Solvency: General Business) Regulations 1977, 1977 Halsbury's Abr para. 1592 and the Insurance Companies (Authorisation and Accounts: General Business) Regulations 1978, para. 1657.

1656   —— changes of director, controller or manager—information to be supplied

The Insurance Companies (Changes of Director, Controller or Manager) Regulations 1978, S.I. 1978 No. 722 (in force on 31st July 1978), prescribe the information to be supplied to the Secretary of State regarding any person proposing to become a managing director, chief executive or controller of an insurance company. They also prescribe the information to be supplied to an insurance company by any person becoming or ceasing to be a controller of the company or becoming a director or manager. The Insurance Companies (Changes of Director, Controller or Manager) Regulations 1975, 1975 Halsbury's Abr para. 1884, are revoked.

1657   —— general business—authorisation and accounts

The Insurance Companies (Authorisation and Accounts: General Business) Regulations 1978, S.I. 1978 No. 720 (in force on 31st July 1978), give effect to the requirements of EEC Council Directive 73/239 that the taking up of the business of direct insurance other than life insurance must be authorised. Under these Regulations, authorisations for general business may be issued to a company having its head office in the United Kingdom, in a member state of the EEC other than the United Kingdom or outside the EEC. The Insurance Companies Act 1974, 1974 Halsbury's Abr para. 1775, which regulates the taking up of all kinds of insurance business, is modified in its application to such companies.

1658   —— —— solvency—deposits

The Insurance Companies (Deposits) Regulations 1978, S.I. 1978 No. 917 (in force on 31st July 1978), contain provisions respecting deposits to be made by certain overseas companies carrying on insurance business or applying for authorisation to do so. These deposits are required by the Insurance Companies (Solvency: General Business) Regulations 1977, 1977 Halsbury's Abr para. 1592, reg. 6.

1659   —— notice of long-term policy

The Insurance Companies (Notice of Long-Term Policy) Regulations 1978, S.I. 1978 No. 1304 (in force on 1st January 1980), prescribe the form and contents of the statutory notice which an insurer is required to send to the other party to an ordinary long-term insurance contract pursuant to the Insurance Companies Act 1974, s. 65 (1). The contents prescribed for statutory notices relating to contracts which are not linked long-term contracts differ from those prescribed for linked long-term contracts. Also prescribed is the form of the notice of cancellation required to be annexed to a statutory notice by the 1974 Act, s. 65 (2) (b). Exemptions are given for certain types of contract.

1660   Liability insurance—carriage of goods by road—carrier's application for indemnity

See *Boughen v Frederick Attwood Ltd and Cryoplants Ltd*, para. 298.

1661   —— employer's liability policy—application for indemnity from insurers—whether employee acting in the course of his employment.

An employee returning from holiday was told by his employers' manager that he was wanted at the building site. He was driven to the site in a staff car, stopping off at the employers' offices some distance from the site. After leaving the offices, the employee was injured in an accident caused by the driver's negligence. The employers admitted liability and claimed an indemnity under two insurance policies in respect of damages they paid to the employee. The first policy, a public liability policy, excluded liability for accidents arising out of and in the course of employment; the second policy, an employer's liability policy, expressly covered such accidents. Therefore, each insurer's liability depended on whether or not the employee had been acting in the course of his employment at the time of the accident. *Held*, the accident arose out of and occurred in the course of employment for two reasons. Firstly the employee was carrying out his duty under express instructions; secondly, as all employees travelling between the offices and the site were taken by staff cars, the employee's journey by staff car was within the sphere of his employment. Accordingly the exclusion clause in the public liability policy applied, but the employers were entitled to an indemnity under the second policy.

PATERSON v COSTAIN & PRESS (OVERSEAS) LTD [1978] 1 Lloyd's Rep 86 (Queen's Bench Division: TALBOT J). *St. Helen's Colliery Co Ltd v Hewitson* [1924] AC 58, HL applied.

1662   —— indemnity in respect of liability for accidental bodily injury—exclusion clause

Australia
An insurance policy covering flying club members provided that the insurer would indemnify the insured in respect of liability for accidental bodily injury (fatal or non-fatal) to passengers w le on board the aircraft. There was an exclusion clause in respect of claims arising as a result of the use of the aircraft for, inter alia, any forms of flying involving abnormal hazards. A club member flew his aircraft with a passenger at a low level in contravention of an Air Navigation regulation, collided with electric power lines and crashed into a river. The passenger was injured in the crash and drowned. It was found that the pilot had been negligent and he sought an indemnity under the policy. *Held*, the passenger's death was within the scope of the indemnity against injury to passengers since he suffered an accidental bodily injury which was a substantial cause of his death by drowning. However, the pilot had engaged in a form of flying which involved abnormal hazards within the meaning of the exclusion clause, and accordingly the insurer was not liable.

MACLEAN v MACLEAN (1977) 15 SASR 306 (Supreme Court of South Australia).

1663   —— subrogation—insured company wound up

See *Re Allobrogia Steamship Corpn*, para. 356.

1664   Life insurance—accidental death—exception for death caused by criminal act—death caused by drinking and driving

Canada
A man was killed in a road accident and evidence showed that he was driving with more than the permitted amount of alcohol in his blood at the time of the accident. His widow was paid $25,000 under a life insurance policy covering his life, but was refused the additional sum of $25,000 which was payable under the policy for death by accident. There was an exclusion in the policy whereby the additional $25,000 was not payable if the death resulted from the insured committing or attempting to commit a criminal offence. The insurance company claimed the case fell within the exclusion and refused to pay the additional sum. The widow brought an action for the additional sum. *Held*, it was clear from the evidence that the insured was committing the criminal offence of driving with excess alcohol in

his blood when the accident happened. The case therefore fell within the exclusion under the policy, and the widow was not entitled to the additional sum.

WYLIE v MUTUAL LIFE ASSURANCE CO OF CANADA (1978) 19 OR (2d) 723 (High Court of Ontario).

1665 —— —— **exception for death caused by disease—death caused by disease contracted in course of employment**

Canada
The terms of a life insurance policy provided for extra benefits payable in case of death caused by "bodily injury effected solely through accidental means". No indemnity was payable if death resulted from "any form of disease or illness". The insured died from hepatitis contracted by his inhaling contaminated air in the course of his employment as a laboratory assistant. On appeal in an action for the additional benefits, *held*, the disease contracted was a bodily injury caused by accidental means. The exception was limited to disease arising from within the insured's body, not to disease accidentally contracted from without.

LUND v GREAT-WEST LIFE ASSURANCE CO (1977) 81 DLR (3d) 487 (Court of Appeal of Saskatchewan).

1666 **Motor insurance—non-disclosure of material fact—whether contract void or voidable**

A motorist obtained an insurance cover note for a motor vehicle by concealing the fact that he was disqualified from driving. An information preferred against him charged him with driving without insurance. Justices found the cover note had been valid because the insurers had not cancelled it. On appeal by the prosecution, *held*, the insurance contract was not void ab initio, but merely voidable. It remained in force until such time as the insurers avoided it. Accordingly, the appeal would be dismissed.

ADAMS v DUNNE [1978] RTR 281 (Queen's Bench Division: MELFORD STEVENSON, CANTLEY and CROOM-JOHNSON JJ).

1667 —— **permitting uninsured person to drive vehicle—mens rea**

The plaintiff bought a car in Holland and brought it to England. As she was not insured the customs authorities told her she would not be able to drive the car herself but would have to find an insured driver to drive it. When the circumstances had been explained to him a neighbour of the plaintiff's offered to drive the car. The plaintiff wrongly assumed that he was insured to drive other people's cars. She was subsequently injured in an accident caused by her neighbour's negligence, and was awarded damages for personal injuries. She sought a declaration that if the judgment was not fully satisfied within seven days the Motor Insurers' Bureau would be liable to pay any amount outstanding on the judgment debt. The Motor Insurers' Bureau disclaimed liability on the basis of a clause in their Agreement exempting them from liability where a vehicle owner had allowed his car to be driven by an uninsured driver, having reason to believe that the driver was uninsured. *Held*, the words "having reason to believe" referred to a rational process of thought. In the present case the plaintiff had made it clear to her neighbour that she needed an insured driver to drive the car. As he had then offered to drive the car, and as she knew he had a car of his own, the plaintiff had made a reasonable assumption that he was insured. The Motor Insurers' Bureau would not be able to rely on the exemption clause.

PORTER v ADDO; PORTER v MOTOR INSURERS' BUREAU (1978) 122 Sol Jo 418 (Queen's Bench Division: FORBES J).

1668 —— **use for social domestic and pleasure purposes—business and domestic trip—extent of cover**

A father, who assisted his son in business, was giving a lift to one of his son's employees in the son's car. The employee was complaining of toothache. The father was going home for lunch and he intended to take the employee to the dentist.

During the journey, there was an accident, as a result of which one person was killed and another injured. The administratrix of the deceased person's estate and the injured person brought actions for damages against the father and his son. The father had an insurance policy which entitled him to drive for social, domestic and pleasure purposes. The father claimed indemnification from his own insurance company against the plaintiff's claims. The insurers denied liability, claiming that at the time of the accident the purpose of the trip had been a business one. *Held*, the purpose of the trip was a business one. The claim would therefore fail. Even if the trip was a combined business and domestic one, the claim still failed for the reason that one of the purposes was not an insured one.

SEDDON v BINIONS; STORK v BINIONS [1978] RTR 163 (Court of Appeal: MEGAW, ROSKILL and BROWNE LJJ).

1669   Non-disclosure—material facts—criminal record—spent conviction

See *Reynolds v Phoenix Assurance Co Ltd*, para. 726.

1670   Policyholders protection scheme—application for reduction of contractual liabilities and benefits—proof of company's inability to pay its debts

An insurance company specialising solely in long term annuity contracts presented its own petition for winding up. Pursuant to the Policyholders Protection Act 1975, s. 16 the Policyholders Protection Board prepared a scheme which inter alia involved an application under the Insurance Companies Act 1974, s. 50 for reduction of the liabilities and benefits under its current policies, including amounts which had accrued due at the date of the petition. *Held*, it was a condition precedent to the exercise of the court's jurisdiction under s. 50 that the company should have been "proved to be unable to pay its debts". This requirement had not been met. The words "unable to pay its debts" had the same meaning as in the Companies Act 1948, ss. 222 and 223. While the company and the board no doubt genuinely believed that the company was commercially insolvent mere evidence that the company had insufficient liquid assets to pay all of its outstanding debts whether or not payment had been demanded was not proof of its inability to pay its debts. Further, the court did not have jurisdiction to order a reduction of the amounts which had accrued due when the petition was presented. A proposed reduction could be ordered without directing meetings of policyholders or any further advertisements or communications with them. The order sought would be declined.

RE CAPITAL ANNUITIES LTD [1978] 3 All ER 704 (Chancery Division: SLADE J). *Re Great Britain Mutual Life Assurance Society* (1882) 20 Ch D 351 applied.

1671   Property insurance—lessor's covenant to insure for full cost of reinstatement—meaning of "full cost of reinstatement".

See *Gleniffer Finance Corporation v Bamar Wood & Products Ltd*, para. 1715.

INTOXICATING LIQUOR

Halsbury's Laws of England (4th edn.), Vol. 26, paras. 1–500.

1672   Beer—regulations

The Beer Regulations 1978, S.I. 1978 No. 893 (in force on 1st September 1978), provide for the revenue control of the brewing of beer liable to excise duty. They substantially reproduce the Beer Regulations 1952, dealing with the manufacture of beer for sale, the use of premises licensed for beer-making processes, the receipt, storage, removal and disposal of sugar by brewers, the warehousing on drawback of beer for exportation, the documents, books and records required by a licensed brewer, the remission or repayment of duty paid on beer accidentally rendered unfit for consumption and substances whose use is prohibited in the manufacture of beer.

1673   The Beer (Amendment) Regulations 1978, S.I. 1978 No. 1186 (in force on 1st September 1978), substitute a new reg. 46 and Sch. 10 in the Beer Regulations 1978, see para. 1672. Saccharin and its salts and glycyrrhizic acid and its salts are now prohibited in the manufacture or preparation for sale of beer.

1674   **Dover hoverport—licensing**

The Dover Hoverport Licensing (Liquor) Order 1978, S.I. 1978 No. 225 (in force 1st March 1978), brings s. 87 of the Licensing Act 1964 into operation at Dover Hoverport. The effect is to allow the sale and consumption of intoxicating liquor outside permitted hours on licensed premises at the hoverport.

1675   **Driving or being in charge with blood-alcohol concentration above prescribed unit**

See ROAD TRAFFIC.

1676   **Licences—fees**

The Licensing (Fees) Order 1978, S.I. 1978 No. 1644 (in force on 1st January 1979), fixes new fees chargeable by justices' clerks in respect of matters arising under the Licensing Act 1964. The Licensing (Fees) Order 1976, 1976 Halsbury's Abr para. 1508 is revoked.

1677   **Licensing hours—exemptions—special order of exemption—"special occasion"**

Justices granted the licensee of a public house special orders of exemption under the Licensing Act 1964, s. 74 (4), extending the permitted hours of opening. The licensee had sought the orders so that he could instal a television set on which his customers could watch World Cup football matches after licensing hours. The police sought an order of certiorari to quash the orders. *Held*, in order to obtain a special order it was necessary for the licensee to show that it was a special occasion within s. 74 (4). The occasion, national or local, had to be special within the ordinary meaning of the word and had to create a potential demand for liquor at the time of the occasion. Although the World Cup might be a national occasion, there was nothing to show that it created a potential demand for liquor by those participating in the occasion. No one in England was participating in the occasion and there was no demand stimulated in this country for the refreshment of the participants. Certiorari would go to quash the order.

R v LEICESTER JUSTICES, EX PARTE WATCHORN (1978) Times, 9th June (Queen's Bench Division: LORD WIDGERY CJ, EVELEIGH LJ and WATKINS J).

1678   **Protection order—criteria for grant—role of justices**

The managing director of a company which owned licensed premises applied for a protection order to allow him to sell liquor pending a transfer of the licence to him from the licensee, who had been dismissed. Justices refused to make the order on the ground that it could prejudice an unfair dismissal action being brought by the licensee. On appeal, *held*, under the Licensing Act 1964, s. 10, justices could make a protection order if they were satisfied the applicant was a person to whom the licence could be transferred by licensing justices. Accordingly, before making an order justices had to be sure that the applicant genuinely proposed to seek a transfer of the licence, that he was a person to whom a licence could be granted, that a transfer was feasible in all the circumstances and that he was a fit and proper person to hold a licence. The applicant satisfied all counts and as the licensee was not in occupation

of the premises an effective order could be and should have been made. Justices'
function was to implement the 1964 Act, not to act as an extension of an industrial
tribunal.

R v MELKSHAM JUSTICES, EX PARTE COLLINS (1978) Times, 10th April (Queen's
Bench Division: MELFORD STEVENSON, CANTLEY and CROOM-JOHNSON JJ).

JUDGMENTS AND ORDERS

Halsbury's Laws of England (4th edn.), Vol. 26, paras. 501–600

1679   Award—currency of award—damages in tort and contract

See *The Despina R; Services Europe Atlantique Sud v Stockholms Rederiaktiebolag Svea*,
para. 841.

**1680   Committal order—validity—failure to follow correct procedure—
whether slip rule applicable**

See *Cinderby v Cinderby; Pekesin v Pekesin*, para. 1518.

1681   Drawing up orders—Chancery Division—Long Vacation

In a case in the Chancery Division MEGARRY V-C stated that there was nothing to
prevent orders made shortly before the Long Vacation and not bespoken by its
commencement being bespoken during it with the leave of the Vacation Registrar.
It was established practice that leave would readily be given if any good reason was
put forward. Costs could also be taxed during the Long Vacation without any
difficulty.

SINGH v NAZEER (1978) Times, 2nd June (Chancery Division).

**1682   Judgment—summary judgment—counterclaim—whether coun-
terclaim sufficiently quantified—effect of plaintiff's insolvency**

A landlord company which was in voluntary liquidation claimed arrears of rent
from tenants who had refused to pay because the company was in breach of repair
covenants. One tenant specified a sum which he had expended in causing certain
repairs to be done, but others merely claimed that they were entitled to an amount
of damages in excess of the amount claimed by way of rent. The tenants alleged that
they should be given unconditional leave to defend the action. *Held*, although as a
general rule tenants could not defeat claims for rent by making unquantified
allegations of breach of repair covenants, in the present case it appeared that the
tenants had genuine claims which had been badly prosecuted. Also it would be
unreasonable if the company could recover arrears of rent while the tenants could
recover nothing because of the company's insolvency. Accordingly the tenants
would be granted unconditional leave to defend the action.

ASCO DEVELOPMENTS LTD v GORDON (1978) 248 Estates Gazette 683 (Chancery
Division: MEGARRY V-C).

**1683   —— —— leave to defend—application—whether applicant's case
arguable**

See *Eagle Star Insurance Co Ltd v Yuval Insurance Co Ltd*, para. 159.

1684   Under the terms of a time charter, a ship was sold to new owners with the charterers'
consent and managing agents appointed. The agents subsequently informed the
charterers that new managers were being appointed. The charterers claimed that on
a true construction of the charter, management of the ship could not be changed after
the sale without their consent and the appointment was a fundamental breach of the
contract which they were entitled to treat as repudiated. The charterers refused to

pay the charter hire and an order under RSC Ord 14 was made against them. They contended that summary judgment was not appropriate and applied for leave to defend. *Held*, the function of the court was not to decide on the correct construction of the charter but to determine whether the charterers had an arguable case. The case against them was not so clear that it could not be defended and accordingly leave to defend would be granted.

THE KATINGO COLOCOTRONIS, EUROPEAN-AMERICAN BANKING CORPORATION v TOTAL TRANSPORT CORPORATION [1978] 1 Lloyd's Rep 20 (Court of Appeal: MEGAW LJ and SIR DAVID CAIRNS).

JURIES

Halsbury's Laws of England (4th edn.), Vol. 26, paras. 601–700

1685   Jurors—allowances

The Jurors' Allowances Regulation 1978, S.I. 1978 No. 1579 (in force on 1st January 1979) revoke and replace the Jurors' Allowances Regulations 1977, 1977 Halsbury's Abr para. 1627 applying to service as a juror in the Crown Court, the High Court or a county court. The Regulations provide that the maximum amounts payable in respect of allowances to jurors are to be calculated in accordance with such rates or scales as may for the time being be determined in accordance with the Juries Act 1974, s. 19 as amended by the Administration of Justice Act 1977, Sch. 2, para. 7.

1686   Oaths Act 1978

See para. 1283.

LAND CHARGES

Halsbury's Laws of England (4th edn.), Vol. 26, paras. 701–900

1687   Article

Pending Land Actions in the Divorce Court, Brenda Hoggett (whether application for adjustment of property order under Matrimonial Causes Act 1973 is registrable as a land charge; consideration of *Whittingham v Whittingham* [1978] 2 WLR 936): 122 Sol Jo 669.

1688   Local land charges—forms

By direction of the Lord Chancellor, use of the local land charges forms used before the coming into force of the Local Land Charges Act 1975 (1st August 1977), see 1975 Halsbury's Abr para. 1990, is to be discontinued from 1st January 1979.

1689   —— rules for registration

The Local Land Charges (Amendment) Rules 1978, S.I. 1978 No. 1638 (in force on 17th November 1978), provide for the temporary use of facsimiles of forms required in connection with local land charges.

1690   Registration—pending land action—whether caution in respect of action registrable

A building company acquired land for the purpose of development. It was contended that when work commenced the support provided by the land to a number of houses adjoining it was withdrawn. The owners of the houses brought actions against the company, claiming a natural right of support or an easement of support to their land plus relief against the company for the reinstatement or the replacement of such support. The plaintiffs registered cautions in respect of the pending actions, against the company's land and the company brought a motion before the court to vacate the entries of these cautions. *Held*, dismissing the case, the actions brought against the company were "pending land actions" within the meaning of the Land Charges Act 1972, s. 17, and were therefore registrable. Any purchaser of the land from the company would not take free of the easement, if the plaintiffs succeeded in establishing such an easement, as it would take effect without registration as an overriding interest. Nevertheless if the land was sold to a third party who had no notice of the claim to the easement and relief sought, there could be very substantial difficulties in obtaining mandatory relief against the third party. It was exactly for this type of purpose that the registration of pending land actions was introduced, so as to ensure that any third party should know of the action that was in progress and the relief claimed in it. A third party knowing of the action would find it very difficult to resist an order enforcing the plaintiffs' rights by mandatory injunction. The registration of the pending actions would therefore stand.

ALLEN v GREENHI BUILDERS LTD [1978] 3 All ER 1163 (Chancery Division: BROWNE-WILKINSON J).

1691   —— unregistered interest in property—execution of legal charge over whole property—validity of charge

A husband owned a property divided into flats, one of which was occupied by his estranged wife. The wife applied to have the flat transferred to her in subsequent divorce proceedings. The husband then executed a legal charge over the whole property in favour of a bank, to secure the overdraft of a company. The wife applied under the Matrimonial Causes Act 1973, s. 37, which avoids certain transactions intended to prevent or reduce financial relief, to have the charge set aside. The application was granted by a district registrar, but this was reversed on the bank's appeal on the ground that the application for a transfer order was a pending land action within the Land Charges Act 1972, s. 5 (1) (a), and as such should have been registered. Because it had not been registered, it was not binding on the bank. Further, the court held that the charge was not a reviewable disposition within s. 37 of the 1973 Act because the bank did not have constructive notice of the husband's intention to defeat the claim for a transfer order at the time the charge was executed. The wife appealed. *Held*, the wife's application for a property transfer order clearly came within the definition of a pending land action contained in the 1972 Act, s. 17 (1) and was therefore registrable. Since the wife had failed to register it, it was not binding on the bank and consequently her application to have the charge set aside had to fail.

WHITTINGHAM v WHITTINGHAM [1978] 3 All ER 805 (Court of Appeal: STAMP, ORR and EVELEIGH LJJ). Decision of Balcombe J (1977) Times, 23rd December, 1977 Halsbury's Abr para. 1647 affirmed.

LAND DRAINAGE AND IMPROVEMENT

Halsbury's Laws of England (3rd edn.), Vol. 39, paras. 892–1051

1692   Drainage rate—assessment—effect of central heating installation

The drainage rate for a number of glasshouses was assessed on the basis that they were heated. It was the practice of the local valuation board to value heated glasshouses in the area at a higher rate than unheated glasshouses. The ratepayer objected on the ground that the heating installation was non-rateable machinery and was not therefore relevant in assessing the rate. The Lands Tribunal decided that the practice of the local valuation board was wrong and reduced the amount of the assessment. The board appealed. *Held*, the heating installation was non-rateable machinery and therefore all the glasshouses in the area had been wrongly valued. The board knew that the basis of their valuation was wrong and should not have continued to make valuations on that basis. The appeal would be dismissed.

WEST OF OUSE INTERNAL DRAINAGE BOARD V H. PRINS LTD (1978) 247 EG 295 (Court of Appeal: MEGAW, LAWTON and BROWNE LJJ).

1693   Land Drainage Act 1976—amendment

The Land Drainage Act 1976 (Amendment) Regulations 1978, S.I. 1978 No. 319 (in force on 1st April 1978), amend the Land Drainage Act 1976, 1976 Halsbury's Abr para. 1532 by replacing imperial units with metric units throughout and by making consequential amendments to associated drainage charges.

1694   Welsh Water Authority—abolition of Valley Drainage District

The Welsh Water Authority (Abolition of the Valley Drainage District) Order 1978, S.I. 1978 No. 1371 (in force on 18th September 1978), confirms a Scheme submitted to the Minister of Agriculture, Fisheries and Food by the Welsh National Water Development Authority for the abolition of the Valley Drainage District and the Valley Drainage Board, which were constituted by the Valley (Anglesey) Drainage Order 1927.

LAND REGISTRATION

Halsbury's Laws of England (4th edn.), Vol. 26, paras. 901–1490

1695   Articles

Security of Title in Registered Land, D. C. Jackson (the effect of *Peffer v Rigg*, 1976 Halsbury's Abr para. 1538 and *Orakpo v Manson Investments Ltd*, 1977 Halsbury's Abr para. 1918): (1978) 94 LQR 239.

Single Trustee for Sale of Registered Land, Martin Davey (certainty afforded by the registered land system in the light of *Peffer v Rigg* [1977] 1 WLR 285, 1976 Halsbury's Abr para. 153): 122 Sol Jo 375.

1696   Chief Land Registrar—annual report

The Report on the Work of HM Land Registry for the year 1977–1978 has been published. In it the Chief Land Registrar refers, inter alia, to the extension of the system of compulsory registration of land, the record number of application for first registration and the increase in the number of dealings in registered land over the previous year. He reports also on the speed of working and computer operations. The report, which also covers the Land Charges Department and Agricultural Credits Department, is available from HMSO, 50p.

1697   District registries—areas served

The Land Registration (District Registries) Order 1978, S.I. 1978 No. 1162 (in force on 30th October 1978), replaces the Land Registration (District Registries) (No. 2) Order 1974, 1974 Halsbury's Abr para. 1915. A new district land registry is constituted at Birkenhead, and responsibility for the registration of titles in the county of Merseyside is transferred from the Lytham District Land Registry to Birkenhead. The areas of the remaining district registries remain unchanged.

1698   Official searches—priority period

The Land Registration (Official Searches) Rules 1978, S.I. 1978 No. 1600 (in force on 1st January 1979), extend the period of priority conferred by an application for an official search from fifteen to twenty working days and make minor and consequential amendments to the Land Registration Rules 1925, S. R. & O. 1925 No. 1093.

The Land Registration (Official Searches) Rules 1969, S.I. 1969 No. 1179 are revoked.

1699 Overriding interest—occupation of matrimonial home by wife—whether actual occupation

See *Bird v Syme Thompson*, para. 1969; *Williams & Glyn's Bank v Boland*, para. 1978.

1700 Rules

The Land Registration Rules 1978, S.I. 1978 No. 1601 (in force on 1st January 1979), amend the Land Registration Rules 1925 by making fresh provision relating to the dates on which applications for registration are treated as having been delivered. They also clarify the provisions relating to competing priorities of applications and to the cancellation of defective applications.

1701 Unregistered interest in property—position of mortgagee claiming possession

See *Bird v Syme Thompson*, para. 1979; *Williams & Glyn's Bank v Boland*, para. 1978.

LANDLORD AND TENANT

Halsbury's Laws of England (3rd edn.), Vol. 23, paras. 985–1746

1702 Articles

Bedsitters and the Rent Act, Trevor M. Aldridge (the effect of *Marchant v Charters* [1977] 3 All ER 918), CA, 1976 Halsbury's Abr para. 2085): 122 Sol Jo 307.

Deductions from Rent, Andrew Waite (when a tenant may make deductions from rent): 128 NLJ 424.

Domestic Violence and the Rent Acts, Jill Martin (whether an injunction under the Domestic Violence and Matrimonial Proceedings Act 1976 excluding a spouse who is sole tenant would terminate a statutory tenancy): 128 NLJ 154.

Incentives to Private Landlords, R. J. Brien: 128 NLJ 864.

The Landlord and Tenant Act 1954; Business Tenancies, H. W. Willkinson (what constitutes a business tenancy?): 128 NLJ 715.

Landlord and Tenant Act 1954 II—Opposing a New Tenancy, H. W. Wilkinson (recent decisions on several of the grounds of opposition to a new tenancy under Landlord and Tenant Act 1954, s. 30): 128 NLJ 826.

The Landlord and Tenant Casebook for 1977, V. G. Wellings, QC (narrative review of the development of the law by the courts during 1977): [1978] JPL 221.

Landlord and Tenant Review, Trevor M. Aldridge (developments in the general law of landlord and tenant): 122 Sol Jo 563.

Occupying for Business Purposes, Henry E. Markson (the effect of *Boyer & Sons Ltd v Adams* 1976 Halsbury's Abr para. 1547): 122 Sol Jo 288.

Owner-Occupiers and the Rent Act 1977, P. F. Smith (consideration of the provisions of the Rent Act 1977 enabling a landlord to recover possession of a dwelling-house let to a residential tenant): 128 NLJ 729.

The Rent Act 1977—A candidate for the Guinness Book of Records, Philip Pettit (a list of printers' and draughtsman's errors in the Act): 128 NLJ 100.

The Rent Acts: Whose Protection?, Andrew Arden (discussion of the rights of flatsharers under the Rent Acts): 128 NLJ 624.

Rights of an Equitable Tenant in Common: a Note, Ian Saunders: Sol Jo 408.

Service Charges in Leases, Brian J. Harding: 247 EG 707.

Tenancies by Estoppel, Equitable Leases and Priorities, Jill Martin (circumstances in which a tenancy by estoppel arises, and whether a tenant by estoppel has any equitable interests): [1978] Conv. 137.

Tenants of Mortgagors, Andrew Walker (examination of the legal rights and liabilities of mortgagees and of tenants in mortgaged property; examination of the relationship between them in view of recent developments in the law of estoppel): 128 NLJ 773.

The Termination of Council House Tenancies, J. F. Garner (jurisdiction of local authorities to evict council tenants and terminate council tenancies): 122 Sol Jo 355.

1703   Business tenancy—application for new tenancy—landlord's intention to occupy

The tenants of a country club applied for a renewal of their business tenancy under the provisions of the Landlord and Tenant Act 1954. The landlords, a religious trust company with wide powers in relation to property and assets of the Roman Catholic Church, wanted to occupy the premises themselves for the purpose of setting up a community centre to be run by the parish priest. They therefore objected on the ground in s. 30 (1) (g) of the Act, namely, that they intended to occupy the holding for the purpose of business to be carried on by them therein. *Held*, first, the proposed activity was clearly one authorised by the trust deed governing the powers of the respondent trust company, and as such could be carried on not only by the trustees themselves but by their agents or other persons duly authorised by them, such as the parish priest. Second, such an activity clearly constituted a 'business' as defined by the Act. The landlords were therefore entitled to resist the grant of a new lease.

PARKES v WESTMINSTER ROMAN CATHOLIC DIOCESE TRUST (1978) 36 P & CR 22 (Court of Appeal: LORD DENNING MR, ORR and BRIDGE LJJ).

1704   ——— —— modification of terms by landlord

In renewing the lease of one of a line of twelve old shops, the landlord wished to insert a break clause, as he had with seven of the others, because he considered it likely that the site would be redeveloped within a few years either by himself or by a purchaser from him. He did not want to be burdened with a lease which would prevent redevelopment or lessen the value of the land if sold. The tenant complained that the clause would decrease the value of his business if he wished to sell. The trial judge rejected this argument but decided that, because there was no prospect of redevelopment, there should be a seven year lease with no break clause. On appeal, *held*, the trial judge had been correct in rejecting the tenant's argument because a tenant was not entitled to a saleable asset but only to the protection of the enjoyment of his business, but he had been wrong to decide that there should be no break clause. It was possible to insert a break clause subject to notice of the landlord's wish to redevelop the site. This would give the tenant the opportunity to contest any notice which was not given with an intention to redevelop. A new lease would be drawn up with a break clause dependent on an intention to redevelop.

ADAMS v GREEN (1978) 247 EG 49 (Court of Appeal: STAMP, ROSKILL and CUMMING-BRUCE LJJ).

1705   ——— —— opposition by landlord—whether reconstruction requires possession

The tenant of a shop applied to renew her lease. The landlord, who wished to transfer his own business to the premises, opposed the renewal on the ground that he wished to carry out reconstruction work which he could not reasonably do without obtaining possession. The lease provided that the landlord could enter the premises to carry out essential structural repairs and therefore the tenant contended that he did not require lawful possession. She also alleged that as she had the temporary use of another shop her business would not suffer and she was therefore entitled to the protection afforded by the Landlord and Tenant Act 1954, s. 31A (1) (a) in that the work would not substantially interfere with her use of the premises. The landlord appealed against the court's finding that he did not require lawful possession even though the work would substantially interfere with the tenant's use of the premises. *Held*, the work which the landlord wished to carry out did not amount to essential structural repair but to reconstruction for which he would require lawful possession. The tenant could not claim the protection of s. 31A (1) (a) because the substantial interference referred to in that section related to physical use of the premises and not to the effect of the work on the tenant's business. The appeal would be allowed.

REDFERN v REEVES (1978) 247 Estates Gazette 991 (Court of Appeal: STEPHENSON, LAWTON and GEOFFREY LANE LJJ).

1706   —— —— **service of application on landlords—extension of time limit for service**

Landlords of business premises gave notice to terminate the tenancy and the tenants made an application in the county court for a new lease, giving as the landlords' address for service the address which had appeared on the notice to quit. The court was unable to effect service because the landlords had moved to new premises. After two requests by the tenants, the landlords' solicitors supplied their new address, which the tenants' solicitors immediately sent to the court. Thereupon the tenants' application was served on the landlords. The landlords applied to the county court to have the tenants' application struck out on the ground that it had not been served within one month of being made as required by CCR. Ord. 8, r. 35. They contended that Ord. 8, r. 35 (4), which provides that where the summons has not been served within the time allowed the action should be struck out, was mandatory and deprived the court of jurisdiction under Ord. 13, r. 5, to extend the time for service. *Held*, the terms of Ord. 8, r. 35 were not mandatory and did not exclude the courts' jurisdiction to grant an extension of time. In the circumstances, the case was a proper one in which to grant an extension of time in which to save the application.

LEWIS v WOLKING PROPERTIES LTD [1978] 1 All ER 427 (Court of Appeal: ORR and GEOFFREY LANE LJJ).

1707   —— —— **tenant liable under lease to pay landlord's costs— whether clause imposed penalty**

The landlord company granted a seven year lease of business premises within the Landlord and Tenant Act 1954. By a clause in the lease the tenant was to reimburse the landlord in respect of all expenses incurred by the landlord in consequence of, inter alia, the serving of notice by the tenant under Part II of the Act requesting a new lease. On the expiry of the lease the tenant duly gave notice requesting renewal and, since he and the landlord company had come to terms, the court made an order by consent granting the tenant a further ten years' tenancy upon the terms of the expired lease. However, the court order made no reference to costs and the landlord subsequently presented the tenant with a substantial bill in respect of all the landlord's expenses. The tenant denied liability, on the ground that the clause in the lease imposed a penalty in the event of him making an application under the Act, and was therefore void under s. 38 (1). The trial judge rejected the argument and the tenant appealed. *Held*, since the effect of the clause was to compel the tenant to pay all costs incurred by the landlord on him making such an application, regardless of any order made by any court as to costs, it was to be construed as imposing a penalty within s. 38 (1). The appeal would be allowed.

STEVENSON & RUSH (HOLDINGS) LTD v LANGDON (1978) 122 Sol Jo 827 (Court of Appeal: MEGAW, BROWNE and WALLER LJJ).

1708   —— —— **terms**

In an application for a new tenancy of a lock-up shop, the landlord sought a modification of the user covenant. The tenant occupied the shop for the purpose of his business as a cutler. This was the only trade or business permitted by the lease. The landlord wanted to widen the user covenant in order to justify an increased rent. *Held*, since the tenant objected to the alteration of the terms, he should not be compelled to accept it. In this respect, the terms of the tenancy would remain as before.

CHARLES CLEMENTS (LONDON) LTD v RANK CITY WALL LTD (1978) 246 EG 739 (Chancery Division: GOULDING J).

1709   —— occupation for business purposes

The owner of a residential hotel had taken the tenancy of a neighbouring cottage, which was occupied by the hotel's head barman and his family. When the owner of the cottage died her administrator served notice to quit on the tenant, the hotel-owner. The hotel-owner contended that it was a business tenancy and that he was protected by the Landlord and Tenant Act 1954, s. 23 of which provides that a business tenancy exists where the premises are occupied for the purposes of a business carried on by the tenant. *Held*, the test for a business tenancy was whether it was necessary for an individual to live in the property to perform his duties in relation to the business. In the present case it was merely convenient, not necessary, for the barman to live in the cottage. It would be extending the meaning of business tenancy too far to hold that it included every house in which an owner of a business housed his staff.

CHAPMAN v FREEMAN [1978] 3 All ER 878 (Court of Appeal: LORD DENNING MR, GEOFFREY LANE and EVELEIGH LJJ).

For discussion of this case, see Justinian, Financial Times, 8th May 1978.

1710   ——— extent of business activity

In two cases the question arose as to whether tenancies of premises were business tenancies or regulated tenancies protected by the Rent Acts.

The first tenant was a doctor who took on a lease of a maisonette. He obtained the landlord's consent to carry on his professional work there. However, he did very little professional work at home, seeing only about one patient a year.

The second tenant was a partner in a business which had no trade premises. When he moved into his apartment, he equipped it for the purposes of his business without his landlord's knowledge and carried out his work from there. Both landlords contended that their tenants were business tenants under the Landlord and Tenant Act 1954, s. 23 (1), since they occupied the premises for business purposes. *Held*, business tenancies within s. 23 (1) did not extend to cover activities merely incidental to residential occupation. Therefore, although the first tenant had intended to use the premises for professional purposes, the intention unaccompanied by any action was insufficient. The only significant purpose for which he occupied the premises was for his home and therefore he was protected by the Rent Acts as a regulated tenant.

The second tenant was in occupation of the premises for the purposes of a business and the business was a significant purpose of his occupation as well as being his home. His case came within s. 23.

ROYAL LIFE SAVING SOCIETY v PAGE; CHERYL INVESTMENTS LTD v SALDANHA [1979] 1 All ER 5 (Court of Appeal: LORD DENNING MR, GEOFFREY LANE and EVELEIGH LJJ).

1711   —— —— taking in lodgers

An elderly woman tenant who took in lodgers but made very little if any profit out of them was served with a notice by her landlords under Landlord and Tenant Act, 1954, s. 25, which purported to terminate her tenancy. The question was whether the tenancy was a business tenancy under the Landlord and Tenant Act 1954, Pt. II, or a protected, regulated tenancy under Rent Act, 1968. The Rent Act 1968, s. 9 (5), provided that a tenancy should not be regulated if it was one to which the Landlord and Tenant Act, 1954, Part II applied. The woman's application under Rent Act, 1968, s. 105, for a declaration that her tenancy was a protected one was dismissed and she appealed. *Held*, to establish that a case came within the definition of a business tenancy in Landlord and Tenant Act 1954, s. 23, the tenant had to have occupied the premises for the purposes of a trade, profession or employment. This exhausted the meaning of "business" in so far as the tenant was a single person and not a body. It was a question of fact and degree whether the tenant carried on a business and nothing in the Act extended it to such activities as providing accommodation for lodgers as was provided in this case. After all the factors were considered, there was nothing to put her in the category of trader as she was not reaping any commercial advantage. The appeal would be allowed.

LEWIS v WELDCREST [1978] 3 All ER 1226 (Court of Appeal: STEPHENSON, ORMROD and WALLER LJJ).

The Rent Act 1968 has been consolidated by the Rent Act 1977.

1712 —— —— whether right of way capable of being occupied

Under a written agreement for seven years a company had a right of way over a private road which was owned by the council and gave access to land owned by the company and used in connection with its waste disposal business. On expiry of the agreement the company applied for an extension under the Landlord and Tenant Act 1954, Part II. The council contended that the tenancy was not a protected business tenancy as the lease was a grant of a term of years in an incorporeal hereditament. *Held*, in the context of the Act the words "used" and "occupied" were not interchangeable. A mere right of way as opposed to the road itself was not capable of being occupied and consequently the security of tenure provisions of the Act did not apply.

LAND RECLAMATION CO LTD v BASILDON DISTRICT COUNCIL [1978] 2 All ER 1162 (Chancery Division: BRIGHTMAN J).

1713 Covenant—covenant against underletting or parting with possession—whether includes assignment

On a preliminary point of law the question for the court was whether a covenant in a lease forbidding underletting or parting with possession also precluded assignment. *Held*, a covenant against assignment, underletting or parting with possession involved three separate covenants which were not mutually exclusive. Although there was no express restriction on assignment in this case, such action necessarily involved parting with possession of the premises and therefore amounted to a breach of covenant.

MARKS v WARREN [1979] 1 All ER 29 (Chancery Division: BROWNE-WILKINSON J).

1714 —— lessee's covenant to pay costs of statutory notice—service of statutory notice—counter-notice by lessee—whether lessor required leave of court to recover costs

A covenant in a lease required the lessee to pay the legal costs and surveyor's fees incidental to any statutory notice relating to a breach of covenant. The lessors served a notice under the Law of Property Act 1925, s. 146 relating to a breach of covenant to repair. The lessee served a counter-notice under the Leasehold Property (Repairs) Act 1938 and subsequently carried out the repairs. The lessors successfully claimed the legal costs and surveyor's fees incidental to the s. 146 notice. The lessee appealed on the ground that as she had served a counter-notice under the 1938 Act, the lessors were required by s. 1 (3) or s. 2 of that Act to obtain leave of the court before taking action to recover the sum claimed. *Held*, (i) s. 1 (3) applied only in relation to a claim for damages; the lessors' claim was for a debt due under the lease not for damages for breach of contract. (ii) Section 2 applied only when the lessor claimed legal costs and surveyor's fees under the Law of Property Act 1925, s. 146 (3); in the present case the lessors were relying on the terms of the lease, not on s. 146 (3). The appeal would be dismissed.

MIDDLEGATE PROPERTIES LTD v GIDLOW-JACKSON (1977) 34 P & CR 4 (Court of Appeal: MEGAW and LAWTON LJJ and SIR DAVID CAIRNS). *Bader Properties Ltd v Linley Property Investments Ltd* (1967) 19 P & CR 621 approved.

1715   —— lessor's covenant to insure for full cost of reinstatement—meaning of "full cost of reinstatement"

A covenant in a lease required the lessee to pay to the lessor each year a sum equal to the premium paid by the lessor in insuring the premises for their full cost of reinstatement following loss or damage by fire or other catastrophe. A dispute arose as to whether the "full cost of reinstatement" meant the cost of reinstatement at the time when the premium was renewed as the lessee contended, or, as the lessor contended, the cost when reinstatement was likely to be completed. *Held*, the words had to be construed according to commercial good sense. The parties must have contemplated that there would be a delay between destruction of the premises and completion of reinstatement during which time the cost of rebuilding would increase. Therefore the lessor was entitled to take account of the likely increase when considering the cost of reinstatement.

GLENIFFER FINANCE CORPORATION v BAMAR WOOD & PRODUCTS LTD [1978] 2 Lloyd's Rep 49 (Queen's Bench Division: FORBES J).

1716   Fair rent—determination—jurisdiction of rent officer—withdrawal of application

The tenant applied to a rent officer to have a fair rent fixed for premises which he occupied. The tenant subsequently left the premises as the result of a county court order granting possession to the landlord. The rent officer treated the rent application as withdrawn, dismissing it on the ground that he had no jurisdiction. An order of mandamus was sought, directing the rent officer to hear and determine the application. *Held*, the rent officer was wrong in treating the application as withdrawn without any intimation from the parties. He was also wrong in thinking that he had no jurisdiction. It did not matter that the tenant had vacated the premises before the hearing. The relevant date for occupation was the date of the application. The order of mandamus would be granted.

R v LAMBETH RENT OFFICER, EX PARTE FOX (1978) 245 EG 569 (Queen's Bench Division: LORD WIDGERY CJ, CUMMING-BRUCE LJ and PARK J). *R v West London Rent Tribunal, ex parte Napper* [1967] 1 QB 169 and *Hanson v Church Commissioners for England* [1977] 3 All ER 404, CA, 1976 Halsbury's Abr para. 2082 applied.

1717   Forfeiture—action by landlord—landlord's claim for interim payment—cross-claim by tenant

In an action for possession of land resulting from an alleged breach of covenant, the defendant cross-claimed against the plaintiff on the ground of harassment. The cross-claim, which was not without substance, was for an amount of damages almost double the amount of the plaintiff's claims for rent outstanding. The plaintiff made an application under RSC Ord. 29, r. 18 (1), for an interim payment for use and occupation of the land and premises pending the trial of the action. *Held*, an interim payment could not properly be ordered in the face of a bone fide cross-claim. The application would be dismissed.

OLD GROVEBURY MANOR FARM LTD v W. SEYMOUR PLANT SALES & HIRE LTD (1978) 122 Sol Jo 457 (Chancery Division: BRIGHTMAN J).

1718   —— breach of condition—bankruptcy of surety—whether landlord required to serve a forfeiture notice

A lease contained a proviso for re-entry by the landlords in the event of a breach of covenant or the bankruptcy of the tenant or surety. The landlords issued a writ to recover possession of the premises for breach of a covenant against underletting. They then sought leave to amend the writ by including the surety's bankruptcy as a further ground for possession. The tenant objected on the ground that the surety's bankruptcy was a breach of condition within the Law of Property Act 1925, s. 146 (1) and therefore the landlords were required to serve a forfeiture notice which they had failed to do. *Held*, the tenant's bankruptcy would have been a breach of condition within s. 146 (1) and there was no reason to distinguish the surety's bankruptcy. As more of the statutory exceptions to s. 146 (1) applied, the landlords were required to serve a forfeiture notice and accordingly leave to amend the writ would be refused.

HALLIARD PROPERTY CO LTD v JACK SEGAL LTD (1978) 245 EG 230 (Chancery Division: GOULDING J).

1719   Lease—assignment—assignment to company—disclaimer of lease by liquidator—effect on liability of original lessees

See *Warnford Investments Ltd v Duckworth*, para. 369.

1720   —— —— consent—subsequent discovery of information about intended assignee—whether consent revocable

A lessee of shop premises requested his landlords' permission to assign his tenancy to a third party. In accordance with the lease which prohibited assignment of the premises without their written consent, the landlords granted conditional consent to the assignment. After the conditions had been fulfilled by the lessee however, the landlords discovered that the intended assignee had been convicted of certain offences. The question arose as to whether the landlords were entitled to revoke their consent to the assignment. *Held*, the lessee had done all that he was duty-bound to do; this was a case where something had come to light after consent had been given through no fault of his. Accordingly, the landlords were not entitled to revoke their consent.

MITTEN v FAGG (1978) 247 EG 901 (Chancery Division: GOULDING J).

1721   —— —— landlord's refusal of consent—right of purchaser to recover deposit

During negotiations for the assignment of a lease the purchaser was unable to provide the landlord with sufficient information about his financial resources so the landlord refused his consent to the assignment. The tenant claimed that the contract imposed a positive obligation on the purchaser to provide sufficient information and that his failure to do so amounted to a breach of covenant. The purchaser counterclaimed that he had done all that he could reasonably be expected to do and that as the tenant could not obtain the landlord's licence to assign he was entitled to the return of his deposit. The trial judge found that the purchaser was in breach of covenant and awarded damages to the tenant. The purchaser appealed. *Held*, the purchaser was not in breach of a positive obligation as the language of the contract did not create a covenant but only a condition and therefore he was not liable in damages. As the tenant could not secure the landlord's licence to assign, the contract was incapable of performance and the purchaser was entitled to the return of his deposit.

SHIRES v BROCK (1977) 247 EG 127 (Court of Appeal: BUCKLEY, SCARMAN and GOFF LJJ).

1722   —— parties—whether statutory tenant's mother an undisclosed principal

See *Hanstown Properties Ltd v Green*, para. 1737.

1723   —— stamp duty—contingent or conditional rent

See *Coventry City Council v Inland Revenue Commissioners*, para 2754.

1724   Leasehold enfranchisement or extension

See LEASEHOLD ENFRANCHISEMENT.

1725   **Licence—licence to occupy—equitable licence for life—effect of licensees' subsequent conduct**

In a county court action in 1972 the defendants were held to have an equitable licence to occupy their cottage for life as the result of a family arrangement. The cottage was later sold to the plaintiff together with an adjoining cottage and a paddock. The defendants created difficulties in relation to the plaintiff's use of the adjoining cottage and paddock and the plaintiff brought an action for possession of the defendants' cottage. Possession was granted on the ground that the defendants' conduct had been so gross as to determine their equitable licence. On appeal by the defendants, *held*, the defendants' established equitable licence to occupy the cottage for life was not determined by their conduct.

LORD DENNING MR considered that such a licence could in extreme cases be revoked but this was not such a case.

GOFF and CUMMING-BRUCE LJJ considered that excessive user or bad behaviour towards the legal owner could not bring to an end or forfeit such an equity once established.

WILLIAMS V STAITE [1978] 2 All ER 928 (Court of Appeal: LORD DENNING MR, GOFF and CUMMING-BRUCE LJJ).

1726   **—— —— licence distinguished from tenancy—exclusive occupation—principles for determining nature of agreement**

The defendants shared a double bed-sitting room under separate licence agreements by which each paid rent separately to the landlord. One defendant applied to a rent officer for a rent reduction, alleging that he was a protected tenant under the Rent Acts. The officer adjourned the hearing pending determination by the county court of the question whether the defendants were tenants at all, and if so whether they were protected. The court found they were regulated joint tenants on the ground that if read as one, their agreements conferred a joint interest in and exclusive occupation of the room. On the landlord's appeal, the defendants contended that there was a simple contract of tenancy and that any permission to occupy residential property exclusively had to be a tenancy unless it came within the category of hotels, hostels, family arrangements, a service occupancy or similar arrangement. *Held*, there was no reason why an ordinary landlord should not be able to grant a licence to occupy an ordinary house. Provided that an agreement was not a lease masquerading as a licence, and that it was the intention of the parties to create a licence, which the evidence in this case clearly supported, it was quite possible for a landlord to create one. It was impossible to reconstruct the obligations contained in the separate agreements into a joint obligation without rewriting the agreements. In the absence of a joint agreement there could be no tenancy because neither occupant had an exclusive right of occupation. Further, even if a joint interest had been created, the existence of a clause enabling the landlord to impose another person on each licence meant that there was no exclusive occupation. Accordingly, the occupants were licensees and the appeal would be allowed.

SOMMA V HAZLEHURST [1978] 2 All ER 1011 (Court of Appeal: STEPHENSON, GEOFFREY LANE and CUMMING-BRUCE LJJ).

1727   The plaintiff was the owner of a property divided into flats. She authorised an estate agent to enter into agreements on her behalf for the occupation of the flats, but told him that she did not want to create tenancies. The agent subsequently entered into an agreement for occupation of one of the flats with the defendants. He asked them to sign a form, purporting to be a licence, which stated that the plaintiff was not willing to grant the defendants exclusive possession and that the occupation of the flat was to be "in common with" the owner or her invitees. The agent assured the defendants that this was merely a legal formality and that there was no question of them having to share the flat with anyone else. The question arose as to whether the agreement was a tenancy or a licence and whether the agent had authority to conclude such an agreement. *Held*, in view of what the agent had told the defendants the agreement created a joint tenancy, giving the defendants exclusive occupation of the flat. The plaintiff's reservation of a right of access did not destroy the defendants' right. The form signed by the defendants was a sham, designed to disguise the true nature of the agreement. Although the agent had been told not to create a tenancy, he had been given authority to make agreements on the plaintiff's behalf, and such agreements would be binding on her.

The court considered that although the granting of exclusive possession might create a licence and not a tenancy, there was no authority for the proposition that there could be no tenancy without a grant of exclusive occupation.

WALSH v GRIFFITHS-JONES [1978] 2 All ER 1002 (Lambeth County Court: JUDGE McDONNELL).

1728   —— —— mistress—nature of licence—notice required for termination—whether constructive trust implied

The defendant and her husband jointly bought a house in 1972. In 1974 the husband left, but continued to make the mortgage payments until 1975. After her husband left, the defendant became the plaintiff's mistress and in 1976 the defendant and her husband sold the house to him. The defendant continued to live there with the children. It was intended that the plaintiff should move in with them after the defendant and her husband were divorced, but soon after the purchase the relationship ended. The plaintiff purported to serve a notice on the defendant terminating her licence and requiring her to quit a month after service. She refused, and the plaintiff brought a claim for possession; the defendant counterclaimed for a declaration that she was a tenant for life, or alternatively a beneficiary under a trust upon terms that she was entitled to remain in the house for as long as she wished. The claim for possession was dismissed on the ground that the defendant was a beneficiary under a trust upon terms that she was entitled to occupy the house for her life. The plaintiff appealed, and the defendant amended her counterclaim by adding that she was a licensee for life or for a period terminable only by reasonable notice. *Held*, it was not challenged that the defendant had an express licence and that the notice could not revoke it. The true dispute arose on the counterclaim. There were two issues; one as to the terms of the licence, and the other as to whether the defendant had an equitable interest arising under a constructive trust, and if so, to what extent. The trial judge had found that there was an express agreement giving rise to a constructive trust, but if the defendant could establish a licence, there was neither room nor need for an equitable interest. If the parties intended that she should have a right of occupation for life, there was a binding contract, and if they did not so agree, there was nothing to give rise to an equitable interest. In this case, there was an intention to create legal relations, but no intention to create a licence for life. The defendant had a contractual licence terminable on reasonable notice, which was twelve calendar months.

CHANDLER v KERLEY [1978] 2 All ER 942 (Court of Appeal: LORD SCARMAN, MEGAW and ROSKILL LJJ).

1729   Mobile home—security of tenure—application for extension of period of security—jurisdiction of the county court

The owners of a caravan site offered the site occupiers an agreement giving them security of tenure for five years, the minimum period required by the Mobile Homes Act 1975, 1975 Halsbury's Abr para. 3292. Under s. 4 (5) of the Act, an occupier who is dissatisfied with the terms offered in an agreement may apply to the court to determine a dispute; the occupiers successfully applied under s. 4 (5) to have the period extended beyond five years. On appeal by the site owners, *held*, an application could only be made under s. 4 (5) when the terms of an agreement did not comply with the Act or else were inconsistent with an existing agreement, with the occupiers. As the terms of the owners' offer complied with the Act, the court had no jurisdiction to extend the period. Accordingly the appeal would be allowed.

TAYLOR v CALVERT [1978] All ER 630 (Court of Appeal: LORD DENNING MR, ORMROD and GEOFFREY LANE LJJ)

1730   **Premiums—returnable deposit and rent payable in advance— illegality**

See *R v Ewing*, para. 641.

1731   **Protected tenancy—agricultural worker—whether gamekeeper a protected tenant.**

See *Normanton (Earl) v Giles*, para. 49.

1732   **Recovery of possession—dwelling-house let on regulated tenancy**

The Rent (County Court Proceedings) (Case 11) Rules 1978, S.I. 1978 No. 1961 (in force on 12th March 1979), provide a summary procedure for the recovery of possession by owner-occupiers as an alternative to the ordinary proceedings in the county court for possession. It is available where the owner-occupier's claim falls within the Rent Act 1977, Sch. 15, Case 11 and the notice required by paragraph (a) of that Case has been given to the tenant.

1733   —— —— **required as residence by only one joint owner-occupier**

One of the two joint owners of a house let on a regulated tenancy applied for an order of possession under the Rent Act 1968, Schedule 3, Case 10 which provided for the making of such an order where, inter alia, a person who occupied the dwelling-house as his residence had let it on a regulated tenancy and the court was satisfied that the dwelling-house was required as a residence for the owner-occupier. *Held*, EVELEIGH LJ dissenting, where a house let on a regulated tenancy was jointly owned the court could make an order under Case 10 only if it was satisfied that the house was required as a residence for both owners. In the context of the language of Case 10 the person who let it and who was referred to as "the owner-occupier" was the applicant and the co-owner.

EVELEIGH LJ considered that it was wholly truthful to say that the applicant had let the house on a regulated tenancy. The fact that two people did a thing together did not prevent either one claiming that he had done it.

TILLING v WHITEMAN [1978] 3 All ER 1103 (Court of Appeal: STEPHENSON, SHAW and EVELEIGH LJJ). *McIntyre v Hardcastle* [1948] 2 KB 82, CA applied.

The Rent Act 1968 has been consolidated by the Rent Act 1977.

This decision was subsequently reversed in the House of Lords.

1734   —— **expiry of fixed term—rent increase—whether new tenancy created**

In 1976, a landlord brought an action for possession of his flat under the Rent Act 1968 on grounds of arrears of rent and the tenants' breach of contractual obligations. The tenants contended that on the expiry of their tenancy agreement in 1975, the landlords had granted them a new contractual tenancy at an increased rent. The landlords' claim for possession was granted on the grounds that no new contractual tenancy had been created, and the tenants appealed. *Held*, from the facts it appeared that there were no variations in the terms of the agreement apart from the rise in rent. It was an established principle that in cases to which the Rent Acts applied, acceptance of rent by the landlord after expiry of the term did not by itself lead to the inference that a new contract had been created. The tenants' appeal would be dismissed.

HARVEY v STAGG (1977) 247 EG 463 (Court of Appeal: STEPHENSON, ORR and BROWNE LJJ).

1735   —— **local authority houses—common law rights of unprotected tenants**

See *Bristol City Council v Rawlins*, para. 1494.

1736 —— mortgage of demised premises—mortgagee's right to obtain possession—evasion of Rent Acts

The owner of a tenanted house charged it to a bank as security for an overdraft. A clause in the mortgage agreement prevented the mortgagor from letting the premises or accepting the surrender of leases without the bank's consent. A fresh tenancy was later made without such consent entitling the bank to bring proceedings for possession. It did not do so but the mortgagor's wife paid off the bank and the charge was transferred to her. She brought proceedings for possession, hoping to sell the house with vacant possession for a high price. *Held*, there was a strict legal right that gave a mortgagee the right to obtain possession of the mortgaged premises. This was, however, subject to equitable considerations; the right to possession had to be exercised bona fide in the interests of enforcing the security. The ulterior motive behind this attempt at repossession had been to evade the Rent Acts and sell the property with vacant possession. In such a situation the court would look behind the formal legal relationship of the parties and look at the true substance of the matter. The order for possession would not be made.

QUENNELL v MALTBY [1979] 1 All ER 568 (Court of Appeal: LORD DENNING MR, BRIDGE AND TEMPLEMAN LJJ).

1737 —— occupation by statutory tenant's mother—whether occupant an undisclosed principal under original lease—rights of landlord

Landlords claimed possession of a flat occupied by the defendant. The defendant was the mother of one of two statutory tenants of the flat, both of whom had departed. She claimed she was a statutory tenant also on the basis that she was an undisclosed principal under the lease out of which the statutory tenancy arose. *Held*, the original lease made no reference to the defendant; in an agreement of the type in issue it was crucial for the landlords to know who the lessees were, both for the enforcement of covenants and because of the possibility of statutory tenancies arising under the Rent Acts. The defendant accordingly could not claim to be a tenant and the landlords were entitled to possession.

HANSTOWN PROPERTIES LTD v GREEN (1977) 246 EG 917 (Court of Appeal: CAIRNS, ROSKILL and BRIDGE LJJ).

1738 Rent—increase after expiry of fixed term—whether new tenancy created

See *Harvey v Stagg*, para. 1734.

1739 —— reasonable rent for premises—evidence of other traders—admissibility

A dispute arose between the landlords and the tenant of business premises as to the amount of rent that should be payable. The matter was referred to the court under Landlord and Tenant Act 1954, s. 34, which provides that the rent is to be that at which the holding might reasonably be expected to be let in the open market by a willing lessor. At the hearing, two of the tenant's neighbours in similar shop premises, gave evidence as to what they thought a reasonable rent for their premises, having regard to their trading position, would be. The trial judge relied heavily on this evidence and also preferred the evidence of the tenant's expert witness to that of the landlords'. The landlords appealed. *Held*, the evidence of the two neighbours was admissible as to the trading position of the area but not as to the rent to be determined for the tenant's premises. The judge had thus wrongly attached importance to the neighbours' views as to reasonable rent for their respective premises. Further, he had relied upon the evidence of the tenant's expert witness which was largely inadmissible, being based on hearsay. Accordingly, the appeal would be allowed and a new trial ordered.

ROGERS v ROSEDIMOND INVESTMENTS (BLAKES MARKET) LTD (1978) 247 EG 467 (Court of Appeal: STAMP, ROSKILL and CUMMING-BRUCE LJJ).

1740   —— registered rent—whether inclusive of rates

The tenant went into occupation of a furnished flat in May 1972. In September 1972 a reduced rent was registered inclusive of rates under the Rent Act 1968, Pt. VI. The tenant remained in possession after the contractual tenancy expired and by virtue of the Rent Act 1974, s. 1, became a protected contractual tenant. In 1976 the landlords gave the tenant a notice to quit, whereupon he became a protected statutory tenant. The landlords brought an action against him claiming that since the expiry of the notice to quit they were entitled to recover from him a sum in respect of rates in addition to the rent. They contended that on the coming into force of the Rent Act 1974, by virtue of s. 5 (1), the rent registered under the 1968 Act, Pt. VI, became deemed to be registered under the 1968 Act, Pt. IV. The 1968 Act, s. 47, provided that rent should be registered under Pt. IV exclusive of rates, and thus what had hitherto been an inclusive rent under Pt. VI became converted into an exclusive rent under Pt. IV. *Held*, s. 5 (1) was not intended to have such an effect. All that it materially said was that the amount registered under Pt. VI should be deemed to be registered under Pt. IV, thus extending to furnished tenancies the same protection as afforded to unfurnished tenancies. There was nothing to say that the registered rent was to be treated as being something which in fact it was not. The landlords' claim would be dismissed.

DOMINAL SECURITIES LTD v McLEOD (1978) 122 Sol Jo 644 (Court of Appeal: MEGAW, BROWNE and SHAW LJJ).

Rent Acts 1968 and 1974 now consolidated in Rent Act 1977.

1741   —— rent increase—whether increase paid under duress—test for duress

Australia

The Commonwealth of Australia, as lessor, increased the rents of its premises in purported compliance with the leases held by the appellant airline companies. The airlines paid the increases because use of the premises was essential for the operation of their businesses, and they believed the leases would be forfeit if the rent was not paid in full. At first instance the judge made a declaration that as the Commonwealth had not acted effectively to increase the rent it had no right to demand payment, but he refused to order repayment of the excess paid. The airline companies appealed, claiming that they were entitled to recover the excess payments as they had paid under duress. *Held*, the authorities indicated that for a payment to be made under compulsion it had to be shown that there was a fear that the payee would take some steps, other than invoking the legal process, which would cause harm to the payer and that this fear was reasonably caused or well founded. In the present case the Commonwealth had made no explicit threat that the leases would be forfeit if the increases were not paid, and had not used its monopolistic position to exact payment. As there was no evidence that the demands for payment had been made by the Commonwealth acting in its governmental capacity the relevant relationship was that of lessor and lessee and the appeal would be dismissed.

AIR INDIA v THE COMMONWEALTH OF AUSTRALIA [1977] 1 NSWLR 449 (Court of Appeal of New South Wales).

1742   —— —— whether service charge included in rent

In an action by landlords for rent, the tenant alleged that certain rent increases authorised by the rent officer had been improperly arrived at. He sought an order for discovery of a summary of the relevant costs of service charges for the flats where he lived under the Housing Finance Act 1972, s. 90, which provides that a tenant is entitled to such a summary where the service charge payable exceeds a specified amount. He alleged that there was a doubt as to the correctness of the figures relating to the service charge element of the rent which had been taken into account by the rent officer and the rent assessment committee in increasing the rent. The lease contained no reference to a service charge, although in it the landlords covenanted to provide certain services. The only liability of the tenant was to pay rent either at the sum stated or such greater sum as might be registered. The county court judge granted the order and the landlords appealed. *Held*, "service charge" was defined in s. 90 (12) as a charge payable as part of or in addition to the rent. The present lease did not create a service charge falling within this definition, even though it provided for contractual services by the landlords. The tenant was not entitled to discovery under s. 90. Nor would the tenant be entitled to discovery under the general law even if the relevant documents were proved to exist as they went to no issue in the proceedings. They would be directed towards challenging figures accepted by the rent officer and the rent assessment committee, and the correct place to do this was before the rent officer and the rent assessment committee, not in the county court. The appeal would be allowed.

LEGAL & GENERAL ASSURANCE SOCIETY LTD v KEANE (1978) 246 EG 827 (Court of Appeal: STAMP, ROSKILL and CUMMING-BRUCE LJJ).

1743   —— rent paid by cheque—cheque posted to landlord by due date—instructions previously given to send rent to agent—whether rent duly paid

The appellant had been tenant of an agricultural holding since 1946. He normally paid his rent by cheque sent through the post to the landlords. In 1974 the landlords instructed an agent to collect the rent on their behalf. The agent wrote to the tenant asking him to pay rent in future direct to him. When the next half-year's rent was not paid on the due date the agent sent the tenant a notice requiring him to pay within two months of service of the notice. Just before the two months expired the tenant sent a cheque by post direct to one of the landlords. It was received after the period had expired. The landlords contended that the tenant had failed to pay the rent within the two month period and that accordingly a notice to quit served by them effectively terminated his tenancy. *Held*, on general principles a landlord should have rent in cash in his hands by the due date. However that requirement might be varied by express arrangement or by necessary implication where the facts established that the landlord had been content to accept payment by cheque posted by the due date. In the present case there had for many years been a course of dealing which showed that the sending of a cheque by post to the landlords was the accepted mode of payment and the request to send the cheque to the agent did no more than provide an alternative destination for it. When the cheque had been put in the post by the appellant not later than the expiry of the two month period the rent had been paid.

BEEVERS v MASON (1978), 122 Sol Jo 610 (Court of Appeal: MEGAW, BROWNE and SHAW LJJ).

1744   —— rent regulation—forms

The Rent Regulation (Forms etc.) Regulations 1978, S.I. 1978 No. 495 (in force on 19th June 1978), supersede the Rent Regulation (Forms etc.) (Consolidation) Regulations 1973, S.I. 1973 No. 176, the Rent Regulation (Forms etc.) (Amendment) Regulations 1973, S.I. 1973 No. 1539, and the Rent Regulation (Forms etc.) Regulations 1975, S.I. 1975 No. 541. The new regulations prescribe the forms to be used for the purposes of Rent Act 1977, Parts III, IV, and Schedule 11.

1745   —— review clause—construction—whether clause applicable where rent frozen by statute

An underlease granted in 1967 for a fixed term of twenty-one years provided for a fixed annual rent of £5,500 for the first seven years, subject to review at the end of that time for the following seven years on the lessor giving written notice. The reviewed rent was to be a "fair rack rent . . . payable for the demised premises" as if they were then to be let for a term of seven years on the terms of the existing lease. Accordingly, on the review date the lessor gave notice, but at that time the Counter-Inflation (Business Rents) Order 1973 was in force under which the rent was frozen at £5,500. However, the lessor contended that the expression "fair rack rent . . . payable" meant the market rental value at the review date, regardless of the freeze. By originating summons the lessee sought, inter alia, an order that a surveyor determining the fair rack rent should apply the provisions of the Order, so that the reviewed yearly rent should not exceed £5,500: he claimed that "fair rack rent . . . payable" was to be construed as meaning the maximum rent permitted by law. He succeeded at first instance and the lessor appealed. *Held*, the rent review clause was to be construed in the light of circumstances existing at the date of the underlease, at which time rents were not subject to any statutory restriction. Accordingly the true meaning of the expression "fair rack rent . . . payable" in the context of the clause and the lease as a whole was the full annual value of the premises reserved or contracted to be paid by the terms of the lease. Therefore, while a surveyor should take account of counter-inflation legislation when making the valuation, he was not thereby precluded from increasing the rent.

The court pointed out that while it was not a function of the court to direct surveyors as to how to make a valuation, the construction of a rent review provision was a question of law to be determined by the court.

COMPTON GROUP LTD v ESTATES GAZETTE LTD (1977) 36 P & CR 148 (Court of Appeal: STEPHENSON and BROWNE LJJ and SIR JOHN PENNYCUICK).

1746   —— —— lessees' improvements—effect on rent

Lessees were granted a twenty-one year lease of a factory. The rent was to be reviewed by an independent surveyor after each seven year period, the new rent to be "a reasonable rent for the demised premises". The factory was burnt down before the first rent review. The lessees incorporated many improvements into the reconstructed building at their own expense. When the rent review became due, a dispute arose as to what amounted to a reasonable rent. The parties agreed that the improvements were now a part of the demised premises but the lessees claimed regard should be had to the fact that they had paid for the improvements. *Held*, LORD WILBERFORCE and LORD SALMON dissenting, in the absence of any provision in the lease to the effect that improvements were to be disregarded in assessing a reasonable rent, it was not possible to disregard them as they were recognised as being part and parcel of the premises. The duty of the independent surveyor was to assess a reasonable rent for the premises, not a reasonable rent for the lessees to pay. Accordingly, their expenditure could not be taken into account when reviewing the rent.

LORD WILBERFORCE considered the effect of the improvement should be disregarded because it was unreasonable for a lessee to have to pay increased rent on top of heavy expenditure of his own; because if a new lease were negotiated in the future the rent would be statutorily barred from reflecting the improvements; and because it was unfair that a lessor could obtain an increase in respect of improvements under a review clause intended to keep the rent in line with inflation if he could not obtain it at the time the improvements were licensed in the first place.

PONSFORD v HMS (AEROSOLS) LTD [1978] 2 All ER 837 (House of Lords: LORD WILBERFORCE, VISCOUNT DILHORNE, LORD SALMON, LORD FRASER OF TULLYBELTON and LORD KEITH OF KINKEL). Majority decision of the Court of Appeal [1977] 3 All ER 651, 1977 Halsbury's Abr para. 1672 affirmed.

1747   Lessees of business premises made improvements to the premises with the landlord's permission. When the lessees sought a new tenancy under the Landlord and Tenant Act 1954, the order for the grant of a new tenancy provided for a rent review clause, the rent disregarding the effect on any improvement carried out by a tenant or his predecessor in title. The lessees then requested the landlords to grant the new tenancy to their subsidiary company. The new lease contained a rent review clause which provided for a specified rent or "such sum as shall be assessed as a reasonable rent". A disagreement arose as to what was to be considered in the surveyor's assessment of a reasonable rent. The landlord sought a declaration that the rent was to be assessed without any regard to the fact that improvements had been carried out by the first lessees or their subsidiary. *Held*, the question was not one of rent which would be reasonable for the tenant to pay but rather that of a reasonable rent for the premises. The surveyor was to take the premises as he found them and then decide upon a reasonable rent regardless of who had paid for the premises or made the improvements.

CUFF V J & F STONE PROPERTY CO LTD (1973) [1978] 2 All ER 833 (Chancery Division: MEGARRY J).

1748   —— —— time limit—non-compliance

A lease provided for the landlord to give notice in writing to the tenant if the landlord wanted to review the rent. Failing an agreement within a certain period, it was provided that the landlord should give the tenant further notice, again within a specified period, stating that the matter would be sent to arbitration. No agreement was reached and no arbitration notice was given within the period. The landlord sought a declaration that time was not of the essence in the rent review clause and that he could therefore validly serve the notice out of time. The basis of his case was a very narrow interpretation of the wording of the lease. *Held*, the wording made time of the essence; a period had been specified and it should have been kept to. The landlord had to comply with the terms of the lease if he wanted to review the rent.

DREBBOND LTD V HORSHAM DISTRICT COUNCIL [1978] LS Gaz R 224 (Chancery Division: MEGARRY V-C).

1749   —— —— willing landlord and tenant—assumptions to be made in assessing full market value

A rent review clause in a lease provided that the reviewed rent should be based on the full market value of the premises at the time of the review as if they were let with vacant possession on the open market by a willing landlord to a willing tenant. The question arose as to what assumptions were to be made in assessing the full market value. *Held*, it had to be assumed that there was a rent on which a willing landlord and tenant would agree. Negotiations would be conducted fairly but with all the appropriate bargaining advantages and disadvantages. The hypothetical willing landlord was neither one who was forced to let the premises nor one who could afford to wait until the market improved, and a hypothetical willing tenant was one who was actively seeking premises like those let but who was not under any pressure to do so. Any circumstance affecting the plaintiff and defendant which would not affect the hypothetical landlord and tenant was irrelevant. The case was remitted to the arbitrator for assessment according to the stated principles.

F. R. EVANS (LEEDS) LTD V ENGLISH ELECTRIC CO LTD (1978) 36 P & CR 185 (Queen's Bench Division: DONALDSON J).

1750   Rent rebate and allowance schemes

See HOUSING.

1751   Service charge—whether included in rent

See *Legal & General Assurance Society Ltd v Keane*, para. 1742.

1752   Statutory tenancy—joint tenant—whether protected by Rent Acts

The landlord granted a tenancy of a flat to two air hostesses. The tenancy was protected under the Rent Act 1968. Rent Act 1968, s. 3 (1) (a), as consolidated by Rent Act 1977, s. 2 (1) (a), gives security of tenure, after the termination of a protected tenancy, to the person who was the protected tenant immediately before that termination. Before the expiry of the protected term, one of the tenants left to get married, with no intention of returning. The other tenant stayed on and, after the expiry of the term, the landlord took proceedings for possession against her. It was contended for the landlord that since the tenancy was a joint tenancy, only an act done by both the individuals together, as joint tenants, had any legal effect. Both the tenants would have to have been in residence on the determination of the protected tenancy, for the provisions of the Act to take effect and create a statutory tenancy in favour of them together as protected tenant. *Held*, in respect of the Rent Act 1968, s. 3 (1) (a), the ordinary law as to joint tenancy ought not to be strictly applied. The single remaining tenant would be treated as the protected tenant immediately before the termination of the contractual tenancy, and as being the statutory tenant thereafter. She therefore had security of tenure under the Act.

LLOYD V SADLER [1978] 2 All ER 529 (Court of Appeal: MEGAW, LAWTON and SHAW LJJ). *Howson v Buxton* [1928] All ER 434 CA, applied.

For a discussion of this case see, Home, sweet secure jointly leased home: Justinian, Financial Times, 23rd January 1978.

1753   —— **right of succession—member of tenant's family—friend treated as nephew**

In 1957 the defendant who was then in his early twenties became friendly with an elderly widow and moved into the flat of which she was the tenant. Their relationship was entirely platonic. They regarded each other as aunt and nephew but were not in fact related. Neither was financially dependent on the other, and expenses, other than the rent, were shared. The rent was paid by the widow. They continued to live together in the flat until the widow died eighteen years later. During that period the contractual tenancy of the flat expired and the widow became a statutory tenant. After her death the landlords sought possession. The defendant claimed that he was a member of the original tenant's family for the purposes of Rent Act 1968, Sch. 1, para. 3 and accordingly had become the statutory tenant on her death. *Held*, two adults who lived together in a platonic relationship without any recognisable family relationship could not be members of each other's family even though they regarded each other as such. Accordingly the landlords were entitled to possession.

JORAM DEVELOPMENTS LTD V SHARRATT [1978] 2 All ER 948 (Court of Appeal: MEGAW, LAWTON and BROWNE LJJ). *Ross v Collins* [1968] 1 All ER 861, CA applied.

The Rent Act 1968 has been consolidated in the Rent Act 1977.

1754   —— —— —— **unmarried couple**

The defendant had lived with a woman in the flat of which she was the statutory tenant for five years. When the woman died the landlord sought possession of the flat. The defendant claimed that he was a member of the woman's family and therefore entitled to protection under the Rent Act 1977, Sch. 1, para. 3 which provides that on the death of the statutory tenant a member of his family who has been living with him for six months shall become the statutory tenant. *Held*, although the meaning of family was not restricted only to relationships of blood and marriage it could not be extended to include casual and intermittent relationships. In the present case the parties had never pretended to be married as the woman had wished to maintain her independence and the freedom to withdraw from the relationship with the minimum formalities. There was no public recognition of the union and therefore the necessary element of permanence was missing. The defendant was not a member of the woman's family for the purposes of the Act.

HELBY V RAFFERTY [1978] 3 All ER 1016 (Court of Appeal: STAMP, ROSKILL and CUMMING-BRUCE LJJ). *Dyson Holdings Ltd v Fox* [1975] 3 All ER 1030, CA 1975 Halsbury's Abr para. 2771 applied.

For discussion of this case, see Justinian, Financial Times, 8th May 1978.

1755   —— **tenancy under the Rent (Agriculture) Act 1976—registration of rent**

The Rent (Agriculture) (Rent Registration) Regulations 1978, S.I. 1978 No. 494 (in force on 19th June 1978), prescribe the application form for the registration of a fair rent for a statutory tenancy under the Rent (Agriculture) Act 1976, and the particulars to be given in that form.

LAW REFORM

1756 Article

Compensation for Personal Injury: Royal Commission's Report (the Pearson report): 122 Sol Jo 241.

The Royal Commission on Civil Liability and Compensation for Personal Injury, Lord Pearson: [1978] 3 LMCLQ 399.

1757 Compensation for personal injury—Pearson report

The Royal Commission on Civil Liability and Compensation for Personal Injury, under the chairmanship of Lord Pearson, has published a three volume report containing 188 recommendations. The commission has been examining most aspects of compensation for personal injury, with the notable exception of accidental injuries in the home. The report proposes a move away from tort towards the provision of no-fault compensation through the social security system, although the abolition of tort is not contemplated. To finance such a scheme a modest additional sum would have to be raised through taxation. Inter alia, the report proposes an extended and improved industrial injuries scheme based on the existing scheme run by the Department of Health and Social Security; the introduction of a no-fault compensation scheme for road accident victims, to be financed by a levy on petrol and run by the Department of Health and Social Security; the extension of benefits payable to handicapped children to children damaged by vaccine; the introduction of strict liability for antenatal drug damage in children but the retention of the general tortious action for antenatal injury conferred by the Congenital Disabilities (Civil Liability) Act 1976, with restrictions on use of the action within the family; the treatment of all severely handicapped children in the same way, by payment to them of a special benefit (the cost to be borne by the Exchequer); changes in the liability of carriers by air, sea, inland waterway and rail; the creation of a system of strict liability for defective products, based on the Council of Europe Convention and draft EEC directive; the close scrutiny of the schemes for no-fault compensation for victims of medical accidents in New Zealand and Sweden but the retention of actions in negligence for the time being; and a review of the existing criminal injuries compensation scheme.

The cost of most proposals should be borne by those creating the risks, but both by removing double compensation and tortious compensation for minor injury, and reducing administrative costs, the short term cost of the new scheme would be less than it currently costs to compensate personal injuries. In due course the costs would increase under the new scheme by an estimated £41m per annum at January 1977 prices: Times, 17th March 1978.

The report of the royal commission (Command 7054), in three volumes priced at £7·60, £3·60 and £3·60 each, is published by the Stationery Office.

1758 Drinking and driving—implementation of proposals of Blennerhassett Committee

In reply to a Parliamentary Question asking whether the effectiveness of the current law relating to the breathalyser and driving under the influence of drink was to be increased, the Secretary of Transport stated that the Government had accepted the recommendations of the Blennerhassett Committee as a basis for legislation to be introduced during a future session of Parliament.

1759 Gambling—report of Royal Commission

See para. 251.

1760 Interest on debts

The Law Commission have published a report entitled Law of Contract—Report on Interest (Law Com. No. 88: Cmnd. 7229).

The Commission concluded that the existing law does not provide adequate means of redress for the creditor who is kept out of his money. The Commission's recommendations are intended to provide a rate of interest at a realistic rate in respect of unpaid contract debts for the period that they have been withheld as if the right had been provided by contract. The Commission have drafted a bill to carry their recommendations into effect.

1761   Joint home ownership—recommendations of Law Commission

The Law Commission recommends that husbands and wives should normally be equal owners of their house by law. This is necessary, it thinks, to reflect the modern view of marriage as a partnership. Statutory co-ownership would also extend to council tenancies, protected tenancies and all leased houses and flats. Detailed amendments are suggested to the Matrimonial Homes Act 1967, which would give statutory tenants joint ownership of the right of occupation: Family Law—Third Report on Family Property: The Matrimonial Home (Co-ownership and occupation rights) and Household Goods (Law Commission, no. 86).

1762   Law Commission

Since its inception in 1965 the Law Commission has made sixty-five reports with recommendations for law reform, fifty-two of which have been implemented in whole or in part by Parliament: 395 HL Official Report, 18th July 1978, *col. 252.*

1763   Official Secrets Act—proposals

See para. 644.

LEASEHOLD ENFRANCHISEMENT
OR EXTENSION

Halsbury's Laws of England (3rd edn.), Vol. 23, Supp. paras. 1747–1845

1764   Acquisition of freehold—concurrent lease interposed—effect to increase purchase price—validity

In 1962 the landlords leased property to the tenant for a term of 87 years. In 1973 the tenant gave notice of her desire to acquire the freehold under the Leasehold Reform Act 1967. Between the date of the tenant's notice and the date of its service, the landlords interposed between their freehold and the tenant's lease a concurrent lease of the premises to a third party for a term of 300 years from 1970, subject to the pre-existing lease. The 1967 Act, s. 23 (1) provides that any agreement relating to a tenancy is void in so far as it purports to exclude or modify any right to acquire the freehold. The tenant contended that the concurrent lease was "an agreement relating to the tenancy" within s. 23 (1), and that it was void in that it purported to modify the tenant's right to acquire the freehold by providing for a purchase price for the freehold of £4,000 compared with the £300 which but for the execution of the concurrent lease would have been payable. *Held*, the effect of the concurrent lease was not to affect or modify the right to enfranchise itself but only the terms upon which that right might be exercised. Since the concurrent lease did not modify that right it was unnecessary to decide whether it was "an agreement relating to the tenancy". Thus the concurrent lease was valid and the price payable for the freehold was £4,000.

JONES v WENTWORTH SECURITIES LTD (1978) 123 Sol Jo 34 LORD DIPLOCK, LORD SALMON, LORD EDMUND-DAVIES, LORD FRASER OF TULLYBELTON and LORD RUSSELL OF KILLOWEN (judgment delivered 13th December)). Decision of Court of Appeal, sub nom *Jones v Wrotham Park Settled Estates,* [1978] 3 All ER 527, reversed. See further 128 NLJ 1246.

1765   —— house and premises—whether paddock part of premises for purposes of enfranchisement

Under the Leasehold Reform Act 1967, the tenant of premises which included a house, garden and paddock sought to acquire the freehold of the property. The landlord claimed he was entitled to exclude the paddock from the conveyance. It was decided that the paddock formed part of the premises as defined in the 1967 Act, s. 2 (3), being an appurtenance. The landlord appealed. *Held*, an appurtenance was something that would pass with the house. The crux of the problem was whether the paddock was within the curtilage of the house. It was a question of fact in each case and the paddock in the present case could not be regarded as being within the curtilage of the house as it was quite extensive and clearly physically divided from it at all material times. The paddock was therefore not an appurtenance and accordingly the appeal would be allowed.

METHUEN-CAMPBELL V WALTERS [1979] 2 WLR 113 (Court of Appeal: BUCKLEY, ROSKILL and GOFF LJJ).

1766   —— rateable value of premises—installation of central heating—structural alteration or addition

A tenant who held a long lease of a house installed a modern gas-fired central heating system, thereby increasing the rateable value of the house to £1,597. He wished to acquire the freehold of the house under the Leasehold Reform Act 1967, which only applies to houses of a rateable value of no more than £1,500. He therefore applied to the county court under the Housing Act 1974, Sch. 8, for a declaration that the installation of a central heating system was an improvement made by the execution of works amounting to a "structural alteration or addition" to the house and that accordingly the rateable value should be reduced to £1,487. The declaration was refused by the county court judge and the tenant applied for an order of certiorari to quash the decision. *Held*, GEOFFREY LANE LJ dissenting, the relevant provisions had been interpreted differently by different judges when applied to the installation of a central heating system. It was necessary in the interests of certainty that the words should always be given the same interpretation. Thus the installation of full central heating, involving a good deal of alterations to the structure of the house, was "an improvement made by the execution of works amounting to structural alteration or addition".

Another question arose as to the jurisdiction of the court to correct the county court judge. Schedule 8, para. 2 (2), made his decision "final and conclusive". These words precluded an appeal proper but did not preclude the High Court from correcting the errors of a lower tribunal by means of certiorari. Certiorari lay in the case of a county court judge's decision under Sch. 8 when he went outside his jurisdiction or there was an error of law on the face of the record. The application would be granted.

GEOFFREY LANE LJ, dissenting, considered that the court had no power to intervene as the County Courts Act 1959 had abolished certiorari for errors of law on the face of the record and the judge had not exceeded his jurisdiction; he had only come to a wrong conclusion on a question of law.

PEARLMAN V KEEPERS AND GOVERNORS OF HARROW SCHOOL [1978] 3 WLR 736 (Court of Appeal: LORD DENNING MR, GEOFFREY LANE and EVELEIGH LJJ).

1767   —— whether tenant occupying house for required period—discovery of documents

A landlord refused his tenant's claim under the Leasehold Reform Act 1967 to purchase the freehold of the tenanted house, on the ground that it had not been the sole or main residence of the tenant for the five year period immediately preceding the application. In order to acquire the information necessary to the determination of the case the county court made an order for discovery of documents. When the evidence was finally produced it was obviously deficient as it failed to mention a bank account which the landlord knew the tenant had held. The landlord made use of the Banker's Books Evidence Act 1879 and discovered that the tenant had had substantial dealings in property and had lived at another address during the relevant five year period. *Held*, the tenant's failure to comply with the order for discovery had been deliberate and he had no excuse that he did not know what was required from him. Without the relevant information no decision could be reached by the court and therefore this was an unusual case where the claim would be dismissed for want of prosecution.

NWOKEJI V NORTHUMBERLAND COURT (STREATHAM) LTD (1978) 247 EG 733 (Court of Appeal: MEGAW, ORMROD and BRIDGE LJJ).

1768   —— —— sub-lease of part of premises—whether landlord had granted a new tenancy

The tenant of a shop and upstairs flat under a ninety-nine year lease which expired in 1973 wished to acquire the freehold. The shop, which was a separate and self contained unit, had been sub-let under a series of tenancies from 1956 and the landlord contended that on the date of expiry of the head lease the tenant was not entitled to Rent Act protection in respect of the whole premises and therefore could not claim the freehold. She insisted that she had always intended to resume full occupation and had not surrendered her tenancy of the shop. She also alleged that the landlord had granted a new tenancy of the whole premises by accepting rent for two years after 1973. On appeal against a county court's decision in favour of the landlord, *held*, the tenant had never evinced an intention to reoccupy the shop and therefore she had not been tenant of the whole building at the material time. Nor could the landlord have been said to have granted a new tenancy by accepting rent after the expiry of the head lease, since this was plainly not his intention. The appeal would be dismissed.

BARON V PHILLIPS (1978) 247 Estates Gazette 1079 (Court of Appeal: STAMP, ORR and GEOFFREY LANE LJJ).

LEGAL AID AND ADVICE

Halsbury's Laws of England (4th edn.), Vol. 11, paras. 751–779; (3rd edn.), Vol. 30, paras. 901–1036

1769   Articles

Criminal Legal Aid in 1976, Howard Levenson (statistics showing the number of refusals and grants of legal aid for 1976): 128 NLJ 52.

Legal Aid in Care Proceedings, N. E. Hickman (whether parents are entitled to legal aid to resist care proceedings brought in respect of their child): 128 NLJ 877.

Legal Aid in the Criminal Courts, James Morton: 128 NLJ 970.

A Question of Interpretation, R. L. Waters (interpretation of "attributable" in legally aided proceedings): 122 Sol Jo 736.

1770   Annual Reports

The Twenty-seventh Legal Aid Annual Reports [1976-77] (HMSO) contain the Report of the Law Society on the operation and finance of Part 1 of the Legal Aid Act 1974 and the Report of the Lord Chancellor's Advisory Committee on Legal Aid. The latter sets out in Appendix A evidence submitted by the Lord Chancellor's Advisory Committee on legal aid to the Royal Commission on Legal Services.

1771   Clergy—vacation of benefices—legal aid

See para. 998.

1772   Costs—unassisted party—award out of Legal Aid Fund—whether just and equitable

The question arose as to the circumstances under which a successful unassisted party could recover his costs against an unsuccessful assisted party from the Legal Aid Fund which had supported the latter. *Held*, the Legal Aid Act 1974, s. 13 provided that where proceedings between legally aided and non-legally aided parties were decided in favour of the unassisted party, the court could make an order for the whole or part of his costs to be paid to him out of the legal aid fund. Such an order, however, would only be made if the court was satisfied that it was just and equitable in all the circumstances for the costs to be made out of public funds. In the present case, it made no difference that the unassisted party was a member of the Police Authority which also received its money from public funds. When the Legal Aid Fund took up cases of assisted persons, it was often just and equitable that it should pay the costs of the other party if the assisted person lost. Accordingly, the costs of the unassisted successful party would be paid out of the legal aid fund.

MAYNARD V OSMOND [1979] 1 WLR 31 (Court of Appeal: LORD DENNING MR, ORR and BRANDON LJJ). For earlier proceedings, see 1976 Halsbury's Abr para. 1915.

1773   The plaintiff's claim for damages for negligent misrepresentation was dismissed. He obtained legal aid to appeal conditional on leading counsel's opinion. This opinion was not favourable, but the defendant's solicitors had not been notified of the limitation. On the question of whether costs should be awarded to the unassisted party when the appeal was dismissed, *held*, the limitation should have been notified to the defendant's solicitors and therefore it would be just and equitable to award costs against the Legal Aid Fund. However, the order would not be drawn up for ten weeks, in order that the Fund might make representations to the court.

SCARTH V JACOBS-PATON (1978) Times, 2nd November (Court of Appeal: LORD DENNING MR, STEPHENSON and SHAW LJJ). *Maynard v Osmond* [1979] 1 WLR 31, CA, para. 1772, applied.

1774   Criminal proceedings—assessment of resources

The Legal Aid in Criminal Proceedings (Assessment of Resources) Regulations 1978, S.I. 1978 No. 30 (in force on 1st March 1978), make provision for the assessment of the resources of any person concerned when a court is considering whether to make a legal aid order in criminal proceedings under the Legal Aid Act 1974, s. 28, or a contribution order under s. 32. The Legal Aid in Criminal Proceedings (Assessment of Resources) Regulations 1968, as amended, are revoked and reenacted with amendments. Resources of persons other than the applicant, such as a spouse or a person liable to maintain an infant, may in certain circumstances be taken into consideration. Provision is made for the assessment of resources on applications for legal aid and contribution orders; the figures for determining whether a person should be required to make a contribution in respect of his legal aid costs are increased. The Regulations also set out the method of calculation of income and capital; in assessing a person's capital the value of any interest in the main or only dwelling in which he resides is to be disregarded.

1775   European agreement—transmission of applications

See para. 1231.

1776   Legal advice and assistance—allowance for dependants

The Legal Advice and Assistance (Amendment) Regulations 1978, S.I. 1978 No. 1569 (in force on 27th November 1978), further amend the Legal Advice and Assistance Regulations 1960 by increasing the allowance for dependants in the assessment of disposable capital. The allowance for the first dependant is increased from £125 to £200, for the second from £80 to £120 and for every other dependant from £40 to £60.

1777   —— financial conditions

The Legal Advice and Assistance (Financial Conditions) Regulations 1978, S.I. 1978 No. 1567 (in force on 27th November 1978), increase from £23 to £25 a week the disposable income above which a person receiving legal advice and assistance under the Legal Aid Act 1974 is required to pay a contribution. The Regulations also make consequential amendments to the scale of contributions.

1778   The Legal Advice and Assistance (Financial Conditions) (No. 2) Regulations 1978, S.I. 1978 No. 1568 (in force on 27th November 1978) increase the disposable income limit for the availability of legal advice and assistance under the Legal Aid Act 1974 from £48 to £52 a week and increase the disposable capital limit from £340 to £365.

1779   Legal aid—financial conditions

The Legal Aid (Financial Conditions) Regulations 1978, S.I. 1978 No. 1571 (in force on 27th November 1978) increase the financial limits of eligibility for legal aid laid down in the Legal Aid Act 1974. Legal aid is available to those with disposable incomes of not more than £2,600 and available without payment of a contribution to those with disposable incomes of not more than £815. The upper limit of disposable capital, above which legal aid may be refused, is increased to £1,700 and the lower limit of disposable capital is increased to £365.

1780   —— resources—assessment

The Legal Aid (Assessment of Resources) (Amendment) Regulations 1978, S.I. 1978 No. 1570 (in force on 27th November 1978), further amend the Legal Aid (Assessment of Resources) Regulations 1960 by increasing the allowances for dependants in the assessment of disposable capital. The allowance for the first dependant is increased from £125 to £200, for the second from £80 to £120 and for every other dependant from £40 to £60.

1781   Legal aid certificate—grant—resources—assessment—change of circumstances

In giving judgment, PAYNE J affirmed the principle, as outlined in *Moss v Moss* [1956] 1 All ER 291, that for the purposes of a legal aid certificate, a notice of an increase in means, given to the area committee concerned by the assisted person, should be treated as an original application and result in a new period of computation, for the purposes of assessment, being brought into effect.

PATEL v PATEL (1978) Times, 29th November (Family Division: PAYNE J).

1782   Proceedings for which aid available—care proceedings—whether legal aid available to parent

A local authority applied under the Children and Young Persons Act 1969, s. 1 (1) for a boy to be taken into care, and brought the boy before the juvenile court to decide what should be done with him. The boy's mother, who wanted her son to stay at home, asked for legal aid so that she could put her case before the juvenile court. The court held that it had no jurisdiction to grant aid as ss. 64, 65 of the Children Act 1975, entitling parents and guardians to legal aid in care proceedings, were not yet in force. Counsel for the mother contended that she was "brought before a juvenile court under s. 1 of the Children and Young Persons Act 1969" and was therefore eligible for legal aid under the Legal Aid Act 1974, s. 28 (3). *Held* (LORD DENNING MR dissenting), under s. 1 of the 1969 Act the person brought before the juvenile court was the boy, and the court was empowered to grant legal aid to him alone. The court did not have jurisdiction to grant legal aid to the mother as the relevant sections of the Children Act were not in force.

LORD DENNING MR considered that as it was desirable for the mother to receive legal aid and as the necessary legislation was merely awaiting implementation, s. 28 (3) should be liberally interpreted so as to allow the mother legal aid.

R v WELWYN JUSTICES, EX PARTE S (1978) Times, 30th November (Court of Appeal: LORD DENNING MR, BRIDGE and TEMPLEMAN LJJ).

LIBEL AND SLANDER

Halsbury's Laws of England (3rd edn.), Vol. 24, paras. 1–257

1783   Article

Qualified Privilege in a Business Context, R. W. Hodgin (when a defamatory letter dictated to a secretary is privileged): 122 Sol Jo 40.

1784   Criminal libel—committal proceedings—evidence—admissibility

At committal proceedings in a case of criminal libel, the defendants, authors and publishers of the book in which the libel was alleged to be contained, sought to adduce evidence of the general bad reputation of the person instituting the proceedings. The evidence was excluded by the magistrate on the ground that she had no jurisdiction to listen to such evidence at that stage in the proceedings. The defendants applied for orders of certiorari setting aside the committal orders on the ground that the evidence had been wrongly excluded. They contended that in deciding whether or not a case was serious enough to justify criminal proceedings, one must look to the extent to which the reputation of the injured party had been damaged, and thus evidence of similar misbehaviour should be admissible. *Held*, the defendants' contention was incorrect. By analogy with the defence of justification introduced by the Libel Act 1843, s. 6, which could not be raised in committal proceedings, evidence of general bad reputation was not admissible. The magistrate was correct in declining jurisdiction to hear the evidence tendered.

R v WELLS STREET JUSTICES, EX PARTE DEAKIN [1978] 3 All ER 252 (Queen's Bench Division: LORD WIDGERY CJ, BOREHAM and DRAKE JJ).

1785   Damages—application to strike out appeal against award as abuse of process of court

See *Obote v Judith, Countess of Listowel*, para. 2218.

1786   —— award by jury—whether award unreasonably high

Canada

In an action against a newspaper for defamation the plaintiff, a prominent public figure, was awarded $135,000 moral damages by the jury. The defendant newspaper moved to have the award reduced, claiming that it was unreasonably high. *Held*, the reasonableness of the award depended largely upon the value which the community was prepared to place on the reputation of its members, particularly those in public life. Juries, representing a cross-section of society, were especially apt at determining the amount which would fairly compensate a person who had been the subject of an extensive libel and, in the light of all the circumstances of the present case, the court was not prepared to say that the jury's estimate of compensation was so grossly inflated as to be unreasonable. The defendant's motion would be dismissed.

SNYDER v MONTREAL GAZETTE LTD (1978) 87 DLR (3d) 5 (Quebec Superior Court).

1787   Defences—fair comment—comment or statement of fact—radio broadcast

Canada

In a radio broadcast dealing with lead poisoning the broadcaster defamed a medical doctor who appeared as an expert witness at an inquiry into lead poisoning, conveying the meaning that the doctor gave untruthful and misleading evidence in wanton disregard of public health. On a question of whether the broadcaster had established the defence of fair comment, *held*, to be comment, fair or unfair, a statement must be a statement of opinion and not a statement of fact. The broadcaster's remarks stated as fact that the doctor was professionally dishonest; he did not state facts from which it might have been inferred that the doctor was dishonest and then expressed that opinion. The defence would accordingly fail. In assessing damages for defamation the court would take into account the serious damage to the doctor's reputation even though no specific loss could be shown.

BARLTROP v CANADIAN BROADCASTING CORPORATION (1978) 86 DLR (3d) 61 (Supreme Court of Nova Scotia).

1788   Exemplary damages—entitlement to bring action—establishment of prima facie case

See *Maudling v Scott*, para. 830.

LIMITATION OF ACTIONS

Halsbury's Laws of England (3rd edn.), Vol. 24, paras. 326–639

1789   Article

Limitation: House Owners v Local Authorities, Patrick Eyre (the date of accrual of the cause of action): 121 Sol Jo 839.

1790   Hague Rules—expiry of time limits—whether remedy or claim extinguished

See *Consolidated Investments and Contracting Co v Sapoaria Shipping Co Ltd*, para. 146.

1791   Limitation period—collection of corporation tax—power of commissioners to obtain information

See *B. & S. Displays Ltd v Inland Revenue Commissioners*, para. 1588.

1792   —— dividend claims—categorisation

See *Re Compania de Electricidad de la Provincia de Buenos Aires Ltd*, para. 382.

1793   —— extension—action for personal injury on behalf of minor—whether minor entitled to commence fresh action within extended time-limit

See *Tolley v Morris*, para. 2225.

1794   —— fraudulent conversion—joinder of defendants—effect of joinder on defence of limitation—when time begins to run

The testatrix died in 1969. Between 1970 and 1973 her solicitor, who was her executor, fraudulently converted much of her estate to his own use and that of his wife, who had no knowledge of the fraud. When he died in 1973, his wife discovered the fraud and on the advice of her solicitor disclosed it to the true beneficiary, who in 1977 brought proceedings to recover the estate. She sought to have the wife's solicitor added as a defendant to the proceedings on the ground that he was a partner of the testator's solicitor at the time the frauds were committed. The order for joinder was made. The solicitor contended that the effect of this would be to deprive him of a defence under the Limitation Act 1939. *Held*, the question was whether when a defendant was added to an existing action time ceased to run in his favour as from the date of the writ or as from the date of the joinder. The joinder did not have any retrospective effect so that time continued to run in the defendant's favour up to the date of the joinder. In any event, time would not start to run until the fraud was discovered or could with reasonable diligence have been discovered, which was in 1973. The joinder would stand.

GAWTHROP v BOULTON [1978] 3 All ER 615 (Chancery Division: WALTON J). *Seabridge v H. Cox & Sons (Plant Hire) Ltd* [1968] 1 All ER 570, CA, applied.

1795   Personal injury—expiry of limitation period—court's power to override time limits

In the first three appeals, the plaintiffs had each suffered personal injury and had at once instructed solicitors who, however, forgot to serve the writs on the defendants within the time limit. The solicitors each issued a new writ out of time and sought to override the time limits under the Limitation Act 1975. On appeal by the defendants against the allowing of the extension, *held*, the 1975 Act, s. 2D, gave the court a general unfettered discretion to extend the time in all cases where the limitation period had expired before the issue of the writ; it was not limited to exceptional or residual cases. In these cases, the discretion should be exercised in favour of the plaintiffs as their solicitors had omitted to serve the writs by the merest slip and as a matter of simple justice the defendants' insurers should pay the claim. The appeals would be dismissed.

In the other appeal, the plaintiff was injured in a car accident in 1970 and wished to join as defendants the company which he claimed had negligently repaired his tyres. By a clerk's mistake the time limit for joinder was overrun and in 1973 the joinder was set aside by a registrar and confirmed by a judge. When the 1975 Act came into operation, the plaintiff's solicitors issued a fresh writ against the company. On appeal by the company against the allowing of the time limit to be overridden, they contended that although the 1975 Act, s. 3, applied to causes of action which accrued before the Act came into force and to actions pending at its commencement it did not apply once a final order or judgment had been made or given, and the judge's order setting aside the joinder, was such a final order. *Held*, the registrar's order in 1973 was nullity and void ab initio. Therefore in law no action had been commenced against the company and s. 3 with its retrospective effect applied to enable the plaintiff to bring an action against the company provided he could persuade the court to exercise its discretion to override the time limit. This was a proper case for the exercise of the discretion in favour of the plaintiff and the appeal would be dismissed.

FIRMAN v ELLIS; INCE v ROGERS; DOWN v HARVEY; PHEASANT v S. T. H. SMITH (TYRES) LTD [1978] 2 All ER 851 (Court of Appeal: LORD DENNING MR, ORMROD and GEOFFREY LANE LJJ). Decision of Kerr J in *Firman v Ellis* (1977) Times, 8th July, 1977 Halsbury's Abr para. 1735 affirmed.

1796   The plaintiff developed thrombosis in 1969, allegedly caused by taking a drug manufactured by the defendants, but she failed to issue a writ claiming damages for negligence until 1976. She contended that although her action was out of time it would be equitable to allow it to proceed. In March 1976 the plaintiff had obtained counsel's opinion and the defendants served an interrogatory to discover whether the opinion indicated that an action against them would be successful. The plaintiff objected on the ground that such matters were protected by privilege but the defendants claimed she was obliged to answer. *Held*, when deciding whether to exercise its discretion to override time limits under the Limitation Act 1939, s. 2D, as added by the Limitation Act 1975, the court had to consider certain matters, including (i) whether the plaintiff acted promptly and reasonably once she knew she might have a cause of action and (ii) whether the plaintiff took legal advice and the nature of any advice received. In some cases, the fact that legal advice had been obtained and indicated the probable outcome of an action could help the court in deciding whether the plaintiff acted promptly and reasonably: to that extent, the words "nature of any advice" required the court to consider all aspects of the plaintiff's legal advice. Such a construction of s. 2D did not encroach upon the doctrine of privilege nor was it intended to suggest that legal advice should be open to discovery or production of documents. Accordingly the plaintiff would be required to answer the defendants' interrogatory.

JONES v G. D. SEARLE & CO LTD [1978] 3 ALL ER 654 (Court of Appeal: ROSKILL and EVELEIGH LJJ and MICHAEL DAVIES J).

1797   —— —— —— **correct procedure**

A National Coal Board employee who was injured while working underground in 1953 sought to bring a claim for damages in 1976. The Board's application to dismiss the application for want of prosecution was refused. On appeal, *held*, the court had a discretion under the Limitation Act 1939, s. 2D not to apply the three year time limit laid down for personal injury cases, but it would not be equitable to exercise the discretion in this case because the Board's evidence had been lost many years earlier and the employee had been receiving all the relevant industrial benefits. In future it would not be necessary to defer a decision on whether the court should exercise its discretion until the trial of the action. Such questions would be best dealt with on a summons with affidavits on either side so that the court could decide whether the action should proceed.

HATTAM v NATIONAL COAL BOARD (1978) 122 Sol Jo 777 (Court of Appeal: LORD DENNING MR, STEPHENSON and SHAW LJJ).

1798   —— —— —— **previous action dismissed for want of prosecution— effect**

The plaintiff was employed by the defendants from 1966 to 1971, during which time he contracted an industrial disease. In October 1971 he issued a writ against the defendants claiming damages for personal injury. The plaintiff's solicitors told him that he did not have a good claim, and no statement of claim was delivered. In 1972 the plaintiff consulted other solicitors who wrote to the defendants in 1973 asserting their liability. The defendants replied that if the claim was proceeded with, they would apply to dismiss it for want of prosecution. The plaintiff then consulted other solicitors, who in 1976 issued another writ asserting the same cause of action as the 1971 writ; the 1971 action was not discontinued. The defendants applied for the second writ to be struck out and the action dismissed on the ground that it was brought in the same matter as the other pending action and was frivolous and vexatious and an abuse of the process of the court. The order was made but the plaintiff's appeal was allowed and the action restored on the plaintiff's undertaking to discontinue the first action. On appeal by the defendants, *held*, the court would have been entitled to dismiss the first action for want of prosecution due to inordinate and inexcusable delay. However, this fact did not debar the plaintiff from the right conferred on him by the Limitation Act 1939, s. 2D, as added by the Limitation Act 1975, to issue a fresh writ outside the limitation period and to have it determined whether it would be equitable to allow the action to proceed. The criteria for so deciding, set out in s. 2D, were not identical with the criteria for deciding whether to dismiss for want of prosecution. Thus an order to dismiss for want of prosecution, even if properly made, would not be conclusive against the plaintiff in respect of the proper exercise of the court's discretion under s. 2D. However, the conduct of the first action and its effect on the prospect of a fair trial and of prejudice to the defendants would be relevant in deciding if it would be equitable to proceed.

However (WALLER LJ dissenting), as there was insufficient evidence to decide whether it would be equitable to proceed, that question should be decided by another court. The appeal would be dismissed.

WALKLEY v PRECISION FORGINGS LTD [1978] 1 WLR 1228 (Court of Appeal: MEGAW, SHAW and WALLER LJJ). *Birkett v James* [1978] AC 297, HL, 1977 Halsbury's Abr para. 2157 applied.

1799   **When time begins to run—time for appeal from industrial tribunal**

See *Firestone Tyre and Rubber Co Ltd v Challoner*, para. 1075.

LOCAL GOVERNMENT

Halsbury's Laws of England (3rd edn.), Vol. 24, paras. 704–1208

1800   Article

Parish Reviews in England: Grass Roots Government, Jonathan Teasdale (position of local councils in local government structure): 128 NLJ 1175.

1801   Boundary commission—revision of electoral arrangements—criteria for revision—equality between voters

A Local Government Boundary Commission recommended in the interests of effective and convenient local government that a borough should have thirty-three electoral wards. The commission acknowledged that this would not result in each elector's vote having the same weight, as required ideally by the Local Government Act 1972, Sch. 11, para. 3 (2) (a), owing to varying ratios of electors to elected members throughout the borough. The borough council contended it should contain two more wards so that the principle was satisfied. *Held*, the principle was not an overriding requirement: the main requirements on local commissions were to comply with the provisions of para. 3 (2) where it was reasonably practicable and to act in the interests of effective and convenient local government. All other considerations were secondary. The commission had settled upon the number of wards for the borough in accordance with the Act and therefore its recommendations would stand.

ENFIELD LONDON BOROUGH COUNCIL V LOCAL GOVERNMENT BOUNDARY COMMISSION FOR ENGLAND AND WALES (1978) Times, 28th July (Court of Appeal: LORD DENNING MR, EVELEIGH LJ and SIR DAVID CAIRNS). Decision of Bristow J, (1978) Times, 28th January reversed.

1802   Byelaw—validity—reasonableness—ban on dogs in parks

In exercise of powers conferred on it by a local Act, a borough council made a byelaw prohibiting a person from causing any dog belonging to him or in his charge from entering or remaining in any scheduled pleasure-ground, other than a guide dog. The byelaw was confirmed by the Home Secretary. Numbers of dog-owners signed a petition objecting to the ban and as a protest walked through a park with their dogs in contravention of the byelaw and in breach of an interlocutory injunction obtained by the council. The council applied for perpetual injunctions against the dog-owners to prevent further breaches. The dog-owners contended that the byelaw was void on the ground of unreasonableness. *Held*, it was established that dogs had been causing a nuisance in the parks. A byelaw was not unreasonable merely because a judge might think it went further than necessary, as elected representatives might be trusted to understand electors' requirements better than judges. The byelaw was not per se unreasonable, nor was it so manifestly unjust or oppressive that no reasonable council could have made it. It was valid and the council was entitled to the relief sought.

BURNLEY BOROUGH COUNCIL V ENGLAND (1978) Times, 15th July (Chancery Division: HUGH FRANCIS QC sitting as a deputy High Court judge).

1803   Employee—loss of office—whether loss attributable to local government reorganisation

The applicant was employed by an urban district council as an airport manager. When the council was replaced by a new district council created by the Local Government Act 1972 that council confirmed his employment. Several months after reorganisation the new council decided that they could no longer run the airport efficiently. The applicant refused alternative employment and applied under the Local Government (Compensation) Regulations 1974 for compensation for loss of employment attributable to the provisions of the 1972 Act. *Held*, compensation was payable only if the applicant could show that the 1972 Act contributed to the circumstances under which he lost his job. However, the new council made its decision not to run the airport due to economic and administrative reasons which would have existed even if the original council had not been replaced. The applicant's loss of employment was due to reasons unconnected with the Act and therefore he was not entitled to compensation.

MALLETT v RESTORMEL BOROUGH COUNCIL [1978] 2 All ER 1057 (Court of Appeal: LORD DIPLOCK, LORD RUSSELL OF KILLOWEN and LORD SCARMAN). Decision of Griffiths J [1978] 1 All ER 503 reversed.

1804   Following the local government reorganisation of 1972, a town clerk became chief executive of a new district council. He was made redundant from his new post in 1976 when the administrative structure of the council was changed in the light of economic restrictions. He claimed compensation for loss of office on the ground that his redundancy was attributable to the provisions of the Local Government Act 1972. *Held,* "attributable to" in the 1972 Act implied a connection. Although there was a clear connection between the Act and his appointment as chief executive, there was none between the former and his loss of employment. The cause of his redundancy was a change in council policy and that alone. Accordingly, he was not entitled to compensation.

WALSH v ROTHER DISTRICT COUNCIL [1978] 3 All ER 881 (Court of Appeal: MEGAW, ORMROD and BRIDGE LJJ). Decision of Donaldson J [1978] 1 All ER 510, 1977 Halsbury's Abr para. 1746 affirmed.

1805   **Inner Urban Areas Act 1978**

See para. 2833.

1806   **Isles of Scilly—constitution of Council**

The Isles of Scilly Order 1978, S.I. 1978 No. 1844 (in force on 1st February 1979), contains a provision for the constitution of the Council of the Isles of Scilly and regulates the application of the Local Government Act 1972, s. 265 (1) to the Isles. The Order also under s. 265 (3) of the 1972 Act provides for payments to the Cornwall County Council in respect of certain expenses of the Council.

1807   **Local authorities—armorial bearings**

The Local Authorities (Armorial Bearings) Order 1978, S.I. 1978 No. 1025 (in force on 21st August 1978), confers on specified local authorities the right to bear and use the armorial bearings formerly borne and used by their predecessors, now defunct by virtue of the Local Government Act 1972.

1808   —— **duties under Housing (Homeless Persons) Act 1977—time at which duties arise**

See *R v Beverley Borough Council, ex parte McPhee*, para. 1486.

1809   —— **duty to facilitate discharge of functions—whether existence of closed shop agreements for employees incompatible with duty**

Local authorities have the same powers as any other employer to negotiate closed shop agreements compelling employees to belong to trade unions.

A Greater London ratepayer objected to the existence of a closed shop for staff of the Greater London Council on the ground that such a policy was not calculated to facilitate the discharge of the council's functions within the meaning of the Local Government Act 1972, s. 111, in that services could be lost to ratepayers, residents and visitors if the council's employees were called upon by their unions to strike. He further contended that compulsory membership was contrary to the European Convention on Human Rights, art. 9, which guarantees freedom of thought and conscience. *Held,* (i) the type of closed shop agreement the council operated, whereby employees had to join a union upon taking up employment or be dismissed, was a perfectly respectable one, sanctioned by Parliament in the Trade Union and Labour Relations Act 1974, Sch. 1, para. 6 (5). It was not apparent whether the agreement's existence made it harder or simpler for the council to discharge its functions.

(ii) The European Convention had not been incorporated in United Kingdom Law. If there was any conflict, the 1974 Act had to prevail.

R v GREATER LONDON COUNCIL, EX PARTE BURGESS [1978] ICR 991 (Queen's Bench Division: LORD WIDGERY CJ, BOREHAM and DRAKE JJ).

1810   —— miscellaneous provisions

The Local Authorities etc. (Miscellaneous Provision) Order 1978, S.I. 1978 No. 440 (in force on 8th May 1978), makes various provisions under the Local Government Acts 1963 and 1972 relating to the name of London borough Corporations where aldermen have ceased to exist, the amendment of the New Forest Acts 1877 and 1949 and the transfer of certain property between specified authorities. The Greater London Council (General Powers) Act 1967, s. 14 is repealed.

1811   —— powers—injunction to restrain breach of tree preservation order

A local authority obtained an interim injunction restraining a farmer from felling, uprooting or damaging trees on his land, which was subject to a tree preservation order. The Court of Appeal quashed a committal order which had been made against the farmer for alleged breaches of the injunction on the ground that there was insufficient evidence against him. When the authority made a second attempt to commit him he sought to have the interim injunction set aside on the ground that the local authority had no locus standi to bring the action. He claimed that the proceedings should have been brought by the Attorney General by way of a relator action, but that such an action would have failed because he could only obtain an injunction in cases concerning criminal acts for which the penalties were inadequate. *Held*, in addition to the fact that the court felt itself compelled to accept that the authority had locus standi because the Court of Appeal had done so, the authority was given the power to institute civil proceedings in its own name by the Local Government Act 1972, s. 222. Nor was the authority's power to obtain injunctions limited to those cases where the Attorney General could have done so because it was not merely concerned with prevention of criminal acts but also with protecting the interests of inhabitants of its area in civil actions.

KENT COUNTY COUNCIL v BATCHELOR [1978] 3 All ER 980 (Queen's Bench Division: TALBOT J).

For proceedings relating to a previous breach of the same injunction see *Kent County Council v Batchelor* (1976) 33 P & CR 185, CA, 1976 Halsbury's Abr para. 445.

1812   Local commissioner—investigation of local government malad-ministration—discretion

A member of the public asked a local councillor to forward four complaints of maladministration to the local commissioner for administration. The complaints related to maladministration by social workers in taking the complainant's children into care. The councillor declined and so the complainant sent the complaints direct to the local commissioner under the Local Government Act 1974, s. 26. After informing the council, the commissioner decided to investigate the complaints. The council applied for a writ of prohibition to stop him from investigating the complaints on the ground that the proposed investigation was contrary to the 1974 Act, s. 26 (2) (c), because the complainant had a remedy by way of proceedings in the local juvenile court and on appeal and had exercised these remedies. The court refused to grant the declarations sought in respect of three of the complaints but decided that the commissioners could not investigate the complaint in relation to the separation of the complainant's children into different foster homes. On appeal by the council and cross-appeal by the commissioner against the granting of the prohibition in relation to one complaint, *held*, SIR DAVID CAIRNS dissenting on the cross-appeal, a local commissioner had a discretion to override a local councillor and to act on his own under the 1974 Act, s. 26. If he decided to investigate a complaint, the courts should not interfere with his decision save on one of the accepted grounds for interference. There was no question of any conflict between the proposed investigation and the jurisdiction of the courts. There had been a sufficient claim of maladministration to justify investigation of all the complaints. It was not necessary for a complainant to specify what the injustice suffered was. The separation of the children was an administrative act and it was open to the claimant to allege that it was improper and to the commissioner to investigate the allegation. The appeal would be dismissed and the cross-appeal allowed.

R v LOCAL COMMISSIONER FOR ADMINISTRATION FOR THE NORTH AND NORTH-EAST AREA OF ENGLAND, EX PARTE BRADFORD CITY METROPOLITAN COUNCIL [1979] 2 WLR 1 (Court of Appeal: LORD DENNING MR, EVELEIGH LJ and SIR DAVID CAIRNS). Decision of May J (1978) Times, 6th July affirmed in part and reversed in part.

1813 Local Government Act 1974—commencement

The Local Government Act 1974 (Commencement No. 3) Order 1978, S.I. 1978 No. 1583, brought the remaining provisions of the 1974 Act into force on 1st April 1979, those being entries in Sch. 8 relating to the National Parks and Access to the Countryside Act 1949, s. 97, Rating Act 1966, ss. 9, 12 (a), Local Government Act 1966, s. 8, and the Countryside Act 1968, ss. 33–36.

1814 Local Government Act 1978

The Local Government Act 1978 amends s. 31 of the Local Government Act 1974 in consequence of a recommendation made by the Commission for Local Administration. The Act received the royal assent on 20th July 1978 and came into force on that date.

Section 1 enables local authorities to make payments to or provide benefits for persons who have suffered injustice as a result of maladministration. Such expenditure is not relevant expenditure for the purposes of the Rate Support Grant. Section 2 deals with citation and extent.

The Act makes similar provision in relation to Scotland.

1815 Officers—allowances

The Local Government (Allowances) (Amendment) Regulations 1978, S.I. 1978 No. 1795 (in force on 29th December 1978), increases the maximum rate of attendance allowance payable for the performance of approved duties to any member of a body to which the Local Government Act 1972 applies. The Local Government (Allowances) (Amendment) (No. 2) Regulations 1977, 1977 Halsbury's Abr para. 1761, reg. 3 (a) is revoked.

1816

The Local Government (Allowances) (Amendment) (No. 2) Regulations 1978, S.I. 1978 No. 1917 (in force on 23rd January 1979) increase the maximum rates of financial loss allowance payable to any member of a body to which the Local Government Act 1972, s. 173 applies, and who is not entitled to attendance allowances for the performance of approved duties.

1817 Pensions

See paras. 2094, 2096.

1818 Rate support grants

The Rate Support Grant Order 1978, S.I. 1978 No. 1867 (in force on 16th December 1978), fixes and prescribes for the year 1979–80 the aggregate amount of the rate support grants payable to local authorities under the Local Government Act 1974,

Part I; the division of the amount between the needs element, the resources element and the domestic element; the amount of supplementary grants to county councils for transport purposes and towards expenditure on National Parks; and the amount by which rates on dwelling-houses are to be reduced in each rating area to take account of the domestic element.

1819　　The Rate Support Grant Regulations 1978, S.I. 1978 No. 1701 (in force on 1st April 1979), provide for carrying into effect the statutory provisions concerning the payment of rate support grants to local authorities for the year 1979–80.

1820　　—— **increase**

The Rate Support Grant (Increase) Order 1978, S.I. 1978 No. 1868 (in force on 16th December 1978), further increases the aggregate amount of supplementary grant for transport purposes for the financial year 1977–78.

1821　　The Rate Support Grant (Increase) (No. 2) Order 1978, S.I. 1978 No. 1869 (in force on 16th December 1978), increases the rate support grants for the financial year 1978–79. It increases the aggregate amount of the rate support grants, increases the aggregate amount of the needs element of rate support grants, specifies the actual aggregate amount of the resources element, and increases the aggregate amount of supplementary grants for transport purposes and National Parks.

1822　　—— **specified bodies**

The Rate Support Grant (Specified Bodies) Regulations 1978, S.I. 1978 No. 171 (in force on 1st April 1978), specify certain bodies in relation to whose services, provided for local authorities, the Secretary of State has power under the Local Government Act 1974, s. 2 (7), to defray expenditure.

1823　　**Reorganisation of local government**

The Local Government Area Changes (Amendment Regulations 1978, S.I. 1978 No. 247 (in force on 30th March 1978), contain incidental, consequential, transitional and supplementary provisions further to those made by the Local Government Area Changes Regulations 1976, 1976 Halsbury's Abr para. 1644. Some of the 1976 provisions have been amended.

LONDON GOVERNMENT

Halsbury's Laws of England (3rd edn.), Vol. 25, paras. 1–182

1824　　**Town and country planning—local planning authorities in Greater London—regulations**

See para. 2788.

MAGISTRATES

Halsbury's Laws of England (3rd edn.), Vol. 25, paras. 183–680

1825　　**Article**

Preparing a Case for the Magistrates' Court, James Morton: 128 NLJ 752.

1826 Appeal to Court of Appeal—restriction on hearing of criminal cause or matter—whether issue of distress for rates a criminal cause or matter

See *Camden London Borough Council v Herwald*, para. 2284.

1827 Committal for trial—application for mandamus—refusal to interfere

The applicant sought an order of mandamus directing a stipendiary magistrate to admit evidence during committal proceedings in which the applicant and two other defendants were charged with conspiracy to defraud their creditors. *Held*, there was a long established tradition that the Divisional Court would not interfere with committal proceedings which had not been concluded. The authority for this was *R v Carden* (1879) 5 QBD 1. The application would be refused.

R v WELLS STREET STIPENDIARY MAGISTRATE, EX PARTE SEILLON [1978] 3 All ER 257 (Queen's Bench Division: LORD WIDGERY CJ, WIEN and KENNETH JONES JJ).

1828 —— evidence—admissibility—criminal libel

See *R v Wells Street Justices, ex parte Deakin*, para. 1784.

1829 —— joinder without consent of defendants—power of magistrate to insist on concurrent committal proceedings

A man and a woman who were living together at the material time were respectively charged with the murder and wilful ill-treatment of the man's child. The magistrate intended to proceed with committal proceedings against both defendants although separate informations were laid against each of them and they did not wish to be joined. The woman applied for an order prohibiting the magistrate from hearing the committal proceedings. *Held*, refusing the application, the principle of joinder was a matter of practice and there was an established practice that where two offenders could be properly tried jointly on indictment, then they could be properly committed jointly without their consent.

R v CAMBERWELL GREEN JUSTICES, EX PARTE CHRISTIE [1978] 2 All ER 377 (Queen's Bench Division: LORD WIDGERY CJ, O'CONNOR and LLOYD JJ).

1830 —— validity—committal of defendant represented by solicitor without practising certificate

See *R v Scott*, para. 2746.

1831 Compensation orders—research study

A Home Office research study (No. 43: HMSO) entitled Compensation Orders in Magistrates' Courts is based on some of the results of the Home Office Research Unit's study of monetary penalties. The study relates to a national sample of defendants convicted by magistrates' courts of selected indictable offences. The report examines the evolution of the power of criminal courts to order offenders to pay compensation, the use of this power by magistrates' courts and the payment by offenders of compensation.

1832 Finger-printing—power to order

See *George v Coombe*, para. 716; *R v Jones*, para. 579.

1833 Information—information charging continuing offence—whether bad for duplicity

In 1975, the district council preferred an information against the appellant that he had since 1972 used certain land in contravention of an enforcement notice dated November 1971 made by the local planning authority. The appellant appealed against conviction contending that the information alleging his infringement of the enforcement notice was bad for duplicity. *Held*, the offence alleged was a continuing one, which implied that a new offence was created every day during the period of default. This meant that there were a large number of offences charged in one information, causing a breach of the principle that an information was bad for duplicity if it alleged more than one offence. The appeal would be allowed.

PARRY v FOREST OF DEAN DISTRICT COUNCIL (1976) 34 P & CR 209 (Queen's Bench Division: LORD WIDGERY CJ, FORBES and SLYNN JJ). *Ex parte Burnby* [1901] 2 KB 458, DC not followed.

1834   Information—information containing misdescription—validity

Two informations were laid before justices in relation to the defendant's alleged contravention of two enforcement notices issued under the Town and Country Planning Act 1971. The charge on the first information was one of storing motor vehicles on a site in contravention of a notice prohibiting the sale and display of vehicles on it. The other information related to a notice prohibiting the use of a site for storing motor vehicles, but since the issue of the notice the site had been used for the sale and display. The defendant appealed against the justices' decision that the misdescriptions did not render the informations ineffective. *Held*, the informations had been defective because the first did not relate to the enforcement notice and the other did not show any offence. The appeal would be allowed.

DRAKES v COLLEY [1978] Crim LR 493 (Queen's Bench Division: LORD WIDGERY CJ, BOREHAM and DRAKE JJ).

1835   Justices—control by High Court—prerogative orders—justices' affidavit

See *R v Daejan Properties Ltd, ex parte Merton London Borough Council*, para. 769.

1836   —— size and chairmanship of bench

The Justices of the Peace (Size and Chairmanship of Bench) (Amendment) Rules 1978, S.I. 1978 No. 1163 (in force on 1st October 1978), amend the Justices of the Peace (Size and Chairmanship of Bench) Rules 1964, r. 4. They provide an alternative ballot for the election of a chairman or of deputy chairman and exclude justices from voting at such elections within twelve months of their appointment.

1837   Justices' clerks—compensation for loss of office

The Justices of the Peace Act 1949 (Compensation) Regulations 1978, S.I. 1978 No. 1682 (in force on 20th December 1978), provide for the payment of compensation to or in respect of justices' clerks and their assistants who suffer loss of office or a diminution in their emoluments as a result of certain administrative changes made under the Justices of the Peace Act 1949. The regulations supersede the Justices of the Peace Act 1949 (Compensation) Regulations 1965, but provide that in assessing compensation account must be taken of any compensation paid under the earlier regulations, subject to the proviso that a claimant must not be placed in a worse position than he was in under the 1965 regulations.

1838   —— rules—amendment

The Justices' Clerks (Amendment) Rules 1978, S.I. 1978 No. 754 (in force on 17th July 1978), amend the Schedule to the Justices' Clerks Rules 1970 so as to provide that a justices' clerk may do the things which a single justice of the peace may do under the Criminal Justice Act 1967, s. 24 (4A), (accepting service of statutory declarations out of time in connection with process for minor offences), and under s. 44A (3) of that Act, (fixing a later day in substitution for a day previously fixed for the appearance of an offender in connection with a means inquiry). These subsections were inserted in the 1967 Act by the Criminal Law Act 1977, Sch. 12, and come into force on the same day as these rules, see para. 693.

1839 Juvenile courts—citing of police cautions

See para. 761.

1840 Licences—fees

See para. 1676.

1841 Magistrates' courts—children and young persons—procedure

See para. 1941.

1842 —— forms

The Magistrates' Courts (Forms) (Amendment) (No. 2) Rules 1978, S.I. 1978 No. 757 (in force on 17th July 1978), amend the Magistrates' Courts (Forms) Rules 1968 in consequence of the coming into force of certain provisions of the Criminal Law Act 1977. New forms are prescribed for use in connection with ss. 26, 41, 42 and 45.

1843 —— —— bail

The Magistrates' Courts (Forms) (Amendment) Rules 1978, S.I. 1978 No. 146 (in force on 17th April 1978), amend the Magistrates' Courts (Forms) Rules 1968 in consequence of the coming into force of the Bail Act 1976. Some existing forms are replaced and some new forms are prescribed for use in connection with bail. These include forms to be used in making records of bail decisions.

1844 The Magistrates' Courts (Amendment) Rules 1978 No. 147 (in force on 17th April 1978), amend the magistrates' Courts Rules 1968 in consequence of the coming into force of the Bail Act 1976. In particular the rules provide that bail decisions are to be recorded by being entered in the court register.

1845 —— rules

The Magistrates' Courts (Amendment) (No. 2) Rules 1978, S.I. 1978 No. 758 (in force on 17th July 1978), amend the Magistrates' Courts Rules 1968 in consequence of the coming into force of certain provisions of the Criminal Law Act 1977. The principal of these are ss. 45 and 41 which deal with remittal of an offender to another magistrates' court for sentence and the transfer of remand hearings.

Other amendments, unconnected with the Criminal Law Act, are also made to the 1968 Rules.

1846 Maintenance order—appeal to Family Division—procedure

See *Practice Direction*, para. 1511.

1847 Petty sessional divisions—Buckinghamshire

The Petty Sessional Divisions (Buckinghamshire) Order 1978, S.I. 1978 No. 1365 (in force 1st December 1978 except for Schedule, para. 2 which came into force on 16th September 1978), gives effect to a draft order submitted by the magistrates' courts committee for the County of Buckinghamshire and provides for the petty sessional divisions of Fenny Stratford, Newport Pagnell and Stony Stratford to be combined to form a new petty sessional division of Milton Keynes.

1848 —— Cambridgeshire

The Petty Sessional Divisions (Cambridgeshire) Order 1978, S.I. 1978 No. 1124 (in force on 1st September 1978, except for Schedule, para. 2, which came into force on 1st August 1978), gives effect to a draft order submitted by the magistrates' courts committee for the county of Cambridgeshire and provides for the abolition of the petty sessional divisions of Huntingdon and Norman Cross, Hurstingstone, Ramsey,

Soke of Peterborough and Whittlesey and the formation from those areas of two new petty sessional divisions to be known as the Huntingdon and the Peterborough divisions.

1849   —— Cheshire

The Petty Sessional Divisions (Cheshire) Order 1978, S.I. 1978 No. 1952 (in force on 1st February 1979), provides for the renaming of the petty sessional division of Ellesmere Port as Ellesmere Port and Neston.

1850   —— Derbyshire

The Petty Sessional Divisions (Derbyshire) Order 1978, S.I. 1978 No. 671 (in force on 1st July 1978 expect for Schedule 3, para. 2 which came into force on 4th May 1978), gives effect to a draft order submitted by the magistrates' courts committee for the county of Derbyshire and provides for the reorganisation of petty sessional divisions in respect of the areas comprised in the existing divisions of Alfreton, Ashbourne, Bakewell, Belper, Derby, Derby County and Appletree, Matlock and South Derbyshire.

1851   —— Gwynedd

The Petty Sessional Divisions (Gwynedd) Order 1978, S.I. 1978 No. 777 (in force on 1st July 1978 except Schedule, para. 2 which came into force on 29th May 1978), gives effect to a draft order submitted by the magistrates' courts committee for Gwynedd and provides for the petty sessional divisions of Caernarvon and Gwyrfai to be combined to form a new division of Caernarvon and Gwyrfai.

1852   —— Nottinghamshire

The Petty Sessional Divisions (Nottinghamshire) Order 1978, S.I. 1978 No. 644 (in force on 1st June 1978 except for Schedule, para. 2 which came into force on 27th April 1978), gives effect to a draft order submitted by the magistrates' courts committee for the county of Nottinghamshire. It provides for the combination of the divisions of Mansfield (Borough) and Mansfield (County) to form the new division of Mansfield and the combination of the divisions of Newark and Southwell to form the new division of Newark and Southwell. It also provides for the transfer of three parishes from the Nottingham (County) division to the new division of Mansfield.

1853   Powers—power to order taking of fingerprints

See *R v Jones*, para. 579; *George v Coombe*, para. 716.

1854   —— power under Road Traffic Acts to prefer lesser charge— limitation period

See *R v Coventry Justices, ex parte Sayers*, para. 2322.

1855   Probation and after-care areas

See PRISONS.

1856   Trial—procedure—plea—discretion to permit change of plea

A haulage company was charged with permitting drivers to work excessive hours, contrary to the Transport Act 1968, s. 96. The company, pleaded guilty, being mistakenly advised by its legal representative that an offence under s. 96 was absolute. The company appealed against conviction to the Crown Court, contending that the fact that there had been a mistake of law by the company's solicitor made the plea equivocal and when this became apparent, the justices were under a duty to treat the plea as one of not guilty. The Crown Court refused to remit the case to the justices, and the company appealed. *Held*, a clear distinction had to be drawn between the duties of a court faced with an equivocal plea at the time it was made and the exercise of the court's jurisdiction to permit a defendant to change an unequivocal plea of guilty at a later stage. The court had no discretion to accept an equivocal plea of guilty; that is, one which had added to it a qualification which, if true, might show that the defendant was not guilty. In such a case, the court had to obtain an unequivocal plea of guilty or enter a plea of not guilty. However, once an unequivocal plea was made, the court had power to permit the plea to be changed. This discretionary power should be exercised only in clear cases and very sparingly.

In this case, there was no doubt that there was an unequivocal plea of guilty. During the proceedings, when it became clear that the company claimed to be unaware that the offences were being committed, the justices should have considered exercising their discretion, and it was no bar to this that the company was legally represented. However, it could not be said that by not inviting a change of plea the justices had exercised their discretion wrongly. They were entitled to come to the conclusion that the company must have known that excessive hours were being worked, and the appeal would be dismissed.

P. FOSTER (HAULAGE) LTD v ROBERTS [1978] 2 All ER 751 (Queen's Bench Division: LORD WIDGERY CJ, O'CONNOR and LLOYD JJ). *S v Manchester City Recorder* [1971] AC 481, HL applied.

MARKETS AND FAIRS

Halsbury's Laws of England (3rd edn.), Vol. 25, paras. 737–870

1857 Market created by statute—application for injunction restraining competition—balance of convenience

Under a statutory power, a town held a market on Wednesdays, Fridays and Saturdays. The defendants, who were landlords of a shopping centre three and a half miles from the market, sought to establish booths on one floor of the centre from which traders would be given licences to trade on Thursdays, Fridays and Saturdays. The town council sought an interlocutory injunction to restrain the defendants from holding a rival market in the shopping centre. *Held*, a person was entitled to prevent the levying of a rival market within six and two-thirds miles of his own market. The question was whether the defendants' activities would constitute carrying on a market, the essential feature of which was causing a congregation or concourse of buyers and sellers. On the evidence, the proposed activities would constitute a market. Any flagrant invasion of a market holder's rights was bound to cause damage, and in the present case such damage existed. As to the balance of convenience, the defendants had known that their activities would be objected to but had nevertheless carried on with the project. The injunction would be granted.

NORTHAMPTON BOROUGH COUNCIL v MIDLAND DEVELOPMENT GROUP OF COMPANIES LTD (1978) 76 LGR 750 (Chancery Division: WALTON J). *Morpeth Corporation v Northumberland Farmers' Auction Mart Co Ltd* [1921] 2 Ch 154 applied.

MEDICINE, PHARMACY, DRUGS AND MEDICINAL PRODUCTS

Halsbury's Laws of England (3rd edn.), Vol. 26, paras. 1–667

1858 Ancillary dental workers

The Ancillary Dental Workers (Amendment) Regulations 1978, S.I. 1978 No. 1128 (in force on 1st December 1978), amend the Ancillary Dental Workers Regulations 1968, S.I. 1968 No. 357 as amended by S.I. 1974 No. 544, 1974 Halsbury's Abr para. 2118, by increasing the enrolment fee to £4 and the fee for retention of a name in the roll to £3.

1859 Dangerous substances—packaging and labelling

See para. 1454.

1860 Committee on Radiation from Radioactive Medicinal Products

The Medicines (Committee on Radiation from Radioactive Medicinal Products) Order 1978, S.I. 1978 No. 1005 (in force on 1st January 1979), establishes the Committee on Radiation from Radioactive Medicinal Products to give advice with respect to the safety, quality and efficacy in relation to radiation of any substance or article for human use to which any provision of the Medicines Act 1968 is applicable.

1861 Dangerous drugs—offences

See CRIMINAL LAW.

1862 General Medical Council—composition

See Medical Act 1978, para. 1864.

1863 ——— disciplinary committee—rules of procedure

The General Medical Council has agreed to proposals to change the rules of procedure for its disciplinary committee. Any party or witness at disciplinary proceedings may apply for the press and public to be excluded. The committee may, of its own accord, exclude the press and public if it thinks it would be in the interests of justice to do so: Times, 26th May 1978.

1864 Medical Act 1978

The Medical Act 1978 provides for the composition of the General Medical Council, establishes new committees and contains provisions relating to professional conduct, medical education and registration of practitioners. The Act received the royal assent on 5th May 1978, and ss. 4, 17 and 32 came into force on that date. Sections 1 (part), 2, 30, 31 (part), Schs. 6 (part), 7 (part), 3 (part) came into force on 23rd August 1978; s. 29 on 1st December 1978, and ss. 22–28, 31 (part), Sch. 6 (part) on 15th February 1979: S.I. 1978 No. 1035.

Sections 1 and 2 provide for the composition of the General Medical Council. Schedule 1 deals with the internal procedure of the General Council. England and Wales each have a separate branch council and the branch council for Ireland is replaced by one for Northern Ireland: s. 3. Section 4 provides for the termination of the office of members elected or appointed for Ireland. Transitional provisions for Ireland are contained in Sch. 2.

Section 5 empowers the General Council to advise the medical profession on standards of professional conduct and medical ethics. The Disciplinary Committee and the Penal Cases Committee are replaced by the Professional Conduct Committee, the Health Committee and the Preliminary Proceedings Committee, except for transitional purposes: s. 6 and Sch. 3. The Professional Conduct Committee is empowered to make a practitioner's registration conditional as an alternative to suspension or striking-off: s. 7. The Committee may restore a name to the register: s. 12. The Health Committee may suspend registration or make it conditional if a practitioner is physically or mentally unfit to practise: s. 8. Either Committee may order immediate suspension if appropriate: s. 9. Cases are referred to each Committee by the Preliminary Proceedings Committee: s. 13. The General Council is empowered to remove a name from the register if entered fraudulently or incorrectly: s. 10. Section 11 deals with the right of appeal. Supplementary provisions relating to professional conduct and fitness to practise are contained in s. 14 and Sch. 4.

Section 15 establishes an Education Committee to promote high standards of medical education and to co-ordinate all its stages. The provisions regarding the experience required for full registration are amended: s. 16.

Sections 17–29 and Sch. 5 contain provisions dealing with the registration of overseas qualified practitioners. Section 17 replaces the Medical Act 1956, Part III. Section 18 provides that certain persons holding recognised overseas qualifications may be fully registered as medical practitioners if they satisfy prescribed requirements. A fully registered person is entitled to have any further recognised overseas qualification he obtains registered: s. 19. Section 20 specifies the experience required for full registration under s. 18. Certain persons may be provisionally registered so as to enable them to obtain the experience necessary for full registration: s. 21. Section 22 provides for the limited registration for not more than five years of certain persons having an acceptable overseas qualification. Details of persons with limited registration are kept in a register and any name may be removed in certain circumstances: ss. 23, 24. Provision for the full registration of persons with limited registration is made in s. 25. Visiting overseas practioners may be fully registered for not more than a year: s. 26. Section 27 provides for the constitution of the Review Board for Overseas Qualified Practioners, the functions of which are specified in s. 28. Section 29 provides that knowledge of English is a condition for registration under the Medical Act 1956, ss. 18, 23.

Supplementary provisions, minor and consequential amendments and repeals are contained in ss. 30–32 and Sch. 6 and 7.

1865 —— departmental circular

The Department of Health and Social Security have issued a circular (No. 78/147) explaining the benefits doctors will gain from the passing of the Medical Act 1978. The circular briefly examines the issues of the reconstitution of the General Medical Council, professional conduct and fitness to practise, medical education and the registration of non-EEC doctors. It also explains that implementation of the provisions relating to all except registration of non-EEC doctors will be dependent on the reconstitution of the General Medical Council, which is expected to take some two years owing to the degree of consultation required.

1866 Medical practitioners—disciplinary committee—procedure

The General Medical Council Disciplinary Committee (Procedure) (Amendment) Rules Order of Council 1978, S.I. 1978 No. 1796 (in force on 1st January 1979), approves rules amending the General Medical Council Disciplinary Committee (Procedure) Rules 1970. They make new provision for the hearing of disciplinary proceedings in private and increase the number of elected members of the Penal Cases Committee of the Council.

1867 —— Newfoundland, Canada

The Medical Practitioners (Newfoundland, Canada) (Revocation) Order 1978, S.I. 1978 No. 283 (made on 1st March 1978), terminates arrangements under the Medical Act 1956, Part III whereby medical practitioners holding recognised qualifications in Newfoundland are eligible for full or provisional registration in the United Kingdom. This does not prejudice the rights of persons already registered. The Order in Council of 19th December 1913 is revoked.

1868 —— registration—General Medical Council

The General Medical Council (Registration (Fees) Regulations) Order of Council 1978, S.I. 1978 No. 1772 (in force on 6th December 1978), prescribe the fees payable to the General Medical Council in respect of the making of entries in the register of medical practitioners, with effect from 15th February 1979, and increase the annual retention fee from £8 to £10 with effect from 1st May 1979.

1869   Medicines—advertising directed to practitioners

The Medicines (Advertising to Medical and Dental Practitioners) Regulations 1978, S.I. 1978 No. 1020 (in force on 1st December 1978), provide that advertisements directed to practitioners for medicinal products administered to human beings must include the name and address of the licence holder, a list of the active ingredients, contra-indications, warnings and precautions and (except in the case of a product advertised in a journal with an overseas circulation of over 15 per cent) the cost of the product. They also provide requirements for graphs and tables, audio-visual advertisements and multi-page advertisements and prohibit the use of certain words and phrases. Offences against the regulations are punishable under criminal sanctions.

1870   —— collection and delivery arrangements—exemption

The Medicines (Collection and Delivery Arrangements Exemption) Order 1978, S.I. 1978 No. 1421 (in force on 30th October 1978), provides exemptions from the restrictions imposed by Medicines Act 1968, ss. 52, 53, where medicines for human use are supplied at premises which are not a registered pharmacy and such medicines have been dispensed in accordance with a prescription as part of certain collection and delivery charges.

1871   —— containers—products for external use

The Medicines (Fluted Bottles) Regulations 1978, S.I. 1978 No. 40 (in force on 1st February 1978), impose a prohibition on the sale or supply of liquid medicinal products for external use unless the bottle containing the product is fluted vertically with ribs or grooves recognisable to the touch. This provision does not apply to, inter alia, medicinal products contained in bottles with a capacity greater than 1·14 litres. The penalty for contravention of these Regulations is on summary conviction a fine not exceeding £400 and on conviction on indictment a fine or imprisonment for a maximum of two years of both.

1872   —— intra-uterine contraceptive devices

The Medicines (Intra-Uterine Contraceptive Devices) (Appointed Day) Order 1978, S.I. 1978 No. 1138, appoints 1st October 1978 as the day on which the licensing restrictions on marketing, manufacture and wholesale dealing imposed by the Medicines Act 1968, ss. 7, 8 and restrictions on clinical trials imposed by s. 31 shall apply to intra-uterine contraceptive devices.

1873   The Medicines (Intra-Uterine Contraceptive Devices) (Amendment to Exemption from Licences) Order 1978, S.I. 1978 No. 1139 (in force on 1st October 1978), amends certain earlier orders containing exemptions from the provisions of the Medicines Act 1968 as to licensing and clinical trials so as to make those Orders applicable to intra-uterine contraceptive devices.

1874   The Medicines (Licensing of Intra-Uterine Contraceptive Devices) (Miscellaneous Amendments) Regulations 1978, S.I. 1978 No. 1140 (in force on 1st October 1978), amend the Medicines (Applications for Manufacturer's and Wholesale Dealer's Licences) Regulations 1971 and the Medicines (Labelling) Regulations 1976, 1976 Halsbury's Abr para. 1687 so as to make them apply to intra-uterine contraceptive devices as they apply to medicinal products.

1875   —— labelling

The Medicines (Labelling) (Special Transitional) Regulations 1978, S.I. 1978 No. 190 (in force on 11th February 1978), provide that, where any container or package of a medicinal product is labelled in a manner which, but for the exemption conferred by the Medicines (Precriptions Only) Order 1977, 1977 Halsbury's Abr para. 1831, as amended (see para. 1882), would have complied with the requirements of the Medicines (Labelling) Regulations 1976, as amended, 1976 Halsbury's Abr para. 1687, such labelling will, for a transitional period of six months, be deemed to satisfy the requirements of the 1976 Regulations.

1876   —— labelling and advertising

The Medicines (Labelling and Advertising to the Public) Regulations 1978, S.I. 1978 No. 41 (in force on 1st February 1978), prohibit advertisements for, or relating to, medicinal products referring to, of for the purpose of treatment of, specified diseases and advertisements for medicinal products available on prescription only. Also prohibited are representations made by a commercially interested party which are likely to lead to the use of medicinal products for specified purposes. Provision is made specifically for the content and form of advertisements for, and the containers and packages of, spermicidal contraceptives and leaflets supplied with them. Exceptions to the requirements are prescribed and penalties specified for breach of the Regulations. The Medicines (Labelling) Regulations 1976, 1976 Halsbury's Abr para. 1687, are amended.

1877   —— licences and certificates—exemption

The Medicines (Exemption from licences) (Importation) Order 1978, S.I. 1978 No. 1461 (in force on 3rd November 1978), exempts from the restrictions imposed by the Medicines Act 1968, s. 7, the importation and sale or supply of certain medicinal products for human use. The exemption is granted in accordance with specified circumstances and conditions provided by the Order.

1878   —— —— fees

The Medicines (Fees) Regulations 1978, S.I. 1978 No. 1121 (in force on 1st September 1978), consolidate the regulations prescribing fees payable in connection with certificates and licences granted under the Medicines Act 1968. They provide for annual fees to be calculated at the standard percentage rate of 0·24 per cent of annual turnover, with certain exceptions for small businesses, and for the payment of lump sums as capital fees. They also include certain administrative provisions and provisions consequential on the extension of licensing to contact lenses, contact lens fluids and intra-uterine contraceptive devices.

1879   —— pharmacy and general sale—exemption

The Medicines (Pharmacy and General Sale—Exemption) Amendment Order 1978, S.I. 1978 No. 988 (in force on 11th August 1978), amends the Medicines (Pharmacy and General Sale—Exemption) Order 1977, 1977 Halsbury's Abr para. 1826 in respect of the restrictions imposed by the Medicines Act 1968 s. 52. It exempts from the restrictions the supply of specified medicinal products by schools, health authorities and those operating occupational health schemes, and it modifies the range of medicinal products which may be supplied by registered ophthalmic opticians free from the restrictions.

1880   —— radioactive substances—administration

The Medicines (Administration of Radioactive Substances) Regulations 1978, S.I. 1978 No. 1006 (regulations 1 and 8 in force on 1st January 1979, remainder in force on 1st July 1980), have been made in pursuance of Euratom Council Directive 76/569. They prohibit the administration of radioactive medicinal substances except by those holding a certificate issued by the Secretaries of State respectively concerned with health in England, Wales and Scotland or the Department of Health and Social Services in Northern Ireland and lay down rules concerning the issue, duration and renewal of such certificates. They also provide a procedure for applicants or holders of such certificates to put their case if the Secretaries of State propose to refuse to grant or renew a certificate or to suspend, vary or revoke it, and provide for the appointment of an advisory committee.

1881   The Medicines (Radioactive Substances) Order 1978, S.I. 1978 No. 1004 (in force on 1st January 1979), extends the application of certain provisions of the Medicines Act 1968 to certain articles containing or generating radioactive substances. Those provisions include s. 60 which enables regulations to be made prohibiting the sale, supply or administration of medicinal products except by practitioners holding a certificate issued under that section. It also modifies the definition of "administrator" for the purposes of the order.

1882   —— **sale or supply**
The Medicines (Prescription Only) Amendment Order 1978, S.I. 1978 No. 189 (in force on 11th February 1978), amends the Medicines (Prescription Only) Order 1977, 1977 Halsbury's Abr para. 1831, by providing a temporary exemption for six months for certain medical products for human and animal use from the restrictions applicable to prescription only medicines imposed by the Medicines Act 1968, s. 58 (2). The exemption applies to those products which became subject to the prescription only requirement under the 1977 Order. Previously, the sale or supply of certain now exempted products was required to be recorded in a register or to be against a signed order under the Pharmacy and Poisons Act 1933. During the transitional exemption period, those procedures must still be followed in relation to such products.

1883   The Medicines (Prescriptions Only) Amendment (No. 2) Order 1978, S.I. 1978 No. 987 (in force on 11th August 1978), amends the Medicines (Prescriptions Only) Order 1977, 1977 Halsbury's Abr para. 1831 as amended by S.I. 1978 No. 189, para. 1882. The Order alters the description and classes of prescription only medicines and modifies the scope of certain exemptions from restrictions applicable to such medicines imposed by the Medicines Act 1968, s. 58 (2). The affected exemptions include those from the restrictions on certain prescription only medicines in an emergency by either persons conducting a retail pharmacy business or other specified persons. The conditions applicable in relation to prescriptions under s. 58 (4) (b) of the 1968 Act are also modified. The Order grants temporary exemptions until 11th February 1979 from the restrictions imposed by the Medicines Act 1968, s. 58 (2), which relate to medicinal products for human and animal use, where the selling, supplying or administering of the medicinal product could have been lawfully done before 11th August 1978 otherwise than in accordance with a prescription.

1884   The Medicines (Sale or Supply) (Miscellaneous Provisions) Amendment Regulations 1978, S.I. 1978 No. 989 (in force on 11th August 1978) amend the Medicines (Sale or Supply) (Miscellaneous Provisions) Regulations 1977, 1977 Halsbury's Abr para. 1833 in respect of the range of prescription only medicines sold by way of wholesale dealings to registered ophthalmic opticians and permits their sale by way of wholesale dealings to persons allowed to administer them under the temporary exemption granted by the Medicines (Prescription Only) Order 1977, 1977 Halsbury's Abr para. 1831. They also alter the requirements relating to pharmacy records by permitting an abridged entry for certain supplies under repeat prescriptions.

1885   ——— **veterinary drugs—exemption**
The Medicines (Exemption from Restrictions on the Retail Sale or Supply of Veterinary Drugs) (Amendment) Order 1978, S.I. 1978 No. 1001 (in force on 11th August 1978), makes it clear that when a person described in the Medicines (Exemption from Restrictions on the Retail Sale or Supply of Veterinary Drugs) Order 1977, art. 3 (1), 1977 Halsbury's Abr para. 1805 lawfully sells a veterinary drug by retail, the subsequent delivery of the drug to the purchaser need not take place on the seller's premises and also clarifies art. 3 (4). In addition it provides for certain exemptions from the restrictions in the Medicines Act 1968, s. 52.

1886   Nurses and midwives

The Nurses Agencies Amendment Regulations 1978, S.I. 1978 No. 1443 (in force on 1st November 1978) amend the Nurses Agencies Regulations 1961, r. 3 which prescribes classes of persons that a nurses agency in England or Wales is authorised to supply. They also increase the fees payable for licences to carry on nurses agencies.

1887   Opticians—General Optical Council—membership

The General Optical Council (Membership) Order of Council 1978, S.I. 1978 No. 1410 (in force on 31st October 1978) increases the number of elected members of the General Optical Council representing registered dispensing opticians from two to three.

1888   Pharmaceutical society—statutory committee—disciplinary procedure

The Pharmaceutical Society (Statutory Committee) Order of Council 1978, S.I. 1978 No. 20 (in force on 1st February 1978), prescribes the procedure to be followed by the statutory committee when dealing with information concerning the criminal conviction of or misconduct by certain persons, including registered pharmaceutical chemists, their employees and employees of a body corporate carrying on a retail pharmacy business. The Pharmaceutical Society (Statutory Committee) Order of Council 1957 is revoked.

1889   Poisons

The Poisons Rules 1978, S.I. 1978 No. 1 (in force on 1st February 1978), made under the Poisons Act 1972, replace the Poisons Rules 1972 as amended. Unlike the 1972 Rules, they have effect only in relation to non-medicinal poisons. The Rules provide for the application and relaxation of the Poisons Act 1972, impose additional restrictions on the sale of poisons, make supplementary provisions with respect to labelling and containers, and make provision as to storage and transport of poisons.

1890   —— list

The Poisons List Order 1978, S.I. 1978 No. 2 (in force on 1st February 1978), made under the Poisons Act 1972, amends the Poisons List as set out in the Poisons List Order 1972, as amended. The List as so amended is set out in the Schedule to the Order.

1891   —— packaging and labelling

See para. 1455.

1892   Pregnancy—medical termination of pregnancy—husband's power to prevent

See *Paton v British Pregnancy Advisory Service*, para. 1507.

1893   Veterinary surgeons and practitioners—registration

The Veterinary Surgeons and Veterinary Practitioners (Registration) (Amendment) Regulations Order of Council 1978, S.I. 1978 No. 1809 (made on 11th December 1978), further amend the Veterinary Surgeons and Veterinary Practitioners Registration Regulations 1967 by increasing various fees payable in respect of registration and retention of names in the registers.

MENTAL HEALTH

Halsbury's Laws of England (3rd edn.), Vol. 29, paras. 790–1125

1894   Guardianship—application of health authority for appointment of guardian—deprivation of spouse of guardianship rights

An area health authority applied for an order placing a terminally ill patient in the care of a local authority welfare officer, to prevent the patient's husband from applying on her behalf for her release from hospital so that she could die at home. *Held*, the husband was an unsuitable person to act as legal guardian for his wife and accordingly the order would be granted: Times, 6th June 1978 (Margate County Court).

The husband was subsequently refused permission by the Court of Appeal to apply to have this decision quashed; see Times, 13th June 1978.

For earlier proceedings in this matter, see para. 765.

1895   Legislation—review—departmental circular

The Department of Health and Social Security has issued a circular to complement a White Paper presented on 12th September 1978 on the Review of the Mental Health Act 1959. It is entitled "A New Deal for the Mentally Disordered" and contains comments on developments since the 1959 Act, a series of questions and answers on the White Paper and a summary of the main proposals for the treatment of mental patients contained in the White Paper.

MINES, MINERALS AND QUARRIES

Halsbury's Laws of England (3rd edn.), Vol. 26, paras. 668–1510

1896   Australia—mining operation on aborigine reserve—distribution of profits of operation

See *Director of Aborigine and Islanders Advancement Corporation v Peinkinna*, para. 321.

1897   Coal industry—redundant workers—concessionary coal

The Redundant Mineworkers and Concessionary Coal (Payments Schemes) Order 1978, S.I. 1978 No. 415 (in force on 25th March 1978), establishes under the Coal Industry Act 1977 schemes for the payment of benefits to mineworkers and other coal industry employees made redundant between 25th March 1978 and 29th March 1981, and for the reimbursement of the National Coal Board for the cost of providing concessionary coal to redundant workers. The schemes prescribe the classes of persons eligible and the conditions they must fulfil in order to qualify for benefit.

1898   —— superannuation

See para. 2086.

1899   Continental shelf—designated areas

The Continental Shelf (Designation of Additional Areas) Order 1978, S.I. 1978 No. 178 (made on 9th February 1978), designates an area of the Continental Shelf north-west of the Shetland Islands as an area in which the United Kingdom may exercise its rights with respect to the sea bed and subsoil and their natural resources.

1900   The Continental Shelf (Designation of Additional Areas) (No. 2) Order 1978, S.I. 1978 No. 1029 (made on 25th July 1978), designates an area of the Continental Shelf in the South-Western Approaches to the English Channel as an area in which the rights of the United Kingdom with respect to the sea bed and subsoil and their natural resources may be exercised.

1901   **—— protection of installations**

See paras. 2615, 2616.

1902   **Employment (Continental Shelf) Act 1978**

See para. 1076.

1903   **Health and safety—coal mines—respirable dust**

The Coal Mines (Respirable Dust) (Amendment) Regulations 1978, S.I. 1978 No. 807 (in force on 4th July 1978), amend the schedules to the Coal Mines (Respirable Dust) Regulations 1975, 1975 Halsbury's Abr para. 2273. They lower the levels of respirable dust indices requiring the taking of additional samples and the ascertainment of the average quartz content in Schedule 1 and the permitted respirable dust indices in Schedule 2.

1904   **—— Mining Qualifications Board—issue of certificates**

The Mines and Quarries Act 1954 (Modification) Regulations 1978, S.I. 1978 No. 1951 (in force on 23rd January 1979), amend the Mines and Quarries Act 1954, s. 148 by providing that the Mining Qualifications Board, which recommends that certain certificates be granted under health and safety regulations, is required to ascertain the fitness of candidates for such certificates. The maximum number of persons who may be appointed to the Board is fifteen.

1905   **Ironstone Restoration Fund**

The Ironstone Restoration Fund (Rates of Contribution) Order 1978, S.I. 1978 No. 195 (in force on 1st April 1978), revokes and re-enacts with amendments the Ironstone Restoration Fund (Rates of Contribution) Order 1977, 1977 Halsbury's Abr para. 1860. It prescribes the full and reduced rates of contributions payable by ironstone operators towards the Ironstone Restoration Fund in respect of ironstone extracted on or after 1st April 1971 and the sums deductible from payments made under mining leases and mineral rights orders in respect of full rate contributions.

1906   The Ironstone Restoration Fund (Standard Rate) Order 1978, S.I. 1978 No. 196 (in force on 1st April 1978), prescribes a standard rate of £708 per acre as the rate of payments to be made to ironstone operators in respect of the restoration of worked ironstone land in compliance with conditions of a planning permission. The Ironstone Restoration Fund (Standard Rate) Order 1977, 1977 Halsbury's Abr para. 1859 is revoked.

1907   **Offshore installations—fire-fighting equipment**

The Offshore Installations (Fire-fighting Equipment) Regulations 1978, S.I. 1978 No. 611 (in force on 1st April 1979), apply to fixed and mobile offshore installations maintained for the underwater exploitation and exploration of mineral resources in waters to which the Mineral Workings (Offshore Installations) Act 1971 applies. They require the provision of specified types of fire-fighting equipment on all such installations which are normally manned. They also prohibit the presence of any person on an offshore installation on or after 1st April 1970 unless the fire-fighting equipment on it has been examined by an authorised person.

1908   —— life-saving appliances

The Offshore Installations (Life-saving Appliances) (Amendment) Regulations 1978, S.I. 1978 No. 931 (in force on 2nd August 1978) amend the Offshore Installations (Life-saving Appliances) Regulations 1977, 1977 Halsbury's Abr para. 1862. They substitute the table set out in the Schedule to the 1977 Regulations, increasing the fee payable for examination of the life-saving appliances on an installation.

1909   Opencast coal—compensation—rate of interest

The Opencast Coal (Rate of Interest on Compensation) (No. 2) Order 1978, S.I. 1978 No. 735 (in force on 21st June 1978) provides for an increase in the rate of interest under the Opencast Coal Act 1958, s. 35 to nine and a half per cent.

This order was subsequently revoked; see para. 1910.

1910   The Opencast Coal (Rate of Interest on Compensation) (No. 3) Order 1978, S.I. 1978 No. 1419 (in force on 26th October 1978) increases the rate of interest payable in addition to compensation under the Opencast Coal Act 1958, s. 35 from nine and a half per cent to ten and a half per cent. The Opencast Coal (Rate of Interest on Compensation) (No. 2) Order 1978, S.I. 1978 No. 735 is revoked.

This order was subsequently revoked; see para. 1911.

1911   The Opencast Coal (Rate of Interest on Compensation) (No. 4) Order 1978, S.I. 1978 No. 1802 (in force on 3rd January 1979), provides for an increase in the rate of interest under the Opencast Coal Act 1958, s. 35 to thirteen per cent.

The Opencast Coal (Rate of Interest on Compensation) (No. 3) Order 1978, see para. 1910, is revoked.

1912   Petroleum—licences

The Petroleum (Production) (Amendment) Regulations 1978, S.I. 1978 No. 929 (in force on 26th July 1978), amend the Petroleum (Production) Regulations 1976, 1976 Halsbury's Abr para. 1720. They provide for an increase in the fee payable by applicants for petroleum production licences for seaward areas, amend the details to be furnished by applicants for production licences for landward and seaward areas and clarify the model clause to be incorporated in production licences for seaward areas relating to the approval of operators.

MINORS

Halsbury's Laws of England (4th edn.), Vol. 24, paras. 401–900

1913   Articles

Access to Children, W. T. West: 122 Sol Jo 425.

Adopted and Legitimated Children, Dr C. H. Sherrin (their entitlement to share in testamentary dispositions, and their eligibility for membership of a class on intestacy): 128 NLJ 101.

Adoption by Parent and Step-Parent, Frank Hopkins and John Benson (Children Act 1975, s. 10 (3)): 128 NLJ 339.

Registration of Children's Maintenance Orders, N. E. Hickman (examination of the objections to registration in magistrates' court of maintenance orders payable directly to children): 128 NLJ 567.

"Womb-Leasing": Some Legal Implications, Douglas J. Cusine (legal implications of situation where a woman agrees to become pregnant and after the birth of the child to hand it over to and surrender all rights to it in favour of another woman): 128 NLJ 824.

1914   **Adoption—application by parent and step-parent—factors to be considered—welfare of child paramount**

After the death of her husband the mother of a young boy married a divorced man with two children. The couple, who had a child of their own and who were a devoted family applied for adoption of the boy. The adoption was opposed by the boy's paternal grandparents, who had always been attached to the boy and who had set up a trust fund for him in the hope that he would join the family business. In making the adoption order the justices had said that the boy should be properly integrated within his new family. Although the mother had stated that on adoption the boy would not sever his links with his grandparents he had in fact not seen them for some time. On appeal *held*, the justices were wrong on the facts and in principle. In severing him from his grandparents they had not considered the boy's welfare now or in the future. The child was already integrated within his new family and making an adoption order added nothing to his welfare. The appeal would be allowed.

RE L A (A MINOR) (1978) 122 Sol Jo 417 (Family Division: SIR GEORGE BAKER P and COMYN J).

1915   —— **application for adoption order in county court—removal of application to High Court—procedure**

The following Practice Direction ([1978] 3 All ER 960) has been issued by the Family Division.

RSC Ord 90, r 10, provides that an application for an order under s. 16(1) of the Guardianship of Minors Act 1971 or s. 101(1) of the Children Act 1975 for the removal of guardianship or adoption proceedings from a county court into the High Court shall be made by originating summons issued out of the Principal Registry. Unless the court otherwise directs, the summons need not be served on any person, and the application for the removal of the proceedings may be heard by a registrar. The following procedure shall apply on any such application:

(1) the originating summons shall be in Form 11 in Appendix A to the Rules of the Supreme Court (ex parte originating summons) suitably amended, and shall be supported by affidavit or other evidence, including where appropriate the written consent of the other party or parties to the application; the fee in respect of an application is £2 (Supreme Court Fees Order 1975, Fee No. 2);

(2) both copies of the summons will be retained in the registry and will be referred, together with the supporting evidence, to the registrar of the day for consideration;

(3) if the registrar requires personal attendance on the summons, the registry will fix a date and will send the sealed copy summons to the applicant's solicitor with a date and time of hearing noted thereon; notice of the hearing must then be given to the other party or parties by the applicant's solicitor;

(4) when the registrar makes an order for the removal of the proceedings to the High Court, the registry will serve a copy on the applicant, but it is the responsibility of the applicant to serve the other party or parties and to send a copy of the order to the registrar of the county court from which the proceedings are to be removed so that he may arrange for the physical removal of the documents referred to in CCR Ord. 16, r. 19, to the "proper officer" of the High Court; for the purposes of RSC Ord. 90, r. 10 (4) the "proper officer" shall be the Senior Registrar of the Principal Registry of the Family Division;

(5) on receipt of the documents referred to in para. (4) above, the registry will give notice to all parties of the removal of the proceedings to the High Court, together with the High Court file reference number.

1916   —— **conflict of laws—international convention**

See para. 415.

1917   —— **convention adoption**

The Convention Adoption Rules 1978, S.I. 1978 No. 417 (in force on 23rd October

1978) prescribes rules for proceedings under the Adoption Act 1968, s. 6 and the Children Act 1975, s. 24, which came into force on the same date, and which relate principally to the Hague Convention on Jurisdiction, Applicable Law and Recognition of Decrees Relating to Adoptions.

1918   The Convention Adoption (Miscellaneous Provisions) Order 1978, S.I. 1978 No. 1432 (in force on 23rd October 1978), contains the definitions of "convention adoption", "British territory", "specified country" and "United Kingdom national" in relation to England and Wales for the purposes of the Adoption Act 1968 and the Children Act 1975 in respect of the Convention on Jurisdiction, Applicable Law and Recognition of Decrees relating to Adoptions concluded at The Hague on 15th November 1965. Evidence of convention adoption, and the provisions of the United Kingdom national law which prohibit adoptions and which have been notified pursuant to the Convention, are also dealt with.

1919   —————— **designated conventions**

The Convention Adoption (Austria and Switzerland) Order 1978, S.I. 1978 No. 1431 (in force on 23rd October 1978), designates Austria and Switzerland as Convention countries for the purposes of the Adoption Act 1968 and the Children Act 1975, 1975 Halsbury's Abr para. 1838. The Order specifies the provisions of Austrian and Swiss national laws which prohibit adoptions and which have been notified to the United Kingdom pursuant to Articles 13, 17 and 24 of the Convention on Jurisdiction, Applicable Law and Recognition of Decrees relating to Adoptions concluded at The Hague on 15th November 1965.

1920   —————— **rules—county court**

The Adoption (County Court) (Amendment) Rules 1978, S.I. 1978 No. 1518 (in force on 20th November 1978), amend the Adoption (County Court) Rules 1976, 1976 Halsbury's Abr para. 1747, by revoking the provisions requiring certain types of adoption proceedings to be heard in chambers. These provisions are superseded by the Domestic Proceedings and Magistrates' Courts Act 1978, para. 1509, which amends The Children Act 1975, s. 21, so as to require all county court adoption proceedings to be heard and determined in camera.

1921   —————— **High Court**

The Adoption (High Court) (Amendment) Rules 1978, S.I. 1978 No. 1519 (in force on 20th November 1978), amend the Adoption (High Court) Rules 1976, 1976 Halsbury's Abr para. 1747, and the Convention Adoption Rules 1978, para. 1917, by revoking the provisions permitting certain types of adoption proceedings to be heard in chambers. These provisions are superseded by the Domestic Proceedings and Magistrates' Courts Act 1978, para. 1509, which amends the Children Act 1975, s. 21, so as to permit all High Court adoption proceedings to be disposed of in chambers.

1922   **Adoption Act 1968—commencement**

The Adoption Act 1968 (Commencement No. 2) Order 1978, S.I. 1978 No. 1430, brought ss. 5–7, 8 (1) and 9 of the 1968 Act into force on 23rd October 1978.

1923   **Adult proceedings—publication of names of children**

The Press Council considers it is usually undesirable to publish the names of children involved in sex cases: Times, 12th June 1978.

1924   **Appeals concerning children—production of documents**

See *In Re B (A minor)*, para. 943.

1925   Child—care—application by parent for writ of habeas corpus—whether issue of writ appropriate

A local authority claimed that under the Children Act 1948, s. 1 it was entitled to take a fifteen year old girl into care. Her father sought leave to issue a writ of habeas corpus. *Held*, the father's application was based on a claim that the local authority were holding the girl against her will, but in fact she did not wish to live with her parents. The use of a writ of habeas corpus was the wrong procedure in the Family Division and the present case would be better dealt with under the wardship jurisdiction.

Re K (A Minor) (1978) 122 Sol Jo 626 (Family Division: Bush J).

1926   —— —— termination—notice by parent

A baby girl was voluntarily placed in care by her mother in 1976. In 1977, the mother requested the local authority to return the child to her. The local authority then passed a resolution under the Children Act 1948, s. 2, assuming parental rights over the child on the ground that the mother had failed to discharge her parental obligations. The mother contended that by virtue of her request to have her child returned, the child was no longer "in care" as required by s. 2, when the resolution was made and the resolution was therefore invalid. *Held*, a local authority's right to keep a child in care ended once the child's parent sought its return and gave the authority notice to this effect. Accordingly, if its right to keep the child under s. 1 (1) of the 1948 Act had ended, then the local authority ceased to have the child in care within the meaning of s. 2 when the resolution was passed. The resolution was thus invalid.

Johns v Jones [1978] 3 All ER 1222 (Court of Appeal: Stamp and Orr LJJ and Sir David Cairns). *Bawden v Bawden* (1975) 74 LGR 347, CA, 1976 Halsbury's Abr para. 1741 applied.

1927   —— —— wardship application—jurisdiction of court where adoption order refused

In dismissing a wardship application, Dunn J stated that where a county court had refused to grant an adoption order the High Court would not hear an application by the proposed adopter under the wardship procedure. To do so would be to allow an appeal from the county court decision by the back door.

Re S (A Minor) (1978) 122 Sol Jo 759 (Family Division: Dunn J).

1928   —— —— —— jurisdiction of court where child already subject of care order

In 1974, at the request of the mother, a local authority received a seven-year-old boy into care. The boy's father was in a mental home at the time and his mother was also receiving treatment in a mental hospital. The boy was put in a foster home and from 1975 he attended a boarding school. In October 1975, a resolution was passed by the local authority assuming parental rights in respect of the boy on the grounds that his mother was suffering from a permanent disability rendering her incapable of caring for him. The mother's objection to the resolution was not upheld. Arrangements made for the mother's access to the boy were unsatisfactory to her and in 1976, she issued an originating summons asking that the boy be made a ward of court and that while he should remain in the care and control of the Local authority, the court should issue directions regarding his education, welfare and mother's access. The court confirmed the boy's wardship and ordered the local authority to file its evidence. The local authority applied to the registrar for directions as to the manner in which it should present its evidence. The registrar referred the application to a judge in chambers and at the hearing the local authority requested the case to be dealt with summarily and applied to have the wardship ended. *Held*, the issue to be considered was the amount of access the mother should be allowed to her child. Once a local authority assumed parental rights under the Children Act 1948, s. 2, the right to control access by other persons including the natural parents was vested in it. Therefore a parent who challenged the local authority's discretion as to access had to show a strong prima facie case for taking such an exceptional course before the court would make a full investigation in wardship proceedings. It would be wrong for the court to override the local authority's views about access unless the court was satisfied that the local authority's view could not be supported. This was a case where the future of the child during his minority could be safely left to be regulated by the local authority. The summons would be dismissed and the child would cease to be a ward of court.

In RE D F (A MINOR) (1977) 76 LGR 133 (Family Division: DUNN J).

1929   A three-year-old girl who had received serious injuries was committed to the care of a local authority by an order under Children and Young Persons Act 1969, ss. 1, 20. Her parents issued a summons making her a ward of court and applied for an order continuing the wardship. The parents were Pakistanis and wished to return to their native country with the child. The local authority opposed the application on the ground that the child's injuries had been caused by one of the parents. The judge decided that the child's injuries were non-accidental but that in the unusual circumstances her future welfare would be best served by allowing her to return to Pakistan with her family. He accordingly ordered that she remain a ward of court. The local authority appealed contending that the court had no jurisdiction to make such an order. *Held,* in deciding whether the High Court had jurisdiction to entertain a wardship application in respect of a child who was subject to a care order under the Children and Young Persons Act 1969 a distinction had to be drawn between the case where the applicant was seeking to challenge the exercise of the local authority's discretion and that where the challenge was directed to the source of the discretionary power. The present case came within the latter category as the parents were seeking to remove the child altogether from the local authority's control. In such a case the most important consideration was the welfare of the child, but it also had to be shown that the circumstances were sufficiently unusual to justify the intervention of the High Court. In all the circumstances the judge had been right to assume jurisdiction.

RE H (A MINOR) (WARDSHIP JURISDICTION) [1978] 2 WLR 608 (Court of Appeal: STAMP, ORR and ORMROD LJJ). *Re M (an infant)* [1961] Ch 328, CA and *Re T (AJJ) (an infant)* [1970] Ch 688, CA distinguished.

1930   A child abandoned by his mother was taken into care by a local authority under its statutory powers and cared for by a foster mother. Although relatives wanted to bring up the child, the local authority assumed parental rights as a result of which the relatives issued a wardship summons. A report by the Official Solicitor as guardian ad litem supported their claim against the local authority. The local authority contended that the court had no jurisdiction to interfere with the exercise of its statutory discretion and in any event the Official Solicitor's views should carry no more weight than the relatives'. *Held,* (i) the court's wardship jurisdiction was not affected by the local authority's exercise of its discretion. Since the authority had not objected to the appointment of the Official Solicitor as guardian ad litem or to his investigations, it could not now object to the court considering his report. (ii) The case was to be decided on its merits for two reasons. Firstly, the Official Solicitor was widely experienced in matters of child welfare and his opinions were to be valued accordingly. Secondly, the committee which passed the resolution assuming parental rights had done so without being aware of the fact that relatives were willing to bring up the child and therefore had not properly exercised its discretion.

RE D (A MINOR) (1978) 122 Sol Jo 193 (Family Division: BALCOMBE J). *Associated Pictures Houses v Wednesbury Corporation* [1948] 1 KB 223, applied.

1931   ———————— **jurisdiction of registrar—practice**

The grandmother of a minor issued an originating summons making the minor a ward of court, and applied for care and control. The deputy district registrar made an order in her favour. The mother appealed, contending that the evidence was insufficient to prove what was in the best interests of the child or, alternatively, on the available evidence, the order should have been made in favour of the mother. *Held*, although the deputy district registrar had jurisdiction to make such an order, it was not the usual practice.   The hearing should have been before the appropriate circuit judge dealing with such matters in the district registry.   The order would be set aside and the case remitted to the district registry.

RE L (A MINOR) [1978] 2 All ER 318 (Court of Appeal: ROSKILL and ORMROD LJJ).

1932   Child benefit

See SOCIAL SECURITY.

1933   Children Act 1975—commencement

The Children Act 1975 (Commencement No. 3) Order 1978, S.I. 1978 No. 1433, brought s. 24 of the 1975 Act into force on 23rd October 1978, and implemented a minor transitional amendment to the Adoption Act 1958, s. 53 (4).

1934   Custody—custody hearing—use of informal discussion

In the course of an appeal against the use of informal discussion to settle a custody case, the Court of Appeal stated that although a degree of informality was permissible in the hearing of cases involving child custody, all such cases presented some difficulty and were consequently to be conducted with great care.   The case in hand could and should have been conducted in the normal contemporary manner.

JENKINS v JENKINS (1978) Times, 30th June (Court of Appeal: STAMP and ORR LJJ).

1935   —— Scottish mother and children temporarily resident in England—jurisdiction of English court

A Scottish mother left her husband and crossed the border into England taking her three children with her.   She applied to an English magistrates' court for an order under the Guardianship of Minors Act 1971, s. 9, seeking custody of and maintenance for the children.   At the hearing, the justices, on the father's application, gave custody of the children to him.   The mother then contended that the justices had no jurisdiction to make the order as she was not resident in England.   *Held*, the extent and quality of the residence necessary to give jurisdiction under any particular Act was a question of fact in the circumstances of each individual case.   Some degree of permanency was usually required.   In this case the mother was expressly doing no more than temporarily taking refuge in England while she sought accommodation in Scotland.   The husband, wife and three children were Scottish.   Their place of work, schooling, and intended permanent residence was Scotland.   The proper forum was clearly a Scottish court.   The custody order, while sound in itself, was made without jurisdiction and would be set aside.

RE IRVING (MINORS) (1978) 122 Sol Jo 348 (Family Division: SIR GEORGE BAKER P and WOOD J).

1936   Employment of minor—illegal employment—liability of employer

See *Portsea Island Mutual Co-operative Society Ltd v Leyland*, para. 1156.

1937   Guardian ad litem—Official Solicitor—wardship application—importance of Official Solicitor's report

See *Re D (A Minor)*, para. 1930.

1938   Guardianship—application for guardianship order in county court—removal of application to High Court—procedure

See para. 1915.

1939   Indecent photographs of children—offences

See Protection of Children Act 1978, para. 652.

1940   Legal proceedings—action for personal injury by next friend— whether minor entitled to commence fresh action within extended limitation period

See *Tolley v Morris*, para. 2225.

1941   Magistrates' courts—children and young persons—procedure

The Magistrates' Courts (Children and Young Persons) (Amendment) Rules 1978, S.I. 1978 No. 869 (in force on 17th July 1978), amend the Magistrates' Courts (Children and Young Persons) Rules 1970, as amended, to take into account the coming into force on the same date of the Criminal Law Act, 1977, ss. 34, 36, 37. These sections amend the law relating to the trial of a juvenile charged jointly with an adult; the enforcement of fines imposed on young offenders; and the requirements which may be included in supervision orders; new rules and forms are introduced to take account of these provisions. Other amendments are consequential on the coming into force on 17th April 1978 of the Bail Act 1976. There are also minor amendments to existing rules.

1942   Maintenance—enforcement order—appeal to High Court— procedure

In the course of a father's appeal on motion against a magistrates' order enforcing payment of arrears of maintenance due under the Guardianship of Minors Act 1971, the Divisional Court of the Family Division stated that the only method of appealing against such an order was by way of case stated on a point of law. The court emphasized that had the appeal not failed on this point, it would in any event have failed on its merits.

RE K (MINORS) (1978) 122 Sol Jo 825 (Family Division: SIR GEORGE BAKER P and COMYN J).

1943   Surname—change by deed poll by one parent—objection by other parent

A pregnant woman left her husband, the father of her child, to live with another man. She executed a deed poll assuming his surname for herself and any children she might have. After her child was born, she registered his surname as that of the man she was living with. The child's father objected and the mother was ordered to execute a fresh deed poll and a statutory declaration amending the entry in the register of births. She was also ordered not to allow the child to be known by any surname except his father's without the consent of the court or the father. On appeal by the mother, *held*, (i) there was nothing she could do about the deed poll. A surname was the name by which a person was known and a deed poll was merely evidential. (ii) Errors of fact on the register of births could be amended by statutory declaration but the Registration of Births, Deaths and Marriages Regulations 1968 defined a child's surname as the name by which he was intended to be known. Therefore, the mother was entitled to argue that there was no error since she had registered the surname by which the child was intended to be known; it was not necessary that both parents should intend that the child should be known by that surname. (iii) A child's surname was of great importance to the father but it was not realistic to litigate over such matters. Providing the child knew his real father and had a close relationship with him, he would not be confused by having a different name. However, he might be confused and embarrassed by having a different name from the people with whom he lived. The appeal would be allowed and the order concerning the child's name would be varied to enable him to be known by his mother's assumed surname.

D v B (OTHERWISE D) (CHILD: SURNAME) [1979] 1 All ER 92 (Court of Appeal:

STAMP and ORMROD LJJ). Decision of Lane J [1977] 3 All ER 751, 1976 Halsbury's Abr para. 1744 varied.

1944 The mother of two children, now aged four and three, who had remarried after divorce from their father, applied for leave to change the children's surname to that of her new husband, their step-father. The children's father objected to the change. *Held*, there were two lines of cases on the problem; one line decided that the question of a change of name was formalistic and of little importance, while the other decided that it was important so far as the children's interests and welfare were concerned. There was thus a conflict of principle, and it was for the courts of first instance to decide which was the correct view. From the point of view of the children's best interests it was essential that the parents' feelings be considered. A change of name could benefit or injure a child, and it was thus a question of importance. In this case the children would have a better sense of security if they were to retain their father's name. Leave would be refused.

L v F (1978) Times, 1st August (Family Division: LATEY J). *Rice v Rice* [1978] 2 All ER 33, CA, 1977 Halsbury's Abr para. 1884 and *Re D (a minor)* (1978) Times, 26th May, CA, para. 1943, not applied. *Re WG* (1976) 6 Family Law 210, CA, applied.

1945 ### Ward of court—attempt to use wardship jurisdiction for purposes of criminal proceedings

A 17½ year old girl was the complainant in criminal proceedings involving a charge of rape. The defendant applied to the judge for an order that the girl be examined by a psychiatrist and that her medical records be made available to the court. The judge refused to make the order, saying it was a matter for the girl's mother to decide. The mother issued a summons making the girl a ward of court. The Official Solicitor, as guardian ad litem, sought directions, in a wardship summons, as to whether a psychiatrist should see the girl and whether her medical records should be made available in the criminal proceedings. *Held*, this was not a matter for a judge in wardship proceedings, but for the judge in the criminal case. It was reasonable for the mother of the girl to decide not to subject her daughter to further medical examination. The mother's decision was the final one. It seemed that the wardship jurisdiction had been used to overcome a procedural difficulty in the criminal case. That was an improper use of the wardship jurisdiction. The wardship summons would be dismissed.

Re D [1978] LS Gaz R 857 (Family Division: DUNN J).

MISREPRESENTATION AND FRAUD

Halsbury's Laws of England (3rd edn.), Vol. 26, paras. 1511–1648

1946 ### Fraud—action for damages—plaintiff in breach of exchange control provisions—effect

See *Shelley v Paddock*, para. 1957.

1947 ### Fraudulent misrepresentation—place where tort committed—service of writ out of jurisdiction

See *Diamond v Bank of London and Montreal Ltd*, para. 428.

1948 ### Innocent misrepresentation—description of premises as offices—representation as to existence of planning permission for use as offices

The lessors obtained planning permission to use part only of a building owned by them as offices. Forgetting the limitation, they offered to let the whole building to the lessees as offices for fifteen years. The lessees accepted the offer on the assumption that planning permission existed for the use of the whole building as offices. They did not make any searches or inquiries. After they had taken possession, their solicitors informed them of the restriction on the planning permission. The parties agreed that the lessors would apply for planning permission to use the whole building as offices. Permission was obtained for two years only, and subject to a review thereafter. After the failure of negotiations for alternative arrangements, the lessees gave notice and left. The lessors brought an action for specific performance of the lease. The lessees claimed to rescind the agreement on the grounds of misrepresentation and common mistake. The lessors contended that the lessees had lost the right to rescind because they had affirmed the contract by remaining in occupation after they had discovered the true facts. *Held*, the lessees were entitled to rescind the agreement on the ground of misrepresentation because the lessors' description of the premises as offices was a representation as to the availability of planning permission for use of the entire building as offices for the full term of fifteen years. The lessors were negligent in making the representation as they had failed to check the facts. The lessees were also entitled to rescind on the ground of common mistake as the parties' belief that unrestricted planning permission was available was a fundamental mistake and the lessees were not at fault as they did not owe a duty of care to the lessors to make searches or inquiries. Their claim was not barred by acquiescence as they had wanted to negotiate for alternative arrangements and were entitled to time for consideration after the breakdown of negotiations.

LAURENCE v LEXCOURT HOLDINGS LTD [1978] 2 All ER 810 (Chancery Division: BRIAN DILLON QC sitting as a deputy High Court judge). *Re Davis and Cavey* (1888) 40 Ch D 607 and *Charles Hunt Ltd v Palmer* [1931] 3 Ch 287 applied.

MISTAKE

Halsbury's Laws of England (3rd edn.), Vol. 26, paras. 1649–1725

1949 Mistake of law—party having no right to enter into contract—compromise made on basis of contract—whether compromise can be set aside

Canada

The receiver-manager of a group of companies advertised them for sale as a going concern. A potential purchaser made an offer for the property and assets of the companies and paid a deposit. Subsequently, negotiations between the parties fell through, and, in a compromise agreement they agreed that the purchaser would forfeit part of his deposit. On an application to the court to approve a later offer to purchase, it was held that the receiver-manager had only power to preserve the assets of the company and not to dispose of them. The purchaser claimed that the remainder of his deposit should be returned on the ground that it was paid under a mistake of law as the receiver-manager had no right to enter into the original contract with him. *Held*, the contract of sale was void ab initio, and, as it was the basis of the later compromise agreement, that compromise although not a legal nullity in itself, was liable to be set aside in equity. Accordingly, the deposit would be returned to the purchaser.

TORONTO-DOMINION BANK v FORTIN [1978] 5 WWR 302 (Supreme Court of British Columbia). *Magee v Pennine Insurance Co* [1969] 2 All ER 891, CA applied.

1950 Rescission—common mistake of fact—existence of planning permission for intended use of premises

See *Laurence v Lexcourt Holdings Ltd*, para. 1948.

1951 Unilateral mistake—mistake by one party not known to other party—contract of salvage

See *The Unique Mariner*, para. 2637.

MONEY AND MONEYLENDERS

Halsbury's Laws of England (3rd edn.), Vol. 27, paras. 1–235

1952   **Asian Development Bank—payments to capital stock**

The Asian Development Bank (Further Payments to Capital Stock) Order 1978, S.I. 1978 No. 154 (in force on 2nd February 1978), provides for the payment of specified sums to the Asian Development Bank as further payments by way of subscription to an issue of shares increasing the authorised stock of the Bank. It also provides for the payment of any sums which may be required to maintain the value of such further payments and for the redemption of non-interest-bearing and non-negotiable notes issued by the Minister of Overseas Development in respect of those further payments.

1953   **Counter-inflation**

See EMERGENCY CONTROLS.

1954   **Exchange control—authorised dealers and depositaries**

The Exchange Control (Authorised Dealers and Depositaries) Order 1978, S.I. 1978 No. 1599 (in force on 28th November 1978), lists those persons authorised under the Exchange Control Act 1947 to deal in gold; to deal in gold and foreign currencies; and to act as authorised depositaries for the purposes of Part III of that Act. The Order supersedes, with amendments, the Exchange Control (Authorised Dealers and Depositaries) Order 1977, as amended, 1977 Halsbury's Abr paras. 1904, 1905, and S.I. 1978 No. 581, para. 1955.

1955   The Exchange Control (Authorised Dealers and Depositaries) (Amendment) Order 1978, S.I. 1978 No. 581 (in force on 8th May 1978), amends the Exchange Control (Authorised Dealers and Depositaries Order 1977, 1977 Halsbury's Abr para. 1904, as amended. The Order amends the lists of banks and other persons authorised under the Exchange Control Act 1947 to deal in gold and foreign currencies and of those who are entitled to act as authorised depositaries for the purpose of the deposit of securities as required by that Act.

This order was subsequently superseded, see para. 1954, supra.

1956   The Exchange Control (Authorised Dealers and Depositaries) (Amendment) (No. 2) Order 1978, S.I. 1978 No. 1942 (in force on 2nd January 1979), amends the list of those who are entitled to act as authorised depositaries for the purpose of the deposit of securities as required by the Exchange Control Act 1947 as prescribed by S.I. 1978 No. 1599, para. 1954, supra.

1957   —— **breach—effect on action for damages for fraud**

The plaintiff paid a deposit in Spain for a house there to the defendants, who purported to be selling it as agents for the owner. It was agreed that the balance of the purchase price would be paid into the defendant's bank account in England, and this was done. The plaintiff, however, failed to obtain the necessary Treasury permission to pay the money to the defendants, who were resident outside the scheduled territories, since she was unaware of the requirements of the Exchange Control Act 1947. The defendants were unable to give the plaintiff any title to the house and they then disappeared. On discovering that she had been swindled, the plaintiff claimed damages for fraud. The defendants contended that she was unable to recover any money paid because the transaction by which the money had been paid was in breach of the 1947 Act. *Held*, although the plaintiff breached the provisions of the Exchange Control Act when she failed to obtain Treasury permission to pay the money to the defendants, that breach had not been deliberate as the plaintiff was unaware of the existence of the Act. As the plaintiff's action was in tort for damages for fraud, and not a claim in contract for the return of her money, public policy did not prevent the court from allowing the plaintiff compensation. She was therefore entitled to recover the sum that she had paid the defendants, her travelling expenses and damages for the distress caused by the fraud.

SHELLEY V PADDOCK [1978] 3 All ER 129 (Queen's Bench Division: BRISTOW J).

1958   —— purchase of foreign currency—cheque card

The Exchange Control (Purchase of Foreign Currency) (Amendment) Order 1978, S.I. 1978 No. 756 (in force on 19th June 1978), amends the Exchange Control (Purchase of Foreign Currency) Order 1970, as amended. The 1970 Order exempts from the Exchange Control Act 1947, s. 1 (1) the purchase abroad by travellers resident in the United Kingdom of foreign currency for travel expenditure if the traveller holds a cheque card issued by a bank named in the Schedule. The present order adds two banks to that Schedule.

1959   The Exchange Control (Purchase of Foreign Currency) (Amendment) (No. 2) Order 1978, S.I. 1978 No. 1683 (in force on 18th December 1978), further amends the Exchange Control (Purchase of Foreign Currency) Order 1970. The 1970 Order exempts from the Exchange Control Act 1947, s. 1 (1), the purchase abroad by travellers resident in the United Kingdom of foreign currency for travel expenditure if the traveller holds a cheque card issued by a bank named in the Schedule. The present order adds a new bank to that Schedule.

1960   —— securities—dealings in breach of exchange regulations— enforceability

See *Swiss Bank Corporation v Lloyds Bank Ltd*, para. 1965.

1961   Incomes and wealth

The standing Royal Commission on the distribution of income and wealth have published the following reports since it was appointed in 1974.

No. 1: Initial report on the standing reference (Cmnd. 6171) 1975.
No. 2: Income from companies and its distribution (Cmnd. 6172) 1975.
No. 3: Higher incomes from employment (Cmnd. 6383) 1976.
No. 4: Second report on the standing reference (Cmnd. 6626) 1976.
No. 5: Third report on the standing reference (Cmnd. 6999) 1977.
No. 6: Lower incomes (Cmnd. 7175) 1978.

1962   Interest—interest on debt—Law Commission report

See para. 1760.

1963   —— lump sum payment in lieu—whether interest payable

The plaintiff executor of an estate was suing the sole executor of another estate for the balance of an unpaid debt. In Order 14 proceedings judgment was given for the plaintiff. A question arose as to whether interest could be awarded under the Law Reform (Miscellaneous Provisions) Act 1934, s. 3 (1). The contract under which the debt arose provided that the sum of £25 per annum should be paid in lieu of interest. It was argued that this provision for interest in the contract prevented interest being awarded under the Act. *Held*, money paid in lieu of interest was, of necessity, not itself interest. There was therefore no provision for interest in the contract. Interest could be awarded.

TOMKINS V TOMKINS (1978) Times, 24th May (Chancery Division: MEGARRY V-C).

1964   International Finance Corporation—payment to capital stock

The International Finance Corporation (Further Payment to Capital Stock) Order 1978, S.I. 1978 No. 1152 (in force on 1st August 1978), provides for the further payment to the Corporation of a specified sum by way of subscription to an issue of shares increasing its authorised stock.

1965   Loan—contract to repay out of specific property—interest of lender in property

The plaintiffs, a Swiss bank lent the defendant company a sum of money subject to Bank of England exchange control conditions. The money was used to acquire securities in a new bank. These were then held by the defendant company's parent company as authorised depositaries. The transaction was subject to Bank of England conditions, one of which was that the loan was to be repaid out of the securities. Later in the year, the parent company was forced to seek financial assistance from the defendant bank and deposited the securities with the bank. The defendant company then executed a charge in favour of the bank on all stocks and shares lodged with the bank. Subsequently, the parent company went into liquidation and when the Swiss bank demanded repayment of the loan out of the securities, the defendant company, without the Swiss bank's knowledge or consent, sold the securities and deposited the proceeds with the defendant bank. The Swiss bank brought an action against the defendant bank, the defendant company and its parent company, contending that it had an equitable interest in the securities, which took priority over the defendant bank's subsequent charge. *Held*, both at the date when the defendant bank took its charge and at the present time, the Swiss bank was entitled to specific performance of the loan agreement requiring service and repayment out of the securities. Accordingly, they had an equitable interest in them that prevailed over the defendant bank's charge. If a contract bound a party to pay a debt out of specific property, such a contract was enforceable and created an equitable interest in the property whether or not the parties knew or intended that legal consequence to follow. Further, the Swiss bank's right prevailed over the defendant bank's charge since that charge was void for illegality as being a breach of the Exchange Control Act 1947, s. 16 and the Swiss bank was entitled, so long as the Bank of England condition prevailed to insist on the repayment of its loan and interest out of the securities. The defendant bank was also liable in damages for converting the securities into sterling with the knowledge that by so doing they were interfering with the Swiss bank's contractual right to have the securities applied in repayment of their loan.

Swiss Bank Corporation v Lloyds Bank Ltd (1978) Times, 16th May (Chancery Division: Browne-Wilkinson J).

1966   Moneylender—temporary loan—whether lender required to be registered

An estate agent, who had a large sum of money, wished to make temporary use of it whilst looking for a suitable long term investment. He knew a solicitor who could put him in touch with the owners of suitable properties on which money could be lent, and he made temporary loans on these properties. He was unable to recover loans he had made to one debtor, but his claim for repayment against the debtor was dismissed at first instance, as the judge held that he was an unregistered moneylender within the meaning of the Moneylenders Act 1900. The estate agent appealed. *Held*, allowing the appeal, on the particular facts of the case the appellant was not a moneylender within the meaning of the Act, in particular considering that the loans were only temporary, pending long term investment, and that they had been made through the solicitor as intermediary.

Offen v Smith (1978) Times, 15th November (Court of Appeal: Lord Denning MR, Bridge and Templeman LJJ).

1967   Premium savings bonds

The Premium Savings Bonds (Amendment) Regulations 1978, S.I. 1978 No. 1297 (in force on 11th September 1978) amend the Premium Savings Bonds Regulations 1972 by increasing the maximum permitted holding of premium savings bonds to 3,000 bond units.

1968   Price code
See EMERGENCY CONTROLS.

1969   Saving certificates
The Savings Certificates (Amendment) Regulations 1978, S.I. 1978 No. 788 (in force on 1st July 1978), amend the Savings Certificates Regulations 1972, by increasing the maximum permitted holding of the holding of the 14th Issue of National Savings Certificates from 1,000 to 3,000 unit certificates.

1970   The Savings Certificates (Amendment) (No. 2) Regulations 1978, S.I. 1978 No. 1334 (in force on 2nd October 1978), amend the Savings Certificates Regulations 1972 by increasing the maximum permitted holding of the 15th Issue of National Savings Certificates to seventy (purchase price £700).

1971   The Savings Certificates (Amendment) (No. 3) Regulations 1978, S.I. 1978 No. 1885 (in force on 29th January 1979), amend the Savings Certificate Regulations 1972 by providing that the maximum permitted holding of the 18th Issue of National Savings Certificates will be 150.

1972   Stocks—stocks held by trustee savings banks
See para. 214.

MORTGAGE

Halsbury's Laws of England (3rd edn.), Vol. 27, paras. 236–896

1973   Article
The Need to Reform the English Law of Mortgages, Paul Jackson: (1978) 94 LQR 571.

1974   Mortgagee—duty of care—extent of duty—whether limited to mortgagor
See *Barclays Bank Ltd v Thienel and Thienel*, para. 3059.

1975   —— —— title deeds—liability for loss
The vendor mortgaged his property to a third party, which received the title deeds as equitable mortgagee. The vendor subsequently contracted to sell the property, but was unable to show title because the deeds had been lost. He was held to be liable in damages and sought indemnity from the third party on the ground that the third party was negligent in losing the title deeds. *Held*, the third party was under no duty of care in relation to the title deeds because as mortgagee it was in law the absolute owner of them subject only to the condition of re-conveyance on repayment. The vendor could seek equitable relief for lost title deeds, but only on redemption. Accordingly, he was not entitled to indemnity.

BROWNING V HANDILAND GROUP LTD AND BUSH INVESTMENTS TRUST LTD (THIRD PARTY) (1976) 35 P & CR 345 (Chancery Division: JUDGE RUBIN sitting as a deputy High Court Judge). *Gilligan and Nugent v National Bank Ltd* [1901] 2 IR 513, DC applied.

1976   —— reliance on valuation—ensuing loss—whether valuers negligent
See *Corisand Investments Ltd v Druce and Co*, para. 3091.

1977   Remedies of mortgagee—action for possession—contents of affidavit in support

In an action by a building society for possession of property mortgaged to it, certain questions arose as to the particulars required to be contained in the affidavit in support. *Held*, RSC Ord. 88, r. 6 (3) (b), in requiring "the amount of the repayments" to be stated, meant that the affidavit should state as at its date the total amount of repayments of principal which had been made under the mortgage. Under r. 6 (4), the affidavit had to give "particulars of every person who to the best of the plaintiff's knowledge is in possession of the mortgaged property". It also had to comply with RSC Ord. 41, r. 51 (1), by containing only such facts as the deponent was able of his own knowledge to prove. Where the plaintiff was a building society, the affidavit had to contain a statement by the deponent showing his place in the society and an unqualified assertion giving the necessary particulars as to the persons in possession to the best of the society's knowledge. The deponent was not required to give the sources of his information or belief.

NATIONWIDE BUILDING SOCIETY v BATEMAN [1978] 1 All ER 999 (Chancery Division: GOULDING J).

The effect of this decision in relation to the particulars of repayment required has been nullified by S.I. 1977 No. 1955, 1977 Halsbury's Abr para. 2150, which amends RSC Ord. 88, r. 6 (3) (b) by substituting "the amount of the periodic repayments required to be made" for "the amount of the repayments".

1978   —— —— effect of unregistered interest of mortgagor's wife

A legal charge over registered residential premises contained a covenant by the mortgagor to pay on demand to the mortgagee, the plaintiff bank, all moneys due at any time. The mortgagor's liabilities to the bank as a guarantor were also included. The bank demanded payment by the mortgagor of the debts of a company in liquidation for which the mortgagor had acted as guarantor. The mortgagor was unable to pay, and the bank sought possession of the mortgaged premises. The mortgagor's wife claimed that she was entitled to remain in possession. She advanced her claim on the basis of her contribution to the purchase price of the house. The property, she said, was held on trust for sale for husband and wife equally, or in shares corresponding to their respective contributions. As a tenant in common in equity entitled to possession and being in actual occupation, she was entitled by virtue of Land Registration Act 1925, s. 70 (1) (g), to an overriding interest which subsisted at the date of the legal charge to the bank and at the date of registration of that charge. The bank took the charge subject to the wife's overriding interest. *Held*, for the purpose of s. 70 (1) (g) "actual occupation" did not include occupation by a wife or husband of the legal owner. A spouse had been given rights capable of registration under the Matrimonial Homes Act 1967. If the wife's contention is this case was allowed, it would make nonsense of the 1967 Act. The wife was not entitled to remain in occupation. Summary judgment for possession would be ordered against both husband and wife in favour of the bank.

WILLIAMS & GLYN'S BANK v BOLAND (1978) 122 Sol Jo 471 (Chancery Division: TEMPLEMAN J).

1979   A beneficiary under a trust purchased the lease of a flat which he intended to use as his matrimonial home. On completion of the purchase he executed a legal charge on the flat in favour of the trustees. The beneficiary's wife alleged that she had contributed to the purchase and understood that the property was to be conveyed into their joint names but this had not been done. When the beneficiary became bankrupt the trustees sought possession of the flat. The wife claimed that as she had been in actual occupation at the time the charge was registered she had an overriding interest under the Land Registration Act 1925, s. 70 (1) (g). *Held*, in registered as well as unregistered land a mortgagor's spouse could not be in actual occupation at the same time as the mortgagor. Thus as the beneficiary had been in actual occupation when the charge was registered the wife had no overriding interest. She had a registrable minor interest because he had held the flat on trust for both of them but no such interest had been registered. The trustees were therefore entitled to possession.

BIRD v SYME THOMPSON [1978] 3 All ER 1027 (Chancery Division: TEMPLEMAN J). *Caunce v Caunce* [1969] 1 All ER 722 applied.

1980 ——— ——— **property subject to tenancy**

See *Quennell v Maltby*, para. 1736.

NATIONAL HEALTH SERVICE

Halsbury's Laws of England (3rd edn.), Vol. 27, paras. 981–1186

1981   Boards of Governors

The National Health Service (Preservation of Boards of Governors) Order 1979, S.I. 1979 No. 51 (in force on 22nd February 1979), preserves from abolition under the National Health Service Reorganisation Act 1973, s. 14, the Boards of Governors of the teaching hospitals specified in the order. This preservation will extend until 31st March 1982 and applies in relation to the Boards' various statutory provisions with or without modification.

1982   Central Health Services Council

The Central Health Services Council (Variation of Constitution) Amendment Order 1978, S.I. 1978 No. 339 (in force on 10th April 1978), amends the Central Health Services Council (Variation of Constitution Order 1974, 1974 Halsbury's Abr para. 2211, by increasing the minimum and maximum numbers of members of the Council to take account of two additional nominated members, who are the President of the Royal College of Radiologists and the Dean of the Faculty of Anaesthetists. This Order has been revoked by The Central Health Services Council (Variation of Constitution) Amendment (No. 2) Order 1978, see para. 1983.

1983   The Central Health Services Council (Variation of Constitution) Amendment (No. 2) Order 1978, S. I. 1978 No. 489 (in force on 1st May 1978), revokes the Central Health Services Council (Variation of Constitution) Amendment Order 1978, see para. 1982, and amends the National Health Service Act 1977, Sched. 4, by increasing the maximum and minimum numbers of members of the Council to take account of two additional nominated members, who are the President of the Royal College of Radiologists and the Dean of the Faculty of Anaesthetists.

1984   Charges

The National Health Service (Dental and Optical Charges) Regulations 1978, S.I. 1978 No. 950 (in force on 7th August 1978), consolidate provisions relating to charges for dental treatment and dental and optical appliances formerly contained in the National Health Service (Charges) Regulations 1971 and other regulations, which are revoked. No changes are made to the amounts of the charges. The regulations also amend the National Health Service (Charges for Drugs and Appliances) Regulations 1974, 1974 Halsbury's Abr para. 2216, by inserting into them provision for the making and recovery of charges for fabric supports and wigs, and for the remission and repayment of such charges, which was formerly contained in the 1971 Regulations. The amounts of the charges are unchanged.

1985   Community health councils—term of office

The National Health Service (Community Health Council) Amendment Regulations 1978, S.I. 1978 No. 21 (in force on 8th February 1978), further amend the National Health Service (Community Health Councils) Regulations 1973 by altering the date of termination of office of members of Community Health Councils in England from 30th June to 31st August and extending the period of office of existing members from 30th June to 31st August.

1986 Health Authorities—membership

The National Health Service (Health Authorities: Membership) Amendment Regulations 1978, S.I. 1978 No. 228 (in force on 21st March 1978), amend the National Health Service (Health Authorities: Membership) Regulations 1977, 1977 Halsbury's Abr para. 1940, by altering the provisions governing the tenure of office of chairmen of Area Health Authorities in Wales so that appointments can be made for periods of less than four years as has been the case with chairmen of Area Health Authorities in England.

1987 Mental health

See MENTAL HEALTH.

1988 Payments by health authorities—reimbursement of wages of doctor's staff—employment by doctor of member of his family—discretion of Secretary of State

A doctor sought a declaration that a term in his contract for services preventing him from receiving a subsidy to cover much of the cost of employing his wife or any other member of his family in his practice, when it was available to pay other staff, was unjust and oppressive. *Held*, although under the Health Services and Public Health Act 1968 the reimbursement of the wages of staff was a matter for the Secretary of State's discretion, the exercise of this discretion had been arbitrary and amounted to a blanket denial of reimbursement in respect of members of doctors' families. The implications and moral effect of that denial had not been properly considered and therefore the Secretary of State's decision had been vitiated. The offending term would be removed from the doctor's contract. Damages were not, however, payable because the term remained valid until proved otherwise.

GLANVILL v SECRETARY OF STATE FOR HEALTH AND SOCIAL SERVICES (1978) 122 Sol Jo 611 (Queen's Bench Division: TALBOT J).

The Health Services and Public Health Act 1968 has been consolidated by the National Health Services Act 1977, see 1977 Halsbury's Abr para. 1945.

1989 Prescription Pricing Authority

The Prescription Pricing Authority Constitution Order 1978, S.I. 1978 No. 331 (in force on 1st April 1978), provides a new Constitution for the Prescription Pricing Authority established by the Prescription Pricing Authority (Establishment and Constitution) Order 1974 as amended, 1974 Halsbury's Abr para. 2247 and 1977 Halsbury's Abr para. 1948. It supersedes that Order with amendments appropriate to the changes in the constitution. These changes mainly involve a reduction in the representation of Family Practitioner Committees, an increase in representation of medical practitioners, and representation of Community Health Councils, academic, research or other expertise, the Department of Health and Social Security and the staff of the Authority.

1990 —— regulations

The Prescription Pricing Authority Regulations 1978, S.I. 1978 No. 332 (in force on 1st April 1978), provide for the consultations to be carried out by the Secretary of State before making appointments to the Prescription Pricing Authority; for the appointment and tenure of office of members; for the termination of and disqualification for office; and the employment of officers by, and the proceedings of, the Authority.

1991 Professions supplementary to medicine

The National Health Service (Professions Supplementary to Medicine) Amendment

Regulations 1978, S.I. 1978 No. 1090 (in force on 1st October 1978), amend the National Health Service (Professions Supplementary to Medicine) Regulations 1974, 1974 Halsbury's Abr para. 2248, relating to employment by health authorities of persons as chiropodists, dietitians, medical laboratory technicians, occupational therapists, physiotherapists, radiographers or remedial gymnasts. A person not registered under the Professions Supplementary to Medicine Act 1960 may be employed by a health authority only if he has never been so registered and was similarly employed on 29th June 1964 and immediately before 1st April 1974.

1992   Superannuation

See para. 2100.

1993   Transfer of trust property

The National Health Service (Transfer of Trust Property—Tooting Bec Hospital) Order 1978, S.I. 1978 No. 1072 (in force on 25th August 1978), provides for the transfer of certain trust property held by South West Thames Regional Health Authority and Merton, Sutton and Wandsworth Area Health Authority (Teaching) to South East Thames Regional Health Authority and Lambeth, Southwark and Lewisham Area Health Authority (Teaching) respectively by reason of a change in the arrangements for the administration of Tooting Bec Hospital.

NEGLIGENCE

Halsbury's Laws of England (3rd edn.), Vol. 28, paras. 1–120

1994   Article

Negligence—A Difficult Landmark, Eric L. Newsome (circumstances in which public authorities should owe a duty in civil law giving rise to an action for damages by a private individual): 128 NLJ 802.

Tort Demolishes Contract in New Construction, I. N. Duncan Wallace (the implications arising for the law of negligence from the liability of developers, builders, designers, contractors and local authority inspectors for defective buildings): (1978) 94 LQR 61.

1995   Barrister—liability for negligence

See *Saif Ali v Sydney Mitchell & Co*, para. 241.

1996   Compensation for personal injury—means of payment

The Royal Commission on Civil Liability and Compensation for Personal Injury (chairman Lord Pearson) has published a report: Cmnd. 7054 (3 vols.). For a summary see para. 1757.

1997   Contributory negligence—defence not pleaded—whether plea necessary

The vehicle which the plaintiff was driving ran into the rear of a parked articulated vehicle. It was dark and the articulated vehicle was unlit. He brought an action for damages for personal injuries. The driver of the articulated vehicle filed no defence and was debarred from defending after failing to comply with a court order to deliver a defence. The judge found that the plaintiff was one-third to blame for the accident and reduced the damages accordingly. On appeal by the plaintiff, *held*, in the absence of pleading by the defendant, the court had no jurisdiction to make a finding of contributory negligence on the plaintiff's part. The defence was only available if it was pleaded. The appeal would be allowed.

FOOKES v SLAYTOR [1979] 1 All ER 137 (Court of Appeal: STAMP and ORR LJJ and SIR DAVID CAIRNS). *Taylor v Simon Carves Ltd* 1958 SLT (Sh Ct) 23 applied.

1998   **Duty of care—architect—duty to advise clients of planning requirements**

See *B.L. Holdings Ltd v Robert J. Wood and Partners*, para. 267.

1999   —— **bailee—duty of garage in relation to customer's vehicle**

See *Cowan v Blackwill Motor Caravan Conversions Ltd*, para. 203.

2000   —— **bank—duty owed to surety**

See *Barclays Bank Ltd v Thienel and Thienel*, para. 205.

2001   —— **collision involving stolen car**

Canada

The defendant escaped from a juvenile detention centre and stole a car and its keys from a garage. The garage reported the theft of the car but not of the keys. When the defendant attempted to use a stolen credit card at a service station, the attendant reported it to the police, who gave chase. A high speed chase ensued, resulting in the defendant colliding with a car driven by the plaintiff. At the time of the collision the police car had slowed down. The plaintiff claimed that the defendant, the police, the juvenile authorities and the garage were all negligent. *Held*, the defendant was clearly negligent. The police were not liable as they had discontinued their active pursuit and had driven with due care having regard to the circumstances. The juvenile authorities were not liable because the accident on the day following the defendant's escape was too far removed from the alleged negligence of custodial care. The garage was not liable as the accident was too remote and could not have been reasonably foreseen.

O'REILLY v C AND THE CANADIAN INDEMNITY CO [1978] 3 WWR 145 (Court of Queen's Bench of Manitoba). *Home Office v Dorset Yacht Co Ltd* [1970] AC 1004, HL considered.

2002   —— **developers and builders—house constructed on steep hillside—landslip**

See *Batty v Metropolitan Property Realisations Ltd*, para. 2433.

2003   —— **driver—disqualified driver—duty to passenger knowing of disqualification**

See *Harrison v Jackson*, para, 2029.

2004   —— —— **emergency vehicle**

See *O'Reilly v C and The Canadian Indemnity Co*, para. 2001.

2005   —— **duty owed to unborn child—extent of duty**

A pregnant woman was involved in an accident; her baby was born prematurely with brain damage which was attributed to injuries sustained in the accident. An action for damages was brought on behalf of the child. Although admitting his negligence, the defendant at first contended that he owed no duty of care towards an unborn child and in any event, the damage suffered was too remote. Subsequently however, the defendant admitted liability and conceded that the child had a good cause of action at common law. Accordingly judgment was entered for damages in favour of the child.

WILLIAMS v LUFF (1978) 122 Sol Jo 164 (Queen's Bench Division: O'CONNOR J).

2006   —— **employer—employee injured in payroll robbery—foreseeability**

See *Charlton v Forrest Printing Ink Co Ltd*, para. 1066.

2007 —— highway authority—road works—obliteration of traffic sign

See *Bird v Pearce*, para. 1467.

2008 —— insurance broker—duty to ensure that assured properly covered

See *McNealy v Pennine Insurance Co Ltd*, para. 1647.

2009 —— —— failure to notify insured of cancellation of policy

See *Cherry Ltd v Allied Insurance Brokers Ltd*, para. 1646.

2010 —— investment counsellor

Canada

Clients of an investment dealer brought an action against the dealer's sales representative alleging that he was in breach of his fiduciary duty in that he had made misrepresentations or negligent misstatements as to the prospects and potential of a company and its shares which influenced the clients to purchase the shares, resulting in financial loss. *Held*, the representative had placed himself in the position of an investment counsellor by representing that he had inside information as to the company and there was thus a fiduciary relationship between the parties imposing a duty on the representative to advise his clients carefully, fully, honestly and in good faith. He was in breach of that duty by making negligent statements. In addition, he was under a duty of care not to be negligent in giving information and advice, the duty arising out of a relationship of the nature described in *Hedley Byrne & Co Ltd v Heller & Partners Ltd*. The representative had a special skill in the investment business and was negligent in the advice or information he gave or failed to give, thereby causing the clients' financial losses.

ELDERKIN V MERRILL LYNCH, ROYAL SECURITIES LTD (1977) 80 DLR (3d) 313 (Supreme Court of Nova Scotia). *Hedley Byrne & Co Ltd v Heller & Partners Ltd* [1964] AC 465, HL, applied.

2011 —— local authority—duty to inspect foundations of building—liability for failure properly to inspect

See *Batty v Metropolitan Property Realisations Ltd*, para. 2433.

2012 —— occupier

See *Hosie v Arbroath Football Club Ltd*, para. 2024.

2013 —— owner of motor vehicle—loan to inexperienced driver—duty to instruct

Canada

The 16 year old defendant allowed the 17 year old plaintiff to ride his powerful motor cycle. The plaintiff, who was unlicensed and who had little experience of motor cycles, lost control of the machine and was seriously injured in the subsequent accident. The plaintiff sued the defendant for negligence, alleging that he had not been properly instructed in the use of the cycle and had not been warned of the dangers inherent in its use. *Held*, the accident was due to the plaintiff's incompetence and not to any mechanical fault. As the defendant was aware of the plaintiff's lack of experience he should not have allowed him to ride the motor cycle without proper instruction. A person who entrusted a vehicle to an inexperienced driver ought to have known that there was a risk of injury, and owed him a duty of care to minimise that risk. Although the plaintiff and defendant were teenagers of equal status there was no evidence to suggest that, because of his youth, the defendant was incapable of appreciating that the plaintiff's inexperience could lead to an accident. The defendant was accordingly liable in negligence, but his liability would be reduced by 50 per cent as the plaintiff had contributed to the accident by riding the motor cycle when he knew he was not properly qualified or experienced.

STERMER v LAWSON (1978) 79 DLR (3d) 366 (Supreme Court of British Columbia).

2014 —— **owner of stolen vehicle**

See *O'Reilly v C and the Canadian Indemnity Co*, para. 2001.

2015 —— **prison authority**

See *O'Reilly v C and The Canadian Indemnity Co*, para. 2001; *Egerton v Home Office*, para. 2238.

2016 —— **school—duty owed to pupil—when duty owed**

Australia

A child was struck on the head while playing games at school. The accident occurred at 8.50 a.m. Children were not supervised before 9.00 a.m. although the school gates were open from 8.15 a.m. onwards. The child claimed damages in negligence from the headmaster and his employers. *Held*, the headmaster had a duty to ensure reasonable measures were taken to prevent physical injury to his pupils. In the absence of supervision, the accident was foreseeable; with adequate supervision it might have been prevented. It was no defence to plead that the accident occurred outside school hours, because the duty extended to all times during which care should reasonably have been taken. Accordingly, the child was entitled to damages.

GEYER v DOWNS (1977) 17 ALR 408 (High Court of Australia).

2017 —— **solicitor—attestation of will**

See *Whittingham v Crease & Co*, para. 2741.

2018 —— —— **conveyancing—measure of damages**

See *Rumsey v Owen White & Catlin*, para. 1670.

2019 —— **valuer**

See *Corisand Investments v Druce*, para. 3091.

2020 **Fatal accident—damages—loss of wife—entitlement to projected cost of housekeeper in lieu of actual loss**

See *Bailey v Barking and Havering Area Health Authority*, para. 851.

2021 **Limitation of actions—expiry of limitation period—court's power to override time limits**

See *Jones v G. D. Searle & Co Ltd*, para. 1796.

2022 **Obstruction of highway—works by electricity board—duty of care to pedestrians**

At dusk one evening the seventy-eight-year-old plaintiff was walking along the pavement. She tripped and fell over the edge of a metal plate which workmen employed by the electricity board had fitted over a hole they had dug in the pavement. The plate projected one-eighth of an inch above the pavement. The plaintiff was awarded damages for personal injuries due to the board's negligence. On appeal, *held*, on the evidence the judge was entitled to find that the metal plate, which projected above the pavement, was an unexpected danger to users of the pavement. The case could be distinguished from cases where injury was caused by the unevenness of flagstones, since the plaintiff was accustomed to the state of the pavement and the metal plate presented a new and unexpected hazard.   The appeal would be dismissed.

PITMAN v SOUTHERN ELECTRICITY BOARD [1978] LS Gaz R 310 (Court of Appeal: MEGAW, LAWTON and BROWNE LJJ).

2023   Occupier's liability—duty owed to neighbour—liability for vandals

Scotland

The plaintiff claimed damages in negligence for loss and damages caused to his printing and stationery business by vandalism in the tenement blocks in which his business was situated.   He claimed that the council, as owners of the tenements, should have secured the empty flats in the tenements to prevent unauthorised entry and subsequent damage to neighbouring property.   The council contended that there was no precedent for the claim that a property owner should fortify his property for the security of adjoining property.   *Held*, although there was no evidence that such a duty existed in law, the court had to consider the proposition in *Donoghue v Stevenson* [1932] All ER 1, that "the categories of negligence are never closed."   In the present case the council was aware that the plaintiff's premises were situated in areas where there was a high risk of vandalism.   In such circumstances there was a duty on property owners or occupiers to take reasonable care to secure their property from vandalism which would affect adjoining properties.

EVANS v GLASGOW DISTRICT COUNCIL 1978 SLT (Notes) 8 (Outer House).

2024   —— duty owed to visitor

Scotland

The plaintiff, who had been waiting to gain entrance to a football match, was knocked down and trampled upon by a crowd of football fans.   The crowd had broken down a gate and surged through, knocking over the plaintiff.   The plaintiff brought an action for damages for personal injuries against the owners as occupiers of the football ground.   He claimed that the owners owed a duty of care to all people entering the grounds in respect of dangers due to the state of the premises.   The gate was a danger as there was evidence to establish that it was not in perfect condition and did not possess a safety device to give it added security; the occupiers therefore knew or ought to have known that it might give way under attack by a crowd. *Held*, it was reasonably foreseeable by the occupiers that an unruly crowd might attempt to force open the gate.   There was a sufficient link between the defects in the gate and the plaintiff's injury.   As the crowd's behaviour could not be regarded as a *novus actus interveniens* breaking the causal link, the occupiers were liable since they had failed to maintain the gate reasonably.   Accordingly, the plaintiff would be awarded damages.

HOSIE v ARBROATH FOOTBALL CLUB LTD 1978 SLT 122 (Outer House).

2025   Product liability—defective towing coupling—liability of owner and driver of vehicle and manufacturer of coupling

The plaintiff's husband and son were killed in a road accident when their car was struck by a trailer which had become detached from a Land Rover when a faulty coupling snapped.   The Land Rover was owned by the first defendant and was being driven by his employee, the second defendant.   The defective coupling had been manufactured by the third defendants and sold to the fourth defendant, who had supplied it to the first defendant.   The plaintiff claimed damages in tort from all four defendants.   The first defendant brought in the fourth defendant as a third party on the ground that the coupling was not fit for the purpose for which it was sold under the Sale of Goods Act 1893, s. 14.   *Held*, the first and second defendants were liable in tort in that they had not taken adequate precautions to ensure the safety of the coupling, and had continued to use it over a period of months in which it was damaged.   The third defendants were liable for faulty and dangerous manufacture of the coupling; a skilled engineer could have foreseen possible dangers from its use.   The fourth defendants were not liable in tort because, as retailers, they had no reason to doubt the suitability of the coupling and were under no duty to inspect it. The fourth defendants were in breach of s. 14 of the Sale of Goods Act 1893, but the first defendant was not entitled to the damages he claimed because it was not contemplated in the contract that he would continue to use the coupling after it was broken.

LAMBERT V LEWIS, LARKIN, DIXON-BATE LTD AND LEXMEAD (BASINGSTOKE) LTD [1978] 1 Lloyd's Rep 610 (Queen's Bench Division: STOCKER J).

2026   Road accident—contributory negligence—duty of passenger in motor vehicle to ensure sobriety of driver

In reducing the damages to be awarded to a road accident victim from £134,000 to £107,000, JUPP J stated that the victim had been guilty of contributory negligence in travelling with the defendant driver knowing he had been drinking. There was an obligation on passengers to ensure that their drivers remained abstemious: Times, 19th July 1978.

2027   —— knowledge of defective brakes—failure to wear seat belt

A passenger was injured when the car in which he was travelling was involved in an accident. The car had no operative foot-brake and the passenger was not wearing a seat belt. The passenger contended that his injuries were due to the driver's negligence. *Held*, the driver was negligent in approaching a corner too fast and in driving when he knew there was no foot-brake. However, the passenger also knew that there was no foot-brake and had failed to wear a seat belt. The driver was deprived of the defence of volenti non fit injuria by the Road Traffic Act 1972, s. 148 (3), but since failure to wear a seat belt was a direct cause of the passenger's injury and he had shown a want of care for his own safety in accepting a lift in a defective car, he was guilty of contributory negligence. The blame would be apportioned sixty per cent to the driver and forty per cent to the passenger.

GREGORY V KELLY (1978) Times, 15th March (Queen's Bench Division: KENNETH JONES J).

2028   —— driver—duty of care

See *O'Reilly v C and The Canadian Indemnity Co*, para. 2001.

2029   —— —— passenger aiding and abetting offence

Australia

A road accident was caused by the negligence of a driver who was disqualified from holding a driving licence. His passenger, who knew of the disqualification, claimed damages for the injuries he sustained during the accident. The trial judge accepted the driver's contention that he owed no duty of care to the passenger because the latter had aided and abetted his offence. The passenger appealed. *Held*, there was a distinction between cases where the offence involved was the lack of a licence or permit and those where a more serious offence, such as theft, had been committed. A negligent driver who had been disqualified from holding a driving licence was not absolved from his duty of care towards a passenger who knew of the disqualification.

HARRISON V JACKSON (1977) 16 SASR 182 (Supreme Court of South Australia).

2030   —— narrow road—whether bus owners bound to take special precautions

The defendants operated a bus service on a country road. Vehicles more than six feet six inches wide were prohibited on the road, but the defendants' buses, which were wider than this, were excepted from the prohibition. One dark evening the plaintiff's car collided with a bus going in the opposite direction. The bus had on its headlights, sidelights and interior lights. The plaintiff alleged that the defendants had been negligent in permitting the bus to be driven on the road without taking special precautions, for example the erection of warning signs, to warn other road users. The defendants were held to have been negligent because they had failed to give special instructions to the driver so that he could take such precautions. On appeal, *held*, any such precautions were either impractical, unlawful or not for the defendants to take. The bus had been driven in a reasonable manner and had been clearly visible. There had been adequate room for the plaintiff's car to pass it safely if he had been alert and therefore negligence had not been established. The appeal would be allowed.

THROWER V THAMES VALLEY AND ALDERSHOT BUS CO LTD [1978] RTR 271 (Court of Appeal: MEGAW, ROSKILL and CUMMING-BRUCE LJJ).

2031   Shipbuilding—safety regulations—extent of employer's duty

See *Lindsay v Vickers*, para. 1457.

2032   Vicarious liability—master and servant—effect of bye-law excluding liability—Singapore

The deceased had been a member of a gang of stevedores, all of whom were employed by the Singapore Port Authority. While the gang was engaged in loading a cargo, the deceased was injured, and subsequently died, as the result of an accident caused by the negligence of another workman. His administrator brought an action for personal damages against the port authority. The port authority disclaimed liability under one of its by-laws, which stated that workmen engaged in the loading or discharging of ships were under the superintendence of the ship's officers. *Held*, the wording of the by-law was not sufficient to discharge the defendants' vicarious liability at common law for the negligent acts of their employees. The appeal would be allowed.

KARUPPAN BHOOMIDAS V PORT OF SINGAPORE AUTHORITY [1978] 1 WLR 189 (Privy Council: LORD SIMON OF GLAISDALE, LORD SALMON, LORD KEITH OF KINKEL, SIR GARFIELD BARWICK and SIR RICHARD WILDE).

NORTHERN IRELAND

Halsbury's Laws of England (4th edn.), Vol. 8, paras. 1637–1647

2033   Northern Ireland Act 1974—interim period extension

The Northern Ireland Act 1974 (Interim Period Extension) Order 1978, S.I. 1978 No. 957 (in force on 10th July 1978), extends until 16th July 1979 the period specified in the Northern Ireland Act 1974, s. 1 (4), as extended by S.I. 1977 No. 1165, 1977 Halsbury's Abr para. 1980, for the operation of the temporary provisions for the government of Northern Ireland contained in Sch. 1 to the Act.

2034   Northern Ireland (Emergency Provisions) Act 1978

The Northern Ireland (Emergency Provisions) Act 1978 consolidates with certain exceptions the Northern Ireland (Emergency Provisions) Act 1973, the Northern Ireland (Young Persons) Act 1974, 1974 Halsbury's Abr para, 2386 and the Northern Ireland (Emergency Provisions) (Amendment) Act 1975, 1975 Halsbury's Abr para. 2417. The Act, which applies to Northern Ireland only, received the royal assent on 23rd March 1978; ss. 32, 33 came into force on that date, the remainder came into force on 1st June 1978.

2035   —— continuance

The Northern Ireland (Emergency Provisions) Act 1978 (Continuance) Order 1978, S.I. 1978 No. 958 (in force on 25th July 1978), continued in force the temporary provisions of the Northern Ireland (Emergency Provisions) Act 1978 for a period of six months from 25th July 1978.

2036   The Northern Ireland (Emergency Provisions) Act 1978 (Continuance) (No. 2) Order 1978, S.I. 1978 No. 1865 (in force on 25th January 1979), continues in force the temporary provisions of the Northern Ireland (Emergency Provisions) Act 1978 for a period of six months from 25th January 1979.

NUISANCE

Halsbury's Laws of England (3rd edn.), Vol. 28, paras. 152–245

2037   Construction work—damage to adjoining premises—measure of damages

See *Dodd Properties (Kent) v Canterbury City Council*, para. 850.

2038   Escape—nuisance stemming from natural causes—liability of owners

Soil and tree stumps falling from the bank of an ancient hill fort, owned by the National Trust, damaged houses backing on to it. The falls, which were the result of natural causes, continued over a long period and a large crack appeared in the bank which caused the houseowners to fear that the bank would fall on to their houses. The National Trust refused to admit any liability. Following further falls the houseowners commenced proceedings against the National Trust for nuisance. Interlocutory relief was granted and the necessary work carried out to prevent further falls. The question for consideration by the court was whether there could be any liability where nuisance stemmed from natural causes rather than from something brought onto the land. *Held*, there was no distinction between land and something brought on to it. On the facts of this case there was danger on the National Trust land of which they were aware; they were under a duty to take reasonable steps to ensure there was no harm to the houseowners' land; and if they did not take these steps they were liable. As to the extent of the National Trust's liability, reasonable behaviour on their part required them to keep an eye on the bank. Any future damage caused by a fall would have to be paid for by the National Trust. As the necessary work had already been done there was no need for a mandatory injunction to deal with the bank. In addition the houseowners would be awarded damages.

LEAKEY v NATIONAL TRUST [1978] 3 All ER 234 (Queen's Bench Division: O'CONNOR J). *Goldman v Hargrave* [1967] 1 AC 645, PC and *Davey v Harrow Corporation* [1958] 1 QB 60, CA applied; *Radstock Co-operative and Industrial Society v Norton Radstock UDC* [1968] 1 Ch 605, CA not followed.

2039   Interests protected—use and enjoyment of land—television reception

Canada

The plaintiffs operated a cable television system relaying television to a locality. The defendants, a public utility, located an electrical power installation very close to the plaintiffs' operation, resulting in interference with the reception and transmission of television broadcast signals. The plaintiffs had to stop supplying one television channel to their subscribers, and brought an action against the defendants for damages for nuisance. *Held*, the plaintiffs' interest which had been interfered with was an interest in the use and enjoyment of their land, as they were unable to use and enjoy their property as before the defendants' intervention or to put it to its full business use. Television viewing, although only a recreational amenity, was an important incident of ordinary enjoyment of property and should be protected as such. The defendants knew or should have known that their activity would adversely affect the cable system. Although a public utility with wide statutory powers, the defendants were not immune from liability in tort. They were accordingly liable in nuisance.

NOR-VIDEO SERVICES LTD v ONTARIO HYDRO (1978) 19 OR (2d) 107 (Supreme Court of Ontario). *Bridlington Relay Ltd v Yorkshire Electricity Board* [1965] 1 All ER 264 disapproved.

OPEN SPACES AND HISTORIC BUILDINGS

Halsbury's Laws of England (3rd edn.), Vol. 28, paras. 246–441

2040   Conservation area—permission for demolition refused—relevance of proposed development

See *Richmond-upon-Thames London Borough Council v Secretary of State for the Environment*, para. 1159.

2041   Public pleasure grounds—byelaws for regulation of grounds—validity

See *Burnley Borough Council v England*, para. 1802.

PARLIAMENT

Halsbury's Laws of England (3rd edn.), Vol. 28, paras. 442–924

2042   House of Commons (Administration) Act 1978

The House of Commons (Administration) Act 1978 implements proposals relating to the organization and staffing of the House of Commons contained in the report of a committee of members of parliament appointed by the Speaker (HC 624). The Act received the royal assent on 20th July 1978 and came into force on that date except s. 2, Sch. 2, paras. 3–5 and Sch. 3 which came into force on 1st January 1979: s. 5.

Section 1 establishes the House of Commons Commission consisting of the Speaker, the Leader of the House of Commons, a member of parliament nominated by the Leader of the Opposition and three other members appointed by the House, none of whom may be ministers. The Commission must make an annual report to the House of Commons. The functions of the Commission are set out in s. 2. These include appointment and determination of terms and conditions of service of staff in the House Departments, defined by s. 4 as the departments of the Clerk of the House of Commons, the Speaker, the Serjeant at Arms, the library, the administration department and the department of the Official Report. Section 4 also provides for future changes in the number and functions of the departments and empowers the Commission to apply provisions of the Act to staff employed in or for the purposes of the House of Commons but who are not members of a House Department. Section 3 requires the Commission to present annual estimates of expenses of the House Departments and makes other financial provisions. Schedule 1 contains detailed provisions relating to the status of the Commission, membership, delegation of functions and procedure. Schedule 2 contains supplementary and consequential provisions and Sch. 3 repeals.

2043   Parliamentary Commissioner

The Parliamentary Commissioners Order 1978, S.I. 1978 No. 616 (in force on 25th May 1978), adds the Forestry Commission to the list of departments and authorities which are subject to investigation by the Parliamentary Commissioner for Administration.

2044   Parliamentary pensions—purchase of added years

The Parliamentary Pensions (Purchase of Added Years) Order 1978, S.I. 1978 No. 1837 (in force on 5th January 1979), makes provision for the purchase of added years of reckonable pensionable service by Members of the House of Commons. The number of years which may be purchased is set out in art. 10. Such purchase may be made by periodical payments, calculation of which is by reference to Schedule, table A, or by lump sum payments. The qualifying conditions and procedure for application to purchase added years are set out in arts. 4 and 5 in the case of purchase by periodical contributions and art. 8 in the case of purchase by lump sum payment. Art. 7 makes provision as to periodical contributions which are interrupted by a Member's death, ill-health or by his ceasing to be a member for other reasons, and provides for the resumption of payment by those who have ceased to be Members and who subsequently resume office.

2045   Parliamentary Pensions Act 1978

The Parliamentary Pensions Act 1978 makes improvements to the Parliamentary Contributory Pensions Scheme following the recommendations of the Review Board on Top Salaries. The Act received the royal assent on 2nd August 1978 and came into force on that date.

Section 1 provides for pensions for Members of Parliament of at least sixty years of age who have an aggregate total of twenty-five years' service and who do not wish to stand for re-election. Sections 2–5 provide for pensions for those forced to retire from Parliament through ill-health. Pensions differ according to whether the individual was a member or an office holder. Medical evidence must be adduced by those seeking pensions under these provisions: s. 5. Section 6 amends the Parliamentary and other Pensions Act 1972, relating to widowers' pensions. Section 7 provides for pensions for widows, widowers and children. Short-term pensions are also provided for widows etc. of members dying in service with less than four years' service: s. 8. Section 9 increases the pension for children of deceased members and also raises the age limit for receipt of such pensions. Death-in-service gratuities are now payable regardless of length of service: s. 10. Section 11 provides that members may purchase additional years of reckonable service. By s. 12, for current members the maximum reckonable service before 1964 for pensions purposes is set at fifteen years and the maximum service at sixty-five at forty years; the absolute maximum is forty-five years reckonable service. Section 13 provides that office-holders are to be included in the pension scheme unless they specifically opt out. Contributions from members' salaries have been increased from five to six per cent: s. 14. Section 15 amends existing provisions relating to members' resolutions on their salaries. Section 16 reduces the qualifying period for a pension under the supplementary scheme for office-holders from four to three years. Section 17 relates to the duration of pensions and provides for partial rather than total abatement of members' pensions should they rise to qualifying office in the House of Lords. Section 18 relates to transfers to and from overseas pensions schemes, s. 19 provides for reduction in lieu of income tax in refunds of contributions to former Prime Ministers, Speakers and Lord Chancellors and s. 20 increases from three to four per cent the rate of interest on refunded contributions. Section 21 contains financial provisions and s. 22 deals with citation, construction, minor and consequential amendments and repeals. Schedule 1 contains those amendments, Sch. 2 repeals.

2046   Pensions—contracting out

See para. 2109.

2047   Statutes—royal assent

During 1978 fifty-nine public General Acts received the royal assent. Of these, eleven related to Scotland or Northern Ireland. Of the remaining forty-eight, six were consolidation Acts. Three General Synod measures also received the royal assent.

PARTNERSHIP

Halsbury's Laws of England (3rd edn.), Vol. 28, paras. 925–1169

2048   Existence of partnership—registration for VAT

Value added tax tribunal decision:

DANIELS AND BLACKMORE v CUSTOMS AND EXCISE COMRS (1978) CAR/78/251 (unreported) (commissioners alleged two builders were working in partnership and therefore their combined taxable supplies rendered them liable to be registered for value added tax; the question whether a partnership existed was one of fact in each case and it did not matter that the parties did not consider themselves as partners; all invoices were made out to one of them but they had a joint bank account to safeguard his interests; jointly owned a car and a van; all accounts listed them as "trading as Daniels and Blackmore" and clearly stated that they shared all profits; they had held themselves out as partners and were therefore liable to be registered for tax).

PATENTS AND INVENTIONS

Halsbury's Laws of England (3rd edn.), Vol. 29, paras. 1–388

2049   Articles

Employee Inventions, Peter Russell (provisions of the Patents Act 1977 relating to employee inventions): 128 NLJ 800.

Patent Pooling and Package Licensing: Some Antitrust Considerations, N. J. Byrne: 128 NLJ 1095.

Right to Repair a Patented Article, Leslie Melville (points arising in *Solar Thomson Engineering Co v Barton* [1977] RPC 537, 1977 Halsbury's Abr para. 2016): 128 NLJ 491

2050   Application—convention application—time limit—whether late delivery could be rectified

A patent agent's employee was entrusted to deliver a convention application on 16th December which was the last day the application could be made if the twelve month time limit was to be complied with. He neglected to do so until the following morning. The application was held to be made on the 17th of December, rendering it too late to obtain the advantages of a convention application. The applicants appealed, contending that the application was still valid as the mode of delivery could be treated as an application by post and would be protected by rule 6 of the Patent Rules 1968, since in the ordinary course, if nothing had gone wrong, the application would have been delivered on 16th December. Alternatively, the late delivery could be considered as an irregularity of procedure that could be rectified under rule 152. *Held*, service by post did not include a delivery service operated by a patent agent for his own convenience. Further, the failure to make an application within the twelve-month period allowed by the Patents Act 1949, s. 1 (2), could not be regarded as a procedural irregularity; rather, it was a failure to fulfil a statutory requirement. Accordingly, the appeal would be dismissed.

FUJISAWA PHARMACEUTICAL CO LTD's APPLICATION [1978] FSR 187 (Court of Appeal: BUCKLEY and GOFF LJJ and Sir DAVID CAIRNS).

2051   —— extension period—time at which application deemed to be abandoned—post dating

A patent application was due to be rendered void on 6th June 1976 under the Patents Act 1949, s. 12 (1) unless the applicants sought an extension of the time limit before 6th September under s. 12 (2). On that date they applied for post dating of one month, but did not seek an extension under s. 12 (2) until 17th September. The Patent Office refused to process the post dating application on the ground that the patent application had been rendered void by virtue of s. 12 (1). The court upheld the decision on the ground that the post dating application could not have been acted upon on 6th September because s. 12 (2) had not been invoked. On appeal, *held*, a patent application would only be rendered void when it became impossible to comply with the requirements of s. 12 (1) or (2). On 6th September it was still possible to invoke s. 12 (2) and therefore the post dating application should have been considered. The appeal would be allowed.

ASSOCIATED BRITISH COMBUSTION LTD's APPLICATION [1978] RPC 581 (Court of Appeal: BUCKLEY and BRIDGE LJJ and SIR DAVID CAIRNS).

2052   **—— manner of manufacture—method of speech instruction**

Patents Appeal Tribunal decision:

DIXON'S APPLICATION [1978] RPC 687: WHITFORD J (patent application claimed method of speech instruction involving conditioning diaphragm and carrying out series of exercises; found that claim did not relate to invention within Patents Act 1949, s. 101; method of speech instruction did not constitute new manner of manufacture).

2053   **Convention country—Korea**

The Patents Etc. (Republic of Korea) (Convention) Order 1978, S.I. 1978 No. 187 (in force on 19th February 1978), made to fulfil an arrangement with the Republic of Korea, and declares that country to be a Convention country for all the purposes of the Acts relating to patents and designs.

2054   **European patents—convention**

The European Patent Convention had been ratified by the United Kingdom and entered into force on 7th October 1977. The convention with related document is published in a white paper: Cmnd. 7090.

The convention establishes a European Patent Organisation which consists of a European Patent Office and an Administration Council. The seat of the Organisation is at Munich.

2055   **—— fees**

The Administration Council of the European Patent Organisation, having regard to the European Patent Convention, Article 33, para. 2 (d), has adopted a table of fees relating to the European Patent Office.

2056   **Infringement—action for infringement—summons for directions—experiments—discovery of documents**

In an infringement action an order was made for discovery and experiments. The defendants sought a further order, first that certain of the plaintiffs' experiments be repeated; secondly, that more extensive discovery of the plaintiffs' documentation relating to every aspect of their work on the patented product, be made. *Held*, the trial judge had decided that the experiments need not be repeated because of a lack of the appropriate material. It had since come to light that the defendants possessed spare material. The experiment relating to this material should therefore be repeated. On the issue of discovery, GOFF LJ dissenting, there would be no order relating to all the experiments and research work leading to the patent. To make such an order would be oppressive and would occasion unreasonable and unnecessary delay and expense. All other documents could be discovered.

GOFF LJ said that in view of the lack of knowledge of the patented process by anyone other than the parties, in order to determine the question of the sufficiency of the patent, full discovery of the experimental and research work was essential.

AMERICAN CYANAMID CO v ETHICON LTD [1978] RPC 667 (Court of Appeal: BUCKLEY, ORR and GOFF LJJ).

2057   **—— imported substance—export of substance in tablet form—no commercial loss to patentee**

The defendants imported certain pharmaceutical products which they turned into tablets and exported, in that form, to purchasers in Nigeria. In an action for infringement of patent, the defendants claimed that the patentee had suffered no loss as a result of what had been done, and that therefore there was no infringement. *Held*, unlicensed possession by a merchant in the UK of patented goods for purposes of supplying customers wherever they may be constitutes infringement. There was no necessity to prove commercial loss on the part of the patentee. The appeal would be dismissed.

SMITHKLINE CORPORATION v D.D.S.A. PHARMACEUTICALS LIMITED [1978] FSR 109 (Court of Appeal: BUCKLEY and BRIDGE LJJ, and SIR DAVID CAIRNS). *Watson, Laidlaw & Co Ltd v Pott* (1914) 31 RPC 104 at 118, and *Hoffman-La Roche v Harris Pharmaceuticals* [1977] FSR 200, 1977 Halsbury's Abr para. 2013 followed.

2058   —— interlocutory injunction—balance of convenience—criteria to be used in deciding balance of convenience

A subsidiary company obtained three patents for the manufacture of plastic cellular board. The parent company incurred heavy capital expenditure and trading losses during the establishment of the manufacturing process and the initial launching of the product on the market, on the understanding that they would have a monopoly of the market for some time to come. Another company imported the same product and put it on the market in Britain. Pending a patent infringement action, the manufacturing company brought interlocutory proceedings against the importer in respect of one of the patents, which had fourteen months to run from the date of the interlocutory proceedings. At first instance the judge held that although the manufacturers had an arguable case, on the balance of convenience they were not likely to be seriously prejudiced by competition from the importers. The injunction was refused and the manufacturers appealed. *Held*, the trial judge had considered the issue purely on the basis of whether the manufacturer's business would be so seriously prejudiced as to put them out of business or cause unemployment among their employees. This was too narrow a view of the question of the balance of convenience. The manufacturers were establishing a new market and attempting to establish themselves in that market. If the importers were allowed to compete the manufacturers would not only lose business during the currency of the patent, but on its expiry they would not have the advantage of being the only established suppliers, and thus would not have the competitive advantage they had calculated on when deciding upon the initial investment. The importers on the other hand would merely be delayed in establishing themselves in a market in which they had made no investment. The business lost to the importers should they win the main action, would be difficult to assess, but it would be even more difficult to assess the continuing damage the manufacturers would suffer if no injunction were granted. Furthermore the manufacturers' loss of competitive advantage on the expiry of the patent, if the injunction was not granted would probably not be recoverable in damages. The injunction would therefore be granted.

CORRUPLAST LTD v GEORGE HARRISON (AGENCIES) LTD [1978] RPC 761 (Court of Appeal: BUCKLEY AND GOFF LJJ and SIR DAVID CAIRNS).

2059   —— order for account of profits—stay of order pending appeal— special circumstances justifying stay

See *J Lucas (Batteries) Ltd v Gaedor Ltd*, para. 2291.

2060   —— sale by foreign seller to English buyer—whether tort committed within jurisdiction

The defendant, a Dutch corporation, sold to an English company quantities of a chemical which was covered by a patent owned by the plaintiffs. The goods were consigned by air from Holland c.i.f. Gatwick and the price was payable when they were received in England. The plaintiffs sued the defendant for infringement of the patent. The defendant denied liability on the ground that it had performed no wrongful act within the jurisdiction, as property in the goods passed to the English buyers when the goods were put aboard the aircraft in Holland. The plaintiffs contended that property passed in England, or alternatively that although the goods were in the custody of the airline they were in the constructive possession of the defendant for purposes of trade, there being infringement on either view. They contended further that the English company had infringed the patent in pursuance of a common design with the defendant and that the defendant and the English company were joint tortfeasors. *Held*, there had been a concerted design to sell the chemical in England. If there was a concerted design by two persons to sell goods which in fact infringed a patent, then the parties were joint tortfeasors and both infringed that patent whether or not they knew that the sale would be an infringement. The English company had sold the chemical in England in pursuance of the common design and the defendant was therefore liable as a joint tortfeasor even if it had done nothing within the jurisdiction.

Property in the goods passed when they were delivered to the airline in Holland, because they were then unconditionally appropriated to the contract under the Sale of Goods Act 1893, s. 18. Therefore the defendant had not sold the goods within the jurisdiction. However, the defendant retained the right to possession of them in transit as against the airline under the Carriage by Air Act 1961 and as against the English buyers because they were not entitled to possession until the price was paid. The defendants' possession for trade purposes continued after the goods entered England and thus the defendants had infringed the patent.

MORTON-NORWICH PRODUCTS INC v INTERCEN LTD [1978] RPC 501 (Chancery Division: GRAHAM J). *British Motor Syndicate v Taylor* (1900) 17 RPC 723 and dictum of Lord Wilberforce in *Pfizer v Ministry of Health* [1965] RPC 261 at 320 applied.

2061   —— specifications—whether specifications essentially similar

See *Catnic Components Ltd v Hill and Smith Ltd*, para. 521.

2062   —— use of confidential information—whether patent invalid on ground of prior user

The plaintiff contended that the defendant lift manufacturers had infringed his patent for a domestic stair lift by using confidential information he had given them. He sought an injunction preventing further manufacture by the defendants of lifts which infringed his patent. Before he had filed his complete specification he had demonstrated his lift to the defendants, who had built one identical lift and 378 embodying a chain and weight system like the plaintiff's. The defendants subsequently devised their own system to replace the chain and weight. They opposed grant of the injunction on the ground that all the features of the plaintiff's lift were drawn from general knowledge. In addition, they claimed the plaintiff's patent should not have been granted on the ground of prior user. *Held*, the alleged prior user amounted to nothing more than reasonable trial and experiment. The defendants had clearly used the plaintiff's design in 378 lifts, and had done so by virtue of the information given them by the plaintiff. The latter deserved payment for this use. He did not, however, have any claim against the defendants with respect to the later lifts because by the time they were being made the plaintiff's information had lost its confidential nature and the lifts did not in any case incorporate any of the plaintiff's designs.

HARRISON v PROJECT & DESIGN CO (REDCAR) LTD [1978] FSR 81 (Chancery Division: GRAHAM J).

2063   International arrangement

The United Kingdom's instrument of ratification of the Patent Co-operation Treaty has been deposited. It entered into force on 24th January 1978 (except for Chapter II which entered into force on 29th March 1978). The treaty provides for an International Patent Co-operation Union with its own Assembly, Executive Committee and International Bureau. Under the treaty, international applications may be made for patents, and international searches may be conducted (Chapter I). International applications may be subjected to international preliminary examination (Chapter II). The treaty and the regulations made under it have been published as Cmnd. 7340.

2064   Inventions—development—increase in assistance

The Development of Inventions (Increase of Limits) Order 1978, S.I. 1978 No. 382 (in force on 24th April 1978), raises from £20,000 to £250,000 the aggregate amount of assistance which the National Research Development Corporation may, without the approval of the Secretary of State, give to any person in any year under the Development of Inventions Act 1967, s. 4 (2) (b), as amended.

2065   —— when made—writing down of formula

See *Beecham Group Ltd v Bristol Laboratories International SA*, para. 2066.

2066   Licence agreement—construction—obligation to disclose secret formulae and to give rights under inventions now existing

Under a licence agreement in 1959, drug manufacturers granted patent licence rights to the licensees. The agreement provided that the manufacturers would disclose to the licensees all information concerning secret processes and other confidential know-how and materials now owned by them. The manufacturers also agreed to add to a list of scheduled patents all new patent applications "hereafter filed on any invention now existing" in any of the eight categories of subject-matter covered by the agreement. Immediately after the agreement, the manufacturers disclosed to the licensees a document listing "acids already used" and "acids being prepared", which were identified only as formulae. The manufacturers were later able to make a penicillin from one of the latter, which was patented in 1962. Another form of the penicillin was patented in 1968 under the name Amoxycillin. The manufacturers brought an action for a declaration that the licensees were not licensed in respect of Amoxycillin. *Held*, the licensees were not so licensed. The information about the acid formula disclosed to them was generally known at the time and did not qualify for disclosure as secret information. Nor did it fall within any of the eight categories of subject-matter covered by the agreement. Even if it did fall within one of those categories, neither of the patents was in respect of an invention existing in 1959, as the drugs derived from the formula had not been invented until they were made and tested; the mere writing down of a formula was not enough to constitute an invention.

BEECHAM GROUP LTD V BRISTOL LABORATORIES INTERNATIONAL SA [1978] RPC 521 (House of Lords: LORD WILBERFORCE, VISCOUNT DILHORNE, LORD DIPLOCK, LORD EDMUND-DAVIES and LORD FRASER OF TULLYBELTON). *I. G. Farbenindustrie AG's Patents* (1930) 47 RPC 283 and dictum of Lord MacDermott in *May and Baker Ltd v Boots Pure Drug Co Ltd* (1950) 67 RPC 23, HL followed.

2067   Patents Act 1977—commencement

The following provisions of the Patents Act 1977, 1977 Halsbury's Abr para. 2023 came into operation on 1st June 1978 by virtue of Patents Act 1977 (Commencement No. 2) Order 1978 (S.I. 1978 No. 586: ss. 1–52, 53 (except s. 53 (1)), 54–59, 60 (except s. 60 (4)), 61–76, 77 (except s. 77 (6), (7), (9)), 78 (except s. 78 (7), (8)), 79–83, 89–113, 115–129, 131, 132 (except s. 132 (5)), Schs. 1–5 and 6 (insofar as it is not already in force).

The only sections not now in force at the end of 1978 were those relating to Community patents.

2068   —— Isle of Man

The Patents Act 1977 (Isle of Man) Order 1978, S.I. 1978 No. 621 (in force on 1st June 1978), modifies specified provisions of the Patents Act 1977, 1977 Halsbury's Abr para. 2023, in their application to the Isle of Man.

2069   Patent agents—rules

The Register of Patent Agents Rules 1978, S.I. 1978 No. 1093 (in force on 1st September 1978), replace the Register of Patent Agents Rules 1950, as amended, and regulate, under the Patents Act 1977, the registration of patent agents and the suspension of the right to act as such an agent.

2070   Patents Court

The Patents Court, established as a new part of the Chancery Division under the Patents Act 1977, s. 96, was inaugurated on June 6th 1978 by the Lord Chancellor. Section 96 came into force on 1st June 1978 by virtue of S.I. 1978 No. 586, see para. 2067: Times, 7th June 1978.

2071   —— appeals from Comptroller—constitution of court

The following Practice Direction ([1978] 2 All ER 464) has been given by GRAHAM J, senior judge of the Patents Court, on behalf of the Lord Chancellor.

Patents Act 1977, s. 97(2) which comes into operation on 1st June 1978, provides that for the hearing of appeals from the Comptroller-General of Patents, Designs and Trade Marks the Patents Court may consist of one or more judges in accordance with directions given by or on behalf of the Lord Chancellor.

For the hearing of such appeals the Patents Court will consist of a single judge unless, in any particular case, the senior judge of the court or, in his absence, another nominated judge directs that it shall consist of two judges.

2072   —— —— practice

The following Practice Direction ([1978] 2 All ER 464) has been issued by the Chancery Division.

1. Under RSC Ord. 104, r. 14 (17) (added by S.I. 1978 No. 579) the Chief Master has nominated Mr D. F. James, at present the Registrar of the Patents Appeal Tribunal, to be the "proper officer" of the Patents Court for the purposes of appeals from the Comptroller-General of Patents, Designs and Trade Marks. He will be known as the Registrar of Patent Appeals. The registrars of the Chancery Division will continue to perform their present duties in infringement actions and other patent business.

2. (a) Appeals from the comptroller must be brought by originating motion (Ord. 104, r. 14 (1)). The originating motion (in r. 14 called "notice of appeal") is issued by lodging copies with the Registrar of Patent Appeals (Room 152). If the Registrar of Patent Appeals and his deputy are not available, the copies may be lodged in the Chief Master's Secretariat (Room 169). (b) Two copies of the originating motion (notice of appeal) will be required, one of which must be stamped with a £10 fee (Fee 8) and the other of which will be sealed and returned to the appellant. (c) A respondent's notice under Ord. 104, r. 14 (9), asking that the decision of the comptroller be varied, must be stamped £5 (Fee 36).

2073

By virtue of Practice Direction [1978] 2 All ER 464, para. 2072 appeals from the Comptroller to the Patents Court must be brought by originating motion called "notice of appeal". For the form of notice of appeal, see [1978] FSR 547.

2074   Priority date—convention application—whether priority date claimed anticipated by earlier application

Two inventors made a convention application for a patent relating to a method of hardening steel cutting edges. They sought a priority date based on a United States application made in 1974 but their application was rejected on the ground that one of the inventors had made a United States application in 1972 which covered the same process. On appeal, *held*, the 1972 application had been made in respect of a process containing all the steps to be found in the latest application; all that the latter had done was to set out the result of putting the former into effect and accordingly the appeal would be dismissed.

ENGEL AND ANDERSON'S APPLICATION [1978] RPC 608 (Patents Appeal Tribunal: WHITFORD J).

2075   Rules—patents rules

The Patents Rules 1978, S.I. 1978 No. 216 (in force 1st June 1978) replace the Patents Rules 1968 as amended. Provision is made for applications by employees for an award of compensation in respect of certain inventions; for applications for European patents (UK) and for international applications for patents. The circumstances in which the deposit of a micro-organism is to be treated as disclosing an invention are prescribed, as are fees and forms.

2076   —— rules of the Supreme Court

See para. 2207.

2077   Specification—amendment to specification—fair basis

A patent application was filed which contained a claim to an encapsulation process by which simulated fruit berries were produced. The process involved treating the drops as they formed from both the inside and the outside to produce a hard skin and a soft centre. The applicants sought amendment without post-dating to remove from the claim the process which hardened the skin from the inside, and sought to introduce this feature in a subsidiary claim. *Held*, the invention related to the production of simulated fruit berries by treating the drops from the inside and the outside. There was no suggestion in the original claim that the same result could be achieved by treating the exterior only. The application for amendment without post-dating would be refused.

UNILEVER LTD (SNEATH'S) APPLICATION [1978] RPC 617 (Patents Appeal Tribunal: WHITFORD J).

2078   —— —— objections—discretion of court to allow amendments

A chemical company sought to amend the specification of an organic compound for photographic use for which it was seeking a patent. The company's intention was to place the specification in a prior claiming relationship with subsequently published specification of a rival company. The rival objected to two of the amendments on the ground that one of them was unjustifiably wide and that another, proposing the introduction of further claims to the specification, was not an amendment by way of disclaimer and should not be allowed. The objection were upheld at first instance on the ground that the main specification itself was unjustifiably wide. On appeal, *held*, the main specification was specifically limited to a compound made of equally specific chemical ingredients and was therefore not unjustifiably wide. The objections to the amendments could not be upheld either. The aim of the first objection was to prevent the main specification from being strengthened against the rival's later specification. However, the amendment itself was unobjectionable and, that being so, there was no reason why the applicant company's prior claiming position should not be allowed to improve. Lastly, it was quite in order for the applicants to introduce by way of amendment subsidiary claims derived from the main specification.

IMPERIAL CHEMICAL INDUSTRIES (WHYTE'S) PATENT [1978] RPC 11 (Patents Appeal Tribunal: GRAHAM and WHITFORD JJ). *Davidson's Patent* (1936) 53 RPC 453 applied.

PENSIONS AND SUPERANNUATION

2079   Articles

The New State Pensions Scheme, L. W. Chapman (the main provisions of the new scheme, its omissions and the contracting-out options): 122 Sol Jo 174.

Pensions for the Self-Employed, John Myers (financial problems of the self-employed when preparing for their retirement): 128 NLJ 642.

Pensions and Insurance (a collection of articles on professional insurance, pensions, life assurance, school fees schemes, CTT and membership of Lloyd's): NJL Supplement, 16th March 1978.

Social Security Pensions Act 1975, Cedric D. Bell (the growth in occupational pension schemes and the objects of the new Act): 128 NLJ 267.

2080   Appeal tribunals—rules

The Pensions Appeal Tribunals (England and Wales) (Amendment) Rules 1978, S.I. 1978 No. 607 (in force on 23rd May 1978), make further amendments to the Pensions Appeal Tribunals (England and Wales) Rules 1971. Rule 27 is revised so that allowances for travel, subsistence and loss of time may be additionally paid to appellants undergoing a medical examination and to necessary witnesses. The level of allowances under rule 27 is increased. Rule 30 is modified so that the maximum fee payable for a copy of a document or a set of documents from a medical expert, hospital or other institutions is £1·25.

2081

The Pensions Appeal Tribunals (England and Wales) (Amendment No. 2) Rules 1978, S.I. 1978 No. 1780 (in force on 15th January 1979) further amend the Pensions Appeal Tribunals (England and Wales) Rules 1971. Rule 9 is revised so that an assessment appeal will be struck out automatically where an increased assessment is made. Rule 23 is modified to enable a Tribunal in certain cases to hear an assessment appeal by an appellant resident abroad without a medical examination. In addition the minimum and maximum fees and expenses allowable by the Tribunal in respect of medical and technical witnesses and reports are increased and the day and night subsistence allowances payable to appellants and witnesses for periods of absence from home are also increased.

2082   British Railways Board—pensions

The British Railways Board (Funding of Pension Schemes) (No. 5) Order 1978, S.I. 1978 No. 1295 (in force on 1st October 1978), prescribes the sum to be provided by the British Railways Board, and to be paid by the Board in instalments during the period beginning on the 1st April 1979 and ending on the 1st April 1986, for the purpose of effecting a partial funding of the Board's obligations in connection with certain of their pension schemes.

2083

The British Railways Board (Funding of Pension Schemes) (No. 6) Order 1978, S.I. 1978 No. 1763 (in force on 1st January 1979), varies the British Railways Board (Funding of Pension Schemes) (No. 1) Order 1974, 1974 Halsbury's Abr para. 2705, as amended, by increasing the sum to be provided by the British Railways Board pursuant to that Order and by making certain changes in the sums apportioned to the various pension schemes to which that order applies. The Order also deals with the funding of the B.R. (1974) Pension Fund.

2084   —— pension funds—contracting out

The British Railways Board (Winding up of Closed Pension Funds) Order 1978, S.I. 1978 No. 1358 (in force on 11th October 1978), amends the terms of the British Railways Superannuation Fund (Amalgamated Sections) and the Great Western Railway Supplemental Pensions Reserve Fund so as to permit the employment of any member of either fund to be contracted-out of the earnings-related component of the State pension scheme provided for in the Social Security Pensions Act 1975.

2085   Clergy—pensions—Channel Islands

The Clergy Pensions (Channel Islands) Order 1978, S.I. 1978 No. 784 (in force on 1st July 1978), applies the Clergy Pensions (Amendment) Measure 1969 and the Clergy Pensions (Amendment) Measure 1972 to the Channel Islands in accordance with a Scheme proposed by the Bishop of Winchester in pursuance of the Channel Islands (Church Legislation) Measures 1931 and 1957.

2086   Coal   industry—mineworkers'   pension   scheme—limit   on contributions

The Mineworkers' Pension Scheme (Limit on Contributions) Order 1978, S.I. 1978 No. 416 (in force on 20th March 1978), amends the National Coal Board (Finance) Act 1976, s. 2 (3) (b) by increasing the maximum aggregate of payments by the Secretary of State to the National Coal Board to reimburse expenditure incurred towards reducing or eliminating deficiencies in the Mineworkers' Pension Scheme to £34 million.

2087   Commutation

The Pensions Commutation (Amendment) Regulations 1978, S.I. 1978 No. 1257 (in force on 1st September 1978), further amend the Pensions Commutation Regulations 1968 by making provision for officers of the armed forces to make application for the commutation of their pensions during the period of twenty-eight days ending on their last day of service. The Regulations substitute new tables which gives the rates for the calculation of the capital sum obtained in commutation and taking account of increases payable under the Pensions (Increase) Act 1971 or a prerogative instrument relating to the armed forces.

2088   Coroners—pensions

The Social Security (Modification of Coroners (Amendment) Act 1926) Order 1978, S.I. 1978 No. 374 (in force on 6th April 1978), modifies the provisions of the Coroners (Amendment) Act 1926 relating to the payment of pensions to coroners by providing that a pension is not payable to a coroner who is appointed on or after 6th April 1978 or who holds office immediately before 6th April 1978 and who elects before 6th July 1978 that the provisions should not apply to him. A pension payable to a coroner under the 1926 Act is reduced by the amount of his additional component of his retirement pension within the meaning of s. 6 (1) (b) of the Social Security Pensions Act 1975.

2089   Firemen—pensions

The Firemen's Pension Scheme (Amendment) Order 1978, S.I. 1978 No. 1228 (in force on 1st October 1978), amends the Firemen's Pension Scheme Order 1973 by providing a new method for transferring superannuation rights where a person enters a fire brigade from certain other forms of pensionable employment or leaves such employment to enter a fire brigade.

2090   The Firemen's Pension Scheme (Amendment) (No. 2) Order 1978, S.I. 1978 No. 1349 (in force on 6th October 1978), amends the Firemen's Pension Scheme 1973 and enables the Scheme to satisfy the requirements for the issue of a contracting-out certificate under the Social Security Pensions Act 1975, s. 31.

2091   The Firemen's Pension Scheme (Amendment) (No. 3) Order 1978, S.I. 1978 No. 1577 (in force on 1st December 1978), amends the Firemen's Pension Scheme 1973, and previous Schemes, in so far as they continue to have effect. Under these Schemes the amounts of certain awards are determined by reference to flat rates which do not qualify for increases under the Pensions (Increase) Act 1971. The Order increases these flat rates with effect from 1st December 1978.

2092   Guaranteed minimum pensions—actuarial tables

The State Scheme Premiums (Actuarial Tables) Regulations 1978, S.I. 1978 No. 134 (in force on 6th April 1978), replace the State Scheme Premiums (Actuarial Tables) Regulations 1976, 1976 Halsbury's Abr para. 1891. They prescribe the table in accordance with which the Secretary of State is required by the Social Security Pensions Act 1975 to calculate the cost of providing or continuing to provide guaranteed minimum pensions, and the difference between the cost of providing guaranteed minimum pensions in accordance with provisions included in a scheme by virtue of the 1975 Act, s. 35 (7), and what would have been the cost of providing them in the absence of such provisions, for the purpose of determining the amount of accrued rights premiums, pensioner's rights premiums and limited revaluation premiums.

2093   Invalidity pension

See SOCIAL SECURITY.

2094   Local government—superannuation

The Local Government Superannuation (Amendment) Regulations 1978, S.I. 1978 No. 266 (in force on 30th March 1978), further amend the Local Government Superannuation Regulations 1974, 1974 Halsbury's Abr para. 2502.

The provisions of the 1974 regulations relating to return of contributions and qualifying service are amended so that they comply with the requirements of the Social Security Act 1973, s. 63, and Sch. 16, Pt. I.

Pensions required by the National Insurance Act 1965 for periods of employment which were non-participating under that Act are provided for persons who would not otherwise be entitled to pensions under the 1974 regulations on retirement and consequential amendments to the 1974 regulations are made.

The provisions of the 1974 regulations relating to modification of benefits under those regulations in connection with the payment of graduated benefit under the National Insurance Act 1965 are amended to take account of the consequential effects of the repeal of Part III (non-participating employments) of that Act and to remedy a small number of omissions and defects.

Provision is made for certain employees who could benefit under the 1974 regulations, to opt to switch to other superannuation arrangements, or to opt not to be superannuable under the regulations and to receive a return of contributions.

2095   The Local Government Superannuation (Amendment) (No. 2) Regulations 1978, S.I. 1978 No. 822 (in force on 6th July 1978), provide for coroners, other than those who elected not to become subject to the Local Government Superannuation Regulations 1974, to become superannuable under the 1974 Regulations and makes the necessary modifications to the 1974 Regulations. In particular, provision is made for the counting of past service as a coroner. The Regulations take effect from 6th April 1978.

2096   The Local Government Superannuation (Amendment) (No. 3) Regulations 1978, S.I. 1978 No. 1739 (in force on 30th December 1978, but having retrospective effect to specified dates, further amend the Local Government Superannuation Regulations 1974, 1974 Halsbury's Abr para. 2502, the Regulations introduce a power to make standard remuneration agreements for superannuation purposes, death gratuities in respect of persons dying while entitled to receive payment of preserved retirement benefits and the compounding of trivial pensions.

2097   The Local Government Superannuation (Social Security—Requirements for Contracting-out) Regulations 1978, S.I. 1978 No. 1738 (in force on 30th December 1978) modify the local government superannuation scheme embodied in the Local Government Superannuation Regulations 1974, 1974 Halsbury's Abr para. 2502, as amended, so as to meet the requirements of the Social Security Pensions Act 1975, 1975 Halsbury's Abr para. 3191 with respect to pension schemes which may be contracted-out of the additional component of the state scheme for old age pensions.

2098   Lord Chancellor—calculation of increases in pension

The Pensions Increase (Judicial Pensions) (Amendment) Regulations 1978, S.I. 1978 No. 1808 (in force on 5th January 1979) amend the Pensions Increase (Judicial Pensions) Regulations 1972 in the calculation of increases in pensions for former Lord Chancellors, their widows and children.

2099   Miscellaneous offices

The Pensions (Miscellaneous Offices) (Requisite Benefits) Order 1978, S.I. 1978 No. 552 (in force on 21st April 1978), modifies the pension schemes of certain office holders so as to comply with the contracting-out requirements laid down by the Social Security Pensions Act 1975, 1975 Halsbury's Abr para. 3191.

2100   National Health Service—superannuation

The National Health Service (Superannuation) (Amendment) Regulations 1978, S.I. 1978 No. 1353 (in force on 6th October 1978), further amend the National Health Service (Superannuation) Regulations 1961 to 1975 which provide for the superannuation of persons engaged in the National Health Service. The scheme is amended so that it complies with the contracting-out requirements of the Social Security Pensions Act 1975. There are other miscellaneous amendments. Regulations 40 and 41 have retrospective effect as from 31st March 1977, regs. 31 and 43 (a) as from 1st July 1977 and regs. 3 to 26, 32, 45, 46 (1) (a), (b) and 46 (2) as from 6th April 1978.

2101   National insurance commissioners—preservation of benefits

The National Insurance Commissioners' Pensions (Preservation of Benefits) Order 1978, S.I. 1978 No. 407 (in force on 6th april 1978), modifies, by virtue of the Social Security Act 1973, ss. 64 and 65, the pension scheme for the Chief and other National Insurance Commissioners appointed under the Social Security Act 1975, s. 97 (3). It enables a reduced pension and derivative benefits (lump sum and widow's and children's pensions) to be preserved for the benefit of a Commissioner who ceases to hold office before the age at which he would otherwise normally become eligible to be granted a pension, and to be paid to or in respect of him thereafter.

2102   —— requisite benefits

The National Insurance Commissioners' Pensions (Requisite Benefits) Order 1978, S.I. 1978 No. 408 (in force on 6th April 1978), modifies, by virtue of the Social Security Act 1973, ss. 64 and 65, the pension scheme for the Chief and other National Insurance Commissioners appointed under the Social Security Act 1975, s. 97 (3). A Commissioner and his wife will be entitled to pensions based on the final salary of the Commissioner and his years of service up to pensionable age. The pensions are not to be less than a guaranteed minimum. The Order relates to any Commissioner who is under pensionable age and who holds office on 6th April 1978, or who is appointed to office when under that age on or after that date.

2103   The National Insurance Commissioners' Pensions (Requisite Benefits) Amendment Order 1978, S.I. 1978 No. 1368 (in force on 13th October 1978), amends the National Insurance Commissioners' Pensions (Requisite Benefits) Order 1978, para. 2102, so as to provide that where a Commissioner dies, after ceasing to hold office, having completed less than five years of qualifying service, his widow shall be entitled to a pension of not less than her guaranteed minimum.

2104   Occupational pension schemes—contracting-out

The Contracted-out Employment (Miscellaneous Provisions) Regulations 1978, S.I. 1978 No. 250 (in force on 6th April 1978), provide that in certain cases and for the purposes only of the Social Security Pensions Act 1975, ss. 35 (7), 42 (1), contracted-out employment is to be treated as not having terminated. They also amend various related regulations in consequence of the Social Security (Miscellaneous Provisions) Act 1977, and, in particular, amend the Contracted-out Employment (Miscellaneous Provisions) Regulations 1977, S.I. 1977 No. 1188, to exempt certain pension schemes from the requirements of the 1975 Act, s. 40 (3), relating to the priority of liabilities.

2105   The Contracted-out Employment (Miscellaneous Provisions) (No. 2) Regulations 1978, S.I. 1978 No. 1827 (in force on 9th January 1979), amend the Occupational

Pensions Schemes (Certification of Employments) Regulations 1975, 1975 Halsbury's Abr para. 2509, by providing that where an election with a view to the issue, variation or surrender of a contracting-out certificate meets the prescribed conditions, the requirements for the giving of notices and for consultation may be dispensed with. The regulations also provide that where an earner's contracted-out employment is to be treated as continuing after the takeover of a business by a new employer the contracting-out certificate is to be treated as issued to the new employer.

2106   The Contracting-out and Preservation (Further Provisions) Regulations 1978, S.I. 1978 No. 1089 (in force on 28th August 1978), amend the Occupational Pensions Schemes (Contracting-out) Regulations 1975 in relation to the transfer of accrued rights and amend the Occupational Pension Schemes (Preservation of Benefit) Regulations 1973 so as to permit the transfer of a member's accrued rights without his consent in certain prescribed cases.

The Occupational Pensions Board is also empowered to require that specified notification and consultation procedures be followed as a condition of their consent to the alteration of the rules of a contracted-out scheme.

2107   —— public service

The Occupational Pension Schemes (Public Service Pension Schemes) Regulations 1978, S.I. 1978 No. 289 (in force on 30th March 1978), provide that the occupational pension schemes referred to in the Schedule to the Regulations are to be treated for the purposes of Part II of the Social Security Act 1973 and of Parts III and IV of the Social Security Pensions Act 1975 as public service pension schemes.

2108   The Occupational Pension Schemes (Public Service Pension Schemes) (Amendment) Regulations 1978, S.I. 1978 No. 1355 (in force on 11th October 1978), amend the Occupational Pension Schemes (Public Service Pension Schemes) Regulations 1978, S.I. 1978 No. 289, para. so as to add three further occupational pension schemes to the Schedule to those regulations.

2109   Parliamentary pensions

The Parliamentary and other Pensions (Contracted-out Provisions) Order 1978, S.I. 1978 No. 891 (in force on 28th June 1978), modifies the Parliamentary and other Pensions Act 1972 to the extent necessary to enable the provisions of the Act to become a contracted-out pension scheme for the purposes of the Social Security Pensions Act 1975, 1975 Halsbury's Abr para. 3191.

See also Parliamentary Pensions Act 1978, para. 2045.

2110   —— purchase of added years

See para. 2044.

2111   Pensions increase—annual review

The Pensions Increase (Annual Review) Order 1978, S.I. 1978 No. 1359 (in force on 1st December 1978), provides for the payment, with effect from 1st December 1978, of public service pension increases resulting from the 1978 review of pensions based on the rise in the cost of living during the twelve month period ending 30th June 1978.

2112   Pensioners Payments Act 1978

The Pensioners Payments Act 1978 received the Royal Assent on 23rd November 1978 and came into force on that date. The Act provided for a lump sum payment of £10 to be made to persons who were entitled to specified benefits for the week beginning 4th December 1978. In certain circumstances provision was also made for an additional payment of £10 in respect of spouses. Conditions of entitlement and ancillary provisions were the same as under the Pensioners Payments Act 1977, 1977 Halsbury's Abr para. 2060.

2113   Police—pensions

The Police Pensions (Amendment) Regulations 1978, S.I. 1978 No. 375 (in force on 6th April 1978), amend provisions of the Police Pensions Regulations 1973 and the Police Pensions (Amendment) (No. 2) Regulations 1977, 1977 Halsbury's Abr para. 2064, relating to the new method of transferring superannuation rights where a person enters a police force from certain other forms of pensionable employment or enters such employment after leaving a police force.   The amendments are consequential upon the change from the old method to the new and ensure that the change does not affect the operation of the 1973 Regs. in relation to a transfer made under the old method.

2114

The Police Pensions (Amendment) (No. 2) Regulations 1978, S.I. 1978 No. 1348 (in force on 6th October 1978), amend the Police Pensions Regulations 1973 by enabling those regulations to satisfy the requirements for the issue of a contracting-out certificate under the Social Security Pensions Act 1975, s. 31.   Provisions are added to the Regulations conferring a right to a deferred pension where an ill-health pension is cancelled in certain circumstances.   A right to a pension is conferred on certain regular policemen who would otherwise not be entitled under the 1973 regulations.

2115

The Police Pensions (Amendment) (No. 3) Regulations 1978, S.I. 1978 No. 1578 (in force on 1st December 1978), amend the Police Pensions Regulations 1973 and in so far as they continue to have effect the Police Pensions Regulations 1971. Under these Regulations the amounts of certain widows' pensions and children's allowances are determined by reference to flat rates which do not qualify for increases under the Pensions (Increase) Act 1971.   The present Regulations increase these flat rates with effect from 1st December 1978.

2116   —— —— payments to widows

The Police Pensions (Lump Sum Payments to Widows) Regulations 1978, S.I. 1978 No. 1691 (in force on 4th December 1978), provide for the payment of a gratuity of £10 to a policeman's widow, in receipt of a police widows' pension under the Police Pensions Regulations 1971, during the week beginning the 4th December 1978 if she is not entitled to a payment by virtue of the Pensioners' Payments Act 1978, s. 1 (1), para. 2112.

2117

The Royal Irish Constabulary (Lump Sum Payments to Widows) Regulations 1978, S.I. 1978 No. 1692 (in force on 4th December 1978), provide for the payment of an additional £10 to a widow, in receipt of an allowance or pension under the Royal Irish Constabulary (Widows' Pensions) Regulations 1971, during the week beginning the 4th December 1978 if she is not entitled to a payment by virtue of the Pensioners' Payments Act 1978, s. 1 (1), para. 2112.

2118   Retirement benefits

See SOCIAL SECURITY.

2119   Retirement pension—surviving spouse

The Social Security (Maximum Additional Component) Regulations 1978, S.I. 1978 No. 949 (in force on 6th April 1979), prescribe a maximum additional component for the purposes of the Social Security Pensions Act 1975, s. 9, 1975 Halsbury's Abr para. 3191, which makes provision for circumstances in which the additional components in the Category A retirement pensions of surviving spouses should be increased up to that maximum.

2120   Royal forces—disablement and death service pensions

The Naval, Military and Air Forces etc. (Disablement and Death) Service Pensions Amendment Order 1978, S.I. 1978 No. 1902 (in force on 24th January 1979) Amends the Naval, Military and Air Forces etc (Disablement and Death) Service Pensions Order 1978 which makes provision for pensions and other grants in respect of disablement and death due to service in the armed forces during the first World War and since the beginning of the second. The Order restores the condition that a woman member of the forces shall not be eligible for an increase of her basic disablement pension in respect of a child of whom her husband is the father unless he is dependent on her and is incapable of self support and in need.

2121   Shipbuilding industry—pension schemes

The Shipbuilding Industry (Pension Schemes) Regulations 1978, S.I. 1978 No. 232 (in force on 20th March 1978), make provision with respect to the pension rights of employees of companies which have become wholly owned subsidiaries of British Shipbuilders, and to those of employees and members of that Corporation. Pension schemes which related partly to employees of vesting companies and partly to employees of non-vesting companies are split. The assets and liabilities of such pension schemes referable to employees of vesting companies are transferred to trustees. All pension schemes providing pensions for employees of wholly owned subsidiaries of British Shipbuilders are modified to enable service as an employee of British Shipbuilders or of any of the Corporation's wholly owned subsidiaries to count as pensionable service with the wholly owned subsidiary in which he previously served as an employee. Such pension schemes are also modified to allow employees who are appointed whole-time members of British Shipbuilders to count their service as service for the purposes of the relevant scheme, subject to any employer's discretionary benefits being conferred on such persons only with the approval of the Secretary of State and the Minister for the Civil Service.

2122   Teachers—superannuation

The Teachers' Superannuation (Amendment) Regulations 1978, S.I. 1978 No. 422 (in force on 17th April 1978), amend the Teachers' Superannuation Regulations 1976. The principal amendments provide that, notwithstanding that a teacher has not attained the age of 60, allowances under the 1976 Regulations shall be immediately payable to him if, having attained the age of 50, his service is terminated by reason of redundancy or in the interests of the efficient discharge of his employer's functions. These amendments are retrospective to the date of termination of a teacher's service if he elects to be dealt with under the 1976 Regulations.

For 1976 Regulations, see 1976 Halsbury's Abr para. 944.

2123   The Teachers' Superannuation (Amendment) (No. 2) Regulations 1978, S.I. 1978 No. 1422 (in force on 6th October 1978 and having effect for the purposes of regs. 5, 19, 26 as from that date and for all other purposes as from 6th April 1978), amend the Teachers' Superannuation Regulations 1976, 1976 Halsbury's Abr para. 944. The present Regulations amend the 1976 Regulations to take account of provisions of the Social Security Pensions Act 1975 relating to requirements to be satisfied by an occupational pension scheme if it is to be a "contracted-out scheme" for the purposes of the 1975 Act.

2124   The Teachers' Superannuation (Amendment) (No. 3) Regulations 1978, S.I. 1978 No. 1512) (in force on 1st December 1978 and having effect for the purposes of regs. 3 (c), 6, as from 1st January 1977, for the purposes of regs. 3 (a), (b), 4, as from 1st May 1978, and for the purposes of reg. 5, as from 1st December 1978), amend the Teachers' Superannuation Regulations 1976, 1976 Halsbury's Abr para. 944. As a result of the termination of the arrangements under which schools were "recognised as efficient", the present Regulations substitute for the criterion "recognised as efficient" in the 1976 Regulations criteria related to registration under the Education Act 1944, s 70.

2125   Transport—National Freight Corporation—pensions

The National Freight Corporation (Central Trust) Order 1978, S.I. 1978 No. 1290 (in force on 1st October 1978), provides for the transfer of the assets and liabilities of certain pension schemes of the National Freight Corporation to the trustees of a central trust established by the Corporation in connection with the funding of pension scheme obligations under the Transport Act 1978, s. 19.

2126   The National Freight Corporation (Funding of Pension Schemes) (No. 1) Order 1978, S.I. 1978 No. 1294 (in force on 1st October), prescribes the sum to be provided by the National Freight Corporation for the partial funding of the obligations of the Corporation and of certain subsidiaries and a former subsidiary of the Corporation in connection with certain of the Corporation's pension schemes.

2127   The National Freight Corporation (Funding of Pension Schemes) (No. 2) Order 1978, S.I. 1978 No. 1764 (in force 1st January 1979) provides for the variation of the sum which the Corporation is to provide for funding its pension schemes.

2128   War—civilians—pensions

The Personal Injuries (Civilians) (Amendment) Scheme 1978, S.I. 1978 No. 384 (in force on 3rd April 1978), further amends the Personal Injuries (Civilians) Scheme 1976 which provides for compensation to or in respect of civilians injured or killed in the 1939–45 war. The present Scheme amends commencing dates of awards in general. The present Scheme also amends rates of pensions and allowances in respect of children of civilians injured or killed in the 1939–45 war and makes transitional provisions in respect of persons who immediately before the coming into operation of the present Scheme were qualified to receive payment of such pensions or allowances at the rate then prescribed, but who are not entitled to benefit under the Child Benefit Act 1975 or corresponding legislation. The present Scheme also increases the maximum daily rate of allowance for part-time treatment.

2129   The Personal Injuries (Civilians) Amendment (No. 2) Scheme 1978, S.I. 1978 No. 1426 (in force on 13th November 1978), further amends the Personal Injuries (Civilians) Scheme 1976, 1976 Halsbury's Abr para. 1910. The 1978 Scheme increases the rates of retired pay, pensions, gratuities and allowances in respect of disablement and death in the 1939–45 war. It also revokes the provisions for an allowance for children who are eligible members of a pensioner's family, save in so far as the allowance is in respect of the first dependent child where the pensioner draws no allowance for a spouse. It further raises the maximum amount which a disabled person may earn each year while deemed unemployable.

2130   —— service pensions

The Injuries in War (Shore Employments) Companies (Amendment) Scheme 1978, S.I. 1978 No. 1629 (in force on 13th November 1978) provides that the maximum weekly allowance payable to ex-members of the Women's Auxiliary Forces who suffered disablement from their services overseas during the 1914–18 War is to be raised from £28·60 to £31·90 and that other allowances are to be increased proportionately.

2131   The War Pensions (Amendment of Previous Instruments) Order 1978, S.I. 1978 No. 278 (in force on 3rd April 1978), further amends the Order in Council of 25th September 1964, the Royal Warrant of 19th September 1964 and the Order by Her Majesty of 24th September 1964.

In each of those Instruments this Order substitutes for references to pension or benefit under the National Insurance Acts 1965 to 1973, or under the corresponding provisions in Northern Ireland, references to pension or benefit under the Social Security Act 1975, under the Widow's Benefit, Retirement Pension and Other Benefits (Transitional) Regulations 1974 or, as the case may be, under the corresponding provisions in Northern Ireland; it also, by amendment of the definition of "regular occupation" for the purposes of an award of allowance for lowered standard of occupation, extends that allowance to members of the naval, military or air forces who, by reason only of their having no regular pre-service occupation, would not otherwise qualify for that allowance. This order also amends commencing dates of awards in general, increases rates of pensions and various allowances, and makes transitional provisions.

2132   The War Pensions (Amendment of Previous Instruments) (No. 2) Order 1978, S.I. 1978 No. 1404 (in force on 13th November 1978), further amends the Order in Council of 25th September 1964, the Royal Warrant of 19th September 1964 and the Order by Her Majesty of 24th September 1964. It increases the rates of retired pay, pensions, gratuities and allowances in respect of disablement and death due to service in the armed forces during the First World War and after 2nd September 1939. It also revokes the provisions for an allowance for children who are eligible members of a pensioner's family, with specified exceptions. It raises the amount of annual earnings which may be received by a disabled person while deemed to be unemployable for the purposes of an award of unemployability allowance, and relaxes the conditions for presuming that the death of a disablement pensioner, who at the time of his death was in receipt of constant attendance allowance, was due to service.

2133   The War Pensions (Pre-Consolidation Amendment) Order 1978, S.I. 1978 No. 1405 (in force on 1st January 1979), revokes the 1919 to 1921 Orders in Council, Royal Warrants and Orders by His Majesty which, in conjunction with the Order in Council of 25th September 1964, the Royal Warrant of 19th September 1964 and the Order by Her Majesty of 24th September 1964, made provision for death and disablement due to service in the armed forces during the First World War. It amends the 1964 instruments to make provision for like cover under those instruments as was previously provided under the revoked instruments. It also makes provision for the date at which the amount of an award of a gratuity is to be calculated and amends the power of the Secretary of State to defray certain expenses.

2134   The Naval, Military and Air Forces etc. (Disablement and Death) Service Pensions Order 1978, S.I. 1978 No. 1525 (in force on 1st January 1979), consolidates into a single instrument the Order in Council of 25th September 1964, the Royal Warrant of 19th September 1964 and the Order of Her Majesty of 24th September 1964, as amended, which made provision for pensions and other awards in respect of disablement or death due to service in the armed forces during the First World War and after 2nd September 1939.

2135   The Naval, Military and Air Forces etc. (Modification of Enactments and other Instruments) Order 1978, S.I. 1978 No. 1526 (in force on 1st January 1979), is made in consequence of the coming into operation of the Naval, Military and Air Forces etc. (Disablement and Death) Service Pensions Order 1978, para. 2134 and the War Pensions (Pre-Consolidation Amendment) Order 1978, para. 2133. It makes provision for references in Acts and instruments to the war pensions instruments which have been consolidated, and to pensions and other benefits provided by them, to be construed, so far as appropriate, as including references to the consolidating order or pensions and other benefits under it.

2136   **Welsh Development Agency—pensions**

The Pensions Increase (Welsh Development Agency) Regulations 1978, S.I. 1978 No. 211 (in force on 17th March 1978), apply the provisions of the Pensions (Increase) Act 1971 to officers of the Council for Small Industries in Rural Wales. The regulations are retrospective to November 1975. They replace the Pensions Increase (Welsh Development Agency) Regulations 1977.

PERPETUITIES AND ACCUMULATIONS

Halsbury's Laws of England (3rd edn.), Vol. 29, paras. 561–709

2137   Accumulations—discretionary power to accumulate—whether within restrictions

See *Baird v Lord Advocate*, para. 1444.

2138   —— statutory restriction on accumulation—trust for accumulation set up by company—whether company a person

A company set up a trust for the benefit of its employees. Under the trust deed the trustees were directed to purchase shares from the company and to distribute the dividends to such employees as the company directed. They were also given power to reserve the dividends to purchase more shares. The trustees sought a declaration that this power was not rendered invalid by the Law of Property Act 1925, s. 164 (1) which prohibits the settlement of property for accumulation except on certain grounds. They contended that the section was not intended to apply to bodies corporate but only to natural persons and that therefore the company was not a person within that section, notwithstanding the provision in the Interpretation Act 1889, s. 19. *Held*, the Law of Property Act 1925 was a consolidating statute and it was clear that, read in the light of the Act from which it was taken, s. 164 (1) was intended to apply only to natural persons. The trustees could not therefore have contravened the section.

RE DODWELL & CO LTD'S TRUST DEED, BAKER v TIMMINS [1978] 3 All ER 738 (Chancery Division: WALTON J).

PLEADING

Halsbury's Laws of England (3rd edn.), Vol. 30, paras. 1–78

2139   Absence of pleading by defendant—jurisdiction of court to make finding of contributory negligence against plaintiff

See *Fookes v Slaytor*, para. 1997.

2140   Amendment of defence after judgment—application to amend defence previously struck out—whether amendment possible

See *Midland Bank Trust Co Ltd v Green (No. 2)*, para. 1290.

2141   Illegality—defence not pleaded—whether issue may be considered where raised at late stage in proceedings

See *Ibbottson v Kushner*, para. 2908.

2142   Litigant in person—necessity for signature on pleadings

See *Greenhouse v Hetherington*, para. 548.

2143   Particularity—degree of particularity required—claim on constructive trust arising from fraud

See *Belmont Finance Corpn Ltd v Williams Furniture Ltd*, para. 351.

2144   Statement of claim—striking out—lack of particularity—whether statement could be redrafted

On appeal against an order of the High Court that a statement of claim for damages for breach of Treaty of Rome arts. 85 and 86 relating to abuse of dominant position should be struck out, *held*, as it stood the statement of claim was embarrassing for lack of particularity and disclosed no cause of action but the claimants would be given the opportunity to redraft it. The appeal would be provisionally allowed until the fresh statement had been made, at which time the hearing would resume on the question whether the action should proceed or be finally dismissed.

VALOR INTERNATIONAL LTD v APPLICATION DES GAZ SA [1978] 3 CMLR 87 (Court of Appeal: BUCKLEY, ROSKILL and GOFF LJJ).

Decision of Whitford J [1978] 1 CMLR 30 provisionally reversed.

POLICE

Halsbury's Laws of England (3rd edn.), Vol. 30, paras. 79–237

2145   Articles

Metropolitan Police Commissioner's Annual Report 1977, Henry E. Markson: 128 NLJ 1176.

Police Powers of Search (in the light of *Frank Truman Export Ltd v Metropolitan Police Commissioner*, 1976 Halsbury's Abr para. 676): 122 Sol Jo 308.

2146   Execution of duty—scope of duty—police intervening in attempted suicide

See *R v Dietrich*, para. 582.

2147   Pay and allowances

The Police (Amendment) Regulations 1978, S.I. 1978 No. 1169 (in force on 1st September 1978), amend the Police Regulations 1971 by increasing rates of pay, conferring a London allowance on members of the City of London and metropolitan police forces and ending the undermanning allowance payable to members of certain police forces.

2148   The Police Cadets (Amendment) Regulations 1978, S.I. 1978 No. 1239 (in force on 1st September 1978), amend the Police Cadets Regulations 1968 by increasing the pay of police cadets and the charges payable by them for board and lodging provided by police authorities.

2149   Pensions

See PENSIONS.

PORTS, HARBOURS AND THE SEASHORE

Halsbury's Laws of England (3rd edn.), Vol. 35, paras. 1247–1311 and Vol. 39, paras. 767–891.

2150   Dock or harbour undertaking—rateable value—assessment

See *Harwich Dock Co Ltd v IRC*, para. 2295.

2151   Port health authorities

See paras. 2258, 2259, 2260.

PRACTICE AND PROCEDURE

Halsbury's Laws of England (3rd edn.), Vol. 30, paras. 547–1036

2152   Articles

Application for Judicial Review (the new RSC Ord 53): 142 JP Jo 80.

Applying for Judicial Review: Practical Points, Henry E. Markson (practical points relating to declaration and injunction, right to be heard, and claims): 122 Sol Jo 495.

The Dismissal of Actions for Want of Prosecution, James P. Corbett (recent developments in the courts): 128 NLJ 351.

Dismissal of Action for Want of Prosecution during Limitation Period (the House of Lords decision in *Birkett v James* [1977] 3 WLR 38, HL 1977 Halsbury's Abr para. 2157): 122 Sol Jo 135.

Possession Proceedings: Interim Payments, Henry E. Markson (whether interim payments may be ordered in actions for possession of land; recent decisions): 122 Sol Jo 446.

Service out of the Jurisdiction, Allan C. Hutchinson (the exercise by the court of its discretion under RSC Ord. 11 to allow service on a defendant who is not in England): 128 NLJ 278.

Unprecedented Judicial Precedents, A. N. Khan (whether House of Lords can depart from precedent where it considers such precedent wrong): 122 Sol Jo 702.

2153   Action in rem—winding-up order made against shipowners—application to continue action—existence of legal nexus between plaintiff and ship

See *Re Aro Co Ltd*, para. 368.

2154   Appeal—appeal to Court of Appeal—application for leave to appeal against finding of contempt in criminal proceedings

See *R v Tibbitts*, para. 470.

2155   Appeal against deportation order—application for judicial review—procedure

A deportation order was made against an Indian husband and wife. They sought a declaration in the Chancery Division that they should not be deported pending the determination of their petition by the European Commission of Human Rights. The declaration was refused and they appealed. *Held*, the application should not have been started in the Chancery Division. They should instead have made an application for judicial review in the Queen's Bench Divisional Court, which was equipped to deal with such matters. The appeal would be dismissed.

UPPAL v HOME OFFICE (1978) Times, 11th November (Court of Appeal: ROSKILL and GEOFFREY LANE LJJ and SIR DAVID CAIRNS). Decision of MEGARRY V-C (1978) Times, 21st October, para. 1536 affirmed on different grounds.

2156   Arbitration

See ARBITRATION.

2157   Barristers

See BARRISTERS.

2158   Chancery Division—bankruptcy—appeals from county courts

See *Practice Direction*, para. 219.

2159   —— **Companies Court—applications in Long Vacation**

The following Practice Direction ([1978] 1 All ER 820) has been issued by the Companies Court.

1. The Practice Direction of 3rd March 1977 ([1977] 1 All ER 688 1977 Halsbury's Abr para. 2108) set out arrangements for hearing in the Long Vacation 1977 certain applications concerning schemes of arrangement and reductions of capital, capital redemption reserve funds and share premium accounts.

2. It has been decided to extend the arrangements set out in that Practice Direction to future Long Vacations, until further notice.

3. The days on which a judge of the Companies Court will be available for sitting will be an early Wednesday in August (this year, 9th August) and each Wednesday in September.

4. It is emphasised that any party wishing to make an application to the Registrar or to have a petition heard by the judge during the Long Vacation under this Practice Direction should give the earliest possible warning of this fact to the office of the Companies Court Registrar before the Long Vacation begins. It will not be necessary at that stage to disclose the name of any company involved.

2160   —— **drawing up orders during the Long Vacation**

See *Singh v Nazeer*, para. 1681.

2161   —— **family provision—application for—appeal from master's decision—procedure**

See *Practice Direction*, 1297.

2162   —— —— **endorsement of consent order on probate and letters of administration**

The following Practice Direction ([1978] 3 All ER 1032) has been issued by the Chancery Division.

1. In June 1953 Vaisey J directed that a consent order made in proceedings under the Inheritance (Family Provision) Act 1938, all parties being sui juris, was not an order under that Act and accordingly that no memorandum of the order should be endorsed on the probate or letters of administration, but that it was otherwise if a compromise was approved by the court on behalf of a party not sui juris. This ruling is equally applicable to consent orders in proceedings in the Chancery Division under the Inheritance (Provision for Family and Dependants) Act 1975.

2. In the Family Division memoranda of all consent orders in proceedings under the 1975 Act are endorsed on the probate or letters of administration, whether or not the parties are all sui juris.

3. To avoid any divergence of practice between two divisions having concurrent jurisdiction, the direction of Vaisey J is now withdrawn. In future, every final order embodying terms of compromise made in proceedings in the Chancery Division under the 1975 Act shall contain a direction that a memorandum thereof shall be endorsed on or permanently annexed to the probate or letters of administration and a copy thereof shall be sent to the Principal Registry of the Family Division with the relevant grant of probate or letters of administration for endorsement, notwithstanding that any particular order may not, strictly speaking, be an order under the 1975 Act.

2163   —— **lists**

In a Practice Note ([1978] 2 All ER 645), MEGARRY V-C said that there would be two improvements in the system of listing cases. The improvements, which were to assist solicitors in forecasting the time when their cases are likely to be heard, took effect from June 6th 1978.

The first improvement concerns the notice of setting down which the clerk of the lists sends to solicitors for all parties as soon as a case in Part 2 of the Witness List or in the Non-Witness List is set down for hearing. In future the notice will state a date on and after which solicitors should watch the weekly Warned List for further information. There is a strong possibility that a case will appear in the Lists soon after the stated date.

Secondly, the Warned List for cases in Part 2 of the Witness List will in future, in addition to the cases for the coming week, list the cases likely to be heard the week after. This will ensure that at least one week's notice is given before the case is listed for hearing.

The improvements do not affect fixed date cases, or "floating" cases in Part 1 of the Witness List.

2164   —— —— warned list

In a Practice Direction ((1978) Times, 28th November), MEGARRY V-C emphasised that solicitors with cases in Part 2 of the Witness List in the Chancery Division who have been advised to watch the Warned List from a certain date under the procedure set out in the Practice Direction of 23rd May 1978 ([1978] 1 WLR 757, para. 2163) must be prepared for their cases to appear in the list at an earlier date. While every effort was made to ensure that the estimated date was reasonably accurate, there would be occasions when cases were disposed of more quickly than envisaged.

2165   —— motion—power to stand motion over to trial—effect on undertakings

Plaintiffs brought an action for copyright infringement and breach of confidence and sought interlocutory relief by motion. The hearing was subject to delay and the plaintiffs alleged that the issues had become contentious. They therefore applied to stand the motion over until the trial, whereupon the defendants sought to have certain undertakings which they had made discharged. *Held*, it would have been wrong to adjourn the motion until trial of the action if this would have bound the defendants to their undertakings for a longer period than that originally contemplated. However, the defendants had offered new undertakings and therefore the motion could be stood over until the time of the trial on terms that the previous undertakings be substituted by those offered later.

WOODSTOCK V DENTON TACKLE CO LTD [1978] FSR 548 (Chancery Division: MEGARRY V-C).

2166   —— setting down for trial—duty of solicitors to be ready for trial

A Chancery action appeared in the warned list. On the day it appeared, the London agents of the plaintiff's solicitors wrote to the clerk of the lists asking that the case be stood out for two months. The defendant's solicitors agreed as the case was not ready. The clerk of the lists referred the application to delay trial to the judge. *Held*, both the plaintiff's and the defendant's solicitors had been wrong to think that all that needed to be done to delay trial was for them to lodge consent. Unless a fixed date was sought, an action was liable to appear in the warned list twenty eight days after setting down. There was a strong obligation on solicitors and litigants to be ready for trial within that time. Failure to be ready would waste the court's time, hinder the efficient listing of cases, and prejudice other litigants who wanted their cases to be heard. In this case, the application to defer the hearing was granted, but the solicitor and client costs of the plaintiff's solicitor would be disallowed under RSC Order 62, rule 8.

RAMAGE-GIBSON V RADCLIFFE (1978) Times, 9th March (Chancery Division: BRIGHTMAN J).

2167   —— transfer of action from Commercial Court

See *Midland Bank Ltd v Stamps*, para. 2223.

2168   Change of parties—court's discretion to add additional defendant

Under the terms of a charterparty, the charterers had a lien on the ship for all claims for damages arising from any breach of the charter by the owners. The ship was mortgaged to the plaintiffs but whilst on charter she sank and the charterers claimed damages from the owners under the charter. When they discovered that insurance money was payable in respect of the lost ship, they successfully applied for an injunction preventing the owners from disposing of that money; the basis of their claim was that they had an equitable charge on the insurance money by virtue of their lien under the charter. The insurance money was held by brokers and the plaintiff mortgagees brought an action against them and the owners to recover the money. The charterers meanwhile applied to be added as a party to the proceedings under RSC Ord. 15, r. 6 (2) (b) (ii) in view of their own claim. *Held*, ROSKILL LJ dissenting, the court was entitled to exercise its discretion under RSC Ord. 15, r. 6 (2) (b) (ii) since the points raised were such that it was just and convenient to determine them as between the plaintiffs and the charterers. Although the use of the word "lien" in the charterparty was inaccurate, it was certainly arguable that the charterers had an equitable charge on the ship and that the insurance money replaced the ship as the subject of that charge. Accordingly, as the charterers' claims could not be dismissed as unsustainable, they would be added as a party to the proceedings.

THE PANGLOBAL FRIENDSHIP, CITIBANK NA v HOBBS SAVILL & CO LTD AND DRAY SHIPPING CO LTD AND A/S SEAHERON [1978] 1 Lloyd's Rep 368 (Court of Appeal: LORD DENNING MR, ROSKILL and BROWNE LJJ).

2169   Committal order—amendment of order—whether slip rule may be applied

See *Cinderby v Cinderby: Pekesin v Pekesin*, para. 1518.

2170   —— application—application by litigant in person

See *Bevan v Hastings Jones*, para. 463.

2171   Compromise of action—power of trustee to accept

See *Re Earl of Strafford, Royal Bank of Scotland v Byng*, para. 2911.

2172   Costs—award in petition for leave to appeal—House of Lords

See *Procedure Direction*, para. 2193.

2173   —— costs of arbitration—discretion of arbitrator—right of court to interfere with order

See *Traumontana Armadora SA v Atlantic Shipping Co SA*, para. 155.

2174   —— criminal cases

See CRIMINAL PROCEDURE.

2175   —— divorce cases

See DIVORCE.

2176   —— exercise of the court's discretion—extension of time for objection

A firm of solicitors, who had acted for the wife in divorce proceedings, claimed costs of £20,000 which the registrar approved. The particular person dealing with the husband's affairs left his firm of solicitors and consequently no objection to this sum was filed within the requisite fourteen days. *Held*, although the rules relating to time were mandatory, the delay had been short and the court would use its discretion to permit the time to be extended. The certificate of taxation would be set aside and the solicitors would be given seven days to lodge their objections.

THORNE v THORNE (1978) Times, 10th November (Family Division: COMYN J). *Maltby v D. J. Freeman* (1976) 120 Sol Jo 284, 1976 Halsbury's Abr para. 1949 followed.

2177   —— order in county court—discretion of judge

See *Greenhouse v Hetherington*, para. 548.

2178   —— taxation—basis—costs incurred in course of liquidation

See *Re Nation Life Insurance Co Ltd (in liquidation)*, para. 367.

2179   —— —— solicitors' fees

See *Martin v Martin*, para. 2739.

2180   —— —— solicitor using computer to record costs—procedure to be followed

The solicitors of a caveator in probate proceedings destroyed their weekly time sheets when they were returned after computer processing, and there was thus no means of resolving the dispute which arose when the amount of time spent on the matter was challenged by the respondent's solicitors. In refusing to disturb the taxation of a bill of costs, PAYNE J said that practising solicitors who made use of computing systems to record costs should retain intact their files, including attendance notes and time sheets until the conclusion of taxation and the review of taxation and probably even until the payment of the bill of costs.

Re KINGLEY, DECEASED (1978) 122 Sol Jo 457 (Family Division).

2181   **County courts**

See COUNTY COURTS (procedure).

2182   **Court of Appeal—appeal from judge in chambers**

LORD DENNING MR has directed that where a judge in chambers has dismissed an appeal under Order 14, in the defendant's absence, the proper course is for him to apply to the judge to set aside his order and hear the appeal. Whilst a right of appeal did lie to the Court of Appeal from a judge in chambers in such circumstances, the above practice should be followed in order to ease the burden on the Court of Appeal.

ROYAL BANK OF CANADA v GHOSH (1978) 122 Sol Jo 827 (Court of Appeal: LORD DENNING MR and BRIDGE LJ).

2183   **Criminal proceedings**

See CRIMINAL PROCEDURE.

2184   **Custody of children—custody hearing—procedure**

See *Jenkins v Jenkins*, para. 1934.

2185   **Discovery**

See DISCOVERY.

2186   **Dismissal for want of prosecution**

See paras. 2225 et seq.

2187   **Documentary evidence—Employment Appeal Tribunal—relevance to issue**

See para. 1073.

2188   **Entry of appearance—court's discretion to allow withdrawal**

A lorry driver claimed damages from a firm of building contractors in respect of an injury received during the unloading of the lorry. The contractors alleged that the accident was caused or contributed to by the suppliers who supervised the unloading and therefore the lorry driver applied to join the suppliers as defendants to the action. Permission was granted outside the limitation period but the suppliers' solicitors failed to notice this fact and entered an unconditional notice of appearance. When they realised their mistake they applied for leave either to withdraw the unconditional appearance or to enter a conditional appearance. The lorry driver appealed against the court's exercise of its discretion to give leave for the solicitors to enter a conditional appearance on the ground that the discretion could only be exercised in the case of a mistake which arose from an absence of authority. *Held*, the court had an unlimited discretion to give leave to withdraw an appearance. As the court in this case had considered all the relevant factors and had exercised its jurisdiction correctly the appeal would be dismissed.

FIRTH v JOHN MOWLEM & CO LTD [1978] 3 All ER 331 (Court of Appeal: MEGAW, SHAW and WALLER LJJ).

2189   Evidence—absence of transcript—admissibility of counsel's notes

See *R v Winter*, para. 1286.

2190   Family Division—appeal from magistrates courts—amount of maintenance order— procedure

See *Practice Direction*, para. 1511.

2191   —— application for grant of representation—production of deed or other instrument

See *Practice Direction*, para. 1301.

2192   —— injunctions—ex parte applications

The President of the Family Division has issued a Practice Note expressing concern at the number of applications for injunctions being made ex parte when they should be made on two clear days' notice to the other side. Nearly half of all recent ex parte applications for injunctions had been shown to be unmeritorious, which resulted in considerable wastage of time and money: (1978) Times, 28th June.

2193   House of Lords—award of costs—petition for leave to appeal

The following Procedure Direction ([1978] 1 All ER 247) has been issued by the Clerk of the Parliaments.

The Appeal Committee have determined:

1. Where a petition for leave to appeal is *not* referred for an oral hearing, costs may be awarded as follows: (*a*) To a legally aided petitioner, reasonable costs incurred in preparing papers for the Appeal Committee (*b*) To a legally aided respondent, only those costs necessarily incurred in attending client, petitioners' agents, perusing petition and entering appearance (*c*) To an unassisted respondent where the petitioner is legally aided, payment out of the legal fund of costs incurred by him at (*b*) above. (*d*) Where neither party is legally aided, respondents will be allowed only the costs at (*b*) above. Applications for such party and party costs must be made in writing to the Judicial Office.

2. Where a petition *is* referred for an oral hearing, application for costs must be made at the conclusion of the hearing.

3. Direction No. 9 in the Directions as to Procedure and Standing Orders is amended accordingly and should be read subject to the terms of this direction.

4. This direction also applies to petitions for leave to appeal in criminal matters.

2194   Legal aid and advice

See LEGAL AID.

2195   Lodgment into court—lodgment by post

The Lord Chancellor's Department has issued a notice stating that lodgment into the High Court may henceforth be effected by post in certain categories of cases; see further 128 NLJ 975.

2196   Matrimonial proceedings—financial provision—appeal—procedure to be followed

See *Adams v Adams*, para. 1514.

2197   Patents Court

See paras. 2070, 2071, 2072, 2075.

2198   Preservation of subject-matter of cause of action—application for immediate disclosure of information—whether such order should be made on ex parte application

The plaintiffs brought an action for a declaration that the defendants were not entitled to remove shellfish from the plaintiffs' fishery. By notice of motion they sought an injunction restraining the defendants from removing the shellfish and an order that the defendants should disclose the identities of other parties who had been involved in removing shellfish. *Held*, the injunction would be granted. As to the order, the question was whether there was any justification for making it on what was in substance an ex parte application before the defendants had had an opportunity to present their case on disputed facts. Taking into account that the plaintiffs' fishery was in great danger from poaching and the giving of the information could do no harm to the defendants, the order should be made.

LOOSE v WILLIAMSON (NOTE) [1978] 3 All ER 89 (Chancery Division: GOULDING J). *EMI Ltd v Sarwar and Haidar* [1977] FSR 146, CA, 1977 Halsbury's Abr para. 2143 applied.

2199   ——application to restrain unauthorised recordings—no infringement of any right—jurisdiction of court to grant application

See *Ex parte Island Records Ltd*, para. 524.

2200   —— ex parte application to search premises—necessity for premises to be precisely described

The plaintiff made an ex parte application for an order of the kind granted in *Anton Piller KG v Manufacturing Processes Ltd*, authorising him to search premises in order to obtain documents which the defendant in a copyright action might otherwise have concealed. He sought permission to enter specified addresses, two of which were in Scotland, and any other premises controlled by the defendant. *Held*, it was unnecessary for the court to decide whether it had jurisdiction to authorise the search of premises in Scotland, but it would exercise its discretion to exclude the Scottish addresses from the order. The references to other premises controlled by the defendant would also be excluded, because an *Anton Piller* order which described the premises to be searched in general terms could only be granted where there was a special reason for doing so, and this had not been shown here.

PROTECTOR ALARMS LTD v MAXIM ALARMS LTD [1978] FSR 442 (Chancery Division: GOULDING J). *Anton Piller KG v Manufacturing Processes Ltd* [1976] Ch 55, 1975 Halsbury's Abr para. 2623 applied.

2201   Proceedings against estate of deceased person—appointment of Official Solicitor to represent estate—duration and scope of appointment

See *Bank Melli, Iran v Personal Representatives of Amirteymour*, para. 1302.

2202   **Queen's Bench Division—Commercial Court—improvement of procedure**

A working party has been established by the Commercial Court Committee to study that court's procedures in order to improve the service provided. Suggestions for improvements from those with experience of the work of the court are welcomed and should be sent to: Mr. J. L. Powel, secretary of the Commercial Court Committee, at the Lord Chancellor's Office, Romney House, Marsham Street, London SW1.

2203   —————— **transfer of action to Chancery Division**

See *Midland Bank Ltd v Stamps*, para. 2223.

2204   —— **masters' summonses—time summonses—arrangements for issue**

The following Practice Direction ([1978] 1 All ER 723) has been issued by the Queen's Bench Division.

1. As from 1st February 1978, a summons for hearing by a master of the Queen's Bench Division asking only for the extension of any period of time will be issued for hearing before the Practice Master of the day at 10.30 a.m. and will be made returnable two days from the date of its issue, excluding Saturdays, Sundays, any bank holidays or other days on which the Central Office is closed.

2. Such a summons must be served at least one day before the day specified therein for its hearing (see RSC Ord 32, r. 3).

3. It should also be emphasised that the mere issue or service of such a summons will not by itself operate to extend any relevant period of time or to stay proceedings.

4. This Practice Direction will not extend to district registries.

2205   **Rules of the Supreme Court**

The Rules of the Supreme Court (Amendment) (Bail) 1978, S.I. 1978 No. 251 (in force 17th April) amend Order 79, r. 9 and Order 59, r. 20 in consequence of the coming into force of the Bail Act 1976. The manner in which bail decisions are to be recorded under s. 5 of that Act and the particulars to be contained in them are prescribed. Jurisdiction in respect of appeals against conviction or sentence by the Crown Court for absconding bail is assigned to the criminal division of the Court of Appeal.

2206   The Rules of the Supreme Court (Amendment No. 2) 1978, S.I. 1978 No. 359 (in force on 24th April 1978), amend the Rules of the Supreme Court 1965 by providing that an appeal from the decision of a master or a registrar of the Family Division in certain proceedings lies to a judge in chambers instead of the Court of Appeal. New fixed costs are substituted for the basic costs allowable under Order 62, App. 3 where not less than £1,200 is recovered and Order 56, r. 2 is revoked.

2207   The Rules of the Supreme Court (Amendment No. 3) 1978, S.I. 1978 No. 579 (in force on 1st June 1978), amend the Rules of the Supreme Court 1965 to take into account the provisions of the Torts (Interference with Goods) Act 1977 and the Patents Act 1977. Appeals to the High Court under the Matrimonial Proceedings (Magistrates' Courts) Act 1960 may now be heard and determined by a single judge instead of a Divisional Court where only the amount of any weekly payment is in issue.

2208   The Rules of the Supreme Court (Amendment No. 4) 1978, S.I. 1978 No. 1066 (in force on 1st September 1978), amend the Rules of the Supreme Court so as to enable the court to allow service of notice of a writ in an EEC member state where the claim is for an agricultural levy or other sum to which EEC Council Directive 76/308 applies. The court is also given express power to order that damages be assessed by a master or in an Admiralty cause or matter or, where appropriate, in a commercial action, by the Admiralty Registrar. Finally, unless otherwise directed, an application for leave to enforce an arbitration award may be made ex parte by affidavit instead of by originating summons.

2209   Service of writ out of jurisdiction—commission of tort within jurisdiction—place where tort committed

See *Diamond v Bank of London and Montreal Ltd*, para. 428.

2210   Solicitors

See SOLICITORS.

2211   Stay of account of profits—patent—infringement—stay pending appeal—special circumstances justifying stay

In infringement actions involving four patents or exclusive licences only one patent was found to be valid and infringed. The other three were found to be invalid. While granting the plaintiffs an injunction and making an order for an account of profits in respect of the infringed patent the trial judge granted the defendants a stay of both pending appeal by both parties. The plaintiffs applied to have the stay on the account of profits set aside. *Held*, courts had a discretion to grant a stay in the special circumstances. The present case involved connected patents in respect of which further orders for amounts of profit could result on appeal; considerable time and expense would be caused by immediate implementation of the order should it not prove final. Therefore, in regarding the circumstances as special, the judge at first instance had exercised his discretion properly and the stay would remain in force.

The court stated the correct procedure for removing a stay once it had been granted was by way of appeal rather than originating motion.

J. LUCAS (BATTERIES) LTD v GAEDOR LTD [1978] RPC 389 (Court of Appeal: BUCKLEY and BRIDGE LJJ and SIR DAVID CAIRNS).

2212   Stay of proceedings—action involving foreign immovables—discretion of the court

See *Cook Industries Incorporated v Galliher*, para. 420.

2213   —— application under Arbitration Acts—action to have defective statement of claim struck out—whether a step in proceedings

See *Eagle Star Insurance Co Ltd v Yuval Insurance Co Ltd*, para. 159.

2214   —— —— discretion of court to grant stay

See *Lonhro Ltd v Shell Petroleum Co Ltd*, para. 160.

2215   —— clause excluding liability of sub-contractors—whether indorsee of bill of lading bound by exemption clause

A cargo of anoraks and pullovers was shipped from Hong Kong to England and bills of lading were issued for and on behalf of the applicants as carriers. The bills of lading provided, inter alia, that any person owning or entitled to possession of the goods or bill of lading would undertake that no claim imposing liability would be brought against any servant, agent or sub-contractor of the carrier and, in the event of any such claim being made, the carriers would be entitled to indemnification. The road transport of the goods in England was sub-contracted to a firm of hauliers. The goods were stolen while in the hauliers' possession and the respondents, as indorsees of the bills of lading, claimed damages in respect of the stolen goods. The carriers applied for an order to stay proceedings under s. 41 of the Judicature Act 1925. They claimed that, as indorsees, the respondents were party to the bills of lading, were therefore bound by the exemption clause and were in breach of it by suing the sub-contractors. *Held*, as the sub-contractors were bailees of the goods at the time of the theft they were, prima facie, liable in tort. The bills of lading established that contractual obligations had arisen between the parties, but it did not necessarily follow from this that the carriers would obtain relief. Under s. 41 the question of relief was for the discretion of the court but, since the carriers could prove that they would suffer financial loss if relief was not granted, the court's discretion should have been exercised in their favour. The fact that the carriers were entitled to indemnification for any claim made did not preclude them from coming to court. Although it was already established that relief would be given to the carriers, a stay of proceedings would be granted to allow the respondents and the sub-contractors to seek legal advice.

THE ELBE MARU, NIPPON YUSEN KAISHA V INTERNATIONAL IMPORT AND EXPORT CO LTD [1978] 1 Lloyd's Rep 206 (Queen's Bench Division: ACKNER J). *Gore v Van der Lann* [1967] 1 All ER 360 applied.

2216   —— **foreign cause of action—selection of forum of action**

See *MacShannon v Rockware Glass Ltd*, etc., para. 422.

2217   —— **reference to arbitration—possibility of award being unsatis-fied—whether grounds for refusal of stay**

See *The Rena K*, para. 22.

2218   **Striking out—application to strike out appeal against award of damages—whether appeal abuse of process of court**

Substantial damages for libel were awarded by a jury against the author of a book. At the trial the author had offered no real defence; the only question had been as to damages. The author appealed against the damages on the basis that they were unreasonable and excessive. The plaintiffs moved to strike out the appeal as an abuse of the process of the court, saying that it would be hopeless to try to upset the jury's verdict. *Held*, the author had a substantial ground of argument. There was no abuse of process and the author should not be prevented from appealing.

OBOTE V JUDITH, COUNTESS OF LISTOWEL (1978) Times, 9th May (Court of Appeal: LORD DENNING MR, GEOFFREY LANE and EVELEIGH LJJ).

2219   **Summary judgment—entitlement**

See *Eagle Star Insurance Co Ltd v Yuval Insurance Co Ltd*, para. 159.

2220   **Supreme Court fees**

The Supreme Court Fees (Amendment) Order 1978, S.I. 1978 No. 1244 (in force on 2nd October 1978) increases from £20.00 to £25.00 the fee payable on the issue of a writ or other originating process in the High Court, except in the case of a writ for a liquidated sum not exceeding £2,000, and replaces all existing fees payable in the Court Funds Office with a new fee payable on a search of the records of unclaimed balances.

2221   **Supreme Court funds**

The Supreme Court Funds (Amendment) Rules 1978, S.I. 1978 No. 751 (in force on 3rd July 1978), amend the Supreme Court Funds Rules 1975, 1975 Halsbury's Abr para. 2639 so as to enable the Accountant General to deal with funds ordered by the Employment Appeal Tribunal to be lodged in court, and to enable the court to order the final disposal of effects which have remained deposited in court unclaimed for more than twenty-five years.

2222   **Transcripts—Court of Appeal Civil Division**

Transcripts of judgments of the Civil Division of the Court of Appeal have been transferred from the Bar Library to the Supreme Court Library. The method of citation is now the following: *Smith v Fraser*, July 19th, 1977, Court of Appeal

(Civil Division) Transcript No. 178 of 1977, CA: Practice Note (Court of Appeal: Transcripts) [1978] 1 WLR 600.

2223   Transfer of proceedings—transfer between divisions of High Court—mortgage and banking action—discretion of judge

Proceedings were brought against the defendant by a bank for payment of moneys secured by a mortgage of real property. The defendant applied for the case to be transferred from the Commercial Court to the Chancery Division on the ground that RSC Ord. 88, r. 2, provided that a case relating to mortgages should be assigned to the Chancery Division. *Held*, the application would be refused. The Supreme Court of Judicature (Consolidation) Act 1925, s. 58, provided that if a matter was begun in a division other than that in which it should have begun, the judge in whose court it was had a complete discretion as to whether to retain it or transfer it. As well as being a mortgage action, the present action was a commercial action within RSC Ord. 72, r. 1 (2), which related to banking. The mortgage in this case was irrelevant as neither the bank nor the defendant needed to refer to it. The matter was primarily a banking dispute appropriate to the Commercial Court and should remain there.

MIDLAND BANK, LTD v STAMPS [1978] 3 All ER 1 (Queen's Bench Division: DONALDSON J).

2224   ——— transfer between judges—objection to original judge

In an appeal involving the Church of Scientology, the Church applied for the appeal to be transferred from the Master of the Rolls' court. The basis of the application was that the church, which had been a frequent litigant, had already appeared before the master of the Rolls eight times. From remarks made by the Master of the Rolls in a previous case, the Church felt that he had decided that scientology was not a religion and that the Church was not entitled to call itself a church, whereas throughout its litigation the Church had maintained that it was a religion and a church. The Church believed that there would be an unconscious influence operating adversely to it in the judgment of a court in which the master of the Rolls was sitting. It was contended that if such a belief was not wholly unreasonable that might be a ground for transferring the matter to another division of the Court of Appeal.

LORD DENNING MR said that if the Church felt that its case would be adversely affected by his hearing it he would see that it came before another court. SHAW and WALLER LJJ said it was almost impossible to resist the application although the grounds were non-existent.

EX PARTE CHURCH OF SCIENTOLOGY OF CALIFORNIA (1978) Times, 21st February (Court of Appeal: LORD DENNING MR, SHAW and WALLER LJJ).

2225   Want of prosecution—dismissal of action—action brought on behalf of minor—whether minor entitled to commence fresh action within extended limitation period

The plaintiff, then aged two, suffered brain damage when struck by the defendant's car in 1964. Her father commenced an action for personal injury on her behalf in 1967 but no further action was taken until 1977 when the case was dismissed for want of prosecution. The plaintiff appealed, contending that even if there had been inordinate and inexcusable delay in prosecuting the action, her legal right under the extended period of limitation conferred on infants by the Limitation Act 1939, s. 22, to issue a fresh writ precluded dismissal of the action for want of prosecution. *Held*, (i) under the Limitation Act 1939, s. 22 as amended, where a minor had a right of action for personal injury, the limitation period for bringing such action was extended until three years after attaining the age of eighteen. The fact that an action had already been brought by the child's father did not affect her statutory right to sue within the extended limitation period. (ii) Where a plaintiff had the right to commence a fresh action because the limitation period had not expired, an action should only be dismissed in exceptional circumstances; delay, however long and inexcusable, was not an exceptional circumstance. Therefore, as the child's right to commence a fresh action was unaffected, it would be wrong and unhelpful to the defendant to dismiss the present action. The appeal would be allowed.

TOLLEY v MORRIS [1979] 1 All ER 71 (Court of Appeal: STEPHENSON and ORR LJJ). *Birkett v James* [1977] 2 All ER 801 HL, 1977 Halsbury's Abr para. 2157 applied.

2226   —— —— application for dismissal by third party

The National Coal Board had engaged an independent contractor to dismantle a monorail system at one of its collieries. An employee of the contractor was injured while working at the colliery and commenced an action for negligence against the board which in turn served a third party notice on the contractor claiming indemnity. Considerable delay ensued and eventually the contractor applied to have both the third party proceedings and the employee's action against the board struck out for want of prosecution although neither party was out of time. *Held*, (i) as the board's claim against the third party was not statute barred it was necessary to show either contumelious conduct or inordinate and inexcusable delay such as created a serious risk of prejudice to a fair trial. The board's failure to take out a third party summons for directions under RSC Order 16, r. 4 was not contumelious conduct as, despite the words "must . . . apply" no time limit was imposed by the rules which in any case enabled the third party to rectify the omission within a short time. Although the board had been guilty of inordinate and inexcusable delay this of itself was not enough. No risk of prejudice to a fair trial (additional to that resulting from delay in commencing the proceedings) had been shown. The application would be dismissed.

(ii) There was no known principle of law or justice upon which a third party should be allowed to prevent the employee from having the board's liability to him or the board's vicarious liability for the third party's employees, determined by the court. This application too would be dismissed.

ENOCH v NATIONAL COAL BOARD (1978) 122 Sol Jo 401 (Queen's Bench Division: MILMO J). *Birkett v James* [1977] 2 All ER 801 HL, 1977 Halsbury's Abr para. 2157 applied.

2227   —— —— delay—plaintiffs' failure to take out summons for directions—prejudicial effect of delay

In 1971 a French television company issued a writ for alleged past and continuing infringements of a patent by an English television marketing company. Pleadings closed the following year, but the plaintiffs failed to take out a summons for directions, although the parties continued discussions as to the possibility of a settlement until the end of 1973. Nothing further happened until the end of 1977, when the plaintiffs gave notice of intention to proceed. The defendants replied with a motion to strike out the action for want of prosecution but the motion was dismissed by the trial judge on the grounds that the delay had been faintly excusable and the defendants had failed to show substantial prejudice. On appeal, *held*, even allowing for the prolonged nature of patent actions, in omitting to take out a summons for directions at the close of pleadings the plaintiffs had failed in their duty both to the defendants and the court, and the delay in proceeding with the action was inexcusable. However the grounds of substantial prejudice caused by the delay submitted by the defendants were equivocal, and the trial judge was perfectly entitled to find that no real prejudice had been shown: the issue was entirely a matter for the discretion of the judge, and in interlocutory proceedings the Court of Appeal should interfere with his exercise of that discretion only where there had been a clear error of principle. The appeal would be dismissed.

ROSKILL LJ pointed out that it would be wrong to engraft a series of qualifications on to the decision in *Birkett v James*.

COMPAGNIE FRANÇAISE DE TELEVISION v THORN CONSUMER ELECTRONICS LTD [1978] RPC 735 (Court of Appeal: BUCKLEY, ROSKILL and GOFF LJJ). *Birkett v James* [1978] AC 297, HL, 1977 Halsbury's Abr para. 2157 applied.

2228   — — — reason for delay—plaintiffs awaiting outcome of connected proceedings

Actions alleging infringement of patents were commenced by the plaintiffs, one in 1969 and one in 1970. The actions took their normal course until 1973 when the defendants sought to amend their defence by contending that if there was an infringement, the plaintiffs were not entitled to relief by virtue of EEC Treaty, arts. 85 and 86, prohibiting restrictive trade agreements and abuse of a dominant market position. At the same time the defendants filed a complaint relating to the plaintiffs' activities with the EC Commission. The plaintiffs took the view that it would be desirable to await the outcome of those proceedings before proceeding with their own action. No steps were therefore taken after August 1974 in the 1969 action nor after November 1975 in the 1970 action. No decision had been given by the Commission by April 1977, and the defendants applied to dismiss the actions against them for want of prosecution. *Held*, it could not sensibly be suggested that the delay was inexcusable. The plaintiffs had a valid excuse for not proceeding, since the result of the proceedings before the Commission might be of great importance to the actions in question. Nor was it likely that the defendants would be seriously prejudiced by the delay. The motion to dismiss the actions would fail.

For previous proceedings in this case, see 1974 Halsbury's Abr para. 2552.

AERO ZIPP FASTENERS LTD v YKK FASTENERS (UK) LTD; OPTI HOLDINGS AG v YOSHSIDA KOGYO KABUSHIKI KAISHA [1978] 2 CMLR 88 (Chancery Division: WHITFORD J).

2229   — — delay in setting down for trial—effect of acquiescence in delay by one of two defendants

The plaintiff brought an action for damages against two defendants. He delayed in supplying further and better particulars of the claim to the second defendants and failed to comply with an order to have the case set down for hearing within a specified time, notwithstanding a written reminder from the second defendants. The second defendants then indicated that they would apply to have the action dismissed for want of prosecution. As a result of this, the plaintiff asked the first defendants, who had failed to give discovery of documents, to co-operate in expediting the case. The action was eventually dismissed for want of prosecution against both defendants; the plaintiff successfully appealed against the dismissal. On appeal by the second defendants, *held,* the first defendants had acquiesced in the plaintiff's delay and contributed to it by their conduct but there was no general rule that acquiescence by one defendant disentitled any other defendant from having the action struck out for want of prosecution. However, the court should consider the requirements of justice before exercising its discretion to dismiss an action against one defendant while allowing it to proceed against another. On the facts of the case, the judge had acted correctly in allowing the case to proceed against both defendants and accordingly the appeal would be dismissed.

KELLY v MARLEY TILE CO LTD (1977) 122 Sol Jo 17 (Court of Appeal: STEPHENSON and BRIDGE LJJ).

2230   — — effect of dismissal of action on new writ issued outside limitation period

See *Walkley v Precision Forgings Ltd*, para. 1798.

2231   — — two actions brought on same issue—whether second action capable of being proceeded with—application of doctrine of laches

The plaintiff began an action in 1974 seeking specific performance of an alleged oral agreement for the purchase of shares in a private company from the defendant. The latter served a defence in 1975. No further steps were taken and in 1977 the defendant sought to have it struck out for want of prosecution. He then died. The plaintiff subsequently brought a second action seeking a declaration that he was absolutely and beneficially entitled to the shares in dispute. The defendant's administratrix applied to have it struck out as an abuse of the process of the court. On the hearing of the summonses to have both actions dismissed, *held*, the plaintiff had failed to establish that the striking out of the first action would be futile in the light of the existence of the second.   For the first to be allowed to continue, he had to show that the second was capable of being proceeded with and that prima facie he could overcome the doctrine of laches, which applied to it in the absence of a fixed limitation period.   As he had not done so, the first action would be dismissed on the ground of inordinate delay.   The second action, however, would be allowed to continue; although it faced great difficulties, it did not amount to an abuse of process.

JOYCE V JOYCE [1978] 1 WLR 1170 (Chancery Division: MEGARRY V-C).   *Birkett v James* [1978] AC 297, HL, 1977 Halsbury's Abr para. 2157 applied.

2232   —— —— **whether dismissal justified where plaintiff entitled to substantial award**

When allowing an appeal against the dismissal of an action for want of prosecution, the Court of Appeal said that although the delay since 1969 was deplorable, a claim by a plaintiff who, on any view, was entitled to a substantial award of damages should not be lightly dismissed.

GREEN V HARDISTY (1978) 122 Sol Jo 281 (Court of Appeal: LORD DENNING MR, ORR and BRIDGE LJJ).

2233   **Winding-up petition—locus standi of petitioner—need for petitioner to show prima facie case**

See *Holt Southey Ltd v Catnic Components Ltd*, para. 377.

PRESS AND PRINTING

Halsbury's Laws of England (3rd edn.), Vol. 30, paras. 1037–1091

2234   **Newspaper—title—likelihood   of   confusion   with   another newspaper**

The plaintiffs were publishers of a newspaper named the *Morning Star*.   They sought an interim injunction to prevent the defendants issuing a newspaper under the name *Daily Star* on the ground that the similarity in names might lead members of the public to believe that there was a connection between the two.   *Held*, the differences between the newspapers as to style, content and price were so marked that only a moron in a hurry would be misled.   The plaintiffs had failed to show that they would have any chance of success and accordingly the claim would be dismissed.   If they had shown that they had an arguable case interlocutory relief would not have been granted because the defendants would have suffered unquantifiable damage.

MORNING STAR CO-OPERATIVE SOCIETY LTD V EXPRESS NEWSPAPERS LTD (1978) Times, 19th October (Chancery Division: FOSTER J).

PRISONS

Halsbury's Laws of England (3rd edn.), Vol. 30, paras. 1092–1231

2235   **Attendance centres**

The Attendence Centre (Amendment) Rules 1978, S.I. 1978 No. 1919 (in force on 1st January 1979), amend the Attendance Centre Rules 1958, so as to make provision for the attendance at attendance centres of female persons.   Provision is made for their supervision by a female member of the staff when participating in physical training and for a female member of staff to be in attendance at all times at a centre provided for the reception of female persons.

2236 Parole—petition for review—procedure

A prisoner petitioned the Secretary of State for an early parole review on 2nd July 1976, claiming that there were new and relevant circumstances which had arisen since his original application for parole had been refused. The Home Office acknowledged receipt of the petition on 10th August. Despite at least six reminders from the prison authorities, however, the Home Office did not reply to the petition until 11th May 1977. This length of delay was criticised by the Parliamentary Commissioner. The Home Office has apologised and stated that a system is being devised to ensure that what went wrong cannot be repeated. (The delay was not found to have resulted in injustice). In the same case the Parliamentary Commissioner describes the procedure following an unfavourable parole recommendation by a local review committee.

See *Case 2/216/77* in the Fifth Report of the Parliamentary Commissioner for Administration for the Session 1977–78 (HC 524), p. 164.

2237 —— statistics

The Report of the Parole Board for 1977 (H of C Paper 497) discloses that 10.3 per cent of prisoners released on licence in 1977 had their licences revoked. This represented an increase of 2.4 per cent over the previous year.

The overall proportion of eligible prisoners receiving parole at some stage of their sentence rose to 62 per cent as compared to 54 per cent in 1976: Times, 16th June 1978.

2238 Prison authority—duty of care owed to prisoner

A prisoner convicted of sexual offences against young girls started his sentence working in isolation under the Prison Rules 1964, r. 43. He was later permitted on his own request, to work with the other prisoners but shortly afterwards he was attacked in a lavatory and injured. He claimed that the prison authority was in breach of its duty of care because the officers supervising the room where he was working had not been told that he was liable to be attacked and therefore had not kept a special watch on him. *Held*, although special steps should have been taken to protect this prisoner from attack, in this case the attack had not been foreseeable as it took place in the lavatory. The prisoner had therefore failed to show that his injury arose from a breach of duty on the part of the prison authority and his claim would be dismissed.

EGERTON v HOME OFFICE [1978] Crim LR 494 (Queens' Bench Division: May J).

2239 Prison rules—legal proceedings

The Home Office has been advised that Prison Rule 37A (1) does not apply to correspondence between a prisoner and his legal adviser in connection with the consideration, examination and investigation of his petition by the European Commission of Human Rights under Articles 25 to 28 of the European Convention on Human Rights, on the grounds that the function performed by the Commission under the Articles do not amount to legal proceedings as that expression is used in the rule: 945 H. of C. Official Report, 27th February 1978, written answers, *col. 6*.

Rule 37A (1) permits a prisoner who is a party to any legal proceedings to correspond with his legal adviser and such correspondence must not be read or stopped unless the Governor suspects that it contains matter unrelated to the proceedings.

2240 Probation and after-care areas

The Combined Probation and After-Care Areas (Buckinghamshire) Order 1978, S.I. 1978 No. 1400 (in force on 1st December 1978 except for Article 3, in force on 12th October 1978), amends the Combined Probation and After-Care Areas Order

1974, 1974 Halsbury's Abr para. 2679, to take account of the continuation of the petty sessional divisions of Fenny Stratford, Newport Pagnell and Stony Stratford in the new petty sessional division of Milton Keynes.

2241   The Combined Probation and After-Care Areas (Nottinghamshire) Order 1978, S.I. 1978 No. 652 (in force on 1st June 1978) amends the Combined Probation and After-Care Areas Order 1974, 1974 Halsbury's Abr para. 2679, to take account of the combination of the petty sessional divisions of Mansfield (Borough) and Mansfield (County) in the new petty sessional division of Mansfield and the combination of the petty sessional divisions of Newark and Southwell in the new petty sessional division of Newark and Southwell.

2242   The Combined Probation and After-Care Areas (Derbyshire) Order 1978. S.I. 1978 No. 813 in force on 1st July 1978, with the exception of decisions taken under Article 3, in which case the Order has effect from 2nd June 1978), amends the Combined Probation and After-Care Areas Order 1974, 1974 Halsbury's Abr para. 2679, to take account of the reorganisation of petty sessional divisions in the county of Derbyshire, effected by the petty sessional divisions (Derbyshire) Order 1978. S.I. 1978 No. 671.

2243   The Combined Probation and After-Care Areas (North Wales) Order 1978, S.I. 1978 No. 814 (in force on 1st July 1978), amends the Combined Probation and After-Care Areas Order 1974, 1974 Halsbury's Abr para. 2679, to take account of the combination of the petty sessional divisions of Caernarvon and Gwyrfai, effected by petty sessional divisions (Gwynedd) Order 1978, S.I. 1978 No. 777.

2244   The Combined Probation and After-Care Areas (Cambridgeshire) Order 1978, S.I. 1978 No. 1192 (in force on 1st September 1978), amends the Combined Probation and After-Care Areas Order 1974, 1974 Halsbury's Abr para. 2679, to take account of the combination of the petty sessional divisions of Huntingdon and Norman Cross, Hurstingstone, Ramsey, Soke of Peterborough and Whittlesey in the new petty sessional divisions of Huntingdon and Peterborough.

PUBLIC HEALTH

Halsbury's Laws of England (3rd edn.), Vol. 31, paras. 1–638

2245   ## Aircraft

The Public Health (Aircraft) (Amendment) Regulations 1978, S.I. 1978 No. 286 (in force on 1st April 1978), amend the Public Health (Aircraft) Regulations 1970 which provide for public health control of aircraft arriving in or leaving England and Wales. The Regulations make provision for the deratting and disinfection of aircraft, and require the crew of an aircraft to inform the commander if anyone on board is suffering from an infectious disease. Surveillance by the medical officer is extended to lassa fever, Viral haemorrhagic fever and marburg.

2246   ## Building regulations

The Building (First Amendment) Regulations 1978, S.I. 1978 No. 723 (in force 1st June 1979) amend the Building Regulations 1976, 1976 Halsbury's Abr para. 2013, by introducing provisions designed to further the conservation of fuel and power.

2247   ## —— inspection of building operations by local authority—failure to inspect properly

See *Batty v Metropolitan Property Realisations Ltd*, para. 2433.

2248   —— type relaxation direction

The Secretary of State for the Environment acting under the Health and Safety at Work etc. Act 1974, s. 66, has further varied type relaxation direction 1 of 16th October 1975 (annexed to Department of Environment circular 105/75 and Welsh Office circular 185/75); see type relaxation direction 1L (Department of Environment circular 48/78 and Welsh office circular 86/78).

2249   Chronically sick and disabled persons—duty of local authority to make arrangements for welfare—enforcement of duty

The appellant suffered from disseminated sclerosis which rendered her incapable of looking after herself. She had been receiving help from the local authority whose duty it was to provide for her welfare under the Chronically Sick and Disabled Persons Act 1970. However the appellant claimed that the authority had failed to provide adequate care and home help causing her to suffer even greater mental distress and anxiety. Her claim was struck out as disclosing no cause of action and she appealed. *Held*, while the Chronically Sick and Disabled Persons Act 1970 dealt with the distribution of benefits or comforts for the sick or disabled, it did not give a right of action to a disappointed sick person. Where a local authority failed to discharge its functions under the Act, the only available remedy was the power of the Minister under the National Assistance Act 1948, s. 36, which provided that he could make an order declaring a local authority to be in default and directing it to remedy the default. The appeal would be dismissed.

WYATT v HILLINGDON LONDON BOROUGH COUNCIL (1978) 76 LGR 727 (Court of Appeal: GEOFFREY LANE and EVELEIGH LJJ). Dicta of Veale J in *Reffell v Surrey County Council* [1964] 1 WLR 358 at 362 and of Lord Denning MR in *Southwark London Borough Council v Williams* [1971] Ch 734 at 742 applied.

For proceedings against the area health authority in this connection, see 1977 Halsbury's Abr para. 1942.

2250   Clean air provisions—authorised fuels

See para. 1164.

2251   Control of Pollution Act 1974—commencement

The Control of Pollution Act 1974 (Commencement No. 13) Order 1978, S.I. 1978 No. 954 brought into force on the 1st August 1978 the Control of Pollution Act 1974, s. 13 (3), (5)–(8). These subsections relate to the provision by occupiers of premises of receptacles for the storage of commercial or industrial waste in cases where the waste, if not so stored, is likely to cause a nuisance or to be detrimental to local amenities.

2252   Dangerous substances—packaging and labelling

See paras 1454, 1455.

2253   Detergents—composition

The Detergents (Composition) Regulations 1978, S.I. 1978 No. 564 (in force on 1st January 1979), give effect to EEC Council Directives 73/404 and 73/405 which relate to the biodegradability of surface active agents in detergents, particularly those which are anionic.

2254   The Detergents (Composition) (Amendment) Regulations 1978, S.I. 1978 No. 1546 (in force on 1st January 1979), amend the definition of "detergent" in the Detergent (Composition) Regulations 1978, see para. 2253.

2255   Local authority—exercise of powers under Public Health Act—compensation for damage

See *George Whitehouse Ltd (t/a Clarke Bros. (Services)) v Anglian Water Authority*, para. 2551.

2256   Nuclear fuels—erection of reprocessing plant—planning permission

See para. 1162.

2257   Pop festivals—public policy

A working group was appointed in 1975 to review Government policies towards pop festivals including free festivals. The group's first report in 1976 stated their view that pop festivals were a reasonable and acceptable form of recreation. In their second and final report entitled Pop Festivals and their Problems (HMSO) the group examine the legislation affecting pop festivals, i.e. licensing powers, general legislation and common law, and conclude that it is doubtful whether the basic problems of festivals can be solved by the introduction of new legislation.

2258   Port health authority—Dover

The Dover Port Health Authority Order 1978, S.I. 1978 No. 819 (in force on 1st August 1978), constitutes the port of Dover as a port health district and constitutes the district council of Dover as port health authority for that district, and provides for the jurisdiction and powers of the council as port health authority. The order supersedes similar orders made under the Public Health Acts and confers on the port health authority functions under general Acts relating to public health and food and drugs.

2259   —— Poole

The Poole Harbour Port Health Authority Order 1978, S.I. 1978 No. 383 (in force on 10th April 1978), constitutes the port of Poole as a port health district and constitutes the borough council of Poole as port health authority for that district, and provides for the jurisdiction and powers of the council as port health authority. Provision is also made for the district council of Purbeck to contribute towards the expenses of the port health authority. This order supersedes similar orders made under the Public Health Acts and confers upon the port health authority functions under general Acts relating to public health and food and drugs.

2260   —— Ramsgate

The Ramsgate Port Health Authority Order 1978, S.I. 1978 No. 1695 (in force on 30th December 1978), constitutes the port of Ramsgate as a port health district and constitutes the district council of Thanet as port health authority for that district.

2261   Rating (Disabled Persons) Act 1978

See para. 2293.

2262   Refuse disposal

Refuse Disposal (Amenity) Act 1978 consolidates certain enactments relating to abandoned vehicles and other refuse; see further para. 1163.

2263   Sewer—ownership of sewer—whether acquired by local authority

See *Royco Homes Ltd v Eatonwill Construction Ltd, Three Rivers District Council* (Third Party), para. 2552.

2264   Ships

The Public Health (Ships) (Amendment) Regulations 1978, S.I. 1978 No. 287 (in force on 1st April 1978), amend the Public Health (Ships) Regulations 1970 which provide for public health control over ships arriving in or leaving England and Wales. The regulations include provisions relating to reports required when there is death or illness aboard ships, and restrictions on the boarding or leaving of an infected ship. The definition of infected ship has been extended, as has the list of diseases in respect of which the medical officer may take precautions in the interests of public health.

2265   Sports grounds—safety

The Safety of Sports Grounds (Designation) Order 1978, S.I. 1978 No. 1091 (in force on 1st January 1979), designates certain sports stadia as stadia requiring safety certificates under the Safety of Sports Grounds Act 1975, 1975 Halsbury's Abr para. 2670.

RACE RELATIONS

Halsbury's Laws of England (4th edn.), Vol. 4, paras. 1034–1100

2266   Article

Public Order and Race Relations, A. N. Khan (the effect of the Public Order Act 1936, ss. 5, 5A and other legislation relating to race relations): 122 Sol Jo 256.

Racially Discriminatory Advertisements, A. N. Khan (discriminatory advertisements and the law relating to race relations): 122 Sol Jo 531.

2267   **Discrimination—advertisement—whether reasonably under-standable as indicating intention to discriminate**

An advertisement was published in a newspaper inviting nurses to apply for jobs in a South African hospital treating "all white patients". The Race Relations Board contended that this amounted to a breach of the Race Relations Act 1968, s. 6 (1), which provides that it is unlawful to publish an advertisement indicating, or which could reasonably be understood as indicating, an intention to do an act of discrimination. *Held*, in asking what could reasonably be understood as an intention to do an act of discrimination, the emphasis was on "reasonably". If the advertisement was capable of being interpreted as meaning that only white nurses need apply, there would have been an infringement of s. 6 (1). However, in this case it was reasonable to conclude that the advertisement was merely telling interested persons about the job, and it was therefore not discrimination within s. 6 (1).

Commission For Racial Equality v Associated Newspapers Group Ltd [1978] 1 WLR 905 (Court of Appeal: Lord Denning MR, Shaw and Waller LJJ). 1968 Act, s. 6 (1), now replaced by Race Relations Act 1976, s. 29 (1).

2268   —— **complaint of discrimination in employment—production of documents—when production of confidential reports should be ordered**

See *Science Research Council v Nasse*; *Vyas v Leyland Cars Ltd*, para. 946; *Rasul v Commission for Racial Equality*, para. 948; *University of Reading v MacCormack*, para. 947.

2269   **Employment—discrimination on racial grounds—barmaid dismissed for serving coloured customers—jurisdiction of industrial tribunal**

A barmaid was dismissed because she refused to obey the publican's instruction not to serve coloured customers. She had claimed before in an industrial tribunal that she had been discriminated against on racial grounds. The publican contended that the facts of the case constituted a breach of the Race Relations Act 1976, s. 30 which could only be remedied by an action brought by the Commission for Racial Equality in the County Court. She appealed against the tribunal's finding that it had no jurisdiction to hear the case. *Held*, it was necessary to look at the intention of Parliament when the Act was made. If they had had the facts of this case in mind they would have made it clear that an industrial tribunal would have jurisdiction. In dismissing the complainant for refusing to obey his instructions not to serve coloured people, the publican had treated her less favourably on racial grounds within the meaning of the 1976 Act, s. 1 (1), and that was an act of unlawful discrimination under s. 4 (2) (c). The appeal would be allowed.

Zarczynska v Levy [1979] 1 WLR 125 (Employment Appeal Tribunal: Kilner Brown J presiding). Dicta of Lord Denning MR and Stephenson LJ in *Race Relations Board v Applin* [1973] QB 815, 828, 831, CA applied.

2270   **Immigration**

See IMMIGRATION.

RAILWAYS, INLAND WATERWAYS AND PIPELINES

Halsbury's Laws of England (3rd edn.), Vol. 31, paras. 639–1403

2271   British Railways Board—pensions

See paras. 2082, 2084.

2272   Transport Act 1978

See para. 2890.

RATING

Halsbury's Laws of England (3rd edn.), Vol. 32, paras. 1–272

2273   Article

Rates and Unused Buildings, Alec Samuels (discussion of rating scheme for empty buildings): [1978] JPL 355.
Recent Rating Decisions, Henry E. Markson: 122 Sol Jo 532.

2274   Company in liquidation—liability for unpaid general rate—date rate due and payable—whether local authority a priority creditor

See *Re Piccadilly Estate Hotels Ltd*, para. 371.

2275   Completion notice—newly erected building—when completion period begins to run

The time for finishing a substantially completed building on which a completion notice has been served for rating purposes runs from the date of substantial completion not the date of service of notice.

A local authority appealed against a decision that a completion notice served by them on a new building was ineffective because it allowed insufficient time for carrying out the outstanding work. The notice had been served some twelve months after substantial completion had been announced by the building's letting agents and allowed seven weeks after service for completion. *Held*, the General Rate Act 1967, Sch. 1, para. 9 clearly stipulated that a local authority was entitled to expect completion of a building within a reasonable time from the date of substantial completion. Time did not run from the date of service of the notice and the appeal would be allowed.

GRAYLAW INVESTMENTS LTD v IPSWICH BOROUGH COUNCIL (1978) Times, 28th June (Court of Appeal: STEPHENSON, WALLER and CUMMING-BRUCE LJJ).

2276   Drainage rate—assessment—greenhouses—effect of central heating installation

See *West of Ouse Internal Drainage Board v H. Prins Ltd*, para. 1692.

2277   Local valuation court—whether a "court"

See *A-G v BBC; Dible v BBC*, para. 467.

2278   Rate rebate scheme

The Rate Rebate Regulations 1978, S.I. 1978 No. 1054 (in force on 13th November 1978) consolidate with amendments the Rate Rebate Regulations 1974, 1974

Halsbury's Abr para. 2763, as amended. The Regulations set out the statutory rate rebate scheme for the grant of rebates from rates by rating authorities or residential occupiers. They set out the method of calculating the rebates with reference to the needs allowance and income of the residential occupier, his reckonable rates and the amount of rebate. They also set out the procedure to be followed to obtain rate rebates, and place a duty on the rating authority receiving an application to determine the eligibility and assess the income of the residential occupier and to notify him of its determinations. Other provisions determine the rebate period and the procedure for applications for further rebates.

The Regulations increase the needs allowances and the amounts to be deducted for any week in a rebate period beginning after 13th November 1978 and increase the minimum rebate from 5p to 10p.

2279 Rate relief—charitable institutions

The Rating (Charitable Institutions) Order 1978, S.I. 1978 No. 218 (in force on 21st March 1978), amends the General Rate Act 1967, Sch. 8, which excludes certain charities from mandatory relief from rating, by omitting from that Schedule the permanent private halls in the University of Oxford. The Order is given retrospective effect to 1st April 1977 under s. 40 (4) of the Act.

2280 Rate support grants

See LOCAL GOVERNMENT.

2281 Rateable occupation—occupation by licensee—house owned by registered charity

A registered charity for ex-servicemen owned a house which was occupied by a disabled ex-serviceman as a licensee. On an application for rates relief on the house under the General Rate Act 1967, s. 40, as it was occupied by a charity and used for charitable purposes, *held*, "occupation" meant legal and not actual occupation. The relevant tests for determining who was in rateable occupation were the degree of control exercised by the owners and the purposes for which the licensee was allowed to reside. Applying those tests, the charity was in rateable occupation and entitled to relief under s. 40.

FORCES HELP SOCIETY AND LORD ROBERTS WORKSHOPS V CANTERBURY CITY COUNCIL (1978) 122 Sol Jo 760 (Chancery Division: SLADE J).

2282 —— occupation by spouse—husband and wife judicially separated—wife sole owner of matrimonial home

After the appellant and his wife married, the wife purchased a matrimonial home in her sole name with her own money. Some years later the parties separated. The wife and children remained in the matrimonial home. The wife petitioned for judicial separation and was granted a decree in May 1976. In her affidavit in support of her application for maintenance she included payment of rates as a necessary expense. The appellant's name remained entered in the records as the rateable occupier of the premises and when he did not pay the rates the rating authority brought a complaint against him. The justices decided that the appellant was the rateable occupier and accordingly was liable for the rates. On appeal the rating authority contended that by reason of the appellant's obligation to maintain his wife and children he was deemed to be in beneficial occupation of the premises and thereby was the rateable occupier. *Held*, it was an established principle that a husband who was separated from his wife was in rateable occupation of the matrimonial home where he had an interest to pass to his wife and by allowing her to remain in the home discharged part of his obligation to maintain. However the appellant had no such interest as his wife owned the house and its contents and had always been responsible for maintaining a home for herself and the children. He was accordingly not in rateable occupation.

BROWN V OXFORD CITY COUNCIL [1978] 3 All ER 1113 (Queen's Bench Division:

LORD WIDGERY CJ, TALBOT and WATKINS JJ). *Cardiff Corporation v Robinson* [1957] 1 QB 39 and *Bromley London Borough Council v Brooks* [1973] RA 137 distinguished.

2283   —— —— rates agreement between absent husband and resident wife—whether husband remained in rateable occupation

A husband and wife jointly owned the matrimonial home. Upon separation, the wife and child continued to live there. An order was made for maintenance in consideration of which the wife accepted responsibility for the payment of the rates. The rating authority brought an action for non-payment of the rates by the husband. On the issue of whether the husband had remained in rateable occupation, *held*, where a husband was using the premises partly to discharge his obligation to maintain his wife and child, the rating authority was not bound by any agreement between the husband and wife. The husband was in rateable occupation of the house.

CHARNWOOD BOROUGH COUNCIL v GARNER (1978) Times, 21st November (Queen's Bench Division: LORD WIDGERY CJ, GRIFFITHS and GIBSON JJ). *Cardiff Corpn v Robinson* [1957] 1 QB 39, applied.

2284   —— occupation of part of premises—whether partial occupation good ground for resisting application for distress warrant in respect of rates on entire property

Magistrates refused to authorise issue of a distress warrant for non-payment of rates. The Divisional Court allowed the local authority's appeal. On appeal by the ratepayer, *held*, the first issue was one of jurisdiction. It was contended for the authority that there was no appeal from a Divisional Court on a case stated by justices relating to the grant of a distress warrant because it was an appeal in a "criminal cause or matter" within the Judicature Act in as much as the proceedings before the magistrates might end in imprisonment. Taking into account the General Rate Act 1967, s. 103 (1), concerning the inquiry as to means before the issue of the warrant of commitment, the present case was not a "criminal cause or matter", and the court had jurisdiction to hear the appeal.

As to the substance of the appeal, the ratepayer contended that the fact that he was only in occupation of part of the hereditament meant that he was only liable for rates in respect of that part, and was a ground for resisting the application for a distress warrant in respect of rates on the whole property. The valuation list showed the entire property as a single hereditament and it was the authority's duty to levy the rates in accordance with the list. The ratepayer's proper remedy was to make a proposal for the alteration of the list. To resist the issue of a warrant, a defendant had to show that the description of the rated property in the valuation list included on its face property that he did not occupy. The description in the valuation list was a "workshop and store", and the ratepayer did not occupy anything which could be described as a store; he also occupied an office which was not covered by the description on the list. He was therefore not liable for any part of the rates claimed and although the magistrates had considered that he was liable for rates on the part of the premises which he occupied, their refusal to authorise the issue of a warrant was right. The appeal would be allowed.

CAMDEN LONDON BOROUGH COUNCIL v HERWALD [1978] 2 All ER 880 (Court of Appeal: MEGAW, LAWTON and BROWNE LJJ). Decision of the Divisional Court of the Queen's Bench Division [1976] 2 All ER 808, 1976 Halsbury's Abr para. 865 reversed. *Manchester Overseers v Headlam* (1888) 21 QBD 96 and *Southwark and Vauxhall Water Co v Hampton UDC* [1899] 1 QB 273, CA applied.

2285   Rateable value—assessment—alteration of valuation list—power of magistrates to go behind list

The plaintiffs purchased a property and made substantial alterations to it as a result of which the valuation officer increased the rateable value. No notice had been given by the plaintiffs to the valuation officer of the change of ownership, so the proposals for increase were sent by him to the old owners. The old owners failed to notify the plaintiffs who were thus unable to object to the proposals for the increase. When a rate demand at the new rate was issued the plaintiffs refused to pay, on the grounds that the procedure for serving notice of the proposals under the General Rate Act 1967, s. 109, had not been complied with. The magistrates, at the request of the rating authority, issued a distress warrant for unpaid rate. The plaintiffs appealed against the issue of the warrant. *Held*, the magistrates could not go behind the valuation list to inquire into such matters as how the figures shown had come into the list. The magistrates were required to judge the position only as between the ratepayer and the rating authority. Since they were satisfied that the ratepayer had been correctly summonsed in accordance with the figure in the list the magistrates had been correct in issuing the warrant.

COUNTY AND NIMBUS ESTATES LTD V EALING LONDON BOROUGH COUNCIL (1978) 76 LGR 624 (Queen's Bench Division: LORD WIDGERY CJ, BOREHAM and DRAKE JJ).

2286   —— —— **installation of central heating—whether a structural alteration or addition**

See *Pearlman v Keepers and Governors of Harrow School*, para. 1766.

2287   —— —— **Lands Tribunal decisions**

BARD V HAYES (VALUATION OFFICER); RIGBY V HAYES (VALUATION OFFICER) (1978) 247 EG 743: E. C. Strathon FRICS (appeals against assessment for rates in respect of two properties situated near motorway on the ground that the valuation officer had not taken sufficient account of noise pollution; valuation officer claimed a hypothetical tenant would accept the noise as a necessary product of modern living and would not reduce his bid for rent; capital values of property in the area had decreased as a result of the noise and a hypothetical tenant would reduce his bid by a similar amount; appeals would be allowed and valuation reduced).

2288   BEAZLEY V COOKE-PRIEST (VALUATION OFFICER) (1977) 247 EG 139: J. H. Emlyn Jones FRICS (hereditament comprised two properties classed as agricultural dwelling-houses in General Rate Act 1967; rates high due to attractive character of village; ratepayer appealed against decision that effect of Act was that 10 per cent be deducted from gross value without first substracting amenity value; market factors were relevant in making valuation; amenity value should not be subtracted before deducting 10 per cent).

2289   F. W. WOOLWORTH & CO LTD V MOORE (VALUATION OFFICER) (1978) 247 Estates Gazette 999: J. H. Emlyn Jones FRICS (tenants of large store in shopping centre appealed against assessment to rates; claimed basis for valuation should have been actual rent; valuation officer based valuation on zone method by reference to smaller shops; considered landlords had accepted low rent from large stores to ensure their presence in shopping centre; rents of small shops only relevant in extreme cases; basis for valuation should be actual rent with adjustments having regard to assessment of other large shops and extra frontage of the store in question).

2290   HAUPTFUHRER V THOMPSON (VALUATION OFFICER) (1978) 246 EG 407: J. D. Russell-Davis FRICS (occupier of Grade 1 listed building appealed against reduction in gross value of only £200 on ground that certain disadvantages not considered; tribunal decided fact that council gave no financial aid or protection against occasional vandalism irrelevant; part of building had to be open to public but only by written appointment so occupier not prevented from using that part as private residence; building well modernised, comfortable and of local importance; competitive market rent easily obtainable; gross value not excessive compared with similar buildings; appeal dismissed).

2291   W. H. SMITH & SON LTD v CLEE (VALUATION OFFICER) [1978] RA 93: R. C. Walmsley FRICS (ratepayers appealed against assessment to rates in respect of shop with frontage on two streets; assessed on basis of full rent; claimed deduction because comparable hereditaments assessed below their rents and further deductions to reflect size and shape; no reason why actual rent should not be starting point for valuation, with discount in relation to rents of comparables; no allowance for size; shop had an excess of frontage so allowance for shape would be made; assessment reduced).

2292   HENRIQUES' v GARLAND (1977) 247 EG 55: V. G. Wellings QC (ratepayer applied for amendment in valuation list; hereditament classed as shop, house and premises, but used as house; change of use to shop would require planning permission; valuation should be based on actual use of premises; description in valuation list should be changed).

2293   MIDLAND BANK LTD v LANHAM (VALUATION OFFICER) (1977) 246 EG 1017: J. H. Emlyn Jones FRICS (bank occupied several floors of building, using part as normal branch of bank, remainder as staff training school; dispute arose as to whether part of building which began as offices but was subsequently given over to training was to be treated as offices or training school for rating purposes; *rebus sic stantibus* rule held to restrict consideration of value not only to physical state of building but also to uses in same class as existing use; accordingly contested part of building, currently used as part of training school, to be treated as such for rating purposes; lower rate therefore applied).

2294   SHEPPARD'S (VALUATION OFFICER) APPEAL (1978) 245 EG 665: R. C. Walmsley FRICS (two adjoining houses; main sewer being sunk nearby; considerable noise, dust and general disturbance for six months; application for temporary rate reduction by owner-occupiers of the houses; period was of sufficient length to allow reduction to be made).

2295   —— —— **provisions to be applied—dock or harbour undertaking**
A limited company, the occupiers of a dock undertaking carried on on premises comprising jetties and ancillary buildings, appealed against a refusal to grant them an order of mandamus requiring the Inland Revenue to calculate the rateable value of the hereditament according to the Docks and Harbours (Valuation) Order 1971 as a dock undertaking carried on under authority conferred by or under any enactment and requiring the valuation officer to make any consequential alteration to the valuation list. They contended that the words "authority conferred by or under any enactment" were wide enough to include the approval by the Customs and Excise Commissioners of the premises on which their dock undertaking was carried on as an "approved wharf" under the Customs and Excise Act 1952, s. 14, since without such approval it would not be lawful for them to carry on a dock undertaking there. *Held*, as a dock company carring out a commercial profit-making business, the appellants were correctly assessed for rating on a profit basis under the General Rate Act 1967. They were not entitled to favourable treatment under the order as they were not carrying out their dock undertaking under authority conferred by an Act of parliament or a statutory instrument, it would be straining the meaning of "under authority" beyond all reasonable bounds to give it the meaning proposed by the appellants, since the approval related to a place and not a particular dock undertaker.
        HARWICH DOCK CO LTD v INLAND REVENUE COMMISSIONERS (1978) 76 LGR 238 (House of Lords: LORD DIPLOCK, LORD SALMON, LORD FRASER OF TULLYBELTON, LORD RUSSELL OF KILLOWEN and LORD KEITH OF KINKEL). Decision of Court of Appeal (1977) 75 LGR 632, 1977 Halsbury's Abr para. 2220 affirmed.

2296   —— —— **tenant in beneficial occupation—whether nil valuation possible**
An occupier appealed against the rating valuation on her flat. She claimed that she

was being harassed by two other families in the building although an order had been made that the maximum number of households in the house should be one. She also said that the valuation should be reduced to nil. The Lands Tribunal held that harassment from neighbours could not affect a rating valuation, and that the valuation could not be nil because the occupier being in beneficial occupation and paying rent, was a hypothetical tenant within the meaning of the General Rate Act 1967, s. 19 (6). On appeal by the occupier *held*, the fact that a tenant was in beneficial occupation did not necessarily preclude a nil valuation. An actual occupier had to be taken into account as one of the hypothetical tenants but any factors which increased the value to her but would not increase it to any other tenant had to be disregarded. Anyone who did not have the occupier's personal reasons for wanting to stay in the flat would not have paid any rent for it. In the present case the existence of troublesome neighbours was a fact which a tenant would take into account when considering a suitable rent. The case would be remitted to the tribunal for rehearing.

BLACK v OLIVER (VALUATION OFFICER) [1978] 3 All ER 408 (Court of Appeal: STEPHENSON, BROWNE and WALLER LJJ).

2297 Rating (Disabled Persons) Act 1978

The Rating (Disabled Persons) Act 1978 amends the law relating to relief from rates in respect of premises used by disabled persons and invalids. The Act received the royal assent on 20th July 1978 and came into force on 1st April 1979: s. 9.

Section 1 requires rating authorities to grant a rebate on the rates chargeable on a hereditament which has special facilities for a disabled person who resides there. Provision is made in Sch. 1 for the regulation of the amount of the rebate. Section 2 requires rating authorities to grant rebates equivalent to the whole of the rates chargeable to an institution occupying a hereditament for a number of specified purposes connected with the care of the disabled. Section 3 lays down the administrative arrangements for applications for rebates, and provides for an appeal to the county court if an application is refused.

Sections 4–7 make similar provision for Scotland, ss. 8 and 9 deal with interpretation, repeals and extent.

2298 —— circular

The Department of the Environment and the Welsh Office have issued a Joint Circular 74/78 (Department of the Environment), 149/78 (Welsh Office), dated 10th November 1978, which provides a brief outline of the new scheme laid down in the Rating (Disabled Persons) Act 1978. It explains how Valuation Officers of the Inland Revenue will be dealing with their functions under the Act and how this will relate to the action of rating authorities on individual cases. Some general advice is offered on points of practice and interpretation which the Secretaries of State wish to commend to rating authorities.

2299 Rating enactments—metrication

The Rating Enactments (Agricultural Land and Agricultural Building) (Amendment) Regulations 1978, S.I. 1978 No. 318 (in force on 1st April 1978), amends the definition of "agricultural land" in the General Rate 1967, s. 26 (3), and that of "agricultural building" in the Rating Act 1971, s. 2, by substituting for references to areas expressed in imperial units references to areas expressed in metric units.

2300 Unoccupied property—levying of rate—hardship cases

The Department of the Environment has issued a circular (No. 34/78) advising local authorities to exercise leniency in the levying of empty property rate in those cases in which hardship would otherwise result.

2301 Valuation list—postponement

The Valuation Lists (Postponement) Order 1978, S.I. 1978 No. 993 (in force on 18th

July 1978) postpones the coming into force of new valuation lists until 1st April 1981.

REAL PROPERTY

Halsbury's Laws of England (3rd edn.), Vol. 32, paras. 273–606

2302   Article

Adverse Possession and Possessory Title, I. G. C. Stratton (the meaning and effect of adverse possession in the light of recent case law): 128 NLJ 367.

2303   Possession—summary proceedings—power to suspend possession order

The applicants applied to the county court under CCR Ord. 26 for an order for the recovery of premises used by them which were occupied by squatters. The order was made but execution was suspended for fourteen days, without the applicants' consent. On appeal by the applicants, *held*, in the absence of consent, the county court judge had no power or discretion under CCR Ord. 26 to grant a suspension of execution of an order for possession against squatters. The appeal would be allowed and the order varied by deleting the suspension of execution.

SWORDHEATH PROPERTIES LTD v FLOYDD [1978] 1 All ER 721 (Court of Appeal: MEGAW, BRIDGE and WALLER LJJ). *McPhail v persons, names unknown* [1973] Ch 447, CA applied.

2304   Sale of land

See SALE OF LAND.

RECEIVERS

Halsbury's Laws of England (3rd edn.), Vol. 32, paras. 607–792

2305   Powers of receiver—power of sale—effect of winding-up of company

A debtor mortgaged his property to a finance company to secure a loan. The company subsequently created a debenture charging all its assets to two banks as security for any present or future debts and giving the banks and their nominees full powers of attorney. At any time after the security became enforceable, the banks had power to appoint a receiver who was to have full powers as the company's agent. The banks demanded repayment of outstanding loans and appointed a receiver. The latter began calling in the assets. However, the company then went into liquidation. Some months after this, the receiver sold the property mortgaged to the company by the debtor to a third party. The conveyance was executed by the receiver and the two banks.

The third party applied to have the conveyance registered but his application was refused on the ground that any conveyance of property of a company in liquidation had to be sealed by that company in the presence of its liquidator. The receiver, third party and both banks issued a summons to establish whether the receiver had the power to sell the property notwithstanding the company's liquidation. *Held*, (i) winding-up deprived the receiver under such a debenture of power to bind the company personally. However, it did not affect his powers to hold and dispose of the company's property comprised in the debenture, for those powers were conferred on him by the disposition made by the debenture itself. Such a disposition could only be of no effect where it was invalidated by the companies Act 1948, or by some provision relating to winding-up, none of which applied in this case.

(ii) The conveyance to the third party had effectively completed the contract because by it the banks, using the powers of attorney vested in them by the debentures, had executed the assurance required to complete a sale validly effected by the receiver. They achieved it in the company's name by exercising the company's power under the mortgage of the property sold. The banks' powers of attorney subsisted in spite of the liquidation both at common law and by statute: the common law maxim of the irrevocable nature of an authority coupled with an interest, and the provisions of the Powers of Attorney Act 1971, s. 4 ensured that.

SOWMAN v DAVID SAMUEL TRUST LTD (IN LIQUIDATION) [1978] 1 WLR 22 (Chancery Division: GOULDING J). *Gaskell v Gosling* [1897] AC 575, HL, and *Gough's Garages Ltd v Pugsley* [1930] 1 KB 615, DC applied.

RENTCHARGES

Halsbury's Laws of England (3rd edn.), Vol. 32, paras. 888–1041

2306   Rentcharges Act 1977—commencement

The Rentcharges Act 1977 (Commencement) Order 1978, S.I. 1978 No. 15, brought into operation on 1st February 1978 the provisions of the Rentcharges Act 1977, 1977 Halsbury's Abr para. 2240 not already in force. These provisions deal mainly with the procedures for the apportionment and redemption of rentcharges and implied covenants affecting rent charges.

2307   Rentcharges—regulations

The Rentcharges Regulations 1978, S.I. 1978 No. 16 (in force on 1st February 1978), prescribe for the purposes of the Rentcharges Act 1977 the forms of application for apportionment of rentcharges and redemption of rentcharges and other rents, and the form of statement of ownership required in connection with an application for redemption. Provision is also made whereby the applicant is responsible for certain expenses incurred on his behalf incidental to an application.

REVENUE

Halsbury's Laws of England (3rd edn.), Vol. 33, paras. 1–622

2308   Articles

Life Assurance Premium Relief, Harold Nisbett (new system for tax relief on life assurance premiums, to be introduced from 6th April 1979): 128 NLJ 705.

Some Thoughts on Tax Avoidance, A. Thompson (examination of the role of tax avoidance in our present system of taxation): 128 NLJ 629.

2309   Appropriation Act 1978

The Appropriation Act 1978 applies a sum out of the Consolidated Fund to the service of the year ending on 31st March 1979, appropriates the supplies granted in the session of Parliament current on the enactment of the Act and repeals certain Consolidated Fund and Appropriation Acts. The Act came into force on receiving the royal assent on 2nd August 1978.

2310   Consolidated Fund Act 1978

The Consolidated Fund Act 1978 applies certain sums out of the Consolidated Fund to the service of the years ending on 31st March 1977 and 1978. The Act came into force on receiving the royal assent on 23rd March 1978.

2311   Customs and Excise

See CUSTOMS AND EXCISE.

2312   Finance Act 1978

The Finance Act 1978 grants and alters certain duties and amends the law relating to the National Debt and the Public Revenue. The Act received the royal assent on 31st July 1978 and came into force on that date.

Part I   Customs and Excise
Section 1 increases the rate of tobacco products duty on certain cigarettes with effect from 4th September 1978. The excise duty on beer, wine, made-wine and imported cider may be repaid in specified circumstances: s. 2. The warehouse regulations in the Finance (No. 2) Act 1975, s. 16 are amended: s. 3. Section 4 enables restrictions to be placed on the free movement of goods. Section 5 imposes penalties for interfering with certain goods. Provisions relating to anti-dumping measures protecting products covered by the European Coal and Steel Community treaty are contained in s. 6 and Sch. 1. Section 7 prescribes the rateable value of land for the purposes of determining gaming licence duty payable for premises in Scotland. From 1st December 1978 certain vehicles used by disabled persons are exempt from duty under the Vehicles (Excise) Act 1971: s. 8. Similar provisions for N. Ireland are contained in s. 9. Section 10 provides for the continuation of Treasury power under the Finance Act 1961, s. 9.

Part II   Value Added Tax
Section 11 amends the provisions of the Finance Act 1972 relating to liability to be registered for value added tax. Under s. 12, a supplier of goods or services may claim bad debt relief.

Part III   Income Tax, Corporation Tax and Capital Gains Tax
Section 13 charges income tax for the year 1978–79 at the basic rate of 33 per cent. A lower rate of 25 per cent will be chargeable on the first £750 of a person's taxable income and higher rate tax will be chargeable on taxable income exceeding £8,000. The investment income surcharge will be 10 per cent on investment income between £1,700 and £2,250 and 15 per cent on the remainder but with a higher threshold for the elderly. Section 14 and Sch. 2 amend various enactments in relation to lower rate income tax. The rate of corporation tax for the financial year 1977 will be 52 per cent: s. 15; the rate of advance corporation tax for the financial year 1978 will be 33/67: s. 16. Section 17 alters the fraction applicable to authorised unit trusts or investment trusts and provides that the rate of advance corporation tax for small companies for the financial year 1977 will be 42 per cent with marginal relief at 1/7. For the year 1978–79 the limit on relief for interest on certain loans for the purchase or improvement of land used as an only or main residence remains at £25,000: s. 18.

Section 19 deals with personal reliefs. A married man's allowance is increased to £1,535 and a single person's to £985; a wife's earned income relief also becomes £985; a married man's age allowance is increased to £2,075 and a single person's to £1,300, with a general limit of income for the full allowance at £4,000. Additional relief for widows and others in respect of children is increased to £550. An allowance may now be claimed for a male or female housekeeper and for the services of a son or daughter.

Section 20 prescribes the child tax allowances and benefits for the year 1978–79, namely for a child over 16 at the commencement of the year of assessment £165, for a child over 11 £135 and for any child under £100. If a child has earned income exceeding £500 or investment income exceeding £115 a year, the allowance is reduced by the excess.

Section 21 exempts maintenance payments from being investment income. Where tax has been deducted from a wife's earned income under the PAYE system, any tax repayment due will be made to her, not to her husband: s. 22. Benefits received by directors and employees earning more than £8,500 a year are taxable: s. 23. Payments of up to £10,000 for loss of employment are not taxable: s. 24.

Section 25 and Sch. 3 amend various enactments relating to relief for premiums payable under a life policy. Section 26 deals with approval of retirement annuity contracts. Tax relief is available to an individual resident in the United Kingdom carrying on a trade or profession partly abroad: s. 27 and Sch. 4. Section 28 grants relief to farmers or market gardeners for fluctuating profits. Divers and diving supervisors working in the United Kingdom and certain areas of the continental shelf are taxable under Sch. D: s. 29. Section 30 grants further relief to individual traders for losses in the early years of trade. However, no relief is allowed for losses under s. 30 or under the Income and Corporation Taxes Act 1970, ss. 168, 177 (2) if they are incurred in dealings in commodity futures: s. 31. Section 32 amends ss. 83, 134 of the 1970 Act. A deduction of 33 per cent must be made from payments to certain sub-contractors in the construction industry: s. 33.

Section 34 provides that certain bodies are exempt from corporation tax in respect of community land transactions with effect from 6th April 1976. Section 35 deals with the power of a close company to apportion part of its income. Section 36 and Sch. 5 make various amendments to the Finance Act 1972, Sch. 16. An industrial buildings allowance may be claimed by a long lessee for capital expenditure on a building: s. 37. Capital expenditure on certain hotels also qualifies for such an allowance: s. 38 and Sch. 6. Section 39 amends the Capital Allowances Act 1968, Part I in relation to allowances for expenditure on agricultural and forestry buildings. Section 40 grants relief for capital expenditure on safety at certain sports grounds. Section 41 postpones the date for payment of income tax charged for 1977–78 which was recalculated to give effect to increased personal allowances and certain other reliefs. Section 42 deals with the deduction of tax from interest payments in 1978–79. Section 43 provides for the repayment of tax paid by police authorities in connection with the provision of free accommodation to police officers.

Sections 44–52 and Schs. 7, 8 relate to capital gains tax. Section 44 and Sch. 7 provide that gains not exceeding £1,000 a year are exempt from tax, gains not exceeding £5,000 are taxed at a reduced rate of 15 per cent and there is marginal relief for gains not exceeding £9,500. Chattels sold for less than £2,000 are exempt from tax: s. 45. Section 46 and Sch. 8 grant relief for gains made on a gift of certain family business assets and shares. Existing relief for replacement of business assets is extended: s. 47. Section 48 increases the relief for gains resulting from the transfer of a business on retirement. Section 49 grants relief for an irrecoverable loan made to a trader. The relief for gains made on the sale of an only or main residence applies although the owner has lived in other accommodation for the purposes of his employment: s. 50. Section 51 grants relief for gains made on a part disposal of land for a sum not exceeding £10,000. Section 52 relates to deeds of family arrangement and disclaimer.

Sections 53–61 and Sch. 9 deal with approved profit sharing schemes. A scheme may only be approved if it limits the initial market value of shares appropriated to each participant in a year to £500; providing the shares also comply with specified conditions they will not be chargeable to tax under Sch. E: s. 53 and Sch. 9, Parts I and II. Certain restrictions on dealings with the shares by a participant are imposed by s. 54. Sections 55 and 56 deal with the tax liability when trustees administering a scheme dispose of shares or receive a capital sum in respect of scheme shares. Section 57 relates to company reconstructions and amalgamations and the treatment of new shares.

No tax relief is available for excess scheme shares when the value of shares appropriated to a participant in a year exceeds £500 or for scheme shares appropriated to an ineligible person: s. 58. Classes of ineligible persons are specified in Sch. 9, Part III. When trustees receive proceeds from a disposal of scheme shares under s. 55 or a capital sum under s. 56, the amount on which tax is due must be paid to the participant after an appropriate PAYE deduction: s. 59. Expenses incurred by a company in making payments to trustees may be deductible from its profits for corporation tax purposes: s. 60. Section 61 deals with the interpretation of various provisions concerning profit sharing schemes.

Part IV   Capital Transfer Tax
For all chargeable transfers after 26th October 1977, s. 62 and Sch. 10 substitute the

following tables for the tables of rates of tax specified in the Finance Act 1975, s. 37:

FIRST TABLE

Portion of value		Rate of tax
Lower limit £	Upper limit £	Per cent.
0	25,000	Nil
25,000	30,000	10
30,000	35,000	15
35,000	40,000	20
40,000	50,000	25
50,000	60,000	30
60,000	70,000	35
70,000	90,000	40
90,000	110,000	45
110,000	130,000	50
130,000	160,000	55
160,000	510,000	60
510,000	1,010,000	65
1,010,000	2,010,000	70
2,010,000	—	75

SECOND TABLE

Portion of value		Rate of tax
Lower limit £	Upper limit £	Per cent.
0	25,000	Nil
25,000	30,000	5
30,000	35,000	$7\frac{1}{2}$
35,000	40,000	10
40,000	50,000	$12\frac{1}{2}$
50,000	60,000	15
60,000	70,000	$17\frac{1}{2}$
70,000	90,000	20
90,000	110,000	$22\frac{1}{2}$
110,000	130,000	$27\frac{1}{2}$
130,000	160,000	35
160,000	210,000	$32\frac{1}{2}$
210,000	260,000	50
260,000	310,000	55
310,000	510,000	60
510,000	1,010,000	65
1,010,000	2,010,000	70
2,010,000	—	75

The limit for an exempt transfer to a non-domiciled spouse is increased to £25,000: s. 63. Business property relief and relief for woodlands is extended: ss. 64, 65. Section 66 amends the definition of control of a company in the Finance Act 1975, Sch. 4. Section 67 and Sch. 11 relate to tax exemption for a transfer of shares by an individual to an employee trust and make consequential amendments to the Finance Acts 1975 and 1976. Section 68 deals with deeds of family arrangement and disclaimer. Transfers of certain interests under a settlement to the settlor, his spouse or widow are not exempt from tax: s. 69. A charge to tax arises when certain bodies become absolutely entitled to property subject to a discretionary trust: s. 70. Section 71 deals with the forfeiture of interests under a protective trust. Section 72 makes minor amendments to the relief for Government securities owned by persons resident abroad. The rule for valuation of life assurance policies and deferred annuity contracts is amended: s. 73. An omission to exercise a right gives rise to a tax liability if it increases the value of property subject to a discretionary trust: s. 74.

Part V Miscellaneous and Supplementary
The surcharge payable under the National Insurance Surcharge Act 1976, s. 1 is increased: s. 75. Section 76 amends the Development Land Tax Act 1976, s. 13 in relation to payment of a reduced rate of tax. Section 77 deals with the disclosure of information to tax authorities in other member states of the EEC. The lending powers of the Public Works Loan Commissioners are extended: s. 78. Miscellaneous supplementary provisions, amendments and repeals are contained in ss. 79, 80 and Schs. 12, 13.

2313　Income tax
See INCOME TAXATION.

2314　Stamp duties
See STAMP DUTIES.

2315　Value added tax
See VALUE ADDED TAX.

ROAD TRAFFIC

Halsbury's Laws of England (3rd edn.), Vol. 33, paras. 623–1383

2316　Article
Dangerous Driving Deceased, Jonathan Fisher (effect of Criminal Law Act 1977, s. 50): 128 NLJ 452.

2317　Accident—failure to stop and report accident—whether one or two offences committed
The defendant's car was involved in an accident. He did not stop, nor did he report the accident at a police station. He was charged with contravening the Road Traffic Act 1972, s. 25 (1), (2). He was convicted on both charges and appealed on the ground that s. 25 created only one offence, relying on *North v Gerrish* (1959) 123 JP 313. *Held*, although there was a reference in *North v Gerrish* to the existence of one offence in s. 25 (1), the decision was that if either element, namely, failing to stop or failing to give name and address, was proved, an offence had been established. Section 25 (2) created a separate offence of failing to report an accident. Although s. 25 (4) referred to "an offence" being committed by a person who failed to comply with s. 25, a person failing to comply with both s. 25 (1) and (2) committed two offences. The appeal would be dismissed.
ROPER v SULLIVAN [1978] Crim LR 233 (Queen's Bench Division: LORD WIDGERY CJ, O'CONNOR and LLOYD JJ).

2318　Carriage by road
See CARRIERS.

2319   Cycle racing

The Cycle Racing on Highways (Special Authorisation) (England and Wales) Regulations 1978, S.I. 1978 No. 254 (in force on 17th March 1978), vary provisions of the Cycle Racing on Highways Regulations 1960 in relation to certain cycle racing events to be held in 1978.

2320   Dangerous driving—disqualification—charge relating to separate incidents during period of driving

A sub-post master was convicted on a charge of dangerous driving, in relation to three separate incidents, and disqualified for twelve months. He appealed against the sentence on the grounds that the offence was not so serious as to demand disqualification and that the jury might have taken one particular incident as the ground for their verdict and, further, that the nature of his occupation required that he be able to drive a car. *Held*, the decision to disqualify was correct. The charge related to his driving throughout the whole period under review. In addition, it was not open to the appellant to plead inconvenience and difficulty if deprived of his licence as he was aware of the penalty involved.

R v KENNEDY [1978] RTR 418 (Court of Appeal: LORD WIDGERY CJ, EVELEIGH LJ and DRAKE J).

2321   —— order to take further driving test—cases in which order appropriate

The appellant was convicted under the Road Traffic Act 1972, s. 2 of dangerous driving and fined £400, disqualified for six months in consequence of three previous convictions for exceeding the speed limit, and ordered under s. 93 (7) of the Act to take a driving test. He appealed against the fine and the order. *Held*, since his driving at excessive speed had caused potential rather than actual danger, the fine was too high and would be reduced to £200. As to the order it was clear that s. 93 (7) was not designed to be punitive and was appropriate only in cases of age or infirmity or where the circumstances of the offence were such as to give rise to a reasonable suspicion that the driver was incompetent. In this case there was no reason to suppose that the driver was incompetent, and the order would be quashed.

R v BANKS (JOHN) [1978] RTR 535 (Court of Appeal: SHAW LJ, LAWSON and SMITH JJ).

The offence of dangerous driving has now been replaced by the offence of reckless driving under the Criminal Law Act 1977, s. 50.

2322   —— preferment of lesser charge by justices—whether limitation period applicable to power to prefer

A bus driver was charged with dangerous driving under the Road Traffic Act 1972, s. 2, following an incident in October 1975 in which a drunken passenger fell from a bus. In June 1976 justices dismissed the charge and, in exercise of their powers under Sch. 4, Pt. IV, para. 4 of that Act, preferred a charge of driving without due care and attention, on which he was convicted. The driver applied for an order of certiorari to quash the decision, on the ground that the justices had no power to prefer a charge more than six months after the event, by virtue of the Magistrates Courts Act 1952, s. 104. Section 104 provides that magistrates may not try an information laid more than six months after the alleged offence. *Held*, MELFORD STEVENSON J dissenting, s. 104 dealt with the trial of informations, while the 1972 Act, Sch. 4 dealt with an entirely separate situation which could only come about under the 1972 Act. Justices could quite properly prefer the lesser charge of driving without due care and attention if they had dismissed one of dangerous driving. Section 104 was wholly irrelevant in such circumstances.

R v COVENTRY JUSTICES, EX PARTE SAYERS [1978] LS Gaz R 346 (Queen's Bench Division: LORD WIDGERY CJ, MELFORD STEVENSON and CANTLEY JJ).

2323   —— **warning of prosecution—whether given at time the offence was committed**

A motorist was arrested following his refusal to take a breath test. Two and a half hours later, he was cautioned and warned that the question of prosecution for dangerous driving would be considered. On conviction of the offence, he appealed, contending that the warning had not been given at the time the offence was committed and was therefore not in accordance with the Road Traffic Act 1972, s. 179 (2) (a). *Held*, literal compliance with the section was virtually impossible in practice. What had to be considered was whether the chain of circumstances was unbroken and all that took place was connected with the accident, bearing in mind that there would always be exceptional circumstances. In the present case, as the lapse of time was neither unreasonable nor unjustified, the appeal would be dismissed.

R v OKIKE (1978) Times, 5th October (Court of Appeal: LORD WIDGERY CJ, EVELEIGH LJ and SMITH J). *Sinclair v Clark* (1962) SLT 307, applied.

2324   **Drivers' hours**

See para. 2396.

2325   —— **community provisions—harmonisation**

The Drivers' Hours (Harmonization with Community Rules) Regulations 1978, S.I. 1978 No. 1157 (in force on 17th August 1978), revoke the Drivers' Hours (Passenger and Goods Vehicles) (International Rules) Regulations 1973, S.I. 1973 No. 379. The Regulations provide that provisions of the Transport Act 1968 regulating the permitted driving times and periods of duty of drivers of passenger and goods vehicles are to be adjusted so as to take account of the European Economic Community rules with respect to international transport operations and national transport operations in Great Britain.

2326   —— —— **temporary modification**

The Community Drivers' Hours Rules (Temporary Modifications) Regulations 1978, S.I. 1978, No. 7 (in force 26th January 1978) modify, in relation to United Kingdom road transport operations, the provisions of EEC Council Regulation 543/69 relating to the hours and conditions of work of drivers in the road transport industry. The modifications will remain in force until 31st December 1980.

2327   —— **goods vehicles**

The Drivers' Hours (Goods Vehicles) (Exemptions) Regulations 1978, S.I. 1978 No. 1364 (in force on 17th October 1978) revoke and replace with amendments the Drivers' Hours (Goods Vehicles) (Exemptions) Regulations 1972, and provide certain exemptions from the requirements of the Transport Act 1968 s. 96 in relation to permitted driving times. The purpose of the regulations is to cover cases of emergency and to meet certain special needs.

2328   —— **records**

The Drivers' Hours (Keeping of Records) (Amendment) Regulations 1978, S.I. 1978 No. 1878 (in force on 1st February 1979), amend the Drivers' Hours (Keeping of Records) Regulations 1976, 1976 Halsbury's Abr para. 2125. They provide for a simplified drivers' record book to be used by short distance freight drivers who do not spend more than four hours each working day in driving. A short distance freight driver is one who operates within a 50 km radius of the vehicle's base.

2329   The Drivers' Hours (Keeping of Records) (Amendment) (No. 2) Regulations 1978, S.I. 1978 No. 1938 (in force on 1st February 1979), amend the Drivers' Hours (Keeping of Records) Regulations 1976, 1976 Halsbury's Abr para. 2125, rendering it unnecessary for the drivers of British passenger vehicles on national transport operations to enter in the weekly reports in their drivers' record books particulars of the time spent in the course of their employment on activities other than driving.

2330   Driving instruction—fees

The Motor Cars (Driving Instruction) (Amendment) Regulations 1978, S.I. 1978 No. 1316 (in force on 1st October 1978) amend the Motor Cars (Driving Instruction) Regulations 1977, r. 13, 1977 Halsbury's Abr para. 2262, with regard to fees.

2331   Driving or being in charge whilst unfit through drink or drugs— blood or urine specimen—procedure—evidence—admissibility

Where a charge is made under the Road Traffic Act 1972, s. 6, of driving with a blood alcohol level above the prescribed limit, a motorist has a technical defence if he can show that the provisions of s. 9 have not been accurately complied with. This section provides that two specimens of blood or urine must be provided within one hour of a request to do so. A motorist who was convicted of an offence under s. 5 of driving while unfit through drink appealed on the ground that the wording of s. 7, which lays down the procedure for provision of specimens for the purpose of a charge under s. 5, was so similar to that of s. 9 that the same technical defence applied. *Held*, s. 6 laid down a technical offence and failure to comply with s. 9 would involve automatic penal consequences, so it was appropriate that a technical defence should be available. The same could not be said of ss. 5 and 7. Nor should the general wording of s. 7, which provided that any specimen given at a material time would be admissible in evidence, be construed as strictly as s. 9 which laid down a one hour time limit.

R v MOORE [1978] RTR 384 (Court of Appeal: BRIDGE LJJ, PARK and EASTHAM JJ). *R v Hyams* [1972] 3 All ER 651 distinguished.

2332   Driving or being in charge with blood-alcohol concentration above prescribed limit—appeal—whether imprisonment and long period of disqualification appropriate

A man who had a number of previous convictions for drunkenness and drinking and driving offences pleaded guilty to two offences of driving with excess alcohol in his blood, one offence of failing to provide a specimen and one offence of driving while unfit through drink. He suffered from a drink problem which he refused to recognise, and the judge at first instance sentenced him to thirty months imprisonment and disqualified him for twenty years. He appealed against both the period of imprisonment and disqualification, maintaining that his anti-social behaviour was not so extreme as to warrant such a severe sentence, that his genuine drink problem and the fact that he was a stepfather to seven children merited some mitigation of the sentence and that the driving ban gave him no real hope of ever driving again. *Held*, the appellant was a menace to the general public and there was a serious risk that before long he would maim or kill someone. It was a serious case and therefore it was not possible to say that the sentence of imprisonment was wrong or the period of disqualification excessive. The appeal would be dismissed.

R v McLAUGHLIN [1978] RTR 452 (Court of Appeal: ROSKILL and BROWNE LJJ and KERR J).

2333   arrest—validity of arrest

The defendant assaulted two police officers to avoid being given a breath test. He was arrested for assault and was given a breath test at the police station, whereupon he was again arrested under the Road Traffic Act 1972, s. 8. He appealed against a conviction for driving with excess alcohol in his blood on the ground that there was no valid arrest under s. 8 because at that time he was already under arrest for assault and so could not have been properly arrested unless he had first been released and then re-arrested. *Held*, the fact that a person was under arrest for one offence did not prevent the imparting to him of a further reason for his arrest, and once that further reason was imparted to him he became arrested for two offences. The appeal would be dismissed.

R v HATTON [1978] Crim LR 95 (Court of Appeal: GEOFFREY LANE LJ, WIEN and MAIS JJ).

2334 —— **blood or urine specimen—agreement to give blood—effect of refusal to allow police doctor to take it**

A motorist required by the police to give a blood or urine specimen requested the presence of his own doctor in addition to the police one. He then refused to allow the police doctor to take blood, although he was willing that his own should. He was convicted for refusing to provide a specimen. On appeal, *held*, the Road Traffic Act 1972 did not specify any particular medical practitioner as having to take specimens. Not every condition imposed by a motorist in such circumstances could be called a refusal and in this case the motorist had complied with the statutory obligations upon him.

BAYLISS v THAMES VALLEY POLICE CHIEF CONSTABLE [1978] LS Gaz R 346 (Queen's Bench Division: MELFORD STEVENSON, CANTLEY and CROOM-JOHNSON JJ).

2335 —— —— **failure to provide specimen—acquittal of being in charge while unfit—effect of acquittal on charge of failing to provide specimen**

The defendant was arrested for being unfit to drive through drink when in charge of a motor vehicle on a road, contrary to the Road Traffic Act 1972, s. 5 (2). He was required to provide a specimen for a laboratory test, which he failed to do. He was charged with contravention of s. 5 (2) and of s. 9 (3), in that "being a person who had been in charge of a motor vehicle on a road" he had failed without reasonable excuse to provide a specimen. He was acquitted of the charge under s. 5 (2). The prosecutor declined to amend the charge under s. 9 (3) so as to delete the reference to his being in charge of a motor vehicle and the justices dismissed the information. On appeal by the prosecutor, *held*, when a person was properly arrested, as here, in respect of an offence under s. 5 (2), it was irrelevant to a charge under s. 9 (3) that the offence under s. 5 (2) was not proved. The allegation that the defendant was in charge of a motor vehicle was mere surplusage. While its deletion might have been convenient, it was not necessary and the case would be remitted to the justices with a direction to convict.

ROBERTS v GRIFFITHS [1978] RTR 362 (Queen's Bench Division: LORD WIDGERY CJ, WIEN and KENNETH JONES JJ).

2336 —— —— **hospital patient—doctor notified of requirement for specimen—validity of notification**

The defendant, who had been injured in a car accident, was admitted to hospital. He refused to provide a specimen for a breath test. The police officer therefore, in accordance with the Road Traffic Act 1972, s. 9 (2), informed the doctor in charge of the defendant's case of his intention to require a blood or urine specimen for a laboratory test. The defendant was within earshot of this conversation. The doctor raised no objection but the defendant failed to provide a specimen and was charged with failing to do so without a reasonable excuse. Justices dismissed the information on the ground that the purpose of s. 9 (2) was negated by the patient being able to overhear the conversation. On appeal by the prosecution, *held*, s. 9 (2) did not require the notification to the doctor to be made in the patient's absence. The fact that the patient was within earshot was immaterial. Section 9 (2) had been complied with and the appeal would be allowed and the case remitted to the justices.

OXFORD v LOWTON [1978] RTR 237 (Queen's Bench Division: LORD WIDGERY CJ and WIEN J).

2337 —— **breath test—defective device—validity of test**

A motorist was required to provide a breath specimen. The bag burst near the end of the test, but not before the crystals had shown a positive result. He was arrested and charged with driving with an excess of alcohol in his blood. At the trial, his only defence was that the bag had burst. He was convicted. On appeal, *held*, since the crystals had changed colour without the bag being fully inflated, there was no risk that the test had been unsatisfactory. The appeal would be dismissed.

R v KAPLAN [1978] RTR 119 (Court of Appeal: LAWTON LJ, MACKENNA and GIBSON JJ). *Rayner v Hampshire Chief Constable* [1971] RTR 15; *R v Parsons* [1972] RTR 425, CA, not applied.

2338 —— —— **failure to inflate bag—duty of constable to inspect crystals**

A motorist was required to provide a breath specimen. He failed to inflate the bag fully. Without checking the crystals in the bag, the constable then arrested the motorist for failing to provide a specimen. The motorist later provided a laboratory test specimen which proved positive. He was charged and convicted with driving with an excess of alcohol in his blood and failing to provide a breath test specimen. He appealed against conviction on the basis of the failure of the constable to check the crystals before arresting him. *Held*, allowing the appeal, that where even a little air had entered the bag, an inspection of the crystals was necessary by the constable, for evaluating whether to arrest on the ground of a positive result or a failure to take the test. The arrest for failure to take the test was therefore unlawful and the conviction would be quashed.

SENEVIRATNE v BISHOP [1978] RTR 92 (Queen's Bench Division: LORD WIDGERY CJ, PARK and MAY JJ). *R v Holah* [1973] 1 All ER 106, CA; *Walker v Lovell* [1975] 3 All ER 107, HL, 1975 Halsbury's Abr para. 2862; *Spicer v Holt* [1976] 3 All ER 71, HL, 1976 Halsbury's Abr para. 2141, applied.

2339 A motorist was required to provide a breath specimen. He did so and the test proved positive. He was arrested and taken to a police station. At the police station he was asked to take another breath test, but on this occasion he failed to inflate the bag. He was asked to take a second test, but again failed to inflate the bag. On neither occasion did the police officer examine the crystals. The motorist was then required to provide a laboratory test specimen, as a result of which he was charged with driving with an excess of alcohol in his blood. The justices dismissed the case on the basis of the failure by the police to inspect the crystals after the breath tests. On appeal, *held*, the laboratory test specimen was correctly required, once it was clear that the breath test could not be evaluated. The case would be remitted to the justices with a direction to convict.

SHEPHERD v KAVULOK [1978] Crim LR 170 (Queen's Bench Division: LORD WIDGERY CJ, CUMMING-BRUCE LJ, and PARK J).

2340 —— —— **failure to provide—validity of arrest**

A police officer arrested a motorist for failure to provide a breath specimen following the latter's inability fully to inflate a breathalyser bag. The officer did not examine the crystals in it before making the arrest. The motorist appealed against his subsequent conviction for driving with excess alcohol in his bloodstream on the ground that he had originally provided a breath specimen and thus should not have been arrested for failure to do so. *Held*, the constable had correctly inferred, from the minimal quantity of breath blown into the bag, that the driver had failed to provide the required breath specimen and the issue had been properly left to the jury as a question of fact. The appeal would be dismissed.

R v REY [1978] RTR 413 (Court of Appeal: SHAW LJ, MAIS and PETER PAIN JJ). *Walker v Lovell* [1975] 3 All ER 107, 1975 Halsbury's Abr para. 2862, distinguished.

2341 —— —— **grounds for requiring**

A police constable, believing that the defendant's car had been involved in an accident, expressly required him to take a breath test under the Road Traffic Act

1972, s. 8 (2). The defendant refused and was charged with failing to provide a breath specimen. The prosecutor conceded that no accident involving the defendant's car had taken place. Justices dismissed the information on the ground that the prosecution had failed to justify the requirement on the footing of s. 8 (2) and could not rely alternatively on s. 8 (1) (a) (suspicion of alcohol) as at the time he required the breath specimen the constable had no thought of alcohol in the defendant's body. On appeal by the prosecutor, *held,* the prosecutor could rely on the alternative ground should the first proposition fall down as long as that alternative proposition was substantiated. In this case, the alternative ground of suspicion of alcohol under s. 8 (1) (a) had not been substantiated and the appeal would be dismissed.

CLEMENTS v DAMS [1978] Crim LR 96 (Queen's Bench Division: LORD WIDGERY CJ, PARK and MAY JJ).

2342   A car which had a defective headlight and was being driven by the defendant was stopped by a police constable. The constable suspected that he had alcohol in his body and required him to take a breath test under the Road Traffic Act 1972, s. 8 (1) (a). The test proved positive and the defendant was charged with driving while the proportion of alcohol in his blood exceeded the prescribed limit. Justices found that s. 8 (1) (a) and not s. 8 (1) (b) (suspicion of a moving traffic offence) had been relied on in requesting the breath test and dismissed the information on the ground that the arrest had been improper since the defendant was not "driving or attempting to drive." On appeal by the prosecutor, *held,* the prosecution could rely alternatively on s. 8 (1) (b), although the constable had had s. 8 (1) (a) in mind when requiring the breath test, since it could be concluded from the reference to s. 8 (1) (b) in the justices' finding that it had been sufficiently relied on and had been present in the justices' minds. The appeal would be allowed and the case remitted to the justices.

RICKWOOD v COCHRANE [1978] Crim LR 97 (Queen's Bench Division: LORD WIDGERY CJ, PARK and MAY JJ).

2343   ——— ——— ——— **proof of occurrence of accident**

The appellant was required by a police officer to take a breath test under the Road Traffic Act 1972, s. 8 (2), which provides that if an accident occurs owing to the presence of a motor vehicle on a road a police officer may require a person whom he has reasonable cause to believe was driving the vehicle at the time of the accident to provide a specimen of breath. He was convicted of driving with a blood-alcohol concentration in excess of the prescribed limit. He appealed against conviction on the grounds that the judge had misdirected the jury by saying that it was open to them to convict him if they were satisfied that the officer had reasonable cause to believe that there had been an accident and that a breath test was required within a reasonable time. *Held,* under s. 8 (2) the prosecution had to establish that an accident had in fact occurred due to the presence of a motor vehicle on the road, and secondly, that an officer had reasonable cause to believe that the appellant was driving the vehicle at the time of the accident. Since the jury were not clearly directed on the actual issues of the case, the appeal would be allowed and the conviction quashed.

R v VARDY [1978] RTR 202 (Court of Appeal: LORD WIDGERY CJ, CANTLEY and PETER PAIN JJ).

2344   ——— ——— **inflation of device not in accordance with manufacturer's instructions—inflation in two breaths—validity of test**

The Attorney General referred to the Court of Appeal a point of law relating to the use of the Alcotest (R) 80 breath test device. The manufacturer's instructions stated that the person being treated had to blow through the mouthpiece and fully inflate the bag with one single breath. The reference asked whether a test was invalid where a police constable told the driver to inflate the device in one breath and the driver, to the constable's knowledge, inflated it in two. *Held,* the requirement of inflation in a single breath was to ensure that the bag would be filled with air which had been fully treated in the lungs. If more than one breath was taken the concentration of alcohol could be diluted and the test could be unduly favourable to the motorist. Where the effect of any breach of the instructions could only be in the motorist's favour there was no reason to regard the test as vitiated. It would be otherwise where the effect of the breach would be to render the result unduly favourable to the Crown.

ATTORNEY GENERAL'S REFERENCE (No. 1 of 1978) (1978) 122 Sol Jo 489 (Court of Appeal: LORD WIDGERY CJ, WALLER LJ and MILMO J). *Webber v Carey* [1970] AC 1072, HL, applied.

2345 —— **driving or attempting to drive—attempting to drive broken down vehicle**

The appellant, who suffered from a heart condition which made strenuous physical exertion inadvisable, was driving his vehicle uphill when it stopped because, unknown to him, the clutch had ceased to function properly. He allowed the car to move backwards downhill until it came to rest and accelerated the engine in the hope that it could be driven a short distance. However, the clutch was burnt out so that the car could no longer be driven by its engine; neither could it be moved by the appellant unaided because of his state of health. Police officers arrived and suspected alcohol in the appellant's body. It was later revealed by a laboratory test that his blood-alcohol proportion exceeded the prescribed limit. The appellant was convicted of attempting to drive with an excess of alcohol in his blood contrary to the Road Traffic Act 1972, s. 6 (1). He appealed against conviction, contending that he could not be found guilty of attempting to drive a car which was incapable of being propelled by its engine and which he could not move unaided. *Held*, a person who sat at the driving seat of a car and attempted to either start it or put it in gear, or accelerated the engine so as to make the car go forward was attempting to drive it and the fact that there was some intervening factor which ultimately would prevent him from fulfilling the attempt did not prevent it from being an attempt to drive. This case differed from circumstances where the commission of the full offence was impossible from the very beginning. Accordingly, the appellant had attempted to drive the car as, apart from the burnt out clutch, there was nothing impossible about driving it in principle. The appeal would be dismissed.

R v FARRANCE [1978] RTR 225 (Court of Appeal: WALLER LJ, MARS-JONES and WATKINS JJ).

2346 The appellant was driving his car when he had to stop it on the side of a road because the tyres had become deflated. He got out of the car and police officers who were patrolling the area smelt alcohol on his breath. A subsequently administered breath test proved positive. The appellant was convicted of driving with an excess of alcohol in his blood contrary to the Road Traffic Act 1972, s. 6 (1). He appealed, contending that there had been a misdirection of the jury in that he had not been driving or attempting to drive his car when the breath test was required, because it was incapable of being driven, having broken down sometime previously. *Held*, the jury had been misdirected because the question of lapse of time was wholly immaterial when they came to consider whether the car was capable of being driven. What was relevant was the state of the car. The jury should have been reminded about its mechanical condition and asked to decide whether it was capable of being driven so that it could be said that the appellant was capable of driving it or whether its condition prevented him from driving it. Accordingly the appeal would be allowed.

R v NEILSON [1978] RTR 232 (Court of Appeal: SHAW LJ, MAIS and PETER PAIN JJ). *Edkins v Knowles* [1973] RTR 257, DC applied.

2347 —— **first offence—whether imprisonment appropriate sentence**

The applicant was arrested while driving in an erratic manner and was given a breath test which proved positive. He resisted arrest and was later charged with driving with a blood alcohol concentration above the prescribed limit. The court found that he had been convicted of several previous road traffic offences and sentenced him to six months' imprisonment. He appealed on the ground that a sentence of imprisonment on a first breathalyser offence was wrong in principle.

Held, there was no principle of sentencing which prohibited a sentence of imprisonment on a first breathalyser offence, but each case would depend on its own facts. The applicant's record showed that he was in the habit of disregarding road traffic laws and on this occasion he had behaved irresponsibly in resisting arrest. In these circumstances a custodial sentence was justified and therefore the appeal would be dismissed.

R v Nokes (1978) 66 Cr App Rep 3 (Court of Appeal: Lawton LJ, Park and Michael Davies JJ).

2348 —— time of driving

The appellant was convicted under the Road Traffic Act 1972, s. 6 (1) of driving with excess alcohol in his blood. Having pleaded guilty to the charge on the basis of agreed facts, he appealed on the grounds that the facts did not establish that he had been driving at the relevant time appropriate to s. 8 (2), the section under which he had been given a breath test prior to providing a specimen under s. 9, namely at the time of the accident in question, as provided by Sch. 4, Part V of the Act. *Held*, the provisions in Sch. 4, Part V were relevant only to the offence under s. 9 (3) of failing to provide a specimen. Therefore, the driving which constituted the offence under s. 6 (1) was not restricted to the driving which justified the breath test requirement under s. 8 (2). The appeal would be dismissed.

R v Wedlake [1978] RTR 529 (Court of Appeal: Bridge LJ, Watkins and Jupp JJ).

2349 Goods vehicles—international journeys—fees

The Goods Vehicles (Authorisation of International Journeys) (Fees) (Amendment) Regulations 1978, S.I. 1978 No. 1801 (in force on 1st January 1979), amend the Goods Vehicles (Authorisation of International Journeys) (Fees) Regulations 1976, 1976 Halsbury's Abr para. 2149. They introduce a fee of £2·50 for the issue of a special permanent permit on behalf of the Spanish government. This permit entitles the holder to use a vehicle exceeding a certain laden weight or dimensions in Spain.

2350 —— loading areas—control of parking

The Control of Parking in Goods Vehicle Loading Areas Orders (Procedure) Regulations 1978, S.I. 1978 No. 1347 (in force on 12th October 1978) lay down the procedure to be followed by the Greater London Council and by county councils when making orders under the Local Government (Miscellaneous Provisions) Act 1976, s. 37, 1976 Halsbury's Abr para. 1633, for controlling the parking of vehicles in designated loading areas.

2351 —— —— removal and disposal of parked vehicles

The Removal and Disposal of Vehicles (Loading Areas) Regulations 1978, S.I. 1978 No. 1345 (in force on 12th October 1978) give power to an authorised officer of a local authority to require the removal of a vehicle parked in a designated loading area in contravention of the Local Government (Miscellaneous Provisions) Act 1976, s. 37, 1976 Halsbury's Abr para. 1633.

2352 —— operators' licences.

The Goods Vehicles (Operators' Licences) (Temporary Use in Great Britain) (Amendment) Regulations 1978, S.I. 1978 No. 1110 (in force on 31st August 1978), amend the Goods Vehicles (Operators' Licences) (Temporary Use in Great Britain) Regulations 1975, 1975 Halsbury's Abr para. 2900 in relation to exemptions for certain vehicles used for the carriage of goods between EEC countries and for vehicles with international authorisations or licences. Also amended are the exemptions and modifications for goods vehicles of certain named European countries.

2353   —— plating and testing

The Goods Vehicles (Plating and Testing) (Amendment) Regulations 1978, S.I. 1978 No. 867 (in force on 1st July 1978), further amend the Goods Vehicles (Plating and Testing) Regulations 1971 by increasing the fees payable for examinations, re-examinations, texts and re-tests of motor vehicles and for the replacement of a test certificate or Ministry Test date disc.

2354   The Vehicles (Plating and Testing). (Amendment) (No. 2) Regulations 1978 S.I. 1978 No. 1018 in force on 30th August 1978), amend the Goods Vehicles (Plating and Testing) Regulations 1971 by introducing a definition of "converter dolly" and providing that these Regulations apply to converter dollies, manufactured on or after 1st January 1979, whose unladen weight does not exceed 1020 kilograms.

2355   Hovercraft—application of enactments

See para. 2630.

2356   Insurance

See INSURANCE (motor insurance).

2357   Licences—drivers

The Motor Vehicles (Driving Licences) (Amendment) Regulations 1978, S.I. 1978 No. 697 (in force on 1st June 1978), amend the Motor Vehicles (Driving Licences) Regulations 1976, 1976 Halsbury's Abr para. 2153, so as to provide an exemption to the conditions attached to provisional licences prescribed by reg. 8 of the 1976 Regulations. The definition of "qualified driver" is extended and the fee for an appointment for a driving test is increased to £7.30.

2358   The Motor Vehicles (Driving Licences) (Amendment) (No. 2) Regulations 1978, S.I. 1978 No. 1109 (in force on 31st August 1978), further amend the Motor Vehicles (Driving Licences) Regulations 1976, 1976 Halsbury's Abr para. 2153, so as to abolish from 1st May 1979 payment of any fee for a driving licence by persons who are sixty-five or over when the licence comes into force. They also add Barra to the category of islands excluded from the exemption from the regulation providing that provisional licence holders must drive under the supervision of a qualified driver.

2359   —— —— heavy goods vehicles—fees

The Heavy Goods Vehicles (Drivers' Licences) (Amendment) Regulations 1978, S.I. 1978 No. 669 (in force on 1st June 1978, further amend the Heavy Goods Vehicles (Drivers' Licences) Regulations 1977, 1977 Halsbury's Abr para. 2291 so as to increase the fee payable by a person who applies for a heavy goods vehicle driving test from £24 to £30.

2360   —— vehicle excise duty—exemptions

The Road Vehicles (Registration and Licensing) (Amendment) Regulations 1978, S.I. 1978 No. 1536 (in force on 17th November 1978) further amend the Road Vehicles (Registration and Licensing) Regulations 1971, in pursuance of the Finance Act 1978, s. 8, which extends the exemptions from vehicle excise duty to persons in receipt of a mobility allowance.

2361   Motor vehicles—approval marks

The Motor Vehicles (Designation of Approval Marks) (Amendment) Regulations 1978, S. I. 1978 No. 1111 (in force on 30th August 1978), amend the Motor Vehicles (Designation of Approval Marks) Regulations 1976, 1976 Halsbury's Abr para. 2166, by adding certain markings to the markings designated as approval marks.

2362   The Motor Vehicles (Designation of Approval Marks) (Amendment) (No. 2) Regulations 1978, S.I. 1978 No. 1870 (in force on 19th January 1979), amend the Motor Vehicles (Designation of Approval Marks) Regulations 1976, 1976 Halsbury's Abr para. 2166 by adding to, and making minor alterations to the markings which are designated as approval marks.

2363   —— **competitions and trials**

The Motor Vehicles (Competitions and Trials) (Amendment) Regulations 1978, S.I. 1978 No. 481 (in force on 26th April 1978), amend the Motor Vehicles (Competitions and Trials) Regulations 1969, as amended, so as to increase the fees payable to the Royal Automobile Club for the authorisation of events in so far as they are to take place, in whole or in part, in England or Wales.

2364   —— **construction and use**

The Motor Vehicles (Construction and Use) Regulations 1978, S.I. 1978 No. 1017 (in force on 30th August 1978), consolidate and further amend the Motor Vehicles (Construction and Use) Regulations 1973 by (i) providing definitions and requirements relating to a composite trailer and converter dolly; (ii) obviating inconsistencies relating to the weights borne by axles and exempting certain agricultural trailers from requirements relating to total laden weight; (iii) exempting vehicles which have been type approved under the Motor Vehicles (Type Approval) (Great Britain) Regulations 1976 from certain requirements in the 1978 Regulations as to marking; (iv) providing for the maintenance of seat belts and anchorages of certain motor vehicles; and (v) in relation to tyres, defining the meanings of "tie-bar", "tread wear indicator" and "stub-axle" and providing requirements as to the types of tyres which may be used on one vehicle.

2365   The Motor Vehicles (Construction and Use) (Amendment) Regulations 1978, S.I. 1978 No. 1233 (in force on 29th September 1978), amend the Motor Vehicles (Construction and Use) Regulations 1978, para. 2364, r. 17, by introducing new provisions as to seat belt anchorage points and seat belts.

2366   The Motor Vehicles (Construction and Use) (Amendment) (No. 2) Regulations 1978, S.I. 1978 No. 1234 (in force on 1st October 1978), amend the Motor Vehicles (Construction and Use) Regulations 1978, para. 2364, r. 26 by making new provisions as to safety glass.

2367   The Motor Vehicles (Construction and Use) (Amendment) (No. 3) Regulations 1978, S.I. 1978 No. 1235 (in force on 1st October 1978), amend the Motor Vehicles (Construction and Use) Regulations 1978, para. 2364, r. 42 by introducing new provisions as to manufacturers' plates.

2368   The Motor Vehicles (Construction and Use) (Amendment) (No. 4) Regulations 1978, S.I. 1978 No. 1263 (in force on 1st October 1978), amend the Motor Vehicles (Constructions and Use) Regulations 1978, para. 2364, r. 36 by introducing new provisions requiring certain vehicles to be marked in relation to the emission of gaseous pollutants.

2369   The Motor Vehicles (Construction and Use) (Amendment) (No. 5) Regulations 1978, S.I. 1978 No. 1317 (in force on 1st October 1978), amend the Motor Vehicles (Construction and Use) Regulations 1978, para. 2364 by introducing a requirement that all motor vehicles in a certain class shall carry a sign indicating an overall travelling height in excess of twelve feet.

2370   —— —— **insecure load—mens rea**

Three coils of steel were loaded for export onto an articulated vehicle. On the way to the docks, one coil fell off and the others rolled to one side of the trailer. All the straps had come loose. The driver and the owner were charged with contravening the Moter Vehicles (Construction and Use) Regulations 1973, reg. 90 (2), in that the load was not secured so that danger was not likely to be caused to any person on a road by reason of the load or part of it falling from the vehicle. Justices found that the coils had been loaded in accordance with normal practice and the load had been secured so that no danger was likely to be caused. On appeal by the prosecutor, *held*, an offence under reg. 90 (2) was one of absolute liability. Although the words "is not likely to be caused" involved an element of foreseeability, it had to be determined according to the factual circumstances as they were, regardless of the knowledge of the person using the vehicle. In this case, the straps were defective and although the defendants had no knowledge of it, when they broke there were circumstances from which it was proper to assume that danger was likely to be caused. The appeal would be allowed.

DENT v COLEMAN [1978] RTR 1 (Queen's Bench Division: LORD WIDGERY CJ, CANTLEY and PETER PAIN JJ). *Cornish v Ferry Masters Ltd* [1975] RTR 292, 1975 Halsbury's Abr para. 2805 followed.

2371   —— —— **tyres**

An employee of a firm in which the defendant was a partner used a motor vehicle which had defective tyres. The defendant was charged with two offences relating to the tyres. The justices found that as the defendant did not take part in the daily management of the firm nor in the maintenance of the vehicle there was no case for him to answer. The prosecution appealed. *Held*, the justices had been misled by the description of the defendant's role in the firm. It was sufficient that he could be classed as the employer of the driver for him to be convicted. The case would be sent back for the hearing to continue.

PASSMOOR v GIBBONS [1978] Crim LR 498 (Queen's Bench Division: LORD WIDGERY CJ, BOREHAM and DRAKE JJ).

2372   —— **lighting**

The Road Vehicles (Rear Fog Lamps) Regulations 1978, S.I. 1978 No. 1260 (in force on 23rd September 1978), provide that certain motor vehicles and trailers should be equipped either with one rear fog lamp or with two rear fog lamps fitted so as to form a pair.

2373   The Road Vehicles Lighting (Amendment) Regulations 1978, S.I. 1978 No. 1261 (in force on 23rd September 1978), amend the Road Vehicles Lighting Regulations 1971 by substituting for all references to fog lamps references to front fog lamps so as to avoid those references including rear fog lamps.

2374   The Road Vehicles (Use of Lights during Daytime) (Amendment) Regulations 1978, S.I. 1978 No. 1262 (in force on 23rd September 1978), amend the Road Vehicles (Use of Lights during Daytime) Regulations 1975, 1975 Halsbury's Abr para. 2811 by substituting for the reference to one fog lamp a reference to one front fog lamp so as to avoid this reference including a rear fog lamp.

2375   —— **removal and disposal**

The Removal and Disposal of Vehicles (Amendment) Regulations 1978, S.I. 1978 No. 1346 (in force on 12th October 1978) increase the charges payable under the Removal and Disposal of Vehicles Regulations 1968, as amended. The charge for removing a vehicle from a motor way is increased to £24, from a place other than a motor way to £22 in London and to £20 elsewhere. The charge for storing a vehicle is increased to £2 a day, and for disposing of a vehicle to £6.

2376	**—— tests**

The Motor Vehicles (Tests) (Amendment) Regulations 1978, S.I. 1978 No. 1574 (in force on 1st December 1978), amend the Motor Vehicles (Tests) Regulations 1976, 1976 Halsbury's Abr para. 2118, by increasing the fee for the examination of a motor bicycle (without sidecar) from £2·50 to £2·70 and the fee for the examination of any other motor vehicle to which the 1976 Regulations apply from £4·10 to £4·50.

2377	**—— type approval**

The Motor Vehicles (Type Approval) (Amendment) Regulations 1978, S.I. 1978 No. 1112 (in force on 30th August 1978), amend the Motor Vehicles (Type Approval) Regulations 1973 by extending the provisions of those Regulations as a result of further EEC Council Directives imposing requirements as to design, construction, equipment and marking of vehicles and their components.

2378	The Motor Vehicles (Type Approval) (Amendment) (No. 2) Regulations 1978, S.I. 1978 No. 1236 (in force on 1st October 1978), extend the provisions of the Motor Vehicles (Type Approval) Regulations 1973 as a result of EEC Council directives relating to the statutory plates and inscriptions for motor vehicles and their trailers, and the location and method of attachment of those trailers.

2379	The Motor Vehicles (Type Approval) (Amendment) (No. 3) Regulations 1978, S.I. 1978 No. 1832 (in force on 12th January 1979), replace Motor Vehicles (Type Approval) Regulations 1973, Sch. 2, S.I. 1973 No. 1199, as amended.

These Regulations revoke Motor Vehicles (Type Approval) (Amendment) Regulations 1976, S.I. 1976 Nos. 316, 1890, 1976 Halsbury's Abr paras. 2173, 2175; S.I. 1977 No. 1402, 1977 Halsbury's Abr para. 2331; S.I. 1978 Nos. 1112, 1236, see paras. 2377, 2378.

2380	The Motor Vehicles (Type Approval) (Great Britain) (Amendment) Regulations 1978, S.I. 1978 No. 293 (in force on 31st March 1978), amend the Motor Vehicles (Type Approval) (Great Britain) Regulations 1976, 1976 Halsbury's Abr para. 2174, as amended, by postponing by four months the coming into operation of the scheme for the compulsory type approval of certain motor vehicles and their parts.

2381	The Motor Vehicles (Type Approval) (Great Britain) (Amendment) (No. 2) Regulations 1978, S.I. 1978 No. 1237 (in force on 1st October 1978), amend the Motor Vehicles (Type Approval) (Great Britain) Regulations 1976, 1976 Halsbury's Abr para. 2174 with regard to vehicle windscreens and exterior windows manufactured in France which are marked with the appropriate French type approval markings. It provides that vehicles with such windscreens and other windows are exempt from the requirements specified in certain British Standards Specifications.

2382	The Motor Vehicles (Type Approval) (Great Britain) (Amendment) (No. 3) Regulations 1978, S.I. 1978 No. 1318 (in force on 1st October 1978), amend the Motor Vehicles (Type Approval) (Great Britain) Regulations 1976, 1976 Halsbury's Abr para. 2174, by postponing for a year the application of the type approval scheme to motor vehicles constructed by persons not ordinarily engaged in the manufacture of motor vehicles.

2383	The Motor Vehicles (Type Approval) (Great Britain) (Amendment) (No. 4) Regulations 1978, S.I. 1978 No. 1319 (in force on 1st October 1978) amend the Motor Vehicles (Type Approval) (Great Britain) Regulations 1976, Sch. 1, 1976 Halsbury's Abr para. 2174. They introduce new requirements relating to seat belts, seat belt anchorage points and the installation of seat belts.

2384   The Motor Vehicles (Type Approval) (Great Britain) (Amendment) (No. 5) Regulations 1978, S.I. 1978 No. 1811 (in force on 10th January 1979), replace Motor Vehicles (Type Approval) (Great Britain) Regulations 1976, Sch. 1, 1976 Halsbury's Abr para. 2174, as replaced by 1977 Regulations, 1977 Halsbury's Abr para. 2332.

2385   The Motor Vehicles (Type Approval) (Great Britain) (Fees) (Amendment) Regulations 1978, S.I. 1978 No. 1320 (in force on 1st October 1978) amend the Motor Vehicles (Type Approval) (Great Britain) (Fees) Regulations 1976, 1976 Halsbury's Abr para. 2177. They provide that where a final examination of a vehicle with a view to the issue of a certificate cannot be completed, the fee charges may be reduced by an appropriate amount. They also replace the 1976 Regulations, Schs. 1–3.

2386   The Motor Vehicles (Type Approval and Approval Marks) (Fees) (Amendment) Regulations 1978, S.I. 1978 No. 1321 (in force on 1st October 1978) amend the Motor Vehicles (Type Approval and Approval Marks) (Fees) Regulations 1976, 1976 Halsbury's Abr para. 2176. They insert a new paragraph which provides that where a vehicle test cannot be completed or the vehicle does not satisfy the requirements of the test and as a result a further partial test has to be made, the fee charged may be reduced by an appropriate amount. They also replace the 1976 Regulations, Schedule 1.

2387   The Motor Vehicles (Type Approval) (Great Britain) (Fees) (Amendment) (No. 2) Regulations 1978, S.I. 1978 No. 1810 (in force on 10th January 1979), amend the Motor Vehicles (Type Approval) (Great Britain) (Fees) Regulations 1976, 1976 Halsbury's Abr para. 2177, by adding fees for examination of seat belts and rear fog lamps.

2388   The Motor Vehicles (Type Approval and Approval Marks) (Fees) (Amendment) (No. 2) Regulations 1978, S.I. 1978 No. 1831 (in force on 12th January 1979), amend the Motor Vehicles (Type Approval and Approval Marks) (Fees) Regulations 1976, 1976 Halsbury's Abr para. 2176, by prescribing the fees payable for the testing of heating systems for the passenger compartment of motor vehicles and the wheel guards of motor vehicles.

2389   —— use of inoperative vehicle—whether excise licence or test certificate required

The defendant was charged with using a moped without an excise licence or test certificate. The justices dismissed the information on the ground that the moped had never worked, had no petrol and was being used as a pedal cycle. The prosecution appealed. *Held*, the justices had misdirected themselves as the test to be applied. The relevant test was not the actual use of the vehicle but the use for which it had been constructed. The moped was constructed as a mechanically propelled vehicle and had to be treated as such unless there was no possibility of its ever being used as one again. There was no evidence of this being the case here, and therefore the appeal would be allowed.

McEACHRAN v HURST [1978] Crim LR 499 (Queen's Bench Division: LORD WIDGERY CJ, CROOM-JOHNSON and STOCKER JJ).

2390   —— weighing

The Weighing of Motor Vehicles (Use of Dynamic Axle Weighing Machines) Regulations 1978, S.I. 1978 No. 1180 (in force on 15th September 1978), provide for the weighing of motor vehicles or trailers and the testing of weights by dynamic axle weighing machines. The Regulations also prescribe a form of certificate of weight when such machine is used.

2391   **Negligence**

See NEGLIGENCE (road accident).

2392   **Parking—off-street parking—licences**

The Control of Off-Street Parking (England and Wales) Order 1978, S.I. 1978 No. 1535 (in force on 1st December 1978) incorporates changes in relation to off-street parking required or permitted by the Transport Act 1978, s. 11, and empowers county councils to designate areas in which the provision of public off-street parking places will require a licence from the relevant district council. The Order prescribes the forms such licences must take and creates offences of contravening the terms and conditions of a licence and of operating a public off-street parking place without a licence.

2393   **Parking place—excess charge—whether order imposing charge valid**

A local council made an order imposing an excess parking charge of £3 in respect of vehicles left in designated car parks for longer than the parking period purchased, but provided that the charge would be reduced to £1.50 if paid within seven days. When they discovered that collecting the charge from those who did not pay was uneconomical they raised the amount to £10 but retained the reduced charge of £1.50. The plaintiff contended that the higher charge was excessive and amounted to a fine for failure to pay the charge of £1.50, and that the council had no power to impose it. *Held*, the council had the power to make an order imposing such a charge and the possibility of a collateral purpose causing the sum to be fixed at £10 did not invalidate the order.

STARTIN v SOLIHULL METROPOLITAN BOROUGH COUNCIL (1978) Times, 7th October (Queen's Bench Division: O'CONNOR J).

2394   **Road-side sales—control orders**

The Control of Road-side Sales Orders (Procedure) Regulations 1978, S.I. 1978 No. 932 (in force 2nd August 1978), prescribe the procedure to be followed by highway authorities in England and Wales when making orders under s. 7 of the Local Government (Miscellaneous Provisions) Act 1976 for controlling road-side sales.

2395   **Road tankers—hazardous substances—labelling**

The Hazardous Substances (Labelling of Road Tankers) Regulations 1978, S.I. 1978 No. 1702 (in force on 28th March 1979), impose requirements for notices to be displayed on road tankers used for the conveyance by road of certain prescribed hazardous substances.

2396   **Road Traffic (Drivers' Ages and Hours of Work) Act 1976—commencement**

The Road Traffic (Drivers, Ages and Hours of Work) Act 1976 (Commencement No. 2) Order 1978, S.I. 1978 No. 6, brought into force, on 26th January 1978, Road Traffic (Drivers, Ages and Hours of Work) Act 1976, s. 2, which is the only provision of that Act not yet in operation.

Section 2 makes certain amendments to Part IV of the Transport Act 1968, which relates to drivers' hours of work, in consequence of the provisions of the regulations of the EEC on this subject.

2397   **Speed circuits**

The 70 miles per hour, 60 miles per hour and 50 miles per hour (Temporary Speed

Limit) (Continuation) Order 1978, S.I. 1978 No. 1548 (in force on 30th November 1978) continues indefinitely the general speed limits of 70 mph on dual carriageway roads (not being motorways), and of 60 mph on single carriageway roads and of 60 mph and 50 mph on certain specified lengths of dual and single carriageway roads respectively.

2398   Traffic orders—London

The London Authorities' Traffic Orders (Procedure) (Amendment) Regulations 1978, S.I. 1978 No. 707 (in force on 15th June 1978), further amend the London Authorities' Traffic Orders (Procedure) Regulations 1972, which prescribe the procedure to be followed in connection with the making of traffic regulation, parking space and speed limit orders under the Road Traffic Regulation Act 1967.

2399   Transport Act 1978

See para. 2890.

2400   Transport operations—EEC regulations—exemptions

The Community Road Transport Rules (Exemptions) Regulations 1978, S.I. 1978 No. 1158 (in force on 17th August 1978), give effect to exemptions, in respect of certain national transport operations, from provisions of EEC Regulations relating to the ages, hours and work conditions of drivers in the road transport industry and recording equipment in road transport.

2401   Vehicles—removal and disposal

The Removal and Disposal of Vehicles (Loading Areas) (Modification of Enactments) Regulations 1978 No. 889 (in force on 19th July 1978), amend the Road Traffic Regulation Act 1967; ss. 20, 52, 53 which relate to the removal, storage and disposal of vehicles left on roads in contravention of a statutory prohibition.

ROYAL FORCES

Halsbury's Laws of England (3rd edn.) Vol. 33, paras. 1348–1866

2402   Army, Air Force and Naval Discipline Acts—continuation

The Army, Air Force and Naval Discipline Acts (Continuation) Order 1978, S.I. 1978 No. 1023 (made on 25th July 1978), continues in force the Army Act 1955, the Air Force Act 1955 and the Naval Discipline Act 1957 until 31st August 1979.

2403   Service pensions—commutation

See para. 2087.

2404   —— disablement and death

See para. 2120.

SALE OF GOODS

Halsbury's Laws of England (3rd edn.), Vol. 34, paras. 1–321

2405   Article

Liability for Defective Products, C. J. Miller (outline of recent developments): 122 Sol Jo 631.

2406   Bill of lading—c and f contract—notation in bill of lading—whether bill clean—liability of buyer to pay for lost cargo

The buyers of a cargo of sugar c. and f. free rejected a bill of lading to which a notation had been attached explaining that the cargo had been destroyed by a fire on board the vessel at the port of loading. The lost goods had not been sent. The sellers contended that the bill of lading as sent was clean and that accordingly the buyers were bound under the contract to pay for the lost sugar. *Held*, whether a bill was or was not clean depended on legal rather than practical and commercial criteria. Under a c. and f. contract both the property and risk passed to the buyer as from the time of shipment whether or not the goods were subsequently lost. The fact that the bill of lading explained the fate of the cargo after it had been loaded rendered it unusual but not unmerchantable. It was for the buyers to ensure that the bill was in the usual form if that was what they wanted. Accordingly, the bill was clean and the buyers were liable to pay the price of the goods destroyed.

M. GOLODETZ and CO INC v CZARNKOW-RIONDA CO INC (1978) Times, 22nd November (Queen's Bench Division: DONALDSON J).

2407   Breach of contract—exclusion clause—whether loss arising from late delivery consequential

See *Croudace Construction Ltd v Cawoods Concrete Products Ltd*, para. 834.

2408   —— force majeure and prohibition clauses—liability of seller

See CONTRACT (frustration).

2409   —— goods not in conformity with contract—resale by buyers—whether damages suffered—whether right of rejection lost

The sellers shipped oil by three shipments in breach of their contracts with the buyers; it was accepted that the oil did not conform with the contract description. The oil on board two ships was resold to Greek buyers who rejected it. The buyers claimed damages from the sellers. The buyers then rejected the oil in the third shipment, although they had taken no steps to analyse the oil when they purported to reject it. In the event, the oil supplied, although of a different description, turned out to be worth no less than the oil contracted for. On the question of whether the buyers had suffered damages as a result of the sellers' breach, *held*, the buyers had failed to show that the goods which they had received and resold were worth less than those they had contracted to buy. They were therefore not entitled to damages. In respect of the third rejected shipment, there had been a reasonable opportunity to examine and analyse the oil before rejection to see whether it was in conformity with the contract description. The buyers had delayed too long in their inspection and had therefore lost their right to reject. Judgment would be given for the sellers.

ALGEMENE OLIEHANDEL INTERNATIONAL BV v BUNGE SA [1978] 2 Lloyd's Rep 207 (Queen's Bench Division: DONALDSON J).

2410   —— stipulations as to time for complaint—defect discovered after expiry of time limit—damages recoverable

The plaintiff firm of seed potato merchants entered into a contract for the sale of several consignments of seed potatoes to the defendants. Thirteen days after delivery of the final consignment, the plaintiffs received a complaint about the condition of the potatoes. They inspected the potatoes but persuaded the defendants that there was insufficient reason for rejecting the consignment. Once the potatoes were planted it soon became obvious that the crop was unhealthy and a subsequent Ministry of Agriculture inspection revealed that it was suffering from a virus. The plaintiffs brought an action for the amount outstanding on the sale of the potatoes. The defendants claimed that this amount could be set off against their loss of profit. The plaintiffs contended that they were protected from such counter-claim by their conditions of sale which provided that time was of the essence of the contract and that complaints should be brought within a maximum of ten days of delivery. The conditions further provided that compensation or damages payable should not amount to more than the contract price of the potatoes. *Held*, the time limit did not apply in the present case as the virus could not have been discovered within the specified time. The damages recoverable were, however, limited to the contract price of the potatoes. That provision applied to all defects and was designed to protect a supplier who inadvertently sold infected potatoes. The contract was of the usual form in such transactions and the risk in so far as damage might exceed the contract price was on the farmer. Although the plaintiffs were in breach of s. 14 of the Sale of Goods Act 1893 in that they supplied goods which were not of merchantable quality or fit for their purpose, they were absolved from liability by the limitation clause.

R. W. GREEN LTD v CADE BROS FARM [1978] 1 Lloyd's Rep 602 (Queen's Bench Division: GRIFFITHS J).

2411   C.i.f. contract—chain of contracts—notice of appropriation—time

See *Bremer Handelsgesellschaft mbH v Toepfer*, para. 484.

2412   Consumer protection

See CONSUMER PROTECTION.

2413   Contract—stipulation as to time—default by seller—effective date of default

Under a contract for sale the sellers were due to ship 300 tons of soya bean meal at a contract price of 158 U.S. dollars per metric ton. The contract provided that the notice of appropriation should be despatched by the shipper to the first buyer within ten days from the date of the bill of lading. Subsequent sellers were under the same obligation but if certain conditions were satisfied the notice of appropriation would be deemed to be in time. Export controls were imposed and the goods were not delivered. By telex on 11th July, the day after the notice of appropriation was due, the buyers gave the sellers seven days to agree that they were in default and to agree a market price for the goods or make a contractual tender. Failing the sellers' agreement to this the buyer claimed arbitration. The market price for a metric ton of meal was, on 10th July, 635 U.S. dollars, and on 11th July, 585 U.S. dollars. On 12th July the sellers gave notice of appropriation in respect of 40 tons only. The buyers were prepared to accept the 40 tons in part fulfilment of the contract on receipt of the shipping documents and proof that the notice of appropriation complied with the specified conditions. Neither the documents nor the proof were tendered. The buyers claimed that the sellers were in default in respect of the entire shipment. The sellers claimed that the buyers' telex of 11th July had extended by seven days the time within which the sellers could give notice of appropriation and therefore any damages awarded in respect of the 260 tons should be assessed by reference to the market price as at 18th July which was 475 U.S. dollars. The sellers further claimed that the buyers had wrongfully refused to accept the shipping documents in respect of the 40 tons and that the damages for that amount should be assessed according to the market price at the date when they would have tendered the documents, which was 440 U.S. dollars. The arbitrator found in favour of the buyers but stated as a special case the questions whether the sellers were liable to the buyers for non-fulfilment of the contract and if so what date was applicable for the calculation of damages. *Held*, the sellers were under an obligation to give notice of appropriation on or before 10th July. The notice given on 12th July was out of time as the sellers had not proved that the specified conditions had been complied with. The buyers' telex of 11th July could not be construed as an invitation to give stale notice. The sellers were therefore in default in respect of the entire consignment and damages would be calculated by reference to the market price on 10th July.

BUNGE GMBH v C. C. V. LANDBOUWBELANG CA [1978] 1 Lloyd's Rep 217 (Queen's Bench Division: DONALDSON J). *Toepfer v Cremer* [1975] 2 Lloyd's Rep 118, 1975 Halsbury's Abr para. 529 applied.

2414 —— **term providing for extension of shipping period on payment by buyer—whether payment constituted a penalty**

See *Thos. P. Gonzalez Corporation v F. R. Waring (International) (Pty) Ltd*, para. 857.

2415 **F.o.b. contract—incorporation of second contract—conflict of terms—extension of time for loading contract goods**

Sellers sold soya beans to be shipped f.o.b. from certain Brazilian ports in July 1974. The contract was the standard Anec f.o.b. contract, which incorporated the terms of the Grain and Feed Trade Association (GAFTA) contract where the latter's terms did not conflict with the Anec contract. The sellers rejected the buyers' nomination of ships because one was due to arrive at the port of loading outside the contract time and they elected to treat the contract as null and void. At first the buyers sought to extend the time for the loading of the vessels under the terms of the GAFTA contract but finally they accepted the sellers' repudiation as an anticipatory breach and claimed damages. A special case was referred to the court on the question whether the provisions as to extension of time in the GAFTA contract were incorporated into the Anec contract. *Held*, the buyers' failure to comply with the terms of the contract as to time for loading was a breach of condition. The Anec contract clearly excluded the extension provisions of the GAFTA contract and so the sellers had been entitled to treat the contract as null and void and the buyers' claim would fail.

BREMER HANDELSGESELLSCHAFT mbH v J. H. RAYNER & CO LTD [1978] 2 Lloyd's Rep 73 (Queen's Bench Division: MOCATTA J). *Finnish Government (Ministry of Food) v H. Ford & Co Ltd* (1921) 6 Ll. L Rep 188, CA, *The Mihalis Angelos* [1971] 1 QB 164, CA and *Tradax Export SA v Andre & Cie SA* [1976] 1 Lloyd's Rep 416 CA applied.

2416 —— **non-acceptance by buyer—whether seller in breach**

The parties in a sale of soya bean meal f.o.b. New Orleans agreed to be bound by the conditions and arbitration provisions of the Grain and Feed Trade Association (GAFTA) contract No. 119, but made specific arrangements as to weight, quality and condition. The buyers did not reserve the right to supervise weighing or to take samples and facilities for doing so were denied them by the elevator operators during loading. They contended that this amounted to a breach of contract by the sellers and refused both to allow loading to continue and to pay for that part of the cargo which had been loaded. The sellers sought to enforce their right to payment in the Italian courts, which the buyers claimed was a breach of the arbitration provisions of the GAFTA contract. On appeal against the arbitrators' award in favour of the sellers, *held*, the sellers had not been in breach of contract because the buyers' right to supervise weighing under the GAFTA contract had been excluded by the specific arrangements of the parties and, although the buyers could request samples, such a request had to be made to the sellers. The award in favour of the sellers would be upheld, but the buyers could recover any loss they had suffered as a result of the Italian proceedings since these were prohibited by the GAFTA contract.

MANTOVANI v CARAPELLI SA [1978] 2 Lloyd's Rep 63 (Queen's Bench Division: DONALDSON J).

2417 **Implied condition—fitness—breach—effect of negligence of buyer**

See *Lambert v Lewis, Larkin, Dixon-Bate Ltd, and Lexmead (Basingstoke) Ltd.*, para. 2025.

2418 —— **fitness and merchantable quality—assessment of damages for breach**

The plaintiff entered into a hire purchase agreement with the defendants to buy a new car, the total hire purchase price being £1,976. He made it clear, before buying it, that he required the car for a holiday in France a few months later, and he hoped to sort out any "teething troubles" before the holiday. The car suffered from many defects, some serious, before, after and during the holiday. The third party dealers carried out many of the repairs, free of charge, under the guarantee. The plaintiff, both before and after his holiday indicated to the dealers, as agents for the defendants, that he wished to return the car in exchange for a return of the money already paid, but his requests were refused. He brought an action in the county court alleging the car had never been of merchantable quality, therefore the defendants were in breach of the hire purchase agreement and he was entitled to a refund of his money. The defendants denied the breach and claimed that in any event the plaintiff had affirmed the contract by paying the instalments for seven months, using the car for at least 6000 miles despite its condition and allowing it to be repaired free of charge by the dealers. At the hearing the judge told the plaintiff that the contract could not be rescinded because of the length of time since the purchase of the car, and that instead his claim lay in damages. The damages awarded were £200 for the defects in the car and £75 for the detrimental effect on the plaintiff's holiday. The plaintiff appealed against the amount of damages awarded. *Held*, allowing the appeal, in order to assess damages it was necessary to assess what the fair market price would have been if the lack of merchantability and lack of suitability for purpose had been known to the plaintiff when the car was purchased. Taking all the factors into account, including the repairs which had been carried out by the dealers free of charge, and the degree to which the holiday had been spoiled, the damages awarded would be £750. The possibility of whether the contract could be rescinded was not considered as the plaintiff stated that he was no longer seeking a rescission of the contract.

JACKSON v CHRYSLER ACCEPTANCES LTD [1978] RTR 474 (Court of Appeal: MEGAW, SHAW and WALLER LJJ).

2419 —— exclusion clause—whether clause in auction conditions carried over to sale by private treaty

A tractor unit was offered for sale at an auction but was withdrawn as its reserve was not reached. The defendant who had bought other vehicles at the auction saw it in the auctioneer's yard a day or two later and bought it by private treaty. It broke down almost immediately with serious faults and the defendant returned it to the sellers. In an action for the price the sellers contended that the condition as to merchantable quality implied by Sale of Goods Act 1893, s. 14 was excluded by a condition of sale at the auction. *Held*, the auction and the sale by private treaty were quite separate transactions and accordingly the sale by private treaty did not have to be on the same terms. The particular auction condition on which the sellers sought to rely was a stringent one excluding the statutory rights of a buyer and could have been incorporated in the contract between the parties only by express notice. The sellers had given no notice of incorporation to the defendant and accordingly were not entitled to rely on the condition.

D & M TRAILERS (HALIFAX) LTD v STIRLING [1978] RTR 468 (Court of Appeal: MEGAW, BROWNE AND SHAW LJJ).

2420 Non-delivery—sellers' failure to tender shipping documents—waiver of right to documents by buyers

Under a contract for the sale of soya bean meal, a shipment was due each month from May to September 1973. Due to the U.S. government's embargo on the export of soya bean meal, the sellers were unable to ship the June instalment. The buyers later accepted a part delivery. The sellers then gave notice of appropriation of the balance, which the buyers rejected as uncontractual. The sellers failed to tender any shipping documents in respect of the balance when it was discharged, arguing that they were relieved of any obligation to do so by the buyers' conduct. On 27th September 1973 the buyers held the sellers to be in default, claimed arbitration and nominated an arbitrator, who was subsequently appointed. The sellers contended that the buyers had waived their contractual right to shipping documents in relation to goods shipped in June, or if they had not, that they were time-barred from raising a claim arising out of the sellers' failure to tender the

documents. The Board of Appeal of GAFTA found in favour of the buyers and stated their award in the form of a special case. *Held*, the buyers had not waived their rights to the shipping documents for the balance, as was clear from their rejection of the notice of appropriation. Moreover, there was no evidence of reliance by the sellers on the buyers' conduct as a waiver. However, the buyers were not entitled to hold the sellers in default for their failure to present the documents since the buyers had never unreservedly accepted the sellers' proposal to fulfil their obligation in regard to the balance constituted by the notice of appropriation, and indeed had rejected that notice. As to the time-bar point, on the construction of the GAFTA Arbitration Rules, the appointment of an arbitrator in this case should have been made within three months of 30th June 1973. The buyers' telex of 27th September was within this period and satisfied the GAFTA rules. The sellers were not in breach of contract for not presenting the documents but they were in default in not having given a valid notice of appropriation in respect of the June instalment. The sellers were thus liable in damages for breach of contract.
BUNGE SA v SCHLESWIG-HOLSTEINISCHE LANDWIRTSCHAFTLICHE HAUPTGENOSSEN-SCHAFT EINGETR GMBH [1978] 1 Lloyds Rep 480 (Queen's Bench Division: MOCATTA J).

2421 —— waiver of right to reject

See *Bremer Handelsgesellschaft mbH v Mackprang*, para. 516.

2422 Passing of property—appropriation of goods—delivery to carrier

See *Morton—Norwich Products Inc v Intercen Ltd*, para. 2060.

2423 Price marking

See FOOD; CONSUMER PROTECTION.

SALE OF LAND

Halsbury's Laws of England (3rd edn.), Vol. 34, paras. 322–668

2424 Articles

The Conveyancer and "If" Contracts, H. W. Wilkinson (consideration of unilateral contracts affecting real property in the light of *Daulia v Four Millbank Nominees Ltd* [1978] 2 All ER 557, 1977 Halsbury's Abr para. 2392): 128 NLJ 1031.

"The Date fixed for Completion . . .," C. T. Emery (remedies for delay in completion of contract for sale of land): [1978] Conv. 144.

House in Return for Services, W. T. West (the doctrine of part performance in the light of *Re Gonin (Deceased), Gonin v Garmeson* [1977] 2 All ER 720, 1977 Halsbury's Abr para. 2391): 122 Sol Jo 272.

Local Authorities' Sales and Purchases, H. W. Wilkinson (consideration of local authorities' attitudes in the light of *Gibson v Manchester City Council*, see para. 2431): 128 NLJ 415.

Avoiding the Misrepresentation Act 1967, H. W. Wilkinson (fair and reasonable exclusions within s. 3 of the Act): 128 NLJ 79).

Conveyancing Practice: the "Normal" and the "Good", H. W. Wilkinson (what practice is, and the consequences of failure to comply with it): 122 Sol Jo 239.

Domestic House Purchase Transactions, D. M. Bows, E. O. Bourne (summary of a Memorandum submitted to the Royal Commission on Legal Services): 122 Sol Jo 87.

How the Lender Can Get His Own Back, W. A. Greene: 122 Sol Jo 91.

Rights of Pre-emption as Interests in Land, Eric Alexander Dumbill (whether a right of pre-emption is an enforceable interest in land): 128 NLJ 227.

Registration and Priorities, H. W. Wilkinson (cases in 1977 on land charges or their equivalent in registered land): 128 NLJ 5.

Should Foreigners be Allowed to Buy Property, Stanley Hamilton (general problems to which alien ownership can give rise, and attitude of individual countries to the situation): 247 EG 623.

2425   Assignment of lease—landlord's refusal of consent—right of purchaser to recover deposit

See *Shires v Brock*, para. 1721.

2426   Completion—notice to complete—whether vendors able and ready to complete

The purchaser agreed to buy a house from the vendor and paid a deposit. He was unable to complete by the agreed date and the vendor served a notice under condition 19 of the Law Society's conditions of sale. The 28 day period allowed under the notice expired without payment of the purchase price. The vendor purported to rescind the contract and forfeit the deposit. The purchaser then brought an action for the return of his deposit. He claimed that when the notice to complete was served, the vendor's solicitors were not themselves able and ready to complete because the abstract of title had referred to only two of the three charges on the land and in a letter accompanying the notice they said they would write later with details of the three charges. The vendor's solicitors contended that they were satisfied before the service of the notice to complete that a title free of charges could be given on completion. *Held*, the solicitors were not ready to complete when they gave notice as they were then uncertain that the entries on the register related to the said charges. They were therefore not ready to complete within condition 19 (2) until they had that confirmation. Accordingly, the notice to complete was ineffective. In all the circumstances it could not be said that the purchasers' delay in completing was so unreasonable as to entitle the vendor to treat the contract as at an end. The purchaser was thus entitled to the return of his deposit. An order would be made accordingly.

COLE v ROSE [1978] 3 All ER 1121 (Chancery Division: MERVYN DAVIES QC sitting as a deputy High Court judge).

2427   Contract—breach—damages—date of assessment of market value

See *Malhotra v Choudhury*, para. 848.

2428   ——— measure of damages—rule in Bain v Fothergill

See *Malhotra v Choudhury*, para. 848.

2429   —— deposit—deposit forfeited on failure to complete—court's discretion to order repayment

Under a contract for the sale of property in London the purchasers paid a substantial deposit, being 10 per cent of the purchase price. However, due to a change in exchange control regulations the purchasers were prevented from transferring funds from Nigeria to London to cover the balance of the purchase price, and were unable to complete on the due date or within the following twenty-eight days pursuant to the completion notice served on them by the vendors under the terms of the contract. The vendors rescinded the contract and purported to forfeit the deposit. The purchasers brought an action claiming repayment of the deposit on the grounds that either the contract had been frustrated or the court should exercise its discretion to order repayment of the deposit under the Law of Property Act 1925, s. 49 (2). The vendors moved to have the action struck out. *Held*, regardless of the question whether a contract for the sale of land could be frustrated, the mere inability of a purchaser to pay the purchase price was not sufficient to attract the application of the doctrine. Further, the exercise of the court's discretion under s. 49 (2) to order the repayment of a deposit was limited to cases where the purchaser could successfully resist an action for specific performance, which excluded the present case in which the vendors clearly would have been granted a decree of specific performance. Accordingly, the purchasers' action was bound to fail and would be struck out.

UNIVERSAL CORPN v FIVE WAYS PROPERTIES LTD [1978] 3 All ER 1131 (Chancery Division: WALTON J).

2430   —— exchange of contracts—exchange by telephone—authority of solicitors to dispense with actual exchange

In an action by the intending purchasers for specific performance of a contract for the sale of a house, the vendor denied that a binding agreement for sale had been concluded. An agreement for sale subject to contract had been made and the vendor and purchasers had each signed their part of the contract and sent it to their respective solicitors. The vendor's part, however, was not sent to the purchasers' solicitors but a telephone conversation took place between the two solicitors, in which they agreed that the contracts would be treated as immediately exchanged by telephone at that moment. The purchasers contended that the conversation was effective in law to dispense with actual exchange and to bind the parties. *Held*, the practice of dispensing with exchange by telephone was a common one when simultaneous exchanges were required where a chain of contracts was concerned. However, the practice was a bad one as it left ample scope for conflicts of evidence. The fundamental rule was that solicitors were not, in the absence of specific authority, agents of their clients to conclude a contract for them. There was no evidence that the parties had specifically authorised their solicitors to exchange contracts by telephone or to dispense with exchange. Thus there was no binding contract and the action would be dismissed.

DOMB v ISOZ (1978) 122 Sol Jo 573 (Chancery Division: BRIAN DILLON QC sitting as a deputy High Court judge).

2431   —— existence of contract—principles for establishing existence— whether decree of specific performance appropriate

The Manchester city council reversed its policy of selling council houses to tenants when the Labour party gained control of it. The plaintiff had previously negotiated for the purchase of his house, although no contract had been exchanged. He applied for a decree of specific performance. *Held* (GEOFFREY LANE LJ dissenting), it was neccessary to look not for strict offer and acceptance but at the relevant correspondence and conduct of the parties to determine whether or not an agreement had been reached. Since the tenant had made improvements at his own expense, and the council had withdrawn his house from its tenants' list, it was fair to infer the existence of an agreement. Furthermore, it would be inequitable if tenants' expectations of house ownership could be ruined by a change in local government policy.

GIBSON v MANCHESTER CITY COUNCIL [1978] 2 All ER 583 (Court of Appeal: LORD DENNING MR, ORMROD and GEOFFREY LANE LJJ).

This decision was reversed subsequently in the House of Lords.

2432   —— house advertised for sale with vacant possession—effect

A house was advertised for sale, subject to a tenancy of the first floor, with vacant possession of the ground floor. The plaintiffs contracted to purchase the house, but then learnt of a local authority statutory notice restricting the number of occupants of the house to one household. The tenancy of the first floor thus precluded occupation of the ground floor. The plaintiffs sought an order for specific performance of the contract in consideration of a sum £1,000 less than the contract price. The vendors counterclaimed for specific performance of the purchase at the original contract price, on the grounds that "vacant possession" meant merely that the ground floor was empty. *Held*, although the meaning of "vacant possession" could vary, in this case there was a contractual obligation on the vendor to convey the property in a state in which the ground floor could be occupied. Accordingly, the plaintiffs' order would be granted, and the defendants' counter-claim dismissed.

TOPFELL LTD v GALLEY PROPERTIES LTD (1978) Times, 27th October (Chancery Division: TEMPLEMAN J).

2433	—— newly built house—warranty of fitness for habitation— house built on hillside—landslip

The plaintiffs purchased a newly built leasehold house from the first defendants, a development company. The house had been built by the second defendants, under arrangements made by them with the first defendants. The house was built on a steep hillside which subsequently proved wholly unsuitable for building. There was a severe landslip. As a result, an investigation was carried out and legal proceedings were commenced. The plaintiffs claimed against the development company in tort for negligence, and for breach of contract; against the builders in tort for negligence; and against the local authority, the third defendants, for negligence or breach of statutory duty in respect of the authority's duty to inspect the foundations. *Held*, the defect lay not in the construction of the house, but in the nature of the hillside on which it was built. The fault could have been detected by experts. The development company was therefore liable for breach of the contractual warranty that the house would be fit for habitation. They were additionally liable in tort for failing properly to inspect the site prior to the decision to build. The builders were also liable in tort, the unsuitability of the land and the outcome being foreseeable by them. The local authority was not liable.

BATTY v METROPOLITAN PROPERTY REALISATIONS LTD [1978] 2 All ER 445 (Court of Appeal: MEGAW, BRIDGE and WALLER LJJ). *Esso Petroleum Co v Mardon* [1976] 1 QB 801, 1976 Halsbury's Abr para. 1830, CA, and *Anns v Merton London Borough Council* [1977] 2 WLR 1024, HL, 1977 Halsbury's Abr para. 2175 applied.

2434	—— order for specific performance—whether order deprived subsequent completion notice of effect

The making of an order for specific performance of a contract for the sale of land deprives of effect a twenty-eight day completion notice served under the contract subsequently.

The purchaser of a house obtained an order for specific performance of the sale. It was not complied with. The purchaser then prevaricated and the vendor issued a twenty-eight day completion notice under a general condition of sale. The purchaser failed to comply, and the vendor instituted proceedings based on that failure. The issue was whether a completion notice served after the making of an order for specific performance was valid. *Held*, although a contract remained extant following the making of an order, the exercise of the rights it conferred were affected; it ceased to be governed by its own terms but was governed by the provisions of the order. Ample remedies were available to either party in the event that an order was not complied with. Furthermore, the general condition under which the completion notice was issued could not be construed as operating in a case where a decree of specific performance had already been made. The vendor and claim would therefore fail.

SINGH v NAZEER [1978] 3 All ER 817 (Chancery Division: MEGARRY V-C).

2435	—— rescission—recoverability of damages

The plaintiffs contracted to purchase a property; the defendants were their solicitors. The plaintiffs paid a deposit but were unable to complete by the completion date. The vendors served on them a notice to complete by 1st December 1973, which provided that upon failure by the plaintiffs to complete by then, the vendors would either rescind the agreement or resell the property and claim any deficiency in the price as damages. The plaintiffs then assigned the contract to a third party. The time for completion was extended twice but the third party failed to complete. On the 7th February 1974, the vendor's solicitors wrote to the defendants rescinding the contract, and the vendors obtained judgment against the plaintiffs for forfeiture of the deposit and damages for loss occasioned by resale of the property. The plaintiffs then commenced an action against the defendants, contending that time had ceased to be of the essence because of the extensions granted to the third party; that by rescinding the contract the vendors were disentitled from claiming damages; and that the defendants were negligent in not perceiving these matters and advising them accordingly. On appeal by the plaintiffs against the dismissal of the action, *held*, as to whether time was of the essence, there was no act of the vendors towards the plaintiffs which constituted a waiver of the requirement to complete; the extensions granted to the third party were granted to him personally and he was not the plaintiffs' agent. Therefore the plaintiffs were in default after 1st December 1973 and the vendors were entitled to rescind. The contract was rescinded, not in the sense of relief granted when a contract was annulled and treated as though it had never been entered into, but in the sense that the vendors had accepted the plaintiffs' repudiation, whereby their rights remained intact. They were therefore entitled to damages. The defendants had not been negligent and the appeal would be dismissed.

BUCKLAND v FARMER & MOODY (A FIRM) [1978] 3 All ER 929 (Court of Appeal: BUCKLEY, GOFF and CUMMING-BRUCE LJJ). Dicta of Lord Sumner in *Hirji Mulji v Cheong Yue SS Co Ltd* [1926] All ER Rep 51 at 58, of Lord Porter in *Heyman v Darwins Ltd* [1942] 1 All ER 337 at 360 and of Farwell J in *Mussen v Van Diemen's Land Co* [1938] 1 All ER 210 at 215 applied.

2436   —— **vendor's obligation to show good title—presumption of facts on which title depends**

The purchasers of freehold premises previously subject to a trust for sale sought to rescind their contract of sale on the ground that the vendors were unable to provide the title contracted for. Examination of the title revealed an option to purchase the premises together with a contract of sale made in 1912, which was suspended by deed in 1930, but remained unperformed. The vendors appealed against a decision that they had not shown a good title. *Held*, it was open to the court to presume facts on which title to the premises depended since, applying the established test, it was a case when a judge would have directed a jury to make such a presumption. The evidence clearly supported a presumption of abandonment of the option and the 1912 contract. A preliminary agreement for a twenty-one year lease of the premises granted in 1933 made no reference to the contract and was prima facie inconsistent with it; a deed of appointment of new trustees reciting the administration of the trust made no reference to the option and finally, the grantee of the option had died over thirty-five years ago, no claim having been made on behalf of his estate in that time. As the option and contract were presumed to be abandoned, there could be no specific performance ordered against the purchasers and the vendors had shown a good title. The appeal would be allowed.

MEPC LTD v CHRISTIAN-EDWARDS [1978] 3 All ER 795 (Court of Appeal: STEPHENSON, ORR and GOFF LJJ). Decision of Goulding J [1978] 1 All ER 295, 1977 Halsbury's Abr para. 2394, reversed. *Emery v Grocock* (1821) 6 Madd 54 and *Hillary v Waller* (1806) 12 Ves 239, applied.

2437   **Conveyance—conveyance by receiver after liquidation of company—whether conveyance registrable**

See *Sowman v David Samuel Trust Ltd (in liquidation)*, para. 2305.

2438   —— **extent of parcels of land—plan for identification purposes only**

In 1921 a vendor sold to a mining company a parcel of land which was coloured yellow on the conveyance plan and was referred to in the particulars of sale by the number 317. This parcel of land was smaller than that numbered 317 in the Ordnance Survey Map which had been drawn up in 1915. The land passed from the mining company's successor to the National Coal Board who in 1965 sold the defendant a parcel of land described as part of the land numbered 317 on the Ordnance Survey Map (1915 edition). In 1972 the original vendor sold to the plaintiffs, who owned certain neighbouring land, the disputed land which comprised that part of the land numbered 317 on the Ordnance Survey Map which had not been the subject of the 1921 conveyance. The defendant built on the disputed land, thinking that it was his property. The plaintiffs brought an action claiming (i) a declaration that the 1972 conveyance entitled them to the disputed land in fee simple absolute, (ii) possession of the disputed land, (iii) an injunction to restrain the defendant from building on the disputed land or using the existing buildings, and (iv) damages.   The defendant claimed that all the land numbered 317 on the Ordnance Survey Map had been sold by the 1921 conveyance and that the disputed land had therefore passed to him.   The court held that the defendant owned the land because (i) although the disputed land had been excluded from the 1921 conveyance plan, the plan was expressed to be used by way of identification only and merely showed the location of the land, (ii) that the use of the number 317 in the particulars of sale showed that all the land marked on the Ordnance Survey Map had been sold.   On appeal, *held*, a conveyance plan could be used to specify the property which was the subject of a conveyance where the particulars of sale were inadequate.   It was clear that the number 317 in the particulars of sale was meant to refer to the yellow coloured area on the plan and that the plan was the only means of discovering the boundary between the land sold and the remainder of the land numbered 317 on the Ordnance Survey Map.   The 1921 conveyance clearly excluded the disputed land which had therefore passed to the plaintiff in 1972.   The appeal would be allowed.

WIGGINTON AND MILNER LTD v WINSTER ENGINEERING LTD [1978] 3 All ER 436 (Court of Appeal: BUCKLEY and BRIDGE LJJ and SIR DAVID CAIRNS).

2439   —— voidable conveyance—transfer of wife's interest in matrimonial home to husband

See *Gresswell v Potter (note)*, para. 1326; *Backhouse v Backhouse*, para. 1327.

2440   Option to purchase—consent of court required—failure to obtain consent—validity of option

New Zealand

The lessor leased a farm to the lessee for five years.   The lease contained an option to purchase at any time during the term upon the lessee's giving notice and filing a declaration under the Land Settlement Promotion and Land Acquisition Act 1952. Under s. 24 of the Act the lessee filed a declaration, which referred to him as lessee of the land but made no reference to the option to purchase.   The lessor subsequently gave notice that he would not continue with the option on the grounds that, under s. 23 of the Act, the court's permission was necessary for the grant of an option and that, as the lessee had not obtained that consent, the option was illegal.   He also claimed that the declaration procedure under s. 24 was not open to an option holder or, alternatively, that the declaration filed did not comply with s. 24.   The lessee applied for a declaration that the option was valid or, alternatively, if it was not valid, for a validating order under the Illegal Contracts Act 1970.   The declaration was granted and the lessor appealed.   *Held*, s. 24 provided a procedure by which a "landless" man could conclude a transaction in land without having to obtain the consent of the court.   The section applied as much to the grant of an option as to ordinary sales and leases.   As the lessee's declaration complied with s. 24 the option was valid, and the appeal would be dismissed.

The court considered that the Illegal Contracts Act 1970 was available to counteract an illegality arising from a declaration which did not sufficiently comply with the requirements of the Land Settlement Act.

ROSS v HENDERSON [1978] 2 WLR 354 (Privy Council: LORD SIMON OF GLAISDALE, LORD SALMON, LORD RUSSELL OF KILLOWEN, LORD KEITH OF KINKEL and SIR GARFIELD BARWICK).

2441   Restrictive covenant—sale resulting in common ownership of benefitted and burdened land—whether covenant extinguished

See *Re Tiltwood, Sussex*; *Barrett v Bond*, para. 1171.

SENTENCING

Halsbury's Laws of England (4th edn.), Vol. 11, paras. 481–573

2442   Articles

Assessing the Value of Community Service, Jenny McEwan: 128 NLJ 772.

Dilemma of Sentencing the "Hungarian Circle", Justinian (the criteria to be applied in sentencing international criminals): Financial Times, 30th May 1978.

Lower Maximum Sentences? (examination of the recommendations and reasoning of the Advisory Council's report on the penal system): 142 JP Jo 409.

Politics and the Suspended Sentence, R. Paul Davis (positions of the two major political parties on the questions of suspended sentences): 128 NLJ 1020.

Sentencing the Mentally Abnormal Offender, Alec Samuels (how to do the best for the patient and protect the public): 128 NLJ 304.

Sentencing the Sex Offender, Alec Samuels (examples of sentences imposed for various sexual offences): 128 NLJ 676.

2443　Appeal—examples

Examples of sentencing appeals are set out under the following headings:
Offences against government and public order
Offences against the person
Offences against property
Offences against decency and morality
Offences relating to drugs
Driving offences

OFFENCES AGAINST GOVERNMENT AND PUBLIC ORDER

2444　*Possessing a firearm with the intent of endangering life; unlawful wounding; possession of a shot gun without a licence*
Sentence: 18 months' imprisonment concurrent suspended for 2 years (possessing a firearm and unlawful wounding); 28 days' imprisonment concurrent (possessing a shot-gun without a licence). (11 month's imprisonment served). Married man, aged 48, with three children. His wife left him, taking the children with her, and went to live with a family friend. The appellant was very distressed and became depressed about the break-up of his marriage. His wife started divorce proceedings. The other man kept going to the appellant's house, in spite of a court undertaking not to do so. On one such visit a quarrel ensued, and the appellant shot the other man through the foot, the latter receiving a number of pellets from the shot. The judge took the view that the appellant intended to alarm rather than injure the victim. Sentenced to 3 years' imprisonment on the first count, 18 months' imprisonment concurrent on the second count, and 28 days imprisonment on the third count. (3 years' imprisonment in all). On appeal it was conceded that he had an excellent work record and was an affectionate father, and that he had acted under the stress caused by the break-up of his marriage and provocation from his wife's lover. *Held*, as the appellant had already served 11 months' imprisonment it was in nobody's interest for him to remain there. He was a hard working, decent man and, as an act of mercy the sentences on the first two counts would be varied as set out above. *R v Archer*, 20th April 1978 (Court of Appeal: Shaw LJ, Lawson and Smith JJ).

2445　*Riot; causing damage to property*
Sentence: 6 months' imprisonment concurrent. Youth, aged 19. Apprenticed at National Coal Board colliery since leaving school. Character and attendance described as good. No previous convictions. A group of young men, including the appellant, went to celebrate the stag night of one of their number. Went to various public houses and, eventually, a night club where fights developed. Two of the youths were thrown out and many of the others left. Rampaged through the streets, shouting, swearing, throwing stones and damaging parked cars. Stopped a car containing two girls and two young men. One of the girls was injured when a stone was thrown through the window of the car. Appellant was one of the youths standing around kicking the car. Sentenced to concurrent terms of 3 years' imprisonment, as were three of the other youths. Those under 17 years old were sent to borstal or detention centres or fined. Appeal on the grounds that an up to date social inquiry report, which had not been before trial judge, showed appellant

had completed 3 years of his apprenticeship, was hardworking, mature and confident for his age, of above average intelligence, came from a respectable family, and expressed remorse for his behaviour. *Held*, appellant had been in prison for 7 months' and if he stayed there would miss the first term of the academic year. Sentence would be varied as set out above. *R v Parsons*, 21st July 1978 (Court of Appeal: Orr and Browne LJJ and Mais J).

2446 *Affray*
Sentence: immediate release (7½ months' imprisonment served). Married man, 60, with a grown up son. No previous convictions. Member of a travelling, if not strictly gypsy, family. Wife gravely ill and himself unemployed since 1971. Lived on caravan site with son and two nephews. The son and nephews became involved in a fight with another family on the site and as a result the appellant was involved in a fist fight. The son accidentally killed a female member of the other family with a shotgun and was convicted of manslaughter. The appellant was sentenced to 15 months' imprisonment for affray. The judge said that he should have used his patriarchal position to stop the fighting. On appeal, *held*, in view of the very limited part the appellant took in the fighting his sentence would be varied to allow his immediate release. *R v James*, 17th January 1978 (Court of Appeal: Lawton LJ, Swanwick and Gibson JJ).

2447 Sentence: 3 years' imprisonment. Youth, aged 19. Had received deferred sentence in November 1976 for assault occasioning actual bodily harm, and had been fined for using obscene language and resisting a police constable in the execution of his duty. The current offence of affray took place on 10th December 1976. With other youths he attacked Iranian students, who were visitors to the United Kingdom, and forcibly entered a bank. Ten days after the affray justices dealt with the deferred sentence by putting him on probation for 2 years. In January 1977 the appellant was involved in a burglary and another assault. In April 1977 he was again involved in a very serious burglary. He was sent to borstal in June 1977 for the two charges of burglary. The affray offences came before the Crown Court in July 1977, and the appellant was sentenced to 3 years' imprisonment. On appeal *held*, there was absolutely no mitigation for this type of mob violence with racial undertones, and for putting the employees of the bank in terror. The appellant's record was the worst the court had seen for a young offender for a long time. The appeal would be dismissed. *R v Lardides*, 3rd March 1978 (Court of Appeal: Roskill LJ, Chapman and Lawson JJ).

2448 Sentence: immediate release (6 months' imprisonment served). Divorced man, aged 35, with one child. Number of previous convictions, all minor and none of which involved imprisonment. Two factions, one white, the other coloured, began a fight inside a public house. Police were called. They interviewed two coloured men but let them go, which caused resentment among the whites. Fight developed outside public house. Appellant was struck by another man with a piece of wood. Appellant snatched wood and hit man on the head, causing a wound. Man was unconscious for a period but there was no fracture of the skull or bone injury. Sentenced to 12 months' imprisonment. On appeal *held*, the sentence imposed was excessive for the part appellant had played in affray. His immediate release would be ordered. *R v Lawlor*, 10th August 1978 (Court of Appeal: Roskill LJ, Ackner and Stocker JJ).

2449 *Possessing a firearm without a certificate*
Sentence: 12 months' imprisonment. Man, aged 28. Bad record for petty crime. Had been sentenced to various terms of imprisonment for house-breaking, theft, burglary etc. but had never carried firearms or been involved in crimes of violence. At 3.15 a.m. he was seen in a cafe with a sawn-off shotgun down his trouser leg. Refused to give the police any explanation as to why he possessed it and what he proposed to do with it. At his trial he said that a prostitute whom he had visited that night had given him the gun to sell for her. Sentenced to 4 years'

imprisonment. Since trial appellant's father said his son was under the influence of drink when he returned home with the gun. Parents treated the gun as a curio but turned son out of the house because of his drunken condition. On appeal *held*, although it was a serious offence, in the circumstances the sentence would be varied to one of 12 months' imprisonment. *R v Wade*, 3rd July 1978 (Court of Appeal: Ormrod LJ, Mais and Peter Pain JJ).

2450   *Drunk and disorderly*
Sentence: conditional discharge for 3 years. Girl, aged 17. In July 1977 when she was subject to a care order she and another girl inmate left their hostel on a legitimate purpose, and did not return at night. In the early hours of the following morning the two girls broke two sheets of plate glass and the police found the appellant lying on the ground in a very drunken state. She was wearing no shoes, and was crying out incoherently. She had drunk too much alcohol and had taken a number of tablets. She had two previous juvenile appearances for, inter alia, burglary and theft. A supervision order had been made in 1976 and a care order in 1977. The appellant came from a disturbed home background, her brothers were unemployed and her sister a delinquent. She was said to be wilful, wayward and defiant. Sentenced to borstal "to undergo some form of custodial training" to cure her anti-social habits. On appeal *held*, primary the function of a court was not one of rehabilitation. It had to look at the offence and see if rehabilitation procedures were apt; they were not in the present case. The later social enquiry report showed that the appellant was at last beginning to show signs of more responsibility. The sentence would be varied as set out above. *R v Sims*, 7th April 1978 (Court of Appeal: Shaw LJ, O'Connor and Lawson JJ).

OFFENCES AGAINST THE PERSON

2451   *Manslaughter*
Sentence: 10 years' imprisonment. Married man, 34, with one child. Fourteen previous convictions, three of which were spent, and many of which involved some sort of violence. Began living with a woman in 1968. In 1969 he was put on probation conditional on hospital treatment for beating her up. They married in 1970. Wife left home on a number of occasions because the appellant ill treated her. In 1976 they had a daughter, to whom the appellant was devoted. Wife left him, claiming that she was too frightened to stay. The appellant bought a gun with the intention of shooting himself, his wife and the baby. He had a telephone conversation with his wife as a result of which she returned to the matrimonial home and he deliberately shot her twice. He said she had provoked him by saying that the baby was not his. He was charged with murder but convicted of manslaughter and sentenced as above. On appeal, *held*, accepting, as the jury did, that there was provocation, the appellant had set up the scene before the provocation began and it could not be said that the sentence was excessive or wrong in principle. *R v Wells*, 17th January 1978 (Court of Appeal: Shaw LJ, Mais and Peter Pain JJ).

2452   Sentence: 6 years' imprisonment. Single man, 47, unemployed. One spent conviction for unlawful wounding. Lived as a lodger in the victim's house. The victim was trying to forcibly evict the appellant from the house and when under the influence of drink had once threatened him with a hammer. The appellant stabbed the victim with a penknife in the pulmonary artery causing his death. Appellant pleaded guilty to manslaughter. Trial judge considered it a very bad case and sentenced him to 10 years' imprisonment, being influenced by his previous conviction in 1974. On appeal *held*, although it was a bad case of manslaughter it was mitigated to a substantial extent both by provocation and antecedent violence shown by the victim. The sentence would be varied to 6 years' imprisonment. *R v Thomas* 27th February 1978 (Court of Appeal: Roskill LJ, Chapman and Lawson JJ).

2453   Sentence: hospital orders under ss. 60 and 65 of the Mental Health Act 1959. Married man, aged 45, with 3 children. Porter on British Railways. Killed wife by cutting her throat. Trial judge sentenced appellant to 10 years' imprisonment. Said that in the opinion of doctors the appellant was a sick man and needed special treatment in secure conditions, but no accommodation was then available. On appeal *held*, that as a place had been found at Broadmoor for the appellant, and as his illness was a mental one, the court would vary the sentence to a s. 60 hospital order with a restriction order, without limit of time, under s. 65 of the Mental Health Act 1959. *R v Gadson*, 25th May 1978 (Court of Appeal: Orr and Cumming-Bruce LJJ, Park J).

2454 Sentence: 9 years' imprisonment. Married man, aged 43. Low intellect. As a juvenile he had gone to approved school, and had spent many years in a mental hospital. Long record of larceny, shop-breaking and drunkenness offences, all of which had been dealt with in magistrates' courts. In 1964 he had been fined for unlawful wounding and in 1967 had been given 3 months' imprisonment for a similar offence. In 1973 he had served a sentence of imprisonment for burglary, and in 1975 had received a suspended sentence for causing grievous bodily harm. Appellant and his wife met a 79 year old woman at a public house. Appellant accompanied the woman to her flat where he punched her, causing extensive bruising, swelling of face and neck and multiple fracture of the jaw. Three days later the woman was discovered dead in her flat. Cause of death was multiple injuries to face and neck. Appellant convicted of murder and sentenced to life imprisonment. On appeal *held*, having regard to appellant's low intellect problem was whether or not to impose an indeterminate sentence. As medical reports showed that appellant's mental condition was not likely to change usual reasons for imposing indeterminate sentence were absent. As the court had varied the conviction for murder to one for manslaughter, it was right that a determinate sentence of 9 years' imprisonment should be imposed. Although no weapon had been used it was a very grave case. *R v O'Grady*, 13th July 1978 (Court of Appeal: Cumming-Bruce LJ, Chapman and Kenneth Jones JJ).

2455 Sentence: detention at a mental hospital. Married man, aged 37, with four children. Various employments including maintenance engineer, fitter and welder. Served in Army 1959–62. Newspaper reporter at time of arrest. In early hours of the morning struck wife with a club hammer when she was in bed. Went to a friend's house and said he had killed his wife, concluding "I've got a shotgun and I'm going to do myself in". He then drove to the police station and admitted the offence, later saying "I was going to kill her with the hammer and shoot the kids, set fire to the house and then shoot myself." He had become depressed due to a union dispute. After being charged with wife's murder pleaded guilty to manslaughter on grounds of diminished responsibility. Medical reports showed that, at the time, he was suffering from a profound psychotic depression and that a s. 60 order under the Mental Health Act 1959 or a s. 3 order under the Powers of Criminal Courts Act 1973 was appropriate. No bed was available at a suitable hospital, so appellant sentenced to 3 years' imprisonment. On appeal *held*, a bed had become available in a suitable hospital so an order would be made under Mental Health Act 1959, s. 60. *R v Cross*, 10th August 1978 (Court of Appeal: Roskill LJ, Ackner and Stocker JJ).

2456 *Causing death by dangerous driving*
Sentence: 12 months' imprisonment suspended for 18 months; disqualified from driving for 6 years. Single man aged 26. Previous convictions for driving offences in the Channel Islands for which he had been fined, and for two offences of false pretences for which he had served 4 months' imprisonment. At night he overtook a car on a main road and knocked down a cyclist who later died from his injuries. Sentenced as above. On appeal *held*, it was a serious case of dangerous driving, not one merely of inadvertence. From his driving record it was clear that he disregarded the law as far as motoring was concerned. The sentence of imprisonment imposed was lenient, and the period of disqualification was neither unreasonable nor unfair. *R v Turner*, 11th January 1978 (Court of Appeal: Lord Widgery CJ, Melford Stevenson and Lloyd JJ).

2457 Sentence: £25 fine: disqualified for 12 months. Man aged 20. No previous convictions and with an excellent work record. When driving his motor cycle along a main road, he overtook a car and killed a woman who was crossing the road. Spectators to the accident assessed his speed "about 30 mph", "45 mph", and an AA patrol man who saw the appellant shortly before the accident assessed it "at between 65 and 70 mph". On this latter assessment the appellant was sentenced to 3 months at a detention centre and disqualified for 15 months. On appeal *held*, as there was doubt as to the appellant's real speed, and as he had probably been driving on a restricted road at least at 40 mph, the sentence passed should have been a substantial fine and the mandatory disqualification of 12 months imposed. In view of the fact that the appellant had been in custody for 12 days, and that the offence was one of dangerous, not reckless, driving, the sentence would be varied as set out above. *R v Yarnold*, 31st January 1978 (Court of Appeal: Lawton LJ, Mars-Jones and Mais JJ).

2458 Sentence: immediate release (3½ months at a detention centre served); disqualified one year. Youth, aged 18. Three summary convictions, two for road traffic offences and one for burglary and theft of drugs from a chemist's shop. Had been fined in respect of each offence. In early morning, when overtaking another car, appellant's car veered across the road and crashed head on with a motor cyclist driving towards him. Motor cyclist subsequently died from his injuries. Appellant sentenced to 6 months at a detention centre and disqualified for 4 years. On appeal on the ground that the appellant had not been drunk and had not been driving at excessive speed *held*, the court could not over-emphasise the seriousness of the result of the appellant's driving. With regard to the fact, however, that the offence was caused by the appellant driving on the wrong side of the road, and the fact that it was a first custodial sentence, the sentence and disqualification would be varied as set out above. *R v Lawless*, 16th June 1978 (Court of Appeal: Eveleigh LJ, O'Connor and Griffiths JJ).

2459 Sentence: £250 fine or 6 months' imprisonment in default; disqualified for 2 years. Man, aged 52, of previous good character. Visitor to U.K. from Sweden. Overlooked the fact that he was required to drive on left side of road in U.K. Drove along a road on the right side for almost a mile and collided with a vehicle coming in the opposite direction, killing its passenger. No evidence of drink or excessive speed. Appellant fined £1,000 and disqualified for 5 years; spent 4 days in custody. Net income of £2,000 per year. On appeal *held*, in all the circumstances the fine of £1,000 was excessive, and the proper fine was £250. The period of disqualification was also excessive and would be varied to 2 years. *R v Olsson*, 26th June 1978 (Court of Appeal: Eveleigh LJ, O'Connor and Griffiths JJ).

2460 *Causing death by dangerous driving: driving while unfit through drink*
Sentence: 3 years' imprisonment concurrent (2 counts); 12 months' imprisonment concurrent; disqualified for 10 years. Married man, 50, with 2 children. Previous convictions, all but one of which were spent. Last conviction in December 1976 for criminal damage and disorderly behaviour for which he had been fined. After drinking heavily in public houses the appellant drove his car at 50 mph in the dark in a street full of people, weaving from side to side. Knocked down four people who were on a pedestrian crossing, killing two of them. In the 9 months awaiting trial for the above offences, the appellant was ostracised by everybody—in effect "having served a very nasty 9 months' imprisonment before his trial took place". Sentenced as above. On appeal *held*, it was a most disgraceful piece of driving. The sentence imposed was in no way too heavy and the appeal would be dismissed *R v Wright*, 6th March 1978 (Court of Appeal: Lord Widgery CJ, Cantley and Drake JJ).

2461 *Unlawful wounding*
Sentence: 3 years' imprisonment. Married man, 29, with one child. Numerous previous convictions including two spent convictions of unlawful wounding, one other of unlawful wounding and one of assault occasioning actual bodily harm.

With co-accused attacked the victim in a dark alley. Knocked him to the ground and hit him twice on the head with a bottle, rendering him unconscious. Co-accused, who was also convicted of robbery, and appellant got identical sentences of 4 years' imprisonment. On appeal *held*, it was a very bad attack although the wound suffered by the victim was not serious. Nevertheless, having regard to the sentence passed on the co-accused the appellant's sentence would be varied to 3 years' imprisonment. *R v Green*, 21st February 1978 (Court of Appeal: Orr LJ, Thompson and Milmo JJ).

2462   Sentence: 3 years' imprisonment. Married man, 20, with one child. Variety of employments since leaving school. Long list of previous convictions—two as a juvenile, and seven summary and three other convictions for theft, burglary and driving offences. Had received conditional discharge, been sent to detention centre, and fined often. Consumed quantity of vodka and beer in a public house. As one of the customers, aged 62, was crossing the car park, the appellant struck him to the ground, causing a wound on his right eyebrow requiring hospital treatment. Sentenced as above. On appeal *held*, a deterrent sentence was called for to discourage such acts of unprovoked violence. There was nothing wrong with the sentence imposed. *R v Barber*, 6th March 1978 (Court of Appeal: Lord Widgery CJ, Drake and Cantley JJ).

2463   Sentence: 9 months' imprisonment concurrent. Man, aged 25. Number of jobs as a labourer. Three convictions for motoring offences, but in the present case he was treated as a man of good character. He had been living with a woman on and off for 5 years. She lost interest in him and began associating with a married man. The appellant saw the couple at a public house, where the man had a private room. The appellant followed them there, and saw the couple naked on the bed. He pulled out a penknife and attacked them both, punching the woman in the face and wounding her in the abdomen. The man had his hand and face slashed. The appellant was sentenced to consecutive terms of 9 months' imprisonment—18 months in all. On appeal *held*, it was a serious situation and a serious offence with a knife, albeit only a penknife. The appellant could be said to be under provocation and had lost his temper. The sentences of 9 months were lenient, but in view of the fact that the two offences were part of the same incident, they would be varied to run concurrently. *R v Gomez*, 20th April 1978 (Court of Appeal: Shaw LJ, Lawson and Smith JJ).

2464   Sentence: 9 months' imprisonment. Married man, aged 64. Criminal record since 1920s. Most serious convictions for robbery in 1948 (7 years' penal servitude) and receiving in 1957 (8 years' imprisonment), but no custodial sentence since release in 1962. After drinking alcohol appellant damaged the wing of another car when overtaking it. The other driver followed the appellant home and, in the ensuing argument, the appellant hit him on the head with a hammer. The injury sustained was not serious, requiring only three stitches. Appellant sentenced to 15 months' imprisonment. On appeal *held*, it was a bad case of assault with a dangerous weapon and an immediate custodial sentence was called for but as the appellant had kept out of trouble for 14 years a measure of leniency would be extended to him. The sentence would be varied to one of 9 months' imprisonment. *R v Monoghan*, 25th May 1978 (Court of Appeal: Bridge LJ, Wien and Eastham JJ).

2465   *Unlawful wounding: breach of suspended sentence*
Sentence: immediate release (3 months' imprisonment served) (first offence); 1 day's imprisonment concurrent (second offence). Single woman, aged 21, with 2 children, and pregnant at time of trial. Unemployed. In December 1976 she had been put on probation for two years for assault on police. Appellant and sister quarrelled with shopkeeper. Appellant later returned to shop and attacked shopkeeper with a knife, causing bruising and a cut requiring stitches. Sentenced to 9 months' imprisonment on the wounding charge, in the mistaken belief that appellant could have children with her in prison. On appeal on ground that if she served her sentence the baby would be born in prison *held*, in view of the pregnancy

and the mistake about the children being allowed in the prison, sentence would be varied as set out above. *R v Wright*, 11th July 1978 (Court of Appeal: Ormrod LJ, Mais and Peter Pain JJ).

2466   *Assault*
Sentence: 6 months' imprisonment concurrent. Nursing assistant, aged 30. No previous convictions. Worked at mental hospital from March to July 1977. Mental ages of patients ranged from 2 to 5 years. Appellant assaulted patients by slapping their faces. First assault pushed patient through a door and second assault reddened patient's face and caused him to fall over a table. Other members of nursing staff reported appellant to authorities. Sentenced as above. On appeal *held*, patients of above mental ages were very vulnerable and were entitled to be treated with consideration and kindness by those who were responsible for them. Appellant had committed grave breach of trust, although assaults were not serious. An immediate custodial sentence was necessary to deter others who might be tempted to behave in the same way. *R v Burb*, 26th October 1978 (Court of Appeal: Bridge LJ, Michael Davies and Stocker JJ).

2467   *Assault occasioning actual bodily harm*
Sentence: immediate release (2 months' imprisonment served). Married man, 39, with 4 daughters. Eight previous court appearances (two as a juvenile) now all spent. Fourteen-year-old daughter had, for years, been causing trouble at home. She was a persistent shoplifter. Appellant had to give up his job to keep daughter in order. He seriously assaulted daughter with a belt. Sentenced to 6 months' imprisonment. On appeal *held*, appellant had been sufficiently punished by term of imprisonment already served. Now that daughter was away from home, the court would reduce the sentence to allow immediate release. *R v Love*, 19th June 1978 (Court of Appeal: Geoffrey Lane and Shaw LJJ, Caulfield J).

2468   *Assault occasioning actual bodily harm: damage to property*
Sentence: borstal training. Youth, aged 20, a labourer. Convicted of four counts of actual bodily harm and damaging property arising from an incident when he threw missiles at a coach containing football supporters. Sentenced as above. On appeal *held*, it had become apparent that sentences such as fines, community service orders and probation, had not curbed football hooliganism; hooligans convicted of offences of violence or damaging property should expect to lose their liberty. The appeal would be dismissed. *R v Motley*, (1978) Times, 25th January (Court of Appeal: Lawton LJ, Swanwick and Gibson JJ).

2469   *Unlawful sexual intercourse*
Sentence: absolute discharge. Youth, aged 19, apprentice mason. Of previous good character. Convicted of unlawful sexual intercourse with a girl under the age of 16, and sentenced to three months in a detention centre. On appeal *held,* only one act of intercourse had taken place and the girl had been a willing participant. Where the parties were in the same age group the court should have regard to current standards of sexual behaviour and should not impose a penalty involving loss of liberty. The sentence would be varied as set out above. *R v O'Grady* (1978) Times, 8th February (Court of Appeal: Shaw LJ, Peter Pain and Mais JJ).

2470   *Incest*
Sentence: 6 years' imprisonment concurrent. Married man, aged 44, with four daughters. Unemployed since 1970; wife went out to work. Since at least 1970 had frequently had sexual intercourse with second daughter, aged 23. Daughter had two children, both of whom died, by her father and had several miscarriages. Trial judge said a more horrific story would be hard to imagine. Appellant had debauched his daughter's body and mind over a period of 6 years. On appeal *held*, it was not an isolated offence but had gone on for several years, the counts in the indictment being specimen ones. Further, at the time, appellant was affected by drink and drugs. In any view, it was a tragic case but it was impossible to say that the sentence imposed

was in any way excessive. *R v Thuruse*, 3rd November 1978 (Court of Appeal: Browne LJ, Phillips and Michael Davies JJ).

2471   *Indecent assault*
Sentence: immediate release (5½ months' imprisonment served). Married school teacher, aged 54. Wife, aged 68, was desperately ill. During 1976 and 1977 he committed offences against 10 and 11 year old girls in his class. Offences consisted of indecently tickling pupils. He pleaded guilty and was sentenced to 18 months' imprisonment concurrent. Lost career as a teacher. If appellant was in prison there was no-one to look after wife. On appeal *held*, as appellant had already served a substantial period of imprisonment, his immediate release would be ordered as an act of mercy. *R v Knight*, 29th June 1978 (Court of Appeal: Eveleigh LJ, O'Connor and Griffiths JJ).

2472   *Indecent assault on girls under 13*
Sentence: 3 years' probation on terms including medical treatment. Man aged 60. Ten previous convictions for indecent assault on young girls and similar offences. In 1974 he was convicted of rape and three indecent assaults and sentenced to 3 years' imprisonment suspended for 2 years. Said to be probably impotent and suffering from a chromosome abnormality. Befriended little girls with the consent of their parents who did not know of his criminal record. Offences consisted of fingering their private parts. Sentenced to 4 years' imprisonment concurrent on the ground that protection of young girls must prevail over the appellant's physical difficulties. On appeal *held*, the court would give the appellant a last chance by putting him on probation on the ground that he would undergo medical treatment for 3 years. *R v Johnson*, 23rd January 1978 (Court of Appeal: Lawton LJ, Swanwick and Gibson JJ).

2473   *Indecent assault, indecency with a child*
Sentence: 3 years' imprisonment (first offence); 2 years' imprisonment concurrent (second offence) (3 years' imprisonment in all). Man, aged 32. No previous convictions and good work record. Befriended a girl, aged 12, and gave her car rides. The counts were specimen counts to which appellant pleaded guilty. The offences took place in the car and other isolated places and consisted of the appellant and girl handling each other's private parts. Appellant contended that girl provoked the conduct. Sentenced to 5 years' imprisonment on first count and 2 years' imprisonment concurrent on second count. Psychiatric report showed no danger to society as a whole. On appeal *held*, bearing appellant's previous good character in mind, 5 years' imprisonment was too long. He should be given credit for the fact that he had pleaded guilty and spared the girl from having to go into the witness box. Sentence would be varied as set out above. *R v Crockford*, 20th June 1978 (Court of Appeal: Eveleigh LJ, O'Connor and Griffiths JJ).

2474   *Buggery*
Sentence: 2 years' imprisonment. Unmarried man, aged 27. Good work record. Employers willing to re-employ him on release from prison. Previous convictions but none for above offence. Last conviction was for burglary and theft (20 cases taken into consideration) in 1974 for which he got 12 months' imprisonment. He met a 16 year old male prostitute in a cafe frequented by homosexuals. The youth stayed at the appellant's flat where various homosexual activities took place between them ending in the appellant buggering the youth, who appeared to have consented. Sentenced as above. The judge remarked that he imposed the sentence to punish the appellant and deter other mature men from committing that sort of offence against teenagers. On appeal *held*, the judge was right in passing such a deterrent sentence. *R v Deighton*, 5th May 1978 (Court of Appeal: Ormrod and Brown LJJ, Willis J).

2475   *Buggery; gross indecency*
Sentence: immediate release (7 months' imprisonment served). Man, aged 40.

Voluntary service officer at a hospital. No previous convictions. Appellant was passive partner in an act of buggery with a boy, aged 15. Boy had said he was 17. Further act of buggery, and other acts giving rise to charge of gross indecency. No question of appellant corrupting boy. Appellant sentenced to 18 months' imprisonment on first count and to one month's imprisonment concurrent on second count. On appeal *held*, after reading testimonials in appellant's favour from youth community centre, YMCA, social workers on local council and Salvation Army member, in view of appellant's previous good record and the fact that he was passive partner, the sentence would be varied as set out above. *R v Parsons*, 26th October 1978 (Court of Appeal: Bridge LJ, Michael Davies and Stocker JJ).

2476   *Living on earnings of prostitution; forgery of valuable security; theft; obtaining money on a forged instrument*
Sentence: 12 months' imprisonment (living on earnings of prostitution); 3 years' imprisonment on all other counts, concurrent to the 12 months (3 years' imprisonment in all); compensation order of £2,180. An unqualified architect, aged 65. Met a prostitute, as her client, in 1959 and lived with her from 1963 to 1977. Between June 1971 and 1972 he forged her signature on her cheques for sums of £30 and £50. In August 1974 she gave him £1,250 to pay into her bank account. He forged the paying in slip and kept the money. In December 1974 the prostitute, wishing to sell a car in part exchange, gave the appellant £2,000 in cash. He kept £650 of it and forged a cheque on her building society account to replace it. Between December 1974 and March 1975 he forged the prostitute's signature to withdrawal slips to her building society and obtained £100 and £1,000. At the trial thirty seven similar cases were taken into consideration, involving a total sum of £8,605. Sentenced to 2 years' imprisonment for the forging of valuable security; 3 years' imprisonment concurrent for the theft; 4 years' and 3 years' imprisonment concurrent for receiving money on a forged instrument, and 12 months' imprisonment consecutive for living on the earnings of prostitution (5 years' imprisonment in all). On appeal it was contended that in view of his plea of guilty and his age, and the fact that his flair with finance had enabled the prostitute to increase her assets to almost £100,000 5 years' imprisonment was excessive. *Held*, the trial judge had not given credit for the fact that the appellant pleaded guilty, that he was a first offender, that it was not an ordinary case of a man living on the earnings of prostitution, and that he had to wait 14 months between arrest and trial. The sentences would be varied as above. *R v Cooper*, 9th March 1978 (Court of Appeal: Ormrod and Waller LJJ, Chapman J).

OFFENCES AGAINST PROPERTY

2477   *Robbery*
Sentence: probation for 2 years. Girl, aged 16. Good middle class family. Normal life until mid 1977 when she met a youth, aged 19, as a result of which she got out of hand. She went to live with the youth. He subsequently invited another man, the victim, to live in the house. The victim had a large sum of money in his pocket. Youth threatened him with a knife, and demanded money. The girl was aiding him. The youth was sentenced to 4 years' imprisonment, and the girl to borstal training. On appeal *held*, it was a very nasty offence, but as the girl had been in Holloway prison for 3 weeks and appeared to have had a change of heart, making a supervision order was likely to be effective, and the court would vary the sentence to 2 years' probation. *R v Dannan*, 9th March 1978 (Court of Appeal: Lord Widgery CJ, Cantley and Drake JJ).

2478   Sentence: 4 years' imprisonment. Man, aged 32. No previous convictions. At 7 p.m. one evening the appellant, armed with an air rifle and with a scarf concealing the lower part of his face, went to a self-service petrol station. Forced attendant to hand over £60. Appellant then drove off and was not traced for 8 months. Then made frank oral confession of what he had done, and later made written confession. Said he had been recently reconciled with his girlfriend and wanted to take her out but had no money. Claimed air rifle was not loaded and expressed remorse. Sentenced as above. On appeal, contended offence was out of character, that appellant was in good employment and had pleaded guilty. *Held*, it was planned robbery, involving a firearm, appellant was in disguise and could have escaped detection. In the early evening petrol stations were particularly vulnerable to the present kind of attack. Such offences had to be severely dealt with. Sentence was not wrong in principle. *R v Moss*, 26th October 1978 (Court of Appeal: Bridge LJ, Michael Davies and Stocker JJ).

2479   *Robbery: blackmail*
Sentence: 3 years' imprisonment; 2 years' imprisonment consecutive (5 years in all) (first defendant); 2 years' imprisonment concurrent (second defendant). First defendant was man, 36, who had been cohabiting for some years with second defendant, woman aged 26. The first defendant had two previous convictions for dishonesty and living on immoral earnings and, jointly with the second defendant, of causing grievous bodily harm for which the man was sentenced to 18 months' imprisonment and the woman to 9 months imprisonment. On release the woman went to live in a probation hostel and formed an association with another man, the victim, who also had a criminal record. On the first defendant's release from prison, the second defendant terminated her relationship with the other man, who was then invited into her room by the first defendant. The first defendant went berserk, robbed the victim of £1 and then punched and hit him. The second defendant kept asking the victim for money and eventually took his rings and watch, worth £350. Sentenced as above. On appeal *held*, in view of the defendants' previous conviction for grievous bodily harm with intent the offences were grave although the victim received only bruising. The sentences imposed were neither wrong in principle nor manifestly excessive. *R v Jackson and Jackson*, 23rd January 1978 (Court of Appeal: Bridge LJ, Michael Davies and Jupp JJ).

2480   *Burglary*
Sentence: borstal training (entering and stealing). Two youths, aged 18 and 19, broke into house, ransacked contents and stole property. Sentenced to borstal training. On appeal, *held*, burglary offences were increasing and caused much distress and insecurity among the public. More and more adolescents were committing such offences. They could only be deterred by being deprived of their liberty. Detention or imprisonment should invariably be imposed in cases of breaking and entering people's homes. *R v Smith* (1978) Times, 18th January (Court of Appeal: Lawton LJ, Swanwick and Gibson JJ).

2481   Sentence: borstal training. Youth, aged 17. In 1975 had received a conditional discharge for two offences of burglary, and in 1976 had received detention for four burglaries. In September 1977 he was made the subject of a supervision order for another burglary. Just prior to that offence he had committed the five burglaries which were the subject matter of the instant appeal. On appeal *held*, in view of the appellant's record there was no reason to interfere with the sentence of borstal training. *R v Curran*, 9th March 1978 (Court of Appeal: Ormrod and Waller LJJ, Chapman J).

2482   Sentence: 4½ years' imprisonment and 4 years' imprisonment respectively. Two defendants first aged 21, second aged 19, both with a record of previous convictions, convicted of burglary with more than 20 offences taken into account. Sentenced as above. On appeal, *held*, burglary in a dwelling house was a very serious matter and was not only an offence of dishonesty but a personal attack. The sentences would stand as a deterrent to other young men in the locality. *R v Jackson, R v Quanbrough* [1978] LS Gaz R 453 (Court of Appeal: Lord Widgery CJ, Cantley and Drake JJ).

2483   Sentence: 3 years' imprisonment. Man, aged 20. Appalling criminal record. Since 1970 before courts eleven times for either burglary or theft, many of these cases asking for a large number of similar offences to be taken into consideration. Every form of remedial treatment had been tried. Committed further offences within weeks of being put on probation. With another young man he broke into a bungalow and ransacked it, but found little to steal. Sentenced as above. On appeal *held*, for the protection of the community a deterrent sentence was properly imposed. *R v Smith*, 20th June 1978 (Court of Appeal: Eveleigh LJ, O'Connor and Griffiths JJ).

2484   Sentence: 18 months' imprisonment consecutive on each indictment (3 years in all). Single man, aged 20. Had done little work since leaving school; had 48 convictions for burglary and 9 convictions for taking vehicles without owners' consent. Had been subject to conditional discharge, probation and care orders and had been in remand home, approved school and borstal. Appellant and his brother broke into a house and stole music centre and jewellery to value of £266. While on bail for this offence appellant rifled another house, where he broke into meters and stole £3.50. Also taken into consideration was the theft of a motor cycle valued at £150. Appellant charged on two indictments with the separate burglaries and sentenced as above. Remand centre report did not recommend return to borstal as appellant was making progress in prison and had shown willingness to co-operate. On appeal *held*, borstal would be inappropriate as appellant needed discipline and training. Burglaries of private houses were too prevalent. Sentences were correct. *R v Gallagher*, 4th July 1978 (Court of Appeal; Ormrod LJ, Mais and Peter Pain JJ).

2485   *Burglary: taking a conveyance*
Sentence: 5 years' imprisonment concurrent; 12 months' imprisonment concurrent. Youth, aged 19. Since 1971 had been before the courts for offences of burglary on eight occasions, for which he had received care orders, conditional discharge, 3 months' detention, borstal training and finally 2 years' imprisonment. With another man ransacked a private house and stole silver etc., worth £550. Two days later with the same man he took a conveyance without the owner's consent. Arrested again two days later. Broke bail and, with the same man, broke into another house and stole equipment, and broke into a garage and stole a car. Sentenced as above. On appeal *held*, that a substantial sentence was called for. The appellant was a persistent criminal and showed no intention of reforming his ways. The appeal would be dismissed. *R v Simmons*, 7th March 1978 (Court of Appeal: Lord Widgery CJ, Cantley and Drake JJ).

2486   *Burglary; breach of probation and conditional discharge*
Sentence: immediate release (9 months' imprisonment served). Registered epileptic, aged 20. Unemployed. Previous convictions, including three for burglary. The present two offences of burglary were committed when the appellant was on probation and subject to a conditional discharge. The articles stolen were all recovered. Sentenced to 18 months' imprisonment for the burglaries, and 6 months' imprisonment concurrent for breach of probation and for breach of conditional discharge. The 6 months was to run consecutive to the 18 months. It was argued that the sentence imposed was excessive, as the appellant had pleaded guilty and co-operated with the police. On appeal *held*, a shorter sentence would be imposed to allow the appellant's immediate release from custody. *R v Allott*, 8th June 1978 (Court of Appeal: Shaw LJ, Jupp and Neill JJ).

2487   *Theft*
Sentence: 9 months' imprisonment consecutive (18 months in all). Single man, aged 28. Painter and decorator earning £60 per week. Previous convictions for burglary, theft and deception for which he had been fined and served two terms of 3 months' imprisonment. In early 1977, in the Midlands, two or three men were persistently stealing electric drills from shops. The appellant was one of these men, but a co-accused was the ringleader. The appellant committed these offences while on bail and had joined the others in organised, persistent shoplifting from two stores. Co-accused had no previous convictions but asked for fifteen cases to be taken into consideration and was sentenced to 6 months' imprisonment suspended and ordered to pay £500 compensation. On appeal on ground of disparity *held*, for

this kind of commercially organised shoplifting 18 months' imprisonment was justified even though his co-accused was treated with undue leniency. There was no reason to interfere on the ground of disparity. *R v Harwood*, 12th January 1978 (Court of Appeal: Lawton LJ, Swanwick and Gibson JJ).

2488   Sentence: 6 months' imprisonment concurrent, suspended for one year. Married man, in early 40's with four children. Previous good character. Worked for a firm of builders' and plumbers' merchants, first as a driver and then as a warehouseman. Could not meet his responsibilities as a warehouseman and was demoted. As a result he stole articles to the value of £276 from the warehouse. Sentenced to concurrent terms of 9 months' imprisonment on grounds that it was a breach of trust and he was in a position to facilitate the thefts which aggravated the offences. On appeal *held*, as the appellant had worked hard and learnt his lesson the sentence would be varied as set out above. *R v Pickford*, 12th January 1978 (Court of Appeal: Shaw LJ, Mais and Peter Pain JJ).

2489   Sentence: 6 months' imprisonment suspended 2 years. Young married woman with two children, boy aged 4, and girl aged 6. Husband was sub postmaster, and the matrimonial home was over the shop. Husband's duties included payment of pensions, etc. under the social security schemes. In assisting husband to discharge duties the appellant falsely inflated the number of vouchers which evidenced how many times people had collected pensions and allowances. In this way she defrauded the Post Office of about £2,000. Trial judge regarded the case as a gross breach of trust, said a deterrent sentence was called for and imposed an immediate sentence of 9 months' imprisonment. The husband was completely innocent of the affair. The appellant was under great emotional strain as her daughter was diabetic. She misappropriated the money to buy gifts for her daughter to compensate for her insulin injections. The husband had to sell the Post Office business and his house. On appeal *held*, the sentence imposed was merciful, but in view of the unusual circumstances and the necessity of the appellant returning home to look after ther daughter, the court would vary the sentence as set out above. *R v Chappell*, 17th January 1978 (Court of Appeal: Bridge LJ, Watkins and Jupp JJ).

2490   Sentence: 28 days' imprisonment. Woman, aged 21. No previous convictions. Employed in the cash office of a magistrates' court. Money disappeared from the office. A marked £5 note was left in a prominent position in the office with the intention of catching a possible thief. Three hours later the note disappeared, and was found in the appellant's handbag. At her trial, after previously confessing to the theft, the appellant claimed the note had been planted in her handbag. Sentenced to 9 months' imprisonment. On appeal *held*, the imposition of an immediate term of imprisonment was correct because theft from offices spreads rapidly and casts suspicion on fellow employees. As the appellant had, however, served 3 weeks of her sentence and the fact of imprisonment was the real punishment, the sentence would be varied as set out above. *R v Reilly*, 16th March 1978 (Court of Appeal: Geoffrey Lane LJ, Thompson and Brown JJ).

2491   Sentence: borstal training. Youth, aged 19. Unemployed since leaving school at 16. With another youth he snatched a handbag from an elderly woman. The bag and contents were worth about £20. Was involved with other youths who committed similar offences. Made a statement: "I have only done one, that was with P, who snatched the bag and I went along with him." Sentenced to borstal training. On appeal *held*, the case clearly called for a custodial sentence as the offence of snatching handbags from elderly women was becoming all too prevalent. The appellant had done well at borstal and the sentence would stand. *R v Jibunoh*, 7th April 1978 (Court of Appeal: Roskill LJ, Swanwick and Michael Davies JJ).

2492   Sentence: £500 fine. Man aged 33 called at a house in answer to an advertisement of a car for sale. He paid a deposit and when the owner went into the house saw that the ignition key had been left in the car and drove off. Found three weeks later and car returned to owner. At time of offence, appellant was on bail on a charge of robbery for which he was acquitted but he had spent some time in custody. Pleaded guilty to theft. Sentenced to fine of £1,500. On appeal, *held*, the judge had taken into account the time which the appellant had spent in custody and did not impose a custodial sentence, but large fines were not to be encouraged and the fine was excessive. The proper sentence would have been a suspended sentence and a fine. The fine would be reduced to £500. *R v Mercer* (1978) Times, 14th April (Court of Appeal: Lord Widgery CJ, Eveleigh LJ and Drake J).

2493 Sentence: 15 months' imprisonment. Single man, aged 25. Lived with a woman and received social security. Had worked for short periods as plumber, factory hand and labourer. Had four findings of guilt and ten previous convictions for burglary, theft, unlawful possession of drugs and, in 1974 and 1976, for shoplifting. Sentenced to various terms of imprisonment from 3 months to 2 years and probation, fined, and sent to approved school and borstal. In December 1977, a month after coming out of prison, he went into a supermarket and loaded a turkey, leg of lamb, two shoulders of lamb and three joints of beef (total value of £13) into his bags. Sentenced as above. Said to have a drink and drugs problem. On appeal *held*, a man with the appellant's record deserved a sentence of 15 months. The time spent in prison would help cure him of his drink and drugs problem. *R v Fleming*, 10th July 1978 (Court of Appeal: Cumming-Bruce LJ, Chapman and Kenneth Jones JJ).

2494 *Theft; assault occasioning actual bodily harm*
Sentence: 4 months' imprisonment suspended for 2 years. Youth, aged 20. In 1977 had been fined £100 for theft and had served 3 months' detention on conviction for conspiracy to steal. Released in December 1977. In June 1978 he and three other youths went into a shop and jostled a man. The man's wallet was stolen. The man chased the youths and captured the appellant who kicked him causing a fractured ankle. Sentenced to 6 months' immediate imprisonment. Since being released from the detention centre the appellant had found a job and resumed cohabition with a woman who had given birth to his child. On appeal that a sentence of imprisonment was wrong in respect of a man who had successfully served 3 months' detention *held*, in the hope that the appellant might redeem himself the proper sentence for the two offences was one of 4 months' imprisonment suspended for 2 years. *R v Curley*, 26th June 1978 (Court of Appeal: Geoffrey Lane and Shaw LJJ, Caulfield J).

2495 *Theft; false accounting*
Sentence: 9 months' imprisonment (4 counts of theft); 10 months imprisonment concurrent (4 counts of theft); 10 months' imprisonment concurrent (4 counts of false accounting); (10 months' imprisonment in all). Married man, aged 48, with one son. Had been employed in the hospital service since 1955, latterly as senior administrator of stores. The offences consisted of stealing from the stores and making false entries to cover up the thefts. A man of previous excellent character Lost his pension rights and career prospects. Sentenced to 9 months' imprisonment on 4 counts of theft, 18 months' imprisonment concurrent on 3 counts of theft and 4 counts of false accounting, and 12 months' imprisonment concurrent on another count of theft (18 months' imprisonment in all). On appeal *held*, sentences as imposed were the proper ones but taking into account the fact that the appellant had been in prison for over 6 months, the court would vary the sentences as set out above. *R v Da Silva*, 27th April 1978 (Court of Appeal: Shaw LJ, Lawson and Smith JJ).

2496 *Conspiracy to commit theft*
Sentence: 9 months imprisonment. Married man, aged 31, with two children. Previous good character. In regular employment with a firm of funiture manufacturers. A checker in the firm enabled furniture to be sent out of the company's factory in the company vans, without making written records. The

drivers then dishonestly disposed of the goods to private purchasers. The appellant stole goods on two occasions, his share of the proceeds being £7 and £20. He lost his job and was sentenced to 18 months' imprisonment. On appeal *held*, as the appellant's involvement in the criminal conspiracy was small, the sentence passed was excessive, and would be varied to 9 month's imprisonment. *R v Howell*, 9th March 1978 (Court of Appeal: Lord Widgery CJ, Cantley and Drake JJ).

2497   *Conspiracy to defraud*
Sentence: 12 months' imprisonment suspended for 2 years; order for defence costs of £5,000. Insurance loss adjuster, aged 57, who also, with his wife, ran a riding school. Indictment with seven other men, four of whom were convicted, of conspiracy to defraud an insurance company. A building was deliberately burnt down and the conspirators attempted to obtain £150,000 from the insurance company. The principal conspirator received a sentence of 7 years' imprisonment, the other three received 4, 4 and 3 years' imprisonment respectively. The judge gave the appellant a suspended sentence of 12 months' imprisonment on the ground that his part in the conspiracy was small, that he joined it at a late stage, and acted in fear of the principal conspirator. In addition the appellant was ordered to pay £5,000 towards his defence costs and £2,000 towards prosecution costs. On appeal *held*, the sentence was in no way excessive. The order for defence costs would stand, but the contribution towards the prosecution costs would be set aside. *R v Jarvis*, 15th May 1978 (Court of Appeal: Bridge LJ, Thompson and Eastham JJ).

2498   Sentence: 9 months' imprisonment suspended for 2 years; compensation orders totalling £200; supervision order (6 weeks' imprisonment served). Woman, aged 21. One minor conviction. Met a criminal (now serving 5 years' imprisonment) and was made the front to a conspiracy. Appellant defrauded banks of substantial sums of money by cashing stolen cheques supported by stolen cheque cards. Offences took place in England in February 1976 and in France and Switzerland in May and June 1976. A total of 126 cheques were cashed at £30 a time, involving a total sum of £3,700. Appellant's share in the proceeds was £400. She went to Wales and was not seen by police until February 1978 when she made a full confession admitting her part in the conspiracy, and she pleaded guilty at the trial. Sentenced to 12 months' immediate imprisonment. On appeal on grounds that appellant had returned £200 of the proceeds to the court as partial restitution and compensation *held*, as appellant was not a hardened criminal, as social inquiry report showed that she was not a dominant personality and as she had already served 6 weeks' imprisonment the court would vary the sentence as set out above. Compensation orders of £100 each were made to two banks who had been defrauded. *R v Richards*, 25th August 1978 (Court of Appeal: Browne LJ, Talbot and Michael Davies JJ).

2499   *Conspiracy to cheat and defraud*
Sentence: £5,000 fine, plus costs, or 12 months' imprisonment in default of payment. Man, aged 48. Chairman of group of companies who were appointed dealers for Volkswagen cars. Volkswagen offered a prize of £5,000 to the dealer who most increased the sale of their cars. Appellant's company produced a figure of sales which was larger than that of any other dealers. Subsequent inquiries revealed 59 sale cards had been falsely completed. Sentenced to fine of £15,000. Principal member of staff involved fined £150. On appeal *held*, as counsel had mistakenly informed the trial judge that appellant's companies' assets were £20 million instead of £2 million, and in view of the disparity of the fine imposed on the staff member, the court would vary the fine as set out above. The order of prosecution costs up to £4,000 would stand. *R v Gupta*, 4th October 1978 (Court of Appeal: Waller LJ, Bristow and Stocker JJ).

2500   *False accounting*
Sentence: 12 months' imprisonment. Married man, 43, with 2 children. No previous convictions but in 1976 he had been found in possession of false exemption

documents for the purposes of the lump system and convicted of going equipped to cheat and possessing a forged instrument for which he was fined and given a conditional discharge. Instant offences took place between September 1975 and May 1976. The appellant was the leader of a gang of men working on the lump system in the construction industry. Obtained forged exemption documents and thereby defrauded the Inland Revenue of £4,000, his personal gain being about £1,200. Sentenced to 2 year's imprisonment. On appeal *held*, the sentence imposed was too long in principle and would be varied as set out above. *R v Phillips*, 13th January 1978 (Court of Appeal: Bridge LJ, Watkins and Jupp JJ).

2501   *Handling stolen goods*
Sentence: immediate release (8 month's imprisonment served). Married man, aged 55. Record of previous convictions of some seriousness, but last conviction was in 1968 when he received a sentence of 12 months' imprisonment suspended for 2 years for receiving. The police found the proceeds of burglaries which had recently taken place in the area in a garage. The appellant and his wife were involved in handling these goods, as some of the thefts had been committed by his stepson. Sentenced to 18 months' imprisonment concurrent on each count. On appeal *held*, that in view of the fact that the appellant had been out of trouble since 1968, that his wife received a suspended sentence although on the whole she had played a more significant part in the assistance offered to the thieves, there was some disparity in sentence. The Court would allow the appeal to the extent of ordering the appellant's immediate release. *R v Chapman* 11th January 1978 (Court of Appeal: Lawton LJ, Swanwick and Gibson JJ).

2502   *Obtaining property by deception*
Sentence: 9 months' imprisonment concurrent. Married man, aged 46, with 5 children. Habitual gambler. Average work record—landscape gardener and general ground worker—since leaving school until 1975 but suffered from ill-health since 1976. Between 1949 and 1966 had three sets of summary convictions including larceny and obtaining money by false pretences. Current offences took place from 1975 until March 1977 when appellant drew unemployment benefit while falsely declaring he was unemployed. At the material times he was doing gardening work for which he was paid £38, £48 and £23. He was drawing unemployment benefit of £41.48. He was seen by police when he was filling in a form for further benefit, and admitted that he could earn £60 per week for regular work. Sentenced as above. On appeal *held*, even though appellant had committed no offences since 1966, 9 months' imprisonment was not excessive for such a calculated and deliberate fraud. It was a widespread offence and an easy fraud to perpetuate so the cases which were detected must be dealt with severely. *R v Springer*, 4th July 1978 (Court of Appeal: Ormrod LJ, Mais and Peter Pain JJ).

2503   *Obtaining property by deception; corruption*
Sentence: 12 months' imprisonment concurrent. Applicant's car, insured for third party, fire and theft only, damaged in accident on 15th November 1975. On same day, applicant's friend injured in separate accident. In collusion with an insurance broker and the friend, applicant agreed to take out a comprehensive policy on his car on 19th November. He stated that the accident took place on 1st December and the friend claimed that he was injured while a passenger in the car. Gave broker £50. On broker's colleague becoming suspicious, applicant tried to withdraw claim. Broker demanded and received another £50. During applicant's absence abroad, friend and broker convicted and sentenced to 12 months' imprisonment each. On his return, applicant pleaded guilty and sentenced as above. On application for leave to appeal, he said he had shown immediate contrition and tried to withdraw claim. *Held*, refusing application, it was essential that people dealing with insurance companies should be persons of integrity and that fraud should not be perpetrated on the companies. If the applicant had been tried with the other two, he would have received the same sentence as them. *R v Halewood* [1978] RTR 341 (Court of Appeal: Browne LJ and Stocker J).

2504   *Obtaining property by deception; attempting to obtain property by deception; uttering a forged document; forgery of a passport; possession of a controlled drug*
Sentence: 2 years' imprisonment concurrent, consecutive to 3 years' already being served. Man, aged 43. Apart from 2 years working as a waiter, unemployed since 1957. Several convictions for dishonesty. Offences arose out of a series of transactions between June and August 1976, when the appellant came into possession of stolen travellers' cheques and participated in cashing them at various banks. The forgery counts involved the forging and production of the necessary documents of identification in order to permit the fraud to take place. Over £1,000 worth of travellers' cheques were dealt with or attempted to be dealt with. There was also a count of possessing a small amount of cannabis. Sentenced as above plus a fine of £1,000 or 6 months' imprisonment in default. On appeal against severity of sentence, particularly as it was consecutive to 3 years' imprisonment for aggravated burglary imposed a month before *held*, it was inevitable that whatever sentence was passed would be consecutive to the 3 years, and the sentence of imprisonment would stand. As it was unlikely that the appellant would ever be able to pay the £1,000 fine that part of the sentence would be quashed. *R v Francis*, 20th June 1978 (Court of Appeal: Eveleigh LJ, O'Connor and Griffiths JJ).

2505   *Obtaining credit while undischarged bankrupt*
Sentence: 1 year's imprisonment concurrent. Married man, 40, with 4 children. Spent convictions. In 1962 when a consultant designer he was adjudicated bankrupt with liabilities of £1,000 and no assets. In May 1972 he set up as an architectural consultant and construction engineer and obtained goods on credit without disclosing that he was an undischarged bankrupt. In 1976 he was again adjudicated bankrupt on a voluntary petition with liabilities of £16,205 and assets of £20. The offences took place between December 1972 and August 1974 and involved a total of £5,000. Between December 1972 and May 1974 he incurred debts of about £2,000 with a building firm; between January 1973 and January 1974 he incurred debts of over £1,000 with a glass firm. He opened a bank account and obtained overdraft facilities without disclosing his bankruptcy. Sentenced to consecutive terms of 6 months' imprisonment—2 years in all. The Insolvency Act 1976, s. 7 discharges a bankrupt automatically after ten years—by 1972, therefore, the appellant could not have been an undischarged bankrupt. On appeal *held*, having regard to the 1976 Act and in all the circumstances of the case the court would vary the sentences to one year's imprisonment concurrent on each count. *R v Hawes*, 19th June 1978 (Court of Appeal: Eveleigh LJ, O'Connor and Caulfield JJ).

2506   *Taking a motor vehicle without authority*
Sentence: 6 months' imprisonment. Man, aged 36. Number of previous convictions, but none since 1962. The car in the present case had been left in a car park by its owner because he could not afford to re-tax it. The appellant took the car and, when stopped by police, could not produce the car's documents. The owner did not know the car had been stolen. The appellant was sentenced to 12 months' imprisonment. On appeal *held*, an immediate term of imprisonment was called for. Owners of motor cars were entitled to the protection of the law for keeping their cars in their own possession, particularly where there was no available garage space and cars had to be left outside houses and in car parks. In the present case, however, the term of imprisonment would be varied as set out above. *R v Pugh*, 8th June 1978 (Court of Appeal: Shaw LJ, Jupp and Neill JJ).

2507   Sentence: 18 months' imprisonment; disqualified 3 years. Man, 25. Substantial criminal record, including 5 years' imprisonment for robbery when aged 19. Shortly after his release from prison he committed current offence of taking a motor vehicle without the owner's permission. Prior to that offence he had committed a number of offences including burglary, theft and twice assaulting police officers, for which he was sentenced to 9 months' imprisonment concurrent, concurrent to the present sentence. On appeal *held*, in view of the appellant's record the sentence imposed was not excessive. *R v Bailey*, 19th June 1978 (Court of Appeal: Geoffrey Lane and Shaw LJJ, Caulfield J).

2508   Sentence: borstal training. Boy, aged 15. One previous conviction when aged 14, on four charges of taking motor vehicles without consent, one of handling stolen goods, one of theft and other charges connected with driving motor vehicles. Asked for thirty-one other cases to be taken into consideration, including nine of taking motor vehicles. Sentenced to 3 months in a detention centre. Current offence committed several weeks after his release. Reports on appellant were conflicting. School report stated he took advantage of lenient approach and salutary action was necessary. Psychiatrists and probation officer took different view and said that he showed some remorse. Sentenced as above. On appeal *held*, subsequent events showed school report to be correct as, within 10 days of going to borstal, appellant and others absconded and committed similar offence. Although appellant was said to be childish and immature, borstal training was correct and sentence would stand. *R v Atkinson*, 21st July 1978 (Court of Appeal: Bridge LJ, Chapman and Kenneth Jones JJ).

2509   *Taking a motor vehicle without authority; driving while disqualified; driving without insurance*
Sentence: 18 months' imprisonment (first offence); 3 months' imprisonment concurrent (second offence); absolute discharge (third offence). Man, aged 26. Numerous convictions since 1968, mainly for road traffic offences but also burglary and theft. Fined numerous times, conditionally discharged, put on probation and given various terms of imprisonment varying from 3 to 9 months. In all disqualified from driving for 16 months. While disqualified and without insurance he saw a parked van with the key left in the ignition switch. Drove the van away. The owner heard appellant driving off and informed police who apprehended appellant. Sent to Crown Court for sentence under Magistrates' Courts Act 1952, s. 29 (taking without consent) and Criminal Justice Act 1967, s. 56 (driving while disqualified and no insurance). Sentenced to 18 months' imprisonment for first offence, 6 months' imprisonment concurrent for second offence and 3 months' imprisonment concurrent on the third count. On appeal *held*, in view of appellant's previous record the sentence for the first offence would stand. The maximum sentence on a s. 56 committal for driving while disqualified was 3 months and that would be substituted. He would be given an absolute discharge on the third count. *R v Hall*, 13th October 1978 (Court of Appeal: Lord Widgery CJ, Eveleigh LJ and Smith J).

2510   *Taking a motor vehicle without authority; assault occasioning actual bodily harm*
Sentence: 3 months' detention (first offence); 2 months' detention consecutive (second offence). Youth, aged 19. Intermittent work record since leaving school. After a drinking session the appellant and another youth stole a car. Their dangerous driving attracted the attention of an off duty police officer who followed them. The car in which the youths were travelling eventually collided with a lamp-post. Police officer identified himself and was assaulted. Shortly afterwards the youths were apprehended. Sentenced as above. On appeal *held*, although the appellant had no previous convictions it was appropriate that a person who attacked a police officer attempting to apprehend him for committing a criminal offence should receive an immediate custodial sentence. Although the taking and driving away and the assault on the officer were part of the same conduct and some judges might have imposed concurrent sentences, in the present case the sentences imposed were correct. *R v Scott*, 29th June 1978 (Court of Appeal: Eveleigh LJ, O'Connor and Griffiths JJ).

2511   *Taking a motor vehicle without authority: burglary*
Sentence: 6 months' detention concurrent; disqualified for 12 months. Youth, aged 16. No previous convictions. After a drinking session appellant and another youth took a car and committed four burglaries. One burglary was at a hardware shop where they smashed a plate glass door and stole £1,000 worth of goods. Also used cutting equipment to enter a cafe, and then burgled two other premises. Sentenced as above. On appeal *held*, the burglaries were sophisticated and carefully planned.

It would be wrong to allow young people to commit such crimes, and then plead their youth as a defence. The sentence imposed was correct. *R v Casey*, 6th June 1978 (Court of Appeal: Lord Widgery CJ, Eveleigh LJ and Watkins J).

2512 *Taking a motor vehicle without authority; burglary; driving with excess alcohol in blood; driving without a licence and while uninsured*
Sentence: 12 months' imprisonment concurrent (counts 1 and 2); 3 months' concurrent (count 3); fined (count 4). Man, aged 27, with a very bad criminal record. Had been before the courts at least once a year for the last 10 years for offences involving motor vehicles, burglary and theft. Burglary first committed while on bail for driving offences. Sentenced as above on counts 1, 2 and 4 and to 3 months' imprisonment consecutive on count 3. The trial judge remarked on count 3 that it was a very bad case for not only did the appellant take other people's cars and drive them while unlicensed and uninsured, but he drove while affected by drink. On appeal against the consecutive term of imprisonment on count 3 *held*, although all the offences were committed while the appellant was on parole, one of the two driving offences did not involve a stolen car. On this basis the court would vary the sentence on count 3 to run concurrently. *R v Fortune*, 8th March 1978 (Court of Appeal: Lord Widgery CJ, Cantley and Drake JJ).

2513 *Taking a motor vehicle without authority; dangerous driving*
Sentence: borstal training; disqualified for 2 years. Youth, aged 19. Had been fined for theft in 1976 and for obtaining a pecuniary advantage in 1977. Stole a car. Drove the wrong way round a roundabout, passed two "keep left" signs on the right and reached speeds of 65 m.p.h. Sentenced as above. Local authority had given him a grant to study for "A" levels and he appealed on ground that he would not be able to pursue his studies if kept in custody. *Held*, offences committed were serious. Appellant did not have a clean record and there was no reason to disturb sentence imposed. *R v Adeniyi*, 20th June 1978 (Court of Appeal: Eveleigh LJ, O'Connor and Griffiths JJ).

2514 *Arson*
Sentences: 6 months' imprisonment (offence of theft taken into consideration) (first appellant); 2 years' probation (second appellant). Appellants were husband and wife, aged 20 and 19 respectively. Husband had 2 previous convictions for assault occasioning actual bodily harm in 1976 and theft in 1978. He was of low intelligence, and had an inadequate personality. She was pregnant by her husband but had 2 children by other men. Appellants set fire to their council flat. Husband told police he wanted to move "because it was haunted" and the reason for setting fire to the flat was that his wife was having trouble with the man who had fathered one of her children. Damage caused to value of £1,291. Husband sentenced as above; wife sentenced to 4 months' imprisonment. On appeal *held*, although of low intelligence, the husband knew what he was doing when he set fire to the flat. Arson was a serious offence, which resulted in a large number of custodial sentences. The offence was committed in a high delinquency area. The sentence imposed on the husband was correct. The wife needed the help of a probation officer in finding a new home, and a probation order for 2 years would be substituted. *R v Brickell*, 25th May 1978 (Court of Appeal: Orr and Cumming-Bruce LJJ and Park J).

2515 Sentence: 3 years' imprisonment. Woman, aged 34, with 2 children. Separated from her husband. Previous convictions for deception, possessing an offensive weapon and arson (this latter offence had been committed in 1975 and she had been put on 2 years' probation). Appellant and a friend spent an afternoon drinking cider in the friend's flat. When the friend fell asleep the appellant set fire to the curtains and sat and watched the flames spread. She then notified a neighbour who summoned the fire brigade. At the time of the offence the appellant was a voluntary in-patient at a hospital undergoing treatment for mental illness. Medical reports showed no treatment was appropriate in present case. Sentenced to life imprisonment. After being sentenced she had swallowed needles and razor blades, but has since become calm and co-operative. On appeal *held*, in view of the appellant's present behaviour a life sentence was not appropriate. Sentence would be varied to one of 3 years' imprisonment. *R v Ryan*, 29th June 1978 (Court of Appeal: Eveleigh LJ, O'Connor and Griffiths JJ).

2516   *Criminal damage*

Sentence: probation for 2 years on conditions. Married man, aged 33, with two children. Drink problem since a teenager. First conviction when aged 16 for breach of the peace. From then until 1968 he had eight convictions for assault, theft of car, theft, driving unfit through drink. Since then had received suspended sentence for number of convictions for assault. Had kept out of trouble since his marriage in 1974. Employment record good. Employed as library attendant at local council at time of offence. After a concert at the library appellant, who was drunk, found himself locked out. Broke windows, cabinets and other fixtures and scattered the books and lending library index on the floor. At 9.00 a.m. next morning he awoke in the library. Admitted offence, saying "I always go like that when I have been drinking." Sentenced to 12 months' imprisonment. On appeal *held*, there was nothing wrong with sentence imposed, but mitigating factors were that he had agreed to take treatment for his alcoholism when in prison, his wife was again pregnant, and a bed was available for him in a hospital specialising in alcoholism and drug dependence treatment. The court would vary the sentence with a condition under Powers of Criminal Courts Act 1973, s. 3. In addition a compensation order would be made in the sum of £250 to be paid at £10 per week. *R v Duncan*, 7th August 1978 (Court of Appeal: Roskill LJ, Ackner and Stocker JJ).

2517   *Criminal damage: theft*

Sentence: borstal training. Youth, aged 20. Unemployed. Numerous convictions for dishonesty and traffic offences, for which he had been sent to a detention centre, conditionally discharged, fined, etc. Offences consisted of removal of lead from a church roof so that rain got in and damaged the timbers. Convicted before justices and committed to Crown Court for sentence. Recorder favoured imposing a community service order but no project was available. Sentenced as above, after postponing sentence. On appeal *held*, that in absence of a community service project the sentence of borstal was right. *R v Creighton*, 6th March 1978 (Court of Appeal: Lord Widgery CJ, Cantley and Drake JJ).

2518   *Receiving stolen goods*

Sentences: £250 fine (6 months' imprisonment in default) (first appellant); £100 fine (6 months' imprisonment in default) (second appellant). First appellant was married man, 34, with 3 children. Self-employed motor mechanic and dealer. Previous good character. Second appellant was married man, 27, with one child. Driver with London Transport, and had some connection with first appellant in motor mechanic business. A clothing factory was burgled and its stock of 400 to 500 car coats stolen. Appellants acquired a number of the coats at £4 each. Charged with others with receiving the stolen coats. Appellants were the only ones convicted and were sentenced to 9 months' imprisonment each. On appeal *held*, in the circumstances the sentences were too severe. The sentences of imprisonment would be quashed, and fines substituted as set out above. *R v De Souza; R v Thomas*, 19th June 1978 (Court of Appeal: Geoffrey Lane and Shaw LJJ, Caulfield J).

2519   *Loitering with intent*

Sentence: probation for 2 years. Youth, aged 17. Unemployed since leaving school and lived with mother. Eleven findings of fault, mainly for dishonesty but two for possessing offensive weapons. Care orders had been imposed, he had been fined and conditionally discharged. Plain clothes police officers saw appellant at an underground station; he twice tried to put his hand into a lady's handbag, and approached another person and tried to do the same thing. Sent to borstal. On appeal *held*, although the sentence imposed was absolutely right, an excellent report from borstal governor showed that appellant had responded well to training, and sentence would be varied as set out above. Appellant needed support and encouragement. *R v Gayle*, 13th October 1978 (Court of Appeal: Waller LJ, Bristow and Stocker JJ).

2520   *Breach of probation*
Sentence: 7 days' imprisonment. Woman, aged 19. Almost subnormal and registered as disabled. Had a personality disorder but did not suffer from any diagnosable mental illness. After leaving school worked for a short time as a machinist but was made redundant in 1976 and had not worked since then. Stole a china rabbit (value of 99p) and a crochet hook (19p). Asked for the theft of a comb to be taken into consideration. Put on probation. Failed to report in accordance with the terms of the probation order. She was bailed for reports to a hostel where her behaviour was so disruptive that other women in the hostel threatened to abscond if she remained. Then she was placed in police custody. Sentenced to borstal training. On appeal *held*, in no circumstances did the offences committed justify a borstal sentence. The sanctions of the criminal law could not be used to supplement public service agencies such as probation service, psychiatric agencies, justices and the Crown Court itself who, through no fault of their own, have been unable to help offenders adequately. Sentence would be varied as set out above. *R v Coe*, 4th October 1978 (Court of Appeal: Waller LJ, Bristow and Stocker JJ).

OFFENCES AGAINST DECENCY AND MORALITY

2521   *Publishing obscene articles for gain*
Sentence: 6 months' imprisonment suspended for 2 years. Man, aged 21. Previous conviction for similar offence for which he had been fined £50 and £25 costs. Tenant of a shop in which obscene books, magazines and films were sold, a substantial number of which were of a homosexual nature. Police raided the shop and found a "mini-movie" where, on inserting ten pence into the machine, the viewer was able to see film of an explicit homosexual act. Film was a specimen of those seized. Sentenced to 6 months' immediate imprisonment, concurrent on each count. On appeal *held*, as the police raid took place in February 1977 and appellant had to wait until July 1978 for sentence, justice would be done by making the sentence a suspended one. *R v Adams*, 10th August 1978 (Court of Appeal: Roskill LJ, Ackner and Stocker JJ).

OFFENCES RELATING TO DRUGS

2522   *Unlawful supply of a controlled drug*
Sentence: 15 months' imprisonment. Married man, aged 24, separated from wife. No previous convictions. Since leaving school had been a mechanic and labourer but unemployed at time of present offence. Police with a search warrant went to appellant's house to search for drugs. Found a pair of scales, a sheath knife and plastic bags. On analysis these items revealed small quantities of cannabis varying from 0.5 milligrammes to 2 milligrammes. Two convictions of unlawful possession of cannabis quashed but sentenced to 4 years' imprisonment for being concerned in unlawful supply. On appeal *held*, sentences for the possession of cannabis were to be distinguished in the criminal courts from sentences for possession of hard drugs. There was no evidence that appellant was heavily involved in the supply of unlawful drugs. Three years' imprisonment was too severe for a young man with no previous convictions. An immediate custodial sentence was appropriate, however, as the courts were determined to punish the social menace of pushing and peddling drugs. The sentence would be varied as set out above. *R v Entwistle*, 10th July 1978 (Court of Appeal: Cumming-Bruce LJ, Chapman and Kenneth Jones JJ).

2523   *Fraudulent evasion of prohibition on importation of controlled drug.*
Sentences: 10 years' imprisonment concurrent (counts 1 and 2) (D); 12 years' imprisonment concurrent (counts 1, 2 and 3) (S); 7 years' imprisonment concurrent (courts 1 and 2) (P). All were recommended for deportation. D, Malaysian, 29, married with one child. A police inspector. No previous convictions. S, Malaysian, 25, single. Worked for a plastics firm. No previous convictions. P, Malaysian, 23, S's fiancée, a secretary. No previous convictions. All three arrived at Heathrow airport from Singapore in April 1976. S and P passed through customs, but D was stopped and searched. In false compartment of his suitcase was found 2,735 grammes of heroin (13 per cent concentration) (count 2). He admitted that he had been approached by S and that this was his second smuggling trip. The first had been in February 1976, when D had been paid by S (count 1). P and S were later arrested at their hotel, and quantities of heroin were found in their cases. S also carried 3.54 grammes of heroin (70 per cent concentration) for his own use (count 3). S confessed to being a heroin addict, and said he had also carried heroin to Amsterdam. P said she had been given the cases by S, and admitted that she had smuggled a case with D and S in February 1976. Total amount of drugs smuggled on the two trips was worth about £1 million and would have provided about 240,000 doses. On arrest each of the appellants had American and Dutch money. S said he had been forced into drug smuggling by his own addiction. P said she had gone along with S because of his health. D said he had suffered a set-back in his police career and that he had infiltrated the heroin smuggling trade to give information to his superiors. He said that S was the leader of the gang. The judge sentenced D and S as above, and P to 10 years' imprisonment, because "heroin smuggling was the worst type of smuggling". On appeal against the length of sentence *held*, it was idle for persons who allow themselves to become involved as carriers in drugs cases to complain. Sentences must be deterrent. Those who succumb to pressure, even if their resistance is weakened by drug addiction, must realise that there can be no mitigation. The sentences of D and S would stand but as P was less involved leniency would be exercised in her case and her sentence varied to 7 years' imprisonment. *R v Dom; R v Phillips; R v Selvadurai*, 21st February 1978 (Court of Appeal: Roskill and Eveleigh LJJ, Stocker J).

2524   Sentence: 3 years' imprisonment. Australian gems trader agreed when he was in Bangkok on his way to West Germany to go to Bogota where he collected cocaine. He stopped at London, where 194 grammes were found in his possession. Pleaded guilty and sentenced as above. On application for leave to appeal, *held*, the fact that the cocaine was not to be used, sold or distributed in the United Kingdom, if not wholly irrelevant, was of little importance. 3 years was a moderate sentence even taking that fact into consideration. The application would be refused. *R v Kence* (1978) Times, 15th April (Court of Appeal: Lord Widgery CJ, Michael Davies and Drake JJ).

2525   *Knowingly concerned in the fraudulent evasion of prohibition on the importation of a controlled drug*
Sentence: 4 years' imprisonment; recommended for deportation. Appellant arrived at Heathrow airport from Pakistan. When his luggage was inspected, a fake compartment was found. It contained 1·95 kilogrammes of cannabis, worth £6,000. He gave the customs officials information which enabled two other collaborators, who were in Switzerland, to be deported from that country. Sentenced to 5 years' imprisonment and recommended for deportation. On appeal on the ground that insufficient recognition was given to his co-operation with the authorities *held*, the sentence imposed was not excessive. In view of his co-operation with the authorities, however, the sentence would be reduced to 4 years. The deportation recommendation would stand. *R v Syed*, 8th June 1978 (Court of Appeal: Geoffrey Lane and Eveleigh LJJ, Watkins J).

2526   *Conspiracy to avoid prohibition on importation of cannabis: illegal exportation of Bank of England notes*
Sentence: 3 years' imprisonment: 18 months' imprisonment concurrent (2 counts)

(3 years' imprisonment in all). Married man, 45, with four children. Self employed as an insurance agent. No previous convictions. With two co-accused, one of whom had a criminal record and was a police informer, the appellant entered into a scheme to illegally import cannabis into the United Kingdom from Morocco. £15,000 was needed to finance the venture. The appellant took £3,000 in a body belt to Morocco as a deposit for the cannabis (second indictment offence) and flew to Morocco where the supplier assured him of a delivery of 150 kilogrammes of cannabis. One of the co-accused was to drive to Morocco, towing the appellant's motor trailer in the false bottom of which was hidden £3,000 (second indictment, second offence). On its return to the United Kingdom customs officials discovered 68 kilogrammes of cannabis in the trailer. The cannabis would have a value of £80,000 in the streets with a wholesale value of £32,000. If the venture had succeeded the total value would have been £148,000. The appellant made a full confession. Offences on second indictment were treated as part of first indictment, and the appellant was sentenced to 5 years' imprisonment. One of the co-accused was sentenced to 2 years' imprisonment, but his conviction was quashed on appeal. The other co-accused was an agent provocateur. On appeal against sentence on first indictment *held*, having regard to the position of the agent provocateur who had played a significant part in bringing the effective conspiracy into existence, the proper tariff sentence for the appellant was one of 3 years' imprisonment. *R v Thompstone*, 16th January 1978 (Court of Appeal: Bridge LJ, Watkins and Jupp JJ).

2527   *Possession of a controlled drug*
Sentence: immediate release (equivalent of 3 months' imprisonment served) American citizen, aged 21, member of United States Air Force. No previous convictions. Found in possession of opium (22 grammes) and cannabis resin (5·9 grammes), both contained in polythene bags. Said the opium cost him 300 dollars and the cannabis cost 30 dollars. First time he had purchased opium. Sentenced to 6 months' imprisonment for the opium offence and 3 months concurrent for the the cannabis offence, the recorder saying that amount of opium required a custodial sentence. Appellant intends to retire from USAF on release from prison and take up career as an architect. On appeal *held*, the USAF had spoken well of the appellant who had appreciated the gravity of the offences and had worked hard and conscientiously in prison. The court would therefore substitute such a sentence as to result in his immediate release. *R v Helfrich*, 16th May 1978 (Court of Appeal: Bridge LJ, Thompson and Eastham JJ).

2528   *Possession of a controlled drug; breach of suspended sentence*
Sentence: 6 months' imprisonment (first offence); 6 months' imprisonment concurrent, consecutive to first sentence (second offence). Woman, 30, with one child. In 1973 sentenced to concurrent terms of imprisonment totalling 2 years for possessing and importing cannabis. That sentence was suspended and she committed no further offence during period of suspension. In 1976 she again received suspended sentences for possessing controlled drugs. She was in breach of these sentences by the present offence, when police drug squad searched her home and found cannabis resin. Sentenced as above. Subject to probation and psychiatric reports which suggested she might benefit from treatment. On appeal *held*, it was impossible to say that the sentence imposed was improper or too severe. Appellant was a woman, not a girl, and had a record of drugs offences. It should be appreciated that suspended sentences meant what they said—if the offender re-offended an immediate prison sentence was likely. *R v Gibbon*, 16th June 1978 (Court of Appeal: Eveleigh LJ, O'Connor and Griffiths JJ).

DRIVING OFFENCES

2529   *Dangerous driving*
Sentence: conditional discharge for 2 years; disqualified for 4 months. Married woman, aged 52, with two children. Two minor convictions in 1977, for which she was fined. The present offence arose out of an argument with neighbours, as a

result of which the appellant drove her car at one of them. Two further similar incidents occurred. In sentencing the appellant to one months' imprisonment and 2 years' disqualification the judge said it was a serious matter which called for a term of imprisonment. On appeal *held*, although the incidents were not trivial, the case did not call for a sentence of imprisonment. An order of conditional discharge would be substituted; the period of disqualification would be varied to one of 4 months. *R v Evans*, 8th June 1978 (Court of Appeal: Shaw LJ, Jupp and Neill JJ).

2530   *Driving with excess alcohol in blood*
Sentence: £50 fine; disqualified for 12 months. Divorced man: aged 38. No previous convictions. At 12.45 a.m. a police constable saw the appellant's car running backwards for about 5 yards down a main street. The appellant, who admitted that he had been drinking until an hour previously, was trying to "bump start the vehicle in reverse". No lights were displayed. A breath test proved positive and a subsequent laboratory test revealed 133 milligrammes of alcohol in 100 millilitres of his blood. The judge found there were special reasons for reducing the period of disqualification they would have imposed—3 years—to one year on the ground that at the time the offence was committed it was early morning with little traffic about. The appellant intended only to park his car, which would not work, at the nearest place where it would be safe from traffic. On appeal that the trial court should not have imposed a disqualification *held*, the sentence imposed was a charitable one and was not a wrong exercise of the court's discretion. *R v Ardalan Raikes*, 16th May 1978 (Court of Appeal: Bridge LJ, Thompson and Eastham JJ).

2531   Sentence: £75 fine; £50 prosecution costs; disqualified for 2 years. Man, aged 47. No previous convictions. While driving he collided with another car; did not stop but drove home where he was interviewed by the police. Agreed to provide a blood specimen which, on analysis, showed a proportion of 203 milligrammes of alcohol in 100 millilitres of blood (2½ times the prescribed limit). Sentenced as above. On appeal against length of disqualification *held*, it was a bad case involving a large amount of alcohol. The sentence imposed was neither manifestly excessive nor wrong in principle. *R v Wilson*, 22nd May 1978 (Court of Appeal: Bridge LJ, Park and Eastham JJ).

2532   *Being carried in a motor vehicle knowing it to be stolen*
Sentence: conditional discharge for 2 years. Youth, aged 16. Living with parents. Five previous court appearances for theft and burglaries. Subject of suspension order for 2 years in 1973 and care orders in 1973 and 1974. Last conviction was for burglary of a dwelling house in 1977, for which he was fined and made subject to a care order until he attained 18. Appellant's brother stole a car from a car-park and, with appellant and another youth, drove off "to look for houses to burgle". Broke into one house which they found empty and left after smashing two windows. Appellant and the other youth successfully broke into another house and removed £750 worth of property. Seen by police, arrested and admitted offences. Pleaded guilty in March 1978. Appellant bound over in sum of £10 to come up for judgment in June 1978, to enable him to take "O" levels. In June a different judge sentenced appellant to 6 months' detention. On appeal *held*, as appellant had behaved well during period of binding over and had taken examinations it was wrong in principle to impose a custodial sentence. In the circumstances (but for the care order) the court would have made a supervision order. The sentence of detention would be quashed and an order for conditional discharge for 2 years would be substituted. *R v O'Neill*, 7th August 1978 (Court of Appeal: Roskill LJ, Ackner and Stocker JJ).

2533   **—— matters to be considered in fixing sentence—comment on earlier sentence by another first instance judge**

The appellant pleaded guilty to a charge of allowing himself to be carried in a vehicle taken without authority, and was sentenced by the Crown Court to eighteen months' imprisonment in view of his substantial record. After receiving the sentence the appellant appeared at another Crown Court on charges of burglary and assault. During the trial, the judge queried the earlier sentence, said that it was very severe and virtually advised the appellant to appeal against it. He then passed sentences of nine months for the burglary and two months for each of the two assaults, all concurrent with the eighteen months' sentence. On appeal against the eighteen months' sentence, *held*, in view of the appellants' record, the sentence could not be described as excessive and the second judge seemed to have adjusted the balance of the sentences. In the rare cases where it was necessary for a judge to comment on a sentence passed by another judge of equal standing, the comments should be made temperately and should not be such as would embarrass an appellate court. The appeal would be dismissed.

R v BAILEY (1978) Times, 22nd June (Court of Appeal: GEOFFREY LANE and SHAW LJJ and CAULFIELD J).

2534   Attendance centres
See para. 2235.

2535   Compensation orders
See CRIMINAL LAW.

2536   Deferred sentence—court's power to adjourn case to another court
The appellant received a deferred sentence from the Crown Court at Croydon after pleading guilty to ten counts of theft, forgery and related offences. He also received a deferred sentence from a Liverpool court on conviction of driving while disqualified and another offence. The Liverpool court immediately transferred the proceedings to Croydon. There was some confusion at the Croydon court as to whether sentence had been deferred by the Liverpool court or whether the proceedings had merely been transferred. In the event the Croydon court decided that it must have been the latter and imposed a three month term of imprisonment for the offence of driving while disqualified. On appeal against sentence, *held*, the Liverpool court had in fact deferred sentence and the appellant had been led to believe that if he committed no further offences he would not be sent to prison. The sentence would therefore be quashed. No problem would have arisen if the case had simply been adjourned to the Croydon court. The power to defer sentence under the Act had not taken away the power to adjourn proceedings to another court.

R v ROBERTS (1978) Times, 19th January (Court of Appeal: LAWTON LJ, SWANWICK and GIBSON JJ).

2537   Deprivation of property used for crime—whether order made by Crown Court may be varied
See *R v Menocal*, para. 610.

2538   —— whether question of ownership determined
The applicant's husband was convicted of several offences and a forfeiture order was made in respect of a car which he had used in connection with the crimes. The applicant claimed that the car was her property, and her husband applied for the order to be rescinded. The order was upheld by the recorder and the applicant applied to the justices under the Police (Property) Act 1897, s. 1. The justices heard no evidence and dismissed the application on the ground that the question of ownership had already been decided and they therefore had no jurisdiction. The applicant sought an order of mandamus to require the justices to hear and determine the matter. *Held*, the justices were wrong in holding that the question of ownership was res judicata and in dismissing the application without hearing any evidence. The application would be granted.

R v CHESTER JUSTICES, EX PARTE SMITH [1978] LS Gaz R 103 (Queen's Bench Division: LORD WIDGERY CJ, CUMMING-BRUCE LJ and PARK J).

2539   Imprisonment—power of Crown Court to vary sentence

The Crown Court convicted a man of malicious wounding, and sentenced him to six months' imprisonment. Within 28 days, the court received reports from two psychiatrists that the man was suffering from a paranoid psychosis and was dangerous. Acting under its power to vary sentence in the Courts Act, 1971, s. 11 (2), the court quashed the sentence of imprisonment and substituted a hospital order for an unlimited period of time. The court's power under section 11 (2) to vary a sentence in this way was questioned on appeal. *Held*, the section gave the court power to vary not only the length of a sentence but also its nature. It was admittedly not usual to substitute an indeterminate period of detention for a short prison sentence, but in this case these were special circumstances which justified such a decision. The man was dangerous, to others as well as to himself. The order would therefore be left to stand and the appeal dismissed.

R v SODHI (1978) Times, 19th January (Court of Appeal: LAWTON LJ, SWANWICK and GIBSON JJ).

2540   —— reduction of sentences—proposals

A report compiled by the Home Secretary's Advisory Council on the Penal System proposes widespread reductions on the length of prison sentences imposed for a variety of offences. A minority of very serious cases would be handled differently, however, with courts retaining the discretion to mete out punishments in excess of the normal maxima. Among the more serious crimes for which lesser penalties are proposed are rape and kidnapping: seven years is the proposed maximum for both offences, rather than life as at present. The council would like to see the new sentencing policy tested and monitored for a trial period.

The main intended consequences of the new approach would be (i) sentencing consistency, because courts would have a clear guide on policy, (ii) wider discretion for courts in sentence the more serious offender; and (iii) a relative reduction in the average length of sentences: Times, 28th June 1978.

The report, entitled "Sentences of Imprisonment—a Review of Maximum Penalties", is obtainable from HMSO, at £4.

2541   Mitigation—duty of justices to hear counsel before passing sentence

The defendant was convicted by justices of using threatening behaviour with intent to provoke a breach of the peace and sentenced to three months' imprisonment. The justices refused to hear counsel in mitigation, and the defendant applied for an order of certiorari to quash the sentence and an order of mandamus directing the justices to hear his submissions in mitigation. *Held*, the sentence would be quashed since by immediately pronouncing sentence after convicting the defendant, the justices had deprived him of the opportunity of putting matters in mitigation before them. The court had power to substitute any sentence it thought appropriate which would have been within the justices' powers. Therefore there would be no order of mandamus but considering all relevant matters including counsel's submissions in mitigation, the court would substitute a sentence of the same length as the original sentence.

R v BILLERICAY JUSTICES, EX PARTE RUMSEY [1978] Crim LR 305 (Queen's Bench Division: LORD WIDGERY CJ, WIEN and KENNETH JONES JJ).

2542   Murder—custody after conviction—duration

The average time spent in custody after sentence by those convicted of murder who were released on licence between 1974 and 1977 was 10 years one month: 948 H. of C. Official Report, 27th April 1978, written answers, *col. 632.*

2543   Probation order—duration of order—reduction in minimum period

The Probation Orders (Variation of Statutory Limits) Order 1978, S.I. 1978 No. 474 (in force 15th May 1978) amends the Powers of the Criminal Courts Act 1973, s. 2 (1) so as to reduce to six months the minimum period of supervision which a court may specify in making a probation order.

2544   Road traffic—driving with blood alcohol concentration above prescribed limit—whether imprisonment appropriate sentence on first offence

See *R v Nokes*, para. 2347.

2545   Young offender—imprisonment—when borstal training mandatory substitute

A twenty-year-old student appealed against a three year prison sentence for a drugs offence. *Held*, an appropriate sentence would have been two years' imprisonment. However, under the Criminal Justice Act 1961, s. 3 a person between the ages of seventeen and twenty-one could only be imprisoned for less than six months or more than three years, so borstal training would be ordered instead, however unsuitable it was. Section 3 was a potent source of injustice: sentences in excess of those appropriate were not to be imposed in order to evade its effect.

R v HARNDEN (1978) Times, 17th January (Court of Appeal: LORD WIDGERY CJ, MELFORD STEVENSON and LLOYD JJ).

SET-OFF AND COUNTER CLAIM

Halsbury's Laws of England (3rd edn.), Vol. 34, paras. 669–755

2546   Set-off against hire under time charter—availability of set-off

See *The Nanfri, The Benfri, The Lorfri*, para. 2609.

2547   Set-off in damages—two heads of damage—benefit accruing to plaintiff in respect of one head—set-off against damages arising from other head

See *Nadreph Ltd v Willmett & Co*, para. 856.

SETTLEMENTS

Halsbury's Laws of England (3rd edn.), Vol. 34, paras. 756–1141

2548   Articles

"Approved Wife", F. Graham Glover (*Re Tuck's Settlement Trusts*, see 1977 Halsbury's Abr para. 2513 and its implications for the future construction of documents): 128 NLJ 504.

2549   Contingent interest—vested interest liable to be divested—gift over on failure or determination of the trusts

Trustees were directed under a settlement to hold one half of the trust fund for the settlor's son if and when he attained the age of 30, but if he died before that age on the trusts of the other half which were for the benefit of the settlor's daughter. There was a trust in corresponding terms relating to the daughter. Clause 5 of the settlement provided that as long as the son or daughter was under 22 years of age, the whole income of his or her half of the trust fund was to be accumulated by way of compound interest by investing it and between the ages of 22 to 25 the income should be applied for their respective maintenance. The settlor died while both his children were still under 21. It was accepted that the express trust to accumulate up to the age of 22 was void, although the income was accumulated up to the age of 21 in accordance with the Trustee Act 1925, s. 31. The son and daughter were both assessed to surtax in respect of the income of their 22nd year on the grounds that, having regard to the gift over in the event of the beneficiary's death before 30, the settlement should be construed as giving the beneficiary a vested interest, and therefore the income formed part of the total income for surtax purposes. The son and daughter appealed against assessment, contending that the gift was a contingent one as the express direction to accumulate, albeit void, showed the settlor's contrary intention to an earlier vesting. Their appeal was allowed and the crown appealed. *Held,* the main question to be considered was whether the income that accrued to the son and daughter between their 21st and 22nd birthdays, belonged to them or was undisposed of by the settlement and resulted to the settlor's estate. It was common ground that the direction to accumulate the income in the beneficiaries' 22nd year was void under the Law of Property Act 1925, s. 164 and under that section income was to be given to the persons who would have been entitled to it if the accumulation had not been directed. If the trust conferred a vested interest on the beneficiaries, he or she would be the person designated by s. 164 as the person to whom the income accruing was to go. What had to be considered therefore, was whether each of the taxpayers took a vested interest liable to be divested or a contingent interest. Clearly but for the provisions in clause 5 each taxpayer would take a vested interest liable to be divested in the event of death under 30. There was nothing in clause 5 which showed the settlor to have had a contrary intention. It followed that the income belonged to the taxpayers in the year between their respective 21st and 22nd birthdays and the assessment had been properly made. Accordingly, the appeal would be allowed.

BROTHERTON v IRC; MEARS v IRC [1978] STC 201 (Court of Appeal: STAMP, ORR and SHAW LJJ). Decision of Foster J [1977] STC 73, 1977 Halsbury's Abr para. 2514 reversed. *Phipps v Ackers* (1842) 9 Cl & Fin 583, applied.

2550   **Settlement on children—income paid to children under deed of release and assignment—whether income assessable as settlor's income.**

See *D'Abreu v Inland Revenue Commissioners,* para. 1553.

SEWERS AND DRAINS

Halsbury's Laws of England (3rd edn.), Vol. 31, paras. 290–397

2551   **Sewer—damage caused by laying sewer—compensation—Lands Tribunal decision**

GEORGE WHITEHOUSE LTD (TRADING AS CLARKE BROS (SERVICES)) v ANGLIAN WATER AUTHORITY (1978) 35 P & CR 230: V. G. Wellings QC (application for compensation under Public Health Act 1936, s. 278, in respect of damage sustained by reason of laying of public sewer in public highway near claimants' garage; claimants sought compensation in respect of dust and mud settling on cars displayed for sale and of loss of profits attributable to motorists being deterred from stopping due to works; authority's contention that s. 278 only applied where damage sustained by reason of construction of sewer on land not forming part of street unjustified; "damage" in s. 278 not limited to damage to land but included damage sustained by a person; enough that use and enjoyment of land materially interfered with; claim for loss of profits good since apart from statutory authority claimants could have brought action for public nuisance; compensation payable).

2552   **—— ownership of sewer—whether acquired by local authority— meaning of acquired**

The plaintiffs intended developing a vacant building site. The local authority informed them a public sewer ran within 100 feet of the site, under a public highway. The plaintiffs used the sewer for soil drainage with the authority's approval.   It then emerged that the sewer had been constructed by the defendants to provide drainage for their housing estate and had never been adopted by the authority.   The defendants cut off the plaintiffs drainage connection.   The plaintiffs claimed the sewer was public and sought damages and an injunction.   On the question of ownership, *held*, the sewer had been acquired by the authority under the Public Health Act 1936, s. 20 (1).   Acquisition under that section included acquisition under the maxim *quicquid plantatur solo, solo cedit*; it was not limited to acquisition by agreement.   The sewer formed part of the land and the defendants had no proprietary interest in it at all nor any right to object to the plaintiffs' using it for drainage purposes.

ROYCO HOMES LTD v EATONWILL CONSTRUCTION LTD, THREE RIVERS DISTRICT COUNCIL (THIRD PARTY) [1978] 2 All ER 821 (Chancery Division: HUGH FRANCIS QC sitting as a deputy High Court Judge).

SEX DISCRIMINATION

Halsbury's Laws of England (4th edn.), Vol. 16, paras. 771:2–771:38

2553   Articles

The Equal Pay Act Interpreted, R. R. Hopkins: 128 NLJ 968.

Sex Discrimination and Employment, John A. Wall (the effect of the 1975 Act through decisions of the Employment Appeal Tribunal): 128 NLJ 179.

Sex Discrimination Laws—Success or Failure?, Jane Fortin (explanation of reasons for introduction of legislation and consideration of reasons for its failure): 128 NLJ 700.

2554   Discovery of documents—power of industrial tribunal to order

See *Science Research Council v Nasse*, para. 946.

2555   Dismissal—dismissal on grounds of pregnancy—whether dismissal discriminatory on grounds of sex

Industrial tribunal decision:

REANEY v KANDA JEAN PRODUCTS LTD [1978] IRLR 427 (female employee dismissed on grounds of her pregnancy; lacked twenty-six weeks continuous service, therefore unable to claim unfair dismissal under Employment Protection Act 1975, s. 34 (1); failed in claim under Sex Discrimination Act 1975; her situation was not the same as or materially similar to that of a hypothetical man, for the purpose of comparison; therefore it could not be held that she had been unlawfully discriminated against on grounds of sex).

2556   Equal pay—exclusion of requirement for equal treatment—contributory pension scheme—whether contributions too closely linked with salary

A bank operated a pension scheme whereby women did not contribute to the fund until the age of twenty-five, but men under twenty-five contributed five per cent of their salary.   In order to compensate the men for this difference there was a five per cent addition to their gross pay.   The women alleged that this practice contravened the provisions of the Equal Pay Act 1970.   An industrial tribunal upheld the bank's claim that the inequality arose from terms related to retirement and therefore an equality clause was inapplicable.   On appeal, *held*, terms relating to pay were distinct from terms relating to pensions.   The bank had failed to separate the two sufficiently for the term to apply only to the pension scheme and therefore an equality clause would be inserted in the contract.

WORRINGHAM v LLOYDS BANK LTD (1978) 122 Sol Jo 825 (Employment Appeal Tribunal: KILNER BROWN J presiding).

2557   —— job evaluation study—failure to implement

Three women claimed that they were discriminated against within the meaning of the Equal Pay Act 1975 in that their jobs had been given an equal rating with those done by men under a job evaluation scheme, but they were still paid less than the men. A merit assessment scheme for banding employees within the different grades had not been completed and the salary structure had never been put into operation. The women appealed against the finding of an industrial tribunal in favour of the employers. *Held*, the job evaluation scheme was valid even though the merit assessment was incomplete and the salary structure had not been applied and therefore the women were entitled to succeed. In the interests of industrial relations the company would be given three months to effect the scheme.

O'Brien v Sim-Chen Ltd [1978] IRLR 398 (Employment Appeal Tribunal: Phillips J presiding).

2558   —— —— validity of study

A council carried out a job evaluation study, adopting the "London Scheme" but varying it by adding points for special factors. Two female committee clerks received additional points for special factors, which entitled them to receive a higher salary than a male committee clerk, who did not receive any additional points. He claimed that he was entitled to equal pay with them because he was either employed on like work within the Equal Pay Act 1970, s. 1 (2) (a) or employed on work rated as equivalent within s. 1 (2) (b), and in considering the evaluation study the special factor points should be disregarded. On appeal against a decision that he was not entitled to equal pay, *held*, under s. 1 (2) (b) the claimant had to show there was in existence an evaluation study satisfying the requirements of s. 1 (5). The only study in force was the London Scheme, as varied, which must be taken as it stood. The employee could not bring himself within s. 1 (2) by contending that the London Scheme without variation should have been adopted, or that the study did not satisfy s. 1 (5). The employee's work was not rated the same as the female employees under the scheme, and the industrial tribunal's conclusion that it was not like work within s. 1 (2) (a) was correct. The appeal would be dismissed.

England v Bromley London Borough Council [1978] ICR 1 (Employment Appeal Tribunal: Phillips J presiding).

2559   —— like work—job comparison—guidelines for tribunals

Ten women whose duties involved the sorting and recording of warehouse stock claimed that they were employed on like work with men whose duties were similar but also included loading and unloading. They made a claim to an industrial tribunal under the Equal Pay Act and on the recommendation of the chairman selected one man whose work they could compare with their own. The tribunal found that both under contract and in fact he was required to perform different duties and it rejected the women's claim. The women appealed. *Held*, in cases where a man had been chosen for comparison he should be regarded as representative of the male workers even though it became apparent that he was not a typical example. It had been suggested that in considering whether male and female employees were employed on like work the terms of the contract were of little importance and it was the actual work done which should be examined. This was not so; although it was true to say that the contract might on some occasions be misleading it should still be examined in addition to the actual situation. This was what the tribunal had done in this case and on the facts they had arrived at the correct decision. The appeal would be dismissed.

Dance v Dorothy Perkins Ltd [1978] ICR 760 (Employment Appeal Tribunal: Kilner Brown J presiding).

For earlier proceedings in the Employment Appeal Tribunal between these parties, see 1977 Halsbury's Abr para. 2531.

2560   —— —— material difference other than sex

An employer operated a large number of betting shops each of which was staffed by two counterhands. In all but a few of the shops both counterhands were female.

In the rest, said to be trouble spots, a male counterhand paid at a higher rate, worked with the female. The employer said that the men were paid at a higher rate because they were needed to cope with trouble if it arose. A female employee working with a male counterhand claimed to be entitled to equal pay. *Held*, in deciding whether the differences between the things done by the employees were of practical importance in relation to terms and conditions of employment the relevant differences were to be ascertained by comparing their observed activities, not their notional contractual obligations. On the evidence the man had never had to deal with any disturbance or attemped violence. The difference in pay between the female and male employees sprang from the undisguised policy of sex discrimination which the employers operated in selecting employees for the trouble spots. The claim would be allowed.

SHIELDS V E. COOMES (HOLDINGS) LTD [1978] 1 WLR 1408 (Court of Appeal: LORD DENNING MR, ORR and BRIDGE LJJ). Decision of Employment Appeal Tribunal [1977] ICR 795, affirmed in part.

2561   Prior to the Equal Pay Act 1970 the appellant company had operated a scheme whereby employees, except married women, who purchased a house on mortgage during their employment were entitled to a mortgage interest allowance. Employees who sold one house and purchased another during their employment were entitled to an allowance in respect of the new mortgage. The scheme was modified so as to comply with the provisions of the Equal Pay Act, and married women were able to claim mortgage interest allowances on the same basis as other employees. The respondent, a married woman, had sold her first house and purchased another during her employment, but before the adoption of the new scheme. As a married woman she was not entitled to an allowance at that time, and the new scheme provided that employees with an existing mortgage were eligible for the allowance only if they had been eligible under the old scheme. The respondent claimed that she was employed on different conditions from men employed on like work. The employers contended that the difference was a material difference other than a difference of sex within the meaning of the Equal Pay Act 1970, s. 1 (3). The industrial tribunal upheld the respondent's claim under the Equal Pay Act and the employers appealed. *Held*, the respondent was entitled to the mortgage allowance because she was employed on like work with the male employees. The difference in treatment was based on sex discrimination. It was irrelevant that the discrimination had been operative before the Equal Pay Act; the new scheme should have included a provision to cover employees who were disqualified under the old scheme solely because they were married women.

SUN ALLIANCE AND LONDON INSURANCE LTD V DUDMAN [1978] ICR 551 (Employment Appeal Tribunal: PHILLIPS J presiding).

2562   A newly-appointed male clerk was paid more than a female doing the same work. He was the only suitable applicant for the vacancy and refused to accept less money than he was already earning. The female employee appealed against a decision that she was not entitled to equal pay. *Held*, under the Equal Pay Act 1970, s. 1 (3) the employers were excused from paying males and females the same wages for like work if there was a material difference other than sex between their cases. In deciding whether there was a material difference, the employers' claim that they did not intend to discriminate and their personal reasons for paying one employee more than another were irrelevant. It was clear that the variation in pay was due to the simple reason that the only suitable applicant demanded more money than the existing employees received and that did not constitute a material difference. The appeal would be allowed.

CLAY CROSS (QUARRY SERVICES) LTD V FLETCHER [1978] 1 WLR 1429 (Court of Appeal: LORD DENNING MR, LAWTON and BROWNE LJJ). Decision of Employment Appeal Tribunal [1977] ICR 868, 1977 Halsbury's Abr para. 2533, reversed. *Shields v E. Coomes (Holdings) Ltd* [1978] 1 WLR 1408, para. 2560 applied.

2563   An employer voluntarily increased the salary of a female employee to cover that part of the difference between her wages and those of a male colleague which was due to sex discrimination. Since the male employee still earned more she made a claim under the Equal Pay Act. An industrial tribunal accepted the employer's contention that the variation was due to a material difference other than that of sex because he was a "red-circled" employee and was on a protected rate, having once been responsible for extra duties. The woman appealed on the ground that, in giving her the increase, the employer could not accurately quantify the amount which was due to the discrimination. *Held*, the tribunal had correctly decided that the variation was due to a material difference other than sex. Nor did the tribunal need to be satisfied that the increase rectifying the discrimination was mathematically accurate. It was sufficient that the employer had proved that there had been a substantial increase in her pay. The appeal would be dismissed.

BOYLE v TENNENT CALEDONIAN BREWERIES LTD [1978] IRLR 321 (Employment Appeal Tribunal: LORD McDONALD MC presiding).

2564   Two women claimed that they were entitled to equal pay with two men employed by the same firm, on the ground that they were employed on like work with the men, as defined in the Equal Pay Act 1970, s. 1 (4). An industrial tribunal found that one of the women who was employed predominantly as a packer and also did some clerical work, was not involved in like work with a man who did mainly packing work plus storeman's duties.

The tribunal also found that the other woman, a machine operator, did not do like work with a male machine operator who could also set his own machine. Both women appealed. *Held*, dismissing the appeals, although the women and the men were employed on broadly similar work, there were differences of practical importance in relation to terms and conditions of employment. When a man performed a job involving different tasks from a woman, those tasks had to be included in a consideration of whether the two employees did like work. They should not be considered and assessed as a separate and distinct job simply in order to arrive at the conclusion that, as regards the main tasks involved, the male and female employees were engaged in like work.

Furthermore, where the gap in remuneration did not reflect a difference in the value of the work performed, the Equal Pay Act did not empower the tribunal to reduce that gap to reflect the true difference.

MAIDMENT AND HARDACRE v COOPER & CO (BIRMINGHAM) LTD [1978] IRLR 462 (Employment Appeal Tribunal: PHILLIPS J presiding).

2565   —— —— —— **burden of proof**

Two female canteen workers complained that they were being discriminated against because they were not entitled to the concessionary coal which was given to a male employee who worked night shift on the same job. The women claimed that they were employed on like work with the man, and that their contracts should be modified so as not to be less favourable than his. An industrial tribunal, disregarding the fact that the man worked at night, found that the women were employed on like work. The employers appealed, on the grounds that there was a material difference other than sex, within the meaning of the Equal Pay Act 1970, s. 1 (3), between the women's work and the man's work. *Held*, the only difference between the women's work and the man's work was the fact that he worked at night. This was not a material difference, and the disadvantage of working at night could be compensated by an additional night shift premium. The appeal would be dismissed, and the women's contracts modified in relation to remuneration and the right to receive concessionary coal.

NATIONAL COAL BOARD v SHERWIN [1978] ICR 700 (Employment Appeal Tribunal: PHILLIPS J presiding).

2566   —— —— —— **grading scheme**

A woman employed by an insurance company as a policy clerk was paid less than a man who was doing the same work but who was in a higher grade. In answer to the woman's claim for equal pay, the employers contended that the variation in pay was due to a material difference other than sex within Equal Pay Act 1970, s. 1 (3), namely that each employee was classified into a different grade. But the woman claimed that the grading system had been operated unfairly against her on the ground of sex. On appeal, *Held*, the Equal Pay Act 1970, as amended by the Sex Discrimination Act 1975, provided for men and women doing like work to receive equal pay. Grading systems were a valid basis for different rates of pay. The employers had to prove on a balance of probabilities that the grading system was based on a proper assessment of an employee's ability, skill and experience and had been fairly applied irrespective of sex. In this case, the employers had successfully discharged that burden of proof.

NATIONAL VULCAN ENGINEERING INSURANCE GROUP LTD v WADE [1978] 3 All ER 121 (Court of Appeal: LORD DENNING MR, ORMROD and GEOFFREY LANE LJJ). Decision of Employment Appeal Tribunal [1977] 3 All ER 634, 1977 Halsbury's Abr para. 2538 reversed.

2567 ————— trainee

In 1970, a bank employee was transferred to the trustee department as a trainee. There, he was supervised by two women who were on a more senior grade with higher pay due to their experience in the work. In 1971, the employee moved to another department. In 1977, he applied to an industrial tribunal for equal pay with the two women in the trustee department under the Equal Pay Act 1970, s. 1 (4), alleging that he had been engaged on "like work" with them. The tribunal dismissed his application and he appealed. *Held*, the fact that the employee was a trainee and the two women were experienced employees meant that they were not employed on "like work" under s. 1 (4) although the work they did may have been similar. The employers could also rely on the defence provided by s. 1 (3) of the Act that the variation in pay was genuinely due to a material difference other than sex, in this case the difference being experience and status. Further, the tribunal had correctly held that it had no jurisdiction to hear the application as the Equal Pay Act came into force in December 1975 and no claims could be made in respect of events before that date. Accordingly, the appeal would be dismissed.

DE BRITO v STANDARD CHARTERED BANK [1978] ICR 650 (Employment Appeal Tribunal: KILNER BROWN J presiding). *Snoxell v Vauxhall Motors Ltd* [1977] ICR 700, EAT, 1977 Halsbury's Abr para. 2542 applied.

2568 —— second application to industrial tribunal—issue estoppel

A woman stock controller made an equal pay claim to an industrial tribunal. The claim was dismissed. The woman appealed out of time. The judge refused leave to appeal, but indicated that in equal pay cases there might not be an inherent objection to a renewal application based upon the facts in existence at the time of the second application. The woman duly made a fresh application, but the industrial tribunal held that the employers succeeded on the basis of issue estoppel. The woman submitted that issue estoppel could not apply to equal pay cases. On appeal, *held*, the basic principle of issue estoppel was that the same facts had been previously adjudicated. Issue estoppel did not apply where the situation was never static; where the facts were never quite the same and, where the position was capable of variation. In equal pay cases the situation was continuous and not static. But there had to be something more than mere potential for change before issue estoppel was ruled out. If the doctrine was not applied an applicant would go on making applications over and over again. There had to be some appreciable difference in the facts if issue estoppel was not to apply to an adjudication. This was not the case here and the appeal would be dismissed.

McLOUGHLIN v GORDONS (STOCKPORT) LTD [1978] ICR 561 (Employment Appeal Tribunal: KILNER BROWN J presiding).

2569 Equal treatment—men and women engaged in like work—women not required to work in colour burst shell shops

Work in a particular shop in a munitions factory which produced colour bursting shells involved wearing protective clothing and taking showers after normal working hours. This necessitated overtime working. A male quality examiner complained that he was being discriminated against because, as women were never required to work in these shops, if he volunteered for overtime he would be required to work there more frequently. An industrial tribunal upheld his complaint and the employers appealed. *Held*, the employers' practice of not requiring women to work in the shops was an act of discrimination because men might be deterred from applying for overtime whereas a woman would not. It also affected the amount of time a man could work in other shops which attracted higher pay and was therefore discriminatory, although it had not been shown that this had direct financial consequences.

MINISTRY OF DEFENCE V JEREMIAH [1978] IRLR 402 (Employment Appeal Tribunal: SLYNN J presiding).

2570   —— **recommendation that employers cease discrimination—failure to end discrimination**

The applicants were women who had not been chosen for promotion. They complained to an industrial tribunal that they had been discriminated against on the ground of sex. The tribunal upheld the complaint and made a recommendation under the Sex Discrimination Act 1975, s. 65 (1), that, within six months, the employers should seriously consider applications for promotion from women. A year later the women complained that the employers had failed to comply with the recommendation. The tribunal found for the employers on the basis that they had reasonable grounds for failing to comply. On appeal, *held*, the tribunal had discretion to award compensation under s. 65 (3) if the employers failed to comply with a recommendation without reasonable justification. "Reasonable justification" was essentially a factual question for the tribunal to decide. The statute took into account the fact that sex discrimination could not be eliminated immediately. The tribunal's decision would be allowed to stand.

NELSON V TYNE AND WEAR PASSENGER TRANSPORT EXECUTIVE [1978] ICR 1183 (Employment Appeal Tribunal: PHILLIPS J presiding).

2571   **Retirement—age of retirement—women retiring earlier than men—effect of EEC provisions**

A Belgian air stewardess complained that a clause in her contract compelling her to retire at the age of forty amounted to sex discrimination as men were not required to retire at that age. The questions arose whether the EEC Treaty, art. 119, which provides for equal pay for men and women doing equal work, also prescribed equal working conditions between the sexes where differences would have financial consequences, and whether there was any general principle of Community law prohibiting sex discrimination in employment in areas other than pay. *Held*, art. 119 was solely concerned with pay; it did not cover dismissal or conditions of retirement even where there might be indirect pecuniary consequences. Community law contained no general principle prohibiting sex discrimination in conditions of work and accordingly the stewardess had no means of redress in the European Court.

Case 149/77: DEFRENNE V SABENA [1978] 3 CMLR 311 (European Court of Justice).

2572   **Selection for appointment—whether occupational qualification necessary**

Industrial tribunal decision:

WYLIE V DEE & CO (MENSWEAR) LTD [1978] IRLR 103 (female applied for job in men's clothing store; management refused to consider her for job as it involved taking inside leg measurements; requirement to take such measurements did not arise very frequently and other assistants could help if necessary; no genuine occupational qualification for the job and applicant was unfairly discriminated against).

2573   Seniority rule—non-application to women—whether discrimination justified

Industrial tribunal decision:

STEEL v THE POST OFFICE [1978] IRLR 198 (a postwoman since 1961 complained of discrimination on grounds of sex in operation of Post Office's seniority rule which did not take into account postwomen's service before coming into force of Sex Discrimination Act 1975; before that date women were not allowed to achieve permanent grade but had to remain temporary, while the temporary grade for men was abolished in 1969; Employment Appeal Tribunal held that she had established a prima facie case of indirect discrimination and remitted case to tribunal to determine whether employers could show that seniority requirement was justifiable irrespective of the sex of the person to whom it applied within 1975 Act, s. 1 (1) (b) (ii); Post Office had failed to discharge burden of proof; applying Employment Appeal Tribunal's guidelines, it was not necessary for the rule to be operated as it was, and there was a feasible non-discriminatory alternative to back-date postwomen's seniority to a reasonable date).

For Employment Appeal Tribunal decision, see [1978] 1 WLR 64, 1977 Halsbury's Abr para. 2552.

SHIPPING AND NAVIGATION

Halsbury's Laws of England (3rd edn.), Vol. 35

2574   Article

"Arrived Ship" (effect of the decision of the House of Lords in *Federal Commerce & Navigation Co Ltd v Tradax Export SA* [1977] 2 All ER 849, 1977 Halsbury's Abr para. 2585): 122 Sol Jo 205.

2575   Admiralty jurisdiction

See ADMIRALTY.

2576   Bill of lading—destruction of cargo—liability of buyers to pay the price

See *M. Golodetz Co Inc v Czarnikow-Rionda Inc*, para. 2406.

2577   —— time charter—right of charterers to order issue of bills of lading

See *The Lorfri; The Nanfri; The Benfri*, para. 2607.

2578   "Blacked" ship—action in furtherance of trade dispute—injunction—balance of convenience

See *The Camilla M*, para 2871.

2579   Carriage of goods by sea—freight—advance payment to owners—whether payment recoverable

The plaintiffs sold a quantity of copra to the buyers. Payment for the shipment was to be made by the plaintiffs as the buyers' agents. Shipment on *The Georgios* was arranged by a firm of shipping agents. The shipowners, the defendants, asked the shipping agents for thirty days hire in advance. The shipping agents asked the plaintiffs to pay this sum. The plaintiffs eventually agreed and sent a draft for the required sum to the defendants' bank. The payment was accompanied by an advice note specifying that it was for the shipment of the cargo of copra on *The Georgios*. The defendants, who had received the plaintiffs' money but not their advice note, pressed the shipping agents for payment of further sums owing. When no further money was forthcoming, *The Georgios* was withdrawn. The shipping agents told the plaintiffs that another vessel would be found and the sum paid returned. But the defendants denied notice of the advice and contended that the payment had been accepted as hire payable by the shipping agents as time charterers. *Held*, the plaintiff's sole interest was in their own cargo of copra. They never intended to do other than make an advance payment in respect of freight. On the terms of the advice note, the defendants were entitled to retain the money until shipment and then to apply it in satisfying any claims they had against the shipping agents. But once a situation arose in which the money could never become due, the defendants were under obligation to return it to the plaintiffs. Judgment would therefore be given for the plaintiffs.

THE GEORGIOS, AFRO PRODUCE (SUPPLIES) LTD v METALFA SHIPPING CO LTD [1978] 2 Lloyd's Rep 197 (Queen's Bench Division: DONALDSON J).

2580 —— Hamburg Rules

The Hamburg Rules have emerged as the final act of the United Nations Conference on the Carriage of Goods by Sea 1978. They cover all aspects of carriers' liability, transport documentation, claims and actions and make supplementary provisions relating to contractual stipulations, general average and the relationship of the Rules to other Conventions. The Rules come into operation on the first of the month following the expiration of one year from receipt of the twentieth instrument of ratification, acceptance, approval or accession.

For a full text of the Rules, see [1978] 3 LMCLQ 439.

2581 —— seaworthiness of ship—liability for maintaining seaworthiness while loading

Canada

Under an agreement for the carriage of a cargo of potatoes, it was the shippers' responsibility to assemble the potatoes on the wharf ready for loading. Stevedores were engaged by the shipowners to load the cargo. While loading was taking place, the temperature dropped and the stevedores provided heaters in the hold of the ship to maintain the required temperature. The stevedores brought an action to recover the cost of heating from the shippers. *Held*, the shippers' responsibility for the safety of the goods ceased when the goods were assembled on the dockside. Responsibility for the goods then passed to the shipowners, who were under a duty to ensure that the space provided for the stowage of cargo was safe. The inherent character of potatoes thus imposed on the shipowners the duty of seeing that heat was provided to protect them in the hold, and the shippers were not liable for the cost of providing the heat.

HENDERSON v COASTAL STEVEDORING AGENCIES LTD (1977) 80 DLR (3d) 354 (Supreme Court of Prince Edward Island).

2582 —— unification of laws—convention countries

The Carriage of Goods by Sea (Parties to Convention) Order 1978, S.I. 1978 No. 1885 (made on 20th December 1978), certifies the contracting states to the 1924 Brussels Convention as amended by the 1968 Brussels Protocol ("the Hague Rules"). The Carriage of Goods by Sea (Parties to Convention) Order 1977, 1977 Halsbury's Abr para. 2571, is revoked.

2583 Certificates of competency—recognition

The Merchant Shipping (Certificates of Competency as A.B.) (Hong Kong) Order 1978, S.I. 1978 No. 1532 (in force on 1st December 1978) provides for the recognition in the United Kingdom of certificates of competency as A.B. granted in Hong Kong.

2584 Charterparty—arbitration—appointment of arbitrator—extension of time limit

See *Consolidated Investment and Contracting Co v Saponaria Shipping Co*, para. 146.

2585   —— —— provision for arbitration in general average clause—whether provision extended to claim for demurrage

Under the provision of a general average clause in a charter in the Gencon form, "general average and arbitration" were "to be settled according to the York-Antwerp Rules 1950, in London". The shipowners subsequently brought a claim for demurrage, and, since the charterers refused to agree to the appointment of an arbitrator, applied to the court for appointment of one. The question for the court was whether the reference in the charter to arbitration was to be construed generally or as being limited solely to disputes as to general average. *Held*, if the parties had intended that all disputes be referred to arbitration, the charter should have contained a separate and general arbitration clause. The clause in question was clearly limited to disputes as to general average, and accordingly the shipowners' application for the appointment of an arbitrator would fail.

THE IOANNA, TRANSAMERICAN OCEAN CONTRACTORS INC v TRANSCHEMICAL ROTTERDAM BV [1978] 1 Lloyd's Rep 238 (Court of Appeal: STEPHENSON and BROWNE LJJ). *Union of India v E. B. Aabys Rederi A/S* [1974] 2 All ER 874, HL, 1974 Halsbury's Abr para. 3025 applied.

2586   —— arbitration clause—guarantee—right of shipowners to claim against guarantor without arbitration first

The defendant guaranteed that he would pay the obligations of the charterers for all sums becoming due under a charterparty. The charterparty contained an arbitration clause which provided that any dispute should be referred to arbitration in London. The guarantee provided that the owners should serve notice of payment on the guarantor, who was under obligation to pay within forty-eight hours unless the liability was contested in good faith by the charterers in appropriate proceedings. In the event, the owners claimed £40,000 against the guarantor, who denied liability, contending that no action lay against him until the owners had first obtained an award against the charterers for the sums due. *Held*, the guarantee specified that the guarantor need not pay where proceedings were being conducted in good faith to settle a dispute between the parties. Since there was no evidence of proceedings in existence in which the charterers were contesting any issue, the guarantor was liable to pay.

THE QUEEN FREDERICA, THERMISTOCLES NAVEGACION SA v LANGTON [1978] 2 Lloyd's Rep 164 (Court of Appeal: LORD DENNING MR, ORMROD and GEOFFREY LANE LJJ).

2587   —— arbitration proceedings—award of costs—matters to be taken into consideration

See *Tramountana Armadora SA v Atlantic Shipping Co SA*, para. 155.

2588   —— breach—warranty as to speed—date at which warranty applies

Owners let a vessel on a time charter for a trip between ports in Japan and South America. The charterparty contained a speed warranty, and provided by cl. 11 (A) that in the event of damage to the hull or other accident hindering or preventing the efficient working of the vessel, no hire was to be paid in respect of any time lost thereby. Cl. 13 provided that the owners were only to be responsible for delay during the currency of the charter if it was caused by want of due diligence by the owner in making the vessel seaworthy. At the date of the charterparty the vessel was capable of steaming at the speed warranted. On delivery to the charterers, her hull was encrusted with molluscs, which was unusual because she had been lying in fresh water and molluscs prefer salt water. During the voyage she was unable to maintain the speed warranted because of the encrustations and on redelivery to the owners the charterers withheld the hire due in respect of the days lost because of the reduction in speed. They claimed either (i) damages for breach of the speed warranty or (ii) that no hire was payable under cl. 11 (A) in respect of the time lost. The owners contended (i) that the speed warranty only applied at the date of the charterparty and not at the date of delivery, alternatively relying on the exception cl. 13, and (ii) that the encrustation did not constitute "damage to the hull or other accident" within cl. 11 (A). *Held,* (i) the speed warranty applied not only at the date of the charterparty but also at the date of delivery. Accordingly the owners were in breach of the warranty. However, they were protected under cl. 13 in that the loss resulting from the breach constituted delay during the currency of the voyage and that delay had not been caused by want of due diligence on the part of the owners in making the vessel seaworthy; (ii) for the purpose of cl. 11 (A) an accident meant something unexpected or out of the ordinary. The encrustation was both and therefore constituted an accident. Since the accident had the effect of hindering the efficient working of the vessel by materially reducing her speed, the charterers were entitled to refuse to pay hire for the days lost in consequence.

Cosmos Bulk Transport Inc v China National Foreign Trade Transportation Corpn [1978] 1 All ER 322 (Queen's Bench Division: Mocatta J). Dictum of Roskill LJ in *Cehave NV v Bremer Handelsgesellschaft GmbH* [1975] 3 All ER 739 at 756, CA, 1975 Halsbury's Abr para. 2955 applied. Dictum of Atkinson J in *Lorentzen v White Shipping Co Ltd* (1942) 74 Ll L Rep 161 at 163 not followed.

2589   —— **consecutive voyage charter—when charterers required to redeliver vessel**

The *Oakwood* was let on a consecutive voyage charter which required her to be redelivered to the disponent owners in November or December 1971. The charterers sought to redeliver her on November 5th but the disponent owners, who could not return her to the owners until November 17th, contended that the charterers were obliged to make another voyage. The court found in favour of the disponent owners and the charterers appealed. *Held,* under the terms of the voyage charter it was clear that the ship could be redelivered on any date in November or December 1971 and therefore the charterers were not obliged to make another voyage. The appeal would be allowed.

The Oakwood, Intermare Transport GmbH v Tradax Export SA [1978] 2 Lloyd's Rep 10 (Court of Appeal: Lord Denning MR, Orr and Scarman LJJ).

2590   —— **construction—charterers' consent required for sale of ship— whether appointment of new manager without charterers' consent amounted to breach of contract**

A clause in a charterparty named the owner-managers of the ship and provided that they were entitled to sell the ship with the charterers' consent; new owners subsequently took over the ship and appointed managing agents with the charterers' consent. The agents then informed the charterers that new managers were being appointed. The charterers refused to pay the charter hire due on the ground that management of the ship could not be changed without their consent and that the appointment was a fundamental breach of contract. *Held,* (i) the clause in the charterparty as to consent applied only with changes in ownership and was clearly not intended to affect changes in management; (ii) there was no reason why the continued management of the ship by the former agents should be necessary for the effective operation of the charter. Accordingly, the charterers were not entitled to treat the appointment as a repudiation of the charter and were liable to pay the hire due.

The Katingo Colocotronis, European-American Banking Corporation v Total Transport Corporation [1978] 1 Lloyd's Rep 388 (Queen's Bench Division: Donaldson J).

For preliminary proceedings in this case, see para. 1684.

2591   —— —— **compliance with description**

The defendants chartered a ship which was described in the charter as to be built at a certain Japanese shipyard and to have a particular hull number. The ship was not built at the specified yard, but at one of its subsidiary yards. The hull number was as specified in the charter. The defendants sought to rescind the charter on the ground that the vessel did not correspond to the contractual description. *Held*, the principles laid down in *The Diana Prosperity, Reardon Smith Line Ltd v Hansen Tangen* (1976) 3 All ER 570 applied in the present case. The words of the charter stating where the ship was to be built were merely words identifying the vessel in question and did not create a contractual obligation. The owners were entitled to offer the vessel built at the subsidiary yard. The defendants had entered into a freely negotiated contract and it was immaterial that they might have hesitated about doing so if they had known where the ship was going to be built.

SANKO STEAMSHIP CO LTD v KANO TRADING LTD [1978] 1 Lloyd's Rep 156 (Court of Appeal: ROSKILL, STEPHENSON and BRIDGE LJJ). *The Diana Prosperity, Reardon Smith Line Ltd v Hansen Tangen* [1976] 3 All ER 570, 1976 Halsbury's Abr para. 2352 applied.

2592   —— —— owner required to pay for all fuel remaining on board—whether owner required to pay for fuel taken on unnecessarily

A time charterparty provided that the shipowners had to pay for all the fuel remaining on board at the port of redelivery at a fixed price. Although there was ample fuel on board to complete the voyage in time, the charterers arranged to redeliver the ship with full oil bunkers and notified the owners that they would be required to pay for all the fuel. The owners instructed the master not to take on any additional bunkers as a result of which the charterers claimed damages for breach of contract. *Held*, although the charterparty required the charterers to provide all the fuel for the voyage, it did not entitle them to take on fuel which was not reasonably necessary to run the ship during the charter period. It was clear that the charterers intended to take on additional fuel shortly before redelivery with the sole object of selling it to the owners at a profit. In such circumstances, the owners were not in breach of contract by instructing the master to refuse the additional bunkers.

THE CAPTAIN DIAMANTIS, MAMMOTH BULK CARRIERS LTD v HOLLAND BULK TRANSPORT BV [1978] 1 Lloyd's Rep 346 (Court of Appeal: LORD DENNING MR, GOFF and CUMMING-BRUCE LJJ). *Darling v Raeburn* [1907] 1 KB 846, applied.

2593   —— —— "safe port"—inordinate delay

A charterparty provided that the charterers were to nominate a safe port to which the vessel was to proceed. The time normally required to sail from the port so nominated was ten to twelve hours, but the vessel was delayed for thirty-seven days due to silting of the river. The shipowners claimed damages for breach of the warranty to nominate a safe port, contending that there had been an inordinate delay which rendered the port unsafe. *Held*, the test which was applicable was whether the delay frustrated the commercial adventure; it was not enough that the delay was commercially unacceptable as that could only be based on the subjective viewpoint of one of the parties. Applying the frustration test, there was no such delay.

UNITRAMP v GARNAC GRAIN CO INC (1978) Times, 13th November (Court of Appeal: ROSKILL and GEOFFREY LANE LJJ and SIR DAVID CAIRNS). *Universal Cargo Carriers Corpn v Citati* [1951] 2 QB 501, *SS Knutsford Ltd v Tullmanns and Co* (1908) AC 406, HL, applied. Decision of Donaldson J [1978] 2 Lloyd's Rep 37 reversed.

2594   —— demurrage—currency in which demurrage payable—appropriate date—rate of exchange

Under three charterparties the rate of demurrage was expressed in US dollars. Demurrage was incurred in each case and calculated in dollars but paid by the charterers in sterling at the rates of exchange prevailing on the dates of the bills of lading. In two cases the arbitrators found that the rates of exchange to be applied were those prevailing on the dates of payment of the amount due, but in the third case the appropriate date was found to be the date on which the cargo was finally discharged. The first two awards were upheld and the third modified in the same terms. The charterers appealed. *Held*, the bills of lading did not apply to demurrage and there was no reason to make demurrage payable at the exchange rates prevailing on the dates of the bills. The clear consequence of the decision in *Miliangos v George Frank (Textiles) Ltd* was that the appropriate rates of exchange were those prevailing on the dates on which demurrage was actually paid. Further, where demurrage was to be calculated in US dollars, in the absence of any contrary provision it was a reasonable inference that it was payable in that currency: the fact that freight was payable in sterling was irrelevant since demurrage was different from freight. The shipowners were therefore entitled to have the balance due awarded in dollars and the appeals would be dismissed.

THE BELLAMI, GEORGE VEFLINGS REDERI A/S v PRESIDENT OF INDIA; THE PEARL MERCHANT, MONROVIA TRAMP SHIPPING CO v PRESIDENT OF INDIA; THE DORIC CHARIOT, MARPERFECTA COMPANIA NAVIERA S/A v PRESIDENT OF INDIA [1979] 1 All ER 380 (Court of Appeal: LORD DENNING MR, GEOFFREY LANE and EVELEIGH LJJ). *Miliangos v George Frank (Textiles) Ltd* [1975] 3 All ER 801, HL, 1975 Halsbury's Abr para. 1916, applied. Decision of Donaldson J [1978] 3 All ER 838 affirmed.

2595   —— —— expiry of lay time—exception clause

The appellants had chartered their vessel to the respondents. The charterparty contained clauses to the effect that time lost in waiting and for discharging cargo was to be counted as discharging time, and that the charterers had an option to fumigate the cargo at any time and that time so used was not to be taken into account. When the vessel arrived at her port of discharge she had to wait her turn for a berth. After the expiry of the laytime the charterers started to fumigate the vessel. The owners claimed demurrage for the whole period after the expiry of laytime. The charterers contended that, by virtue of the exclusion clause, they were not liable to pay demurrage for the period when the fumigation was taking place. At first instance it was held that demurrage was payable for that period, but that decision was reversed by the Court of Appeal. On appeal by the owners *held*, the exclusion clause with regard to fumigation applied only to the duration of laytime. Where laytime had already expired and demurrage had begun before fumigation took place the clause had no further application. The charterers were therefore liable to pay demurrage during the fumigation period and the appeal would be allowed.

THE DIAS, DIAS COMPANIA NAVIERA SA v LOUIS DREYFUS CORPORATION [1978] 1 All ER 724 (House of Lords: LORD DIPLOCK, VISCOUNT DILHORNE, LORD EDMUND-DAVIES, LORD FRASER OF TULLYBELTON and LORD SCARMAN). Decision of Court of Appeal [1977] 1 Lloyd's Rep 485, 1977 Halsbury's Abr para. 2577, reversed.

2596   —— freight—calculation of freight payable according to variable scale—whether variation in scale affected charter

In 1973 the plaintiffs chartered their vessel to the defendants for two years. Freight was to be payable at the Worldscale rate, which both parties knew varied annually. For the first eighteen months the charterers paid up at the appropriate rate, but in 1975 contended that the 1973 rates applied and paid up on that basis. The owners sought the balance of the 1975 rate. *Held*, the Worldscale rate was specifically designed to be revised annually, and the charter specified that it should apply, as amended from time to time. Accordingly, it was perfectly clear that the owners were entitled to the balance.

THE BUNGAMAWAR, MITSUI OSK LINES LTD v AGIP SPA [1978] 1 Lloyd's Rep 263 (Queen's Bench Division: GOFF J).

2597   —— —— part delivery—whether freight payable on cargo delivered or cargo loaded

A vessel carrying a bulk cargo of petroleum lost part of her cargo while stranded in the Magellan Straits. The charter provided that freight was to be computed on the intaken quantity, but that payment was to be made upon delivery. The charterers only paid freight on the delivered quantity plus five per cent for transit losses. The court upheld the owners' claim for payment for the whole quantity loaded. On appeal by the charterers, *held*, although under the charter freight was to be paid upon delivery there was no provision for adjustment in the event of a shortage of cargo. The provision that freight should be computed on the intaken quantity clearly indicated that it should be finally ascertained then. The appeal would be dismissed.

THE METULA, SHELL INTERNATIONAL PETROLEUM LTD v SEABRIDGE SHIPPING LTD [1978] 2 Lloyd's Rep 5 (Court of Appeal: LORD DENNING MR, ROSKILL and BROWNE LJJ). Decision of Donaldson J, 1977 Halsbury's Abr para. 2607 affirmed.

2598   —— general average contribution clause—loss due to unseaworthiness of ship—whether owner acted diligently to make ship seaworthy—charterer's liability for contribution

A ship was chartered to take a cargo across the Pacific; she ran out of fuel on the way and had to be towed to the nearest bunkering port at considerable expense. A clause in the charterparty provided that if the owners acted diligently to make the ship seaworthy, the charterers were required to make a general average contribution towards any loss caused by the ship being unseaworthy on shipment or at the beginning of the voyage. The owners claimed a general average contribution towards the cost of towage; the charterers contended that the owners, through persons acting on their behalf, had failed to use due diligence to make the ship seaworthy. *Held*, due to miscalculations by the ship's master, there was insufficient fuel on board to take the ship across the Pacific in winter. In addition, he had taken on oil which was obviously unsuitable for the engine and inadequate for the voyage. The loss incurred through the cost of towage was clearly due to the ship being unseaworthy from the outset and could have been avoided if the owners had acted with due diligence. Accordingly the owners were prevented by the clause from recovering a general average contribution.

THE EVJE (NO. 2), E. B. AABY's REDERI A/S v THE UNION OF INDIA [1978] 1 Lloyd's Rep 351 (Court of Appeal: LORD DENNING MR, LAWTON and GOFF LJJ).

2599   —— hire—cesser of hire in event of accident—meaning of accident

See *Cosmos Bulk Transport Inc. v China National Foreign Trade Transportation Corpn*, para. 2588.

2600   —— —— non-payment—right of owners to withdraw vessel temporarily—rights of charterers

A charter in Baltime form provided for the payment of hire monthly in advance, with a right of withdrawal in default of payment. The charterers were required to deposit a further thirty days hire, "the escrow hire payment". The owners would become entitled to this sum if hire was due and unpaid for seven days. The charter also provided that the owners would only be responsible for delay during the currency of the charter caused by want of due diligence. The charterers delayed in paying both the advance hire and the escrow. The owners instructed the master to refuse to load until the hire had been paid. Delay occurred. The owners then instructed the master not to sail until the escrow had been paid. Further delay occurred. Eventually the owners withdrew the vessel for non-payment of another instalment of hire, at the same time forfeiting the escrow. The charterers claimed repayment of hire for the periods of delay, and part of the escrow for the remainder of the month following the withdrawal of the vessel. *Held*, the delay caused by the owners' refusal to load and sail amounted to a temporary withdrawal of the vessel. Temporary withdrawal for non-payment of hire was a right which had to be expressly conferred by the charter. No such right was reserved to the owners, who therefore could not justify the refusal to load or to sail. The owners were only entitled to keep that part of the advance payment of hire in the form of the escrow which had been earned. They had to account to the charterers for the balance.

THE MIHALIOS XILAS, INTERNATIONAL BULK CARRIERS (BEIRUT) SARL v EVLOGIA SHIPPING CO SA [1978] 2 Lloyd's Rep 186 (Queen's Bench Division: DONALDSON J). *Aegnoussiotis Shipping Corporation v A/S Kristian Jebsens Rederi* [1977] 1 Lloyd's Rep 268, and *The Agios Giorgis* [1976] 2 Lloyd's Rep 192, 1976 Halsbury's Abr para. 2365, applied.

2601   —— **laytime—meaning of "weather permitting working day"**

A charterparty provided that cargo was to be discharged "at the average rate of 750 metric tons per day of 24 consecutive hours per weather permitting working day." The ship arrived in the roads and notice of readiness was tendered and accepted. In accordance with the charterparty, laytime then began, although the ship did not reach her berth until much later. During the intervening time there was one period when rain would have prevented discharge if the ship had been in berth. The owners claimed demurrage which was calculated without making allowance for the period of rain. On the question of whether the period of rain before the ship reached her berth should have been deducted from laytime, *held*, the expression "weather permitting working day" meant the same as the expression "working day weather permitting". Both expressions meant a working day which counted unless work was prevented by the weather. The charterparty provided for the period of laytime to begin even though cargo was not actually being discharged. The period of rain which would have prevented discharge should therefore have been taken into account. Demurrage would be recalculated.

THE CAMELIA, MAGNOLIA SHIPPING CO LTD V INTERNATIONAL TRADING & SHIPPING ENTERPRISES AND KINSHIP MANAGEMENT CO LTD [1978] 2 Lloyd's Rep 182 (Queen's Bench Division: BRANDON J). *The Darrah* [1976] 2 All ER 963, HL, 1976 Halsbury's Abr para. 2364, applied.

2602   —— —— **time lost waiting for berth—whether non-working days to count**

A charterparty provided that time lost by a ship in waiting for a berth was to count as laytime. When the ship reached port, there was considerable delay before a berth was free and she could be unloaded. A dispute arose as to when the permitted laytime expired and as to the amount of demurrage payable. The charterers contended that non-working days were to be excluded when computing time lost waiting for a berth; the shipowners wanted non-working days included so that the permitted laytime would be exhausted at an earlier date and increased demurrage would be payable. An arbitrator made an interim award in the form of a special case for the sum claimed by the shipowners with interest. The charterers, who had already paid the shipowners a lesser sum, contended that the lesser sum was the correct sum and also that the arbitrator had no jurisdiction to award interest on the lesser sum since he had not given judgment for it. *Held*, (i) non-working days were to be excluded when computing time lost waiting for a berth in the same way as they would be excluded when computing permitted laytime if the ship had been in a berth. (ii) Under the Law Reform (Miscellaneous Provisions) Act 1934, s. 3 (1) interest may only be awarded on a sum for which judgment has been given. If the arbitrator had made on award in the form of an alternative between the greater and the lesser sum, it would have been a final judgment within the meaning of s. 3 (1). The form of the actual interim award was sufficiently close to a judgment to come within s. 3 (1) and accordingly the matter would be remitted to the arbitrator with a direction to award interest on the lesser sum already paid.

THE FINIX, NEA TYHI MARITIME CO LTD OF PIRAEUS V COMPAGNIE GRAINIERE SA OF ZURICH [1978] 1 Lloyd's Rep 16 (Court of Appeal: LORD DENNING MR, GEOFFREY LANE and CUMMING-BRUCE LJJ). Decision of Donaldson J [1975] 2 Lloyd's Rep 417 reversed. *The Darrah* [1976] 2 All ER 963, HL, 1976 Halsbury's Abr para. 2364, applied.

2603   —— —— **when laytime begins to run**

One clause of a charterparty provided that laytime should begin the morning after the vessel was ready to load and was in free pratique, having obtained a clean bill of health and satisfied any other local requirements. A second clause provided that if loading was held up by unavoidable congestion, laytime would "commence to count" as per the first clause, but not until thirty-six hours after the vessel's arrival. In the event the vessel was delayed by unavoidable congestion at an offshore anchorage while not in free pratique. The owners claimed that the vessel was on laytime for most of that period by virtue of the second clause, the charterers that it was not because it was not in free pratique. The court upheld the owners' claim. On appeal, *held*, the court had been correct in holding that the requirements of the first clause did not relate to the second. The reference in the second clause to laytime commencing to count referred to the counting of laytime, not to its commencement. The first clause made it plain that where the ship could not commence loading because it was delayed by congestion the burden was to fall on the charterers. The appeal would de dismissed.

THE FREIJO, LOGS AND TIMBER PRODUCTS (SINGAPORE) PTE LTD v KEELEY GRANITE (PTY) LTD [1978] 2 Lloyd's Rep 1 (Court of Appeal: MEGAW and ROSKILL LJJ).

2604   A vessel was chartered on terms such that laytime was to commence when the recipients of the cargo were notified of the vessel's arrival at the port of discharge and customs clearance was obtained. When the vessel was still outside the port of discharge and before it had received customs clearance, the recipients accepted notice of arrival. Considerable time elapsed before the vessel could berth and obtain customs clearance and more delay occurred when she had to move to a different berth to unload. On the questions of when laytime began to run and whether time spent moving berth could be included in it, *held*, (i) the recipients' premature acceptance of the notice of arrival effectively estopped any claim that laytime had not begun until customs clearance had been obtained. (ii) The carrying voyage had ended when the notice of arrival was accepted. Therefore, all subsequent moves during the discharging stage were to be included in the computation of laytime.

THE SHACKLEFORD, SURREY SHIPPING CO LTD v COMPAGNIE CONTINENTALE (FRANCE) SA [1978] 1 WLR 1080 (Court of Appeal: BUCKLEY and BRIDGE LJJ and SIR DAVID CAIRNS). Decision of Donaldson J [1978] 1 Lloyd's Rep 191, affirmed. Dicta of Buckley and Roskill LJJ in *E. L. Oldendorff & Co GmbH v Tradax Export SA* [1974] AC 479, at 501, 515, CA applied.

2605   Shipowners chartered their vessel to carry grain from South America to Liverpool. Laytime at Liverpool was to run from the start of the first business day after both the vessel had reported to customs and the charterers' agents had received written notice of readiness to unload. In the event of congestion preventing immediate berthing, the vessel was to issue notice of readiness on arrival outside Liverpool docks, laytime to run from the next working day. The only suitable berth for unloading the grain was occupied on the ship's arrival, and accordingly she moored outside Liverpool docks, where it was impossible to report to customs. The owners issued notice of readiness. The charterers refused to accept it. The owners then moved the vessel to a lay-by berth within the docks, reported to customs and issued a second notice while still maintaining the validity of the first. The question of when laytime began to run came to the court as a special case. *Held*, the charterers could not reject the first notice of readiness for the owners' failure to report to customs when that was impossible. The contingency clause relating to congestion at the port of discharge clearly applied, and laytime accordingly ran from the morning after the first notice was issued. For the charterers to require a vessel waiting to unload to proceed to a lay-by berth, report to customs, and then issue notice of readiness, was unreasonable and uncommercial.

The PUERTO ROCCA, COMPANIA ARGENTINA DE NAVEGACION DE ULTRAMAR v TRADAX EXPORT SA [1978] 1 Lloyd's Rep 252 (Queen's Bench Division: MOCATTA, J).

2606   —— loss of ship—action to recover insurance money—court's discretion to add additional defendant

See *Citibank NA v Hobbs Savill & Co Ltd and Dray Shipping Co Ltd and A/S Seaheron (The "Panglobal Friendship")*, para. 2168.

2607   —— time charter—right of charterers to order issue of appropriate bills of lading—issue of contrary instructions by owners—whether owners' conduct repudiatory

By identical time charterparties three ships were chartered for six years. Under the charters, which gave the owners a right of lien over bills of lading issued by the masters, the charterers were entitled to make deductions from hire in respect of expenses incurred as a result of slow steaming. The charterers made such a deduction, notwithstanding the objections of the owners, who then instructed the masters to refuse to sign freight pre-paid bills of lading and informed the charterers that they would withdraw the instructions only if the deductions were paid. The charterers told the owners that they regarded their conduct as repudiating the charters, and treated them as terminated. However, a "without prejudice" agreement was then negotiated and the owners' instructions were never carried out. The Court of Appeal reversed a decision that the owners' conduct was not repudiatory, and the owners appealed. *Held*, since the nature and purpose of time charters was to enable charterers to use vessels during the charter period for trading in whatever manner they chose, charterers had to have the unfettered right to instruct masters to issue bills of lading appropriate to the trade in which they are engaged. In this case the charterers were engaged in a trade which, as the owners knew, required the issue of freight pre-paid bills. The owners were therefore not entitled to require claused bills, since to do so would be contrary to the whole commercial purpose of the charters and would have ruined the charterers' trade. Further the owners' claim that the charterers could not issue bills of lading which would defeat the owners' lien could not be supported since the lien clause was not to be read as interfering with the charterers' primary right to use the ship and direct the master. Accordingly, although there had been no actual breach of the charters, the issue of the owners' instructions constituted an anticipatory breach which went to the root of the contract in depriving the charterers of substantially the whole benefit of the charters.

In the absence of definite findings of fact, their lordships were unable to consider the validity of the deductions, either under the charters or by way of equitable set-off.

THE NANFRI, THE BENFRI, THE LORFRI [1979] 1 All ER 307 (House of Lords: LORD WILBERFORCE, VISCOUNT DILHORNE, LORD FRASER OF TULLYBELTON, LORD RUSSELL OF KILLOWEN and LORD SCARMAN). Decision of Court of Appeal [1978] 3 All ER 1066, para. 2609 affirmed in part.

2608 —— —— **time lost through medical inspection**

The owners let their vessel to the charterers. One clause of the charter provided that if time was lost from "any other cause whatsoever preventing the full working of the vessel" the payment of hire was to cease during that period. In the course of a voyage two members of the crew were taken ashore with suspected typhus. The vessel then sailed on to another port to load a cargo. On its arrival there the vessel was inspected by health officers but free pratique was not granted for another seventeen hours. The charterers subsequently deducted from hire the amount which would have been payable during those seventeen hours. The owners claimed that as the delay was due to outside interference from the port health authorities the charterers were not able to rely on the exemption clause. The arbitrators stated their award in the form of a consultative case the question for the court being whether the charterers were liable for the hire charges during all or part of that period. *Held*, although the exemption clause made reference to "any other cause whatsoever" it had to be taken in context and was limited to reasons of a similar kind to those already enumerated in the clause. It applied to any cause "preventing the full working of the vessel". Due to the illness among the crew it was necessary for the vessel to be properly inspected and disinfected, and as this action had prevented the full working of the vessel the off hire clause applied. The charterers would, however, be liable to pay hire for a period of several hours during which the vessel was waiting for a berth as this time would have been lost whether or not a free pratique was granted.

THE APOLLO, SIDERMAR SPA V APOLLO CORPORATION [1978] 1 Lloyd's Rep 200 (Queen's Bench Division: MOCATTA J).

2609 —— —— **whether charterer entitled to deduct from hire**

Shipowners let their ships to the charterers on a time charter. The charter provided

that no hire was payable for time lost due to the breakdown of machinery and that
any expenses incurred due to such loss could be deducted from the hire. The owners
were also given a lien on any bill of lading freight. The charterers made several
deductions from hire to which the owners objected. They informed the charterers
that sole authority to sign bills of lading would be taken from them and vested in the
master of each ship who would indorse the bills of lading, which were normally
issued "freight pre-paid", with the owners' lien on freight. The charterers appealed
against a decision that the owners' conduct was not a repudiation of the charter.
Held, (i) the charterers were entitled to deduct from hire without the owners'
consent valid claims arising under the charterparty. (ii) CUMMING-BRUCE LJ
dissenting, the rule of law that freight payable under a voyage charterparty was
payable without deduction did not extend to hire payable under a time charterparty,
and therefore the charterers were entitled to deduct claims which constituted an
equitable set-off. (iii) The owners' conduct evinced an intention not to be bound by
the terms of the charterparty and amounted to an anticipatory breach. The
charterers had accepted the repudiation and had validly terminated the charterparty. The appeal would be allowed.

THE NANFRI, THE BENFRI, THE LORFRI [1978] 3 All ER 1066 (Court of Appeal:
LORD DENNING MR, GOFF and CUMMING-BRUCE LJJ). *The Teno* [1977] 2 Lloyd's
Rep 289, 1977 Halsbury's Abr para. 2592 approved; *The Satya Kamal* [1975] 2
Lloyd's Rep 188 and *The Agios Giorgis* [1976] 2 Lloyd's Rep 192, 1976 Halsbury's
Abr para. 2365 disapproved.

On appeal to the House of Lords [1978] 3 WLR 991, para. 2607 the question of
the validity of the deductions was not considered.

2610   Collision—apportionment of liability—negligence of both ships

During fog a collision occurred between the plaintiffs' ship and the defendants'
ship. Neither ship was keeping a sufficiently careful radar lookout, and both were
going too fast for the weather conditions. When the ships sighted each other a few
minutes before the collision, both changed course and sounded warning signals.
Neither ship heard the other signal, and the change of course resulted in the stem of
the defendants' ship striking the side of the plaintiffs' ship and causing a large hole.
The master ordered the ship to be abandoned and it subsequently sank with the
complete loss of its cargo. The plaintiffs brought an action in rem against the
defendants for liability for the collision. The defendants counter-claimed that the
master of the plaintiffs' ship had been negligent in abandoning the ship and not
taking proper measures to prevent its sinking. *Held,* in view of the weather
conditions both ships were at fault in going at too great a speed, keeping insufficient
radar lookout and failing to change course before getting so close. Initially the
plaintiffs' ship had been setting too southerly a course, but this was of less causative
effect than the defendants' change of course when the plaintiffs' ship was sighted. As
the defendants' speed was greater than the plaintiffs' liability would be apportioned
60 per cent to the defendants and 40 per cent to the plaintiffs. Whether or not the
master had contributed to the loss of the ship depended on the requirements of good
seamanship. In the circumstances the master might have abandoned the ship later
than he did, but the loss was due to the collision and not to any causative negligence
on the master's part.

THE ZAGLEBIE DABROWSKIE [1978] 1 Lloyd's Rep 564 (Queen's Bench Division:
BRANDON J).

2611   —— narrow channel—rules applicable

The plaintiff's ship, the *Pasteur*, was damaged when taking action to avoid an
imminent collision in a narrow channel with the defendants' ship, the *Stella Antares*.
At the time of the accident, the *Stella Antares* was steering to port in accordance with
local navigation rules. The plaintiffs claimed that the near collision was caused by
the *Stella Antares* failing to signal her first alteration to port and failing to alter course
to starboard in accordance with the Collision Regulations r. 25. *Held,* (i) there was
no evidence to show that the failure of the *Stella Antares* to signal her first alteration
to port caused the near collision. (ii) The relative position of the ships in the channel

was such that the local navigation rules prevailed over the Collision Regulations. The masters of both ships were familiar with the local rules and the *Stella Antares* had acted correctly in complying with them. The master of the *Pasteur* was at fault in failing to appreciate that the local rules were operative.

THE STELLA ANTARES [1978] 1 Lloyd's Rep 41 (Queen's Bench Division: BRANDON J).

2612   —— regulations—distress signals

The Collision Regulations and Distress Signals (Amendments) Order 1978, S.I. 1978 No. 462 (in force on 1st May 1978), further amends the Collision Regulations and Distress Signals Order 1977, 1977 Halsbury's Abr para. 2597, by changing references to certain editions of Admiralty notices and manuals references to later editions, and by adding further countries to the list of those to whose vessels the Collision Regulations and Distress Signals Rules apply.

2613   The Collision Regulations and Distress Signals (Amendment No. 2) Order 1978, S.I. 1978 No. 1059 (in force on 1st September 1978), further amends the Collision Regulations and Distress Signals Order 1977, 1977 Halsbury's Abr para. 2597. The Order makes the necessary amendment in respect of the traffic separation scheme adopted by IMCO, and adds Saudi Arabia and the Dominican Republic to the list of foreign countries to whose vessels the Regulations apply.

2614   ——— Mersey Channel

The Mersey Channel (Collision Rules) Order 1978, S.I. 1978 No. 1914 (in force on 11th March 1979), revokes the Mersey Channel (Collision Rules) Orders 1960 and 1970 and makes new rules concerning the lights and signals to be exhibited and the steps for avoiding collision to be taken by vessels navigating in the Mersey and the sea channels or approaches to it.

2615   Continental shelf—protection of installations

The Continental Shelf (Protection of Installations) Order 1978, S.I. 1978 No. 260 (in force on 31st March 1978), the Continental Shelf (Protection of Installations) (No. 2) Order 1978, S.I. 1978 No. 673 (in force on 6th March 1978), the Continental Shelf (Protection of Installations) (No. 3) Order 1978, S.I. 1978 No. 733 (in force on 19th May 1978), the Continental Shelf (Protection of Installations) (No. 4) Order 1978, S.I. 1978 No. 890 (in force on 22nd June 1978) and the Continental Shelf (Protection of Installations) (No. 5) Order 1978, S.I. 1978 No. 935 (in force on 6th July 1978), specify as safety zones certain sea areas (being areas within a radius of 500 metres of an offshore installation) and prohibits ships from entering the zone except with the permission of the Secretary of State or in specified circumstances. All previous orders, 1976 Halsbury's Abr para. 2374 and 1977 Halsbury's Abr paras. 2599 and 2600 are replaced.

2616   The Continental Shelf (Protection of Installations) (Variation) Order 1978, S.I. 1978 No. 1411 (in force on 3rd October 1978), varies the Continental Shelf (Protection of Installations) Order 1978, para. 2615, by deleting one zone from the list of safety zones specified in the order.

2617   Contract—ship's master—authority to conclude necessary contracts

See *The Polyduke, Bahamas Oil Refining Co v Kristiansands Tankrederie A/S and Shell International Marine Ltd*, para. 2636; *The Unique Mariner*, para. 2637.

2618   Crew accommodation

The Merchant Shipping (Crew Accommodation) Regulations 1978, S.I. 1978 No. 795 (in force on 1st July 1978), revoke the Merchant Shipping (Crew

Accommodation) Regulations 1953 as amended. The Regulations govern the crew accommodation to be provided in new ships which are either registered in the United Kingdom or unregistered but owned by United Kingdom residents, and existing foreign-registered ships transferred to the United Kingdom register.

2619   Dangerous goods

The Merchant Shipping (Dangerous Goods) Rules 1978, S.I. 1978 No. 1543 (in force on 29th December 1978), supersede the Merchant Shipping (Dangerous Goods) Rules, as amended. The principal changes relate to the definition of dangerous goods, the packing of dangerous goods in freight containers and compliance with IMCO codes and IMDG codes.

2620   Deck officers—certification

The Merchant Shipping (Certification of Deck Officers) (Amendment) Regulations 1978, S.I. 1978 No. 430 (in force on 1st September 1981), amend the provisions of the Merchant Shipping (Certification of Deck Officers) Regulations 1977, 1977 Halsbury's Abr para. 2603, which relate to certificates of competency and certificates of service.

2621   Disciplinary offences

The Merchant Shipping (Disciplinary Offences) (Amendment) Regulations 1978, S.I. 1978 No. 1754 (in force on 1st January 1979), amend the Merchant Shipping (Disciplinary Offences) Regulations 1972, S.I. 1972 No. 1294. Those regulations are not to apply to seamen who are employed in a ship, in respect of which the crew agreement approved by the Secretary of State is one to which the National Maritime Board agreement on disciplinary procedures applies and which requires the seamen to comply with the Code of Conduct for the Merchant Navy which is published by the Board.

2622   —— deductions from wages

The Merchant Shipping (Seamen's Wages and Accounts) (Amendment) Regulations 1978, S.I. 1978 No. 1757 (in force on 1st January 1979), amend the Merchant Shipping (Seamen's Wages and Accounts) Regulations 1972, S.I. 1972 No. 1700, by authorising a deduction from the wages of a seaman who is required to comply with the Code of Conduct of the National Maritime Board and who has committed one of the acts of misconduct specified in para. 9 of the Code. The deduction is a contribution towards the seaman's repatriation expenses incurred by his employer.

2623   —— discharge of seamen—procedure

The Merchant Shipping (Crew Agreements, Lists of Crew and Discharge of Seamen) (Amendment) Regulations 1978, S.I. 1978 No. 1756 (in force on 1st January 1979), amend the Merchant Shipping (Crew Agreements, Lists of Crew and Discharge of Seamen) Regulations 1972, S.I. 1972 No. 918, by providing that a seaman who is required to comply with the Code of Conduct of the National Maritime Board may be discharged from a ship outside the United Kingdom without the consent of a proper officer if the master is satisfied that he has committed one of the acts of misconduct set out in para. 9 of the Code.

2624   —— entries in official log books

The Merchant Shipping (Official Log Books) (Amendment) Regulations 1978, S.I. 1978 No. 1755 (in force on 1st January 1979), amend the Merchant Shipping (Official Log Books) Regulations 1972, S.I. 1972 No. 1874, by prescribing additional particulars to be entered in official log books by masters when a seaman who is required to comply with the Code of Conduct of the National Maritime Board is charged with one of the acts of misconduct set out in the Code.

2625   —— **surrender of discharge books**

The Merchant Shipping (Seamen's Documents) (Amendment No. 3) Regulations 1978, S.I. 1978 No. 1758 (in force on 1st January 1979), amend the Merchant Shipping (Seamen's Documents) Regulations 1972, S.I. 1972 No. 1295, by providing that a seaman who is required to comply with the Code of Conduct of the National Maritime Board and who has committed one of the acts of misconduct specified in para. 9 of the Code shall surrender his discharge book to the Secretary of State upon the recommendation of a shore-based disciplinary committee. Such a person may not apply for another discharge book.

2626   **Fees—merchant shipping**

The Merchant Shipping (Fees) Regulations 1978, S.I. 1978 No. 600 (reg. 3 (2) and Schedule, Part XI, in force on 1st July 1978, remainder in force on 22nd May 1978), revoke the Merchant Shipping (Fees) Regulations 1977, 1977 Halsbury's Abr para. 2633 and the Merchant Shipping (Fees for Seamen's Documents) Regulations 1975, 1975 Halsbury's Abr para. 3094. The fees laid down in those Regulations are mostly re-enacted, and fees in respect of specified matters are increased.

2627   **Fishing vessels**

See FISHERIES.

2628   **Government ships—registration**

The Merchant Shipping (Registration of Government Ships) Order 1978, S.I. 1978 No. 1533 (in force on 22nd November 1978) amends Orders in Council of 1911 and 1921 by applying the provisions of the Merchant Shipping (Mercantile Marine Fund) Act 1898, s. 3 to such ships. The Amendment provides for the payment of fees under the 1898 Act by the Ministry of Defence and the Departments of Trade, Prices and Consumer Protection, Energy, Environment and Transport upon the registration, transfer and mortgage of ships in their service.

2629   **Hong Kong—confirmation of legislation**

The Merchant Shipping (Confirmation of Legislation) (Hong Kong) Order 1978, S.I. 1978 No. 1061 (in force on 1st September 1978), confirms the Merchant Shipping (Amendment) Ordinance 1978 of Hong Kong, by which the legislature of Hong Kong has repealed the Merchant Shipping Act 1894, s. 126 and the Merchant Shipping Act 1906, s. 58 and substituted corresponding provisions of the Merchant Shipping Act 1948. These provisions relate to the qualifications for the engagement of able-bodied seamen in British ships registered in Hong Kong and the recognition of Commonwealth certificates of competency as A.B.

2630   **Hovercraft—application of enactments**

The Hovercraft (Application of Enactments) (Amendment) Order 1978, S.I. 1978 No. 1913 (in force on 29th December 1978), amends the Hovercraft (Application of Enactments) Order 1972, Sch. 1, S.I. 1972 No. 971, by adding references to amendments of both the Collision and Distress Signals Order 1977, contained in S.I. 1977 No. 1301, 1977 Halsbury's Abr para. 2597, and S.I. 1978 No. 462, para. 2612, and also of the Merchant Shipping (Dangerous Goods) Rules 1965, S.I. 1965 No. 1067, contained in S.I. 1978 No. 1543, para. 2619.

2631   —— **fees**

The Hovercraft (Fees) Regulations 1978, S.I. 1978 No. 483 (in force on 20th April 1978), revoke and replace the Hovercraft (Fees) Regulations 1972, as amended. They prescribe increased fees to be paid to the Civil Aviation Authority in respect of matters under the Hovercraft (General) Order 1972. Fees payable to the Secretary of State for the issue of certificates of registration of hovercraft and for operating permits are not increased.

2632   **Hoverport—Dover hoverport—sale of intoxicating liquor**

See para. 1674.

2633   **Life-saving appliances**

The Merchant Shipping (Life-Saving Appliances) (Amendment) Rules 1978, S.I. 1978 No. 1874 (in force on 1st February 1979), further amend the Merchant Shipping (Life-Saving Appliances) Rules 1965 by prescribing requirements for lifebuoy marker smoke signals, different requirements for line-throwing appliances, different requirements for parachute distress rocket signals for lifeboats and liferafts and for ships, different requirements for hand-held distress flare signals for lifeboats and liferafts, and different requirements for buoyant smoke signals for lifeboats.

2634   **Limitation of liability—sterling equivalents**

The Merchant Shipping (Sterling Equivalents) (Various Enactments) Order 1978, S.I. 1978 No. 54 (in force on 1st February 1978), specifies the sterling equivalents of the amounts expressed in gold francs in various enactments as being the limit of liability in certain circumstances. The Merchant Shipping (Limitation of Liability) (Sterling Equivalents) (No. 2) Order 1976, 1976 Halsbury's Abr para. 2378 and the Carriage of Goods by Sea (Sterling Equivalents Order 1977, 1977 Halsbury's Abr para. 2570, are revoked.

2635   **Maritime lien—priority between salvage and wages**

Following the salvage of the *Lyrma* under bad weather conditions the salvors obtained an order for sale of the ship and remuneration for the salvage valued at £22,000. This sum represented forty per cent of the true salved value, which was considerably higher than the price obtained because there had been a delay in the sale. The master and crew of the ship brought an action claiming unpaid wages earned before and after the salvage. The salvors applied to the court to determine the priorities between their salvage lien and the lien for wages, as the fund available for distribution was insufficient to satisfy both claims. *Held*, the court would uphold the equitable principle that a maritime lien on a ship for salvage had priority over all earlier liens. This principle was founded on the basis that the salvage had preserved the property to which the earlier lien had attached. The contention of the master and crew that no property had been preserved in this case because there were insufficient funds to satisfy both claims could not be upheld, as the wages claim could have been satisfied if the ship had realised her true salved value. Nor could the court draw any distinction between wages earned before and after salvage and therefore the salvor's lien would rank before the lien for wages.

THE LYRMA (No 1) and (No 2) [1978] 2 Lloyd's Rep 27, 30 (Queen's Bench Division: BRANDON J).

2636   **Master—authority to make contracts—validity of contract indemnifying harbour owner against damage**

The defendant shipowners chartered their vessel to the second defendants who ordered her to go to the plaintiffs' terminal to load a cargo. Before being allowed to berth the ship's master had to sign a document indemnifying the plaintiffs against any damage to their berths, premises or facilities. The indemnity extended to damage contributed to or by the plaintiffs' negligence. The plaintiffs' jetty was damaged when there was a high wind and the defendants' vessel hit against it. The plaintiffs' claimed compensation on the basis of the clause entitling them to indemnification. The defendants contended that the clause had no contractual effect and, even if it had, the ship's master had no authority to conclude such a contract. *Held*, in the tanker trade it was usual for ships' masters to be required to sign documents such as the document in question, and these documents were generally regarded as having contractual effect. Taking the document as a whole it was meant to be contractual and, unless the master expressly repudiated the effect of his signature, the court could not assume that he had not intended to enter a binding contract. The master had an implied authority to sign documents which were necessary for the proper performance of his duties. He had not exceeded this authority and his signature must be taken as agreement to the terms contained in the document. The plaintiff's claim would be allowed.

THE POLYDUKE, BAHAMAS OIL REFINING CO V KRISTIANSANDS TANKREDERIE A/S AND SHELL INTERNATIONAL MARINE LTD [1978] 1 Lloyd's Rep 211 (Queen's Bench Division: KERR J).

2637   —— —— validity of salvage contract

The plaintiffs' ship ran aground and the master informed the managers that assistance would be required to refloat her. The managers replied that a tug was being sent. Meanwhile, the captain of the defendants' tug saw the plaintiffs' ship aground and offered to salve her. Mistakenly believing that the defendants' tug was the one sent by the managers, the master signed the Lloyd's Standard Form of Salvage Agreement, and the captain commenced salvage of the ship. On receipt of telegrams from the managers, the master realised his error and refused to allow the captain to continue his operations. The plaintiffs brought an action contending that the Lloyds form was not a valid contract on the grounds of, inter alia, want of authority of the master, mistake, and non-disclosure by the captain that he had found the ship by chance. *Held*, the master of a stranded ship had implied authority to accept the services of a suitable tug. The effect of the communication received by the master from the managers was to limit his actual authority to acceptance of the tug sent by them. However, the master had ostensible authority to accept the services of the defendants' tug since the captain was not aware, and had no reason to be aware, of the restriction on the master's actual authority.

As to the mistake, a contract could only be vitiated by a unilateral mistake if the party who was not mistaken was, or ought to have been, aware that the other party was mistaken. Since the captain did not know, and had no reason to know, of the master's mistake, the mistake could not, even if it were sufficiently fundamental, adversely affect the validity of the contract.

As to the plea of non-disclosure, there was no reason why contracts for the rendering of salvage services should be treated as contracts uberrimae fidei. Therefore the failure of the captain of the defendants' tug to disclose that he had come across the ship by chance did not render the contract voidable. The plaintiffs' claim would fail.

THE UNIQUE MARINER [1978] 1 Lloyd's Rep 438 (Queen's Bench Division: BRANDON J).

2638   Merchant shipping—registration of colonial government ships

The Merchant Shipping (Registration of Colonial Government Ships) (Amendment) Order 1978, S.I. 1978 No. 1628 (in force on 14th December 1978) extends the provisions of the Merchant Shipping (Registration of Colonial Government Ships 1963, relating to the registration of ships belonging to or operated by the governments of certain overseas territories as British ships, to Saint Vincent.

2639   Merchant Shipping Act 1970—commencement

The Merchant Shipping Act 1970 (Commencement No. 5) Order 1978, S.I. 1978 No. 797 brings into force on 1st July 1979 s. 100 (3) and Sch. 5 of the 1970 Act so far as they relate to the repeals of the Merchant Shipping Act 1948, ss. 1–4, the Merchant Shipping Act 1950, s. 1, Sch. 1, and the Merchant Shipping Act 1952.

2640   Merchant Shipping Act 1974—commencement

The Merchant Shipping Act 1974 (Commencement No. 3) Order 1978, S.I. 1978 No. 1466, brought into force on 16th October 1978, ss. 1, 2, 4–8 of the 1974 Act, in consequence of the coming into force on that date of the International Convention on the Establishment of an International Fund for Compensation for Oil Pollution Damage 1971.

2641   Oil pollution—convention countries

The Prevention of Oil Pollution (Convention Countries) (Additional Countries) Order 1978, S.I. 1978 No. 188 (in force on 10th March 1978), declares that Argentina, Bulgaria, Surinam and Chile have accepted the International Convention for the Prevention of Pollution of the Sea by Oil 1954.

2642   —— indemnification of shipowners

The Merchant Shipping (Indemnification of Shipowners) Order 1978, S.I. 1978 No. 1467 (in force on 16th October 1978) prescribes the requirements with which a ship must comply if the International Fund for Compensation for Oil Pollution Damage is to indemnify shipowners in respect of their liability under the Merchant Shipping (Oil Pollution) Act 1971.

2643   Pilotage

The London Pilotage (Amendment) Order 1978, S.I. 1978 No. 1540 (in force on 8th December 1978) further amends the Pilotage Order (London) Confirmation Act 1913 by providing for the reconstitution of the Pilotage Committee of the Trinity House for the London Pilotage District, and by amending the powers and duties delegated by the Trinity House to the Pilotage Committee.

2644   Pilotage authorities—returns

The Pilotage Authorities (Returns) Order 1978, S.I. 1978 No. 852 (in force on 1st August 1978), revokes the Pilotage Authorities (Returns) Order 1965. It prescribes revised forms of returns to be furnished to the Secretary of State by pilotage authorities. The principal changes are that the tonnage of ships piloted during the year may now be expressed in net or gross tons, and additional information in respect of the pilot boat account is to be furnished in the statement of account.

2645   Port authority—goods in custody of port authority—liability of port authority as bailees

See *Port Swettenham Authority v T. W. Wu & Co*, para. 200.

2646   Protection of wrecks—restricted areas

The Protection of Wrecks (Designation No. 1) Order 1978, S.I. 1978 No. 199 (in force on 8th March 1978), designates areas at Pwll Fanog, Menai Straits and off Moor Sands, Salcombe round the sites of what are believed to be wrecked vessels of historical and archaeological importance as a restricted area for the purposes of the Protection of Wrecks Act 1973.

2647   The Protection of Wrecks (Designation No. 2) Order 1978, S.I. 1978 No. 321 (in force on 31st March 1978), designates an area off Rame Head, Plymouth round the site of what is believed to be a wrecked vessel of historical and archaeological importance as a restricted area for the purposes of the Protection of Wrecks Act 1973.

2648   The Protection of Wrecks (Designation No. 3) Order 1978, S.I. 1978 No. 664 (in force on 1st June 1978), designates an area in the South Mouth of the Out Skerries, Shetland Isles round the site of what is believed to be a wrecked vessel of historical and archeological importance as a restricted area for the purposes of the Protection of Wrecks Act 1973.

2649   The Protection of Wrecks (Designation No. 4) Order 1978, S.I. 1978 No. 764 (in force on 26th May 1978), designates an area off Langdon Bay, Dover, round the site of what is believed to be a wreck of historical and archaeological importance for the purpose of the Protection of Wrecks Act 1973.

2650   **Provisions and water**

The Merchant Shipping (Provisions and Water) (Amendment) Regulations 1978, S.I. 1978 No. 36 (in force on 1st March 1978), further amend the Merchant Shipping (Provisions and Water) Regulations 1972 by altering the quantities of certain provisions to be carried in ships for seamen ordinarily resident in Bangladesh.

2651   **Public health regulations—ships**

See para. 2264.

2652   **Registrar of British ships—Bermuda**

The Merchant Shipping (Registrar of British Ships in Bermuda) Order 1978, S.I. 1978 No. 1522 (in force on 22nd November 1978) provides that the Registrar of British ships in Bermuda shall be the Registrar of Shipping, Bermuda, or if that office is vacant or the Registrar is unable to act, the Principal Marine Surveyor, Bermuda.

2653   **Seamen's documents**

The Merchant Shipping (Seamen's Documents) (Amendment) Regulations 1978, S.I. 1978 No. 107 (in force on 1st March 1978), further amend the Merchant Shipping (Seamen's Documents) Regulations 1972, by amending the requirements relating to photographs on application for a British Seamen's Card or discharge book.

2654   The Merchant Shipping (Seamen's Documents) (Amendment No. 2) Regulations 1978, S.I. 1978 No. 979 (in force on 1st September 1978), further amend the merchant Shipping (Seamen's Documents) Regulations 1972 by providing that details of any pension fund of which a British seaman may be a member may be recorded in discharge books by an official of the Merchant Navy Establishment Administration.

2655   **Shipbuilding (Redundancy Payments) Act 1978**

See para. 1145.

2656   **Smooth and partially smooth waters**

The Merchant Shipping (Smooth and Partially Smooth Waters) (Amendment) Rules 1978, S.I. 1978 No. 801 (in force on 30th June 1978), amend the Merchant Shipping (Smooth and Partially Smooth Waters) Rules 1977, 1977 Halsbury's Abr para. 2631 by specifying Sullom Vae and Newport as additional areas of smooth and partially smooth waters.

2657   **State immunity—Union of Soviet Socialist Republics**

The State Immunity (Merchant Shipping) (Union of Soviet Socialist Republics) Order 1978, S.I. 1978 No. 1524 (in force on 22nd November 1978), preserves the immunity from execution of ships and cargoes of the Union of Soviet Socialist Republics, and requires that before a warrant of arrest is issued in an action in rem against a Soviet ship notice should be given to a Soviet consul.

2658   **Sterling equivalents**

The Merchant Shipping (Sterling Equivalents) (Various Enactments) (No. 2) Order 1978, S.I. 1978 No. 1468 (in force on 16th October 1978) specifies the sterling amounts which are to be taken as equivalent to the amounts expressed in gold francs in specified enactments.

SOCIAL SECURITY

Halsbury's Laws of England (3rd edn.), Vol. 27, paras. 897–980, 1187–1570

2659   Accommodation—provision by local authority—charges

The National Assistance (Charges for Accommodation) Regulations 1978, S.I. 1978 No. 1073 (in force on 13th November 1978), increase the minimum weekly amounts which a person is required to pay for accommodation managed by a local authority. The regulations also increase the weekly sum for personal requirements which the local authority will allow in assessing a person's ability to pay for accommodation. The National Assistance (Charges for Accommodation) Regulations, 1977, 1977 Halsbury's Abr para. 2636, were revoked.

2660   Attendance allowance—entitlement—effect of Community legislation on national legislation

See *Re Residence Conditions*, para. 1250.

2661   —— whether deductible from damages for personal injuries

See *Bowker v Rose*, para. 860.

2662   Benefit—computation of earnings

The Social Security Benefit (Computation of Earnings) Regulations 1978, S.I. 1978 No. 1698 (in force on 1st January 1979) consolidate earlier regulations in providing for the way in which the earnings of a person to whom a benefit is or may be payable or of such a person's dependants are to be calculated or estimated for the purposes of the Social Security Act 1975. The Social Security Benefit (Computation of Earnings) Regulations 1974, 1974 Halsbury's Abr para. 3092 and certain other regulations are revoked.

2663   —— married women and widows

The Social Security Pensions (Home Responsibilities and Miscellaneous Amendments) Regulations 1978, S.I. 1978 No. 508 (in force on 6th April 1979) define the expression "precluded from regular employment by responsibilities at home" in para. 5 (6) and (7) of Sch. 3 to the Social Security Act 1975. They also modify or revoke certain provisions of the Social Security (Benefit) (Married Women and Widows Special Provisions) Regulations 1974 and the Social Security Benefit (Married Women and Widows) (Amendments and Transitional Provisions) Regulations 1975 relating to Category A and B retirement pensions, widow's pension and widowed mother's allowance for women whose marriages have terminated.

2664   —— overlapping benefits

The Social Security (Overlapping Benefits) Amendment Regulations 1978, S.I. 1978 No. 524 (in force on 6th April 1979) amend the Social Security (Overlapping Benefits) Regulations 1975 so as to make provision is respect of benefits payable under the Social Security Pensions Act 1975.

2665   The Social Security (Overlapping Benefits) Amendment (No. 2) Regulations 1978, S.I. 1978 No. 1511 (in force on 16th November 1978) amend the Social Security (Overlapping Benefits) Regulations 1975, regulation 2, as amended, so as to provide that where more than one person is entitled to receive an increase in benefit in respect of the same child, priority of entitlement shall be given to the person who has been awarded child benefit in respect of the child for the relevant period.

2666   **—— unemployment, sickness and invalidity**

The Social Security (Unemployment, Sickness and Invalidity Benefit) Amendment Regulations 1978, S.I. 1978 No. 394 (in force on 17th March 1978) amend the Social Security (Unemployment, Sickness and Invalidity Benefit) Regulations 1975, 1975 Halsbury's Abr para. 3117 so as to provide that medical certificates deeming people incapable of work should indicate that absence from work consequential on disease or disablement is for precautionary or convalescent reasons.

2667   The Social Security (Unemployment, Sickness and Invalidity Benefit) Amendment (No. 2) Regulations 1978, S.I. 1978 No. 608 (in force on 15th May 1978), amend the Social Security (Unemployment, Sickness and Invalidity Benefit) Regulations 1975, 1975 Halsbury's Abr para. 3117, by providing that any day on which a payment is received under a scheme set up under the Employment Subsidies Act 1978 is not to be treated as a day of unemployment.

2668   The Social Security (Unemployment, Sickness and Invalidity Benefit) Amendment (No. 3) Regulations 1978 S.I. 1978 No. 1213 (in force on 11th September 1978), further amend the Social Security (Unemployment, Sickness and Invalidity Benefit) Regulations 1975, 1975 Halsbury's Abr para. 3117, so as to include an officer of the Manpower Services Commission as one of the Officers to whom a person claiming unemployment benefit may be required to report by the Secretary of State.

2669   **—— up-rating**

The Social Security Benefits Up-rating Order 1978, S.I. 1978 No. 912 (in force on 13th November 1978), increases with effect from specified dates in the week beginning 13th November 1978 the rates and amounts of the benefits and increases of benefit (except age addition and mobility allowance) specified in the Social Security Act 1975, Sch. 4, Parts I, III, IV, and V. It also alters the rate of graduated retirement benefit under the National Insurance Act 1965, increases the rates laid down in the Industrial Injuries and Diseases (Old Cases) Act 1975 for the maximum weekly rate of lesser incapacity allowance supplementing workmen's compensation and increases the weekly allowance for partial disability under the Industrial Diseases Benefit Scheme.

The Order additionally reduces weekly child benefits under the 1975 Act from 2nd April 1979, see further the Child Benefits and Social Security (Fixing and Adjustment of Rates) Amendment Regulations 1978, para. 2675.

The Social Security Benefits Up-rating Orders 1977, 1977 Halsbury's Abr para. 2638, is revoked.

2670   The Social Security Benefits Up-rating Regulations 1978, S.I. 1978 No. 1128 (in force on 13th November 1978, except reg. 8 which comes into force on 6th April 1979) are made in consequence of the Social Security Benefits Up-rating Order 1978, see para. 2669. They set out circumstances in which the rate of benefit which is awarded before the date from which altered rates become payable is not automatically altered by the Social Security Act 1975, Sch. 14, para. 2. They apply the provisions of the Social Security Benefit (Persons Abroad) Regulations 1975, 1975 Halsbury's Abr para. 3116 to the increases of benefit provided by the Up-rating order. They also amend the Social Security (Unemployment, Sickness and Invalidity Benefit) Regulations 1975, 1975 Halsbury's Abr para. 3117, the Social Security (Non-Contributory Invalidity Pension) Regulations 1975, 1975 Halsbury's Abr para. 3171 and the Social Security (Industrial Injuries) (Benefit) Regulations 1975, 1975 Halsbury's Abr para. 3154, raising the limit on permitted earnings of a person in receipt of benefit. The provisions of the National Insurance Act 1965 ss. 36, 37 relating to graduated retirement benefit are modified.

The Social Security Benefits Up-rating Regulations 1977, 1977 Halsbury's Abr para. 2639 are revoked.

2671 —— —— **review of rates by Secretary of State—reconsideration of previous assessment**

The Secretary of State in accordance with the Social Security Act 1975, s. 125, carried out a review of pensions in order to determine whether they had retained their value in relation to the general level of earnings and prices. In consequence, he made an up-rating order. Later, he undertook another review and, having regard to the changes that had occurred since the first order, made a further up-rating order. The plaintiffs, who were recipients of the pension, brought an action for a declaration that the second order was not made in accordance with the Act. Their action was dismissed and they appealed, contending that on a review following an up-rating order, the Secretary of State was under a duty to ascertain whether the first order had been properly estimated and to make good any under-estimation or loss in value in the subsequent order. *Held*, under the 1975 Act, the Secretary of State's duty on a review was to ascertain whether the previous up-rating order had retained its value from the date it came into force. He had to estimate the general level of earnings and prices in any manner he thought fit. While there was nothing to preclude him considering whether the first order had been under-estimated and compensating for it in the second order, there was no duty on him to do so. In the present case, the second up-rating order had been made with regard to the changes that had occurred since the first order and was therefore valid.

METZGER V DEPARTMENT OF HEALTH AND SOCIAL SECURITY [1978] 3 All ER 753 (Court of Appeal: STAMP, ORR and EVELEIGH LJJ). Decision of Megarry V-C [1977] 3 All ER 444, 1977 Halsbury's Abr para. 2644 affirmed.

2672 —— **widow's benefit and retirement pensions**

The Social Security (Widow's Benefit and Retirement Pensions) Amendment Regulations 1978, S.I. 1978 No. 392 (in force on 6th April 1979) and the Social Security (Widow's Benefit and Retirement Pensions) Regulations 1974, consequential to the Social Security Pensions Act 1975. The amendments relate to elections to be treated as not having retired, increments to retirement pensions for deferred retirement, benefit at reduced rates for those who do not fully satisfy the contribution conditions and, in certain cases, provide for substitution of the contribution record of a former spouse to give title to Category A retirement pension.

2673 **Child benefit**

The Child Benefit (General) Amendment Regulations 1978, S.I. 1978 No. 1275 (in force on 31st August 1978) amend the Child Benefit (General) Regulations 1976 so as to provide that child benefit under the Child Benefit Act 1975 shall not be payable in respect of a child who is receiving financial support under the Employment and Training Act 1973, s 2, or during a period of interruption of full-time education immediately prior to receiving such financial support. The Regulations further provide that a child is to be treated as receiving education by virtue of his employment where he is receiving financial support from his employment is consideration of such education.

2674 —— **claims and questions—amendment**

The Child Benefit (Miscellaneous Amendments) Regulations 1978, S.I. 1978 No. 540 (in force on 5th May 1978), amend the Child Benefit (Determination of Claims and Questions) Regulations 1976, 1976 Halsbury's Abr para 2415, so as to correct an omission from the definition of "special questions" and to clarify both the time for appeals against insurance officers' decisions and the means of ascertaining the date of an application for review of a decision. The regulations also amend the Child Benefit (General) Regulations 1976, 1976 Halsbury's Abr para. 2418, and the Child Benefit (Claims and Payments) Regulations 1976, 1976 Halsbury's Abr para. 2416.

2675 —— **rates**

The Child Benefit and Social Security (Fixing and Adjustment of Rates) Amendment

Regulations 1978, S.I. 1978 No. 914 (in force on 13th November 1978, except reg. 2 (4), which comes into force on 2nd April 1979), provide for higher rates of child benefit under the Child Benefit Act 1975 and Child Benefit and Social Security (Fixing and Adjustment of Rates) Regulations 1976, 1976 Halsbury's Abr para. 2417.

1976 Regulations, reg. 3, dealing with variations and increases in weekly benefits, is revoked in the light of the Social Security Benefits Up-rating Order 1978, see para. 2669.

2676 Contributions

The Social Security (Contributions, Re-rating) Consequential Amendment Regulations 1978, S.I. No. 70 (in force 6th April 1978), further amend the Social Security (Contributions) Regulations 1975, 1975 Halsbury's Abr para. 3126. They increase the percentage rates of primary and secondary Class 1 contributions in respect of serving members of the forces, increase the percentage rate of secondary Class 1 contributions in respect of mariners employed on a foreign-going or partly foreign-going ship, and reduce the special rate of Class 2 contributions payable by share fishermen.

2677   The Social Security (Contributions) Amendment Regulations 1978, S.I. 1978 No. 423 (in force on 6th April 1978) amend the Social Security (Contributions) Regulations 1975, 1975 Halsbury's Abr para.3126. The amendments prescribe the circumstances in which and the amount which an employer may deduct from subsequent earnings in relation to Class 1 contributions underdeducted at the contracted-out employment rate when the employment ceases to be contracted-out. The Regulations also make provision for the refund of Class 1 contributions wrongly paid at the non-contracted-out rate in respect of employment which is contracted-out. There are other minor amendments.

2678   The Social Security (Credits) Amendment and (Earnings Factor) Transitional Regulations 1978, S.I. 1978 No. 409 (in force on 6th April 1978), make minor amendments to the Social Security (Credits) Regulations 1975, 1975 Halsbury's Abr para. 3130, resulting from amendments relating to the satisfaction of contribution conditions and rates of contributions made to the Social Security Act 1975 by the Social Security Pensions Act 1975, 1975 Halsbury's Abr para. 3191. They also make transitional provisions in relation to the derivation of earnings factors from contracted-out contributions for the purposes of Social Security Act 1975, Sch. 3, Part II, para. 8 (satisfaction of contribution conditions in early years of contribution).

2679 —— categorisation of earners

The Social Security (Categorisation of Earners) Amendment Regulations 1978, S.I. 1978 No. 1462 (in force on 3rd November 1978) further amend the Social Security (Categorisation of Earners) Regulations 1975 by substituting a new provision which disregards, for contribution purposes, employment as a returning officer or counting on of persons appointed by such officers for the purpose of any election or referendum authorised by Act of Parliament.

These regulations were subsequently consolidated, see para. 2680.

2680   The Social Security (Categorisation of Earners) Regulations 1978, S.I. 1978 No. 1689 (in force on 27th December 1978), consolidate the Social Security (Categorisation of Earners) Regulations 1975, 1975 Halsbury's Abr para. 3118 and subsequent amending Regulations. The present Regulations provide for persons in certain prescribed employments to be treated for the purposes of the Social Security Act 1975 as falling within another category of earners and provide for certain other prescribed employments to be disregarded. Provision is also made for the circumstances in which employment as a self-employed earner is treated as continuing; and, for prescribed persons to be treated for the purposes of the 1975 Act as Secondary Class I Contributors.

2681   —— destination of contributions

The Social Security (Contributions) Amendment (No. 2) Regulations 1978, S.I. 1978 No. 821 (in force on 1st July 1978), modify Social Security Act 1975, s. 134 (4) by providing that no allocation is to be made to the Maternity Pay Fund from secondary Class I contributions paid in respect of members of the forces.

2682   —— earnings limits

The Social Security (Contributions) (Earnings Limits) Amendment Regulations 1978, S.I. 1978 No. 1669 (in force on 6th April 1979) further amend the Social Security (Contributions) Regulations 1975, 1975 Halsbury's Abr para. 3127, by substituting new lower and upper earnings limits for Class 1 of £19·50 and £135·00 respectively for the tax year beginning 6th April 1979.

2683   —— earnings related contributions

The Social Security (Contributions) Amendment (No. 3) Regulations 1978, S.I. 1978 No. 1703 (regulations 1, 3 and 4 in force on 4th January 1979, regulation 2 in force on 6th April 1979) further amend the Social Security (Contributions) Regulations 1975, 1975 Halsbury's Abr para. 3126, by providing that a payment to defray or a contribution towards travelling expenses paid to a disabled person under the Disabled Persons (Employment) Act 1944, s. 15 and earnings derived from a profit-sharing scheme to which the Finance Act 1978, para. 2312, applies are to be disregarded for the purposes of earnings-related contributions. They also except divers and diving supervisors in employment to which the Finance Act 1978, para. 2312, applies from class 4 contributions.

2684   —— mariners

The Social Security (Contributions) (Mariners) Amendment Regulations 1978, S.I. 1978 No. 1877 (in force on 6th April 1979), further amend the Social Security (Contributions) Regulations 1975, 1975 Halsbury's Abr para. 3126. They provide for mariners employed on British ships to be treated as employed earners and, in relation to them, excludes the provision that the person by whom the mariner's earnings are paid or the owner of the ship should have a place of business in Great Britain. Transitional provisions relating to mariners, which are spent, are revoked and new provision is made for the calculation of earnings-related contributions payable by mariners in respect of a voyage period which falls partly in two or more tax years. Provision is also made as to the tax years in respect of which contributions paid in respect of the voyage period may be treated as paid.

2685   —— re-rating

The Social Security (Contributions, Re-rating) Order 1978, S.I. 1978 No. 1840 (in force on 6th April 1979), substitutes increased rates of Class 2 and 3 contributions payable under the Social Security Act 1975, 1975 Halsbury's Abr para. 3187. The upper and lower limits of profits between which Class 4 contributions are payable and the amount of earnings below which an earner may be exempted from liability for Class 2 contributions are raised.

2686   In a written parliamentary reply the national insurance contribution rate increases for 1979/80 have been announced. The employee Class 1 contribution (not contracted out) rate remains at 6·5 per cent but the upper limit of reckonable earnings will be increased from £120 per week to £135. This increase will also affect the employer's contribution (which will remain at 10 per cent excluding the surcharge). The new upper limit will also be applied to contracted-out Class 1 contributions. Class 2 (self-employed) contributions will rise from £1·90 per week to £2·10 but the small earnings exemption will be increased to £1050 per annum. See The Times, 23rd November 1978.

2687 —— **special annual maximum**

The Social Security (Contributions) (Special Annual Maximum) Regulations 1978, S.I. 1978 No. 410 (in force on 6th April 1978) prescribe a special annual maximum of primary Class 1 contributions payable at the rate of 6·5 per cent in respect of employment which is not contracted-out employment by earners who reach pensionable age in the year ending 5th April 1979. The Regulations also provide for the repayment of amounts paid in excess of the special maximum, and for disregarding such repayment for the purposes of the annual maximum of Class 4 and special Class 4 contributions.

2688 **Distribution of income and wealth—effect on living standards of the poor**

Contrary to what has been suggested, the poor people in Britain are not becoming poorer. Over the last fifteen years the living standards of the poorest people have stayed stable. This has been largely due to changing social policies which have resulted in higher social security payments and lower tax rates: Royal Commission on the Distribution of Income and Wealth: Sixth Report, Times, 25th May 1978.

2689 **Family income supplement—qualifications**

To qualify for family-income supplement, the man in the family or the single mother must be normally engaged in work for not less than 30 hours in a week. In a written reply to a question, the Secretary of State for Social Services has stated that regulations will be introduced to take effect in April 1979 to reduce the number of hours to 24 which a lone parent must normally work each week to qualify for family income supplement (The Times, 8th November 1978).

2690 —— **rates—increase**

The Family Income Supplements (Computation) Regulations 1978, S.I. 1978 No. 1137 (in force on 14th November 1978) raise the income level below which the supplement is paid to £46.00 for a family with one child plus £4.00 for each additional child. They also provide that the maximum weekly rate of benefit shall not exceed £10.50 for a family with one child plus £1.00 for each additional child.

The Family Income Supplements (Computation) (No. 2) Regulations 1977, 1977 Halsbury's Abr para. 2671, are revoked.

2691 **Industrial injury—prescribed diseases—occupational deafness**

National Insurance Commissioner's decision:

R (I) 1/78 (claim for industrial disablement benefit in respect of occupational deafness; claimant employed from 1938 to 1961 and from 1965 to date of claim in 1976 as boiler engineer; required to use pneumatic percussive tools on fittings for boilers made of rough cast metal requiring finishing; claimant entitled to benefit although use of tools diminished since 1965; as conditions for prescription of disease do not specify any degree of frequency of use of prescribed tools in prescribed processes, degree must be such that claimant's occupation might reasonably be described as involving use of such tools in one or more of prescribed processes and use must not be so infrequent as to be negligible).

2692 —— **special hardship allowance—meaning of regular occupation**

A miner was diagnosed as suffering from pneumoconiosis in 1959 and a medical board found him able to work in approved dust conditions. In 1975 the miner gave up working as a faceworker and took another underground job at a lower wage. He claimed a special hardship allowance under the Social Security Act 1975, s. 60, which was refused. He applied for an order of certiorari to quash that decision. *Held* under s. 60 (1) (a) an applicant had to show that he was incapable of following his regular occupation; "regular occupation" referred only to the generality of the occupation under any conditions, and did not include any restrictions such as having to work in approved dust conditions. The applicant satisfied this condition as he could only work in dust-free conditions. Under s. 60 (1) (b) he had to show that he was incapable of following employment of an equivalent standard. Since the applicant could carry on as a miner in dust-free conditions, he failed to satisfy that condition and the application would be refused.

R v NATIONAL INSURANCE COMMISSIONERS, EX PARTE STEEL [1978] 3 All ER 78 (Queen's Bench Division; LORD WIDGERY CJ, WIEN and KENNETH JONES JJ).

2693 Invalidity benefit

See paras. 2666–2668.

2694 —— entitlement—claim made in another EEC member state

See *Re An Italian Claimant*, para. 1251.

2695 —— —— claimant not totally incapacitated for work

National Insurance Commissioner's decision:

R (S) 2/78 (former furniture salesman aged forty-eight suffered from osteo-arthritis of the spine and hypertension; received sickness or invalidity benefit continuously from 23rd August 1976; in January and February 1977 he was examined by medical officers who concluded that he was incapable of work at his former occupation but capable of work within specified limits; claimant had failed to prove that in February and March 1977 he was incapable of work which he could reasonably be expected to do within Social Security Act 1975, s. 17 (1) (a) (ii); not too early to consider whether claimant capable of alternative work other than his normal occupation; invalidity benefit thus not payable for that period).

2696 —— non-contributory invalidity pension

The Social Security (Non-Contributory Invalidity Pension) Amendment Regulations 1978, S.I. 1978 No. 1340 (in force 13th September 1978), amend the 1975 Regulations, 1975 Halsbury's Abr para. 3171 by specifying not only the circumstances in which a woman is to be treated as incapable of performing normal household duties but also the circumstances in which she is to be treated as not incapable of performing such duties.

2697

The Social Security (Non-Contributory Invalidity Pension) Amendment (No. 2) Regulations 1978, S.I. 1978 No. 1845 (in force on 5th January 1979), amend the Social Security (Non-Contributory Invalidity Pension) Regulations 1975, 1975 Halsbury's Abr para. 3171, reg. 4 (2), which relates to days for which persons are to be regarded as incapable of work, so as to provide an exception to the requirement that in determining whether a person has been incapable of work for 196 consecutive days, a day is not to be treated as one on which he was incapable of work if he was absent from Great Britain. The exception applies if during the period of 196 days there were at least 168 days on which he was present in Great Britain.

2698 —— —— entitlement—days of incapacity

The claimant had suffered from poliomyelitis since infancy and had never been able to work. In 1975, for health reasons he went to the West Indies until 3rd December of that year. On the 20th of November 1975, a new long-term non-contributory invalidity pension was introduced. To qualify for it, the Social Security Act 1975, s. 36, provided that a claimant had to be incapable of work on the day he made his claim as well as for 196 consecutive days immediately preceding that day. However, by the Social Security (Non-Contributory Invalidity Pension) Regulations 1975, reg. 4 (2) Halsbury's Abridgment 1975 para. 3171, a day on which a claimant was absent from Great Britain did not rank as a day of incapacity. It was decided by the National Insurance Commissioner that reg. 4 (2) was ultra vires the Secretary of State so that the claimant was entitled to benefit from 20th November 1975 notwithstanding his absence from Britain during that time. The national insurance officer applied to quash that decision. *Held*, the Secretary of State had sufficiently wide regulation-making powers to empower her to make reg. 4 (2). The regulation was thus intra vires the Secretary of State and valid, so the National Insurance Commissioner had been wrong in upholding the claimant's entitlement to benefit from 20th November 1975. Accordingly, his decision would be quashed.

R v NATIONAL INSURANCE COMMISSIONER, EX PARTE FLEETWOOD (1978) 122 Sol Jo 146 (Queen's Bench Division: LORD WIDGERY CJ, WIEN and KENNETH JONES JJ).

2699   —— —— incapacity to work—officer's discretion

The Social Security (Unemployment, Sickness and Invalidity Benefit) Regulations 1975, reg. 3 (1), provide that a person who is not incapable of work may be deemed to be incapable of work by reason of some specific disease or bodily or mental disablement for any day on which certain requirements are met. A national insurance commissioner had held that the word "may" in reg. 3 (1) was equivalent to "must"; thus he had no discretion to find that a claimant who had fullfilled the requirements of the regulation was not to be deemed to be incapable of work. The Department of Health and Social Security sought an order of certiorari to quash the decision. *Held*, the word "may" was to be construed in its literal meaning, thus conferring on those who decided whether an invalidity pension was payable a discretion to decide whether or not an individual was incapable of work, even though he fulfilled all the requirements of the regulation.

R v NATIONAL INSURANCE COMMISSIONER, EX PARTE DEPARTMENT OF HEALTH AND SOCIAL SECURITY (1978) 122 Sol Jo 812 (Queen's Bench Division: LORD WIDGERY CJ, WIEN and SMITH JJ).

2700   Invalidity pension

The Social Security (Widow's and Widower's Invalidity Pensions) Regulations 1978, S.I. 1978 No. 529 (in force on 6th April 1979) make provision for providing rates of invalidity pension and Catetory A retirement pension to certain classes of widows and widowers to whom ss. 15 and 16 of the Social Security Pensions Act 1975 apply. They also prescribe periods in connection with entitlement to benefit under s. 16.

2701   Miscellaneous provisions

The Social Security (Miscellaneous Amendments) Regulations 1978, S.I. 1978 No. 433 (in force on 3rd April 1978) contain miscellaneous amendments to regulations made, or having effect as made, under the Social Security Act 1975, 1975 Halsbury's Abr para. 3187. The amendments relate to dependency benefit and child benefit, the prescribed times for claiming dependency benefit, and the circumstances in which a person is to be treated as entitled to child benefit during temporary periods of residence. The regulations also include minor and drafting amendments and revocations.

2702   Mobility allowance—payment to someone other than benefici- ary—Motability arrangements

The Mobility Allowance (Motability Payment Arrangements) Regulations 1978, S.I. 1978 No. 1131 (in force on 31st August 1978), prescribe the circumstances in which mobility allowance may be paid to someone other than the beneficiary where that beneficiary is provided with a vehicle under arrangements made by the charitable organisation known as "Motability".

2703   —— up-rating

The Mobility Allowance Up-rating Order 1978, S.I. 1978 No. 475 (in force on 5th July 1978), increases the weekly mobility allowance payable under the Social Security Act 1975, Sch. 4, as amended, from £7 to £10.

2704   —— vehicle scheme beneficiary

The Mobility Allowance (Vehicle Scheme Beneficiaries) Amendment Regulations 1978, S.I. 1978 No. 743 (in force on 26th May 1978), amend the Mobility Allowance (Vehicle Scheme Beneficiaries) Regulations 1977, 1977 Halsbury's Abr para. 2687 by providing that a vehicle scheme beneficiary includes certain persons who have been provided with or have applied for an invalid carriage or other vehicle, being a power driven road vehicle controlled by the occupant.

2705   —— whether deductible from damages for personal injuries

See *Bowker v Rose*, para. 860.

2706   National insurance commissioners—pensions

See paras. 2101–2103.

2707   Pensions

See PENSIONS.

2708   Retirement benefit—deferred retirement graduated benefit

The Social Security (Graduated Retirement Benefit) Regulations 1978, S.I. 1978 No. 391 (in force on 5th April 1978) make provision for certain people who, on 5th April 1975, had rights or prospective rights to graduated retirement benefit under the National Insurance Act 1965, ss. 36, 37 and who have deferred their retirement beyond pensionable age. Where a person has deferred his retirement beyond pensionable age all graduated contributions paid by him in the year in which he attained that age are to be treated as if they had been paid earlier. The Regulations preserve the entitlement of a woman who has been widowed more than once and who has deferred her retirement beyond pensionable age to receive additional graduated retirement in respect of a former husband.

2709   The Social Security (Graduated Retirement Benefit) (No. 2) Regulations 1978, S.I. 1978 No. 393 (regs. 1 and 2 in force on 6th April 1978; remainder for purposes specified in reg. 1 (3) on 6th December 1978; and for all other purposes on 6th April 1979) revoke the Social Security (Graduated Retirement Benefit) Regulations 1975 and contain provision for the continuance in force of ss. 36 and 37 of the National Insurance Act 1965 and related regulations. These regulations also provide that the Social Security Act 1975, ss. 124–126 relating to increases in rates of benefit apply to graduated retirement benefit.

2710   Sickness benefit

See paras. 2666–2668.

2711   —— entitlement—disqualifying act by worker outside United Kingdom

National Insurance Commissioner's decision:

KENNY V INSURANCE OFFICER [1978] 1 CMLR 181 (Irish national claimed sickness benefit in England; whole period of illness spent in prison or hospital in Ireland; claimant not disqualified by absence from United Kingdom due to EEC Council Regulation 1408/71, art 22; person in prison or detained in custody disqualified from benefit by National Insurance Act 1965, s. 49 (1) (b); although in hospital, claimant still in prison or custody; only imprisonment or detention in Great Britain disqualifying act under s. 49 (1) (b); reference to European Court of Justice to determine whether, notwithstanding Regulation 1408/71, arts. 19 or 22, member state could treat act by Community national in different member state as disqualifying act when it would be disqualifying act in its own territory and ground for withholding benefit).

For decision of European Court see para. 1264.

2712 —— —— **person taken ill outside the United Kingdom**

National Insurance Commissioner's decision:

R (S) 1/78 (claimant had records of contributions in United Kingdom as employed person, then as self-employed person, then as non-employed person; in March 1975, while non-employed, went to France on holiday; injured and remained incapable of work till May 1975, when returned to England; claimed sickness benefit for period he was in France; claimant entitled to benefit since prior to coming into force of Social Security Act 1975 on 5th April 1975 he was a "worker" within EEC Council Regulation 1408/71, art. 1 (a) (ii), as a person compulsorily insured under a social security scheme; after that date, claimant's insurance as non-employed person ceased to be compulsory and became voluntary and he was a "worker" under art. 1 (a) (iii) as a person voluntarily insured under a social security scheme). *Brack v Insurance Officer* [1976] ECR 1429, ECJ, 1976 Halsbury's Abr para. 1159 and *Decision R (S) 2/77*, 1977 Halsbury's Abr para. 2698 applied.

2713 **Social Security Pensions Act 1975—commencement**

The Social Security Pensions Act 1975 (Commencement No. 12) Order 1978, S.I. 1978 No. 367, brings provisions relating to mobility allowance into force for persons born on or after 14th January 1921 but before 2nd February 1922 and for persons born on or after 21st December 1919, but before 14th January 1921. The days appointed for the coming into force of ss. 22, 65 (part) and Sch. 4 (part) for the purpose of making claims for and the determination of claims and questions relating to mobility allowance is 7th June 1978 in relation to the former class of persons and 20th September 1978 in relation to the latter. For all other purposes the days appointed are 6th September 1978 in relation to the former and 20th December 1978 in relation to the latter.

2714 **Supplementary benefit**

The Supplementary Benefits (General) Amendment Regulations 1978, S.I. 1978 No. 1459 (in force on 13th November 1978) further amend the Supplementary Benefits (General) Regulations 1977. The amendments make changes in respect of the day when changes in the amount of, or terminations of entitlement to, benefit take effect, and include the Manpower Services Commission among the bodies with which a person may register for employment within the meaning of the 1977 Regulations.

2715 —— **application for increase as "householder"—whether applicant a "householder"**

The tenant of a house, who had agreed not to assign or sub-let or part with possession, allowed the two applicants to live in the house on payment of £8 per week each. The applicants claimed increased allowances as householders in respect of supplementary benefit under the Supplementary Benefits Act 1976, Sch. 1, para. 11(1) (a). *Held*, the mere fact that a sub-tenancy was unlawful did not mean that the sub-tenant was not a householder. However, since the tenant had no right to sub-let, it was reasonable to assume that the applicants were licensees or guests or friends and were thus not householders. The applications would be dismissed.

HOLLAND v SOUTH LONDON SUPPLEMENTARY BENEFITS APPEAL TRIBUNAL (1978) 122 Sol Jo 626 (Court of Appeal: LORD DENNING MR, GEOFFREY LANE and EVELEIGH LJJ).

2716 —— **cost of running electrical aids for handicapped person—whether cost a medical requirement—discretion of tribunal**

The husband of a woman suffering from multiple sclerosis applied to the Department of Health and Social Security for special payments towards the cost of running electrical equipment provided for her use. The application was refused by a tribunal on the ground that the provision of electricity was a medical requirement excluded by the Supplementary Benefits Act 1976, s. 1 (3). The claimant applied for an order of certiorari to quash the decision. *Held*, the tribunal should have considered each item of equipment for the running of which assistance was sought before it had generically termed the requirements medical requirements. Not to have done so was an error of law. In any event, the tribunal had an ultimate discretion to make exceptional payments under the 1976 Act, Sch. 1, para. 4, which it should have considered exercising. Accordingly, the order sought would be granted.

R v WEST LONDON SUPPLEMENTARY BENEFITS APPEAL TRIBUNAL EX PARTE WYATT [1978] 2 All ER 315 (Queen's Bench Division; LORD WIDGERY CJ, PARK and MAY JJ).

The 1976 Act consolidated the Supplementary Benefits Act 1966 and related enactments.

2717 —— determination of requirements

The Supplementary Benefits (Determination of Requirements) Regulations 1978, S.I. 1978 No. 913 (in force on 13th November 1978), vary the provisions relating to the calculation of requirements contained in the Supplementary Benefits Act 1976, Sch. 1, Part II.

2718 —— entitlement—salary in advance during strike—whether constituting "resources"

During a firemen's strike, a fire officer applied for supplementary benefit for his family. His salary was paid on the fifteenth day of every month for the whole month. His salary for November was paid to him on 15th November, the day after he went on strike. The Supplementary Benefits Commission refused to grant him an allowance before 15th December. Its decision was upheld by the Supplementary Benefits Appeal Tribunal on the ground that he was not entitled to it any earlier because the salary he received in November constituted his resources for the period ending 14th December as it was the money which he would have had to use if he had not gone on strike. The officer appealed, contending that part of the sum had not been earned as it had been repaid to his employers at a later date because of the strike. *Held*, the question was whether the officer had resources to maintain his family for the first two weeks of December. The Supplementary Benefits Act 1976, Sch. 1, Part III showed that one's "resources" were composed of three elements; capital, earnings and other income such as child benefits. It could not be said that the salary fell into either the category of "capital" or "other income." Neither could the salary be treated as earnings as they were a product of a man's work and the money in question was not earned as it had been repaid at a later stage. The tribunal ought to have disregarded the officer's salary received over the strike period when it determined his resources for the purposes of supplementary benefit. Accordingly, its decision would be quashed.

R v BOLTON SUPPLEMENTARY BENEFITS APPEAL TRIBUNAL, EX PARTE FORDHAM (1978) Times, 28th November (Queen's Bench Division: SHEEN J). *R v Preston Supplementary Benefits Appeal Tribunal, ex parte Moore* [1975] 2 All ER 207, CA, 1975 Halsbury Abr para. 3202 applied.

2719 —— resources—wages paid in arrears

A student received a week's supplementary benefit payment during his first week of employment, because he was paid his wages a week in arrears. On terminating his employment and receiving his final week's wages plus holiday pay, he made another claim for benefit, which the Supplementary Benefit Commission refused on the grounds that he had sufficient resources. The claimant appealed to a tribunal who held that he should be paid benefit for the two weeks immediately following his claim on the basis that the final week's wages paid by his employer should not be taken into account as resources. The Commission appealed. *Held*, allowing the appeal, the decision of the tribunal was wrong in law. The purpose of supplementary benefit was to provide financial support to those in need. In deciding whether an individual was in need, his capital resources over £1200 and his income from earnings or investment had to be taken into account. In this case the claimant's wages and holiday pay fell into the latter category. The claimant had received benefit during his first week of employment, because his wages were paid in arrears, but he could not expect benefit during the two weeks following the termination of that employment as he had resources in excess of £11·35 per week.

R v SUPPLEMENTARY BENEFITS COMMISSION, EX PARTE RILEY (1978) 123 Sol Jo 80 (Queen's Bench Division: SHEEN J).

2720 Unemployment benefit

See paras. 2666–2668.

2721 —— claims and payments

The Social Security (Claims and Payments) (Unemployment Benefit Transitory Provisions) Amendment Regulations 1978, S.I. 1978 No. 1000 (in force on 1st September 1978), amend the Social Security (Claims and Payments) (Unemployment Benefit Transitory Provisions) Regulations 1977, 1977 Halsbury's Abr para. 2720, so as to increase to two years the period during which claims for unemployment benefit may be made at specified unemployment benefit offices for a period falling partly after the date on which the claim is made.

2722 —— entitlement—absence abroad

National Insurance Commissioner's decisions:

Decision CU 13/77: RE SEARCH FOR WORK IN IRELAND [1978] 2 CMLR 174 (claimant for unemployment benefit, registered as unemployed at a British office, went to Ireland for five days to look for work and missed signing-on day at unemployment benefit office; insurance officer contended claimant disqualified from receiving benefit because not available for employed earner's employment during absence; claimant entitled to benefit by virtue of EEC Council Regulation 1408/71, art. 69, which enabled a person registered as unemployed in one member state to retain right to benefit if he went to another member state to look for work; requirement that he signed on at office of place where he went within seven days; claimant failed to sign on in Ireland but did not lose benefit since he returned home before expiry of seven-day period).

2723

Decision CU 4/78: RE AN ABSENCE IN GERMANY [1978] 2 CMLR 603 (claimant registered as unemployed in England; informed unemployment benefit office of intention to seek work in W. Germany; not informed of right to claim unemployment benefit while abroad and advised to sign off register; on return, claimed benefit for period of absence; not entitled to benefit since he had not signed on with German employment services as required by EEC Council Regulation 1408/71, art. 69; requirement mandatory; irrelevant that reason for not doing so was due to wrong advice given by authorities).

2724 —— —— days of unemployment

National Insurance Commissioner's decisions:

R (U) 3/77 (claimant while in full-time employment also owned share in a farm on which there were three cottages let to ordinary tenants; farm was run by employee and claimant's wife, claimant working at weekends and early mornings; claimant became unemployed and sought unemployment benefit for period of unemployment during which he continued working on the farm to broadly same extent as before; claimant was entitled to benefit under Social Security (Unemployment, Sickness and Invalidity) Regulations 1975, 1975 Halsbury's Abr para. 3117, reg. 7 (1) (h), as he satisfied all conditions including condition of consistency with full-time employment, since he worked on farm no more than he had done when employed; daily earnings did not exceed 75p after deducting rents of cottages, since they were let separately and were not part of farming business).

R (U) 4/77 (claim for unemployment benefit in respect of period in which claimant ran gift shop with wife; claimed period should be treated as days of unemployment under Social Security (Unemployment, Sickness and Invalidity

Benefit) Regulations 1975, 1975 Halsbury's Abr para. 3117, reg. 7 (1) (h); claimant satisfied conditions that he remain available for full-time employment and that his employment in shop was not employed earner's employment; failed to satisfy earnings condition in part as earnings exceeded 75p per day in six out of fourteen weeks; consistency condition was satisfied as employment in shop was consistent with full-time employment elsewhere since as part proprietor of shop he could do as much or as little work as he thought fit; thus entitled to benefit except for weeks in which daily earnings exceeded 75p).

R (U) 6/77 (claim for unemployment benefit for a period of sixty-four days in which claimant attended meetings of a local authority of which he was a member; for each attendance he received an attendance allowance of £5 or £10; on days in question, claimant was engaged to a significant extent in employment, therefore days were not days of unemployment; employment could not be disregarded under Social Security (Unemployment, Sickness and Invalidity Benefit) Regulations 1975, 1975 Halsbury's Abr para. 3117, reg. 7 (1) (h), because attendance allowance constituted earnings derived from next employment and exceeded 75p per day; therefore benefit not payable).

2725   —— —— overlapping benefits

National Insurance Commissioner's decision:

Decision CU 14/77: RE AN IRISH WIDOW [1978] 2 CMLR 178 (claimant for unemployment benefit in Great Britain already entitled to widow's pension under Irish law; claim disallowed on ground that payments were overlapping and EEC Council Regulation 1408/71, art. 12 (2), provided that legislative provisions of a member state for reduction of benefit in cases of overlapping with other social security benefits might be invoked even though the right to such benefit was acquired under the legislation of another member state; provisions in the legislation of one member state for reduction of benefit in cases of plurality only applied by virtue of art. 12 (2) of the regulation to insured persons if they were in receipt of benefits acquired through the application of that regulation; thus art. 12 (2) did not operate to reduce benefits obtained under the national law of a member state without recourse to the regulation; claimant thus entitled to unemployment benefit without adjustment under rules on overlapping benefits).

2726   —— —— receipt of special payment—whether payment a bar to unemployment benefit

A member of the Armed Forces received a special capital payment on the termination of his employment in 1975 due to compulsory redundancy. When he subsequently applied for unemployment benefit, it was held by the Chief National Insurance Commissioner that the said payment disqualified him from entitlement to unemployment benefit for a year after the termination of his employment under the Social Security (Unemployment, Sickness and Invalidity Benefit) Regulations 1975, reg. 7 (1) (d). 1975 Halsbury's Abr para. 3117, which provides that a day shall not be treated as a day of unemployment if it is a day in respect of which a person receives a payment in lieu of, inter alia, the remuneration which he would have received for that day had his employment not been terminated. An application was made to quash the decision of the Chief National Insurance Commissioner. *Held*, the question to be considered was whether the payment had been made in lieu of the remuneration the officer would have received for that period had his employment not been terminated. In the Armed Services the special payment was based on factors which were not susceptible of precise evaluation such as the loss of a way of life and chosen profession. The payment was a composite one and while it possibly contained an element of payment in lieu of remuneration, the extent of that element was speculative and unascertainable. Therefore the redundancy payment was not a payment in lieu of the remuneration he would have received for some specified period within reg. 7 (1) (d) and the officer was entitled to unemployment benefit. The application would be granted.

R v NATIONAL INSURANCE COMMISSIONER, EX PARTE STRATTON [1978] 1 WLR 1041 (Queen's Bench Division: LORD WIDGERY CJ, MELFORD STEVENSON and CANTLEY JJ).

2727   —— —— **satisfaction of contribution conditions**

National Insurance Commissioner's decision:

RE WORK IN GERMANY [1978] 2 CMLR 169 (claim in United Kingdom for unemployment benefit; claimant working in Germany throughout relevant contribution period and had paid German contributions but no British ones; question was whether contribution conditions for benefit were satisfied, which under Social Security Act 1975, s. 93 (1) (b), fell to be determined by Secretary of State; preliminary questions of EEC law arising, on which answer to basic contribution question might well be based, were also questions relating to a person's contributions within s. 93 (1) (b); they were thus to be dealt with by the Secretary of State in his determination of the question and not by the statutory authorities).

2728   —— —— **whether disqualified due to trade dispute**

National Insurance Commissioner's decision:

R (U) 5/77 (claimants employed at power station claimed free provision of protective clothing by employer, who refused; HM Factory Inspectorate advised that provision of clothing was not a specific requirement of Health and Safety at Work etc. Act 1974 but an arrangement for welfare within s. 2 (2) (e); breakdown of negotiations led to withdrawal of labour and stoppage of work; in claim for unemployment benefit, claimants contended that dispute was not a trade dispute within Social Security Act 1975, s. 19 (2) (b), as it was not connected with terms or conditions of employment but with statutory provisions of 1974 Act; 1974 Act imposed obligations and conferred rights which were connected with the employment or the conditions of employment of the employees; any dispute concerning such obligations and rights was thus by definition a trade dispute; stoppage was due to a trade dispute and claimants not entitled to benefit).

2729   —— **forward disallowance—grounds for imposition**

National Insurance Commissioner's decision:

R(U) 1/78 (short-time working in claimant's normal full-time employment caused alternate Mondays and Fridays to be non-working days for him; on one Monday he worked for two hours as a table-tennis coach at a youth centre, for which he was paid £3.23 per hour; unemployment benefit was not payable for that day as he was engaged in employment from which his earnings exceeded 75p; however, there was no sufficiently continuing feature in the grounds of disallowance to justify the imposition of a forward disallowance for other days under Social Security (Claims and Payments) Regulations 1975, 1975 Halsbury's Abr para. 3125).

2730   **Welfare food**

See para. 2733.

2731   **Workmen's compensation—scheme**

The Workmen's Compensation (Supplementation) (Amendment) Scheme 1978, S.I. 1978 No. 1460 (in force on 15th November 1978) amends the Workmen's Compensation (Supplementation) Scheme 1966 by making adjustments to the intermediate rates of lesser incapacity allowance consequential upon the increase in the maximum rate of that allowance made by the Social Security Benefits Up-rating Order 1978.

SOCIAL WELFARE

2732   **Article**

The Government and the Voluntary Sector: A Consultative Document (government's proposed review of the relationship between the statutory and voluntary sectors in the field of social welfare).

2733   Welfare food

The Welfare Food (Amendment) Order 1978, S.I. 1978 No. 269 (in force on 3rd April 1978) and the Welfare Food (Amendment No. 2) Order 1978, S.I. 1978, No. 1786 (in force on 15th January 1979) further amend the Welfare Food Order 1977, S.I. 1977 No. 25, 1977 Halsbury's Abr para. 1016, as amended.

SOLICITORS

Halsbury's Laws of England (3rd edn.), Vol. 36, paras. 1–358

2734   Articles

The Duty Solicitor Scheme: Distribution of Criminal Work, Philip A. Thomas and Penny Smith (a survey carried out in Cardiff to see whether the scheme has led to a redistribution of criminal work): 128 NLJ 324.

Finance and Investment (a selection of articles on the management of solicitors' offices and accounts, and the provision of financial and investment advice by solicitors): NLJ supplement, 2nd November 1978

Remuneration: Solicitors in Private Practice (extracts from the Law Society's Remuneration Survey of all solicitors in private practice): 128 NLJ 398.

Research as a Way to Improve the Quality of Legal Work, Michael Zander: 128 NLJ 576.

Who Speaks for Solicitors?, S. P. Best: 128 NLJ 1060.

Who Speaks for Solicitors? Who Indeed! Graham Lee (defence of the Law Society): 128 NLJ 1084.

2735   Advertising—relaxation of prohibition—form of advertising to be allowed

Law Societies in England and Wales are to be allowed to publish information about individual firms in local newspapers, according to a Parliamentary answer given by the Minister of State for Prices and Consumer Protection. New entrants to the profession, and firms establishing new branches, will also be allowed to make appropriate announcements.

Similar provisions will apply in Scotland.

2736   Articled clerk—articles containing covenant in restraint of trade—validity of covenant

An articled clerk's articles contained a covenant that he would not practise the profession of a solicitor at any place in the Borough of Ealing for a three year period following the expiry of the articles. He left his principal on the expiry of his articles and was offered employment with a firm of solicitors close to one of his principal's offices. He then offered an undertaking that he would not be concerned with clients of the principal's firm, apart from a few of his own personal clients, for the following three years. The principal did not accept his undertaking and obtained an interim injunction restraining him from practising in the area until the trial of the action. On appeal, *held*, from the facts it appeared that the clause was too wide. The Borough covered twenty-one square miles and to restrain the former articled clerk from competing for three years in that large and populated area might be in restraint of trade. On the balance of convenience, the principal should accept the undertaking. The injunction would be discharged and the matter could still go to trial.

RICHARDS v LEVY (1978) 122 Sol Jo 713 (Court of Appeal: LORD DENNING MR, SHAW and BRANDON LJJ).

2737   Authority—authority to conclude contracts—exchange of contracts by telephone

See *Domb v Isoz*, para. 2430.

2738   Conduct in court—finding of deliberate lying—finding based on evidence of one witness alone—whether finding satisfactory

A solicitor who was seriously unwell and who was the defendant in an action, opposed the adjournment of the hearing to a particular day claiming that it had been set aside for a very important meeting. At a later date he was cross-examined on whether the meeting ever took place. He named a particular person as being present at the meeting and also said that a colleague present had no recollection of it. The person named testified that no meeting had been arranged with him or held on the day in question. He had been out of the country at the time. On an application to the court under the Solicitor's Act 1974, ss. 50 and 51 the solicitor was found guilty of deliberately lying to the court and ordered to be struck off. On appeal *held*, the requirement in the Perjury Act 1911, s. 13 that there should be no conviction for perjury on the evidence of one witness alone was in accordance with the long-standing practice of the common law. It would not be proper to convict the solicitor of perjury or its equivalent on the evidence of the one witness. The solicitor's statement regarding his colleague's lack of recollection of the meeting was hearsay and could not be corroboration. The appeal would be allowed.

RE A SOLICITOR (1978) 122 Sol Jo 264 (Court of Appeal: LORD DENNING MR, ORR and BRIDGE LJJ).

2739   Costs—taxation—whether fees greater than maximum scale allowable

Solicitors submitted a bill for costs for taxation in respect of a case heard in the Court of Appeal. The amount allowed was greater than the maximum set down by the scale contained in RSC Ord. 62, Appendix 2, Pt V, but considerably less than the sum claimed. The solicitors applied for a review of the taxation. *Held*, a review of the scale was in progress because inflation had rendered the fees allowed under it too low. Until that review had been completed assessment should be left to the registrars. There was authority for allowing fees above the maximum contained in the scale.

MARTIN V MARTIN [1978] LS Gaz R 589 (Family Division: PAYNE J). *Smith v Church of Scientology* (1972) (unreported) applied.

2740   Disciplinary proceedings—unbefitting conduct—criminal trial—attempt to pervert the course of justice

During a criminal trial involving charges of conspiracy to live on immoral earnings and related offences a solicitor acting for one of the defendants arranged for the defendant's uncle to be placed in the well of the court among the solicitors. Subsequently the prosecution complained to the Solicitors Disciplinary Tribunal alleging that the uncle had been placed in such a position that some of the prosecution witnesses were put in fear and unable to give their evidence frankly. The tribunal found the solicitor guilty of conduct unbefitting a solicitor and struck him off. On appeal *held*, the tribunal's finding that the incident although apparently trivial was in reality an attempt to pervert the course of justice, involved no error or misdirection. The application for leave to appeal would be refused.

RE A SOLICITOR (1978) Times, 31st January (Court of Appeal: LORD DENNING MR, ORMROD and GEOFFREY LANE LJJ).

2741   Duty of care—attestation of will

Canada

A solicitor drew up a will for a testator. Under the provisions of the will, the plaintiff was the residuary beneficiary. The plaintiff and his wife were present when the testator executed the will. They both gave evidence that the solicitor had requested the plaintiff's wife to witness the will despite the fact that she had asked whether it was possible for her, as a beneficiary's spouse, to do so. Following the testator's death, the gift to the plaintiff was declared void. The plaintiff sued the solicitor in negligence. *Held*, the solicitor had failed to exercise the reasonable degree of skill and knowledge to be expected from a lawyer undertaking to supervise the execution of a will. He was liable to the plaintiff in damages for the difference between the amount which the plaintiff received under the intestacy rules and what he would have received, not under the terms of the will but, had a petition under the Canadian counterpart of the Inheritance (Provision for Family and Dependants) Act 1975 been heard.

WHITTINGHAM V CREASE & CO [1978] 5 WWR 45 (Supreme Court of British Columbia). *Hedley Byrne & Co Ltd v Heller & Partners Ltd* [1963] 2 All ER 575, applied.

2742   —— delay—liability of solicitor

Solicitors took six months to obtain counsel's opinion over a pending action which was subsequently dismissed for want of prosecution. Some of the delay was caused by the solicitors themselves and some by counsel. Their clients, the plaintiffs in the action, claimed damages against them. *Held*, in the exercise of his duty towards a client, a solicitor was always expected to use a reasonable degree of skill, care and knowledge. He had to act expeditiously, particularly in stale actions, to protect his client's case from being struck out due to delay caused by his neglect. Further, the solicitors were accountable not only for themselves, but also for the counsel's delay in the matter, as they could have rectified the situation by seeking advice elsewhere. The clients would be awarded damages.

MAINZ V JAMES AND CHARLES DODD (1978) 122 Sol Jo 645 (Queen's Bench Division: WATKINS J).

2743   Law Society—treatment of complaints

The lay observer of the Law Society states in his third annual report that solicitors should be providing a better service for ordinary people. They have failed to remove three basic areas of complaint against the profession, namely delay, expense and incomplete explanation. The Law Society had, however, dealt thoroughly and competently with cases of serious dishonesty or deceit: Times, 26th May 1978.

2744   Legal services—provisions governing EEC lawyers practising in UK

See para. 1225.

2745   Liability for costs—delay in matrimonial proceedings

In November 1972, following the separation of the parties to a marriage, the husband presented a petition for divorce on the ground of irretrievable breakdown based on the wife's behaviour. In 1973 the solicitors representing the parties came to an agreement on financial matters. The wife's solicitor then resiled from the agreement and a delay of four and a half years followed. In 1977, in an undefended suit, the husband was granted a decree nisi and applied under the Rules of the Supreme Court, Ord. 62, r. 8 for an order that his former wife's solicitor should personally indemnify him against his costs incurred from 1973. The wife's solicitor submitted that any order made could only be on a party and party basis. *Held*, the wife's solicitor had no authority to resile from the agreement. By doing so he was acting against his client's express instructions and contrary to her interests. The court's discretion as to the scale of costs applicable was not limited and there was no reason why the husband should be left with a sum against which he was not indemnified. The wife's solicitor would therefore be ordered to pay three-quarters of the husband's solicitor and own client costs from November 1973.

S v S (1978) 122 Sol Jo 541 (Family Division: LATEY J).

2746   Practising certificate—failure to renew—instruction of counsel— validity of instruction

At committal proceedings, the defendant's solicitor, who instructed counsel to represent the defendant, did not have a practising certificate. The defendant was committed for trial under the Criminal Justice Act 1967, s. 1 (1), which provides that a magistrates court may commit a defendant for trial without consideration of statements, unless the defendant is not represented by counsel or a solicitor. The defendant was subsequently convicted and appealed, contending that the trial was a nullity as the committal was irregular and did not comply with s. 1 (1); he was in fact not represented as his instructing solicitor did not hold a practising certificate. *Held*, the question was whether in fact counsel was there to discharge the function of representing the defendant. Counsel did represent the defendant and the fact that the instructing solicitor had failed to comply with the statutory requirements as to the holding of a practising certificate could not alter that, nor did it cause any detriment to the defendant. The Solicitors Act 1974, while imposing penalties for non-compliance with practising requirements, did not vitiate acts done by a solicitor in those circumstances. The appeal would be dismissed.

R v Scott (1978) 122 Sol Jo 523 (Court of Appeal: Geoffrey Lane and Shaw LJJ and Caulfield J).

2747   Remuneration — non-contentious business — probate — calculation of remuneration

The plaintiff executors instructed the defendant solicitors to act in the administration of an estate valued at £1·8m. The first plaintiff assisted the defendants in his capacity as a surveyor by valuing certain properties. Following a grant of probate and some work in the administration of the estate, the plaintiffs dispensed with the defendants' services. The defendants' bill amounted to some £11,000. The plaintiffs requested them to obtain a certificate of fairness and reasonableness from the Law Society. The Society recommended a charge of £8,500. The plaintiffs then had the bill taxed, whereupon it was fixed at £10,500. On a review of the taxation, *held*, in determining a fair charge under the Supreme Court (Non-Contentious Probate Costs) Rules 1956, care had to be taken to ensure that the same work was not included under more than one of the seven heads of costs listed in r. 1. In view of the fact that the plaintiffs had dispensed with the defendants' services early, and that the first plaintiff had provided professional assistance a charge of £8,500 was fair.

Maltby v D. J. Freeman and Co [1978] 2 All ER 913 (Chancery Division: Walton J).

For earlier proceedings in this case, see 1976 Halsbury's Abr para. 1949.

SPECIFIC PERFORMANCE

Halsbury's Laws of England (3rd edn.), Vol. 36, paras. 359–529

2748   Article

Specific Performance—Mutuality, F. Graham Glover (time at which test of mutuality is to be applied): 128 NLJ 569.

2749   Contract for sale of land—order for specific performance—whether order deprived subsequently issued completion notice of effect

See *Singh v Nazeer*, para. 2434.

2750   —— sale of local authority house—whether agreement for sale concluded

See *Gibson v Manchester City Council*, para. 2431.

STAMP DUTIES

Halsbury's Laws of England (3rd edn.), Vol. 33, paras. 480–622

2751   Companies—amalgamation—relief from duty

See *Chelsea Land & Investment Co Ltd v Inland Revenue Commissioners*, para. 347.

2752   Company—issue of loan capital—sums advanced to company without issue of written evidence—whether "issue" of "loan capital"

The taxpayer company issued debenture stocks in order to raise money to lend on agricultural mortgages. Under a series of agreements the company raised money on loan from the Minister of Agriculture and Fisheries to establish and maintain a guarantee fund which secured the debenture stocks issued. In the event of a winding up, it was provided that the company's liability to the Minister would rank after that to the other creditors but, in the event of a deficiency, would rank pari passu with the paid-up share capital. The company requested several advances under the agreements and the money was paid into the company's bank account. No certificate of any kind was issued to the Minister. The company appealed against a decision that its acceptance of liability to the Minister for the advances was an "issue of loan capital" within the Finance Act 1899, s. 8 (1), being "capital raised by the company which is borrowed money" within s. 8 (5) and so attracted stamp duty. *Held*, the advances were loan capital within s. 8 (5) but there had been no "issue" within s. 8 (1). There had to be an overt act by the company as debtor showing its acceptance of the Minister's offer, recognising his rights as creditor and perfecting his title. The mere acceptance of money on loan did not constitute such an act. Furthermore, the term "issue" applied only to commercial transactions at arm's length which these transactions were not. Accordingly the appeal would be allowed.

AGRICULTURAL MORTGAGE CORPORATION LTD v INLAND REVENUE COMMISSIONERS [1978] STC 11 (Court of Appeal: BUCKLEY, SCARMAN and GOFF LJJ). Dicta of Walton J in *A-G v London and India Docks Co* (1906) 95 LT 536 at 538, and Lord Sands in *Canada Permanent Mortgage Corporation v IRC* 1932 SC 123 at 129, applied. Decision of Walton J [1975] 2 All ER 155, 1975 Halsbury's Abr para. 3230 reversed.

Finance Act 1899, s. 8 is now repealed by the Finance Act 1973, ss. 49 (2), 59 (2), Sch. 22, Part V.

2753   Conveyance in consideration of a debt—measure of consideration

Stamp duty on an instrument transferring property in consideration of the discharge of a debt owing to the transferee is governed by the Stamp Act 1891, s. 57. The Inland Revenue take the view that where the value of the property transferred is less than the amount of the indebtedness agreed to be discharged, the latter is the proper measure of the consideration for stamp duty purposes: Inland Revenue Press Release dated 8th November 1978 and Statement of Practice 5/78

2754   Lease or tack—rent reserved by lease—contingent or conditional rent—whether contingent rent to be taken into account in assessing duty

As part of a scheme to secure the development of a site, a corporation granted a head lease of the site to a company for a term of 125 years at an annual rent of £17,500. On the same day, the company granted an underlease of the site to the corporation for the same term less one day. A building was to be erected on the site and paid for by the corporation, who were to be reimbursed by the company up to a maximum of £1,300,000. The rent payable in the underlease included by cl. 3 (A) a yearly rent equivalent to 8·142 per cent of the company's total expenditure up to £1,300,000 on specified items including the company's legal costs, quantified at

£2,500 and the cost of erecting the building. The underlease was assessed to ad valorem stamp duty under para. (3) of the head of charge "Lease or Tack" in the Stamp Act 1891, Sch. 1, on the basis of a rent of £105, 846, being 8·142 per cent of £1,300,000 which was the maximum rent payable under cl. 3 (A). The corporation contended that the only duty payable under cl. 3 (A) was 8·142 per cent of the quantified legal costs, because, at the date of execution of the underlease, the total amount of rent under cl. 3 (A) was unquantifiable, being expressed by reference to a formula incapable of solution at that date. *Held*, the sum of £105,846 was rent payable on a contingency or conditionally, since it was the maximum amount payable under cl. 3 (A). The existence of a contingency or condition in relation to money payable periodically or a security for any sum or sums of money at stated periods, or security for the payment or repayment of money was of no relevance in assessing ad valorem duty. The existence of a contingency ought also to be disregarded in relation to rent reserved, since it was nevertheless rent reserved by the lease under para (3) of the head of charge "Lease of Tack" in the 1891 Act, Sch. 1, since the 1891 Act, s. 77 (1), clearly assumed that rent payable on a particular contingency was prima facie within the charge to duty and since a lease reserving a rent was only a particular type of obligation securing the payment of a sum of money at stated periods, and it was already established that contingencies were to be disregarded in relation to sums of money at stated periods. The assessment would be upheld.

COVENTRY CITY COUNCIL v INLAND REVENUE COMMISSIONERS [1978] STC 151 (Chancery Division: BRIGHTMAN J). Dicta of Collins MR in *Underground Electric Railways Co of London Ltd v Inland Revenue Commissioners* [1905] 1 KB 174 at 182 and of Lord Radcliffe in *Independent Television Authority v Inland Revenue Commissioners* [1960] 1 All ER 481 at 485, 486 applied.

STATUTES

Halsbury's Laws (3rd edn.), Vol. 36, paras. 530–750

2755 ### Construction—alleged breach of statutory duty—no provision in statute for remedy—whether private person has right of action

The National Enterprise Board, the first defendant, was set up under the Industry Act 1975 to develop or assist the economy of the United Kingdom. The Board has wide powers to reorganise industrial undertakings. The Secretary of State has power to direct the Board to exercise any of its functions in a particular way. In 1976 the Secretary of State issued directions on matters which the Board should take into account when making acquisitions and investing in companies. As the result of a recession in the tanning industry, the Secretary of State ordered the Board to make certain acquisitions with a view to an industrial reorganisation. The acquisitions were made and the reorganisation carried out. The plaintiff companies objected to the Board's activities on the basis that they had helped some companies at the expense of the trade as a whole. They sought a declaration that the Board had acted in breach of its statutory duty in that it had not acted in accordance with the 1976 directive. In turn, the Board applied to have the action struck out, contending that even if there had been a breach of statutory duty, the plaintiffs, as private persons, had no locus standi. They claimed that it was not the intention of the 1975 Act to give private persons any such right to sue. *Held*, the Board's application would be dismissed. It was possible that the Board was in breach of its obligations by virtue of not having followed certain aspects of the directive. It was arguable that as the 1975 Act provided no remedy for breach of statutory duty, private persons who were aggrieved by an alleged breach could sue if they were able to show peculiar injury over and above injury suffered by the public at large. In any case, the Board would suffer no great detriment if the actions were allowed to continue.

BOOTH & CO (INTERNATIONAL) LTD v NATIONAL ENTERPRISE BOARD [1978] 3 All ER 624 (Queen's Bench Division: FORBES J).

2756　Interpretation Act 1978

The Interpretation Act 1978 consolidates the Interpretation Act 1889 and certain other enactments relating to the construction and operation of statutes and other instruments. Relevant tables appear below.

DESTINATION TABLE

This table shows in column (1) the enactments repealed by the Interpretation Act 1978, and in column (2) the provisions of that Act corresponding to the repealed provisions.

In certain cases, the enactment in column (1), though having a corresponding provision in column (2), is not, or is not wholly, repealed, as it is still required, or partly required, for the purposes of other legislation.

(1)	(2)	(1)	(2)
Wales and Berwick Act 1746 (c. 42)	Interpretation Act 1978 (c. 30)	Interpretation Act 1889 (c. 63)	Interpretation Act 1978 (c. 30)
s. 3	Sch. 2, para. 5 (a)	s. 12 (5)	Sch. 1, Sch. 2, para. 4 (1)
Acts of Parliament (Commencement) Act 1793 (c. 13)†		(6)–(11)	—
	s. 4	(12)	Sch. 1, Sch. 2, para. 4 (1)
		(13)	—
Statutes (Definition of Time) Act 1880 (c. 9) —		(14)–(20)	Sch. 1, Sch. 2, para. 4 (1)
s. 1	ss. 9, 23 (3), Sch. 2, paras. 1, 6.	13 (1)–(3)	Sch. 1, Sch. 2, para. 4 (1)
2	—	(4), (5)	Rep. 1971 c. 23, s. 56 (4), Sch. 11, Part IV, and 1978 c. 23, s. 122 (2), Sch. 7, Part I
Revenue Act 1884 (c. 62) —		(6), (7)	—
		(8)	Sch. 2, para. 5 (c)
s. 14†	Sch. 1, Sch. 2, para. 4 (1)	(9)	Rep., 1962 c. 30, s. 30 (3), Sch. 4, Part IV
		(10)	—
Interpretation Act 1889 (c. 63) —		(11)	Sch. 1, Sch. 2, para. 4 (1)
s. 1 (1)	s. 6, Sch. 2, para. 2	(12), (13)	—
(2)	Sch. 2, para. 1	(14)	Rep. 1971 c. 23, s. 56 (4), Sch. 11, Part IV, and 1978 c. 23, s. 122 (2), Sch. 7, Part I
2 (1)	Sch. 1, Sch. 2, para. 4 (5)	14	Sch. 1, Sch. 2, para. 4 (1)
(2)	—	15 (1), (2)	—
3	Sch. 1, Sch. 2, paras. 4 (1), 5 (b)	(3)	Rep., 1948 c. 65, s. 80 (7), Sch. 13
4	—	(4)	Sch. 1, Sch. 2, para. 4 (1)
5	Rep., 1925 c. 90, s. 69, Sch. 8, and 1963 c. 33, s. 93 (1), Sch. 18, Part II	16	—
6	Sch. 1, Sch. 2, paras. 4 (1), 7	17 (1)	Sch. 1, Sch. 2, para. 4 (1)
7	Applied to Scotland	(2), (3)	Rep., 1948 c. 65, s. 80 (7), Sch. 13
8	s. 1, Sch. 2, para. 2	18 (1), (2)	Sch. 1, Sch. 2, para. 4 (1)
9	3, Sch. 2, para. 2	(3)	Sch. 1, Sch. 2, para. 4 (1), (3)
10	s. 2, Sch. 2, para. 2	(4), (5)	Rep., S.R. & O. 1937 No. 230, art. 2, Schedule, Part I
11 (1)	15, Sch. 2, para. 2	(6), (7)	Sch. 1, Sch. 2, para. 4 (1)
(2)	17 (1), Sch. 2, para. 2		
12 (1)	Sch. 1, Sch. 2, paras. 4 (1), (4)	18A ss. 19, 19A, 20–23	Sch. 1, Sch. 2, para. 4 (1)
(2), (3)	Sch. 1, Sch. 2, para. 4 (1)		
(4)	Rep. S.I. 1964 No. 488, art. 2, Sch. 1, Part II	s. 24	—

(1)	(2)	(1)	(2)
Interpretation Act 1889 (c. 63)	Interpretation Act 1978 (c. 30)	Irish Free State (Consequential Adaptation of Enactments) Order 1923, S.R. & O. 1923 No. 405	Interpretation Act 1978 (c. 30)
s. 25	Sch. 1, Sch. 2, para. 4 (1)		
26	s. 7, Sch. 2, para. 3		
27	Sch. 1, Sch. 2, para. 4 (1)	art. 2★	Sch. 1, Sch. 2, para. 4 (2)
28	Applied to Scotland	Schedule†	Sch. 1, Sch. 2, para. 4 (2)
29	Sch. 1, Sch. 2, para. 4 (1)		
30	ss. 10, 21 (2), Sch. 2, para. 1	Interpretation Measure 1925 (No. 1)	
31	11, 21 (1), Sch. 2, para. 1		
32 (1), (2)	s. 12, Sch. 2, para. 3	s. 1	s. 22 (3)
(3)	16, Sch. 2, para. 3		
33	18, Sch. 2, para. 1	Royal and Parliamentary Titles Act 1927 (c. 4)	
34	8, Sch. 2, para. 3		
35 (1)	Omitted as recommended by the Law Commissions; see Cmnd. 7235, para. 7A	s. 2 (2)†	Sch. 1, Sch. 2, paras. 4 (1), 6
(2)	s. 19 (1), Sch. 2, paras. 3, 6	Statute of Westminster 1931 (c. 4)	
(3)	20 (1), Sch. 2, para. 3		
36 (1)	Sch. 1, Sch. 2, para. 4 (1)	s. 11	Sch. 1, Sch. 2, para. 4 (3)
(2)	s. 4, Sch. 2, paras. 3, 6		
37	ss. 13, 21 (1), Sch. 2, para. 3	Public Health Act 1936 (c. 49)	
38 (1)	s. 17 (2) (a), Sch. 2, para. 3	s. 61 (1)★	Sch. 1, Sch. 2, para. 4 (1)
(2)	16 (1), Sch. 2, para. 3		
39	21 (1)	Ceylon Independence Act 1947 (c. 7)	
40	25 (3)		
41	Rep., S.L.R.A. 1908	s. 4 (2)	Sch. 1, Sch. 2, para. 4 (3)
ss. 42, 43	—		
Schedule	Rep., S.L.R.A. 1908	Church Commissioners Measure 1947 (No. 2)	
Inland Revenue Regulation Act 1890 (c. 21)		s. 1★	Sch. 1
s. 38 (1)†	—	British Nationality Act 1948 (c. 56)	
Short Titles Act 1896 (c. 14)		s. 1 (1),★ (2)†	s. 24 (4), Sch. 1, Sch. 2, paras. 4 (1), 6
s. 3	s. 19 (2), Sch. 2, para. 1	Magistrates' Courts Act 1962 (c. 55)	
		s. 124★	Sch. 1, Sch. 2, para. 4 (1)
General Adaptation of Enactments (Northern Ireland) Order 2921, S.R. & O. 1921 No. 1804		Sch. 5†	Sch. 1
		Medical Act 1956 (c. 76)	
art. 5★	Sch. 4, para. 4 (4)	s. 52 (3)	Sch. 1, Sch. 2, para. 4 (1)

(1)	(2)	(1)	(2)
Ghana Independence Act 1957 (c. 6)	Interpretation Act 1978 (c. 30)	London Government Act 1963 (c. 33)	Interpretation Act 1978 (c. 30)
s. 4 (1)	Sch. 1, Sch. 2, para. 4 (3)	s. 1 (1), † (6) †	Sch. 1, Sch. 2, para. 4 (1)
County Courts Act 1959 (c. 22)		Kenya Independence Act 1963 (c. 54)	
s. 205 (4)	Sch. 1	s. 4 (1)	Sch. 1, Sch. 2, para. 6 (3)
Nigeria Independence Act 1960 (c. 55)		Malawi Independence Act 1964 (c. 46)	
s. 3 (1)	Sch. 1, Sch. 2, para. 4 (3)	s. 4 (1)	Sch. 1, Sch. 2, para. 4 (3)
Charities Act 1960 (c. 58)		Police Act 1964 (c. 48)	
s. 1 (1)*	Sch. 1	s. 62†	Sch. 1, Sch. 2, para. 4 (1)
Sierra Leone Independence Act 1961 (c. 16)		Malta Independence Act 1964 (c. 86)	
s. 3 (1)	Sch. 1, Sch. 2, para. 4 (3)	s. 4 (1)	Sch. 1, Sch. 2, para. 4 (3)
Crown Estate Act 1961 (c. 55)		Gambia Independence Act 1964 (c. 93)	
s. 1*	Sch. 1	s. 4 (1)	Sch. 1, Sch. 2, para. 4 (3)
Tanganyika Independence Act 1961 (c. 1)		Guyana Independence Act 1966 (c. 14)	
s. 3 (1)	Sch. 1, Sch. 2, para. 4 (3)	s. 5 (1)	Sch. 1, Sch. 2, para. 4 (3)
Northern Ireland Act 1962 (c. 30)		Barbados Independence Act 1966 (c. 37)	
s. 27	Sch. 1, Sch. 2, para. 4 (1)	s. 4 (1)	Sch. 1, Sch. 2, para. 4 (3)
Jamaica Independence Act 1962 (c. 40)		West Indies Act 1967 (c. 66)	
s. 3 (1)	Sch. 1, Sch. 2, para. 4 (3)	s. 1 (3)*	Sch. 1, Sch. 2, para. 4 (1)
		3 (5)	Sch. 1, Sch. 2, para. 4 (3)
Trinidad and Tobago Independence Act 1962 (c. 54)		Welsh Language Act 1967 (c. 66)	
s. 3 (1)	Sch. 1, Sch. 2, para. 4 (3)	s. 4	Sch. 2, para. 5 (a)
Uganda Independence Act 1962 (c. 57)		Mauritius Independence Act 1968 (c. 8)	
s. 3 (1)	Sch. 1, Sch. 2, para. 4 (3)	s. 4 (1)	Sch. 1, Sch. 2, para. 4 (3)

(1)	(2)	(1)	(2)
National Loans Act 1968 (c. 13)	Interpretation Act 1978 (c. 30)	National Health Service Reorganisation Act 1973 (c. 32)	Interpretation Act 1978 (c. 30)
s. 1 (6)	Sch. 1		
Consular Relations Act 1968 (c. 18)		s. 55 (2)†	Sch. 2, para. 4 (6)
Sch. 1, Art. 1★	Sch. 1	Water Act 1973 (c. 37)	
Synodical Government Measure 1969 (No. 2)		s. 2 (3)†	Sch. 1, Sch. 2, para. 4 (1)
		38 (2)	Sch. 2, para. 4 (6)
s. 2 (2)★	s. 22 (3)	Health and Safety at Work Act 1974 (c. 37)	
Income and Corporation Taxes Act 1970 (c. 10)		s. 61 (1)★	Sch. 1
s. 526 (1),† (2)†	s. 24 (4), Sch. 1, Sch. 2, para. 4 (1)	Children Act 1975 (c. 72)	
		s. 89	Sch. 1, Sch. 2, para. 4 (1)
Fiji Independence Act 1970 (c. 50)		Local Land Charges Act 1978 (c. 76)	
s. 4 (1)	Sch. 1, Sch. 2, para. 4 (3)	s. 4†	Sch. 1, Sch. 2, paras. 4 (1), 6
Courts Act 1971 (c. 23)		Bail Act 1976 (c. 63)	
s. 1 (1)★	Sch. 1, Sch. 2, para. 4 (1)	Sch. 2†	Sch. 1
4 (1)★	Sch. 1, Sch. 2, para. 4 (1)	Criminal Law Act 1977 (c. 45)	
European Communities Act 1972 (c. 68)		s. 64 (1),† (2)†	Sch. 1, Sch. 2, para. 4 (1)
s. 1 (2)†	s. 24 (4), Sch. 1, Sch. 2, para. 4 (1)	Medical Act 1978 (c. 12)	
Local Government Act 1972 (c. 70)		Sch. 5, para. 48†	Sch. 1
		Solomon Islands Act 1978 (c. 15)	
s. 269†	Sch. 1, Sch. 2, paras. 4 (1), 6	s. 7 (1)	Sch. 1, Sch. 2, para. 4 (3)
Costs in Criminal Cases Act 1973 (c. 14)		Tuvalu Act 1978 (c. 20)	
s. 13 (1)†	Sch. 1, Sch. 2, para. 4 (1)	s. 4 (1)	Sch. 1, Sch. 2, para. 4 (3)
Bahamas Independence Act 1973 (c. 27)		Judicature (Northern Ireland) Act 1978 (c. 23)	
s. 4 (1)	Sch. 1, Sch. 2, para. 4 (3)	s. 4 (1)	Sch. 1, Sch. 2, para. 4 (1)

† Repealed in part.   ★ Not repealed.

TABLE OF DERIVATIONS

This table shows in the right hand column the legislative source from which the sections of the Interpretation Act 1978 have been derived. In the table the following abbreviations are used:

1889 = The Interpretation Act 1889
      (52 & 53 Vict. c. 63)

R (followed by = The recommendation set out in the paragraph of that number in the
a number   Appendix to the Report of the Law Commission and the Scottish Law
      Commission (Cmnd. 7235).

Section of Act	Derivation
1	1889 s. 8.
2	1889 s. 10.
3	1889 s. 9.
4	Acts of Parliament (Commencement) Act 1793 (c. 13); 1889 s. 36 (2); R.I.
5	—
6	1889 s. 1 (1); R.2.
7	1889 s. 26.
8	1889 s. 34.
9	Statutes (Definition of Time) Act 1880 (c. 9) s. 1; Summer Time Act 1972 (c. 6) s. 1.
10	1889 s. 30.
11	1889 s. 31.
12 (1)	1889 32 (1).
(2)	1889 32 (2).
13	1889 s. 37; R.3.
14	1889 s. 32 (3); R.4.
15	1889 s. 11 (1).
16 (1)	1889 s. 38 (2).
(2)	R.5.
17 (1)	1889 s. 11 (2).
(2)	1889 s. 38 (1); R.6.
18	1889 s. 33.
19 (1)	1889 s. 35 (2); R.7.
(2)	Short Titles Act 1896 (c. 14) s. 3.
20 (1)	1889 s. 35 (3).
(2)	R.8.
21 (1)	1889 s. 39.
(2)	1889 s. 30.
22 (1) (2)	—
(3)	Interpretation Measure 1925 (No. 1) s. 1; Synodical Government Measure 1969 (No. 2) s. 2 (2).
23 (1) (2)	R.9.
(3)	See derivation of provisions referred to; R.6.
(4)	R.9.

Section of Act	Derivation
24 (1)	—
(2)	R.10.
(3)	R.4.
(4)	See derivation of provisions referred to.
(5)	—
25 (1) (2)	—
(3)	1889 s. 40.
26	—
27	—
Sch. 1	"Associated state": West Indies Act 1967 (c. 4) s. 1 (3).
	"Bank of England": 1889 s. 12 (18).
	"Bank of Ireland": 1889 s. 12 (19).
	"British Islands": 1889 s. 18 (1); Irish Free State (Consequential Adaptation of Enactments) Order 1923 (No. 405) Art. 2, Sch.
	"British possession": 1889 s. 18 (2).
	"British subject" and "Commonwealth citizen": British Nationality Act 1948 (c. 56) s. 1.
	"Building regulations": Public Health Act 1936 (c. 49) s. 61; Health and Safety at Work etc. Act 1974 (c. 37) s. 61.
	"Central funds": Costs in Criminal Cases Act 1973 (c. 14) s. 13 (1).
	"Charity Commissioners": 1889 s. 12 (14); Charities Act 1960 (c. 58) s. 1.
	"Church Commissioners": 1889 s. 12 (15) (16); Church Commissioners Measure 1947 (No. 2).
	"Colonial legislature" and "legislature": 1889 s. 18 (7).
	"Colony": 1889 s. 18 (3); Statute of Westminster 1931 (c. 4) s. 11; Independence Acts from 1947 to date; West Indies Act 1967 (c. 4) s. 3 (5).
	"Commencement": 1889 s. 36 (1).
	"Committed for trial": 1889 s. 27; Magistrates' Courts Act 1952 (c. 55) s. 131, Sch. 5; Bail Act 1976 (c. 63) s. 12, Sch. 2; R.11.
	"The Communities", "the Treaties" and "the Community Treaties": European Communities Act 1972 (c. 68) s. 1 (2).
	"Comptroller and Auditor General": Revenue Act 1884 (c. 62) s. 14.
	"Consular officer": 1889 s. 12 (20); Consular Relations Act 1968 (c. 18) s. 1, Sch. 1.
	"The Corporation Tax Acts": Income and Corporation Taxes Act 1970 (c. 10) s. 526 (1) (a).
	"County court": 1889 ss. 6, 29; County Courts Act 1959 (c. 22) s. 205 (4); County Courts Act (Northern Ireland) 1959 (c. 25) s. 152 (3).
	"Court of Appeal": 1889 s. 13 (3).
	"Court of summary jurisdiction", "summary conviction" and "Summary Jurisdiction Acts": Northern Ireland Act 1962 (c. 30) s. 27.
	"Crown Court": 1889 s. 13 (4); Courts Act 1971 (c. 23) ss. 1 (2), 6 (1); Judicature (Northern Ireland) Act 1978 (c. 23) ss. 1, 4 (1).
	"Crown Estate Commissioners": 1889 s. 12 (12); Crown Estate Act 1961 (c. 55) s. 1.
	"England": Local Government Act 1972 (c. 70) s. 269.
	"Financial year": 1889 s. 22; National Loans Act 1968 (c. 13) s. 1 (6).
	"Governor-General": 1889 s. 18 (6).
	"High Court": 1889 s. 13 (3).
	"The Income Tax Acts": Income and Corporation Taxes Act 1970 (c. 10) s. 526 (1) (6).
	"Land": 1889 s. 3; R.12.
	"Lands Clauses Acts": 1889 s. 23; Interpretation Act (Northern Ireland) 1954 (c. 33) s. 46 (1).
	"Local land charges register" and "appropriate local land charges register"; Local Land Charges Act 1975 (c. 76) s. 4.
	"London borough": 1889 s. 15 (4); London Government Act 1963 (c. 33) s. 1.
	"Lord Chancellor": 1889 s. 12 (1).
	"Magistrates' Court: 1889 s. 13 (11); Magistrates' Courts Act 1952 (c. 55) s. 124; Magistrates Courts Act (Northern Ireland) 1964 (c. 21) s. 1.
	"Month": 1889 s. 3.
	"National Debt Commissioners": 1889 s. 12 (17).

Section of Act	Derivation
Sch. 1	"Northern Ireland legislation": R.10.
	"Oath" and "Affidavit": 1889 s. 3; Administration of Justice Act 1977 (c. 38) s. 8, Sch. 5 Part III.
	"Ordnance Map": 1889 s. 25.
	"Parliamentary Election": 1889 s. 17 (1).
	"Person": 1889 s. 19.
	"Police area", "police authority" and other expressions relating to the police: Police Act 1964 (c. 48) s. 62; Police (Scotland) Act 1967 (c. 77) ss. 50 and 51 (4).
	"The Privy Council": 1889 s. 12 (5).
	"Registered medical practitioner": Medical Act 1956 (c. 76) s. 52 (3); Medical Act 1978 (c. 12) Sch. 5, para. 48 (b).
	"Rules of Court": 1889 s. 14.
	"Secretary of State": 1889 s. 12 (3).
	"Sheriff": 1889 s. 28; Sheriff Courts (Scotland) Act 1971 (c. 58) s. 4 (3).
	"Statutory declaration": 1889 s. 21.
	"Supreme Court": 1889 s. 13 (1); Courts Act 1971 (c. 23) s. 1 (1).
	"The Tax Acts": Income and Corporation Taxes Act 1970 (c. 10) s. 526 (2).
	"The Treasury": 1889 s. 12 (2).
	"United Kingdom": Royal and Parliamentary Titles Act 1927 (c. 4) s. 2 (2).
	"Wales": Local Government Act 1972 (c. 70) s. 269.
	"Water authority" and "water authority area": Water Act 1973 (c. 37) s. 2 (3).
	"Writing": 1889 s. 20.
	Construction of certain expressions relating to children: 1889 s. 19A: Children Act 1975 (c. 72) s. 89.
	Construction of certain expressions relating to offences: Criminal Law Act 1977 (c. 45) s. 64 (1) (2).
Sch. 2 paras.	
1–3	See derivation of provisions referred to.
4 (1)	See derivation of provisions referred to.
	Irish Free State (Consequential Adaptation of Enactments) Order 1923 (No. 405) Art. 2, Sch.
(3)	1889 s. 18 (3); Statute of Westminster 1931 (c. 4) s. 11; Independence Acts from 1947 to date; West Indies Act 1967 (c. 4) s. 3 (5).
(4)	Wales and Berwick Act 1746 (c. 42) s. 3.
(5)	1889 s. 12 (1); General Adaptation of Enactments (Northern Ireland) Order 1921 (No. 1804) Art. 5.
(6)	1889 s. 2 (1).
(7)	National Health Service Reorganisation Act 1973 (c. 32) s. 55 (2); Water Act 1973 (c. 37) s. 38 (2).
5	1889 s. 3; 1889 s. 13 (8); Criminal Procedure (Scotland) Act 1975 (c. 21) Sch. 9 para. 6.
6	See derivation of provisions referred to.
7	1889 s. 6.
8	Local Government Act 1972 (c. 70) s. 269.
Sch. 3	—

2757   **Statute Law (Repeals) Act 1978**

The Statute Law (Repeals) Act 1978 received the royal assent on 31st July 1978 and came into force on that date. The Act promotes the reform of statute law by the repeal, in accordance with recommendations of the Law Commission and the Scottish Law Commission, of certain enactments which (except in so far as their effect is preserved) are no longer of practical utility, and facilitates the citation of statutes.

TELECOMMUNICATIONS AND TELEVISION

Halsbury's Laws of England (3rd edn.), Vol. 36, paras. 971–1123

2758   **Article**

Satellite Broadcasting and Freedom of Information, Lucia S. Orth (regulation of satellite broadcasting to reduce threats to national security, cultural integrity and national goals): (1977) II Human Rights Review 157.

2759   **Future of broadcasting**

The government has announced its proposals for the future of broadcasting. These include the creation of an Open Broadcasting Authority which would operate a fourth television channel catering mainly for minority interests. It is intended that the existing channels should continue to be operated by the BBC and IBA. It is also intended to create a new complaints commission to deal with complaints against the BBC, the IBA and the OBA, in relation to misrepresentation, unfair treatment, invasions of privacy etc: Broadcasting (Cmnd. 7294).

2760   **Independent Broadcasting Authority Act 1978**

The Independent Broadcasting Authority Act 1978 received the royal assent on 31st July 1978 and came into force on that date.

The Act extends until 31st December 1981, the period during which the Independent Broadcasting Authority is, under s. 2 (1) of the Independent Broadcasting Act 1973, required to provide television and local sound broadcasting services: s. 1. The restriction on the expression of opinion on political or industrial controversy, or current public policy and the exclusion of certain religious matter from broadcast programmes does not apply to broadcasts of parliamentary and local authority proceedings: s. 2.

2761   **Licence charges**

The Wireless Telegraphy (Broadcast Licence Charges and Exemption) (Amendment) Regulations 1978, S.I. 1978 No. 1680 (in force on 25th November 1978) increase the basic fee for television licences from £9 to £10 in the case of monochrome and from £21 to £25 in the case of colour.

2762   The Wireless Telegraphy (General Licence Charges) (Amendment) Regulations 1978, S.I. 1978 No. 12 (in force on 1st February 1978), amend the Wireless Telegraphy (General Licence Charges) Regulations 1968, as amended. The Regulations increase the fees payable on the issue, renewal and variation of certain wireless telegraphy licences, other than television broadcast receiving licences and broadcast relay station licences. The Wireless Telegraphy (General Licence Charges) (Amendment) Regulations 1975, 1975 Halsbury's Abr para. 3245 are revoked.

2763   **Offences—Isle of Man**

The Wireless Telegraphy (Isle of Man) Order 1978, S.I. 1978 No. 1055 (in force on 1st August 1978), extends to the Isle of Man, with exceptions, adaptations and modifications, the Wireless Telegraphy Act 1967, s. 11, as amended by the Criminal Law Act 1977. Section 11 of the 1967 Act amends the provisions relating to penalties for offences under the Wireless Telegraphy Act 1949.

2764   Radio interference—electrical appliances

The Wireless Telegraphy (Control of Interference from Household Appliances, Portable Tools etc.) Regulations 1978, S.I. 1978 No. 1267 (in force on 1st April 1979 except in relation to any lighting dimmer where the date is 1st November 1979), implements ECC Council Directive 76/889, 1976 Halsbury's Abr para. 1105. Regulation 5 further provides that the requirements to be complied with are satisfied if the apparatus conformed to those requirements at the date of its manufacture or assembly, is maintained in good working order and is not likely to interfere with wireless telegraphy used for safety of life services. The Order revokes S.I. 1955 Nos. 291, 292 and S.I. 1957 Nos. 348, 349 (relating to the control of interference from electric motors and refrigerators).

THEATRES AND OTHER PLACES OF ENTERTAINMENT

Halsbury's Laws of England (3rd edn.), Vol. 37, paras. 1–132

2765   Cinemas—licence fees

The Fees for Cinematograph Licences (Variation) Order 1978, S.I. 1978 No. 1387 in force on 1st November 1978) raises the maximum fees payable for the grant, renewal and transfer of licences issued under the Cinematograph Act 1909, s. 2 for the use of premises for cinematograph exhibitions.

2766   Films—application for registration

The Films (Registration) (Amendment) Regulations 1978, S.I. 1978 No. 1632 (in force on 1st January 1979) amend the Films (Registration) Regulations 1970 by prescribing a new form of application for the registration of films.

2767   —— levy

The Cinematograph Films (Collection of Levy) (Amendment No. 6) Regulations 1978, S.I. 1978 No. 1092 (in force on 24th September 1978), increases to 17½p the portion of the payment for admission (net of VAT) which is not liable to levy, and increases to £1,100 the amount by reference to which total or partial exemption from payment of levy is allowed in respect of cinemas at which takings or average takings are small.

2768   Theatres—licence fees

The Theatres (Licence Application Fees) (Amendment) Order 1978, S.I. 1978 No. 1388 (in force on 1st November 1978) amends the Theatres (Licence Application Fees) Order 1968 by raising the fees payable for the grant, renewal or transfer of licences for the use of premises for the public performance of a play under the Theatres Act 1968.

TIME

Halsbury's Laws of England (3rd edn.), Vol. 37, paras. 133–185

2769   Sunset—time—judicial notice

See *R v Crush*, para. 1285.

TORT

Halsbury's Laws of England (3rd edn.), Vol. 37, paras. 186–280

2770   Articles

An Account of US Product Liability Claim, Professor Derrick Owles: 128 NLJ 91.

Compensation for Detention, Carolyn Shelbourn (the possibility of establishing a scheme to provide compensation other than ex gratia payments for persons wrongly detained): [1978] Crim LR 22.

Injuries to Unborn Children, Peter F. Crane: (1977) 51 ALJ 704.

Liability for Defective Premises, Charles Bennett (remedies open to purchaser of defective premises): 128 NLJ 25.

2771   Damages—causation—subsequent non-tortious act

See *Hodgson v General Electricity Co Ltd*, para. 854.

2772   Joint tortfeasors—patent infringement

See *Morton-Norwich Products Inc v Intercen Ltd*, para. 2060.

2773   Location of tort—fraudulent misrepresentation—service of writ out of jurisdiction

See *Diamond v Bank of London and Montreal Ltd*, para. 428.

TOWN AND COUNTRY PLANNING

Halsbury's Laws of England (3rd edn.), Vol. 37, paras. 281–816

2774   Articles

Bargaining as a Tool of Department Control: A Case of All Gain and No Loss? Martin Loughlin: [1978] JPL 290.

Challenging Enforcement Notices, J. F. Alder (the procedures facing a would-be challenger): [1978] JPL 160.

Developers' Contributions and Planning Gains: Ethics and Legalities, Malcolm Grant: [1978] JPL 8.

2775   Caravan site—gypsy encampments

The Gypsy Encampments (Designation of the County of Dorset) Order 1978, S.I. 1978 No. 1221 (in force on 21st September 1978), designates the county of Dorset under the Caravan Sites Act 1968, s. 12, as an area in which it is an offence for a gypsy to station a caravan for the purpose of residing for any period on any land situated within the boundaries of a highway, on any other unoccupied land, or on any occupied land without the occupier's consent.

2776   —— site not licensed—whether provisions for protection of occupiers apply to unlicensed site

See *Hooper v Eaglestone*, para. 593.

2777   Community land—local authorities—finance

The Department of the Environment, in a guidance note to local authorities, has stated that local authorities will in future be given block loan sanctions for approved land acquisition programmes and will not need specific approval for each project.

Also for an experimental five-year period they will be able to retain 50 per cent (formerly 30 per cent) of the surplus on their land accounts. See *The Times*, 28th November 1978.

2778   Community Land Act 1975—building licences—income tax relief

See para. 1610.

2779   Derelict land clearance areas

The Derelict Land Clearance Areas Order 1978, S.I. 1978 No. 691 (in force on 8th June 1978), specifies certain areas as derelict land clearance areas for the purposes of the Local Employment Act 1972.

2780   Development—conditional planning permission—imposition of condition limiting new use to one specified body—validity of condition

The Secretary of State attached a condition to a grant of planning permission which restricted the use of a building owned by the plaintiffs to one public body. The condition was a repeat of an identical one contained in an office development permit issued one month earlier for the same building, but, for the restriction now being contained in the grant of planning permission, it was permanent. The inference could be drawn from the grant that if the plaintiffs were to convert other office premises they owned to residential use, the restriction would be lifted. They contended that the ulterior motive rendered the condition ultra vires. *Held*, the facts did not show that the motive behind the condition was the desire to persuade the plantiffs to change the use of their other premises. It appeared that the condition had been imposed because the area in which the building was situated was scheduled for general industry, not office use, and it was only because of the particular needs of the public body intending to occupy the building that any office use at all had been sanctioned. Had any other body or persons wished to use the building as offices, planning permission would have been refused.

RKT INVESTMENTS LTD v HACKNEY LONDON BOROUGH COUNCIL (1978) 246 EG 919 (Queen's Bench Division: SIR DOUGLAS FRANK QC sitting as a deputy High Court judge).

2781   —— —— validity of condition

In 1962 a company was granted planning permission to use two hangers as warehouses for storing synthetic rubber on condition that the buildings were to be removed by the end of 1972. The buildings were not removed and the local authority served enforcement notices. The notices were quashed by the Secretary of State on the ground that the condition was void as being extraneous to the proposed use. The local authority's appeal was dismissed. On further appeal, *held*, the planning permission granted to the company was for temporary change of use and the condition requiring removal of the buildings at the end of the period of use related fairly and reasonably to the permitted development. The condition was accordingly valid and the appeal would be allowed.

NEWBURY DISTRICT COUNCIL v SECRETARY OF STATE FOR THE ENVIRONMENT [1978] 1 All ER 243 (Court of Appeal: LORD DENNING MR, LAWTON and BROWNE LJJ). Decision of Divisional Court of the Queen's Bench Division (1977) 75 LGR 608, 1977 Halsbury's Abr para. 2783, reversed.

**2782   **A local authority appealed against a decision of the Secretary of State that conditions it had imposed on a grant of planning permission for the extension of a factory were ultra vires in so far as they imposed new conditions on the existing factory as to the hours of use and noise. *Held*, as the purpose of the proposed extension was to enable the existing factory to operate twenty-four hours a day and as any noise would emanate from both factory and extension, the local authority's conditions related to the permitted development. Accordingly the authority was empowered to impose them and the appeal would be allowed.

PENWITH DISTRICT COUNCIL v SECRETARY OF STATE FOR THE ENVIRONMENT (1977) 34 P & CR 269 (Queen's Bench Division: SIR DOUGLAS FRANK QC, sitting as a deputy High Court judge).

2783   In 1950, a local authority granted planning permission for the use of a quarry as a tip subject to its surveyor's approval of the materials to be deposited. However, no formal selection of the materials was made by the surveyor. In 1976, in a letter from a planning officer, the owners of the quarry were informed that only certain approved materials could be deposited in it and that the depositing of any other materials would be considered a breach of planning control. The owners were served with an enforcement notice alleging such a breach. They appealed against the Secretary of State's decision to uphold the order, on the ground that as the dumping of other materials had been going on for many years prior to the 1976 letter, it could be assumed that it was done lawfully, therefore the subsequent restrictions could not be effective. *Held*, merely because the tipping had been going on in the quarry for many years, it could not be assumed that it had been done lawfully, since the tipping had started prior to the granting of the planning permission. The only materials that were now permitted to be tipped were those mentioned in the 1976 letter and as the owners had deposited other materials, they were in breach of planning control. The appeal would therefore be dismissed.

BILBOE v SECRETARY OF STATE FOR THE ENVIRONMENT (1978) 248 Estates Gazette 229 (Queen's Bench Division: LORD WIDGERY CJ, MILMO and TUDOR EVANS JJ).

2784   —— —— —— **powers of Secretary of State**

Two building firms appealed against the deemed refusal of a local authority to grant planning permission for the construction of two housing estates. The parties subsequently came to an agreement on the development subject to the builders' providing play areas for children, public open spaces and a social/shopping centre. In the light of this agreement the local authority asked the Secretary of State to allow the appeal. He nevertheless dismissed it on the grounds that he could not grant permission subject to conditions which did not relate to the development applied for, that he could not require land to be dedicated to public use and could not enforce a condition as vague as the one relating to a social/shopping centre. *Held*, the Secretary of State was wrong in thinking his powers were so limited because (i) the conditions were ancillary to the proposed development and would not render the permitted development substantially different, (ii) the conditions did not require that space be dedicated to the public, only that it should be available to the public when the council adopted it, (iii) the term social/shopping centre could be given a sensible meaning and so was not incapable of definition. The conditions could therefore be imposed.

ROBERT HITCHINS BUILDERS LTD v SECRETARY OF STATE FOR THE ENVIRONMENT; BRITANNIA (CHELTENHAM) LTD v SECRETARY OF STATE FOR THE ENVIRONMENT (1978) 247 EG 301 (Queen's Bench Division: SIR DOUGLAS FRANK QC, sitting as a deputy High Court judge).

2785   —— **outline planning permission—application for approval of reserved matters—whether second application in respect of same matters possible**

A local planning authority granted outline planning permission for the development of a site, which involved demolishing buildings. The permission did not extend to the proposed lay-out which was left to be dealt with later when detailed plans were submitted. Detailed plans were later submitted for the first phase of the development and were approved. Certain of the buildings due to be demolished were then listed as being of special historical or architectural interest, and the development was redesigned to avoid demolishing them. The developers were anxious to retain the original grant of outline permission, and therefore applied to the authority under the heading of "approval of reserved matters following grant of outline permission" in respect of the first phase of the redesigned development. The authority refused approval on the ground that a new application for outline permission should have been made; once reserved matters had been approved, they could not be revised or varied by a further consideration of reserved matters under the same outline consent. The developers were granted a declaration that their application was valid, and the authority appealed. *Held*, there was no reason why an applicant should not make another and different application for approval in respect of reserved matters for which the planning authority had already given its approval. A second application could be granted, leaving the first still standing, and the applicant could then use whichever he liked. The only restriction was that when an application was made for approval of a reserved matter, it had to be within the ambit of the outline permission and in accordance with the conditions annexed to it. If it was not, new permission had to be applied for. In this case the judge was right to grant the declaration and the appeal would be dismissed.

HERON CORPORATION LTD V MANCHESTER CITY COUNCIL [1978] 3 All ER 1240 (Court of Appeal: LORD DENNING MR, ORR and BRIDGE LJJ). Decision of Sir Douglas Frank QC sitting as a deputy High Court judge (1976) 33 P & CR 268, 1976 Halsbury's Abr para. 2543 affirmed.

2786 —— —— **grounds   for   refusal   of   application—economic considerations**

An inspector was appointed by the Secretary of State for Wales to determine an appeal against a local planning authority's refusal to grant outline planning permission for the erection of dwelling houses. The appeal was dismissed and the applicant applied to quash the decision on the ground that the inspector's decision had been based on the irrelevant factor that it was not economically viable to develop on that particular plot. *Held*, it was true to say that the grant of planning permission did not depend on the resources and intentions of the applicant. It was for the developer, not the local planning authority, to make the economic decision whether to carry out the development. However, the inspector had not determined the issue on economic grounds but on the grounds that it was, with regard to economic, marketing and road safety considerations, impossible to devise a suitable scheme for which permission ought to have been granted. The application would be refused.

WALTERS V SECRETARY OF STATE FOR WALES (1978) Times, 8th November (Queen's Bench Division: SIR DOUGLAS FRANK QC sitting as a deputy High Court judge).

2787 —— **permitted development—facing of dwelling house with stone tiles—whether permission required**

The respondent householders wished to face their houses with stone tiles. They applied for planning permission, which was refused on the basis of the aesthetic unacceptability of the proposed alteration. The Secretary of State decided that planning permission was not required by virtue of the Town and Country Planning General Development Order 1977, Sch. 1, which obviates the necessity for an application where the alterations do not cause the front wall to project further forward towards the highway than previously. On appeal by the local planning authority, *held*, upholding the Secretary of State's decision, the alterations would not cause the wall to project beyond the original wall, the moulded surrounds, and window sills, which were regarded as part of the wall. Planning permission for the stone cladding was therefore not required.

BRADFORD METROPOLITAN DISTRICT COUNCIL V SECRETARY OF STATE FOR THE ENVIRONMENT (1977) 76 LGR 454 (Queen's Bench Division: GRIFFITHS J). *Brutus v Cozens* [1973] AC 855, HL, and *LTSS Print & Supply Services Ltd v Hackney Borough Council* [1976] QB 663, 1975 Halsbury's Abr para. 3287 applied.

2788 —— **planning authorities—Greater London**

The Town and Country Planning (Local Planning Authorities in Greater London) Regulations 1978, S.I. 1978 No. 602 (in force on 19th May 1978), re-enact with amendments the provisions of the Town and Country Planning (Local Planning

Authorities in Greater London) Regulations 1965 to 1974. The Regulations set out the development for which the GLC shall be the local planning authority; the classes of development to be referred to the GLC; the GLC's power of direction in respect of applications referred to it; provisions relating to development conflicting with the development plans; and the areas to which the regulations apply. The Town and Country Planning (Local Planning Authorities in Greater London) Regulations 1965, S.I. 1965 No. 679; 1967 No. 430; and 1974 No. 450, 1974 Halsbury's Abr para. 3198, are revoked.

2789   —— planning permission—access to highway—common land

A planning authority refused to grant permission for the construction of a means of access to the applicant's land from a public highway. The access would have had to cut across a grass verge, which formed part of a common, between the highway and the applicant's land. The planning authority required unimpeded visibility on either side of the access. This effectively meant that the grass verge would have to be kept clear for 300 yards in both directions. The application was turned down because the grass verge was common land over which the applicant had no control to ensure that the visibility would be kept clear. On appeal, the applicant argued that the conveyance of the common land to the present owners reserved him a right of way from the highway to his own land. He contended that it was implicit in the reservation that he also had a right to maintain clear visibility if this was required. *Held*, the provision of clear visibility would effectively sterilize far more common land than was envisaged by the original right of way. In any case, there was no evidence that the applicant had a right of way in the first place. The appeal would be dismissed.

HAYNS V SECRETARY OF STATE FOR THE ENVIRONMENT (1978) 245 EG 53 (Queen's Bench Division: SIR DOUGLAS FRANK QC sitting as a deputy High Court judge).

2790   —— —— exercise of powers of Secretary of State—material considerations

Planning permission for the development of two pieces of land was refused by a local planning authority on the grounds of water drainage problems. The owners of the first site, together with the owners of the second site, then put forward schemes for the improvement of the land and the construction of a balancing lagoon. However, before the agreement concerning the cost of the improvements under the Town and Country Planning Act 1971, s. 52, could be carried out, the owners of the second site went into liquidation. The appeal by the owners of the first site against the local planning authority's decision was dismissed by the Secretary of State on the grounds that as the improvements could no longer be carried out without the contribution of the owners of the second site, there was no permanent solution available. The owners of the first site appealed. *Held*, the Secretary of State should have considered the application relating to the first site on its own and the question of whether the provision of a balancing lagoon by the owners of the first site alone should have been accepted as a permanent solution to the problem. Accordingly, his decision would be quashed.

GEORGE WIMPEY & CO LTD V SECRETARY OF STATE FOR THE ENVIRONMENT (1978) 247 EG 470 (Queen's Bench Division: SIR DOUGLAS FRANK QC sitting as a deputy High Court judge).

2791   —— —— failure to obtain office development permit—liability of architect

See *B. L. Holdings Ltd v Robert J. Wood and Partners*, para. 267.

2792   —— —— inquiry—matters to be considered in inspector's report

An application for planning permission to develop an area for residential use was refused. The applicant appealed, and at the inquiry the inspector found that there was a need for an increased allocation of development land due to an anticipated population increase in the area. The Secretary of State accordingly allowed the appeal. The local planning authority appealed, contending that the inspector had failed to report that the population increase was anticipated because of the taking up of already existing planning permissions and would not require the allocation of additional land; as a result, the minister had failed to have regard to a material consideration. *Held*, the Town and Country Planning (Inquiries Procedure) Rules 1974, 1974 Halsbury's Abr para. 3213, r. 12, provided that the inspector had to include in his report his findings of fact and his recommendations. It was for the inspector to find the principal facts, and the court would not usually intervene. It was however permissible to bring evidence to show that a matter of real importance had been wholly ignored or completely misunderstood, so that the Secretary of State was given the wrong picture. In such a case the court could consider if there had been a breach of r. 12. It was open to the inspector to consider the evidence and reject it, but in this case he had failed to consider it at all. The report was thus misleading and there was a failure to comply with r. 12. The decision of the Secretary of State would be quashed and the matter remitted to him.

EAST HAMPSHIRE DISTRICT COUNCIL V SECRETARY OF STATE FOR THE ENVIRONMENT (1977) 248 Estates Gazette 43 (Queen's Bench Division: SLYNN J).

2793   —— —— material change of use

A large house and stable block formed one planning unit for the purposes of the Town and Country Planning Act 1971. It was proposed to divide the unit into two, so that one family could use the house, and another family could use the modernized stable block as an entirely separate dwelling. Planning permission was refused on the basis that the division of the unit into two was an unreasonable material change of use. On appeal, *held*, where the house remained one entity and the stable block was turned into a separate unit for entirely separate occupation, that was a material change of use. In finding that the change of use was unreasonable the inspector had not erred in law. The appeal would be dismissed.

WAKELIN V SECRETARY OF STATE FOR THE ENVIRONMENT (1978) Times, 15th June (Court of Appeal: LORD DENNING MR, LAWTON and BROWNE LJJ).

2794   —— —— material considerations

In 1968, after consultation with the gypsies of Sheffield the defendant council granted planning permission for a caravan site. A suitable site was found in 1976 when the defendant, as the local planning authority, granted itself planning permission to develop the site. Both the gypsy council and the applicant, who lived near the proposed site, were opposed to the choice. The applicant sought an order of certiorari to quash the decision granting the planning permission contending that, by failing to consult the gypsy community, the defendant had not given proper regard to a material consideration in contravention of the Town and Country Planning Act 1971, s. 39 (1). *Held*, although there had been no consultations between the authority and the gypsies immediately before the granting of planning permission, there had been an interchange of views since 1968. In planning law there was no general obligation to have formal consultations, and the authority had a discretion as to whom it consulted. In the present case no consultation was necessary. The application would be dismissed.

R V SHEFFIELD CITY COUNCIL, EX PARTE MANSFIELD (1978) Times, 28th January (Queen's Bench Division: LORD WIDGERY CJ, O'CONNOR and LLOYD JJ).

2795   —— —— —— existing permitted development rights

The applicants, a water company, applied for planning permission to erect certain buildings contending that the land in question was operational land of a statutory undertaker and they thus had Class XVIII.C permitted development rights under the Town and Country Planning General Development Order 1973. On the refusal of their application, they appealed to the Secretary of State and an inquiry was held. The inspector recommended that subject to the Secretary of State being satisfied that the land was operational land of a statutory undertaker, the appeal should be allowed. The Secretary of State dismissed their appeal on the grounds that the decision did not depend on whether the site was operational land but on the merits of the proposals. The applicants appealed contending that the inspector had failed to record certain of the applicants' arguments which it had been his duty to do and that the Secretary of State had erred in law in deliberately excluding from his consideration their Class XVIII.C rights under the 1973 Order, as they were a material consideration. *Held,* while natural justice required legal arguments to be set out comprehensively for the Secretary of State to deal with, the matter was at the discretion of the inspector. There was no absolute duty to record every submission which was made. All that was required was an intelligible account of the applicant's argument. However, the Secretary of State had misdirected himself in deciding that he should not regard the possible existence of Class XVIII.C rights and the position which could arise if those rights were exercised as being relevant as matters of law and therefore his decision was erroneous in point of law. The Secretary of State's decision would be quashed and the appeal allowed.

NORTH SURREY WATER CO v SECRETARY OF STATE FOR THE ENVIRONMENT (1976) 34 P & CR 140 (Queens' Bench Division: SLYNN J). *Wells v Minister of Housing and Local Government* [1967] 2 All ER 1041, CA applied.

1973 Order now replaced by the Town and Country Planning General Development Order 1977, 1977 Halsbury's Abr para. 2787.

2796   —— —— reference of application to Secretary of State—effect of failure to serve notice on applicant

The applicant applied for planning permission to extend a caravan site. The Secretary of State directed that the application be referred to him for decision. The local planning authority failed to serve notice of the direction on the applicant, in breach of the Town and Country Planning General Development Order 1973, art. 15. Nor did it serve on him a statement under the Town and Country Planning (Inquiries Procedure) Rules 1969, r. 6(2). The Secretary of State subsequently served notice on the applicant that an inquiry would be held and on request by the applicants' solicitors the Welsh Office sent them a copy of a statement under the Town and Country Planning (Inquiries Procedure) Rules 1974, which had meanwhile replaced the 1969 Rules, r. 6(2). The inquiry was held and planning permission refused. The applicant applied under the Town and Country Planning Act 1971, s. 245, for the decision to be quashed on the ground that there had been a failure to comply with the 1973 Order, art. 15, and the 1974 Rules, r. 6(2). *Held,* failure to serve notice under art. 15 could not be the subject of an application under s. 245. Moreover, failure to serve notice did not deprive the applicant of rights which would have accrued if it had been served; he had not been substantially prejudiced and thus failed to satisfy s. 245(4) (b). Nor had he been substantially prejudiced by failure to serve a statement under r. 6 within the time required. The application would be refused.

DAVIES v SECRETARY OF STATE FOR WALES (1976) 33 P & CR 330 (Queen's Bench Division: SIR DOUGLAS FRANK QC sitting as a deputy High Court judge).

1973 Order, art. 15, now Town and Country Planning General Development Order 1977, art. 19.

2797   —— —— refusal—application of rules of natural justice

Appellants were given outline permission to build twenty-three houses on a site on condition that they preserved the character of a bridleway across the site. Approval of other matters was reserved for later consideration. When the appellants sought consideration of these matters and permission to increase the number of houses to be built, the inspector rejected their proposed layout on grounds that the estate road should have been aligned with an existing road and that the urbanisation of the area would have an undesirable effect on the bridleway. On appeal, *held,* the appellants had been unaware that there might be any difficulty with regard to the estate road and the fact that they had not been given any opportunity to discuss the point ran contrary to the rules of natural justice. The urbanisation of the area had been inevitable when the outline planning permission was granted and therefore the objection on that ground was irrelevant. Accordingly the appeal would be dismissed.

LEWIS THIRKELL LTD v SECRETARY OF STATE FOR THE ENVIRONMENT (1978) 248 Estates Gazette 685 (Queen's Bench Division: WILLIS J).

2798 —— —— **representations by planning officer—whether public body estopped from performing its statutory duty**

See *Western Fish Products Ltd v Penwith District Council*, para. 1173.

2799 —— —— **special development order—reprocessing plant for nuclear fuels**

See para. 1162.

2800 —— —— **subsequent sale of part of complex—whether new unit created**

The owners of a petrol station and garage were granted planning permission for, inter alia, the conversion of an existing workshop to a retail showroom. There was no condition restricting the character or nature of the goods to be sold there. Subsequently a company acquired an interest in the workshop, but not in the rest of the premises. They used it for the purpose of a retail supermarket selling food, confectionery and cigarettes. The planning authority, considering that an unauthorised change of use had occurred, served an enforcement notice requiring the company to discontinue the use. The company appealed against the dismissal by the Secretary of State of its appeal against the notice. They contended that on the severance of the workshop from the rest of the site so far as activity and control were concerned, there came into existence a new planning unit comprising the former workshop. Treated as a separate unit, and since there were no express restrictions on the activities that could be carried on there, the workshop could be used as a retail shop of any kind. *Held*, there could be no creation of a new and separate unit simply by selling one of a complex of buildings to an owner and occupier different from those of the rest of the site. The boundaries of new planning units were not primarily matters of title but of activity. There was an implied restriction in the planning permission restricting the sale of goods in the retail showroom to automobile goods. The appeal would be dismissed.

KWIK SAVE DISCOUNT GROUP LTD v SECRETARY OF STATE FOR WALES (1978) Times, 29th June (Queen's Bench Division: LORD WIDGERY CJ, TALBOT and ACKNER JJ).

2801 —— **structure and local plans—East Sussex**

The Town and Country Planning Act 1971 (Commencement No. 40) (East Sussex) Order 1978, S.I. 1978 No. 727, brought into force on 28th June 1978 s. 20 and Sch. 23, Part I (part) for the county of East Sussex. These provisions relate to structure and local plans.

The above provisions replace the provisions of the 1971 Act relating to development plans which are repealed by the Town and Country Planning (Repeal of Provisions No. 12) (East Sussex) Order 1978, S.I. 1978 No. 726 (in force on 28th June 1978).

2802 —— —— **Staffordshire**

The Town and Country Planning Act 1971 (Commencement No. 39) (Staffordshire) Order 1978, S.I. 1978 No. 557 bring into force on 23rd May 1978 s. 20 and Sch. 23, Part I (part) for the counties of Staffordshire and West Midlands. These provisions relate to structure and local plans.

2803 —— —— **West Midlands**

The Town and Country Planning Act 1971 (Commencement No. 41) (West

Midlands (Part)) Order 1978, S.I. 1978 No. 725, brought into force on 28th June 1978 s. 20 and Sch. 23, Part I (part) for certain areas of the West Midlands. These provisions relate to structure and local plans.

The above provisions replace the provisions of the 1971 Act relating to development plans which are repealed by the Town and Country Planning (Repeal of Provisions No. 13) (West Midlands (Part)) Order 1978, S.I. 1978 No. 724 (in force on 28th June 1978).

2804   Discontinuance order—use of land—meaning of "use"

Land in a national park had been used for storing and sorting scrap metal for over 30 years. The planning board made a discontinuance order requiring the use of the land for that purpose to be discontinued. Town and Country Planning Act 1971, s. 290, provides that use of land does not include its use for the carrying out of any building or other operations on the land. The owner successfully appealed against the order on the ground that the activities fell within "other operations" and could not form the subject of a discontinuance order. On further appeal by the Secretary of State, *held*, "operations" meant operations that resulted in some permanent physical alteration in the land itself whereas "use" referred to things which were done in, alongside or on the land which were not interfering with the actual physical characteristics of the land. Storing and processing scrap was plainly the use of land and did not alter the physical characteristics of the land. The appeal would be allowed.

PARKES v SECRETARY OF STATE FOR THE ENVIRONMENT [1978] 1 ALL ER 211 (Court of Appeal: LORD DENNING MR, GEOFFREY LANE and EVELEIGH LJJ).

2805   Enforcement notice—material change of use—date of change of use

Landowners were served with an enforcement notice alleging breach of planning control and requiring them to discontinue the use of their farm for the storing of scrap metal. Their appeal to the Secretary of State under the Town and Country Planning Act 1971, s. 88 (1) (d), on the ground that the breach had occurred before the beginning of 1964, was dismissed. The landowners appealed, contending that the Secretary of State had misdirected himself by not amending the notice to take account of the extent to which the activities forbidden by the notice had taken place before the beginning of 1964. *Held*, the Secretary of State had found that the landowners had failed to discharge the onus of proof on them as to commencement of the use. As it appeared that he had considered all the matters that were relevant it could not be said that he had erred in law. Accordingly, the appeal would be dismissed.

STANTON v SECRETARY OF STATE FOR THE ENVIRONMENT (1978) 248 Estates Gazette 227 (Queen's Bench Division: LORD WIDGERY CJ, TALBOT and WATKINS JJ).

2806   ———— intensification of use

The owner of a farm obtained planning permission to erect a building on condition that it would only be used for the storage of agricultural produce from the farm and farm implements and not for any other purpose. The local authority then decided that he had intensified his activities and served an enforcement notice on him alleging a material change of use in that the building was being used for the wholesale distribution of fruit and vegetables not produced on the farm. On appeal against the Secretary of State's decision to uphold the enforcement notice, it was held that there had been an intensification of the use, which had so affected the character of the land as to amount to a material change of use. The landowner appealed. *Held*, from the evidence available it could not be established that there had been such an intensification of the use of the building to result in a material change in the use of the farm as a whole. Accordingly, the appeal would be allowed and the decision of the Secretary of State would be remitted to him for further consideration.

HILLIARD v SECRETARY OF STATE FOR THE ENVIRONMENT (1978) 248 Estates Gazette 225 (Court of Appeal: MEGAW, BROWNE and SHAW LJJ). Decision of Divisional Court of the Queen's Bench Division (1977) 34 P & C R 193 reversed.

2807   —— —— **permission granted for warehouse use and storage— whether parking of caravans permitted—meaning of "warehouse"**

The respondent was granted planning permission for use of land for warehousing and as a storage depot. An enforcement notice was served on him, requiring him to remove two caravans from the land. The respondent failed to comply with the notice, claiming that the use for warehousing and storage covered any kind of storage. On a case stated to the High Court, *held*, use of the land for parking caravans was clearly not within the sanctioned use for warehousing and storage. Warehouse use implied covered storage. The case would be remitted to the justices with a direction to continue the hearing.

HOOPER V SLATER (1977) 245 EG 573 (Queen's Bench Division: LORD WIDGERY CJ, CUMMING-BRUCE LJ and PARK J).

2808   —— **non-compliance—information charging continuing offence— whether information bad for duplicity**

See *Parry v Forest of Dean District Council*, para. 1833.

2809   —— **service of notice—different notices served on owner and occupiers—substantial prejudice**

The owner of a site let the four buildings on it separately to four individuals. The local authority served an enforcement notice on the owner in respect of the whole site and served individual enforcement notices on the occupiers, copies of which were not served on the owner. On appeal by the owner against the notice, the Secretary of State decided that he was entitled under the Town and Country Planning Act 1971, s. 88 (4) (b), to disregard the authority's failure to serve on the owner the notices served on the occupiers, since the owner had not been substantially prejudiced by the failure. On further appeal by the owner, *held*, unless it could be shown that there was no evidence on which the Secretary of State's conclusion could be based or that he had accepted an erroneous principle by leaving out some relevant factor or including an irrelevant one, the court could not interfere with his finding. The appeal would be dismissed.

SKINNER V SECRETARY OF STATE FOR THE ENVIRONMENT (1978) 247 Estates Gazette 1179 (Queen's Bench Division: LORD WIDGERY CJ, TALBOT and WATKINS JJ).

2810   —— **validity—appeal to Secretary of State—matters to be considered**

An area was zoned in an initial development plan as primarily for commercial purposes. Planning permission was subsequently granted for the development of the area for residential purposes. The occupiers of one of the properties began to use it as an estate agency and the local authority served an enforcement notice requiring them to discontinue the use of the land for office purposes. The notice was upheld by the Secretary of State, who extended the period for compliance. The occupiers appealed. *Held*, the occupiers had correctly drawn a distinction between the results obtaining if the Secretary of State granted an extension of time for compliance under the Town and Country Planning Act 1971, s. 89 (6), and if he granted temporary planning permission under s. 88 (5); however, it was entirely a matter for the Secretary of State to decide which course to adopt, having taken into account all relevant matters. He was obliged to consider the initial development plan but was entitled to set it aside as having no bearing on the matter. There was nothing to show that he had taken into account irrelevant material or failed to take into account relevant material. The appeal would be dismissed.

MOLDENE LTD V SECRETARY OF STATE FOR THE ENVIRONMENT (1978) 248 Estates Gazette 43 (Queen's Bench Division: LORD WIDGERY CJ, TALBOT and WATKINS JJ).

2811   **Footpath—obstruction—discretion of council to take proceedings to prevent**

See *R v Lancashire County Council, ex parte Guyer*, para. 1466.

2812   Inner Urban Areas Act 1978

See para. 2833.

2813   Inquiry—duty of inspector to record all submissions

See *North Surrey Water Co v Secretary of State for the Environment*, para. 2795.

2814   —— duty to comply with procedural rules

See *Performance Cars Ltd v Secretary of State for the Environment*, para. 11.

2815   Mineral working—controls

The Department of the Environment has issued a circular outlining the Secretary of State's conclusions on the Report of the Committee on Planning Control over Mineral Working (the Stevens Report). The report was published in 1976. For a full summary of those conclusions, see DoE Circular 58/78.

2816   Welsh Development Agency—pensions

See para. 2136.

TRADE AND INDUSTRY

Halsbury's Laws of England (3rd edn.), Vol. 38, paras. 1–600

2817   Article

Licensing Industrial Property Rights, B.I. Cawthra (scope of the British law on competition): 128 NLJ 648.

2818   Aircraft and shipbuilding industries—shipbuilding industry—pension schemes

See para. 2121.

2819   Census of production

The Census of Production (1979) (Returns and Exempted Persons) Order 1978, S.I. 1978 No. 1573 (in force on 31st December 1978), prescribes the matters about which a person carrying on an undertaking may be required to furnish returns for the Census of Production being taken in 1979, and exempts from such an obligation any person carrying on an undertaking in the exploration for and extraction of petroleum on land and offshore.

2820   Co-operative Development Agency Act 1978

The Co-operative Development Agency Act 1978 gives effect to the majority report of the Working Group on a Co-operative Development Agency. The Act received the royal assent on 30th June 1978 and came into force on that date.

The Act provides for the establishment of the Co-operative Development Agency and provides that the chairman and members of the Agency are to be appointed by the Secretary of State: s. 1. The Agency's functions are to promote the adoption and better understanding of co-operative principles, and to represent the interests of the co-operative movement: s. 2. Subject to certain qualifications the Agency is empowered to do anything necessary for the performance of its functions. The main qualification is that its borrowing limit is £100,000 and that sum may only be borrowed temporarily. The Secretary of State may make grants to the Agency of amounts not exceeding £900,000, or may specify amounts up to £1·5 million by statutory instrument: ss. 3 and 4. The Agency must prepare statements of account, which must be audited by the Comptroller and Auditor General who has a duty to lay them, together with his auditor's report, before Parliament. The Agency has to make an annual report of its operations to the Secretary of State who has a duty to lay that report before Parliament: ss. 5 and 6. Section 7 contains financial provisions. Section 8 contains the citation and extends the application of the Act to Northern Ireland.

Members of the Agency are disqualified from membership of the House of Commons and the Northern Ireland Assembly. Detailed provisions are laid down as to the appointment, tenure of office and remuneration of members of the Agency, and as to the proceedings of the Agency: Sch. 1. Schedule 2 contains the alternative provisions for accounts and audit to which effect can be given by the Secretary of State under s. 5.

2821   Counter-inflation

See EMERGENCY CONTROLS.

2822   Employer; employment

See EMPLOYMENT; UNFAIR DISMISSAL.

2823   Employment agencies and businesses—licence—fee

The Employment Agencies and Employment Businesses Licence Fee Regulations 1978, S.I. 1978 No. 390 (in force on 1st June 1978), revoke the Employment Agencies and Employment Businesses Licence Fee Regulations 1976, 1976 Halsbury's Abr para. 2572, and prescribe the increased fees payable on the grant or renewal of a licence under the Employment Agencies Act 1973 to carry on an employment agency or business.

2824   Exports—control

See CUSTOMS AND EXCISE.

2825   Export guarantees—subsidies to exporters—extension of period

The Export Guarantees (Extension of Period) (No. 2) Order 1978, S.I. 1978 No. 322 (in force on 4th March 1978), extends to 26th March 1979, the period during which arrangements for export subsidies may be made by the Secretary of State.

2826   Export Guarantees and Overseas Investment Act 1978

The Export Guarantees and Overseas Investment Act 1978 received the royal assent on 30th June 1978 and came into force on 30th July 1978. The Act consolidates the Export Guarantees Act 1975, as amended by s. 4 of the International Finance, Trade and Aid Act 1977, and ss. 1 and 2 of the Overseas Investment and Export Guarantees Act 1972.

Tables showing the destination of enactments consolidated and the deviation of the Act are set out on pp. 627, 628 following.

DESTINATION TABLE

This table shows in column (1) the enactments repealed by the Export Guarantees and Overseas Investment Act 1978, and in column (2) the provisions of that Act corresponding to the repealed provisions.

In certain cases the enactment in column (1), though having a corresponding provision in column (2), is not repealed as it is still required for the purposes of other legislation.

(1)	(2)	(1)	(2)
Overseas Investment and Export Guarantees Act 1972 (c. 40)	Export Guarantees and Overseas Investment Act 1978 (c. 18)	Export Guarantees Act 1975 (c. 38)	Export Guarantees and Overseas Investment Act 1978 (c. 18)
s. 1 (1)	s. 11 (1)	s. 6 (7)	s. 15 (2)
(2)	ss. 11 (2), 15 (5)	6A	7
(3)	s. 11 (3)	6B	8
(4)	12 (1)	7	9
(5), (6)	11 (6), (7)	8	ss. 10, 15 (4)
2 (1), (2)	14	9	12
(3)	11 (4)	10	14
(4)	ss. 11 (5), 13	11 (1)	15 (1)
5 (2) (a)★	s. 15 (1)	(2), (3)	(5), (6)
(b)★	(4)	(4)	———
(3)★	14 (1)	(5)	(7)
Export Guarantees Act 1975 (c. 38)		12	———
s. 1	1	**International Finance, Trade and Aid Act 1977 (c. 6)**	
2	2		
3	3	s. 4 (1)	See against 1977 c. 6, Sch. 1, below
4 (1)–(3)	4		
(4)	15 (1)	(2), (3)	———
5 (1)–(4)	5 (1)–(4)	Sch. 1, para. 1	ss. 6–8, 13, 15 (1)–(3)
(5)	13	2	s. 9
6 (1)–(4)	6	3	12 (1)
(5)	13	4	15 (1)
(6)	15 (1), (3)		

★ Not repealed

TABLE OF DERIVATIONS

This table shows in the right hand column the legislative source from which the sections of the 1978 Act in the left hand column have been derived. In the table the following abbreviations are used:

1972 = The Overseas Investment and Export Guarantees Act 1972 (c. 40)
1975 = The Export Guarantees Act 1975 (c. 38)
1977 = The International Finance, Trade and Aid Act 1977 (c. 6)

Section of Act	Derivation
1–4	1975 ss. 1–4.
5 (1), (2) (3) (4)	1975 s. 5 (1), (2). 1975 s. 5 (3); Export Guarantees (Extension of Period) (No. 2) Order 1978. 1975 s. 5 (4).
6	1975 s. 6 (1)–(4); 1977 s. 4, Sch. 1 para. 1.
7, 8	1975 ss. 6A, 6B; 1977 s. 4 Sch. 1 para. 1.
9	1975 s. 7; 1977 s. 4 Sch. 1 para. 2.
10	1975 s. 8
11 (1)–(3) (4), (5) (6), (7)	1972 s. 1 (1)–(3). 1972 s. 2 (3), (4). 1972 s. 1 (5), (6).
12	1975 s. 9.
13	1972 s. 2 (4); 1975 ss. 5 (5), 6 (5); 1977 s. 4 Sch. 1 para. 1.
14 (1) (2)	1972 ss. 2 (1), 5 (3); 1975 s. 10 (1). 1972 s. 2 (2); 1975 s. 10 (2).
15 (1) (2) (3) (4) (5), (6) (7)	1972 s. 5 (2) (*a*), 1975 s. 11 (1), (definition of "business"); 1975 s. 11 (1), (definition of "export contracts"); 1975 ss. 6 (6), 11 (1); 1975 s. 6 (6); 1977 s. 4 Sch. 1 para. 1 (definition of "foreign currency"); 1977 s. 4 Sch. 1 para. 1 (definition of "foreign currency liabilities"); 1975 s. 11 (1) (definition of "guarantee"); 1975 s. 11 (1); 1977 s. 4 Sch. 1 para. 4 (definition of "quarter"); 1975 ss. 6A (6), 11 (1); 1977 s. 4 Sch. 1 paras. 1, 4 (definition of "quarterly revaluation"); 1975 s. 4 (4) (definition of "securities"); 1975 ss. 6 (6), 11 (1); 1977 s. 4 Sch. 1 paras. 1, 4 (definition of "sterling liabilities"); 1975 s. 11 (1), (definition of "trade with other countries"). 1975 s. 6 (7); 1977 s. 4 Sch. 1 para. 1. 1975 ss. 6 (6), 11 (1); 1977 s. 4 Sch. 1 para. 1. 1975 s. 8. 1975 s. 11 (2), (3). 1975 s. 11 (5).
16	[Short title, repeals, revocation, commencement and extent.]
Sch.	[Enactments repealed.]

2827   **Health and safety at work**

See HEALTH AND SAFETY AT WORK.

2828   **Imports—control**

See CUSTOMS AND EXCISE.

2829   **Industrial relations**

See EMPLOYMENT; UNFAIR DISMISSAL.

2830   **Industrial training levy—construction industry**

The Industrial Training Levy (Construction Board) Order 1978, S.I. 1978 No. 1471 (in force on 22nd November 1978), gives effect to proposals made by the Construction Industry Training Board for the imposition of a levy on employers in the construction industry to encourage adequate training. The levy is to be assessed by the Board with a right of appeal against the assessment to an industrial tribunal.

2831   **—— wool, jute and flax industry**

The Industrial Training Levy (Wool, Jute and Flax) Order 1978, S.I. 1978 No. 1305 (in force on 16th October 1978), gives effect to proposals made by the Wool, Jute and Flax Industry Training Board for the imposition of a levy on employers in the wool, jute and flax industry to encourage adequate training. The levy is to be assessed by the Board with a right of appeal against the assessment to an industrial tribunal.

2832   **Industry—financial assistance**

The Financial Assistance for Industry (Increase of Limit) Order 1978, S.I. 1978 No. 812 (in force on 3rd June 1978), increases the limit of the aggregate of the sums paid by the Secretary of State under the Industry Act 1972, s. 8, and the liabilities of the Secretary of State under guarantees given under that section, from £850 million to £1,100 million.

2833   **Inner Urban Areas Act 1978**

The Inner Urban Areas Act 1978 gives effect to the proposals contained in paragraph 54 of the White Paper on Policy for the Inner Cities (Cmnd. 6845) to enhance the powers of local authorities with serious inner area problems. The Act received the royal assent on 31st July 1978 and came into force on that date.

The Act defines "designated district" as an inner urban area in which the Secretary of State is satisfied that special social need may be alleviated by the exercise of the powers under the Act. "Designated district authorities" are then the relevant county, regional and district councils: s. 1. Designated district authorities may make loans for the acquisition of land or the carrying out of works on land situated within a designated district; terms and conditions of the loans are prescribed: s. 2. Loans and grants may also be made to establish common ownership and co-operative enterprises: s. 3. The authorities may declare industrial improvement areas. The procedure for such declarations is prescribed and the Secretary of State is given power to negative the declaration of an area: s. 4; Sch. Designated district authorities may make loans and grants to assist with improvements to amenities in improvement areas: s. 5; and may make grants for the conversion or improvement of industrial or commercial buildings in improvement areas. The grants may be up to 50 per cent of the work carried out or £1,000 for each job that is likely to be created or preserved as a result of the carrying out of the works: s. 6. The Secretary of State may give directions as to the making of the grants. The Secretary of State and other ministers may enter into arrangements with local authorities and other persons in designated districts if they are satisfied that a concerted effort should be made to alleviate the conditions giving rise to a special social need: s. 7. Section 8 provides that where arrangements are made with designated district authorities under s. 7 the

Secretary of State may specify parts of the designated districts as "special areas" in which the powers contained in ss. 9, 10 and 11 may be exercised. These sections provide that designated district authorities may make loans, interest free for up to two years, for site preparation in special areas: s. 9, grants, payable to persons taking new leases, towards rents of industrial or commercial premises in special areas: s. 10, and grants towards the interest payable in respect of any loan made to a small firm (an industrial or commercial undertaking with no more than 50 employees) for the acquisition of land or the carrying out of works on land situated within a special area: s. 11. The Secretary of State may give directions as to the making of grants under ss. 9, 10 and 11. If the Secretary of State so directs, local authorities in England and Wales with serious inner urban problems can adopt a local plan in advance of the approval or alteration of a structure plan: s. 12. Sections 13 and 14 provide for minor amendments to the Local Government Act 1972, s. 137 (1), the Local Government (Scotland) Act 1973, s. 83 (1) and the Local Employment Act 1972, s. 8. Sections 15 to 18 are miscellaneous provisions dealing with the making of orders under the Act financial provisions and interpretation.

2834 —— designated districts

The Inner Urban Areas (Designated Districts) (England and Wales) Order 1978, S.I. 1978 No. 1314 (in force on 29th September 1978), specifies designated districts, the district authorities of which are given additional powers under the Inner Urban Areas Act 1978, see para. 2833.

2835

The Inner Urban Areas (Designated Districts) (England and Wales) (No. 2) Order 1978, S.I. 1978 No. 1486 (in force on 13th November 1978), specifies the district of Wolverhampton as a designated district for the purposes of the Inner Urban Areas Act 1978.

2836 Investment grants—termination

The Investment Grants Termination (No. 8) Order 1978, S.I. 1978 No. 73 (in force on 20th February 1978), specifies further dates by which applications for investment grants must be made. It also provides for the making of directions as to the form and contents of such applications.

2837 Iron and Steel (Amendment) Act 1978

The Iron and Steel (Amendment) Act 1978 received the royal assent on 20th July 1978 and came into force on that date. The Act increases the limit on the sums which the British Steel Corporation may borrow to £4,750 million and provides that the limit may be further increased up to £5,500 million by order of the Secretary of State.

2838 National Enterprise Board—alleged breach of statutory duty— action by private individual

See *Booth & Co (International) Ltd v National Enterprise Board*, para. 2755.

2839 —— increase in financial limits

The National Enterprise Board (Financial Limit) Order 1978, S.I. 1978 No. 580 (in force on 15th April 1978), raises the maximum permissible limit under the Industry Act 1975, s. 8 (2), to £1,000 million. This sum is in respect of general external borrowing, guarantees of external borrowing by the Board. Government investment in the Board, and offers by the Board of selective financial assistance.

2840 Participation Agreements Act 1978

The Participation Agreements Act 1978 exempts agreements providing for majority state participation in United Kingdom offshore petroleum from the Restrictive Trade Practices Acts 1956 and 1976. The Act, which has retrospective effect, received the royal assent on 23rd February 1978 and came into force on that date.

An agreement which is certified as a participation agreement by the Secretary of State is exempt from the 1956 and 1976 Acts: s. 1 (1), (2). A participation agreement is defined as an agreement which provides for participation by the United Kingdom Government, the British National Oil Corporation or any other body on behalf of the Government in activities connected with petroleum found in the United Kingdom territorial sea or certain other designated areas: s. 1 (3).

2841   Price code

See EMERGENCY CONTROLS.

2842   Prices

See FOOD; CONSUMER PROTECTION.

2843   —— footwear

The Distribution of Footwear (Prices) Order 1978, S.I. 1978 No. 1307 (in force on 1st October 1978), requires certain distributors who specialise in the retail distribution of footwear to restrict retail prices so that their gross margins do not exceed a level determined by reference to those achieved in specified earlier periods.

2844   Redundancy

See EMPLOYMENT.

2845   Restraint of trade—covenant not to compete—validity

Canada

An employee covenanted with the firm that employed him not to compete with that firm for a period of three years after leaving his employment. The restriction applied to fields in which the firm carried on business or in which it would carry on business during the period of employment. After the employee had left, the firm applied for an injunction restraining him from breaching his agreement. *Held*, the terms of agreement were unreasonably wide since it was not possible for the employee to know at the time of execution of the agreement what business the employer might later carry on. The agreement was therefore unenforceable.

CREDITEL OF CANADA LTD v FAULTLESS (1977) 81 DLR (3d) 567 (High Court of Ontario).

2846   —— covenant restraining solicitor from practising in area for three years—validity of covenant

See *Richards v Levy*, para. 2736.

2847   Restrictive trade practices—exemptions

See para. 2840.

2848   Shipbuilding industry—redundancy payments scheme

See para. 1142.

2849   Special development areas

The Special Development Areas Order 1978, S.I. 1978 No. 1141 (in force on 24th August 1978), amends the Special Development Areas Order 1972 so as to designate specified areas as special development areas for the purposes of the Industry Act 1972, s. 1. It also contains a description of the Scottish Special Development Area incorporating the changes made to it by the Assisted Areas Order 1977, as amended, 1977 Halsbury's Abr para. 2823.

2850 Unfair dismissal

See UNFAIR DISMISSAL.

TRADE DESCRIPTIONS

2851 Article

Misdescriptions of Goods, Services and Property, Deborah L. Rudkin (a look at the Review of the Trade Descriptions Act 1968 (Cmnd 6628)): 122 Sol Jo 119.

2852 False indication as to price—discharge of purchase price in part by exchange

Motorcycle retailers advertised a Yamaha motorcycle for sale "list price £580, our price £540". In response to the advertisement a potential customer visited the retailers and offered to trade in his motorcycle in part exchange for a Yamaha. The salesman invoiced the price as £580 before the reduction for part exchange. The customer was told that the special price only applied to sales for cash or hire purchase, not to part exchange. The retailers were convicted of offering to supply a motorcycle having given, by mean of a statement in writing, an indication likely to be taken as an indication that it was being offered at a price less than that at which it was in fact being offered contrary to Trade Descriptions Act 1968, s. 11 (2). The prosecuting authority appealed against a decision of the Crown Court allowing an appeal against conviction. The retailers contended that a trader was entitled to insist on cash, that there was nothing in the advertisement to show that anything else was contemplated, and that the part exchange gave rise to completely fresh negotiations. *Held*, s. 11 (2) was concerned with an offer which induced a subsequent sale. The fact that the purchase price was discharged in part by exchange could not affect the situation which existed when the advertisement appeared. If the retailers had wished to limit the offer to sale by cash or hire purchase they could easily have worded the advertisement accordingly. They had not done so and the effect on the customer was that he took the advertisement as an indication that goods were being offered at a price lower than that at which they were offered. The case would be remitted to the Crown Court.

READ BROS CYCLES (LEYTON) LTD v WALTHAM FOREST LONDON BOROUGH COUNCIL (1978) 76 LGR 741 (Queen's Bench Division: LORD WIDGERY CJ, CROOM-JOHNSON and STOCKER JJ). *Doble v David Greig Ltd* [1972] 2 All ER 195 applied.

2853 False trade description—disclaimer—effectiveness

The defendants, second-hand car dealers, offered for sale a car with a false mileage recorded on the odometer. Displayed in the office was a notice stating that no guarantee was given with regard to mileage. The defendants were charged with contravening the Trade Descriptions Act 1968, s. 1 (1) (b), by offering to supply a car to which a false trade description was applied by means of a false odometer reading. Justices dismissed the information on the ground that the notice was sufficient to exclude liability. On appeal by the prosecutor, *held*, for the notice to be effective, it would have to be displayed beside the false description. The notice in this case was not sufficiently proximate. The appeal would be allowed and the case sent back to the justices with a direction to convict.

WALTHAM FOREST LONDON BOROUGH COUNCIL v T. G. WHEATLEY (CENTRAL GARAGE) LTD (No. 2) (1978) Times, 22nd April (Queen's Bench Division: LORD WIDGERY CJ, BOREHAM and DRAKE JJ).

2854 Indication of origin

The Trade Descriptions (Indication of Origin) (Exemptions No. 11) Directions

1978, S.I. 1978 No. 1153 (in force on 1st September 1978), exclude the Trade Descriptions Act 1972, s. 1 (2), which requires a United Kingdom name or mark applied to imported goods to be accompanied by an indication of the country of origin of those goods, in relation to gramophone records.

TRADE MARKS, TRADE NAMES AND DESIGNS

Halsbury's Laws of England (3rd edn.), Vol. 38, paras. 811–1135

2855 Designs rules

The Designs (Amendment No. 2) Rules 1978, S.I. 1978 No. 1151 (in force on 10th August 1978, except r. 3, which is in force on 2nd October 1978), further amend the Designs Rules 1949 so as to increase certain fees payable under them with effect from 2nd October 1978. In the case of fees paid in advance for the extension of the copyright period in a design in respect of any period beginning on or after 2nd October 1978, the fees are increased with effect from 10th August 1978. The Designs (Amendment No. 3) Rules 1975, 1975 Halsbury's Abr para. 3352, are revoked, as are the Designs (Amendment) Rules 1978, S.I. 1978 No. 907, which made similar provisions.

2856 Gun Barrel Proof Act 1978

The Gun Barrel Proof Act 1978 makes provisions for the United Kingdom to accede to the 1969 Convention for the Reciprocal Recognition of Proof Marks, the purpose of which is to promote common standards of proof. The Act also makes minor amendments to the Gun Barrel Proof Act 1868 and increases penalties under that Act so as to bring them into line with the penalties for other offences of similar gravity. The Act received the royal assent on 5th May 1978 and ss. 2–7, 8 (1) (so far as it relates to Sch. 3), 8 (2), 9, Sch. 3, paras. 1 (part), 2–9, 10 (1), 11–14, 15 (1), (2), 16 (part), 17–20 and Sch. 4 came into force on 1st December 1978.

Sections 129–137 of the 1868 Act are replaced by three new sections which provide for the Two Companies to keep a copy of and to publicise the register of convention proof marks published by the International Commission, exempt barrels bearing convention proof marks from the requirements as to proof of the 1868 Act, and modify the offence creating provisions of the 1868 Act: s. 1, Sch. 1. Schedule 2 contains transitional provisions relating to the register of foreign proof marks kept by the Two Companies, and provides that certain foreign barrels shall be exempt from the requirement for proof under the 1868 Act.

A person who commits an offence under ss. 30, 122 or 143 of the 1868 Act is liable on summary conviction to a fine not exceeding the statutory maximum and on conviction on indictment to a fine. The categories of offences under ss. 87, 100 and 142 of the 1868 Act are removed: s. 2. Restrictions on the siting of a branch proof house within ten miles of Birmingham or the City of London are removed: s. 3. The Guardians of the Birmingham Proof House have the power to make rules and regulations under s. 106 of the 1868 Act, and ss. 101–105 of that Act are revoked: s. 4. Rules of Proof may be expressed in either imperial or metric units: s. 5.

The Gun Barrel Proof Acts of 1868 and 1950 are extended to Scotland and Northern Ireland: s. 6. Section 7 deals with interpretation; s. 8 and Schs. 3 and 4 provide for minor and consequential amendments and repeals. The formal provisions are contained in s. 9.

2857 Hallmarking

The United Kingdom deposited its instrument of ratification of the Convention on the Control and Marking of Articles of Precious Metals signed at Vienna in 1972 (Cmnd. 7219) on 1st April 1976 and the convention entered into force for the

United Kingdom on 1st June 1976; it was presented to Parliament in July 1978. The convention provides for the mutual recognition of assay and other marks on articles of precious metals (i.e. silver, gold, platinum or alloys of those metals). The convention prescribes the methods of analysis, the marks to be applied and a common control mark.

2858   Passing-off—interlocutory injunction—balance of convenience

The defendants' business included the supply and installation of bulk liquefied petroleum gas dispensing units. On occasions the defendants had filled empty Calor Gas cylinders with gas which was not Calor Gas. They had done this at the request of the customers. The plaintiffs sought an injunction to restrain the defendants from filling Calor Gas cylinders with other gas and so passing off that other gas as Calor Gas. It was also argued that, by doing this, the defendants were inducing customers to break their contracts with Calor Gas. On appeal against a refusal to grant an injunction, *held*, by coming to the defendants, the customers were already in breach of their contracts with Calor Gas so that there was no inducement to breach. It could not be said that the judge had been plainly wrong in deciding that on the balance of convenience no injunction was required. The appeal would be dismissed and no injunction would be granted.

CALOR GAS LTD v CARGOES CARGAS LTD [1978] FSR 182 (Court of Appeal: STEPHENSON and SHAW LJJ).

2859   —— —— —— likelihood of damage to both parties

The plaintiffs were whisky dealers with an extensive reputation in the name "Red Label" for whisky. The defendants were tobacco manufacturers who were about to launch a new brand of cigarettes under the name of "Red Label". The plaintiffs applied for an interlocutory injunction to restrain the defendants' use of the name "Red Label", alleging that it was likely to mislead the public into believing that the cigarettes were associated with Red Label Whisky. *Held*, there was a serious question to be tried because the plaintiffs' claim was neither frivolous not vexatious. There was a risk of unquantifiable damage to the plaintiffs if no interlocutory injunction was granted and they were successful in obtaining a permanent injunction at the trial; and a certainty of unquantifiable damage to the defendants if the plaintiffs obtained an interlocutory injunction but failed at the trial. Where both parties might suffer unquantifiable damage, the status quo should be maintained unless there were compelling reasons to the contrary. In the present case, the main reason was that there was only a risk of unquantifiable damage to the plaintiffs yet a certainty of unquantifiable damage to the defendants. Accordingly, the application would be refused.

JOHN WALKER & SONS LTD v ROTHMANS INTERNATIONAL LTD AND JOHN SINCLAIR LTD [1978] FSR 357 (Chancery Division: BRIGHTMAN J). *American Cyanamid Co v Ethicon Ltd* [1975] 1 All ER 504, HL, 1975 Halsbury's Abr para. 1864 applied.

2860   —— —— likelihood of confusion—distinctiveness of trade name

The plaintiffs prepared a drink in the Netherlands known as advocaat the alcoholic content of which was the spirit "brandewijn". It was imported and sold in the United Kingdom. The defendants began to manufacture and sell in the United Kingdom a drink known as "Keeling's Old English Advocaat" the alcoholic content of which was a fortified Cypriot wine. The plaintiffs' alleged that the defendants' mixture could not honestly be called advocaat since it contained fortified wine instead of spirit and that the defendants' mixture had injured the plaintiffs' business and goodwill. The plaintiffs' were granted an injunction restraining the defendants from advertising and selling their product as advocaat. The defendants appealed. *Held*, although the defendants had not intended to pass off their advocaat as that of the plaintiffs the tort of passing off did not only consist of a representation to the public by the defendant that his goods were in fact the plaintiffs'; it was only necessary that there should be a relevant misrepresentation and consequent damage or likelihood of damage to the plaintiff's goodwill. In the case of a trade name there could be no proprietary right in one which was purely descriptive; some measure of distinctiveness was essential for it to be capable of giving rise to a passing off action. The plaintiffs' contention that advocaat was a name distinctive of a particular type of product, namely a drink consisting of egg yolks and spirit, was incorrect. A trade name could only be protected in passing off proceedings if it was distinctive of the goods of one particular producer, or a number of identified producers. Alternatively, if it was distinctive of the goods of a class of producers whose products had a particular character and reputation. Further, where a name was purely descriptive of a kind of goods, a person who used it accurately to describe his goods had no cause of action against another who misused it to describe his goods inaccurately, notwithstanding that by the inaccurate description the public was misled in a way injurious to the user. The plaintiffs could not succeed either upon the ground of passing off or upon any wider ground of unfair competition. The appeal would be allowed.

ERVEN WARNINK BV v J. TOWNEND & SONS (HULL) LTD (1978) Times, 20th April (Court of Appeal: BUCKLEY and GOFF LJJ and SIR DAVID CAIRNS). Decision of Goulding J [1978] FSR 1, reversed. *H. P. Bulmer Ltd v J. Bollinger.SA* [1977] 2 CMLR 625, CA, 1977 Halsbury's Abr para. 2872 and *Bollinger v Costa Brava Wine Co Ltd* [1960] Ch 262, *Vine Products Ltd v Mackenzie & Co Ltd* [1969] RPC 1, applied.

2861   The plaintiffs manufactured mechanical excavators including a series known as the '580' series. The basis of the name was that the capacity of the excavation bucket on the machine was ⅝ cubic yard. The defendants began to market an excavator for which the number '580' was used for identification; in their machines, the designation bore no relation to bucket capacity. In a passing off action the plaintiffs sought an interlocutory injunction restraining the defendants from using the designation, arguing that it was distinctive of their machines alone. The defendants claimed that the number was merely descriptive and available for anyone to use. *Held*, '580' was not obviously descriptive of any feature of the plaintiffs' machines but part of a private numerology. No satisfactory reason had been advanced by the defendants to show why they had selected that designation. Thus on the balance of convenience the injunction would be granted.

HYMAC LTD v PRIESTMAN BROTHERS LTD [1978] RPC 495 (Chancery Division: WALTON J).

2862   —— newspaper—title—likelihood of confusion with another newspaper

See *Morning Star Co-operative Society Ltd v Express Newspapers Ltd*, para. 2234.

2863   —— sale of unnamed goods with known brand—whether packaging suggested authorisation of known brand's manufacturer

The plaintiffs sought an interlocutory injunction to restrain the defendants from marketing a gift package containing a bottle of their perfumed foam-bath and an unnamed bottle of scent. The plaintiffs feared their reputation could suffer if the public thought either that the scent was theirs or that they had authorised its sale together with the foam-bath. *Held*, it was arguable that the packaging suggested the plaintiffs' authorisation of the side-by-side sale, although it was fanciful to suggest the scent was being represented as the plaintiffs' product. Equally arguably, the plaintiffs' goodwill could be damaged. As the plaintiffs had applied for relief as soon as the gift pack appeared in advertisements, an injunction would be granted to preserve the status quo.

MORNY LTD v BALL & ROGERS (1975) LTD [1978] FSR 91 (Chancery Division: GOULDING J).

2864   Rectification of the register—assignment of associated mark—partial assignment—validity

An application was made for rectification of the register by cancellation of the registration of a trade mark. The mark had been assigned to the proprietors in respect of some only of the classes of goods described in it. It had at all times been associated with two other marks of the assignors and had never been dissociated from them. The application for rectification was made under the Trade Marks Act 1938, s. 23 (1), which prohibits partial assignment of associated marks; the applicants contended that no application had been made to dissociate the mark and the assignment was therefore a nullity. The proprietors argued that there was no reason or requirement to dissociate associated marks before assignment unless the whole of the mark was to be transferred. It was held that the entry should be removed. On appeal, *held*, s. 23 applied only to an assignment of a mark in respect of all the goods to which it related. The case of a partial assignment was dealt with by s. 22, without regard to the restriction in s. 23 (1). The registration complied with the provisions of s. 22 and was valid. The appeal would be allowed.

PHANTOM TRADE MARK [1978] RPC 245 (Court of Appeal: BUCKLEY and GOFF LJJ and SIR DAVID CAIRNS). Decision of Graham J [1978] RPC 64, reversed.

2865   Registration—Convention application for registration—failure to comply with time limits—whether post-dating of application possible

An application to register a design was made in France. Subsequently a Convention application for United Kingdom registration was made claiming priority as from the date of the first application. The Convention documents to support the claim were filed one day outside the statutory period of three months from the application. As there was no discretionary power to enlarge the period, the applicants applied to post-date the filing of their United Kingdom application by one day and thereby upheld their claim to priority. The application was rejected and they appealed. *Held*, the power to permit an application to be post-dated did not exist under the Registered Designs Act 1949. The appeal would be dismissed.

ALLIBERT EXPLOITATION'S APPLICATION [1978] RPC 261 (Registered Designs Appeal Tribunal: WHITFORD J).

2866   —— descriptive word—whether word capable of distinguishing the goods

Dog food traders applied to have the word "chunky" registered as a trade mark. The application was opposed on the ground that the word was inherently incapable of distinguishing the particular goods from any other similar products. *Held*, at the date of the application the word had been little used; its subsequent wider use was attributable in the main to an advertising campaign mounted by the applicants. None of the evidence suggested that other traders had used the word before the applicants had and accordingly the latter had discharged their onus of proof and the objection would fail.

CHUNKY TRADE MARK [1978] FSR 322 (Chancery Division: WHITFORD J).

2867   —— design—principles governing registration

The designers of a computer print-out featuring coloured bands applied to have the design registered. Their application was refused on the ground that the design was of a literary or artistic character and thus not registrable under the Designs Rules 1949. On appeal, *held*, on the facts the design was not of a literary or artistic nature. Nonetheless, the Registered Designs Act 1949, s.1 precluded registration because the coloured bands were not features which in the finished article would be judged solely by the eye.

LAMSON INDUSTRIES LIMITED'S APPLICATION [1978] RPC 1 (Registered Designs Appeal Tribunal: WHITFORD J).

2868   A designer applied for registration of a design for a chocolate egg, the novelty of which was that the shell had a chocolate coloured outer layer and a white inner layer. The hearing officer accepted that, while the Registered Designs Act 1949 s. 1 laid down that the sole judge of novelty was the eye, it was not necessary that the feature could be seen on examination of the exterior. However he refused the application on the ground that in this case the novelty could only be seen if the egg was broken, after which it would not be a finished article within s. 1 (3). On appeal, *held*, the Act required only that the novelty be a feature of the finished article which would appeal to the eye when seen, not that a consumer should be able to see the feature when the article was in a finished state. The appeal would be allowed.

P. FERRERO AND CSPA'S APPLICATION [1978] RPC 473 (Registered Designs Appeal Tribunal: WHITFORD J.) *Amp Incorporated v Utilux Property Ltd* [1972] RPC 103 explained.

2869   Trade Marks Rules

The Trade Marks (Amendment) Rules 1978, S.I. 1978 No. 1120 (rule 3 in force on 1st November 1978, remainder in force on 8th August 1978) further amend the Trade Marks Rules 1938 so as to increase certain fees payable under them. The new fees become payable on or after 1st November 1978, except in the case of renewal fees paid in advance in respect of any period beginning on or after 1st November 1978, which are increased with effect from 8th August 1978. The Rules revoke S.I. 1975 No. 1532, 1975 Halsbury's Abr para. 3375.

TRADE UNIONS

Halsbury's Laws of England (3rd edn.), Vol. 38, paras. 601–677

2870   Articles

Shop Stewards and the Law, Nicola Squire (statement of problem concerning legal position of a shop steward): 128 NLJ 765.

Union Recognition Procedure Reviewed, Henry E. Markson (points arising out of the judgments of the Court of Appeal and House of Lords in *Grunwick Processing Laboratories Ltd v ACAS*, 1977 Halsbury's Abr para. 2887: 122 Sol Jo 39.

2871   Action in furtherance of trade dispute—interlocutory injunction to restrain action—balance of convenience

The owners of a Liberian vessel recruited Indian seamen at a low rate of pay which was mutually convenient to both sides. At the insistence of the International Federation of Transport Workers (ITF), a federation of seamen's unions, who had "blacked" the vessel and had threatened to prohibit it from sailing, the owners agreed that they would increase the pay to the higher ITF scale. The Indian seamen however, refused to agree to the increase because they did not want to prejudice their position with their own union and government. The crew were consequently repatriated and a new Greek crew were taken on who also refused to sign the ITF agreement as they preferred Greek union terms. The ITF continued to "black" the vessel. The owners' application for an interlocutory injunction to restrain the "blacking" was refused and they appealed. *Held*, statutory immunity from actions in tort was granted to trade unions by the Trade Union and Labour Relations Act 1974, s. 13, which covered acts done in contemplation or furtherance of a trade dispute. Section 17 of the Act provided that where an application for an interlocutory injunction was made to restrain such an act, the court had to consider whether s. 13 would provide a defence to the action. In the present case however, as there was a very arguable point of law mixed up with facts, the balance of convenience had also to be considered in deciding whether or not to grant an injunction. The vessel had been prevented from sailing and the owners had suffered greater loss than the ITF whose only loss was a bargaining counter. While s. 17 was an important factor, it was not decisive and on the balance of convenience the ship should be allowed to sail and the ban lifted. The injunction would therefore be granted.

THE CAMILLA M, (1978) Times, 14th October (Court of Appeal: LORD DENNING MR, STEPHENSON and BRANDON LJJ).

2872   Advisory, Conciliation and Arbitration Service—statutory duties—validity of decision to defer inquiries pending judicial proceedings

The Engineers' and Managers' Association (EMA) referred its case of recognition to the Advisory, Conciliation and Arbitration Service (ACAS). Meanwhile, the Trade Union Congress instructed the EMA to cease recruitment and not to seek recognition for itself. The EMA then brought an action seeking a declaratory injunction against the TUC to the effect that the TUC's instructions were invalid. In deference to these proceedings, ACAS delayed its own inquiries as the outcome of the trial would be a material factor in the recognition issue. The EMA then brought an action against ACAS for failing to observe its statutory duties to carry out inquiries on the recognition issue. *Held*, ACAS had a discretion, subject to the test of reasonableness, to defer its inquiries if circumstances rendered it desirable to do so. At the time ACAS made its decision to defer, an early disposal of the trial was probable and it was reasonable in those circumstances to defer its inquiries. The courts would not interfere with their decision.

ENGINEERS' AND MANAGERS' ASSOCIATION v ADVISORY, CONCILIATION AND ARBITRATION SERVICE [1978] ICR 875 (Chancery Division: OLIVER J).

2873   Amalgamations—trade unions and employers' associations

The Trade Unions and Employers' Associations (Amalgamations, etc.) (Amendment) Regulations 1978, S.I. 1978 No. 1344 (in force on 1st November 1978) amend the Trade Unions and Employers' Associations (Amalgamations, etc.) Regulations 1975, 1975 Halsbury's Abr para. 3377. They increase the fees payable in connection with amalgamations and transfers of engagements, name changes and inspection of documents.

2874   Certificate of independence—criteria for grant

A staff association was refused a certificate of independence by the Certification Officer on the ground that although it was not under the domination or control of the employer, it was liable to interference by him tending towards such control, contrary to the definition of an independent trade union in the Trade Union and Labour Relations Act 1974, s. 30 (1). The Certification Officer considered that the association was particularly vulnerable because of the extensive facilities provided for it by the employer, without which he considered that the association would find it difficult to operate. On appeal from a decision by the Employment Appeal Tribunal that the association was independent, *held*, there was a risk that the association was liable to interference by the employer. The degree of likelihood of the risk was irrelevant so long as it was not insignificant or de minimis. In this instance, the employer merely had to withdraw the facilities which he provided, for the association to be weakened. The appeal would be allowed.

SQUIBB UNITED KINGDOM STAFF ASSOCIATION v CERTIFICATION OFFICER (1978) Times, 11th October (Court of Appeal: LORD DENNING MR, SHAW and BRANDON LJJ). Decision of Forbes J, [1978] ICR 115, 1977 Halsbury's Abr para. 2879, reversed.

2875   —— fees

The Certification Officer (Amendment of Fees) Regulations 1978, S.I. 1978 No. 1329 (in force on 1st November 1978), increase the fee payable to the Certification Officer, by a trade union on application for a certificate of independence, from £21 to £50.

2876   Closed shop agreement—application to local authority employees—whether incompatible with duties of authority

See *R v Greater London Council, ex parte Burgess*, para. 1809.

2877   Income tax—exemption—provident benefits

See para. 1586.

2878   Members—union duties and activities—absence from employment for performance of duties—entitlement to pay

See *Vine v DRG Ltd*, para. 1149.

2879   Recognition—acts amounting to recognition—whether employer's correspondence and meeting with union amounted to recognition

See *National Union of Gold, Silver and Allied Trades v Albury Brothers Ltd*, para. 1128.

2880   —— recommendation by Advisory Conciliation and Arbitration Service—validity of recommendation

The Advisory Conciliation and Arbitration Service were asked to decide a question of recognition involving a union that wished to represent the professionally qualified engineers working within a company. There were already a number of unions representing the company's employees, and these unions opposed the recognition of the union. ACAS recommended that the union should not be recognised. The union appealed to the Divisional Court, which found the ACAS report a nullity and of no effect because ACAS had failed to discharge its duties under the Employment Protection Act. ACAS appealed to the Court of Appeal. *Held*, dismissing the appeal, ACAS had not fulfilled its obligations under s 12 (4) of the Act because it had not set out its findings in the form of an objective assessment of the case, but merely stated the views of the parties. In particular it had not established whether the engineers were an effective group for collective bargaining purposes, who needed separate representation. Furthermore ACAS had not fulfilled its obligations under s. 1 (2). This section laid upon ACAS two duties, namely the improvement of industrial relations and the development and, where necessary, the reform of collective bargaining machinery. Where the two duties clashed it was necessary to weigh the two against each other. LORD DENNING considered the special duty to encourage the development of collective bargaining took priority over the general duty to improve industrial relations under the maxim *generalia specialibus non derogant*. ACAS had not considered the need to reform the collective bargaining machinery, but had instead based its recommendation entirely upon the objections of the other unions and the possible consequences recognition might have for industrial relations.

UNITED KINDGOM ASSOCIATION OF PROFESSIONAL ENGINEERS V ADVISORY CONCILIATION AND ARBITRATION SERVICE (1979) 123 Sol Jo 79 (Court of Appeal: LORD DENNING MR, BRANDON and LAWTON LJJ (judgment delivered on 17th January)). Decision of MAY J (1978) Times, 1st July, affirmed.

2881   Rules—construction—amendment of rules—power of council to hold referendum

An action was brought by a union to determine the effect of its rules governing the alteration of the rules. Rule 43 provided that alterations should be made at general meetings and that a two-thirds majority of those present was necessary to effect an alteration. Rule 34 (1) empowered the governing council to conduct a vote of the entire association on "any question or resolution" whenever it was deemed necessary. By r. 34 (2), the members could present a petition demanding a vote of the entire association on any resolution passed at a general meeting. On appeal to the House of Lords, *held*, LORD FRASER OF TULLYBELTON dissenting, the union's contention that a rule could only be altered if r. 43 was complied with was incorrect. Reading r. 34 (2) and r. 43 together, if an alteration to a rule was made at a general meeting, on presentation of a petition a referendum could be taken on that resolution. Rule 34 (2) should be given its full effect, since otherwise a rule could be altered by a minority contrary to the wishes of the majority. Additionally, if an alteration in the rules was put to a meeting but did not get a two-thirds majority, a referendum could take place at the instance of the council if it considered it desirable in the members' interests. The rules showed that it was intended that any change of rules should be initiated at a general meeting and r. 34 gave a right of appeal to the entire association to a member who disapproved of a rule or alteration to a rule passed at such a meeting, and to the council, both in relation to a resolution which had been passed and one which had not been passed.

BRITISH ACTORS' EQUITY ASSOCIATION V GORING (1978) Times, 14th April (House of Lords: VISCOUNT DILHORNE, LORD PEARSON, LORD SALMON, LORD FRASER OF TULLYBELTON and LORD SCARMAN). Decision of the Court of Appeal [1977] ICR 393, 1977 Halsbury's Abr para. 2890, reversed in part.

2882 —— —— **power to hold fresh elections**

The plaintiff was a candidate for the post of national officer in an election held by a trade union. Due to a clerical error, an incorrect number of votes was returned in favour of another candidate, who was declared to have been duly elected. When the error was noticed, the head office informed all branches that another ballot would be held, the first being regarded as null and void. The plaintiff contended that while the union had acted fairly and honestly, the rules of the union did not empower the national council to declare an election invalid. Its only power was to call for and recount the voting papers and declare the result on the basis of such recount. *Held,* the trade union rules did not lay down a detailed code of conduct for ballots and made no attempt to deal with problems which might arise due to irregularities. However, they were wide enough to give the national council complete discretion as to how it should proceed. The decision to hold a fresh election was therefore valid.

SALTS V NATIONAL GRAPHICAL ASSOCIATION (1978) Times, 16th May (Queen's Bench Division: JUDGE LEWIS HAWSER QC sitting as a deputy High Court judge).

TRANSPORT

Halsbury's Laws of England (3rd edn.), Vol. 31, paras. 639–1403

2883 **London Transport—lost property**

The London Transport (Lost Property) (Amendment) Regulations 1978, S.I. 1978 No. 1791 (in force on 1st January 1979), amend the London Transport (Lost Property) Regulations 1971, S.I. 1971 No. 2125, by introducing a new scale of charges payable on the return of property accidentally left in or on vehicles or premises of the London Transport Executive.

2884 **Minibus—permit—grant by designated body**

The Minibus (Designated Bodies) (Amendment) Order 1978, S.I. 1978 No. 1930 (in force on 26th January 1979), amends the Minibus (Designated Bodies) Order 1977, 1977 Halsbury's Abr para. 2898. That Order designated the bodies which, in addition to the Traffic Commissioners, may grant permits under the Minibus Act 1977, 1977 Halsbury's Abr para. 2895, for the use of certain minibuses. The 1978 Order designates further bodies and classes of bodies.

2885 —— —— **prescribed form**

The Minibus (Permits) (Amendment) Regulations 1978, S.I. 1978 No. 1931 (in force on 26th January 1979), amend the Minibus (Permits) Regulations 1977 by prescribing more extensively the conditions which must be fulfilled by the driver of a minibus.

2886 **National Freight Corporation—pensions**

See paras 2125, 2126.

2887   **Public service vehicles—community buses**

The Community Bus Regulations 1978, S.I. 1978 No. 1313 (in force on 1st November 1978) apply to vehicles being used to provide a community bus service under the Transport Act 1978, ss. 5 and 6. Such vehicles, although exempt from the requirements relating to public service vehicle licensing, must comply with the conditions laid down in the Regulations whenever they are being used to provide a community bus service, unless the particular vehicle is one in respect of which a public service licence is in force. The Regulations also lay down conditions which must be satisfied by a driver of a community bus who does not hold a public service vehicle driver's licence, and prescribe the disc to be displayed on a vehicle to indicate that it is being used as a community bus.

2888   —— **lost property**

The Public Service Vehicles (Lost Property) Regulations 1978, S.I. 1978 No. 1684 (in force on 1st January 1979), replace the Public Service Vehicles (Lost Property) Regulations 1934, as amended. The principal changes are that awards are no longer to be made to conductors who find property or to whom property is handed and that charges to be paid by the owners of property are to be calculated according to specified rates set out in Schedule 2 of the Regulations, rather than being calculated by reference to the value of the property.

2889   —— **licences and certificates**

The Public Service Vehicles (Licences and Certificates) (Amendment) Regulations 1978, S.I. 1978 No. 1315 (in force on 1st November 1978) amend the Public Service Vehicles (Licences and Certificates) Regulations 1952. They provide that the 1952 Regulations, regs. 37–39, 41 and 43–45 shall not apply in relation to an application for a short term road service licence.

2890   **Transport Act 1978**

The Transport Act 1978 makes various changes in the law relating to transport and road traffic. It received the royal assent on 2nd August 1978 and came into force as follows: ss. 15, 17, 18, 21, 23, 24 (part) and Sch. 4 (part) came into force on 4th August 1978 (S.I. 1978 No. 1150); ss. 1–4, 7, 8 (part), 10–14, 16, 22, 24 (part), Schs. 1, 2 (part) and 4 (part) came into force on 1st September 1978, ss. 5, 6, 8 (part), 9, 24 (part), Schs. 2 (part), 3, 4 (part) came into force on 1st November 1978 (S.I. 1978 No. 1187); ss. 19 (part) and 20 (part) came into force on 1st October 1978 (S.I. 1978 No. 1289); the remaining parts of ss. 19 and 20 came into force on 1st October 1978 (S.I. 1978 No. 1289).

County transport planning
Section 1 provides that non-metropolitan county councils in England and Wales are under a duty to promote a co-ordinated and efficient system of public passenger transport to meet the county's needs. Such county councils must publish annually a five-year public passenger transport plan containing a review of the county's needs, a description of the council's policies and intended measures, estimates of the financial resources required and an account of how far previous forecasts have been realised: s. 2. County councils are required to enter into agreements with public passenger transport undertakings to provide financial support for services required by the plan which would not otherwise be provided: s. 3. They are also required to include in their public passenger transport plans a description of the concessionary fare schemes in their area or if there are none, the reasons for this: s. 4.

Public service vehicle licensing
Section 5 provides that the provision of community bus services using volunteer drivers may be authorised, and such vehicles are to be exempt from the requirement of public service vehicle licences providing certain conditions are met. Section 6 authorises the use of a community bus for contract work. Section 7 and Schedule 1 substitute new conditions in the Road Traffic Act 1960, Sch. 12, which completely

exempt vehicles carrying a maximum of seven passengers from public service vehicle licensing. The conditions concerning previous advertisement to the public are also amended. Section 8 and Schedule 2 amend the criteria in the 1960 Act to which traffic commissioners must have regard in exercising their road service licensing functions.

Road traffic regulation
Section 9 and Schedule 3 amend the provisions of the Road Traffic Acts governing the loading and maintenance of lorries, especially those relating to weighbridges and testing stations. A new defence to contravention of provisions restricting drivers' hours is provided by s. 10. The discretionary power to license public off-street parking places may be extended to county councils in England and Wales by Order in Council: s. 11. Section 12 states that the power of authorities to provide parking places extends to the provision of stands and racks for bicycles.

Waterway transport and railways
Section 13 provides that it is the duty of the Secretary of State to promote a national policy for the use of inland waterways for commercial transport. Section 14 continues the system of financial support for British Rail's public service obligations under the Railways Act 1974 and introduces new monetary limits. Section 15 provides for the transfer to the British Railways Board of all the securities in Freightliners Ltd which were previously vested in the National Freight Corporation. Section 16 amends the Railways Act 1974, s. 8, by expressly providing that grants towards rail freight facilities may be made for privately owned rolling stock.

National Freight Corporation
Sections 17–21 deal with the financial reconstruction of the National Freight Corporation, including the reduction of its capital debt to £100 m; capital grants to the Corporation; arrangements to be made by order of the Secretary of State for the funding of pension obligations of the Corporation, National Carriers Ltd and Freightliners Ltd; and travel concessions for employees transferred from British Rail.

Section 22 amends the Local Government Act 1974, s. 6, dealing with transport supplementary grants. Section 23 deals with financial matters arising from the Act, s. 24 with commencement, interpretation and the repeals specified in Sch. 4, and s. 25 with citation and extent.

TRESPASS

Halsbury's Laws of England (3rd edn.), Vol. 38, paras. 1194–1282

2891   Trespass to land—rights of trespasser—whether trespasser entitled to let property

The appellant, a squatter, occupied property belonging to the Greater London Council and paid towards the rates. She let a room to a married couple and continued to receive rent from them after leaving. She was convicted of obtaining property by deception by falsely pretending that it was lawful for her to let the room and collect the rent. On appeal against conviction on the ground that having dispossessed the Council she could do anything with the property that the owner could, *held*, the Council had not been dispossessed. As a trespasser, the appellant could exclude anyone except the true owner and probably charge them for admittance. The one thing she could not do was let the property for rent.

R v EDWARDS [1978] Crim LR 49 (Court of Appeal: GEOFFREY LANE LJ, THESIGER and DAVIES JJ).

2892   Trespass to property abroad—immovable property and chattels—jurisdiction of English courts

See *Hesperides Hotels Ltd v Muftizade*, para. 424.

TROVER AND DETINUE

Halsbury's Laws of England (3rd edn.), Vol. 38, paras. 1283–1345

2893   Articles

The Application of the Torts (Interference with Goods) Act 1977 to Actions in Bailment, N. E. Palmer (circumvention of 1977 Act by bringing actions for breach of bailment): (1978) 41 MLR 629.

The Law of Treasure and Treasure Hunters, Michael Leyland Nash: 128 NLJ 1163.

2894   Conversion—knowingly   misapplying   cheques—liability   in conversion

The plaintiffs agreed to purchase all the debts of a company, and the company agreed to execute an assignment to the plaintiffs in respect of each debt. The agreement further provided that if an assigned debt was paid directly to the company, the company was to hold it in trust for the plaintiffs, and hand to the plaintiffs an identical amount of money. The company was in financial difficulties and the defendant, one of its directors, arranged for a number of cheques to be paid into the company's bank account. He knew that the money should have been paid directly to the plaintiffs. The plaintiffs brought an action against him for conversion, and claimed the face value of the cheques as damages. At first instance judgment was for the plaintiffs and the defendant appealed, contending that the plaintiffs were not entitled to sue in conversion because they did not have a proprietary right to the cheques and that he could not be liable in conversion unless the company was liable. *Held*, the plaintiffs were entitled to sue in conversion because the agreement expressly gave them a right to immediate possession of the cheques. The defendant could not claim that he had acted on the company's behalf. He was the primary tortfeasor because he had misapplied the cheques in a manner which he knew would conflict with the plaintiffs' rights.

INTERNATIONAL FACTORS LTD v RODRIGUEZ [1979] 1 All ER 17 (Court of Appeal: BUCKLEY and BRIDGE LJJ and SIR DAVID CAIRNS).

2895   —— liability of auctioneer

See *Union Transport Finance Ltd v British Car Auctions Ltd*, para. 162.

2896   —— —— liability where seller has no title

See *R. H. Willis and Son v British Car Auctions Ltd*, para. 161.

2897   Torts (Interference with Goods) Act 1977—commencement

The Torts (Interference with Goods) Act 1977 (Commencement No. 2) Order 1978, S.I. 1978 No. 627 brought into force on 1st June 1978 the 1977 Act, 1977 Halsbury's Abr para. 2912 so far as it was not already in force.

2898   —— rules of the Supreme Court—amendment

See para. 2207.

TRUSTS

Halsbury's Laws of England (3rd edn.), Vol. 38, paras. 1346–1833

2899   Articles

Actuarial Valuations of Trust Interests, Vernon Harding (examination of an actuary's job in relation to the valuation of an interest in a trust or settlement): 128 NLJ 691.

Certainty of Words in the Creation of Trusts, M. J. Griffiths (the effect of *Paul v Constance* [1977] 1 All ER 195, CA, 1977 Halsbury's Abr para. 2918): 122 Sol Jo 287.

Delay in Distribution of Trust Income, F. Graham Glover (points arising from *Re Locker's Settlement, Meachem v Sacks* [1978] 1 All ER 216): 128 NLJ 1032.

Treatment of Income in Probate, R. Meads: 122 Sol Jo 689.

2900   Breach of trust—duties of trustees—causal connection between breach of duty and loss

In 1964 the settlor executed two deeds of settlement for the benefit of his sons. Two friends agreed to act as trustees together with a third trustee. The first two trustees were told that they would have nothing to do with the running of the trust, which would be done by the third trustee. Neither of them read the trust documents, or knew what the trusts were, except that they were in favour of the settlor's sons, or were given a copy of the deeds. In 1966 shares constituting a controlling interest in a company were vested in the trustees, although the first two trustees did not know of this until 1969. In 1969 the company appointed a receiver and its shares became valueless. The settlor's sons claimed damages for breach of trust and replacement of the value of the shares. *Held*, the first two trustees were clearly in breach of trust in not inquiring into the precise nature of the trusts, but it could not be claimed that their failure to do so led to the damage that occurred. The third trustee had to be considered as the embodiment of all the trustees, so if there was no breach of duty by him there was none by the others. There was no duty on trustees having a controlling interest in a private company that one of them or a nominee should be on the board of directors. The third trustee was in breach of duty in not keeping the others informed of the company's progress, but the result would not have been different had he done so. There was no causal connection between the breach of duty and the loss, and the action would be dismissed.

Re MILLER's DEED TRUSTS [1978] LS Gaz R 454 (Chancery Division: OLIVER J). *Re Lucking* [1968] 1 WLR 866 applied.

2901   Charitable trusts

See CHARITIES.

2902   Constructive trust—unmarried couple—purchase of house in joint names—no financial contribution to purchase by one party

See *Ruff v Strobel*, para. 2909

2903   —— whether need to infer where contractual licence in existence

See *Chandler v Kerley*, para. 1728.

2904   Express trust—purchase of property in joint names—express declaration of joint tenancy—whether doctrine of constructive trusts applicable

Under a contract for the sale and purchase of the freehold of a house, the property was transferred to the plaintiff and defendant as joint tenants in law and equity, the transfer containing a declaration to that effect. Six years later the plaintiff brought an action seeking a declaration that the property was held by himself and the defendant on trust for himself absolutely, on the grounds that the defendant had made no contribution to the purchase price of the house, and had been joined as a purchaser merely to satisfy the mortgagees of the property. He also sought an order that the defendant should do all that was necessary to transfer all his estate and interest in the property to the plaintiff, to give effect to the plaintiff's rights. The defendant claimed that he was entitled to an interest in the property on the ground that he had contributed £500 towards the purchase price. The Master who heard the case concluded that it was for the defendant to show that he had made the payment at the time of and for the purpose of contributing to the purchase of the house: he found that the defendant had failed to show this and gave judgment for the plaintiff. On appeal by the defendant, *held*, where there was a voluntary express declaration of trust the doctrine of constructive trusts did not apply. An effective declaration of trust could only be removed either by rescission on the grounds of fraud or mistake or appropriate rectification to vary or delete the declaration of trust. In the latter case the onus was on the plaintiff to show the existence of circumstances justifying rectification. Since the Master had not considered this aspect of the case, it should be remitted to the Chancery Division for a new trial.

PINK v LAWRENCE (1977) 36 P & CR 98 (Court of Appeal: BUCKLEY and EVELEIGH LJJ and SIR JOHN PENNYCUICK). *Pettit v Pettit* [1970] AC 777 and *Wilson v Wilson* [1969] 1 WLR 1470 applied.

2905   Fiduciary relationship—investment counsellor and client

See *Elderkin v Merrill Lynch, Royal Securities Ltd*, para. 2010.

2906   Public trustee—fees

The Public Trustee (Fees) (Amendment) Order 1978, S.I. 1978 No. 373 (in force on 1st April 1978), amends the Public Trustee (Fees) Order 1977, 1977 Halsbury's Abr para. 2919, by increasing the rates of the administration fee, investment fee and income collection fee; it also restates the requirement for a fee for audits.

2907   Rectification—onus of establishing justifiable circumstances

See *Pink v Lawrence* para. 2904.

2908   Resulting trust—unmarried couple—land owned by man transferred into woman's name 'in trust'

Canada

A married man and his mistress lived together for some time with the intention of eventually marrying. When the man acquired a plot of land they proposed to build a house on it and the man had it conveyed into his mistress' name "in trust" to avoid the possibility of his existing wife making a claim against it. He subsequently built a pre-fabricated house on the plot and his mistress moved in with him, but she left for good some six weeks later. The man brought an action seeking a declaration that his mistress held the land on trust for him and an order that it should be conveyed into his name. The mistress claimed a one-half interest in the land on the grounds that she had provided him with financial support during the period of their cohabitation, had worked on the land, had contributed to the deposit paid on the building materials and had guaranteed a mortgage of the land executed by the man to raise the balance of the cost of the building materials. *Held*, on the evidence the intention of the parties was that the mistress should acquire a beneficial interest in the land only in the event of their marriage: should the marriage not take place, the man had intended that he should be able to recover the whole interest in the land.

Further, the contention of the mistress that by conveying the land to her in order to protect it from possible claims of his wife the man was estopped from recovering the land could not be considered: since the conveyance was not prima facie illegal, the defence had been raised at too late a stage in the proceedings, thereby precluding the man from bringing evidence on the issue.

IBOTTSON v KUSHNER (1978) 84 DLR (3d) 417 (Supreme Court of Canada). *North Western Salt Co Ltd v Electrolytic Alkali Co Ltd* [1914] AC 461 applied.

2909   —— —— purchase of house in joint names—no financial contribution by one party

Canada

An unmarried couple living together bought a home in their joint names but separated shortly afterwards. The respondent paid the deposit, the mortgage repayments and all the legal fees herself. The appellant, who had paid nothing, appealed against a decision that there was a resulting trust in the respondent's favour and that he held his interest in the house as constructive trustee for her. *Held*, (i) there was a presumption of a resulting trust in the respondent's favour, arising from the fact that she had paid for everything. However, the presumption was rebutted as all the legal documents were signed by both parties and it was clearly their intention to hold the beneficial interest in the house equally. (ii) A constructive trust was a proprietary remedy available against a party who had been unjustly enriched provided that personal remedies were inadequate. There could be no constructive trust in the respondent's favour since adequate personal remedies were available to her. She could have commenced an action for an appropriate contribution from the appellant in respect of the payments made or alternatively for the sale of the house and compensation from the proceeds of sale. (iii) By signing the mortgage deed, the appellant accepted liability for payment of a debt. He made a contribution to the purchase and was therefore entitled to a beneficial interest in the property. The appeal would be allowed.

RUFF v STROBEL [1978] 3 WWR 588 (Supreme Court of Alberta, Appellate Division). *Shephard v Cartwright* [1955] AC 431, HL applied.

2910   Trust for accumulation of income—statutory restriction on accumulation—trust set up by company—whether company a person

See *Re Dodwell & Co Ltd's Trust Deed*, para. 2138.

2911   Trustee—powers—power to compromise litigation

In a dispute over the terms of trusts on which a considerable number of valuable chattels had been settled, a preliminary point arose as to whether the trustees were entitled under the Trustee Act 1925, s. 15 to accept a compromise designed to avoid lengthy litigation. *Held*, trustees (or the court in cases where they had waived their discretion) were fully empowered to accept any compromise if they considered it desirable and fair to all the beneficiaries: they were under no express or implied obligation to obtain the beneficiaries' consent. Each case depended on its facts and it was prima facie within the powers of the trustees in the case in hand to accept the projected compromise.

RE EARL OF STRAFFORD, ROYAL BANK OF SCOTLAND v BYNG [1978] 3 All ER 18 (Chancery Division: MEGARRY V-C). *Re Ezekiel's Settlement Trusts* [1942] Ch 230 applied.

2912   —— remuneration—court's inherent jurisdiction to award remuneration

The settlor conveyed properties to trustees, including a trustee company, on discretionary trusts. The settlement provided for the professional trustees to charge for their services and for the trustee company to charge its normal fees at the date of the settlement. Further properties were subsequently added to the settlement and the whole site was redeveloped, involving unforeseen work for the trustees. The trust company and one of its former directors took out a summons asking for increased remuneration for their services. *Held*, the court had an inherent jurisdiction to award remuneration to a trustee in exceptional cases, which was to be exercised sparingly; for example, if it were necessary to obtain the services of a particular trustee or kind of trustee. Remuneration might also be awarded if the circumstances of the case raised an implied promise to pay it on behalf of the beneficiaries. There had been a marked reluctance to award any remuneration unless the application was made promptly on assumption of office or there had been a radical change of circumstances. As the plaintiffs in dealing with the redevelopment had performed services wholly outside the scope of any duties which could reasonably have been expected to be rendered by trustees in the normal course of their duties, they were entitled to additional remuneration in connection with that task on the basis that there was an implied promise to pay it.   There had been no fundamental change in the nature or assets of the trust so as to justify altering the general level of the trust company's fees.   There should, however, be a revaluation of the settlement properties upon which the trust company's charges allowed by the trust instrument were based, since the existing valuation was out of date.

RE DUKE OF NORFOLK'S SETTLEMENT TRUSTS; EARL OF PERTH V FITZALAN-HOWARD [1978] 3 WLR 655 (Chancery Division: WALTON J). Dictum of Lord Simonds LC in *Chapman v Chapman* [1954] AC 439, 443, 444, HL; *Marshall v Holloway* (1918) 2 Swan 432; *Re Salmen* (1912) 107 LT 108, CA and *Forster v Ridley* (1864) 4 DeGJ & S 452 applied.

UNFAIR DISMISSAL

Halsbury's Laws of England (4th edn.), Vol. 16, paras. 615–639:15

2913   Articles

Collective Agreements and Unfair Dismissal, H. M. G. Concannon (position of employer who has made a dismissal in conformity with a relevant collective agreement): 128 NLJ 900.

Taxation, Damages and Compensation for Unfair Dismissal, O. P. Wylie and J. E. McGlyne (assessment of damages and compensation, with regard to reductions for income tax; application of the principle in *British Transport Commission v Gourley* [1955] 3 All ER 796): 128 NLJ 550.

Unfair Dismissal Cases and Evidence, Stephen Cooke (the best approach to be taken by those representing respondents before industrial tribunals): 122 Sol Jo 156.

Unfair Dismissal for Union Activities, Thomas Poole: 128 NLJ 930.

Victimisation for Strike, A. N. Khan (interpretation of statutory provisions relating to dismissals in connection with industrial action): 122 Sol Jo 737.

2914   Capability of employee—pregnancy—employer's duty to offer suitable available vacancy

See *Martin v BSC Footwear (Supplies) Ltd*, para. 2993.

2915   Compensation—assessment—basis for assessment under Trade Union and Labour Relations Act 1974

On an employee's appeal against an award of nil compensation for unfair dismissal, the Employment Appeal Tribunal stated that, as regards those appeals outstanding under the Trade Union and Labour Relations Act 1974, the employee's loss arising from the dismissal should first be calculated and from that sum any deduction for the employee's contributory fault should then be made.

NUDDS V W. AND J. B. EASTWOOD LTD [1978] ICR 171 (Employment Appeal Tribunal: PHILLIPS J presiding).

2916   —— —— basic award—injustice of statutory provision

See *British Midland Airways Ltd v Lewis*, para. 1099.

2917   —— —— calculation of basic award—calculation of compensatory award

An industrial tribunal found that the employee had been unfairly dismissed, and awarded him compensation consisting of a basic award and a compensatory award. The awards were calculated on the basis of a normal working week of $44\frac{1}{2}$ hours. The employee appealed, contending that the awards should have taken his hours of overtime into consideration, and submitting evidence of the amount of overtime he had worked in the three months prior to his dismissal. *Held*, the Employment

Protection Act 1975, Sch. 4 provided that the basic award was to be calculated on the basis of a week's pay for "normal working hours". A week's pay was what an employee received working the normal working hours under his contract of employment. The basic award had been correctly assessed on a 44½ hour week. The industrial tribunal had, however, erred in law by excluding the overtime payments from the calculation of the compensatory award. A compensatory award should include everything that the employee would have received had he not been dismissed, and involved as assessment of the amount of overtime he would have earned during the period he was unemployed.

BROWNSON V HIRE SERVICE SHOPS LTD [1978] IRLR 73 (Employment Appeal Tribunal: BRISTOW J presiding).

1975 Act, Sch. 4, now Employment Protection (Consolidation) Act 1978, Sch. 14.

2918   —— —— principles for reduction of award

See *Brown's Cycles Ltd v Brindley*, para. 2956

2919   —— —— —— employee's capability

The employee was held by an industrial tribunal to have been unfairly dismissed on grounds of lack of capability; however, as he had been forty per cent to blame for his dismissal, his compensation would be reduced by that proportion. On appeal, *held*, the tribunal had not erred when they held him forty per cent to blame for his dismissal and reduced his compensation. Distinctions between conduct which was under the control of the employee and matters which were beyond his control were relevant but difficult to draw in practice. The matters that the tribunal relied on in coming to their decision could not be said to be outside the employee's control. The assessment of contribution was a question for the tribunal to decide. The appeal would be dismissed.

MONCUR V INTERNATIONAL PAINT CO LTD [1978] IRLR 223 (Employment Appeal Tribunal: PHILLIPS J presiding).

2920   —— —— —— employee charged with theft—delay of trial by employee

See *Harris (Ipswich) Ltd v Harrison*, para. 2939.

2921   —— —— —— employee's conduct

The employee was promoted to factory manager. He subsequently admitted to his employers that he had improperly arranged for bonus payments to be made to him. He was told that he would be summarily dismissed before being given an opportunity to explain his conduct. On his complaint of unfair dismissal, the industrial tribunal found that the real reason for the dismissal was not dishonesty but incompetence and that it was unfair. The tribunal deducted ten per cent from the compensation awarded on the ground that the employee had contributed to his own dismissal within the Employment Protection Act 1975, s. 76 (6). On appeal by the employers, *held*, the tribunal was correct in holding that the dismissal was unfair. The dismissal towards which the employee was alleged to have contributed permitted a broad consideration of the real reason and the alleged reason for dismissal. Thus the employee's conduct should be considered not only with reference to incompetence but also with reference to misconduct, as factors contributing to the dismissal. The award would be reduced by twenty per cent and the appeal allowed to that extent.

ROBERT WHITING DESIGNS LTD V LAMB [1978] ICR 89 (Employment Appeal Tribunal: KILNER BROWN J presiding).

1975 Act, s. 76 now Employment Protection (Consolidation) Act 1978, s. 74.

2922   —— —— —— offer of reinstatement

Having dismissed the employee, the employers made her an offer of reinstatement which she refused. She complained of unfair dismissal and was awarded compensation. On appeal, the employers contended that the industrial tribunal, when assessing compensation, had failed to consider whether the refusal to accept the offer of reinstatement constituted a failure to mitigate her loss. *Held*, an unreasonable refusal to take up an offer of reinstatement was a relevant factor in the assessment of compensation. Since the tribunal did not expressly say that it had considered the question, the appeal would be allowed and the case remitted to the tribunal.

HEPWORTHS LTD v COMERFORD [1978] LS Gaz R 308 (Employment Appeal Tribunal: PHILLIPS J presiding).

2923 —— —— —— relevance of employee's belief in honesty of his conduct

See *Ladbroke Racing Ltd v Mason*, para. 2941.

2924 —— —— whether employee under duty to mitigate loss—loss of pension rights

An industrial tribunal had found that an employee was unfairly dismissed. The amount of compensation was agreed except for loss of pension rights. The employee opted to take his own pension contributions rather than a deferred pension, which would have resulted in a larger sum. The employers contended that there was no loss of pension rights and even if there was, the employee was under a duty to mitigate his loss by accepting the deferred pension. *Held*, the employee had lost his pension position as a result of the unfair dismissal and had therefore suffered loss. There was no duty on his part to mitigate that loss. However, the employers were relieved from paying a pension for the dismissed employee and the amount in the fund would go towards topping up the fund for other employees.

STURDY FINANCE LTD v BARDSLEY (1978) Times, 21st November (Employment Appeal Tribunal: SLYNN J presiding). *Copson v Eversure Accessories Ltd* [1974] ICR 636, approved.

2925 —— contracting out of right to claim

See *The Open University v Triesman*, para. 1134

2926 —— increase of limit

The Unfair Dismissal (Increase of Compensation Limit) Order 1978, S.I. 1978 No. 1778 (in force on 1st February 1979), increases from £5,200 to £5,750, the limit on the amount of compensation which can be awarded by an industrial tribunal in unfair dismissal claims as the compensatory award or as compensation for failure to comply with the terms of an order for reinstatement or re-engagement.

2927 —— liability—employee lent to subsidiary company—whether holding or subsidiary company liable to pay compensation

A company sent one of its employees to work on a project for a second company, its subsidiary, and his contract of employment was modified to include terms necessary to the change in his position. He was to be under the general control of the second company which could dismiss him from the project for specified reasons but he received his salary and service-related benefits from the first company. It was provided that when his employment on the project ceased he would return to work for the first company. He claimed that his subsequent dismissal from the project by the second company was unfair, or alternatively that he had been unfairly selected for redundancy by the first company. An industrial tribunal found that he had been employed by the second company and that his dismissal from the project had been unfair, but that he had no claim against the first company as it was not his employer. On appeal by both the second company and the employee, *held*, the industrial tribunal had erred in finding that the second company was the employer. Although it had had control over the employee to the extent that it would have been vicariously liable for any tort committed by him against a third party, the first company had remained his employer at all times. Prior to the appeal it had been agreed between the two companies that the employee should receive compensation for unfair dismissal, and liability for payment would fall on the first company.

CROSS V REDPATH DORMAN LONG LTD [1978] ICR 730 (Employment Appeal Tribunal: PHILLIPS J presiding).

2928   Complaint to industrial tribunal—agreement to preclude—validity of agreement—duty of conciliation officer

An employee who had been arrested on suspicion of theft was suspended without pay and his employers sought the advice of an officer of the Advisory, Conciliation and Arbitration Service. This officer, in his capacity as conciliation officer, arranged a settlement between the employer and employee on the termination of his employment. On the employee's claim that he had been unfairly dismissed, the employers contended that, as the settlement had been arranged by a conciliation officer, the employee was precluded from subsequently bringing an action for unfair dismissal by virtue of the Trade Union and Labour Relations Act 1974, Sch. 1, para. 32. The employers appealed against an industrial tribunal's finding in favour of the employee. *Held*, the ACAS officer's role could have been made more clear to the employee. However, para. 32 was intended to facilitate agreements between employers and employees, and ACAS officers clearly understood that they had a duty to act impartially in all disputes. The settlement had complied with the requirements of para. 32 and accordingly the appeal would be dismissed.

DUPORT FURNITURE PRODUCTS LTD V MOORE (1978) Times, 18th October (Employment Appeal Tribunal: KILNER BROWN J presiding).

2929   —— agreement to withdraw—validity

An employee complained to an industrial tribunal that he had been unfairly dismissed. As he wished to obtain a reference from his employers, he agreed with them to withdraw the complaint provided that they would reinstate him, after which he would voluntarily terminate his employment. The Secretary of Industrial Tribunals was informed that the employee wished to withdraw his complaint. The following day, the employee informed the Secretary that he had changed his mind. He claimed that his agreement with the employers was void under the Trade Union and Labour Relations Act 1974, Sch. 1, para. 32 (1), which invalidated agreements precluding a person from presenting a complaint to or bringing proceedings before an industrial tribunal. The tribunal dismissed his claim and he appealed. *Held*, while the words "presenting a complaint" in para. 32 (1) (b) were limited to the initiation of proceedings before the tribunal, "bringing any proceedings before" could be extended to proceedings after a complaint had been made. The tribunal had erred in law in holding that the agreement to withdraw the complaint was not avoided by para. 32 (1) (b) and the case would be reconsidered by a new tribunal.

NAQVI V STEPHENS JEWELLERS LTD [1978] ICR 631 (Employment Appeal Tribunal: ARNOLD J presiding).

1974 Act, Sch. 1, para. 32 (1) (b) now Employment Protection (Consolidation) Act 1978, s. 140.

2930   —— complaint made out of time—whether reasonably practicable to make complaint within time limit

An employee resigned from his job and presented a complaint of unfair dismissal over six weeks outside the three month time limit. An industrial tribunal decided that it was not reasonably practicable for the complaint to be presented within the time limit as the employee was unaware of his rights. On appeal by the employers, *held*, ignorance of the law was not a complete defence in every case. Taking a common sense approach, it was reasonably practicable to present a complaint in time if the employee ought to have known of his rights even if he did not actually do so. The employee was an intelligent and well educated man who ought to have been aware of his rights and the necessity to act in time. Accordingly, the appeal would be allowed.

AVON COUNTY COUNCIL V HAYWOOD-HICKS [1978] IRLR 118 (Employment Appeal Tribunal: KILNER BROWN J presiding).

2931 A warehouse manager was charged with stealing from his employers' warehouse and dismissed in May 1976. In March 1977, he was tried, but no evidence was offered by the prosecution. His claim for unfair dismissal, filed in April 1977, was dismissed by an industrial tribunal on the ground that it was not satisfied that it was not reasonably practicable for the claim to have been presented within the three month time limit. The Employment Appeal Tribunal upheld the tribunal's decision and the employee appealed. *Held*, (ORMROD LJ dissenting) the onus of proving that it was not reasonably practicable to present a complaint within three months was upon the employee, who had to show why it was not presented. The tribunal had to be satisfied that the employee did not know of his rights during the relevant period and that he had no reason to make inquiries about them. In the present case therefore, the tribunals were entitled to decide that the employee ought to have known about his rights in time to present his case within the time limit.

ORMROD LJ considered that the words "reasonably practicable" should not be construed strictly in relation to the time limit for starting unfair dismissal proceedings. Further, as the employee was unaware of the existence of his rights, there could be no duty on him to make inquiries about them.

PORTER V BANDRIDGE LTD [1978] IRLR 271 (Court of Appeal: STEPHENSON, ORMROD and WALLER LJJ). *Dedman v British Building and Engineering Appliances Ltd* [1974] 1 All ER 520, CA applied.

2932 After her dismissal in 1976 on suspicion of theft, the employee was advised by a Citizens Advice Bureau that nothing could be done about an unfair dismissal claim until her trial was over. Her complaint was finally submitted in 1977. An industrial tribunal found it had no jurisdiction to hear her complaint of unfair dismissal because it had been reasonably practicable for the complaint to have been filed within the three month time limit prescribed by the Trade Union and Labour Relations Act 1974. The tribunal considered that the Bureau had acted as a skilled adviser and the employee had to take the consequences of its incorrect advice. The employee appealed. *Held*, the industrial tribunal was right to conclude that the employee had engaged the Bureau as a skilled advisor. As the employee had consulted the Bureau in time and its incorrect advice had resulted in the complaint being presented out of time, the employee could not claim that it was not reasonably practicable to have made the complaint within the time limit. The tribunal was not deciding a dispute between an applicant and his skilled advisor. Accordingly, the appeal would be dismissed.

RILEY V TESCO STORES LTD (1978) Times, 13th November (Employment Appeal Tribunal: SLYNN J presiding). *Dedman v British Building and Engineering Appliances Ltd* [1974] 1 All ER 520, CA applied.

1974 Act now Employment Protection (Consolidation) Act 1978.

2933 —— —— —— **reasonableness of excess period**

The employee was dismissed following a fight with a fellow employee. On claiming unemployment benefit he was told that a tribunal would consider the matter, which he misinterpreted as meaning the matter of his dismissal, being unaware of the existence of separate tribunals. He realised his error two weeks after the expiry of the three month statutory time limit for presenting complaints of unfair dismissal. He instructed solicitors who presented his complaint a month later. The industrial tribunal permitted him to proceed, applying the proviso to the statutory requirement as to time and holding that it had not been reasonably practicable for the complaint to have been made within the prescribed period. The Employment Appeal Tribunal dismissed the employers' appeal and they appealed to the Court of Appeal. *Held*, a distinction should be drawn between deciding whether it was not reasonably practicable for the complaint to have been presented within the time limit, and whether the length of the further period before which the complaint was in fact presented was reasonable. The first question was a question of law and the test was whether the employee had just cause or excuse for not presenting his complaint within the time limit in the light of the relevant circumstances: in this case, the employee mistakenly but reasonably believed that his complaint was already being dealt with and was thus afforded such just cause or excuse. The second question, as to the reasonableness of the length of the further period, was a question of fact exclusively for the industrial tribunal before which the complaint was finally presented, and as such could not be the subject of appeal, since appeals to the Employment Appeal Tribunal lay only on questions of law. The employers' appeal would be dismissed.

WALL'S MEAT CO v KHAN [1979] ICR 52 (Court of Appeal: LORD DENNING MR, SHAW and BRANDON LJJ). *Dedman v British Building and Engineering Appliances Ltd* [1974] 1 All ER 520, CA, applied. Decision of Employment Appeal Tribunal (1977) 12 ITR 497 affirmed.

2934   —— right to make complaint—whether director an employee

See *Parsons v Albert J. Parsons & Sons Ltd*, para. 1091.

2935   Conduct of employee—breach of safety rules

An employee was dismissed for interfering with the mechanism of a machine, so that it could be operated without the safety device. An industrial tribunal held the dismissal to be fair. The employee appealed. *Held*, dismissing the appeal, the dismissal was fair. It was not clear whether the incident was covered by the employer's rule, namely that dismissal for a first breach of the rules would apply to disorderly conduct likely to endanger other employees. Nevertheless it was clear from his own admission that the employee was aware that neglect of safety devices would result in dismissal.

MARTIN v YORKSHIRE IMPERIAL METALS LTD [1978] IRLR 440 (Employment Appeal Tribunal: ARNOLD J presiding).

2936   —— capability—opportunity to explain conduct

An electrician was dismissed from his job whilst on holiday, on the grounds of lack of capability. He was never given a chance to offer an explanation for his conduct and consequently complained he had been unfairly dismissed. *Held*, there was a distinction to be made between two kinds of lack of capability; the one caused by an inherent incapacity to do the work and the other by laziness or carelessness. In the latter kind, of which the present case was an example, an employee should be warned and given a chance to improve his performance before being finally interviewed and dismissed. The employer's failure to give the electrician a chance to explain his conduct rendered his dismissal unfair, although in assessing compensation the employee's degree of culpability should be taken into consideration.

SUTTON AND GATES (LUTON) LTD v BOXALL [1978] IRLR 486 (Employment Appeal Tribunal: KILNER BROWN J presiding).

2937   —— dishonesty—reasonableness of employer's suspicions

The employee was a shop assistant in the defendant firm of retail fruiterers and florists. As the result of a minor incident which caused him to doubt the employee's integrity the employer introduced a till roll in the cash register. Subsequently the employee recorded a transaction in a book kept for that purpose, but no corresponding amount was shown on the till roll. The employee was dismissed for "industrial misconduct". There was a conflict of evidence as to what took place when the employer confronted the employee prior to her dismissal but the industrial tribunal felt that the employer had discharged the onus of proving that he had acted reasonably, and that the dismissal was not unfair. On appeal *held*, where the employee is dismissed for alleged dishonesty it must be shown that the employer had reasonable grounds for his suspicions. In the present case there were a number of ways in which the money could have disappeared and the employer had not made a sufficient investigation of those other possibilities. As there was a conflict of evidence as to what had happened prior to the dismissal, the industrial tribunal could not claim that there was sufficient evidence to justify the finding that the employer had given the employee a reasonable opportunity of explaining the alleged dishonesty before her dismissal. The appeal would be allowed and the case remitted to the industrial tribunal for assessment of compensation.

LEES v THE ORCHARD [1978] IRLR 20 (Employment Appeal Tribunal: LORD McDONALD presiding).

2938   Employers investigating a series of suspicious staff purchases were led to the conclusion that a number of employees had been involved in acts of dishonesty. They dismissed an employee who had been said by one of her colleagues to have taken part in those activities. An industrial tribunal upheld her claim that the dismissal had been unfair. On appeal by the employers, *held*, the tribunal had misunderstood the distinction between the sort of evidence which could justify a reasonable conclusion of management and that required in a criminal prosecution, and had placed too heavy a burden on the employers. When an employer had dismissed an employee for suspected acts of dishonesty he had to establish three factors: that he believed the employee had committed the acts, that he had reasonable grounds for that belief and that he had investigated the matter sufficiently. These factors had been established in this case and accordingly the appeal would be allowed.

BRITISH HOME STORES LTD v BURCHELL [1978] IRLR 397 (Employment Appeal Tribunal: ARNOLD J presiding).

2939   An employer who was charged with stealing from his employers was suspended with pay, but when he elected for trial by jury, thus delaying the trial, he was dismissed. An industrial tribunal found that the dismissal was unfair. The employers appealed both against the finding and the assessment of compensation. *Held*, although it was not necessary for an employer who had dismissed an employee for theft to prove that the employee had been stealing he had to show that he had reasonable grounds to believe that he had. The employers in this case had failed to make sufficient inquiries to satisfy themselves that the employee should be dismissed and therefore the dismissal had been unfair. However, the industrial tribunal had failed to consider the question of the employee's own contribution to the dismissal and so the question of compensation would be referred to them for reconsideration.

HARRIS (IPSWICH) LTD v HARRISON [1978] IRLR 382 (Employment Appeal Tribunal: PHILLIPS J presiding).

2940   —— —— **theft from fellow employee**

An employee with fifteen years unblemished service, was found in possession of a watch belonging to another employee. His employers decided, before his appeal to a director was heard, that he would be dismissed in any event. His claim for unfair dismissal was upheld by an industrial tribunal on the grounds that his long blameless service warranted a more thorough investigation of the matter by the employers, who should also have given him a chance to call evidence. The employers appealed. *Held*, although stealing was a serious offence, its gravity depended on the circumstances. It was important to distinguish between theft of employer's property, causing a breach of confidence between employer and employee and other forms of theft such as that in the present case. Taking all matters into consideration, the tribunal had not erred in reaching its decision and the appeal would be dismissed.

JOHNSON MATTHEY METALS LTD v HARDING [1978] IRLR 248 (Employment Appeal Tribunal: PHILLIPS J presiding).

2941   —— **employees trading on own account—breach of trust—opportunity to be heard**

The employees, who were senior managers in betting shops, planned to buy two of the employer's shops and operate them on their own account, while still working for the employers. The firm's security officer, who was instructed to investigate the matter, wrongly suspected that they were involved in a criminal conspiracy, and cautioned them. The employees were summarily dismissed. An industrial tribunal found that the dismissals were unfair, but deducted twenty per cent in the case of one employee and twenty-five per cent in the case of the other from the total awards on the grounds of their misconduct, taking into account the fact that they had not believed they were acting wrongly. On appeal by the employers, *held*, notwithstanding that the employees had committed a grave breach of trust, they were not given a reasonable opportunity to put their side of the case, particularly in view of the fact that they were wrongly treated as suspects of a criminal offence. The dismissal was therefore unfair. With regard to the reduction of compensation, under the Trade Union and Labour Relations Act 1974, Sch. 1, para. 19 (3), it was irrelevant that the employees did not think that they were doing anything wrong, since their actions plainly contributed to the matters to which the complaints related. The appeal would be allowed to the extent that the amount to be deducted from the compensation would be increased to fifty per cent in each case.

LADBROKE RACING LTD v MASON [1978] ICR 49 (Employment Appeal Tribunal: KILNER BROWN J presiding).

Trade Union and Labour Relations Act 1974, Sch. 1, para. 19 (3), as replaced by Employment Protection Act 1975, s. 74 (1) (b), (7), now Employment Protection (Consolidation) Act 1978, s. 73.

2942   The employees, who were managers, started a company similar to their employers' without the employers' knowledge. The employers, suspecting dishonesty, asked the police to investigate. The employees were suspended and, when asked to a meeting to discuss the situation, refused to attend. They were dismissed and complained that the dismissal was unfair. On appeal by the employers against a decision that the dismissal was unfair, subject to a reduction in compensation of seventy-five per cent on the ground of the employees' misconduct, *held*, this was a relationship involving mutual confidence and trust, and the mere fact that there was a breach of trust justified dismissal, the employers had acted reasonably in requiring the employees to attend a meeting during their suspension and had given them a reasonable opportunity of stating their case. The dismissals were not unfair and the appeal would be allowed.

MANSARD PRECISION ENGINEERING CO LTD v TAYLOR [1978] ICR 44 (Employment Appeal Tribunal: KILNER BROWN J presiding).

2943   ——fight between employees—whether justification for dismissal

The employee was dismissed following a fight with another employee, who was also dismissed. An industrial tribunal found that the dismissal was unfair as it was not due to "gross misconduct". The tribunal defined gross misconduct as misconduct which is tantamount to the employee's repudiation of the contract of employment. On appeal by the employers *held*, the industrial tribunal had used the wrong test in assessing the conduct of the employee. The proper test was whether the employee's conduct was of such a kind that the reasonable employer would regard it as sufficient reason for dismissal. It was essentially for the employers to decide whether a fight between employees justified their dismissal. As the employers had made a proper investigation of the facts, and had come to the conclusion that the dismissals were justified, the appeal would be allowed.

C. A. PARSONS & CO LTD v MCLOUGHLIN [1978] IRLR 65 (Employment Appeal Tribunal: KILNER BROWN J presiding).

2944   ——refusal to carry out instructions—dispute over scope of duties

A dispute arose as to whether it was part of the duties of the employee, a public lighting maintenance attendant, to paint lamp posts. No agreement was reached, but the employee continued to do some painting of lamp posts. A year later, the employee was told he was doing insufficient painting. He was asked to give an undertaking to carry out instructions which might include painting lamp posts. He failed to reply and was dismissed. An industrial tribunal found that the dismissal was unfair. On appeal by the employers, *held*, although there had been a dispute, the employee had in fact continued to do painting work; it could thus be said that he had given the impression that he was accepting the painting as part of his duties, and the employers had acted reasonably in dismissing him for failing to carry out the work. The appeal would be allowed and the case remitted for rehearing.

WEST YORKSHIRE METROPOLITAN DISTRICT COUNCIL v PLATTS [1978] ICR 33 (Employment Appeal Tribunal: KILNER BROWN J presiding).

2945   —— refusal to co-operate with management—reasonableness of dismissal

The employee wrote to her employers claiming that she was being demoted from her job as chief nursing officer, and making vague complaints against the chief medical officer. The employers wanted to put their grievance procedure into operation but the employee insisted on a "full impartial enquiry". The employee's solicitor started discussions with the employers but before the conclusion of the discussions the employee was dismissed. An industrial tribunal held that the dismissal amounted to an act of bad faith and was therefore unfair, but that the employee had contributed to her dismissal to the extent of 70 per cent. The employee appealed against the finding as to contribution. *Held*, the industrial tribunal had correctly decided that the employee's conduct contributed to the dismissal. Even after the appointment of the solicitor and the start of the discussions, the employee had maintained her position and continued to demand an external enquiry. There was nothing in her behaviour to indicate acquiescence with the employers.

BROWN v ROLLS-ROYCE (1971) LTD (1977) 12 ITR 382 (Employment Appeal Tribunal: PHILLIPS J presiding).

2946   —— refusal to work overtime—whether breach of contract of employment

From 1966, the employee worked as a council driver/attendant. There was no express provision in his contract for overtime, but he frequently worked late in order to complete his rounds, and was paid overtime. In 1968, the council entered into an agreement with the union concerned recognising that the drivers worked overtime. In 1976 the employee refused to do any more overtime. He was dismissed and complained that the dismissal was unfair. An industrial tribunal found that he was in breach of contract and the council had acted reasonably in treating that breach as sufficient grounds for dismissal; even if there were no breach, his refusal to co-operate was also sufficient ground. On appeal, *held*, no term that the employee would work overtime could be read into the contract at the time it was entered into in 1966. Although the employee had worked overtime, there was insufficient evidence to imply such a term into the contract subsequent to his entering into it. Nevertheless, the industrial tribunal's conclusion that the employers were entitled to treat his refusal as sufficient reason for dismissal was correct and the appeal would be dismissed.

HORRIGAN v LEWISHAM LONDON BOROUGH COUNCIL [1978] ICR 15 (Employment Appeal Tribunal: ARNOLD J presiding).

2947   —— safety petition organised by unionist—whether trade union activity

A member of a trade union was dismissed after organising a petition complaining about the unsafe condition of certain machinery. He alleged that he had been dismissed for taking part in the activities of an independent trade union within the terms of the Trade Union and Labour Relations Act 1974, Sch. 1, para 6 (4) (b) and that therefore the dismissal had been unfair. *Held*, the dismissal was not unfair. The mere fact that an employee making representations was a trade unionist did not make the representations trade union activity. Although the petition had been vetted by a union official it was not a communication from the union to the employer. Accordingly the petition was not union activity and the employee had not been dismissed for taking part in trade union activities.

CHANT V AQUABOATS LTD [1978] 3 All ER 102 (Employment Appeal Tribunal: KILNER BROWN J presiding).

1974 Act, Sch. 1, para. 6(4) as amended by Employment Protection Act 1975, now Employment Protection (Consolidation) Act 1978, s. 58.

2948   —— sleeping on night shift

Industrial tribunal decision:

AYUB V VAUXHALL MOTORS LTD [1978] IRLR 428 (male employee dismissed for sleeping on night shift; had already completed work quota for shift; dismissal unfair under Trade Union and Labour Relations Act 1974; the conduct complained of did not constitute an act of gross misconduct and no reasonable employer would regard it as such, although different considerations would have applied had the employee known it was regarded as gross misconduct; in addition, where another employee had been suspended for a similar offence, such a discrepancy between penalties was unfair).

1974 Act now Employment Protection (Consolidation) Act 1978.

2949   Constructive dismissal—circumstances entitling employee to terminate employment—calculation of awards—tips

A night club employee arranged with other staff, according to custom, to start work at 8.30 p.m. instead of 7 p.m. The manager alleged that he was late and used abusive language. When the employee complained about the language the manager told him that if he did not like it he could leave and continued to swear at him. The employee left and claimed that he had been unfairly dismissed. An industrial tribunal found that there had been a constructive dismissal and calculated his basic award on his gross basic wage including tips and his compensatory award on his net basic wage plus the gross value of the tips. The employers appealed. *Held*, even allowing for the manager's anger, his conduct had been so unreasonable as to amount to a constructive dismissal. In calculating the basic award the tribunal should not have included the tips as they were not payable by the employer. They could however be included in the compensatory award, but the tribunal should have deducted the tax that would have been payable on them.

PALMANOR LTD (TRADING AS CHAPLINS NIGHT CLUB) V CEDRON [1978] IRLR 303 (Employment Appeal Tribunal: SLYNN J presiding).

2950   —— —— dismissal for participating in strike

See *Wilkins v Cantrell and Cochrane (GB) Ltd*, para. 2992.

2951   —— —— test to be applied

The employee resigned and claimed that she had been constructively dismissed because other employees had received pay increases and she had not received an increase for two years. An industrial tribunal found that she had been unfairly dismissed and that, within the meaning of the Trade Union and Labour Relations Act 1974, Sch. I, para. 5 (2) (c), she was entitled to resign by reason of the employer's conduct. On appeal *held*, in the light of the recent decision in *Western Excavating (ECC) Ltd v Sharp* [1978] 1 All ER 713, 1977 Halsbury's Abr para. 2960, the correct test for constructive dismissal was whether the employer was guilty of a significant breach going to the root of the contract, not whether his conduct was unreasonable. The case would be remitted to the same industrial tribunal on the same evidence to be decided on this new test.

F. C. GARDNER LTD V BERESFORD [1978] IRLR 63 (Employment Appeal Tribunal: PHILLIPS J presiding).

1974 Act, Sch. 1, para. 5 now Employment Protection (Consolidation) Act 1978, s. 55.

2952   An employee works manager was on bad terms with his superior who failed to
consult him over the appointment of an assistant or inform him of pay increases
awarded to junior staff. Although never given a preliminary warning, the employee
received a formal warning of dismissal from his superior, who made a number of
complaints about his performance. The employee resigned and told his employers
that he had been offered a better job although the real reason was that he was
unhappy with his superior's conduct. The employee appealed against the decision
of an industrial tribunal that he had not been constructively dismissed. *Held*, (i)
applying the contractual test, the tribunal had decided correctly since the superior's
conduct did not constitute a significant breach going to the root of the contract of
employment. (ii) To claim constructive dismissal, an employee must have left
because of the employers' conduct, whereas the employee clearly indicated that he
was leaving to take up a better job. Accordingly the appeal would be dismissed.

WALKER V JOSIAH WEDGWOOD & SONS LTD [1978] IRLR 105 (Employment
Appeal Tribunal: ARNOLD J presiding). *Western Excavating (ECC) Ltd v Sharp*
[1978] 1 All ER 713, CA, 1977 Halsbury's Abr para. 2960 and *Logabax Ltd v
Titherley* [1977] ICR 369, 1977 Halsbury's Abr para. 2983 applied.

2953   An employee was provided with goggles to protect her eyes while she was working
but was unable to use them because she wore spectacles. She complained about this
and the safety manager concluded that the employers should be asked to provide her
with goggles fitted with lenses made according to her prescription. Nothing was
done and so she resigned. An industrial tribunal, in considering her claim that she
had been unfairly dismissed, applied the test of reasonableness of the employer's
conduct and concluded that she had been constructively dismissed. The employers
appealed on the ground that the correct test in such cases was whether the employer
was in breach of contract. *Held*, the contractual test of constructive dismissal could
and should have been applied because the employers' failure to investigate her
problem was a breach of their duty to take reasonable care of the safety of their
employees. This was a fundamental breach of contract which put the employee in
a position where her only choice was to risk damage to her eyesight or resign.
Accordingly the appeal would be dismissed.

The Employment Appeal Tribunal considered the two tests of constructive
dismissal and concluded that they did not conflict. The question of unreasonableness
was part of the contractual test which was the correct test to be applied in such cases.

BRITISH AIRCRAFT CORPORATION LTD v AUSTIN [1978] IRLR 332 (Employment
Appeal Tribunal: PHILLIPS J presiding). *Western Excavating (ECC)Ltd v Sharp*
[1978] 1 All ER 713, CA, 1977 Halsbury's Abr para. 2960 applied.

2954   **—— test to be applied where employee has given notice**

Following a disagreement with his employer, a sales manager gave three months
notice of his departure. Because he intended going to a rival company, his employer
then took away many of his duties and told him to vacate his office. There was some
discussion about this but as no agreement was reached the employee left before his
period of notice expired. An industrial tribunal found that the changes in his
employment amounted to a repudiation of the contract by the employer and that he
had been unfairly dismissed. The employer appealed. *Held*, the tribunal was
justified in finding that the employer's conduct amounted to a constructive
dismissal. It was not important to that finding that the contract had been repudiated
after the employee had given notice, as the employer's conduct would in any case
have amounted to a constructive dismissal. However, the question was relevant in
deciding whether the dismissal was fair. The tribunal had correctly decided that the
repudiation did not of itself make the dismissal unfair, but there were sufficient facts
for it to conclude that there had been an unfair dismissal.

MILTHORN TOLEMAN LTD v FORD [1978] IRLR 306 (Employment Appeal
Tribunal: PHILLIPS J presiding).

2955   **Dismissal procedure—defects**

A meat inspector employed by a council was charged with conspiracy to assault a
rent collector also employed by the council. His contract of employment provided

for a dismissal procedure. However, the employee, after being suspended, was dismissed without the prescribed procedure being followed on the ground that he had committed a serious offence. The employee claimed that his dismissal was unfair. An industrial tribunal upheld his claim on the ground that the council had not complied with its own procedure. The employers appealed. *Held*, the tribunal had misdirected itself in concluding that the dismissal was unfair because the council had failed to comply with its own dismissal procedure. The tribunal should have considered whether the exceptional nature of the employee's misconduct was such as to override the necessity for compliance with the prescribed procedure. It was irrelevant that the failure to comply with the dismissal procedure was a breach of a contractual term. The case would be remitted to another industrial tribunal.

CARDIFF CITY COUNCIL v CONDE [1978] IRLR 218 (Employment Appeal Tribunal: ARNOLD J presiding). *Carr v Alexander Russel Ltd* [1976] IRLR 220, 1976 Halsbury's Abr para. 2725 and *Lowndes v Specialist Heavy Engineering Ltd* [1976] IRLR 246, 1976 Halsbury's Abr para. 2680 applied.

2956   —— —— sufficiency of warning of dismissal

The employee, the manager of a shop, was dismissed for incompetence. On his complaint of unfair dismissal, the tribunal found that he was incapable of performing his duties but that the employers had failed to give him any warning and thus the dismissal was unfair within the Trade Union and Labour Relations Act 1974, Sch. 1, para. 6 (8). The compensation awarded was reduced by one-third on the ground that the employee had contributed to his dismissal by his own conduct. The employers appealed against the finding of unfair dismissal and the employee cross-appealed against the reduction of compensation. *Held*, the question of whether a sufficient warning had been given was a question of fact for the industrial tribunal; the tribunal's finding that an adequate warning had not been given was justified and the employee was entitled to compensation. The compensatory amount had been calculated correctly and the tribunal was entitled to reduce the amount on the basis of the employee's conduct. The appeal and the cross-appeal would be dismissed.

BROWN'S CYCLES LTD v BRINDLEY [1978] ICR 467 (Employment Appeal Tribunal: PHILLIPS J presiding).

1974 Act, Sch. 1, para. 6 (8) now Employment Protection (Consolidation) Act 1978, s. 57.

2957   An employee was dismissed because he refused to accept the duties and responsibilities of his position as deputy head of his department. An industrial tribunal held that because he had never been warned that he risked dismissal, had he been unfairly dismissed, but found that he had been 50 per cent to blame for his own dismissal, and reduced his compensation award accordingly. The employers appealed. *Held*, the dismissal was unfair because a letter written to him before his dismissal did not amount to a warning of dismissal, in that it only stated that he would lose his job as deputy head if he did not fulfil his duties, and not that he would be offered no further employment at all by the employers.

Furthermore, the employee could not be said to be 100 per cent to blame for the dismissal, because the unfairness was not purely technical; he was dismissed for a continuing course of action which he might have reconsidered if he had been warned of the consequences. The tribunal's assessment was correct.

UBAF BANK LTD v DAVIS [1978] IRLR 442 (Employment Appeal Tribunal: ARNOLD J presiding).

2958   —— —— —— employee's right to be heard

The employee, who was a shop manager, received a written warning of complaints concerning his bad language, losses of temper and the making of suggestive remarks to staff. The warning was issued without hearing what he had to say on the issue; he wrote a protesting letter to the employers about this, but never received a reply. The employee was subsequently dismissed after using bad language to a young employee. An industrial tribunal found that the employee had received the correct prior warning and that the dismissal was fair. The employee appealed. *Held*, the decision of the tribunal would be upheld. Although the warning was unsatisfactory, the same consideration did not apply in considering whether a warning should be taken into account on a later occasion, as applied in deciding whether a dismissal was unfair. It was necessary to examine the prior warning having regard to the merits and reality of the case, and despite the employee's protest, he had done nothing more to have the warning removed from his records.

WOOD v KETTERING CO-OPERATIVE CHEMISTS LTD [1978] IRLR 438 (Employment Appeal Tribunal: PHILLIPS J presiding).

2959   Employment Appeal Tribunal—costs

See *TVR Engineering Ltd v Johnson*, para. 1071.

2960   Excluded employment—age limit—normal retiring age

Under an agreed scheme, Post Office employees reaching the age of sixty could retire with a pension, be re-employed under a temporary contract, or continue under their existing contract thereby increasing their pension entitlement. There was no automatic right for an employee to continue working after sixty, that being regarded as the normal retiring age for the purposes of the re-employment and pension schemes. The employee was re-employed under a temporary contract. On his dismissal be applied to an industrial tribunal. The tribunal refused to hear his case on the basis that he was over the normal retiring age; in this case, sixty. On appeal, *held*, the tribunal had correctly refused to hear the case. From the employee's contract and the pension scheme provisions, sixty was the normal retiring age for Post Office employees.

SMITH v POST OFFICE [1978] ICR 283 (Employment Appeal Tribunal: PHILLIPS J presiding).

2961   —— —— normal retiring age above state pension age

A woman teacher aged sixty-one was dismissed. An industrial tribunal and the Employment Appeal Tribunal decided that they were precluded by the Trade Union and Labour Relations Act 1974, Sch. 1, para. 10 (b) from hearing her complaint of unfair dismissal. Paragraph 10 (b) provides that the right not to be unfairly dismissed does not apply to an employee who has attained the age which, in the undertaking in which he was employed, is the normal retiring age, or, if a man, has attained the age of sixty-five, or, if a woman, the age of sixty. The Court of Appeal reversed the decision, holding that the teacher was entitled to make a claim for unfair dismissal. The Borough Council appealed. *Held*, (LORD DIPLOCK and LORD FRASER OF TULYBELTON dissenting) upholding the decision of the Court of Appeal, where the normal retiring age was over sixty, that age was the appropriate limit, not sixty. As the contractual retiring age for teachers of both sexes was sixty-five, the teacher was entitled to make a claim for unfair dismissal.

NOTHMAN v BARNET LONDON BOROUGH COUNCIL [1979] 1 WLR 67 (House of Lords: LORD DIPLOCK, LORD SALMON, LORD EDMUND-DAVIES, LORD FRASER OF TULLYBELTON and LORD RUSSELL OF KILLOWEN). Decision of the Court of Appeal [1979] 1 All ER 142, 1977 Halsbury's Abr para. 2973 affirmed.

For a discussion of this case see "Women over 60 can sue for unfair sacking", Terence Shaw, Daily Telegraph, 14th December 1978.

2962   —— employment for less than twenty-one hours per week—meaning of employment—retained fireman

A retained fireman who had been required under his contract of employment to be in attendance at the fire station for two hours a week but on standby for 102 hours claimed compensation for unfair dismissal. The employers appealed against the Employment Appeal Tribunal's finding in his favour on the ground that he was only employed during the hours when he actually worked which were less than twenty-one hours a week. *Held*, the fact that the fireman was not present at the fire station while he was on call did not mean that he was not employed during that time. He was under the control of his employer because his activities were restricted for the full 102 hours under his contract of employment and therefore he was entitled to claim compensation.

BULLOCK v MERSEYSIDE COUNTY COUNCIL (1978) Times, 8th November (Court of Appeal: LORD DENNING MR, STEPHENSON and SHAW LJJ). Decision of the Employment Appeal Tribunal, 1977 Halsbury's Abr para. 2977, affirmed.

2963   Fixed term contract—effective date of termination

A part-time teacher, who was employed under a fresh contract each academic year, complained that she had been unfairly dismissed when her contract was not renewed for the year 1977/78. She had finished working before the last day of the academic year, when she had finished her courses. The employer appealed against an industrial tribunal's decision that she had been dismissed within the definition in the Trade Union and Labour Relations Act 1974, Sch. 1, para. 5 (2) (b). *Held*, although the duration of the contract was not fixed by an agreed date, it was understood to terminate on a specified event, namely the completion of her courses. Failure to renew her contract therefore amounted to a dismissal.

WILTSHIRE COUNTY COUNCIL v NATIONAL ASSOCIATION OF TEACHERS IN FURTHER AND HIGHER EDUCATION [1978] IRLR 301 (Employment Appeal Tribunal: PHILLIPS J presiding).

1974 Act, Sch. 1, para. 5 now Employment Protection (Consolidation) Act 1978, s. 55.

2964   —— meaning—contract for fixed term determinable by notice— failure to renew

Two employees were employed in 1974 under contracts which expired on a particular day, but provided that they might be terminated before the date of expiry by notice. The contracts were not renewed at the expiry of the fixed term. The Employment Appeal Tribunal held that the employees had been dismissed in accordance with Trade Union and Labour Relations Act 1974, Sch. 1, para. 5 (2) (b), as they were employed under fixed term contracts even though there was provision for determination by notice. The employers appealed. *Held*, the Employment Appeal Tribunal had correctly concluded that the employees' contracts were fixed term contracts within para. 5 (2) (b). A contract for a stated period, determinable by either party giving a specified period of notice, was a contract for a fixed term. The phrase meant a specified term even though it was terminable by notice within that term and had the same meaning in para. 5 (2) (b) as para. 12 of the Act which provided that the right to bring an unfair dismissal claim did not apply to certain contracts for fixed term of two years or more. The Court of Appeal had incorrectly held in *British Broadcasting Corporation v Ioannou* [1975] 2 All ER 999, 1975 Halsbury's Abr para. 1293, that a contract which was determinable by notice was not for a fixed term in relation to para. 12. Accordingly, the appeal would be dismissed.

DIXON v BRITISH BROADCASTING CORPORATION: CONSTANTI v BRITISH BROADCASTING CORPORATION (1978) Times, 6th October (Court of Appeal: LORD DENNING MR, SHAW and BRANDON LJJ). Decision of Employment Appeal Tribunal [1978] 2 WLR 50, 1977 Halsbury's Abr para. 2980, affirmed.

1974 Act, Sch. 1, para. 5 now Employment Protection (Consolidation) Act 1978, s. 55.

2965   Industrial action—dismissal of only one participating employee

Employees went on strike after other workers had been dismissed for taking part in union activities. Two strikers returned to work but the others did not and were dismissed. The employers appealed against a decision that one of the employees had been unfairly dismissed. *Held*, the matter was governed by the Trade Union and Labour Relations Act 1974, Sch 1, para. 8 (2), which provided that if the principal reason for the dismissal was that the employee was taking part in industrial action, the dismissal should not be regarded as unfair unless one or more other employees who also took part in that action were not dismissed, or if they were, were offered re-engagement, and the employee was not offered re-engagement, the reason for the dismissal being an inadmissible one. The 1974 Act, Sch 1, para. 6, provided that if the principal reason for the dismissal was that the employee had taken part at any appropriate time in the activities of an independent trade union, it was an inadmissible reason. Since other employees who also took part in the strike were not dismissed, and the reason for the employee's dismissal was inadmissible within para. 6, the two conditions precedent in para. 8 (2) were satisfied and the dismissal was unfair. The employer's contention that para. 8 (2) should be read as if it said that the other employees who took part in the strike but were not dismissed must still have been taking part in the strike at the time of the employee's dismissal to render it unfair was incorrect. There was no justification for reading in such words, as to do so would be to limit the scope of the protection against victimisation given by the paragraph. The fact that the paragraph as it stood might give rise to anomalies could not limit the meaning to be attached to clear language in a statute. The appeal would be dismissed.

STOCK v FRANK JONES (TIPTON) LTD [1978] 1 All ER 948 (House of Lords: VISCOUNT DILHORNE, LORD SIMON OF GLAISDALE, LORD EDMUND-DAVIES, LORD FRASER OF TULLYBELTON and LORD SCARMAN). Decision of the Court of Appeal [1977] 3 All ER 58, 1977 Halsbury's Abr para. 2982 affirmed.

1974 Act, Sch. 1, para. 6, 8 now Employment Protection (Consolidation) Act 1978, ss. 57–59, 62.

2966 ——— employee not on strike at time of dismissal—whether dismissed for inadmissible reason

See *Winnett v Seamarks Bros Ltd*, para. 2990.

2967 ——— participation in strike—whether striking employees fairly dismissed

See *Wilkins v Cantrell and Cochrane (GB) Ltd*, para. 2992.

2968 Industrial tribunal—costs

At the hearing of a complaint for unfair dismissal, the employee alleged that the employer's reason for dismissal was inadequate. As a result, the employer made five specific allegations against the employee two of which were new. An adjournment was then requested by the employee in order that the new matters should be considered. The industrial tribunal granted the adjournment, but ordered the employee to pay the employer's costs of the day under Industrial Tribunals (Labour Relations) Regulations 1974, r. 10 (2) (a), on the ground that there should have been a request for further and better particulars of the employer's case at an earlier stage. The employee appealed against the order as to costs. *Held*, it was not reasonable to have expected further and better particulars to be asked for at an earlier stage as there was no need to resort to procedural process in such litigation. Further, the failure to ask for further and better particulars was more relevant to the question of whether an adjournment should have been granted than to the question of costs. The tribunal was wrong to subject the adjournment to an award of costs and accordingly, the order would be ineffective.

RAJGURU v TOP ORDER LTD [1978] ICR 565 (Employment Appeal Tribunal: KILNER BROWN J presiding).

2969 ——— ——— compensation—assessment

An employee was dismissed without notice for paying staff for overtime in goods rather than in cash. She was given no opportunity to state her case and in their notice of appearance before an industrial tribunal the employers described her as a criminal. The tribunal found that she had been unfairly dismissed and made an order for costs and a high award for compensation in respect of future loss. The employers appealed against both the order for costs and the assessment of compensation. *Held*, the employers' conduct had led the employee to believe that the allegations were serious and had caused her the unnecessary expense of instructing counsel. They should have realised that their case was hopeless and that the only real issue was the amount of compensation she should receive. Therefore the tribunal were correct in awarding costs on the ground that the employers had acted frivolously and vexatiously. Nor were there any grounds for finding that the tribunal had misdirected itself as to the assessment of compensation. They were entitled to consider all uncertain future events and reduce them into a single multiplier. The appeal would be dismissed.

CARTIERS SUPERFOODS LTD v LAWS [1978] IRLR 315 (Employment Appeal Tribunal: PHILLIPS J presiding).

2970   —— decision based on ground not introduced by applicant— validity of decision

An employee was dismissed for redundancy and applied for relief based on the ground that he had been unfairly dismissed. An industrial trubunal found that the dismissal was unfair, not on the basis of the selection for redundancy, but because the employers had not attempted to find the employee another job within their group of companies, and had not assisted him in finding work outside. On appeal by the employers *held*, the industrial tribunal had erred in law in finding that the dismissal of the employee was unfair on the grounds that the employers had not attempted to find the employee another job as this argument had not been raised before the tribunal. There was no evidence as to whether the employers had tried to help the employee find work, and it was not legitimate to regard as evidence, the lack of evidence to the contrary. The case would be remitted to a different industrial tribunal for reconsideration.

BARWORTH FLOCKTON LTD v KIRK [1978] IRLR 18 (Employment Appeal Tribunal: ARNOLD J presiding).

2971   —— decision based on wrong test—proper test to be applied

An employee was dismissed from his job after 49 years' service. On a complaint of unfair dismissal the industrial tribunal considered whether the employee had suffered any injustice and whether the employer had been shown to have acted patently unreasonably. It held that the dismissal was fair. On appeal by the employee *held*, the test applied by the industrial tribunal incorrectly put the onus of proving that the dismissal was unfair on the employee. It was for the employer to show that he had acted reasonably. An industrial tribunal should focus its attention on the conduct of the employer and not on whether the employee had in fact suffered any injustice. The case would be remitted to a differently constituted tribunal for rehearing.

MITCHELL v THE OLD HALL EXCHANGE AND PALATINE CLUB LTD [1978] IRLR 160 (Employment Appeal Tribunal: KILNER BROWN J presiding). *Vickers Ltd v Smith* [1977] IRLR 11 explained; *Devis & Sons Ltd v Atkins* [1977] AC 931, H.L., 1977 Halsbury's Abr para. 3001 applied.

2972   —— duty to give reason for decision

The respondent employees had expressed dissatisfaction at the way in which their shop steward was handling their interests. As a result of this the shop committees would not allow the employees to work in their usual department. For the next three months the employees continued to receive their wages but were not allowed to work. They refused several offers of jobs in other departments and were eventually dismissed. An industrial tribunal found that the dismissals were unfair. On appeal *held*, the industrial tribunal had not made clear in its decision whether it thought that para. 15 of Sch. 1 of the Trade Union and Labour Relations Act 1974, relating to pressure on the employers, applied or whether it thought the reason for the dismissals was industrial pressure or the employees' refusal to work elsewhere. The proper test to be applied with regard to industrial pressure was whether the pressure on the employers was such that it could reasonably be foreseen that it might result is dismissals. In the present case it was also necessary to consider the likely attitude of reasonable employees if asked to move for no other reason than that their fellow employees refused to work with them. If para. 15 did not apply it was for the industrial tribunal to consider whether there was a substantial reason justifying the dismissal under para. 6 (8) of the 1974 Act. The case would be remitted to the industrial tribunal for reconsideration.

FORD MOTOR CO LTD v HUDSON [1978] IRLR 66 (Employment Appeal Tribunal: PHILLIPS J presiding).

1974 Act Sch. 1, paras. 6 (8), 15 now Employmennt Protection (Consolidation) Act 1978, ss. 57, 63.

2973   The employee was dismissed, allegedly on grounds of redundancy. An industrial tribunal found that the dismissal was on grounds of redundancy, and was not unfair. On appeal by the employee, the employers contended that even if there was no redundancy, the dismissal fell within Sch. 1, para. 6 (1) (b) of the Trade Union and Labour Relations Act 1974; as being due to "some other substantial reason". *Held*, the decision was defective in that it did not set out the facts found by the industrial tribunal and it did not state the reasoning by which the tribunal reached its decision. The case would be remitted to the same industrial tribunal. It would hear the submissions of the parties, but would not hear further evidence. The Appeal Tribunal considered that if, for technical reasons, a dismissal did not constitute redundancy within the meaning of the Redundancy Payments Act 1965, s. 1 (2) (b), on remission it was for the employers to argue that the same reason constituted "some other substantial reason of a kind such as to justify the dismissal". When considering whether there was proper warning and consultation in advance of an impending redundancy the correct approach was set out in *British United Shoe Machinery Co Ltd v Clarke* [1977] ICR 70, EAT, 1977 Halsbury's Abr para. 3022.

GORMAN v LONDON COMPUTER TRAINING CENTRE [1978] ICR 394 (Employment Appeal Tribunal: PHILLIPS J presiding).

1974 Act, Sch. 1, para. 6 (1) now Employment Protection (Consolidation) Act 1978, s. 57.

2974   —— **duty of tribunal to hear evidence of both sides**

The employers had accused the employee of theft and he had been prosecuted by the police. The employee gave the employers an opportunity to apologise for the prosecution, but when no apology was forthcoming, he handed in his resignation. The employee was subsequently acquitted on the theft charge, and brought an action for unfair dismissal against the employers contending that he had been constructively dismissed. An industrial tribunal dismissed the complaint, without hearing the employers' evidence, on the basis that the employee had not discharged the burden of showing that he was entitled to resign by reason of the employers' conduct. On appeal *held*, in a contract of employment there was mutual trust and confidence between the employer and the employee, and breach of this confidence by the employer might entitle the employee to claim he had been constructively dismissed. An industrial tribunal could not decide whether such a claim was justified without hearing all the evidence. As the industrial tribunal had not heard the employers' evidence the case would be remitted for reconsideration.

ROBINSON v CROMPTON PARKINSON LTD [1978] ICR 401 (Employment Appeal Tribunal: KILNER BROWN J presiding).

2975   —— **jurisdiction—agreement to withdraw complaint—validity**

See *Naqvi v Stephens Jewellers Ltd*, para. 2929.

2976   —— —— **employee ordinarily working inside and outside Great Britain**

From May 1976 the employee worked on an oil rig which moved from position to position in the North Sea. In June 1976, the Employment Protection (Offshore Employment) Order 1976, 1976 Halsbury's Abr para. 985 came into force, which provided that in designated areas, employment in activities carried on on or from oil rigs carried the same rights as employment in Great Britain for unfair dismissal purposes. Some of the areas in which the employees' rig was situated were designated areas while others were not. The employee was dismissed and his claim of unfair dismissal was held under the Trade Union and Labour Relations Act 1974, Sch. 1, para. 9 (2), not to be within the jurisdiction of the industrial tribunal; as he was employed both inside and outside Great Britain. He appealed. *Held*, in order to bring a claim for unfair dismissal, the employee would have to show that he ordinarily worked inside Great Britain or in the designated areas. One method of ascertaining where an employee ordinarily worked would be to look at his base as stated in the contract. In the present case, the employees' working base was the rig and as he had been unable to show that he was ordinarily employed inside Great Britain or the designated areas, his appeal would fail.

CLAISSE v HOSTETTER, STEWART & KEYDRIL LTD [1978] IRLR 205 (Employment Appeal Tribunal: BRISTOW J presiding). *Wilson v Maynard Shipping Consultants AB* [1978] 2 WLR 466, CA, 1977 Halsbury's Abr para. 2989, applied.

This case was overruled in *Todd v British Midland Airways* (1978) Times, 22nd July, para. 2977.

1974 Act, Sch. 1, para. 9 (2) now Employment Protection (Consolidation) Act 1978, ss. 141, 144.

2977   An airline pilot appealed against a decision of the Employment Appeal Tribunal, upholding an industrial tribunal, that he ordinarily worked outside Great Britain and therefore was not entitled to lodge a claim for unfair dismissal. *Held*, the correct approach was to look at the express and implied terms of the employee's contract to ascertain where his base was. The pilot operated from Great Britain and accordingly was entitled to make a claim for unfair dismissal. The case would be remitted to the industrial tribunal for a full hearing.

TODD v BRITISH MIDLAND AIRWAYS [1978] ICR 959 (Court of Appeal: LORD DENNING MR, EVELEIGH LJ and SIR DAVID CAIRNS). *Wilson v Maynard Shipbuilding Consultants AB* [1978] 2 WLR 466, CA, 1977 Halsbury's Abr para. 2989 applied, *Claisse v Hostetter Stewart and Keydril Ltd* [1978] IRLR 205, para. 2976 overruled.

2978   The employee was transferred from a bank in Dacca to its London branch. He then lived in London but spent 45 per cent of his working time in Europe. When the bank subsequently closed down, the employee was dismissed. An industrial tribunal held that it had no jurisdiction to hear his complaint of unfair dismissal because, having regard to the number of days the employee had spent abroad, he ordinarily worked outside Great Britain within the meaning of Trade Union and Labour Relations Act 1974, Sch. 1, para. 9 (2). The employee appealed. *Held*, the correct approach was to pay greater attention to the requirements of the contract of employment than to the geographical test of where the employee spent his working hours. The bank's contention that the employee's base was Dacca could not be upheld. As the contract was not specific, the pragmatic and geographical approach had to be taken. While under the contract his original base was Dacca, subsequent events had the effect of varying it. A man who spent 55 per cent of his time in London and the remainder in Europe could not be held to have been ordinarily working in Dacca. The industrial tribunal had failed to apply the contractual test and had erred in their consideration of the geographical test and accordingly the appeal would be allowed.

AHMED v JANATA BANK [1978] LS Gaz R 795 (Employment Appeal Tribunal: KILNER BROWN J presiding). *Wilson v Maynard Shipbuilding Consultants AB* [1978] ICR 376, CA, 1977 Halsbury's Abr para. 2989, applied.

1974 Act, Sch. 1, para. 9 (2) now Employment Protection (Consolidation) Act 1978, ss. 141, 144.

2979   —— procedure—effect of employer's failure to comply with rules of procedure—whether grounds for resisting application for review

An employee was awarded compensation for unfair dismissal. The employers applied for a review because they had not attended the hearing. The tribunal refused to review its decision on the ground that a review had no reasonable prospect of success since the employers had failed to state in their formal notice of appearance on what grounds they resisted the claim, as required by the Industrial Tribunals (Labour Relations) Regulations 1974, 1974 Halsbury's Abr para. 1834, r. 3 (1). On appeal by the employers against the refusal, *held*, r. 3 (1) was directory and mandatory. There were grounds for allowing a review and the appeal would be allowed.

SELDUN TRANSPORT SERVICES LTD v BAKER [1978] ICR 1035 (Employment Appeal Tribunal: SLYNN J presiding).

2980   Interim relief

An employee, contending that he had been dismissed for taking part in union activities, sought interim relief under the Employment Protection Act 1975, s. 78 (5). An industrial tribunal turned down the application, considering that it was not "likely" that the employee would succeed in showing that he had been dismissed for an inadmissible reason. "Likely" was defined as connoting "a degree nearer certainty than would be the case if the word 'probable' had been used". The employee appealed. *Held*, dismissing the appeal, that, in the particular context of the Act, it was not intended that an employee should be able to receive interim relief, without first showing that he had a higher degree of certainty of success than just a reasonable prospect of success. He must have a "pretty good" chance of success.

TAPLIN v C. SHIPPAM LTD [1978] IRLR 450 (Employment Appeal Tribunal: SLYNN J presiding).

1975 Act, s. 78 now Employment Protection (Consolidation) Act 1978, s. 77.

2981   Reason for dismissal—dismissal pursuant to closed shop agreement—employee a member of another union—whether second union specified

In 1972 employers entered into a recognition agreement with the Transport and General Workers' Union. In 1976 they implemented a closed shop agreement whereby any employee who had joined the company since 1972 was to become a member of the union. An employee, who had joined the company in 1974, refused on the ground that he was already a member of another union. He contended that his dismissal was unfair on the ground that he was a member of an appropriate trade union within the Trade Union and Labour Relations Act 1974, s. 30 and that the subsequent amendment of the word "appropriate" to "specified" did not apply retrospectively. *Held*, and employee could only allege that he had been unfairly dismissed for failure to comply with a closed shop agreement if he was a member of a specified trade union. It was no longer sufficient to be a member of an appropriate union and accordingly the employee's dismissal had been fair.

BEAUMONT v LIBBY NCNEILL & LIBBY LTD (1978) Times, 10th October (Employment Appeal Tribunal: SLYNN J presiding).

2982   —— —— employers' genuine belief that employee not a union member

The employee was expelled from his union and as a result was dismissed by his employers, who operated a closed shop. He obtained a court ruling that the union had acted in excess of their powers and a declaration that he had at all times been a union member. He also claimed that the dismissal was unfair. Trade Union and Labour Relations Act 1974, Sch 1, para. 6 (5), provides that where there is a closed shop, the dismissal of an employee is fair if the reason for dismissal is that he is not a union member. The employee contended that since he was a union member, the dimissal was unfair, the employer's genuine belief that he was not a union member being irrelevant. On appeal against the dismissal of his claim, *held*, "reason for dismissal" had been defined as a set of facts known to the employer, or genuine beliefs held by him, which caused him to dismiss the employee. The employers' genuine belief that the employee was no longer a union member entitled them to dismiss him under para. 6 (5). The appeal would be dismissed.

The court added that industrial tribunals should leave the correction of ambiguity or injustice in legislation to the Court of Appeal or House of Lords.

LAKHANI v HOOVER LTD [1978] ICR 1063 (Employment Appeal Tribunal: KILNER BROWN J presiding). Dicta of Cairns LJ in *Abernethy v Mott, Hay and Anderson* [1974] ICR 323, 1974 Halsbury's Abr para. 1890, applied.

1974 Act, Sch. 1, para. 6 (5) now Employment Protection (Consolidation) Act 1978, s. 58.

2983   —— —— whether all employees belong to specified trade union

Employers decided that their sixty employees should be organised by an independent trade union and after discussions as to the suitability of the TGWU or USDAW, the employees were told that they could join a union of their choice. The employers then signed a closed shop agreement with USDAW and informed the employees that membership of USDAW was a condition of employment. By then, thirty-one employees had joined TGWU. Due to a reduction of the workforce, there were finally thirty-three USDAW members and nine TGWU members. The TGWU members refused to join USDAW and were not allowed to work. They claimed that they had been unfairly dismissed. On appeal against the dismissal of their application, *held*, allowing the appeal, for the dismissal to be regarded as fair under the Trade Union and Labour Relations Act 1974, Sch. 1, para. 6 (5), as taking place pursuant to a closed shop agreement the employers had to show that it was the practice, in accordance with a union membership agreement, for all the employees of the same class as a dismissed employee to belong to the specified union. Since nine out of forty-two employees did not belong to USDAW, it could not be said that almost all the relevant employees were members of the specified union and thus the employers could not rely on para. 6 (5).

HIMPFEN v ALLIED RECORDS LTD [1978] IRLR 154 (Employment Appeal Tribunal: ARNOLD J presiding). Dictum of Bristow J in *Home Counties Dairies Ltd v Woods* [1977] 1 All ER 869 at 873, EAT, 1976 Halsbury's Abr para. 2722 applied.

1974 Act, Sch. 1, para. 6 (5) now Employment Protection (Consolidation) Act 1978, s. 58.

2984   —— employees' complaint to trade union—whether complaint a trade union activity

The appellants had made complaints about the safety of the conditions in which they worked, and had contacted their trade unions. The unions had consulted the factory inspector with the result that the union representative and factory inspector made an unannounced visit to the factory premises. In the resulting disagreement the employers announced their intention of reducing the appellants' wages. The appellants resigned and claimed constructive dismissal on the basis that their dismissals were due to the fact that they had taken part in the activities of an independent trade union. An industrial tribunal held that, within the Trade Union and Labour Relations Act 1974, Sch. I, para. 6 (4), the meaning of activities of an independent trade union was confined to membership meetings and activities involving status as trade unionists, and that the appellants' behaviour was not within this definition. It also held that reporting the safety conditions was not the principal reason for the dismissals. On appeal *held*, the industrial tribunal had not erred in law in holding that the dismissals were not due to trade union activities. On the evidence it was a decision which any reasonable industrial tribunal could have reached, and the appeals would be dismissed.

The Employment Appeal Tribunal considered that the definition which the industrial tribunal had applied to "activities of an independent trade union" was too narrow.

DIXON AND SHAW v WEST ELLA DEVELOPMENTS LTD [1978] IRLR 151 (Employment Appeal Tribunal: PHILLIPS J presiding).

1974 Act, Sch. 1, para. 6 (4) now Employment Protection (Consolidation) Act 1978, s. 58.

2985   —— **failure to comply with condition of continued employment**

After his firm had been taken over, an employee was required by his new employers to obtain a fidelity bond from their insurers to remain in employment. He failed to obtain one and was dismissed. On his claim that the dismissal was unfair, *held*, as the obtaining of the bond was a condition of his continued employment, his failure to obtain one amounted to a substantial reason for his dismissal within the Trade Union and Labour Relations Act 1974 Sch. 1, para. 6 (1) (b). Accordingly, the claim would be dismissed.

MOODY v TELEFUSION LTD [1978] IRLR 311 (Employment Appeal Tribunal: PHILLIPS J presiding).

1974 Act, Sch. 1, para. 6 (1) now Employment Protection (Consolidation) Act 1978, s. 57.

2986   —— **finding by tribunal—duty of tribunal to state basis of finding**

See paras. 2972, 2973.

2987   —— **inadmissible reason—burden of proof**

After less than twenty-six weeks of service, the applicant, who was employed as a town clerk, was dismissed by a six to five vote at a council meeting. One councillor, who voted for the dismissal, indicated that he would have voted the other way had it not been for the fact that the applicant proposed to join a trade union. The applicant claimed that this was an inadmissible reason within the Trade Union and Labour Relations Act 1974, Sch. 1, para. 6, and therefore, under para. 11 (1), it did not matter that the period of service was less than twenty-six weeks. *Held*, LORD DENNING MR dissenting, the wording of para. 11 (1) placed the burden of proof on the employee. But the applicant had been unable to show that anti-union prejudice was the principal reason for his dismissal by the whole council. There was no evidence that the applicant had been dismissed for an inadmissible reason. There was therefore no jurisdiction to hear the complaint.

LORD DENNING MR said that it was wrong to place the burden of proof on the employee. On the merits and evidence the clerk's dismissal was unfair.

SMITH v HAYLE TOWN COUNCIL [1978] IRLR 413 (Court of Appeal: LORD DENNING MR, EVELEIGH LJ and SIR DAVID CAIRNS).

1974 Act, Sch. 1, para. 11, now Employment Protection (Consolidation) Act 1978, s. 64.

2988   —— —— **taking part in independent trade union activities at an appropriate time—meaning of "appropriate time"**

The employee, a trade union shop steward, called a meeting of employees during working hours to discuss a pay grievance without the employers' consent. The employee was dismissed and the employers appealed against the decision of an industrial tribunal that the dismissal was unfair. *Held*, a dismissal was unfair if it was for an inadmissible reason, which included taking part in independent trade union activities at an appropriate time. Under the Trade Union and Labour Relations Act 1974, Sch. 1, para. 6 (4A), activities held during working hours with the employers' consent were held at an "appropriate time." The fact that the employee did not have the employers' express consent to hold the meeting in working hours was irrelevant as their consent was implied by the general relationship between management and unions in industry. Therefore, the employee was unfairly dismissed since the meeting took place at an "appropriate time." The appeal would be dismissed.

MARLEY TILE CO LTD v SHAW (1978) Times, 27th April (Employment Appeal Tribunal: PHILLIPS J presiding).

1974 Act, Sch. 1, para. 6 (4A) now Employment Protection (Consolidation) Act 1978, s. 58.

2989   An employee who spoke to her colleagues about trade union activities in the course of conversations while they were working and during lunch and tea breaks was dismissed. She claimed that she had been dismissed for an inadmissible reason, namely taking part in trade union activities and alleged that the conversations had taken place at an appropriate time. The employers contended that the time had been inappropriate and that she had been dismissed for disruptive activities. An industrial tribunal found that any time for which the employee was paid by the employer and was required to be on the premises was a time when she could be required to work and as such was an inappropriate time for such conversations unless the employers' consent had been obtained. On appeal by the employee, *held*, the tribunal had misdirected itself as to the meaning of appropriate time. There would in all cases be times when an employee could be required to be on the employers' premises but could not be required to work, and these might have been appropriate times for discussion about trade union activities. Also, without considering whether there was any restriction on employees conversing while they were working it could not be said that any of the employees' discussions had taken place at an inappropriate time. The case would be remitted to a differently constituted tribunal for reconsideration.

ZUCKER V ASTRID JEWELS LTD [1978] IRLR 385 (Employment Appeal Tribunal: PHILLIPS J presiding).

2990   —— whether dismissal for participating in trade union activities or industrial action

Employers paid their coach drivers according to length of service. The drivers received the impression that a previous employee who was returning was to be paid at the highest rate and asked for a meeting with the managing director. He insisted on following a newly instituted procedure whereby two days' notice was required before any meeting could be called. Several of the drivers declared that they would not work the next day and were dismissed. On a claim by one of them that he had been unfairly dismissed for taking part in trade union activities an industrial tribunal found that he had been dismissed for taking part in a strike and therefore the dismissal had been fair. On appeal, *held*, in order for an employee to be taking part in a strike it was not necessary for him to be striking at the time of his dismissal. It was sufficient that he had made it clear that he intended to strike on the following day and therefore the tribunal's decision had been correct.

WINNETT V SEAMARKS BROS LTD [1978] IRLR 387 (Employment Appeal Tribunal: SLYNN J presiding).

2991   —— matters to be taken into consideration—employee's misconduct not known at time of dismissal

An employee was awarded compensation for unfair dismissal by an industrial tribunal. His employers were subsequently informed that the employee had received illegal payments in the course of his work. They appealed against the finding of unfair dismissal and the refusal by the tribunal to review its finding in view of the fresh evidence. *Held*, (i) the employers could not rely on misconduct unknown to them at the time of dismissal to show that the dismissal was reasonable. (ii) Similarly, such conduct did not affect the employee's right to the basic award of compensation. Under the Employment Protection Act 1975, s. 75 (7) the basic award could only be reduced when dismissal was caused or contributed to by the employee's conduct which was known to the employers at the time of dismissal. However, s. 76 empowered a tribunal to make such compensatory award as it considered just and equitable: if evidence of misconduct previously unknown to the employers had been available to the tribunal, it might have affected their assessment of the compensatory award. Accordingly the appeal would be allowed in part so as to allow the fresh evidence to be heard.

D. G. MONCRIEFF (FARMERS) V MACDONALD [1978] IRLR 112 (Employment Appeal Tribunal: LORD MCDONALD MC presiding). *W. Devis & Sons Ltd v Atkins* [1977] 3 All ER 40, HL, 1977 Halsbury's Abr para. 3001 applied.

1975 Act, ss. 75, 76 now Employment Protection (Consolidation) Act 1978, ss. 73, 74.

2992   —— **participation in strike—whether contract of employment repudiated**

Lorry drivers employed by the respondent company went on strike after repeatedly complaining of overloading of the lorries at their depot. They were subsequently dismissed. On their complaint that they had been dismissed unfairly, *held*, going on strike gave an employer the right to regard an employee's conduct as a breach of contract and to dismiss him. The act of going on strike did not terminate the contract of employment as the whole aim of such industrial action was to remedy faults in the existing contract. Although overloading could in some cases constitute a fundamental breach of contract by an employer, in this case it did not and the employees consequently could not treat their contracts of employment as having ended. Accordingly, the dismissals were fair.

WILKINS v CANTRELL AND COCHRANE (GB) LTD [1978] IRLR 483 (Employment Appeal Tribunal: KILNER BROWN J presiding).

2993   —— **pregnancy—employer's duty to offer suitable available vacancy**

Industrial tribunal decision:

MARTIN v BSC FOOTWEAR (SUPPLIES) LTD [1978] IRLR 95 (pregnant employee advised by doctor not to carry out part of her job involving physical strain; employers refused to allow her to do paper work full time; employee dismissed on ground she was incapable due to pregnancy; during notice she did light work in another department in place of employee in hospital for unknown time; dismissal unfair since Employment Protection Act 1975, s. 34 (2) required employers to offer her any suitable available vacancy; they should have kept her on light work until beginning of pregnancy leave or return of other employee from hospital, whichever earlier).

1975 Act, s. 34 (2) now Employment Protection (Consolidation) Act 1978, s. 60.

2994   —— **refusal to join designated union—dismissal pursuant to closed shop agreement**

A company concluded a union membership agreement, making membership of that union a condition of employment. All existing non-members were required to join the union within the allotted time or pay an amount equal to union dues into a charity to be mutually agreed. The appellant refused to do either and he was dismissed pursuant to the Trade Union and Labour Relations Act 1974, Sch. 1, para. 6 (5) which provides that a dismissal is to be deemed fair if it is on account of the employee's not being a member of the union, where there is a recognised membership agreement. *Held*, the obligation to pay into a charity was an alternative open to employees who did not want to join the union, it did not render para. 6 (5) inapplicable. The employee was dismissed because he refused to join the union and accordingly the dismissal was automatically fair under para. 6 (5).

RAWLINGS v LIONWELD LTD [1978] IRLR 481 (Employment Appeal Tribunal: PHILLIPS J presiding).

1974 Act, Sch. 1, para. 6 (5), now Employment Protection (Consolidation) Act 1978, s. 58.

2995   —— —— **religious belief**

The employee, a Jehovah's Witness, refused to join a union on the ground that his Christian convictions and his conscience did not permit him to do so, and was dismissed. An industrial tribunal held that since the creed of Jehovah's Witnesses permitted followers to belong to a union, the employee's objection on the ground of his own personal belief did not enable him to complain that the dismissal was unfair. He appealed to the Employment Appeal Tribunal, who remitted the case for rehearing on the grounds that the tribunal had erred in concluding that a religious belief had to be an identifiable belief shared by an employee and his sect: under the Trade Union and Labour Relations Act 1974, Sch. 1, para. 6 (5), the objection had to be an objection of the employee and the word "belief" suggested a belief which was actually held by the person in question. On remission, an industrial tribunal held that although they accepted the sincerity of the employee's claim that his objection to joining a trade union was based on his religious beliefs, his objection was in fact on more general grounds of conscience, and therefore the dismissal remained fair. On appeal by the employee to the Employment Appeal Tribunal, *held*, on the employee's own evidence of his personal beliefs, which it had accepted as genuine, the industrial tribunal had reached a conclusion which no reasonable tribunal could have reached. The appeal would be allowed.

SAGGERS v BRITISH RAILWAYS BOARD (No. 2) [1978] IRLR 435 (Employment Appeal Tribunal: KILNER BROWN J presiding). For earlier proceedings see 1977 Halsbury's Abr para. 3010.

1974 Act, Sch. 1, para. 6 (5) now Employment Protection (Consolidation) Act 1978, s. 58.

2996   —— refusal to perform duties other than those for which engaged—teacher

A teacher was employed at a school to direct a resources centre to provide modern teaching aids. She agreed to give twelve English lessons per week as well. When it was proposed that she should give eighteen English lessons per week, she refused and was dismissed. The local education authority appealed against a decision of an industrial tribunal that the dismissal was unfair. *Held*, the appropriate test was whether the local authority had acted reasonably in treating the teacher's refusal to give eighteen English lessons per week as sufficient reason for dismissing her within the Trade Union and Labour Relations Act 1974, Sch. 1, para. 6 (8). A head teacher was entitled to require teachers to do work other than that for which they were engaged provided the request was reasonable. The request in this case was unreasonable and the dismissal unfair. The appeal would be dismissed.

REDBRIDGE LONDON BOROUGH COUNCIL v FISHMAN (1978) Times, 27th January (Employment Appeal Tribunal: PHILLIPS J presiding).

1974 Act, Sch. 1, para. 6 (8) now Employment Protection (Consolidation) Act 1978, s. 57.

2997   —— reorganisation of business—whether substantial reason

A trade union dismissed one of its group secretaries who refused to accept various proposed changes in the organisation and wage structure in local branches. He claimed that he had been unfairly dismissed and that he should have been consulted about the changes. An industrial tribunal rejected his claim on the ground that a failure to accept a reorganisation which was necessary for business reasons amounted to some other substantial reason for dismissal within the Trade Union and Labour Relations Act 1974, Sch. 1, para. 6 (1) (b) and stated that in such a case consultation with the employee was unnecessary. The employee appealed. *Held*, where reorganisation was necessary for business reasons an employer could rely on an employee's refusal to accept the changes as forming some other substantial reason for dismissal provided that the employer acted reasonably. It was not necessary to show that failure to reorganise would have resulted in total disaster, nor need there have been any consultation with the employee. However, the union in this case had failed to establish that it had acted reasonably in dismissing the employee and so the dismissal had been unfair.

HOLLISTER v NATIONAL FARMERS' UNION [1978] ICR 712 (Employment Appeal Tribunal: ARNOLD J presiding).

1974 Act Sch. 1, para. 6 (1) now Employment Protection (Consolidation) Act 1978, s. 57.

2998   —— replacement of employee with employer's son—whether replacement a substantial reason justifying dismissal

An employee was taken on in the knowledge that he would eventually be replaced by his employer's son. When he was, he claimed his dismissal was unfair. An industrial tribunal found that his replacement had been for a substantial reason justifying dismissal within the Trade Union and Labour Relations Act 1974, Sch. 1, para. 6 (1) (b). On the employee's appeal, *held*, the "some other substantial reason justifying dismissal" in para. 6 (1) (b) did not have to be construed eiusdem generis with the reasons for dismissal cited in para. 6 (2). Accordingly, it was for tribunals to consider reasons for dismissal and whether they were reasonable in all the circumstances. In this case the tribunal had acted properly and the appeal would be dismissed.

PRIDDLE V DIBBLE [1978] 1 All ER 1058 Employment Appeal Tribunal: BRISTOW J presiding).

1974 Act, Sch. 1, para. 6 (1), (2) now Employment Protection (Consolidation) Act 1978, s. 57.

2999 —— strike by employees—reinstatement pending inquiry— whether employer's right of dismissal waived

After a strike by the plaintiff school teachers, an education officer made complaints about them to a disciplinary tribunal. In accordance with the teachers' staff code, he also made a report and was available to assist the tribunal. On its recommendation, the teachers were subsequently dismissed by their education authority. Their claim of unfair dismissal was not upheld by an industrial tribunal. The teachers appealed, contending that as the strike had constituted a fundamental breach of their contract of employment, the education authority had waived the breach by not acting upon it and dismissing them immediately after the strike. They also contended that the dual role of the education officer in relation to the disciplinary tribunal was a breach of natural justice. *Held*, (i) while the teachers were taken back after the strike, it would be wrong to say that the education authority had thereby waived its right to dismiss them. They were accepted back subject to the tribunal's findings and subsequently fairly dismissed on account of their misconduct in going on strike. (ii) Although the dual role of the education officer as prosecutor in laying the complaints, and rapporteur in preparing the report and in his availability for consultation was unsatisfactory, the main question was whether the tribunal had acted fairly and justly. As the tribunal had acted fairly, the appeals would be dismissed.

ELLIS V INNER LONDON EDUCATION AUTHORITY (1978) Times, 7th November (Employment Appeal Tribunal: KILNER BROWN J presiding). For earlier proceedings, see 1977 Halsbury's Abr para. 8.

3000 —— sufficiency of reason—findings of internal disciplinary hearing

The employee was a nurse employed by an area health authority. As a result of written complaints by several patients about her conduct, a disciplinary hearing was held and it was resolved that she should be dismissed. This decision was confirmed at an internal appeal hearing. The employee's claim of unfair dismissal was dismissed by an industrial tribunal. She appealed on the ground that the decision was wrong in law, as the authority had acted unreasonably in relying on the findings of the disciplinary hearings when no oral evidence had been received from the patients who had complained against her. *Held*, the authority was entitled to rely on the findings of disciplinary hearings to justify its decision to dismiss the employee. Failure to call patients to give oral evidence did not render the hearings unfair as being contrary to natural justice. The only requirements of natural justice which had to be complied with at a domestic disciplinary hearing were that the accused should know the nature of the accusation made, that he should be given an opportunity to state his case and that the tribunal should act in good faith. As all three requirements had been met, the appeal would be dismissed.

KHANUM V MID-GLAMORGAN AREA HEALTH AUTHORITY [1978] IRLR 215 (Employment Appeal Tribunal: BRISTOW J presiding).

3001 —— —— onus of proof

The employers closed the factory at which the plaintiff was employed. As the particular post occupied by the plaintiff had been abolished and there was no suitable vacancy in the same grade he was dismissed for redundancy. He claimed that the dismissal was unfair in that the employers had failed to bring satisfactory proof under the Trade Union and Labour Relations Act 1974, Sch. 1, para. 6 that they had acted reasonably in dismissing the employee. *Held*, where it was admitted that the employee's job was redundant the question was whether the employers had made reasonable efforts to find the employee another job in their organisation. In the present case there had been no complaint about the employer's failure to find the employee another job, and it was therefore sufficient that the employers had called reliable witnesses to explain the circumstances of the redundancy.

Cox v Wildt Mellor Bromley Ltd [1978] ICR 736 (Employment Appeal Tribunal: Phillips J presiding). *Bristol Channel Ship Repairers Ltd v O'Keefe* [1977] 2 All ER 258, 1977 Halsbury's Abr para. 3018 considered.

1974 Act, Sch. 1, para. 6 now Employment Protection (Consolidation) Act 1978, ss. 57–59.

3002 —— —— statutory restriction on employment

The employee, a probationary teacher, was found to be unsuitable as a teacher by the Department of Education and Science and was subsequently dismissed. The local education authority who dismissed him claimed that it was compelled to do so by the Schools Regulations 1959, the Secretary of State having determined him to be unsuitable. The dismissal was held to be fair by an industrial tribunal who considered that once the local authority had established that it was unlawful to employ the employee as a teacher after he had been found unsuitable, it had discharged the burden of proof under para. 6 (8) of Sch. 1 to the Trade Union and Labour Relations Act 1974. On appeal by the employee, *held*, the industrial tribunal had construed para. 6 (8) too narrowly. It did not follow that merely because the local education authority could not have lawfully continued to employ the employee that he was fairly dismissed. He had contended that there was an element of racial discrimination in that he was treated unreasonably during the probationary period and not given the chance to prove himself. These matters had to be considered by the industrial tribunal in deciding whether or not his employers had acted reasonably in dismissing him. The appeal would be allowed against the local authority as employers but not against the Department of Education and Science, who were not his employers.

Sandhu v Department of Education and Science and London Borough of Hillingdon [1978] IRLR 208 (Employment Appeal Tribunal: Phillips J presiding).

1974 Act, Sch. 1, para. 6 (8) now Employment Protection (Consolidation) Act 1978, s. 57.

3003 —— whether dismissal by reason of redundancy—guidelines for tribunals

Following the takeover of the company by which he had been employed as a branch manager, an employee was retained by the new company as assistant manager with the prospect of promotion if he adapted well to the new system of working. He received no training and the company decided his work was unsatisfactory. As they wished to reduce the managerial costs of that branch to bring them in line with those at other branches they abolished the post of assistant manager and declared the employee redundant. An industrial tribunal rejected his claim that he had been unfairly dismissed on the ground that there had been a "redundancy situation" and he had not been unfairly selected for redundancy. The employee appealed. *Held*, tribunals should avoid the use of general expressions such as "redundancy situation" and explain their decisions in terms similar to the relevant statutory provision, which in this case was the Redundancy Payments Act 1965 s. 1 (2). Applying that provision it was impossible to say that the requirement for an assistant manager had ceased or diminished since there had never been any such requirement. Accordingly, as the dismissal had not been by reason of redundancy, it was unfair.

Ranson v G & W Collins Ltd [1978] ICR 765 (Employment Appeal Tribunal: Bristow J presiding).

1965 Act, s. 1 now Employment Protection (Consolidation) Act 1978, s. 81.

3004   —— whether employee a member of designated union— qualifications

An employee who was employed onshore as a donkeyman, was asked by his employers to sail on a voyage for which they were a man short. He agreed, but pointed out that he was not a registered seafarer. After he had completed three voyages the National Union of Seamen, with whom there was a closed shop agreement, asked the employers whether he was a union member, whereupon the employers made a few inquiries and then dismissed the employee. On the employee's complaint to an industrial tribunal that he had been unfairly dismissed the employers stated that the dismissal had resulted from his not being a union member within the Trade Union and Labour Relations Act 1974, Sch. 1, para. 6 (5) or, alternatively, that as he was not a registered seafarer he was not qualified to perform the work. Later in the proceedings they asked the tribunal to consider whether there had been some other substantial reason for the dismissal but this was refused and the tribunal found that the employee had been unfairly dismissed. The employers appealed. *Held*, (i) the employers had failed to prove that they had made sufficient inquiries about the employee's membership of the union and could not justify a dismissal within para. 6 (5); (ii) for the purpose of para. 6 (9) the word "qualifications" related to aptitude or ability and so the fact that an employee was not authorised to work in a particular job was not a lack of qualification; (iii) the tribunal had not failed to exercise its discretion in refusing to consider whether there was some other substantial reason for the dismissal. Such an amendment would have substantially altered the nature of the case and the tribunal was correct to refuse to allow it. Accordingly the appeal would be dismissed.

BLUE STAR SHIP MANAGEMENT LTD v WILLIAMS [1978] ICR 770 (Employment Appeal Tribunal: PHILLIPS J presiding).

1974 Act, Sch. 1, paras. 6 (5), (8) now Employment Protection (Consolidation) Act 1978, ss. 57, 58.

3005   —— winding up of company

On the winding up of a company, the employee was instantly dismissed while other employees were retained. She was awarded compensation for unfair dismissal. On appeal by the employers, the question arose as to whether a dismissal pursuant to a declared voluntary liquidation could be unfair. *Held*, selection for redundancy might constitute unfair dismissal if unreasonably carried out. In the present case however, where some people were reasonably and temporarily retained in order to achieve an orderly winding up, it did not follow that the dismissal of others not so retained was unfair. Further, while upon voluntary liquidation an expressed instant dismissal, in the event of an unexpired contract of service, constituted a breach of contract giving rise to a claim for damages, such right to damages was not synonymous with unfair dismissal, and it was doubtful whether, in the case of a properly conducted entry into liquidation, whether there could be on an unfair dismissal. The appeal would be allowed.

FOX BROTHERS (CLOTHES) LTD v BRYANT [1979] ICR 64 (Employment Appeal Tribunal: KILNER BROWN J presiding).

3006   Redundancy—selection of redundant employees

The employee was employed on general maintenance duties on the employer's estate. Following a dispute with another employee, the employee exchanged duties with a third employee who had been employed for a shorter time than himself. He was subsequently made redundant when the third employee was not. He complained of unfair dismissal on the grounds that he had been unfairly selected for redundancy. An industrial tribunal found that the dismissal was unfair and the employers appealed. *Held*, the tribunal had found that the dismissal was not unfair within the Trade Union and Labour Relations Act 1974, Sch. 1, para. 6 (7), and had then gone on to consider whether it was unfair within para. 6 (8) in that the employer had acted unreasonably in treating the redundancy as sufficient reason for dismissal. This was a correct approach. The tribunal had considered the plain words of para. 6 (8) and was not bound to consider whether the employer's decision as to which employee to make redundant was so wrong that no reasonable employer could have made the same choice. It could not be said that no tribunal properly directing itself could have come to the same conclusion and the appeal would be dismissed.

JOWETT V EARL OF BRADFORD (No. 2) [1978] ICR 431 (Employment Appeal tribunal: BRISTOW J presiding).

1974 Act, Sch. 1, paras. 6 (7), (8) now Employment Protection (Consolidation) Act 1978, ss. 57, 59.

3007   —— —— agreed procedure—meaning

Under an agreed redundancy procedure of "last in, first out, all other things being equal", a semi-skilled employee of twenty-five was dismissed instead of a skilled man of sixty-five who had been employed for longer. An industrial tribunal decided that the employee had been unfairly selected for redundancy, since having regard to the difference in ages, all other things were not equal. On appeal by the employers, *held*, "all other things being equal" meant equal in the view of a fair and reasonable employer applying proper industrial considerations. The employers did not automatically retire men at sixty-five and believed it was reasonable to retain the more experienced man. The tribunal had erred by substituting its own views for the employers' and the case would be remitted for further consideration.

CAMPER & NICHOLSON LTD V SHAW [1978] ICR 520 (Employment Appeal Tribunal: ARNOLD J presiding).

3008   —— —— burden of proof

The employee was an electrician employed by a firm of electrical contractors. He worked on two main contract sites until he was made redundant on the ground that one of the contracts had terminated. He claimed that the dismissal was unfair because the employers had engaged two additional electricians shortly before his dismissal, who were retained in preference to himself. An industrial tribunal found in his favour, holding that a redundancy situation did not exist at the time of the dismissal. The employers appealed. *Held*, the Trade Union and Labour Relations Act 1974, Sch. 1, para. 6 (8), imposed the burden of showing that the dismissal was fair upon the employers. In this case, the employers had failed to discharge the onus upon them to show that it was fair to dismiss the employee on grounds of redundancy, as it was not reasonable to dismiss an employee who had worked for a substantial period of time in preference to a newcomer. While the industrial tribunal had erred in failing to consider specifically para. 6 (8), they had come to the right conclusion and the appeal would be dismissed.

N. C. WATLING & CO LTD V RICHARDSON [1978] IRLR 255 (Employment Appeal Tribunal: PHILLIPS J presiding).

1974 Act, Sch. 1, para. 6 (8) now Employment Protection (Consolidation) Act 1978, s. 57.

3009   —— —— degree of consultation required

An employee complained that his selection for redundancy was unfair. There was an agreed procedure for selections for redundancy between his employer and the recognised trade union, based on absenteeism, timekeeping, capability and seniority. An industrial tribunal decided that the dismissal was unfair because there was insufficient consultation with the union about the points system used for assessing absenteeism. The employer appealed. *Held*, the tribunal had erred in law in deciding that there had been insufficient consultation with the union and had placed an unduly heavy burden on the employer. In making selections for redundancy it was enough that the employer's method of selection was approved by the union as fair. The final choice as to who should be dismissed lay with the employer.

CLYDE PIPEWORKS LTD V FOSTER [1978] IRLR 313 (Employment Appeal Tribunal: LORD MCDONALD MC presiding).

3010   —— —— grounds of selection—participation in industrial action

There was a strike at the employer's premises and the strikers were dismissed. After the strike a shortage of work arose and only some of the employees were re-engaged. One employee was not re-engaged on the grounds of poor conduct prior to the strike, about which he had received warnings. An industrial tribunal found that his dismissal was fair. The employee appealed. *Held*, the employee would not have been dismissed for his conduct prior to the strike. Consequently, for the employers to treat his prior conduct as the reason for not re-engaging him meant that he was not being re-engaged, unlike other employees, because he had gone on strike. The dismissal was therefore unfair. Had the reason for failing to re-engage him been that there were not enough jobs for the employees to fill, then his previous conduct would have been relevant in deciding whether the employers were acting reasonably in not re-engaging him.

The supervisors did not go on strike, but when asked to carry out work which they would normally have supervised some refused, including the employee in question. They were suspended without pay. Later, when the redundancy situation arose the redundancy selection was based upon the criterion of who had been "loyal" to the company during the strike. The employee was not retained, and an industrial tribunal found that she had not been unfairly dismissed. The employee appealed. *Held* whilst loyalty was a valid matter to be considered, in the absence of a redundancy procedure, the employer should have consulted with the union and the candidates for redundancy. Consequently, the dismissal was unfair.

LAFFIN AND CALLAGHAN v FASHION INDUSTRIES (HARTLEPOOL) LTD [1978] IRLR 448 (Employment Appeal Tribunal: PHILLIPS J presiding).

3011   **Reinstatement—employer's non-compliance with reinstatement order—additional award of compensation**

A married couple were dismissed from their positions as cooks in a small hotel. The industrial tribunal, holding that the dismissals were unfair, awarded them certain payments and made an order for their reinstatement by a certain date. By letter the hotel duly agreed to reinstate them, but informed them that on the final date for reinstatement they would be made redundant since in the light of a change of policy, the hotel no longer required cooks. The matter then came before the same tribunal, which found that the hotel had not complied with the reinstatement order and had failed to satisfy the tribunal that such compliance was not practicable. The tribunal therefore made an award to the employees under the Employment Protection Act 1975, s. 72 (2), which provides for additional awards of compensation for non-compliance with a reinstatement order. On appeal by the employers *held*, the proposal to make the employees redundant from the last date for reinstatement negatived any apparently serious genuine attempt to comply with the order, and the tribunal was entitled to find that reinstatement had not taken place. Further, the evidence justified the tribunal's conclusion that the hotel had failed to show that compliance with the order was not practicable: the employer might have done more in attempting to comply such as interviewing the employees and discussing their future with them. Accordingly, although s. 72 (2) was in effect a penal provision to be applied with care and scrupulous fairness, the tribunal were entitled to make the additional award of compensation. The appeal would be dismissed.

LORD McDONALD pointed out that it had not been appropriate to make a reinstatement order in the first place: this was a case where the parties were in close personal relationship, and it was wrong to enforce such an order upon a reluctant employer.

ENESSY CO SA (trading as THE TULCHAN ESTATE) v MINOPRIO [1978] IRLR 489 (Employment Appeal Tribunal: Lord McDonald presiding).

1975 Act, s. 72 now Employment Protection (Consolidation) Act 1978, s. 71.

3012   **Termination of employment—dismissal or resignation—test**

See *Gale Ltd v Gilbert*, para. 1146.

VALUE ADDED TAX

Halsbury's Laws of England (4th edn.), Vol. 12, paras. 846–1053

3013   Article

A VAT Trap, John F. Avery Jones (distinction between business and investment for value added tax purposes): 122 Sol Jo 547.

3014   Appeal—appeal against assessment—assessment subject of final judgment

Value added tax tribunal decision:

DIGWA v CUSTOMS AND EXCISE COMMISSIONERS [1978] VATTR 119 (taxpayer applied for extension of time within which to serve notice of appeal against assessments; subsequently applied to set aside decision given on that application; assessments against which he sought to appeal were subject of final High Court judgment in default of appearance; tribunal decided that effect of judgment was to exclude any appeal against assessment unless and until judgment set aside by court; application otherwise without merits and would be dismissed).

3015   —— appeal to tribunal—jurisdiction of tribunal

Value added tax tribunal decision:

BIRD v CUSTOMS AND EXCISE COMRS (1978) CAR/78/170 (unreported) (appeal against assessment for value added tax before appellant had paid all amounts shown as payable in tax return; refused to pay on the ground that he had not received tax payable to him by the commissioners; commissioners showed they had repaid tax due to him; tribunal had no jurisdiction to hear the appeal because he had not made all payments due).

3016   —— costs

It has been customary for HM Customs and Excise not to ask for costs in proceedings before VAT tribunals. In a written reply to a parliamentary question, the Financial Secretary to the Treasury has announced a change to the present practice. Although costs will not be sought as a general rule against unsuccessful appellants, in future costs will be sought at any hearings which prove complex and involve large sums or where the proceedings amount to a misuse of the appeal procedure. He further indicated that costs would not be sought where a general point of law requiring clarification was involved. See The Times, 14th November 1978.

3017   —— time for service of notice—discretion of tribunal to extend time—factors to be taken into consideration

Value added tax tribunal decision:

ROGER KYFFIN TRADING AS DISCOUNT CYCLES v CUSTOMS AND EXCISE COMMISSIONERS (1978) MAN/78/89 (unreported) (applicant paid assessment to tax in full; subsequent tribunal decision suggested deduction might have been permissible; appeal out of time; application for extension of time for service of notice of appeal; tribunal's discretion not fettered by fact tax had been paid but applicant had to have reasonable chance of recovering money; no general right to recover money paid voluntarily under mistake of law; judicial decision reversing former understanding of law did not give right to recover money already paid; application refused).

3018   Assessment—assessment by Commissioners—failure to specify accounting periods—effect of failure

The Customs and Excise Commissioners, acting under the Finance Act 1972, s. 31 (1), made a lump sum assessment to VAT in respect of incomplete or incorrect returns covering a period of twenty-one months. On appeal by the taxpayers, *held*, although s. 31 did not in terms require an assessment in respect of incomplete or incorrect returns to be made by reference to prescribed accounting periods, s. 31 (2) and (4) imposed limitation periods after which an assessment of "an amount of tax due for any prescribed accounting period" could not be made. It was a necessary implication that the assessment had to show what tax was due for specific periods. The assessment was thus invalid and the appeal would be allowed.

S. J. GRANGE LTD V CUSTOMS AND EXCISE COMMISSIONERS (1978) Times, 26th July (Queen's Bench Division: NEILL J).

This decision was reversed on appeal, see para. 3055.

3019 —— **mistake by commissioners—liability of taxpayer**

Value added tax tribunal decision:

MAIDSTONE SAILING CLUB V CUSTOMS AND EXCISE COMMISSIONERS (1978) LON/77/359 (unreported) (unincorporated members' club became liable for registration; date for registration agreed with tax office; when certificate of registration delivered, a later date had been inserted by mistake; assessment then made for period running from earlier agreed date; club tried to claim liability from date in certificate only; under Finance Act 1972, s. 31, club was liable for tax from earlier agreed date).

3020 **Charge to tax—by whom tax payable—circulation of tax**

Value added tax tribunal decision:

PETER DALY TRADING AS PENNINE VARIETY AGENCY V CUSTOMS AND EXCISE COMMISSIONERS (1978) MAN/78/85 (unreported) (entertainment agent had never issued tax invoices to clubs to which he supplied artists; claimed he should not be liable for tax because clubs could recover tax payable by them; tax would be circular and revenue would suffer no loss; loss to revenue was no concern of tribunal; agent was liable for tax but could still recover from clubs for whole period if he could trace them; circularity of tax irrelevant provided ultimate taxpayer was final consumer, here the club audiences).

3021 **Exempt supply—betting, gaming and lotteries—charge for admission to premises**

Value added tax tribunal dicision:

TYNEWYDD LABOUR WORKING MEN'S CLUB AND INSTITUTE LTD V CUSTOMS AND EXCISE COMMISSIONERS (1977) CAR /76/195 (unreported) (working men's club with premises at which various facilities provided; hall used for playing bingo and provision of entertainments; bingo played on two thirds of nights of the week; club contended that payments for admission on occasions when bingo was played were not chargeable to tax, the provision of facilities for the placing of bets or playing of games of chance being exempt applies under Finance Act 1972, Sch. 5, Group 4; tribunal found that payments for admission varied either because of cost of entertainments or because club funds were low; payments to be apportioned, part exempt under Sch. 5, Group 4 and part not exempt being additional charges made for admission to premises).

3022 —— **education—examiner**

Value added tax tribunal decision:

HOLLAND V CUSTOMS AND EXCISE COMMISSIONERS [1978] VATTR 108 (appellant chief examiner for Royal Society of Arts; first appointed when employed by a college of technology; later started her own tuition centre; assessed to value added tax on fees for setting and marking papers for society; tribunal found appellant was part-time employee of society and that services she supplied in setting and marking papers were exempt under Finance Act 1972, Sch. 5, Group 6 (provision of education).

3023 —— **land—grant of interest in redeveloped property**

Value added tax tribunal decision:

TRUSTEES FOR HULME TRUST EDUCATIONAL FOUNDATION V CUSTOMS AND EXCISE

COMMISSIONERS (1978) MAN/77/104 (unreported) (educational foundation held headleases of re-developed property; contended it was "a person constructing a building" for purposes of Finance Act 1972, Sch. 4. Group 8, item 1 and that consequently the supply by it of major interests in buildings was a zero-rated supply rendering it liable to registration but entitling it to claim as input tax all tax paid on supplies made to it; commissioners contended that "a person constructing a building" had to be interpreted literally, that foundation was not such a being and thus that its supply of interests in land was exempt under Sch. 5, Group 1, item 1; words had to be given their normal everyday meaning; accordingly, construction had to have been done either by foundation, its servants or agents, or to have been contracted out to another directly by it; neither of these was the case, thus supply of interests exempt).

3024   —— —— permission to use building for meetings—whether grant of licence

Value added tax tribunal decision:

SWINDON MASONIC ASSOCIATION v CUSTOMS AND EXCISE COMRS (1978) LON/77/313 (unreported) (commissioners claimed that a masonic association which comprised twelve lodges had not declared all its taxable supplies; supplies in question were payments by lodges for use of the association's buildings, donations by the lodges to the association and money raised by the Entertainments Committee; association contended supplies exempt because the permission to use the building was a grant of a licence to occupy land and the donations from the lodges and Entertainments Committee revenues were voluntary donations like those from individual members; contentions upheld; supplies exempt).

3025   —— —— proportion of exempt to total supplies

Value added tax tribunal decision:

WENDY FAIR MARKET CLUB v CUSTOMS AND EXCISE COMRS (1978) LON/77/400 (unreported) (company which carried on business trading in markets formed a club to enable people to buy from traders on Sundays; club appealed against assessment for value added tax relating to a repayment of input tax; commissioners claimed no deduction could be made because the club had not taken account of the proportions of exempt supplies to total supplies; relevant supplies were supplies of land between company and club under agreements covering three separate periods; club had only made exempt supplies during one period because on construction of the agreements the company had made the supplies during the other two; order for re-assessment made).

3026   Finance Act 1978

Finance Act 1978, Part II deals with value added tax; see further para. 2312.

3027   Higher rated goods—boat—whether imported or supplied in United Kingdom

Value added tax tribunal decision:

HARRIS v CUSTOMS AND EXCISE COMMISSIONERS (1978) LON/78/354 (unreported) (boat made in Norway and delivered to South of France; registered in London and flying British flag; later brought to England; for purposes of Finance Act 1972 s. 1, boat never delivered to United Kingdom, supplied outside United Kingdom and imported; subject to tax at higher rate).

3028   —— boats and boat accessories—goods suitable for use as parts— couplings and winches

The supply of certain couplings and winches was assessed to higher rate VAT on the grounds that the goods fell within Finance (No. 2) Act 1975, Sch. 7, Group 3, item 6. On appeal from the VAT tribunal the Divisional Court upheld the commissioners' assessment and the supplier appealed. *Held*, on a true construction of the words "goods of a kind suitable for use" in the context of the schedule, to fall within item 6 the goods must have been made exclusively or primarily for use as parts of boats or trailers: mere incidental suitability for such use was not sufficient, as goods could not be of more than one kind for the purpose of item 6. Since the couplings and winches in question had been used primarily for purposes other than in connection with boats or trailers, they could not be assessed to higher rate VAT under item 6. The appeal would be allowed.

CUSTOMS AND EXCISE COMRS v MECHANICAL SERVICES (TRAILER ENGINEERS) LTD [1979] STC 79 (Court of Appeal: MEGAW, BROWNE and WALLER LJJ). Decision of Divisional Court [1978] 1 All ER 204, 1977 Halsbury's Abr para. 3049 reversed.

3029   —— **radio receivers or transmitters—personal alarm—whether suitable for domestic use**

Value added tax tribunal decision:

EMERALD ELECTRONICS LTD v CUSTOMS AND EXCISE COMMISSIONERS (1978) MAN/78/73 (unreported) (supply of radio transmitter to be worn on wrist which emits alarm plus receiver usually sited in neighbour's house; used to alert others to fact that elderly or distressed person needs assistance; appeal against Commissioners' decision that supply chargeable at higher rate as comprised radio transmitter and receiver suitable for domestic use; appellants contended alarm was not for "domestic" use but for use in any situation not necessarily in the home; appeal dismissed as principal use of appliance was to summon assistance to person in distress at home; thus suitable for domestic use).

3030   —— **swivel television platform—whether accessory or furniture**

Value added tax tribunal decision:

GOMME v CUSTOMS AND EXCISE COMRS (1978) LON/78/281 (unreported) (appellant firm of furniture manufacturers made an item described as "swivel TV platform" on which it charged VAT at the standard rate; commissioners contended that the platform, which fixed on to a base unit, was an accessory to a television and therefore should be charged VAT at a higher rate; company claimed that it was a piece of furniture; tribunal held that the normal meaning of accessory was an article designed or adapted to aid or contribute to the use or enjoyment of something else; on the evidence the swivel platform was designed to contribute to the use and enjoyment of a television and was therefore an accessory and chargeable to VAT at the higher rate).

3031   **Imposition of VAT**

The Value Added Tax (General) (Amendment) Regulations 1978, S.I. 1978 No. 532 (Regs. 1, 2 and 8 in force on 29th April 1978, and the remainder in force on 4th May 1978), amend the various provisions of, and add a new Part to, the Value Added Tax (General) Regulations 1977, 1977 Halsbury's Abr para. 3052. The amended provisions relate to cancellation of registration, less detailed tax invoices, the giving of security for the release of imported goods without payment of tax, increase of sheriff's fees, and the giving of certain directions in writing. The new part deals with partial exemption and import tax.

3032   —— **Isle of Man**

The Value Added Tax (United Kingdom and Isle of Man) Order 1978, S.I. 1978 No. 1621 (in force on 15th November 1978), makes the necessary provisions to secure that in respect of certain specified instruments, value added tax is not charged both under the Finance Act 1972 and the Value Added Tax and Other Taxes Act 1973 (an Act of Tynwald) in respect of the same transaction.

3033   —— **consolidation**

The Value Added Tax (United Kingdom and Isle of Man) (Consolidation) Order 1978, S.I. 1978 No. 273 ensures that value added tax is chargeable under either the

Finance Act 1972, or the Value Added Tax and Other Taxes Act 1973 (an Act of Tynwald), but not under both. Persons who are taxable persons under one Act are automatically so under the other. The 1974 Order of the same name, 1974 Halsbury's Abr para. 3350 has been revoked.

3034   —— —— **reliefs and rate of tax**

The Value Added Tax (Consolidation) Order 1978, S.I. 1978 No. 1064 (in force on 4th September 1978), consolidates and revokes the following Orders: S.I. 1976 Nos. 128, 2024–2027, 2029, 1976 Halsbury's Abr paras. 2783, 2738, 2785, 2784, 2749, 2788, and S.I. 1977 Nos. 1786–1789, 1791–1794, 1797, 1849, 1977 Halsbury's Abr paras. 3047, 3038, 3045, 3102, 3104, 3098, 3108, 3043, 3106.

The Order specifies the supplies of goods or services which are either zero-rated or exempt for value added tax purposes and those which are higher rated. The Value Added Tax (Consolidation) Order 1977 Halsbury's Abr para. 3036, is revoked.

3035   **Input tax—deduction—business entertainment**

Value added tax tribunal decision:
BRITISH CAR AUCTIONS LIMITED v CUSTOMS AND EXCISE COMMISSIONERS (1978) LON/77/86 (unreported) (company dealt successfully in the sale of second-hand cars at auction sales; two racehorses were bought and raced in the company's name; company claimed deduction as input tax of value added tax paid on purchase of horses and on expenses for their upkeep, training fees and similar matters; company claimed expenses were for purpose of its business as being for purpose of advertising; advertisement took form of entertaining big clients at races on day one of company's horses were running; horses were therefore bought for purpose of business entertainment within meaning of Input Tax (Exceptions) (No. 3) Order 1972, and input tax was not deductible).

3036   —— —— **guarantee payment**

Value added tax tribunal decision:
NORMAL MOTOR FACTORS LTD v CUSTOMS AND EXCISE COMMISSIONERS [1978] VATTR 56 (guarantee scheme for car owners who had treated vehicles with company's lubrication products, company deducted as input tax amounts charged as tax by repairing garages: tax not deductible by company; not a supply of services to it for purposes of its business but a supply to car owner who was then indemnified by company on supplies of goods and services in effecting repairs and repaid to owners by company under scheme).

3037   —— —— **purchase tax rebate**

Value added tax tribunal decision:
JASON RUSSELL LIMITED v CUSTOMS AND EXCISE COMMISSIONERS (1978) LON/77/446 (unreported) (Finance Act 1973, s. 4, provided that purchase tax charged in respect of goods at the beginning of April 1973 was to be treated as an account to be deducted as input tax; trader submitted a claim within time for purchase tax rebate; later, trader sought to increase the sum claimed; VAT tribunal decided that it had no jurisdiction to hear an appeal against the Commissioners' refusal to sanction the late increase in amount of claim; trader argued that the original notification, albeit for a lesser sum, had been made within time and that was sufficient; tribunal decided that there was no right of appeal against the Commissioners' refusal to accept the late increase unless there was a very exceptional and compelling reason to the contrary; appeal was dismissed).

3038   —— —— **supply of professional services to pension fund**

Value added tax tribunal decision
LINOTYPE AND MACHINERY LTD v CUSTOMS AND EXCISE COMMISSIONERS [1978] VATTR 123 (appellant company set up pension fund for employees; fund managed

and administered by trustees; company bound by deed establishing fund to pay all administrative costs; value added tax paid on professional fees for auditing and advisory services to pension fund; company and trustees separate legal persons; professional services rendered to trustees, not company, accordingly company not entitled to deduct tax relating to supply of such services as input tax; *Customs and Excise Commissioners v British Railways Board* [1976] 3 All ER 100, CA 1976 Halsbury's Abr para. 2769 distinguished).

3039   —— —— supply for purpose of business

Value added tax tribunal decisions:

HILLINGDON SHIRT CO LTD v CUSTOMS AND EXCISE COMRS (1978) MAN/78/26 (unreported) (shirt manufacturing company appealed against assessment to input tax on the import of a racehorse; company had purchased a number of racehorses with the intention of using them for the purposes of advertising and promoting the company's products; company contended that it had obtained the horses for the purposes of its business; tribunal held that the horses had been purchased as a means of advertising the company's products and as part of an integrated advertising campaign; the horses had been supplied to the company for the purposes of a business and the appeal would be allowed).

3040   ASHTREE HOLDINGS LTD v CUSTOMS AND EXCISE COMMISSIONERS (1978) LON/78/141 (unreported) (appellant company, incorporated in Eire, dealt in publication of records, tapes and books, as well as carrying on the business of popular entertainment and the promotion of theatrical productions; company altered Memorandum of Association to include object of buying, dealing in and racing horses; six horses were bought in England on behalf of company for purpose of racing them and advertising the company's trade name; but at time of purchase Jockey Club rules prevented horses owned by an Irish company from being raced in England; tribunal therefore found no evidence that purchase of horses was either for benefit of the Irish company or for the purpose of a business carried on by it; value added tax paid on their acquisition could not be claimed as input tax).

3041   Liability to tax—charge for tax already arisen—subsequent issue of credit note—effect

Value added tax tribunal decision:

PETER CRIPWELL AND ASSOCIATES v CUSTOMS AND EXCISE COMMISSIONERS (1978) CAR/78/131 (unreported) (firm supplied services to a company, issued tax invoices in respect of them and accounted for tax in returns; company subsequently went into liquidation; firm unlikely to receive payment, so issued credit note for total amount shown in invoices and sought repayment of tax by deducting it from return for period in which credit note issued; credit note not issued bona fide in order to correct genuine mistake or overcharge, but to seek to recover tax for which charge had arisen when invoices issued after services performed and which had been duly accounted for in tax returns for relevant periods; firm not entitled to deduct tax).

3042   Refund—"do-it-yourself" housebuilders' scheme goods and services

Value added tax tribunal decision:

LORD KARL WOOD v CUSTOMS AND EXCISE COMMISSIONERS (1978) LON/77/268 (unreported) (retired professional builder decided to build himself a new house; applied for planning permission; in order to apply he enlisted services of an architect; in the course of the erection of the house, the builder hired labour from an agency; hiring charges included VAT; certain fixtures were installed which commissioners claimed were not usual; tribunal found that "do-it-yourself" scheme did not apply to services, but only to goods; refund of tax on goods ordinarily installed was allowable, otherwise not; for instance, tax on cooker hoods was allowed; on audio equipment, not).

3043 —— —— reconstruction—estoppel

Value added tax tribunal decision:

MEDLAM v CUSTOMS AND EXCISE COMMISSIONERS (1978) LON/77/304 (unreported) (appellant, owner of stables and garage with walls but no roof and floor obtained planning permission to "improve existing living accommodation"; sought advice on claiming a refund on VAT under do-it-yourself housebuilders' scheme; local VAT official said "I think you have a good case, I would certainly recommend it"; appellant built house within existing walls, as required by planning permission, but not supported by them, and submitted claim for refund on goods used in course of construction; refund refused on ground that it was not construction of a new dwelling but conversion, alteration or reconstruction of an existing building; Commissioners' decision upheld on account of wording of planning permission; VAT official's words would give rise to a promissory estoppel but estoppel could not arise in relation to the duty imposed by statute on the Commissioners to collect VAT).

3044 Registration—educational establishment—failure to register when exempt status removed—effective date of registration

Value added tax tribunal decision:

WATSON v CUSTOMS AND EXCISE COMMISSIONERS (1978) LON/78/33 (unreported) (owner of higher education establishment failed to register it for value added tax when exempt status taken away by Value Added Tax (Education) Order 1976, see 1976 Halsbury's Abr para. 2738; owner claimed he was not informed of change in law, that local value added tax office had failed to advise him properly and that 1st April 1977, the date of registration notified to him by the commissioners, was unreasonably early; owner should have registered himself by 1st April; failure due partly to himself, partly to other factors; in any event, commissioners had no choice but to register him and tribunal had no power to vary registration).

3045 —— exemption from registration—zero-rated supplies—exercise of commissioners' discretion

Value added tax tribunal decision:

FONG v CUSTOMS AND EXCISE COMMISSIONERS [1978] VATTR 75 (proprietress of Chinese chip restaurant registered for value added tax purposes as taxable supplier exceeded £5,000; nearly all outputs zero-rated (supply of chips for consumption off the premises); appellant accordingly repayment trader receiving amount by which deductible input tax exceeded output tax; commissioners decided they had no discretion to exempt her from registration as not all supplies were zero-rated; tribunal found commissioners did have discretion to exempt any trader who made zero-rated supplies and that as grant of exemption was in the interests of the Revenue discretion should be exercised in appellant's favour).

3046 —— group of companies—application to be treated as part of group—application out of time

The respondents transferred their unit trust business to a subsidiary company in 1973. Inadvertently no application was made to register the subsidiary for value added tax. When the failure was discovered application was made for registration and for group treatment. The commissioners agreed to retrospective registration but decided that as the application was not made within the ninety day time limit laid down by Finance Act 1972, s. 21 (7) they had no power to include the subsidiary in the group retrospectively. Section 21 (7) provides that an application must be made not less than ninety days before the date from which it is to take effect or at such later time as the commissioners may allow. On appeal a value added tax tribunal decided that the commissioners did have jurisdiction to determine the application. It then went on to determine the application in favour of the respondents. On appeal by the commissioners *held*, the tribunal had correctly decided that s. 21 (7) empowered the commissioners to hear an application made the ninety days. However it should not have determined the application itself and it would be ordered to send it back to the commissioners for consideration.

CUSTOMS AND EXCISE COMMISSIONERS V SAVE AND PROSPER GROUP LTD (1978) Times, 13th July (Queen's Bench Division: NEILL J). Decision of value added tax tribunal (1978) LON/77/245 (unreported), affirmed in part and reversed in part.

3047   —— liability to be registered—non-profit making society

Value added tax tribunal decision:

THE ROYAL PHOTOGRAPHIC SOCIETY OF GREAT BRITAIN V CUSTOMS AND EXCISE COMMISSIONERS (1978) LON/78/156 (unreported) (appellant a non-profit making society and a registered charity: membership open to anyone interested in photography: membership in fact both amateur and professional; purpose of society to promote photography generally; society claimed exemption from registration on basis that it was a non-profit making professional association and an association with the primary purpose of advancing a particular branch of knowledge; claim failed because membership not restricted to individuals whose present or previous professions or employments were directly connected with photography).

3048   —— —— separate registration in respect of activities as trustee

Value added tax tribunal decision:

BRITISH INSTITUTE OF MANAGEMENT V CUSTOMS AND EXCUSE COMMISSIONERS [1978] VATTR 101 (British Institute of Management, company limited by guarantee, main object to act as central institute for those interested in management and to promote art and science of management; also represented interests of members; British Institute of Management Foundation set up by BIM in 1977 as charitable trust to carry out educational functions; BIM sole trustee; commissioners decided that BIM should be separately registered in respect of activities as sole trustee of Foundation; tribunal found reality of position was that BIM supplied part of services through company which was not restricted to charitable services and other part through Foundation of which it was the sole trustee; accordingly no justification for separate registration in respect of activities as charitable trustee).

3049   —— partnership—existence of partnership

See *Daniels and Blackmore v Customs and Excise Comrs*, para. 2048.

3050   Relief—bad debts

The Value Added Tax (Bad Debt Relief) Regulations 1978, S.I. 1978 No. 1129 (in force on 2nd October 1978), are made under the Finance Act 1978, s. 12. They regulate generally the administration of relief from VAT included in bad debts incurred on supplies where the debtor becomes formally insolvent after 1st October 1978. They describe the procedure for claiming relief and the evidence to be held in support of claims; prescribe the minimum period for retention of evidence; prescribe how the outstanding consideration is to be calculated in cases of mutual debts and part payments; and provide for repayment by the claimant to Customs and Excise where conditions are breached after relief has been obtained.

3051   —— second-hand goods—boats

Under the Value Added Tax (Boats and Outboard Motors) Order 1975 tax is only payable on the difference between the consideration for which the second-hand boat was acquired and the consideration for which it was sold. A company which bought bare hulls and after fully fitting them out sold the resulting product at a profit contended that the cost of acquisition included the cost of refitting and commissioning. *Held*, such costs were not included. The 1975 Order envisaged only one supply. Acquisition was not a continuing process extending from the basic hull through the various parts added to the finished boat. What had been acquired was simply a hull which was a boat for the purpose of calculating the taxable difference.

WYVERN SHIPPING LTD v CUSTOMS AND EXCISE COMMISSIONERS [1979] STC 91 (Queen's Bench Division: NEILL J). Decision of VAT tribunal (unreported), 1977 Halsbury's Abr para. 3075 affirmed.

3052   —— —— works of art

Value added tax tribunal decision:

JOCELYN FEILDING FINE ARTS LTD v CUSTOMS AND EXCISE COMMISSIONERS (1978) LON/78/81 (unreported) (fine art dealers used the London auction houses, Christie's and Sotheby's; under scheme laid down by Customs and Excise Commissioners dealer was to pay value added tax on difference between price at which he bought an article and the purchase price at the auction; Christie's and Sotheby's both included premium paid to them by buyers in purchase price for tax purposes; dealer contended as premium was paid to auctioneers in consideration of their service to the buyers it was not part of the purchase price; value added tax could only be levied on money representing consideration for the goods which reached the dealer, not on consideration for services which was retained by the auctioneer; buyer's premium not part of purchase price for purpose of dealer's assessment to tax).

3053   —— —— —— antiques and scientific collections

See *Customs and Excise Commissioners v J. H. Corbitt (Numismatists) Ltd,* para. 3072.

3054   Return—failure to make return—taxpayer no longer trading— whether taxpayer required to make return

A haulage contractor, who was registered for the purpose of value added tax under the Finance Act 1972, failed to furnish a return under Value Added Tax (General) Regulations 1975, 1975 Halsbury's Abr para. 3429, reg. 51, when directed to do so by the Customs and Excise Commissioners. He contended that as he had ceased to trade before the commencement of the relevant period of the return, he was not required to make a return. The Commissioners claimed that notwithstanding the circumstances, he should have furnished a nil return for the relevant period. The justices held that a nil return was not a legal requirement and the Commissioners appealed. *Held,* reg. 51 provided that every registered person should furnish a return. As the contractor had remained registered notwithstanding the fact that he had ceased to trade, the regulation still applied to him. He was therefore guilty of an offence under the 1972 Act. The case would be remitted to the justices with an order for conviction.

KEOGH v GORDON [1978] STC 340 (Queen's Bench Division: LORD WIDGERY CJ, BOREHAM AND DRAKE JJ).

3055   —— incomplete or incorrect returns—failure to specify accounting periods—effect

The Customs and Excise Commissioners made an assessment under the Finance Act 1972, s. 31 (1) of the amount of additional VAT payable by the taxpayer company in respect of a period of twenty-one months, spanning several of the company's three-month accounting periods, for which the company's returns were incomplete or incorrect. The company's appeal against the assessment was upheld, on the grounds that it was a necessary implication of the limitation periods prescribed by s. 31 (2) that such an assessment should show the amount of tax due for specific periods. On appeal by the Commissioners, *held,* an assessment under s. 31 (1) could relate to a period covering more than one prescribed accounting period, although in such a case the two-year limitation period provided for by s. 31 (2) ran from the end of the first prescribed accounting period included in the period covered by the assessment. The appeal would be allowed.

S. J. GRANGE LTD v CUSTOMS AND EXCISE COMMISSIONERS [1979] 1 WLR 239 (Court of Appeal: LORD DENNING MR, BRIDGE and TEMPLEMAN LJJ). Decision of Neill J (1978) Times, 26th July reversed.

3056   Sale of business—transfer of fixtures and fittings—whether sale as going concern or in course of business

Value added tax tribunal decision:

WENSUE COACHWORKS v CUSTOMS AND EXCISE COMMISSIONERS (1978) LON/78/128 (unreported) (sale of business; vendor thought it was a sale as going concern and that purchaser would be responsible for value added tax; helped purchaser set up business and introduced clients; customs and excise asked for information on sale of fixtures; purchasers alleged vendors liable for tax because fixtures sold in course of business; facts showed sale was complete transfer of business and assets; purchasers liable to pay tax).

3057   Solicitor's costs

Discussions between the Law Society and HM Customs and Excise concerning the value added tax treatment of costs payable to an employed solicitor have yielded guidelines to be applied in all cases where the costs of an employed solicitor are payable by a third party.   For a summary of these principles, see [1978] LS Gaz 963.

3058   Supply of goods and services—company's gift to employee for long service

A company had a long-standing practice of making presentations of clocks and other valuable articles worth over £10 to employees with more that twenty-five years' service.   A value added tax tribunal upheld the commissioners' assessment that the company was liable to value added tax on the articles because they were supplied in the course of its business under Finance Act 1972, s. 2 (2) (b).   The company appealed, contending that the goods were outside the scope of value added tax because they were subject to income tax as emoluments of the employees, and that the words "goods supplied . . . in the course of a business" in s. 2 (2) (b) should be construed narrowly so as not to include gifts to employees.   *Held*, income and value added tax were not mutually exclusive, and therefore the fact that the gifts attracted income tax did not remove them from the scope of value added tax.   The words in s 2 (2) (b) should be given their ordinary and natural meaning and would include gifts to employees which were designed to promote good industrial relations. Accordingly the appeal would be dismissed.

RHM BAKERIES (NORTHERN) LTD v CUSTOMS AND EXCISE COMMISSIONERS [1979] STC 72 (Queen's Bench Division: NEILL J).   Decision of value added tax tribunal (1977) MAN/77/37 (unreported), 1977 Halsbury's Abr para. 3078 affirmed.

3059   ——contract for supply imposing several obligations on taxpayer—whether each obligation to be treated as a separate supply

The taxpayer, a farmer, included among his activities the keeping of two stallions at stud.   He entered into contracts with mare owners, for a fixed fee, to have the mares served at the stud by the stallions.   The contracts imposed on the taxpayer various duties such as pregnancy tests, the provision of accommodation for the mare, and observation of her.   The value added tax tribunal treated the farmer's obligations under the contract as separate, and assessed to tax the various activities accordingly. For instance, part of the fee for feeding from growing grass was said by the tribunal to be zero-rated.   On appeal, *held*, the transaction for the fee was one transaction, not a collection of several different ones.   The tribunal had been in error in assessing each of the activities separately.   The appeal would be allowed.

CUSTOMS AND EXCISE COMMISSIONERS v SCOTT [1978] STC 191 (Queen's Bench Division: LORD WIDGERY CJ, CUMMING-BRUCE LJ and PARK J).   *British Railways Board v Customs and Excise Commissioners* [1977] 2 All ER 873, 1977 Halsbury's Abr para. 3085 applied.

3060   Value added tax tribunal decision:

RIVER BARGE HOLIDAYS LTD v CUSTOMS AND EXCISE COMMISSIONERS (1978) LON/77/345 (unreported) (company ran river barge cruises on Thames; took up to twelve passengers for several days; price included accommodation, food, river and road transport; supplies by company to be divided into categories; supply of cabins and passenger catering (both standard rated); road transport and river transport (both zero rated); indefinite category (overheads) to be divided in proportion to the first four categories on a cost basis).

3061   —— jewellery—remodelling of old articles

Value added tax tribunal decision:

SHARUNA JEWELLERS V CUSTOMS AND EXCISE COMMISSIONERS (1977) MAN/77/195 (unreported) (jewellers remodelled jewellery from gold articles bought in by individual customers; claimed tax payable only on labour charge; inspectors contended articles went into general gold stock, new jewellery was made out of stockpile, and that consequently tax was payable on market value of finished article; found as fact, jewellers used customer's own gold to remake article adding extra if necessary from stockpile; tax payable on labour charge and extra gold).

3062   —— place of supply—supply by agents

See *Interbet Trading Ltd v Customs and Excise Comrs*, para. 3070.

3063   —— provision of garage accommodation—whether taxable supply in course of business

Value added tax tribunal decision:

R. W. AND A. A. W. WILLIAMSON V CUSTOMS AND EXCISE COMMISSIONERS [1978] VATTR 90 (business of letting garage accommodation was carried on by a partnership which also owned a company responsible for the management of those properties; management involved collection of rents and taking care of tenants on a day to day basis; partnership assessed to tax on lettings as taxable supplies; tribunal decided the letting of garage accommodation was by definition a taxable supply in the course of a business, as partnership actively concerned in management and letting of garages; therefore tax payable on supplies).

3064   Value added tax tribunal decision;

WILCOX V CUSTOMS AND EXCISE COMMISSIONERS (1978) MAN/77/269 (unreported) (appellant assessed to VAT on income from rents of garages owned by him but managed by estate agents; appellant contended supply of garage accommodation was not a supply made by him in the course of a business carried on by him since he only received income and played no active role in management, and income was treated as investment income for income tax purposes; although activity was not a "trade, profession or vocation" within Finance Act 1972, s. 45 (1), it was nevertheless a business carried on by the appellant notwithstanding his passive role, the test being who had the power of overall control; treatment of income for income tax purposes was irrelevant; assessment upheld).

3065   —— secondment of employees

Value added tax tribunal decision:

BRITISH AIRWAYS BOARD V CUSTOMS AND EXCISE COMMISSIONERS; BRITISH AIRWAYS HOUSING TRUST LTD V CUSTOMS AND EXCISE COMMISSIONERS (1978) LON/78/191A, 191B (unreported) (British Airways Board established housing society to provide accommodation for employees and Trust to assist the society; Board, society and Trust registered separately as taxable persons; staff seconded by Board to Trust and by Trust to society in return for reimbursement of employees' salaries which were paid by the Board; in allowing employees to work for Trust and society, Board was supplying services for consideration consisting of reimbursement of salaries; although main business was that of airline operator, assisting employees to obtain housing was incidental to business; supply thus made in course of business; tax chargeable on supplies).

3066   —— self-supply—car built by second-hand motor dealer for own use

Value added tax tribunal decision:

NICHOL V CUSTOMS AND EXCISE COMMISSIONERS (1978) MAN/77/322 (unreported) (second-hand car dealer built car for himself from new and second-hand parts; later sold it for a profit; dealer liable for value added tax on the value of car when built; on sale of car again liable to tax but with benefit of concessionary scheme; dealer wrongly advised by local value added tax office before sale; commissioners not estopped from recovering sum due on sale as dealer responsible in law for not advising himself properly as to the effect of the statutory provisions).

3067   —— supply in the course of business—club or association with objects in public domain—whether club carrying on business

Value added tax tribunal decision:

SOUTH CHURCH WORKMEN'S CLUB AND INSTITUTE LTD V CUSTOMS AND EXCISE COMMISSIONERS (1978) MAN/78/40 (unreported) (workmen's club incorporated under Industrial and Provident Societies Act providing means of social intercourse, recreation and other advantages of a club; facilities included drink on payment, bingo and concert room for entertainment; members held one share each and paid annual subscription; club appealed against decision that subscription was consideration for taxable supply of services made by it in the course or furtherance of its business; tribunal rejected contention that in accordance with Finance Act 1972, s. 45 (3); Finance Act 1977, Sch. 6 club was not to be treated a carrying on business; club not within that provision as part of consideration for subscription was recreational facilities and advantages.

3068   —— —— food sold at cost price in employees' canteen

Value added tax tribunal decision:

M. B. METALS LTD V CUSTOMS AND EXCISE COMMISSIONERS (1978) LON/77/466 (unreported) (company appealed against assessment for value added tax in respect of meals served in employees' canteen; commissioners contended this was a supply in the course of business; company claimed that meals were bought by employees at cost price to cover raw materials only and therefore employees were providing meals; as company assumed responsibility for running canteen and purchasing food they were making a supply in the course of business and were liable to pay tax).

3069   —— time of supply—whether goods supplied when condition as to passing of property not fulfilled

Value added tax tribunal decision:

VERNITRON LTD V CUSTOMS AND EXCISE COMMISSIONERS (1978) LON/77/428 (unreported) (appellants supplied equipment to company subject to conditions of sale on invoices; conditions specified that property not to pass until price paid; date of tax point on invoice left blank; equipment then resold to customers; in 1976 purchasing company transferred equipment to holding company without paying for it and holding company sold it to customers; both companies registered for value added tax as part of same group; tribunal held that equipment supplied by appellants to purchasing company on date invoice issued despite condition as to passing of property; fact that purchasing company had no right to transfer goods to holding company before payment immaterial for tax purposes because of group registration).

3070   Tribunals—jurisdiction

Value added tax tribunal decision:

INTERBET TRADING LTD V CUSTOMS AND EXCISE COMRS (1978) MAN/78/93 (unreported) (appeal against two decisions of the Commissioners; first addressed to appellant at registered office in Jersey; no appeal lay in respect of it because it was not a decision as such but merely an intimation of the Commissioners' intention to put into effect earlier decision, appeal against which had been previously struck out (see

1977 Halsbury's Abr para. 3086); alternatively, tribunal had no jurisdiction to hear it because no tribunal appointed for any area outside UK; second decision addressed to appellant at York; Commissioners contended appellants liable to registration for VAT purposes as they were making taxable supplies in UK by means of an agent; appellants were making supplies in UK and were liable to register; fact that registered office was in Jersey irrelevant).

3071   —— —— questions of equity and natural justice

Value added tax tribunal decision:

COOLISLE LTD v CUSTOMS AND EXCISE COMRS (1978) LON/78/242 (unreported) (trader failed to account for VAT on service charges; appealed against assessment, contending that records showed that VAT had not been so charged and VAT officers failed to notice this; as he had been misled by officers, it would be contrary to natural justice and equity to require him to account for tax; failure to point out error not an adequate ground for saying assessment contrary to natural justice; tribunal had no equitable jurisdiction, thus unable to apply rules or maxims of equity; appellant also contended that circumstances fell within terms of letter from Chairman of Board of Customs and Excise published in newspaper, stating that where an officer knowing the full facts misled a trader to his detriment, some tax would be waived; question also fell outside tribunal's jurisdiction; in any event, officer's conduct did not amount to representation; appeal dismissed).

3072   —— —— review of commissioners' discretion

Numismatists dealing in fine coins, medals and militaria appealed against an assessment to VAT in respect of items which had been disallowed under the Value Added Tax (Works of Art, Antiques and Scientific Collections) Order 1972. The items had been disallowed as the commissioners were not satisfied that proper records had been kept in respect of them and thus the items did not qualify for the margin scheme set out in the Order. The tribunal found that it had express jurisdiction over the assessment and had power to go into all matters relating to the appeal de novo, including re-examining the records. The commissioners applied for an order that the tribunal's decision be set aside. *Held*, as authorised by the Finance Act 1972, s. 14 (1), the commissioners had in pursuance of the 1972 Order published a notice laying down the outline of the margin scheme and details as to the records to be maintained by a trader in order to come within the scheme. The 1972 Order provided that where records did not comply with the terms of the notice they might still be recognised as sufficient. The question was whether it was possible for the tribunal to substitute its view as to the sufficiency of the records for that of the commissioners. It had no such right. Once the commissioners had laid down conditions, it was a subject entirely within their control and discretion and was not open to review by the tribunal. The application would be granted and the matter remitted to the tribunal for reconsideration.

CUSTOMS AND EXCISE COMMISSIONERS v J. H. CORBITT (NUMISMATISTS) LTD [1978] STC 531 (Queen's Bench Division: NEILL J). Decision of VAT tribunal [1977] VATTR 194, 1977 Halsbury's Abr para. 3087 reversed.

3073   Zero-rating—books, leaflets and pamphlets—advertising material

Value added tax tribunal decision:

PAGE GROUP (COMMUNICATIONS) LTD v CUSTOMS AND EXCISE COMMISSIONERS (1978) MAN/77/210 (unreported) (appellant claimed that supply if stiff folded paper advertising boards was zero-rated under the Finance Act 1972, Sch. 4, Group 3, as falling within the definition of pamphlets; they were pamphlets and therefore zero-rated; window banners and door stickers were not leaflets and therefore not within the section).

3074   —— building work—boundary wall

Value added tax tribunal decision:

SAYER v CUSTOMS AND EXCISE COMRS (1978) LON/78/211 (unreported) (applicant built wall for purchaser of a house affected by road-widening scheme; wall built on grounds of house, behind local authority markers set along new boundary; applicant agreed price for the work on understanding that construction of wall would be zero-rated; tribunal held tax chargeable at standard rate; wall not a building and consequently supply not zero-rated as construction of building; no decision on whether wall was civil engineering work as such work excluded for zero-rating if private residence involved).

3075   —— —— repair or maintenance

Value added tax tribunal decision:

MAJOR AND PARTINGTON v CUSTOMS AND EXCISE COMMISSIONERS (1978) MAN/77/258 (unreported) (houses built in 1966; in 1976 concrete floors subsided due to lack of compaction of infill material; original concrete removed and replaced by new concrete bed involving letting new concrete pillars through floor; appellants contended supplies made by builder carrying out work were zero-rated since work amounted to construction or alteration of the buildings and was not a work of repair or maintenance; work was not construction as houses were ten years old; nor was it alteration, although a new floor had been laid, since the house still had a concrete floor as it had originally and any physical differences were due to the impossibility of merely replacing the old concrete; work thus amounted to repair or maintenance and was liable to tax at standard rate).

3076   —— —— —— remedying inherent defect

Value added tax tribunal decision:

WHYMAN v CUSTOMS AND EXCISE COMMISSIONERS (1978) CAR/77/361 (unreported) (appellant contended that supply of goods to remedy inherent defect in roof was made in the course of alteration of the building; not repair or maintenance; test was whether work was carried out in the course of alteration; here work corrected defects over only one quarter of the roof and so could not be held to be an alteration).

3077   —— —— —— restoration after fire

Value added tax tribunal decision:

PAROCHIAL CHURCH COUNCIL OF ST LUKES v CUSTOMS AND EXCISE COMRS (1978) MAN/78/59 (unreported) (church destroyed by fire; completely redesigned for restoration, involving further demolition and substantial reconstruction; church council's contention that at least part of the work constituted alterations and was therefore zero-rated for purposes of value added tax failed; test to be applied was to compare the state of the building immediately before restoration with its condition and completion of the work; comparison showed work to be in the nature of repairs; tax at standard rate).

3078   —— —— —— underpinning of foundations

Value added tax tribunal decision:

ACT CONSTRUCTION LTD v CUSTOMS AND EXCISE COMMISSIONERS (1978) LON/78/144 (unreported) (builders carried out underpinning on house foundations to prevent subsidence; inserted new foundations under old; accountants advised them that as no work was done on existing structure it was not a work of maintenance; claimed underpinning was supply in the course of alteration and was zero-rated; although premises had been altered work was work of maintenance; maintenance could be carried out by improvements; tax at standard rate).

3079   —— —— whether claimant a person constructing a building

See *Royal Exchange Theatre Trust v Customs and Excise Commissioners*, para. 3086; *Trustees for Hulme Trust Educational Foundation v Customs and Excise Commissioners*, para. 3023.

3080 —— civil engineering work

Value added tax tribunal decision:

Rawlins Davy and Wells v Customs and Excise Commissioners (1978) LON/77/251 (unreported) (appellants owned building and private car parking space in front of it; kerbway was raised between pavement and carriageway thus causing inconvenience to users of car park; appellants requested local authority to lower kerbway; work was carried out and local authority billed appellants; appellants claimed supply was zero-rated on basis work constituted supply of services in alteration of civil engineering works; tribunal found that lowering eighteen metres of kerbway by a few inches was not a sufficient alteration of civil engineering works to satisfy Finance Act 1972, Sch. 4, Grp. 8; tax had been properly charged).

3081 —— construction of buildings

Value added tax tribunal decision:

Monsell Youell Developments Ltd v Customs and Excise Commissioners [1978] VATTR 1 (company purchased land for development, laid out roads and sewers and sold off plots with houses; claimed supply on sale of houses zero-rated as company was "person constructing a building" within Finance Act 1972, Sch. 4, Group 8, item 1; all houses built by a second company in same group but with separate VAT registration; on a question of fact, first company's activities did not constitute "constructing a building" so supply not zero-rated).

3082 —— exports

The Value Added Tax (General) (Amendment) (No. 2) Regulations 1978, S.I. 1978 No. 972 (in force on 1st October 1978), amend the Value Added Tax (General) Regulations 1977, S.I. 1977 No. 1759, 1977 Halsbury's Abr para. 3052. The Regulations specify the earliest date on which overseas visitors and other persons may apply for permission to acquire new motor vehicles for subsequent export without payment of tax and the earliest date both parties may acquire such vehicles before departure from the United Kingdom. The requirement upon a body corporate acting as a representative member of a group to make an annual return of the trading figures of the associated businesses in that group is removed. The removal, simplification and shortening of certain forms are also provided for.

3083 —— —— necessity for documentary proof of export

Value added tax tribunal decision:

Robbins of Putney Ltd v Customs and Excise Commissioners (1978) LON/77/220 (unreported) (company sold used cars in United Kingdom to customers with overseas addresses for them to drive back to their homes abroad; supplies not zero-rated as company had no satisfactory proof of export; evidence had to be at least bill of lading, certificate of shipment or other similar document; tribunal expressed view that conditions imposed by Commissioners as to export of used cars obscure).

3084 —— food

Value added tax tribunal decision:

Burnham Radio Recreational & Welfare Club v Customs & Excise Commissioners (1978) CAR/77/157 (unreported) (supply of hot drinks from coin-operated vending machines in members' club; claimed supply was of food and therefore zero-rated; commissioners objected that under Finance Act 1972, s. 12 (2), Sch. 4, Group 1, supply was excepted from zero-rating as being a supply in the course of catering of goods consumed on the premises; supply was so excluded and liable to tax at standard rate).

3085 —— footwear for young children

Value added tax tribunal decision:

Brays of Glastonbury Ltd v Customs and Excise Commissioners (1978)

CAR/78/95 (unreported) (appellant manufacturer of footwear produced indoor and outdoor moccasins known as "Young Moccs" and "Young Mokashoos"; commissioners contended that the shoes ought not to fall within the zero-rating exemption for children's footwear because they were also suitable for wear by older persons; tribunal decided that they were so suitable and that therefore they were taxable at the standard rate).

3086 ——— grant of building constructed within existing building

Value added tax tribunal decision:

ROYAL EXCHANGE THEATRE TRUST V CUSTOMS AND EXCISE COMMISSIONERS (1978) MAN/76/62 (unreported) (theatre trust appealed against de-registration as it needed to be registered in order to deduct input tax on erection of theatre module within an existing building; commissioners claimed erection was merely an alteration, that the grant of any interest in the alteration would be an exempt supply under Finance Act 1972, Sch. 5, Group 1, and thus that registration was unnecessary; module did amount to a permanent building notwithstanding its implantation within another building; any assignment would therefore be zero-rated under Sch. 4, Group 8 and the trust was entitled to be registered).

3087 ——— overseas services—tutorial services for overseas students

Value added tax tribunal decision:

WEBB V CUSTOMS AND EXCISE COMRS (1978) LON/77/463 (unreported) (appellant practised as barrister and as law tutor to overseas students; claimed tutorial services not used by students in UK, therefore should be zero-rated; tribunal held attendance of students amounted to use of his service in UK, therefore not zero-rated; when VAT first became effective, appellant had mistakenly applied for registration for both his practice as barrister and separately for his business as law tutor; registration as tutor cancelled by commissioners; appellent misled into thinking tax not payable as tutor and claimed this estopped commissioners from levying tax; tribunal held no representation made to appellant entitling him to plead estoppel; *Pierre's Coiffure (Manchester) Ltd v Customs and Excise Comrs* (1978) MAN/77/198 (unreported), para. 3088 followed.)

3088 ——— service to overseas traders or for overseas purposes

Value added tax tribunal decisions:

PIERRE'S COIFFURE (MANCHESTER) LTD V CUSTOMS AND EXCISE COMMISSIONERS (1978) MAN/77/198 (unreported) (tuition courses and seminars were organised by a hairdresser for students of hairdressing, some of whom were overseas students; hairdresser contended that course fees paid by overseas students were zero-rated for purposes of VAT, as falling within the provisions of Finance Act 1972, Schedule 4, Group 9 item 6, as amended, supply to an overseas resident of services not used by a person present in the UK; overseas students attended courses in their capacity as individuals in the same way as UK students; supply of tuition was complete on termination of course and was therefore "used" by person present in the UK for purposes of the legislation; supply did not fall within zero-rating provisions and was liable to tax).

3089   TECHNICARE INTERNATIONAL LTD V CUSTOMS AND EXCISE COMMISSIONERS (1978) LON/78/112 (unreported) (company registered in Channel Islands agreed to supply equipment for use on an oil field to a Libyan company; arranged training programme to teach Libyan nationals to use and maintain equipment; when they invoiced the Libyan company in respect of the training scheme no charge was made for value added tax; claimed supply of training course was zero-rated as a supply by an agent to a principal trading overseas; clear that Channel Islands company had acted as agents when arranging training programme, even where it had not disclosed the principal's existence).

VALUERS AND APPRAISERS

Halsbury's Laws of England (3rd Edn.), Vol. 39, paras. 1–17

3090   Companies—production of papers for examination by auditors— responsibility of external valuer

See para. 345.

3091   Negligence—duty owed to persons relying on valuation—over- valuation

Moneylenders employed a firm of valuers to make a valuation of a hotel for mortgage purposes. The valuation, which was made in September 1973, towards the end of a property boom, was relied upon by the moneylenders, who made a loan on the basis of it. Overvaluation of the hotel led to a complete loss of security and the moneylenders brought an action alleging negligence. The main points of their claim for damages were that; (i) the valuers failed to take account of certain fire precautions which would have materially affected the lenders' decision to make the loan, had they known of the added expense in conforming to the regulations and (ii) the highly speculative market value, based on the recent buoyant market, ought not to have been included in the valuation, or if it were included it ought to be separable and recognisable as such. *Held* (i) the valuers had a duty to make allowances for fire regulations of which the purchasers would have had to conform before the hotel could be operative and (ii) the valuers ought to have been aware of market trends and in September 1973 there had been every indication that the open market would not continue to maintain such high prices as it had previously. Consequently the valuers ought not to have been so optimistic in relation to the speculative element of their valuation. The moneylenders would succeed in their claim for damages.

CORISAND INVESTMENTS LTD V DRUCE AND CO (1978) 248 Estates Gazette 315 (Queen's Bench Division: GIBSON J).

3092   Professional body—byelaws—alteration of chartered designation

The Royal Institution of Chartered Surveyors was constituted by the unification of three societies. Some former members of one of these societies, the Chartered Auctioneers and Estate Agents Institute, sought a declaration that a certain amendment to the byelaws of the Royal Institution were void or invalid. The amendment concerned the right to use the chartered designation "auctioneer". This designation was to be dropped and the plaintiff members felt resentment at being required to abandon it. It was established that many of the plaintiffs did not in fact use this designation. *Held*, as the plaintiffs were still able to use the description "auctioneers", as a by-line, they could not be described as an oppressed minority, nor would the public be in any doubt as to their function. The plaintiffs were not, therefore, entitled to the declaration nor to a mandatory injunction ordering a new meeting to be called, as the earlier meeting, during which the amendment had been passed, had been duly and properly convened according to the constitution of the institution.

MERRILLS V ROYAL INSTITUTION OF CHARTERED SURVEYORS (1978) Times, 1st November (Chancery Division: TEMPLEMAN J).

WAR AND ARMED CONFLICT

Halsbury's Laws of England (3rd Edn.), Vol. 39, paras. 18–240

3093   Pensions—personal injuries of civilians

See paras. 2128, 2129.

3094   —— **personal injuries due to war service**

See paras. 2131 et seq.

WATER SUPPLY

Halsbury's Laws of England (3rd edn.), Vol. 39, paras. 241–652

3095   **Land drainage**

See LAND DRAINAGE.

3096   **Statutory water undertakers—duty to provide domestic supply to new dwellings—contribution towards cost of construction— "necessary mains"**

A firm of developers had built dwellings on a site where there was no existing mains water supply. The water authority demanded a contribution to the cost of laying a new main which the developers paid without prejudice to their contention that the amount claimed was not exigible. The developers contended that although they had to pay for any necessary mains on the site, they were, by the Water Act 1945, s. 37, required only to pay the cost of an off-site main from the boundary of the site to the nearest place off-site where a distribution main existed. This was so even if that main was so over-committed that it would be unable to provide adequate supplies to the site. If it were necessary to supplement the supply as a result the cost had to fall on the water authority. *Held*, a necessary main within s. 37 meant one necessary for the purpose of conveying water from the existing distribution system to the site. The point at which the new main was to connect to the existing system was not necessarily the nearest off-site main; rather it was the point from which, according to good water engineering practice, it was possible to charge the main with sufficient water to supply the proposed development. Further, the fact that the new main, once constructed, might be used for some purpose other than supplying the developer's site did not prevent the main being necessary within s. 37. It was the purpose for which the main was laid and not the purpose for which the water in it might subsequently be used that was the criterion. The water authority could therefore lawfully demand a contribution from the developers for the laying of a new off-site main to a point in the distribution system which they thought suitable.

ROYCO HOMES LTD v SOUTHERN WATER AUTHORITY [1978] 2 All ER 821 (Queen's Bench Division: FORBES J). *Charwell DC v Thames Water Board* [1975] 1 All ER 763, 1975 Halsbury's Abr para. 3496 considered.

Leave to appeal direct to the House of Lords was granted.

3097   **Water charges—equalisation**

The Water Charges Equalisation Order 1978, S.I. 1978 No. 1921 (in force on 21st December 1978), relates to the calendar year 1979. It directs specified statutory water undertakers to pay to the National Water Council a specified equalisation levy. It also directs the National Water Council to pay out the aggregate of those levies in the form of equalisation payments to specified undertakers, to the specified limits. These levies and equalisation payments are to be made in equal quarterly payments.

WATERS AND WATERCOURSES

Halsbury's Laws of England (3rd edn.), Vol. 39, paras. 653–1128

3098   **Drainage rate—assessment—effect of central heating installation**

See *West of Ouse Internal Drainage Board v H Prins Ltd*, para. 1692.

3099   **High seas—pollution from land based sources—convention**

See para. 1401

3100   **Water authorities—control of discharges**

The Water Authorities (Control of Discharges) Order 1978, S.I. 1978 No. 1210 (in force on 15th September 1978), lays down procedures for the granting of consent for the making of discharges of trade or sewage effluent where such discharges are made, or proposed to be made, by water authorities to streams, controlled waters or underground strata. It also provides for the imposition, variation and revocation of conditions attached to such consent.

3101   **Water charges—collection by local authorities**

The Water Authorities (Collection of Charges) Order 1978, S.I. 1978 No. 285 (in force on 31st March 1978), provides for the collection and recovery by local authorities who are rating authorities, on behalf of water authorities, of charges made by water authorities for the supply of water and sewerage and environmental services during the year beginning 1st April 1978.

WEIGHTS AND MEASURES

Halsbury's Laws of England (3rd edn.), Vol. 39, paras. 1129–1272

3102   **Coffee and chicory extracts**

The Weights and Measures Act 1963 (Coffee Extracts and Chicory Extracts) Order 1978, S.I. 1978 No. 1081 (in force on 1st July 1979), implements the requirements of EEC Council Directive 77/436 as to the metric quantities and quantity marking relating to coffee and chicory extracts. The order supersedes Weights and Measures Act 1936, Sch. 4, Parts VIII and XI as respects solid, paste and liquid coffee and chicory products.

3103   **Cubic measures—ballast and agricultural materials**

The Cubic Measures (Ballast and Agricultural Materials) Regulations 1978, S.I. 1978 No. 1962 (in force on 1st February 1979), replace the Cubic Measures (Sand, Ballast and Agricultural Materials) Regulations 1970, as amended. The only major change is the deletion of all reference to imperial measures, consequent on the requirement in EEC Council Directive 71/354 that the cubic yard is no longer authorised for use in specified circumstances.

3104   **Imperial quantities—termination**

The Weights and Measures Act 1963 (Various Goods) (Termination of Imperial Quantities) Order 1978, S.I. 1978 No. 1080 (in force on 28th July 1978), amends various statutory provisions by providing that after certain dates, the prescribed ranges of imperial weights in which various specified goods may be pre-packed are withdrawn. The specified foods are pasta, flour and flour products, dried vegetables and dried fruits.

3105   **Measuring instruments—fees—EEC requirements**

The Measuring Instruments (EEC Requirements) (Amendment) Regulations 1978, S.I. 1978 No. 25 (in force on 20th February 1978), amend the Measuring Instruments (EEC Requirements) Regulations 1975, S.I. 1975, No. 1173. The Regulations provide that the fee payable on examinations of patterns of measuring instruments in order to ascertain conformity to EEC pattern approval requirements, is no longer payable on making the application for the examination.

See also Measuring Instruments (EEC Requirements) (Fees) Regulations 1978, S.I. 1978 No. 26, para. 3106.

3106   The Measuring Instruments (EEC Requirements) (Fees) Regulations 1978, S.I. 1978 No. 26 (in force on 20th February 1978), prescribe the fees (or the method of determining them) payable in connection with services provided by the Department of Prices and Consumer Protection in respect of EEC pattern approval of certain measuring instruments.

3107   **Potatoes**

The Weights and Measures Act 1963 (Potatoes) Order 1978, S.I. 1978 No. 741 (in force on 1st June 1978), revokes the Weights and Measures (Potatoes) (Exemption) Order 1976, S.I. 1976 No. 1296, 1976 Halsbury's Abr para. 2812. The Order substitutes new regulations for those provided by the Weights and Measures Act 1963, Sch. 4, Pt. VII requiring potatoes to be pre-packed in prescribed imperial quantities.

3108   **Solid fuel—display of information**

The Weights and Measures (Solid Fuel) Regulations 1978, S.I. 1978 No. 238 (in force on 1st April 1978) prescribe the manner in which information required to be displayed on a vehicle is to be displayed where solid fuel is carried on the highway for sale in open containers. The information relates to the indication of quantity of solid fuel carried in the containers on the vehicle. The Regulations also prescribe the form in which the name and address of the seller is to be displayed.

3109   **Units of measurement**

The Units of Measurement Regulations 1978, S.I. 1978 No. 484 (in force on 27th April 1978), implement the requirement of EEC Council Directive 71/354 as amended by EEC Council Directive 76/770, that certain units of measurement are no longer to be authorised for use. The units which cease to be authorised include the dram, the cubic yard and the bushel.

3110   —— **metrication—agriculture**

See paras. 99–102.

3111   ——— **rating enactments**

See para. 2299.

3112   —— **use in mines—metrication**

See para. 1140.

3113   **Wine—prepackaging and labelling—EEC requirements**

The Pre-packaging and Labelling of Wine and Grape Must (EEC Requirements) Regulations 1978, S.I. 1978 No. 463 (in force on 15th May 1978), implement certain requirements relating to the prepackaging and labelling of wine and grape must imposed by the Community provisions.

WILLS

Halsbury's Laws of England (3rd edn.), Vol. 39, paras. 1273–1720

3114   **Articles**

Gift of Residue: Persons Entitled, F. Graham Glover (application of a residuary clause in the light of the decision in *Re Osoba* [1978] 2 All ER 1099, para. 3118): 128 NLJ 918.

A Non-Defining Relative Clause, F. Graham Glover (problems of construing relative clauses in wills): 128 NLJ 962.

Probate Problem, Henry E. Markson (difficulties arising from revocation of wills): 128 NLJ 1077.

The Rule in *Andrews v Partington*, F. Graham Glover (review of the rule of construction known as the rule in *Andrews v Partington* (1791) 3 Bro CC 401): 128 NLJ 776.

3115 Attestation—beneficiary's spouse as witness—liability of solicitor supervising execution

See *Whittingham v Crease & Co*, para. 2741.

3116 Construction—gift of "cash"—whether cash includes bonds

Canada

The testator left his "money in the banks and in cash" to his children and the residue of his estate to his executors to be used as they thought fit. The amount of cash and money on deposit was negligible but the residue consisted of valuable bonds. The children claimed that the bonds should be treated as cash and distributed between them. *Held*, it was unreasonable to suggest that the testator intended to give his executors absolute discretion to dispose of a large sum of money whilst leaving only a small sum to his children. On a true construction of his will, the testator had treated the bonds as cash and they should be distributed accordingly.

RE COWAN AND BARRY (1978) 82 DLR (3d) 419 (Court of Queen's Bench of Manitoba). *Perrin v Morgan* [1943] AC 399, applied.

3117 —— question arising on punctuation in original will—words of qualification or of explanation

The testator's will, written in his own hand consisted of legacies of between £25 and £250. It also provided that "any residue remaining [was] to be divided between those beneficiaries who have only received small amounts". Two constructions of this provision were possible. The first was that the words "who have only received small amounts" were words of qualification or exclusion, meaning that only those would receive who belonged to the category of those who received small amounts. The second was that the words were words of explanation, referring to all the legatees, so that the testator was acknowledging that he had given small amounts to them all. *Held*, only a comma was needed between "beneficiaries" and "who" to make the words words of explanation. The handwritten will contained very little punctuation, but the phrase beginning "who have only" was begun on a fresh line, thus producing a gap or "comma substitute". This indicated that the words were words of explanation, and therefore all the legatees should take. The division between them should be made equally, not in proportion to the size of their legacies. The gift was not void for uncertainty, as the words were not words of qualification, and thus there was no need to decide what was meant by "small amounts".

RE STEEL WILL TRUSTS (1978) Times, 13th February (Chancery Division: MEGARRY V-C).

3118 —— residuary gift on trusts—trusts accomplished—entitlement to residue

A testator bequeathed all rents from his leasehold properties in Nigeria for the maintenance of his second wife and for their daughter until she finished university. The residue of the estate was left to his second wife on trust for the above purposes. The testator died in 1965, his residuary estate including a house in London. His daughter graduated in 1975, her mother having died in 1970. The testator's son by his first marriage sought to determine whether, the specified purposes having come to an end, his father's residuary estate in England was an absolute gift in equal shares between his second wife and daughter or was held as on partial intestacy. *Held*, although the specified purposes could no longer be carried out, the court would readily construe such a residuary gift as being effective rather than leave it to pass as on intestacy. While such expressions of purpose indicated a motive to make an absolute gift, they did not restrict the gift to those purposes. The testator's overriding intention was to provide for his immediate dependants. Accordingly, although the maintenance of the wife might be expected to consume more of the residue than the training of the daughter, there could be equality of gifts without equality of motive; the residuary estate would thus be divided equally between the daughter and her mother's personal representatives.

RE OSOBA [1978] 1 WLR 791 (Chancery Division: MEGARRY V-C). *Re St. Andrew's Trust* [1905] 2 Ch. 48 and dictum of Page Wood V-C in *Re Sanderson's Trust* (1857) 3 K & J 497, at 503–505 applied.

This decision was reversed in part on appeal: [1979] 1 WLR 247.

3119 Deposit of wills

The Wills (Deposit for Safe Custody) Regulations 1978, S.I. 1978 No. 1724 (in force on 1st February 1979), provide that, pursuant to the Supreme Court of Judicature (Consolidation) Act 1925, s. 172, the Principal Registry of the Family Division is the depository for the safe custody of testamentary documents of living persons under the control of the High Court, and regulate the procedure for the lodgment and withdrawal of such documents.

3120 Election against will—effect on protected life interest of beneficiary under will—applicability of doctrine

See *Re Gordon's Will Trusts, National Westminster Bank Ltd v Gordon*, para. 1167.

3121 Gift—gift to particular institution—institution no longer in existence—applicability of cy-près doctrine

See *Re Spence (Deceased), Ogden v Shackleton*, para. 300.

3122 —— residuary gift—gift subject to life interest—date of distribution of estate

Canada

A testator provided by his will that, subject to a life interest in favour of his wife, his estate should be divided between certain named beneficiaries. In the event of any of them dying before the division and distribution of the estate, other named persons were to take the named beneficiaries' place. The testator's wife subsequently died and was followed some three months later by one the primary beneficiaries. At the time of the latter's death, the testator's executor had not distributed the estate. The beneficiary's administrator claimed that the date of distribution should be taken as being the date on the death of the testator's wife and consequently the beneficiary's heirs should receive his share in preference to the alternative persons cited in the will. On the executor's petition for directions, *held*, although it was true that the capital of the testator's estate had vested in the primary beneficiaries at the date of the testator's death, that vesting was contingent on the beneficiaries' not dying before distribution. The proper date of distribution had to be taken as the earlier of the end of the testator's executor's year or the date of completion of the estate; neither of these had occurred by the time the benefeary died and accordingly the alternative beneficiaries would take in lieu of the deceased beneficiary's estate.

ROYAL TRUST COMPANY V EAST [1978] 5 WWR 444 (Supreme Court of British Columbia).

3123 Revocation—revocation by subsequent marriage—lack of consent to marriage

In 1973 the deceased had executed a will under which his brother was a beneficiary. Eighteen months later he married. After his death his widow sought to obtain letters of administration in respect of his estate contending that the will was revoked by the marriage in accordance with the Wills Act 1837, s. 18. The brother alleged that the deceased had been unable to consent to the marriage as he had been suffering from senile dementia and that accordingly the ceremony did not revoke the will. *Held*, until 1971 lack of consent made a marriage void. However, a marriage which took place after the commencement of Nullity of Marriage Act 1971 was merely voidable on the ground of lack of consent and was to be treated as valid up to the time of a decree of nullity avoiding it. No such decree had been obtained in this case, but even if it had, the marriage would still have subsisted to the date of that decree. A voidable, as opposed to a void marriage, must therefore operate in every case to revoke an earlier will of a party to that marriage. The brother's contention failed.

RE ROBERTS, DECEASED [1978] 3 All ER 225 (Court of Appeal: BUCKLEY and GOFF LJJ). Decision of Walton J [1978] 1 WLR 653, 1977 Halsbury's Abr para. 3143 affirmed.

3124   —— revocation by subsequent will—intention of testator—power of court to ignore revocation

A testatrix added a codicil to her will which provided that should her sister, who was sole beneficiary under the will, predecease her, her estate should pass to her niece. On the sister's death the testatrix made a new will, revoking all previous wills and bequeathing her whole estate to the niece, who was also to be executrix. The niece's husband witnessed the will. After the death of the testatrix probate was granted for the second will. The Wills Act 1837 s. 15 precluded the niece from benefiting under the second will because her husband had witnessed it and the revocation clause in the second will precluded her from benefiting under the codicil to the first will. She therefore asked the court to revoke the grant of probate and pronounce in solemn form for the second will without the revocation clause and for the codicil to the first will. *Held*, the granting of probate for the second will clearly ran contrary to the testatrix's intention that her niece should inherit her whole estate. In the circumstances the court could ignore the express revocation clause because it was dependent on the second will's being effective to pass on the estate to the niece, which it had failed to do. The court would pronounce in solemn form for the second will and declare that both the wills and the codicil were to be regarded as the last will and testament of the testatrix.

MANSELL V CRANNIS [1978] LS Gaz R 589 (Chancery Division: BROWNE-WILKINSON J).

3125   —— will not found on death of testator—presumption of destruction animus revocandi

In 1969 a solicitor drew up a will on the deceased's instructions and she executed it. Six months later she discussed the will with a bank official who had witnessed her signature. There was general discussion and mention of relations but she did not say that she wanted to change it. Later that year she deposited at her bank a case which after her death was found to contain two unexpected copies of the will. Shortly afterwards she went into an old people's home. After her death her will could not be found and her niece, who was executrix and the main beneficiary, sought to obtain probate on the basis of the copy in the case, but the deceased's illegitimate daughter as next of kin refused to consent. The niece entered a caveat and the daughter who had applied for letters of administration issued a warning. Because of a probate registry error the date for appearance by the caveator was wrongly stated and letters of administration were granted. The niece brought an action for probate in solemn form and revocation of the letters of administration. *Held*, as the will was last traced to the possession of the deceased and could not be found at her death there was a presumption that she had destroyed it animus revocandi. The presumption could however be rebutted by the person seeking the grant. The evidence showed that the will had been carefully made, that the deceased had provided reasonably for all for whom she might be expected to provide and that she would not have destroyed her will in secret and without telling her solicitor. There was no doubt that the deceased had not revoked her will and the court would pronounce for it in solemn form. The letters of administration would be revoked under Administration of Justice Act 1956, s. 17 as there had been an irregularity in their issue.

RE DAVIES (DECEASED), PANTON V JONES (1978) Times, 23rd May (Chancery Division: JUDGE MERVYN DAVIES, sitting as a deputy High Court judge).

INDEX

WORDS AND PHRASES

able and ready to complete (Law Society's conditions of sale)..2426
accident..2588
acquired (Public Health Act 1936, s. 20 (1))..2552
actual occupation (Land Registration Act 1925, s. 70)..1978
actual occupation (Land Registration Act 1925, s. 70 (1))..1969
agreement (Taxes Management Act 1970, s. 54 (1))..277
agreement relating to the tenancy (Leasehold Reform Act 1967, s. 23 (1))..1764
agriculture (Rent (Agriculture) Act 1976, S.I.)..48
aggrieved person (Commons Registration Act 1965, s. 18 (1))..319
annual payments (Finance Act 1965, Sch. 7, para. 12)..283
any annuity or other annual payment (Income and Corporation Taxes Act 1970, s. 52)..1599
appropriate time (Trade Union and Labour Relations Act 1974, Sch. 1, para. 6 (4A))..2988
attempting to drive (Road Traffic Act 1972, s. 6 (1))..2345, 2346
attributable to (Local Government Act 1972)..1804
attributable (Local Government (Compensation) Regulations 1974)..1803
belief (Trade Union and Labour Relations Act 1974, Sch. 1, para. 6 (5))..2995
benefit service for victims of war (EEC Council Regulation 1408/71)..1260
building (Housing Act 1957, s. 105 (4), (4A))..1482
business (Criminal Evidence Act 1965, s. 1 (4))..731
carrying on any business (Companies Act 1948, s. 332)..364
cash (will)..3116
causing grievous bodily harm (Offences against the Person Act 1861, s. 18)..758
commercial reasons (Income and Corporation Taxes Act 1970, s. 460 (1))..1622
competitive bidding (Mock Auctions Act 1961, s. 3 (1))..163
cost of reinstatement (insurance policy)..1715
custody (Courts Act 1971, s. 13 (4))..590
debt on a security..276, 284
dishonestly (Theft Act 1968, s. 13)..620
due and payable (rates) (Companies Act 1948, s. 319)..371
due under covenant (Finance Act 1965, Sch. 7, para. 12)..283
earnings (Attachment of Earnings Act 1971, s. 24 (2) (b))..971
evade (customs and Excise Act 1952, s. 56 (2))..822
expenditure on provision of plant..1562
express agreement (Copyright Act 1911, s. 24 (1))..525
fair rack rent ... payable..1745
fixed term (Trade Union and Labour Relations Act 1974, Sch. 1, para. 5 (2) (b))..2964
from time to time as work progresses (building contracts)..270
full cost of reinstatement (for purposes of insuring building)..1715
full cost of reinstatement (leasehold covenant)..1715
goods supplied ... in the course of a business (Finance Act 1972, s. 2 (2) (b))..3058
house or other building (Lands Clauses Consolidation Act 1845, s. 92)..409
householder (Supplementary Benefits Act 1976, Sch. 1, para. 11 (1) (a))..2715
impossible (carrying out of conspiracy)..601
included car parking (Land Compensation Act 1961, s. 17)..389
inferior court (RSC Ord. 52, v. 1.)..467
issue of loan capital (Finance Act 1899, s. 8 (1))..2752
learning (Obscene Publications Act 1959, s. 4 (1))..639
likely (Employment Protection Act 1975, s. 78 (5))..2980
loan capital (Finance Act 1899, s. 8 (5))..2752
loss (Powers of Criminal Courts Act 1973, s. 35 (1))..595
maintenance (Inheritance (Provision for Family and Dependants) Act 1975, s. 1 (2) (b))..1294
may (Social Security (Unemployment, Sickness and Invalidity Benefit) Regulations 1975, reg. 3 (1))..2699
medical requirement (Supplementary Benefits Act 1976, s. 1 (3))..2716
member of the family (Rent Act 1977, Sch. 1, para. 3)..1754

nature of legal advice (Limitation Act 1939, s. 2D)..1796
necessary main (Water Act 1945, s. 37)..3096
nominee property (Finance Act 1976, s. 22 (5))..289
occupied (Housing Act 1964, s. 73 (1))..1483
of a manor (Commons Registration Act 1965, s. 22 (1) (b)..320
operations (Town and Country Planning Act 1971, s. 290)..2804
particular existing company (Finance Act 1927, s. 55)..347
payment (Income and Corporation Taxes Act 1970, s. 204)..1593
pending land transaction (Land Charges Act 1972, s. 17)..2699
poverty (charitable trust)..302
producers of olive oil (EEC Council Regulation 136/66)..82
property . . . which is situate out of Great Britain (Finance Act 1949, s. 28 (2))..1445
proved to be unable to pay its debts (Insurance Companies Act 1974, s. 50)..1670
public place (Public Order Act 1936, s. 5)..653
reason for dismissal (Trade Union and Labour Relations Act 1974, Sch. 1, para. 6 (5))..2982
reasonably (Race Relations Act 1968, s. 6 (1))..2267
regular occupation (Social Security Act 1975, s. 60)..2692
safe port (charterparty)..2513
same offence (Criminal Evidence Act 1898, s. 1 (f) (iii))..722
scientific instrument or apparatus (EEC Council Regulation 1798/75)..1213
service charge (Housing Finance Act 1972, s. 90)..1742
social security benefit (EEC Council Regulation 1408/71)..1260
special occasion (Licensing Act 1964, s. 74 (4))..1677
step in the proceedings (Arbitration Act 1950, s. 4 (1); Arbitration Act 1975, s. 1)..159
structural alteration or addition (Housing Act 1974, Sch. 8)..1766
supply (building contracts)..270
unable to pay its debts (Insurance Companies Act 1974, s. 50)..1670
undertakings (EEC Council Regulation 543/69)..1198
unlawful wounding (Offences against the Person Act 1861, s. 20)..758
use (Town and Country Planning Act 1971, s. 51)..2804
vacant possession (sale of land)..2432
warehouse (in grant of planning permission)..2807
warehouse use (Town and Country Planning (Use Classes) Order 1972)..2881
whole family (Statement of Immigration Rules for Control on Entry, para. 44)..1539
wife (Inheritance (Provision for Family and Dependants) Act 1975, s. 1 (1) a)..1293
work (Health and Safety at Work etc. Act 1974, Part I)..1459
worthy causes (charitable trust)..305

Typeset by CCC and printed and bound at William Clowes & Sons Limited, Beccles and London